The Settlement of International Disputes: Basic Documents
Second Edition

This collection of documents brings together a large number of primary sources on the peaceful settlement of disputes in a usable and affordable format. The documents included reflect the diverse techniques of international dispute settlement, as recognised in Articles 2(3) and 33 of the UN Charter, such as negotiation, mediation, arbitration, and judicial settlement. The book comprises the most relevant multilateral treaties establishing dispute settlement regimes, as well as examples of special agreements, compromissory clauses, optional clause declarations, and other relevant documents. It covers both diplomatic and adjudicative methods of dispute settlement and follows a basic division between general dispute settlement mechanisms and sectoral regimes in fields such as human rights, WTO law, investment, law of the sea, environmental law, and arms control. The book is aimed at teachers, students, and practitioners of international law and related disciplines.

DOCUMENTS IN INTERNATIONAL LAW

GENERAL EDITOR: PROFESSOR STEFAN TALMON
Director at the Institute of Public International Law, University of Bonn, and Supernumerary Fellow of St. Anne's College, Oxford

ALSO IN THIS SERIES

THE LEGAL ORDER OF THE OCEANS
Vaughan Lowe and Stefan Talmon (2009)

THE IRAN NUCLEAR ISSUE
Yaël Ronen (2010)

TERRORISM
Ben Saul (2012)

THE OCCUPATION OF IRAQ: VOLUME 2
Stefan Talmon (2013)

ANTARCTICA IN INTERNATIONAL LAW
Ben Saul and Tim Stephens (2015)

THE ARCTIC IN INTERNATIONAL LAW AND POLICY
Kristina Schönfeldt (2017)

BASIC DOCUMENTS ON INTERNATIONAL INVESTMENT PROTECTION, Second Edition
Martins Paparinskis (2019)

THE SETTLEMENT OF INTERNATIONAL DISPUTES: BASIC DOCUMENTS, Second Edition
Christian J Tams and Antonios Tzanakopoulos (2022)

The Settlement of International Disputes: Basic Documents
Second Edition

Christian J Tams and
Antonios Tzanakopoulos

•HART•
OXFORD • LONDON • NEW YORK • NEW DELHI • SYDNEY

HART PUBLISHING

Bloomsbury Publishing Plc

Kemp House, Chawley Park, Cumnor Hill, Oxford, OX2 9PH, UK

1385 Broadway, New York, NY 10018, USA

29 Earlsfort Terrace, Dublin 2, Ireland

HART PUBLISHING, the Hart/Stag logo, BLOOMSBURY and the Diana logo are trademarks of Bloomsbury Publishing Plc

First published in Great Britain 2022

A catalogue record for this book is available from the British Library.

Library of Congress Cataloging-in-Publication data

Names: Tams, Christian J, editor. | Tzanakopoulos, Antonios, editor.

Title: The settlement of international disputes : basic documents / edited by Christian J Tams and Antonios Tzanakopoulos.

Description: Second edition. | Oxford ; New York : Hart, 2022. | Series: Documents in international law | Includes bibliographical references and index.

Identifiers: LCCN 2022001592 (print) | LCCN 2022001593 (ebook) | ISBN 9781509942213 (paperback) | ISBN 9781509942237 (pdf) | ISBN 9781509942220 (Epub)

Subjects: LCSH: Pacific settlement of international disputes. | Arbitration (International law) | International commercial arbitration. | LCGFT: Treaties.

Classification: LCC KZ6010 .S48 2022 (print) | LCC KZ6010 (ebook) | DDC 347.09—dc23/eng/20220429

LC record available at https://lccn.loc.gov/2022001592

LC ebook record available at https://lccn.loc.gov/2022001593

ISBN: PB: 978-1-50994-221-3
ePDF: 978-1-50994-223-7
ePub: 978-1-50994-222-0

Typeset by Compuscript Ltd, Shannon
Printed and bound in Great Britain by CPI Group (UK) Ltd, Croydon CR0 4YY

FSC www.fsc.org MIX Paper from responsible sources FSC® C013604

To find out more about our authors and books visit www.hartpublishing.co.uk. Here you will find extracts, author information, details of forthcoming events and the option to sign up for our newsletters.

Preface

The first edition of this collection was published in 2012. The decade since has been a turbulent one in international dispute settlement. The 'business' of settling disputes continues apace (if not always successfully). International courts and tribunals, in particular, have remained much in demand. Human rights courts and investment tribunals have addressed more disputes than in any previous decade. The ICJ and PCA, by their standards, remain very busy as well, as do the judicial branches of regional integration frameworks. At the same time, the tone of the debate seems to have changed. Narratives stressing the rise of binding dispute settlement – measured by the growth of courts and cases, and perhaps presented as a sign of inevitable progress in international organisation – have become less prevalent. Discontent with international arbitration and judicial settlement (or at least with certain of its emanations) has become more palpable. It is reflected in the burgeoning literature organised around topoi such as 'backlash', 'pushback', and 'resistance'. In many fields, this discontent is felt in the practice of dispute settlement; in some (WTO law chiefly among them) it has left its mark on the primary rules governing proceedings. Against this background, however, the practice of international dispute settlement continues unabated, and 'backlash' in some areas or fora can be contrasted to a rise in attempts to engage in dispute settlement in others, in part through seeking to 'shoehorn' particular disputes in existing compromissory clauses.

The present collection is addressed to students, users, observers, and critics of dispute settlement. As the first edition, it brings together key primary documents governing diplomatic and adjudicatory procedures. The material is divided into a 'General Part' (bringing together techniques and institutions of general scope as well as 'foundational documents' of general or historical relevance) and a number of 'Sectoral Regimes' (comprising dispute settlement in special areas of international law, such as human rights, the law of the sea, etc.). In order to be able to provide a meaningful survey of dispute settlement in its near-infinite variety, we have only included those provisions of a document that bear on the dispute settlement process. Our choice is, needless to say, subjective. A single-volume collection cannot present the full picture. But we hope to have made plausible choices that illustrate the diversity of contemporary dispute settlement and that provide readers of the volume with easy access to a set of representative, practically relevant, or historically influential documents.

Our aims in presenting this material remain the same as a decade ago, when the first edition was published. In selecting primary documents and making them available in a single volume, we hope to provide a guide through the maze of dispute settlement, inform discussion about it, and above all, encourage engagement with the governing texts. And so, we hope that that this volume will actually be used – read, marked-up, annotated, perhaps graced with post-it notes (for those still appreciating the 'analogue' experience).

Readers who have read (and perhaps worked their way through) the first edition will find much that looks familiar. But this may be deceptive. While many of the basic texts remain in force, below the surface of continuity there have been many changes and adjustments. A surprising number of dispute settlement bodies have revised their rules of procedure or internal practice directions – e.g. to permit virtual hearings, to regulate electronic filings, or to facilitate the transparency of proceedings. States have agreed on new jurisdictional clauses that warrant close scrutiny – e.g. in the Canada-EU Trade Agreement (CETA), or the Greece-North Macedonia Prespa Agreement. New documents reflect changes brought about by the United Kingdom's decision to leave the European Union, and responses to the above-mentioned discontent with binding dispute settlement – among them, the WTO Multi-Party Interim Appeal Arbitration Agreement, but also the ICJ's attempts to address concerns about 'moonlighting judges' engaged in arbitration. All of this we have tried to capture in an updated edition that reflects the state of the law as of August 2021. In addition, we have taken the opportunity modestly to expand the coverage, including by adding the text of the 1958 New York Convention and the dispute settlement clauses of the ICAO Convention prompting recent ICJ proceedings.

To facilitate navigation within the book, each of the documents has been given a document number, which can be found on the top outside corner of each page. The detailed Table of Contents lists documents by their official title and introduces shorthand titles where the official ones are not well known or inconveniently long. The Table of Contents is complemented by a list of documents in chronological order, and by an Index which we have sought to make as user-friendly as any Index can ever be.

In updating and modestly expanding the collection, we have benefited from comments by Professor Stefan Talmon, the General Editor of the Hart Documents Series, and from feedback received from generations of students taking classes on dispute settlement at our academic homes, the Universities of Oxford and Glasgow. Ms Tsvetelina van Benthem has provided valuable research assistance. Ms Sinead Moloney and Mr. Tom Adams at Bloomsbury have expertly seen the book through the production process. To all of them, we are grateful.

Christian J Tams and Antonios Tzanakopoulos
Cologne and Tinos, August 2021

Contents

Detailed Table of Contents

A GENERAL PART

B SELECTED SECTORAL REGIMES

5 Human Rights

List of Documents in Chronological Order

[Document numbers can be found in the top outside corner of each page]

OTHER DOCUMENTS

A

General Part

1 Foundational Documents

1 Treaty of Amity, Commerce, and Navigation, between His Britannick Majesty and The United States of America (The Jay Treaty)

Date: 19 November 1794

Source: D Hunter Miller (ed), Treaties and Other International Acts of the United States of America (vol 2, 1776–1818)
http://avalon.law.yale.edu/18th_century/jay.asp

Preamble

His Britannick Majesty and the United States of America, being desirous by a Treaty of Amity, Commerce and Navigation to terminate their Differences in such a manner, as without reference to the Merits of Their respective Complaints and Pretensions, may be the best calculated to produce mutual satisfaction and good understanding: And also to regulate the Commerce and Navigation between Their respective Countries, Territories and People, in such a manner as to render the same reciprocally beneficial and satisfactory; They have respectively named their Plenipotentiaries, and given them Full powers to treat of, and conclude, the said Treaty, that is to say; His Brittanick Majesty has named for His Plenipotentiary, The Right Honourable William Wyndham Baron Grenville of Wotton, One of His Majesty's Privy Council, and His Majesty's Principal Secretary of State for Foreign Affairs; and The President of the said United States, by and with the advice and Consent of the Senate thereof, hath appointed for Their Plenipotentiary The Honourable John Jay, Chief Justice of the said United States and Their Envoy Extraordinary to His Majesty, who have agreed on, and concluded the following Articles

…

Article 4.

Whereas it is uncertain whether the River Mississippi extends so far to the Northward as to be intersected by a Line to be drawn due West from the Lake of the woods in the manner mentioned in the Treaty of Peace between His Majesty and the United States, it is agreed, that measures shall be taken in Concert between His Majesty's Government in America, and the Government of the United States, for making a joint Survey of the said River, from one Degree of Latitude below the falls of St Anthony to the principal Source or Sources of the said River, and also of the parts adjacent thereto, And that if on the result of such Survey it should appear that the said River would not be intersected by such a Line as is above mentioned; The two Parties will thereupon proceed by amicable negotiation to regulate the Boundary Line in that quarter as well as all other Points to be adjusted between the said Parties, according to Justice and mutual Convenience, and in Conformity, to the Intent of the said Treaty.

Article 5.

Whereas doubts have arisen what River was truly intended under the name of the River St Croix mentioned in the said Treaty of Peace and forming a part of the boundary therein described, that question shall be referred to the final Decision of Commissioners to be appointed in the following Manner.

One Commissioner shall be named by His Majesty, and one by the President of the United States, by and with the advice and Consent of the Senate thereof, and the said two Commissioners shall agree on the choice of a third, or, if they cannot so agree, They shall each propose one Person, and of the two names so proposed one shall be drawn by Lot, in the presence of the two original Commissioners. And the three Commissioners so appointed shall be Sworn impartially to examine and decide the said question according to such Evidence as shall respectively be laid before Them on the part of the British Government and of the United States. The said Commissioners shall meet at Halifax and shall have power to adjourn to such other place or places as they shall think fit. They shall have power to appoint a Secretary, and to employ such Surveyors or other Persons as they shall judge necessary. The said Commissioners shall by a Declaration under their Hands and Seals, decide what River is the River St Croix intended by the Treaty.

The said Declaration shall contain a description of the said River, and shall particularize the Latitude and Longitude of its mouth and of its Source. Duplicates of this Declaration ant of the State meets of their Accounts, and of the Journal of their proceedings, shall be delivered by them to the Agent of His Majesty, and to the Agent of the United States, who may be respectively appointed and authorized to manage the business on behalf of the respective Governments. And both parties agree to consider such decision as final and conclusive, so as that the same shall never thereafter be called into question, or made the subject of dispute or difference between them.

Article 6.

Whereas it is alleged by divers British Merchants and others His Majesty's Subjects, that Debts to a considerable amount which were bona fide contracted before the Peace, still remain owing to them by Citizens or Inhabitants of the United States, and that by the operation of various lawful Impediments since the Peace, not only the full recovery of the said Debts has been delayed, but also the Value and Security thereof, have been in several instances impaired and lessened, so that by the ordinary course of Judicial proceedings the British Creditors, cannot now obtain and actually have and receive full and adequate Compensation for the losses and damages which they have thereby sustained: It is agreed that in all such Cases where full Compensation for such losses and damages cannot, for whatever reason, be actually obtained had and received by the said Creditors in the ordinary course of Justice, The United States will make full and complete Compensation for the same to the said Creditors; But it is distinctly understood, that this provision is to extend to such losses only, as have been occasioned by the lawful impediments aforesaid, and is not to extend to losses occasioned by such Insolvency of the Debtors or other Causes as would equally have operated to produce such loss, if the said impediments had not existed, nor to such losses or damages as have been occasioned by the manifest delay or negligence, or wilful omission of the Claimant.

For the purpose of ascertaining the amount of any such losses and damages, Five Commissioners shall be appointed and authorized to meet and act in manner following. Two of them shall be appointed by His Majesty, Two of them by the President of the United States by and with the advice and consent of the Senate thereof, and the fifth, by the unanimous voice of the other Four; and if they should not agree in such Choice, then the Commissioners named by the two parties shall respectively propose one person, and of the two names so proposed, one shall be drawn by Lot in the presence of the Four Original Commissioners. When the Five Commissioners thus appointed shall first meet, they shall before they proceed to act respectively, take the following Oath or Affirmation in the presence of each other, which Oath or Affirmation, being so taken, and duly attested, shall be entered on the Record of their Proceedings, -viz.- I, A:B: One of the Commissioners appointed in pursuance of the 6th Article of the Treaty of Amity, Commerce and Navigation between His Britannic Majesty and The United States of America, do solemnly swear (or affirm) that I will honestly, diligently, impartially, and carefully examine, and to the best of my Judgement, according to Justice and Equity decide all such Complaints, as under the said Article shall be preferred to the said Commissioners; and that I will forbear to act as a Commissioner in any Case in which I may be personally interested.

Three of the said Commissioners shall constitute a Board, and shall have power to do any act appertaining to the said Commission, provided that one of the Commissioners named on each side, and the Fifth Commissioner shall be present, and all decisions shall be made by the Majority of the Voices of the Commissioners then present. Eighteen Months from the Day on which the said Commissioners shall form a Board, and be ready to proceed to Business are assigned for receiving Complaints and applications, but they are nevertheless authorized in any particular Cases in which it shall appear to them to be reasonable and just to extend the said Term of Eighteen Months, for any term not exceeding Six Months after the expiration thereof. The said Commissioners shall first meet at Philadelphia, but they shall have power to adjourn from Place to Place as they shall see Cause.

The said Commissioners in examining the Complaints and applications so preferred to them, are empowered and required in pursuance of the true intent and meaning of this article to take into their Consideration all claims whether of principal or interest, or balances of principal and interest, and to determine the same respectively according to the merits of the several Cases, due regard being had to all the Circumstances thereof, and as Equity and Justice shall appear to them to require. And the said Commissioners shall have power to examine all such Persons as shall come before them on Oath or Affirmation touching the premises; and also to receive in Evidence according as they may think most consistent with Equity and Justice all written positions, or Books or Papers, or Copies or Extracts thereof. Every such Deposition, Book or Paper or Copy or Extract being duly authenticated either according to the legal Forms now respectively existing in the two Countries, or in such other manner as the said Commissioners shall see cause to require or allow.

The award of the said Commissioners or of any three of them as aforesaid shall in all Cases be final and conclusive both as to the Justice of the Claim, and to the amount of the Sum to be paid to the Creditor or Claimant. And the United States undertake to cause the Sum so awarded to be paid in Specie to such Creditor or Claimant without deduction; and at such Time or Times, and at such Place or Places, as shall be awarded by the said Commissioners, and on Condition of such Releases or assignments to be given by the Creditor or Claimant as by the said Commissioners may be directed; Provided always that no such payment shall be fixed by the said Commissioners to take place sooner then twelve months from the Day of the Exchange of the Ratifications of this Treaty.

Article 7.

Whereas Complaints have been made by divers Merchants and others, Citizens of the United States, that during the course of the War in which His Majesty is now engaged they have sustained considerable losses and damage by reason of irregular or illegal Captures or Condemnations of their vessels and other property under Colour of authority or Commissions from His Majesty, and that from various Circumstances belonging to the said Cases adequate Compensation for the losses and damages so sustained cannot now be actually obtained, had and received by the ordinary Course of Judicial proceedings; It is agreed that in all such Cases where adequate Compensation cannot for whatever reason be now actually obtained, had and received by the said Merchants and others in the ordinary course of Justice, full and Complete Compensation for the same will be made by the British Government to the said Complainants. But it is distinctly understood, that this provision is not to extend to such losses or damages as have been occasioned by the manifest delay or negligence, or wilful omission of the Claimant. That for the purpose of ascertaining the amount of any such losses and damages Five Commissioners shall be appointed and authorized to act in London exactly in the manner directed with respect to those mentioned in the preceding Article, and after having taken the same Oath or Affirmation (mutatis mutandis). The same term of Eighteen Months is also assigned for the reception of Claims, and they are in like manner authorised to extend the same in particular Cases. They shall receive Testimony, Books, Papers and Evidence in the same latitude, and exercise the like discretion, and powers respecting that subject, and shall decide the Claims in question, according to the merits of the several Cases, and to Justice Equity and the Laws of Nations. The award of the said Commissioners or any such three of them as aforesaid, shall in all Cases be final and conclusive both as to the Justice of the Claim and the amount of the Sum to be paid to the Claimant; and His Britannic Majesty undertakes to cause the same to be paid to such Claimant in Specie, without any Deduction, at such place or places, and at such Time or Times as shall be awarded by the said Commissioners and on Condition of such releases or assignments to be given by the Claimant, as by the said Commissioners may be directed. And whereas certain merchants and others, His Majesty's Subjects, complain that in the course of the war they have sustained Loss and Damage by reason of the Capture of their Vessels and Merchandize taken within the Limits and Jurisdiction of the States, and brought into the Ports of the same, or taken by Vessels originally armed in Ports of the said States:

It is agreed that in all such cases where Restitution shall not have been made agreeably to the tenor of the letter from Mr. Jefferson to Mr. Hammond dated at Philadelphia September 5th 1793. A Copy of which is annexed to this Treaty, the Complaints of the parties shall be, and hereby are referred to the Commissioners to be appointed by virtue of this article, who are hereby authorized and required to proceed in the like manner relative to these as to the other Cases committed to them, and the United States undertake to pay to the Complainants or Claimants in specie without deduction the amount of such Sums as shall be awarded to them respectively by the said Commissioners and at the times and places which in such awards shall be specified, and on Condition of such Releases or assignments to be given by the Claimants as in the said awards may be directed: And it is further agreed that not only to be now existing Cases of both descriptions, but also all such as shall exist at the Time, of exchanging the Ratifications of this Treaty shall be considered as being within the provisions intent and meaning of this article.

…

2 Treaty between Great Britain and the United States for the Amicable Settlement of All Causes of Difference between the Two Countries (The Treaty of Washington)

Date: 8 May 1871
Source: C Parry, *Consolidated Treaty Series* (vol 143, 145) (1969) 145
http://www.archive.org/stream/treatyofwashingt00cush/treatyofwashingt00cush_djvu.txt

Article I.

Whereas differences have arisen between the Government of the United States and the Government of Her Britannic Majesty, and still exist, growing out of the acts committed by the several vessels which have given rise to the claims generically known as the "*Alabama* Claims":

And whereas Her Britannic Majesty has authorized her High Commissioners and Plenipotentiaries to express, in a friendly spirit, the regret felt by Her Majesty's Government for the escape, under whatever circumstances, of the *Alabama* and other vessels from British ports, and for the depredations committed by those vessels:

Now, in order to remove and adjust all complaints and claims on the part of the United States, and to provide for the speedy settlement of such claims, which are not admitted by Her Britannic Majesty's Government, the High Contracting Parties agree that all the said claims, growing out of acts committed by the aforesaid vessels and generically known as the "*Alabama* Claims," shall be referred to a Tribunal of Arbitration to be composed of five Arbitrators, to be appointed in the following manner, that is to say: One shall be named by the President of the United States; one shall be named by Her Britannic Majesty; His Majesty the King of Italy shall be requested to name one; the President of the Swiss Confederation shall be requested to name one; and His Majesty the Emperor of Brazil shall be requested to name one.

In case of the death, absence, or incapacity to serve of any or either of the said Arbitrators, or, in the event of either of the said Arbitrators omitting or declining or ceasing to act as such, the President of the United States, or Her Britannic Majesty, or His Majesty the King of Italy, or the President of the Swiss Confederation, or His Majesty the Emperor of Brazil, as the case may be, may forthwith name another person to act as Arbitrator in the place and stead of the Arbitrator originally named by such Head of a State.

And in the event of the refusal or omission for two months after receipt of the request from cither of the High Contracting Parties of His Majesty the King of Italy, or the President of the Swiss Confederation, or His Majesty the Emperor of Brazil, to name an Arbitrator either to fill the original appointment or in the place of one who may have died, be absent, or incapacitated, or who may omit, decline, or from any cause cease to act as such Arbitrator, His Majesty the King of Sweden and Norway shall he requested to name one or more persons, as the case may be, to act as such Arbitrator or Arbitrators.

Article II.

The Arbitrators shall meet at Geneva, in Switzerland, at the earliest convenient day after they shall have been named, and shall proceed impartially and carefully to examine and decide all questions that shall be laid before them on the part of the Governments of the United States and Her Britannic Majesty respectively. All questions considered by the Tribunal, including the final award, shall be decided by a majority of all the Arbitrators.

Each of the High Contracting Parties shall also name one person to attend the Tribunal as its agent to represent it generally in all matters connected with the arbitration.

Article III.

The written or printed case of each of the two Parties, accompanied by the documents, the official correspondence, and other evidence on which each relies, shall be delivered in duplicate to each of the Arbitrators and to the agent of the other Party as soon as may be after the organization of the Tribunal, but within a period not exceeding six months from the date of the exchange of the ratifications of this Treaty.

Article IV.

Within four months after the delivery on both sides of the written or printed case, either Party may, in like manner, deliver in duplicate to each of the said Arbitrators, and to the agent of the other Party, a counter-case, and additional documents, correspondence, and evidence, in reply to the case, documents, correspondence, and evidence so presented by the other Party.

The Arbitrators may, however, extend the time for delivering such counter-case, documents, correspondence, and evidence, when, in their judgment, it becomes necessary, in consequence of the distance of the place from which the evidence to be presented is to be procured.

If in the case submitted to the Arbitrators either Party shall have specified or alluded to any report or document in its own exclusive possession without annexing a copy, such Party shall be bound, if the other Party thinks proper to apply for it, to furnish that Party with a copy thereof; and either Party may call upon the other, through the Arbitrators, to produce the originals or certified copies of any papers adduced as evidence, giving in each instance such reasonable notice as the Arbitrators may require.

Article V.

It shall be the duty of the agent of each Party, within two months after the expiration of the time limited for the delivery of the counter-case on both sides, to deliver in duplicate to each of the said Arbitrators and to the agent of the other party a written or printed argument showing the points and referring to the evidence upon which his Government relies; and the Arbitrators may, if they desire further elucidation with regard to any point, require a written or printed statement or argument, or oral argument by counsel upon it; but in such case the other Party shall be entitled to reply either orally or in writing, as the case may be.

Article VI.

In deciding the matters submitted to the Arbitrators, they shall be governed by the following three rules, which are agreed upon by the High Contracting Parties as rules to be taken as applicable to the case, and by such principles of International Law not inconsistent therewith as the Arbitrators shall determine to have been applicable to the case.

Rules.

A neutral Government is bound —

First, to use due diligence to prevent the fitting out, arming, or equipping, within its jurisdiction, of any vessel which it has reasonable ground to believe is intended to cruise or to carry on war against a Power with which it is at peace; and also to use like diligence to prevent the departure from its jurisdiction of any vessel intended to cruise or carry on war as above, such vessel having been specially adapted, in whole or in part, within such jurisdiction, to war-like use.

Secondly, not to permit or suffer either belligerent to make use of its ports or waters as the base of naval operations against the other, or for the purpose of the renewal or augmentation of military supplies or arms, or the recruitment of men.

Thirdly, to exercise due diligence in its own ports and waters, and, as to all persons within its jurisdiction, to prevent any violation of the foregoing obligations and duties.

Her Britannic Majesty has commanded her High Commissioners and Plenipotentiaries to declare that Her Majesty's Government cannot assent to the foregoing rules as a statement of principles of International Law which were in force at the time when the claims mentioned in Article I. arose; but that Her Majesty's Government, in order to evince its desire of strengthening the friendly relations between the two countries and of making satisfactory provision for the future, agrees that, in deciding the questions between the two countries arising out of those claims, the Arbitrators should assume that Her Majesty's Government had undertaken to act upon the principles set forth in these rules.

And the High Contracting Parties agree to observe these rules as between themselves in future, and to bring them to the knowledge of other maritime Powers, and to invite them to accede to them.

Article VII.

The decision of the Tribunal shall, if possible, be made within three months from the close of the argument on both sides.

It shall be made in writing and dated, and shall be signed by the Arbitrators who may assent to it.

The said Tribunal shall first determine as to each vessel separately whether Great Britain has, by any act or omission, failed to fulfill any of the duties set forth in the foregoing three rules, or recognized by the principles of International Law not inconsistent with such rules, and shall certify such fact as to each of the said vessels. In case the Tribunal find that Great Britain has failed to fulfill any duty or duties as aforesaid, it may, if it think proper, proceed to award a sum in gross to be paid by Great Britain to the United States for all the claims referred to it; and in such case the gross sum so awarded shall be paid in coin by the Government of Great Britain to the Government of the United States, at Washington, within twelve months after the date of the award.

The award shall be in duplicate, one copy whereof shall be delivered to the agent of the United States for his Government, and the other copy shall be delivered to the agent of Great Britain for his Government.

Article VIII.

Each Government shall pay its own agent, and provide for the proper remuneration of the counsel employed by it and of the Arbitrator appointed by it, and for the expense of preparing and submitting its case to the Tribunal. All other expenses connected with the arbitration shall be defrayed by the two Governments in equal moieties.

Article IX.

The Arbitrators shall keep an accurate record of their proceedings, and may appoint and employ the necessary officers to assist them.

Article X.

In case the Tribunal finds that Great Britain has failed to fulfill any duty or duties as aforesaid, and does not award a sum in gross, the High Contracting Parties agree that a Board of Assessors shall be appointed to ascertain and determine what claims are valid, and what amount or amounts shall be paid by Great Britain to the United States on account of the liability arising from such failure, as to each vessel, according to the extent of such liability as decided by the Arbitrators.

The Board of Assessors shall be constituted as follows: One member thereof shall be named by the President of the United States, one member thereof shall be named by Her Britannic Majesty, and one member thereof shall be named by the Representative at Washington of His Majesty the King of Italy, and in case of a vacancy happening from any cause, it shall be filled in the same manner in which the original appointment was made.

As soon as possible after such nominations the Board of Assessors shall be organized in Washington, with power to hold their sittings there, or in New York, or in Boston. The members thereof shall severally subscribe a solemn declaration that they will impartially and carefully examine and decide, to the best of their judgment and according to justice and equity, all matters submitted to them, and shall forthwith proceed, under such rules and regulations as they may prescribe, to the investigation of the claims which shall be presented to them by the Government of the United States, and shall examine and decide upon them in such order and manner as they may think proper, but upon such evidence or information only as shall be furnished by or on behalf of the Governments of the United States and of Great Britain respectively. They shall be bound to hear on each separate claim, if required, one person on behalf of each Government, as counsel or agent. A majority of the Assessors in each case shall be sufficient for a decision.

The decision of the Assessors shall be given upon each claim in writing, and shall be signed by them respectively and dated.

Every claim shall be presented to the Assessors within six months from the day of their first meeting; but they may, for good cause shown, extend the time for the presentation of any claim to a further period not exceeding three months.

The Assessors shall report to each Government at or before the expiration of one year from the date of their first meeting the amount of claims decided by them up to the date of such report; if further claims then remain undecided, they shall make a further report at or before the expiration of two years from the date of such first meeting; and in case any claims remain undetermined at that time, they shall make a final report within a further period of six months.

The report or reports shall be made in duplicate, and one copy thereof shall be delivered to the Secretary of State of the United States, and one copy thereof to the Representative of Her Britannic Majesty at Washington.

All sums of money which may be awarded under this article shall be payable at Washington, in coin, within twelve months after the delivery of each report.

The Board of Assessors may employ such clerks as they shall think necessary.

The expenses of the Board of Assessors shall be borne equally by the two Governments, and paid from time to time, as may be found expedient, on the production of accounts certified by the Board. The remuneration of the Assessors shall also be paid by the two Governments in equal moieties in a similar manner.

Article XI.

The High Contracting Parties engage to consider the result of the proceedings of the Tribunal of Arbitration and of the Board of Assessors, should such Board be appointed, as a full, perfect, and final settlement of all the claims hereinbefore referred to; and further engage that every such claim, whether the same may or may not have been presented to the notice of, made, preferred, or laid before the Tribunal or Board, shall, from and after the conclusion of the proceedings of the Tribunal or Board, be considered and treated as finally settled, barred, and thenceforth inadmissible.

Article XII.

The High Contracting Parties agree that all claims on the part of corporations, companies, or private individuals, citizens of the United States, upon the Government of Her Britannic Majesty, arising out of acts committed against the persons or property of citizens of the United States during the period between the thirteenth of April, eighteen hundred and sixty-one, and the ninth of April, eighteen hundred and sixty-five, inclusive, not being claims growing out of the acts of the vessels referred to in Article I. of this Treaty, and all claims, with the like exception, on the part of corporations, companies, or private individuals, subjects of Her Britannic Majesty, upon the Government of the United States, arising out of acts committed against the persons or property of subjects of Her Britannic Majesty during the same period, which may have been presented to either Government for its interposition with the other, and which yet remain unsettled, as well as any other such claims which may be presented within the time specified in Article XIV. of this Treaty, shall be referred to three Commissioners, to be appointed in the following manner, that is to say: One Commissioner shall be named by the President of the United States, one by Her Britannic Majesty, and a third by the President of the of United States and Her Britannic Majesty conjointly; and in case the third Commissioner shall not have been so named within a period of three months from the date of the exchange of the ratifications of this Treaty, then the third Commissioner shall be named by the Representative at Washington of His Majesty the King of Spain. In case of the death, absence, or incapacity of any Commissioner, or in the event of any Commissioner omitting or ceasing to act, the vacancy shall be filled in the manner hereinbefore provided for making the original appointment; the period of three months in case of such substitution being calculated from the date of the happening of the vacancy.

The Commissioners so named shall meet at Washington at the earliest convenient period after they have been respectively named; and shall, before proceeding to any business, make and subscribe a solemn declaration that they will impartially and carefully examine and decide, to the best of their judgment, and according to justice and equity, all such claims as shall be laid before them on the part of the Governments of the United States and of Her Britannic Majesty, respectively; and such declaration shall be entered on the record of their proceedings.

Article XIII.

The Commissioners shall then forthwith proceed to the investigation of the claims which shall be presented to them. They shall investigate and decide such claims in such order and such manner as they may think proper, but upon such evidence or information only as shall be furnished by or on behalf of the respective Governments. They shall be bound to receive and consider all written documents or statements which may be presented to them by or on behalf of the respective Governments in support of, or in answer to, any claim, and to hear, if required, one person on each side, on behalf of each Government, as counsel or agent for such Government, on each and every separate claim. A majority of the Commissioners shall be sufficient for an award in each case. The award shall be given upon each claim in writing, and shall be signed by the Commissioners assenting to it. It shall be competent for each Government to name one person to attend the Commissioners as its agent, to present and support claims on its behalf, and to answer claims made upon it, and to represent it generally in all matters connected with the investigation and decision thereof.

The High Contracting Parties hereby engage to consider the decision of the Commissioners, as absolutely final and conclusive upon each claim decided upon by them, and to give full effect to such decisions without any objection, evasion, or delay whatsoever.

Article XIV.

Every claim shall be presented to the Commissioners within six months from the day of their first meeting, unless in any case where reasons for delay shall be established to the satisfaction of the Commissioners, and then, and in any such case, the period for presenting the claim may be extended by them to any time not exceeding three months longer.

The Commissioners shall be bound to examine and decide upon every claim within two years from the day of their first meeting. It shall be competent for the Commissioners to decide in each case whether any claim has or has not been duly made, preferred, and laid before them, either wholly or to any and what extent, according to the true intent and meaning of this Treaty.

Article XV.

All sums of money which may be awarded by the Commissioners on account of any claim shall be paid by the one Government to the other, as the case may be, within twelve months after the date of the final award, without interest, and without any deduction save as specified in Article XVI. of this Treaty.

Article XVI.

The Commissioners shall keep an accurate record and correct minutes or notes of all their proceedings, with the dates thereof, and may appoint and employ a secretary, and any other necessary officer or officers, to assist them in the transaction of the business which may come before them.

Each Government shall pay its own Commissioner and agent or counsel. All other expenses shall be defrayed by the two Governments in equal moieties.

The whole expenses of the Commission, including contingent expenses, shall be defrayed by a ratable deduction on the amount of the sums awarded by the Commissioners, provided always that such deduction shall not exceed the rate of five per cent, on the sums so awarded.

Article XVII.

The High Contracting Parties engage to consider the result of the proceedings of this Commission as a full, perfect, and final settlement of all such claims as are mentioned in Article XII. of this Treaty upon either Government; and further engage that every such claim, whether or not the same may have been presented to the notice of, made, preferred, or laid before the said Commission, shall, from and after the conclusion of the proceedings of the said Commission, be considered and treated as finally settled, barred, and thenceforth inadmissible.

Article XVIII.

It is agreed by the High Contracting Parties that, in addition to the liberty secured to the United States fishermen by the Convention between Great Britain and the United States, signed at London on the 20th day of October, 1818, of taking, curing, and drying fish on certain coasts of the British North American Colonies therein defined, the inhabitants of the United States shall have, in common with the subjects of Her Britannic Majesty, the liberty, for the term of years mentioned in Article XXXIII. of this Treaty, to take fish of every kind, except shell-fish, on the sea coasts and shores, and in the bays, harbors, and creeks, of the Provinces of Quebec, Nova Scotia, and New Brunswick, and the Colony of Prince Edward's Island, and of the several islands thereunto adjacent, without being restricted to any distance from the shore, with permission to land upon the said coasts and shores and islands, and also upon the Magdalen Islands, for the purpose of drying their nets and curing their fish; provided that, in so doing, they do not interfere with the rights of private property, or with British fishermen, in the peaceable use of any part of the said coasts in their occupancy for the same purpose.

It is understood that the above-mentioned liberty applies solely to the sea fishery, and that the Salmon and shad fisheries, and all other fisheries in rivers and the mouths of rivers, are hereby reserved exclusively for British fishermen.

Article XIX.

It is agreed by the High Contracting Parties that British subjects shall have, in common with the citizens of the United States, the liberty, for the terrm of years mentioned in Article XXXIII. of this Treaty, to take fish of every kind, except shellfish, on the eastern sea-coasts and shores of the United States north of the thirty-ninth parallel of north latitude, and on the shores of the several inlands thereunto adjacent, and in the bays, harbors, and creeks of the said sea-coasts and shores of the United States and of the said islands, without being restricted to any distance from the shore, with permission to land upon the said, coasts of the United States and of the Islands aforesaid for the purpose of drying their nets and curing their fish; provided that, in so doing, they do not interfere with the rights of private property, or with the fishermen of the United States, in the peaceable use of any part of the said coasts in their occupancy for the same purpose.

It is understood that the above-mentioned liberty applies solely to the sea fishery, and that salmon and shad fisheries and all other fisheries in rivers and mouths of rivers, are hereby reserved exclusively for fishermen of the United States.

Article XX.

It is agreed that the places designated by the Commissioners appointed under the First Article of the Treaty between Great Britain and the United States, concluded at Washington on the 5th of June, 1854, upon the coasts of Her Britannic Majesty's Dominions and the United States, as places reserved from the common right of fishing under that Treaty, shall be regarded as in like manner reserved from the common right of fishing under the preceding articles. In case any question should arise between the Governments of the United States and of Her Britannic Majesty as to the common right of fishing in places not thus designated as reserved, it is agreed that a Commission shall be appointed to designate such places and shall be constituted in the same manner, and have the same powers, duties, and authority as the Commission appointed under the said First Article of the Treaty of the 5th of June, 1854.

Article XXI.

It is agreed that, for the term of years mentioned in Article XXXIII. of this Treaty, fish-oil and fish of all kinds, (except fish of the inland lakes and of the rivers falling into them, and except fish preserved in oil), being the produce of the fisheries of the United States, or of the Dominion of Canada, or of Prince Edward's Island, shall be admitted into each country, respectively, free of duty.

Article XXII.

Inasmuch as it is asserted by the Government of Her Britannic Majesty that the privilege accorded to the citizens of the United States under Article XVIII. of this Treaty are of greater value than those accorded by Articles XIX. and XXI. of this Treaty to the subjects of Her Britannic Majesty, and this assertion is not admitted by the Government of the United States, it is further agreed that Commissioners shall be appointed to determine, having regard to the privileges accorded to the United States to the subjects of Her Britannic Majesty, as stated in Articles XIX. and XXI. of this Treaty, the amount of any compensation which, in their opinion, ought to be paid by the Government of the United States to the Government of Her Britannic Majesty in return for the privileges accorded to the citizens of the United States under Article XVIII. of this Treaty; and that any sum of money which the said Commissioners may so award shall be paid by the United States Government, in a gross sum, within twelve months after such award shall have been given.

Article XXIII.

The Commissioners referred to in the preceding article shall be appointed in the following manner, that is to say: One Commissioner shall be named by Her Britannic Majesty, one by the President of the United States and a third by Her Britannic Majesty and the President of the United States conjointly; and in case the third Commissioner shall not have been so named within a period' of three months from the date, when this article shall take effect, then the third Commissioner shall be named by the Representative at London of His Majesty the Emperor of Austria and King of Hungary. In case of the death, absence, or incapacity of any Commissioner, or in the event of any Commissioner omitting or ceasing to act, the vacancy shall be filled in the manner hereinbefore provided for making the original appointment, the period of three months in case of such substitution being calculated from the date of the happening of the vacancy.

The Commissioners so named shall meet in the City of Halifax, in the Province of Nova Scotia, at the earliest convenient period, after they have been respectively named, and shall, before proceeding to any business, make and subscribe a solemn declaration that they will impartially and carefully examine and decide the matters referred to them to the best of their judgment, and according to justice and equity; and such declaration shall be entered on the record of their proceedings.

Each of the High Contracting Parties shall also name one person to attend the Commission as its agent, to represent it generally in all matters connected with the Commission.

Article XXIV.

The proceedings shall be conducted in such order as the Commissioners appointed under Articles XXII. and XXIII. of this Treaty shall determine. They shall be bound to receive such oral or written testimony as either Government may present. If either Party shall offer oral testimony, the other Party shall have the right of cross-examination, under such rules as the Commissioners shall prescribe.

If in the case submitted to the Commissioners either Party shall have specified or alluded to any report or document in its own exclusive possession, without annexing a copy, such Party shall be bound, if the other Party thinks proper to apply for it, to furnish that Party with a copy thereof; and either Party may call upon the other, through the Commissioners, to produce the originals or certified copies of any papers adduced as evidence, giving in each instance such reasonable notice as the Commissioners may require.

The case on either side shall be closed within a period of six months from the date of the organization of the Commission, and the Commissioners shall be requested to give their award as soon as possible thereafter. The aforesaid period of six months may be extended for three months in case of a vacancy occurring among the Commissioners under the circumstances contemplated in Article XXIII. of this Treaty.

Article XXV.

The Commissioners shall keep an accurate record and correct minutes or notes of all their proceedings, with the dates thereof, and may appoint and employ a secretary and any other necessary officer or officers, to assist them in the transaction of the business which may come before them.

Each of the High Contracting Parties shall pay its own Commissioner and agent or counsel; all other expenses shall be defrayed by the two Governments in equal moieties.

Article XXVI.

The navigation of the river St. Lawrence, ascending and descending, from the forty-fifth parallel of north latitude, where it ceases to form the boundary between the two countries, from, to, and into the sea, shall forever remain free and open for purposes of commerce to the citizens of the United States, subject to any laws and regulations of Great Britain, or of the Dominion of Canada, not inconsistent with such privilege of free navigation.

The navigation of the Rivers Yukon, Porcupine, and Stikine, ascending and descending, from, to, and into the sea, shall forever remain free and open for the purposes of commerce to the subjects of Her Britannic Majesty and to the citizens of the United States, subject to any laws and regulations of either country within its own territory, not inconsistent with such privilege of free navigation.

Article XXVII.

The Government of Her Britannic Majesty engages to urge upon the Government of the Dominion of Canada to secure to the citizens of the United States the use of the Welland, St. Lawrence, and other canals in the Dominion on terms of equality with the inhabitants of the Dominion; and the Government of the United States engages that the subjects of Her Britannic Majesty shall enjoy the use of the St. Clair Flats' Canal on terms of equality with the inhabitants of the United States, and further engages to urge upon the State Governments to secure to the subjects of Her Britannic Majesty the use of the several State canals connected with the navigation of the lakes or rivers traversed by or contiguous to the boundary-line between the possessions of the High Contracting Parties, on terms of equality with the inhabitants of the United States.

Article XXVIII.

The navigation of Lake Michigan shall also, for the term of years mentioned in Article XXXIII. of this Treaty, be free and open for the purposes of commerce to the subjects of Her Britannic Majesty, subject to any laws and regulations of the United States or of the States bordering thereon not inconsistent with such privilege of free navigation.

Article XXIX.

It is agreed that, for the term of years mentioned in Article XXXIII. of this Treaty, goods, wares, or merchandise arriving at the ports of New York, Boston, and Portland, and any other ports in the United States which have been or may from time to time be specially designated by the President of the United States, and destined for Her Britannic Majesty's Possessions in North America, may be entered at the proper custom-house and conveyed in transit, without the payment of duties, through the territory of the United States, under such rules, regulations, and conditions, for the protection of the revenue as the Government of the United States may from time to time prescribe; and, under like rules, regulations, and conditions, goods, wares, or merchandise may be conveyed in transit, without the payment of duties, from such Possessions through the territory of the United States for export from the said ports of the United States.

It is further agreed that, for the like period, goods, wares, or merchandise arriving at any of the ports of Her Britannic Majesty's Possessions in North America and destined for the United States may be entered at the proper custom-house and conveyed in transit, without the payment of duties, through the said Possessions, under such rules, regulations, and conditions for the protection of the revenue as the Governments of the said Possessions may from time to time prescribe; and, under like rules, regulations, and conditions, goods, wares, or merchandise may be conveyed in transit, without payment of duties, from the United States through the said Possessions to other places in the United States, or for export from ports in the said Possessions.

Article XXX.

It is agreed that, for the term of years mentioned in Article XXXIII. of this Treaty, subjects of Her Britannic Majesty may carry in British vessels, without payment of duty, goods, wares, or merchandise from one port or place within the territory of the United States upon the St. Lawrence, the Great Lakes, and the rivers connecting the same, to another port or place within the territory of the United States as aforesaid: Provided, that a portion of such transportation is made through the Dominion of Canada by land carriage and in bond, under such rules and regulations as may be agreed upon between the Government of Her Britannic Majesty and the Government of the United States.

Citizens of the United States may for the like period carry in United States vessels, without payment of duty, goods, wares, or merchandise from one port or place within the Possessions of Her Britannic Majesty in North America, to another port or place within the said Possessions: Provided, that a portion of such transportation is made through the territory of the United States by land carriage, and in bond, under such rules and regulations as may be agreed upon between the Government of Her Britannic Majesty and the Government of the United States.

The Government of the United States further engages not to impose any export duties on goods, wares, or merchandise carried under this Article through the territory of the United States; and Her Majesty's Government engages to urge the Parliament of the Dominion of Canada and the Legislatures of the other Colonies not to impose any export duties on goods, wares, or merchandise carried under this Article; and the Government of the United States may, in case such export duties are imposed by the Dominion of Canada, suspend, during the period that such duties are imposed, the right of carrying granted under this article in favor of the subjects of Her Britannic Majesty.

The Government of the United States may suspend the right of carrying granted in favor of the subjects of Her Britannic Majesty under this article in case the Dominion of Canada should at any time deprive the citizens of the United States of the use of the canals in the said Dominion on terms of equality with the inhabitants of the Dominion, as provided in Article XXVII.

Article XXXI.

The Government of Her Britannic Majesty further engages to urge upon the Parliament of the Dominion of Canada and the Legislature of New Brunswick, that no export duty, or other duty, shall be levied on lumber or timber of any kind cut on that portion of the American territory in the State of Maine watered by the River St. John and its tributaries, and floated down that river to the sea, when the same is shipped to the United States from the Province of New Brunswick. And, in case any such export or other duty continues to be levied after the expiration of one year from the date of the exchange of the ratifications of this Treaty, it is agreed that the Government of the United States may suspend the right of carrying hereinbefore granted under Article XXX. of this Treaty for such period as such export or other duty may be levied.

Article XXXII.

It is further agreed that the provisions and stipulations of Articles XVII. to XXV. of this Treaty, inclusive, shall extend to the Colony of Newfoundland, so far as they are applicable. But if the Imperial Parliament, the Legislature of Newfoundland, or the Congress of the United States, shall not embrace the Colony of Newfoundland in their laws enacted for carrying the foregoing articles into effect, then this article shall be of no effect; but the omission to make provision by law to give it effect, by either of the legislative bodies aforesaid, shall not in any way impair any other articles of this Treaty.

Article XXXIII.

The foregoing Articles XVIII. to XXV., inclusive, and Article XXX., of this Treaty, shall take effect as soon as the laws required to carry them into operation shall have been passed by the Imperial Parliament of Great Britain by the Parliament of Canada, and by the Legislature of Prince Edward's Island on the one hand, and by the Congress of the United

States on the other. Such assent having been given, the said articles shall remain in force for the period of ten years from the date at which they may come into operation; and further until the expiration of two years after either of the High Contracting Parties shall have given notice to the other of its wish to terminate the same; each of the High Contracting Parties being at liberty to give such notice to the other at the end of the said period of ten years or at any time afterward.

Article XXXIV.

Whereas it was stipulated by Article I. of the Treaty concluded at Washington on the 15th of June, 1846, between the United States and Her Britannic Majesty, that the line of boundary between the territories of the United States and those of Her Britannic Majesty from the point on the forty-ninth parallel of north latitude up to which it had already been ascertained, should be continued westward along the said parallel of north latitude "to the middle of the channel which separates the continent from Vancouver's Island, and thence southerly through the middle of the said channel and of Fuca Straits, to the Pacific Ocean;" and whereas the Commissioners appointed by the two High Contracting Parties to determine that portion of the boundary which runs southerly through the middle of the channel aforesaid, were unable to agree upon the same; and whereas the Government of Her Britannic Majesty claims that such boundary-line should, under the terms of the Treaty above recited, be run through the Rosario Straits, and the Government of the United States claims that it should be run through the Canal de Haro, it is agreed that the respective claims of the Government of the United States and the Government of Her Britannic Majesty shall be submitted to the arbitration and award of His Majesty the Emperor of Germany, who, having regard to the above-mentioned article of the said Treaty, shall decide thereupon, finally and without appeal, which of those claims is most in accordance with the true interpretation of the Treaty of June 15, 1846.

Article XXXV.

The award of His Majesty the Emperor of Germany shall be considered as absolutely final and conclusive; and full effect shall be given to such award without any objection, evasion, or delay whatsoever. Such decision shall be given in writing and dated; it shall be in whatsoever form His Majesty may choose to adopt it shall be delivered to the Representatives or other public agents of the United States and of Great Britain, respectively, who may be actually at Berlin, and shall be considered as operative from the day of the date of the delivery thereof.

Article XXXVI.

The written or printed case of each of the two Parties, accompanied by the evidence offered in support of the same, shall be laid before His Majesty the Emperor of Germany within six months from the date of the exchange of the ratifications of this Treaty, and a copy of such case and evidence shall be communicated by each Party to the other, through their respective Representatives at Berlin.

The High Contracting Parties may include in the evidence to be considered by the Arbitrator such documents, official correspondence, and other official or public statements bearing on the subject of the reference as they may consider necessary to the support of their respective cases.

After the written or printed case shall have been communicated by each Party to the other, each Party shall have the power of drawing up and laying before the Arbitrator a second and definitive statement, if it think fit to do so, in reply to the case of the other party so communicated, which definitive statement shall be so laid before the Arbitrator, and also be mutually communicated in the same manner as aforesaid, by each Party to the other, within six months from the date of laying the first statement of the case before the Arbitrator.

Article XXXVII.

If, in the case submitted to the Arbitrator, either Party shall specify or allude to any report or document in its own exclusive possession without annexing a copy, such Party shall be bound, if the other Party thinks proper to apply for it, to furnish that Party with a copy thereof, and either Party may call upon the other, through the Arbitrator, to produce the originals or certified copies of any papers adduced as evidence, giving in each instance such reasonable notice as the Arbitrator may require. And if the Arbitrator should desire further elucidation or evidence with regard to any point contained in the statements laid before him, he shall be at liberty to require it from either Party, and he shall be at liberty to hear one counsel or agent for each Party, in relation to any matter, and at such time, and in such manner, as he may think fit.

Article XXXVIII.

The Representatives or other public Agents of Great Britain and of the United States at Berlin respectively shall be considered as the agents of their respective Governments to conduct their cases before the Arbitrator, who shall be requested to address all his communications, and give all his notices, to such Representatives or other public Agents, who shall represent their respective Governments generally in all matters connected with the arbitration.

Article XXXIX.

It shall be competent to the Arbitrator to proceed in the said arbitration, and all matters relating thereto, as and when he shall see fit, either in person, or by a person or persons named by him for that purpose, either in the presence or absence of either or both agents, and either orally or by written discussion or otherwise.

Article XL.

The Arbitrator may, if he think fit, appoint a secretary or clerk, for the purposes of the proposed arbitration, at such rate of remuneration as he shall think proper. This, and all other expenses of and connected with the said arbitration, shall be provided for as hereinafter stipulated.

Article XLI.

The Arbitrator shall be requested to deliver, together with his award, an account of all the costs and expenses which he may have been put to, in relation to this matter, which shall forthwith be repaid by the two Governments in equal moieties.

Article XLII.

The Arbitrator shall be requested to give his award in writing as early as convenient after the whole case on each side shall have been laid before him, and to deliver one copy thereof to each of the said agents.

Article XLIII.

The present Treaty shall be duly ratified by the President of the United States of America, by and with the advice and consent of the Senate thereof, and by Her Britannic Majesty; and the ratifications shall be exchanged either at Washington or at London within six months from the date thereof, or earlier if possible.

In faith whereof, we, the respective Plenipotentiaries, have signed this Treaty and have hereunto affixed our seals.

Done in duplicate at Washington the eighth day of May, in the year of our Lord one thousand eight hundred and seventy-one.

3 Convention for the Pacific Settlement of International Disputes (The 1907 Hague Convention on Pacific Settlement)*

Date: 18 October 1907
Source: JB Scott (ed), *The Hague Conventions and Declarations of 1899 and 1907* (1915) http://avalon.law.yale.edu/20th_century/pacific.asp

His Majesty the German Emperor, King of Prussia; the President of the United States of America ….

Animated by the sincere desire to work for the maintenance of general peace;

Resolved to promote by all the efforts in their power the friendly settlement of international disputes;

Recognizing the solidarity uniting the members of the society of civilized nations;

Desirous of extending the empire of law and of strengthening the appreciation of international justice;

Convinced that the permanent institution of a Tribunal of Arbitration accessible to all, in the midst of independent Powers, will contribute effectively to this result;

Having regard to the advantages attending the general and regular organization of the procedure of arbitration;

Sharing the opinion of the august initiator of the International Peace Conference that it is expedient to record in an International Agreement the principles of equity and right on which are based the security of States and the welfare of peoples;

Being desirous, with this object, of insuring the better working in practice of Commissions of Inquiry and Tribunals of Arbitration, and of facilitating recourse to arbitration in cases which allow of a summary procedure;

Have deemed it necessary to revise in certain particulars and to complete the work of the First Peace Conference for the pacific settlement of international disputes;

The High Contracting Parties have resolved to conclude a new Convention for this purpose, and have appointed the following as their Plenipotentiaries:

* N.B.: The 1907 Hague Convention expands upon the provisions of the Convention on the Pacific Settlement of International Disputes signed at the First Hague Peace Conference of 1899 (in: JB Scott (ed), *The Hague Conventions and Declarations of 1899 and 1907* [1915]; http://avalon.law.yale.edu/19th_century/hague01.asp), eg by providing more detailed provisions on commissions of inquiry and introducing the possibility of summary procedure. In most other respects, the two Conventions are identical.

[List of Plenipotentiaries]

Who, after deposited their full powers, found in good and due form, have agreed upon the following:

Part I. The maintenance of General Peace

Article 1

With a view to obviating as far as possible recourse to force in the relations between States, the Contracting Powers agree to use their best efforts to ensure the pacific settlement of international differences.

Part II. Good Offices and Mediation

Article 2

In case of serious disagreement or dispute, before an appeal to arms, the Contracting Powers agree to have recourse, as far as circumstances allow, to the good offices or mediation of one or more friendly Powers.

Article 3

Independently of this recourse, the Contracting Powers deem it expedient and desirable that one or more Powers, strangers to the dispute, should, on their own initiative and as far as circumstances may allow, offer their good offices or mediation to the States at variance.

Powers strangers to the dispute have the right to offer good offices or mediation even during the course of hostilities.

The exercise of this right can never be regarded by either of the parties in dispute as an unfriendly act.

Article 4

The part of the mediator consists in reconciling the opposing claims and appeasing the feelings of resentment which may have arisen between the States at variance.

Article 5

The functions of the mediator are at an end when once it is declared, either by one of the parties to the dispute or by the mediator himself, that the means of reconciliation proposed by him are not accepted.

Article 6

Good offices and mediation undertaken either at the request of the parties in dispute or on the initiative of Powers strangers to the dispute have exclusively the character of advice, and never have binding force.

Article 7

The acceptance of mediation cannot, unless there be an agreement to the contrary, have the effect of interrupting, delaying, or hindering mobilization or other measures of preparation for war.

If it takes place after the commencement of hostilities, the military operations in progress are not interrupted in the absence of an agreement to the contrary.

Article 8

The Contracting Powers are agreed in recommending the application, when circumstances allow, of special mediation in the following form:

In case of a serious difference endangering peace, the States at variance choose respectively a Power, to which they entrust the mission of entering into direct communication with the Power chosen on the other side, with the object of preventing the rupture of pacific relations.

For the period of this mandate, the term of which, unless otherwise stipulated, cannot exceed thirty days, the States in dispute cease from all direct communication on the subject of the dispute, which is regarded as referred exclusively to the mediating Powers, which must use their best efforts to settle it.

In case of a definite rupture of pacific relations, these Powers are charged with the joint task of taking advantage of any opportunity to restore peace.

Part III. International Commissions of Inquiry

Article 9

In disputes of an international nature involving neither honour nor vital interests, and arising from a difference of opinion on points of facts, the Contracting Powers deem it expedient and desirable that the parties who have not been able to come to an agreement by means of diplomacy, should, as far as circumstances allow, institute an International Commission of Inquiry, to facilitate a solution of these disputes by elucidating the facts by means of an impartial and conscientious investigation.

Article 10

International Commissions of Inquiry are constituted by special agreement between the parties in dispute.

The Inquiry convention defines the facts to be examined; it determines the mode and time in which the Commission is to be formed and the extent of the powers of the Commissioners.

It also determines, if there is need, where the Commission is to sit, and whether it may remove to another place, the language the Commission shall use and the languages the use of which shall be authorized before it, as well as the date on which each party must deposit its statement of facts, and, generally speaking, all the conditions upon which the parties have agreed.

If the parties consider it necessary to appoint Assessors, the Convention of Inquiry shall determine the mode of their selection and the extent of their powers.

Article 11

If the Inquiry Convention has not determined where the Commission is to sit, it will sit at The Hague.

The place of meeting, once fixed, cannot be altered by the Commission except with the assent of the parties.

If the Inquiry Convention has not determined what languages are to be employed, the question shall be decided by the Commission.

Article 12

Unless an undertaking is made to the contrary, Commissions of Inquiry shall be formed in the manner determined by Articles 45 and 57 of the present Convention.

Article 13

Should one of the Commissioners or one of the Assessors, should there be any, either die, or resign, or be unable for any reason whatever to discharge his functions, the same procedure is followed for filling the vacancy as was followed for appointing him.

Article 14

The parties are entitled to appoint special agents to attend the Commission of Inquiry, whose duty it is to represent them and to act as intermediaries between them and the Commission.

They are further authorized to engage counsel or advocates, appointed by themselves, to state their case and uphold their interests before the Commission.

Article 15

The International Bureau of the Permanent Court of Arbitration acts as registry for the Commissions which sit at The Hague, and shall place its offices and staff at the disposal of the Contracting Powers for the use of the Commission of Inquiry.

Article 16

If the Commission meets elsewhere than at The Hague, it appoints a Secretary-General, whose office serves as registry.

It is the function of the registry, under the control of the President, to make the necessary arrangements for the sittings of the Commission, the preparation of the Minutes, and, while the inquiry lasts, for the charge of the archives, which shall subsequently be transferred to the International Bureau at The Hague.

Article 17

In order to facilitate the constitution and working of Commissions of Inquiry, the Contracting Powers recommend the following rules, which shall be applicable to the inquiry procedure in so far as the parties do not adopt other rules.

Article 18

The Commission shall settle the details of the procedure not covered by the special Inquiry Convention or the present Convention, and shall arrange all the formalities required for dealing with the evidence.

Article 19

On the inquiry both sides must be heard.

At the dates fixed, each party communicates to the Commission and to the other party the statements of facts, if any, and, in all cases, the instruments, papers, and documents which it considers useful for ascertaining the truth, as well as the list of witnesses and experts whose evidence it wishes to be heard.

Article 20

The Commission is entitled, with the assent of the Powers, to move temporarily to any place where it considers it may be useful to have recourse to this means of inquiry or to send one or more of its members. Permission must be obtained from the State on whose territory it is proposed to hold the inquiry.

Article 21

Every investigation, and every examination of a locality, must be made in the presence of the agents and counsel of the parties or after they have been duly summoned.

Article 22

The Commission is entitled to ask from either party for such explanations and information as it considers necessary.

Article 23

The parties undertake to supply the Commission of Inquiry, as fully as they may think possible, with all means and facilities necessary to enable it to become completely acquainted with, and to accurately understand, the facts in question.

They undertake to make use of the means at their disposal, under their municipal law, to insure the appearance of the witnesses or experts who are in their territory and have been summoned before the Commission.

If the witnesses or experts are unable to appear before the Commission, the parties will arrange for their evidence to be taken before the qualified officials of their own country.

Article 24

For all notices to be served by the Commission in the territory of a third Contracting Power, the Commission shall apply direct to the Government of the said Power. The same rule applies in the case of steps being taken on the spot to procure evidence.

The requests for this purpose are to be executed so far as the means at the disposal of the Power applied to under its municipal law allow. They cannot be rejected unless the Power in question considers they are calculated to impair its sovereign rights or its safety.

The Commission will equally be always entitled to act through the Power on whose territory it sits.

Article 25

The witnesses and experts are summoned on the request of the parties or by the Commission of its own motion, and, in every case, through the Government of the State in whose territory they are.

The witnesses are heard in succession and separately in the presence of the agents and counsel, and in the order fixed by the Commission.

Article 26

The examination of witnesses is conducted by the President.

The members of the Commission may however put to each witness questions which they consider likely to throw light on and complete his evidence, or get information on any point concerning the witness within the limits of what is necessary in order to get at the truth.

The agents and counsel of the parties may not interrupt the witness when he is making his statement, nor put any direct question to him, but they may ask the President to put such additional questions to the witness as they think expedient.

Article 27

The witness must give his evidence without being allowed to read any written draft. He may, however, be permitted by the President to consult notes or documents if the nature of the facts referred to necessitates their employment.

Article 28

A Minute of the evidence of the witness is drawn up forthwith and read to the witness. The latter may make such alterations and additions as he thinks necessary, which will be recorded at the end of his statement.

When the whole of his statement has been read to the witness, he is asked to sign it.

Article 29

The agents are authorized, in the course of or at the close of the inquiry, to present in writing to the Commission and to the other party such statements, requisitions, or summaries of the facts as they consider useful for ascertaining the truth.

Article 30

The Commission considers its decisions in private and the proceedings are secret.

All questions are decided by a majority of the members of the Commission.

If a member declines to vote, the fact must be recorded in the Minutes.

Article 31

The sittings of the Commission are not public, nor the Minutes and documents connected with the inquiry published except in virtue of a decision of the Commission taken with the consent of the parties.

Article 32

After the parties have presented all the explanations and evidence, and the witnesses have all been heard, the President declares the inquiry terminated, and the Commission adjourns to deliberate and to draw up its Report.

Article 33

The Report is signed by all the members of the Commission.

If one of the members refuses to sign, the fact is mentioned; but the validity of the Report is not affected.

Article 34

The Report of the Commission is read at a public sitting, the agents and counsel of the parties being present or duly summoned.

A copy of the Report is given to each party.

Article 35

The Report of the Commission is limited to a statement of facts, and has in no way the character of an Award. It leaves to the parties entire freedom as to the effect to be given to the statement.

Article 36

Each party pays its own expenses and an equal share of the expenses incurred by the Commission.

Part IV. International Arbitration
Chapter I. The System of Arbitration

Article 37

International arbitration has for its object the settlement of disputes between States by Judges of their own choice and on the basis of respect for law.

Recourse to arbitration implies an engagement to submit in good faith to the Award.

Article 38

In questions of a legal nature, and especially in the interpretation or application of International Conventions, arbitration is recognized by the Contracting Powers as the most effective, and, at the same time, the most equitable means of settling disputes which diplomacy has failed to settle.

Consequently, it would be desirable that, in disputes about the above-mentioned questions, the Contracting Powers should, if the case arose, have recourse to arbitration, in so far as circumstances permit.

Article 39

The Arbitration Convention is concluded for questions already existing or for questions which may arise eventually.

It may embrace any dispute or only disputes of a certain category.

Article 40

Independently of general or private Treaties expressly stipulating recourse to arbitration as obligatory on the Contracting Powers, the said Powers reserve to themselves the right of concluding new Agreements, general or particular, with a view to extending compulsory arbitration to all cases which they may consider it possible to submit to it.

Chapter II. The Permanent Court of Arbitration

Article 41

With the object of facilitating an immediate recourse to arbitration for international differences, which it has not been possible to settle by diplomacy, the Contracting Powers undertake to maintain the Permanent Court of Arbitration, as established by the First Peace Conference, accessible at all times, and operating, unless otherwise stipulated by the parties, in accordance with the rules of procedure inserted in the present Convention.

Article 42

The Permanent Court is competent for all arbitration cases, unless the parties agree to institute a special Tribunal.

Article 43

The Permanent Court sits at The Hague.

An International Bureau serves as registry for the Court. It is the channel for communications relative to the meetings of the Court; it has charge of the archives and conducts all the administrative business.

The Contracting Powers undertake to communicate to the Bureau, as soon as possible, a certified copy of any conditions of arbitration arrived at between them and of any Award concerning them delivered by a special Tribunal.

They likewise undertake to communicate to the Bureau the laws, regulations, and documents eventually showing the execution of the Awards given by the Court.

Article 44

Each Contracting Power selects four persons at the most, of known competency in questions of international law, of the highest moral reputation, and disposed to accept the duties of Arbitrator.

The persons thus elected are inscribed, as Members of the Court, in a list which shall be notified to all the Contracting Powers by the Bureau.

Any alteration in the list of Arbitrators is brought by the Bureau to the knowledge of the Contracting Powers.

Two or more Powers may agree on the selection in common of one or more Members.

The same person can be selected by different Powers. The Members of the Court are appointed for a term of six years. These appointments are renewable.

Should a Member of the Court die or resign, the same procedure is followed for filling the vacancy as was followed for appointing him. In this case the appointment is made for a fresh period of six years.

Article 45

When the Contracting Powers wish to have recourse to the Permanent Court for the settlement of a difference which has arisen between them, the Arbitrators called upon to form the Tribunal with jurisdiction to decide this difference must be chosen from the general list of Members of the Court.

Failing the direct agreement of the parties on the composition of the Arbitration Tribunal, the following course shall be pursued:

Each party appoints two Arbitrators, of whom one only can be its national or chosen from among the persons selected by it as Members of the Permanent Court. These Arbitrators together choose an Umpire.

If the votes are equally divided, the choice of the Umpire is intrusted to a third Power, selected by the parties by common accord.

If an agreement is not arrived at on this subject each party selects a different Power, and the choice of the Umpire is made in concert by the Powers thus selected.

If, within two months' time, these two Powers cannot come to an agreement, each of them presents two candidates taken from the list of Members of the Permanent Court, exclusive of the members selected by the parties and not being nationals of either of them. Drawing lots determines which of the candidates thus presented shall be Umpire.

Article 46

The Tribunal being thus composed, the parties notify to the Bureau their determination to have recourse to the Court, the text of their '*Compromis*', and the names of the Arbitrators.

The Bureau communicates without delay to each Arbitrator the '*Compromis*', and the names of the other members of the Tribunal.

The Tribunal assembles at the date fixed by the parties. The Bureau makes the necessary arrangements for the meeting.

The members of the Tribunal, in the exercise of their duties and out of their own country, enjoy diplomatic privileges and immunities.

Article 47

The Bureau is authorized to place its offices and staff at the disposal of the Contracting Powers for the use of any special Board of Arbitration.

The jurisdiction of the Permanent Court may, within the conditions laid down in the regulations, be extended to disputes between non-Contracting Powers or between Contracting Powers and non-Contracting Powers, if the parties are agreed on recourse to this Tribunal.

Article 48

The Contracting Powers consider it their duty, if a serious dispute threatens to break out between two or more of them, to remind these latter that the Permanent Court is open to them.

Consequently, they declare that the fact of reminding the parties at variance of the provisions of the present Convention, and the advice given to them, in the highest interests of peace, to have recourse to the Permanent Court, can only be regarded as friendly actions.

In case of dispute between two Powers, one of them can always address to the International Bureau a note containing a declaration that it would be ready to submit the dispute to arbitration.

The Bureau must at once inform the other Power of the declaration.

Article 49

The Permanent Administrative Council, composed of the Diplomatic Representatives of the Contracting Powers accredited to The Hague and of the Netherland Minister for Foreign Affairs, who will act as President, is charged with the direction and control of the International Bureau.

The Council settles its rules of procedure and all other necessary regulations.

It decides all questions of administration which may arise with regard to the operations of the Court.

It has entire control over the appointment, suspension, or dismissal of the officials and employees of the Bureau.

It fixes the payments and salaries, and controls the general expenditure.

At meetings duly summoned the presence of nine members is sufficient to render valid the discussions of the Council. The decisions are taken by a majority of votes.

The Council communicates to the Contracting Powers without delay the regulations adopted by it. It furnishes them with an annual Report on the labours of the Court, the working of the administration, and the expenditure. The Report likewise contains a résumé of what is important in the documents comunicated to the Bureau by the Powers in virtue of Article 43, paragraphs 3 and 4.

Article 50

The expenses of the Bureau shall be borne by the Contracting Powers in the proportion fixed for the International Bureau of the Universal Postal Union.

The expenses to be charged to the adhering Powers shall be reckoned from the date on which their adhesion comes into force.

Chapter III. Arbitration Procedure

Article 51

With a view to encouraging the development of arbritation, the Contracting Powers have agreed on the following rules, which are applicable to arbitration procedure, unless other rules have been agreed on by the parties.

Article 52

The Powers which have recourse to arbitration sign a '*Compromis*', in which the subject of the dispute is clearly defined, the time allowed for appointing Arbitrators, the form, order, and time in which the communication referred to in Article 63 must be made, and the amount of the sum which each party must deposit in advance to defray the expenses.

The '*Compromis*' likewise defines, if there is occasion, the manner of appointing Arbitrators, any special powers which may eventually belong to the Tribunal, where it shall meet, the language it shall use, and the languages the employment of which shall be authorized before it, and, generally speaking, all the conditions on which the parties are agreed.

Article 53

The Permanent Court is competent to settle the '*Compromis*', if the parties are agreed to have recourse to it for the purpose.

It is similarly competent, even if the request is only made by one of the parties, when all attempts to reach an understanding through the diplomatic channel have failed, in the case of:

1. A dispute covered by a general Treaty of Arbitration concluded or renewed after the present Convention has come into force, and providing for a '*Compromis*' in all disputes and not either explicitly or implicitly excluding the settlement of the '*Compromis*' from the competence of the Court. Recourse cannot, however, be had to the Court if the other party declares that in its opinion the dispute does not belong to the category of disputes which can be submitted to compulsory arbitration, unless the Treaty of Arbitration confers upon the Arbitration Tribunal the power of deciding this preliminary question.

2. A dispute arising from contract debts claimed from one Power by another Power as due to its nationals, and for the settlement of which the offer of arbitration has been accepted. This arrangement is not applicable if acceptance is subject to the condition that the '*Compromis*' should be settled in some other way.

Article 54

In the cases contemplated in the preceding Article, the '*Compromis*' shall be settled by a Commission consisting of five members selected in the manner arranged for in Article 45, paragraphs 3 to 6.

The fifth member is President of the Commission *ex officio*.

Article 55

The duties of Arbitrator may be conferred on one Arbitrator alone or on several Arbitrators selected by the parties as they please, or chosen by them from the Members of the Permanent Court of Arbitration established by the present Convention.

Failing the constitution of the Tribunal by direct agreement between the parties, the course referred to in Article 45, paragraphs 3 to 6, is followed.

Article 56

When a Sovereign or the Chief of a State is chosen as Arbitrator, the arbitration procedure is settled by him.

Article 57

The Umpire is President of the Tribunal *ex officio*.

When the Tribunal does not include an Umpire, it appoints its own President.

Article 58

When the '*Compromis*' is settled by a Commission, as contemplated in Article 54, and in the absence of an agreement to the contrary, the Commission itself shall form the Arbitration Tribunal.

Article 59

Should one of the Arbitrators either die, retire, or be unable for any reason whatever to discharge his functions, the same procedure is followed for filling the vacancy as was followed for appointing him.

Article 60

The Tribunal sits at The Hague, unless some other place is selected by the parties.

The Tribunal can only sit in the territory of a third Power with the latter's consent.

The place of meeting once fixed cannot be altered by the Tribunal, except with the consent of the parties.

Article 61

If the question as to what languages are to be used has not been settled by the '*Compromis*', it shall be decided by the Tribunal.

Article 62

The parties are entitled to appoint special agents to attend the Tribunal to act as intermediaries between themselves and the Tribunal.

They are further authorized to retain for the defence of their rights and interests before the Tribunal counsel or advocates appointed by themselves for this purpose.

The Members of the permanent Court may not act as agents, counsel, or advocates except on behalf of the Power which appointed them Members of the Court.

Article 63

As a general rule, arbitration procedure comprises two distinct phases: pleadings and oral discussions.

The pleadings consist in the communication by the respective agents to the members of the Tribunal and the opposite party of cases, counter-cases, and, if necessary, of replies; the parties annex thereto all papers and documents called for in the case. This communication shall be made either directly or through the intermediary of the International Bureau, in the order and within the time fixed by the '*Compromis*'.

The time fixed by the '*Compromis*' may be extended by mutual agreement by the parties, or by the Tribunal when the latter considers it necessary for the purpose of reaching a just decision.

The discussions consists in the oral development before the Tribunal of the arguments of the parties.

Article 64

A certified copy of every document produced by one party must be communicated to the other party.

Article 65

Unless special circumstances arise, the Tribunal does not meet until the pleadings are closed.

Article 66

The discussions are under the control of the President. They are only public if it be so decided by the Tribunal, with the assent of the parties.

They are recorded in minutes drawn up by the Secretaries appointed by the President. These minutes are signed by the President and by one of the Secretaries and alone have an authentic character.

Article 67

After the close of the pleadings, the Tribunal is entitled to refuse discussion of all new papers or documents which one of the parties may wish to submit to it without the consent of the other party.

Article 68

The Tribunal is free to take into consideration new papers of documents to which its attention may be drawn by the agents or counsel of the parties.

In this case, the Tribunal has the right to require the production of these papers or documents, but is obliged to make them known to the opposite party.

Article 69

The Tribunal can, besides, require from the agents of the parties the production of all papers, and can demand all necessary explanations. In case of refusal the Tribunal takes note of it.

Article 70

The agents and the counsel of the parties are authorized to present orally to the Tribunal all the arguments they may consider expedient in defence of their case.

Article 71

They are entitled to raise objections and points. The decisions of the Tribunal on these points are final and cannot form the subject of any subsequent discussion.

Article 72

The members of the Tribunal are entitled to put questions to the agents and counsel of the parties, and to ask them for explanations on doubtful points.

Neither the questions put, nor the remarks made by members of the Tribunal in the course of the discussions, can be regarded as an expression of opinion by the Tribunal in general or by its members in particular.

Article 73

The Tribunal is authorized to declare its competence in interpreting the '*Compromis*', as well as the other Treaties which may be invoked, and in applying the principles of law.

Article 74

The Tribunal is entitled to issue rules of procedure for the conduct of the case, to decide the forms, order, and time in which each party must conclude its arguments, and to arrange all the formalities required for dealing with the evidence.

Article 75

The parties undertake to supply the Tribunal, as fully as they consider possible, with all the information required for deciding the case.

Article 76

For all notices which the Tribunal has to serve in the territory of a third Contracting Power, the Tribunal shall apply direct to the Government of that Power. The same rule applies in the case of steps being taken to procure evidence on the spot.

The requests for this purpose are to be executed as far as the means at the disposal of the Power applied to under its municipal law allow. They cannot be rejected unless the Power in question considers them calculated to impair its own sovereign rights or its safety.

The Court will equally be always entitled to act through the Power on whose territory it sits.

Article 77

When the agents and counsel of the parties have submitted all the explanations and evidence in support of their case the President shall declare the discussion closed.

Article 78

The Tribunal considers its decisions in private and the proceedings remain secret.

All questions are decided by a majority of the members of the Tribunal.

Article 79

The Award must give the reasons on which it is based. It contains the names of the Arbitrators; it is signed by the President and Registrar or by the Secretary acting as Registrar.

Article 80

The Award is read out in public sitting, the agents and counsel of the parties being present or duly summoned to attend.

Article 81

The Award, duly pronounced and notified to the agents of the parties, settles the dispute definitively and without appeal.

Article 82

Any dispute arising between the parties as to the interpretation and execution of the Award shall, in the absence of an Agreement to the contrary, be submitted to the Tribunal which pronounced it.

Article 83

The parties can reserve in the '*Compromis*' the right to demand the revision of the Award.

In this case and unless there be an Agreement to the contrary, the demand must be addressed to the Tribunal which pronounced the Award. It can only be made on the ground of the discovery of some new fact calculated to exercise a decisive influence upon the Award and which was unknown to the Tribunal and to the party which demanded the revision at the time the discussion was closed.

Proceedings for revision can only be instituted by a decision of the Tribunal expressly recording the existence of the new fact, recognizing in it the character described in the preceding paragraph, and declaring the demand admissible on this ground.

The 'Compromis' fixes the period within which the demand for revision must be made.

Article 84

The Award is not binding except on the parties in dispute.

When it concerns the interpretation of a Convention to which Powers other than those in dispute are parties, they shall inform all the Signatory Powers in good time. Each of these Powers is entitled to intervene in the case. If one or more avail themselves of this right, the interpretation contained in the Award is equally binding on them.

Article 85

Each party pays its own expenses and an equal share of the expenses of the Tribunal.

Chapter IV. Arbitration by Summary Procedure

Article 86

With a view to facilitating the working of the system of arbitration in disputes admitting of a summary procedure, the Contracting Powers adopt the following rules, which shall be observed in the absence of other arrangements and subject to the reservation that the provisions of Chapter III apply so far as may be.

Article 87

Each of the parties in dispute appoints an Arbitrator. The two Arbitrators thus selected choose an Umpire. If they do not agree on this point, each of them proposes two candidates taken from the general list of the Members of the Permanent Court exclusive of the members appointed by either of the parties and not being nationals of either of them; which of the candidates thus proposed shall be the Umpire is determined by lot.

The Umpire presides over the Tribunal, which gives its decisions by a majority of votes.

Article 88

In the absence of any previous agreement the Tribunal, as soon as it is formed, settles the time within which the two parties must submit their respective cases to it.

Article 89

Each party is represented before the Tribunal by an agent, who serves as intermediary between the Tribunal and the Government who appointed him.

Article 90

The proceedings are conducted exclusively in writing. Each party, however, is entitled to ask that witnesses and experts should be called. The Tribunal has, for its part, the right to demand oral explanations from the agents of the two parties, as well as from the experts and witnesses whose appearance in Court it may consider useful.

Part V. Final Provisions

Article 91

The present Convention, duly ratified, shall replace, as between the Contracting Powers, the Convention for the Pacific Settlement of International Disputes of the 29th July, 1899.

Article 92

The present Convention shall be ratified as soon as possible.

The ratifications shall be deposited at The Hague.

The first deposit of ratifications shall be recorded in a procès-verbal signed by the Representatives of the Powers which take part therein and by the Netherland Minister for Foreign Affairs.

The subsequent deposits of ratifications shall be made by means of a written notification, addressed to the Netherland Government and accompanied by the instrument of ratification.

A duly certified copy of the procès-verbal relative to the first deposit of ratifications, of the notifications mentioned in the preceding paragraph, and of the instruments of ratification, shall be immediately sent by the Netherland Government, through the diplomatic channel, to the Powers invited to the Second Peace Conference, as well as to those Powers which have adhered to the Convention. In the cases contemplated in the preceding paragraph, the said Government shall at the same time inform the Powers of the date on which it received the notification.

Article 93

Non-Signatory Powers which have been invited to the Second Peace Conference may adhere to the present Convention.

The Power which desires to adhere notifies its intention in writing to the Netherland Government, forwarding to it the act of adhesion, which shall be deposited in the archives of the said Government.

This Government shall immediately forward to all the other Powers invited to the Second Peace Conference a duly certified copy of the notification as well as of the act of adhesion, mentioning the date on which it received the notification.

Article 94

The conditions on which the Powers which have not been invited to the Second Peace Conference may adhere to the present Convention shall form the subject of a subsequent Agreement between the Contracting Powers.

Article 95

The present Convention shall take effect, in the case of the Powers which were not a party to the first deposit of ratifications, sixty days after the date of the procès-verbal of this deposit, and, in the case of the Powers which ratify subsequently or which adhere, sixty days after the notification of their ratification or of their adhesion has been received by the Netherland Government.

Article 96

In the event of one of the Contracting Parties wishing to denounce the present Convention, the denunciation shall be notified in writing to the Netherland Government, which shall immediately communicate a duly certified copy of the notification to all the other Powers informing them of the date on which it was received.

The denunciation shall only have effect in regard to the notifying Power, and one year after the notification has reached the Netherland Government.

Article 97

A register kept by the Netherland Minister for Foreign Affairs shall give the date of the deposit of ratifications effected in virtue of Article 92, paragraphs 3 and 4, as well as the date on which the notifications of adhesion (Article 93, paragraph 2) or of denunciation (Article 96, paragraph 1) have been received.

Each Contracting Power is entitled to have access to this register and to be supplied with duly certified extracts from it.

In faith whereof the Plenipotentiaries have appended their signatures to the present Convention.

Done at The Hague, the 18th October 1907, in a single copy, which shall remain deposited in the archives of the Netherland Government, and duly certified copies of which shall be sent, through the diplomatic channel, to the Contracting Powers.

4 Convention for the Establishment of a Central American Court of Justice

Date: 20 December 1907
Source: (1908) 2 American Journal of International Law (Suppl) 231

Preamble

The Governments of the Republics of Costa Rica, Guatemala, Honduras, Nicaragua and Salvador, for the purpose of efficaciously guaranteeing their rights and maintaining peace and harmony inalterably in their relations, without being obliged to resort in any case to the employment of force, have agreed to conclude a Convention for the constitution of a Court of Justice charged with accomplishing such high aims, and, to that end, have named as Delegates:

[Names of delegates.]

Article I.

The High Contracting Parties agree by the present Convention to constitute and maintain a permanent tribunal which shall be called the "Central American Court of Justice," to which they bind themselves to submit all controversies or questions which may arise among them, of whatsoever nature and no matter what their origin may be, in case the respective Departments of Foreign Affairs should not have been able to reach an understanding.

Article II.

This Court shall also take cognizance of the questions which individuals of one Central American country may raise against any of the other contracting Governments, because of the violation of treaties or conventions, and other cases of an international character; no matter whether their own Government supports said claim or not; and provided that the remedies which the laws of the respective country provide against such violation shall have been exhausted or that denial of justice shall have been shown.

Article III.

It shall also take cognizance of the cases which by common accord the contracting Governments may submit to it, no matter whether they arise between two or more of them or between one of said Governments and individuals.

It shall also have jurisdiction over cases arising between any of the Contracting Governments and individuals, when by common accord they are submitted to it.

Article IV.

The Court can likewise take cognizance of the international questions which by special agreement any one of the Central American Governments and a foreign Governments may have determined to submit to it.

Article V.

The Central American Court of Justice shall sit at the City of Cartago in the Republic of Costa Rica, but it may temporarily transfer its residence to another point in Central America whenever it deems it expedient for reasons of health, or in order to insure the exercise of its functions, or of the personal safety of its members.

Article VI.

The Central American Court of Justice shall consist of five Justices, one being appointed by each Republic and selected from among the jurists who possess the qualifications which the laws of each country prescribe for the exercise of high judicial office, and who enjoy the highest consideration, both because of their moral character and their professional ability.

Vacancies shall be filled by substitute Justices, named at the same time and in the same manner as the regular Justices and who shall unite the same qualifications as the latter.

The attendance of the five justices who constitute the Tribunal is indispensable in order to make a legal quorum in the decisions of the Court.

Article VII.

The Legislative Power of each one of the five contracting Republics shall appoint their respective Justices, one regular and two substitutes.

The salary of each Justice shall be eight thousand dollars, gold, per annum, which shall be paid them by the Treasury of the Court. The salary of the Justice of the country where the Court resides shall be fixed by the Government thereof. Furthermore each State shall contribute two thousand dollars, gold, annually toward the ordinary and extraordinary expenses of the Tribunal. The Governments of the contracting Republics bind themselves to include their respective contributions in their estimates of expenses and to remit quarterly in advance to the Treasury of the Court the share they may have to bear on account of such services.

Article VIII.

The regular and substitute Justices shall be appointed for a term of five years, which shall be counted from the day on which they assume the duties of their office, and they may be reelected.

In case of death, resignation or permanent incapacity of any of them, the vacancy shall be filled by the respective Legislature, and the Justice elected shall complete the term of his predecessor.

Article IX.

The regular and substitute Justices shall take oath or make affirmation prescribed by law before the authority that may have appointed them, and from that moment they shall enjoy the immunities and prerogatives which the present Convention confers upon them. The regular Justices shall likewise enjoy thenceforth the salary fixed in Article VII.

Article X.

Whilst they remain in the country of their appointment the regular and substitute Justices shall enjoy the personal immunity which the respective laws grant to the magistrates of the Supreme Court of Justice, and in the other contracting Republics they shall have the privileges and immunities of Diplomatic Agents.

Article XI.

The office of Justice whilst held is incompatible with the exercise of his profession, and with the holding of public office. The same incompatibility applies to the substitute Justices so long as they may actually perform their duties.

Article XII.

At its first annual session the Court shall elect from among its own members a President and Vice-President; it shall organize the personnel of its office by designating a Clerk, a Treasurer, and such other subordinate employees as it may deem necessary, and it shall draw up the estimate of its expenses.

Article XIII.

The Central American Court of Justice represents the national conscience of Central America, wherefore the Justices who compose the Tribunal shall not consider themselves barred from the discharge of their duties because of the interest which the Republics, to which they owe their appointment, may have in any case or question. With regard to allegations of personal interest, the rules of procedure which the Court may fix, shall make proper provision.

Article XIV.

When differences or questions subject to the jurisdiction of the Tribunal arise, the interested party shall present a complaint which shall comprise all the points of fact and law relative to the matter, and all pertinent evidence. The Tribunal shall communicate without loss of time a copy of the complaint to the Governments or individuals interested, and shall invite them to furnish their allegations and evidence within the term that it may designate to them, which, in no case, shall exceed sixty days counted from the date of notice of the complaint.

Article XV.

If the term designated shall have expired without answer having been made to the complaint, the Court shall require the complainant or complainants to do so within a further term not to exceed twenty days, after the expiration of which and in view of the evidence presented and of such evidence as it may *ex officio* have seen fit to obtain, the Tribunal shall render its decision in the case, which decision shall be final.

Article XVI.

If the Government, Governments, or individuals sued shall have appeared in time before the Court, presenting their allegations and evidence, the Court shall decide the matter within thirty days following, without further process or proceedings; but if a new term for the presentation of evidence be solicited, the Court shall decide whether or not there is occasion to grant it; and in the affirmative it shall fix therefore a reasonable time. Upon the expiration of such term, the Court shall pronounce its final judgment within thirty days.

Article XVII.

Each one of the Governments or individuals directly concerned in the questions to be considered by the Court has the right to be represented before it by a trustworthy person or persons, who shall present evidence, formulate arguments, and shall, within the terms fixed by this Convention and by the rules of the Court of Justice do everything that in their judgment shall be beneficial to the defense of the rights they represent.

Article XVIII.

From the moment in which any suit is instituted against any one or more governments up to that in which a final decision has been pronounced, the court may at the solicitation of any one of the parties fix the situation in which the contending parties must remain, to the end that the difficulty shall not be aggravated and that things shall be conserved in *statu quo* pending a final decision.

Article XIX.

For all the effects of this Convention, the Central American Court of Justice may address itself to the Governments or tribunals of justice of the contracting States, through the medium of the Ministry of Foreign Relations or the office of the Clerk of the Supreme Court of Justice of the respective country, according to the nature of the requisite proceeding, in order to have the measures that it may dictate within the scope of its jurisdiction carried out.

Article XX.

It may also appoint special commissioners to carry out the formalities above referred to, when it deems it expedient for their better fulfillment. In such case, it shall ask of the Government where the proceeding is to be had, its cooperation and assistance, in order that the Commissioner may fulfill his mission. The contracting Governments formally bind themselves to obey and to enforce the orders of the Court, furnishing all the assistance that may be necessary for their best and most expeditious fulfillment.

Article XXI.

In deciding points of fact that may be raised before it, the Central American Court of Justice shall be governed by its free judgment, and with respect to points of law, by the principles of international law. The final judgment shall cover each one of the points in litigation.

Article XXII.

The Court is competent to determine its jurisdiction, interpreting the Treaties and Conventions germane to the matter in dispute, and applying the principles of international law.

Article XXIII.

Every final or interlocutory decision shall be rendered with the concurrence of at least three of the Justices of the Court. In case of disagreement, one of the substitute Justices shall be chosen by lot, and if still a majority of three be not thus obtained other Justices shall be successively chosen by lot until three uniform votes shall have been obtained.

Article XXIV.

The decisions must be in writing and shall contain a statement of the reasons upon which they are based. They must be signed by all the Justices of the Court and countersigned by the Clerk. Once they have been notified they can not be altered on any account; but, at the request of any of the parties, the Tribunal may declare the interpretation which must be given to its judgments.

Article XXV.

The judgments of the Court shall be communicated to the five Governments of the contracting Republics. The interested parties solemnly bind themselves to submit to said judgments, and all agree to lend all moral support that may be necessary in order that they may be properly fulfilled, thereby constituting a real and positive guarantee of respect for this Convention and for the Central American Court of Justice.

Article XXVI.

The Court is empowered to make its rules, to formulate the rules of procedure which may be necessary, and to determine the forms and terms not prescribed in the present Convention. All the decisions which may be rendered in this respect shall be communicated immediately to the High Contracting Parties.

Article XXVII.

The High Contracting Parties solemnly declare that on no ground nor in any case will they consider the present Convention as void; and that, therefore, they will consider it as being always in force during the term of ten years counted from the last ratification. In the event of the change or alteration of the political status of one or more of the Contracting Republics, the functions of the Central American Court of Justice created by this Convention shall be suspended *ipso facto*; and a conference to adjust the constitution of said Court to the new order of things shall be forthwith convoked by the respective Governments; in case they do not unanimously agree the present Convention shall be considered as rescinded.

Article XXVIII.

The exchange of ratifications of the present Convention shall be made in accordance with Article XXI of the General Treaty of Peace and Amity concluded on this date.

Provisional Article.

As recommended by the five Delegations an Article is annexed which contains an amplification of the jurisdiction of the Central American Court of Justice, in order that the Legislatures may, if they see fit, include it in this Convention upon ratifying it.

Annexed Article.

The Central American Court of Justice shall also have jurisdiction over the conflicts which may arise between the Legislative, Executive and Judicial Powers, and when as a matter of fact the judicial decisions and resolutions of the National Congress are not respected.

Signed at the city of Washington on the twentieth day of December, one thousand nine hundred and seven.

5 General Act (Pacific Settlement of International Disputes)*

Date: 26 September 1928
Source: 93 LNTS 344

CHAPTER I.
Conciliation.

Article 1.

Disputes of every kind between two or more Parties to the present General Act which it has not been possible to settle by diplomacy shall, subject to such reservations as may be made under Article 39, be submitted, under the conditions laid down in the present Chapter, to the procedure of conciliation.

Article 2.

The disputes referred to in the preceding article shall be submitted to a permanent or special Conciliation Commission constituted by the parties to the dispute.

Article 3.

On a request to that effect being made by one of the Contracting Parties to another Party, a permanent Conciliation Commission shall be constituted within a period of six months.

Article 4.

Unless the parties concerned agree otherwise, the Conciliation Commission shall be constituted as follows:

* N.B.: In 1949, the UN General Assembly 'instruct[ed] the Secretary-General to prepare a revised text of the [1928] General Act … and to hold it open to accession by States, under the title "Revised General Act for the Pacific Settlement of International Disputes" (GA Res 268 [III]). The 'Revised Act', which—but for references to UN organs—is almost identical to the initial General Act included here, can be found in 71 UNTS 101.

(1) The Commission shall be composed of five members. The parties shall each nominate one commissioner, who must be chosen from among their respective nationals. The three other commissioners shall be appointed by agreement from among the nationals of third Powers. These three commissioners must be of different nationalities and must not be habitually resident in the territory nor be in the service of the parties. The parties shall appoint the President of the Commission from among them.

(2) The commissioners shall be appointed for three years. They shall be re-eligible. The commissioners appointed jointly may be replaced during the course of their mandate by agreement between the parties. Either party may, however, at any time replace a commissioner whom it has appointed. Even if replaced, the commissioners shall continue to exercise their functions until the termination of the work in hand.

(3) Vacancies which may occur as a result of death, resignation or any other cause shall be filled within the shortest possible time in the manner fixed for the nominations.

Article 5.

If, when a dispute arises, no permanent Conciliation Commission appointed by the parties is in existence, a special commission shall be constituted for the examination of the dispute within a period of three months from the date at which a request to that effect is made by one of the parties to the other party. The necessary appointments shall be made in the manner laid down in the preceding article, unless the parties decide otherwise.

Article 6.

1. If the appointment of the commissioners to be designated jointly is not made within the periods provided for in Articles 3 and 5, the making of the necessary appointments shall be entrusted to a third Power, chosen by agreement between the parties, or on request of the parties, to the Acting President of the Council of the League of Nations.

2. If no agreement is reached on either of these procedures, each party shall designate a different Power, and the appointment shall be made in concert by the Powers thus chosen.

3. If, within a period of three months, the two Powers have been unable to reach an agreement, each of them shall submit a number of candidates equal to the number of members to be appointed. It shall then be decided by lot which of the candidates thus designated shall be appointed.

Article 7.

1. Disputes shall be brought before the Conciliation Commission by means of an application addressed to the President by the two parties acting in agreement, or in default thereof by one or other of the parties.

2. The application, after giving a summary account of the subject of the dispute, shall contain the invitation to the Commission to take all necessary measures with a view to arriving at an amicable solution.

3. If the application emanates from only one of the parties, the other party shall, without delay, be notified by it.

Article 8.

1. Within fifteen days from the date on which a dispute has been brought by one of the parties before a permanent Conciliation Commission, either party may replace its own commissioner, for the examination of the particular dispute, by a person possessing special competence in the matter.

2. The party making use of the right shall immediately notify the other party; the latter shall, in such case, be entitled to take similar action within fifteen days from the date on which it received the notification.

Article 9.

1. In the absence of agreement to the contrary between the parties, the Conciliation Commission shall meet at the seat of the League of Nations, or at some other place selected by its President.

2. The Commission may in all circumstances request the Secretary-General of the League of Nations to afford it his assistance.

Article 10.

The work of the Conciliation Commission shall not be conducted in public unless a decision to that effect is taken by the Commission with the consent of the parties.

Article 11.

1. In the absence of agreement to the contrary between the parties, the Conciliation Commission shall lay down its own procedure, which in any case must provide for both parties being heard. In regard to enquiries, the Commission, unless it decides unanimously to the contrary, shall act in accordance with the provisions of Part III of the Hague Convention of October 18, 1907, for the Pacific Settlement of International Disputes.

2. The parties shall be represented before the Conciliation Commission by agents, whose duty shall be to act as intermediaries between them and the Commission; they may, moreover, be assisted by counsel and experts appointed by them for that purpose and may request that all persons whose evidence appears to them desirable shall be heard.

3. The Commission, for its part, shall be entitled to request oral explanations from the agents, counsel and experts of both parties, as well as from all persons it may think desirable to summon with the consent of their governments.

Article 12.

In the absence of agreement to the contrary between the parties, the decisions of the Conciliation Commission shall be taken by a majority vote, and the Commission may only take decisions on the substance of the dispute if all its members are present.

Article 13.

The parties undertake to facilitate the work of the Conciliation Commission, and particularly to supply it to the greatest possible extent with all the relevant documents and information, as well as to use the means at their disposal to allow it to proceed in their territory, and in accordance with their law, to the summoning and hearing of witnesses or experts and to visit the localities in question.

Article 14.

1. During the proceedings of the Commission, each of the commissioners shall receive emoluments the amount of which shall be fixed by agreement between the parties, each of which shall contribute an equal share.

2. The general expenses arising out of the working of the Commission shall be divided in the same manner.

Article 15.

1. The task of the Conciliation Commission shall be to elucidate the questions in dispute, to collect with that object all necessary information by means of enquiry or otherwise, and to endeavour to bring the parties to an agreement. It may, after the case has been examined, inform the parties of the terms of settlement which seem suitable to it, and lay down the period within which they are to make their decisions.

2. At the close of the proceedings the Commission shall draw up a procès-verbal stating, as the case may be, either that the parties have come to an agreement and, if need arises, the terms of the agreement, or that it has been impossible to effect a settlement. No mention shall be made in the procès-verbal of whether the Commission's decisions were taken unanimously or by a majority vote.

3. The proceedings of the Commission must, unless the parties otherwise agree, be terminated within six months from the date on which the Commission shall have been given cognizance of the dispute.

Article 16.

The Commission's procès-verbal shall be communicated without delay to the parties. The parties shall decide whether it shall be published.

CHAPTER II.
Judicial Settlement.

Article 17.

All disputes with regard to which the parties are in conflict as to their respective rights shall, subject to any reservations which may be made under Article 39, be submitted for decision to the Permanent Court of International Justice, unless the parties agree, in the manner hereinafter provided, to have resort to an arbitral tribunal.

It is understood that the disputes referred to above include in particular those mentioned in Article 36 of the Statute of the Permanent Court of International Justice.

Article 18.

If the parties agree to submit the disputes mentioned in the preceding article to an arbitral tribunal, they shall draw up a special agreement in which they shall specify the subject of the dispute, the arbitrators selected, and the procedure to be followed. In the absence of sufficient particulars in the special agreement, the provisions of the Hague Convention of October 18th, 1907, for the Pacific Settlement of International Disputes shall apply so far as is necessary. If nothing is laid down in the special agreement as to the rules regarding the substance of the dispute to be followed by the arbitrators, the tribunal shall apply the substantive rules enumerated in Article 38 of the Statute of the Permanent Court of International Justice.

Article 19.

If the parties fail to agree concerning the special agreement referred to in the preceding article, or fail to appoint arbitrators, either party shall be at liberty, after giving three months' notice, to bring the dispute by an application direct before the Permanent Court of International Justice.

Article 20.

1. Notwithstanding the provisions of Article 1, disputes of the kind referred to in Article 17 arising between parties who have acceded to the obligations contained in the present chapter shall only be subject to the procedure of conciliation if the parties so agree.

2. The obligation to resort to the procedure of conciliation remains applicable to disputes which are excluded from judicial settlement only by the operation of reservations under the provisions of Article 39.

3. In the event of recourse to and failure of conciliation, neither party may bring the dispute before the Permanent Court of International Justice or call for the constitution of the arbitral tribunal referred to in Article 18 before the expiration of one month from the termination of the proceedings of the Conciliation Commission.

CHAPTER III.
Arbitration.

Article 21.

Any dispute not of the kind referred to in Article 17 which does not, within the month following the termination of the work of the Conciliation Commission provided for in Chapter I, form the object of an agreement between the parties, shall, subject to such reservations as may be made under Article 39, be brought before an arbitral tribunal which, unless the parties otherwise agree, shall be constituted in the manner set out below.

Article 22.

The Arbitral Tribunal shall consist of five members. The parties shall each nominate one member, who may be chosen from among their respective nationals. The two other arbitrators and the Chairman shall be chosen by common agreement from among the nationals of third Powers. They must be of different nationalities and must not be habitually resident in the territory nor be in the service of the parties.

Article 23.

1. If the appointment of the members of the Arbitral Tribunal is not made within a period of three months from the date on which one of the parties requested the other party to constitute an arbitral tribunal, a third Power, chosen by agreement between the parties, shall be requested to make the necessary appointments.

2. If no agreement is reached on this point, each party shall designate a different Power, and the appointments shall be made in concert by the Powers thus chosen.

3. If, within a period of three months, the two Powers so chosen have been unable to reach an agreement, the necessary appointments shall be made by the President of the Permanent Court of International Justice. If the latter is prevented from acting or is a subject of one of the parties, the nominations shall be made by the Vice-President. If the

latter is prevented or is a subject of one the parties, the appointments shall be made by the oldest member of the Court who is not a subject of either party.

Article 24.

Vacancies which may occur as a result of death, resignation or any other cause shall be filled within the shortest possible time in the manner fixed for the nominations.

Article 25.

The parties shall draw up a special agreement determining the subject of the disputes and the details of the procedure.

Article 26.

In the absence of sufficient particulars in the special agreement regarding the matters referred to in the preceding article, the provisions of the Hague Convention of October 18th, 1907, for the Pacific Settlement of International Disputes shall apply so far as is necessary.

Article 27.

Failing the conclusion of a special agreement within a period of three months from the date on which the Tribunal was constituted, the dispute may be brought before the Tribunal by an application by one or other party.

Article 28.

If nothing is laid down in the special agreement or no special agreement has been made, the Tribunal shall apply the rules in regard to the substance of the dispute enumerated in Article 38 of the Statute of the Permanent Court of International Justice. In so far as there exists no such rule applicable to the dispute, the Tribunal shall decide *ex aequo et bono*.

CHAPTER IV.
General Provisions.

Article 29.

1. Disputes for the settlement of which a special procedure is laid down in other conventions in force between the parties to the dispute shall be settled in conformity with the provisions of those conventions.

2. The present General Act shall not affect any agreements in force by which conciliation procedure is established between the Parties or they are bound by obligations to resort to arbitration or judicial settlement which ensure the settlement of the dispute. If, however, these agreements provide only for a procedure of conciliation, after such procedure has been followed without result, the provisions of the present General Act concerning judicial settlement or arbitration shall be applied in so far as the parties have acceded thereto.

Article 30.

If a party brings before a Conciliation Commission a dispute which the other party, relying on conventions in force between the parties, has submitted to the Permanent Court of International Justice or an Arbitral Tribunal, the Commission shall defer consideration of the dispute until the Court or the Arbitral Tribunal has pronounced upon the conflict of competence. The same rule shall apply if the Court of the Tribunal is seized of the case by one of the parties during the conciliation proceedings.

Article 31.

1. In the case of a dispute the occasion of which, according to the municipal law of one of the parties, falls within the competence of its judicial or administrative authorities, the party in question may object to the matter in dispute being submitted for settlement by the different methods laid down in the present General Act until a decision with final effect has been pronounced, within a reasonable time, by the competent authority.

2. In such a case, the party which desires to resort to the procedures laid down in the present General Act must notify the other party of its intention within a period of one year from the date of the aforementioned decision.

Article 32.

If, in a judicial sentence or arbitral award, it is declared that a judgment, or a measure enjoined by a court of law or other authority of one of the parties of the dispute, is wholly or in part contrary to international law, and if the constitutional law of that party does not permit or only partially permits the consequences of the judgment of measure in question to be annulled, the parties agree that the judicial sentence or arbitral award shall grant the injured party equitable satisfaction.

Article 33.

1. In all cases where a dispute forms the object of arbitration or judicial proceedings, and particularly if the question on which the parties differ arises out of acts already committed or on the point of being committed, the Permanent Court of International Justice, acting in accordance with Article 41 of its Statute, or the Arbitral Tribunal, shall lay down within the shortest possible time the provisional measures to be adopted. The parties to the dispute shall be bound to accept such measures.

2. If the dispute is brought before a Conciliation Commission, the latter may recommend to the parties the adoption of such provisional measures as it considers suitable.

3. The parties undertake to abstain from all measures likely to react prejudicially upon the execution of the judicial or arbitral decision or upon the arrangements proposed by the Conciliation Commission and, in general, to abstain from any sort of action whatsoever which may aggravate or extend the dispute.

Article 34.

Should a dispute arise between more than two Parties to the present General Act, the following rules shall be observed for the application of the forms of procedure described in the foregoing provisions:

(a) In the case of conciliation procedure, a special commission shall invariably be constituted. The composition of such commission shall differ according as the parties all have separate interests or as two or more of their number act together.

In the former case, the parties shall each appoint one commissioner and shall jointly appoint commissioners nationals of third Powers not parties to the dispute, whose number shall always exceed by one the number of commissioners appointed separately by the parties.

In the second case, the parties who act together shall appoint their commissioner jointly by agreement between themselves and shall combine with the other party or parties in appointing third commissioners.

In either event, the parties, unless they agree otherwise, shall apply Article 5 and the following articles of the present Act, so far as they are compatible with the provisions of the present article.

(b) In the case of judicial procedure, the Statute of the Permanent Court of International Justice shall apply.

(c) In the case of arbitral procedure, if agreement is not secured as to the composition of the tribunal, in the case of the disputes mentioned in Article 17, each party shall have the right, by means of an application, to submit the dispute to the Permanent Court of International Justice; in the case of the disputes mentioned in Article 21, the above Article 22 and following articles shall apply, but each party having separate interests shall appoint one arbitrator and the number of arbitrators separately appointed by the parties to the dispute shall always be one less than that of the other arbitrators.

Article 35.

1. The present General Act shall be applicable as between the Parties thereto, even though a third Power, whether a party to the Act or not, has an interest in the dispute.

2. In conciliation procedure, the parties may agree to invite such third Power to intervene.

Article 36.

1. In judicial or arbitral procedure, if a third Power should consider that it has an interest of a legal nature which may be affected by the decision in the case, it may submit to the Permanent Court of International Justice or to the arbitral tribunal a request to intervene as a third party.

2. It will be for the Court or the tribunal to decide upon this request.

Article 37.

1. Whenever the construction of a convention to which States other than those concerned in the case are parties is in question, the Registrar of the Permanent Court of International Justice or the arbitral tribunal shall notify all such States forthwith.

2. Every State so notified has the right to intervene in the proceedings; but, if it uses this right, the construction given by the decision will be binding upon it.

Article 38.

Accessions to the present General Act may extend:

A. Either to all the provisions of the Act (Chapters I, II, II and IV);

B. Or to those provisions only which relate to conciliation and judicial settlement (Chapters I and II), together with the general provisions dealing with these procedures (Chapter IV);

C. Or to those provisions only which relate to conciliation (Chapter I), together with the general provisions concerning that procedure (Chapter IV).

The Contracting Parties may benefit by the accessions of other Parties only in so far as they have themselves assumed the same obligations.

Article 39.

1. In addition to the power given in the preceding article, a Party, in acceding to the present General Act, may make his acceptance conditional upon the reservations exhaustively enumerated in the following paragraph. These reservations must be indicated at the time of accession.

2. These reservations may be such as to exclude from the procedure described in the present Act:

(a) Disputes arising out of facts prior to the accession either of the Party making the reservation or of any other Party with whom the said Party may have a dispute;

(b) Disputes concerning questions which by international law are solely within the domestic jurisdiction of States;

(c) Disputes concerning particular cases or clearly specified subject-matters, such as territorial status, or disputes falling within clearly defined categories.

3. If one of the parties to a dispute has made a reservation, the other parties may enforce the same reservation in regard to that party.

4. In the case of Parties, who have acceded to the provisions of the present General Act relating to judicial settlement or to arbitration, such reservations as they may have made shall, unless otherwise expressly stated, be deemed not to apply to the procedure of conciliation.

Article 40.

A Party whose accession has been only partial, or was made subject to reservations, may at any moment, by means of a simple declaration, either extend the scope of his accession or abandon all or part of his reservations.

Article 41.

Disputes relating to the interpretation or application of the present General Act, including those concerning the classification of disputes and the scope of reservations, shall be submitted to the Permanent Court of International Justice.

Article 42.

The present General Act, of which the French and English texts shall both be authentic, shall bear the date of the 26th of September, 1928.

Article 43.

1. The present General Act shall be open to accession by all the Heads of States or other competent authorities of the Members of the League of Nations and the non-Member States to which the Council of the League of Nations has communicated a copy of this purpose.

2. The instruments of accession and the additional declarations provided for by Article 40 shall be transmitted to the Secretary-General of the League of Nations, who shall notify their receipt to all the Members of the League and the non-Member States referred to in the preceding paragraph.

3. The Secretary-General of the League of Nations shall draw up three lists, denominated respectively by the letters A, B and C, corresponding to the three forms of accession to the present Act provided for in Article 38, in which shall be shown the accessions and additional declarations of the Contracting Parties. These lists, which shall be continually

kept up to date, shall be published in the annual report presented to the Assembly of the League of Nations by the Secretary-General.

Article 44.

1. The present General Act shall come into force on the ninetieth day following the receipt by the Secretary-General of the League of Nations of the accession of not less than two Contracting Parties.

2. Accessions received after the entry into force of the Act, in accordance with the previous paragraph, shall become effective as from the ninetieth day following the date of receipt by the Secretary-General of the League of Nations. The same rule shall apply to the additional declaration provided for by Article 40.

Article 45.

1. The present General Act shall be concluded for a period of five years, dating from its entry into force.

2. It shall remain in force for further successive periods of five years in the case of Contracting Parties which do not denounce it at least six months before the expiration of the current period.

3. Denunciation shall be effected by a written notification addressed to the Secretary-General of the League of Nations, who shall inform all the Members of the League and the non-Member States referred to in Article 43.

4. A denunciation may be partial only, or may consist in notification of reservations not previously made.

5. Notwithstanding denunciation by one of the Contracting Parties concerned in a dispute, all proceedings pending at the expiration of the current period of the General Act shall be duly completed.

Article 46.

A copy of the present General Act, signed by the President of the Assembly and by the Secretary-General of the League of Nations, shall be deposited in the archives of the Secretariat; a certified true copy shall be delivered by the Secretary-General to all the Members of the League of Nations and to the non-Member States indicated by the Council of the League of Nations.

Article 47.

The present General Act shall be registered by the Secretary-General of the League of Nations on the date of its entry into force.

The President of the ninth ordinary session of the Assembly of the League of Nations:
(Signed) Herluf Zahle.

The Secretary-General:
(Signed) Eric Drummond.

6 Charter of the United Nations

Date: 26 June 1945
Source: United Nations Conference on International Organization, Documents, vol XV (1945) 335
http://www.un.org/en/documents/charter/

Preamble

WE THE PEOPLES OF THE UNITED NATIONS DETERMINED

to save succeeding generations from the scourge of war, which twice in our lifetime has brought untold sorrow to mankind, and

to reaffirm faith in fundamental human rights, in the dignity and worth of the human person, in the equal rights of men and women and of nations large and small, and

to establish conditions under which justice and respect for the obligations arising from treaties and other sources of international law can be maintained, and

to promote social progress and better standards of life in larger freedom,

AND FOR THESE ENDS

to practice tolerance and live together in peace with one another as good neighbors, and

to unite our strength to maintain international peace and security, and

to ensure, by the acceptance of principles and the institution of methods, that armed force shall not be used, save in the common interest, and

to employ international machinery for the promotion of the economic and social advancement of all peoples,

HAVE RESOLVED TO COMBINE OUR EFFORTS TO ACCOMPLISH THESE AIMS.

...

CHAPTER I
PURPOSES AND PRINCIPLES

Article 1

The Purposes of the United Nations are:

1. To maintain international peace and security, and to that end: to take effective collective measures for the prevention and removal of threats to the peace, and for the suppression of acts of aggression or other breaches of the peace, and to bring about by peaceful means, and in conformity with the principles of justice and international law, adjustment or settlement of international disputes or situations which might lead to a breach of the peace;

2. To develop friendly relations among nations based on respect for the principle of equal rights and self-determination of peoples, and to take other appropriate measures to strengthen universal peace;

3. To achieve international co-operation in solving international problems of an economic, social, cultural, or humanitarian character, and in promoting and encouraging respect for human rights and for fundamental freedoms for all without distinction as to race, sex, language, or religion; and

4. To be a centre for harmonizing the actions of nations in the attainment of these common ends.

Article 2

The Organization and its Members, in pursuit of the Purposes stated in Article 1, shall act in accordance with the following Principles.

1. The Organization is based on the principle of the sovereign equality of all its Members.

2. All Members, in order to ensure to all of them the rights and benefits resulting from membership, shall fulfill in good faith the obligations assumed by them in accordance with the present Charter.

3. All Members shall settle their international disputes by peaceful means in such a manner that international peace and security, and justice, are not endangered.

4. All Members shall refrain in their international relations from the threat or use of force against the territorial integrity or political independence of any state, or in any other manner inconsistent with the Purposes of the United Nations.

5. All Members shall give the United Nations every assistance in any action it takes in accordance with the present Charter, and shall refrain from giving assistance to any state against which the United Nations is taking preventive or enforcement action.

6. The Organization shall ensure that states which are not Members of the United Nations act in accordance with these Principles so far as may be necessary for the maintenance of international peace and security.

7. Nothing contained in the present Charter shall authorize the United Nations to intervene in matters which are essentially within the domestic jurisdiction of any state or shall require the Members to submit such matters to settlement under the present Charter; but this principle shall not prejudice the application of enforcement measures under Chapter VII.

…

CHAPTER III
ORGANS

Article 7

1. There are established as the principal organs of the United Nations: a General Assembly, a Security Council, an Economic and Social Council, a Trusteeship Council, an International Court of Justice, and a Secretariat.

2. Such subsidiary organs as may be found necessary may be established in accordance with the present Charter.

…

CHAPTER VI
PACIFIC SETTLEMENT OF DISPUTES

Article 33

1. The parties to any dispute, the continuance of which is likely to endanger the maintenance of international peace and security, shall, first of all, seek a solution by negotiation, enquiry, mediation, conciliation, arbitration, judicial settlement, resort to regional agencies or arrangements, or other peaceful means of their own choice.

2. The Security Council shall, when it deems necessary, call upon the parties to settle their dispute by such means.

Article 34

The Security Council may investigate any dispute, or any situation which might lead to international friction or give rise to a dispute, in order to determine whether the continuance of the dispute or situation is likely to endanger the maintenance of international peace and security.

Article 35

1. Any Member of the United Nations may bring any dispute, or any situation of the nature referred to in Article 34, to the attention of the Security Council or of the General Assembly.

2. A state which is not a Member of the United Nations may bring to the attention of the Security Council or of the General Assembly any dispute to which it is a party if it accepts in advance, for the purposes of the dispute, the obligations of pacific settlement provided in the present Charter.

3. The proceedings of the General Assembly in respect of matters brought to its attention under this Article will be subject to the provisions of Articles 11 and 12.

Article 36

1. The Security Council may, at any stage of a dispute of the nature referred to in Article 33 or of a situation of like nature, recommend appropriate procedures or methods of adjustment.

2. The Security Council should take into consideration any procedures for the settlement of the dispute which have already been adopted by the parties.

3. In making recommendations under this Article the Security Council should also take into consideration that legal disputes should as a general rule be referred by the parties to the International Court of Justice in accordance with the provisions of the Statute of the Court.

Article 37

1. Should the parties to a dispute of the nature referred to in Article 33 fail to settle it by the means indicated in that Article, they shall refer it to the Security Council.

2. If the Security Council deems that the continuance of the dispute is in fact likely to endanger the maintenance of international peace and security, it shall decide whether to take action under Article 36 or to recommend such terms of settlement as it may consider appropriate.

Article 38

Without prejudice to the provisions of Articles 33 to 37, the Security Council may, if all the parties to any dispute so request, make recommendations to the parties with a view to a pacific settlement of the dispute.

CHAPTER VII
ACTION WITH RESPECT TO THREATS TO THE PEACE, BREACHES OF THE PEACE, AND ACTS OF AGGRESSION

Article 39

The Security Council shall determine the existence of any threat to the peace, breach of the peace, or act of aggression and shall make recommendations, or decide what measures shall be taken in accordance with Articles 41 and 42, to maintain or restore international peace and security.

Article 40

In order to prevent an aggravation of the situation, the Security Council may, before making the recommendations or deciding upon the measures provided for in Article 39, call upon the parties concerned to comply with such provisional measures as it deems necessary or desirable. Such provisional measures shall be without prejudice to the rights, claims, or position of the parties concerned. The Security Council shall duly take account of failure to comply with such provisional measures.

Article 41

The Security Council may decide what measures not involving the use of armed force are to be employed to give effect to its decisions, and it may call upon the Members of the United Nations to apply such measures. These may include complete or partial interruption of economic relations and of rail, sea, air, postal, telegraphic, radio, and other means of communication, and the severance of diplomatic relations.

Article 42

Should the Security Council consider that measures provided for in Article 41 would be inadequate or have proved to be inadequate, it may take such action by air, sea, or land forces as may be necessary to maintain or restore international peace and security. Such action may include demonstrations, blockade, and other operations by air, sea, or land forces of Members of the United Nations.

Article 43

1. All Members of the United Nations, in order to contribute to the maintenance of international peace and security, undertake to make available to the Security Council, on its call and in accordance with a special agreement or agreements, armed forces, assistance, and facilities, including rights of passage, necessary for the purpose of maintaining international peace and security.
2. Such agreement or agreements shall govern the numbers and types of forces, their degree of readiness and general location, and the nature of the facilities and assistance to be provided.
3. The agreement or agreements shall be negotiated as soon as possible on the initiative of the Security Council. They shall be concluded between the Security Council and Members or between the Security Council and groups of Members and shall be subject to ratification by the signatory states in accordance with their respective constitutional processes.

Article 44

When the Security Council has decided to use force it shall, before calling upon a Member not represented on it to provide armed forces in fulfillment of the obligations assumed under Article 43, invite that Member, if the Member so desires, to participate in the decisions of the Security Council concerning the employment of contingents of that Member's armed forces.

Article 45

In order to enable the United Nations to take urgent military measures Members shall hold immediately available national air-force contingents for combined international enforcement action. The strength and degree of readiness of these contingents and plans for their combined action shall be determined, within the limits laid down in the special agreement or agreements referred to in Article 43, by the Security Council with the assistance of the Military Staff Committee.

Article 46

Plans for the application of armed force shall be made by the Security Council with the assistance of the Military Staff Committee.

Article 47

1. There shall be established a Military Staff Committee to advise and assist the Security Council on all questions relating to the Security Council's military requirements for the maintenance of international peace and security, the employment and command of forces placed at its disposal, the regulation of armaments, and possible disarmament.

2. The Military Staff Committee shall consist of the Chiefs of Staff of the permanent members of the Security Council or their representatives. Any Member of the United Nations not permanently represented on the Committee shall be invited by the Committee to be associated with it when the efficient discharge of the Committee's responsibilities requires the participation of that Member in its work.

3. The Military Staff Committee shall be responsible under the Security Council for the strategic direction of any armed forces placed at the disposal of the Security Council. Questions relating to the command of such forces shall be worked out subsequently.

4. The Military Staff Committee, with the authorization of the Security Council and after consultation with appropriate regional agencies, may establish regional subcommittees.

Article 48

1. The action required to carry out the decisions of the Security Council for the maintenance of international peace and security shall be taken by all the Members of the United Nations or by some of them, as the Security Council may determine.

2. Such decisions shall be carried out by the Members of the United Nations directly and through their action in the appropriate international agencies of which they are members.

Article 49

The Members of the United Nations shall join in affording mutual assistance in carrying out the measures decided upon by the Security Council.

Article 50

If preventive or enforcement measures against any state are taken by the Security Council, any other state, whether a Member of the United Nations or not, which finds itself confronted with special economic problems arising from the carrying out of those measures shall have the right to consult the Security Council with regard to a solution of those problems.

Article 51

Nothing in the present Charter shall impair the inherent right of individual or collective self-defense if an armed attack occurs against a Member of the United Nations, until the Security Council has taken measures necessary to maintain international peace and security. Measures taken by Members in the exercise of this right of self-defense shall be immediately reported to the Security Council and shall not in any way affect the authority and responsibility of the Security Council under the present Charter to take at any time such action as it deems necessary in order to maintain or restore international peace and security.

CHAPTER VIII
REGIONAL ARRANGEMENTS

Article 52

1. Nothing in the present Charter precludes the existence of regional arrangements or agencies for dealing with such matters relating to the maintenance of international peace and security as are appropriate for regional action, provided that such arrangements or agencies and their activities are consistent with the Purposes and Principles of the United Nations.
2. The Members of the United Nations entering into such arrangements or constituting such agencies shall make every effort to achieve pacific settlement of local disputes through such regional arrangements or by such regional agencies before referring them to the Security Council.
3. The Security Council shall encourage the development of pacific settlement of local disputes through such regional arrangements or by such regional agencies either on the initiative of the states concerned or by reference from the Security Council.
4. This Article in no way impairs the application of Articles 34 and 35.

Article 53

1. The Security Council shall, where appropriate, utilize such regional arrangements or agencies for enforcement action under its authority. But no enforcement action shall be taken under regional arrangements or by regional agencies without the authorization of the Security Council, with the exception of measures against any enemy state, as defined in paragraph 2 of this Article, provided for pursuant to Article 107 or in regional arrangements directed against renewal of aggressive policy on the part of any such state, until such time as the Organization may, on request of the Governments concerned, be charged with the responsibility for preventing further aggression by such a state.
2. The term enemy state as used in paragraph 1 of this Article applies to any state which during the Second World War has been an enemy of any signatory of the present Charter.

Article 54

The Security Council shall at all times be kept fully informed of activities undertaken or in contemplation under regional arrangements or by regional agencies for the maintenance of international peace and security.

…

CHAPTER XIV
THE INTERNATIONAL COURT OF JUSTICE

Article 92

The International Court of Justice shall be the principal judicial organ of the United Nations. It shall function in accordance with the annexed Statute, which is based upon the Statute of the Permanent Court of International Justice and forms an integral part of the present Charter.

Article 93

1. All Members of the United Nations are ipso facto parties to the Statute of the International Court of Justice.

2. A state which is not a Member of the United Nations may become a party to the Statute of the International Court of Justice on conditions to be determined in each case by the General Assembly upon the recommendation of the Security Council.

Article 94

1. Each Member of the United Nations undertakes to comply with the decision of the International Court of Justice in any case to which it is a party.

2. If any party to a case fails to perform the obligations incumbent upon it under a judgment rendered by the Court, the other party may have recourse to the Security Council, which may, if it deems necessary, make recommendations or decide upon measures to be taken to give effect to the judgment.

Article 95

Nothing in the present Charter shall prevent Members of the United Nations from entrusting the solution of their differences to other tribunals by virtue of agreements already in existence or which may be concluded in the future.

Article 96

1. The General Assembly or the Security Council may request the International Court of Justice to give an advisory opinion on any legal question.

2. Other organs of the United Nations and specialized agencies, which may at any time be so authorized by the General Assembly, may also request advisory opinions of the Court on legal questions arising within the scope of their activities.

CHAPTER XV
THE SECRETARIAT

Article 97

The Secretariat shall comprise a Secretary-General and such staff as the Organization may require. The Secretary-General shall be appointed by the General Assembly upon the recommendation of the Security Council. He shall be the chief administrative officer of the Organization.

Article 98

The Secretary-General shall act in that capacity in all meetings of the General Assembly, of the Security Council, of the Economic and Social Council, and of the Trusteeship Council, and shall perform such other functions as are entrusted to him by these organs.

The Secretary-General shall make an annual report to the General Assembly on the work of the Organization.

Article 99

The Secretary-General may bring to the attention of the Security Council any matter which in his opinion may threaten the maintenance of international peace and security.

Article 100

1. In the performance of their duties the Secretary-General and the staff shall not seek or receive instructions from any government or from any other authority external to the Organization. They shall refrain from any action which might reflect on their position as international officials responsible only to the Organization.

2. Each Member of the United Nations undertakes to respect the exclusively international character of the responsibilities of the Secretary-General and the staff and not to seek to influence them in the discharge of their responsibilities.

Article 101

1. The staff shall be appointed by the Secretary-General under regulations established by the General Assembly.

2. Appropriate staffs shall be permanently assigned to the Economic and Social Council, the Trusteeship Council, and, as required, to other organs of the United Nations. These staffs shall form a part of the Secretariat.

3. The paramount consideration in the employment of the staff and in the determination of the conditions of service shall be the necessity of securing the highest standards of efficiency, competence, and integrity. Due regard shall be paid to the importance of recruiting the staff on as wide a geographical basis as possible.

…

General Assembly Resolutions Addressing Issues of Dispute Settlement

7.a Declaration on Principles of International Law Concerning Friendly Relations and Cooperation Among States in Accordance with the Charter of the United Nations (Friendly Relations Declaration)

Date: 24 October 1970
Source: UN Doc A/RES/2625 (XXV) (Annex)
https://legal.un.org/avl/ha/dpilfrcscun/dpilfrcscun.html

Preamble

The General Assembly,

Reaffirming in the terms of the Charter of the United Nations that the maintenance of international peace and security and the development of friendly relations and co-operation between nations are among the fundamental purposes of the United Nations,

Recalling that the peoples of the United Nations are determined to practise tolerance and live together in peace with one another as good neighbours,

Bearing in mind the importance of maintaining and strengthening international peace founded upon freedom, equality, justice and respect for fundamental human rights and of developing friendly relations among nations irrespective of their political, economic and social systems or the levels of their development,

Bearing in mind also the paramount importance of the Charter of the United Nations in the promotion of the rule of law among nations,

Considering that the faithful observance of the principles of international law concerning friendly relations and co-operation among States and the fulfillment in good faith of the obligations assumed by States, in accordance with the Charter, is of the greatest importance for the maintenance of international peace and security and for the implementation of the other purposes of the United Nations,

Noting that the great political, economic and social changes and scientific progress which have taken place in the world since the adoption of the Charter give increased importance to these principles and to the need for their more effective application in the conduct of States wherever carried on,

Recalling the established principle that outer space, including the Moon and other celestial bodies, is not subject to national appropriation by claim of sovereignty, by means of use or occupation, or by any other means, and mindful of the fact that consideration is being given in the United Nations to the question of establishing other appropriate provisions similarly inspired,

Convinced that the strict observance by States of the obligation not to intervene in the affairs of any other State is an essential condition to ensure that nations live together in peace with one another, since the practice of any form of intervention not only violates the spirit and letter of the Charter, but also leads to the creation of situations which threaten international peace and security,

Recalling the duty of States to refrain in their international relations from military, political, economic or any other form of coercion aimed against the political independence or territorial integrity of any State,

Considering it essential that all States shall refrain in their international relations from the threat or use of force against the territorial integrity or political independence of any State, or in any other manner inconsistent with the purposes of the United Nations,

Considering it equally essential that all States shall settle their international disputes by peaceful means in accordance with the Charter,

Reaffirming, in accordance with the Charter, the basic importance of sovereign equality and stressing that the purposes of the United Nations can be implemented only if States enjoy sovereign equality and comply fully with the requirements of this principle in their international relations,

Convinced that the subjection of peoples to alien subjugation, domination and exploitation constitutes a major obstacle to the promotion of international peace and security, Convinced that the principle of equal rights and self-determination of peoples constitutes a significant contribution to contemporary international law, and that its effective application is of paramount importance for the promotion of friendly relations among States, based on respect for the principle of sovereign equality,

Convinced in consequence that any attempt aimed at the partial or total disruption of the national unity and territorial integrity of a State or country or at its political independence is incompatible with the purposes and principles of the Charter,

Considering the provisions of the Charter as a whole and taking into account the role of relevant resolutions adopted by the competent organs of the United Nations relating to the content of the principles,

Considering that the progressive development and codification of the following principles:

(a) The principle that States shall refrain in their international relations from the threat or use of force against the territorial integrity or political independence of any State, or in any other manner inconsistent with the purposes of the United Nations,

(b) The principle that States shall settle their international disputes by peaceful means in such a manner that international peace and security and justice are not endangered,

(c) The duty not to intervene in matters within the domestic jurisdiction of any State, in accordance with the Charter,

(d) The duty of States to co-operate with one another in accordance with the Charter,

(e) The principle of equal rights and self-determination of peoples,

(f) The principle of sovereign equality of States,

(g) The principle that States shall fulfil in good faith the obligations assumed by them in accordance with the Charter, so as to secure their more effective application within the international community, would promote the realization of the purposes of the United Nations,

Having considered the principles of international law relating to friendly relations and co-operation among States,

1. Solemnly proclaims the following principles:

The principle that States shall refrain in their international relations from the threat or use of force against the territorial integrity or political independence of any State or in any other manner inconsistent with the purposes of the United Nations

Every State has the duty to refrain in its international relations from the threat or use of force against the territorial integrity or political independence of any State, or in any other manner inconsistent with the purposes of the United Nations. Such a threat or use of force constitutes a violation of international law and the Charter of the United Nations and shall never be employed as a means of settling international issues.

A war of aggression constitutes a crime against the peace, for which there is responsibility under international law.

In accordance with the purposes and principles of the United Nations, States have the duty to refrain from propaganda for wars of aggression.

Every State has the duty to refrain from the threat or use of force to violate the existing international boundaries of another State or as a means of solving international disputes, including territorial disputes and problems concerning frontiers of States.

Every State likewise has the duty to refrain from the threat or use of force to violate international lines of demarcation, such as armistice lines, established by or pursuant to an international agreement to which it is a party or which it is otherwise bound to respect. Nothing in the foregoing shall be construed as prejudicing the positions of the parties concerned with regard to the status and effects of such lines under their special regimes or as affecting their temporary character.

States have a duty to refrain from acts of reprisal involving the use of force.

Every State has the duty to refrain from any forcible action which deprives peoples referred to in the elaboration of the principle of equal rights and self-determination of their right to self-determination and freedom and independence.

Every State has the duty to refrain from organizing or encouraging the organization of irregular forces or armed bands, including mercenaries, for incursion into the territory of another State.

Every State has the duty to refrain from organizing, instigating, assisting or participating in acts of civil strife or terrorist acts in another State or acquiescing in organized activities within its territory directed towards the commission of such acts, when the acts referred to in the present paragraph involve a threat or use of force.

The territory of a State shall not be the object of military occupation resulting from the use of force in contravention of the provisions of the Charter. The territory of a State shall not be the object of acquisition by another State resulting from the threat or use of force. No territorial acquisition resulting from the threat or use of force shall be recognized as legal. Nothing in the foregoing shall be construed as affecting:

(a) Provisions of the Charter or any international agreement prior to the Charter régime and valid under international law; or

(b) The powers of the Security Council under the Charter.

All States shall pursue in good faith negotiations for the early conclusion of a universal treaty on general and complete disarmament under effective international control and strive to adopt appropriate measures to reduce international tensions and strengthen confidence among States.

All States shall comply in good faith with their obligations under the generally recognized principles and rules of international law with respect to the maintenance of international peace and security, and shall endeavour to make the United Nations security system based on the Charter more effective.

Nothing in the foregoing paragraphs shall be construed as enlarging or diminishing in any way the scope of the provisions of the Charter concerning cases in which the use of force is lawful.

The principle that States shall settle their international disputes by peaceful means in such a manner that international peace and security and justice are not endangered

Every State shall settle its international disputes with other States by peaceful means in such a manner that international peace and security and justice are not endangered.

States shall accordingly seek early and just settlement of their international disputes by negotiation, inquiry, mediation, conciliation, arbitration, judicial settlement, resort to regional agencies or arrangements or other peaceful means of their choice. In seeking such a settlement the parties shall agree upon such peaceful means as may be appropriate to the circumstances and nature of the dispute.

The parties to a dispute have the duty, in the event of failure to reach a solution by any one of the above peaceful means, to continue to seek a settlement of the dispute by other peaceful means agreed upon by them.

States parties to an international dispute, as well as other States shall refrain from any action which may aggravate the Situation so as to endanger the maintenance of international peace and security, and shall act in accordance with the purposes and principles of the United Nations.

International disputes shall be settled on the basis of the Sovereign equality of States and in accordance with the principle of free choice of means. Recourse to, or acceptance of, a settlement procedure freely agreed to by States with regard to existing or future disputes to which they are parties shall not be regarded as incompatible with sovereign equality.

Nothing in the foregoing paragraphs prejudices or derogates from the applicable provisions of the Charter, in particular those relating to the pacific settlement of international disputes.

The principle concerning the duty not to intervene in matters within the domestic jurisdiction of any State, in accordance with the Charter

No State or group of States has the right to intervene, directly or indirectly, for any reason whatever, in the internal or external affairs of any other State. Consequently, armed intervention and all other forms of interference or attempted threats against the personality of the State or against its political, economic and cultural elements, are in violation of international law.

No State may use or encourage the use of economic, political or any other type of measures to coerce another State in order to obtain from it the subordination of the exercise of its sovereign rights and to secure from it advantages of any kind. Also, no State shall organize, assist, foment, finance, incite or tolerate subversive, terrorist or armed activities directed towards the violent overthrow of the régime of another State, or interfere in civil strife in another State.

The use of force to deprive peoples of their national identity constitutes a violation of their inalienable rights and of the principle of non-intervention.

Every State has an inalienable right to choose its political, economic, social and cultural systems, without interference in any form by another State.

Nothing in the foregoing paragraphs shall be construed as reflecting the relevant provisions of the Charter relating to the maintenance of international peace and security.

…

7.b Manila Declaration on the Peaceful Settlement of International Disputes (Manila Declaration)

Date: 15 November 1982
Source: UN Doc A/RES/37/10 (Annex)
https://legal.un.org/avl/ha/mdpsid/mdpsid.html

The General Assembly,

Reaffirming the principle of the Charter of the United Nations that all States shall settle their international disputes by peaceful means in such a manner that international peace and security, and justice, are not endangered,

Conscious that the Charter of the United Nations embodies the means and an essential framework for the peaceful settlement of international disputes, the continuance of which is likely to endanger the maintenance of international peace and security,

Recognizing the important role of the United Nations and the need to enhance its effectiveness in the peaceful settlement of international disputes and the maintenance of international peace and security, in accordance with the principles of justice and international law, in conformity with the Charter of the United Nations,

Reaffirming the principle of the Charter of the United Nations that all States shall refrain in their international relations from the threat or use of force against the territorial integrity or political independence of any State, or in any other manner inconsistent with the purposes of the United Nations,

Reiterating that no State or group of States has the right to intervene directly or indirectly, for any reason whatsoever, in the internal or external affairs of any other State,

Reaffirming the Declaration on Principles of International Law concerning Friendly Relations and Co-operation among States in accordance with the Charter of the United Nations,

Bearing in mind the importance of maintaining and strengthening international peace and security and the development of friendly relations among States, irrespective of their political, economic and social systems or levels of economic development,

Reaffirming the principle of equal rights and self-determination of peoples as enshrined in the Charter of the United Nations and referred to in the Declaration on Principles of International Law concerning Friendly Relations and Co-operation among States in accordance with the Charter of the United Nations and in other relevant resolutions of the General Assembly,

Stressing the need for all States to desist from any forcible action which deprives peoples, particularly peoples under colonial and racist régimes or other forms of alien domination, of their inalienable right to self-determination, freedom and independence, as referred to in the Declaration on Principles of International Law concerning Friendly Relations and Co-operation among States in accordance with the Charter of the United Nations,

Mindful of existing international instruments as well as respective principles and rules concerning the peaceful settlement of international disputes, including the exhaustion of local remedies whenever applicable,

Determined to promote international co-operation in the political field and to encourage the progressive development of international law and its codification, particularly in relation to the peaceful settlement of international disputes,

Solemnly declares that:

I

1. All States shall act in good faith and in conformity with the purposes and principles enshrined in the Charter of the United Nations with a view to avoiding disputes among themselves likely to affect friendly relations among States, thus contributing to the maintenance of international peace and security. They shall live together in peace with one another as good neighbours and strive for the adoption of meaningful measures for strengthening international peace and security.

2. Every State shall settle its international disputes exclusively by peaceful means in such a manner that international peace and security, and justice, are not endangered.

3. International disputes shall be settled on the basis of the sovereign equality of States and in accordance with the principle of free choice of means in conformity with obligations under the Charter of the United Nations and with the principles of justice and international law. Recourse to, or acceptance of, a settlement procedure freely agreed to by States with regard to existing or future disputes to which they are parties shall not be regarded as incompatible with the sovereign equality of States.

4. States parties to a dispute shall continue to observe in their mutual relations their obligations under the fundamental principles of international law concerning the

sovereignty, independence and territorial integrity of States, as well as other generally recognized principles and rules of contemporary international law.

5. States shall seek in good faith and in a spirit of co-operation an early and equitable settlement of their international disputes by any of the following means: negotiation, inquiry, mediation, conciliation, arbitration, judicial settlement, resort to regional arrangements or agencies or other peaceful means of their own choice, including good offices. In seeking such a settlement, the parties shall agree on such peaceful means as may be appropriate to the circumstances and the nature of their dispute.

6. States parties to regional arrangements or agencies shall make every effort to achieve pacific settlement of their local disputes through such regional arrangements or agencies before referring them to the Security Council. This does not preclude States from bringing any dispute to the attention of the Security Council or of the General Assembly in accordance with the Charter of the United Nations.

7. In the event of failure of the parties to a dispute to reach an early solution by any of the above means of settlement, they shall continue to seek a peaceful solution and shall consult forthwith on mutually agreed means to settle the dispute peacefully. Should the parties fail to settle by any of the above means a dispute the continuance of which is likely to endanger the maintenance of international peace and security, they shall refer it to the Security Council in accordance with the Charter of the United Nations and without prejudice to the functions and powers of the Council set forth in the relevant provisions of Chapter VI of the Charter.

8. States parties to an international dispute, as well as other States, shall refrain from any action whatsoever which may aggravate the situation so as to endanger the maintenance of international peace and security and make more difficult or impede the peaceful settlement of the dispute, and shall act in this respect in accordance with the purposes and principles of the United Nations.

9. States should consider concluding agreements for the peaceful settlement of disputes among them. They should also include in bilateral agreements and multilateral conventions to be concluded, as appropriate, effective provisions for the peaceful settlement of disputes arising from the interpretation or application thereof.

10. States should, without prejudice to the right of free choice of means, bear in mind that direct negotiations are a flexible and effective means of peaceful settlement of their disputes. When they choose to resort to direct negotiations, States should negotiate meaningfully, in order to arrive at an early settlement acceptable to the parties. States should be equally prepared to seek the settlement of their disputes by the other means mentioned in the present Declaration.

11. States shall in accordance with international law implement in good faith all the provisions of agreements concluded by them for the settlement of their disputes.

12. In order to facilitate the exercise by the peoples concerned of the right to self-determination as referred to in the Declaration on Principles of International Law concerning Friendly Relations and Co-operation among States in accordance with the Charter of the United Nations, the parties to a dispute may have the possibility, if they agree to do so and as appropriate, to have recourse to the relevant procedures mentioned in the present Declaration, for the peaceful settlement of the dispute.

13. Neither the existence of a dispute nor the failure of a procedure of peaceful settlement of disputes shall permit the use of force or threat of force by any of the States parties to the dispute.

II

1. Member States should make full use of the provisions of the Charter of the United Nations, including the procedures and means provided for therein, particularly Chapter VI, concerning the peaceful settlement of disputes.

2. Member States shall fulfil in good faith the obligations assumed by them in accordance with the Charter of the United Nations. They should, in accordance with the Charter, as appropriate, duly take into account the recommendations of the Security Council relating to the peaceful settlement of disputes. They should also, in accordance with the Charter, as appropriate, duly take into account the recommendations adopted by the General Assembly, subject to Articles 11 and 12 of the Charter, in the field of peaceful settlement of disputes.

3. Member States reaffirm the important role conferred on the General Assembly by the Charter of the United Nations in the field of peaceful settlement of disputes and stress the need for it to discharge effectively its responsibilities. Accordingly, they should:

(a) Bear in mind that the General Assembly may discuss any situation, regardless of origin, which it deems likely to impair the general welfare or friendly relations among nations and, subject to Article 12 of the Charter, recommend measures for its peaceful adjustment;

(b) Consider making use, when they deem it appropriate, of the possibility of bringing to the attention of the General Assembly any dispute or any situation which might lead to international friction or give rise to a dispute;

(c) Consider utilizing, for the peaceful settlement of their disputes, the subsidiary organs established by the General Assembly in the performance of its functions under the Charter;

(d) Consider, when they are parties to a dispute brought to the attention of the General Assembly, making use of consultations within the framework of the Assembly, with a view to facilitating an early settlement of their dispute.

4. Member States should strengthen the primary role of the Security Council so that it may fully and effectively discharge its responsibilities, in accordance with the Charter of the United Nations, in the area of the settlement of disputes or of any situation the continuance of which is likely to endanger the maintenance of international peace and security. To this end they should:

(a) Be fully aware of their obligation to refer to the Security Council such a dispute to which they are parties if they fail to settle it by the means indicated in Article 33 of the Charter;

(b) Make greater use of the possibility of bringing to the attention of the Security Council any dispute or any situation which might lead to international friction or give rise to a dispute;

(c) Encourage the Security Council to make wider use of the opportunities provided for by the Charter in order to review disputes or situations the continuance of which is likely to endanger the maintenance of international peace and security;

(d) Consider making greater use of the fact-finding capacity of the Security Council in accordance with the Charter;

(e) Encourage the Security Council to make wider use, as a means to promote peaceful settlement of disputes, of the subsidiary organs established by it in the performance of its functions under the Charter;

(f) Bear in mind that the Security Council may, at any stage of a dispute of the nature referred to in Article 33 of the Charter or of a situation of like nature, recommend appropriate procedures or methods of adjustment;

(g) Encourage the Security Council to act without delay, in accordance with its functions and powers, particularly in cases where international disputes develop into armed conflicts.

5. States should be fully aware of the role of the International Court of Justice, which is the principal judicial organ of the United Nations. Their attention is drawn to the facilities offered by the International Court of Justice for the settlement of legal disputes, especially since the revision of the Rules of the Court.

States may entrust the solution of their differences to other tribunals by virtue of agreements already in existence or which may be concluded in the future.

States should bear in mind:

(a) That legal disputes should as a general rule be referred by the parties to the International Court of Justice, in accordance with the provisions of the Statute of the Court;

(b) That it is desirable that they:

(i) Consider the possibility of inserting in treaties, whenever appropriate, clauses providing for the submission to the International Court of Justice of disputes which may arise from the interpretation or application of such treaties;

(ii) Study the possibility of choosing, in the free exercise of their sovereignty, to recognize as compulsory the jurisdiction of the International Court of Justice in accordance with Article 36 of its Statute;

(iii) Review the possibility of identifying cases in which use may be made of the International Court of Justice.

The organs of the United Nations and the specialized agencies should study the advisability of making use of the possibility of requesting advisory opinions of the International Court of Justice on legal questions arising within the scope of their activities, provided that they are duly authorized to do so.

Recourse to judicial settlement of legal disputes, particularly referral to the International Court of Justice, should not be considered an unfriendly act between States.

6. The Secretary-General should make full use of the provisions of the Charter of the United Nations concerning the responsibilities entrusted to him. The Secretary-General may bring to the attention of the Security Council any matter which in his opinion may threaten the maintenance of international peace and security. He shall perform such other functions as are entrusted to him by the Security Council or by the General Assembly. Reports in this connection shall be made whenever requested to the Security Council or the General Assembly.

Urges all States to observe and promote in good faith the provisions of the present Declaration in the peaceful settlement of their international disputes;

Declares that nothing in the present Declaration shall be construed as prejudicing in any manner the relevant provisions of the Charter or the rights and duties of States, or the scope of the functions and powers of the United Nations organs under the Charter, in particular those relating to the peaceful settlement of disputes;

Declares that nothing in the present Declaration could in any way prejudice the right to self-determination, freedom and independence, as derived from the Charter, of peoples forcibly deprived of that right and referred to in the Declaration on Principles of International Law concerning Friendly Relations and Co-operation among States in accordance with the Charter of the United Nations, particularly peoples under colonial and racist regimes or other forms of alien domination; nor the right of these peoples to struggle to that end and to seek and receive support, in accordance with the principles of the Charter and in conformity with the above-mentioned Declaration;

Stresses the need, in accordance with the Charter, to continue efforts to strengthen the process of the peaceful settlement of disputes through progressive development and codification of international law, as appropriate, and through enhancing the effectiveness of the United Nations in this field.

7.c Declaration on the Prevention and Removal of Disputes and Situations Which May Threaten International Peace and Security and on the Role of the United Nations in this Field (Declaration on the Prevention and Removal of Disputes)

Date: 5 December 1988
Source: UN Doc A/RES/43/51 (Annex)
https://legal.un.org/avl/ha/dprds/dprds.html

The General Assembly,

Recognizing the important role that the United Nations and its organs can play in the prevention and removal of international disputes and situations which may lead to international friction or give rise to an international dispute, the continuance of which may threaten the maintenance of international peace and security (hereafter: "disputes" or "situations"), within their respective functions and powers under the Charter of the United Nations,

Convinced that the strengthening of such a role of the United Nations will enhance its effectiveness in dealing with questions relating to the maintenance of international peace and security and in promoting the peaceful settlement of international disputes,

Recognizing the fundamental responsibility of States for the prevention and removal of disputes and situations,

Recalling that the peoples of the United Nations are determined to practise tolerance and live together in peace with one another as good neighbours,

Bearing in mind the right of all States to resort to peaceful means of their own choice for the prevention and removal of disputes or situations,

Reaffirming the Declaration on Principles of International Law concerning Friendly Relations and Co-operation among States in accordance with the Charter of the United Nations, the Manila Declaration on the Peaceful Settlement of International Disputes and the Declaration on the Enhancement of the Effectiveness of the Principle of Refraining from the Threat or Use of Force in International Relations,

Recalling that it is the duty of States to refrain in their international relations from military, political, economic or any other form of coercion against the political independence or territorial integrity of any State,

Calling upon States to co-operate fully with the relevant organs of the United Nations and to support actions taken by them in accordance with the Charter relating to the prevention or removal of disputes and situations,

Bearing in mind the obligation of States to conduct their relations with other States in accordance with international law, including the principles of the United Nations,

Reaffirming the principle of equal rights and self-determination of peoples,

Recalling that the Charter confers on the Security Council the primary responsibility for the maintenance of international peace and security, and that the Member States have agreed to accept and carry out its decisions in accordance with the Charter,

Recalling also the important role conferred by the Charter on the General Assembly and the Secretary-General in the maintenance of international peace and security,

1. Solemnly declares that:

1. States should act so as to prevent in their international relations the emergence or aggravation of disputes or situations, in particular by fulfilling in good faith their obligations under international law;

2. In order to prevent disputes or situations, States should develop their relations on the basis of the sovereign equality of States and in such a manner as to enhance the effectiveness of the collective security system through the effective implementation of the provisions of the Charter of the United Nations;

3. States should consider the use of bilateral or multilateral consultations in order better to understand each other's views, positions and interests;

4. States party to regional arrangements or members of agencies referred to in Article 52 of the Charter should make every effort to prevent or remove local disputes or situations through such arrangements and agencies;

5. States concerned should consider approaching the relevant organs of the United Nations in order to obtain advice or recommendations on preventive means for dealing with a dispute or situation;

6. Any State party to a dispute or directly concerned with a situation, particularly if it intends to request a meeting of the Security Council, should approach the Council, directly or indirectly, at an early stage and, if appropriate, on a confidential basis;

7. The Security Council should consider holding from time to time meetings, including at a high level with the participation, in particular, of Ministers for Foreign Affairs, or consultations to review the international situation and search for effective ways of improving it;

8. In the course of the preparation for the prevention or removal of particular disputes or situations, the Security Council should consider making use of the various means at its disposal, including the appointment of the Secretary-General as rapporteur for a specified question;

9. When a particular dispute or situation is brought to the attention of the Security Council without a meeting being requested, the Council should consider holding consultations with a view to examining the facts of the dispute or situation and keeping it under review, with the assistance of the Secretary-General when needed; the States concerned should have the opportunity of making their views known;

10. In such consultations, consideration should be given to employing such informal methods as the Security Council deems appropriate, including confidential contacts by its President;

11. In such consultations the Security Council should consider, inter alia:

(a) Reminding the States concerned to respect their obligations under the Charter;

(b) Making an appeal to the States concerned to refrain from any action which might give rise to a dispute or lead to the deterioration of the dispute or situation;

(c) Making an appeal to the States concerned to take action which might help to remove, or to prevent the continuation or deterioration of, the dispute or situation.

12. The Security Council should consider sending, at an early stage, fact-finding or good offices missions or establishing appropriate forms of United Nations presence, including observers and peace-keeping operations, as a means of preventing the further deterioration of the dispute or situation in the areas concerned;

13. The Security Council should consider encouraging and, where appropriate, endorsing efforts at the regional level by the States concerned or by regional arrangements or agencies to prevent or remove a dispute or situation in the region concerned;

14. Taking into consideration any procedures that have already been adopted by the States directly concerned, the Security Council should consider recommending to them appropriate procedures or methods of settlement of disputes or adjustment of situations, and such terms of settlement as it deems appropriate;

15. The Security Council, if it is appropriate for promoting the prevention and removal of disputes or situations, should, at an early stage, consider making use of the provisions of the Charter concerning the possibility of requesting the International Court of Justice to give an advisory opinion on any legal question;

16. The General Assembly should consider making use of the provisions of the Charter in order to discuss disputes or situations, when appropriate, and, in accordance with Article 11 and subject to Article 12 of the Charter, making recommendations;

17. The General Assembly should consider, where appropriate, supporting efforts undertaken at the regional level by the States concerned or by regional arrangements or agencies, to prevent or remove a dispute or situation in the region concerned;

18. If a dispute or situation has been brought before it, the General Assembly should consider, including in its recommendations making more use of fact-finding capabilities, in accordance with Article 11 and subject to Article 12 of the Charter;

19. The General Assembly, if it is appropriate for promoting the prevention and removal of disputes or situations, should consider making use of the provisions of the Charter concerning the possibility of requesting the International Court of Justice to give an advisory opinion on any legal question;

20. The Secretary-General, if approached by a State or States directly concerned with a dispute or situation, should respond swiftly by urging the States to seek a solution or adjustment by peaceful means of their own choice under the Charter and by offering his good offices or other means at his disposal, as he deems appropriate;

21. The Secretary-General should consider approaching the States directly concerned with a dispute or situation in an effort to prevent it from becoming a threat to the maintenance of international peace and security;

22. The Secretary-General should, where appropriate, consider making full use of fact-finding capabilities, including, with the consent of the host State, sending a representative or fact-finding missions to areas where a dispute or a situation exists; where necessary, the Secretary-General should also consider making the appropriate arrangements;

23. The Secretary-General should be encouraged to consider using, at as early a stage as he deems appropriate, the right that is accorded to him under Article 99 of the Charter;

24. The Secretary-General should, where appropriate, encourage efforts undertaken at the regional level to prevent or remove a dispute or situation in the region concerned;

25. Should States fail to prevent the emergence or aggravation of a dispute or situation, they shall continue to seek a settlement by peaceful means in accordance with the Charter;

2. Declares that nothing in the present Declaration shall be construed as prejudicing in any manner the provisions of the Charter, including those contained in Article 2, paragraph 7, thereof, or the rights and duties of States, or the scope of the functions and the powers of United Nations organs under the Charter, in particular those relating to the maintenance of international peace and security;

3. Also declares that nothing in the present Declaration could in any way prejudice the right to self-determination, freedom and independence of peoples forcibly deprived of that right and referred to in the Declaration on Principles of International Law concerning Friendly Relations and Co-operation among States in accordance with the Charter of the United Nations, particularly peoples under colonial or racist regimes or other forms of alien domination.

8 American Treaty on Pacific Settlement (Pact of Bogotá)

Date: 30 April 1948
Source: 30 UNTS 55
http://www.oas.org/juridico/english/treaties/a-42.html

CHAPTER ONE
GENERAL OBLIGATION TO SETTLE DISPUTES BY PACIFIC MEANS

ARTICLE I. The High Contracting Parties, solemnly reaffirming their commitments made in earlier international conventions and declarations, as well as in the Charter of the United Nations, agree to refrain from the threat or the use of force, or from any other means of coercion for the settlement of their controversies, and to have recourse at all times to pacific procedures.

ARTICLE II. The High Contracting Parties recognize the obligation to settle international controversies by regional procedures before referring them to the Security Council of the United Nations.

Consequently, in the event that a controversy arises between two or more signatory states which, in the opinion of the parties, cannot be settled by direct negotiations through the usual diplomatic channels, the parties bind themselves to use the procedures established in the present Treaty, in the manner and under the conditions provided for in the following articles, or, alternatively, such special procedures as, in their opinion, will permit them to arrive at a solution.

ARTICLE III. The order of the pacific procedures established in the present Treaty does not signify that the parties may not have recourse to the procedure which they consider most appropriate in each case, or that they should use all these procedures, or that any of them have preference over others except as expressly provided.

ARTICLE IV. Once any pacific procedure has been initiated, whether by agreement between the parties or in fulfillment of the present Treaty or a previous pact, no other procedure may be commenced until that procedure is concluded.

ARTICLE V. The aforesaid procedures may not be applied to matters which, by their nature, are within the domestic jurisdiction of the state. If the parties are not in agreement as to whether the controversy concerns a matter of domestic jurisdiction, this preliminary question shall be submitted to decision by the International Court of Justice, at the request of any of the parties.

ARTICLE VI. The aforesaid procedures, furthermore, may not be applied to matters already settled by arrangement between the parties, or by arbitral award or by decision of an international court, or which are governed by agreements or treaties in force on the date of the conclusion of the present Treaty.

ARTICLE VII. The High Contracting Parties bind themselves not to make diplomatic representations in order to protect their nationals, or to refer a controversy to a court of international jurisdiction for that purpose, when the said nationals have had available the means to place their case before competent domestic courts of the respective state.

ARTICLE VIII. Neither recourse to pacific means for the solution of controversies, nor the recommendation of their use, shall, in the case of an armed attack, be ground for delaying the exercise of the right of individual or collective self-defense, as provided for in the Charter of the United Nations.

CHAPTER TWO
PROCEDURES OF GOOD OFFICES AND MEDIATION

ARTICLE IX. The procedure of good *offices* consists in the attempt by one or more American Governments not parties to the controversy, or by one or more eminent citizens of any American State which is not a party to the controversy, to bring the parties together, so as to make it possible for them to reach an adequate solution between themselves.

ARTICLE X. Once the parties have been brought together and have resumed direct negotiations, no further action is to be taken by the states or citizens that have offered their good offices or have accepted an invitation to offer them; they may, however, by agreement between the parties, be present at the negotiations.

ARTICLE XI. The procedure of mediation consists in the submission of the controversy to one or more American Governments not parties to the controversy, or to one or more eminent citizens of any American State not a party to the controversy. In either case the mediator or mediators shall be chosen by mutual agreement between the parties.

ARTICLE XII. The functions of the mediator or mediators shall be to assist the parties in the settlement of controversies in the simplest and most direct manner, avoiding formalities and seeking an acceptable solution. No report shall be made by the mediator and, so far as he is concerned, the proceedings shall be wholly confidential.

ARTICLE XIII. In the event that the High Contracting Parties have agreed to the procedure of mediation but are unable to reach an agreement within two months on the selection of, the mediator or mediators, or no solution to the controversy has been reached within five months after mediation has begun, the parties shall have recourse without delay to any one of the other procedures of peaceful settlement established in the present Treaty.

ARTICLE XIV. The High Contracting Parties may offer their mediation, either individually or jointly, but they agree not to do so while the controversy is in process of settlement by any of the other procedures established in the present Treaty.

CHAPTER THREE
PROCEDURE OF INVESTIGATION AND CONCILIATION

ARTICLE XV. The procedure of investigation and conciliation consists in the submission of the controversy to a Commission of Investigation and Conciliation, which shall be established in accordance with the provisions established in subsequent articles of the present Treaty, and which shall function within the limitations prescribed therein.

ARTICLE XVI. The party initiating the procedure of investigation and conciliation shall request the Council of the Organization of American States to convoke the Commission of Investigation and Conciliation. The Council for its part shall take immediate steps to convoke it.

Once the request to convoke the Commission has been received, the controversy between the parties shall immediately be suspended, and the parties shall refrain from any act that might make conciliation more difficult. To that end, at the request of one of the parties, the Council of the Organization of American States may, pending the convocation of the Commission, make appropriate recommendations to the parties.

ARTICLE XVII. Each of the High Contracting Parties may appoint, by means of a bilateral agreement consisting of a simple exchange of notes with each of the other signatories, two members of the Commission of Investigation and Conciliation, only one of whom may be of its own nationality. The fifth member, who shall perform the functions of chairman, shall be selected immediately by common agreement of the members thus appointed.

Any one of the contracting parties may remove members whom it has appointed, whether nationals or aliens; at the same time it shall appoint the successor. If this is not done, the removal shall be considered as not having been made. The appointments and substitutions shall be registered with the Pan American Union, which shall endeavor to ensure that the commissions maintain their full complement of five members.

ARTICLE XVIII. Without prejudice to the provisions of the foregoing article, the Pan American Union shall draw up a permanent panel of American conciliators, to be made up as follows:

a) Each of the High Contracting Parties shall appoint, for three year periods, two of their nationals who enjoy the highest reputation for fairness, competence and integrity; b) The Pan American Union shall request of the candidates notice of their formal acceptance, and it shall place on the panel of conciliators the names of the persons who so notify it; c) The governments may, at any time, fill vacancies occurring among their appointees; and they may reappoint their members.

ARTICLE XIX. In the event that a controversy should arise between two or more American States that have not appointed the Commission referred to in Article XVII, the following procedure shall be observed:

a) Each party shall designate two members from the permanent panel of American conciliators, who are not of the same nationality as the appointing party.
b) These four members shall in turn choose a fifth member, from the permanent panel, not of the nationality of either party.
c) If, within a period of thirty days following the notification of their selection, the four members are unable to agree upon a fifth member, they shall each separately list the conciliators composing the permanent panel, in order of their preference, and upon comparison of the lists so prepared, the one who first receives a majority

of votes shall be declared elected. The person so elected shall perform the duties of chairman of the Commission.

ARTICLE XX. In convening the Commission of Investigation and Conciliation, the Council of the Organization of American States shall determine the place where the Commission shall meet. Thereafter, the Commission may determine the place or places in which it is to function, taking into account the best facilities for the performance of its work.

ARTICLE XXI. When more than two states are involved in the same controversy, the states that hold similar points of view shall be considered as a single party. If they have different interests they shall be entitled to increase the number of conciliators in order that all parties may have equal representation. The chairman shall be elected in the manner set forth in Article XIX.

ARTICLE XXII. It shall be the duty of the Commission of Investigation and Conciliation to clarify the points in dispute between the parties and to endeavor to bring about an agreement between them upon mutually acceptable terms. The Commission shall institute such investigations of the facts involved in the controversy as it may deem necessary for the purpose of proposing acceptable bases of settlement.

ARTICLE XXII. It shall be the duty of the parties to facilitate the work of the Commission and to supply it, to the fullest extent possible, with all useful documents and information, and also to use the means at their disposal to enable the Commission to summon and hear witnesses or experts and perform other tasks in the territories of the parties, in conformity with their laws.

ARTICLE XXIV. During the proceedings before the Commission, the parties shall be represented by plenipotentiary delegates or by agents, who shall serve as intermediaries between them and the Commission. The parties and the Commission may use the services of technical advisers and experts.

ARTICLE XXV. The Commission shall conclude its work within a period of six months from the date of its installation; but the parties may, by mutual agreement, extend the period.

ARTICLE XXVI. If, in the opinion of the parties, the controversy relates exclusively to questions of fact, the Commission shall limit itself to investigating such questions, and shall conclude its activities with an appropriate report.

ARTICLE XXVII. If an agreement is reached by conciliation, the final report of the Commission shall be limited to the text of the agreement and shall be published after its transmittal to the parties, unless the parties decide otherwise. If no agreement is reached, the final report shall contain a summary of the work of the Commission; it shall be delivered to the parties, and shall be published after the expiration of six months unless the parties decide otherwise. In both cases, the final report shall be adopted by a majority vote.

ARTICLE XXVIII. The reports and conclusions of the Commission of Investigation and Conciliation shall not be binding upon the parties, either with respect to the statement of facts or in regard to questions of law, and they shall have no other character than that of recommendations submitted for the consideration of the parties in order to facilitate a friendly settlement of the controversy.

ARTICLE XXIX. The Commission of Investigation and Conciliation shall transmit to each of the parties, as well as to the Pan American Union, certified copies of the minutes of its proceedings. These minutes shall not be published unless the parties so decide.

ARTICLE XXX. Each member of the Commission shall receive financial remuneration, the amount of which shall be fixed by agreement between the parties. If the parties do not agree thereon, the Council of the Organization shall determine the remuneration. Each government shall pay its own expenses and an equal share of the common expenses of the Commission, including the aforementioned remunerations.

CHAPTER FOUR
JUDICIAL PROCEDURE

ARTICLE XXXI. In conformity with Article 36, paragraph 2, of the Statute of the International Court of Justice, the High Contracting Parties declare that they recognize, in relation to any other American State, the jurisdiction of the Court as compulsory *ipso facto*, without the necessity of any special agreement so long as the present Treaty is in force, in all disputes of a juridical nature that arise among them concerning:

a) The interpretation of a treaty;
b) Any question of international law;
c) The existence of any fact which, if established, would constitute the breach of an international obligation;
d) The nature or extent of the reparation to be made for the breach of an international obligation.

ARTICLE XXXII. When the conciliation procedure previously established in the present Treaty or by agreement of the parties does not lead to a solution, and the said parties have not agreed upon an arbitral procedure, either of them shall be entitled to have recourse to the International Court of Justice in the manner prescribed in Article 40 of the Statute thereof. The Court shall have compulsory jurisdiction in accordance with Article 36, paragraph 1, of the said Statute.

ARTICLE XXXIII. If the parties fail to agree as to whether the Court has jurisdiction over the controversy, the Court itself shall first decide that question.

ARTICLE XXXIV. If the Court, for the reasons set forth in Articles V, VI and VII of this Treaty, declares itself to be without jurisdiction to hear the controversy, such controversy shall be declared ended.

ARTICLE XXXV. If the Court for any other reason declares itself to be without jurisdiction to hear and adjudge the controversy, the High Contracting Parties obligate themselves to submit it to arbitration, in accordance with the provisions of Chapter Five of this Treaty.

ARTICLE XXXVI. In the case of controversies submitted to the judicial procedure to which this Treaty refers, the decision shall devolve upon the full Court, or, if the parties so request, upon a special chamber in conformity with Article 26 of the Statute of the Court. The parties may agree, moreover, to have the controversy decided *ex aequo et bono.*

ARTICLE XXXVII. The procedure to be followed by the Court shall be that established in the Statute thereof.

CHAPTER FIVE
PROCEDURE OF ARBITRATION

ARTICLE XXXVIII. Notwithstanding the provisions of Chapter Four of this Treaty, the High Contracting Parties may, if they so agree, submit to arbitration differences of any kind, whether juridical or not, that have arisen or may arise in the future between them.

ARTICLE XXXIX. The Arbitral Tribunal to which a controversy is to be submitted shall, in the cases contemplated in Articles XXXV and XXXVIII of the present Treaty, be constituted in the following manner, unless there exists an agreement to the contrary.

ARTICLE XL. (1) Within a period of two months after notification of the decision of the Court in the case provided for in Article XXXV, each party shall name one arbiters of recognized competence in questions of international law and of the highest integrity, and shall transmit the designation to the Council of the Organization. At the same time, each party shall present to the Council a list of ten jurists chosen from among those on the general panel of members of the Permanent Court of Arbitration of The Hague who do not belong to its national group and who are willing to be members of the Arbitral Tribunal.

(2) The Council of the Organization shall, within the month following the presentation of the lists, proceed to establish the Arbitral Tribunal in the following manner:

a) If the lists presented by the parties contain three names in common, such persons, together with the two directly named by the parties, shall constitute the Arbitral Tribunal;
b) In case these lists contain more than three names in common, the three arbiters needed to complete the Tribunal shall be selected by lot;
c) In the circumstances envisaged in the two preceding clauses, the five arbiters designated shall choose one of their number as presiding officer;
d) If the lists contain only two names in common, such candidates and the two arbiters directly selected by the parties shall by common agreement choose the fifth arbiter, who shall preside over the Tribunal. The choice shall devolve upon a jurist on the aforesaid general panel of the Permanent Court of Arbitration of The Hague who has not been included in the lists drawn up by the parties;
e) If the lists contain only one name in common, that person shall be a member of the Tribunal, and another name shall be chosen by lot from among the eighteen jurists remaining on the above-mentioned lists. The presiding officer shall be elected in accordance with the procedure established in the preceding clause;
f) If the lists contain no names in common, one arbiter shall be chosen by lot from each of the lists; and the fifth arbiter, who shall act as presiding officer, shall be chosen in the manner previously indicated;
g) If the four arbiters cannot agree upon a fifth arbiter within one month after the Council of the Organization has notified them of their appointment, each of them shall separately arrange the list of jurists in the order of their preference and, after comparison of the lists so formed, the person who first obtains a majority vote shall be declared elected.

ARTICLE XLI. The parties may by mutual agreement establish the Tribunal in the manner they deem most appropriate; they may even select a single arbiter, designating in such case a chief of state, an eminent jurist, or any court of justice in which the parties have mutual confidence.

ARTICLE XLII. When more than two states are involved in the same controversy, the states defending the same interests shall be considered as a single party. If they have opposing interests they shall have the right to increase the number of arbiters so that all parties may have equal representation. The presiding officer shall be selected by the method established in Article XL.

ARTICLE XLIII. The parties shall in each case draw up a special agreement clearly defining the specific matter that is the subject of the controversy, the seat of the Tribunal, the rules of procedure to be observed, the period within which the award is to be handed down, and such other conditions as they may agree upon among themselves.

If the special agreement cannot be drawn up within three months after the date of the installation of the Tribunal, it shall be drawn up by the International Court of Justice through summary procedure, and shall be binding upon the parties.

ARTICLE XLIV. The parties may be represented before the Arbitral Tribunal by such persons as they may designate.

ARTICLE XLV. If one of the parties fails to designate its arbiter and present its list of candidates within the period provided for in Article XL, the other party shall have the right to request the Council of the Organization to establish the Arbitral Tribunal. The Council shall immediately urge the delinquent party to fulfill its obligations within an additional period of fifteen days, after which time the Council itself shall establish the Tribunal in the following manner

a) It shall select a name by lot from the list presented by the petitioning party.
b) It shall choose, by absolute majority vote, two jurists from the general panel of the Permanent Court of Arbitration of The Hague who do not belong to the national group of any of the parties.
c) The three persons so designated, together with the one directly chosen by the petitioning party, shall select the fifth arbiter, who shall act as presiding officer, in the manner provided for in Article XL.
d) Once the Tribunal is installed, the procedure established in article XLIII shall be followed.

ARTICLE XLVI. The award shall be accompanied by a supporting opinion, shall be adopted by a majority vote, and shall be published after notification thereof has been given to the parties. The dissenting arbiter or arbiters shall have the right to state the grounds for their dissent. The award, once it is duly handed down and made known to the parties, shall settle the controversy definitively, shall not be subject to appeal, and shall be carried out immediately.

ARTICLE XLVII. Any differences that arise in regard to the interpretation or execution of the award shall be submitted to the decision of the Arbitral Tribunal that rendered the award.

ARTICLE XLVIII. Within a year after notification thereof, the award shall be subject to review by the same Tribunal at the request of one of the parties, provided a previously existing fact is discovered unknown to the Tribunal and to the party requesting the review, and provided the Tribunal is of the opinion that such fact might have a decisive influence on the award.

ARTICLE XLIX. Every member of the Tribunal shall receive financial remuneration, the amount of which shall be fixed by agreement between the parties. If the parties do not agree on the amount, the Council of the Organization shall determine the remuneration. Each Government shall pay its own expenses and an equal share of the common expenses of the Tribunal, including the aforementioned remunerations.

CHAPTER SIX
FULFILLMENT OF DECISIONS

ARTICLE L. If one of the High Contracting Parties should fail to carry out the obligations imposed upon it by a decision of the International Court. of Justice or by an arbitral award, the other party or parties concerned shall, before resorting to the Security Council of the United Nations, propose a Meeting of Consultation of Ministers of Foreign Affairs to agree upon appropriate measures to ensure the fulfillment of the judicial decision or arbitral award.

CHAPTER SEVEN
ADVISORY OPINIONS

ARTICLE LI. The parties concerned in the solution of a controversy may, by agreement, petition the General Assembly or the Security Council of the United Nations to request an advisory opinion of the International Court of Justice on any juridical question.

The petition shall be made through the Council of the Organization of American States.

CHAPTER EIGHT
FINAL PROVISIONS

ARTICLE LII. The present Treaty shall be ratified by the High Contracting Parties in accordance with their constitutional procedures. The original instrument shall be deposited in the Pan American Union, which shall transmit an authentic certified copy to each Government for the purpose of ratification. The instruments of ratification shall be deposited in the archives of the Pan American Union, which shall notify the signatory governments of the deposit. Such notification shall be considered as an exchange of ratifications.

ARTICLE LIII. This Treaty shall come into effect between the High Contracting Parties in the order in which they deposit their respective ratifications.

ARTICLE LIV. Any American State which is not a signatory to the present Treaty, or which has made reservations thereto, may adhere to it, or may withdraw its reservations in whole or in part, by transmitting an official instrument to the Pan American Union, which shall notify the other High Contracting Parties in the manner herein established.

ARTICLE LV. Should any of the High Contracting Parties make reservations concerning the present Treaty, such reservations shall, with respect to the state that makes them, apply to all signatory states on the basis of reciprocity.

ARTICLE LVI. The present Treaty shall remain in force indefinitely, but may be denounced upon one year's notice, at the end of which period it shall cease to be in force with respect to the state denouncing it, but shall continue in force for the remaining signatories. The denunciation shall be addressed to the Pan American Union, which shall transmit it to the other Contracting Parties.

The denunciation shall have no effect with respect to pending procedures initiated prior to the transmission of the particular notification.

ARTICLE LVII. The present Treaty shall be registered with the Secretariat of the United Nations through the Pan American Union.

ARTICLE VLIII. As this Treaty comes into effect through the successive ratifications of the High Contracting Parties, the following treaties, conventions and protocols shall cease to be in force with respect to such parties:

Treaty to Avoid or Prevent Conflicts between the American States, of May 3, 1923;

General Convention of Inter-American Conciliation, of January 5, 1929;

General Treaty of Inter-American Arbitration and Additional Protocol of Progressive Arbitration, of January 5, 1929;

Additional Protocol to the General Convention of Inter-American Conciliation, of December 26, 1933;

Anti-War Treaty of Non-Aggression and Conciliation, of October 10, 1933;

Convention to Coordinate, Extend and Assure the Fulfillment of the Existing Treaties between the American States, of December 23, 1936;

Inter-American Treaty on Good Offices and Mediation, of December 23, 1936;

Treaty on the Prevention of Controversies, of December 23, 1936.

ARTICLE LIX. The provisions of the foregoing Article shall not apply to procedures already initiated or agreed upon in accordance with any of the above-mentioned international instruments.

ARTICLE LX. The present Treaty shall be called the "PACT OF BOGOTÁ."

IN WITNESS WHEREOF, the undersigned Plenipotentiaries, having deposited their full powers, found to be in good and due form, sign the present Treaty, in the name of their respective Governments, on the dates appearing below their signatures.

Done at the City of Bogotá, in four texts, in the English, French, Portuguese and Spanish languages respectively, on the thirtieth day of April, nineteen hundred forty-eight.

9 European Convention for the Peaceful Settlement of Disputes

Date: 29 April 1957
Source: 320 UNTS 243
https://www.coe.int/en/web/conventions/full-list/-/conventions/treaty/023

Preamble

The governments signatory hereto, being members of the Council of Europe,

Considering that the aim of the Council of Europe is to achieve a greater unity between its members;

Convinced that the pursuit of peace based upon justice is vital for the preservation of human society and civilisation;

Resolved to settle by peaceful means any disputes which may arise between them,

Have agreed as follows:

Chapter I – Judicial settlement

Article 1

The High Contracting Parties shall submit to the judgement of the International Court of Justice all international legal disputes which may arise between them including, in particular, those concerning:

(a) the interpretation of a treaty;
(b) any question of international law;
(c) the existence of any fact which, if established, would constitute a breach of an international obligation;
(d) the nature or extent of the reparation to be made for the breach of an international obligation.

Article 2

1. The provisions of Article 1 shall not affect undertakings by which the High Contracting Parties have accepted or may accept the jurisdiction of the International Court of Justice for the settlement of disputes other than those mentioned in Article 1.

2. The parties to a dispute may agree to resort to the procedure of conciliation before that of judicial settlement.

Article 3

The High Contracting Parties which are not parties to the Statute of the International Court of Justice shall carry out the measures necessary to enable them to have access thereto.

Chapter II – Conciliation

Article 4

1. The High Contracting Parties shall submit to conciliation all disputes which may arise between them, other than disputes falling within the scope of Article 1.

2. Nevertheless, the parties to a dispute falling within the scope of this article may agree to submit it to an arbitral tribunal without prior recourse to the procedure of conciliation.

Article 5

When a dispute arises which falls within the scope of Article 4, it shall be referred to a Permanent Conciliation Commission competent in the matter, previously set up by the parties concerned. If the parties agree not to have recourse to that Commission, or if there is no such Commission, the dispute shall be referred to a special Conciliation Commission, which shall be set up by the parties within a period of three months from the date on which a request to that effect is made by one of the parties to the other party.

Article 6

In the absence of agreement to the contrary between the parties concerned, the Special Conciliation Commission shall be constituted as follows:

The Commission shall be composed of five members. The parties shall each nominate one Commissioner, who may be chosen from among their respective nationals. The three other Commissioners, including the President, shall be chosen by agreement from among the nationals of third States. These three Commissioners shall be of different nationalities and shall not be habitually resident in the territory nor be in the service of the parties.

Article 7

If the nomination of the Commissioners to be designated jointly is not made within the period provided for in Article 5, the task of making the necessary nominations shall be entrusted to the government of a third State, chosen by agreement between the parties, or, failing such agreement being reached within three months, to the President of the International Court of Justice. Should the latter be a national of one of the parties to the dispute, this task shall be entrusted to the Vice-President of the Court or to the next senior judge of the Court who is not a national of the parties.

Article 8

Vacancies which may occur as a result of death, resignation or any other cause shall be filled within the shortest possible time in the manner fixed for the nominations.

Article 9

1. Disputes shall be brought before the Special Conciliation Commission by means of an application addressed to the President by the two parties acting in agreement or, in default thereof, by one or other of the parties.

2. The application, after giving a summary account of the subject of the dispute, shall contain the invitation to the Commission to take all necessary measures with a view to arriving at an amicable solution.

3. If the application emanates from only one of the parties, the other party shall, without delay, be notified of it by that party.

Article 10

1. In the absence of agreement to the contrary between the parties, the Special Conciliation Commission shall meet at the seat of the Council of Europe or at some other place selected by its President.

2. The Commission may at all times request the Secretary General of the Council of Europe to afford it his assistance.

Article 11

The work of the Special Conciliation Commission shall not be conducted in public unless the Commission with the consent of the parties so decides.

Article 12

1. In the absence of agreement to the contrary between the parties, the Special Conciliation Commission shall lay down its own procedure, which in any case must provide for both parties being heard. In regard to enquiries, subject to the provisions of this Convention, the Commission, unless it decides unanimously to the contrary, shall act in accordance with the provisions of Part III of The Hague Convention for the Pacific Settlement of International Disputes of 18th October 1907.

2. The parties shall be represented before the Conciliation Commission by agents whose duty shall be to act as intermediaries between them and the Commission; they may be assisted by counsels and experts appointed by them for that purpose and may request that all persons whose evidence appears to them desirable shall be heard.

3. The Commission shall be entitled to request oral explanations from the agents, counsels and experts of both parties, as well as from all persons it may think desirable to summon with the consent of their governments.

Article 13

In the absence of agreement to the contrary between the parties, the decisions of the Special Conciliation Commission shall be taken by a majority vote and, except in relation to questions of procedure, decisions of the Commission shall be valid only if all its members are present.

Article 14

The parties shall facilitate the work of the Special Conciliation Commission and, in particular, shall supply it to the greatest possible extent with all relevant documents and information. They shall use the means at their disposal to allow it to proceed in their territory, and in accordance with their law, to the summoning and hearing of witnesses or experts and to visit the localities in question.

Article 15

1. The task of the Special Conciliation Commission shall be to elucidate the questions in dispute, to collect with that object all necessary information by means of enquiry or otherwise, and to endeavour to bring the parties to an agreement. It may, after the case has been examined, inform the parties of the terms of settlement which seem suitable to it and lay down the period within which they are to make their decision.

2. At the close of its proceedings, the Commission shall draw up a *procès-verbal* stating, as the case may be, either that the parties have come to an agreement and, if need arises, the terms of the agreement, or that it has been impossible to effect a settlement. No mention shall be made in the *procès-verbal* of whether the Commission's decisions were taken unanimously or by a majority vote.

3. The proceedings of the Commission shall, unless the parties otherwise agree, be terminated within six months from the date on which the Commission shall have been given cognisance of the dispute.

Article 16

The Commission's *procès-verbal* shall be communicated without delay to the parties. It shall only be published with their consent.

Article 17

1. During the proceedings of the Commission, each of the Commissioners shall receive emoluments, the amount of which shall be fixed by agreement between the parties, each of which shall contribute an equal share.

2. The general expenses arising out of the working of the Commission shall be divided in the same manner.

Article 18

In the case of a mixed dispute involving both questions for which conciliation is appropriate and other questions for which judicial settlement is appropriate, any party to the dispute shall have the right to insist that the judicial settlement of the legal questions shall precede conciliation.

Chapter III – Arbitration

Article 19

The High Contracting Parties shall submit to arbitration all disputes which may arise between them other than those mentioned in Article 1 and which have not been settled by conciliation, either because the parties have agreed not to have prior recourse to it or because conciliation has failed.

Article 20

1. The party requesting arbitration shall inform the other party of the claim which it intends to submit to arbitration, of the grounds on which such claim is based and of the name of the arbitrator whom it has nominated.

2. In the absence of agreement to the contrary between the parties concerned, the Arbitral Tribunal shall be constituted as follows:

The Arbitral Tribunal shall consist of five members. The parties shall each nominate one member, who may be chosen from among their respective nationals. The other three arbitrators, including the President, shall be chosen by agreement from among the nationals of third States. They shall be of different nationalities and shall not be habitually resident in the territory nor be in the service of the parties.

Article 21

If the nomination of the members of the Arbitral Tribunal is not made within a period of three months from the date on which one of the parties requested the other party to constitute an Arbitral Tribunal, the task of making the necessary nominations shall be entrusted to the government of a third State, chosen by agreement between the parties, or, failing agreement within three months, to the President of the International Court of Justice. Should the latter be a national of one of the parties to the dispute, this task shall be entrusted to the Vice-President of the Court, or to the next senior judge of the Court who is not a national of the parties.

Article 22

Vacancies which may occur as a result of death, resignation or any other cause shall be filled within the shortest possible time in the manner fixed for the nomination.

Article 23

The parties shall draw up a special agreement determining the subject of the dispute and the details of procedure.

Article 24

In the absence of sufficient particulars in the special agreement regarding the matters referred to in Article 23, the provisions of Part IV of The Hague Convention of 18th October 1907 for the Pacific Settlement of International Disputes shall apply so far as possible.

Article 25

Failing the conclusion of a special agreement within a period of three months from the date on which the Arbitral Tribunal was constituted, the dispute may be brought before the Tribunal upon application by one or other party.

Article 26

If nothing is laid down in the special agreement or no special agreement has been made, the Tribunal shall decide *ex aequo et bono*, having regard to the general principles of international law, while respecting the contractual obligations and the final decisions of international tribunals which are binding on the parties.

Chapter IV – General provisions

Article 27

The provisions of this Convention shall not apply to:

(a) disputes relating to facts or situations prior to the entry into force of this Convention as between the parties to the dispute;

(b) disputes concerning questions which by international law are solely within the domestic jurisdiction of States.

Article 28

1. The provisions of this Convention shall not apply to disputes which the parties have agreed or may agree to submit to another procedure of peaceful settlement. Nevertheless, in respect of disputes falling within the scope of Article 1, the High Contracting Parties shall refrain from invoking as between themselves agreements which do not provide for a procedure entailing binding decisions.

2. This Convention shall in no way affect the application of the provisions of the Convention for the Protection of Human Rights and Fundamental Freedoms signed on 4th November 1950, or of the Protocol thereto signed on 20th March 1952.

Article 29

1. In the case of a dispute the subject of which, according to the municipal law of one of the parties, falls within the competence of its judicial or administrative authorities, the party in question may object to the dispute being submitted for settlement by any of the procedures laid down in this Convention until a decision with final effect has been pronounced, within a reasonable time, by the competent authority.

2. If a decision with final effect has been pronounced in the State concerned, it will no longer be possible to resort to any of the procedures laid down in this Convention after the expiration of a period of five years from the date of the aforementioned decision.

Article 30

If the execution of a judicial sentence or arbitral award would conflict with a judgement or measure enjoined by a court of law or other authority of one of the parties to the dispute, and if the municipal law of that party does not permit or only partially permits the consequences of the judgement or measure in question to be annulled, the Court or the Arbitral Tribunal shall, if necessary, grant the injured party equitable satisfaction.

Article 31

1. In all cases where a dispute forms the subject of arbitration or judicial proceedings, and particularly if the question on which the parties differ arises out of acts already committed or on the point of being committed, the International Court of Justice, acting in accordance with Article 41 of its Statute, or the Arbitral Tribunal, shall lay down within the shortest possible time the provisional measures to be adopted. The parties to the dispute shall be bound to accept such measures.

2. If the dispute is brought before a Conciliation Commission the latter may recommend to the parties the adoption of such provisional measures as it considers suitable.

3. The parties shall abstain from all measures likely to react prejudicially upon the execution of the judicial or arbitral decision or upon the arrangements proposed by the Conciliation Commission and, in general, shall abstain from any sort of action whatsoever which may aggravate or extend the dispute.

Article 32

1. This Convention shall remain applicable as between the Parties thereto, even though a third State, whether a Party to the Convention or not, has an interest in the dispute.

2. In the procedure of conciliation the parties may agree to invite such a third State to intervene.

Article 33

1. In judicial or arbitral procedure, if a third State should consider that its legitimate interests are involved, it may submit to the International Court of Justice or to the Arbitral Tribunal a request to intervene as a third party.

2. It will be for the Court or the Tribunal to decide upon this request.

Article 34

1. On depositing its instrument of ratification, any one of the High Contracting Parties may declare that it will not be bound by:

(a) Chapter III relating to arbitration; or

(b) Chapters II and III relating to conciliation and arbitration.

2. A High Contracting Party may only benefit from those provisions of this Convention by which it is itself bound.

Article 35

1. The High Contracting Parties may only make reservations which exclude from the application of this Convention disputes concerning particular cases or clearly specified subject matters, such as territorial status, or disputes falling within clearly defined categories. If one of the High Contracting Parties has made a reservation, the other Parties may enforce the same reservation in regard to that Party.

2. Any reservation made shall, unless otherwise expressly stated, be deemed not to apply to the procedure of conciliation.

3. Except as provided in paragraph 4 of this article, any reservations must be made at the time of depositing instruments of ratification of the Convention.

4. If a High Contracting Party accepts the compulsory jurisdiction of the International Court of Justice under paragraph 2 of Article 36 of the Statute of the said Court, subject to reservations, or amends any such reservations, that High Contracting Party may by a simple declaration, and subject to the provisions of paragraphs 1 and 2 of this article, make the same reservations to this Convention. Such reservations shall not release the High Contracting Party concerned from its obligations under this Convention in respect of disputes relating to facts or situations prior to the date of the declaration by which they are made. Such disputes shall, however, be submitted to the appropriate procedure under the terms of this Convention within a period of one year from the said date.

Article 36

A Party which is bound by only part of this Convention, or which has made reservations, may at any time, by a simple declaration, either extend the scope of its obligations or abandon all or part of its reservations.

Article 37

The declarations provided for in paragraph 4 of Article 35 and in Article 36 shall be addressed to the Secretary General of the Council of Europe, who shall transmit copies to each of the other High Contracting Parties.

Article 38

1. Disputes relating to the interpretation or application of this Convention, including those concerning the classification of disputes and the scope of reservations, shall be submitted

to the International Court of Justice. However, an objection concerning the obligation of a High Contracting Party to submit a particular dispute to arbitration can only be submitted to the Court within a period of three months after the notification by one party to the other of its intention to resort to arbitration. Any such objection made after that period shall be decided upon by the arbitral tribunal. The decision of the Court shall be binding on the body dealing with the dispute.

2. Recourse to the International Court of Justice in accordance with the above provisions shall have the effect of suspending the conciliation or arbitration proceedings concerned until the decision of the Court is known.

Article 39

1. Each of the High Contracting Parties shall comply with the decision of the International Court of Justice or the award of the Arbitral Tribunal in any dispute to which it is a party.

2. If one of the parties to a dispute fails to carry out its obligations under a decision of the International Court of Justice or an award of the Arbitral Tribunal, the other party to the dispute may appeal to the Committee of Ministers of the Council of Europe. Should it deem necessary, the latter, acting by a two-thirds majority of the representatives entitled to sit on the Committee, may make recommendations with a view to ensuring compliance with the said decision or award.

Article 40

1. This Convention may be denounced by a High Contracting Party only after the conclusion of a period of five years from the date of its entry into force for the Party in question. Such denunciation shall be subject to six months' notice, which shall be communicated to the Secretary General of the Council of Europe, who shall inform the other Contracting Parties.

2. Denunciation shall not release the High Contracting Party concerned from its obligations under this Convention in respect of disputes relating to facts or situations prior to the date of the notice referred to in the preceding paragraph. Such dispute shall, however, be submitted to the appropriate procedure under the terms of this Convention within a period of one year from the said date.

3. Subject to the same conditions, any High Contracting Party which ceases to be a member of the Council of Europe shall cease to be a party to this Convention within a period of one year from the said date.

Article 41

1. This Convention shall be open for signature by the members of the Council of Europe. It shall be ratified. Instruments of ratification shall be deposited with the Secretary General of the Council of Europe.

2. This Convention shall enter into force on the date of the deposit of the second instrument of ratification.

3. As regards any signatory ratifying subsequently, the Convention shall enter into force on the date of the deposit of its instrument of ratification.

4. The Secretary General of the Council of Europe shall notify all the members of the Council of Europe of the entry into force of the Convention, the names of the High Contracting Parties who have ratified it and the deposit of all instruments of ratification which may be effected subsequently.

In witness whereof the undersigned, being duly authorised thereto, have signed the present Convention.

Done at Strasbourg, this 29th day of April 1957, in English and French, both texts being equally authoritative, in a single copy which shall remain deposited in the archives of the Council of Europe. The Secretary General shall transmit certified copies to each of the signatories.

10 United Nations Convention on the Recognition and Enforcement of Foreign Arbitral Awards

Date: 10 June 1958
Source: http://www.newyorkconvention.org/english

Article I

1. This Convention shall apply to the recognition and enforcement of arbitral awards made in the territory of a State other than the State where the recognition and enforcement of such awards are sought, and arising out of differences between persons, whether physical or legal. It shall also apply to arbitral awards not considered as domestic awards in the State where their recognition and enforcement are sought.

2. The term "arbitral awards" shall include not only awards made by arbitrators appointed for each case but also those made by permanent arbitral bodies to which the parties have submitted.

3. When signing, ratifying or acceding to this Convention, or notifying extension under article X hereof, any State may on the basis of reciprocity declare that it will apply the Convention to the recognition and enforcement of awards made only in the territory of another Contracting State. It may also declare that it will apply the Convention only to differences arising out of legal relationships, whether contractual or not, which are considered as commercial under the national law of the State making such declaration.

Article II

1. Each Contracting State shall recognize an agreement in writing under which the parties undertake to submit to arbitration all or any differences which have arisen or which may arise between them in respect of a defined legal relationship, whether contractual or not, concerning a subject matter capable of settlement by arbitration.

2. The term "agreement in writing" shall include an arbitral clause in a contract or an arbitration agreement, signed by the parties or contained in an exchange of letters or telegrams.

3. The court of a Contracting State, when seized of an action in a matter in respect of which the parties have made an agreement within the meaning of this article, shall, at the request of one of the parties, refer the parties to arbitration, unless it finds that the said agreement is null and void, inoperative or incapable of being performed.

Article III

Each Contracting State shall recognize arbitral awards as binding and enforce them in accordance with the rules of procedure of the territory where the award is relied upon, under the conditions laid down in the following articles. There shall not be imposed substantially more onerous conditions or higher fees or charges on the recognition or enforcement of arbitral awards to which this Convention applies than are imposed on the recognition or enforcement of domestic arbitral awards.

Article IV

1. To obtain the recognition and enforcement mentioned in the preceding article, the party applying for recognition and enforcement shall, at the time of the application, supply:

(a) The duly authenticated original award or a duly certified copy thereof;

(b) The original agreement referred to in article II or a duly certified copy thereof.

2. If the said award or agreement is not made in an official language of the country in which the award is relied upon, the party applying for recognition and enforcement of the award shall produce a translation of these documents into such language. The translation shall be certified by an official or sworn translator or by a diplomatic or consular agent.

Article V

1. Recognition and enforcement of the award may be refused, at the request of the party against whom it is invoked, only if that party furnishes to the competent authority where the recognition and enforcement is sought, proof that:

(a) The parties to the agreement referred to in article II were, under the law applicable to them, under some incapacity, or the said agreement is not valid under the law to which the parties have subjected it or, failing any indication thereon, under the law of the country where the award was made; or

(b) The party against whom the award is invoked was not given proper notice of the appointment of the arbitrator or of the arbitration proceedings or was otherwise unable to present his case; or

(c) The award deals with a difference not contemplated by or not falling within the terms of the submission to arbitration, or it contains decisions on matters beyond the scope of the submission to arbitration, provided that, if the decisions on matters submitted to arbitration can be separated from those not so submitted, that part of the award which contains decisions on matters submitted to arbitration may be recognized and enforced; or

(d) The composition of the arbitral authority or the arbitral procedure was not in accordance with the agreement of the parties, or, failing such agreement, was not in accordance with the law of the country where the arbitration took place; or

(e) The award has not yet become binding on the parties, or has been set aside or suspended by a competent authority of the country in which, or under the law of which, that award was made.

2. Recognition and enforcement of an arbitral award may also be refused if the competent authority in the country where recognition and enforcement is sought finds that:

(a) The subject matter of the difference is not capable of settlement by arbitration under the law of that country; or

(b) The recognition or enforcement of the award would be contrary to the public policy of that country.

Article VI

If an application for the setting aside or suspension of the award has been made to a competent authority referred to in article V (1) (e), the authority before which the award is sought to be relied upon may, if it considers it proper, adjourn the decision on the enforcement of the award and may also, on the application of the party claiming enforcement of the award, order the other party to give suitable security.

Article VII

1. The provisions of the present Convention shall not affect the validity of multilateral or bilateral agreements concerning the recognition and enforcement of arbitral awards entered into by the Contracting States nor deprive any interested party of any right he may have to avail himself of an arbitral award in the manner and to the extent allowed by the law or the treaties of the country where such award is sought to be relied upon.

2. The Geneva Protocol on Arbitration Clauses of 1923 and the Geneva Convention on the Execution of Foreign Arbitral Awards of 1927 shall cease to have effect between Contracting States on their becoming bound and to the extent that they become bound, by this Convention.

Article VIII

1. This Convention shall be open until 31 December 1958 for signature on behalf of any Member of the United Nations and also on behalf of any other State which is or hereafter becomes a member of any specialized agency of the United Nations, or which is or hereafter becomes a party to the Statute of the International Court of Justice, or any other State to which an invitation has been addressed by the General Assembly of the United Nations.

2. This Convention shall be ratified and the instrument of ratification shall be deposited with the Secretary-General of the United Nations.

Article IX

1. This Convention shall be open for accession to all States referred to in article VIII.

2. Accession shall be effected by the deposit of an instrument of accession with the Secretary-General of the United Nations.

Article X

1. Any State may, at the time of signature, ratification or accession, declare that this Convention shall extend to all or any of the territories for the international relations of which it is responsible. Such a declaration shall take effect when the Convention enters into force for the State concerned.

2. At any time thereafter any such extension shall be made by notification addressed to the Secretary-General of the United Nations and shall take effect as from the ninetieth day after the day of receipt by the Secretary-General of the United Nations of this notification, or as from the date of entry into force of the Convention for the State concerned, whichever is the later.

3. With respect to those territories to which this Convention is not extended at the time of signature, ratification or accession, each State concerned shall consider the possibility of taking the necessary steps in order to extend the application of this Convention to such territories, subject, where necessary for constitutional reasons, to the consent of the Governments of such territories.

Article XI

In the case of a federal or non-unitary State, the following provisions shall apply:

(a) With respect to those articles of this Convention that come within the legislative jurisdiction of the federal authority, the obligations of the federal Government shall to this extent be the same as those of Contracting States which are not federal States;

(b) With respect to those articles of this Convention that come within the legislative jurisdiction of constituent states or provinces which are not, under the constitutional system of the federation, bound to take legislative action, the federal Government shall bring such articles with a favourable recommendation to the notice of the appropriate authorities of constituent states or provinces at the earliest possible moment;

(c) A federal State Party to this Convention shall, at the request of any other Contracting State transmitted through the Secretary-General of the United Nations, supply a statement of the law and practice of the federation and its constituent units in regard to any particular provision of this Convention, showing the extent to which effect has been given to that provision by legislative or other action.

Article XII

1. This Convention shall come into force on the ninetieth day following the date of deposit of the third instrument of ratification or accession.

2. For each State ratifying or acceding to this Convention after the deposit of the third instrument of ratification or accession, this Convention shall enter into force on the ninetieth day after deposit by such State of its instrument of ratification or accession.

Article XIII

1. Any Contracting State may denounce this Convention by a written notification to the Secretary-General of the United Nations. Denunciation shall take effect one year after the date of receipt of the notification by the Secretary-General.

2. Any State which has made a declaration or notification under article X may, at any time thereafter, by notification to the Secretary-General of the United Nations, declare that this Convention shall cease to extend to the territory concerned one year after the date of the receipt of the notification by the Secretary-General.

3. This Convention shall continue to be applicable to arbitral awards in respect of which recognition and enforcement proceedings have been instituted before the denunciation takes effect.

Article XIV

A Contracting State shall not be entitled to avail itself of the present Convention against other Contracting States except to the extent that it is itself bound to apply the Convention.

Article XV

The Secretary-General of the United Nations shall notify the States contemplated in article VIII of the following:

(a) Signatures and ratifications in accordance with article VIII;

(b) Accessions in accordance with article IX;

(c) Declarations and notifications under articles I, X and XI;

(d) The date upon which this Convention enters into force in accordance with article XII;
(e) Denunciations and notifications in accordance with article XIII.

Article XVI

1. This Convention, of which the Chinese, English, French, Russian and Spanish texts shall be equally authentic, shall be deposited in the archives of the United Nations.

2. The Secretary-General of the United Nations shall transmit a certified copy of this Convention to the States contemplated in article VIII.

2 Diplomatic Means

11 Permanent Court of Arbitration Optional Rules for Fact-Finding Commissions of Inquiry

Date: 15 December 1997
Source: https://docs.pca-cpa.org/2016/01/Permanent-Court-of-Arbitration-Optional-Rules-for-Fact-finding-Commissions-of-Inquiry.pdf

Application of the Rules

Article 1

1. These Rules shall apply when the parties have agreed to have recourse to a Fact-finding Commission of Inquiry ('Commission') pursuant to the Permanent Court of Arbitration ('PCA') Optional Rules for Fact-finding Commissions of Inquiry, to establish, by means of an impartial and independent investigation, facts with respect to which there is a difference of opinion between them.

2. The parties may agree to exclude or vary any of these Rules at any time.

Initiation of Fact-finding Proceedings

Article 2

1. The party initiating fact-finding shall send to the other party a written invitation to engage in fact-finding under these Rules, briefly identifying the facts to be established. A copy of the invitation shall also be sent to the International Bureau of the PCA ('International Bureau').

2. If the other party rejects the invitation, there will be no fact-finding proceedings under these Rules.

3. If the party initiating fact-finding does not receive a reply within sixty days from the date on which the invitation was sent, or within such other period of time as specified in the invitation, it may elect to treat this as a rejection of the invitation to engage in fact-finding. If it so elects, it shall inform the other party accordingly.

4. The parties may also jointly request in writing, addressed to the Secretary-General of the Permanent Court of Arbitration (the 'Secretary-General'), that a Commission be established. The request shall, to the extent possible, specify the facts to be established, without excluding any relevant new facts that may come up in the course of the fact-finding.

Number of Commissioners

Article 3

The Commission may consist of one, three, or five commissioners.[1] Unless the parties agree otherwise there shall be one commissioner.

[1] Throughout these Rules, the fact-finding body is referred to as the 'Commission', irrespective of the number of commissioners.

Appointment of Commissioners

Article 4

1. (a) In fact-finding proceedings with one commissioner, the parties shall endeavour to reach agreement on the name of a sole commissioner;
   (b) In fact-finding proceedings with three or five commissioners, each party shall appoint one or two commissioners, as the case may be. Within two months of the last appointment, the party-appointed commissioners shall designate a third or fifth commissioner, as the case may be, who will act as President of the Commission.

2. The parties may enlist the assistance of an appropriate institution or person in connection with the appointment of commissioners. In particular,
   (a) A party may request such an institution or person to recommend the names of suitable individuals to act as commissioner; or
   (b) The parties may agree that the appointment of one or more commissioners be made directly by such an institution or person.

3. The parties may also enlist the assistance of the Secretary-General in connection with the appointment of commissioners. In particular,
   (a) A party may request the Secretary-General to designate an institution or person to perform the function set forth in paragraph 2(a) of this article;
   (b) The parties may request the Secretary-General to designate an institution or person to perform the function set forth in paragraph 2(b) of this article; or
   (c) The Secretary-General may be the 'person' performing the functions set forth in paragraphs 2(a) and (b) of this article, pursuant to a request or agreement.

4. In recommending or appointing individuals to act as commissioners, the institution or person shall have regard to such considerations as are likely to secure the appointment of an independent and impartial commissioner, and, with respect to a sole, third or fifth commissioner, shall take into account the advisability of appointing a commissioner of a nationality other than the nationalities of the parties.

5. Any vacancy on the Commission shall be filled in the manner in which the original appointment of the commissioner being replaced was made.

Independence of Commissioners

Article 5

Commissioners shall act in strict conformity with their mandate and perform their task in an impartial manner. Upon accepting appointment, each commissioner shall submit to the International Bureau a declaration confirming his or her independence from the parties.

Place of Meeting of the Commission

Article 6

1. Unless the parties have agreed otherwise, the Commission shall meet in The Hague. The International Bureau shall act as Registry, keep the Commission's archives, and place its offices and staff at the disposal of the Commission.

2. If the fact-finding proceedings are held at a place other than The Hague, the Commission may, in consultation with the International Bureau, appoint a secretary.

3. The Commission may determine the locale of the fact-finding proceedings within the country agreed upon by the parties. It may hold meetings for consultation among its

members at any place it deems appropriate, having regard to the circumstances of the fact-finding.

4. The Commission may meet at any place it deems appropriate for the inspection of goods, property, documents, or sites, or for the interrogation of witnesses. The parties shall be given sufficient notice to enable them to be present at such inspection.

5. For purposes of the activities contemplated in paragraphs 2–4 of this article, the Commission or the International Bureau shall, where necessary, seek the permission of, and any requisite assistance from, the country in which these activities are to be undertaken.

Representation and Assistance

Article 7

The parties may be represented or assisted by persons of their choice. The names and addresses of such persons shall be communicated in writing to the other party and to the Commission; such communication shall specify whether the appointment is made for purposes of representation or of assistance.

Language

Article 8

Subject to an agreement by the parties, the Commission shall determine the language or languages to be used in the proceedings. The Commission may request that any documents submitted in the course of the proceedings be accompanied by a translation into the language or languages agreed upon by the parties or determined by the Commission.

Co-operation of Parties with the Commission

Article 9

1. The parties shall co-operate with the Commission in good faith and shall, in particular, comply with requests by the Commission to submit written materials, provide evidence and attend meetings. All such documents submitted to the Commission shall, at the same time, be transmitted to the other party and to the International Bureau.

2. The parties undertake to make use of all means at their disposal to insure the appearance of witnesses and experts before the Commission. If witnesses or experts are unable to appear before the Commission, the parties shall arrange for their evidence to be taken before qualified officials in the place where the witnesses or experts are located, and speedily transmit the evidence thus obtained to the Commission.

3. A State that agrees to engage in fact-finding pursuant to these Rules shall be deemed to have granted its permission for the conduct in its territory of any of the activities set forth in article 6, paragraphs 2–4, and further undertakes to use all means at its disposal to provide the Commission with whatever assistance it may require in the conduct of the fact-finding proceedings, including but not limited to, ensuring the appearance or written testimony of witnesses and experts, as contemplated in paragraph 1 of this article.

4. In the event that the Commission requires the permission or cooperation of a third State, for example, as contemplated in article 6 of these Rules, the parties shall use all reasonable means at their disposal to obtain such permission and/or co-operation. A State that is a party to fact-finding undertakes to make the necessary request to the State concerned.

Confidentiality

Article 10

Unless the parties agree otherwise, or unless disclosure is required by the law applicable to a party, the members of the Commission and the parties shall keep confidential all matters relating to the fact-finding proceedings, including the investigations, hearings, deliberations and findings of the Commission. Unless the parties agree otherwise, the Commission shall meet *in camera*.

Submission of Statements to the Commission

Article 11

1. Upon its establishment, the Commission shall request each party to submit to it a brief written statement describing the general nature of the facts to be established and the points at issue. The Commission shall have the discretion to determine whether these statements are to be submitted simultaneously or responsively.

2. The Commission may request the parties to submit further written statements of their respective positions and the facts and grounds in support thereof, supplemented by any documents and other evidence that each party deems appropriate.

3. At any stage of the fact-finding proceedings, the Commission may request a party to submit such additional information as the Commission deems appropriate.

4. All documents, statements, information or evidence supplied by one party shall at the same time be provided to the other party, and a copy shall be filed with the International Bureau.

Conduct of the Fact-finding Proceedings

Article 12

1. Subject to these Rules and the agreement of the parties, the Commission may conduct the fact-finding proceedings in such manner as it considers appropriate, provided that the parties are treated with equality and that at any stage of the proceedings each party is given a full opportunity to present its case.

2. The Commission shall give the parties every opportunity to be present at hearings and investigations, and to submit documents, present evidence and have witnesses and experts called. The Commission may also take initiative in asking for documents and calling witnesses and experts. The method for obtaining oral testimony from witnesses and experts shall be determined by the Commission.

3. Unless the parties have decided otherwise, and having regard to the circumstances of the case, the Commission shall determine the scope and type of any record to be made of the hearings and other meetings of the Commission.

Decision-making

Article 13

When the Commission consists of three or five members, all decisions of the Commission shall be made by a majority of its members.

Termination of Fact-finding Proceedings

Article 14

1. Unless agreed otherwise, the fact-finding proceedings shall terminate upon the issuance of a written report by the Commission.

2. Unless the parties have agreed otherwise, the report of the Commission shall not be binding on the parties.

Article 15

The report shall be signed by the sole commissioner or the President of the Commission, as the case may be, and signed for acknowledgment by the Secretary-General. Individual opinions may be attached to the report. The report shall state in detail the facts established by the Commission, and the reason why certain facts may not be considered as having been established. Unless the parties agree to make it public, the report shall remain confidential.

Costs

Article 16

1. Upon termination of the fact-finding proceedings, the Commission shall, in consultation with the International Bureau, fix the costs of the fact-finding and give written notice thereof to the parties. The term 'costs' shall include:

(a) The fees of the commissioners, which shall be reasonable in amount;
(b) The travel and other expenses of the commissioners;
(c) The travel and other expenses of witnesses requested by the Commission;
(d) The costs of any expert advice requested by the Commission;
(e) The costs of any services of the Secretary-General and the International Bureau, including costs related to the holding of proceedings outside The Hague.

2. The costs, as defined above, shall be borne equally by the parties unless the Commission provides for a different apportionment. All other expenses incurred by a party, including those related to the written or oral testimony of any witnesses or experts that it presents, shall be borne by that party.

Deposits

Article 17

1. The Commission, on its establishment, may request the parties to deposit equal amounts as an advance for the costs referred to in article 16. All amounts deposited by the parties pursuant to this paragraph and paragraph 2 of this article shall be paid to the International Bureau, and shall be disbursed by it for such costs.

2. During the course of the fact-finding proceedings the Commission may request supplementary deposits from the parties.

3. If the required deposits under paragraphs 1 and 2 of this article are not paid in full by both parties within sixty days of a request therefore, the Commission may suspend the proceedings or may make a written declaration of termination to the parties, effective thirty days after the date of that declaration.

4. Upon termination of the fact-finding proceedings, the Commission shall render an accounting to the parties of the deposits received and amounts disbursed, and shall return any unexpended balance to the parties.

12 The International Commission of Inquiry between Great Britain and Russia Arising out of the North Sea Incident: Agreement of Submission (The Dogger Bank Incident)

Date: 25 (12) November 1904
Source: (1908) *2 American Journal of International Law 929*

Agreement of submission

His Britannic Majesty's Government and the Imperial Russian Government having agreed to intrust to an International Commission of Inquiry, assembled conformably to Articles IX to XIV of the Hague convention of the 29th (17th) July, 1899, for the pacific settlement of international disputes, the task of elucidating by means of an impartial and conscientious investigation the questions of fact connected with the incident which occurred during the night of the 21st–22d (8th–9th) October, 1904, in the North Sea (on which occasion the firing of the guns of the Russian fleet caused the loss of a boat and the death of two persons belonging to a British fishing fleet, as well as damages to other boats of that fleet and injuries to the crews of some of those boats), the undersigned, being duly authorized thereto, have agreed upon the following provisions:

ARTICLE I

The International Commission of Inquiry shall be composed of five members (commissioners), of whom two shall be officers of high rank in the British and Imperial Russian navies, respectively. The Governments of France and of the United States of America shall each be requested to select one of their naval officers of high rank as a member of the commission. The fifth member shall be chosen by agreement between the four members above mentioned.

In the event of no agreement being arrived at between the four commissioners as to the selection of the fifth member of the commission, His Imperial and Royal Majesty the Emperor of Austria, King of Hungary, shall be invited to select him.

Each of the two High Contracting Parties shall likewise appoint a legal assessor to advise the commissioners, and an agent officially empowered to take part in the labors of the commission.

ARTICLE II

The commission shall inquire into and report on all the circumstances relative to the North Sea incident, and particularly on the question as to where the responsibility lies and the degree of blame attaching to the subjects of the two High Contracting Parties or to the subjects of other countries in the event of their responsibility being established by the inquiry.

ARTICLE III

The commission shall settle the details of the procedure which it will follow for the purpose of accomplishing the task with which it has been intrusted.

ARTICLE IV

The two High Contracting Parties undertake to supply the International Commission of Inquiry, to the utmost extent which they may find possible, with all the means and facilities necessary, in order to enable it to acquaint itself thoroughly with and appreciate correctly the matters in dispute.

ARTICLE V

The commission shall assemble at Paris as soon as possible after the signature of this agreement.

ARTICLE VI

The commission shall present its report to the two High Contracting Parties signed by all the members of the commission.

ARTICLE VII

The commission shall take all its decisions by a majority of the votes of the five commissioners.

ARTICLE VIII

The two High Contracting Parties undertake each to bear, on reciprocal terms, the expenses of the inquiry made by it previous to the assembly of the commission. The expenses incurred by the International Commission, after the date of its assembly, in organizing its staff and in conducting the investigations which it will have to make, shall be shared equally by the two Governments.

In witness whereof the undersigned have signed the present declaration and have affixed thereto their seals.

Done in duplicate at St. Petersburgh, November 25 (12), 1904.

(Signed) CHARLES HARDINGE.
(Signed) COMTE LAMSDORFF.

13 Declaration of the Government of the Democratic and Popular Republic of Algeria (General Declaration)* (Mediated Algiers Accords)

Date: 19 January 1981
Source: (1981) 20 ILM 224

The Government of the Democratic and Popular Republic of Algeria, having been requested by the Governments of the Islamic Republic of Iran and the United States of

* N.B.: The Undertakings by the Governments of the United States of America and of the Islamic Republic of Iran with Respect to the Declaration, and the Escrow Agreement, have been omitted. The Declaration concerning the Settlement of Claims is reproduced as Document No. 66.a below.

America to serve as an intermediary in seeking a mutually acceptable resolution of the crisis in their relations arising out of the detention of the 52 United States nationals in Iran, has consulted extensively with the two governments as to the commitments which each is willing to make in order to resolve the crisis within the framework of the four points stated in the resolution of November 2, 1980, of the Islamic Consultative Assembly of Iran. On the basis of formal adherences received from Iran and the United States, the Government of Algeria now declares that the following interdependent commitments have been made by the two governments:

General Principles

The undertakings reflected in this Declaration are based on the following general principles:

A. Within the framework of and pursuant to the provisions of the two Declarations of the Government of the Democratic and Popular Republic of Algeria, the United States will restore the financial position of Iran, in so far as possible, to that which existed prior to November 14, 1979. In this context, the United States commits itself to ensure the mobility and free transfer of all Iranian assets within its jurisdiction, as set forth in Paragraphs 4–9.

B. It is the purpose of both parties, within the framework of and pursuant to the provisions of the two Declarations of the Government of the Democratic and Popular Republic of Algeria, to terminate all litigation as between the Government of each party and the nationals of the other, and to bring about the settlement and termination of all such claims through binding arbitration. Through the procedures provided in the Declaration, relating to the Claims Settlement Agreement, the United States agrees to terminate all legal proceedings in United States courts involving claims of United States persons and institutions against Iran and its state enterprises, to nullify all attachments and judgments obtained therein, to prohibit all further litigation based on such claims, and to bring about the termination of such claims through binding arbitration.

Point I: Non-Intervention in Iranian Affairs

1. The United States pledges that it is and from now on will be the policy of the United States not to intervene, directly or indirectly, politically or militarily, in Iran's internal affairs.

Points II and III: Return of Iranian Assets and Settlement of U.S. Claims

2. Iran and the United States (hereinafter "the parties") will immediately select a mutually agreeable central bank (hereinafter "the Central Bank") to act, under the instructions of the Government of Algeria and the Central Bank of Algeria (hereinafter "The Algerian Central Bank") as depositary of the escrow and security funds hereinafter prescribed and will promptly enter into depositary arrangements with the Central Bank in accordance with the terms of this declaration. All funds placed in escrow with the Central Bank pursuant to this declaration shall be held in an account in the name of the Algerian Central Bank. Certain procedures for implementing the obligations set forth in this Declaration and in the Declaration of the Democratic and Popular Republic of Algeria concerning the settlement of claims by the Government of the United States and the Government of the Islamic Republic of Iran (hereinafter "the Claims Settlement Agreement") are separately set forth in certain Undertakings of the Government of the United States of America and the Government of

the Islamic Republic of Iran with respect to the Declaration of the Democratic and Popular Republic of Algeria.

3. The depositary arrangements shall provide that, in the event that the Government of Algeria certifies to the Algerian Central Bank that the 52 U.S. nationals have safely departed from Iran, the Algerian Central Bank will thereupon instruct the Central Bank to transfer immediately all monies or other assets in escrow with the Central Bank pursuant to this declaration, provided that at any time prior to the making of such certification by the Government of Algeria, each of the two parties, Iran and the United States, shall have the right on seventy-two hours notice to terminate its commitments under this declaration. If such notice is given by the United States and the foregoing certification is made by the Government of Algeria within the seventy-two hour period of notice, the Algerian Central Bank will thereupon instruct the Central Bank to transfer such monies and assets. If the seventy-two hour period of notice by the United States expires without such a certification having been made, or if the notice of termination is delivered by Iran, the Algerian Central Bank will thereupon instruct the Central Bank to return all such monies and assets to the United States, and thereafter the commitments reflected in this declaration shall be of no further force and effect.

Assets in the Federal Reserve Bank

4. Commencing upon completion of the requisite escrow arrangements with the Central Bank, the United States will bring about the transfer to the Central Bank of all gold bullion which is owned by Iran and which is in the custody of the Federal Reserve Bank of New York, together with all other Iranian assets (or the cash equivalent thereof) in the custody of the Federal Reserve Bank of New York, to be held by the Central Bank in escrow until such time as their transfer or return is required by Paragraph 3 above.

Assets in Foreign Branches of U.S. Banks

5. Commencing upon the completion of the requisite escrow arrangements with the Central Bank, the United States will bring about the transfer to the Central Bank, to the account of the Algerian Central Bank, of all Iranian deposits and securities which on or after November 14, 1979, stood upon the books of overseas banking offices of U.S. banks, together with interest thereon through December 31, 1980, to be held by the Central Bank, to the account of the Algerian Central Bank, in escrow until such time as their transfer or return is required in accordance with Paragraph 3 of this Declaration.

Assets in U.S. Branches of U.S. Banks

6. Commencing with the adherence by Iran and the United States to this declaration and the claims settlement agreement attached hereto, and following the conclusion of arrangements with the Central Bank for the establishment of the interest-bearing security account specified in that agreement and Paragraph 7 below, which arrangements will be concluded within 30 days from the date of this Declaration, the United States will act to bring about the transfer to the Central Bank, within six months from such date, of all Iranian deposits and securities in U.S. banking institutions in the United States, together with interest thereon, to be held by the Central Bank in escrow until such time as their transfer or return is required by Paragraph 3.

7. As funds are received by the Central Bank pursuant to Paragraph 6 above, the Algerian Central Bank shall direct the Central Bank to (1) transfer one-half of each such receipt to

Iran and (2) place the other half in a special interest-bearing security account in the Central Bank, until the balance in the security account has reached the level of $1 billion. After the $1 billion balance has been achieved, the Algerian Central Bank shall direct all funds received pursuant to Paragraph 6 to be transferred to Iran. All funds in the security account are to be used for the sole purpose of securing the payment of, and paying, claims against Iran in accordance with the claims settlement agreement. Whenever the Central Bank shall thereafter notify Iran that the balance in the security account has fallen below $500 million, Iran shall promptly make new deposits sufficient to maintain a minimum balance of $500 million in the account. The account shall be so maintained until the President of the Arbitral Tribunal established pursuant to the claims settlement agreement has certified to the Central Bank of Algeria that all arbitral awards against Iran have been satisfied in accordance with the claims settlement agreement, at which point any amount remaining in the security account shall be transferred to Iran.

Other Assets in the U.S. and Abroad

8. Commencing with the adherence of Iran and the United States to this declaration and the attached claims settlement agreement and the conclusion of arrangements for the establishment of the security account, which arrangements will be concluded within 30 days from the date of this Declaration, the United States will act to bring about the transfer to the Central Bank of all Iranian financial assets (meaning funds or securities) which are located in the United States and abroad, apart from those assets referred to in Paragraph 5 and 6 above, to be held by the Central Bank in escrow until their transfer or return is required by Paragraph 3 above.

9. Commencing with the adherence by Iran and the United States to this declaration and the attached claims settlement agreement and the making by the Government of Algeria of the certification described in Paragraph 3 above, the United States will arrange, subject to the provisions of U.S. law applicable prior to November 14, 1979, for the transfer to Iran of all Iranian properties which are located in the United States and abroad and which are not within the scope of the preceding paragraphs.

Nullification of Sanctions and Claims

10. Upon the making by the Government of Algeria of the certification described in Paragraph 3 above, the United States will revoke all trade sanctions which were directed against Iran in the period November 4, 1979, to date.

11. Upon the making by the Government of Algeria of the certification described in Paragraph 3 above, the United States will promptly withdraw all claims now pending against Iran before the International Court of Justice and will thereafter bar and preclude the prosecution against Iran of any pending or future claim of the United States or a United States national arising out of events occurring before the date of this declaration related to (A) the seizure of the 52 United States nationals on November 4, 1979, (B) their subsequent detention, (C) injury to United States property or property of the United States nationals within the United States Embassy compound in Tehran after November 3, 1979, and (D) injury to the United States nationals or their property as a result of popular movements in the course of the Islamic Revolution in Iran which were not an act of the Government of Iran. The United States will also bar and preclude the prosecution against

Iran in the courts of the United States of any pending or future claim asserted by persons other than the United States nationals arising out of the events specified in the preceding sentence.

Point IV: Return of the Assets of the Family of the Former Shah

12. Upon the making by the Government of Algeria of the certification described in Paragraph 3 above, the United States will freeze, and prohibit any transfer of, property and assets in the United States within the control of the estate of the former Shah or of any close relative of the former Shah served as a defendant in U.S. litigation brought by Iran to recover such property and assets as belonging to Iran. As to any such defendant, including the estate of the former Shah, the freeze order will remain in effect until such litigation is finally terminated. Violation of the freeze order shall be subject to the civil and criminal penalties prescribed by U.S. law.

13. Upon the making by the Government of Algeria of the certification described in Paragraph 3 above, the United States will order all persons within U.S. jurisdiction to report to the U.S. Treasury within 30 days, for transmission to Iran, all information known to them, as of November 3, 1979, and as of the date of the order, with respect to the property and assets referred to in Paragraph 12. Violation of the requirement will be subject to the civil and criminal penalties prescribed by U.S. law.

14. Upon the making by the Government of Algeria of the certification described in Paragraph 3 above, the United States will make known, to all appropriate U.S. courts, that in any litigation of the kind described in Paragraph 12 above the claims of Iran should not be considered legally barred either by sovereign immunity principles or by the act of state doctrine and that Iranian decrees and judgments relating to such assets should be enforced by such courts in accordance with United States law.

15. As to any judgment of a U.S. court which calls for the transfer of any property or assets to Iran, the United States hereby guarantees the enforcement of the final judgment to the extent that the property or assets exist within the United States.

16. If any dispute arises between the parties as to whether the United States has fulfilled any obligation imposed upon it by Paragraphs 12–15, inclusive, Iran may submit the dispute to binding arbitration by the tribunal established by, and in accordance with the provisions of, the claims settlement agreement. If the tribunal determines that Iran has suffered a loss as a result of a failure by the United States to fulfill such obligation, it shall make an appropriate award in favor of Iran which may be enforced by Iran in the courts of any nation in accordance with its laws.

Settlement of Disputes

17. If any other dispute arises between the parties as to the interpretation or performance of any provision of this declaration, either party may submit the dispute to binding arbitration by the tribunal established by, and in accordance with the provisions of, the claims settlement agreement. Any decision of the tribunal with respect to such dispute, including any award of damages to compensate for a loss resulting from a breach of this declaration or the claims settlement agreement, may be enforced by the prevailing party in the courts of any nation in accordance with its laws.

14 United Nations Model Rules for the Conciliation of Disputes between States

Date: 11 December 1995
Source: UN Doc A/RES/50/50 (Annex)
https://legal.un.org/avl/ha/unmrcdbs/unmrcdbs.html

CHAPTER I
APPLICATION OF THE RULES

Article 1

1. These rules apply to the conciliation of disputes between States where those States have expressly agreed in writing to their application.

2. The States which agree to apply these rules may at any time, through mutual agreement, exclude or amend any of their provisions.

CHAPTER II
INITIATION OF THE CONCILIATION PROCEEDINGS

Article 2

1. The conciliation proceedings shall begin as soon as the States concerned (henceforth: the parties) have agreed in writing to the application of the present rules, with or without amendments, as well as on a definition of the subject of the dispute, the number and emoluments of members of the conciliation commission, its seat and the maximum duration of the proceedings, as provided in article 24. If necessary, the agreement shall contain provisions concerning the language or languages in which the proceedings are to be conducted and the linguistic services required.

2. If the States cannot reach agreement on the definition of the subject of the dispute, they may by mutual agreement request the assistance of the Secretary-General of the United Nations to resolve the difficulty. They may also by mutual agreement request his assistance to resolve any other difficulty that they may encounter in reaching an agreement on the modalities of the conciliation proceedings.

CHAPTER III
NUMBER AND APPOINTMENT OF CONCILIATORS

Article 3

There may be three conciliators or five conciliators. In either case the conciliators shall form a commission.

Article 4

If the parties have agreed that three conciliators shall be appointed, each one of them shall appoint a conciliator, who may not be of its own nationality. The parties shall appoint by mutual agreement the third conciliator, who may not be of the nationality of any of the parties or of the other conciliators. The third conciliator shall act as president of the commission. If he is not appointed within two months of the appointment of the conciliators appointed individually by the parties, the third conciliator shall be appointed by the Government of a third State chosen by agreement between the parties or, if such agreement is not obtained within two months, by the President of the International Court of Justice. If the President is a national of one of the parties, the appointment shall be made by the Vice-President or the next member of the Court in order of seniority who is not a national of the parties. The third conciliator shall not reside habitually in the territory of the parties or be or have been in their service.

Article 5

1. If the parties have agreed that five conciliators should be appointed, each one of them shall appoint a conciliator who may be of its own nationality. The other three conciliators, one of whom shall be chosen with a view to his acting as president, shall be appointed by agreement between the parties from among nationals of third States and shall be of different nationalities. None of them shall reside habitually in the territory of the parties or be or have been in their service. None of them shall have the same nationality as that of the other two conciliators.

2. If the appointment of the conciliators whom the parties are to appoint jointly has not been effected within three months, they shall be appointed by the Government of a third State chosen by agreement between the parties or, if such an agreement is not reached within three months, by the President of the International Court of Justice. If the President is a national of one of the parties, the appointment shall be made by the Vice-President or the next judge in order of seniority who is not a national of the parties. The Government or member of the International Court of Justice making the appointment shall also decide which of the three conciliators shall act as president.

3. If, at the end of the three-month period referred to in the preceding paragraph, the parties have been able to appoint only one or two conciliators, the two conciliators or the conciliator still required shall be appointed in the manner described in the preceding paragraph. If the parties have not agreed that the conciliator or one of the two conciliators whom they have appointed shall act as president, the Government or member of the International Court of Justice appointing the two conciliators or the conciliator still required shall also decide which of the three conciliators shall act as president.

4. If, at the end of the three-month period referred to in paragraph 2 of this article, the parties have appointed three conciliators but have not been able to agree which of them shall act as president, the president shall be chosen in the manner described in that paragraph.

Article 6

Vacancies which may occur in the commission as a result of death, resignation or any other cause shall be filled as soon as possible by the method established for appointing the members to be replaced.

CHAPTER IV
FUNDAMENTAL PRINCIPLES

Article 7

The commission, acting independently and impartially, shall endeavour to assist the parties in reaching an amicable settlement of the dispute. If no settlement is reached during the consideration of the dispute, the commission may draw up and submit appropriate recommendations to the parties for consideration.

CHAPTER V
PROCEDURES AND POWERS OF THE COMMISSION

Article 8

The commission shall adopt its own procedure.

Article 9

1. Before the commission begins its work, the parties shall designate their agents and shall communicate the names of such agents to the president of the commission. The president shall determine, in agreement with the parties, the date of the commission's first meeting, to which the members of the commission and the agents shall be invited.

2. The agents of the parties may be assisted before the commission by counsel and experts appointed by the parties.

3. Before the first meeting of the commission, its members may meet informally with the agents of the parties, if necessary, accompanied by the appointed counsel and experts to deal with administrative and procedural matters.

Article 10

1. At its first meeting, the commission shall appoint a secretary.

2. The secretary of the commission shall not have the nationality of any of the parties, shall not reside habitually in their territory and shall not be or have been in the service of any of them. He may be a United Nations official if the parties agree with the Secretary-General on the conditions under which the official will exercise these functions.

Article 11

1. As soon as the information provided by the parties so permits, the commission, having regard, in particular, to the time-limit laid down in article 24, shall decide in consultation with the parties whether the parties should be invited to submit written pleadings and, if so, in what order and within what time-limits, as well as the dates when, if necessary, the agents and counsel will be heard. The decisions taken by the commission in this regard may be amended at any later stage of the proceedings.

2. Subject to the provisions of article 20, paragraph 1, the commission shall not allow the agent or counsel of one party to attend a meeting without having also given the other party the opportunity to be represented at the same meeting.

Article 12

The parties, acting in good faith, shall facilitate the commission's work and, in particular, shall provide it to the greatest possible extent with whatever documents, information and explanations may be relevant.

Article 13

1. The commission may ask the parties for whatever relevant information or documents, as well as explanations, it deems necessary or useful. It may also make comments on the arguments advanced as well as the statements or proposals made by the parties.

2. The commission may accede to any request by a party that persons whose testimony it considers necessary or useful be heard, or that experts be consulted.

Article 14

In cases where the parties disagree on issues of fact, the commission may use all means at its disposal, such as the joint expert advisers mentioned in article 15, or consultation with experts, to ascertain the facts.

Article 15

The commission may propose to the parties that they jointly appoint expert advisers to assist it in the consideration of technical aspects of the dispute. If the proposal is accepted, its implementation shall be conditional upon the expert advisers being appointed by the parties by mutual agreement and accepted by the commission and upon the parties fixing their emoluments.

Article 16

Each party may at any time, at its own initiative or at the initiative of the commission, make proposals for the settlement of the dispute. Any proposal made in accordance with this article shall be communicated immediately to the other party by the president, who may, in so doing, transmit any comment the commission may wish to make thereon.

Article 17

At any stage of the proceedings, the commission may, at its own initiative or at the initiative of one of the parties, draw the attention of the parties to any measures which in its opinion might be advisable or facilitate a settlement.

Article 18

The commission shall endeavour to take its decisions unanimously but, if unanimity proves impossible, it may take them by a majority of votes of its members. Abstentions are not allowed. Except in matters of procedure, the presence of all members shall be required in order for a decision to be valid.

Article 19

The commission may, at any time, ask the Secretary-General of the United Nations for advice or assistance with regard to the administrative or procedural aspects of its work.

CHAPTER VI
CONCLUSION OF THE CONCILIATION PROCEEDINGS

Article 20

1. On concluding its consideration of the dispute, the commission may, if full settlement has not been reached, draw up and submit appropriate recommendations to the parties for consideration. To that end, it may hold an exchange of views with the agents of the parties, who may be heard jointly or separately.

2. The recommendations adopted by the commission shall be set forth in a report communicated by the president of the commission to the agents of the parties, with a request that the agents inform the commission, within a given period, whether the

parties accept them. The president may include in the report the reasons which, in the commission's view, might prompt the parties to accept the recommendations submitted. The commission shall refrain from presenting in its report any final conclusions with regard to facts or from ruling formally on issues of law, unless the parties have jointly asked it to do so.

3. If the parties accept the recommendations submitted by the commission, a procès-verbal shall be drawn up setting forth the conditions of acceptance. The procès-verbal shall be signed by the president and the secretary. A copy thereof signed by the secretary shall be provided to each party. This shall conclude the proceedings.

4. Should the commission decide not to submit recommendations to the parties, its decision to that effect shall be recorded in a procès-verbal signed by the president and the secretary. A copy thereof signed by the secretary shall be provided to each party. This shall conclude the proceedings.

Article 21

1. The recommendations of the commission will be submitted to the parties for consideration in order to facilitate an amicable settlement of the dispute. The parties undertake to study them in good faith, carefully and objectively.

2. If one of the parties does not accept the recommendations and the other party does, it shall inform the latter, in writing, of the reasons why it could not accept them.

Article 22

1. If the recommendations are not accepted by both parties but the latter wish efforts to continue in order to reach agreement on different terms, the proceedings shall be resumed. Article 24 shall apply to the resumed proceedings, with the relevant time-limit, which the parties may, by mutual agreement, shorten or extend, running from the commission's first meeting after resumption of the proceedings.

2. If the recommendations are not accepted by both parties and the latter do not wish further efforts to be made to reach agreement on different terms, a procès-verbal signed by the president and the secretary of the commission shall be drawn up, omitting the proposed terms and indicating that the parties were unable to accept them and do not wish further efforts to be made to reach agreement on different terms. The proceedings shall be concluded when each party has received a copy of the procès-verbal signed by the secretary.

Article 23

Upon conclusion of the proceedings, the president of the commission shall, with the prior agreement of the parties, deliver the documents in the possession of the secretariat of the commission either to the Secretary-General of the United Nations or to another person or entity agreed upon by the parties. Without prejudice to the possible application of article 26, paragraph 2, the confidentiality of the documents shall be preserved.

Article 24

The commission shall conclude its work within the period agreed upon by the parties. Any extension of this period shall be agreed upon by the parties.

CHAPTER VII
CONFIDENTIALITY OF THE COMMISSION'S WORK AND DOCUMENTS

Article 25

1. The commission's meetings shall be closed. The parties and the members and expert advisers of the commission, the agents and counsel of the parties, and the secretary and the secretariat staff, shall maintain strictly the confidentiality of any documents or statements, or any communication concerning the progress of the proceedings unless their disclosure has been approved by both parties in advance.

2. Each party shall receive, through the secretary, certified copies of any minutes of the meetings at which it was represented.

3. Each party shall receive, through the secretary, certified copies of any documentary evidence received and of experts' reports, records of investigations and statements by witnesses.

Article 26

1. Except with regard to certified copies referred to in article 25, paragraph 3, the obligation to respect the confidentiality of the proceedings and of the deliberations shall remain in effect for the parties and for members of the commission, expert advisers and secretariat staff after the proceedings are concluded and shall extend to recommendations and proposals which have not been accepted.

2. Notwithstanding the foregoing, the parties may, upon conclusion of the proceedings and by mutual agreement, make available to the public all or some of the documents that in accordance with the preceding paragraph are to remain confidential, or authorize the publication of all or some of those documents.

CHAPTER VIII
OBLIGATION NOT TO ACT IN A MANNER WHICH MIGHT HAVE AN ADVERSE EFFECT ON THE CONCILIATION

Article 27

The parties shall refrain during the conciliation proceedings from any measure which might aggravate or widen the dispute. They shall, in particular, refrain from any measures which might have an adverse effect on the recommendations submitted by the commission, so long as those recommendations have not been explicitly rejected by either of the parties.

CHAPTER IX
PRESERVATION OF THE LEGAL POSITION OF THE PARTIES

Article 28

1. Except as the parties may otherwise agree, neither party shall be entitled in any other proceedings, whether in a court of law or before arbitrators or before any other body, entity or person, to invoke any views expressed or statements, admissions or proposals made by the other party in the conciliation proceedings, but not accepted, or the report of the commission, the recommendations submitted by the commission or any proposal made by the commission, unless agreed to by both parties.

2. Acceptance by a party of recommendations submitted by the commission in no way implies any admission by it of the considerations of law or of fact which may have inspired the recommendations.

CHAPTER X
COSTS

Article 29

The costs of the conciliation proceedings and the emoluments of expert advisers appointed in accordance with article 15, shall be borne by the parties in equal shares.

15 Permanent Court of Arbitration Optional Conciliation Rules

Date: 1 July 1996

Source: https://docs.pca-cpa.org/2016/01/Permanent-Court-of-Arbitration-Optional-Conciliation-Rules.pdf

Application of the Rules

Article 1

1. These Rules apply to conciliation of disputes arising out of or relating to a contractual legal relationship or other circumstances where the parties seeking an amicable settlement of their disputes have agreed that the Permanent Court of Arbitration Optional Conciliation Rules apply.

2. The parties may agree to exclude or vary any of these Rules at any time.

3. Where any of these Rules is in conflict with a provision of law from which the parties cannot derogate, that provision prevails.

Commencement of Conciliation Proceedings

Article 2

1. The party initiating conciliation sends to the other party a written invitation to conciliate under these Rules, briefly identifying the subject of the dispute.

2. Conciliation proceedings commence when the other party accepts the invitation to conciliate. If the acceptance is made orally, it is advisable that it be confirmed in writing.

3. If the other party rejects the invitation, there will be no conciliation proceedings.

4. If the party initiating conciliation does not receive a reply within thirty days from the date on which it sends the invitation, or within such other period of time as specified in the invitation, it may elect to treat this as a rejection of the invitation to conciliate. If it so elects, it informs the other party accordingly.

Number of Conciliators

Article 3

There shall be one conciliator unless the parties agree that there shall be two or three conciliators. Where there is more than one conciliator, they ought, as a general rule, to act jointly.

Appointment of Conciliators

Article 4

1. (a) In conciliation proceedings with one conciliator, the parties shall endeavour to reach agreement on the name of a sole conciliator;
   (b) In conciliation proceedings with two conciliators, each party appoints one conciliator;
   (c) In conciliation proceedings with three conciliators, each party appoints one conciliator. The parties shall endeavour to reach agreement on the name of the third conciliator.

2. Parties may enlist the assistance of an appropriate institution or person in connection with the appointment of conciliators. In particular,
   (a) A party may request such an institution or person to recommend the names of suitable individuals to act as conciliator; or
   (b) The parties may agree that the appointment of one or more conciliators be made directly by such an institution or person.

3. Parties may also enlist the assistance of the Secretary-General of the Permanent Court of Arbitration in connection with the appointment of conciliators. In particular,
   (a) A party may request the Secretary-General of the Permanent Court of Arbitration to designate an institution or person to perform the function set forth in paragraph 2(a) of this article 4;
   (b) The parties may request the Secretary-General of the Permanent Court of Arbitration to designate an institution or person to perform the function set forth in paragraph 2(b) of this article 4; or
   (c) The Secretary-General may be the 'person' performing the functions set forth in paragraphs 2(a) and (b) of this article 4, pursuant to a request or agreement.

In recommending or appointing individuals to act as conciliator, the institution or person shall have regard to such considerations as are likely to secure the appointment of an independent and impartial conciliator, and, with respect to a sole or third conciliator, shall take into account the advisability of appointing a conciliator of a nationality other than the nationalities of the parties.

Submission of Statements to Conciliator

Article 5

1. The conciliator,[1] upon his appointment requests each party to submit to him a brief written statement describing the general nature of the dispute and the points at issue. Each party sends a copy of its statement to the other party.

2. The conciliator may request each party to submit to him a further written statement of its position and the facts and grounds in support thereof, supplemented by any documents and other evidence that such party deems appropriate. The party sends a copy of its statement to the other party.

3. At any stage of the conciliation proceedings the conciliator may request a party to submit to him such additional information as he deems appropriate.

[1] In this and all following articles, the term 'conciliator' applies to a sole conciliator, two or three conciliators, and masculine terms include the feminine, as the case may be.

Representation and Assistance

Article 6

The parties may be represented or assisted by persons of their choice. The names and addresses of such persons are to be communicated in writing to the other party and to the conciliator; such communication is to specify whether the appointment is made for purposes of representation or of assistance.

Role of Conciliator

Article 7

1. The conciliator assists the parties in an independent and impartial manner in their attempt to reach an amicable settlement of their dispute.
2. The conciliator will be guided by principles of objectivity, fairness and justice, giving consideration to, among other things, the rights and obligations of the parties and the circumstances surrounding the dispute, including any previous practices between the parties.
3. The conciliator may conduct the conciliation proceedings in such a manner as he considers appropriate, taking into account the circumstances of the case, the wishes the parties may express, including any request by a party that the conciliator hear oral statements, and any special need for a speedy settlement of the dispute.
4. The conciliator may, at any stage of the conciliation proceedings, make proposals for a settlement of the dispute. Such proposals need not be in writing and need not be accompanied by a statement of the reasons therefor.

Administrative Assistance

Article 8

In order to facilitate the conduct of the conciliation proceedings, the parties, or the conciliator with the consent of the parties, may arrange for administrative assistance by a suitable institution or person. The parties, or the conciliator with the consent of the parties, may request the International Bureau of the Permanent Court of Arbitration to provide such administrative assistance.

Communication between Conciliator and Parties

Article 9

1. The conciliator may invite the parties to meet with him or may communicate with them orally or in writing. He may meet or communicate with the parties together or with each of them separately.
2. Unless the parties have agreed upon the place where meetings with the conciliator are to be held, such place will be determined by the conciliator, after consultation with the parties, having regard to the circumstances of the conciliation proceedings. The conciliator may request the International Bureau of the Permanent Court of Arbitration to arrange for the place where such meetings will be held.

Disclosure of Information

Article 10

When the conciliator receives factual information concerning the dispute from a party, he discloses the substance of that information to the other party in order that the other party may have the opportunity to present any explanation which he considers appropriate. However, when a party gives any information to the conciliator subject to a specific condition that it be kept confidential, the conciliator does not disclose that information to the other party.

Co-operation of Parties with Conciliator

Article 11

The parties will in good faith co-operate with the conciliator and, in particular, will endeavour to comply with requests by the conciliator to submit written materials, provide evidence and attend meetings.

Suggestions by Parties for Settlement of Dispute

Article 12

Each party may, on its own initiative or at the invitation of the conciliator, submit to the conciliator suggestions for the settlement of the dispute.

Settlement Agreement

Article 13

1. When it appears to the conciliator that there exist elements of a settlement which would be acceptable to the parties, he formulates the terms of a possible settlement and submits them to the parties for their observations. After receiving the observations of the parties, the conciliator may reformulate the terms of a possible settlement in the light of such observations.

2. If the parties reach agreement on a settlement of the dispute, they draw up and sign a written settlement agreement.[2] If requested by the parties, the conciliator draws up, or assists the parties in drawing up, the settlement agreement.

3. The parties by signing the settlement agreement put an end to the dispute and are bound by the agreement.

Confidentiality

Article 14

Unless the parties agree otherwise, or the disclosure is required in connection with judicial proceedings pursuant to article 16 hereof, the conciliator and the parties shall keep confidential all matters relating to the conciliation proceedings. Confidentiality extends also to the settlement agreement, except where its disclosure is necessary for purposes of implementation and enforcement.

[2] The parties may wish to consider including in the settlement agreement a clause that any dispute arising out of or relating to the settlement agreement shall be submitted to arbitration.

Termination of Conciliation Proceedings

Article 15

The conciliation proceedings are terminated:

(a) By the signing of the settlement agreement by the parties, on the date of the agreement; or

(b) By a written declaration of the conciliator, after consultation with the parties, to the effect that further efforts at conciliation are no longer justified, on the date of the declaration; or

(c) By a written declaration of the parties addressed to the conciliator to the effect that the conciliation proceedings are terminated, on the date of the declaration; or

(d) By a written declaration of a party to the other party and the conciliator, if appointed, to the effect that the conciliation proceedings are terminated, on the date of the declaration.

Resort to Arbitral or Judicial Proceedings

Article 16

The parties undertake not to initiate, during the conciliation proceedings, any arbitral or judicial proceedings in respect of a dispute that is the subject of the conciliation proceedings, except that a party may initiate arbitral or judicial proceedings where, in its opinion, such proceedings are necessary for preserving its rights.

Costs

Article 17

1. Upon termination of the conciliation proceedings, the conciliator fixes the costs of the conciliation and gives written notice thereof to the parties. The term ‘costs’ includes only:

(a) The fee of the conciliator which shall be reasonable in amount;

(b) The travel and other expenses of the conciliator;

(c) The travel and other expenses of witnesses requested by the conciliator with the consent of the parties;

(d) The costs of any expert advice requested by the conciliator with the consent of the parties;

(e) The cost of any assistance provided pursuant to articles 4, paragraph (2) and 8 of these Rules;

(f) The costs of any services of the Secretary-General and the International Bureau of the Permanent Court of Arbitration.

2. The costs, as defined above, are borne equally by the parties unless the settlement agreement provides for a different apportionment. All other expenses incurred by a party are borne by that party.

Deposits

Article 18

1. The conciliator, upon his appointment, may request each party to deposit an equal amount as an advance for the costs referred to in article 17, paragraph 1 which he expects will be incurred.

2. During the course of the conciliation proceedings the conciliator may request supplementary deposits in an equal amount from each party.

3. If the required deposits under paragraphs 1 and 2 of this article are not paid in full by both parties within thirty days, the conciliator may suspend the proceedings or may make a written declaration of termination to the parties, effective on the date of that declaration.

4. Upon termination of the conciliation proceedings, the conciliator renders an accounting to the parties of the deposits received and returns any unexpended balance to the parties.

Role of Conciliator in Other Proceedings

Article 19

The parties and the conciliator undertake that, unless the parties agree otherwise, the conciliator will not act as an arbitrator or as a representative or counsel of a party in any arbitral or judicial proceedings in respect of a dispute that is the subject of the conciliation proceedings. The parties also undertake that they will not present the conciliator as a witness in any such proceedings.

Admissibility of Evidence in Other Proceedings

Article 20

The parties undertake not to rely on or introduce as evidence in arbitral or judicial proceedings, whether or not such proceedings relate to the dispute that is the subject of the conciliation proceedings:

(a) Views expressed or suggestions made by the other party in respect of a possible settlement of the dispute;
(b) Admissions made by the other party in the course of the conciliation proceedings;
(c) Proposals made by the conciliator;
(d) The fact that the other party had indicated its willingness to accept a proposal for settlement made by the conciliator.

16 Vienna Convention on the Law of Treaties: Annex on Conciliation

Date: 23 May 1969
Source: 1155 UNTS 331
https://treaties.un.org/doc/publication/unts/volume%201155/volume-1155-i-18232-english.pdf

1. A list of conciliators consisting of qualified jurists shall be drawn up and maintained by the Secretary-General of the United Nations. To this end, every State which is a Member

of the United Nations or a party to the present Convention shall be invited to nominate two conciliators, and the names of the persons so nominated shall constitute the list. The term of a conciliator, including that of any conciliator nominated to fill a casual vacancy, shall be five years and may be renewed. A conciliator whose term expires shall continue to fulfil any function for which he shall have been chosen under the following paragraph.

2. When a request has been made to the Secretary-General under article 66, the Secretary-General shall bring the dispute before a conciliation commission constituted as follows:

The State or States constituting one of the parties to the dispute shall appoint:

(a) one conciliator of the nationality of that State or of one of those States, who may or may not be chosen from the list referred to in paragraph 1; and

(b) one conciliator not of the nationality of that State or of any of those States, who shall be chosen from the list.

The State or States constituting the other party to the dispute shall appoint two conciliators in the same way. The four conciliators chosen by the parties shall be appointed within sixty days following the date on which the Secretary-General receives the request.

The four conciliators shall, within sixty days following the date of the last of their own appointments, appoint a fifth conciliator chosen from the list, who shall be chairman.

If the appointment of the chairman or of any of the other conciliators has not been made within the period prescribed above for such appointment, it shall be made by the Secretary-General within sixty days following the expiry of that period. The appointment of the chairman may be made by the Secretary-General either from the list or from the membership of the International Law Commission. Any of the periods within which appointments must be made may be extended by agreement between the parties to the dispute.

Any vacancy shall be filled in the manner prescribed for the initial appointment.

3. The Conciliation Commission shall decide its own procedure. The Commission, with the consent of the parties to the dispute, may invite any party to the treaty to submit to it its views orally or in writing. Decisions and recommendations of the Commission shall be made by a majority vote of the five members.

4. The Commission may draw the attention of the parties to the dispute to any measures which might facilitate an amicable settlement.

5. The Commission shall hear the parties, examine the claims and objections, and make proposals to the parties with a view to reaching an amicable settlement of the dispute.

6. The Commission shall report within twelve months of its constitution. Its report shall be deposited with the Secretary-General and transmitted to the parties to the dispute. The report of the Commission, including any conclusions stated therein regarding the facts or questions of law, shall not be binding upon the parties and it shall have no other character than that of recommendations submitted for the consideration of the parties in order to facilitate an amicable settlement of the dispute.

7. The Secretary-General shall provide the Commission with such assistance and facilities as it may require. The expenses of the Commission shall be borne by the United Nations.

The OSCE Conciliation Framework

17.a Convention on Conciliation and Arbitration within the Conference on Security and Co-operation in Europe*

Date: 15 December 1992
Source: 1842 UNTS 150
https://www.osce.org/files/f/documents/a/0/111409_0.pdf

The States parties to this Convention, being States participating in the Conference on Security and Co-operation in Europe,

Conscious of their obligation, as provided for in Article 2, paragraph 3, and Article 33 of the Charter of the United Nations, to settle their disputes peacefully;

Emphasizing that they do not in any way intend to impair other existing institutions or mechanisms, including the International Court of Justice, the European Court of Human Rights, the Court of Justice of the European Communities and the Permanent Court of Arbitration;

Reaffirming their solemn commitment to settle their disputes through peaceful means and their decision to develop mechanisms to settle disputes between participating States;

Recalling that full implementation of all CSCE principles and commitments constitutes in itself an essential element in preventing disputes between the CSCE participating States; Concerned to further and strengthen the commitments stated, in particular, in the Report of the Meeting of Experts on Peaceful Settlement of Disputes adopted at Valletta and endorsed by the CSCE Council of Ministers of Foreign Affairs at its meeting in Berlin on 19 and 20 June 1991,

Have agreed as follows:

CHAPTER I – GENERAL PROVISIONS

Article 1 Establishment of the Court

A Court of Conciliation and Arbitration shall be established to settle, by means of conciliation and, where appropriate, arbitration, disputes which are submitted to it in accordance with the provisions of this Convention.

Article 2 Conciliation Commissions and Arbitral Tribunals

1. Conciliation shall be undertaken by a Conciliation Commission constituted for each dispute. The Commission shall be made up of conciliators drawn from a list established in accordance with the provisions of Article 3.

2. Arbitration shall be undertaken by an Arbitral Tribunal constituted for each dispute. The Tribunal shall be made up of arbitrators drawn from a list established in accordance with the provisions of Article 4.

3. Together, the conciliators and arbitrators shall constitute the Court of Conciliation and Arbitration within the CSCE, hereinafter referred to as "the Court".

* N.B.: The Financial Protocol is omitted.

Article 3 Appointment of Conciliators

1. Each State party to this Convention shall appoint, within two months following its entry into force, two conciliators of whom at least one is a national of that State. The other may be a national of another CSCE participating State. A State which becomes party to this Convention after its entry into force shall appoint its conciliators within two months following the entry into force of this Convention for the State concerned.

2. The conciliators must be persons holding or having held senior national or international positions and possessing recognized qualifications in international law, international relations, or the settlement of disputes.

3. Conciliators shall be appointed for a renewable period of six years. Their functions may not be terminated by the appointing State during their term of office. In the event of death, resignation or inability to attend recognized by the Bureau, the State concerned shall appoint a new conciliator; the term of office of the new conciliator shall be the remainder of the term of office of the predecessor.

4. Upon termination of their period of office, conciliators shall continue to hear any cases that they are already dealing with.

5. The names of the conciliators shall be notified to the Registrar, who shall enter them into a list, which shall be communicated to the CSCE Secretariat for transmission to the CSCE participating States.

Article 4 Appointment of Arbitrators

1. Each State party to this Convention shall appoint, within two months following its entry into force, one arbitrator and one alternate, who may be its nationals or nationals of any other CSCE participating State. A State which becomes Party to this Convention after its entry into force shall appoint its arbitrator and the alternate within two months of the entry into force of this Convention for that State.

2. Arbitrators and their alternates must possess the qualifications required in their respective countries for appointment to the highest judicial offices or must be jurisconsults of recognized competence in international law.

3. Arbitrators and their alternates are appointed for a period of six years, which may be renewed once. Their functions may not be terminated by the appointing State party during their term of office. In the event of death, resignation or inability to attend, recognized by the Bureau, the arbitrator shall be replaced by his or her alternate.

4. If an arbitrator and his or her alternate die, resign or are both unable to attend, the fact being recognized by the Bureau, new appointments will be made in accordance with paragraph 1. The new arbitrator and his or her alternate shall complete the term of office of their predecessors.

5. The Rules of the Court may provide for a partial renewal of the arbitrators and their alternates.

6. Upon expiry of their term of office, arbitrators shall continue to hear any cases that they are already dealing with.

7. The names of the arbitrators shall be notified to the Registrar, who shall enter them into a list, which shall be communicated to the CSCE Secretariat for transmission to the CSCE participating States.

Article 5 Independence of the Members of the Court and of the Registrar

The conciliators, the arbitrators and the Registrar shall perform their functions in full independence. Before taking up their duties, they shall make a declaration that they will exercise their powers impartially and conscientiously.

Article 6 Privileges and Immunities

The conciliators, the arbitrators, the Registrar and the agents and counsel of the parties to a dispute shall enjoy, while performing their functions in the territory of the States parties to this Convention, the privileges and immunities accorded to persons connected with the International Court of Justice.

Article 7 Bureau of the Court

1. The Bureau of the Court shall consist of a President, a Vice-President and three other members.
2. The President of the Court shall be elected by the members of the Court from among their number. The President presides over the Bureau.
3. The conciliators and the arbitrators shall each elect from among their number two members of the Bureau and their alternates.
4. The Bureau shall elect its Vice-President from among its members. The Vice-President shall be a conciliator if the President is an arbitrator, and an arbitrator if the President is a conciliator.
5. The Rules of the Court shall establish the procedures for the election of the President as well as of the other members of the Bureau and their alternates.

Article 8 Decision-Making Procedure

1. The decisions of the Court shall be taken by a majority of the members participating in the vote. Those abstaining shall not be considered participating in the vote.
2. The decisions of the Bureau shall be taken by a majority of its members.
3. The decisions of the Conciliation Commissions and the Arbitral Tribunals shall be taken by a majority of their members, who may not abstain from voting.
4. In the event of a tied vote, the vote of the presiding officer shall prevail.

Article 9 Registrar

The Court shall appoint its Registrar and may provide for the appointment of such other officers as may be necessary. The staff regulations of the Registry shall be drawn up by the Bureau and adopted by the States parties to this Convention.

Article 10 Seat

1. The seat of the Court shall be established in Geneva.
2. At the request of the parties to the dispute and in agreement with the Bureau, a Conciliation Commission or an Arbitral Tribunal may meet at another location.

Article 11 Rules of the Court

1. The Court shall adopt its own Rules, which shall be subject to approval by States parties to this Convention.
2. The Rules of the Court shall establish, in particular, the rules of procedure to be followed by the Conciliation Commissions and Arbitral Tribunals constituted pursuant to

this Convention. They shall state which of these rules may not be waived by agreement between the parties to the dispute.

Article 12 Working Languages

The Rules of the Court shall establish rules on the use of languages.

Article 13 Financial Protocol

Subject to the provisions of Article 17, all the costs of the Court shall be met by the States parties to this Convention. The provisions for the calculation of the costs; for the drawing up and approval of the annual budget of the Court; for the distribution of the costs among the States parties to this Convention; for the audit of the accounts of the Court; and for related matters, shall be contained in a Financial Protocol to be adopted by the Committee of Senior Officials. A State becomes bound by the Protocol on becoming a party to this Convention.

Article 14 Periodic Report

The Bureau shall annually present to the CSCE Council through the Committee of Senior Officials a report on the activities under this Convention.

Article 15 Notice of Requests for Conciliation or Arbitration

The Registrar of the Court shall give notice to the CSCE Secretariat of all requests for conciliation or arbitration, for immediate transmission to the CSCE participating States.

Article 16 Conduct of Parties – Interim Measures

1. During the proceedings, the parties to the dispute shall refrain from any action which may aggravate the situation or further impede or prevent the settlement of the dispute.

2. The Conciliation Commission may draw the attention of the parties to the dispute submitted to it to the measures the parties could take in order to prevent the dispute from being aggravated or its settlement made more difficult.

3. The Arbitral Tribunal constituted for a dispute may indicate the interim measures that ought to be taken by the parties to the dispute in accordance with the provisions of Article 26, paragraph 4.

Article 17 Procedural Costs

The parties to a dispute and any intervening party shall each bear their own costs.

CHAPTER II – COMPETENCE

Article 18 Competence of the Commission and of the Tribunal

1. Any State party to this Convention may submit to a Conciliation Commission any dispute with another State party which has not been settled within a reasonable period of time through negotiation.

2. Disputes may be submitted to an Arbitral Tribunal under the conditions stipulated in Article 26.

Article 19 Safeguarding the Existing Means of Settlement

1. A Conciliation Commission or an Arbitral Tribunal constituted for a dispute shall take no further action in the case:

(a) If, prior to being submitted to the Commission or the Tribunal, the dispute has been submitted to a court or tribunal whose jurisdiction in respect of the dispute the parties thereto are under a legal obligation to accept, or if such a body has already given a decision on the merits of the dispute;

(b) If the parties to the dispute have accepted in advance the exclusive jurisdiction of a jurisdictional body other than a Tribunal in accordance with this Convention which has jurisdiction to decide, with binding force, on the dispute submitted to it, or if the parties thereto have agreed to seek to settle the dispute exclusively by other means.

2. A Conciliation Commission constituted for a dispute shall take no further action if, even after the dispute has been submitted to it, one or all of the parties refer the dispute to a court or tribunal whose jurisdiction in respect of the dispute the parties thereto are under a legal obligation to accept.

3. A Conciliation Commission shall postpone examining a dispute if this dispute has been submitted to another body which has competence to formulate proposals with respect to this dispute. If those prior efforts do not lead to a settlement of the dispute, the Commission shall resume its work at the request of the parties or one of the parties to the dispute, subject to the provisions of Article 26, paragraph 1.

4. A State may, at the time of signing, ratifying or acceding to this Convention, make a reservation in order to ensure the compatibility of the mechanism of dispute settlement that this Convention establishes with other means of dispute settlement resulting from international undertakings applicable to that State.

5. If, at any time, the parties arrive at a settlement of their dispute, the Commission or Tribunal shall remove the dispute from its list, on receiving written confirmation from all the parties thereto that they have reached a settlement of the dispute.

6. In the event of disagreement between the parties to the dispute with regard to the competence of the Commission or the Tribunal, the decision in the matter shall rest with the Commission or the Tribunal.

CHAPTER III – CONCILIATION

Article 20 Request for the Constitution of a Conciliation Commission

1. Any State party to this Convention may lodge an application with the Registrar requesting the constitution of a Conciliation Commission for a dispute between it and one or more other States parties. Two or more States parties may also jointly lodge an application with the Registrar.

2. The constitution of a Conciliation Commission may also be requested by agreement between two or more States parties or between one or more States parties and one or more other CSCE participating States. The agreement shall be notified to the Registrar.

Article 21 Constitution of the Conciliation Commission

1. Each party to the dispute shall appoint, from the list of conciliators established in accordance with Article 3, one conciliator to sit on the Commission.

2. When more than two States are parties to the same dispute, the States asserting the same interest may agree to appoint one single conciliator. If they do not so agree, each of

the two sides to the dispute shall appoint the same number of conciliators up to a maximum decided by the Bureau.

3. Any State which is a party to a dispute submitted to a Conciliation Commission and which is not a party to this Convention, may appoint a person to sit on the Commission, either from the list of conciliators established in accordance with Article 3, or from among other persons who are nationals of a CSCE participating State. In this event, for the purpose of examining the dispute, such persons shall have the same rights and the same obligations as the other members of the Commission. They shall perform their functions in full independence and shall make the declaration required by Article 5 before taking their seats on the Commission.

4. As soon as the application or the agreement whereby the parties to a dispute have requested the constitution of a Conciliation Commission is received, the President of the Court shall consult the parties to the dispute as to the composition of the rest of the Commission.

5. The Bureau shall appoint three further conciliators to sit on the Commission. This number can be increased or decreased by the Bureau, provided it is uneven. Members of the Bureau and their alternates, who are on the list of conciliators, shall be eligible for appointment to the Commission.

6. The Commission shall elect its Chairman from among the members appointed by the Bureau.

7. The Rules of the Court shall stipulate the procedures applicable if an objection is raised to one of the members appointed to sit on the Commission or if that member is unable to or refuses to sit at the commencement or in the course of the proceedings.

8. Any question as to the application of this article shall be decided by the Bureau as a preliminary matter.

Article 22 Procedure for the Constitution of a Conciliation Commission

1. If the constitution of a Conciliation Commission is requested by means of an application, the application shall state the subject of the dispute, the name of the party or parties against which the application is directed, and the name of the conciliator or conciliators appointed by the requesting party or parties to the dispute. The application shall also briefly indicate the means of settlement previously resorted to.

2. As soon as an application has been received, the Registrar shall notify the other party or parties to the dispute mentioned in the application. Within a period of fifteen days from the notification, the other party or parties to the dispute shall appoint the conciliator or conciliators of their choice to sit on the Commission. If, within this period, one or more parties to the dispute have not appointed the member or members of the Commission whom they are entitled to appoint, the Bureau shall appoint the appropriate number of conciliators. Such appointment shall be made from among the conciliators appointed in accordance with Article 3 by the party or each of the parties involved or, if those parties have not yet appointed conciliators, from among the other conciliators not appointed by the other party or parties to the dispute.

3. If the constitution of a Conciliation Commission is requested by means of an agreement, the agreement shall state the subject of the dispute. If there is no agreement, in whole or in part, concerning the subject of the dispute, each party thereto may formulate its own position in respect of such subject.

4. At the same time as the parties request the constitution of a Conciliation Commission by agreement, each party shall notify the Registrar of the name of the conciliator or conciliators whom it has appointed to sit on the Commission.

Article 23 Conciliation Procedure

1. The conciliation proceedings shall be confidential and all parties to the dispute shall have the right to be heard. Subject to the provisions of Articles 10 and 11 and the Rules of the Court, the Conciliation Commission shall, after consultation with the parties to the dispute, determine the procedure.

2. If the parties to the dispute agree thereon, the Conciliation Commission may invite any State party to this Convention which has an interest in the settlement of the dispute to participate in the proceedings.

Article 24 Objective of Conciliation

The Conciliation Commission shall assist the parties to the dispute in finding a settlement in accordance with international law and their CSCE commitments.

Article 25 Result of the Conciliation

1. If, during the proceedings, the parties to the dispute, with the help of the Conciliation Commission, reach a mutually acceptable settlement, they shall record the terms of this settlement in a summary of conclusions signed by their representatives and by the members of the Commission. The signing of the document shall conclude the proceedings. The CSCE Council shall be informed through the Committee of Senior Officials of the success of the conciliation.

2. When the Conciliation Commission considers that all the aspects of the dispute and all the possibilities of finding a solution have been explored, it shall draw up a final report. The report shall contain the proposals of the Commission for the peaceful settlement of the dispute.

3. The report of the Conciliation Commission shall be notified to the parties to the dispute, which shall have a period of thirty days in which to examine it and inform the Chairman of the Commission whether they are willing to accept the proposed settlement.

4. If a party to the dispute does not accept the proposed settlement, the other party or parties are no longer bound by their own acceptance thereof.

5. If, within the period prescribed in paragraph 3, the parties to the dispute have not accepted the proposed settlement, the report shall be forwarded to the CSCE Council through the Committee of Senior Officials.

6. A report shall also be drawn up which provides immediate notification to the CSCE Council through the Committee of Senior Officials of circumstances where a party fails to appear for conciliation or leaves a procedure after it has begun.

CHAPTER IV – ARBITRATION

Article 26 Request for the Constitution of an Arbitral Tribunal

1. A request for arbitration may be made at any time by agreement between two or more States parties to this Convention or between one or more States parties to this Convention and one or more other CSCE participating States.

2. The States parties to this Convention may at any time by a notice addressed to the Depositary declare that they recognize as compulsory, *ipso facto* and without special agreement, the jurisdiction of an Arbitral Tribunal, subject to reciprocity. Such a declaration may be made for an unlimited period or for a specified time. It may cover all disputes or exclude disputes concerning a State's territorial integrity, national defence,

title to sovereignty over land territory, or competing claims with regard to jurisdiction over other areas.

3. A request for arbitration against a State party to this Convention which has made the declaration specified in paragraph 2 may be made by means of an application to the Registrar only after a period of thirty days after the report of the Conciliation Commission which has dealt with the dispute has been transmitted to the CSCE Council in accordance with the provisions of Article 25, paragraph 5.

4. When a dispute is submitted to an Arbitral Tribunal in accordance with this article, the Tribunal may, on its own authority or at the request of one or all of the parties to the dispute, indicate interim measures that ought to be taken by the parties to the dispute to avoid an aggravation of the dispute, greater difficulty in reaching a solution, or the possibility of a future award of the Tribunal becoming unenforceable owing to the conduct of one or more of the parties to the dispute.

Article 27 Cases Brought before an Arbitral Tribunal

1. If a request for arbitration is made by means of an agreement, it shall indicate the subject of the dispute. If there is no agreement, in whole or in part, concerning the subject of the dispute, each party thereto may formulate its own position in respect of such subject.

2. If a request for arbitration is made by means of an application, it shall indicate the subject of the dispute, the States party or parties to this Convention against which it is directed, and the main elements of fact and law on which it is grounded. As soon as the application is received, the Registrar shall notify the other States party or parties mentioned in the application.

Article 28 Constitution of the Arbitral Tribunal

1. When a request for arbitration is submitted, an Arbitral Tribunal shall be constituted.

2. The arbitrators appointed by the parties to the dispute in accordance with Article 4 are *ex officio* members of the Tribunal. When more than two States are parties to the same dispute, the States asserting the same interest may agree to appoint one single arbitrator.

3. The Bureau shall appoint, from among the arbitrators, a number of members to sit on the Tribunal so that the members appointed by the Bureau total at least one more than the ex officio members. Members of the Bureau and their alternates, who are on the list of arbitrators, shall be eligible for appointment to the Tribunal.

4. If an *ex officio* member is unable to attend or has previously taken part in any capacity in the hearings of the case arising from the dispute submitted to the Tribunal, that member shall be replaced by his or her alternate. If the alternate is in the same situation, the State involved shall appoint a member to examine the dispute pursuant to the terms and conditions specified in paragraph 5. In the event of a question arising as to the capacity of a member or of his or her alternate to sit on the Tribunal, the matter shall be decided by the Bureau.

5. Any State, which is a party to a dispute submitted to an Arbitral Tribunal and which is not party to this Convention, may appoint a person of its choice to sit on the Tribunal, either from the list of arbitrators established in accordance with Article 4 or from among other persons who are nationals of a CSCE participating State. Any person thus appointed must meet the conditions specified in Article 4, paragraph 2, and for the purpose of examining the dispute, shall have the same rights and obligations as the other members of the Tribunal. The person shall perform his or her functions in full independence and shall make the declaration required by Article 5 before sitting on the Tribunal.

6. The Tribunal shall appoint its Chairman from among the members appointed by the Bureau.

7. In the event that one of the members of the Tribunal appointed by the Bureau is unable to attend the proceedings, that member shall not be replaced unless the number of members appointed by the Bureau falls below the number of *ex officio* members, or members appointed by the parties to the dispute in accordance with paragraph 5. In this event, one or more new members shall be appointed by the Bureau pursuant to paragraphs 3 and 4 of this article. A new Chairman will not be elected if one or more new members are appointed, unless the member unable to attend is the Chairman of the Tribunal.

Article 29 Arbitration Procedure

1. All the parties to the dispute shall have the right to be heard during the arbitration proceedings, which shall conform to the principles of a fair trial. The proceedings shall consist of a written part and an oral part.

2. The Arbitral Tribunal shall have, in relation to the parties to the dispute, the necessary fact-finding and investigative powers to carry out its tasks.

3. Any CSCE participating State which considers that it has a particular interest of a legal nature likely to be affected by the ruling of the Tribunal may, within fifteen days of the transmission of the notification by the CSCE Secretariat as specified in Article 15, address to the Registrar a request to intervene. This request shall be immediately transmitted to the parties to the dispute and to the Tribunal constituted for the dispute.

4. If the intervening State establishes that it has such an interest, it shall be authorized to participate in the proceedings in so far as may be required for the protection of this interest. The relevant part of the ruling of the Tribunal is binding upon the intervening State.

5. The parties to the dispute have a period of thirty days in which to address their observations regarding the request for intervention to the Tribunal. The Tribunal shall render its decision on the admissibility of the request.

6. The hearings in the Tribunal shall be held in camera, unless the Tribunal decides otherwise at the request of the parties to the dispute.

7. In the event that one or more parties to the dispute fail to appear, the other party or parties thereto may request the Tribunal to decide in favour of its or their claims. Before doing so, the Tribunal must satisfy itself that it is competent and that the claims of the party or parties taking part in the proceedings are well-founded.

Article 30 Function of the Arbitral Tribunal

The function of the Arbitral Tribunal shall be to decide, in accordance with international law, such disputes as are submitted to it. This provision shall not prejudice the power of the Tribunal to decide a case *ex aequo et bono*, if the parties to the dispute so agree.

Article 31 Arbitral Award

1. The award of the Arbitral Tribunal shall state the reasons on which it is based. If it does not represent in whole or in part the unanimous opinion of the members of the Arbitral Tribunal, any member shall be entitled to deliver a separate or dissenting opinion.

2. Subject to Article 29, paragraph 4, the award of the Tribunal shall have binding force only between the parties to the dispute and in respect of the case to which it relates.

3. The award shall be final and not subject to appeal. However, the parties to the dispute or one of them may request that the Tribunal interpret its award as to the meaning or scope.

Unless the parties to the dispute agree otherwise, such request shall be made at the latest within six months after the communication of the award. After receiving the observations of the parties to the dispute, the Tribunal shall render its interpretation as soon as possible.

4. An application for revision of the award may be made only when it is based upon the discovery of some fact which is of such a nature as to be a decisive factor and which, when the award was rendered, was unknown to the Tribunal and to the party or parties to the dispute claiming revision. The application for revision must be made at the latest within six months of the discovery of the new fact. No application for revision may be made after the lapse of ten years from the date of the award.

5. As far as possible, the examination of a request for interpretation or an application for revision should be carried out by the Tribunal which made the award in question. If the Bureau should find this to be impossible, another Tribunal shall be constituted in accordance with the provisions of Article 28.

Article 32 Publication of the Arbitral Award

The award shall be published by the Registrar. A certified copy shall be communicated to the parties to the dispute and to the CSCE Council through the Committee of Senior Officials.

CHAPTER V – FINAL PROVISIONS

Article 33 Signature and Entry into Force

1. This Convention shall be open for signature with the Government of Sweden by the CSCE participating States until 31 March 1993. It shall be subject to ratification.

2. The CSCE participating States which have not signed this Convention may subsequently accede thereto.

3. This Convention shall enter into force two months after the date of deposit of the twelfth instrument of ratification or accession.

4. For every State which ratifies or accedes to this Convention after the deposit of the twelfth instrument of ratification or accession, the Convention shall enter into force two months after its instrument of ratification or accession has been deposited.

5. The Government of Sweden shall serve as depositary of this Convention.

Article 34 Reservations

This Convention may not be the subject of any reservation that it does not expressly authorize.

Article 35 Amendments

1. Amendments to this Convention must be adopted in accordance with the following paragraphs.

2. Amendments to this Convention may be proposed by any State party thereto, and shall be communicated by the Depositary to the CSCE Secretariat for transmission to the CSCE participating States.

3. If the CSCE Council adopts the proposed text of the amendment, the text shall be forwarded by the Depositary to States parties to this Convention for acceptance in accordance with their respective constitutional requirements.

4. Any such amendment shall come into force on the thirtieth day after all States parties to this Convention have informed the Depositary of their acceptance thereof.

Article 36 Denunciation

1. Any State party to this Convention may, at any time, denounce this Convention by means of a notification addressed to the Depositary.

2. Such denunciation shall become effective one year after the date of receipt of the notification by the Depositary.

3. This Convention shall, however, continue to apply for the denouncing party with respect to proceedings which are under way at the time the denunciation enters into force. Such proceedings shall be pursued to their conclusion.

Article 37 Notifications and Communications

The notifications and communications to be made by the Depositary shall be transmitted to the Registrar and to the CSCE Secretariat for further transmission to the CSCE participating States.

Article 38 Non-Parties

In conformity with international law, it is confirmed that nothing in this Convention shall be interpreted to establish any obligations or commitments for CSCE participating States that are not parties to this Convention if not expressly provided for and expressly accepted by such States in writing.

Article 39 Transitional Provisions

1. The Court shall proceed, within four months of the entry into force of this Convention, to elect the Bureau, to adopt its rules and to appoint the Registrar in accordance with the provisions of Articles 7, 9 and 11. The host Government of the Court shall, in co-operation with the Depositary, make the arrangements required.

2. Until a Registrar is appointed, the duties of the Registrar under Article 3, paragraph 5, and Article 4, paragraph 7 shall be performed by the Depositary.

Done at in the English, French, German, Italian, Russian and Spanish languages, all six language versions being equally authentic, on 15th December 1992.

17.b Rules of the Court of Conciliation and Arbitration within the OSCE

Date: 1 February 1997
Source: http://www.osce.org/cca/40108

CHAPTER I: GENERAL AND INSTITUTIONAL PROVISIONS

1. General Provision

Article 1: Rules of the Court

1. The present Rules, adopted by the Court of Conciliation and Arbitration (hereinafter: the Court) and approved by the States Parties to the Stockholm Convention of 15 December 1992 on Conciliation and Arbitration within the OSCE (hereinafter: the Convention), shall govern, in accordance with Article 11, paragraph 1, of the Convention, the activities of the Court and of the organs established within the Court.

2. In the event of a conflict between provisions of the Convention and of the Rules, the former shall prevail.

2. The Court

Article 2: Solemn Declaration

Upon taking up their duties, conciliators, arbitrators and their alternates shall make the following solemn declaration: "I solemnly declare that I shall fulfil impartially and conscientiously, to the best of my ability, my duties as member of the Court of Conciliation and Arbitration established by the Convention on Conciliation and Arbitration within the OSCE."

Article 3: Working Languages

1. The languages of the Court and of the organs established within the Court shall be the official languages of the OSCE (English, French, German, Italian, Russian and Spanish).

2. From among those languages, in each case, the conciliation commission or the arbitral tribunal concerned, after hearing the parties, shall determine, in its rules of procedure, the language or languages to be used.

3. Any party to a dispute may however request to express itself in another language. In that event, it shall bear the additional expenses arising from the use of that language.

Article 4: Notice of Requests and List of Cases

1. In accordance with Article 15 of the Convention, all requests for conciliation or arbitration addressed to the Court shall be communicated by the Registrar to the Secretariat of the OSCE, which shall transmit them forthwith to the States participating in the OSCE.

2. The Court shall establish a list of the cases brought before it. The List shall be kept by the Registrar.

Article 5: Decision-Making

1. The decision-making procedure of the Court, the Bureau and the organs established within the Court shall be governed by Article 8 of the Convention.

2. The Court, the Bureau and the organs established within the Court may decide to take decisions by correspondence or facsimile.

Article 6: Procedural Costs

1. In accordance with Article 17 of the Convention, the parties to a dispute and any intervening party shall each bear their own costs.

2. This rule shall apply to the circumstances contemplated in Article 23, paragraph 2, of the Convention.

Article 7: Publications of the Court

1. In accordance with Article 32 of the Convention, the Court shall publish the awards rendered by arbitral tribunals established within it.

2. The Court may also publish the Annual Report on its activities submitted by the Bureau to the OSCE Council pursuant to Article 14 of the Convention.

3. The Court shall not publish the final reports of conciliation commissions established within it, unless the parties so agree.

3. The Bureau of the Court

Article 8: Composition

1. The Bureau of the Court shall consist of the President of the Court, the Vice-President of the Bureau and three other members of the Court.

2. The alternates of the four members of the Bureau other than the President shall participate in the work of the Bureau without vote.

Article 9: Election of the President of the Court, the Other Members of the Bureau and the Vice-President of the Bureau

1. Nominations for President of the Court and for membership of the Bureau may be submitted by any member of the Court. They shall be announced to the Depositary State twenty days at least before the date set for the election.

2. In accordance with Article 7, paragraph 2, of the Convention, the President of the Court shall be elected for a six-year term by all the members of the Court. The candidate obtaining the highest number of votes shall be elected. In the event of a tie, a second ballot shall be held. In the event of a further tie, the election shall be decided by lot. The election of the President shall take place under the chairmanship of a representative of the Depositary State.

3. In accordance with Article 7, paragraph 3, of the Convention, the conciliators and the arbitrators shall then each elect, from among their number, two members of the Bureau for six-year terms. The two candidates obtaining the highest number of votes shall be elected. In the event of a tie, a second ballot shall be held. In the event of a further tie, the election shall be decided by lot. Elections under this paragraph shall take place under the chairmanship of the President of the Court.

4. Two alternates each shall be elected by the conciliators and by the arbitrators from among their number, following the procedure laid down in the preceding paragraph. The Bureau shall subsequently indicate which alternate would be called upon to take the place of which member of the Bureau.

5. The Vice-President shall be elected by the Bureau from among its members, in accordance with Article 7, paragraph 4, of the Convention.

6. The President, the other members of the Bureau and the alternates may be re-elected.

7. In the event of the death, resignation or prolonged inability of the President to fulfil his or her duties, a new President shall be elected, following the procedure laid down in paragraphs 1 and 2 of this Article, to serve out the term of the former President.

8. In the event of the death, resignation or prolonged inability of a member of the Bureau other than the President to fulfil his or her duties, the alternate appointed under paragraph 4 of this Article shall serve out the term of the member concerned. In the event of the death, resignation or prolonged inability of an alternate to fulfil his or her duties, a new alternate shall be elected, following the procedure laid down in paragraph 4 of this Article, to serve out the former alternate's term.

Article 10: Functions of the Bureau

1. The Bureau is the permanent executive body of the Court. It shall meet regularly to ensure the satisfactory operation of the Court and carry out the duties entrusted to it under the Convention, the Financial Protocol and the present Rules.

2. The Bureau shall appoint the conciliators and arbitrators as provided by Articles 21 and 28 of the Convention.

3. An exchange of letters shall take place between the Bureau and the host State concerning the obligations assumed by that State in accordance with Article 1 of the Financial Protocol. A further exchange of letters between the Bureau and that State shall specify the legal status, on the territory of the host State, of the members, the Registrar and the officials of the Court, as well as of the agents, counsel and experts of the States parties to a dispute brought before the Court. Such exchanges of letters shall be approved by the States Parties.

4. The Registrar

Article 11: Appointment of the Registrar and of Registry Officials

1. The Registrar shall be appointed by the Court for a maximum term of six years on the proposal of the Bureau of the Court.

2. The Court may appoint such other officials as it requires and its financial ressources permit. It may delegate that function to the Bureau.

Article 12: Functions of the Registrar

1. The Registrar shall supervise the Court's officials under the authority and control of the Bureau of the Court.

2. The Registrar and, under his or her authority, the officials of the Court shall perform all the duties laid upon them by the Convention, the Financial Protocol and the present Rules.

3. The Registrar shall serve as secretary of the Court, of its Bureau, and of the conciliation commissions and arbitral tribunals established within the Court. The Registrar shall draw up the minutes of the meetings of such organs.

4. The Registrar shall be responsible for the Archives of the Court.

5. The Registrar shall fulfil such other duties as may be entrusted to him or her by the Court, its Bureau or the conciliation commissions and arbitral tribunals established within the Court.

6. The Registrar may, as necessary, delegate duties to other officials of the Court.

Article 13: Solemn Declaration

Upon taking up their duties, the Registrar and the other officials of the Court shall make the following solemn declaration: "I solemnly declare that I shall fulfil impartially and conscienciously, to the best of my ability, my duties at the Court of Conciliation and Arbitration established by the Convention on Conciliation and Arbitration within the OSCE."

CHAPTER II: CONCILIATION

Article 14: Purpose

1. The purpose of conciliation is to assist the parties to a dispute in finding a settlement in accordance with international law and their OSCE commitments. The conciliation commission may submit to the parties proposals with a view to bringing about a settlement of the dispute.

2. The parties may request the conciliation commission to clarify questions of fact. Its findings shall not be binding upon the parties, unless they otherwise agree.

3. Conciliation proceedings may be initiated only after a fact-finding procedure set in motion under paragraph 2 of this Article has been concluded.

Article 15: Request for Conciliation

1. Any dispute between States Parties to the Convention may be submitted to conciliation by unilateral or joint application, as laid down in Articles 18, paragraph 1, and 20, paragraph 1, of the Convention. The application shall specify the facts, the subject of the dispute, the parties thereto, the name or names of the conciliator or conciliators appointed by the applicant or applicants, and the means of settlement previously used.

2. Disputes between two or more States Parties to the Convention, or between one or more States Parties to the Convention and one or more other OSCE participating States, may be submitted to conciliation by an agreement notified to the Registrar, in accordance with Article 20, paragraph 2, of the Convention. That agreement shall specify the subject of the dispute; in the event of total or partial disagreement concerning the subject of the dispute, each party shall state its own position. When notifying the agreement, the parties shall inform the Registrar of the name or names of the conciliator or conciliators appointed by them.

Article 16: Composition and Constitution of Conciliation Commissions

1. The conciliation commission shall be composed and constituted in accordance with Articles 21 and 22 of the Convention.

2. If more than two States are parties to a dispute, and the parties in the same interest are unable to agree on the appointment of a single conciliator, as contemplated by Article 21, paragraph 2, of the Convention, each of the two sides shall appoint the same number of conciliators, up to a maximum decided by the Bureau of the Court.

3. If more than two States are parties to a dispute, and there are no parties in the same interest, each State may appoint one conciliator.

4. In accordance with Article 21, paragraph 5, of the Convention, the Bureau shall appoint three conciliators. It may increase or decrease this number after consulting the parties. If more than two States are parties to the dispute, the number of members appointed to the conciliation commission by the Bureau shall total one more than the members appointed by the parties.

5. When all its members have been appointed, the conciliation commission shall hold its constitutive meeting. At that meeting, it shall elect its chairman in accordance with Article 21, paragraph 6, of the Convention.

Article 17: Objection and Refusal or Inability to Sit

1. If a party to the dispute objects to a conciliator, the Bureau of the Court shall rule on the objection. Any objection shall be made within thirty days of the notification of the conciliator's appointment. If the objection is upheld, the conciliator concerned shall be replaced according to the provisions laid down for his or her own appointment.

2. If a conciliator, having previously taken part in the case or for any other reason, refuses to sit, he or she shall be replaced according to the provisions laid down for his or her own appointment.

3. In the event of death or of a prolonged inability or refusal to sit during the proceedings, the conciliator concerned shall be replaced according to the provisions laid down for his or her own appointment if this is considered necessary by the Bureau.

Article 18: Safeguarding Existing Means of Settlement

1. In the situations referred to by Article 19, paragraphs 1 and 2, of the Convention, the conciliation commission shall take no further action and have the case removed from the List.

2. In the situation referred to by Article 19, paragraph 3, of the Convention, the commission shall suspend the conciliation proceedings. The proceedings shall be resumed, at the request of the parties or one of them, if the procedure resulting in the suspension failed to produce a settlement of the dispute.

3. In the situation referred to by Article 19, paragraph 4, of the Convention, the commission shall take no further action and have the case removed from the List upon the request of one of the parties if it is satisfied that the dispute is covered by the reservation.

Article 19: Rules of Procedure

In accordance with Article 23, paragraph 1, of the Convention, the conciliation commission shall determine its own rules of procedure after consulting the parties to the dispute. The rules of procedure laid down by the commission, which are subject to approval by the Bureau of the Court, may not derogate from the following rules:

(a) Each party shall appoint a representative to the commission no later than at the time of its constitution.

(b) The parties shall participate in all the proceedings and co-operate with the commission, in particular by providing the documents and information it may require.

Article 20: Interlocutory Matters

1. The conciliation commission may, *proprio motu* or at the request of the parties to the dispute or one of them, call the parties' attention to the measures they could take in order to prevent the dispute from being aggravated or its settlement made more difficult.

2. In accordance with Article 23, paragraph 2, of the Convention, the commission may, with the parties' consent, invite to participate in the proceedings any other State Party to the Convention which has an interest in the settlement of the dispute.

Article 21: Result of Conciliation

1. The conciliation proceedings shall be concluded by the signature, by the representatives of the parties, of the summary of conclusions referred to in Article 25, paragraph 1, of the Convention. The summary of conclusions shall be tantamount to an agreement settling the dispute.

2. Failing such an agreement, the conciliation commission shall draw up a final report when it considers that all possibilities of reaching an amicable settlement have been exhausted. The report, which shall be communicated to the parties, shall include a statement of the facts and claims of the parties, a record of the proceedings and proposals made by the commission for the peaceful settlement of the dispute.

3. The parties may agree in advance to accept the proposals of the commission. Failing such an agreement, they shall, within thirty days of the notification of the report under Article 25, paragraph 3, of the Convention, inform the chairman of the commission whether they accept the proposals for a settlement contained in the final report.

4. The acceptance of such proposals by the parties shall be tantamount to an agreement settling the dispute. If one of the parties rejects the proposals, the other party or parties shall

no longer be bound by their own acceptance, in accordance with Article 25, paragraph 4, of the Convention.

5. In the event of a party failing to appear, the commission shall draw up a report for the OSCE Council in accordance with Article 25, paragraph 6, of the Convention.

CHAPTER III: ARBITRATION

Article 22: Purpose

The role of an arbitral tribunal is to settle, in accordance with international law, such disputes as are submitted to it. If the parties to the dispute agree, the tribunal may decide *ex aequo et bono.*

Article 23: Institution of Proceedings

1. Any dispute between two or more States Parties to the Convention, or between one or more States Parties to the Convention and one or more States participating in the OSCE, may be submitted to arbitration, as provided by Article 26 of the Convention.

2. When a request for arbitration is made by means of an agreement, in accordance with Article 26, paragraph 1, of the Convention, such agreement, notified to the Registrar by the parties to the dispute or by one of them, shall indicate the subject of the dispute. In the event of total or partial disagreement concerning the subject of the dispute, each party may state its own position in that respect.

3. When a request for arbitration is made by means of an application addressed to the Registrar, in accordance with Article 26, paragraphs 2 and 3, of the Convention, the application shall indicate the facts giving rise to the dispute, the subject of the dispute, the parties, the means of settlement previously used and the main legal arguments invoked.

Article 24: Composition and Constitution of Arbitral Tribunals

1. The arbitral tribunal shall be composed and constituted in accordance with Article 28 of the Convention.

2. If more than two States are parties to a dispute and the parties in the same interest are unable to agree on the appointment of a single arbitrator, as contemplated by Article 28, paragraph 2, of the Convention, the arbitrators designated by each party under Article 28, paragraphs 2, 4 or 5, of the Convention shall be *ex officio* members of the tribunal.

3. In accordance with Article 28, paragraph 3, of the Convention, the Bureau of the Court shall appoint a number of members to sit on the tribunal totalling at least one more than the *ex officio* members under paragraph 2 of this Article. The Bureau may consult the parties in this matter.

4. When all its members have been appointed, the tribunal shall hold its constitutive meeting. At that meeting, it shall elect its chairman in accordance with Article 28, paragraph 6, of the Convention.

Article 25: Objection and Refusal or Inability to Sit

1. If a party to the dispute objects to an arbitrator, the Bureau of the Court shall rule on the objection. Any objection shall be made within thirty days of the notification of the arbitrator's appointment. If the objection is upheld, the arbitrator concerned shall be replaced according to the provisions laid down for his or her own appointment, except for *ex officio* members of the tribunal who shall be replaced by their alternates. If the

alternate is in the same situation, the State concerned shall appoint a member according to the procedure laid down in Article 28, paragraph 5, of the Convention.

2. If an arbitrator, having previously taken part in the case or for any other reason, refuses to sit, he or she shall be replaced according to the procedure laid down for his or her own appointment, except for *ex officio* members of the tribunal who shall be replaced by their alternates. If the alternate is in the same situation, the State concerned shall appoint a member according to the procedure laid down in Article 28, paragraph 5, of the Convention.

3. In the event of death, or of a prolonged inability or refusal to sit during the proceedings, an *ex officio* member of the tribunal shall be replaced by his or her alternate. If the alternate is in the same situation, the State concerned shall appoint a member according to the procedure laid down in Article 28, paragraph 5, of the Convention. A member appointed by the Bureau shall only be replaced, in accordance with Article 28, paragraph 7, of the Convention, if the number of members appointed by the Bureau falls below the number of *ex officio* members or members appointed by the parties to the dispute under paragraph 5 of the same Article. If the member concerned was the chairman of the tribunal, a new chairman shall then be elected.

Article 26: Safeguarding Existing Means of Settlement

1. In the situations referred to by Article 19, paragraph 1, of the Convention, the arbitral tribunal shall take no further action and have the case removed from the List.

2. In the situation referred to by Article 19, paragraph 4, of the Convention, the tribunal shall take no further action and have the case removed from the List upon the request of one of the parties or if it is satisfied that the dispute is covered by the reservation. To be admissible, the request must be formulated within the time-limit set under Article 29, paragraph 1, of the present Rules.

Article 27: Rules of Procedure

1. The arbitral tribunal shall lay down its own rules of procedure after consulting the parties to the dispute. The rules of procedure laid down by the tribunal, which are subject to approval by the Bureau of the Court, may not derogate from the rules that follow.

2. All the parties to the dispute shall have the right to be heard in the course of the proceedings, which shall conform to the principles of a fair trial.

3. Each party shall appoint an agent to represent it before the tribunal no later than at the time of its constitution.

4. The parties shall participate in all the proceedings and co-operate with the tribunal, in particular by providing the documents and information it may require.

5. A certified copy of every document produced by one party shall immediately be communicated to the other party or parties.

6. The proceedings shall consist of a written phase and hearings. The hearings shall be held *in camera*, unless the tribunal decides otherwise at the request of the parties.

7. The tribunal shall have all the necessary fact-finding and investigative powers to carry out its task. It may, in particular:

(a) make any orders necessary for the good conduct of the proceedings;
(b) determine the number and order of, and the time-limits for, the written phase;
(c) order the production of evidence and make all other arrangements for the taking of evidence;
(d) refuse to admit, after the closure of the written phase, any new documents a party may wish to submit without the consent of the other party or parties;

(e) visit the site;
(f) appoint experts;
(g) examine witnesses and request clarifications from the agents, counsel or experts of the parties.

8. As soon as the hearings have been completed, the tribunal shall declare the proceedings closed and begin its deliberations. It may however, during its deliberations, request the parties to provide any additional information or clarification it considers necessary.

Article 28: Interim Measures

1. Before indicating any interim measures under Article 26, paragraph 4, of the Convention, the arbitral tribunal shall hear the parties to the dispute.

2. The tribunal may at any time request the parties to provide information on the implementation of the measures indicated by it.

3. The tribunal may at any time examine, *proprio motu* or at the request of the parties or one of them, whether the situation requires the maintenance, modification or cancellation of the measures indicated. Before taking any decision, it shall hear the parties.

4. The measures indicated by the tribunal shall cease to apply upon the rendering of the arbitral award.

Article 29: Objections Concerning Jurisdiction and Admissibility

1. Any objection concerning jurisdiction or admissibility shall be made in writing to the Registrar within thirty days of the transmission of the notice of the request for arbitration referred to in Article 15 of the Convention. The preliminary objection shall set out the facts and the law on which the objection is based, the submissions of the objecting party and any evidence it may wish to produce. The other party shall have a period of thirty days to communicate its written observations on the objection.

2. The tribunal shall decide, in an order, whether it upholds or rejects the objection, or declare that the objection is not, in the circumstances of the case, exclusively preliminary in character. If it upholds the objection, the tribunal shall have the case removed from the List. If it rejects the objection or considers that it is not exclusively preliminary in character, the tribunal shall fix time-limits for the further proceedings.

Article 30: Counter-claims

1. The tribunal may examine counter-claims directly connected with the subject-matter of the main claim if they are within its jurisdiction.

2. Counter-claims shall be submitted within the time-limit set for the filing of the Counter-Memorial.

3. After hearing the parties, the tribunal shall decide on the admissibility of the counter-claim in the form of an order.

Article 31: Intervention

1. In accordance with Article 29, paragraph 3, of the Convention, any OSCE participating State which considers that it has a particular interest of a legal nature likely to be affected by the award of the tribunal may, within fifteen days of the transmission of the notice of the request for arbitration, as referred to in Article 15 of the Convention, address to the Registrar of the Court a request to intervene indicating the legal interest concerned and the precise object of its intervention. Such request, which shall be immediately transmitted to

the tribunal and the parties to the dispute, shall also include, as appropriate, a list of the documents submitted in support of the request and which shall be attached to the request.

2. The parties shall have thirty days to comment in writing on the request for intervention.

3. The tribunal shall decide on the request for intervention in the form of an order. If the request is granted, the intervening State shall participate in the proceedings to the extent required to protect its interest. The relevant part of the award shall be binding upon the intervening State in accordance with Article 29, paragraph 4, of the Convention.

Article 32: Failure to Appear

In the event that one or more parties to the dispute fail to appear, the tribunal shall apply Article 29, paragraph 7, of the Convention.

Article 33: Discontinuance of Proceedings

1. If, at any time prior to the rendering of the arbitral award, all the parties to the dispute, jointly or separately, notify the arbitral tribunal in writing that they have agreed to discontinue the proceedings, the tribunal shall make an order noting the discontinuance and have the case removed from the List.

2. If, in the course of proceedings initiated by an application, the applicant informs the tribunal that it wishes to discontinue the proceedings, the tribunal shall set a time-limit for the respondent to state its position. If the respondent does not object to the discontinuance, the tribunal shall make an order noting the discontinuance and have the case removed from the List.

Article 34: The Arbitral Award

1. When the tribunal has concluded its deliberations, which shall be secret, and adopted the arbitral award, it shall render the award by communicating to the agent of each party to the dispute an authentic copy bearing the seal of the Court and the signatures of the chairman of the tribunal and the Registrar of the Court. A further authentic copy shall be placed in the Archives of the Court.

2. The award, which shall mention the names of all the arbitrators, shall state the reasons on which it is based. Any member of the tribunal may, if he or she so desires, attach a dissenting or separate opinion. The same shall apply to the orders of the tribunal.

3. The award shall have binding force only between the parties to the dispute and in respect of the case to which it relates, subject to Article 29, paragraph 4, of the Convention and Article 30, paragraph 3, of the present Rules. The same shall apply to the orders of the tribunal.

4. The award shall be final and not subject to appeal. The same shall apply to orders made by the tribunal under Articles 2, 30, paragraph 3, 31, paragraph 3, and 37, paragraph 3, as well as to the awards rendered under Articles 35 and 36 of the present Rules.

Article 35: Interpretation of the Arbitral Award

1. Any request for interpretation of the arbitral award the meaning or scope of which is in dispute shall be in the form of a written application made under the conditions laid down by Article 31, paragraph 3, of the Convention. The application shall indicate the precise point or points in dispute.

2. Requests for interpretation shall be examined by the arbitral tribunal which rendered the award. If the Bureau of the Court should find this to be impossible, a new arbitral

tribunal shall be constituted in accordance with Article 28 of the Convention and Article 24 of the present Rules.

3. Before interpreting the award by means of an additional award, the tribunal shall set a time-limit for the parties to communicate their written observations.

4. It is up to the tribunal to decide whether and to what extent the implementation of the award is to be suspended pending the communication of the additional award.

Article 36: Revision

1. Any request for revision of the arbitral award shall be in the form of a written application made under the conditions laid down by Article 31, paragraph 4, of the Convention. The application shall indicate the precise grounds for revision according to the party claiming revision.

2. A request for revision shall be examined by the arbitral tribunal which rendered the award. If the Bureau of the Court should find this to be impossible, a new arbitral tribunal shall be constituted in accordance with Article 28 of the Convention and Article 24 of the present Rules.

3. The other party or parties may, within a time-limit set by the tribunal, make written observations on the admissibility of the request for revision.

4. If the tribunal, by an order, declares the application admissible, it shall set time-limits for the subsequent proceedings on the merits.

5. At the request of the party claiming revision, and if the circumstances so justify, the tribunal may suspend the implementation of the award pending its revision.

6. The tribunal shall decide on the merits in the form of a new arbitral award.

CHAPTER IV: FINAL PROVISIONS

Article 37: Amendments

1. The Court, any member of the Court and any State Party to the Convention may propose amendments to the present Rules.

2. Proposals for amendment shall be communicated to the Court for comment and approved by consensus of the States Parties to the Convention.

3. Amendments shall come into force upon their approval by the States Parties to the Convention but shall not apply to cases pending at the time of their entry into force.

Article 38: Entry into Force of the Present Rules

The present Rules shall enter into force on 1 February 1997, date of their approval by consensus of the States Parties to the Convention.

17.c Provisions for a CSCE Conciliation Commission

Date: 15 December 1992
Source: CSCE Doc 3STOCK92.e (Annex 3)
http://www.osce.org/mc/40342

The participating States in the Conference on Security and Co-operation Europe (CSCE) hereby establish a procedure to complement the Valletta Procedure for the

Peaceful Settlement of Disputes endorsed by the Berlin Meeting, by the establishment of a Conciliation Commission ("the Commission") in accordance with the following provisions.

Section I

A dispute between two CSCE participating States may be brought before the Commission if the parties to it so agree.

Section II

A participating State may at any time declare that it will accept, on condition of reciprocity, conciliation by the Commission for disputes between it and other participating States. The declaration may not include conditions which would affect the procedures described in Sections III to XVII below. The declaration will be deposited with the Secretary of the Commission ("the Secretary") who will transmit copies to all the participating States.

Section III

1. Where the parties to a dispute have agreed to bring it before the Commission, the procedure will be invoked by a joint written request by the parties to the Secretary.

2. Where both parties to a dispute have made declarations under Section II which apply to that dispute, the procedure may be invoked by a written request by either party to the other and to the Secretary.

Section IV

As soon as the Secretary has received a request made in accordance with Section III, the Commission will be constituted in accordance with Section V.

Any question as to the application of Section II with respect to the dispute, and in particular as to reciprocity of the declaration made thereunder, will be decided by the Commission as a preliminary question. For this purpose the parties will proceed directly to the appointment of the conciliators.

Section V

1. The parties to the dispute will, within 20 days of the receipt by the Secretary of a written request under Section III, appoint one conciliator from the Register maintained for the purposes of the Valletta Procedure for the Peaceful Settlement of Disputes ("the Valletta Register"). A party which invokes the procedure in accordance with Section III, paragraph 2, should name its conciliator in its written request.

2. The conciliators will within 20 days of the date of the second of their own appointments, appoint a third conciliator chosen from the Valletta Register, who will act as Chairman of the Commission. He will not be a national of either of the parties or have been nominated by either of them to the Register.

3. If the appointment of the Chairman, or of any of the other conciliators, has not been made within the prescribed period, it will be made within 20 days of the expiry of the relevant period by the Secretary-General of the Permanent court of Arbitration, after consultations with the parties.

4. Any vacancies will be filled in the manner prescribed for the initial appointment.

Section VI

1. The Commission will consult the parties on the procedure to be followed in the exercise of its responsibilities as described herein. The Commission will give effect to any

agreement between the parties on procedure. In the absence of agreement on any point, the Commission may decide the matter.

2. Decision and recommendations of the Commission will be made by a majority vote of the members.

Section VII

The Commission may, with the consent of the parties, invite any participating State to submit its views orally or in writing.

Section VIII

The parties will refrain throughout the course of the procedure from any action which may aggravate the situation and make more difficult or impede the peaceful settlement of the dispute. In this connection, the Commission may draw the attention of the parties to any measures which it considers might facilitate an amicable settlement.

Section IX

The Commission will seek to clarify the points in dispute between the parties and endeavour to bring about a resolution of the dispute on mutually agreeable terms.

Section X

If the Commission considers that to do so will facilitate an amicable settlement of the dispute, it may suggest possible terms of settlement and set a time limit within which the parties should inform the Commission whether they accept such recommendations.

Section XI

Each party will, within the time limit set under Section X, inform the Secretary and the other party whether or not it accepts the proposed terms of settlement. If both parties have notified such acceptance within such time limit the Secretary will forward a report from the Commission to the Committee of Senior Officials of the CSCE. The report will not include the matters referred to in Section XII.

Section XII

Any measures recommended under Section VIII, and any information and comments provided to the Commission by the parties in confidence, will remain confidential unless the parties agree otherwise.

Section XIII

Each party to the dispute will bear its own costs and the costs of the conciliator appointed by it. The rest of the costs of the Commission will be shared equally by the parties.

Section XIV

A participating State may at any time, whether before or after a dispute has been referred to the Commission, declare, either generally or in relation to a particular dispute, that it will accept as binding, on condition of reciprocity, any terms of settlement proposed by the Commission. Such declaration will be deposited with the Secretary who will transmit copies to all the participating States.

Section XV

A declaration made under Section II or Section XIV may be withdrawn or modified by written notification to the Secretary who will transmit copies to all the participating States. A declaration made under Section II of Section XIV may not be withdrawn or modified in relation to a dispute to which it applies once a written request for conciliation of the dispute has been made under Section II, and the other party to the dispute has already made such a declaration.

Section XVI

The parties may agree to modify the procedure set out in the preceding sections with respect to their particular dispute.

Section XVII

The Director of the Conflict Prevention Centre will act as Secretary of the Commission. In carrying out his functions the Director may consult the Committee of Senior Official as and when he deems necessary. If the Director is a national of one the parties to a dispute, his functions in respect of that dispute will be performed by the next most senior official of the Conflict Prevention Centre who is not such a national.

17.d Provisions for Directed Conciliation

Date: 15 December 1992
Source: CSCE Doc 3STOCK92.e (Annex 4)
http://www.osce.org/mc/40342

The Council of Ministers or the Committee of Senior Officials (CSO) may direct any two participating States to seek conciliation to assist them in resolving a dispute that they have not been able to settle within a reasonable period of time.

1. In using this authority, the Council or the CSO may direct that the parties to the dispute use the provisions for conciliation described in Annex 3, on the same basis as if the parties had made a joint request to bring the dispute before the Conciliation Commission established by that Annex. However, in such situations:

a) the Council or the CSO may decide, in view of the nature of the particular dispute or other relevant factors, either to increase or to decrease any of the twenty-day periods for appointment by the parties of the two members of the Conciliation Commission or for selection of the Chairman; and

b) the work of the Commission will not be conducted in public, unless the parties agree otherwise.

2. Moreover, in cases involving disputes between two parties to the Convention on the Conciliation and Arbitration within the CSCE, the Council or the CSO may direct that they parties use the provisions for conciliation established under that Convention, once that Convention enters into force.

3. The parties to the dispute may exercise any rights they otherwise have to participate in all discussion within the Council or CSO regarding the dispute, but they will not take

part in the decision by the Council or the CSO directing the parties to conciliation, or in decisions described in paragraph 2(a).

4. The Council or the CSO will not direct parties to a dispute to seek conciliation under this Annex:

a) if the dispute is being addressed under some other procedure for the peaceful settlement of disputes;
b) if the dispute is covered by any process outside the CSCE which the parties to the dispute have accepted, including under an agreement in which the parties have undertaken to address certain disputes only through negotiations; or
c) if either party to the dispute considers that, because the dispute raises issues concerning its territorial integrity, or national defence, title to sovereignty over land territory, or competing claims with regard to the jurisdiction over other areas, the provisions of this Annex should not be applied.

5. The parties to the dispute will bear their own expenses. Except for disputes covered in paragraph 3, any other expenses incurred under the procedure will be shared by all participating States in accordance with the CSCE scale of distribution, subject to any procedures that the CSO may adopt to ensure that expenses are limited to those reasonable. With respect to disputes covered by paragraph 3, responsibility for such other expenses will be borne in accordance with the provisions of the Convention on Conciliation and Arbitration within the CSCE.

6. In addition to any reports otherwise provided for under the conciliation provision described in paragraphs 2 and 3, the Council or the CSO may request the Commission to report on the results of the conciliation. The report will not reflect matters that are considered confidential under the applicable provisions, unless the parties agree otherwise.

3 The International Court of Justice

The Framework*

18.a Statute of the International Court of Justice

Date: 26 June 1945
Source: 33 UNTS 993
https://www.icj-cij.org/en/statute

Article 1

The International Court of Justice established by the Charter of the United Nations as the principal judicial organ of the United Nations shall be constituted and shall function in accordance with the provisions of the present Statute.

CHAPTER I – ORGANIZATION OF THE COURT

Article 2

The Court shall be composed of a body of independent judges, elected regardless of their nationality from among persons of high moral character, who possess the qualifications required in their respective countries for appointment to the highest judicial offices, or are jurisconsults of recognized competence in international law.

Article 3

1. The Court shall consist of fifteen members, no two of whom may be nationals of the same state.

2. A person who for the purposes of membership in the Court could be regarded as a national of more than one state shall be deemed to be a national of the one in which he ordinarily exercises civil and political rights.

Article 4

1. The members of the Court shall be elected by the General Assembly and by the Security Council from a list of persons nominated by the national groups in the Permanent Court of Arbitration, in accordance with the following provisions.

2. In the case of Members of the United Nations not represented in the Permanent Court of Arbitration, candidates shall be nominated by national groups appointed for this purpose by their governments under the same conditions as those prescribed for members of the Permanent Court of Arbitration by Article 44 of the Convention of The Hague of 1907 for the pacific settlement of international disputes.

3. The conditions under which a state which is a party to the present Statute but is not a Member of the United Nations may participate in electing the members of the Court shall, in the absence of a special agreement, be laid down by the General Assembly upon recommendation of the Security Council.

* N.B.: See also Articles 7, 92–96 of the Charter of the United Nations (Document No. 6).

Article 5

1. At least three months before the date of the election, the Secretary-General of the United Nations shall address a written request to the members of the Permanent Court of Arbitration belonging to the states which are parties to the present Statute, and to the members of the national groups appointed under Article 4, paragraph 2, inviting them to undertake, within a given time, by national groups, the nomination of persons in a position to accept the duties of a member of the Court.

2. No group may nominate more than four persons, not more than two of whom shall be of their own nationality. In no case may the number of candidates nominated by a group be more than double the number of seats to be filled.

Article 6

Before making these nominations, each national group is recommended to consult its highest court of justice, its legal faculties and schools of law, and its national academies and national sections of international academies devoted to the study of law.

Article 7

1. The Secretary-General shall prepare a list in alphabetical order of all the persons thus nominated. Save as provided in Article 12, paragraph 2, these shall be the only persons eligible.

2. The Secretary-General shall submit this list to the General Assembly and to the Security Council.

Article 8

The General Assembly and the Security Council shall proceed independently of one another to elect the members of the Court.

Article 9

At every election, the electors shall bear in mind not only that the persons to be elected should individually possess the qualifications required, but also that in the body as a whole the representation of the main forms of civilization and of the principal legal systems of the world should be assured.

Article 10

1. Those candidates who obtain an absolute majority of votes in the General Assembly and in the Security Council shall be considered as elected.

2. Any vote of the Security Council, whether for the election of judges or for the appointment of members of the conference envisaged in Article 12, shall be taken without any distinction between permanent and non-permanent members of the Security Council.

3. In the event of more than one national of the same state obtaining an absolute majority of the votes both of the General Assembly and of the Security Council, the eldest of these only shall be considered as elected.

Article 11

If, after the first meeting held for the purpose of the election, one or more seats remain to be filled, a second and, if necessary, a third meeting shall take place.

Article 12

1. If, after the third meeting, one or more seats still remain unfilled, a joint conference consisting of six members, three appointed by the General Assembly and three by the Security Council, may be formed at any time at the request of either the General Assembly or the Security Council, for the purpose of choosing by the vote of an absolute majority one name for each seat still vacant, to submit to the General Assembly and the Security Council for their respective acceptance.

2. If the joint conference is unanimously agreed upon any person who fulfills the required conditions, he may be included in its list, even though he was not included in the list of nominations referred to in Article 7.

3. If the joint conference is satisfied that it will not be successful in procuring an election, those members of the Court who have already been elected shall, within a period to be fixed by the Security Council, proceed to fill the vacant seats by selection from among those candidates who have obtained votes either in the General Assembly or in the Security Council.

4. In the event of an equality of votes among the judges, the eldest judge shall have a casting vote.

Article 13

1. The members of the Court shall be elected for nine years and may be re-elected; provided, however, that of the judges elected at the first election, the terms of five judges shall expire at the end of three years and the terms of five more judges shall expire at the end of six years.

2. The judges whose terms are to expire at the end of the above-mentioned initial periods of three and six years shall be chosen by lot to be drawn by the Secretary-General immediately after the first election has been completed.

3. The members of the Court shall continue to discharge their duties until their places have been filled. Though replaced, they shall finish any cases which they may have begun.

4. In the case of the resignation of a member of the Court, the resignation shall be addressed to the President of the Court for transmission to the Secretary-General. This last notification makes the place vacant.

Article 14

Vacancies shall be filled by the same method as that laid down for the first election, subject to the following provision: the Secretary-General shall, within one month of the occurrence of the vacancy, proceed to issue the invitations provided for in Article 5, and the date of the election shall be fixed by the Security Council.

Article 15

A member of the Court elected to replace a member whose term of office has not expired shall hold office for the remainder of his predecessor's term.

Article 16

1. No member of the Court may exercise any political or administrative function, or engage in any other occupation of a professional nature.

2. Any doubt on this point shall be settled by the decision of the Court.

Article 17

1. No member of the Court may act as agent, counsel, or advocate in any case.

2. No member may participate in the decision of any case in which he has previously taken part as agent, counsel, or advocate for one of the parties, or as a member of a national or international court, or of a commission of enquiry, or in any other capacity.

3. Any doubt on this point shall be settled by the decision of the Court.

Article 18

1. No member of the Court can be dismissed unless, in the unanimous opinion of the other members, he has ceased to fulfill the required conditions.

2. Formal notification thereof shall be made to the Secretary-General by the Registrar.

3. This notification makes the place vacant.

Article 19

The members of the Court, when engaged on the business of the Court, shall enjoy diplomatic privileges and immunities.

Article 20

Every member of the Court shall, before taking up his duties, make a solemn declaration in open court that he will exercise his powers impartially and conscientiously.

Article 21

1. The Court shall elect its President and Vice-President for three years; they may be re-elected.

2. The Court shall appoint its Registrar and may provide for the appointment of such other officers as may be necessary.

Article 22

1. The seat of the Court shall be established at The Hague. This, however, shall not prevent the Court from sitting and exercising its functions elsewhere whenever the Court considers it desirable.

2. The President and the Registrar shall reside at the seat of the Court.

Article 23

1. The Court shall remain permanently in session, except during the judicial vacations, the dates and duration of which shall be fixed by the Court.

2. Members of the Court are entitled to periodic leave, the dates and duration of which shall be fixed by the Court, having in mind the distance between The Hague and the home of each judge.

3. Members of the Court shall be bound, unless they are on leave or prevented from attending by illness or other serious reasons duly explained to the President, to hold themselves permanently at the disposal of the Court.

Article 24

1. If, for some special reason, a member of the Court considers that he should not take part in the decision of a particular case, he shall so inform the President.

2. If the President considers that for some special reason one of the members of the Court should not sit in a particular case, he shall give him notice accordingly.

3. If in any such case the member of the Court and the President disagree, the matter shall be settled by the decision of the Court.

Article 25

1. The full Court shall sit except when it is expressly provided otherwise in the present Statute.

2. Subject to the condition that the number of judges available to constitute the Court is not thereby reduced below eleven, the Rules of the Court may provide for allowing one or more judges, according to circumstances and in rotation, to be dispensed from sitting.

3. A quorum of nine judges shall suffice to constitute the Court.

Article 26

1. The Court may from time to time form one or more chambers, composed of three or more judges as the Court may determine, for dealing with particular categories of cases; for example, labour cases and cases relating to transit and communications.

2. The Court may at any time form a chamber for dealing with a particular case. The number of judges to constitute such a chamber shall be determined by the Court with the approval of the parties.

3. Cases shall be heard and determined by the chambers provided for in this article if the parties so request.

Article 27

A judgment given by any of the chambers provided for in Articles 26 and 29 shall be considered as rendered by the Court.

Article 28

The chambers provided for in Articles 26 and 29 may, with the consent of the parties, sit and exercise their functions elsewhere than at The Hague.

Article 29

With a view to the speedy dispatch of business, the Court shall form annually a chamber composed of five judges which, at the request of the parties, may hear and determine cases by summary procedure. In addition, two judges shall be selected for the purpose of replacing judges who find it impossible to sit.

Article 30

1. The Court shall frame rules for carrying out its functions. In particular, it shall lay down rules of procedure.

2. The Rules of the Court may provide for assessors to sit with the Court or with any of its chambers, without the right to vote.

Article 31

1. Judges of the nationality of each of the parties shall retain their right to sit in the case before the Court.

2. If the Court includes upon the Bench a judge of the nationality of one of the parties, any other party may choose a person to sit as judge. Such person shall be chosen preferably from among those persons who have been nominated as candidates as provided in Articles 4 and 5.

3. If the Court includes upon the Bench no judge of the nationality of the parties, each of these parties may proceed to choose a judge as provided in paragraph 2 of this Article.

4. The provisions of this Article shall apply to the case of Articles 26 and 29. In such cases, the President shall request one or, if necessary, two of the members of the Court forming the chamber to give place to the members of the Court of the nationality of the parties concerned, and, failing such, or if they are unable to be present, to the judges specially chosen by the parties.

5. Should there be several parties in the same interest, they shall, for the purpose of the preceding provisions, be reckoned as one party only. Any doubt upon this point shall be settled by the decision of the Court.

6. Judges chosen as laid down in paragraphs 2, 3, and 4 of this Article shall fulfill the conditions required by Articles 2, 17 (paragraph 2), 20, and 24 of the present Statute. They shall take part in the decision on terms of complete equality with their colleagues.

Article 32

1. Each member of the Court shall receive an annual salary.

2. The President shall receive a special annual allowance.

3. The Vice-President shall receive a special allowance for every day on which he acts as President.

4. The judges chosen under Article 31, other than members of the Court, shall receive compensation for each day on which they exercise their functions.

5. These salaries, allowances, and compensation shall be fixed by the General Assembly. They may not be decreased during the term of office.

6. The salary of the Registrar shall be fixed by the General Assembly on the proposal of the Court.

7. Regulations made by the General Assembly shall fix the conditions under which retirement pensions may be given to members of the Court and to the Registrar, and the conditions under which members of the Court and the Registrar shall have their travelling expenses refunded.

8. The above salaries, allowances, and compensation shall be free of all taxation.

Article 33

The expenses of the Court shall be borne by the United Nations in such a manner as shall be decided by the General Assembly.

CHAPTER II – COMPETENCE OF THE COURT

Article 34

1. Only states may be parties in cases before the Court.

2. The Court, subject to and in conformity with its Rules, may request of public international organizations information relevant to cases before it, and shall receive such information presented by such organizations on their own initiative.

3. Whenever the construction of the constituent instrument of a public international organization or of an international convention adopted thereunder is in question in a case before the Court, the Registrar shall so notify the public international organization concerned and shall communicate to it copies of all the written proceedings.

Article 35

1. The Court shall be open to the states parties to the present Statute.

2. The conditions under which the Court shall be open to other states shall, subject to the special provisions contained in treaties in force, be laid down by the Security Council, but in no case shall such conditions place the parties in a position of inequality before the Court.

3. When a state which is not a Member of the United Nations is a party to a case, the Court shall fix the amount which that party is to contribute towards the expenses of the Court. This provision shall not apply if such state is bearing a share of the expenses of the Court.

Article 36

1. The jurisdiction of the Court comprises all cases which the parties refer to it and all matters specially provided for in the Charter of the United Nations or in treaties and conventions in force.

2. The states parties to the present Statute may at any time declare that they recognize as compulsory *ipso facto* and without special agreement, in relation to any other state accepting the same obligation, the jurisdiction of the Court in all legal disputes concerning:

   a. the interpretation of a treaty;
   b. any question of international law;
   c. the existence of any fact which, if established, would constitute a breach of an international obligation;
   d. the nature or extent of the reparation to be made for the breach of an international obligation.

3. The declarations referred to above may be made unconditionally or on condition of reciprocity on the part of several or certain states, or for a certain time.

4. Such declarations shall be deposited with the Secretary-General of the United Nations, who shall transmit copies thereof to the parties to the Statute and to the Registrar of the Court.

5. Declarations made under Article 36 of the Statute of the Permanent Court of International Justice and which are still in force shall be deemed, as between the parties to the present Statute, to be acceptances of the compulsory jurisdiction of the International Court of Justice for the period which they still have to run and in accordance with their terms.

6. In the event of a dispute as to whether the Court has jurisdiction, the matter shall be settled by the decision of the Court.

Article 37

Whenever a treaty or convention in force provides for reference of a matter to a tribunal to have been instituted by the League of Nations, or to the Permanent Court of International Justice, the matter shall, as between the parties to the present Statute, be referred to the International Court of Justice.

Article 38

1. The Court, whose function is to decide in accordance with international law such disputes as are submitted to it, shall apply:

   a. international conventions, whether general or particular, establishing rules expressly recognized by the contesting states;

b. international custom, as evidence of a general practice accepted as law;
c. the general principles of law recognized by civilized nations;
d. subject to the provisions of Article 59, judicial decisions and the teachings of the most highly qualified publicists of the various nations, as subsidiary means for the determination of rules of law.

2. This provision shall not prejudice the power of the Court to decide a case *ex aequo et bono*, if the parties agree thereto.

CHAPTER III – PROCEDURE

Article 39

1. The official languages of the Court shall be French and English. If the parties agree that the case shall be conducted in French, the judgment shall be delivered in French. If the parties agree that the case shall be conducted in English, the judgment shall be delivered in English.

2. In the absence of an agreement as to which language shall be employed, each party may, in the pleadings, use the language which it prefers; the decision of the Court shall be given in French and English. In this case the Court shall at the same time determine which of the two texts shall be considered as authoritative.

3. The Court shall, at the request of any party, authorize a language other than French or English to be used by that party.

Article 40

1. Cases are brought before the Court, as the case may be, either by the notification of the special agreement or by a written application addressed to the Registrar. In either case the subject of the dispute and the parties shall be indicated.

2. The Registrar shall forthwith communicate the application to all concerned.

3. He shall also notify the Members of the United Nations through the Secretary-General, and also any other states entitled to appear before the Court.

Article 41

1. The Court shall have the power to indicate, if it considers that circumstances so require, any provisional measures which ought to be taken to preserve the respective rights of either party.

2. Pending the final decision, notice of the measures suggested shall forthwith be given to the parties and to the Security Council.

Article 42

1. The parties shall be represented by agents.

2. They may have the assistance of counsel or advocates before the Court.

3. The agents, counsel, and advocates of parties before the Court shall enjoy the privileges and immunities necessary to the independent exercise of their duties.

Article 43

1. The procedure shall consist of two parts: written and oral.

2. The written proceedings shall consist of the communication to the Court and to the parties of memorials, counter-memorials and, if necessary, replies; also all papers and documents in support.

3. These communications shall be made through the Registrar, in the order and within the time fixed by the Court.
4. A certified copy of every document produced by one party shall be communicated to the other party.
5. The oral proceedings shall consist of the hearing by the Court of witnesses, experts, agents, counsel, and advocates.

Article 44

1. For the service of all notices upon persons other than the agents, counsel, and advocates, the Court shall apply direct to the government of the state upon whose territory the notice has to be served.
2. The same provision shall apply whenever steps are to be taken to procure evidence on the spot.

Article 45

The hearing shall be under the control of the President or, if he is unable to preside, of the Vice-President; if neither is able to preside, the senior judge present shall preside.

Article 46

The hearing in Court shall be public, unless the Court shall decide otherwise, or unless the parties demand that the public be not admitted.

Article 47

1. Minutes shall be made at each hearing and signed by the Registrar and the President.
2. These minutes alone shall be authentic.

Article 48

The Court shall make orders for the conduct of the case, shall decide the form and time in which each party must conclude its arguments, and make all arrangements connected with the taking of evidence.

Article 49

The Court may, even before the hearing begins, call upon the agents to produce any document or to supply any explanations. Formal note shall be taken of any refusal.

Article 50

The Court may, at any time, entrust any individual, body, bureau, commission, or other organization that it may select, with the task of carrying out an enquiry or giving an expert opinion.

Article 51

During the hearing any relevant questions are to be put to the witnesses and experts under the conditions laid down by the Court in the rules of procedure referred to in Article 30.

Article 52

After the Court has received the proofs and evidence within the time specified for the purpose, it may refuse to accept any further oral or written evidence that one party may desire to present unless the other side consents.

Article 53

1. Whenever one of the parties does not appear before the Court, or fails to defend its case, the other party may call upon the Court to decide in favour of its claim.

2. The Court must, before doing so, satisfy itself, not only that it has jurisdiction in accordance with Articles 36 and 37, but also that the claim is well founded in fact and law.

Article 54

1. When, subject to the control of the Court, the agents, counsel, and advocates have completed their presentation of the case, the President shall declare the hearing closed.

2. The Court shall withdraw to consider the judgment.

3. The deliberations of the Court shall take place in private and remain secret.

Article 55

1. All questions shall be decided by a majority of the judges present.

2. In the event of an equality of votes, the President or the judge who acts in his place shall have a casting vote.

Article 56

1. The judgment shall state the reasons on which it is based.

2. It shall contain the names of the judges who have taken part in the decision.

Article 57

If the judgment does not represent in whole or in part the unanimous opinion of the judges, any judge shall be entitled to deliver a separate opinion.

Article 58

The judgment shall be signed by the President and by the Registrar. It shall be read in open court, due notice having been given to the agents.

Article 59

The decision of the Court has no binding force except between the parties and in respect of that particular case.

Article 60

The judgment is final and without appeal. In the event of dispute as to the meaning or scope of the judgment, the Court shall construe it upon the request of any party.

Article 61

1. An application for revision of a judgment may be made only when it is based upon the discovery of some fact of such a nature as to be a decisive factor, which fact was, when the judgment was given, unknown to the Court and also to the party claiming revision, always provided that such ignorance was not due to negligence.

2. The proceedings for revision shall be opened by a judgment of the Court expressly recording the existence of the new fact, recognizing that it has such a character as to lay the case open to revision, and declaring the application admissible on this ground.

3. The Court may require previous compliance with the terms of the judgment before it admits proceedings in revision.

4. The application for revision must be made at latest within six months of the discovery of the new fact.

5. No application for revision may be made after the lapse of ten years from the date of the judgment.

Article 62

l. Should a state consider that it has an interest of a legal nature which may be affected by the decision in the case, it may submit a request to the Court to be permitted to intervene.

2 It shall be for the Court to decide upon this request.

Article 63

1. Whenever the construction of a convention to which states other than those concerned in the case are parties is in question, the Registrar shall notify all such states forthwith.

2. Every state so notified has the right to intervene in the proceedings; but if it uses this right, the construction given by the judgment will be equally binding upon it.

Article 64

Unless otherwise decided by the Court, each party shall bear its own costs.

CHAPTER IV – ADVISORY OPINIONS

Article 65

1. The Court may give an advisory opinion on any legal question at the request of whatever body may be authorized by or in accordance with the Charter of the United Nations to make such a request.

2. Questions upon which the advisory opinion of the Court is asked shall be laid before the Court by means of a written request containing an exact statement of the question upon which an opinion is required, and accompanied by all documents likely to throw light upon the question.

Article 66

1. The Registrar shall forthwith give notice of the request for an advisory opinion to all states entitled to appear before the Court.

2. The Registrar shall also, by means of a special and direct communication, notify any state entitled to appear before the Court or international organization considered by the Court, or, should it not be sitting, by the President, as likely to be able to furnish information on the question, that the Court will be prepared to receive, within a time-limit to be fixed by the President, written statements, or to hear, at a public sitting to be held for the purpose, oral statements relating to the question.

3. Should any such state entitled to appear before the Court have failed to receive the special communication referred to in paragraph 2 of this Article, such state may express a desire to submit a written statement or to be heard; and the Court will decide.

4. States and organizations having presented written or oral statements or both shall be permitted to comment on the statements made by other states or organizations in the form, to the extent, and within the time-limits which the Court, or, should it not be sitting, the President, shall decide in each particular case. Accordingly, the Registrar shall in due time communicate any such written statements to states and organizations having submitted similar statements.

Article 67

The Court shall deliver its advisory opinions in open court, notice having been given to the Secretary-General and to the representatives of Members of the United Nations, of other states and of international organizations immediately concerned.

Article 68

In the exercise of its advisory functions the Court shall further be guided by the provisions of the present Statute which apply in contentious cases to the extent to which it recognizes them to be applicable.

CHAPTER V – AMENDMENT

Article 69

Amendments to the present Statute shall be effected by the same procedure as is provided by the Charter of the United Nations for amendments to that Charter, subject however to any provisions which the General Assembly upon recommendation of the Security Council may adopt concerning the participation of states which are parties to the present Statute but are not Members of the United Nations.

Article 70

The Court shall have power to propose such amendments to the present Statute as it may deem necessary, through written communications to the Secretary-General, for consideration in conformity with the provisions of Article 69.

18.b Rules of Court

Date: 14 April 1978
Source: Acts and Documents Concerning the Organization of the Court (No 6)
https://www.icj-cij.org/en/rules

PREAMBLE*

The Court,

Having regard to Chapter XIV of the Charter of the United Nations;
Having regard to the Statute of the Court annexed thereto;
Acting in pursuance of Article 30 of the Statute;
Adopts the following Rules.

*N.B.: as last amended, 25 June 2020. Articles amended since 1 July 1978 are marked with an asterisk and appear in their amended form.

PART I THE COURT

SECTION A. JUDGES AND ASSESSORS

Subsection 1. The Members of the Court

Article 1

1. The Members of the Court are the judges elected in accordance with Articles 2 to 15 of the Statute.

2. For the purposes of a particular case, the Court may also include upon the Bench one or more persons chosen under Article 31 of the Statute to sit as judges *ad hoc*.

3. In the following Rules, the term "Member of the Court" denotes any elected judge; the term "judge" denotes any Member of the Court, and any judge *ad hoc*.

Article 2

1. The term of office of Members of the Court elected at a triennial election shall begin to run from the sixth of February* in the year in which the vacancies to which they are elected occur.

2. The term of office of a Member of the Court elected to replace a Member whose term of office has not expired shall begin to run from the date of the election.

Article 3

1. The Members of the Court, in the exercise of their functions, are of equal status, irrespective of age, priority of election or length of service.

2. The Members of the Court shall, except as provided in paragraphs 4 and 5 of this Article, take precedence according to the date on which their terms of office respectively began, as provided for by Article 2 of these Rules.

3. Members of the Court whose terms of office began on the same date shall take precedence in relation to one another according to seniority of age.

4. A Member of the Court who is re-elected to a new term of office which is continuous with his previous term shall retain his precedence.

5. The President and the Vice-President of the Court, while holding these offices, shall take precedence before all other Members of the Court.

6. The Member of the Court who, in accordance with the foregoing paragraphs, takes precedence next after the President and the Vice-President is in these Rules designated the "senior judge". If that Member is unable to act, the Member of the Court who is next after him in precedence and able to act is considered as senior judge.

Article 4

1. The declaration to be made by every Member of the Court in accordance with Article 20 of the Statute shall be as follows:

"I solemnly declare that I will perform my duties and exercise my powers as judge honourably, faithfully, impartially and conscientiously."

2. This declaration shall be made at the first public sitting at which the Member of the Court is present. Such sitting shall be held as soon as practicable after his term of office begins and, if necessary, a special sitting shall be held for the purpose.

* This is the date on which the terms of office of the Members of the Court elected at the first election began in 1946.

3. A Member of the Court who is re-elected shall make a new declaration only if his new term is not continuous with his previous one.

Article 5

1. A Member of the Court deciding to resign shall communicate his decision to the President, and the resignation shall take effect as provided in Article 13, paragraph 4, of the Statute.

2. If the Member of the Court deciding to resign from the Court is the President, he shall communicate his decision to the Court, and the resignation shall take effect as provided in Article 13, paragraph 4, of the Statute.

Article 6

In any case in which the application of Article 18 of the Statute is under consideration, the Member of the Court concerned shall be so informed by the President or, if the circumstances so require, by the Vice-President, in a written statement which shall include the grounds therefor and any relevant evidence. He shall subsequently, at a private meeting of the Court specially convened for the purpose, be afforded an opportunity of making a statement, of furnishing any information or explanations he wishes to give, and of supplying answers, orally or in writing, to any questions put to him. At a further private meeting, at which the Member of the Court concerned shall not be present, the matter shall be discussed; each Member of the Court shall state his opinion, and if requested a vote shall be taken.

Subsection 2. Judges ad hoc

Article 7

1. Judges *ad hoc*, chosen under Article 31 of the Statute for the purposes of particular cases, shall be admitted to sit on the Bench of the Court in the circumstances and according to the procedure indicated in Article 17, paragraph 2, Articles 35, 36, 37, Article 91, paragraph 2, and Article 102, paragraph 3, of these Rules.

2. They shall participate in the case in which they sit on terms of complete equality with the other judges on the Bench.

3. Judges *ad hoc* shall take precedence after the Members of the Court and in order of seniority of age.

Article 8

1. The solemn declaration to be made by every judge *ad hoc* in accordance with Articles 20 and 31, paragraph 6, of the Statute shall be as set out in Article 4, paragraph 1, of these Rules.

2. This declaration shall be made at a public sitting in the case in which the judge *ad hoc* is participating. If the case is being dealt with by a chamber of the Court, the declaration shall be made in the same manner in that chamber.

3. Judges *ad hoc* shall make the declaration in relation to any case in which they are participating, even if they have already done so in a previous case, but shall not make a new declaration for a later phase of the same case.

Subsection 3. Assessors

Article 9

1. The Court may, either *proprio motu* or upon a request made not later than the closure of the written proceedings, decide, for the purpose of a contentious case or request for advisory opinion, to appoint assessors to sit with it without the right to vote.

2. When the Court so decides, the President shall take steps to obtain all the information relevant to the choice of the assessors.

3. The assessors shall be appointed by secret ballot and by a majority of the votes of the judges composing the Court for the case.

4. The same powers shall belong to the chambers provided for by Articles 26 and 29 of the Statute and to the presidents thereof, and may be exercised in the same manner.

5. Before entering upon their duties, assessors shall make the following declaration at a public sitting:

> "I solemnly declare that I will perform my duties as an assessor honourably, impartially and conscientiously, and that I will faithfully observe all the provisions of the Statute and of the Rules of the Court."

SECTION B. THE PRESIDENCY

Article 10

1. The term of office of the President and that of the Vice-President shall begin to run from the date on which the terms of office of the Members of the Court elected at a triennial election begin in accordance with Article 2 of these Rules.

2. The elections to the presidency and vice-presidency shall be held on that date or shortly thereafter. The former President, if still a Member of the Court, shall continue to exercise his functions until the election to the presidency has taken place.

Article 11

1. If, on the date of the election to the presidency, the former President is still a Member of the Court, he shall conduct the election. If he has ceased to be a Member of the Court, or is unable to act, the election shall be conducted by the Member of the Court exercising the functions of the presidency by virtue of Article 13, paragraph 1, of these Rules.

2. The election shall take place by secret ballot, after the presiding Member of the Court has declared the number of affirmative votes necessary for election; there shall be no nominations. The Member of the Court obtaining the votes of a majority of the Members composing it at the time of the election shall be declared elected, and shall enter forthwith upon his functions.

3. The new President shall conduct the election of the Vice-President either at the same or at the following meeting. The provisions of paragraph 2 of this Article shall apply equally to this election.

Article 12

The President shall preside at all meetings of the Court; he shall direct the work and supervise the administration of the Court.

Article 13

1. In the event of a vacancy in the presidency or of the inability of the President to exercise the functions of the presidency, these shall be exercised by the Vice-President, or failing him, by the senior judge.

2. When the President is precluded by a provision of the Statute or of these Rules either from sitting or from presiding in a particular case, he shall continue to exercise the functions of the presidency for all purposes save in respect of that case.

3. The President shall take the measures necessary in order to ensure the continuous exercise of the functions of the presidency at the seat of the Court. In the event of his absence, he may, so far as is compatible with the Statute and these Rules, arrange for these functions to be exercised by the Vice-President, or failing him, by the senior judge.

4. If the President decides to resign the presidency, he shall communicate his decision in writing to the Court through the Vice-President, or failing him, the senior judge. If the Vice-President decides to resign his office, he shall communicate his decision to the President.

Article 14

If a vacancy in the presidency or the vice-presidency occurs before the date when the current term is due to expire under Article 21, paragraph 1, of the Statute and Article 10, paragraph 1, of these Rules, the Court shall decide whether or not the vacancy shall be filled during the remainder of the term.

SECTION C. THE CHAMBERS

Article 15

1. The Chamber of Summary Procedure to be formed annually under Article 29 of the Statute shall be composed of five Members of the Court, comprising the President and Vice-President of the Court, acting ex officio, and three other members elected in accordance with Article 18, paragraph 1, of these Rules. In addition, two Members of the Court shall be elected annually to act as substitutes.

2. The election referred to in paragraph 1 of this Article shall be held as soon as possible after the sixth of February in each year. The members of the Chamber shall enter upon their functions on election and continue to serve until the next election; they may be re- elected.

3. If a member of the Chamber is unable, for whatever reason, to sit in a given case, he shall be replaced for the purposes of that case by the senior in precedence of the two substitutes.

4. If a member of the Chamber resigns or otherwise ceases to be a member, his place shall be taken by the senior in precedence of the two substitutes, who shall thereupon become a full member of the Chamber and be replaced by the election of another substitute. Should vacancies exceed the number of available substitutes, elections shall be held as soon as possible in respect of the vacancies still existing after the substitutes have assumed full membership and in respect of the vacancies in the substitutes.

Article 16

1. When the Court decides to form one or more of the Chambers provided for in Article 26, paragraph 1, of the Statute, it shall determine the particular category of cases

for which each Chamber is formed, the number of its members, the period for which they will serve, and the date at which they will enter upon their duties.

2. The members of the Chamber shall be elected in accordance with Article 18, paragraph 1, of these Rules from among the Members of the Court, having regard to any special knowledge, expertise or previous experience which any of the Members of the Court may have in relation to the category of case the Chamber is being formed to deal with.

3. The Court may decide upon the dissolution of a Chamber, but without prejudice to the duty of the Chamber concerned to finish any cases pending before it.

Article 17

1. A request for the formation of a Chamber to deal with a particular case, as provided for in Article 26, paragraph 2, of the Statute, may be filed at any time until the closure of the written proceedings. Upon receipt of a request made by one party, the President shall ascertain whether the other party assents.

2. When the parties have agreed, the President shall ascertain their views regarding the composition of the Chamber, and shall report to the Court accordingly. He shall also take such steps as may be necessary to give effect to the provisions of Article 31, paragraph 4, of the Statute.

3. When the Court has determined, with the approval of the parties, the number of its Members who are to constitute the Chamber, it shall proceed to their election, in accordance with the provisions of Article 18, paragraph 1, of these Rules. The same procedure shall be followed as regards the filling of any vacancy that may occur on the Chamber.

4. Members of a Chamber formed under this Article who have been replaced, in accordance with Article 13 of the Statute following the expiration of their terms of office, shall continue to sit in all phases of the case, whatever the stage it has then reached.

Article 18

1. Elections to all Chambers shall take place by secret ballot. The Members of the Court obtaining the largest number of votes constituting a majority of the Members of the Court composing it at the time of the election shall be declared elected. If necessary to fill vacancies, more than one ballot shall take place, such ballot being limited to the number of vacancies that remain to be filled.

2. If a Chamber when formed includes the President or Vice-President of the Court, or both of them, the President or Vice-President, as the case may be, shall preside over that Chamber. In any other event, the Chamber shall elect its own president by secret ballot and by a majority of votes of its members. The Member of the Court who, under this paragraph, presides over the Chamber at the time of its formation shall continue to preside so long as he remains a member of that Chamber.

3. The president of a Chamber shall exercise, in relation to cases being dealt with by that Chamber, all the functions of the President of the Court in relation to cases before the Court.

4. If the president of a Chamber is prevented from sitting or from acting as president, the functions of the presidency shall be assumed by the member of the Chamber who is the senior in precedence and able to act.

SECTION D. INTERNAL FUNCTIONING OF THE COURT

Article 19

The internal judicial practice of the Court shall, subject to the provisions of the Statute and these Rules, be governed by any resolutions on the subject adopted by the Court.*

Article 20

1. The quorum specified by Article 25, paragraph 3, of the Statute applies to all meetings of the Court.

2. The obligation of Members of the Court under Article 23, paragraph 3, of the Statute, to hold themselves permanently at the disposal of the Court, entails attendance at all such meetings, unless they are prevented from attending by illness or for other serious reasons duly explained to the President, who shall inform the Court.

3. Judges *ad hoc* are likewise bound to hold themselves at the disposal of the Court and to attend all meetings held in the case in which they are participating. They shall not be taken into account for the calculation of the quorum.

4. The Court shall fix the dates and duration of the judicial vacations and the periods and conditions of leave to be accorded to individual Members of the Court under Article 23, paragraph 2, of the Statute, having regard in both cases to the state of its General List and to the requirements of its current work.

5. Subject to the same considerations, the Court shall observe the public holidays customary at the place where the Court is sitting.

6. In case of urgency the President may convene the Court at any time.

Article 21

1. The deliberations of the Court shall take place in private and remain secret. The Court may however at any time decide in respect of its deliberations on other than judicial matters to publish or allow publication of any part of them.

2. Only judges, and the assessors, if any, take part in the Court's judicial deliberations. The Registrar, or his deputy, and other members of the staff of the Registry as may be required shall be present. No other person shall be present except by permission of the Court.

3. The minutes of the Court's judicial deliberations shall record only the title or nature of the subjects or matters discussed, and the results of any vote taken. They shall not record any details of the discussions nor the views expressed, provided however that any judge is entitled to require that a statement made by him be inserted in the minutes.

PART II
THE REGISTRY

*Article 22***

1. The Court shall elect its Registrar by secret ballot. The Registrar shall be elected for a term of seven years. The Registrar may be re-elected.

2. The Court shall give public notice of a vacancy or impending vacancy, either forthwith upon the vacancy arising, or, where the vacancy will arise on the expiration of the term

* The resolution now in force was adopted on 12 April 1976. [N.B.: See Document No. 18.d.]
** Amendment entered into force on 21 October 2019.

of office of the Registrar, not less than six months prior thereto. The Court shall fix a date for the closure of the list of candidates so as to enable information concerning the candidates to be received in sufficient time. Interested persons shall be invited to submit their applications by the date so fixed by the Court.

3. Applications shall indicate the relevant information concerning the candidate, and in particular information as to the candidate's age, nationality, present occupation, university qualifications, knowledge of languages, and any previous experience in public international law, diplomacy, or the work of international organizations and institutional management.

4. The candidate obtaining the votes of the majority of the Members of the Court composing it at the time of the election shall be declared elected.

*Article 23**

The Court shall elect a Deputy-Registrar: the provisions of Article 22 of these Rules shall apply to the Deputy-Registrar's election and term of office.

Article 24

1. Before taking up his duties, the Registrar shall make the following declaration at a meeting of the Court:

"I solemnly declare that I will perform the duties incumbent upon me as Registrar of the International Court of Justice in all loyalty, discretion and good conscience, and that I will faithfully observe all the provisions of the Statute and of the Rules of the Court."

2. The Deputy-Registrar shall make a similar declaration at a meeting of the Court before taking up his duties.

Article 25

1. The staff-members of the Registry shall be appointed by the Court on proposals submitted by the Registrar. Appointments to such posts as the Court shall determine may however be made by the Registrar with the approval of the President.

2. Before taking up his duties, every staff-member shall make the following declaration before the President, the Registrar being present:

"I solemnly declare that I will perform the duties incumbent upon me as an official of the International Court of Justice in all loyalty, discretion and good conscience, and that I will faithfully observe all the provisions of the Statute and of the Rules of the Court."

Article 26

1. The Registrar, in the discharge of his functions, shall:

(a) be the regular channel of communications to and from the Court, and in particular shall effect all communications, notifications and transmission of documents required by the Statute or by these Rules and ensure that the date of despatch and receipt thereof may be readily verified;

(b) keep, under the supervision of the President, and in such form as may be laid down by the Court, a General List of all cases, entered and numbered in the order in which the documents instituting proceedings or requesting an advisory opinion are received in the Registry;

(c) have the custody of the declarations accepting the jurisdiction of the Court made by States not parties to the Statute in accordance with any resolution adopted by the

* Amendment entered into force on 21 October 2019.

Security Council under Article 35, paragraph 2, of the Statute, and transmit certified copies thereof to all States parties to the Statute, to such other States as shall have deposited declarations, and to the Secretary-General of the United Nations;

(d) transmit to the parties copies of all pleadings and documents annexed upon receipt thereof in the Registry;

(e) communicate to the government of the country in which the Court or a Chamber is sitting, and any other governments which may be concerned, the necessary information as to the persons from time to time entitled, under the Statute and relevant agreements, to privileges, immunities, or facilities;

(f) be present, in person or by his deputy, at meetings of the Court, and of the Chambers, and be responsible for the preparation of minutes of such meetings;

(g) make arrangements for such provision or verification of translations and interpretations into the Court's official languages as the Court may require;

(h) sign all judgments, advisory opinions and orders of the Court, and the minutes referred to in subparagraph *(f)*;

(i) be responsible for the printing and publication of the Court's judgments, advisory opinions and orders, the pleadings and statements, and minutes of public sittings in cases, and of such other documents as the Court may direct to be published;

(j) be responsible for all administrative work and in particular for the accounts and financial administration in accordance with the financial procedures of the United Nations;

(k) deal with enquiries concerning the Court and its work;

(l) assist in maintaining relations between the Court and other organs of the United Nations, the specialized agencies, and international bodies and conferences concerned with the codification and progressive development of international law;

(m) ensure that information concerning the Court and its activities is made accessible to governments, the highest national courts of justice, professional and learned societies, legal faculties and schools of law, and public information media;

(n) have custody of the seals and stamps of the Court, of the archives of the Court, and of such other archives as may be entrusted to the Court.*

2. The Court may at any time entrust additional functions to the Registrar.

3. In the discharge of his functions the Registrar shall be responsible to the Court.

Article 27

1. The Deputy-Registrar shall assist the Registrar, act as Registrar in the latter's absence and, in the event of the office becoming vacant, exercise the functions of Registrar until the office has been filled.

2. If both the Registrar and the Deputy-Registrar are unable to carry out the duties of Registrar, the President shall appoint an official of the Registry to discharge those duties for such time as may be necessary. If both offices are vacant at the same time, the President, after consulting the Members of the Court, shall appoint an official of the Registry to discharge the duties of Registrar pending an election to that office.

* The Registrar also keeps the Archives of the Permanent Court of International Justice, entrusted to the present Court by decision of the Permanent Court of October 1945 (*I.C.J. Yearbook 1946–1947*, p. 26). and the Archives of the Trial of the Major War Criminals before the International Military Tribunal at Nuremberg (1945–1946), entrusted to the Court by decision of that Tribunal of 1 October 1946; the Court authorized the Registrar to accept the latter Archives by decision of 19 November 1949.

Article 28

1. The Registry shall comprise the Registrar, the Deputy-Registrar, and such other staff as the Registrar shall require for the efficient discharge of his functions.

2. The Court shall prescribe the organization of the Registry, and shall for this purpose request the Registrar to make proposals.

3. Instructions for the Registry shall be drawn up by the Registrar and approved by the Court.

4. The staff of the Registry shall be subject to Staff Regulations drawn up by the Registrar, so far as possible in conformity with the United Nations Staff Regulations and Staff Rules, and approved by the Court.

*Article 29**

1. The Registrar may be removed from office only if, in the opinion of two-thirds of the Members of the Court composing it at the time of the decision to be taken, the incumbent has either become permanently incapacitated from exercising his or her functions, or has committed a serious breach of duty. Such decision shall be taken by secret ballot.

2. Before a decision is taken under this Article, the Registrar shall be informed by the President of the action contemplated, in a written statement which shall include the grounds therefor and any relevant evidence. The Registrar shall subsequently, at a private meeting of the Court, be afforded an opportunity of making a statement, of furnishing any information or explanations, and of supplying answers, orally or in writing, to any questions.

3. The Deputy-Registrar may be removed from office only on the same grounds and by the same procedure.

PART III
PROCEEDINGS IN CONTENTIOUS CASES

SECTION A. COMMUNICATIONS TO THE COURT AND CONSULTATIONS

Article 30

All communications to the Court under these Rules shall be addressed to the Registrar unless otherwise stated. Any request made by a party shall likewise be addressed to the Registrar unless made in open court in the course of the oral proceedings.

Article 31

In every case submitted to the Court, the President shall ascertain the views of the parties with regard to questions of procedure. For this purpose he shall summon the agents of the parties to meet him as soon as possible after their appointment, and whenever necessary thereafter.

SECTION B. THE COMPOSITION OF THE COURT FOR PARTICULAR CASES

Article 32

1. If the President of the Court is a national of one of the parties in a case he shall not exercise the functions of the presidency in respect of that case. The same rule applies to the Vice-President, or to the senior judge, when called on to act as President.

* Amendment entered into force on 21 October 2019.

2. The Member of the Court who is presiding in a case on the date on which the Court convenes for the oral proceedings shall continue to preside in that case until completion of the current phase of the case, notwithstanding the election in the meantime of a new President or Vice-President. If he should become unable to act, the presidency for the case shall be determined in accordance with Article 13 of these Rules, and on the basis of the composition of the Court on the date on which it convened for the oral proceedings.

Article 33

Except as provided in Article 17 of these Rules, Members of the Court who have been replaced, in accordance with Article 13, paragraph 3, of the Statute following the expiration of their terms of office, shall discharge the duty imposed upon them by that paragraph by continuing to sit until the completion of any phase of a case in respect of which the Court convenes for the oral proceedings prior to the date of such replacement.

Article 34

1. In case of any doubt arising as to the application of Article 17, paragraph 2, of the Statute or in case of a disagreement as to the application of Article 24 of the Statute, the President shall inform the Members of the Court, with whom the decision lies.

2. If a party desires to bring to the attention of the Court facts which it considers to be of possible relevance to the application of the provisions of the Statute mentioned in the previous paragraph, but which it believes may not be known to the Court, that party shall communicate confidentially such facts to the President in writing.

Article 35

1. If a party proposes to exercise the power conferred by Article 31 of the Statute to choose a judge *ad hoc* in a case, it shall notify the Court of its intention as soon as possible. If the name and nationality of the judge selected are not indicated at the same time, the party shall, not later than two months before the time-limit fixed for the filing of the Counter-Memorial, inform the Court of the name and nationality of the person chosen and supply brief biographical details. The judge *ad hoc* may be of a nationality other than that of the party which chooses him.

2. If a party proposes to abstain from choosing a judge *ad hoc*, on condition of a like abstention by the other party, it shall so notify the Court which shall inform the other party. If the other party thereafter gives notice of its intention to choose, or chooses, a judge *ad hoc*, the time-limit for the party which has previously abstained from choosing a judge may be extended by the President.

3. A copy of any notification relating to the choice of a judge *ad hoc* shall be communicated by the Registrar to the other party, which shall be requested to furnish, within a time-limit to be fixed by the President, such observations as it may wish to make. If within the said time-limit no objection is raised by the other party, and if none appears to the Court itself, the parties shall be so informed.

4. In the event of any objection or doubt, the matter shall be decided by the Court, if necessary after hearing the parties.

5. A judge *ad hoc* who has accepted appointment but who becomes unable to sit may be replaced.

6. If and when the reasons for the participation of a judge *ad hoc* are found no longer to exist, he shall cease to sit on the Bench.

Article 36

1. If the Court finds that two or more parties are in the same interest, and therefore are to be reckoned as one party only, and that there is no Member of the Court of the nationality of any one of those parties upon the Bench, the Court shall fix a time-limit within which they may jointly choose a judge *ad hoc*.

2. Should any party amongst those found by the Court to be in the same interest allege the existence of a separate interest of its own, or put forward any other objection, the matter shall be decided by the Court, if necessary after hearing the parties.

Article 37

1. If a Member of the Court having the nationality of one of the parties is or becomes unable to sit in any phase of a case, that party shall thereupon become entitled to choose a judge *ad hoc* within a time-limit to be fixed by the Court, or by the President if the Court is not sitting.

2. Parties in the same interest shall be deemed not to have a judge of one of their nationalities upon the Bench if the Member of the Court having one of their nationalities is or becomes unable to sit in any phase of the case.

3. If the Member of the Court having the nationality of a party becomes able to sit not later than the closure of the written proceedings in that phase of the case, that Member of the Court shall resume his seat on the Bench in the case.

SECTION C. PROCEEDINGS BEFORE THE COURT

Subsection 1. Institution of Proceedings

Article 38

1. When proceedings before the Court are instituted by means of an application addressed as specified in Article 40, paragraph 1, of the Statute, the application shall indicate the party making it, the State against which the claim is brought, and the subject of the dispute.

2. The application shall specify as far as possible the legal grounds upon which the jurisdiction of the Court is said to be based; it shall also specify the precise nature of the claim, together with a succinct statement of the facts and grounds on which the claim is based.

3. The original of the application shall be signed either by the agent of the party submitting it, or by the diplomatic representative of that party in the country in which the Court has its seat, or by some other duly authorized person. If the application bears the signature of someone other than such diplomatic representative, the signature must be authenticated by the latter or by the competent authority of the applicant's foreign ministry.

4. The Registrar shall forthwith transmit to the respondent a certified copy of the application.

5. When the applicant State proposes to found the jurisdiction of the Court upon a consent thereto yet to be given or manifested by the State against which such application is made, the application shall be transmitted to that State. It shall not however be entered in the General List, nor any action be taken in the proceedings, unless and until the State against which such application is made consents to the Court's jurisdiction for the purposes of the case.

Article 39

1. When proceedings are brought before the Court by the notification of a special agreement, in conformity with Article 40, paragraph 1, of the Statute, the notification may be effected by the parties jointly or by any one or more of them. If the notification is not a joint one, a certified copy of it shall forthwith be communicated by the Registrar to the other party.

2. In each case the notification shall be accompanied by an original or certified copy of the special agreement. The notification shall also, in so far as this is not already apparent from the agreement, indicate the precise subject of the dispute and identify the parties to it.

Article 40

1. Except in the circumstances contemplated by Article 38, paragraph 5, of these Rules, all steps on behalf of the parties after proceedings have been instituted shall be taken by agents. Agents shall have an address for service at the seat of the Court to which all communications concerning the case are to be sent. Communications addressed to the agents of the parties shall be considered as having been addressed to the parties themselves.

2. When proceedings are instituted by means of an application, the name of the agent for the applicant shall be stated. The respondent, upon receipt of the certified copy of the application, or as soon as possible thereafter, shall inform the Court of the name of its agent.

3. When proceedings are brought by notification of a special agreement, the party making the notification shall state the name of its agent. Any other party to the special agreement, upon receiving from the Registrar a certified copy of such notification, or as soon as possible thereafter, shall inform the Court of the name of its agent if it has not already done so.

Article 41

The institution of proceedings by a State which is not a party to the Statute but which, under Article 35, paragraph 2, thereof, has accepted the jurisdiction of the Court by a declaration made in accordance with any resolution adopted by the Security Council under that Article,* shall be accompanied by a deposit of the declaration in question, unless the latter has previously been deposited with the Registrar. If any question of the validity or effect of such declaration arises, the Court shall decide.

Article 42

The Registrar shall transmit copies of any application or notification of a special agreement instituting proceedings before the Court to: *(a)* the Secretary-General of the United Nations; *(b)* the Members of the United Nations; *(c)* other States entitled to appear before the Court.

*Article 43***

1. Whenever the construction of a convention to which States other than those concerned in the case are parties may be in question within the meaning of Article 63, paragraph 1, of the Statute, the Court shall consider what directions shall be given to the Registrar in the matter.

* The resolution now in force was adopted on 15 October 1946. [N.B.: See Document No. 18.f.]

** Amendment entered into force on 29 September 2005: Article 43, paragraph 1, as amended, repeats unchanged the text of Article 43, as adopted on 14 April 1978. Paragraphs 2 and 3 of the amended Article 43 are new.

2. Whenever the construction of a convention to which a public international organization is a party may be in question in a case before the Court, the Court shall consider whether the Registrar shall so notify the public international organization concerned. Every public international organization notified by the Registrar may submit its observations on the particular provisions of the convention the construction of which is in question in the case.

3. If a public international organization sees fit to furnish its observations under paragraph 2 of this Article, the procedure to be followed shall be that provided for in Article 69, paragraph 2, of these Rules.

Subsection 2. The Written Proceedings

Article 44

1. In the light of the information obtained by the President under Article 31 of these Rules, the Court shall make the necessary orders to determine, *inter alia*, the number and the order of filing of the pleadings and the time-limits within which they must be filed.

2. In making an order under paragraph 1 of this Article, any agreement between the parties which does not cause unjustified delay shall be taken into account.

3. The Court may, at the request of the party concerned, extend any time-limit, or decide that any step taken after the expiration of the time-limit fixed therefor shall be considered as valid, if it is satisfied that there is adequate justification for the request. In either case the other party shall be given an opportunity to state its views.

4. If the Court is not sitting, its powers under this Article shall be exercised by the President, but without prejudice to any subsequent decision of the Court. If the consultation referred to in Article 31 reveals persistent disagreement between the parties as to the application of Article 45, paragraph 2, or Article 46, paragraph 2, of these Rules, the Court shall be convened to decide the matter.

Article 45

1. The pleadings in a case begun by means of an application shall consist, in the following order, of: a Memorial by the applicant; a Counter-Memorial by the respondent.

2. The Court may authorize or direct that there shall be a Reply by the applicant and a Rejoinder by the respondent if the parties are so agreed, or if the Court decides, *proprio motu* or at the request of one of the parties, that these pleadings are necessary.

Article 46

1. In a case begun by the notification of a special agreement, the number and order of the pleadings shall be governed by the provisions of the agreement, unless the Court, after ascertaining the views of the parties, decides otherwise.

2. If the special agreement contains no such provision, and if the parties have not subsequently agreed on the number and order of pleadings, they shall each file a Memorial and Counter-Memorial, within the same time-limits. The Court shall not authorize the presentation of Replies unless it finds them to be necessary.

Article 47

The Court may at any time direct that the proceedings in two or more cases be joined. It may also direct that the written or oral proceedings, including the calling of witnesses, be in common; or the Court may, without effecting any formal joinder, direct common action in any of these respects.

Article 48

Time-limits for the completion of steps in the proceedings may be fixed by assigning a specified period but shall always indicate definite dates. Such time-limits shall be as short as the character of the case permits.

Article 49

1. A Memorial shall contain a statement of the relevant facts, a statement of law, and the submissions.

2. A Counter-Memorial shall contain: an admission or denial of the facts stated in the Memorial; any additional facts, if necessary; observations concerning the statement of law in the Memorial; a statement of law in answer thereto; and the submissions.

3. The Reply and Rejoinder, whenever authorized by the Court, shall not merely repeat the parties' contentions, but shall be directed to bringing out the issues that still divide them.

4. Every pleading shall set out the party's submissions at the relevant stage of the case, distinctly from the arguments presented, or shall confirm the submissions previously made.

Article 50

1. There shall be annexed to the original of every pleading certified copies of any relevant documents adduced in support of the contentions contained in the pleading.

2. If only parts of a document are relevant, only such extracts as are necessary for the purpose of the pleading in question need be annexed. A copy of the whole document shall be deposited in the Registry, unless it has been published and is readily available.

3. A list of all documents annexed to a pleading shall be furnished at the time the pleading is filed.

Article 51

1. If the parties are agreed that the written proceedings shall be conducted wholly in one of the two official languages of the Court, the pleadings shall be submitted only in that language. If the parties are not so agreed, any pleading or any part of a pleading shall be submitted in one or other of the official languages.

2. If in pursuance of Article 39, paragraph 3, of the Statute a language other than French or English is used, a translation into French or English certified as accurate by the party submitting it, shall be attached to the original of each pleading.

3. When a document annexed to a pleading is not in one of the official languages of the Court, it shall be accompanied by a translation into one of these languages certified by the party submitting it as accurate. The translation may be confined to part of an annex, or to extracts therefrom, but in this case it must be accompanied by an explanatory note indicating what passages are translated. The Court may however require a more extensive or a complete translation to be furnished.

*Article 52**

1. The original of every pleading shall be signed by the agent and filed in the Registry. It shall be accompanied by a certified copy of the pleading, documents annexed, and

* Amendment entered into force on 14 April 2005. The agents of the parties are requested to ascertain from the Registry the usual format of the pleadings. The text of Article 52, as adopted on 14 April 1978, contained a paragraph 3 concerning the procedure to be followed where the Registrar arranges for the printing of a pleading; this paragraph has been deleted and the footnote to the Article has been amended. Former paragraph 4 has been renumbered and is now paragraph 3.

any translations, for communication to the other party in accordance with Article 43, paragraph 4, of the Statute, and by the number of additional copies required by the Registry, but without prejudice to an increase in that number should the need arise later.

2. All pleadings shall be dated. When a pleading has to be filed by a certain date, it is the date of the receipt of the pleading in the Registry which will be regarded by the Court as the material date.

3. The correction of a slip or error in any document which has been filed may be made at any time with the consent of the other party or by leave of the President. Any correction so effected shall be notified to the other party in the same manner as the pleading to which it relates.

Article 53

1. The Court, or the President if the Court is not sitting, may at any time decide, after ascertaining the views of the parties, that copies of the pleadings and documents annexed shall be made available to a State entitled to appear before it which has asked to be furnished with such copies.

2. The Court may, after ascertaining the views of the parties, decide that copies of the pleadings and documents annexed shall be made accessible to the public on or after the opening of the oral proceedings.

Subsection 3. The Oral Proceedings

Article 54

1. Upon the closure of the written proceedings, the case is ready for hearing. The date for the opening of the oral proceedings shall be fixed by the Court, which may also decide, if occasion should arise, that the opening or the continuance of the oral proceedings be postponed.

2. When fixing the date for, or postponing, the opening of the oral proceedings the Court shall have regard to the priority required by Article 74 of these Rules and to any other special circumstances, including the urgency of a particular case.

3. When the Court is not sitting, its powers under this Article shall be exercised by the President.

Article 55

The Court may, if it considers it desirable, decide pursuant to Article 22, paragraph 1, of the Statute that all or part of the further proceedings in a case shall be held at a place other than the seat of the Court. Before so deciding, it shall ascertain the views of the parties.

Article 56

1. After the closure of the written proceedings, no further documents may be submitted to the Court by either party except with the consent of the other party or as provided in paragraph 2 of this Article. The party desiring to produce a new document shall file the original or a certified copy thereof, together with the number of copies required by the Registry, which shall be responsible for communicating it to the other party and shall inform the Court. The other party shall be held to have given its consent if it does not lodge an objection to the production of the document.

2. In the absence of consent, the Court, after hearing the parties, may, if it considers the document necessary, authorize its production.

3. If a new document is produced under paragraph 1 or paragraph 2 of this Article, the other party shall have an opportunity of commenting upon it and of submitting documents in support of its comments.

4. No reference may be made during the oral proceedings to the contents of any document which has not been produced in accordance with Article 43 of the Statute or this Article, unless the document is part of a publication readily available.

5. The application of the provisions of this Article shall not in itself constitute a ground for delaying the opening or the course of the oral proceedings.

Article 57

Without prejudice to the provisions of the Rules concerning the production of documents, each party shall communicate to the Registrar, in sufficient time before the opening of the oral proceedings, information regarding any evidence which it intends to produce or which it intends to request the Court to obtain. This communication shall contain a list of the surnames, first names, nationalities, descriptions and places of residence of the witnesses and experts whom the party intends to call, with indications in general terms of the point or points to which their evidence will be directed. A copy of the communication shall also be furnished for transmission to the other party.

Article 58

1. The Court shall determine whether the parties should present their arguments before or after the production of the evidence; the parties shall, however, retain the right to comment on the evidence given.

2. The order in which the parties will be heard, the method of handling the evidence and of examining any witnesses and experts, and the number of counsel and advocates to be heard on behalf of each party, shall be settled by the Court after the views of the parties have been ascertained in accordance with Article 31 of these Rules.

*Article 59**

1. The hearing in Court shall be public, unless the Court shall decide otherwise, or unless the parties demand that the public be not admitted. Such a decision or demand may concern either the whole or part of the hearing, and may be made at any time.

2. The Court may decide, for health, security or other compelling reasons, to hold a hearing entirely or in part by video link. The parties shall be consulted on the organization of such a hearing.

Article 60

1. The oral statements made on behalf of each party shall be as succinct as possible within the limits of what is requisite for the adequate presentation of that party's contentions at the hearing. Accordingly, they shall be directed to the issues that still divide the parties, and shall not go over the whole ground covered by the pleadings, or merely repeat the facts and arguments these contain.

2. At the conclusion of the last statement made by a party at the hearing, its agent, without recapitulation of the arguments, shall read that party's final submissions. A copy of the written text of these, signed by the agent, shall be communicated to the Court and transmitted to the other party.

* Amendment entered into force on 25 June 2020.

Article 61

1. The Court may at any time prior to or during the hearing indicate any points or issues to which it would like the parties specially to address themselves, or on which it considers that there has been sufficient argument.

2. The Court may, during the hearing, put questions to the agents, counsel and advocates, and may ask them for explanations.

3. Each judge has a similar right to put questions, but before exercising it he should make his intention known to the President, who is made responsible by Article 45 of the Statute for the control of the hearing.

4. The agents, counsel and advocates may answer either immediately or within a time-limit fixed by the President.

Article 62

1. The Court may at any time call upon the parties to produce such evidence or to give such explanations as the Court may consider to be necessary for the elucidation of any aspect of the matters in issue, or may itself seek other information for this purpose.

2. The Court may, if necessary, arrange for the attendance of a witness or expert to give evidence in the proceedings.

Article 63

1. The parties may call any witnesses or experts appearing on the list communicated to the Court pursuant to Article 57 of these Rules. If at any time during the hearing a party wishes to call a witness or expert whose name was not included in that list, it shall so inform the Court and the other party, and shall supply the information required by Article 57. The witness or expert may be called either if the other party makes no objection or if the Court is satisfied that his evidence seems likely to prove relevant.

2. The Court, or the President if the Court is not sitting, shall, at the request of one of the parties or *proprio motu*, take the necessary steps for the examination of witnesses otherwise than before the Court itself.

Article 64

Unless on account of special circumstances the Court decides on a different form of words,

(a) every witness shall make the following declaration before giving any evidence: "I solemnly declare upon my honour and conscience that I will speak the truth, the whole truth and nothing but the truth";

(b) every expert shall make the following declaration before making any statement: "I solemnly declare upon my honour and conscience that I will speak the truth, the whole truth and nothing but the truth, and that my statement will be in accordance with my sincere belief."

Article 65

Witnesses and experts shall be examined by the agents, counsel or advocates of the parties under the control of the President. Questions may be put to them by the President and by the judges. Before testifying, witnesses shall remain out of court.

Article 66

The Court may at any time decide, either *proprio motu* or at the request of a party, to exercise its functions with regard to the obtaining of evidence at a place or locality to which the case relates, subject to such conditions as the Court may decide upon after ascertaining the views of the parties. The necessary arrangements shall be made in accordance with Article 44 of the Statute.

Article 67

1. If the Court considers it necessary to arrange for an enquiry or an expert opinion, it shall, after hearing the parties, issue an order to this effect, defining the subject of the enquiry or expert opinion, stating the number and mode of appointment of the persons to hold the enquiry or of the experts, and laying down the procedure to be followed. Where appropriate, the Court shall require persons appointed to carry out an enquiry, or to give an expert opinion, to make a solemn declaration.

2. Every report or record of an enquiry and every expert opinion shall be communicated to the parties, which shall be given the opportunity of commenting upon it.

Article 68

Witnesses and experts who appear at the instance of the Court under Article 62, paragraph 2, and persons appointed under Article 67, paragraph 1, of these Rules, to carry out an enquiry or to give an expert opinion, shall, where appropriate, be paid out of the funds of the Court.

Article 69

1. The Court may, at any time prior to the closure of the oral proceedings, either *proprio motu* or at the request of one of the parties communicated as provided in Article 57 of these Rules, request a public international organization, pursuant to Article 34 of the Statute, to furnish information relevant to a case before it. The Court, after consulting the chief administrative officer of the organization concerned, shall decide whether such information shall be presented to it orally or in writing, and the time-limits for its presentation.

2. When a public international organization sees fit to furnish, on its own initiative, information relevant to a case before the Court, it shall do so in the form of a Memorial to be filed in the Registry before the closure of the written proceedings. The Court shall retain the right to require such information to be supplemented, either orally or in writing, in the form of answers to any questions which it may see fit to formulate, and also to authorize the parties to comment, either orally or in writing, on the information thus furnished.

3. In the circumstances contemplated by Article 34, paragraph 3, of the Statute, the Registrar, on the instructions of the Court, or of the President if the Court is not sitting, shall proceed as prescribed in that paragraph. The Court, or the President if the Court is not sitting, may, as from the date on which the Registrar has communicated copies of the written proceedings and after consulting the chief administrative officer of the public international organization concerned, fix a time-limit within which the organization may submit to the Court its observations in writing. These observations shall be communicated to the parties and may be discussed by them and by the representative of the said organization during the oral proceedings.

4. In the foregoing paragraph, the term "public international organization" denotes an international organization of States.

Article 70

1. In the absence of any decision to the contrary by the Court, all speeches and statements made and evidence given at the hearing in one of the official languages of the Court shall be interpreted into the other official language. If they are made or given in any other language, they shall be interpreted into the two official languages of the Court.

2. Whenever, in accordance with Article 39, paragraph 3, of the Statute, a language other than French or English is used, the necessary arrangements for interpretation into one of the two official languages shall be made by the party concerned; however, the Registrar shall make arrangements for the verification of the interpretation provided by a party of evidence given on the party's behalf. In the case of witnesses or experts who appear at the instance of the Court, arrangements for interpretation shall be made by the Registry.

3. A party on behalf of which speeches or statements are to be made, or evidence given, in a language which is not one of the official languages of the Court, shall so notify the Registrar in sufficient time for him to make the necessary arrangements.

4. Before first interpreting in the case, interpreters provided by a party shall make the following declaration in open court:

"I solemnly declare upon my honour and conscience that my interpretation will be faithful and complete."

Article 71

1. A verbatim record shall be made by the Registrar of every hearing, in the official language of the Court which has been used. When the language used is not one of the two official languages of the Court, the verbatim record shall be prepared in one of the Court's official languages.

2. When speeches or statements are made in a language which is not one of the official languages of the Court, the party on behalf of which they are made shall supply to the Registry in advance a text thereof in one of the official languages, and this text shall constitute the relevant part of the verbatim record.

3. The transcript of the verbatim record shall be preceded by the names of the judges present, and those of the agents, counsel and advocates of the parties.

4. Copies of the transcript shall be circulated to the judges sitting in the case, and to the parties. The latter may, under the supervision of the Court, correct the transcripts of speeches and statements made on their behalf, but in no case may such corrections affect the sense and bearing thereof. The judges may likewise make corrections in the transcript of anything they may have said.

5. Witnesses and experts shall be shown that part of the transcript which relates to the evidence given, or the statements made by them, and may correct it in like manner as the parties.

6. One certified true copy of the eventual corrected transcript, signed by the President and the Registrar, shall constitute the authentic minutes of the sitting for the purpose of Article 47 of the Statute. The minutes of public hearings shall be printed and published by the Court.

Article 72

Any written reply by a party to a question put under Article 61, or any evidence or explanation supplied by a party under Article 62 of these Rules, received by the Court after the closure of the oral proceedings, shall be communicated to the other party, which shall be given the opportunity of commenting upon it. If necessary the oral proceedings may be reopened for that purpose.

SECTION D. INCIDENTAL PROCEEDINGS

Subsection 1. Interim Protection

Article 73

1. A written request for the indication of provisional measures may be made by a party at any time during the course of the proceedings in the case in connection with which the request is made.

2. The request shall specify the reasons therefor, the possible consequences if it is not granted, and the measures requested. A certified copy shall forthwith be transmitted by the Registrar to the other party.

Article 74

1. A request for the indication of provisional measures shall have priority over all other cases.

2. The Court, if it is not sitting when the request is made, shall be convened forthwith for the purpose of proceeding to a decision on the request as a matter of urgency.

3. The Court, or the President if the Court is not sitting, shall fix a date for a hearing which will afford the parties an opportunity of being represented at it. The Court shall receive and take into account any observations that may be presented to it before the closure of the oral proceedings.

4. Pending the meeting of the Court, the President may call upon the parties to act in such a way as will enable any order the Court may make on the request for provisional measures to have its appropriate effects.

Article 75

1. The Court may at any time decide to examine *proprio motu* whether the circumstances of the case require the indication of provisional measures which ought to be taken or complied with by any or all of the parties.

2. When a request for provisional measures has been made, the Court may indicate measures that are in whole or in part other than those requested, or that ought to be taken or complied with by the party which has itself made the request.

3. The rejection of a request for the indication of provisional measures shall not prevent the party which made it from making a fresh request in the same case based on new facts.

*Article 76**

1. At the request of a party or *proprio motu*, the Court may, at any time before the final judgment in the case, revoke or modify any decision concerning provisional measures if, in its opinion, some change in the situation justifies such revocation or modification.

2. Any application by a party proposing such a revocation or modification shall specify the change in the situation considered to be relevant.

3. Before taking any decision under paragraph 1 of this Article the Court shall afford the parties an opportunity of presenting their observations on the subject.

Article 77

Any measures indicated by the Court under Articles 73 and 75 of these Rules, and any decision taken by the Court under Article 76, paragraph 1, of these Rules, shall forthwith

* Amendment entered into force on 21 October 2019.

be communicated to the Secretary-General of the United Nations for transmission to the Security Council in pursuance of Article 41, paragraph 2, of the Statute.

Article 78

The Court may request information from the parties on any matter connected with the implementation of any provisional measures it has indicated.

Subsection 2. Preliminary Objections

*Article 79**

1. Following the submission of the application and after the President has met and consulted with the parties, the Court may decide, if the circumstances so warrant, that questions concerning its jurisdiction or the admissibility of the application shall be determined separately.

2. Where the Court so decides, the parties shall submit pleadings concerning jurisdiction or admissibility within the time-limits fixed, and in the order determined, by the Court. Each pleading shall contain the party's observations and submissions, including any evidence on which it relies, and shall attach copies of supporting documents.

Article 79 bis**

1. When the Court has not taken any decision under Article 79, an objection by the respondent to the jurisdiction of the Court or to the admissibility of the application, or other objection the decision upon which is requested before any further proceedings on the merits, shall be made in writing as soon as possible, and not later than three months after the delivery of the Memorial. Any such objection made by a party other than the respondent shall be filed within the time-limit fixed for the delivery of that party's first pleading.

2. The preliminary objection shall set out the facts and the law on which the objection is based, the submissions and a list of the documents in support; it shall include any evidence on which the party relies. Copies of the supporting documents shall be attached.

3. Upon receipt by the Registry of a preliminary objection, the proceedings on the merits shall be suspended and the Court, or the President if the Court is not sitting, shall fix the time-limit for the presentation by the other party of a written statement of its observations and submissions, which shall include any evidence on which the party relies. Copies of the supporting documents shall be attached.

4. The Court shall give effect to any agreement between the parties that an objection submitted under paragraph 1 be heard and determined within the framework of the merits.

Article 79 ter***

1. Pleadings with respect to preliminary questions, or objections filed pursuant to Article 79, paragraph 2, or Article 79bis, paragraphs 1 and 3, shall be confined to those matters that are relevant to the preliminary questions or objections.

* Amendment entered into force on 1 February 2001. Article 79 of the Rules of Court as adopted on 14 April 1978 has continued to apply to all cases submitted to the Court prior to 1 February 2001. In Article 79, paragraph 1, as amended, the words "as soon as possible, and not later than three months after the delivery of the Memorial" have been substituted for the words "within the time-limit fixed for the delivery of the Counter-Memorial" contained in the text of this paragraph as adopted on 14 April 1978. Paragraphs 2 and 3 of the amended Article 79 are new. The former paragraphs 2 to 8 have been renumbered, respectively, as paragraphs 4 to 10. Subsequent amendment entered into force on 21 October 2019.

** Amendment entered into force on 21 October 2019.

*** Amendment entered into force on 21 October 2019.

2. Unless otherwise decided by the Court, the further proceedings shall be oral.

3. The Court, whenever necessary, may request the parties to argue all questions of law and fact, and to adduce all evidence, which bear on the preliminary questions or objections.

4. After hearing the parties, the Court shall decide upon a preliminary question or uphold or reject a preliminary objection. The Court may however declare that, in the circumstances of the case, a question or objection does not possess an exclusively preliminary character.

5. The Court shall give its decision in the form of a judgment. If the judgment does not dispose of the case, the Court shall fix time-limits for the further proceedings.

Subsection 3. Counter-Claims

*Article 80**

1. The Court may entertain a counter-claim only if it comes within the jurisdiction of the Court and is directly connected with the subject-matter of the claim of the other party.

2. A counter-claim shall be made in the Counter-Memorial and shall appear as part of the submissions contained therein. The right of the other party to present its views in writing on the counter-claim, in an additional pleading, shall be preserved, irrespective of any decision of the Court, in accordance with Article 45, paragraph 2, of these Rules, concerning the filing of further written pleadings.

3. Where an objection is raised concerning the application of paragraph 1 or whenever the Court deems necessary, the Court shall take its decision thereon after hearing the parties.

Subsection 4. Intervention

Article 81

1. An application for permission to intervene under the terms of Article 62 of the Statute, signed in the manner provided for in Article 38, paragraph 3, of these Rules, shall be filed as soon as possible, and not later than the closure of the written proceedings. In exceptional circumstances, an application submitted at a later stage may however be admitted.

2. The application shall state the name of an agent. It shall specify the case to which it relates, and shall set out:

(a) the interest of a legal nature which the State applying to intervene considers may be affected by the decision in that case;

(b) the precise object of the intervention;

(c) any basis of jurisdiction which is claimed to exist as between the State applying to intervene and the parties to the case.

3. The application shall contain a list of the documents in support, which documents shall be attached.

*Amendment entered into force on 1 February 2001. Article 80 of the Rules of Court as adopted on 14 April 1978 has continued to apply to all cases submitted to the Court prior to 1 February 2001.

Article 80 of the Rules of Court as adopted on 14 April 1978 read as follows: "*Article 80*

1. A counter-claim may be presented provided that it is directly connected with the subject-matter of the claim of the other party and that it comes within the jurisdiction of the Court.

2. A counter-claim shall be made in the Counter-Memorial of the party presenting it, and shall appear as part of the submissions of that party.

3. In the event of doubt as to the connection between the question presented by way of counter-claim and the subject-matter of the claim of the other party the Court shall, after hearing the parties, decide whether or not the question thus presented shall be joined to the original proceedings."

Article 82

1. A State which desires to avail itself of the right of intervention conferred upon it by Article 63 of the Statute shall file a declaration to that effect, signed in the manner provided for in Article 38, paragraph 3, of these Rules. Such a declaration shall be filed as soon as possible, and not later than the date fixed for the opening of the oral proceedings. In exceptional circumstances a declaration submitted at a later stage may however be admitted.

2. The declaration shall state the name of an agent. It shall specify the case and the convention to which it relates and shall contain:

(a) particulars of the basis on which the declarant State considers itself a party to the convention;

(b) identification of the particular provisions of the convention the construction of which it considers to be in question;

(c) a statement of the construction of those provisions for which it contends;

(d) a list of the documents in support, which documents shall be attached.

3. Such a declaration may be filed by a State that considers itself a party to the convention the construction of which is in question but has not received the notification referred to in Article 63 of the Statute.

Article 83

1. Certified copies of the application for permission to intervene under Article 62 of the Statute, or of the declaration of intervention under Article 63 of the Statute, shall be communicated forthwith to the parties to the case, which shall be invited to furnish their written observations within a time-limit to be fixed by the Court or by the President if the Court is not sitting.

2. The Registrar shall also transmit copies to: *(a)* the Secretary-General of the United Nations; *(b)* the Members of the United Nations; *(c)* other States entitled to appear before the Court; *(d)* any other States which have been notified under Article 63 of the Statute.

Article 84

1. The Court shall decide whether an application for permission to intervene under Article 62 of the Statute should be granted, and whether an intervention under Article 63 of the Statute is admissible, as a matter of priority unless in view of the circumstances of the case the Court shall otherwise determine.

2. If, within the time-limit fixed under Article 83 of these Rules, an objection is filed to an application for permission to intervene, or to the admissibility of a declaration of intervention, the Court shall hear the State seeking to intervene and the parties before deciding.

Article 85

1. If an application for permission to intervene under Article 62 of the Statute is granted, the intervening State shall be supplied with copies of the pleadings and documents annexed and shall be entitled to submit a written statement within a time-limit to be fixed by the Court. A further time-limit shall be fixed within which the parties may, if they so desire, furnish their written observations on that statement prior to the oral proceedings. If the Court is not sitting, these time-limits shall be fixed by the President.

2. The time-limits fixed according to the preceding paragraph shall, so far as possible, coincide with those already fixed for the pleadings in the case.

3. The intervening State shall be entitled, in the course of the oral proceedings, to submit its observations with respect to the subject-matter of the intervention.

Article 86

1. If an intervention under Article 63 of the Statute is admitted, the intervening State shall be furnished with copies of the pleadings and documents annexed, and shall be entitled, within a time-limit to be fixed by the Court, or by the President if the Court is not sitting, to submit its written observations on the subject-matter of the intervention.

2. These observations shall be communicated to the parties and to any other State admitted to intervene. The intervening State shall be entitled, in the course of the oral proceedings, to submit its observations with respect to the subject-matter of the intervention.

Subsection 5. Special Reference to the Court

Article 87

1. When in accordance with a treaty or convention in force a contentious case is brought before the Court concerning a matter which has been the subject of proceedings before some other international body, the provisions of the Statute and of the Rules governing contentious cases shall apply.

2. The application instituting proceedings shall identify the decision or other act of the international body concerned and a copy thereof shall be annexed; it shall contain a precise statement of the questions raised in regard to that decision or act, which constitute the subject of the dispute referred to the Court.

Subsection 6. Discontinuance

Article 88

1. If at any time before the final judgment on the merits has been delivered the parties, either jointly or separately, notify the Court in writing that they have agreed to discontinue the proceedings, the Court shall make an order recording the discontinuance and directing that the case be removed from the list.

2. If the parties have agreed to discontinue the proceedings in consequence of having reached a settlement of the dispute and if they so desire, the Court may record this fact in the order for the removal of the case from the list, or indicate in, or annex to, the order, the terms of the settlement.

3. If the Court is not sitting, any order under this Article may be made by the President.

Article 89

1. If in the course of proceedings instituted by means of an application, the applicant informs the Court in writing that it is not going on with the proceedings, and if, at the date on which this communication is received by the Registry, the respondent has not yet taken any step in the proceedings, the Court shall make an order officially recording the discontinuance of the proceedings and directing the removal of the case from the list. A copy of this order shall be sent by the Registrar to the respondent.

2. If, at the time when the notice of discontinuance is received, the respondent has already taken some step in the proceedings, the Court shall fix a time-limit within which the respondent may state whether it opposes the discontinuance of the proceedings. If no objection is made to the discontinuance before the expiration of the time-limit, acquiescence will be presumed and the Court shall make an order officially recording the discontinuance of the proceedings and directing the removal of the case from the list. If objection is made, the proceedings shall continue.

3. If the Court is not sitting, its powers under this Article may be exercised by the President.

SECTION E. PROCEEDINGS BEFORE THE CHAMBERS

Article 90

Proceedings before the Chambers mentioned in Articles 26 and 29 of the Statute shall, subject to the provisions of the Statute and of these Rules relating specifically to the Chambers, be governed by the provisions of Parts I to III of these Rules applicable in contentious cases before the Court.

Article 91

1. When it is desired that a case should be dealt with by one of the Chambers which has been formed in pursuance of Article 26, paragraph 1, or Article 29 of the Statute, a request to this effect shall either be made in the document instituting the proceedings or accompany it. Effect will be given to the request if the parties are in agreement.

2. Upon receipt by the Registry of this request, the President of the Court shall communicate it to the members of the Chamber concerned. He shall take such steps as may be necessary to give effect to the provisions of Article 31, paragraph 4, of the Statute.

3. The President of the Court shall convene the Chamber at the earliest date compatible with the requirements of the procedure.

Article 92

1. Written proceedings in a case before a Chamber shall consist of a single pleading by each side. In proceedings begun by means of an application, the pleadings shall be delivered within successive time-limits. In proceedings begun by the notification of a special agreement, the pleadings shall be delivered within the same time-limits, unless the parties have agreed on successive delivery of their pleadings. The time-limits referred to in this paragraph shall be fixed by the Court, or by the President if the Court is not sitting, in consultation with the Chamber concerned if it is already constituted.

2. The Chamber may authorize or direct that further pleadings be filed if the parties are so agreed, or if the Chamber decides, *proprio motu* or at the request of one of the parties, that such pleadings are necessary.

3. Oral proceedings shall take place unless the parties agree to dispense with them, and the Chamber consents. Even when no oral proceedings take place, the Chamber may call upon the parties to supply information or furnish explanations orally.

Article 93

Judgments given by a Chamber shall be read at a public sitting of that Chamber.

SECTION F. JUDGMENTS, INTERPRETATION AND REVISION

Subsection 1. Judgments

*Article 94**

1. When the Court has completed its deliberations and adopted its judgment, the parties shall be notified of the date on which it will be read.

* Amendment entered into force on 25 June 2020.

2. The judgment shall be read at a public sitting of the Court. The Court may decide, for health, security or other compelling reasons, that the judgment shall be read at a sitting of the Court accessible to the parties and the public by video link. The judgment shall become binding on the parties on the day of the reading.

Article 95

1. The judgment, which shall state whether it is given by the Court or by a Chamber, shall contain:

the date on which it is read;
the names of the judges participating in it;
the names of the parties;
the names of the agents, counsel and advocates of the parties;
a summary of the proceedings;
the submissions of the parties; a statement of the facts;
the reasons in point of law;
the operative provisions of the judgment;
the decision, if any, in regard to costs;
the number and names of the judges constituting the majority;
a statement as to the text of the judgment which is authoritative.

2. Any judge may, if he so desires, attach his individual opinion to the judgment, whether he dissents from the majority or not; a judge who wishes to record his concurrence or dissent without stating his reasons may do so in the form of a declaration. The same shall also apply to orders made by the Court.

3. One copy of the judgment duly signed and sealed, shall be placed in the archives of the Court and another shall be transmitted to each of the parties. Copies shall be sent by the Registrar to: *(a)* the Secretary-General of the United Nations; *(b)* the Members of the United Nations; *(c)* other Sates entitled to appear before the Court.

Article 96

When by reason of an agreement reached between the parties, the written and oral proceedings have been conducted in one of the Court's two official languages, and pursuant to Article 39, paragraph 1, of the Statute the judgment is to be delivered in that language, the text of the judgment in that language shall be the authoritative text.

Article 97

If the Court, under Article 64 of the Statute, decides that all or part of a party's costs shall be paid by the other party, it may make an order for the purpose of giving effect to that decision.

Subsection 2. Requests for the Interpretation or Revision of a Judgment

Article 98

1. In the event of dispute as to the meaning or scope of a judgment any party may make a request for its interpretation, whether the original proceedings were begun by an application or by the notification of a special agreement.

2. A request for the interpretation of a judgment may be made either by an application or by the notification of a special agreement to that effect between the parties; the precise point or points in dispute as to the meaning or scope of the judgment shall be indicated.

3. If the request for interpretation is made by an application, the requesting party's contentions shall be set out therein, and the other party shall be entitled to file written observations thereon within a time-limit fixed by the Court, or by the President if the Court is not sitting.

4. Whether the request is made by an application or by notification of a special agreement, the Court may, if necessary, afford the parties the opportunity of furnishing further written or oral explanations.

Article 99

1. A request for the revision of a judgment shall be made by an application containing the particulars necessary to show that the conditions specified in Article 61 of the Statute are fulfilled. Any documents in support of the application shall be annexed to it.

2. The other party shall be entitled to file written observations on the admissibility of the application within a time-limit fixed by the Court, or by the President if the Court is not sitting. These observations shall be communicated to the party making the application.

3. The Court, before giving its judgment on the admissibility of the application may afford the parties a further opportunity of presenting their views thereon.

4. If the Court finds that the application is admissible it shall fix time-limits for such further proceedings on the merits of the application as, after ascertaining the views of the parties, it considers necessary.

5. If the Court decides to make the admission of the proceedings in revision conditional on previous compliance with the judgment, it shall make an order accordingly.

Article 100

1. If the judgment to be revised or to be interpreted was given by the Court, the request for its revision or interpretation shall be dealt with by the Court. If the judgment was given by a Chamber, the request for its revision or interpretation shall be dealt with by that Chamber.

2. The decision of the Court, or of the Chamber, on a request for interpretation or revision of a judgment shall itself be given in the form of a judgment.

SECTION G. MODIFICATIONS PROPOSED BY THE PARTIES

Article 101

The parties to a case may jointly propose particular modifications or additions to the rules contained in the present Part (with the exception of Articles 93 to 97 inclusive), which may be applied by the Court or by a Chamber if the Court or the Chamber considers them appropriate in the circumstances of the case.

PART IV
ADVISORY PROCEEDINGS

Article 102

1. In the exercise of its advisory functions under Article 65 of the Statute, the Court shall apply, in addition to the provisions of Article 96 of the Charter and Chapter IV of the Statute, the provisions of the present Part of the Rules.

2. The Court shall also be guided by the provisions of the Statute and of these Rules which apply in contentious cases to the extent to which it recognizes them to be applicable.

For this purpose, it shall above all consider whether the request for the advisory opinion relates to a legal question actually pending between two or more States.

3. When an advisory opinion is requested upon a legal question actually pending between two or more States, Article 31 of the Statute shall apply, as also the provisions of these Rules concerning the application of that Article.

Article 103

When the body authorized by or in accordance with the Charter of the United Nations to request an advisory opinion informs the Court that its request necessitates an urgent answer, or the Court finds that an early answer would be desirable, the Court shall take all necessary steps to accelerate the procedure, and it shall convene as early as possible for the purpose of proceeding to a hearing and deliberation on the request.

Article 104

All requests for advisory opinions shall be transmitted to the Court by the Secretary-General of the United Nations or, as the case may be, the chief administrative officer of the body authorized to make the request. The documents referred to in Article 65, paragraph 2, of the Statute shall be transmitted to the Court at the same time as the request or as soon as possible thereafter, in the number of copies required by the Registry.

Article 105

1. Written statements submitted to the Court shall be communicated by the Registrar to any States and organizations which have submitted such statements.

2. The Court, or the President if the Court is not sitting, shall:

(a) determine the form in which, and the extent to which, comments permitted under Article 66, paragraph 4, of the Statute shall be received, and fix the time-limit for the submission of any such comments in writing;

(b) decide whether oral proceedings shall take place at which statements and comments may be submitted to the Court under the provisions of Article 66 of the Statute, and fix the date for the opening of such oral proceedings.

Article 106

The Court, or the President if the Court is not sitting, may decide that the written statements and annexed documents shall be made accessible to the public on or after the opening of the oral proceedings. If the request for advisory opinion relates to a legal question actually pending between two or more States, the views of those States shall first be ascertained.

Article 107

1. When the Court has completed its deliberations and adopted its advisory opinion, the opinion shall be read at a public sitting of the Court.

2. The advisory opinion shall contain:

the date on which it is delivered in Art 107(2);
the names of the judges participating;
a summary of the proceedings;
a statement of the facts;
the reasons in point of law;
the reply to the question put to the Court;

the number and names of the judges constituting the majority;
a statement as to the text of the opinion which is authoritative.

3. Any judge may, if he so desires, attach his individual opinion to the advisory opinion of the Court, whether he dissents from the majority or not; a judge who wishes to record his concurrence or dissent without stating his reasons may do so in the form of a declaration.

Article 108

The Registrar shall inform the Secretary-General of the United Nations, and, where appropriate, the chief administrative officer of the body which requested the advisory opinion, as to the date and the hour fixed for the public sitting to be held for the reading of the opinion. He shall also inform the representatives of the Members of the United Nations and other States, specialized agencies and public international organizations immediately concerned.

Article 109

One copy of the advisory opinion, duly signed and sealed, shall be placed in the archives of the Court, another shall be sent to the Secretary-General of the United Nations and, where appropriate, a third to the chief administrative officer of the body which requested the opinion of the Court. Copies shall be sent by the Registrar to the Members of the United Nations and to any other States, specialized agencies and public international organizations immediately concerned.

18.c Practice Directions

Date: as amended on 20 January 2009
Source: https://www.icj-cij.org/en/practice-directions

Practice Direction I

The Court wishes to discourage the practice of simultaneous deposit of pleadings in cases brought by special agreement.

The Court would expect future special agreements to contain provisions as to the number and order of pleadings, in accordance with Article 46, paragraph 1, of the Rules of Court. Such provisions shall be without prejudice to any issue in the case, including the issue of burden of proof.

If the special agreement contains no provisions on the number and order of pleadings, the Court will expect the parties to reach agreement to that effect, in accordance with Article 46, paragraph 2, of the Rules of Court.

Practice Direction II

Each of the parties is, in drawing up its written pleadings, to bear in mind the fact that these pleadings are intended not only to reply to the submissions and arguments of the other party, but also, and above all, to present clearly the submissions and arguments of the party which is filing the proceedings.

In the light of this, at the conclusion of the written pleadings of each party, there is to appear a short summary of its reasoning.

Practice Direction III

The parties are strongly urged to keep the written pleadings as concise as possible, in a manner compatible with the full presentation of their positions.

In view of an excessive tendency towards the proliferation and protraction of annexes to written pleadings, the parties are also urged to append to their pleadings only strictly selected documents. The number of pages of annexes attached by a party to its written pleadings shall not exceed 750 in total, unless the Court decides, upon request of a party, that a number in excess of that limit is warranted, in the particular circumstances of the cases. Amendment promulgated on 30 January 2009. Further amendment, establishing the page limit, promulgated on 20 January 2021, applicable to proceedings instituted after that date.

Practice Direction IV

Where one of the parties has a full or partial translation of its own pleadings or of those of the other party in the other official language of the Court, these translations should as a matter of course be passed to the Registry of the Court. The same applies to the annexes.

These translations will be examined by the Registry and communicated to the other party. The latter will also be informed of the manner in which they were prepared.

Practice Direction V*

With the aim of accelerating proceedings on preliminary objections made by one party under Article 79*bis*, paragraph 1, of the Rules of Court, the time-limit for the presentation by the other party of a written statement of its observations and submissions under Article 79*bis*, paragraph 3, shall generally not exceed four months from the date of the filing of the preliminary objections.

Practice Direction VI**

The Court requires full compliance with Article 60, paragraph 1, of the Rules of Court and observation of the requisite degree of brevity in oral pleadings. In that context, the Court will find it very helpful if the parties focus in the first round of the oral proceedings on those points which have been raised by one party at the stage of written proceedings but which have not so far been adequately addressed by the other, as well as on those which each party wishes to emphasize by way of winding up its arguments. Where objections of lack of jurisdiction or of inadmissibility are being considered, oral proceedings are to be limited to statements on the objections.

Practice Direction VII***

The Court considers that it is not in the interest of the sound administration of justice that a person sit as judge *ad hoc* in one case who is also acting or has recently acted as agent, counsel or advocate in another case before the Court. Accordingly, parties, when choosing a judge *ad hoc* pursuant to Article 31 of the Statute and Article 35 of the Rules of Court, should refrain from nominating persons who are acting as agent, counsel or advocate in

* Amendments promulgated on 30 July 2004 and 11 December 2019.

** Amendment promulgated on 30 January 2009.

*** Practice Directions VII and VIII do not affect a choice or designation made by the parties prior to 7 February 2002, the date of the adoption by the Court of those Directions.

another case before the Court or have acted in that capacity in the three years preceding the date of the nomination. Furthermore, parties should likewise refrain from designating as agent, counsel or advocate in a case before the Court a person who sits as judge *ad hoc* in another case before the Court.

Practice Direction VIII*

The Court considers that it is not in the interest of the sound administration of justice that a person who until recently was a Member of the Court, judge *ad hoc*, Registrar, Deputy-Registrar or higher official of the Court (principal legal secretary, first secretary or secretary), appear as agent, counsel or advocate in a case before the Court. Accordingly, parties should refrain from designating as agent, counsel or advocate in a case before the Court a person who in the three years preceding the date of the designation was a Member of the Court, judge *ad hoc*, Registrar, Deputy-Registrar or higher official of the Court.

Practice Direction IX**

1. The parties to proceedings before the Court should refrain from submitting new documents after the closure of the written proceedings.

2. A party nevertheless desiring to submit a new document after the closure of the written proceedings, including during the oral proceedings, pursuant to Article 56, paragraphs 1 and 2, of the Rules, shall explain why it considers it necessary to include the document in the case file and shall indicate the reasons preventing the production of the document at an earlier stage.

3. In the absence of consent of the other party, the Court will authorize the production of the new document only in exceptional circumstances, if it considers it necessary and if the production of the document at this stage of the proceedings appears justified to the Court.

4. If a new document has been added to the case file under Article 56 of the Rules of Court, the other party, when commenting upon it, shall confine the introduction of any further documents to what is strictly necessary and relevant to its comments on what is contained in this new document.

Practice Direction IX*bis*****

1. Any recourse to Article 56, paragraph 4, of the Rules of Court, is not to be made in such a manner as to undermine the general rule that all documents in support of a party's contentions shall be annexed to its written pleadings or produced in accordance with Article 56, paragraphs 1 and 2, of the Rules of Court.

2. While the Court will determine, in the context of a particular case, whether a document referred to under Article 56, paragraph 4, of the Rules of Court, can be considered "part of a publication readily available", it wishes to make it clear to the parties that both of the following two criteria must be met whenever that provision is applied.

(i) First, the document should form "part of a publication", i.e. should be available in the public domain. The publication may be in any format (printed or electronic), form (physical or online, such as posted on the internet) or on any data medium (on paper, on digital or any other media).

* Adopted on 7 February 2002.
** Promulgated on 4 April 2002; amendment promulgated on 13 December 2006.
*** Promulgated on 13 December 2006.

(ii) Second, the requirement of a publication being "readily available" shall be assessed by reference to its accessibility to the Court as well as to the other party. Thus the publication or its relevant parts should be accessible in either of the official languages of the Court, and it should be possible to consult the publication within a reasonably short period of time. This means that a party wishing to make reference during the oral proceedings to a new document emanating from a publication which is not accessible in one of the official languages of the Court should produce a translation of that document into one of these languages certified as accurate.

3. In order to demonstrate that a document is part of a publication readily available in conformity with paragraph 2 above and to ensure the proper administration of the judicial process, a party when referring to the contents of a document under Article 56, paragraph 4, of the Rules of Court, should give the necessary reference for the rapid consultation of the document, unless the source of the publication is well known (e.g. United Nations documents, collections of international treaties, major monographs on international law, established reference works, etc.).

4. If during the oral proceedings a party objects to the reference by the other party to a document under Article 56, paragraph 4, of the Rules of Court, the matter shall be settled by the Court.

5. If during the oral proceedings a party refers to a document which is part of a publication readily available, the other party shall have an opportunity of commenting upon it.

Practice Direction IX*ter**

The Court has noted the practice by the parties of preparing folders of documents for the convenience of the judges during the oral proceedings. The Court invites parties to exercise restraint in this regard and recalls that the documents included in a judge's folder should be produced in accordance with Article 43 of the Statute or Article 56, paragraphs 1 and 2, of the Rules of Court. No other documents may be included in the folder except for any document which is part of a publication readily available in conformity with Practice Direction IX*bis* and under the conditions specified therein. In addition, parties should indicate from which annex to the written pleadings or which document produced under Article 56, paragraphs 1 and 2, of the Rules, the documents included in a judge's folder originate.

Practice Direction IX*quater***

1. Having regard to Article 56 of the Rules of Court, any party wishing to present audio-visual or photographic material at the hearings which was not previously included in the case file of the written proceedings shall submit a request to that effect sufficiently in advance of the date on which that party wishes to present that material to permit the Court to take its decision after having obtained the views of the other party.

2. The party in question shall explain in its request why it wishes to present the audio-visual or photographic material at the hearings.

3. A party's request to present audio-visual or photographic material must be accompanied by information as to the source of the material, the circumstances and date of its making

* Promulgated on 13 December 2006.

** Promulgated on 11 April 2013.

and the extent to which it is available to the public. The party in question must also specify, wherever relevant, the geographic co-ordinates at which that material was taken.

4. The audio-visual or photographic material which the party in question is seeking to present shall be filed in the Registry in five copies. The Registrar shall communicate a copy to the other party and inform the Court accordingly.

5. It shall be for the Court to decide on the request, after considering any views expressed by the other party and taking account of any question relating to the sound administration of justice which might be raised by that request.

Practice Direction X*

Whenever a decision on a procedural issue needs to be made in a case and the President deems it necessary to call a meeting of the agents to ascertain the views of the parties in this regard pursuant to Article 31 of the Rules of Court, agents are expected to attend that meeting as early as possible.

Practice Direction XI**

In the oral pleadings on requests for the indication of provisional measures parties should limit themselves to what is relevant to the criteria for the indication of provisional measures as stipulated in the Statute, Rules and jurisprudence of the Court. They should not enter into the merits of the case beyond what is strictly necessary for that purpose.

Practice Direction XII***

1. Where an international nongovernmental organization submits a written statement and/or document in an advisory opinion case on its own initiative, such statement and/or document is not to be considered as part of the case file.

2. Such statements and/or documents shall be treated as publications readily available and may accordingly be referred to by States and intergovernmental organizations presenting written and oral statements in the case in the same manner as publications in the public domain.

3. Written statements and/or documents submitted by international nongovernmental organizations will be placed in a designated location in the Peace Palace. All States as well as intergovernmental organizations presenting written or oral statements under Article 66 of the Statute will be informed as to the location where statements and/or documents submitted by international nongovernmental organizations may be consulted.

Practice Direction XIII****

The reference in Article 31 of the Rules of Court to ascertaining the views of the parties with regard to questions of procedure is to be understood as follows:

After the initial meeting with the President, and in the context of any further ascertainment of the parties' views relating to questions of procedure, the parties may, should they agree on the procedure to be followed, inform the President by letter accordingly.

The views of the parties as to the future procedure may also, should they agree, be ascertained by means of a video or telephone conference.

* Promulgated on 30 July 2004.

** Promulgated on 30 July 2004; amendment promulgated on 13 December 2006.

*** Promulgated on 30 July 2004.

**** Promulgated on 30 January 2009.

18.d Resolution concerning the Internal Judicial Practice of the Court

Date: 12 April 1976
Source: https://www.icj-cij.org/en/other-texts/resolution-concerning-judicial-practice

The Court decides to revise its Resolution concerning the Internal Judicial Practice of the Court of 5 July 1968. Prior to 1968, the internal judicial practice of the Court was governed by the Resolution of the Permanent Court of International Justice of 20 February 1931 (as amended on 17 March 1936), by virtue of a decision of the International Court of Justice of 1946 to adopt provisionally the practice of the Permanent Court and to adopt the articles concerning its internal judicial practice which are set out in the present Resolution. The Court remains entirely free to depart from the present Resolution, or any part of it, in a given case, if it considers that the circumstances justify that course.

Article 1

(i) After the termination of the written proceedings and before the beginning of the oral proceedings, a deliberation is held at which the judges exchange views concerning the case, and bring to the notice of the Court any point in regard to which they consider it may be necessary to call for explanations during the course of the oral proceedings.

(ii) In cases where two exchanges of oral arguments take place, after the first such exchange has been concluded, a further deliberation is held having the same objects.

(iii) The Court also meets in private from time to time during the oral proceedings to enable judges to exchange views concerning the case and to inform each other of possible questions which they may intend to put in the exercise of their right under Article 61, paragraph 3, of the Rules.

Article 2

After the termination of the oral proceedings, an appropriate period is allowed to the judges in order that they may study the arguments presented to the Court.

Article 3

(i) At the expiration of this period a deliberation is held at which the President outlines the issues which in his opinion will require discussion and decision by the Court. Any judge may then comment on the statement or call attention to any other issue or question which he considers relevant, and may at any time during or at the close of the deliberation cause to be distributed a text formulating a new question or reformulating a question already brought to notice.

(ii) During this deliberation any judge may comment on the pertinence of any issues or questions arising in the case. The President also invites judges to indicate their preliminary impressions regarding any issue or question.

(iii) Judges will be called on by the President in the order in which they signify their desire to speak.

Article 4

(i) At a suitable interval of time after this deliberation, each judge prepares a written note which is distributed to the other judges.

(ii) The written note expresses the judge's views on the case, indicating, inter alia:

(a) whether any questions which have been called to notice should be eliminated from further consideration or should not, or need not, be decided by the Court;

(b) the precise questions which should be answered by the Court;

(c) his tentative opinion as to the answers to be given to the questions in (b) and his reasons therefor;

(d) his tentative conclusion as to the correct disposal of the case.

Article 5

(i) After the judges have had an opportunity to examine the written notes, a further deliberation is held, in the course of which all the judges, called upon by the President as a rule in inverse order of seniority, must declare their views. Any judge may address comments to or ask for further explanations from a judge concerning the latter's statement declaring his views.

(ii) During this deliberation any judge may circulate an additional question or a reformulation of a question already brought to notice.

(iii) On the request of any judge the President shall ask the Court to decide whether a vote shall be taken on any question.

Article 6

(i) On the basis of the views expressed in the deliberations and in the written notes, the Court proceeds to choose a drafting committee by secret ballot and by an absolute majority of votes of the judges present. Two members are elected who should be chosen from among those judges whose oral statements and written notes have most closely and effectively reflected the opinion of the majority of the Court as it appears then to exist.

(ii) The President shall ex officio be a member of the drafting committee unless he does not share the majority opinion of the Court as it appears then to exist, in which case his place shall be taken by the Vice-President. If the Vice-President is ineligible for the same reason, the Court shall proceed, by the process already employed, to the election of a third member, in which case the senior of the elected judges shall preside in the drafting committee.

(iii) If the President is not a member of the drafting committee, the committee shall discuss its draft with him before submitting it to the Court. If the President proposes amendments which the committee does not find it possible to adopt, it shall submit the President's proposals to the Court together with its own draft.

Article 7

(i) A preliminary draft of the decision is circulated to the judges, who may submit amendments in writing. The drafting committee, having considered these amendments, submits a revised draft for discussion by the Court in first reading.

(ii) Judges who wish to deliver separate or dissenting opinions make the text thereof available to the Court after the first reading is concluded and within a time-limit fixed by the Court.

(iii) The drafting committee circulates an amended draft of the decision for the second reading, at which the President enquires whether any judge wishes to propose further amendments.

(iv) Judges who are delivering separate or dissenting opinions may make changes in or additions to their opinions only to the extent that changes have been made in the draft decision. During the second reading they inform the Court of any changes in or additions to their opinions which they propose to make for that reason. A time-limit is fixed by the

Court for the filing of the revised texts of separate or dissenting opinions, copies of which are distributed to the Court.

Article 8

(i) At or after a suitable interval following upon the termination of the second reading, the President calls upon the judges to give their final vote on the decision or conclusion concerned in inverse order of seniority, and in the manner provided for by paragraph (v) of this Article.

(ii) Where the decision deals with issues that are separable, the Court shall in principle, and unless the exigencies of the particular case require a different course, proceed on the following basis, namely that:

(a) any judge may request a separate vote on any such issue;

(b) wherever the question before the Court is whether the Court is competent or the claim admissible, any separate vote on particular issues of competence or admissibility shall (unless such vote has shown some preliminary objection to be well-founded under the Statute and the Rules of Court) be followed by a vote on the question of whether the Court may proceed to entertain the merits of the case or, if that stage has already been reached, on the global question of whether, finally, the Court is competent or the claim admissible.

(iii) In any case coming under paragraph (ii) of this Article, or in any other case in which a judge so requests, the final vote shall take place only after a discussion on the need for separate voting, and whenever possible after a suitable interval following upon such discussion.

(iv) Any question whether separate votes as envisaged in paragraph (ii) of this Article should be recorded in the decision shall be decided by the Court.

(v) Every judge, when called upon by the President to record his final vote in any phase of the proceedings, or to vote upon any question relative to the putting to the vote of the decision or conclusion concerned, shall do so only by means of an affirmative or negative.

Article 9

(i) Although because of illness or other reason deemed adequate by the President, a judge may have failed to attend part of the public hearing or of the Court's internal proceedings under Articles 1 to 7 inclusive of this Resolution, he may nevertheless participate in the final vote provided that:

(a) during most of the proceedings, he shall have been, or remained, at the seat of the Court or other locality in which the Court is sitting and exercising its functions for the purposes of the case under paragraph 1 of Article 22 of the Statute;

(b) as regards the public hearing, he shall have been able to read the official transcript of the proceedings;

(c) as regards the internal proceedings under Articles 1 to 7 inclusive, he shall have been able at least to submit his own written note, read those of the other judges, and study the drafts of the drafting committee; and

(d) as regards the proceedings as a whole, he shall have taken a sufficient part in the public hearing and in the internal proceedings under Articles 1 to 7 inclusive to enable him to arrive at a judicial determination of all issues of fact and law material to the decision of the case.

(ii) A judge who is qualified to participate in the final vote must record his vote in person. In the event of a judge who is otherwise in a fit condition to record his vote being unable because of physical incapacity or other compelling reason to attend the meeting at which the vote is to be taken, the vote shall, if the circumstances permit, be postponed until he can attend. If, in the opinion of the Court, the circumstances do not permit of such a postponement, or render it inadvisable, the Court may, for the purpose of enabling the judge to record his vote, decide to convene elsewhere than at its normal meeting place. If neither of these alternatives is practicable, the judge may be permitted to record his vote in any other manner which the Court decides to be compatible with the Statute.

(iii) In the event of any doubt arising as to whether a judge may vote in the circumstances contemplated by paragraphs (i) and (ii) hereof – and if this doubt cannot be resolved in the course of discussion – the matter shall, upon the proposal of the President, or at the request of any other Member of the Court, be decided by the Court.

(iv) When a judge casts his final vote in the circumstances contemplated by paragraphs (i) and (ii) of the present Article, paragraph (v) of Article 8 shall apply.

Article 10

The foregoing provisions shall apply whether the proceedings before the Court are contentious or advisory.

Article 11*

(i) Where the Court indicates provisional measures, it shall elect three judges to form an *ad hoc* committee which will assist the Court in monitoring the implementation of provisional measures. This committee shall include neither a Member of the Court of the nationality of one of the parties nor any judges *ad hoc*.

(ii) The *ad hoc* committee shall examine the information supplied by the parties in relation to the implementation of provisional measures. It shall report periodically to the Court, recommending potential options for the Court.

(iii) Any decision in this respect shall be taken by the Court.

18.e Compilation of decisions adopted by the Court concerning the external activities of its members

Source: https://icj-cij.org/public/files/basic-documents/compilation-of-decisions-en.pdf

A. Arbitration activities of Members of the Court

1. Members of the Court may only participate in inter-State arbitration cases.

2. Members of the Court may accept an appointment by a State party in inter-State arbitration, including the State of which the judge is a national.

3. Members of the Court must however decline to be appointed as arbitrators by a State that is a party in a case pending before the Court, even if there is no substantial interference between that case and the case submitted to arbitration.

4. Members of the Court may participate in inter-State arbitration without necessarily having to be appointed President of the arbitral tribunal in question.

* Article adopted by the Court on 21 December 2020.

5. Members of the Court may only participate in one inter-State arbitration procedure at a time.

6. Prior authorization must have been granted to a Member of the Court wishing to participate in an arbitration by a panel made up of the President, the Vice-President and the Chairman of the Rules Committee. If the Member of the Court requesting the authorization is a member of the group, the decision shall be taken by the other two judges. The panel will inform the Court once a year on the authorizations given during the course of that year, and at any time as necessary.

7. Any participation of Members of the Court in inter-State arbitrations is subject to the strict condition that their judicial activities must take absolute precedence.

B. External activities of Members of the Court other than arbitration

(a) General guidelines

1. Members of the Court are required to give absolute priority to the exercise of their judicial functions over their external activities. An external activity may be undertaken only if it does not affect the exercise of the Members' judicial functions.

2. When undertaking an external activity, Members of the Court shall ensure that it does not impinge on their independence or place their impartiality at risk.

3. Members of the Court shall preserve the confidentiality of the Court's deliberations.

(b) Teaching activities and academic discussions

4. A Member of the Court shall refrain from engaging in regular teaching. He or she may give the occasional lecture and take part as an external examiner in a jury for a doctoral thesis. He or she may participate in discussions of an academic character in conferences, seminars, workshops or meetings of learned societies.

(c) Publications

5. A Member of the Court may publish writings of a literary, academic or scientific character.

(d) Professional contacts

6. A Member of the Court may maintain professional contacts established prior to the assumption of his or her duties and acquire new ones, provided that he or she avoids interactions that might be seen as undermining his or her independence or impartiality in pending or future cases.

(e) Positions in external entities

7. A Member of the Court may be a member of a learned society and may hold a position in its governing or scientific board, including presidency.

8. A Member of the Court shall not hold a position in a non-governmental organization if his or her engagement might call into question or appear to call into question his or her impartiality or independence.

9. A Member of the Court shall not hold a position in a law firm or on the board of directors of a commercial company.

(f) Implementation

10. Members of the Court are invited to inform the President periodically of their commitments relating to the different external activities covered in the present guidelines and of other external activities that may also be relevant.

C. Invitations from State entities to Members of the Court

1. Invitations to visit from States that have cases pending before the Court may not be accepted by Members of the Court, including when the Member concerned is not sitting in a particular case under Article 24 of the Statute.

2. All other invitations by State entities may be accepted if the Member of the Court concerned considers them useful and in line with the independence and moral integrity expected from Members of the Court.

3. For the sake of transparency and orderly record-keeping, it would be desirable for Members of the Court who receive invitations from State entities to provide, through the President, a short account of these invitations and visits, if any, for the archives. Such an account would be useful for building up a record of the practice of the Court in this area.

4. This text does not apply to invitations from universities and other institutions exercising activities of an academic character.

5. The Registrar of the Court shall also draw guidance from the above when deciding whether to accept invitations from State entities.

18.f SC Res 9 (1946) (Admission of States Not Parties to the Statute of the Court)

Date: 15 October 1946
Source: UN Doc S/RES/9 (1946)
https://www.icj-cij.org/en/other-texts/resolution-9

The Security Council,

In virtue of the powers conferred upon it by Article 35, paragraph 2, of the Statute of the International Court of Justice, and subject to the provisions of that Article,

Resolves that:

1. The International Court of Justice shall be open to a State which is not a party to the Statute of the International Court of Justice, upon the following condition, namely, that such State shall previously have deposited with the Registrar of the Court a declaration by which it accepts the jurisdiction of the Court, in accordance with the Charter of the United Nations and with the terms and subject to the conditions of the Statute and Rules of the Court, and undertakes to comply in good faith with the decision or decisions of the Court and to accept all the obligations of a Member of the United Nations under Article 94 of the Charter;

2. Such declaration may be either particular or general. A particular declaration is one accepting the jurisdiction of the Court in respect only of a particular dispute or disputes which have already arisen. A general declaration is one accepting the jurisdiction generally in respect of all disputes or of a particular class or classes of disputes which have already arisen or which may arise in the future. A state, in making such a general declaration, may, in accordance with Article 36, paragraph 2, of the Statute, recognize as compulsory, *ipso facto* and without special agreement, the jurisdiction of the Court, provided, however, that such acceptance may not, without explicit agreement, be relied upon vis-à-vis States parties

to the Statute which have made the declaration in conformity with Article 36, paragraph 2, of the Statute of the International Court of Justice;

3. The original declarations made under the terms of this resolution shall be kept in the custody of the Registrar of the Court, in accordance with the practice of the Court. Certified true copies thereof shall be transmitted, in accordance with the practice of the Court, to all States parties to the Statute of the International Court of Justice, and to such other States as shall have deposited a declaration under the terms of this resolution, and to the Secretary-General of the United Nations;

4. The Security Council reserves the right to rescind or amend this resolution by a resolution which shall be communicated to the Court, and on the receipt of such communication and to the extent determined by the new resolution, existing declarations shall cease to be effective except in regard to disputes which are already before the Court;

5. All questions as to the validity or the effect of a declaration made under the terms of this resolution shall be decided by the Court.

18.g Secretary-General's Trust Fund to Assist States in the Settlement of Disputes through the International Court of Justice (Revised Terms of Reference, Guidelines and Rules)

Date: 7 October 1989 as revised 21 September 2004
Source: UN Doc A/47/444 (Annex) as revised by UN Doc A/59/372 (Annex)
http://www.un.org/law/trustfund/trustfund.htm

Revised Terms of Reference, Guidelines and Rules of the Secretary-General's Trust Fund to Assist States in the Settlement of Disputes through the International Court of Justice

Reasons for establishing the Trust Fund

1. The United Nations has a special role in the maintenance of peace and security. The Charter of the United Nations recognizes settlement of international disputes "by peaceful means, and in conformity with the principles of justice and international law" as a basic purpose of the United Nations and as an essential tool for the maintenance of international peace and security. The importance of peaceful settlement of disputes has been reiterated in numerous legal instruments of the United Nations, including the Declaration on Principles of International Law concerning Friendly Relations and Cooperation among States in accordance with the Charter of the United Nations of 24 October 1970 and the Manila Declaration on the Peaceful Settlement of International Disputes of 15 November 1982. In the Manila Declaration, the General Assembly stressed once again that States should be encouraged to settle disputes by making full use of the provisions of the Charter of the United Nations, in particular those concerning the peaceful settlement of disputes. The Assembly also stated that recourse to judicial settlement of legal disputes, particularly referral to the International Court of Justice, should not be considered an unfriendly act between States.

2. The Court is the principal judicial organ of the United Nations. Its judgments represent the most authoritative pronouncement on international law. As follows from Article 36, paragraph 3, of the Charter, the Court is also the principal organ for resolving legal disputes between States. The Secretary-General, as the Chief Administrative Officer of the Organization, has, therefore, a special responsibility to promote judicial settlement through the Court.

3. Legal disputes may arise in various parts of the world over a wide variety of issues. There are occasions where the parties concerned are prepared to seek settlement of their disputes through the International Court of Justice, but cannot proceed because of the lack of legal expertise or funds. There may also be cases where the parties are unable to implement a decision of the Court for the same reasons. In all such cases, the availability of funds would advance the peaceful settlement of disputes.

4. The cost which may be incurred by ICJ proceedings is a factor which may in some instances discourage States from resorting to the Court. In arbitration, the parties bear the costs of the arbitrators and the maintenance of the tribunal (e.g. the registry etc.). The administrative costs of the International Court of Justice are borne by the United Nations. However, as in arbitration, the parties must remunerate their counsel, reimburse, where applicable, the costs of their agents, experts and witnesses and bear the expense of the preparation of memorials and countermemorials. The total costs may be considerable. Thus, cost considerations may be a factor in the decision whether or not to refer a dispute to the Court. The availability of funds would therefore be helpful for States which lack the necessary funds.

5. The United Nations has extensive experience in raising and managing voluntary contributions for purposes of providing assistance to countries for their industrial and economic development. This experience could be utilized in raising and managing financial resources which would be used to assist States in obtaining the necessary legal and other expertise to facilitate resolution of their disputes by peaceful means through the International Court of Justice.

Object and purpose of the Trust Fund

6. The Trust Fund (hereinafter referred to as "the Fund") is established by the Secretary-General under the Financial Regulations and Rules of the United Nations in accordance with the terms and conditions specified in the present Terms of Reference, Guidelines and Rules (hereinafter referred to as "the Terms of Reference"). The purpose of the Fund is to provide financial assistance to States for expenses incurred in connection with:

- (a) A dispute submitted to the International Court of Justice under Article 40, paragraph 1, of its Statute:
  - (i) By way of a special agreement on the basis of Article 36, paragraph 1, of the Statute;
  - (ii) By way of an application on the basis of Article 36, paragraphs 1 and 2, of the Statute provided that:
    - (a) In a case in which preliminary objections have been filed by one or both parties to the case under Article 79 of the Rules of the Court, such objections have been either rejected by the Court or definitively withdrawn by the party or parties concerned;

(b) In a case in which no preliminary objections have been filed, the State requesting financial assistance gives the Secretary-General an undertaking not to present any preliminary objection under Article 79 of the Rules of the Court and to plead the case on the merits; such an undertaking shall be duly notified to the Court by the Secretary-General;

(b) The execution of a Judgment of the International Court of Justice.

Contributions to the Fund

7. The Secretary-General invites States, intergovernmental organizations, national institutions and non-governmental organizations, as well as natural and juridical persons, to make voluntary financial contributions to the Fund.

Application for financial assistance

8. Subject to the requirements of paragraph 6 of the Terms of Reference, an application for financial assistance from the Fund may be submitted by any Member State of the United Nations, any other State party to the Statute of the International Court of Justice or any State not party to the Statute of the Court having complied with Article 35, paragraph 2, of the Statute (hereinafter referred to as "the requesting State"). The application shall be accompanied by:

(a) If financial assistance is sought under paragraph 6 (a) (i) of the Terms of Reference, a copy of the special agreement;

(b) If financial assistance is sought under paragraph 6 (a) (ii) (a.) of the Terms of Reference, a copy of the judgment of the Court rejecting preliminary objections in the case, and/or a copy of a document confirming the withdrawal of preliminary objections, as appropriate;

(c) If financial assistance is sought under paragraph 6 (a) (ii) (b.) of the Terms of Reference, the undertaking referred to in that paragraph;

(d) An itemized statement of the estimated costs for which financial assistance is requested from the Fund;

(e) An undertaking that the requesting State shall:

(i) Supply a final statement of account providing details of the expenditures made from the approved amounts, to be certified by an auditor acceptable to the United Nations;

(ii) Refund, where applicable, any unused advance which may have been made to it;

(f) An indication by the requesting State of the amount of the advance it wishes to receive under the provisions of paragraph 13 of the Terms of Reference.

Establishment of a Panel of Experts

9. Once the request for financial assistance is determined to be admissible, the Secretary-General shall establish a Panel of Experts composed of three persons of the highest judicial and moral standing. The task of the Panel shall be to examine the application in order to recommend to the Secretary-General the amount of the financial assistance to be awarded, the amount of the advance to be allocated under the provisions of paragraph 13 of the Terms of Reference and the types of expenses to be covered by the assistance: preparation of memorials, counter-memorials and replies; fees for counsel and payment,

where applicable, of the expenses of agents, experts or witnesses; legal research fees; costs related to oral proceedings (e.g., interpretation in the case of languages other than English and French); expenses of producing technical materials (e.g., reproduction of cartographic evidence) and costs relating to the execution of a judgment of the Court (e.g., demarcation of boundaries).

10. The deliberations of the Panel of Experts shall be conducted in strict confidentiality.

11. In considering an application, the Panel of Experts shall be guided solely by the financial needs of the requesting State and the availability of funds.

12. Travel expenses and subsistence allowance are payable to members of the Panel of Experts from the Fund.

Granting of assistance

13. On the basis of the evaluation and recommendations of the Panel of Experts, the Secretary-General shall make a final determination regarding the financial assistance to be awarded from the Fund and the amount of the advance to be allocated. The latter is not to exceed 50 per cent of the awarded financial assistance. Payments of the advance and of the final payment of the awarded financial assistance shall be made by means of a wire transfer from the Secretary-General's Trust Fund. The final payment shall be made against receipts evidencing actual expenditures for the total amount of the approved costs.

14. The requesting State shall not be eligible to receive the final portion of the award, and shall be liable for the reimbursement of the advance, if the final payment of the award is not claimed:

(a) Within two years from the date of the judgment, in cases referred to in paragraph 6 (a) above; or

(b) Within a reasonable period of time from the date of the judgment which should, under no circumstances, exceed five years, in the case referred to in paragraph 6 (b) above.

Application of the Financial Regulations and Rules of the United Nations

15. The Financial Regulations and Rules of the United Nations shall apply to the administration of the Trust Fund. The Fund shall be subject to the auditing procedures provided therein.

Reporting

16. An annual report on the activities of the Fund shall be made to the General Assembly.

Implementing office

17. The Office of Legal Affairs shall be the implementing office for the Trust Fund and shall provide the services required for the operation of the Fund.

Revision

18. The Secretary-General shall revise the above provisions if circumstances so require.

Activating ICJ Jurisdiction (1): Examples of Special Agreements (*compromis*)

19.a Special Agreement between the Republic of Hungary and the Slovak Republic for Submission to the International Court of Justice of the Differences between Them concerning the Gabčíkovo-Nagymaros Project (*Gabčíkovo-Nagymaros Project* Special Agreement)

Date: 7 April 1993
Source: https://www.icj-cij.org/public/files/case-related/92/10835.pdf

The Republic of Hungary and the Slovak Republic,

Considering that differences have arisen between the Czech and Slovak Federal Republic and the Republic of Hungary regarding the implementation and the termination of the Treaty on the Construction and Operation of the Gabcikovo-Nagymaros Barrage System signed in Budapest on 16 September 1977 and related instruments (hereinafter referred to as "the Treaty"), and on the construction and operation of the "provisional solution";

Bearing in mind that the Slovak Republic is one of the two successor Stares of the Czech and Slovak Federal Republic and the sole successor State in respect of rights and obligations relating to the Gabcikovo-Nagymaros Project;

Recognizing that the Parties concerned have been unable to settle these differences by negotiations;

Having in mind that both the Czechoslovak and Hungarian delegations expressed their commitment to submit the differences connected with the Gabcikovo-Nagymaros Project in all its aspects to binding international arbitration or to the International Court of Justice;

Desiring that these differences should be settled by the International Court of Justice;

Recalling their commitment to apply, pending the Judgment of the International Court of Justice, such a temporary water management regime of the Danube as shall be agreed between the Parties;

Desiring further to define the issues to be submitted to the International Court of Justice,

Have agreed as follows:

Article 1

The Parties submit the questions contained in Article 2 to the International Court of Justice pursuant to Article 40, paragraph 1, of the Statute of the Court.

Article 2

(1) The Court is requested to decide on the basis of the Treaty and rules and principles of general international law, as well as such other treaties as the Court may find applicable,

(a) whether the Republic of Hungary was entitled to suspend and subsequently abandon, in 1989, the works on the Nagymaros Project and on the part of the Gabcikovo Project for which the Treaty attributed responsibility to the Republic of Hungary;

(b) whether the Czech and Slovak Federal Republic was entitled to proceed, in November 1991, to the "provisional solution" and to put into operation from October 1992 this system, described in the Report of the Working Group of Independent Experts of the Commission of the European Communities, the Republic of Hungary and the Çzech and Slovak Federal Republic dated 23 November 1992 (damming up of the Danube at river kilometre 185 1.7 on Çzechoslovak territory and resulting consequences on water and navigation course);

(c) what are the legal effects of the notification, on 19 May 1992, of the termination of the Treaty by the Republic of Hungary.

(2) The Court is also requested to determine the legal consequences, including the rights and obligations for the Parties, arising from its Judgment on the questions in paragraph 1 of this Article.

Article 3

(1) All questions of procedure and evidence shall be regulated in accordance with the provisions of the Statute and the Rules of Court.

(2) However, the Parties request the Court to order that the written proceedings should consist of:

(a) a Memorial presented by each of the Parties not later than ten months after the date of notification of this Special Agreement to the Registrar of the International Court of Justice;

(b) a Counter-Memorial presented by each of the Parties not later than seven months after the date on which each has received the certified copy of the Memorial of the other Party;

(c) a Reply presented by each of the Parties within such time-limits as the Court may order.

(d) the Court may request additional written pleadings by the Parties if it so determines.

(3) The above-mentioned parts of the written proceedings and their annexes presented to the Registrar will not be transmitted to the other Party until the Registrar has received the corresponding part of the proceedings from the said Party.

Article 4

(1) The Parties agree that, pending the final Judgment of the Court, they will establish and implement a temporary water management régime for the Danube.

(2) They further agree that, in the period before such a régime is established or implemented, if either Party believes its rights are endangered by the conduct of the other, it may request immediate consultation and reference, if necessary, to experts, including the Commission of the European Communities, with a view to protecting those rights; and that protection shall not be sought through a request to the Court under Article 41 of the Statute.

(3) This commitment is accepted by both Parties as fundamental to the conclusion and continuing validity of the Special Agreement.

Article 5

(1) The Parties shall accept the Judgment of the Court as final and binding upon them and shall execute it in its entirety and in good faith.

(2) Immediately after the transmission of the Judgment the Parties shall enter into negotiations on the modalities for its execution.

(3) If they are unable to reach agreement within six months, either Party may request the Court to render an additional judgment to determine the modalities of executing its Judgment.

Article 6

(1) The present Special Agreement shall be subject to ratification.

(2) The instruments of ratification shall be exchanged as soon as possible in Brussels.*

(3) The present Special Agreement shall enter into force on the date of exchange of instruments of ratification. Thereafter it will be notified jointly to the Registrar of the Court.

In witness whereof the undersigned, being duly authorized thereto, have signed the present Special Agreement and have affixed thereto their seals.

Done in Brussels, this 7th day of April 1993, in triplicate in English.

19.b Special Agreements and Protocol for the Submission to the International Court of Justice of Differences between the Kingdom of Denmark, the Kingdom of the Netherlands and the Federal Republic of Germany concerning the Delimitation, as between Them, of the Continental Shelf in the North Sea (*North Sea Continental Shelf* Special Agreements)

Date: 2 February 1967
Source: https://www.icj-cij.org/public/files/case-related/52/9331.pdf

A. Danish-German Special Agreement

The Government of the Kingdom of Denmark and the Government of the Federal Republic of Germany,

Considering that the delimitation of the coastal continental shelf in the North Sea between the Kingdom of Denmark and the Federal Republic of Germany has been laid down by a Convention concluded on 9 June 1965,

Considering that in regard to the further course of the boundary disagreement exists between the Danish and German Governments, which could not be settled by detailed negotiations,

Intending to settle the open questions in the spirit of the friendly and goodneighbourly relations existing between them,

Recalling the obligation laid down in Article 1 of the Danish-German Treaty of Conciliation and Arbitration of 2 June 1926 to submit to a procedure of conciliation or to judicial settlement all controversies which cannot be settled by diplomacy,

Bearing in mind the obligation assumed by them under Articles 1 and 28 of the European Convention for the Peaceful Settlement of Disputes of 29 April 1957 to submit to the judgment of the International Court of Justice all international legal controversies to the extent that no special arrangement has been or will be made,

* N.B.: This exchange took place on 28 June 1993. The text of the Protocol is available at http://www.icj-cij.org/docket/files/92/10835.pdf.

By virtue of the fact that the Kingdom of Denmark is a party to the Statute of the International Court of Justice, and of the Declaration of acceptance of the jurisdiction of the International Court of Justice made by the Federal Republic of Germany on 29 April 1961 in conformity with Article 3 of the Convention of 29 April 1957 and with the Resolution adopted by the Security Council of the United Nations on 15 October 1946 concerning the "Condition under which the International Court of Justice shall be open to States not Parties to the Statute of the International Court of Justice",

Have agreed as follows:

Article 1

(1) The International Court of Justice is requested to decide the following question: What principles and rules of international law are applicable to the delimitation as between the Parties of the areas of the continental shelf in the North Sea which appertain to each of them beyond the partial boundary determined by the above-mentioned Convention of 9 June 1965?

(2) The Governments of the Kingdom of Denmark and of the Federal Republic of Germany shall delimit the continental shelf in the North Sea as between their countries by agreement in pursuance of the decision requested from the International Court of Justice.

Article 2

(1) The Parties shall present their written pleadings to the Court in the order stated below:

1. a Memorial of the Federal Republic of Germany to be submitted within six months from the notification of the present Agreement to the Court;
2. a Counter-Memorial of the Kingdom of Denmark to be submitted within six months from the delivery of the German Memorial;
3. a German Reply followed by a Danish Rejoinder to be delivered within such time-limits as the Court may order.

(2) Additional written pleadings may be presented if this is jointly proposed by the Parties and considered by the Court to be appropriate to the case and the circumstances.

(3) The foregoing order of presentation is without prejudice to any question of burden of proof which might arise.

Article 3

The present Agreement shall. enter into force on the day of signature thereof. Done at Bonn on 2 February 1967 in triplicate in the English language.

B. Dutch-German Special Agreement

The Government of the Federal Republic of Germany and the Government of the Kingdom of the Netherlands,

Considering that the delimitation of the coastal continental shelf in the North Sea between the Federal Republic of Germany and the Kingdom of the Netherlands has been laid down by a Convention concluded on 1 December 1964,

Considering that in regard to the further course of the boundary disagreement exists between the German and the Netherlands Governments, which could not be settled by detailed negotiations,

Intending to settle the open questions in the spirit of the friendly and goodneighbourly relations existing between them,

Recalling the obligation laid down in Article 1 of the German-Netherlands Treaty of Conciliation and Arbitration of 20 May 1926 to submit to a procedure of conciliation or to judicial settlement all controversies which cannot be settled by diplomacy,

Bearing in mind the obligation assumed by them under Articles 1 and 28 of the European Convention for the Peaceful Settlement of Disputes of 29 April 1957 to submit to the judgment of the International Court of Justice all international legal controversies to the extent that no special arrangement has been or will be made,

By virtue of the fact that the Kingdom of the Netherlands is a party to the Statute of the International Court of Justice, and of the Declaration of acceptance of the jurisdiction of the International Court of Justice made by the Federal Republic of Germany on 29 April 1961 in conformity with Article 3 -if the Convention of 29 April 1957 and with the Resolution adopted by the Security Council of the United Nations on 15 October 1946 concerning the "Conditions under which the International Court of Justice shall be open to States not Parties to the Statute of the International Court of Justice", Have agreed as follows:

Article 1

(1) The International Court of Justice is requested to decide the following question: What principles and rules of international law are applicable to the delimitation as between the Parties of the areas of the continental shelf in the North Sea which appertain to each of them beyond the partial boundary determined by the above- mentioned Convention of 1 December 1964?

(2) The Governments of the Federal Republic of Germany and of the Kingdom of the Netherlands shall delimit the continental shelf in the North Sea as between their countries by agreement in pursuance of the decision requested from the International Court of Justice.

Article 2

(1) The Parties shall present their written pleadings to the Court in the order stated below:

1. a Memorial of the Federal Republic of Germany to be submitted within six months from the notification of the present Agreement to the Court;
2. a Counter-Memorial of the Kingdom of the Netherlands to be submitted within six months from the delivery of the German Memorial;
3. a German Reply followed by a Netherlands Rejoinder to be delivered within such time-limits as the Court may order.

(2) Additional written pleadings may be presented if this is jointly proposed by the Parties and considered by the Court to be appropriate to the case and the circumstances.

(3) The foregoing order of presentation is without prejudice to any question of burden of proof which might arise.

Article 3

The present Agreement shall enter into force on the day of signature thereof. Done at Bonn on 2 February 1967 in triplicate in the English language.

C. Annexed Protocol

NORTH SEA CONTINENTAL SHELF PROTOCOL

At the signature of the Special Agreement of today's date between the Government of the Federal Republic of Germany and the Governments of the Kingdom of Denmark and the Kingdom of the Netherlands respectively, on the submission to the International Court of Justice of the differences between the Parties concerning the delimitation of the continental shelf in the North Sea, the three Governments wish to state their agreement on the following:

1. The Government of the Kingdom of the Netherlands will, within a month from the signature, notify the two Special Agreements together with the present Protocol to the International Court of Justice in accordance with Article 40, paragraph 1, of the Statute of the Court.

2. After the notification in accordance with item 1 above the Parties will ask the Court to join the two cases.

3. The three Governments agree that, for the purpose of appointing a judge *ad hoc*, the Governments of the Kingdom of Denmark and the Kingdom of the Netherlands shall be considered parties in the same interest within the meaning of Article 31, paragraph 5, of the Statute of the Court.

Activating ICJ Jurisdiction (2): Examples of Compromissory Clauses*

20.a Convention for the Suppression of Unlawful Acts Against the Safety of Civil Aviation (The 1971 Montreal Convention)

Date: 23 September 1971
Source: 974 UNTS 178
http://treaties.un.org/doc/db/Terrorism/Conv3-english.pdf

...

Article XIV

1. Any dispute between two or more Contracting States concerning the interpretation or application of this Convention which cannot be settled through negotiation, shall, at the request of one of them, be submitted to arbitration. If within six months from the date of the request for arbitration the parties are unable to agree on the organization of the arbitration,

* N.B.: Recourse to the International Court of Justice is envisaged under many documents included in this collection, often subject to further conditions: see, eg, Documents Nos. 7.a, 7.b, 7.c (general encouragement to submit disputes to the Court); Nos. 8, 9 (disputes under the regional dispute settlement agreements); Nos. 25, 26, 29.a, 30 (disputes under human rights treaties), No. 37.a (inter-State disputes under the ICSID Convention), Nos. 50.a, 52 (disputes relating to the law of the sea), 53.a, No. 54.a (disputes relating to the environment). A list of treaties containing references to the International Court of Justice can be found at http://www.icj-cij.org/jurisdiction/index.php?p1=5&p2=1&p3=4. See also Art 37 ICJ Statute (Document No. 18.a), pursuant to which compromissory clauses envisaging recourse to the Permanent Court of International Justice are 'transferred' to the ICJ.

any one of those Parties may refer the dispute to the International Court of Justice by request in conformity with the Statute of the Court.

2. Each State may at the time of signature or ratification of the this Convention or accession thereto, declare that it does not consider itself bound by the preceding paragraph. The other Contracting State shall not be bound by the preceding paragraph with respect to any Contracting State having made such a reservation.

3. Any Contracting State having made a reservation in accordance with the preceding paragraph may at any time withdraw this reservation by notification to the Depositary Governments.

...

20.b Vienna Convention on Diplomatic Relations: Optional Protocol concerning the Compulsory Settlement of Disputes

Date: 18 April 1961
Source: 500 UNTS 241
https://treaties.un.org/doc/Treaties/1964/06/19640624%2010-27%20PM/Ch_III_5p.pdf

...

Article I

Disputes arising out of the interpretation or application of the Convention[1] shall lie within the compulsory jurisdiction of the International Court of Justice and may accordingly be brought before the Court by an application made by any party to the dispute being a Party to the present Protocol.

Article II

The parties may agree, within a period of two months after one party has notified its opinion to the other that a dispute exists, to resort not to the International Court of Justice but to an arbitral tribunal. After the expiry of the said period, either party may bring the dispute before the Court by an application.

Article III

1. Within the same period of two months, the parties may agree to adopt a conciliation procedure before resorting to the International Court of Justice.

2. The conciliation commission shall make its recommendations within five months after its appointment. If its recommendations are not accepted by the parties to the dispute within two months after they have been delivered either party may bring the dispute before the Court by an application.

Article IV

States Parties to the Convention, to the Optional Protocol concerning acquisition of Nationality[2], and to the present Protocol may at any time declare that they will extend the

[1] 500 UNTS 95.
[2] 500 UNTS 223.

provisions of the present Protocol to disputes arising out of the interpretation or application of the Optional Protocol concerning Acquisition of Nationality. Such declarations shall be notified to the Secretary-General of the United Nations.

…

20.c Treaty of Amity, Economic Relations and Consular Rights (United States–Iran)

Date: 15 August 1955
Source: 284 UNTS 93

…

Article XXI

1. Each High Contracting Party shall accord sympathetic consideration to, and shall afford adequate opportunity for consultation regarding, such representations as the other High Contracting Party may make with respect to any matter affecting the operation of the present Treaty.

2. Any dispute between the High Contracting Parties as to the interpretation or application of the present Treaty, not satisfactorily adjusted by diplomacy, shall be submitted to the International Court of Justice, unless the High Contracting Parties agree to settlement by some other pacific means.

…

20.d Convention on International Civil Aviation

Date: 7 December 1944
Source: https://www.icao.int/publications/Documents/7300_9ed.pdf (ninth edition, 2006)

…

Article 84

Settlement of disputes

If any disagreement between two or more contracting States relating to the interpretation or application of this Convention and its Annexes cannot be settled by negotiation, it shall, on the application of any State concerned in the disagreement, be decided by the Council. No member of the Council shall vote in the consideration by the Council of any dispute to which it is a party. Any contracting State may, subject to Article 85, appeal from the decision of the Council to an ad hoc arbitral tribunal agreed upon with the other parties to the dispute or to the Permanent Court of International Justice. Any such appeal shall be notified to the Council within sixty days of receipt of notification of the decision of the Council.

Article 85

Arbitration procedure

If any contracting State party to a dispute in which the decision of the Council is under appeal has not accepted the Statute of the Permanent Court of International Justice and the contracting States parties to the dispute cannot agree on the choice of the arbitral tribunal, each of the contracting States parties to the dispute shall name a single arbitrator who shall name an umpire. If either contracting State party to the dispute fails to name an arbitrator within a period of three months from the date of the appeal, an arbitrator shall be named on behalf of that State by the President of the Council from a list of qualified and available persons maintained by the Council. If, within thirty days, the arbitrators cannot agree on an umpire, the President of the Council shall designate an umpire from the list previously referred to. The arbitrators and the umpire shall then jointly constitute an arbitral tribunal. Any arbitral tribunal established under this or the preceding Article shall settle its own procedure and give its decisions by majority vote, provided that the Council may determine procedural questions in the event of any delay which in the opinion of the Council is excessive.

Article 86

Appeals

Unless the Council decides otherwise any decision by the Council on whether an international airline is operating in conformity with the provisions of this Convention shall remain in effect unless reversed on appeal. On any other matter, decisions of the Council shall, if appealed from, be suspended until the appeal is decided. The decisions of the Permanent Court of International Justice and of an arbitral tribunal shall be final and binding.

...

20.e United Nations Convention against Transnational Organised Crime

Date: 12 December 2000

Source: https://www.unodc.org/documents/middleeastandnorthafrica/organised-crime/UNITED_NATIONS_CONVENTION_AGAINST_TRANSNATIONAL_ORGANIZED_CRIME_AND_THE_PROTOCOLS_THERETO.pdf

...

Article 35. Settlement of disputes

1. States Parties shall endeavour to settle disputes concerning the interpretation or application of this Convention through negotiation.

2. Any dispute between two or more States Parties concerning the interpretation or application of this Convention that cannot be settled through negotiation within a reasonable time shall, at the request of one of those States Parties, be submitted to arbitration. If, six months after the date of the request for arbitration, those States Parties are unable to agree on the organization of the arbitration, any one of those States Parties may refer the

dispute to the International Court of Justice by request in accordance with the Statute of the Court.

3. Each State Party may, at the time of signature, ratification, acceptance or approval of or accession to this Convention, declare that it does not consider itself bound by paragraph 2 of this article. The other States Parties shall not be bound by paragraph 2 of this article with respect to any State Party that has made such a reservation.

4. Any State Party that has made a reservation in accordance with paragraph 3 of this article may at any time withdraw that reservation by notification to the Secretary-General of the United Nations.

…

20.f Final Agreement for the Settlement of the Differences as Described in the United Nations Security Council Resolutions 817 (1993) and 845 (1993), the Termination of the Interim Accord of 1995, and the Establishment of a Strategic Partnership between the Parties ('Prespa Agreement')

Date: 17 June 2018
Source: https://www.un.org/pga/73/wp-content/uploads/sites/53/2019/02/14-February-Letter-dated-14-February-2019.pdf

…

Article 19

1. The Parties shall settle any disputes exclusively by peaceful means in accordance with the Charter of the United Nations.

2. In the event that a Party considers that the other Party is not acting in accordance with the provisions of this Agreement, this Party shall first notify the other Party of its concerns and shall seek a solution by negotiation. If the Parties are unable to resolve the matter bilaterally, the Parties may agree to request the Secretary-General of the United Nations to use his good offices to resolve the matter.

3. Any dispute that arises between the Parties concerning the interpretation or implementation of this Agreement and not resolved according to the procedures referred to under Article 19(2), may be submitted to the International Court of Justice. The Parties should first seek to agree upon a joint submission to said Court regarding any such dispute. However, if agreement is not reached within six months, or such longer period as the Parties shall mutually agree, then any such dispute may be submitted by either Party individually.

…

* N.B.: A full list of all declarations submitted can be found at https://www.icj-cij.org/en/declarations. For a list of States having submitted a declaration see Document No. 21.f below.

Activating ICJ Jurisdiction (3): Examples of Optional Clause Declarations*

21.a Declaration of Uganda

Date: 3 October 1963
Source: https://www.icj-cij.org/en/declarations/ug

I hereby declare on behalf of the Government of Uganda that Uganda recognizes as compulsory ipso facto and without special agreement, in relation to any other State accepting the same obligation, and on condition of reciprocity, the jurisdiction of the International Court of Justice in conformity with paragraph 2 of Article 36 of the Statute of the Court.

New York, 3rd October, 1963.

(Signed) Apollo K. KIRONDE,
Ambassador and Permanent Representative of Uganda to the United Nations.

21.b Declaration of the United Kingdom

Date: 22 February 2017
Source: https://www.icj-cij.org/en/declarations/gb

1. The Government of the United Kingdom of Great Britain and Northern Ireland accepts as compulsory ipso facto and without special convention, on condition of reciprocity, the jurisdiction of the International Court of Justice, ln conformity with paragraph 2 of Article 36 of the Statute of the Court, until such time as notice may be given to terminate the acceptance, over all disputes arising after 1 January 1987, with regard to situations or facts subsequent to the same date, other than:

(i) any dispute which the United Kingdom has agreed with the other Party or Parties thereto to settle by some other method of peaceful settlement;

(ii) any dispute with the government of any other country which is or has been a Member of the Commonwealth;

(iii) any dispute in respect of which any other Party to the dispute has accepted the compulsory jurisdiction of the International Court of Justice only in relation to or for the purpose of the dispute; or where the acceptance of the Court's compulsory jurisdiction on behalf of any other Party to the dispute was deposited or ratified less than twelve months prior to the filing of the application bringing the dispute before the Court;

(iv) any claim or dispute which is substantially the same as a claim or dispute previously submitted to the Court by the same or another Party;

(v) any claim or dispute in respect of which the claim or dispute in question has not been notified to the United Kingdom by the State or States concerned in writing, including of an Intention to submit the claim or dispute to the Court failing an amicable settlement, at least six months in advance of the submission of the claim or dispute to the Court;

(vi) any claim or dispute that arises from or is connected with or related to nuclear disarmament and/or nuclear weapons, unless all of the other nuclear-weapon States Party to the Treaty on the Non-Proliferation of Nuclear Weapons have also consented to the jurisdiction of the Court and are party to the proceedings in question.

2. The Government of the United Kingdom also reserves the right at any time, by means of a notification addressed to the Secretary-General of the United Nations, and with effect as from the moment of such notification, either to add to, amend or withdraw any of the foregoing reservations, or any that may hereafter be added.

22 February 2017

21.c Declaration of India

Date: 27 September 2019
Source: https://www.icj-cij.org/en/declarations/in

I have the honour to declare, on behalf of the Government of the Republic of India, that they accept, in conformity with paragraph 2 of Article 36 of the Statute of the Court, until such time as notice may be given to terminate such acceptance, as compulsory ipso facto and without special agreement, and on the basis and condition of reciprocity, the jurisdiction of the International Court of Justice over all disputes other than:

(1) disputes in regard to which the parties to the dispute have agreed or shall agree to have recourse to some other method or methods of settlement;

(2) disputes with the government of any State which is or has been a Member of the Commonwealth of Nations;

(3) disputes in regard to matters which are essentially within the domestic jurisdiction of the Republic of India;

(4) disputes relating to or connected with facts or situations of hostilities, armed conflicts, individual or collective actions taken in self-defence, resistance to aggression, fulfilment of obligations imposed by international bodies, and other similar or related acts, measures or situations in which India is, has been or may in future be involved, including the measures taken for protection of national security and ensuring national defence;

(5) disputes with regard to which any other party to a dispute has accepted the compulsory jurisdiction of the International Court of Justice exclusively for or in relation to the purposes of such dispute; or where the acceptance of the Court's compulsory jurisdiction on behalf of a party to the dispute was deposited or ratified less than 12 months prior to the filing of the application bringing the dispute before the Court;

(6) disputes where the jurisdiction of the Court is or may be founded on the basis of a treaty concluded under the auspices of the League of Nations, unless the Government of India specially agree to jurisdiction in each case;

(7) disputes concerning the interpretation or application of a multilateral treaty to which India is not a party; and disputes concerning the interpretation or application of a multilateral

treaty to which India is a party, unless all the parties to the treaty are also parties to the case before the Court or the Government of India specially agree to jurisdiction;

(8) disputes with the Government of any State with which, on the date of an application to bring a dispute before the Court, the Government of India has no diplomatic relations or which has not been recognized by the Government of India;

(9) disputes with non-sovereign States or territories;

(10) disputes with India concerning or relating to:

(a) the status of its territory or the modification or delimitation of its frontiers or any other matter concerning boundaries;

(b) the territorial sea, the continental shelf and the margins, the exclusive fishery zone, the exclusive economic zone, and other zones of national maritime jurisdiction including for the regulation and control of marine pollution and the conduct of scientific research by foreign vessels;

(c) the condition and status of its islands, bays and gulfs and that of the bays and gulfs that for historical reasons belong to it;

(d) the airspace superjacent to its land and maritime territory; and

(e) the determination and delimitation of its maritime boundaries.

(11) disputes prior to the date of this declaration, including any dispute the foundations, reasons, facts, causes, origins, definitions, allegations or bases of which existed prior to this date, even if they are submitted or brought to the knowledge of the Court hereafter.

(12) This declaration revokes and replaces the previous declaration submitted by the Government of India on 18 September, 1974.

(13) The Government of India reserves the right at any time, by means of a written notification addressed to the Secretary-General of the United Nations, and with effect as from the moment of such notification, either to amend or terminate the present declaration.

(*Signed*) Dr. S. Jaishankar
Minister of External Affairs
New Delhi, 18 September 2019

21.d Declaration of Canada

Date: 10 May 1994
Source: https://www.icj-cij.org/en/declarations/ca

On behalf of the Government of Canada,

(1) I give notice that I hereby terminate the acceptance by Canada of the compulsory jurisdiction of the International Court of Justice hitherto effective by virtue of the declaration made on 10 September 1985 in conformity with paragraph 2 of Article 36 of the Statute of the Court.

(2) I declare that the Government of Canada accepts as compulsory ipso facto and without special convention, on condition of reciprocity, the jurisdiction of the International Court of Justice, in conformity with paragraph 2 of Article 36 of the Statute of the Court, until such time as notice may be given to terminate the acceptance, over all disputes arising

after the present declaration with regard to situations or facts subsequent to this declaration, other than:

(a) disputes in regard to which the parties have agreed or shall agree to have recourse to some other method of peaceful settlement;

(b) disputes with the government of any other country which is a member of the Commonwealth, all of which disputes shall be settled in such manner as the parties have agreed or shall agree;

(c) disputes with regard to questions which by international law fall exclusively within the jurisdiction of Canada; and

(d) disputes arising out of or concerning conservation and management measures taken by Canada with respect to vessels fishing in the NAFO Regulatory Area, as defined in the Convention on Future Multilateral Co-operation in the Northwest Atlantic Fisheries, 1978, and the enforcement of such measures.

(3) The Government of Canada also reserves the right at any time, by means of a notification addressed to the Secretary-General of the United Nations, and with effect as from the moment of such notification, either to add to, amend or withdraw any of the foregoing reservations, or any that may hereafter be added.

It is requested that this notification be communicated to the governments of all the States that have accepted the Optional Clause and to the Registrar of the International Court of Justice.

New York, 10 May 1994.

(Signed) Louise FRECHETTE,
Ambassador and Permanent Representative

21.e Declaration of Nicaragua

Date: 24 September 1929
Source: https://www.icj-cij.org/en/declarations/ni

[Translation from the French]

On behalf of the Republic of Nicaragua I recognize as compulsory unconditionally the jurisdiction of the Permanent Court of International Justice.

Geneva, 24 September 1929.

(Signed) T. F. MEDINA.

24 October 2001

Reservation

Nicaragua will not accept the jurisdiction or competence of the International Court of Justice in relation to any matter or claim based on interpretations of treaties or arbitral awards that were signed and ratified or made, respectively, prior to 31 December 1901.

Managua, 23 October 2001.

(Signed) Francisco X. AGUIRRE SACASA

21.f List of States that Have Submitted Optional Clause Declarations

Source: https://www.icj-cij.org/en/declarations

- Australia *(22 March 2002)*
- Austria *(19 May 1971)*
- Barbados *(1 August 1980)*
- Belgium *(17 June 1958)*
- Botswana *(16 March 1970)*
- Bulgaria *(27 November 2015)*
- Cambodia *(19 September 1957)*
- Cameroon *(3 March 1994)*
- Canada *(10 May 1994)*
- Costa Rica *(20 February 1973)*
- Côte d'Ivoire *(29 September 2001)*
- Cyprus *(3 September 2002)*
- Democratic Republic of the Congo *(8 February 1989)*
- Denmark *(10 December 1956)*
- Djibouti *(2 September 2005)*
- Dominica, Commonwealth of *(31 March 2006)*
- Dominican Republic *(30 September 1924)*
- Egypt *(22 July 1957)*
- Equatorial Guinea *(11 August 2017)*
- Estonia *(31 October 1991)*
- Finland *(25 June 1958)*
- Gambia *(22 June 1966)*
- Georgia *(20 June 1995)*
- Germany *(30 April 2008)*
- Greece *(14 January 2015)*
- Guinea, Republic of *(4 December 1998)*
- Guinea-Bissau *(7 August 1989)*
- Haiti *(4 October 1921)*
- Honduras *(6 June 1986)*
- Hungary *(22 October 1992)*
- India *(27 September 2019)*
- Ireland *(15 December 2011)*
- Italy *(25 November 2014)*

- Japan *(6 October 2015)*
- Kenya *(19 April 1965)*
- Latvia, Republic of *(24 September 2019)*
- Lesotho *(6 September 2000)*
- Liberia *(20 March 1952)*
- Liechtenstein *(29 March 1950)*
- Luxembourg *(15 September 1930)*
- Madagascar *(2 July 1992)*
- Malawi *(12 December 1966)*
- Malta *(2 September 1983)*
- Marshall Islands *(24 April 2013)*
- Mauritius *(23 September 1968)*
- Mexico *(28 October 1947)*
- Netherlands *(21 February 2017)*
- New Zealand *(22 September 1977)*
- Nicaragua *(24 September 1946)*
- Nigeria *(30 April 1998)*
- Norway *(24 June 1996)*
- Pakistan *(29 March 2017)*
- Panama *(25 October 1921)*
- Paraguay *(25 September 1996)*
- Peru *(7 July 2003)*
- Philippines *(18 January 1972)*
- Poland *(25 March 1996)*
- Portugal *(25 February 2005)*
- Romania *(23 June 2015)*
- Senegal *(2 December 1985)*
- Slovakia *(28 May 2004)*
- Somalia *(11 April 1963)*
- Spain *(29 October 1990)*
- Sudan *(2 January 1958)*
- Suriname *(31 August 1987)*
- Swaziland *(26 May 1969)*
- Sweden *(6 April 1957)*
- Switzerland *(28 July 1948)*
- Timor-Leste *(21 September 2012)*
- Togo *(25 October 1979)*
- Uganda *(3 October 1963)*
- United Kingdom of Great Britain and Northern Ireland *(22 February 2017)*
- Uruguay *(28 January 1921)*

Activating ICJ Jurisdiction (4): Examples of Resolutions Requesting an Advisory Opinion

22.a Request for an Advisory Opinion from the International Court of Justice on the Legality of the Threat or Use of Nuclear Weapons

Date: 15 December 1994
Source: UN Doc A/RES/49/75
https://www.icj-cij.org/public/files/case-related/95/7646.pdf

...

The General Assembly,

Conscious that the continuing existence and development of nuclear weapons pose serious risks to humanity,

Mindful that States have an obligation under the Charter of the United Nations to refrain from the threat or use of force against the territorial integrity or political independence of any State,

Recalling its resolutions 1653 (XVI) of 24 November 1961, 33/71 B of 14 December 1978, 34/83 G of 11 December 1979, 35/152 D of 12 December 1980, 36/92 I of 9 December 1981, 45/59 B of 4 December 1990 and 46/37 D of 6 December 1991, in which it declared that the use of nuclear weapons would be a violation of the Charter and a crime against humanity,

Welcoming the progress made on the prohibition and elimination of weapons of mass destruction, including the Convention on the Prohibition of the Development, Production and Stockpiling of Bacteriological (Biological) and Toxin Weapons and on Their Destruction and the Convention on the Prohibition of the Development, Production, Stockpiling and Use of Chemical Weapons and on Their Destruction,

Convinced that the complete elimination of nuclear weapons is the only guarantee against the threat of nuclear war,

Noting the concerns expressed in the Fourth Review Conference of the Parties to the Treaty on the Non-Proliferation of Nuclear Weapons that insufficient progress had been made towards the complete elimination of nuclear weapons at the earliest possible time,

Recalling that, convinced of the need to strengthen the rule of law in international relations, it has declared the period 1990–1999 the United Nations Decade of International Law,

Noting that Article 96, paragraph 1, of the Charter empowers the General Assembly to request the International Court of Justice to give an advisory opinion on any legal question,
Recalling the recommendation of the Secretary-General, made in his report entitled "An Agenda for Peace", that United Nations organs that are authorized to take advantage of the advisory competence of the International Court of Justice turn to the Court more frequently for such opinions,

Welcoming resolution 46/40 of 14 May 1993 of the Assembly of the World Health Organization, in which the organization requested the International Court of Justice to give an advisory opinion on whether the use of nuclear weapons by a State in war or other armed conflict would be a breach of its obligations under international law, including the Constitution of the World Health Organization,

Decides, pursuant to Article 96, paragraph 1, of the Charter of the United Nations, to request the International Court of Justice urgently to render its advisory opinion on the following question:

"Is the threat or use of nuclear weapons in any circumstance permitted under international law?".

22.b Health and Environmental Effects of Nuclear Weapons

Date: 14 May 1993
Source: Doc WHA 46.40
https://www.icj-cij.org/public/files/case-related/93/7648.pdf

The Forty-sixth World Health Assembly,

Bearing in mind the principles laid down in the WHO Constitution;

Noting the report of the Director-General on health and environmental effects of nuclear weapons;[1]

Recalling resolutions WHA 34.38 WHA 36.28 and WHA40.24 on the effects of nuclear war on health and health services;

Recognizing that it has been established that no health service in the world can alleviate in any significant way a situation resulting from the use of even one single nuclear weapon;[2]

Recalling resolutions WHA42.26 on WHO's contribution to the international efforts towards sustainable development and WHA45.31 which draws attention to the effects on health of environmental consequences of the use of nuclear weapons that would affect human health for generations;

Recalling that primary prevention is the only appropriate means to deal with the health and environmental effects of the use of nuclear weapons;[3]

Noting the concern of the world health community about the continued threat to health and the environment from nuclear weapons;

Mindful of the role of WHO as defined in its Constitution to act as the directing and coordinating authority on international health work (Article 2(a)); to propose conventions, agreements and regulations (Article 2(k)) to report on administrative and social techniques affecting public health from preventive and curative points of view (Article 2 (p)); and to take all necessary action to attain the objectives of the Organization (Article 2 (v));

Realising that primary prevention of the health hazards of nuclear weapons requires clarity about the status in international law of their use, and that over the last 48 years marked differences of opinion have been expressed by Member States about the lawfulness of the use of nuclear weapons;

1. *Decides*, in accordance with Article 96(2) of the Charter of the United Nations, Article 76 of the Constitution of the World Health Organization and Article X of the Agreement between the United Nations and the World Health Organization approved by the

[1] Document A46/30

[2] See effects of Nuclear War on Health and Health Services (2nd ed.), Geneva, WHO, 1987

[3] Ibid.

General Assembly of the United Nations on 15 November 1947 in its resolution 124 (II), to request the International Court of Justice to give an advisory opinion on the following question:

"In view of the health and environmental effects, would the use of nuclear weapons by a State in war or other armed conflict be a breach of its obligations under international law including the WHO Constitution?"

2. *Requests* the Director General to transmit this resolution to the International Court of Justice, accompanied by all documents likely to throw light upon the question, in accordance with Article 65 of the Statute of the Court.

22.c The Situation in Namibia

Date: 29 July 1970
Source: UN Doc S/RES/284 (1970) https://www.icj-cij.org/public/files/case-related/53/9361.pdf

The Security Council,

Reaffirming the special responsibility of the United Nations with regard to the Territory and the people of Namibia,

Recalling its resolution 276 (1970) of 30 January 1970 on the question of Namibia,

Taking note of the report and recommendations submitted by the *Ad Hoc* Sub-Committee established in pursuance of Security Council resolution 276 (1970),

Taking further note of the recommendation of the *Ad Hoc* Sub-Committee on the possibility of requesting an advisory opinion from the International Court of Justice,

Considering that an advisory opinion from the International Court of Justice would be useful for the Security Council in its further consideration of the question of Namibia and in furtherance of the objectives the Council is seeking,

1. *Decides* to submit, in accordance with Article 96, paragraph 1, of the Charter of the United Nations, the following question to the International Court of Justice, with the request for an advisory opinion which shall be transmitted to the Security Council at an early date:

"What are the legal consequences for States of the continued presence of South Africa in Namibia, notwithstanding Security Council resolution 276 (1970)?"

2. *Requests* the Secretary-General to transmit the present resolution to the International Court of Justice, in accordance with Article 65 of the Statute of the Court, accompanied by all documents likely to throw light upon the question.

22.d Request for an Advisory Opinion from the International Court of Justice on the legal consequences of the separation of the Chagos Archipelago from Mauritius in 1965

Date: 22 June 2017
Source: UN Doc A/RES/71/292 (2017)
https://www.icj-cij.org/public/files/case-related/169/169-20170623-REQ-01-00-EN.pdf

The General Assembly,

Reaffirming that all peoples have an inalienable right to the exercise of their sovereignty and the integrity of their national territory,

Recalling the Declaration on the Granting of Independence to Colonial Countries and Peoples, contained in its resolution 1514 (XV) of 14 December 1960, and in particular paragraph 6 thereof, which states that any attempt aimed at the partial or total disruption of the national unity and the territorial integrity of a country is incompatible with the purposes and principles of the Charter of the United Nations,

Recalling also its resolution 2066 (XX) of 16 December 1965, in which it invited the Government of the United Kingdom of Great Britain and Northern Ireland to take effective measures with a view to the immediate and full implementation of resolution 1514 (XV) and to take no action which would dismember the Territory of Mauritius and violate its territorial integrity, and its resolutions 2232 (XXI) of 20 December 1966 and 2357 (XXII) of 19 December 1967,

Bearing in mind its resolution 65/118 of 10 December 2010 on the fiftieth anniversary of the Declaration on the Granting of Independence to Colonial Countries and Peoples, reiterating its view that it is incumbent on the United Nations to continue to play an active role in the process of decolonization, and noting that the process of decolonization is not yet complete,

Recalling its resolution 65/119 of 10 December 2010, in which it declared the period 2011–2020 the Third International Decade for the Eradication of Colonialism, and its resolution 71/122 of 6 December 2016, in which it called for the immediate and full implementation of the Declaration on the Granting of Independence to Colonial Countries and Peoples,

Noting the resolutions on the Chagos Archipelago adopted by the Organization of African Unity and the African Union since 1980, most recently at the twenty-eighth ordinary session of the Assembly of the Union, held in Addis Ababa on 30 and 31 January 2017, and the resolutions on the Chagos Archipelago adopted by the Movement of Non-Aligned Countries since 1983, most recently at the Seventeenth Conference of Heads of State or Government of Non-Aligned Countries, held on Margarita Island, Bolivarian Republic of Venezuela, from 13 to 18 September 2016, and in particular the deep concern expressed therein at the forcible removal by the United Kingdom of Great Britain and Northern Ireland of all the inhabitants of the Chagos Archipelago,

Noting also its decision of 16 September 2016 to include in the agenda of its seventy-first session the item entitled “Request for an advisory opinion of the International Court of Justice on the legal consequences of the separation of the Chagos Archipelago from Mauritius in 1965", on the understanding that there would be no consideration of this item before June 2017,

Decides, in accordance with Article 96 of the Charter of the United Nations, to request the International Court of Justice, pursuant to Article 65 of the Statute of the Court, to render an advisory opinion on the following questions:

(a) "Was the process of decolonization of Mauritius lawfully completed when Mauritius was granted independence in 1968, following the separation of the Chagos Archipelago from Mauritius and having regard to international law, including obligations reflected in General Assembly resolutions 1514 (XV) of 14 December 1960, 2066 (XX) of 16 December 1965, 2232 (XXI) of 20 December 1966 and 2357 (XXII) of 19 December 1967?";

(b) "What are the consequences under international law, including obligations reflected in the above-mentioned resolutions, arising from the continued administration by the United Kingdom of Great Britain and Northern Ireland of the Chagos Archipelago, including with respect to the inability of Mauritius to implement a programme for the resettlement on the Chagos Archipelago of its nationals, in particular those of Chagossian origin?"

4 Ad Hoc Inter-State Arbitration:* the Permanent Court of Arbitration**

The Framework

23.a Permanent Court of Arbitration Arbitration Rules

Date: 17 December 2012
Source: https://docs.pca-cpa.org/2015/11/PCA-Arbitration-Rules-2012.pdf

SECTION I. INTRODUCTORY RULES

Scope of application

Article 1

1. Where a State, State-controlled entity, or intergovernmental organization has agreed with one or more States, State-controlled entities, intergovernmental organizations, or private parties that disputes between them in respect of a defined legal relationship, whether contractual, treaty-based, or otherwise, shall be referred to arbitration under the Permanent Court of Arbitration Arbitration Rules 2012 (hereinafter the "Rules"), then such disputes shall be settled in accordance with these Rules subject to such modification as the parties may agree.

2. Agreement by a State, State-controlled entity, or intergovernmental organization to arbitrate under these Rules with a party that is not a State, State-controlled entity, or intergovernmental organization constitutes a waiver of any right of immunity from jurisdiction in respect of the proceedings relating to the dispute in question to which such party might otherwise be entitled. A waiver of immunity relating to the execution of an arbitral award must be explicitly expressed.

3. The International Bureau of the Permanent Court of Arbitration at the Hague (hereinafter the "International Bureau") shall serve as registry for the proceedings and provide secretariat services.

4. The involvement of at least one State, State-controlled entity, or intergovernmental organization as a party to the dispute is not necessary for jurisdiction where all the parties have agreed to settle a dispute under these Rules. However, where the Secretary-General of the Permanent Court of Arbitration determines that no State, State-controlled entity, or intergovernmental organization is a party to the dispute, the Secretary-General may decide to limit the Permanent Court of Arbitration's role in the proceedings to the function of the

* N.B.: Arbitration is envisaged under many other sections in this set of documents: see, eg, Document Nos. 17.a and 17.b on arbitration within the context of the OSCE; Document Nos. 36.b and 36.e on arbitration in the context of the WTO; Document Nos. 37-44 on investment arbitration; Document Nos. 50.a, 50.e, and 50.f on arbitration in the context of the law of the sea.

** N.B.: The Permanent Court of Arbitration is established by virtue of the provisions in Title IV of the 1899 Hague Convention, which are identical to those in the corresponding Part IV in the 1907 Hague Convention: see Document No. 3.

Secretary-General as appointing authority, with the role of the International Bureau under these Rules to be assumed by the arbitral tribunal.

Notice and calculation of periods of time

Article 2

1. A notice, including a notification, communication or proposal, may be transmitted by any means of communication that provides or allows for a record of its transmission.

2. If an address has been designated by a party specifically for this purpose or authorized by the arbitral tribunal, any notice shall be delivered to that party at that address, and if so delivered shall be deemed to have been received. Delivery by electronic means such as facsimile or e-mail may only be made to an address so designated or authorized.

3. In the absence of such designation or authorization, a notice is:

(a) Received if it is physically delivered to the addressee; or

(b) Deemed to have been received if it is delivered at the place of business, habitual residence or mailing address of the addressee.

4. If, after reasonable efforts, delivery cannot be effected in accordance with paragraphs 2 or 3, a notice is deemed to have been received if it is sent to the addressee's last-known place of business, habitual residence or mailing address by registered letter or any other means that provides a record of delivery or of attempted delivery.

5. A notice shall be deemed to have been received on the day it is delivered in accordance with paragraphs 2, 3 or 4, or attempted to be delivered in accordance with paragraph 4. A notice transmitted by electronic means is deemed to have been received on the day it is sent, except that a notice of arbitration so transmitted is only deemed to have been received on the day when it reaches the addressee's electronic address.

6. For the purpose of calculating a period of time under these Rules, such period shall begin to run on the day following the day when a notice is received. If the last day of such period is an official holiday or a non-business day at the residence or place of business of the addressee, the period is extended until the first business day which follows. Official holidays or non-business days occurring during the running of the period of time are included in calculating the period.

Notice of arbitration

Article 3

1. The party or parties initiating recourse to arbitration (hereinafter the "claimant") shall communicate to the other party or parties (hereinafter the "respondent") and the International Bureau a notice of arbitration.

2. Arbitral proceedings shall be deemed to commence on the date on which the notice of arbitration is received by the respondent.

3. The notice of arbitration shall include the following:

(a) A demand that the dispute be referred to arbitration;

(b) The names and contact details of the parties;

(c) Identification of the arbitration agreement that is invoked;

(d) Identification of any rule, decision, agreement, contract, convention, treaty, constituent instrument of an organization or agency, or relationship out of, or in relation to which, the dispute arises;

(e) A brief description of the claim and an indication of the amount involved, if any;

(f) The relief or remedy sought;
(g) A proposal as to the number of arbitrators, language and place of arbitration, if the parties have not previously agreed thereon.

4. The notice of arbitration may also include:
(a) A proposal for the appointment of a sole arbitrator referred to in article 8, paragraph 1;
(b) Notification of the appointment of an arbitrator referred to in articles 9 or 10.

5. The constitution of the arbitral tribunal shall not be hindered by any controversy with respect to the sufficiency of the notice of arbitration, which shall be finally resolved by the arbitral tribunal.

Response to the notice of arbitration

Article 4

1. Within 30 days of the receipt of the notice of arbitration, or such other period as may be set by the International Bureau, the respondent shall communicate to the claimant and the International Bureau a response to the notice of arbitration, which shall include:
(a) The name and contact details of each respondent;
(b) A response to the information set forth in the notice of arbitration, pursuant to article 3, paragraphs 3 (c) to (g).

2. The response to the notice of arbitration may also include:
(a) Any plea that an arbitral tribunal to be constituted under these Rules lacks jurisdiction;
(b) A proposal for the appointment of a sole arbitrator referred to in article 8, paragraph 1;
(c) Notification of the appointment of an arbitrator referred to in articles 9 or 10;
(d) A brief description of counterclaims or claims for the purpose of a set-off, if any, including where relevant, an indication of the amounts involved, and the relief or remedy sought;
(e) A notice of arbitration in accordance with article 3 in case the respondent formulates a claim against a party to the arbitration agreement other than the claimant.

3. The constitution of the arbitral tribunal shall not be hindered by any controversy with respect to the respondent's failure to communicate a response to the notice of arbitration, or an incomplete or late response to the notice of arbitration, which shall be finally resolved by the arbitral tribunal.

Representation and assistance

Article 5

1. In disputes involving only States and/or intergovernmental organizations, each party shall appoint an agent. Each party may also be assisted by persons of its choice.

2. In other disputes under these Rules, each party may be represented or assisted by persons chosen by it.

3. The names and addresses of agents, party representatives, and other persons assisting the parties must be communicated to all parties, to the International Bureau, and to the arbitral tribunal. Such communication must specify whether the appointment is being made for purposes of representation or assistance. Where a person is to act as an agent or representative of a party, the arbitral tribunal, on its own initiative or at the request of any

party, may at any time require proof of authority granted to the agent or representative in such a form as the arbitral tribunal may determine.

Appointing authority

Article 6

1. The Secretary-General of the Permanent Court of Arbitration shall serve as appointing authority.

2. In exercising its functions under these Rules, the appointing authority may require from any party and the arbitrators the information it deems necessary and it shall give the parties and, where appropriate, the arbitrators, an opportunity to present their views in any manner it considers appropriate.

3. The appointing authority shall have regard to such considerations as are likely to secure the appointment of an independent and impartial arbitrator and shall take into account the advisability of appointing an arbitrator of a nationality other than the nationalities of the parties.

SECTION II. COMPOSITION OF THE ARBITRAL TRIBUNAL

Number of arbitrators

Article 7

1. If the parties have not previously agreed on the number of arbitrators, and if within 30 days after the receipt by the respondent of the notice of arbitration the parties have not agreed on the number of arbitrators, three arbitrators shall be appointed.

2. Notwithstanding paragraph 1, if no other parties have responded to a party's proposal to appoint a sole arbitrator within the time limit provided for in paragraph 1 and the party or parties concerned have failed to appoint a second arbitrator in accordance with articles 9 or 10, the appointing authority may, at the request of a party, appoint a sole arbitrator pursuant to the procedure provided for in article 8, paragraph 2 if it determines that, in view of the circumstances of the case, this is more appropriate.

Appointment of arbitrators (articles 8 to 10)

Article 8

1. If the parties have agreed that a sole arbitrator is to be appointed and if within 30 days after receipt by all other parties of a proposal of an individual who would serve as a sole arbitrator the parties have not reached agreement thereon, a sole arbitrator shall, at the request of a party, be appointed by the appointing authority.

2. The appointing authority shall appoint the sole arbitrator as promptly as possible. In making the appointment, the appointing authority shall use the following list-procedure, unless the parties agree that the list-procedure should not be used or unless the appointing authority determines in its discretion that the use of the list-procedure is not appropriate for the case:

(a) The appointing authority shall communicate to each of the parties an identical list containing at least three names;

(b) Within 15 days after the receipt of this list, or such other period as may be set by the International Bureau, each party may return the list to the appointing authority, without copying the other party, after having deleted the name or names to which it objects and numbered the remaining names on the list in the order of its preference;

(c) After the expiration of the above period of time the appointing authority shall appoint the sole arbitrator from among the names approved on the lists returned to it and in accordance with the order of preference indicated by the parties;

(d) If for any reason the appointment cannot be made according to this procedure, the appointing authority may exercise its discretion in appointing the sole arbitrator.

Article 9

1. If three arbitrators are to be appointed, each party shall appoint one arbitrator. The two arbitrators thus appointed shall choose the third arbitrator who will act as the presiding arbitrator of the arbitral tribunal. If five arbitrators are to be appointed, the two party-appointed arbitrators shall choose the remaining three arbitrators and designate one of those three as the presiding arbitrator of the tribunal.

2. If within 30 days after the receipt of a party's notification of the appointment of an arbitrator the other party has not notified the first party of the arbitrator it has appointed, the first party may request the appointing authority to appoint the second arbitrator.

3. If within 30 days after the appointment of the second arbitrator, or such other period as may be set by the International Bureau, the two arbitrators have not agreed on the choice of the remaining arbitrators and/or the presiding arbitrator, the remaining arbitrators and/or the presiding arbitrator shall be appointed by the appointing authority in the same way as a sole arbitrator would be appointed under article 8, paragraph 2.

Article 10

1. For the purposes of article 9, paragraph 1, where three or five arbitrators are to be appointed and there are multiple parties as claimant or as respondent, unless the parties have agreed to another method of appointment of arbitrators, the multiple parties jointly, whether as claimant or as respondent, shall appoint an arbitrator.

2. If the parties have agreed that the arbitral tribunal is to be composed of a number of arbitrators other than one, three, or five, the arbitrators shall be appointed according to the method agreed upon by the parties.

3. In the event of any failure to constitute the arbitral tribunal under these Rules, the appointing authority shall, at the request of any party, constitute the arbitral tribunal and, in doing so, may revoke any appointment already made and appoint each of the arbitrators and designate one of them as the presiding arbitrator. The appointing authority may, if it deems it appropriate, reappoint previous appointees.

4. In appointing arbitrators pursuant to these Rules, the parties and the appointing authority are free to choose persons who are not Members of the Permanent Court of Arbitration.

Disclosures by and challenge of arbitrators* (articles 11 to 13)

Article 11

When a person is approached in connection with his or her possible appointment as an arbitrator, he or she shall disclose any circumstances likely to give rise to justifiable doubts as to his or her impartiality or independence. An arbitrator, from the time of his or

* Model statements of independence pursuant to article 11 can be found in the annex to the Rules.

her appointment and throughout the arbitral proceedings, shall without delay disclose any such circumstances to the parties and the other arbitrators unless they have already been informed by him or her of these circumstances.

Article 12

1. Any arbitrator may be challenged if circumstances exist that give rise to justifiable doubts as to the arbitrator's impartiality or independence.

2. A party may challenge the arbitrator appointed by it only for reasons of which it becomes aware after the appointment has been made.

3. In the event that an arbitrator fails to act or in the event of the *de jure* or *de facto* impossibility of his or her performing his or her functions, the procedure in respect of the challenge of an arbitrator as provided in article 13 shall apply.

4. If an arbitrator on a tribunal of three, five, or more persons fails to participate in the arbitration, the other arbitrators shall, unless the parties agree otherwise, have the power in their sole discretion to continue the arbitration and to make any decision, ruling or award, notwithstanding the failure of one arbitrator to participate. In determining whether to continue the arbitration or to render any decision, ruling or award without the participation of an arbitrator, the other arbitrators shall take into account the stage of the arbitration, the reason, if any, expressed by the arbitrator for such non-participation, and such other matters as they consider appropriate in the circumstances of the case. In the event that the other arbitrators determine not to continue the arbitration without the non-participating arbitrator, the arbitral tribunal shall declare the office vacant, and, subject to article 14, paragraph 2, a substitute arbitrator shall be appointed pursuant to the provisions of articles 8 to 11, unless the parties agree on a different method of appointment.

Article 13

1. A party that intends to challenge an arbitrator shall send notice of its challenge within 30 days after it has been notified of the appointment of the challenged arbitrator, or within 30 days after the circumstances mentioned in articles 11 and 12 became known to that party.

2. The notice of challenge shall be communicated to all other parties, to the arbitrator who is challenged, to the other arbitrators, and to the International Bureau. The notice of challenge shall state the reasons for the challenge.

3. When an arbitrator has been challenged by a party, all parties may agree to the challenge. The arbitrator may also, after the challenge, withdraw from his or her office. In neither case does this imply acceptance of the validity of the grounds for the challenge.

4. If, within 15 days from the date of the notice of challenge, all parties do not agree to the challenge or the challenged arbitrator does not withdraw, the party making the challenge may elect to pursue it. In that case, within 30 days from the date of the notice of challenge, it shall seek a decision on the challenge by the appointing authority.

5. In rendering a decision on the challenge, the appointing authority may indicate the reasons for the decision, unless the parties agree that no reasons shall be given.

Replacement of an arbitrator

Article 14

1. Subject to paragraph 2 of this article, in any event where an arbitrator has to be replaced during the course of the arbitral proceedings, a substitute arbitrator shall be appointed or

chosen pursuant to the procedure provided for in articles 8 to 11 that was applicable to the appointment or choice of the arbitrator being replaced. This procedure shall apply even if during the process of appointing the arbitrator to be replaced, a party had failed to exercise its right to appoint or to participate in the appointment.

2. If, at the request of a party, the appointing authority determines that, in view of the exceptional circumstances of the case, it would be justified for a party to be deprived of its right to appoint a substitute arbitrator, the appointing authority may, after giving an opportunity to the parties and the remaining arbitrators to express their views, appoint the substitute arbitrator.

Repetition of hearings in the event of the replacement of an arbitrator

Article 15

If an arbitrator is replaced, the proceedings shall resume at the stage where the arbitrator who was replaced ceased to perform his or her functions, unless the arbitral tribunal decides otherwise.

Exclusion of liability

Article 16

The parties waive, to the fullest extent permitted under the applicable law, any claim against the arbitrators and any person appointed by the arbitral tribunal based on any act or omission in connection with the arbitration.

SECTION III. ARBITRAL PROCEEDINGS

General provisions

Article 17

1. Subject to these Rules, the arbitral tribunal may conduct the arbitration in such manner as it considers appropriate, provided that the parties are treated with equality and that at an appropriate stage of the proceedings each party is given a reasonable opportunity of presenting its case. The arbitral tribunal, in exercising its discretion, shall conduct the proceedings so as to avoid unnecessary delay and expense and to provide a fair and efficient process for resolving the parties' dispute.

2. As soon as practicable after its constitution and after inviting the parties to express their views, the arbitral tribunal shall establish the provisional timetable of the arbitration. The arbitral tribunal may, at any time, after inviting the parties to express their views, extend or abridge any period of time prescribed under these Rules or agreed by the parties.

3. If at an appropriate stage of the proceedings any party so requests, the arbitral tribunal shall hold hearings for the presentation of evidence by witnesses, including expert witnesses, or for oral argument. In the absence of such a request, the arbitral tribunal shall decide whether to hold such hearings or whether the proceedings shall be conducted on the basis of documents and other materials.

4. All communications to the arbitral tribunal by one party shall be communicated by that party to all other parties and the International Bureau. Such communications shall be made at the same time, except as otherwise permitted by the arbitral tribunal if it may do so under applicable law.

5. The arbitral tribunal may, at the request of any party, allow one or more third persons to be joined in the arbitration as a party provided such person is a party to the arbitration agreement, unless the arbitral tribunal finds, after giving all parties, including the person or persons to be joined, the opportunity to be heard, that joinder should not be permitted because of prejudice to any of those parties. The arbitral tribunal may make a single award or several awards in respect of all parties so involved in the arbitration.

Place of arbitration

Article 18

1. If the parties have not previously agreed on the place of arbitration, the place of arbitration shall be determined by the arbitral tribunal having regard to the circumstances of the case. The award shall be deemed to have been made at the place of arbitration.

2. The arbitral tribunal may meet at any location it considers appropriate for deliberations. Unless otherwise agreed by the parties, the arbitral tribunal may also meet at any location it considers appropriate for any other purpose, including hearings.

Language

Article 19

1. Subject to an agreement by the parties, the arbitral tribunal shall, promptly after its appointment, determine the language or languages to be used in the proceedings. This determination shall apply to the statement of claim, the statement of defence, and any further written statements and, if oral hearings take place, to the language or languages to be used in such hearings.

2. The arbitral tribunal may order that any documents annexed to the statement of claim or statement of defence, and any supplementary documents or exhibits submitted in the course of the proceedings, delivered in their original language, shall be accompanied by a translation into the language or languages agreed upon by the parties or determined by the arbitral tribunal.

Statement of claim

Article 20

1. The claimant shall communicate its statement of claim in writing to the respondent, to the International Bureau, and to each of the arbitrators within a period of time to be determined by the arbitral tribunal. The claimant may elect to treat its notice of arbitration referred to in article 3 as a statement of claim, provided that the notice of arbitration also complies with the requirements of paragraphs 2 to 4 of this article.

2. The statement of claim shall include the following particulars:

(a) The names and contact details of the parties;
(b) A statement of the facts supporting the claim;
(c) The points at issue;
(d) The relief or remedy sought;
(e) The legal grounds or arguments supporting the claim.

3. A copy of any rule, decision, agreement, contract, convention, treaty, constituent instrument of an organization or agency, or relationship out of, or in relation to which, the dispute arises, and of the arbitration agreement shall be annexed to the statement of claim.

4. The statement of claim should, as far as possible, be accompanied by all documents and other evidence relied upon by the claimant, or contain references to them.

Statement of defence

Article 21

1. The respondent shall communicate its statement of defence in writing to the claimant, to the International Bureau, and to each of the arbitrators within a period of time to be determined by the arbitral tribunal. The respondent may elect to treat its response to the notice of arbitration referred to in article 4 as a statement of defence, provided that the response to the notice of arbitration also complies with the requirements of paragraph 2 of this article.

2. The statement of defence shall reply to the particulars (b) to (e) of the statement of claim (article 20, paragraph 2). The statement of defence should, as far as possible, be accompanied by all documents and other evidence relied upon by the respondent, or contain references to them.

3. In its statement of defence, or at a later stage in the arbitral proceedings if the arbitral tribunal decides that the delay was justified under the circumstances, the respondent may make a counterclaim or rely on a claim for the purpose of a set-off provided that the arbitral tribunal has jurisdiction over it.

4. The provisions of article 20, paragraphs 2 to 4 shall apply to a counterclaim, a claim under article 4, paragraph 2(e), and a claim relied on for the purpose of a set-off.

Amendments to the claim or defence

Article 22

During the course of the arbitral proceedings, a party may amend or supplement its claim or defence, including a counterclaim or a claim for the purpose of a set-off, unless the arbitral tribunal considers it inappropriate to allow such amendment or supplement having regard to the delay in making it or prejudice to other parties or any other circumstances. However, a claim or defence, including a counterclaim or a claim for the purpose of a set-off, may not be amended or supplemented in such a manner that the amended or supplemented claim or defence falls outside the jurisdiction of the arbitral tribunal.

Pleas as to the jurisdiction of the arbitral tribunal

Article 23

1. The arbitral tribunal shall have the power to rule on its own jurisdiction, including any objections with respect to the existence or validity of the arbitration agreement. For that purpose, an arbitration clause that forms part of a contract, treaty, or other agreement shall be treated as an agreement independent of the other terms of the contract, treaty, or other agreement. A decision by the arbitral tribunal that the contract, treaty, or other agreement is null, void, or invalid shall not entail automatically the invalidity of the arbitration clause.

2. A plea that the arbitral tribunal does not have jurisdiction shall be raised no later than in the statement of defence or, with respect to a counterclaim or a claim for the purpose of a set-off, in the reply to the counterclaim or to the claim for the purpose of a set-off. A party is not precluded from raising such a plea by the fact that it has appointed, or participated

in the appointment of, an arbitrator. A plea that the arbitral tribunal is exceeding the scope of its authority shall be raised as soon as the matter alleged to be beyond the scope of its authority is raised during the arbitral proceedings. The arbitral tribunal may, in either case, admit a later plea if it considers the delay justified.

3. The arbitral tribunal may rule on a plea referred to in paragraph 2 either as a preliminary question or in an award on the merits. The arbitral tribunal may continue the arbitral proceedings and make an award, notwithstanding any pending challenge to its jurisdiction before a competent authority.

Further written statements

Article 24

The arbitral tribunal shall decide which further written statements, in addition to the statement of claim and the statement of defence, shall be required from the parties or may be presented by them and shall fix the periods of time for communicating such statements.

Periods of time

Article 25

The periods of time fixed by the arbitral tribunal for the communication of written statements (including the statement of claim and statement of defence) should not exceed 45 days. However, the arbitral tribunal may extend the time limits if it concludes that an extension is justified.

Interim measures

Article 26

1. The arbitral tribunal may, at the request of a party, grant interim measures.

2. An interim measure is any temporary measure by which, at any time prior to the issuance of the award by which the dispute is finally decided, the arbitral tribunal orders a party, for example and without limitation, to:

(a) Maintain or restore the status quo pending determination of the dispute;

(b) Take action that would prevent, or refrain from taking action that is likely to cause, (i) current or imminent harm or (ii) prejudice to the arbitral process itself;

(c) Provide a means of preserving assets out of which a subsequent award may be satisfied; or

(d) Preserve evidence that may be relevant and material to the resolution of the dispute.

3. The party requesting an interim measure under paragraphs 2 (a) to (c) shall satisfy the arbitral tribunal that:

(a) Harm not adequately reparable by an award of damages is likely to result if the measure is not ordered, and such harm substantially outweighs the harm that is likely to result to the party against whom the measure is directed if the measure is granted; and

(b) There is a reasonable possibility that the requesting party will succeed on the merits of the claim. The determination on this possibility shall not affect the discretion of the arbitral tribunal in making any subsequent determination.

4. With regard to a request for an interim measure under paragraph 2 (d), the requirements in paragraphs 3 (a) and (b) shall apply only to the extent the arbitral tribunal considers appropriate.

5. The arbitral tribunal may modify, suspend or terminate an interim measure it has granted, upon application of any party or, in exceptional circumstances and upon prior notice to the parties, on the arbitral tribunal's own initiative.

6. The arbitral tribunal may require the party requesting an interim measure to provide appropriate security in connection with the measure.

7. The arbitral tribunal may require any party promptly to disclose any material change in the circumstances on the basis of which the interim measure was requested or granted.

8. The party requesting an interim measure may be liable for any costs and damages caused by the measure to any party if the arbitral tribunal later determines that, in the circumstances then prevailing, the measure should not have been granted. The arbitral tribunal may award such costs and damages at any point during the proceedings.

9. A request for interim measures addressed by any party to a judicial authority shall not be deemed incompatible with the agreement to arbitrate, or as a waiver of that agreement.

Evidence

Article 27

1. Each party shall have the burden of proving the facts relied on to support its claim or defence.

2. Witnesses, including expert witnesses, who are presented by the parties to testify to the arbitral tribunal on any issue of fact or expertise may be any individual, notwithstanding that the individual is a party to the arbitration or in any way related to a party. Unless otherwise directed by the arbitral tribunal, statements by witnesses, including expert witnesses, may be presented in writing and signed by them.

3. At any time during the arbitral proceedings the arbitral tribunal may require the parties to produce documents, exhibits or other evidence within such a period of time as the arbitral tribunal shall determine. The arbitral tribunal may also, after consultation with the parties, perform a site visit.

4. The arbitral tribunal shall determine the admissibility, relevance, materiality and weight of the evidence offered.

Hearings

Article 28

1. In the event of an oral hearing, the arbitral tribunal shall give the parties adequate advance notice of the date, time and place thereof.

2. Witnesses, including expert witnesses, may be heard under the conditions and examined in the manner set by the arbitral tribunal.

3. Hearings shall be held *in camera* unless the parties agree otherwise. The arbitral tribunal may require the retirement of any witness or witnesses, including expert witnesses, during the testimony of such other witnesses, except that a witness, including an expert witness, who is a party to the arbitration shall not, in principle, be asked to retire.

4. The arbitral tribunal may direct that witnesses, including expert witnesses, be examined through means of telecommunication that do not require their physical presence at the hearing (such as videoconference).

Experts appointed by the arbitral tribunal

Article 29

1. After consultation with the parties, the arbitral tribunal may appoint one or more independent experts to report to it, in writing, on specific issues to be determined by the arbitral tribunal. A copy of the expert's terms of reference, established by the arbitral tribunal, shall be communicated to the parties.

2. The expert shall, in principle before accepting appointment, submit to the arbitral tribunal and to the parties a description of his or her qualifications and a statement of his or her impartiality and independence. Within the time ordered by the arbitral tribunal, the parties shall inform the arbitral tribunal whether they have any objections as to the expert's qualifications, impartiality or independence. The arbitral tribunal shall decide promptly whether to accept any such objections. After an expert's appointment, a party may object to the expert's qualifications, impartiality or independence only if the objection is for reasons of which the party becomes aware after the appointment has been made. The arbitral tribunal shall decide promptly what, if any, action to take.

3. The parties shall give the expert any relevant information or produce for his or her inspection any relevant documents or goods that he or she may require of them. Any dispute between a party and such expert as to the relevance of the required information or production shall be referred to the arbitral tribunal for decision.

4. Upon receipt of the expert's report, the arbitral tribunal shall communicate a copy of the report to the parties, which shall be given the opportunity to express, in writing, their opinion on the report. A party shall be entitled to examine any document on which the expert relied in his or her report.

5. If a party so requests or if the arbitral tribunal considers it necessary, the expert shall, after delivery of the report, participate in a hearing where the parties have the opportunity to put questions to him or her and to present expert witnesses in order to testify on the points at issue. The provisions of article 28 shall be applicable to such proceedings.

Default

Article 30

1. If, within the period of time fixed by these Rules or the arbitral tribunal, without showing sufficient cause:

(a) The claimant has failed to communicate its statement of claim, the arbitral tribunal shall issue an order for the termination of the arbitral proceedings, unless there are remaining matters that may need to be decided and the arbitral tribunal considers it appropriate to do so;

(b) The respondent has failed to communicate its response to the notice of arbitration or its statement of defence, the arbitral tribunal shall order that the proceedings continue, without treating such failure in itself as an admission of the claimant's allegations; the provisions of this subparagraph also apply to a claimant's failure to submit a defence to a counterclaim or to a claim for the purpose of a set-off.

2. If a party, duly notified under these Rules, fails to appear at a hearing, without showing sufficient cause for such failure, the arbitral tribunal may proceed with the arbitration.

3. If a party, duly invited by the arbitral tribunal to produce documents, exhibits or other evidence, fails to do so within the established period of time, without showing sufficient cause for such failure, the arbitral tribunal may make the award on the evidence before it.

Closure of proceedings

Article 31

1. When it is satisfied that the parties have had a reasonable opportunity to present their cases, the arbitral tribunal shall declare the proceedings closed.

2. The arbitral tribunal may, if it considers it necessary owing to exceptional circumstances, decide, on its own initiative or upon application of a party, to reopen the proceedings at any time before the award is made.

Waiver of right to object

Article 32

A failure by any party to object promptly to any non-compliance with these Rules or with any requirement of the arbitration agreement shall be deemed to be a waiver of the right of such party to make such an objection, unless such party can show that, under the circumstances, its failure to object was justified.

SECTION IV. THE AWARD

Decisions

Article 33

1. When there is more than one arbitrator, any award or other decision of the arbitral tribunal shall be made by a majority of the arbitrators.

2. In the case of questions of procedure, when there is no majority or when the arbitral tribunal so authorizes, the presiding arbitrator may decide alone, subject to revision, if any, by the arbitral tribunal.

Form and effect of the award

Article 34

1. The arbitral tribunal may make separate awards on different issues at different times.

2. All awards shall be made in writing and shall be final and binding on the parties. The parties shall carry out all awards without delay.

3. The arbitral tribunal shall state the reasons upon which the award is based, unless the parties have agreed that no reasons are to be given.

4. An award shall be signed by the arbitrators and it shall contain the date on which the award was made and indicate the place of arbitration. Where there is more than one arbitrator and any of them fails to sign, the award shall state the reason for the absence of the signature.

5. An award may be made public with the consent of all parties or where and to the extent disclosure is required of a party by legal duty, to protect or pursue a legal right or in relation to legal proceedings before a court or other competent authority.

6. Copies of the award signed by the arbitrators shall be communicated to the parties by the International Bureau.

7. In cases involving only States, the parties shall communicate to the International Bureau the laws, regulations, or other documents evidencing the execution of the award.

Applicable law, *amiable compositeur*

Article 35

1. The arbitral tribunal shall apply the rules of law designated by the parties as applicable to the substance of the dispute. Failing such designation by the parties, the arbitral tribunal shall:
   (a) In cases involving only States, decide such disputes in accordance with international law by applying:
      i. International conventions, whether general or particular, establishing rules expressly recognized by the contesting States;
      ii. International custom, as evidence of a general practice accepted as law;
      iii. The general principles of law recognized by civilized nations;
      iv. Judicial and arbitral decisions and the teachings of the most highly qualified publicists of the various nations, as subsidiary means for the determination of rules of law.
   (b) In cases involving only States and intergovernmental organizations, apply the rules of the organization concerned and the law applicable to any agreement or relationship between the parties, and, where appropriate, the general principles governing the law of intergovernmental organizations and the rules of general international law.
   (c) In cases involving intergovernmental organizations and private parties, have regard both to the rules of the organization concerned and to the law applicable to the agreement or relationship out of or in relation to which the dispute arises, and, where appropriate, to the general principles governing the law of intergovernmental organizations and to the rules of general international law. In such cases, the arbitral tribunal shall decide in accordance with the terms of the agreement and shall take into account relevant trade usages.
   (d) In all other cases, apply the law which it determines to be appropriate. In such cases, the arbitral tribunal shall decide in accordance with the terms of the agreement and shall take into account relevant trade usages.

2. The arbitral tribunal shall decide as *amiable compositeur* or *ex aequo et bono* only if the parties have expressly authorized the arbitral tribunal to do so.

Settlement or other grounds for termination

Article 36

1. If, before the award is made, the parties agree on a settlement of the dispute, the arbitral tribunal shall either issue an order for the termination of the arbitral proceedings or, if requested by the parties and accepted by the arbitral tribunal, record the settlement in the form of an arbitral award on agreed terms. The arbitral tribunal is not obliged to give reasons for such an award.

2. If, before the award is made, the continuation of the arbitral proceedings becomes unnecessary or impossible for any reason not mentioned in paragraph 1, the arbitral tribunal shall inform the parties of its intention to issue an order for the termination of the proceedings. The arbitral tribunal shall have the power to issue such an order unless there

are remaining matters that may need to be decided and the arbitral tribunal considers it appropriate to do so.

3. Copies of the order for termination of the arbitral proceedings or of the arbitral award on agreed terms, signed by the arbitrators, shall be communicated by the arbitral tribunal to the parties. Where an arbitral award on agreed terms is made, the provisions of article 34, paragraphs 2, 4 and 5 shall apply.

Interpretation of the award

Article 37

1. Within 30 days after the receipt of the award, a party, with notice to the other parties and the International Bureau, may request that the arbitral tribunal give an interpretation of the award.

2. The interpretation shall be given in writing within 45 days after the receipt of the request. The interpretation shall form part of the award and the provisions of article 34, paragraphs 2 to 6, shall apply.

Correction of the award

Article 38

1. Within 30 days after the receipt of the award, a party, with notice to the other parties and the International Bureau, may request the arbitral tribunal to correct in the award any error in computation, any clerical or typographical error, or any error or omission of a similar nature. If the arbitral tribunal considers that the request is justified, it shall make the correction within 45 days of receipt of the request.

2. The arbitral tribunal may within 30 days after the communication of the award make such corrections on its own initiative.

3. Such corrections shall be in writing and shall form part of the award. The provisions of article 34, paragraphs 2 to 6, shall apply.

Additional award

Article 39

1. Within 30 days after the receipt of the termination order or the award, a party, with notice to the other parties and the International Bureau, may request the arbitral tribunal to make an award or an additional award as to claims presented in the arbitral proceedings but not decided by the arbitral tribunal.

2. If the arbitral tribunal considers the request for an award or additional award to be justified, it shall render or complete its award within 60 days after the receipt of the request. The arbitral tribunal may extend, if necessary, the period of time within which it shall make the award.

3. When such an award or additional award is made, the provisions of article 34, paragraphs 2 to 6, shall apply.

Definition of costs

Article 40

1. The arbitral tribunal shall fix the costs of arbitration in the final award and, if it deems appropriate, in another decision.

2. The term "costs" includes only:

(a) The fees of the arbitral tribunal to be stated separately as to each arbitrator and to be fixed by the tribunal itself in accordance with article 41;
(b) The reasonable travel and other expenses incurred by the arbitrators;
(c) The reasonable costs of expert advice and of other assistance required by the arbitral tribunal;
(d) The reasonable travel and other expenses of witnesses to the extent such expenses are approved by the arbitral tribunal;
(e) The legal and other costs incurred by the parties in relation to the arbitration to the extent that the arbitral tribunal determines that the amount of such costs is reasonable;
(f) The fees and expenses of the International Bureau, including the fees and expenses of the appointing authority.

3. In relation to interpretation, correction or completion of any award under articles 37 to 39, the arbitral tribunal may charge the costs referred to in paragraphs 2 (b) to (f), but no additional fees.

Fees and expenses of arbitrators

Article 41

1. The costs referred to in article 40, paragraphs 2 (a), (b) and (c) shall be reasonable in amount, taking into account the amount in dispute, the complexity of the subject matter, the time spent by the arbitrators and any experts appointed by the arbitral tribunal, and any other relevant circumstances of the case.

2. Promptly after its constitution, the arbitral tribunal shall inform the parties as to how it proposes to determine its fees and expenses, including any rates it intends to apply. Within 15 days of receiving that proposal, any party may refer the proposal to the appointing authority for review. If the appointing authority finds that the proposal of the arbitral tribunal is inconsistent with paragraph 1, it shall make any necessary adjustments thereto, which shall be binding upon the arbitral tribunal.

3.
(a) Before fixing the costs of arbitration pursuant to article 40, the arbitral tribunal shall submit its determination of the costs referred to in article 40, paragraphs 2 (a), (b) and (c), with an explanation of the manner in which the corresponding amounts have been calculated, to the appointing authority for review;
(b) If the appointing authority finds that the arbitral tribunal's determination is inconsistent with the criteria in paragraph 1 or with the arbitral tribunal's proposal (and any adjustments thereto) under paragraph 2, it shall make any necessary adjustments to the arbitral tribunal's determination. Any such adjustments shall be binding upon the arbitral tribunal when it fixes the costs of arbitration pursuant to article 40.

4. Throughout the procedure under paragraphs 2 and 3 of this article, the arbitral tribunal shall proceed with the arbitration, in accordance with article 17, paragraph 1.

Allocation of costs

Article 42

1. The costs of arbitration shall in principle be borne by the unsuccessful party or parties. However, the arbitral tribunal may apportion each of such costs between the parties if it determines that apportionment is reasonable, taking into account the circumstances of the case.

2. The arbitral tribunal shall in the final award or, if it deems appropriate, in any other award, determine any amount that a party may have to pay to another party as a result of the decision on allocation of costs.

Deposit of costs

Article 43

1. The International Bureau, following the commencement of the arbitration, may request the parties to deposit an equal amount as an advance for the costs referred to in article 40, paragraphs 2 (a), (b), (c), and (f). All amounts deposited by the parties pursuant to this paragraph and paragraph 2 of this article shall be directed to the International Bureau, and disbursed by it for such costs, including, *inter alia*, fees to the arbitrators, to the appointing authority, and to the International Bureau. The International Bureau shall ensure that any disbursements of arbitral tribunal fees and expenses made prior to the fixing of the costs of arbitration pursuant to article 40 are consistent with the criteria in article 41, paragraph 1 and with the arbitral tribunal's proposal (and any adjustments thereto) under article 41, paragraph 2.

2. During the course of the arbitral proceedings the International Bureau may request supplementary deposits from the parties.

3. Any deposit of security for costs ordered by the arbitral tribunal pursuant to article 26 shall be directed to the International Bureau and disbursed by it upon order from the arbitral tribunal.

4. If the requested deposits are not paid in full within 30 days after the receipt of the request or such other period as may be set by the International Bureau, the International Bureau shall so inform the parties in order that one or more of them may make the required payment. If such payment is not made, the arbitral tribunal may order the suspension or termination of the arbitral proceedings.

5. After a termination order or final award has been made, the International Bureau shall render an accounting to the parties of the deposits received and return any unexpended balance to the parties.

Annex

Model arbitration clause for contracts

Any dispute, controversy or claim arising out of or relating to this contract, or the breach, termination or invalidity thereof, shall be settled by arbitration in accordance with the PCA Arbitration Rules 2012.

Model arbitration clause for treaties and other agreements

Any dispute, controversy or claim arising out of or in relation to this [agreement] [treaty], or the existence, interpretation, application, breach, termination, or invalidity thereof, shall be settled by arbitration in accordance with the PCA Arbitration Rules 2012.

Note – Parties should consider adding:

(a) The number of arbitrators shall be … (one, three, or five);

(b) The place of arbitration shall be … (town and country);

(c) The language to be used in the arbitral proceedings shall be ….

Possible waiver statement

Note – If the parties wish to exclude recourse against the arbitral award that may be available under the applicable law, they may consider adding a provision to that effect as suggested below, considering, however, that the effectiveness and conditions of such an exclusion depend on the applicable law.

Waiver: The parties hereby waive their right to any form of recourse against an award to any court or other competent authority, insofar as such waiver can validly be made under the applicable law.

Model statements of impartiality and independence pursuant to article 11 of the Rules

No circumstances to disclose: I am impartial and independent of each of the parties and intend to remain so. To the best of my knowledge, there are no circumstances, past or present, likely to give rise to justifiable doubts as to my impartiality or independence. I shall promptly notify the parties and the other arbitrators of any such circumstances that may subsequently come to my attention during this arbitration.

Circumstances to disclose: I am impartial and independent of each of the parties and intend to remain so. Attached is a statement made pursuant to article 11 of the PCA Arbitration Rules 2012 of (a) my past and present professional, business and other relationships with the parties and (b) any other relevant circumstances. [Include statement] I confirm that those circumstances do not affect my independence and impartiality. I shall promptly notify the parties and the other arbitrators of any such further relationships or circumstances that may subsequently come to my attention during this arbitration.

Note – Any party may consider requesting from the arbitrator the following addition to the statement of impartiality and independence:

I confirm, on the basis of the information presently available to me, that I can devote the time necessary to conduct this arbitration diligently, efficiently and in accordance with the time limits in the Rules.

23.b Model Arbitration Clauses for Use in Connection with the Permanent Court of Arbitration Optional Rules for Arbitrating Disputes between Two States

Source: https://docs.pca-cpa.org/2016/02/Model-Arbitration-Clauses-for-Use-in-Connection-with-the-Permanent-Court-of-Arbitration-Optional-Rules-for-Arbitrating-Disputes-between-Two-States.pdf

Future Disputes

Parties to a bilateral treaty or other agreement who wish to have any dispute referred to arbitration under these Rules may insert in the treaty or agreement an arbitration clause in the following form:

1. *If any dispute arises between the parties as to the interpretation, application or performance of this [treaty] [agreement], including its existence, validity or*

termination, either party may submit the dispute to final and binding arbitration in accordance with the Permanent Court of Arbitration Optional Rules for Arbitrating Disputes between Two States, as in effect on the date of this [treaty] [agreement].

Parties may wish to consider adding:

2. *The number of arbitrators shall be ...* [insert '*one*', '*three*', or '*five*'].
3. *The language(s) to be used in the arbitral proceedings shall be ...* [insert choice of one or more languages].
4. *The appointing authority shall be the Secretary-General of the Permanent Court of Arbitration.*
5. *The place of arbitration shall be ...* [insert city and country].

Existing Disputes

If the parties have not already entered into an arbitration agreement, or if they mutually agree to change a previous agreement in order to provide for arbitration under these Rules, they may enter into an agreement in the following form:

The parties agree to submit the following dispute to final and binding arbitration in accordance with the Permanent Court of Arbitration Optional Rules for Arbitrating Disputes between Two States, as in effect on the date of this agreement:... [insert brief description of dispute].

Parties may wish to consider adding paragraphs 2-5 of the arbitration clause for future disputes as set forth above.

NOTES

1. Parties may agree to vary this model clause. If they consider doing so, they may consult with the Secretary-General of the Permanent Court of Arbitration to ensure that the clause to which they agree will be appropriate in the context of the Rules, and that the functions of the Secretary-General and the International Bureau can be carried out effectively.

2. If the parties do not agree on the number of arbitrators, the number shall be three, in accordance with article 5 of the Rules.

3. If the parties do not agree on the language, or languages, to be used in the arbitral proceedings, this shall be determined by the arbitral tribunal in accordance with article 17 of the Rules.

Activating PCA Jurisdiction

24.a Agreement Relating to the Arbitration of Differences Respecting Sovereignty over the Island of Palmas

Date: 23 January 1925
Source: II UNRIA 831
https://legal.un.org/riaa/cases/vol_II/829-871.pdf

The United States of America and Her Majesty the Queen of the Netherlands,

Desiring to terminate in accordance with the principles of International Law and any applicable treaty provisions the differences which have arisen and now subsist between them with respect to the sovereignty over the Island of Palmas (or Miangas) situated approximately fifty miles south-east from Cape San Augustin, Island of Mindanao, at about five degrees and thirty-five minutes (5° 35') north latitude, one hundred and twenty-six degrees and thirty-six minutes (126° 36') longitude east from Greenwich;

Considering that these differences belong to those which, pursuant to Article I of the Arbitration Convention concluded by the two high contracting parties on May 2, 1908, and renewed by agreements, dated May 9, 1914, March 8, 1919, and February 13, 1924, respectively, might well be submitted to arbitration, Have appointed as their respective plenipotentiaries for the purpose of concluding the following special agreement:

The President of the United States of America: CHARLES EVANS HUGHES, Secretary of State of the United States of America, and Her Majesty the Queen of the Netherlands: JONKHEER Dr. A. C. D. DE GRAEFF, Her Majesty's Envoy Extraordinary and Minister Plenipotentiary at Washington.

Who, after exhibiting to each other their respective full powers, which were found to be in due and proper form, have agreed upon the following articles:

Article I

The United States of America and Her Majesty the Queen of the Netherlands hereby agree to refer the decision of the above-mentioned differences to the Permanent Court of Arbitration at The Hague. The arbitral tribunal shall consist of one arbitrator.

The sole duty of the Arbitrator shall be to determine whether the Island of Palmas (or Miangas) in its entirety forms a part of territory belonging to the United States of America or of Netherlands territory.

The two Governments shall designate the Arbitrator from the members of the Permanent Court of Arbitration. If they shall be unable to agree on such designation, they shall unite in requesting the President of the Swiss Confederation to designate the Arbitrator.

Article II

Within six months after the exchange of ratifications of this special agreement, each Government shall present to the other party two printed copies of a memorandum containing a statement of its contentions and the documents in support thereof. It shall be sufficient for this purpose if the copies aforesaid are delivered by the Government of the United States at the Netherlands Legation at Washington and by the Netherlands Government at the American Legation at The Hague, for transmission. As soon thereafter as possible and within thirty days, each party shall transmit two printed copies of its memorandum to the International Bureau of the Permanent Court of Arbitration for delivery to the Arbitrator.

Within six months after the expiration of the period above fixed for the delivery of the memoranda to the parties, each party may, if it is deemed advisable, transmit to the other two printed copies of a counter-memorandum and any documents in support thereof in answer to the memorandum of the other party. The copies of the counter-memorandum shall be delivered to the parties, and within thirty days thereafter to the Arbitrator, in the manner provided for in the foregoing paragraph respecting the delivery of memoranda.

At the instance of one or both of the parties, the Arbitrator shall have authority, after hearing both parties and for good cause shown, to extend the above-mentioned periods.

Article III

After the exchange of the counter-memoranda, the case shall be deemed closed unless the Arbitrator applies to either or both of the parties for further written explanations.

In case the Arbitrator makes such a request on either party, he shall do so through the International Bureau of the Permanent Court of Arbitration which shall communicate a copy of his request to the other party. The party addressed shall be allowed for reply three months from the date of the receipt of the Arbitrator's request, which date shall be at once communicated to the other party and to the International Bureau. Such reply shall be communicated to the other party and within thirty days thereafter to the Arbitrator in the manner provided for above for the delivery of memoranda, and the opposite party may if it is deemed advisable, have a further period of three months to make rejoinder thereto, which shall be communicated in like manner.

The Arbitrator shall notify both parties through the International Bureau of the date upon which, in accordance with the foregoing provisions, the case is closed, so far as the presentation of memoranda and evidence by either party is concerned.

Article IV

The parties shall be at liberty to use, in the course of arbitration, the English or Netherlands language or the native language of the Arbitrator. If either party uses the English or Netherlands language, a translation into the native language of the Arbitrator shall be furnished if desired by him.

The Arbitrator shall be at liberty to use his native language or the English or Netherlands language in the course of the arbitration and the award and opinion accompanying it may be in any one of those languages.

Article V

The Arbitrator shall decide any questions of procedure which may arise during the course of the arbitration.

Article VI

Immediately after the exchange of ratifications of this special agreement each party shall place in the hands of the Arbitrator the sum of one hundred pounds sterling by way of advance of costs.

Article VII

The Arbitrator shall, within three months after the date upon which he declares the case closed for the presentation of memoranda and evidence, render his award in writing and deposit three signed copies thereof with the International Bureau at The Hague, one copy to be retained by the Bureau and one to be transmitted to each party, as soon as this may be done.

The award shall be accompanied by a statement of the grounds upon which it is based. The Arbitrator shall fix the amount of the costs of procedure in his award. Each party shall defray its own expenses and half of said costs of procedure and of the honorarium of the Arbitrator.

Article VIII

The parties undertake to accept the award rendered by the Arbitrator within the limitations of this special agreement, as final and conclusive and without appeal. All disputes connected with the interpretation and execution of the award shall be submitted to the decision of the Arbitrator.

Article IX

This special agreement shall be ratified in accordance with the constitutional forms of the contracting parties and shall take effect immediately upon the exchange of ratifications, which shall take place as soon as possible at Washington. In witness whereof the respective plenipotentiaries have signed this special agreement and have hereunto affixed their seals.

Done in duplicate in the City of Washington in the English and Netherlands languages this 23rd day of January, 1925.

(L. S.) CHARLES EVANS HUGHES.
(L. S.) DE GRAEFF.

24.b Arbitration Agreement between the United Kingdom of Belgium and the Kingdom of the Netherlands* (*The Iron Rhine* Special Agreement)

Date: 22-23 July 2003
Source: https://pcacases.com/web/sendAttach/469

The Embassy of Kingdom of Belgium presents its compliments to the Ministry of Foreign Affairs and, with reference to the official agreement resulting from the negotiations of 11 April 2003 concerning the so-called Iron Rhine railway line, has the honour to suggest the following:

The Kingdom of Belgium and the Kingdom of the Netherlands have agreed to submit the dispute concerning the reactivation of the Iron Rhine to an arbitral tribunal they are to set up under the auspices of the Permanent Court of Arbitration in the Hague, by requesting a binding decision on the following jointly formulated statement of questions.

"Belgium and the Netherlands agree that Belgium has the right to use, restore, adapt and modernise the Dutch section of the historical route of the Iron Rhine, for the benefit of all Belgian and other rail operators that comply with the rules for access to the market.

With a view to the future investments in the Iron Rhine the two Parties have decided to submit the following questions to an arbitral tribunal under the auspices of the Permanent Court of Arbitration in The Hague:

1. To what extent is Dutch legislation and the decision-making power based thereon in respect of the use, restoration, adaption and modernisation of railway lines on Dutch territory applicable, in the same way, to the use, restoration, adaption and modernisation of the historical route of the Iron Rhine on Dutch territory?
2. To what extent does Belgium have the right to perform or commission work with a view to the use, restoration, adaption and modernisation of the historical route of the Iron Rhine on Dutch territory, and to establish plans, specifications and procedures related to it according to Belgian law and the decision-making power based thereon? Should a distinction be drawn between requirement, standards,

* N.B.: Exchange of diplomatic notes, as translated by the PCA.

plans, specification and procedures related to, on the one hand, the land use planning and the integration of the rail infrastructure, and, if so, what are the implications of this? Can the Netherlands unilaterally impose the building of underground and above-ground tunnels, diversions and the like as well as the proposed associated construction and safety standards?

3. In light of the answers to the previous questions, to what extent should the cost items and financial risks associated with the use, restoration, adaptation and modernisation of the historical route of the Iron Rhine on Dutch territory be borne by Belgium or by the Netherlands? Is Belgium obliged to fund investments over and above those that are necessary for the functionality of the historical route of the railway line?

The Arbitral Tribunal is requested to render its decision on the basis of international law, including European law if necessary, while taking into account the Parties' obligations under article 292 of the EC Treaty."

The Kingdom of Belgium and the Kingdom of the Netherland have agreed to jointly draw up the rules of procedure for the arbitration on the basis of the "Permanent Court of Arbitration Optional Rules for Arbitrating Disputes between Two States". These rules of procedure will be laid down in a joint document.

The Kingdom of Belgium and the Kingdom of the Netherlands have agreed to execute the Arbitral Tribunal's decision as soon as possible by taking a decision on the definitive route, and on the temporarily and restricted re-use of the historical route.

The Embassy proposes that this Note and the affirmative Note from the Ministry shall together constitute an agreement between the Kingdom of Belgium and the Kingdom of the Netherlands which shall be applied provisionally from the day on which the Ministry's affirmative Note is received, and which shall enter into force on the first day of the second month following the date on which both Governments have informed each other via diplomatic channels that the constitutional formalities required for its entry into force have been completed.

The Embassy of the Kingdom of Belgium avails itself of this opportunity to renew the Ministry Foreign Affairs the assurances of its highest consideration.

The Hague, 22 July 2003

The Ministry of Foreign Affairs for the Kingdom of the Netherlands presents its compliments to the Embassy of the Kingdom of Belgium and has the honour to acknowledge the receipt of Note nr. A.71.92/3110 dated 22 July 2003 of the Embassy, of which the content is as follows:

... [reproduced above]

The Ministry of Foreign Affairs has the honour to confirm that the Government of the Kingdom of the Netherlands can agree with the above-mentioned proposals and that the Note of the Embassy of Belgium and this affirmative Note together constitute an agreement between the Kingdom of the Netherland and the Kingdom of Belgium, which shall be applied provisionally from the day on which this affirmative Note is received, and which shall enter into force on the first day of the second month following the date on which both Governments have informed each other via diplomatic channels that the constitutional formalities requires for its entry into force have been completed.

The Embassy of the Kingdom of the Netherlands avails itself of this opportunity to renew to the Ministry of Foreign Affairs the assurances of its highest consideration.

B

Selected Sectoral Regimes

5 Human Rights

(a) Universal Human Rights Treaties and Related Monitoring Mechanisms

25. Convention on the Prevention and Punishment of the Crime of Genocide

Date: 9 December 1948
Source: 78 UNTS 277
http://www.un.org/ga/search/view_doc.asp?symbol=a/res/260(III)

...

Article IX

Disputes between the Contracting Parties relating to the interpretation, application or fulfilment of the present Convention, including those relating to the responsibility of a State for genocide or any of the other acts enumerated in Article 3, shall be submitted to the International Court of Justice at the request of any of the parties to the dispute.

26. International Convention on the Elimination of All Forms of Racial Discrimination*

Date: 21 December 1965
Source: 660 UNTS 195
https://www.ohchr.org/Documents/ProfessionalInterest/cerd.pdf

...

PART II

Article 8

1. There shall be established a Committee on the Elimination of Racial Discrimination (hereinafter referred to as the Committee) consisting of eighteen experts of high moral standing and acknowledged impartiality elected by States Parties from among their nationals, who shall serve in their personal capacity, consideration being given to equitable geographical distribution and to the representation of the different forms of civilization as well as of the principal legal systems.

2. The members of the Committee shall be elected by secret ballot from a list of persons nominated by the States Parties. Each State Party may nominate one person from among its own nationals.

* N.B.: The Rules of Procedure of the Committee on the Elimination of All Forms of Racial Discrimination are not included in this document set, as they are largely similar, though in no way identical, to those of the Human Rights Committee, reproduced in Document No. 27.c below.

3. The initial election shall be held six months after the date of the entry into force of this Convention. At least three months before the date of each election the Secretary-General of the United Nations shall address a letter to the States Parties inviting them to submit their nominations within two months. The Secretary-General shall prepare a list in alphabetical order of all persons thus nominated, indicating the States Parties which have nominated them, and shall submit it to the States Parties.

4. Elections of the members of the Committee shall be held at a meeting of States Parties convened by the Secretary-General at United Nations Headquarters. At that meeting, for which two thirds of the States Parties shall constitute a quorum, the persons elected to the Committee shall be nominees who obtain the largest number of votes and an absolute majority of the votes of the representatives of States Parties present and voting.

5.

(a) The members of the Committee shall be elected for a term of four years. However, the terms of nine of the members elected at the first election shall expire at the end of two years; immediately after the first election the names of these nine members shall be chosen by lot by the Chairman of the Committee;

(b) For the filling of casual vacancies, the State Party whose expert has ceased to function as a member of the Committee shall appoint another expert from among its nationals, subject to the approval of the Committee.

6. States Parties shall be responsible for the expenses of the members of the Committee while they are in performance of Committee duties.

Article 9

1. States Parties undertake to submit to the Secretary-General of the United Nations, for consideration by the Committee, a report on the legislative, judicial, administrative or other measures which they have adopted and which give effect to the provisions of this Convention:

(a) within one year after the entry into force of the Convention for the State concerned; and

(b) thereafter every two years and whenever the Committee so requests. The Committee may request further information from the States Parties.

2. The Committee shall report annually, through the Secretary-General, to the General Assembly of the United Nations on its activities and may make suggestions and general recommendations based on the examination of the reports and information received from the States Parties. Such suggestions and general recommendations shall be reported to the General Assembly together with comments, if any, from States Parties.

Article 10

1. The Committee shall adopt its own rules of procedure.

2. The Committee shall elect its officers for a term of two years.

3. The secretariat of the Committee shall be provided by the Secretary General of the United Nations.

4. The meetings of the Committee shall normally be held at United Nations Headquarters.

Article 11

1. If a State Party considers that another State Party is not giving effect to the provisions of this Convention, it may bring the matter to the attention of the Committee. The Committee

shall then transmit the communication to the State Party concerned. Within three months, the receiving State shall submit to the Committee written explanations or statements clarifying the matter and the remedy, if any, that may have been taken by that State.

2. If the matter is not adjusted to the satisfaction of both parties, either by bilateral negotiations or by any other procedure open to them, within six months after the receipt by the receiving State of the initial communication, either State shall have the right to refer the matter again to the Committee by notifying the Committee and also the other State.

3. The Committee shall deal with a matter referred to it in accordance with paragraph 2 of this article after it has ascertained that all available domestic remedies have been invoked and exhausted in the case, in conformity with the generally recognized principles of international law. This shall not be the rule where the application of the remedies is unreasonably prolonged.

4. In any matter referred to it, the Committee may call upon the States Parties concerned to supply any other relevant information.

5. When any matter arising out of this article is being considered by the Committee, the States Parties concerned shall be entitled to send a representative to take part in the proceedings of the Committee, without voting rights, while the matter is under consideration.

Article 12

1. (a) After the Committee has obtained and collated all the information it deems necessary, the Chairman shall appoint an ad hoc Conciliation Commission (hereinafter referred to as the Commission) comprising five persons who may or may not be members of the Committee. The members of the Commission shall be appointed with the unanimous consent of the parties to the dispute, and its good offices shall be made available to the States concerned with a view to an amicable solution of the matter on the basis of respect for this Convention;

(b) If the States parties to the dispute fail to reach agreement within three months on all or part of the composition of the Commission, the members of the Commission not agreed upon by the States parties to the dispute shall be elected by secret ballot by a two-thirds majority vote of the Committee from among its own members.

2. The members of the Commission shall serve in their personal capacity. They shall not be nationals of the States parties to the dispute or of a State not Party to this Convention.

3. The Commission shall elect its own Chairman and adopt its own rules of procedure.

4. The meetings of the Commission shall normally be held at United Nations Headquarters or at any other convenient place as determined by the Commission.

5. The secretariat provided in accordance with article 10, paragraph 3, of this Convention shall also service the Commission whenever a dispute among States Parties brings the Commission into being.

6. The States parties to the dispute shall share equally all the expenses of the members of the Commission in accordance with estimates to be provided by the Secretary-General of the United Nations.

7. The Secretary-General shall be empowered to pay the expenses of the members of the Commission, if necessary, before reimbursement by the States parties to the dispute in accordance with paragraph 6 of this article.

8. The information obtained and collated by the Committee shall be made available to the Commission, and the Commission may call upon the States concerned to supply any other relevant information.

Article 13

1. When the Commission has fully considered the matter, it shall prepare and submit to the Chairman of the Committee a report embodying its findings on all questions of fact relevant to the issue between the parties and containing such recommendations as it may think proper for the amicable solution of the dispute.

2. The Chairman of the Committee shall communicate the report of the Commission to each of the States parties to the dispute. These States shall, within three months, inform the Chairman of the Committee whether or not they accept the recommendations contained in the report of the Commission.

3. After the period provided for in paragraph 2 of this article, the Chairman of the Committee shall communicate the report of the Commission and the declarations of the States Parties concerned to the other States Parties to this Convention.

Article 14

1. A State Party may at any time declare that it recognizes the competence of the Committee to receive and consider communications from individuals or groups of individuals within its jurisdiction claiming to be victims of a violation by that State Party of any of the rights set forth in this Convention. No communication shall be received by the Committee if it concerns a State Party which has not made such a declaration.

2. Any State Party which makes a declaration as provided for in paragraph I of this article may establish or indicate a body within its national legal order which shall be competent to receive and consider petitions from individuals and groups of individuals within its jurisdiction who claim to be victims of a violation of any of the rights set forth in this Convention and who have exhausted other available local remedies.

3. A declaration made in accordance with paragraph 1 of this article and the name of any body established or indicated in accordance with paragraph 2 of this article shall be deposited by the State Party concerned with the Secretary-General of the United Nations, who shall transmit copies thereof to the other States Parties. A declaration may be withdrawn at any time by notification to the Secretary-General, but such a withdrawal shall not affect communications pending before the Committee.

4. A register of petitions shall be kept by the body established or indicated in accordance with paragraph 2 of this article, and certified copies of the register shall be filed annually through appropriate channels with the Secretary-General on the understanding that the contents shall not be publicly disclosed.

5. In the event of failure to obtain satisfaction from the body established or indicated in accordance with paragraph 2 of this article, the petitioner shall have the right to communicate the matter to the Committee within six months.

6. (a) The Committee shall confidentially bring any communication referred to it to the attention of the State Party alleged to be violating any provision of this Convention, but the identity of the individual or groups of individuals concerned shall not be revealed without his or their express consent. The Committee shall not receive anonymous communications;

(b) Within three months, the receiving State shall submit to the Committee written explanations or statements clarifying the matter and the remedy, if any, that may have been taken by that State.

7. (a) The Committee shall consider communications in the light of all information made available to it by the State Party concerned and by the petitioner. The Committee shall not consider any communication from a petitioner unless it has ascertained that the petitioner has exhausted all available domestic remedies. However, this shall not be the rule where the application of the remedies is unreasonably prolonged;

(b) The Committee shall forward its suggestions and recommendations, if any, to the State Party concerned and to the petitioner.

8. The Committee shall include in its annual report a summary of such communications and, where appropriate, a summary of the explanations and statements of the States Parties concerned and of its own suggestions and recommendations.

9. The Committee shall be competent to exercise the functions provided for in this article only when at least ten States Parties to this Convention are bound by declarations in accordance with paragraph I of this article.

Article 15

1. Pending the achievement of the objectives of the Declaration on the Granting of Independence to Colonial Countries and Peoples, contained in General Assembly resolution 1514 (XV) of 14 December 1960, the provisions of this Convention shall in no way limit the right of petition granted to these peoples by other international instruments or by the United Nations and its specialized agencies.

2. (a) The Committee established under article 8, paragraph 1, of this Convention shall receive copies of the petitions from, and submit expressions of opinion and recommendations on these petitions to, the bodies of the United Nations which deal with matters directly related to the principles and objectives of this Convention in their consideration of petitions from the inhabitants of Trust and Non-Self-Governing Territories and all other territories to which General Assembly resolution 1514 (XV) applies, relating to matters covered by this Convention which are before these bodies;

(b) The Committee shall receive from the competent bodies of the United Nations copies of the reports concerning the legislative, judicial, administrative or other measures directly related to the principles and objectives of this Convention applied by the administering Powers within the Territories mentioned in subparagraph (a) of this paragraph, and shall express opinions and make recommendations to these bodies.

3. The Committee shall include in its report to the General Assembly a summary of the petitions and reports it has received from United Nations bodies, and the expressions of opinion and recommendations of the Committee relating to the said petitions and reports.

4. The Committee shall request from the Secretary-General of the United Nations all information relevant to the objectives of this Convention and available to him regarding the Territories mentioned in paragraph 2 (a) of this article.

Article 16

The provisions of this Convention concerning the settlement of disputes or complaints shall be applied without prejudice to other procedures for settling disputes or complaints in the field of discrimination laid down in the constituent instruments of, or conventions adopted by, the United Nations and its specialized agencies, and shall not prevent the States Parties from having recourse to other procedures for settling a dispute in accordance with general or special international agreements in force between them.

...

PART III

...

Article 22

Any dispute between two or more States Parties with respect to the interpretation or application of this Convention, which is not settled by negotiation or by the procedures expressly provided for in this Convention, shall, at the request of any of the parties to the dispute, be referred to the International Court of Justice for decision, unless the disputants agree to another mode of settlement.

The ICCPR Framework

27.a International Covenant on Civil and Political Rights

Date: 16 December 1966
Source: 999 UNTS 171
https://www.ohchr.org/Documents/ProfessionalInterest/ccpr.pdf

...

PART IV

Article 28

1. There shall be established a Human Rights Committee (hereafter referred to in the present Covenant as the Committee). It shall consist of eighteen members and shall carry out the functions hereinafter provided.

2. The Committee shall be composed of nationals of the States Parties to the present Covenant who shall be persons of high moral character and recognized competence in the field of human rights, consideration being given to the usefulness of the participation of some persons having legal experience.

3. The members of the Committee shall be elected and shall serve in their personal capacity.

Article 29

1. The members of the Committee shall be elected by secret ballot from a list of persons possessing the qualifications prescribed in article 28 and nominated for the purpose by the States Parties to the present Covenant.

2. Each State Party to the present Covenant may nominate not more than two persons. These persons shall be nationals of the nominating State.

3. A person shall be eligible for re-nomination.

Article 30

1. The initial election shall be held no later than six months after the date of the entry into force of the present Covenant.

2. At least four months before the date of each election to the Committee, other than an election to fill a vacancy declared in accordance with article 34, the Secretary-General of the United Nations shall address a written invitation to the States Parties to the present Covenant to submit their nominations for membership of the Committee within three months.

3. The Secretary-General of the United Nations shall prepare a list in alphabetical order of all the persons thus nominated, with an indication of the States Parties which have nominated them, and shall submit it to the States Parties to the present Covenant no later than one month before the date of each election.

4. Elections of the members of the Committee shall be held at a meeting of the States Parties to the present Covenant convened by the Secretary General of the United Nations at the Headquarters of the United Nations. At that meeting, for which two thirds of the States Parties to the present Covenant shall constitute a quorum, the persons elected to the Committee shall be those nominees who obtain the largest number of votes and an absolute majority of the votes of the representatives of States Parties present and voting.

Article 31

1. The Committee may not include more than one national of the same State.

2. In the election of the Committee, consideration shall be given to equitable geographical distribution of membership and to the representation of the different forms of civilization and of the principal legal systems.

Article 32

1. The members of the Committee shall be elected for a term of four years. They shall be eligible for re-election if re-nominated. However, the terms of nine of the members elected at the first election shall expire at the end of two years; immediately after the first election, the names of these nine members shall be chosen by lot by the Chairman of the meeting referred to in article 30, paragraph 4.

2. Elections at the expiry of office shall be held in accordance with the preceding articles of this part of the present Covenant.

Article 33

1. If, in the unanimous opinion of the other members, a member of the Committee has ceased to carry out his functions for any cause other than absence of a temporary character, the Chairman of the Committee shall notify the Secretary-General of the United Nations, who shall then declare the seat of that member to be vacant.

2. In the event of the death or the resignation of a member of the Committee, the Chairman shall immediately notify the Secretary-General of the United Nations, who shall declare the seat vacant from the date of death or the date on which the resignation takes effect.

Article 34

1. When a vacancy is declared in accordance with article 33 and if the term of office of the member to be replaced does not expire within six months of the declaration of the vacancy, the Secretary-General of the United Nations shall notify each of the States Parties

to the present Covenant, which may within two months submit nominations in accordance with article 29 for the purpose of filling the vacancy.

2. The Secretary-General of the United Nations shall prepare a list in alphabetical order of the persons thus nominated and shall submit it to the States Parties to the present Covenant. The election to fill the vacancy shall then take place in accordance with the relevant provisions of this part of the present Covenant.

3. A member of the Committee elected to fill a vacancy declared in accordance with article 33 shall hold office for the remainder of the term of the member who vacated the seat on the Committee under the provisions of that article.

Article 35

The members of the Committee shall, with the approval of the General Assembly of the United Nations, receive emoluments from United Nations resources on such terms and conditions as the General Assembly may decide, having regard to the importance of the Committee's responsibilities.

Article 36

The Secretary-General of the United Nations shall provide the necessary staff and facilities for the effective performance of the functions of the Committee under the present Covenant.

Article 37

1. The Secretary-General of the United Nations shall convene the initial meeting of the Committee at the Headquarters of the United Nations.

2. After its initial meeting, the Committee shall meet at such times as shall be provided in its rules of procedure.

3. The Committee shall normally meet at the Headquarters of the United Nations or at the United Nations Office at Geneva.

Article 38

Every member of the Committee shall, before taking up his duties, make a solemn declaration in open committee that he will perform his functions impartially and conscientiously.

Article 39

1. The Committee shall elect its officers for a term of two years. They may be re-elected.

2. The Committee shall establish its own rules of procedure, but these rules shall provide, inter alia, that:

(a) Twelve members shall constitute a quorum;

(b) Decisions of the Committee shall be made by a majority vote of the members present.

Article 40

1. The States Parties to the present Covenant undertake to submit reports on the measures they have adopted which give effect to the rights recognized herein and on the progress made in the enjoyment of those rights:

(a) Within one year of the entry into force of the present Covenant for the States Parties concerned;

(b) Thereafter whenever the Committee so requests.

2. All reports shall be submitted to the Secretary-General of the United Nations, who shall transmit them to the Committee for consideration. Reports shall indicate the factors and difficulties, if any, affecting the implementation of the present Covenant.

3. The Secretary-General of the United Nations may, after consultation with the Committee, transmit to the specialized agencies concerned copies of such parts of the reports as may fall within their field of competence.

4. The Committee shall study the reports submitted by the States Parties to the present Covenant. It shall transmit its reports, and such general comments as it may consider appropriate, to the States Parties. The Committee may also transmit to the Economic and Social Council these comments along with the copies of the reports it has received from States Parties to the present Covenant.

5. The States Parties to the present Covenant may submit to the Committee observations on any comments that may be made in accordance with paragraph 4 of this article.

Article 41

1. A State Party to the present Covenant may at any time declare under this article that it recognizes the competence of the Committee to receive and consider communications to the effect that a State Party claims that another State Party is not fulfilling its obligations under the present Covenant. Communications under this article may be received and considered only if submitted by a State Party which has made a declaration recognizing in regard to itself the competence of the Committee. No communication shall be received by the Committee if it concerns a State Party which has not made such a declaration. Communications received under this article shall be dealt with in accordance with the following procedure:

(a) If a State Party to the present Covenant considers that another State Party is not giving effect to the provisions of the present Covenant, it may, by written communication, bring the matter to the attention of that State Party. Within three months after the receipt of the communication the receiving State shall afford the State which sent the communication an explanation, or any other statement in writing clarifying the matter which should include, to the extent possible and pertinent, reference to domestic procedures and remedies taken, pending, or available in the matter;

(b) If the matter is not adjusted to the satisfaction of both States Parties concerned within six months after the receipt by the receiving State of the initial communication, either State shall have the right to refer the matter to the Committee, by notice given to the Committee and to the other State;

(c) The Committee shall deal with a matter referred to it only after it has ascertained that all available domestic remedies have been invoked and exhausted in the matter, in conformity with the generally recognized principles of international law. This shall not be the rule where the application of the remedies is unreasonably prolonged;

(d) The Committee shall hold closed meetings when examining communications under this article;

(e) Subject to the provisions of subparagraph (c), the Committee shall make available its good offices to the States Parties concerned with a view to a friendly solution of the matter on the basis of respect for human rights and fundamental freedoms as recognized in the present Covenant;

(f) In any matter referred to it, the Committee may call upon the States Parties concerned, referred to in subparagraph (b), to supply any relevant information;

(g) The States Parties concerned, referred to in subparagraph (b), shall have the right to be represented when the matter is being considered in the Committee and to make submissions orally and/or in writing;

(h) The Committee shall, within twelve months after the date of receipt of notice under subparagraph (b), submit a report:

(i) If a solution within the terms of subparagraph (e) is reached, the Committee shall confine its report to a brief statement of the facts and of the solution reached;

(ii) If a solution within the terms of subparagraph (e) is not reached, the Committee shall confine its report to a brief statement of the facts; the written submissions and record of the oral submissions made by the States Parties concerned shall be attached to the report. In every matter, the report shall be communicated to the States Parties concerned.

2. The provisions of this article shall come into force when ten States Parties to the present Covenant have made declarations under paragraph I of this article. Such declarations shall be deposited by the States Parties with the Secretary-General of the United Nations, who shall transmit copies thereof to the other States Parties. A declaration may be withdrawn at any time by notification to the Secretary-General. Such a withdrawal shall not prejudice the consideration of any matter which is the subject of a communication already transmitted under this article; no further communication by any State Party shall be received after the notification of withdrawal of the declaration has been received by the Secretary-General, unless the State Party concerned has made a new declaration.

Article 42

1. (a) If a matter referred to the Committee in accordance with article 41 is not resolved to the satisfaction of the States Parties concerned, the Committee may, with the prior consent of the States Parties concerned, appoint an ad hoc Conciliation Commission (hereinafter referred to as the Commission). The good offices of the Commission shall be made available to the States Parties concerned with a view to an amicable solution of the matter on the basis of respect for the present Covenant;

(b) The Commission shall consist of five persons acceptable to the States Parties concerned. If the States Parties concerned fail to reach agreement within three months on all or part of the composition of the Commission, the members of the Commission concerning whom no agreement has been reached shall be elected by secret ballot by a two-thirds majority vote of the Committee from among its members.

2. The members of the Commission shall serve in their personal capacity. They shall not be nationals of the States Parties concerned, or of a State not Party to the present Covenant, or of a State Party which has not made a declaration under article 41.

3. The Commission shall elect its own Chairman and adopt its own rules of procedure.

4. The meetings of the Commission shall normally be held at the Headquarters of the United Nations or at the United Nations Office at Geneva. However, they may be held at such other convenient places as the Commission may determine in consultation with the Secretary-General of the United Nations and the States Parties concerned.

5. The secretariat provided in accordance with article 36 shall also service the commissions appointed under this article.

6. The information received and collated by the Committee shall be made available to the Commission and the Commission may call upon the States Parties concerned to supply any other relevant information.

7. When the Commission has fully considered the matter, but in any event not later than twelve months after having been seized of the matter, it shall submit to the Chairman of the Committee a report for communication to the States Parties concerned:

(a) If the Commission is unable to complete its consideration of the matter within twelve months, it shall confine its report to a brief statement of the status of its consideration of the matter;

(b) If an amicable solution to the matter on tie basis of respect for human rights as recognized in the present Covenant is reached, the Commission shall confine its report to a brief statement of the facts and of the solution reached;

(c) If a solution within the terms of subparagraph (b) is not reached, the Commission's report shall embody its findings on all questions of fact relevant to the issues between the States Parties concerned, and its views on the possibilities of an amicable solution of the matter. This report shall also contain the written submissions and a record of the oral submissions made by the States Parties concerned;

(d) If the Commission's report is submitted under subparagraph (c), the States Parties concerned shall, within three months of the receipt of the report, notify the Chairman of the Committee whether or not they accept the contents of the report of the Commission.

8. The provisions of this article are without prejudice to the responsibilities of the Committee under article 41.

9. The States Parties concerned shall share equally all the expenses of the members of the Commission in accordance with estimates to be provided by the Secretary-General of the United Nations.

10. The Secretary-General of the United Nations shall be empowered to pay the expenses of the members of the Commission, if necessary, before reimbursement by the States Parties concerned, in accordance with paragraph 9 of this article.

Article 43

The members of the Committee, and of the ad hoc conciliation commissions which may be appointed under article 42, shall be entitled to the facilities, privileges and immunities of experts on mission for the United Nations as laid down in the relevant sections of the Convention on the Privileges and Immunities of the United Nations.

Article 44

The provisions for the implementation of the present Covenant shall apply without prejudice to the procedures prescribed in the field of human rights by or under the constituent instruments and the conventions of the United Nations and of the specialized agencies and shall not prevent the States Parties to the present Covenant from having recourse to other procedures for settling a dispute in accordance with general or special international agreements in force between them.

Article 45

The Committee shall submit to the General Assembly of the United Nations, through the Economic and Social Council, an annual report on its activities.

27.b Optional Protocol to the International Covenant on Civil and Political Rights

Date: 16 December 1966
Source: 999 UNTS 171
https://www.ohchr.org/Documents/ProfessionalInterest/ccpr-one.pdf

The States Parties to the present Protocol,

Considering that in order further to achieve the purposes of the International Covenant on Civil and Political Rights (hereinafter referred to as the Covenant) and the implementation of its provisions it would be appropriate to enable the Human Rights Committee set up in part IV of the Covenant (hereinafter referred to as the Committee) to receive and consider, as provided in the present Protocol, communications from individuals claiming to be victims of violations of any of the rights set forth in the Covenant.

Have agreed as follows:

Article 1

A State Party to the Covenant that becomes a Party to the present Protocol recognizes the competence of the Committee to receive and consider communications from individuals subject to its jurisdiction who claim to be victims of a violation by that State Party of any of the rights set forth in the Covenant. No communication shall be received by the Committee if it concerns a State Party to the Covenant which is not a Party to the present Protocol.

Article 2

Subject to the provisions of article 1, individuals who claim that any of their rights enumerated in the Covenant have been violated and who have exhausted all available domestic remedies may submit a written communication to the Committee for consideration.

Article 3

The Committee shall consider inadmissible any communication under the present Protocol which is anonymous, or which it considers to be an abuse of the right of submission of such communications or to be incompatible with the provisions of the Covenant.

Article 4

1. Subject to the provisions of article 3, the Committee shall bring any communications submitted to it under the present Protocol to the attention of the State Party to the present Protocol alleged to be violating any provision of the Covenant.
2. Within six months, the receiving State shall submit to the Committee written explanations or statements clarifying the matter and the remedy, if any, that may have been taken by that State.

Article 5

1. The Committee shall consider communications received under the present Protocol in the light of all written information made available to it by the individual and by the State Party concerned.

2. The Committee shall not consider any communication from an individual unless it has ascertained that:

(a) The same matter is not being examined under another procedure of international investigation or settlement;

(b) The individual has exhausted all available domestic remedies. This shall not be the rule where the application of the remedies is unreasonably prolonged.

3. The Committee shall hold closed meetings when examining communications under the present Protocol.

4. The Committee shall forward its views to the State Party concerned and to the individual.

Article 6

The Committee shall include in its annual report under article 45 of the Covenant a summary of its activities under the present Protocol.

Article 7

Pending the achievement of the objectives of resolution 1514(XV) adopted by the General Assembly of the United Nations on 14 December 1960 concerning the Declaration on the Granting of Independence to Colonial Countries and Peoples, the provisions of the present Protocol shall in no way limit the right of petition granted to these peoples by the Charter of the United Nations and other international conventions and instruments under the United Nations and its specialized agencies.

Article 8

1. The present Protocol is open for signature by any State which has signed the Covenant.

2. The present Protocol is subject to ratification by any State which has ratified or acceded to the Covenant. Instruments of ratification shall be deposited with the Secretary- General of the United Nations.

3. The present Protocol shall be open to accession by any State which has ratified or acceded to the Covenant.

4. Accession shall be effected by the deposit of an instrument of accession with the Secretary-General of the United Nations.

5. The Secretary-General of the United Nations shall inform all States which have signed the present Protocol or acceded to it of the deposit of each instrument of ratification or accession.

Article 9

1. Subject to the entry into force of the Covenant, the present Protocol shall enter into force three months after the date of the deposit with the Secretary-General of the United Nations of the tenth instrument of ratification or instrument of accession.

2. For each State ratifying the present Protocol or acceding to it after the deposit of the tenth instrument of ratification or instrument of accession, the present Protocol shall enter into force three months after the date of the deposit of its own instrument of ratification or instrument of accession.

Article 10

The provisions of the present Protocol shall extend to all parts of federal States without any limitations or exceptions.

Article 11

1. Any State Party to the present Protocol may propose an amendment and file it with the Secretary-General of the United Nations. The Secretary-General shall thereupon communicate any proposed amendments to the States Parties to the present Protocol with a request that they notify him whether they favour a conference of States Parties for the purpose of considering and voting upon the proposal. In the event that at least one third of the States Parties favours such a conference, the Secretary-General shall convene the conference under the auspices of the United Nations. Any amendment adopted by a majority of the States Parties present and voting at the conference shall be submitted to the General Assembly of the United Nations for approval.

2. Amendments shall come into force when they have been approved by the General Assembly of the United Nations and accepted by a two-thirds majority of the States Parties to the present Protocol in accordance with their respective constitutional processes.

3. When amendments come into force, they shall be binding on those States Parties which have accepted them, other States Parties still being bound by the provisions of the present Protocol and any earlier amendment which they have accepted.

Article 12

1. Any State Party may denounce the present Protocol at any time by written notification addressed to the Secretary-General of the United Nations. Denunciation shall take effect three months after the date of receipt of the notification by the Secretary-General.

2. Denunciation shall be without prejudice to the continued application of the provisions of the present Protocol to any communication submitted under article 2 before the effective date of denunciation.

Article 13

Irrespective of the notifications made under article 8, paragraph 5, of the present Protocol, the Secretary-General of the United Nations shall inform all States referred to in article 48, paragraph I, of the Covenant of the following particulars:

(a) Signatures, ratifications and accessions under article 8;

(b) The date of the entry into force of the present Protocol under article 9 and the date of the entry into force of any amendments under article 11;

(c) Denunciations under article 12.

Article 14

1. The present Protocol, of which the Chinese, English, French, Russian and Spanish texts are equally authentic, shall be deposited in the archives of the United Nations.

2. The Secretary-General of the United Nations shall transmit certified copies of the present Protocol to all States referred to in article 48 of the Covenant.

27.c Rules of Procedure of the Human Rights Committee

Date: 22 September 2005
Source: UN Doc CCPR/C/3/Rev.12
https://docstore.ohchr.org/SelfServices/FilesHandler.ashx?enc=6QkG1d%2fPPRiCAqhKb7yhspSfzoplnqcaRnZEWMKfe1tSjisL%2bhNIzkeCc5clygMh1XamAcX%2bzhX5iH9rw32CjJiNv7NZevXmcJHbSF9HqoPw%2fAlNZAeEcyCPymBEAkMs

PART I. GENERAL RULES

I. SESSIONS

Rule 1

The Human Rights Committee shall hold sessions as may be required for the satisfactory performance of its functions in accordance with the International Covenant on Civil and Political Rights.

Rule 2

1. The Committee shall normally hold three regular sessions each year.
2. Regular sessions of the Committee shall be convened at dates decided by the Committee in consultation with the Secretary-General of the United Nations, taking into account the calendar of conferences and meetings.

Rule 3

1. Special sessions of the Committee shall be convened by decision of the Committee. When the Committee is not in session, the Chair may convene special sessions after consulting with the other officers of the Committee. The Chair of the Committee shall also convene special sessions at the request of a majority of the members of the Committee and may do so at the request of a State party to the Covenant.
2. Special sessions shall be convened as soon as possible at a date fixed by the Chair in consultation with the Secretary-General and with the other officers of the Committee, taking into account the calendar of conferences as approved by the General Assembly.

Rule 4

The Secretary-General shall notify the members of the Committee of the date and place of each session. Such notification shall be sent, in the case of a regular session, at least 6 weeks in advance and, in the case of a special session, at least 18 days in advance.

Rule 5

Sessions of the Committee shall normally be held at United Nations Headquarters or at the United Nations Office at Geneva. Another place for a session may be designated by the Committee in consultation with the Secretary-General.

II. AGENDA

Rule 6

The provisional agenda for each regular session shall be prepared by the Secretary-General in consultation with the Chair of the Committee, in conformity with the relevant provisions of the Covenant and of the first Optional Protocol to the International Covenant on Civil and Political Rights, and shall include:

(a) Any item the inclusion of which has been decided upon by the Committee at a previous session;
(b) Any item proposed by the Chair of the Committee;
(c) Any item proposed by a State party to the Covenant;
(d) Any item proposed by a member of the Committee;
(e) Any item proposed by the Secretary-General relating to functions of the Secretary-General under the Covenant, the Optional Protocol or the present rules.

Rule 7

The provisional agenda for a special session of the Committee shall consist only of those items which are proposed for consideration at that special session.

Rule 8

The first item on the provisional agenda for any session shall be the adoption of the agenda, except for the election of officers when required under rule 16 of the present rules.

Rule 9

During a session, the Committee may revise the agenda and may, as appropriate, add, defer or delete items.

Rule 10

The provisional agenda and the basic documents relating to each item appearing thereon shall be transmitted to the members of the Committee by the Secretary-General, who shall endeavour to have the documents transmitted to the members at least six weeks prior to the opening of the session.

III. MEMBERS OF THE COMMITTEE

Rule 11

The members of the Committee shall be the 18 persons elected in accordance with articles 28 to 34 of the Covenant.

Rule 12

The term of office of the members of the Committee elected shall begin on the day after the date of expiry of the term of office of the members whom they replace.

Rule 13

1. If, in the unanimous opinion of the other members, a member of the Committee has ceased to carry out his or her functions for any reason other than absence of a temporary character, the Chair of the Committee shall notify the Secretary-General, who shall then declare the seat of that member to be vacant.

2. In the event of the death or the resignation of a member of the Committee, the Chair shall immediately notify the Secretary-General, who shall declare the seat vacant from the date of death or the date on which the resignation takes effect. The resignation of a member of the Committee shall be notified by that member in writing directly to the Chair or to the Secretary-General and action shall be taken to declare the seat of that member vacant only after such notification has been received.

3. A vacancy declared in accordance with paragraphs 1 and 2 of the present rule shall be dealt with in accordance with article 34 of the Covenant.

4. Any member of the Committee elected to fill a vacancy declared in accordance with article 33 of the Covenant shall hold office for the remainder of the term of the member who vacated the seat on the Committee under the provisions of that article.

Rule 14

Before assuming duties as a member, each member of the Committee shall make the following solemn undertaking in open Committee:

> "I solemnly undertake to discharge my duties as a member of the Human Rights Committee independently, impartially and conscientiously."

Rule 15

The guidelines on the independence and impartiality of members of the human rights treaty bodies (the Addis Ababa guidelines), excepting the preamble, replace the Committee's own 1998 guidelines on the exercise of the functions of the Committee.

IV. OFFICERS

Rule 16

The Committee shall elect from among its members a Chair, three Vice-Chairs and a Rapporteur, who is responsible for preparing the Committee's annual report. In electing its officers, the Committee shall give consideration to equitable geographical distribution and appropriate gender balance and, to the extent possible, rotation among members.

Rule 17

The Chair, the three Vice-Chairs and the Rapporteur shall constitute the Bureau of the Committee. The Chair shall consult with the other members of the Bureau on matters relating to the organization of work of the Committee, and the Bureau shall determine the agenda for meetings dedicated to reviewing the Committee's methods of work and shall approve the programme of work for future sessions of the Committee. All recommendations and decisions adopted by the Bureau shall be notified to the Committee and, where requested by any member of the Committee, shall be reviewed by the Committee, which may approve or reject them.

Rule 18

The officers of the Committee shall be elected for a term of two years. They shall be eligible for re-election. None of them, however, may hold office after ceasing to be a member of the Committee.

Rule 19

1. The Chair shall perform the functions conferred upon him or her by the Covenant, the rules of procedure and the decisions of the Committee. In the exercise of those functions, the Chair shall remain under the authority of the Committee and shall consult as broadly as possible with the officers of the Committee (Bureau) and other members of the Committee.

2. The Chair shall represent the Committee at United Nations meetings in which the Committee is officially invited to participate. If the Chair is unable to represent the Committee at such a meeting, he or she may designate another officer of the Committee or, if no officer is available, another member of the Committee, to attend on his or her behalf.

Rule 20

If during a session the Chair is unable to be present at a meeting or any part thereof, the Chair, or if he or she is unable to do so, the remaining members of the Bureau, shall designate one of the Vice-Chairs to act as Chair.

Rule 21

A Vice-Chair acting as Chair shall have the same powers and duties as the Chair.

Rule 22

If any of the officers of the Committee ceases to serve or declares himself or herself unable to continue serving as a member of the Committee or for any reason is no longer able to act as an officer, a new officer shall be elected for the unexpired term of the predecessor.

Rule 23

When the Committee is working in two chambers, the Chair shall act as Chair of one of the chambers, and one of the Vice-Chairs shall act as Chair of the other chamber. The Chair, in consultation with the Bureau, will designate the Vice-Chair who will chair the second chamber.

V. SECRETARIAT

Rule 24

1. The secretariat of the Committee and of such subsidiary bodies as may be established by the Committee shall be provided by the Secretary-General.

2. The Secretary-General shall provide the necessary staff and facilities for the effective performance of the functions of the Committee under the Covenant.

Rule 25

The Secretary-General or a representative of the Secretary-General shall attend all meetings of the Committee. Subject to rule 40 of the present rules, the Secretary-General or the representative may make oral or written statements at meetings of the Committee or its subsidiary bodies.

Rule 26

The Secretary-General shall be responsible for all the necessary arrangements for meetings of the Committee and its subsidiary bodies.

Rule 27

The Secretary-General shall be responsible for informing the members of the Committee without delay of any questions which may be brought before it for consideration.

Rule 28

Before any proposal that involves expenditure is approved by the Committee or by any of its subsidiary bodies, the Secretary-General shall prepare and circulate to the members of the Committee or subsidiary body, as early as possible, an estimate of the cost involved in the proposal. It shall be the duty of the Chair to draw the attention of members to this estimate and to invite discussion on it when the proposal is considered by the Committee or a subsidiary body.

VI. LANGUAGES

Rule 29

Arabic, Chinese, English, French, Russian and Spanish shall be the official languages of the Committee. The working languages of the Committee, relating both to translation of documentation and interpretation, will be determined by the Committee depending on the membership of the Committee. This is without prejudice to the right of each State party and authors of communications to provide information to the Committee in any of the six official languages of the United Nations.

Rule 30

Interpretation shall be provided by the Secretariat of the United Nations. Speeches made in any of the working languages shall be interpreted into the other working languages. Speeches made in an official language shall be interpreted into the working languages.

Rule 31

Any speaker addressing the Committee and using a language other than one of the official languages shall normally provide for interpretation into one of the working languages. Interpretation into the other working languages may be based on the interpretation given in the first working language.

Rule 32

Summary records of the meetings of the Committee shall be drawn up in the working languages, as determined by the Committee.

Rule 33

All official documents and formal decisions of the Committee shall be made available in the official languages and in accessible formats.

Rule 34

Any draft document relating to the Committee's activities under the Covenant and requiring discussion and adoption by the Committee must be translated into the working languages of the Committee. Such documents include any document relating to reporting (such as draft concluding observations, draft lists of issues, draft lists of issues prior to reporting and draft reports on follow-up to concluding observations), individual and inter-State communications (such as draft decisions and Views and draft reports on follow-up to Views), legal interpretations (such as draft general comments) and working methods and other matters (such as draft working methods, draft annual reports, draft rules of procedure and draft guidelines).

VII. MEETINGS OF THE COMMITTEE

Rule 35

The meetings of the Committee and its subsidiary bodies shall be held in public unless the Committee decides otherwise or it appears from the relevant provisions of the Covenant or the Optional Protocol that the meeting should be held in private. The adoption of concluding observations under article 40 of the Covenant shall take place in closed meetings.

Rule 36

At the close of each private meeting, the Committee or its subsidiary body may issue a communiqué.

VIII. RECORDS

Rule 37

Summary records of the public and private meetings of the Committee and its subsidiary bodies shall be prepared by the Secretariat. They shall be distributed as soon as possible to the members of the Committee and to any others participating in the meeting. All such participants may, within six working days after receipt of the record of the meeting, submit corrections to the Secretariat. Any disagreement concerning such corrections shall be settled by the Chair of the Committee or the Chair of the subsidiary body to which the record relates or, in the case of continued disagreement, by decision of the Committee or of the subsidiary body.

Rule 38

1. The summary records of public meetings of the Committee in their final form and recordings of public meetings shall be accessible to the public unless, in exceptional circumstances, the Committee decides otherwise.

2. The summary records of private meetings shall be distributed to the members of the Committee and to other participants in the meetings. They may be made available to others upon the decision of the Committee at such time and under such circumstances as the Committee may decide.

IX. CONDUCT OF BUSINESS

Rule 39

Twelve members of the Committee shall constitute a quorum for plenary meetings of the Committee. The Committee may decide to conduct meetings dedicated to the examination of State reports or communications in chambers and determine, in that case, the quorum requirements for such meetings.

Rule 40

The Chair shall declare the opening and closing of each meeting of the Committee, direct the discussion, ensure observance of the present rules, accord the right to speak, put questions to the vote and announce decisions. The Chair, subject to the present rules, shall have control over the proceedings of the Committee and over the maintenance of order at its meetings. The Chair may, in the course of the discussion of an item, propose to the Committee the limitation of the time to be allowed to speakers, the limitation of the number of times each speaker may speak on any question and the closure of the list of speakers. The Chair shall rule on points of order and shall have the power to propose adjournment or closure of the debate, or adjournment or suspension of a meeting. Debate shall be confined to the question before the Committee and the Chair may call a speaker to order if that speaker's remarks are not relevant to the subject under discussion.

Rule 41

During the discussion of any matter, a member may, at any time, raise a point of order and the point of order shall immediately be decided by the Chair in accordance with the rules of procedure. Any appeal against the ruling of the Chair shall immediately be put to the vote, and the ruling of the Chair shall stand unless overruled by a majority of the members present. A member may not, in raising a point of order, speak on the substance of the matter under discussion.

Rule 42

During the discussion of any matter, a member may make a motion for the adjournment of the debate on the item under discussion. In addition to the proposer of the motion, one member may speak in favour of and one against the motion, after which the motion shall immediately be put to the vote.

Rule 43

The Committee may limit the time allowed to each speaker on any question. When debate is limited and a speaker exceeds his or her allotted time, the Chair shall call that speaker to order without delay.

Rule 44

1. When the debate on an item is concluded because there are no other speakers, the Chair shall declare the debate closed. Such closure shall have the same effect as closure by the consent of the Committee.

2. A member may, at any time, make a motion for the closure of the debate on the item under discussion, regardless of whether any other member or representative has signified a wish to speak. Permission to speak on the closure of the debate shall be accorded only to two speakers opposing the closure, after which the motion shall immediately be put to the vote.

Rule 45

During the discussion of any matter, a member may make a motion for the suspension or the adjournment of the meeting. No discussion on such motions shall be permitted, and they shall immediately be put to the vote.

Rule 46

Subject to rule 41 of the present rules, the following motions shall have precedence, in the following order, over all other proposals or motions before the meeting:

(a) To suspend the meeting;
(b) To adjourn the meeting;
(c) To adjourn the debate on the item under discussion;
(d) For the closure of the debate on the item under discussion.

Rule 47

Unless otherwise decided by the Committee, proposals and substantive amendments or motions submitted by members shall be introduced in writing and handed to the Secretariat, and their consideration shall, if so requested by any member, be deferred until the next meeting on the following day, or to a later date decided by the Committee.

Rule 48

Subject to rule 46 of the present rules, any motion by a member calling for a decision on the competence of the Committee to adopt a proposal submitted to it shall be put to the vote immediately before a vote is taken on the proposal in question.

Rule 49

A motion may be withdrawn by its proposer at any time before voting on it has commenced, provided that the motion has not been amended. A motion which has thus been withdrawn may be reintroduced by another member.

Rule 50

When a proposal has been adopted or rejected, it may not be reconsidered at the same session unless the Committee so decides. Permission to speak on a motion to reconsider shall be accorded only to two speakers in favour of the motion and two speakers opposing the motion, after which it shall immediately be put to the vote.

X. VOTING

Rule 51

Each member of the Committee shall have one vote.

Rule 52

Except as otherwise provided in the Covenant or elsewhere in the present rules, decisions of the Committee shall be made by a majority of the members present.

Rule 53

If a vote is equally divided on a matter addressed in this section, other than an election, the proposal shall be regarded as rejected.

Rule 54

Subject to rule 60 of the present rules, the Committee shall normally vote by show of hands, except that any member may request a roll call, which shall then be taken in the alphabetical order of the names of the members of the Committee, beginning with the member whose name is drawn by lot by the Chair.

Rule 55

The vote of each member participating in a roll call shall be inserted in the record.

Rule 56

After the voting has commenced, it shall not be interrupted unless a member raises a point of order in connection with the actual conduct of the voting. Brief statements by members consisting solely of explanations of their votes may be permitted by the Chair before the voting has commenced or after the voting has been completed.

Rule 57

Parts of a proposal shall be voted on separately if a member requests that the proposal be divided. Those parts of the proposal which have been approved shall then be put to the vote as a whole; if all the operative parts of a proposal have been rejected, the proposal shall be considered to have been rejected as a whole.

Rule 58

1. When an amendment to a proposal is moved for, the amendment shall be voted on first. When two or more amendments to a proposal are moved, the Committee shall first vote on the amendment furthest removed in substance from the original proposal and then on the amendment next furthest removed therefrom and so on until all the amendments have been put to the vote. If one or more amendments are adopted, the amended proposal shall then be voted upon.

2. A motion is considered an amendment to a proposal if it adds to, deletes from or revises part of that proposal.

Rule 59

1. If two or more proposals relate to the same question, the Committee shall, unless it decides otherwise, vote on the proposals in the order in which they have been submitted.

2. The Committee may, after each vote on a proposal, decide whether to vote on the next proposal.

3. Any motions requiring that no decision be taken on the substance of such proposals shall, however, be considered as previous questions and shall be put to the vote before them.

XI. ELECTIONS

Rule 60

Elections shall be held by secret ballot, unless the Committee decides otherwise in the case of an election to fill a place for which there is only one candidate.

Rule 61

1. When only one person or member is to be elected and no candidate obtains the required majority in the first ballot, a second ballot shall be taken, which shall be restricted to the two candidates who obtained the greatest number of votes.

2. If the second ballot is inconclusive and a majority vote of members present is required, a third ballot shall be taken in which votes may be cast for any eligible candidate. If the third ballot is inconclusive, the next ballot shall be restricted to the two candidates who obtained the greatest number of votes in the third ballot and so on, with unrestricted and restricted ballots alternating, until a person or member is elected.

3. If the second ballot is inconclusive and a two-thirds majority is required, the balloting shall be continued until one candidate secures the necessary two-thirds majority. In the next three ballots, votes may be cast for any eligible candidate. If three such unrestricted ballots are inconclusive, the next three ballots shall be restricted to the two candidates who obtained the greatest number of votes in the third unrestricted ballot, and the following three ballots shall be unrestricted, and so on until a person or member is elected.

Rule 62

When two or more elective places are to be filled at one time under the same conditions, those candidates obtaining the required majority in the first ballot shall be elected. If the number of candidates obtaining such majority is less than the number of persons or members to be elected, there shall be additional ballots to fill the remaining places, the voting being restricted to the candidates obtaining the greatest number of votes in the previous ballot, whose number shall not be more than twice the number of places remaining to be filled; however, after the third inconclusive ballot, votes may be cast for any eligible candidate. If three such unrestricted ballots are inconclusive, the next three ballots shall be restricted to the candidates who obtained the greatest number of votes in the third of the unrestricted ballots, whose number shall not be more than twice the number of places remaining to be filled; the following three ballots shall be unrestricted, and so on until all the places have been filled.

XII. SUBSIDIARY BODIES

Rule 63

1. The Committee may, taking into account the provisions of the Covenant and the first Optional Protocol, set up such subcommittees and other ad hoc subsidiary bodies as it deems necessary for the performance of its functions and define their composition and powers.

2. Subject to the provisions of the Covenant and the Optional Protocol and unless the Committee decides otherwise, each subsidiary body shall elect its own officers and may adopt its own rules of procedure. Failing such rules, the present rules of procedure shall apply mutatis mutandis.

3. The Committee may also designate one or more of its members as rapporteurs to assist it in any manner in which the Committee may decide, including by making recommendations to the Committee.

XIII. ANNUAL REPORT OF THE COMMITTEE

Rule 64

As prescribed in article 45 of the Covenant, the Committee shall submit to the General Assembly of the United Nations an annual report on its activities, including a summary of its activities under the Optional Protocol as prescribed in article 6 thereof. The report shall be prepared by the Bureau member designated as Committee Rapporteur.

XIV. INFORMATION AND DOCUMENTATION

Rule 65

1. Without prejudice to the provisions of rule 38 of the present rules and subject to paragraphs 2 and 3 of the present rule, reports, formal decisions and all other official documents of the Committee and its subsidiary bodies shall be documents of general distribution unless the Committee decides otherwise.

2. All reports, formal decisions and other official documents of the Committee and its subsidiary bodies relating to articles 41 and 42 of the Covenant and to the Optional Protocol shall be distributed by the Secretariat to all members of the Committee, to the States parties concerned and, as may be decided by the Committee, to members of its subsidiary bodies and to others concerned.

3. Reports and additional information submitted by States parties pursuant to article 40 of the Covenant shall be documents of general distribution. The same applies to other information provided by a State party unless the State party concerned requests otherwise.

PART II. RULES RELATING TO THE FUNCTION OF THE COMMITTEE

XV. REPORTS FROM STATES PARTIES UNDER ARTICLE 40 OF THE COVENANT

Rule 66

1. The States parties to the Covenant shall submit reports on the measures they have adopted which give effect to the rights recognized in the Covenant and on the progress made in the enjoyment of those rights. Reports shall indicate the factors and difficulties, if any, affecting the implementation of the Covenant.

2. Requests for submission of a report under article 40 (1) (b) of the Covenant may be made in accordance with the periodicity decided by the Committee or at any other time the Committee may deem appropriate. In particular, the Committee may request a State to submit a special report in situations requiring immediate attention to appropriately address serious violations of the Covenant. In the case of an exceptional situation when the Committee is not in session, a request may be made through the Chair, acting in consultation with the members of the Committee.

3. Whenever the Committee requests States parties to submit reports under article 40 (1) (b) of the Covenant, it shall determine the dates by which such reports shall be submitted.

4. The Committee may, through the Secretary-General, inform the States parties of its wishes regarding the form and content of the reports to be submitted under article 40 of the Covenant.

Rule 67

1. The Secretary-General may, after consultation with the Committee, transmit to the specialized agencies concerned copies of such parts of the reports of States members of those agencies as may fall within their field of competence.

2. The Committee may invite the specialized agencies to which the Secretary-General has transmitted parts of the reports to submit comments on those parts within such time limits as it may specify.

Rule 68

1. The Committee shall, through the Secretary-General, notify the States parties of the opening date, duration and place of the session at which their respective reports will be examined. Representatives of the States parties are expected to be present at the meetings of the Committee when their reports are examined. The Committee shall, during the meetings in which State reports are examined, seek further information about the implementation of the Covenant from the State representatives present at the meeting. Such representatives should be able to answer questions which may be put to them by the Committee and make statements on reports already submitted by the State party concerned. They may also submit additional information from that State party during the meeting or in a brief written memorandum submitted within two working days after the meeting.

2. If a State party has submitted a report but fails to send any representative to the session at which it has been notified that its report will be examined, the Committee may, at its discretion, notify the State party through the Secretary-General that at the session originally specified, or at a later one that is indicated, it intends to examine the report and present its concluding observations under rule 74, paragraph 1, of the present rules. The concluding observations will specify the date of the following periodic report that shall be submitted under rule 66 of the present rules.

Rule 69

The Committee may conduct examinations of reports in plenary or in chambers, according to the decision of the Committee. The concluding observations composed pursuant to rule 74, paragraph 1, shall be approved in all cases by the plenary of the Committee.

Rule 70

1. At each session the Secretary-General shall notify the Committee of all cases of non-submission of reports or additional information requested under rules 66, 72 and 75 of the present rules. In such cases the Committee may transmit to the State party concerned, through the Secretary-General, a reminder concerning the submission of the report or additional information.

2. If, after the reminder referred to in paragraph 1 of the present rule, the State party does not submit the report or additional information required under rules 66, 72 and 75 of the present rules, the Committee shall so state in the annual report which it submits to the General Assembly.

Rule 71

1. In cases where the Committee has been notified under rule 70, paragraph 1, of the present rules of the failure of a State to submit under rule 66, paragraph 3, any report under article 40 (1) (a) or (b) of the Covenant and has sent the corresponding reminders to the State party, the Committee may, at its discretion, notify the State party through the Secretary-General that it intends, on a date or at a session specified in the notification, to examine in a public session the measures taken by the State party to give effect to the rights recognized in the Covenant, and to proceed by adopting concluding observations.

2. Where the Committee acts under paragraph 1 of the present rule, it shall transmit to the State party, in advance of the date or session specified, a list of issues, indicating the topics relating to the implementation of the Covenant on which the Committee wishes the State to provide specific information, in accordance with rule 73, paragraph 1, of the present rules.

3. The concluding observations shall be communicated to the State party, in accordance with rule 74, paragraph 1, of the present rules, and made public. The State party shall present its next report within two years of the adoption of the concluding observations.

Rule 72

1. When considering a report submitted by a State party under article 40 of the Covenant, the Committee shall first satisfy itself that the report provides all the information required under rule 66 of the present rules.

2. If a report of a State party under article 40 of the Covenant does not, in the opinion of the Committee, contain sufficient information, the Committee may request that State

to furnish the additional information which is required, indicating by what date that information should be submitted.

Rule 73

1. In order to facilitate a constructive dialogue between the Committee and the representatives of the State party which is to be reviewed, the Committee shall prepare a list of issues prior to reporting, in accordance with the simplified reporting procedure, and request the State party to provide replies by a specified date. The replies of the State party to the list of issues prior to reporting shall constitute for the period under review the State party report required under article 40 of the Covenant. The meeting with representatives of the State party shall take place in principle within 12 months of the date on which its replies to the list of issues prior to reporting were submitted to the Committee.

2. States parties may notify the Secretary-General that they do not wish to opt for the simplified reporting procedure. In that case, the State party should submit an initial or periodic report by a specified date. The Committee shall then, prior to the meeting at which the State party report is to be reviewed, forward to it a list of issues indicating the topics relating to the implementation of the Covenant on which the Committee wishes the State party to provide further specific information. The State party will be invited to submit its responses to the list of issues in writing by a specified date, prior to the meeting with the Committee.

Rule 74

1. On the basis of its examination of any report or information supplied by a State party, the Committee may make appropriate concluding observations which shall be communicated to the State party, together with notification of the date by which the next report under article 40 of the Covenant shall be submitted.

2. No member of the Committee shall participate in the examination of State party reports or the discussion and adoption of concluding observations if they involve the State party in respect of which he or she was elected to the Committee.

Rule 75

1. The Committee may request the State party to give priority to certain aspects of its concluding observations and, thus, request the State party to provide the Committee with follow-up information by a specified date. For that purpose, the Committee may designate one or more of its members as rapporteurs to follow up with the State party on its implementation of the concluding observations.

2. The follow-up rapporteur(s) shall assess the information provided by the State party and from other sources and report to the Committee on his or her activities. The Committee may set guidelines for such assessments.

XVI. GENERAL COMMENTS

Rule 76

1. The Committee may decide to prepare and adopt general comments on specific topics addressing aspects of the Covenant or its Optional Protocols with a view to assisting States parties in fulfilling their obligations under the Covenant and its Optional Protocols.

2. Before work on the formulation of a general comment begins, the Chair shall invite members of the Committee to propose suitable topics for a general comment.

The Committee shall select from among the proposals a topic and appoint one or more members of the Committee to serve as rapporteur(s) entrusted with facilitating the preparation of the general comment.

3. The rapporteur(s) will submit an initial proposal for a general comment to the Committee, which will then discuss the proposal and approve it in first reading, in a preliminary manner, with any necessary changes.

4. The preliminary draft of the general comment will be circulated to the States parties and other relevant stakeholders for comments. The Committee will discuss, in a second reading, any further changes in the general comment. It shall then consider formally adopting the general comment.

Rule 77

The Committee shall communicate to States parties, through the Secretary-General, the general comments it has adopted.

XVII. PROCEDURE FOR THE CONSIDERATION OF COMMUNICATIONS RECEIVED UNDER ARTICLE 41 OF THE COVENANT

Rule 78

1. A communication under article 41 of the Covenant may be referred to the Committee by either State party concerned by notice given in accordance with paragraph 1 (b) of that article.

2. The notice referred to in paragraph 1 of the present rule shall contain or be accompanied by information regarding:

(a) Steps taken to seek adjustment of the matter in accordance with article 41 (1) (a) and (b) of the Covenant, including the text of the initial communication and of any subsequent written explanations or statements by the States parties concerned which are pertinent to the matter;

(b) Steps taken to exhaust domestic remedies;

(c) Any other procedure of international investigation or settlement resorted to by the States parties concerned.

Rule 79

The Secretary-General shall maintain and publish a permanent register of all communications received by the Committee under article 41 of the Covenant.

Rule 80

The Secretary-General shall inform the members of the Committee without delay of any notice given under rule 78 of the present rules and shall transmit to them as soon as possible copies of the notice and relevant information.

Rule 81

1. The Committee shall examine communications under article 41 of the Covenant at closed meetings.

2. The Committee may, after consultation with the States parties concerned, issue communiqués, through the Secretary-General, for the use of the information media and the general public regarding the activities of the Committee at its closed meetings.

Rule 82

A communication shall not be considered by the Committee unless:

(a) Both States parties concerned have made declarations under article 41 (1) of the Covenant that are applicable to the communication;

(b) The time limit prescribed in article 41 (1) (b) of the Covenant has expired;

(c) The Committee has ascertained that all available domestic remedies have been invoked and exhausted in the matter in conformity with the generally recognized principles of international law, or that the application of the remedies is unreasonably prolonged.

Rule 83

Subject to the provisions of rule 78 of the present rules, the Committee shall proceed to make its good offices available to the States parties concerned with a view to a friendly resolution of the matter on the basis of respect for human rights and fundamental freedoms as recognized in the Covenant.

Rule 84

The Committee may, through the Secretary-General, request the States parties concerned, or either of them, to submit additional information or observations orally or in writing. The Committee shall indicate a time limit for the submission of such written information or observations.

Rule 85

1. The States parties concerned shall have the right to be represented when the matter is being considered in the Committee and to make submissions orally and/or in writing.

2. The Committee shall, through the Secretary-General, notify the States parties concerned as early as possible of the opening date, duration and place of the session at which the matter will be examined.

3. The procedure for making oral and/or written submissions shall be decided by the Committee, after consultation with the States parties concerned.

Rule 86

1. Within 12 months of the date on which the Committee received the notice referred to in rule 78 of the present rules, the Committee shall adopt a report in accordance with article 41 (1) (h) of the Covenant.

2. The provisions of paragraph 1 of rule 85 shall not apply to the deliberations of the Committee concerning the adoption of the report.

3. The Committee's report shall be communicated, through the Secretary-General, to the States parties concerned.

Rule 87

If a matter referred to the Committee in accordance with article 41 of the Covenant is not resolved to the satisfaction of the States parties concerned, the Committee may, with their prior consent, proceed to apply the procedure prescribed in article 42 of the Covenant.

XVIII. PROCEDURE FOR THE CONSIDERATION OF COMMUNICATIONS RECEIVED UNDER THE OPTIONAL PROTOCOL

A. Transmission of communications to the Committee

Rule 88

1. The Secretary-General shall bring to the attention of the Committee, in accordance with the present rules, communications which are or appear to be submitted for consideration by the Committee under article 1 of the Optional Protocol.

2. The Secretary-General, when necessary, may request clarification from the author of a communication as to whether the author wishes to have the communication submitted to the Committee for consideration under the Optional Protocol. In case there is still doubt as to the wish of the author, the Committee shall be seized of the communication.

3. No communication shall be received by the Committee if it (a) concerns a State which is not a party to the Optional Protocol; (b) is not in writing; or (c) is anonymous.

4. Communications shall be submitted in one of the official languages of the Committee indicated in rule 29, preferably the official language of the United Nations most commonly used in the State party against which the communication is addressed.

Rule 89

1. The Secretary-General shall maintain a permanent record of all communications submitted under the Optional Protocol.

2. The Secretary-General shall prepare a list of the communications registered by the Committee, together with a brief summary of their contents, and will make it public while keeping the author's name confidential.

3. The full text of any registered communication may be made available in the language of submission to any member of the Committee upon request by that member.

Rule 90

1. The Secretary-General may request clarification or additional information from the author of a communication, including:

(a) The name, address, date of birth and occupation of the author and the verification of the author's identity;

(b) The name of the State party against which the communication is directed;

(c) The object of the communication;

(d) The provision or provisions of the Covenant alleged to have been violated;

(e) The facts of the claim and evidence to substantiate them;

(f) Steps taken by the author to exhaust domestic remedies;

(g) The extent to which the same matter is being or has been examined under another procedure of international investigation or settlement.

2. When requesting clarification or information, the Secretary-General shall indicate an appropriate time limit to the author of the communication with a view to avoiding undue delays in the procedure under the Optional Protocol.

3. The Committee may approve a questionnaire for the purpose of requesting the above-mentioned information from the author of the communication.

Rule 91

Communications may be submitted by or on behalf of one or several individuals, whose names should be provided. Where a communication is submitted on behalf of one or several individuals, this shall be with their consent, unless the author(s) can justify acting on their behalf without such consent.

B. Registration of communications and submission of observations and comments by the parties

Rule 92

1. As soon as possible after the communication has been received, the Committee, through its special rapporteur designated under rule 107, paragraph 2, of the present rules, shall decide whether the communication brought to its attention should be registered.

2. After the decision to register has been taken, the communication shall be brought to the attention of the State party concerned, with a request that the State party submit a written reply within six months.

3. The special rapporteur may decide that in order to reach a determination on the admissibility of a registered communication, its transmission to the State party is not required. However, the decision shall be transmitted to the Committee plenary for discussion. Inadmissibility decisions on registered cases can be taken by the Committee without prior transmission of the communication to the State concerned for observations.

4. A request addressed to a State party under paragraph 2 of the present rule shall include a statement of the fact that such a request does not imply that any decision has been reached on the question of admissibility or the merits of the communication.

5. Within six months of receipt of the Committee's request under the present rule, the State party shall submit to the Committee written explanations or statements that shall relate both to the admissibility of the communication and its merits, as well as to any remedy that may have been provided in the matter, unless the Committee or the special rapporteur decides, in view of the circumstances of the case and any remedy requested by the author, to request a written reply that relates only to the question of admissibility. A State party that has been requested to submit a written reply that relates only to the question of admissibility is not precluded thereby from submitting, within the six-month period, a written reply that relates to both the admissibility and the merits of the communication.

6. The author may submit a reply and the State party a rejoinder.

7. Upon the request of one of the parties, additional written submissions may be authorized by the special rapporteur, on an exceptional basis, with due consideration given to the circumstances of the case.

8. The reply and the rejoinder, and additional submissions that may be authorized by the special rapporteur, shall focus on addressing the issues still in contention.

9. Notwithstanding the six-month period for the State party's first submission, as set out in article 4 of the Optional Protocol, the Committee will establish a definite date for the completion of further steps in the proceedings.

10. No written observations or other documents filed outside the time limit for their submission shall be included in the case file, unless the special rapporteur decides otherwise.

11. A party seeking an extension of the time limit must make a request as soon as it has become aware of the circumstances justifying such an extension and, in any event, before

the expiry of the time limit. It should state the reason for the request for an extension. The decision to extend the time limit is at the discretion of the special rapporteur.

12. Before draft Views are presented to the working group for discussion, the special rapporteur may request the parties to provide updates on the current status of the case.

Rule 93

1. A State party that has received a request for a written reply under paragraph 2 of rule 92 on both admissibility and the merits of the communication may apply in writing, within two months, for the question of admissibility to be examined separately from the merits. The Committee, through its special rapporteur, will decide on the State party's request. If the special rapporteur agrees to the request, the State party will not need to submit explanations or statements on the merits until the Committee decides otherwise.

2. The author may submit a reply to the State party's objection on admissibility.

3. Upon the request of one of the parties, additional written submissions may be authorized by the special rapporteur, on an exceptional basis, with due consideration for the circumstances of the case.

Rule 94

1. At any time after the registration of a communication and before a determination on the merits has been reached, the Committee may request that the State party concerned take on an urgent basis such interim measures as the Committee considers necessary to avoid possible actions which could have irreparable consequences for the rights invoked by the author.

2. When the Committee requests interim measures under the present rule, it will indicate that the request does not imply a determination on the admissibility or the merits of the communication, but that failure to implement such measures is incompatible with the obligation to respect in good faith the procedure of individual communications established under the Optional Protocol.

3. At any stage of the proceedings, the Committee will examine any arguments presented by the State concerned on the request to take interim measures, including reasons that would justify the lifting of the measures.

4. The Committee may withdraw a request for interim measures on the basis of information submitted by the State party and the author(s) of the communication.

Rule 95

Upon receiving information from the author of the communication, the Committee may also request the State party to take protection measures in favour of individuals, including the author(s), his or her counsel and family members, who might suffer acts of intimidation or reprisals as a result of the submission of the communication or cooperation with the Committee. The Committee may seek from the State party written explanations or statements clarifying the matter and describing any action taken in that regard.

Rule 96

1. When considering communications under the Optional Protocol, the Committee or its special rapporteur may accept information and documentation submitted by third parties which may be relevant for the proper determination of the case.

2. The Committee will establish guidelines for the requirements to be observed for third-party submissions.

3. The Committee shall forward third-party submissions to the parties to the communication, who are entitled to submit written observations and comments in reply.

4. Individuals or entities that are third parties shall not be considered parties to the communication.

C. Procedure to determine the admissibility and the merits of communications

Rule 97

1. Communications shall be examined by the Committee, as to their admissibility and/or merits in the order in which they were received by the Secretariat, unless the Committee decides otherwise in view of the circumstances and issues involved.

2. Prior to examining the merits of a communication, the Committee shall decide whether the communication is admissible.

3. Two or more communications may be dealt with jointly, if deemed appropriate by the Committee.

4. Decisions on admissibility and the merits shall be taken by the Committee by a simple majority, in accordance with the present rules. A majority of members present and voting shall be required for finding a communication admissible and for any finding of violation of the Covenant.

5. The Committee may decide to review communications in chambers.

Rule 98

1. Prior to their examination by the Committee plenary, communications will be examined by one or more working groups established under rule 107, paragraph 1, of the present rules and consisting of at least five members. A rapporteur from among the members of the working group will be designated to assist in the handling of communications.

2. The rules of procedure of the Committee shall apply as relevant to the meetings of the working group. Four members constitute a quorum for the meetings.

3. The working group shall make recommendations to the Committee concerning the fulfilment of the conditions of admissibility laid down in the Optional Protocol. The working group may also make recommendations to the Committee concerning the merits of the communications under examination.

4. The working group may declare a communication inadmissible when all the members so agree. However, the decision will be transmitted to the Committee plenary, which may confirm it without formal discussion. If any Committee member requests a plenary discussion, the plenary will examine the communication and take a decision.

5. Decisions to declare a communication admissible separate from its examination on the merits may be taken by the working group when all its members so agree, provided that the number of voting members is at least five.

Rule 99

With a view to reaching a decision on the admissibility of a communication, the Committee, or a working group established under rule 107, paragraph 1, of the present rules shall ascertain:

(a) That the communication is not anonymous and that it emanates from an individual, or individuals, subject to the jurisdiction of a State party to the Optional Protocol;

(b) That the individual claims, in a manner sufficiently substantiated, to be a victim of a violation by that State party of any of the rights set forth in the Covenant. Normally, the communication should be submitted by the individual personally or by that individual's representative. A communication submitted on behalf of an alleged victim may, however, be accepted when it appears that the individual in question is unable to submit the communication personally;

(c) That the communication does not constitute an abuse of the right of submission. An abuse of the right of submission is not, in principle, a basis of a decision of inadmissibility *ratione temporis* on grounds of delay in submission. However, a communication may constitute an abuse of the right of submission, when it is submitted five years after the exhaustion of domestic remedies by the author of the communication, or, where applicable, three years from the conclusion of another procedure of international investigation or settlement, unless there are reasons justifying the delay, taking into account all the circumstances of the communication;

(d) That the communication is not incompatible with the provisions of the Covenant;

(e) That the same matter is not being examined under another procedure of international investigation or settlement;

(f) That the individual has exhausted all available domestic remedies.

Rule 100

1. Where the Committee decides that a communication is inadmissible under the Optional Protocol, it shall as soon as possible communicate its decision, through the Secretary-General, to the author of the communication and, where the communication has been transmitted to a State party concerned, to that State party.

2. If the Committee has declared a communication inadmissible under article 5 (2) of the Optional Protocol, that decision may be reviewed at a later date by the Committee upon a written request by or on behalf of the individual concerned, containing information to the effect that the reasons for inadmissibility referred to in article 5 (2) no longer apply.

Rule 101

1. In those cases in which the issue of admissibility is decided before receiving the State party's reply on the merits and the Committee, or a working group established under rule 107, paragraph 1, of the present rules, decides that the communication is admissible, that decision shall be transmitted, through the Secretary-General, to the author of the communication and the State party concerned.

2. Within six months, the State party concerned shall submit to the Committee written explanations or statements on the merits and the remedy, if any, that may have been taken by that State party.

3. Any explanations or statements submitted by a State party pursuant to the present rule shall be communicated, through the Secretary-General, to the author of the communication, who may submit any additional written information or observations within fixed time limits.

4. The Committee may decide in exceptional cases to invite the parties to comment on each other's submissions orally, in accordance with its guidelines on making oral comments concerning communications (CCPR/C/159/Rev.1).

5. Upon consideration of the merits, the Committee may review a decision that a communication is admissible in the light of any explanations or statements submitted by the State party pursuant to the present rule.

Rule 102

1. In those cases in which the parties have submitted information relating both to the questions of admissibility and the merits, or in which a decision on admissibility has already been taken and the parties have submitted information on the merits, the Committee shall consider the communication in the light of all the information made available to it and shall formulate its Views thereon.

2. The Committee shall not decide on the merits of the communication without having considered the applicability of all the grounds of admissibility referred to in the Optional Protocol.

3. The Committee's findings on the merits shall be known as "Views". The Secretary-General shall transmit the Views of the Committee to the author of the communication and to the State party concerned.

Rule 103

Any member of the Committee who has participated in a decision may write a separate opinion that should be appended to the Committee's Views or decision.

Rule 104

The Committee may discontinue the consideration of a communication when the reasons for its submission under the Optional Protocol have become moot, or on other relevant grounds.

Rule 105

1. The Committee may appoint one or two members as rapporteur(s) for repetitive communications.

2. The rapporteur(s) for new communications and interim measures may refer cases which raise facts and legal questions of substantially the same nature as those already decided by the Committee in previous cases to the rapporteur(s) for repetitive communications.

3. The rapporteur(s) for repetitive communications shall propose a draft recommendation to the Working Group established under rule 107, paragraph 1. Unless one or more members of the Working Group objects, the recommendation of the rapporteur(s) for repetitive communications shall be submitted to the Committee for adoption. The Working Group may, if it so decides, modify or reject the recommendation.

4. Unless one or more members of the Committee objects, recommendations of the rapporteur(s) for repetitive communications shall be considered to be adopted as Views of the Committee.

Rule 106

1. The Committee shall designate a Special Rapporteur for follow-up on Views adopted under article 5 (4) of the Optional Protocol, for the purpose of ascertaining the measures taken by States parties to give effect to the Committee's Views.

2. The Special Rapporteur may make such contacts and take such action as appropriate for performance of the follow-up mandate. The Special Rapporteur shall make such recommendations for further action by the Committee as may be necessary.

3. The Special Rapporteur shall regularly report to the Committee on follow-up activities.

4. The Committee shall include information on follow-up activities in its annual report.

D. General provisions regarding the consideration of communications by the Committee or its subsidiary bodies

Rule 107

1. In any matter relating to communications under the Optional Protocol, the Committee may establish a working group and may designate a rapporteur to assist in any manner in which the Committee decides.

2. The Committee will designate one or more special rapporteurs to process new communications and requests for interim measures as they are received, as well as to deal with other procedural matters as authorized by the Committee.

Rule 108

1. A member shall not take part in the examination of a communication by the Committee:

(a) If he or she is a national of the State party or has the same nationality as the alleged victim;

(b) If he or she has any personal or professional conflict of interest in the case;

(c) If he or she has participated in any capacity in the making of any decision on the case covered by the communication.

2. Any question which may arise under paragraph 1 of the present rule shall be decided by the Committee. The member concerned shall not take part in the decision.

Rule 109

If, for any reason, a member considers that he or she should not take part or continue to take part in the examination of a communication, the member shall inform the Chair of his or her withdrawal.

Rule 110

Meetings of the Committee or its subsidiary bodies during which communications under the Optional Protocol will be examined shall be closed. Meetings during which the Committee may consider general issues, such as procedures for the application of the Optional Protocol, may be public if the Committee so decides.

Rule 111

1. Communications under the Optional Protocol shall be examined by the Committee and a working group established pursuant to rule 107, paragraph 1, of the present rules in closed session. Oral deliberations and summary records shall remain confidential.

2. The Committee may decide ex officio or upon request of the author or alleged victim that the names of the author or the alleged victim be kept confidential in the final decision of the Committee disposing of the communication.

3. All working documents issued by the Secretariat for the Committee, the Working Group established pursuant to rule 107, paragraph 1, or the Special Rapporteur designated pursuant to rule 107, paragraph 2, shall remain confidential, unless the Committee decides otherwise.

4. Paragraph 1 of the present rule shall not affect the right of the author of a communication or the State party concerned to make public any submissions or information bearing on the proceedings. However, the Committee, the Working Group or the Special Rapporteur may, as deemed appropriate, request the author of a communication or the State party concerned to keep confidential the whole or part of any such submissions or information.

5. When a decision has been taken on confidentiality, pursuant to paragraph 4 of the present rule, the Committee may decide that all or part of the submissions shall remain confidential after the Committee's decision on inadmissibility, the merits or discontinuance has been adopted.

6. The Committee's decisions on inadmissibility, the merits and discontinuance shall be made public after having been brought to the attention of the author and the State party concerned. Decisions taken under rule 94 of the present rules by the Committee or the Special Rapporteur designated pursuant to rule 107, paragraph 2, shall be made public if the Committee or the Special Rapporteur consider it appropriate.

7. The Secretariat is responsible for the distribution of the Committee's final decisions. The Secretariat shall not be responsible for the reproduction and distribution of submissions concerning communications.

Rule 112

Information furnished by the parties within the framework of follow-up to the Committee's Views is not subject to confidentiality, unless the Committee decides otherwise. Decisions of the Committee relating to follow-up activities are equally not subject to confidentiality, unless the Committee decides otherwise.

Rule 113

The Committee may issue communiqués, through the Secretary-General, for the use of the information media and the general public regarding the activities of the Committee at its closed meetings.

XIX. AMENDMENTS

Rule 114

The present rules of procedure may be amended by a decision of the Committee, without prejudice to the relevant provisions of the Covenant and the Optional Protocol.

The ICESCR Framework

28.a International Covenant on Economic, Social and Cultural Rights

Date: 16 December 1966
Source: 993 UNTS 3
https://www.ohchr.org/Documents/ProfessionalInterest/cescr.pdf

…

PART IV

Article 16

1. The States Parties to the present Covenant undertake to submit in conformity with this part of the Covenant reports on the measures which they have adopted and the progress made in achieving the observance of the rights recognized herein.

2.
(a) All reports shall be submitted to the Secretary-General of the United Nations, who shall transmit copies to the Economic and Social Council for consideration in accordance with the provisions of the present Covenant;
(b) The Secretary-General of the United Nations shall also transmit to the specialized agencies copies of the reports, or any relevant parts therefrom, from States Parties to the present Covenant which are also members of these specialized agencies in so far as these reports, or parts therefrom, relate to any matters which fall within the responsibilities of the said agencies in accordance with their constitutional instruments.

Article 17

1. The States Parties to the present Covenant shall furnish their reports in stages, in accordance with a programme to be established by the Economic and Social Council within one year of the entry into force of the present Covenant after consultation with the States Parties and the specialized agencies concerned.
2. Reports may indicate factors and difficulties affecting the degree of fulfilment of obligations under the present Covenant.
3. Where relevant information has previously been furnished to the United Nations or to any specialized agency by any State Party to the present Covenant, it will not be necessary to reproduce that information, but a precise reference to the information so furnished will suffice.

Article 18

Pursuant to its responsibilities under the Charter of the United Nations in the field of human rights and fundamental freedoms, the Economic and Social Council may make arrangements with the specialized agencies in respect of their reporting to it on the progress made in achieving the observance of the provisions of the present Covenant falling within the scope of their activities. These reports may include particulars of decisions and recommendations on such implementation adopted by their competent organs.

Article 19

The Economic and Social Council may transmit to the Commission on Human Rights for study and general recommendation or, as appropriate, for information the reports concerning human rights submitted by States in accordance with articles 16 and 17, and those concerning human rights submitted by the specialized agencies in accordance with article 18.

Article 20

The States Parties to the present Covenant and the specialized agencies concerned may submit comments to the Economic and Social Council on any general recommendation under article 19 or reference to such general recommendation in any report of the Commission on Human Rights or any documentation referred to therein.

Article 21

The Economic and Social Council may submit from time to time to the General Assembly reports with recommendations of a general nature and a summary of the information received from the States Parties to the present Covenant and the specialized agencies on the measures taken and the progress made in achieving general observance of the rights recognized in the present Covenant.

Article 22

The Economic and Social Council may bring to the attention of other organs of the United Nations, their subsidiary organs and specialized agencies concerned with furnishing technical assistance any matters arising out of the reports referred to in this part of the present Covenant which may assist such bodies in deciding, each within its field of competence, on the advisability of international measures likely to contribute to the effective progressive implementation of the present Covenant.

Article 23

The States Parties to the present Covenant agree that international action for the achievement of the rights recognized in the present Covenant includes such methods as the conclusion of conventions, the adoption of recommendations, the furnishing of technical assistance and the holding of regional meetings and technical meetings for the purpose of consultation and study organized in conjunction with the Governments concerned.

Article 24

Nothing in the present Covenant shall be interpreted as impairing the provisions of the Charter of the United Nations and of the constitutions of the specialized agencies which define the respective responsibilities of the various organs of the United Nations and of the specialized agencies in regard to the matters dealt with in the present Covenant.

28.b Optional Protocol to the International Covenant on Economic, Social and Cultural Rights

Date: 10 December 2008
Source: UN Doc A/RES/63/117
https://www.ohchr.org/Documents/HRBodies/CESCR/OProtocol_en.pdf

Preamble

The States Parties to the present Protocol,

Considering that, in accordance with the principles proclaimed in the Charter of the United Nations, recognition of the inherent dignity and of the equal and inalienable rights of all members of the human family is the foundation of freedom, justice and peace in the world,

Noting that the Universal Declaration of Human Rights proclaims that all human beings are born free and equal in dignity and rights and that everyone is entitled to all the rights and freedoms set forth therein, without distinction of any kind, such as race, colour, sex, language, religion, political or other opinion, national or social origin, property, birth or other status,

Recalling that the Universal Declaration of Human Rights and the International Covenants on Human Rights recognize that the ideal of free human beings enjoying freedom from fear and want can only be achieved if conditions are created whereby everyone may enjoy civil, cultural, economic, political and social rights,

Reaffirming the universality, indivisibility, interdependence and interrelatedness of all human rights and fundamental freedoms,

Recalling that each State Party to the International Covenant on Economic, Social and Cultural Rights (hereinafter referred to as the Covenant) undertakes to take steps, individually and through international assistance and cooperation, especially economic and technical, to the maximum of its available resources, with a view to achieving progressively the full realization of the rights recognized in the Covenant by all appropriate means, including particularly the adoption of legislative measures,

Considering that, in order further to achieve the purposes of the Covenant and the implementation of its provisions, it would be appropriate to enable the Committee on Economic, Social and Cultural Rights (hereinafter referred to as the Committee) to carry out the functions provided for in the present Protocol,

Have agreed as follows:

Article 1 Competence of the Committee to receive and consider communications

1. A State Party to the Covenant that becomes a Party to the present Protocol recognizes the competence of the Committee to receive and consider communications as provided for by the provisions of the present Protocol.

2. No communication shall be received by the Committee if it concerns a State Party to the Covenant which is not a Party to the present Protocol.

Article 2 Communications

Communications may be submitted by or on behalf of individuals or groups of individuals, under the jurisdiction of a State Party, claiming to be victims of a violation of any of the economic, social and cultural rights set forth in the Covenant by that State Party. Where a communication is submitted on behalf of individuals or groups of individuals, this shall be with their consent unless the author can justify acting on their behalf without such consent.

Article 3 Admissibility

1. The Committee shall not consider a communication unless it has ascertained that all available domestic remedies have been exhausted. This shall not be the rule where the application of such remedies is unreasonably prolonged.

2. The Committee shall declare a communication inadmissible when:

(a) It is not submitted within one year after the exhaustion of domestic remedies, except in cases where the author can demonstrate that it had not been possible to submit the communication within that time limit;

(b) The facts that are the subject of the communication occurred prior to the entry into force of the present Protocol for the State Party concerned unless those facts continued after that date;

(c) The same matter has already been examined by the Committee or has been or is being examined under another procedure of international investigation or settlement;

(d) It is incompatible with the provisions of the Covenant;

(e) It is manifestly ill-founded, not sufficiently substantiated or exclusively based on reports disseminated by mass media;
(f) It is an abuse of the right to submit a communication; or when
(g) It is anonymous or not in writing.

Article 4 Communications not revealing a clear disadvantage

The Committee may, if necessary, decline to consider a communication where it does not reveal that the author has suffered a clear disadvantage, unless the Committee considers that the communication raises a serious issue of general importance.

Article 5 Interim measures

1. At any time after the receipt of a communication and before a determination on the merits has been reached, the Committee may transmit to the State Party concerned for its urgent consideration a request that the State Party take such interim measures as may be necessary in exceptional circumstances to avoid possible irreparable damage to the victim or victims of the alleged violations.

2. Where the Committee exercises its discretion under paragraph 1 of the present article, this does not imply a determination on admissibility or on the merits of the communication.

Article 6 Transmission of the communication

1. Unless the Committee considers a communication inadmissible without reference to the State Party concerned, the Committee shall bring any communication submitted to it under the present Protocol confidentially to the attention of the State Party concerned.

2. Within six months, the receiving State Party shall submit to the Committee written explanations or statements clarifying the matter and the remedy, if any, that may have been provided by that State Party.

Article 7 Friendly settlement

1. The Committee shall make available its good offices to the parties concerned with a view to reaching a friendly settlement of the matter on the basis of the respect for the obligations set forth in the Covenant.

2. An agreement on a friendly settlement closes consideration of the communication under the present Protocol.

Article 8 Examination of communications

1. The Committee shall examine communications received under article 2 of the present Protocol in the light of all documentation submitted to it, provided that this documentation is transmitted to the parties concerned.

2. The Committee shall hold closed meetings when examining communications under the present Protocol.

3. When examining a communication under the present Protocol, the Committee may consult, as appropriate, relevant documentation emanating from other United Nations bodies, specialized agencies, funds, programmes and mechanisms, and other international organizations, including from regional human rights systems, and any observations or comments by the State Party concerned.

4. When examining communications under the present Protocol, the Committee shall consider the reasonableness of the steps taken by the State Party in accordance with Part II

of the Covenant. In doing so, the Committee shall bear in mind that the State Party may adopt a range of possible policy measures for the implementation of the rights set forth in the Covenant.

Article 9 Follow-up to the views of the Committee

1. After examining a communication, the Committee shall transmit its views on the communication, together with its recommendations, if any, to the parties concerned.

2. The State Party shall give due consideration to the views of the Committee, together with its recommendations, if any, and shall submit to the Committee, within six months, a written response, including information on any action taken in the light of the views and recommendations of the Committee.

3. The Committee may invite the State Party to submit further information about any measures the State Party has taken in response to its views or recommendations, if any, including as deemed appropriate by the Committee, in the State Party's subsequent reports under articles 16 and 17 of the Covenant.

Article 10 Inter-State communications

1. A State Party to the present Protocol may at any time declare under this article that it recognizes the competence of the Committee to receive and consider communications to the effect that a State Party claims that another State Party is not fulfilling its obligations under the Covenant. Communications under this article may be received and considered only if submitted by a State Party that has made a declaration recognizing in regard to itself the competence of the Committee. No communication shall be received by the Committee if it concerns a State Party which has not made such a declaration. Communications received under this article shall be dealt with in accordance with the following procedure:

(a) If a State Party to the present Protocol considers that another State Party is not fulfilling its obligations under the Covenant, it may, by written communication, bring the matter to the attention of that State Party. The State Party may also inform the Committee of the matter. Within three months after the receipt of the communication the receiving State shall afford the State that sent the communication an explanation, or any other statement in writing clarifying the matter which should include, to the extent possible and pertinent, reference to domestic procedures and remedies taken, pending or available in the matter;

(b) If the matter is not settled to the satisfaction of both States Parties concerned within six months after the receipt by the receiving State of the initial communication, either State shall have the right to refer the matter to the Committee, by notice given to the Committee and to the other State;

(c) The Committee shall deal with a matter referred to it only after it has ascertained that all available domestic remedies have been invoked and exhausted in the matter. This shall not be the rule where the application of the remedies is unreasonably prolonged;

(d) Subject to the provisions of subparagraph (*c*) of the present paragraph the Committee shall make available its good offices to the States Parties concerned with a view to a friendly solution of the matter on the basis of the respect for the obligations set forth in the Covenant;

(e) The Committee shall hold closed meetings when examining communications under the present article;

(f) In any matter referred to it in accordance with subparagraph (*b*) of the present paragraph, the Committee may call upon the States Parties concerned, referred to in subparagraph (*b*), to supply any relevant information;

(g) The States Parties concerned, referred to in subparagraph (*b*) of the present paragraph, shall have the right to be represented when the matter is being considered by the Committee and to make submissions orally and/or in writing;

(h) The Committee shall, with all due expediency after the date of receipt of notice under subparagraph (*b*) of the present paragraph, submit a report, as follows:

(i) If a solution within the terms of subparagraph (*d*) of the present paragraph is reached, the Committee shall confine its report to a brief statement of the facts and of the solution reached;

(ii) If a solution within the terms of subparagraph (*d*) is not reached, the Committee shall, in its report, set forth the relevant facts concerning the issue between the States Parties concerned. The written submissions and record of the oral submissions made by the States Parties concerned shall be attached to the report. The Committee may also communicate only to the States Parties concerned any views that it may consider relevant to the issue between them.

In every matter, the report shall be communicated to the States Parties concerned.

2. A declaration under paragraph 1 of the present article shall be deposited by the States Parties with the Secretary-General of the United Nations, who shall transmit copies thereof to the other States Parties. A declaration may be withdrawn at any time by notification to the Secretary-General. Such a withdrawal shall not prejudice the consideration of any matter that is the subject of a communication already transmitted under the present article; no further communication by any State Party shall be received under the present article after the notification of withdrawal of the declaration has been received by the Secretary-General, unless the State Party concerned has made a new declaration.

Article 11 Inquiry procedure

1. A State Party to the present Protocol may at any time declare that it recognizes the competence of the Committee provided for under this article.

2. If the Committee receives reliable information indicating grave or systematic violations by a State Party of any of the economic, social and cultural rights set forth in the Covenant, the Committee shall invite that State Party to cooperate in the examination of the information and to this end to submit observations with regard to the information concerned.

3. Taking into account any observations that may have been submitted by the State Party concerned as well as any other reliable information available to it, the Committee may designate one or more of its members to conduct an inquiry and to report urgently to the Committee. Where warranted and with the consent of the State Party, the inquiry may include a visit to its territory.

4. Such an inquiry shall be conducted confidentially and the cooperation of the State Party shall be sought at all stages of the proceedings.

5. After examining the findings of such an inquiry, the Committee shall transmit these findings to the State Party concerned together with any comments and recommendations.

6. The State Party concerned shall, within six months of receiving the findings, comments and recommendations transmitted by the Committee, submit its observations to the Committee.

7. After such proceedings have been completed with regard to an inquiry made in accordance with paragraph 2, the Committee may, after consultations with the State Party concerned, decide to include a summary account of the results of the proceedings in its annual report provided for in article 15.

8. Any State Party having made a declaration in accordance with paragraph 1 of the present article may, at any time, withdraw this declaration by notification to the Secretary-General.

Article 12 Follow-up to the inquiry procedure

1. The Committee may invite the State Party concerned to include in its report under articles 16 and 17 of the Covenant details of any measures taken in response to an inquiry conducted under article 11 of the present Protocol.

2. The Committee may, if necessary, after the end of the period of six months referred to in article 11, paragraph 6, invite the State Party concerned to inform it of the measures taken in response to such an inquiry.

Article 13 Protection measures

A State Party shall take all appropriate measures to ensure that individuals under its jurisdiction are not subjected to any form of ill-treatment or intimidation as a consequence of communicating with the Committee pursuant to the present Protocol.

Article 14 International assistance and cooperation

1. The Committee shall transmit, as it may consider appropriate, and with the consent of the State Party concerned, to United Nations specialized agencies, funds and programmes and other competent bodies, its views or recommendations concerning communications and inquiries that indicate a need for technical advice or assistance, along with the State Party's observations and suggestions, if any, on these views or recommendations.

2. The Committee may also bring to the attention of such bodies, with the consent of the State Party concerned, any matter arising out of communications considered under the present Protocol which may assist them in deciding, each within its field of competence, on the advisability of international measures likely to contribute to assisting States Parties in achieving progress in implementation of the rights recognized in the Covenant.

3. A trust fund shall be established in accordance with the relevant procedures of the General Assembly, to be administered in accordance with the financial regulations and rules of the United Nations, with a view to providing expert and technical assistance to States Parties, with the consent of the State Party concerned, for the enhanced implementation of the rights contained in the Covenant, thus contributing to building national capacities in the area of economic, social and cultural rights in the context of the present Protocol.

4. The provisions of this article are without prejudice to the obligations of each State Party to fulfil its obligations under the Covenant.

Article 15 Annual report

The Committee shall include in its annual report a summary of its activities under the present Protocol.

Article 16 Dissemination and information

Each State Party undertakes to make widely known and to disseminate the Covenant and the present Protocol and to facilitate access to information about the views and recommendations of the Committee, in particular, on matters involving that State Party, and to do so in accessible formats for persons with disabilities.

Article 17 Signature, ratification and accession

1. The present Protocol is open for signature by any State that has signed, ratified or acceded to the Covenant.
2. The present Protocol is subject to ratification by any State that has ratified or acceded to the Covenant. Instruments of ratification shall be deposited with the Secretary-General of the United Nations.
3. The present Protocol shall be open to accession by any State that has ratified or acceded to the Covenant.
4. Accession shall be effected by the deposit of an instrument of accession with the Secretary-General of the United Nations.

Article 18 Entry into force

1. The present Protocol shall enter into force three months after the date of the deposit with the Secretary-General of the United Nations of the tenth instrument of ratification or accession.
2. For each State ratifying or acceding to the present Protocol, after the deposit of the tenth instrument of ratification or accession, the protocol shall enter into force three months after the date of the deposit of its instrument of ratification or accession.

Article 19 Amendments

1. Any State Party may propose an amendment to the present Protocol and submit it to the Secretary-General of the United Nations. The Secretary-General shall communicate any proposed amendments to States Parties, with a request to be notified whether they favour a meeting of States Parties for the purpose of considering and deciding upon the proposals. In the event that, within four months from the date of such communication, at least one third of the States Parties favour such a meeting, the Secretary-General shall convene the meeting under the auspices of the United Nations. Any amendment adopted by a majority of two thirds of the States Parties present and voting shall be submitted by the Secretary-General to the General Assembly for approval and thereafter to all States Parties for acceptance.
2. An amendment adopted and approved in accordance with paragraph 1 of this article shall enter into force on the thirtieth day after the number of instruments of acceptance deposited reaches two thirds of the number of States Parties at the date of adoption of the amendment. Thereafter, the amendment shall enter into force for any State Party on the thirtieth day following the deposit of its own instrument of acceptance. An amendment shall be binding only on those States Parties which have accepted it.

Article 20 Denunciation

1. Any State Party may denounce the present Protocol at any time by written notification addressed to the Secretary-General of the United Nations. Denunciation shall take effect six months after the date of receipt of the notification by the Secretary-General.

2. Denunciation shall be without prejudice to the continued application of the provisions of the present Protocol to any communication submitted under articles 2 and 10 or to any procedure initiated under article 11 before the effective date of denunciation.

Article 21 Notification by the Secretary-General

The Secretary-General of the United Nations shall notify all States referred to in article 26, paragraph 1 of the Covenant of the following particulars:

(a) Signatures, ratifications and accessions under the present Protocol;
(b) The date of entry into force of the present Protocol and of any amendment under article 19;
(c) Any denunciation under article 20.

Article 22 Official languages

1. The present Protocol, of which the Arabic, Chinese, English, French, Russian and Spanish texts are equally authentic, shall be deposited in the archives of the United Nations.

2. The Secretary-General of the United Nations shall transmit certified copies of the present Protocol to all States referred to in article 26 of the Covenant.

The CEDAW Framework*

29.a Convention on the Elimination of All Forms of Discrimination against Women

Date: 18 December 1979
Source: 1249 UNTS 13
https://www.ohchr.org/Documents/ProfessionalInterest/cedaw.pdf

...

PART V

Article 17

1. For the purpose of considering the progress made in the implementation of the present Convention, there shall be established a Committee on the Elimination of Discrimination against Women (hereinafter referred to as the Committee) consisting, at the time of entry into force of the Convention, of eighteen and, after ratification of or accession to the Convention by the thirty-fifth State Party, of twenty-three experts of high moral standing and competence in the field covered by the Convention. The experts shall be elected by States Parties from among their nationals and shall serve in their personal capacity, consideration being given to equitable geographical distribution and to the representation of the different forms of civilization as well as the principal legal systems.

* N.B.: The Rules of Procedure of the Committee on the Elimination of All Forms of Discrimination against Women are not included in this document set, as they are largely similar, though in no way identical, to those of the Human Rights Committee, reproduced in Document No. 27.c above.

2. The members of the Committee shall be elected by secret ballot from a list of persons nominated by States Parties. Each State Party may nominate one person from among its own nationals.

3. The initial election shall be held six months after the date of the entry into force of the present Convention. At least three months before the date of each election the Secretary-General of the United Nations shall address a letter to the States Parties inviting them to submit their nominations within two months. The Secretary-General shall prepare a list in alphabetical order of all persons thus nominated, indicating the States Parties which have nominated them, and shall submit it to the States Parties.

4. Elections of the members of the Committee shall be held at a meeting of States Parties convened by the Secretary-General at United Nations Headquarters. At that meeting, for which two thirds of the States Parties shall constitute a quorum, the persons elected to the Committee shall be those nominees who obtain the largest number of votes and an absolute majority of the votes of the representatives of States Parties present and voting.

5. The members of the Committee shall be elected for a term of four years. However, the terms of nine of the members elected at the first election shall expire at the end of two years; immediately after the first election the names of these nine members shall be chosen by lot by the Chairman of the Committee.

6. The election of the five additional members of the Committee shall be held in accordance with the provisions of paragraphs 2, 3 and 4 of this article, following the thirty-fifth ratification or accession. The terms of two of the additional members elected on this occasion shall expire at the end of two years, the names of these two members having been chosen by lot by the Chairman of the Committee.

7. For the filling of casual vacancies, the State Party whose expert has ceased to function as a member of the Committee shall appoint another expert from among its nationals, subject to the approval of the Committee.

8. The members of the Committee shall, with the approval of the General Assembly, receive emoluments from United Nations resources on such terms and conditions as the Assembly may decide, having regard to the importance of the Committee's responsibilities.

9. The Secretary-General of the United Nations shall provide the necessary staff and facilities for the effective performance of the functions of the Committee under the present Convention.

Article 18

1. States Parties undertake to submit to the Secretary-General of the United Nations, for consideration by the Committee, a report on the legislative, judicial, administrative or other measures which they have adopted to give effect to the provisions of the present Convention and on the progress made in this respect:

(a) Within one year after the entry into force for the State concerned;

(b) Thereafter at least every four years and further whenever the Committee so requests.

2. Reports may indicate factors and difficulties affecting the degree of fulfilment of obligations under the present Convention.

Article 19

1. The Committee shall adopt its own rules of procedure.

2. The Committee shall elect its officers for a term of two years.

Article 20

1. The Committee shall normally meet for a period of not more than two weeks annually in order to consider the reports submitted in accordance with article 18 of the present Convention.

2. The meetings of the Committee shall normally be held at United Nations Headquarters or at any other convenient place as determined by the Committee. (amendment, status of ratification)

Article 21

1. The Committee shall, through the Economic and Social Council, report annually to the General Assembly of the United Nations on its activities and may make suggestions and general recommendations based on the examination of reports and information received from the States Parties. Such suggestions and general recommendations shall be included in the report of the Committee together with comments, if any, from States Parties.

2. The Secretary-General of the United Nations shall transmit the reports of the Committee to the Commission on the Status of Women for its information.

Article 22

The specialized agencies shall be entitled to be represented at the consideration of the implementation of such provisions of the present Convention as fall within the scope of their activities. The Committee may invite the specialized agencies to submit reports on the implementation of the Convention in areas falling within the scope of their activities.

PART VI

...

Article 29

1. Any dispute between two or more States Parties concerning the interpretation or application of the present Convention which is not settled by negotiation shall, at the request of one of them, be submitted to arbitration. If within six months from the date of the request for arbitration the parties are unable to agree on the organization of the arbitration, any one of those parties may refer the dispute to the International Court of Justice by request in conformity with the Statute of the Court.

2. Each State Party may at the time of signature or ratification of the present Convention or accession thereto declare that it does not consider itself bound by paragraph I of this article. The other States Parties shall not be bound by that paragraph with respect to any State Party which has made such a reservation.

3. Any State Party which has made a reservation in accordance with paragraph 2 of this article may at any time withdraw that reservation by notification to the Secretary-General of the United Nations.

29.b Optional Protocol to the Convention on the Elimination of All Forms of Discrimination against Women

Date: 6 October 1999
Source: 2131 UNTS 83
https://www.ohchr.org/Documents/HRBodies/CEDAW/OP_CEDAW_en.pdf

The States Parties to the present Protocol,

Noting that the Charter of the United Nations reaffirms faith in fundamental human rights, in the dignity and worth of the human person and in the equal rights of men and women,

Also noting that the Universal Declaration of Human Rights. proclaims that all human beings are born free and equal in dignity and rights and that everyone is entitled to all the rights and freedoms set forth therein, without distinction of any kind, including distinction based on sex,

Recalling that the International Covenants on Human Rights. and other international human rights instruments prohibit discrimination on the basis of sex,

Also recalling the Convention on the Elimination of All Forms of Discrimination against Women ("the Convention"), in which the States Parties thereto condemn discrimination against women in all its forms and agree to pursue by all appropriate means and without delay a policy of eliminating discrimination against women,

Reaffirming their determination to ensure the full and equal enjoyment by women of all human rights and fundamental freedoms and to take effective action to prevent violations of these rights and freedoms,

Have agreed as follows:

Article 1

A State Party to the present Protocol ("State Party") recognizes the competence of the Committee on the Elimination of Discrimination against Women ("the Committee") to receive and consider communications submitted in accordance with article 2.

Article 2

Communications may be submitted by or on behalf of individuals or groups of individuals, under the jurisdiction of a State Party, claiming to be victims of a violation of any of the rights set forth in the Convention by that State Party. Where a communication is submitted on behalf of individuals or groups of individuals, this shall be with their consent unless the author can justify acting on their behalf without such consent.

Article 3

Communications shall be in writing and shall not be anonymous. No communication shall be received by the Committee if it concerns a State Party to the Convention that is not a party to the present Protocol.

Article 4

1. The Committee shall not consider a communication unless it has ascertained that all available domestic remedies have been exhausted unless the application of such remedies is unreasonably prolonged or unlikely to bring effective relief.

2. The Committee shall declare a communication inadmissible where:

(a) The same matter has already been examined by the Committee or has been or is being examined under another procedure of international investigation or settlement;

(b) It is incompatible with the provisions of the Convention;

(c) It is manifestly ill-founded or not sufficiently substantiated;

(d) It is an abuse of the right to submit a communication;

(e) The facts that are the subject of the communication occurred prior to the entry into force of the present Protocol for the State Party concerned unless those facts continued after that date.

Article 5

1. At any time after the receipt of a communication and before a determination on the merits has been reached, the Committee may transmit to the State Party concerned for its urgent consideration a request that the State Party take such interim measures as may be necessary to avoid possible irreparable damage to the victim or victims of the alleged violation.

2. Where the Committee exercises its discretion under paragraph 1 of the present article, this does not imply a determination on admissibility or on the merits of the communication.

Article 6

1. Unless the Committee considers a communication inadmissible without reference to the State Party concerned, and provided that the individual or individuals consent to the disclosure of their identity to that State Party, the Committee shall bring any communication submitted to it under the present Protocol confidentially to the attention of the State Party concerned.

2. Within six months, the receiving State Party shall submit to the Committee written explanations or statements clarifying the matter and the remedy, if any, that may have been provided by that State Party.

Article 7

1. The Committee shall consider communications received under the present Protocol in the light of all information made available to it by or on behalf of individuals or groups of individuals and by the State Party concerned, provided that this information is transmitted to the parties concerned.

2. The Committee shall hold closed meetings when examining communications under the present Protocol.

3. After examining a communication, the Committee shall transmit its views on the communication, together with its recommendations, if any, to the parties concerned.

4. The State Party shall give due consideration to the views of the Committee, together with its recommendations, if any, and shall submit to the Committee, within six months, a written response, including information on any action taken in the light of the views and recommendations of the Committee.

5. The Committee may invite the State Party to submit further information about any measures the State Party has taken in response to its views or recommendations, if any, including as deemed appropriate by the Committee, in the State Party's subsequent reports under article 18 of the Convention.

Article 8

1. If the Committee receives reliable information indicating grave or systematic violations by a State Party of rights set forth in the Convention, the Committee shall invite that State Party to cooperate in the examination of the information and to this end to submit observations with regard to the information concerned.

2. Taking into account any observations that may have been submitted by the State Party concerned as well as any other reliable information available to it, the Committee may designate one or more of its members to conduct an inquiry and to report urgently to the Committee. Where warranted and with the consent of the State Party, the inquiry may include a visit to its territory.

3. After examining the findings of such an inquiry, the Committee shall transmit these findings to the State Party concerned together with any comments and recommendations.

4. The State Party concerned shall, within six months of receiving the findings, comments and recommendations transmitted by the Committee, submit its observations to the Committee.

5. Such an inquiry shall be conducted confidentially and the cooperation of the State Party shall be sought at all stages of the proceedings.

Article 9

1. The Committee may invite the State Party concerned to include in its report under article 18 of the Convention details of any measures taken in response to an inquiry conducted under article 8 of the present Protocol.

2. The Committee may, if necessary, after the end of the period of six months referred to in article 8.4, invite the State Party concerned to inform it of the measures taken in response to such an inquiry.

Article 10

1. Each State Party may, at the time of signature or ratification of the present Protocol or accession thereto, declare that it does not recognize the competence of the Committee provided for in articles 8 and 9.

2. Any State Party having made a declaration in accordance with paragraph 1 of the present article may, at any time, withdraw this declaration by notification to the Secretary-General.

Article 11

A State Party shall take all appropriate steps to ensure that individuals under its jurisdiction are not subjected to ill treatment or intimidation as a consequence of communicating with the Committee pursuant to the present Protocol.

Article 12

The Committee shall include in its annual report under article 21 of the Convention a summary of its activities under the present Protocol.

Article 13

Each State Party undertakes to make widely known and to give publicity to the Convention and the present Protocol and to facilitate access to information about the views and recommendations of the Committee, in particular, on matters involving that State Party.

Article 14

The Committee shall develop its own rules of procedure to be followed when exercising the functions conferred on it by the present Protocol.

Article 15

1. The present Protocol shall be open for signature by any State that has signed, ratified or acceded to the Convention.

2. The present Protocol shall be subject to ratification by any State that has ratified or acceded to the Convention. Instruments of ratification shall be deposited with the Secretary-General of the United Nations.

3. The present Protocol shall be open to accession by any State that has ratified or acceded to the Convention.

4. Accession shall be effected by the deposit of an instrument of accession with the Secretary-General of the United Nations.

Article 16

1. The present Protocol shall enter into force three months after the date of the deposit with the Secretary-General of the United Nations of the tenth instrument of ratification or accession.

2. For each State ratifying the present Protocol or acceding to it after its entry into force, the present Protocol shall enter into force three months after the date of the deposit of its own instrument of ratification or accession.

Article 17

No reservations to the present Protocol shall be permitted.

Article 18

1. Any State Party may propose an amendment to the present Protocol and file it with the Secretary-General of the United Nations. The Secretary-General shall thereupon communicate any proposed amendments to the States Parties with a request that they notify her or him whether they favour a conference of States Parties for the purpose of considering and voting on the proposal. In the event that at least one third of the States Parties favour such a conference, the Secretary-General shall convene the conference under the auspices of the United Nations. Any amendment adopted by a majority of the States Parties present and voting at the conference shall be submitted to the General Assembly of the United Nations for approval.

2. Amendments shall come into force when they have been approved by the General Assembly of the United Nations and accepted by a two-thirds majority of the States Parties to the present Protocol in accordance with their respective constitutional processes.

3. When amendments come into force, they shall be binding on those States Parties that have accepted them, other States Parties still being bound by the provisions of the present Protocol and any earlier amendments that they have accepted.

Article 19

1. Any State Party may denounce the present Protocol at any time by written notification addressed to the Secretary-General of the United Nations. Denunciation shall take effect six months after the date of receipt of the notification by the Secretary-General.

2. Denunciation shall be without prejudice to the continued application of the provisions of the present Protocol to any communication submitted under article 2 or any inquiry initiated under article 8 before the effective date of denunciation.

Article 20

The Secretary-General of the United Nations shall inform all States of:

(a) Signatures, ratifications and accessions under the present Protocol;

(b) The date of entry into force of the present Protocol and of any amendment under article 18;

(c) Any denunciation under article 19.

Article 21

1. The present Protocol, of which the Arabic, Chinese, English, French, Russian and Spanish texts are equally authentic, shall be deposited in the archives of the United Nations.

2. The Secretary-General of the United Nations shall transmit certified copies of the present Protocol to all States referred to in article 25 of the Convention.

30. Convention against Torture and Other Cruel, Inhuman or Degrading Treatment or Punishment*

Date: 10 December 1984
Source: 1465 UNTS 85
https://www.ohchr.org/Documents/ProfessionalInterest/cat.pdf

...

PART II

Article 17

1. There shall be established a Committee against Torture (hereinafter referred to as the Committee) which shall carry out the functions hereinafter provided. The Committee shall consist of ten experts of high moral standing and recognized competence in the field of human rights, who shall serve in their personal capacity. The experts shall be elected by the States Parties, consideration being given to equitable geographical distribution and to the usefulness of the participation of some persons having legal experience.

2. The members of the Committee shall be elected by secret ballot from a list of persons nominated by States Parties. Each State Party may nominate one person from among its own nationals. States Parties shall bear in mind the usefulness of nominating persons who

* N.B.: The Rules of Procedure of the Committee against Torture are not included in this document set, as they are largely similar, though in no way identical, to those of the Human Rights Committee, reproduced in Document No. 27.c above.

are also members of the Human Rights Committee established under the International Covenant on Civil and Political Rights and who are willing to serve on the Committee against Torture.

3. Elections of the members of the Committee shall be held at biennial meetings of States Parties convened by the Secretary-General of the United Nations. At those meetings, for which two thirds of the States Parties shall constitute a quorum, the persons elected to the Committee shall be those who obtain the largest number of votes and an absolute majority of the votes of the representatives of States Parties present and voting.

4. The initial election shall be held no later than six months after the date of the entry into force of this Convention. At least four months before the date of each election, the Secretary-General of the United Nations shall address a letter to the States Parties inviting them to submit their nominations within three months. The Secretary-General shall prepare a list in alphabetical order of all persons thus nominated, indicating the States Parties which have nominated them, and shall submit it to the States Parties.

5. The members of the Committee shall be elected for a term of four years. They shall be eligible for re-election if re-nominated. However, the term of five of the members elected at the first election shall expire at the end of two years; immediately after the first election the names of these five members shall be chosen by lot by the chairman of the meeting referred to in paragraph 3 of this article.

6. If a member of the Committee dies or resigns or for any other cause can no longer perform his Committee duties, the State Party which nominated him shall appoint another expert from among its nationals to serve for the remainder of his term, subject to the approval of the majority of the States Parties. The approval shall be considered given unless half or more of the States Parties respond negatively within six weeks after having been informed by the Secretary-General of the United Nations of the proposed appointment.

7. States Parties shall be responsible for the expenses of the members of the Committee while they are in performance of Committee duties.

Article 18

1. The Committee shall elect its officers for a term of two years. They may be re-elected.

2. The Committee shall establish its own rules of procedure, but these rules shall provide, inter alia, that:

(a) Six members shall constitute a quorum;

(b) Decisions of the Committee shall be made by a majority vote of the members present.

3. The Secretary-General of the United Nations shall provide the necessary staff and facilities for the effective performance of the functions of the Committee under this Convention.

4. The Secretary-General of the United Nations shall convene the initial meeting of the Committee. After its initial meeting, the Committee shall meet at such times as shall be provided in its rules of procedure.

5. The States Parties shall be responsible for expenses incurred in connection with the holding of meetings of the States Parties and of the Committee, including reimbursement to the United Nations for any expenses, such as the cost of staff and facilities, incurred by the United Nations pursuant to paragraph 3 of this article.

Article 19

1. The States Parties shall submit to the Committee, through the Secretary-General of the United Nations, reports on the measures they have taken to give effect to their undertakings under this Convention, within one year after the entry into force of the Convention for the State Party concerned. Thereafter the States Parties shall submit supplementary reports every four years on any new measures taken and such other reports as the Committee may request.

2. The Secretary-General of the United Nations shall transmit the reports to all States Parties.

3. Each report shall be considered by the Committee which may make such general comments on the report as it may consider appropriate and shall forward these to the State Party concerned. That State Party may respond with any observations it chooses to the Committee.

4. The Committee may, at its discretion, decide to include any comments made by it in accordance with paragraph 3 of this article, together with the observations thereon received from the State Party concerned, in its annual report made in accordance with article 24. If so requested by the State Party concerned, the Committee may also include a copy of the report submitted under paragraph I of this article.

Article 20

1. If the Committee receives reliable information which appears to it to contain well-founded indications that torture is being systematically practised in the territory of a State Party, the Committee shall invite that State Party to co-operate in the examination of the information and to this end to submit observations with regard to the information concerned.

2. Taking into account any observations which may have been submitted by the State Party concerned, as well as any other relevant information available to it, the Committee may, if it decides that this is warranted, designate one or more of its members to make a confidential inquiry and to report to the Committee urgently.

3. If an inquiry is made in accordance with paragraph 2 of this article, the Committee shall seek the co-operation of the State Party concerned. In agreement with that State Party, such an inquiry may include a visit to its territory.

4. After examining the findings of its member or members submitted in accordance with paragraph 2 of this article, the Commission shall transmit these findings to the State Party concerned together with any comments or suggestions which seem appropriate in view of the situation.

5. All the proceedings of the Committee referred to in paragraphs I to 4 of the is article shall be confidential, and at all stages of the proceedings the co-operation of the State Party shall be sought. After such proceedings have been completed with regard to an inquiry made in accordance with paragraph 2, the Committee may, after consultations with the State Party concerned, decide to include a summary account of the results of the proceedings in its annual report made in accordance with article 24.

Article 21

1. A State Party to this Convention may at any time declare under this article that it recognizes the competence of the Committee to receive and consider communications to the effect that a State Party claims that another State Party is not fulfilling its obligations

under this Convention. Such communications may be received and considered according to the procedures laid down in this article only if submitted by a State Party which has made a declaration recognizing in regard to itself the competence of the Committee. No communication shall be dealt with by the Committee under this article if it concerns a State Party which has not made such a declaration. Communications received under this article shall be dealt with in accordance with the following procedure;

(a) If a State Party considers that another State Party is not giving effect to the provisions of this Convention, it may, by written communication, bring the matter to the attention of that State Party. Within three months after the receipt of the communication the receiving State shall afford the State which sent the communication an explanation or any other statement in writing clarifying the matter, which should include, to the extent possible and pertinent, reference to domestic procedures and remedies taken, pending or available in the matter;

(b) If the matter is not adjusted to the satisfaction of both States Parties concerned within six months after the receipt by the receiving State of the initial communication, either State shall have the right to refer the matter to the Committee, by notice given to the Committee and to the other State;

(c) The Committee shall deal with a matter referred to it under this article only after it has ascertained that all domestic remedies have been invoked and exhausted in the matter, in conformity with the generally recognized principles of international law. This shall not be the rule where the application of the remedies is unreasonably prolonged or is unlikely to bring effective relief to the person who is the victim of the violation of this Convention;

(d) The Committee shall hold closed meetings when examining communications under this article; (e) Subject to the provisions of subparagraph

(e) the Committee shall make available its good offices to the States Parties concerned with a view to a friendly solution of the matter on the basis of respect for the obligations provided for in this Convention. For this purpose, the Committee may, when appropriate, set up an ad hoc conciliation commission;

(f) In any matter referred to it under this article, the Committee may call upon the States Parties concerned, referred to in subparagraph (b), to supply any relevant information;

(g) The States Parties concerned, referred to in subparagraph (b), shall have the right to be represented when the matter is being considered by the Committee and to make submissions orally and/or in writing;

(h) The Committee shall, within twelve months after the date of receipt of notice under subparagraph (b), submit a report:

(i) If a solution within the terms of subparagraph (e) is reached, the Committee shall confine its report to a brief statement of the facts and of the solution reached;

(ii) If a solution within the terms of subparagraph (e) is not reached, the Committee shall confine its report to a brief statement of the facts; the written submissions and record of the oral submissions made by the States Parties concerned shall be attached to the report.

In every matter, the report shall be communicated to the States Parties concerned.

2. The provisions of this article shall come into force when five States Parties to this Convention have made declarations under paragraph 1 of this article. Such declarations shall

be deposited by the States Parties with the Secretary-General of the United Nations, who shall transmit copies thereof to the other States Parties. A declaration may be withdrawn at any time by notification to the Secretary-General. Such a withdrawal shall not prejudice the consideration of any matter which is the subject of a communication already transmitted under this article; no further communication by any State Party shall be received under this article after the notification of withdrawal of the declaration has been received by the Secretary-General, unless the State Party concerned has made a new declaration.

Article 22

1. A State Party to this Convention may at any time declare under this article that it recognizes the competence of the Committee to receive and consider communications from or on behalf of individuals subject to its jurisdiction who claim to be victims of a violation by a State Party of the provisions of the Convention. No communication shall be received by the Committee if it concerns a State Party which has not made such a declaration.

2. The Committee shall consider inadmissible any communication under this article which is anonymous or which it considers to be an abuse of the right of submission of such communications or to be incompatible with the provisions of this Convention.

3. Subject to the provisions of paragraph 2, the Committee shall bring any communications submitted to it under this article to the attention of the State Party to this Convention which has made a declaration under paragraph I and is alleged to be violating any provisions of the Convention. Within six months, the receiving State shall submit to the Committee written explanations or statements clarifying the matter and the remedy, if any, that may have been taken by that State.

4. The Committee shall consider communications received under this article in the light of all information made available to it by or on behalf of the individual and by the State Party concerned.

5. The Committee shall not consider any communications from an individual under this article unless it has ascertained that:

(a) The same matter has not been, and is not being, examined under another procedure of international investigation or settlement;

(b) The individual has exhausted all available domestic remedies; this shall not be the rule where the application of the remedies is unreasonably prolonged or is unlikely to bring effective relief to the person who is the victim of the violation of this Convention.

6. The Committee shall hold closed meetings when examining communications under this article.

7. The Committee shall forward its views to the State Party concerned and to the individual.

8. The provisions of this article shall come into force when five States Parties to this Convention have made declarations under paragraph 1 of this article. Such declarations shall be deposited by the States Parties with the Secretary-General of the United Nations, who shall transmit copies thereof to the other States Parties. A declaration may be withdrawn at any time by notification to the Secretary-General. Such a withdrawal shall not prejudice the consideration of any matter which is the subject of a communication already transmitted under this article; no further communication by or on behalf of an individual shall be received under this article after the notification of withdrawal of the declaration has been received by the Secretary-General, unless the State Party has made a new declaration.

Article 23

The members of the Committee and of the ad hoc conciliation commissions which may be appointed under article 21, paragraph I (e), shall be entitled to the facilities, privileges and immunities of experts on mission for the United Nations as laid down in the relevant sections of the Convention on the Privileges and Immunities of the United Nations.

Article 24

The Committee shall submit an annual report on its activities under this Convention to the States Parties and to the General Assembly of the United Nations.

PART III

...

Article 30

1. Any dispute between two or more States Parties concerning the interpretation or application of this Convention which cannot be settled through negotiation shall, at the request of one of them, be submitted to arbitration. If within six months from the date of the request for arbitration the Parties are unable to agree on the organization of the arbitration, any one of those Parties may refer the dispute to the International Court of Justice by request in conformity with the Statute of the Court.
2. Each State may, at the time of signature or ratification of this Convention or accession thereto, declare that it does not consider itself bound by paragraph I of this article. The other States Parties shall not be bound by paragraph I of this article with respect to any State Party having made such a reservation.
3. Any State Party having made a reservation in accordance with paragraph 2 of this article may at any time withdraw this reservation by notification to the Secretary-General of the United Nations.

Model Communication Forms

31.a Model Complaint Form for Communications under ICCPR-OP I, CAT, CERD

Source: http://www2.ohchr.org/english/bodies/docs/annex1.pdf

Model Complaint Form

For communications under:

• Optional Protocol to the International Covenant on Civil and Political Rights
• Convention against Torture, or
• International Convention on the Elimination of Racial Discrimination

Please indicate which of the above procedures you are invoking: ....
Date: ....

Information on the complainant:

Name: .... First name(s): ....
Nationality: .... Date and place of birth: ....
Address for correspondence on this complaint: ....
Submitting the communication:
on the author's own behalf: ....
on behalf of another person: ....

[If the complaint is being submitted on behalf of another person:]
Please provide the following personal details of that other person
Name: .... First name(s): ....
Nationality: .... Date and place of birth: ....
Address or current whereabouts: ....
If you are acting with the knowledge and consent of that person, please provide that person's authorization for you to bring this complaint ....
Or
If you are not so authorized, please explain the nature of your relationship with that person: .... and detail why you consider it appropriate to bring this complaint on his or her behalf: ....

II. State concerned/Articles violated

Name of the State that is either a party to the Optional Protocol (in the case of a complaint to the Human Rights Committee) or has made the relevant declaration (in the case of complaints to the Committee against Torture or the Committee on the Elimination of Racial Discrimination): ....
Articles of the Covenant or Convention alleged to have been violated: ....

III. Exhaustion of domestic remedies/Application to other international procedures

Steps taken by or on behalf of the alleged victims to obtain redress within the State concerned for the alleged violation – detail which procedures have been pursued, including recourse to the courts and other public authorities, which claims you have made, at which times, and with which outcomes: ....
If you have not exhausted these remedies on the basis that their application would be unduly prolonged, that they would not be effective, that they are not available to you, or for any other reason, please explain your reasons in detail: ....
Have you submitted the same matter for examination under another procedure of international investigation or settlement (e.g. the Inter-American Commission on Human Rights, the European Court of Human Rights, or the African Commission on Human and Peoples' Rights)?...............
If so, detail which procedure(s) have been, or are being, pursued, which claims you have made, at which times, and with which outcomes: ....

IV. Facts of the complaint

Detail, in chronological order, the facts and circumstances of the alleged violations. Include all matters which may be relevant to the assessment and consideration of your particular case. Please explain how you consider that the facts and circumstances described violate your rights. ....

....

Author's signature: ....

[The blanks under the various sections of this model communication simply indicate where your responses are required. You should take as much space as you need to set out your responses.]

V. Checklist of supporting documentation (copies, not originals, to be enclosed with your complaint):

– Written authorization to act (if you are bringing the complaint on behalf of another person and are not otherwise justifying the absence of specific authorization): ....
– Decisions of domestic courts and authorities on your claim (a copy of the relevant national legislation is also helpful): ......
– Complaints to and decisions by any other procedure of international investigation or settlement: ....
– Any documentation or other corroborating evidence you possess that substantiates your description in Part IV of the facts of your claim and/or your argument that the facts described amount to a violation of your rights: ......

If you do not enclose this information and it needs to be sought specifically from you, or if accompanying documentation is not provided in the working languages of the Secretariat, the consideration of your complaint may be delayed.

31.b Model Form for Submission of Communications to the Committee on the Elimination of Discrimination against Women under the Optional Protocol of the Convention

Source: https://www.ohchr.org/documents/HRBodies/CEDAW/InfoNote_OP_en.doc

The Optional Protocol to the Convention on the Elimination of All Forms of Discrimination against Women entered into force on 22 December 2000. It entitles the Committee on the Elimination of Discrimination against Women, a body of 23 independent experts, to receive and consider communications (complaint) from, or on behalf of, individuals or a group of individuals who claim to be victims of violations of the rights protected by the Convention.

To be considered by the Committee, a communication:

- shall be in writing;
- shall not be anonymous;
- must refer to a State which is a party to both the Convention on the Elimination of All Forms of Discrimination against Women and the Optional Protocol;
- must be submitted by, or on behalf of, an individual or a group of individuals under the jurisdiction of a State which is a party to the Convention and the Optional Protocol. In cases where a communication is submitted on behalf of an individual or a group of individuals, their consent is necessary unless the person submitting the communication can justify acting on their behalf without such consent.

A communication will *not* normally be considered by the Committee:

- unless all available domestic remedies have been exhausted;
- where the same matter is being or has already been examined by the Committee or another international procedure;
- if it concerns an alleged violation occurring before the entry into force of the Optional Protocol for the State.

In order for a communication to be considered the victim or victims must agree to disclose her/their identity to the State against which the violation is alleged. The communication, if admissible, will be brought confidentially to the attention of the State party concerned.

If you wish to submit a communication, please follow the guidelines below as closely as possible. Also, please submit any relevant information which becomes available after you have submitted this form.

Further information on the Convention on the Elimination of All Forms of Discrimination against Women and its Optional Protocol, as well as the rules of procedure of the Committee can be found at: [obsolete; now at: http://www.un.org/womenwatch/daw/cedaw/]

Guidelines for submission

The following questionnaire provides a guideline for those who wish to submit a communication for consideration by the Committee on the Elimination of Discrimination against Women under the Optional Protocol to the Convention on the Elimination of All Forms of Discrimination against Women. Please provide as much information as available in response to the items listed below.

Send your communication to:
Petitions Team
Office of the High Commissioner for Human Rights United Nations Office at Geneva
1211 Geneva 10, Switzerland
E-Mail: tb-petitions@ohchr.org

1. Information concerning the author(s) of the communication

- Family name
- First name
- Date and place of birth
- Nationality/citizenship
- Passport/identity card number (if available)
- Sex
- Marital status/children
- Profession
- If relevant, ethnic background, religious affiliation, social group
- Present address
- Mailing address for confidential correspondence (if other than present address)
- Telephone/e-mail
- Indicate whether you are submitting the communication as:
  - Alleged victim(s). If there is a group of individuals alleged to be victims, provide basic information about each individual.
  - On behalf of the alleged victim(s). Provide evidence showing the consent of the victim(s), or reasons that justify submitting the communication without such consent.

2. Information concerning the alleged victim(s) (if other than the author)

- Family name
- First name
- Date and place of birth
- Nationality/citizenship
- Passport/identity card number (if available)
- Sex
- Marital status/children
- Profession
- Ethnic background, religious affiliation, social group (if relevant)
- Present address
- Mailing address for confidential correspondence (if other than present address)
- Telephone/e-mail

3. Information on the State party concerned

- Name of the State party (country)

4. Facts of the complaint and nature of the alleged violation(s)

Please detail, in chronological order, the facts and circumstances of the alleged violations, including:

- Description of alleged violation(s) and alleged perpetrator(s)
- Date(s)
- Place(s)
- Provisions of the Convention on the Elimination of All Forms of Discrimination against Women that were allegedly violated. If the communication refers to more than one provision, describe each issue separately.

5. Steps taken to exhaust domestic remedies

Describe the action taken to exhaust domestic remedies; for example, attempts to obtain legal, administrative, legislative, policy or programme remedies, including:

- Type(s) of remedy sought
- Date(s)
- Place(s)
- Who initiated the action
- Which authority or body was addressed
- Name of court hearing the case (if any)
- If you have not exhausted domestic remedies on the ground that their application would be unduly prolonged, that they would not be effective, that they are not available to you, or for any other reason, please explain your reasons in detail.

Please note: Enclose copies of all relevant documentation.

6. Other international procedures

Has the same matter already been examined or is it being examined under another procedure of international investigation or settlement? If yes, explain:

- Type of procedure(s)
- Date(s)
- Place(s)
- Results (if any)

Please note: Enclose copies of all relevant documentation.

7. Disclosure of your name (s)

Do you consent to the disclosure of your name(s) to the State party should your communication be registered by the Committee in accordance with article 6, paragraph 1 of the Optional Protocol and rule 69, paragraph 1 of the Committee's rules of procedure?

8. Date and signature

Date/place:

Signature of author(s) and/or victim(s):

9. List of documents attached (do not send originals, only copies)

(b) Regional Human Rights Treaties and Related Monitoring Mechanisms

The ECHR Framework

32.a Convention for the Protection of Human Rights and Fundamental Freedoms*

Date: 4 November 1950
Source: CETS No 005
https://rm.coe.int/1680a2353d

Section II – European Court of Human Rights

Article 19 – Establishment of the Court

To ensure the observance of the engagements undertaken by the High Contracting Parties in the Convention and the Protocols thereto, there shall be set up a European Court of Human Rights, hereinafter referred to as "the Court". It shall function on a permanent basis.

Article 20 – Number of judges

The Court shall consist of a number of judges equal to that of the High Contracting Parties.

Article 21 – Criteria for office**

1. The judges shall be of high moral character and must either possess the qualifications required for appointment to high judicial office or be jurisconsults of recognised competence.

* N.B.: As amended by Protocols No. 11 and No. 14.

A number of further changes were made by Protocol No. 15, which, upon ratification by all member States, entered into force on 1 August 2021. These changes are reflected as footnotes to the articles of the Convention reproduced below.

See further below, at Document No. 32.b, for the text of Protocol No. 16, which introduces an advisory procedure. While not ratified by all Member States, Protocol No. 16 entered into force in 2018.

** As per Protocol 15:

Article 2:

1. In Article 21 of the Convention, a new paragraph 2 shall be inserted, which shall read as follows:

"Candidates shall be less than 65 years of age at the date by which the list of three candidates has been requested by the Parliamentary Assembly, further to Article 22."

2. The judges shall sit on the Court in their individual capacity.

3. During their term of office the judges shall not engage in any activity which is incompatible with their independence, impartiality or with the demands of a full-time office; all questions arising from the application of this paragraph shall be decided by the Court.

Article 22 – Election of judges

The judges shall be elected by the Parliamentary Assembly with respect to each High Contracting Party by a majority of votes cast from a list of three candidates nominated by the High Contracting Party.

Article 23 – Terms of office and dismissal

1. The judges shall be elected for a period of nine years. They may not be re-elected.

2. The terms of office of judges shall expire when they reach the age of 70.

3. The judges shall hold office until replaced. They shall, however, continue to deal with such cases as they already have under consideration.

4. No judge may be dismissed from office unless the other judges decide by a majority of two-thirds that that judge has ceased to fulfil the required conditions.

Article 24 – Registry and rapporteurs

1. The Court shall have a registry, the functions and organisation of which shall be laid down in the rules of the Court.

2. When sitting in a single-judge formation, the Court shall be assisted by rapporteurs who shall function under the authority of the President of the Court. They shall form part of the Court's registry.

Article 25 – Plenary Court

The plenary Court shall

(a) elect its President and one or two Vice-Presidents for a period of three years; they may be re-elected;

(b) set up Chambers, constituted for a fixed period of time;

(c) elect the Presidents of the Chambers of the Court; they may be re-elected;

(d) adopt the rules of the Court;

(e) elect the Registrar and one or more Deputy Registrars;

(f) make any request under Article 26, paragraph 2.

Article 26 – Single-judge formation, committees, Chambers and Grand Chamber

1. To consider cases brought before it, the Court shall sit in a single-judge formation, in committees of three judges, in Chambers of seven judges and in a Grand Chamber of seventeen judges. The Court's Chambers shall set up committees for a fixed period of time.

2. At the request of the plenary Court, the Committee of Ministers may, by a unanimous decision and for a fixed period, reduce to five the number of judges of the Chambers.

2. Paragraphs 2 and 3 of Article 21 of the Convention shall become paragraphs 3 and 4 of Article 21 respectively.

3. Paragraph 2 of Article 23 of the Convention shall be deleted. Paragraphs 3 and 4 of Article 23 shall become paragraphs 2 and 3 of Article 23 respectively.

3. When sitting as a single judge, a judge shall not examine any application against the High Contracting Party in respect of which that judge has been elected.

4. There shall sit as an *ex officio* member of the Chamber and the Grand Chamber the judge elected in respect of the High Contracting Party concerned. If there is none or if that judge is unable to sit, a person chosen by the President of the Court from a list submitted in advance by that Party shall sit in the capacity of judge.

5. The Grand Chamber shall also include the President of the Court, the Vice-Presidents, the Presidents of the Chambers and other judges chosen in accordance with the rules of the Court. When a case is referred to the Grand Chamber under Article 43, no judge from the Chamber which rendered the judgment shall sit in the Grand Chamber, with the exception of the President of the Chamber and the judge who sat in respect of the High Contracting Party concerned.

Article 27 – Competence of single judges

1. A single judge may declare inadmissible or strike out of the Court's list of cases an application submitted under Article 34, where such a decision can be taken without further examination.

2. The decision shall be final.

3. If the single judge does not declare an application inadmissible or strike it out, that judge shall forward it to a committee or to a Chamber for further examination.

Article 28 – Competence of committees

1. In respect of an application submitted under Article 34, a committee may, by a unanimous vote,

(a) declare it inadmissible or strike it out of its list of cases, where such decision can be taken without further examination; or

(b) declare it admissible and render at the same time a judgment on the merits, if the underlying question in the case, concerning the interpretation or the application of the Convention or the Protocols thereto, is already the subject of well-established case-law of the Court.

2. Decisions and judgments under paragraph 1 shall be final.

3. If the judge elected in respect of the High Contracting Party concerned is not a member of the committee, the committee may at any stage of the proceedings invite that judge to take the place of one of the members of the committee, having regard to all relevant factors, including whether that Party has contested the application of the procedure under paragraph 1.b.

Article 29 – Decisions by Chambers on admissibility and merits

1. If no decision is taken under Article 27 or 28, or no judgment rendered under Article 28, a Chamber shall decide on the admissibility and merits of individual applications submitted under Article 34. The decision on admissibility may be taken separately.

2. A Chamber shall decide on the admissibility and merits of inter-State applications submitted under Article 33. The decision on admissibility shall be taken separately unless the Court, in exceptional cases, decides otherwise.

Article 30 – Relinquishment of jurisdiction to the Grand Chamber

Where a case pending before a Chamber raises a serious question affecting the interpretation of the Convention or the protocols thereto, or where the resolution of a question before the Chamber might have a result inconsistent with a judgment previously delivered by the Court, the Chamber may, at any time before it has rendered its judgment, relinquish jurisdiction in favour of the Grand Chamber, unless one of the parties to the case objects.*

Article 31 – Powers of the Grand Chamber

The Grand Chamber shall

(a) determine applications submitted either under Article 33 or Article 34 when a Chamber has relinquished jurisdiction under Article 30 or when the case has been referred to it under Article 43;

(b) decide on issues referred to the Court by the Committee of Ministers in accordance with Article 46, paragraph 4; and

(c) consider requests for advisory opinions submitted under Article 47.

Article 32 – Jurisdiction of the Court

1. The jurisdiction of the Court shall extend to all matters concerning the interpretation and application of the Convention and the protocols thereto which are referred to it as provided in Articles 33, 34, 46 and 47.

2. In the event of dispute as to whether the Court has jurisdiction, the Court shall decide.

Article 33 – Inter-State cases

Any High Contracting Party may refer to the Court any alleged breach of the provisions of the Convention and the protocols thereto by another High Contracting Party.

Article 34 – Individual applications

The Court may receive applications from any person, non-governmental organisation or group of individuals claiming to be the victim of a violation by one of the High Contracting Parties of the rights set forth in the Convention or the protocols thereto. The High Contracting Parties undertake not to hinder in any way the effective exercise of this right.

Article 35 – Admissibility criteria

1. The Court may only deal with the matter after all domestic remedies have been exhausted, according to the generally recognised rules of international law, and within a period of six months from the date on which the final decision was taken.**

2. The Court shall not deal with any application submitted under Article 34 that

(a) is anonymous; or

* As per Protocol 15:
Article 3
In Article 30 of the Convention, the words "unless one of the parties to the case objects" shall be deleted.

** As per Protocol 15:
Article 4
In Article 35, paragraph 1 of the Convention, the words "within a period of six months" shall be replaced by the words "within a period of four months".

(b) is substantially the same as a matter that has already been examined by the Court or has already been submitted to another procedure of international investigation or settlement and contains no relevant new information.

3. The Court shall declare inadmissible any individual application submitted under Article 34 if it considers that:

(a) the application is incompatible with the provisions of the Convention or the Protocols thereto, manifestly ill-founded, or an abuse of the right of individual application; or

(b) the applicant has not suffered a significant disadvantage, unless respect for human rights as defined in the Convention and the Protocols thereto requires an examination of the application on the merits and provided that no case may be rejected on this ground which has not been duly considered by a domestic tribunal.*

4. The Court shall reject any application which it considers inadmissible under this Article. It may do so at any stage of the proceedings.

Article 36 – Third party intervention

1. In all cases before a Chamber or the Grand Chamber, a High Contracting Party one of whose nationals is an applicant shall have the right to submit written comments and to take part in hearings.

2. The President of the Court may, in the interest of the proper administration of justice, invite any High Contracting Party which is not a party to the proceedings or any person concerned who is not the applicant to submit written comments or take part in hearings.

3. In all cases before a Chamber or the Grand Chamber, the Council of Europe Commissioner for Human Rights may submit written comments and take part in hearings.

Article 37 – Striking out applications

1. The Court may at any stage of the proceedings decide to strike an application out of its list of cases where the circumstances lead to the conclusion that

(a) the applicant does not intend to pursue his application; or

(b) the matter has been resolved; or

(c) for any other reason established by the Court, it is no longer justified to continue the examination of the application.

However, the Court shall continue the examination of the application if respect for human rights as defined in the Convention and the protocols thereto so requires.

2. The Court may decide to restore an application to its list of cases if it considers that the circumstances justify such a course.

Article 38 – Examination of the case

The Court shall examine the case together with the representatives of the parties and, if need be, undertake an investigation, for the effective conduct of which the High Contracting Parties concerned shall furnish all necessary facilities.

* As per Protocol 15:
Article 5
In Article 35, paragraph 3, sub-paragraph b of the Convention, the words "and provided that no case may be rejected on this ground which has not been duly considered by a domestic tribunal" shall be deleted.

Article 39 – Friendly settlements

1. At any stage of the proceedings, the Court may place itself at the disposal of the parties concerned with a view to securing a friendly settlement of the matter on the basis of respect for human rights as defined in the Convention and the Protocols thereto.

2. Proceedings conducted under paragraph 1 shall be confidential.

3. If a friendly settlement is effected, the Court shall strike the case out of its list by means of a decision which shall be confined to a brief statement of the facts and of the solution reached.

4. This decision shall be transmitted to the Committee of Ministers, which shall supervise the execution of the terms of the friendly settlement as set out in the decision.

Article 40 – Public hearings and access to documents

1. Hearings shall be in public unless the Court in exceptional circumstances decides otherwise.

2. Documents deposited with the Registrar shall be accessible to the public unless the President of the Court decides otherwise.

Article 41 – Just satisfaction

If the Court finds that there has been a violation of the Convention or the protocols thereto, and if the internal law of the High Contracting Party concerned allows only partial reparation to be made, the Court shall, if necessary, afford just satisfaction to the injured party.

Article 42 – Judgments of Chambers

Judgments of Chambers shall become final in accordance with the provisions of Article 44, paragraph 2.

Article 43 – Referral to the Grand Chamber

1. Within a period of three months from the date of the judgment of the Chamber, any party to the case may, in exceptional cases, request that the case be referred to the Grand Chamber.

2. A panel of five judges of the Grand Chamber shall accept the request if the case raises a serious question affecting the interpretation or application of the Convention or the protocols thereto, or a serious issue of general importance.

3. If the panel accepts the request, the Grand Chamber shall decide the case by means of a judgment.

Article 44 – Final judgments

1. The judgment of the Grand Chamber shall be final.

2. The judgment of a Chamber shall become final

(a) when the parties declare that they will not request that the case be referred to the Grand Chamber; or

(b) three months after the date of the judgment, if reference of the case to the Grand Chamber has not been requested; or

(c) when the panel of the Grand Chamber rejects the request to refer under Article 43.

3. The final judgment shall be published.

Article 45 – Reasons for judgments and decisions

1. Reasons shall be given for judgments as well as for decisions declaring applications admissible or inadmissible.

2. If a judgment does not represent, in whole or in part, the unanimous opinion of the judges, any judge shall be entitled to deliver a separate opinion.

Article 46 – Binding force and execution of judgments

1. The High Contracting Parties undertake to abide by the final judgment of the Court in any case to which they are parties.

2. The final judgment of the Court shall be transmitted to the Committee of Ministers, which shall supervise its execution.

3. If the Committee of Ministers considers that the supervision of the execution of a final judgment is hindered by a problem of interpretation of the judgment, it may refer the matter to the Court for a ruling on the question of interpretation. A referral decision shall require a majority vote of two thirds of the representatives entitled to sit on the Committee.

4. If the Committee of Ministers considers that a High Contracting Party refuses to abide by a final judgment in a case to which it is a party, it may, after serving formal notice on that Party and by decision adopted by a majority vote of two thirds of the representatives entitled to sit on the Committee, refer to the Court the question whether that Party has failed to fulfil its obligation under paragraph 1.

5. If the Court finds a violation of paragraph 1, it shall refer the case to the Committee of Ministers for consideration of the measures to be taken. If the Court finds no violation of paragraph 1, it shall refer the case to the Committee of Ministers, which shall close its examination of the case.

Article 47 – Advisory opinions

1. The Court may, at the request of the Committee of Ministers, give advisory opinions on legal questions concerning the interpretation of the Convention and the protocols thereto.

2. Such opinions shall not deal with any question relating to the content or scope of the rights or freedoms defined in Section I of the Convention and the protocols thereto, or with any other question which the Court or the Committee of Ministers might have to consider in consequence of any such proceedings as could be instituted in accordance with the Convention.

3. Decisions of the Committee of Ministers to request an advisory opinion of the Court shall require a majority vote of the representatives entitled to sit on the Committee.

Article 48 – Advisory jurisdiction of the Court

The Court shall decide whether a request for an advisory opinion submitted by the Committee of Ministers is within its competence as defined in Article 47.

Article 49 – Reasons for advisory opinions

1. Reasons shall be given for advisory opinions of the Court.

2. If the advisory opinion does not represent, in whole or in part, the unanimous opinion of the judges, any judge shall be entitled to deliver a separate opinion.

3. Advisory opinions of the Court shall be communicated to the Committee of Ministers.

Article 50 – Expenditure on the Court

The expenditure on the Court shall be borne by the Council of Europe.

Article 51 – Privileges and immunities of judges

The judges shall be entitled, during the exercise of their functions, to the privileges and immunities provided for in Article 40 of the Statute of the Council of Europe and in the agreements made thereunder.

Section III – Miscellaneous provisions

...

Article 55 – Exclusion of other means of dispute settlement

The High Contracting Parties agree that, except by special agreement, they will not avail themselves of treaties, conventions or declarations in force between them for the purpose of submitting, by way of petition, a dispute arising out of the interpretation or application of this Convention to a means of settlement other than those provided for in this Convention.

32.b Protocol 16 to the Convention on the Protection of Human Rights and Fundamental Freedoms

Date: 2 October 2013
Source: CETS No 214
https://www.echr.coe.int/Documents/Protocol_16_ENG.pdf

Preamble

The member States of the Council of Europe and other High Contracting Parties to the Convention for the Protection of Human Rights and Fundamental Freedoms, signed at Rome on 4 November 1950 (hereinafter referred to as "the Convention"), signatories hereto,

Having regard to the provisions of the Convention and, in particular, Article 19 establishing the European Court of Human Rights (hereinafter referred to as "the Court");

Considering that the extension of the Court's competence to give advisory opinions will further enhance the interaction between the Court and national authorities and thereby reinforce implementation of the Convention, in accordance with the principle of subsidiarity;

Having regard to Opinion No. 285 (2013) adopted by the Parliamentary Assembly of the Council of Europe on 28 June 2013,

Have agreed as follows:

Article 1

1. Highest courts and tribunals of a High Contracting Party, as specified in accordance with Article 10, may request the Court to give advisory opinions on questions of principle

relating to the interpretation or application of the rights and freedoms defined in the Convention or the protocols thereto.

2. The requesting court or tribunal may seek an advisory opinion only in the context of a case pending before it.

3. The requesting court or tribunal shall give reasons for its request and shall provide the relevant legal and factual background of the pending case.

Article 2

1. A panel of five judges of the Grand Chamber shall decide whether to accept the request for an advisory opinion, having regard to Article 1. The panel shall give reasons for any refusal to accept the request.

2. If the panel accepts the request, the Grand Chamber shall deliver the advisory opinion.

3. The panel and the Grand Chamber, as referred to in the preceding paragraphs, shall include ex officio the judge elected in respect of the High Contracting Party to which the requesting court or tribunal pertains. If there is none or if that judge is unable to sit, a person chosen by the President of the Court from a list submitted in advance by that Party shall sit in the capacity of judge.

Article 3

The Council of Europe Commissioner for Human Rights and the High Contracting Party to which the requesting court or tribunal pertains shall have the right to submit written comments and take part in any hearing. The President of the Court may, in the interest of the proper administration of justice, invite any other High Contracting Party or person also to submit written comments or take part in any hearing.

Article 4

1. Reasons shall be given for advisory opinions.

2. If the advisory opinion does not represent, in whole or in part, the unanimous opinion of the judges, any judge shall be entitled to deliver a separate opinion.

3. Advisory opinions shall be communicated to the requesting court or tribunal and to the High Contracting Party to which that court or tribunal pertains.

4. Advisory opinions shall be published.

Article 5

Advisory opinions shall not be binding.

Article 6

As between the High Contracting Parties the provisions of Articles 1 to 5 of this Protocol shall be regarded as additional articles to the Convention, and all the provisions of the Convention shall apply accordingly.

Article 7

1. This Protocol shall be open for signature by the High Contracting Parties to the Convention, which may express their consent to be bound by:

(a) signature without reservation as to ratification, acceptance or approval; or

(b) signature subject to ratification, acceptance or approval, followed by ratification, acceptance or approval.

2. The instruments of ratification, acceptance or approval shall be deposited with the Secretary General of the Council of Europe.

Article 8

1. This Protocol shall enter into force on the first day of the month following the expiration of a period of three months after the date on which ten High Contracting Parties to the Convention have expressed their consent to be bound by the Protocol in accordance with the provisions of Article 7.

2. In respect of any High Contracting Party to the Convention which subsequently expresses its consent to be bound by it, the Protocol shall enter into force on the first day of the month following the expiration of a period of three months after the date of the expression of its consent to be bound by the Protocol in accordance with the provisions of Article 7.

Article 9

No reservation may be made under Article 57 of the Convention in respect of the provisions of this Protocol.

Article 10

Each High Contracting Party to the Convention shall, at the time of signature or when depositing its instrument of ratification, acceptance or approval, by means of a declaration addressed to the Secretary General of the Council of Europe, indicate the courts or tribunals that it designates for the purposes of Article 1, paragraph 1, of this Protocol. This declaration may be modified at any later date and in the same manner.

Article 11

The Secretary General of the Council of Europe shall notify the member States of the Council of Europe and the other High Contracting Parties to the Convention of:

(a) any signature;

(b) the deposit of any instrument of ratification, acceptance or approval;

(c) any date of entry into force of this Protocol in accordance with Article 8;

(d) any declaration made in accordance with Article 10; and

(e) any other act, notification or communication relating to this Protocol.

In witness whereof the undersigned, being duly authorised thereto, have signed this Protocol.

Done at Strasbourg, this 2nd day of October 2013, in English and French, both texts being equally authentic, in a single copy which shall be deposited in the archives of the Council of Europe. The Secretary General of the Council of Europe shall transmit certified copies to each member State of the Council of Europe and to the other High Contracting Parties to the Convention.

32.c Rules of Court*

Date: 1 April 2011**
Source: https://www.echr.coe.int/documents/rules_court_eng.pdf

The European Court of Human Rights,

Having regard to the Convention for the Protection of Human Rights and Fundamental Freedoms and the Protocols thereto,

Makes the present Rules:

Rule 1 – Definitions

For the purposes of these Rules unless the context otherwise requires:

(a) the term "Convention" means the Convention for the Protection of Human Rights and Fundamental Freedoms and the Protocols thereto;
(b) the expression "plenary Court" means the European Court of Human Rights sitting in plenary session;
(c) the expression "Grand Chamber" means the Grand Chamber of seventeen judges constituted in pursuance of Article 26 § 1 of the Convention;
(d) the term "Section" means a Chamber set up by the plenary Court for a fixed period in pursuance of Article 25 (b) of the Convention and the expression "President of the Section" means the judge elected by the plenary Court in pursuance of Article 25 (c) of the Convention as President of such a Section;
(e) the term "Chamber" means any Chamber of seven judges constituted in pursuance of Article 26 § 1 of the Convention and the expression "President of the Chamber" means the judge presiding over such a "Chamber";
(f) the term "Committee" means a Committee of three judges set up in pursuance of Article 26 § 1 of the Convention and the expression "President of the Committee" means the judge presiding over such a "Committee";
(g) the expression "single-judge formation" means a single judge sitting in accordance with Article 26 § 1 of the Convention;
(h) the term "Court" means either the plenary Court, the Grand Chamber, a Section, a Chamber, a Committee, a single judge or the panel of five judges referred to in Article 43 § 2 of the Convention and in Article 2 of Protocol No. 16 thereto;
(i) the expression "ad hoc judge" means any person chosen in pursuance of Article 26 § 4 of the Convention and in accordance with Rule 29 to sit as a member of the Grand Chamber or as a member of a Chamber;
(j) the terms "judge" and "judges" mean the judges elected by the Parliamentary Assembly of the Council of Europe or ad hoc judges;
(k) the expression "Judge Rapporteur" means a judge appointed to carry out the tasks provided for in Rules 48 and 49;
(l) the term "non-judicial rapporteur" means a member of the Registry charged with assisting the single-judge formations provided for in Article 24 § 2 of the Convention;

* N.B.: Footnotes have been omitted.

** This new edition of the Rules of Court incorporates amendments made by the Plenary Court on 4 November 2019.

The new edition entered into force on 2 June 2021.

(m) the term "delegate" means a judge who has been appointed to a delegation by the Chamber and the expression "head of the delegation" means the delegate appointed by the Chamber to lead its delegation;
(n) the term "delegation" means a body composed of delegates, Registry members and any other person appointed by the Chamber to assist the delegation;
(o) the term "Registrar" denotes the Registrar of the Court or the Registrar of a Section according to the context;
(p) the terms "party" and "parties" mean
   - the applicant or respondent Contracting Parties;
   - the applicant (the person, non-governmental organisation or group of individuals) that lodged a complaint under Article 34 of the Convention;

(q) the expression "third party" means any Contracting Party or any person concerned or the Council of Europe Commissioner for Human Rights who, as provided for in Article 36 §§ 1, 2 and 3 of the Convention and in Article 3 of Protocol No. 16, has exercised the right to submit written comments and take part in a hearing, or has been invited to do so;
(r) the terms "hearing" and "hearings" mean oral proceedings held on the admissibility and/or merits of an application or in connection with a request for revision or an advisory opinion, a request for interpretation by a party or by the Committee of Ministers, or a question whether there has been a failure to fulfil an obligation which may be referred to the Court by virtue of Article 46 § 4 of the Convention;
(s) the expression "Committee of Ministers" means the Committee of Ministers of the Council of Europe;
(t) the terms "former Court" and "Commission" mean respectively the European Court and European Commission of Human Rights set up under former Article 19 of the Convention.

TITLE I – ORGANISATION AND WORKING OF THE COURT

Chapter I: Judges

Rule 2 – Calculation of term of office

1. Where the seat is vacant on the date of the judge's election, or where the election takes place less than three months before the seat becomes vacant, the term of office shall begin as from the date of taking up office which shall be no later than three months after the date of election.

2. Where the judge's election takes place more than three months before the seat becomes vacant, the term of office shall begin on the date on which the seat becomes vacant.

3. In accordance with Article 23 § 3 of the Convention, an elected judge shall hold office until a successor has taken the oath or made the declaration provided for in Rule 3.

Rule 3 – Oath or solemn declaration

1. Before taking up office, each elected judge shall, at the first sitting of the plenary Court at which the judge is present or, in case of need, before the President of the Court, take the following oath or make the following solemn declaration:

> "I swear" – or "I solemnly declare" – "that I will exercise my functions as a judge honourably, independently and impartially and that I will keep secret all deliberations."

2. This act shall be recorded in minutes.

Rule 4 – Incompatible activities

1. In accordance with Article 21 § 3 of the Convention, the judges shall not during their term of office engage in any political or administrative activity or any professional activity which is incompatible with their independence or impartiality or with the demands of a full-time office. Each judge shall declare to the President of the Court any additional activity. In the event of a disagreement between the President and the judge concerned, any question arising shall be decided by the plenary Court.

2. A former judge shall not represent a party or third party in any capacity in proceedings before the Court relating to an application lodged before the date on which he or she ceased to hold office. As regards applications lodged subsequently, a former judge may not represent a party or third party in any capacity in proceedings before the Court until a period of two years from the date on which he or she ceased to hold office has elapsed.

Rule 5 – Precedence

1. Elected judges shall take precedence after the President and Vice-Presidents of the Court and the Presidents of the Sections, according to the date of their taking up office in accordance with Rule 2 §§ 1 and 2.

2. Vice-Presidents of the Court elected to office on the same date shall take precedence according to the length of time they have served as judges. If the length of time they have served as judges is the same, they shall take precedence according to age. The same rule shall apply to Presidents of Sections.

3. Judges who have served the same length of time shall take precedence according to age. 4. Ad hoc judges shall take precedence after the elected judges according to age.

Rule 6 – Resignation

Resignation of a judge shall be notified to the President of the Court, who shall transmit it to the Secretary General of the Council of Europe. Subject to the provisions of Rules 24 § 4 in fine and 26 § 3, resignation shall constitute vacation of office.

Rule 7 – Dismissal from office

No judge may be dismissed from his or her office unless the other judges, meeting in plenary session, decide by a majority of two-thirds of the elected judges in office that he or she has ceased to fulfil the required conditions. He or she must first be heard by the plenary Court. Any judge may set in motion the procedure for dismissal from office.

Chapter II: Presidency of the Court and the role of the Bureau

Rule 8 – Election of the President and Vice-Presidents of the Court and the Presidents and Vice-Presidents of the Sections

1. The plenary Court shall elect its President and two Vice-Presidents for a period of three years as well as the Presidents of the Sections for a period of two years, provided that such periods shall not exceed the duration of their terms of office as judges.

2. Each Section shall likewise elect a Vice-President for a period of two years, provided that such period shall not exceed the duration of his or her term of office as judge.

3. A judge elected in accordance with paragraphs 1 or 2 above may be re-elected but only once to the same level of office.

4. The Presidents and Vice-Presidents shall continue to hold office until the election of their successors.

5. The elections referred to in paragraph 1 of this Rule shall be by secret ballot. Only the elected judges who are present shall take part. If no candidate receives an absolute majority of the votes cast, an additional round or rounds shall take place until one candidate has achieved an absolute majority. After the first round, any candidate receiving fewer than five votes shall be eliminated, and the vote shall take place between the remaining candidates. In each subsequent round, the candidate who has received the least number of votes shall be eliminated. If there is more than one candidate in this position, only the candidate who is lowest in the order of precedence in accordance with Rule 5 shall be eliminated. If there are only two candidates left and in two rounds of voting neither of them has achieved an absolute majority of the votes cast, the candidate who obtains a majority of the votes cast in the next round, excluding blank and invalid votes, shall be elected. In the event of a tie between two candidates in the final round, preference shall be given to the judge having precedence in accordance with Rule 5.

6. The rules set out in the preceding paragraph shall apply to the elections referred to in paragraph 2 of this Rule. However, where more than one round of voting is required until one candidate has achieved the required majority, only the candidate who has received the least number of votes shall be eliminated after each round.

Rule 9 – Functions of the President of the Court

1. The President of the Court shall direct the work and administration of the Court. The President shall represent the Court and, in particular, be responsible for its relations with the authorities of the Council of Europe.

2. The President shall preside at plenary meetings of the Court, meetings of the Grand Chamber and meetings of the panel of five judges.

3. The President shall not take part in the consideration of cases being heard by Chambers except where he or she is the judge elected in respect of a Contracting Party concerned.

Rule 9A – Role of the Bureau

1. (a) The Court shall have a Bureau, composed of the President of the Court, the Vice-Presidents of the Court and the Section Presidents. Where a Vice-President or a Section President is unable to attend a Bureau meeting, he or she shall be replaced by the Section Vice-President or, failing that, by the next most senior member of the Section according to the order of precedence established in Rule 5.

(b) The Bureau may request the attendance of any other member of the Court or any other person whose presence it considers necessary.

2. The Bureau shall be assisted by the Registrar and the Deputy Registrars.

3. The Bureau's task shall be to assist the President in carrying out his or her function in directing the work and administration of the Court. To this end the President may submit to the Bureau any administrative or extra-judicial matter which falls within his or her competence.

4. The Bureau shall also facilitate coordination between the Court's Sections.

5. The President may consult the Bureau before issuing practice directions under Rule 32 and before approving general instructions drawn up by the Registrar under Rule 17 § 4.

6. The Bureau may report on any matter to the Plenary. It may also make proposals to the Plenary.

7. A record shall be kept of the Bureau's meetings and distributed to the Judges in both the Court's official languages. The secretary to the Bureau shall be designated by the Registrar in agreement with the President.

Rule 10 – Functions of the Vice-Presidents of the Court

The Vice-Presidents of the Court shall assist the President of the Court. They shall take the place of the President if the latter is unable to carry out his or her duties or the office of President is vacant, or at the request of the President. They shall also act as Presidents of Sections.

Rule 11 – Replacement of the President and the Vice-Presidents of the Court

If the President and the Vice-Presidents of the Court are at the same time unable to carry out their duties or if their offices are at the same time vacant, the office of President of the Court shall be assumed by a President of a Section or, if none is available, by another elected judge, in accordance with the order of precedence provided for in Rule 5.

Rule 12 – Presidency of Sections and Chambers

The Presidents of the Sections shall preside at the sittings of the Section and Chambers of which they are members and shall direct the Sections' work. The Vice-Presidents of the Sections shall take their place if they are unable to carry out their duties or if the office of President of the Section concerned is vacant, or at the request of the President of the Section. Failing that, the judges of the Section and the Chambers shall take their place, in the order of precedence provided for in Rule 5.

Rule 13 – Inability to preside

Judges of the Court may not preside in cases in which the Contracting Party of which they are nationals or in respect of which they were elected is a party, or in cases where they sit as a judge appointed by virtue of Rule 29 § 1 (a) or Rule 30 § 1.

Rule 14 – Balanced representation of the sexes

In relation to the making of appointments governed by this and the following chapter of the present Rules, the Court shall pursue a policy aimed at securing a balanced representation of the sexes.

Chapter III: The Registry

Rule 15 – Election of the Registrar

1. The plenary Court shall elect its Registrar. The candidates shall be of high moral character and must possess the legal, managerial and linguistic knowledge and experience necessary to carry out the functions attaching to the post.

2. The Registrar shall be elected for a term of five years and may be re-elected. The Registrar may not be dismissed from office, unless the judges, meeting in plenary session, decide by a majority of two-thirds of the elected judges in office that the person concerned has ceased to fulfil the required conditions. He or she must first be heard by the plenary Court. Any judge may set in motion the procedure for dismissal from office.

3. The elections referred to in this Rule shall be by secret ballot; only the elected judges who are present shall take part. If no candidate receives an absolute majority of the votes

cast, an additional round or rounds of voting shall take place until one candidate has achieved an absolute majority. After each round, any candidate receiving fewer than five votes shall be eliminated; and if more than two candidates have received five votes or more, the one who has received the least number of votes shall also be eliminated. In the event of a tie in an additional round of voting, preference shall be given, firstly, to the female candidate, if any, and, secondly, to the older candidate.

4. Before taking up office, the Registrar shall take the following oath or make the following solemn declaration before the plenary Court or, if need be, before the President of the Court:

> "I swear" – or "I solemnly declare" – "that I will exercise loyally, discreetly and conscientiously the functions conferred upon me as Registrar of the European Court of Human Rights."

This act shall be recorded in minutes.

Rule 16 – Election of the Deputy Registrars

1. The plenary Court shall also elect one or more Deputy Registrars on the conditions and in the manner and for the term prescribed in the preceding Rule. The procedure for dismissal from office provided for in respect of the Registrar shall likewise apply. The Court shall first consult the Registrar in both these matters.

2. Before taking up office, a Deputy Registrar shall take an oath or make a solemn declaration before the plenary Court or, if need be, before the President of the Court, in terms similar to those prescribed in respect of the Registrar. This act shall be recorded in minutes.

Rule 17 – Functions of the Registrar

1. The Registrar shall assist the Court in the performance of its functions and shall be responsible for the organisation and activities of the Registry under the authority of the President of the Court.

2. The Registrar shall have the custody of the archives of the Court and shall be the channel for all communications and notifications made by, or addressed to, the Court in connection with the cases brought or to be brought before it.

3. The Registrar shall, subject to the duty of discretion attaching to this office, reply to requests for information concerning the work of the Court, in particular to enquiries from the press.

4. General instructions drawn up by the Registrar, and approved by the President of the Court, shall regulate the working of the Registry.

Rule 18 – Organisation of the Registry

1. The Registry shall consist of Section Registries equal to the number of Sections set up by the Court and of the departments necessary to provide the legal and administrative services required by the Court.

2. The Section Registrar shall assist the Section in the performance of its functions and may be assisted by a Deputy Section Registrar.

3. The officials of the Registry shall be appointed by the Registrar under the authority of the President of the Court. The appointment of the Registrar and Deputy Registrars shall be governed by Rules 15 and 16 above.

Rule 18A – Non-judicial rapporteurs

1. When sitting in a single-judge formation, the Court shall be assisted by non-judicial rapporteurs who shall function under the authority of the President of the Court. They shall form part of the Court's Registry.

2. The non-judicial rapporteurs shall be appointed by the President of the Court on a proposal by the Registrar. Section Registrars and Deputy Section Registrars, as referred to in Rule 18 § 2, shall act ex officio as non-judicial rapporteurs.

Rule 18B – Jurisconsult

For the purposes of ensuring the quality and consistency of its case-law, the Court shall be assisted by a Jurisconsult. He or she shall be a member of the Registry. The Jurisconsult shall provide opinions and information, in particular to the judicial formations and the members of the Court.

Chapter IV: The Working of the Court

Rule 19 – Seat of the Court

1. The seat of the Court shall be at the seat of the Council of Europe at Strasbourg. The Court may, however, if it considers it expedient, perform its functions elsewhere in the territories of the member States of the Council of Europe.

2. The Court may decide, at any stage of the examination of an application, that it is necessary that an investigation or any other function be carried out elsewhere by it or one or more of its members.

Rule 20 – Sessions of the plenary Court

1. The plenary sessions of the Court shall be convened by the President of the Court whenever the performance of its functions under the Convention and under these Rules so requires. The President of the Court shall convene a plenary session if at least one-third of the members of the Court so request, and in any event once a year to consider administrative matters.

2. The quorum of the plenary Court shall be two-thirds of the elected judges in office.

3. If there is no quorum, the President shall adjourn the sitting.

Rule 21 – Other sessions of the Court

1. The Grand Chamber, the Chambers and the Committees shall sit full time. On a proposal by the President, however, the Court shall fix session periods each year.

2. Outside those periods the Grand Chamber and the Chambers shall be convened by their Presidents in cases of urgency.

Rule 22 – Deliberations

1. The Court shall deliberate in private. Its deliberations shall remain secret.

2. Only the judges shall take part in the deliberations. The Registrar or the designated substitute, as well as such other officials of the Registry and interpreters whose assistance is deemed necessary, shall be present. No other person may be admitted except by special decision of the Court.

3. Before a vote is taken on any matter in the Court, the President may request the judges to state their opinions on it.

Rule 23 – Votes

1. The decisions of the Court shall be taken by a majority of the judges present. In the event of a tie, a fresh vote shall be taken and, if there is still a tie, the President shall have a casting vote. This paragraph shall apply unless otherwise provided for in these Rules.

2. The decisions and judgments of the Grand Chamber and the Chambers shall be adopted by a majority of the sitting judges. Abstentions shall not be allowed in final votes on the admissibility and merits of cases.

3. As a general rule, votes shall be taken by a show of hands. The President may take a roll-call vote, in reverse order of precedence.

4. Any matter that is to be voted upon shall be formulated in precise terms.

Rule 23A – Decision by tacit agreement

Where it is necessary for the Court to decide a point of procedure or any other question other than at a scheduled meeting of the Court, the President may direct that a draft decision be circulated among the judges and that a deadline be set for their comments on the draft. In the absence of any objection from a judge, the proposal shall be deemed to have been adopted at the expiry of the deadline.

Chapter V: The Composition of the Court

Rule 24 – Composition of the Grand Chamber

1. The Grand Chamber shall be composed of seventeen judges and at least three substitute judges.

2. (a) The Grand Chamber shall include the President and the Vice-Presidents of the Court and the Presidents of the Sections. Any Vice-President of the Court or President of a Section who is unable to sit as a member of the Grand Chamber shall be replaced by the Vice-President of the relevant Section.

(b) The judge elected in respect of the Contracting Party concerned or, where appropriate, the judge designated by virtue of Rule 29 or Rule 30 shall sit as an ex officio member of the Grand Chamber in accordance with Article 26 §§ 4 and 5 of the Convention.

(c) In cases referred to the Grand Chamber under Article 30 of the Convention, the Grand Chamber shall also include the members of the Chamber which relinquished jurisdiction.

(d) In cases referred to it under Article 43 of the Convention, the Grand Chamber shall not include any judge who sat in the Chamber which rendered the judgment in the case so referred, with the exception of the President of that Chamber and the judge who sat in respect of the State Party concerned, or any judge who sat in the Chamber or Chambers which ruled on the admissibility of the application.

(e) The judges and substitute judges who are to complete the Grand Chamber in each case referred to it shall be designated from among the remaining judges by a drawing of lots by the President of the Court in the presence of the Registrar. The modalities for the drawing of lots shall be laid down by the Plenary Court, having due regard to the need for a geographically balanced composition reflecting the different legal systems among the Contracting Parties.

(f) In examining a request under Article 46 § 4 of the Convention, the Grand Chamber shall include, in addition to the judges referred to in paragraph 2 (a) and (b) of this Rule, the members of the Chamber or Committee which rendered the judgment in the case concerned. If the judgment was rendered by a Grand Chamber, the Grand Chamber shall be constituted as the original Grand Chamber. In all cases, including those where it is not possible to reconstitute the original Grand Chamber, the judges and substitute judges who are to complete the Grand Chamber shall be designated in accordance with paragraph 2 (e) of this Rule.

(g) In examining a request for an advisory opinion under Article 47 of the Convention, the Grand Chamber shall be constituted in accordance with the provisions of paragraph 2 (a) and (e) of this Rule.

(h) In examining a request for an advisory opinion under Protocol No. 16 to the Convention, the Grand Chamber shall be constituted in accordance with the provision of paragraph 2 (a), (b) and (e) of this Rule.

3. If any judges are prevented from sitting, they shall be replaced by the substitute judges in the order in which the latter were selected under paragraph 2 (e) of this Rule.

4. The judges and substitute judges designated in accordance with the above provisions shall continue to sit in the Grand Chamber for the consideration of the case until the proceedings have been completed. Even after the end of their terms of office, they shall continue to deal with the case if they have participated in the consideration of the merits. These provisions shall also apply to proceedings relating to advisory opinions.

5. (a) The panel of five judges of the Grand Chamber called upon to consider a referral request submitted under Article 43 of the Convention shall be composed of

- the President of the Court. If the President of the Court is prevented from sitting, he or she shall be replaced by the Vice-President of the Court taking precedence;
- two Presidents of Sections designated by rotation. If the Presidents of the Sections so designated are prevented from sitting, they shall be replaced by the Vice-Presidents of their Sections;
- two judges designated by rotation from among the judges elected by the remaining Sections to serve on the panel for a period of six months;
- at least two substitute judges designated in rotation from among the judges elected by the Sections to serve on the panel for a period of six months.

(b) When considering a referral request, the panel shall not include any judge who took part in the consideration of the admissibility or merits of the case in question.

(c) No judge elected in respect of, or who is a national of, a Contracting Party concerned by a referral request may be a member of the panel when it examines that request. An elected judge appointed pursuant to Rules 29 or 30 shall likewise be excluded from consideration of any such request.

(d) Any member of the panel unable to sit, for the reasons set out in (b) or (c) shall be replaced by a substitute judge designated in rotation from among the judges elected by the Sections to serve on the panel for a period of six months.

(e) When considering a request for an advisory opinion submitted under Article 1 of Protocol No. 16 to the Convention, the panel shall be composed in accordance with the provisions of Rule 93.

Rule 25 – Setting-up of Sections

1. The Chambers provided for in Article 25 (b) of the Convention (referred to in these Rules as "Sections") shall be set up by the plenary Court, on a proposal by its President, for

a period of three years with effect from the election of the presidential office-holders of the Court under Rule 8. There shall be at least four Sections.

2. Each judge shall be a member of a Section. The composition of the Sections shall be geographically and gender balanced and shall reflect the different legal systems among the Contracting Parties.

3. Where a judge ceases to be a member of the Court before the expiry of the period for which the Section has been constituted, the judge's place in the Section shall be taken by his or her successor as a member of the Court.

4. The President of the Court may exceptionally make modifications to the composition of the Sections if circumstances so require.

5. On a proposal by the President, the plenary Court may constitute an additional Section.

Rule 26 – Constitution of Chambers

1. The Chambers of seven judges provided for in Article 26 § 1 of the Convention for the consideration of cases brought before the Court shall be constituted from the Sections as follows.

(a) Subject to paragraph 2 of this Rule and to Rule 28 § 4, last sentence, the Chamber shall in each case include the President of the Section and the judge elected in respect of any Contracting Party concerned. If the latter judge is not a member of the Section to which the application has been assigned under Rules 51 or 52, he or she shall sit as an ex officio member of the Chamber in accordance with Article 26 § 4 of the Convention. Rule 29 shall apply if that judge is unable to sit or withdraws.

(b) The other members of the Chamber shall be designated by the President of the Section in rotation from among the members of the relevant Section.

(c) The members of the Section who are not so designated shall sit in the case as substitute judges.

2. The judge elected in respect of any Contracting Party concerned or, where appropriate, another elected judge or ad hoc judge appointed in accordance with Rules 29 and 30 may be dispensed by the President of the Chamber from attending meetings devoted to preparatory or procedural matters. For the purposes of such meetings the first substitute judge shall sit.

3. Even after the end of their terms of office, judges shall continue to deal with cases in which they have participated in the consideration of the merits.

Rule 27 – Committees

1. Committees composed of three judges belonging to the same Section shall be set up under Article 26 § 1 of the Convention. After consulting the Presidents of the Sections, the President of the Court shall decide on the number of Committees to be set up.

2. The Committees shall be constituted for a period of twelve months by rotation among the members of each Section, excepting the President of the Section.

3. The judges of the Section, including the President of the Section, who are not members of a Committee may, as appropriate, be called upon to sit. They may also be called upon to take the place of members who are unable to sit.

4. The President of the Committee shall be the member having precedence in the Section.

Rule 27A – Single-judge formation

1. A single-judge formation shall be introduced in pursuance of Article 26 § 1 of the Convention. After consulting the Bureau, the President of the Court shall decide on the number of single judges to be appointed and shall appoint them in respect of one or more Contracting Parties.

2. The following shall also sit as single judges

(a) the Presidents of the Sections when exercising their competences under Rule 54 §§ 2 (b) and 3;

(b) Vice-Presidents of Sections appointed to decide on requests for interim measures in accordance with Rule 39 § 4.

3. In accordance with Article 26 § 3 of the Convention, a judge may not examine as a single judge any application against the Contracting Party in respect of which that judge has been elected. In addition, a judge may not examine as a single judge any application against a Contracting Party of which that judge is a national.

4. Single judges shall be appointed for a period of twelve months. They shall continue to carry out their other duties within the Sections of which they are members in accordance with Rule 25 § 2.

5. Pursuant to Article 24 § 2 of the Convention, when deciding, each single judge shall be assisted by a non-judicial rapporteur.

Rule 28 – Inability to sit, withdrawal or exemption

1. Any judge who is prevented from taking part in sittings which he or she has been called upon to attend shall, as soon as possible, give notice to the President of the Chamber.

2. A judge may not take part in the consideration of any case if

(a) he or she has a personal interest in the case, including a spousal, parental or other close family, personal or professional relationship, or a subordinate relationship, with any of the parties;

(b) he or she has previously acted in the case, whether as the Agent, advocate or adviser of a party or of a person having an interest in the case, or as a member of another national or international tribunal or commission of inquiry, or in any other capacity;

(c) he or she, being an ad hoc judge or a former elected judge continuing to sit by virtue of Rule 26 §3, engages in any political or administrative activity or any professional activity which is incompatible with his or her independence or impartiality;

(d) he or she has expressed opinions publicly, through the communications media, in writing, through his or her public actions or otherwise, that are objectively capable of adversely affecting his or her impartiality;

(e) for any other reason, his or her independence or impartiality may legitimately be called into doubt.

3. If a judge withdraws for one of the said reasons, he or she shall notify the President of the Chamber, who shall exempt the judge from sitting.

4. In the event of any doubt on the part of the judge concerned or the President as to the existence of one of the grounds referred to in paragraph 2 of this Rule, that issue shall be decided by the Chamber. After hearing the views of the judge concerned, the Chamber shall deliberate and vote, without that judge being present. For the purposes of the Chamber's deliberations and vote on this issue, he or she shall be replaced by the first substitute judge

in the Chamber. The same shall apply if the judge sits in respect of any Contracting Party concerned in accordance with Rules 29 and 30.

5. The provisions above shall apply also to a judge's acting as a single judge or participation in a Committee, save that the notice required under paragraphs 1 or 3 of this Rule shall be given to the President of the Section.

Rule 29 – *Ad hoc* judges

1. (a) If the judge elected in respect of a Contracting Party concerned is unable to sit in the Chamber, withdraws, or is exempted, or if there is none, the President of the Chamber shall appoint an ad hoc judge, who is eligible to take part in the consideration of the case in accordance with Rule 28, from a list submitted in advance by the Contracting Party containing the names of three to five persons whom the Contracting Party has designated as eligible to serve as ad hoc judges for a renewable period of four years and as satisfying the conditions set out in paragraph 1 (c) of this Rule.

The list shall include both sexes and shall be accompanied by biographical details of the persons whose names appear on the list. The persons whose names appear on the list may not represent a party or a third party in any capacity in proceedings before the Court.

(b) The procedure set out in paragraph 1 (a) of this Rule shall apply if the person so appointed is unable to sit or withdraws.

(c) An ad hoc judge shall possess the qualifications required by Article 21 § 1 of the Convention and must be in a position to meet the demands of availability and attendance provided for in paragraph 5 of this Rule. For the duration of their appointment, an ad hoc judge shall not represent any party or third party in any capacity in proceedings before the Court.

2. The President of the Chamber shall appoint another elected judge to sit as an ad hoc judge where

(a) at the time of notice being given of the application under Rule 54 § 2 (b), the Contracting Party concerned has not supplied the Registrar with a list as described in paragraph 1 (a) of this Rule, or

(b) the President of the Chamber finds that less than three of the persons indicated in the list satisfy the conditions laid down in paragraph 1 (c) of this Rule.

3. The President of the Chamber may decide not to appoint an ad hoc judge pursuant to paragraph 1 (a) or 2 of this Rule until notice of the application is given to the Contracting Party under Rule 54 § 2 (b). Pending the decision of the President of the Chamber, the first substitute judge shall sit.

4. An ad hoc judge shall, at the beginning of the first sitting held to consider the case after the judge has been appointed, take the oath or make the solemn declaration provided for in Rule 3. This act shall be recorded in minutes.

5. Ad hoc judges are required to make themselves available to the Court and, subject to Rule 26 § 2, to attend the meetings of the Chamber.

6. The provisions of this Rule shall apply mutatis mutandis to proceedings before a panel of the Grand Chamber in connection with a request for an advisory opinion submitted under Article 1 of Protocol No. 16 to the Convention, as well as to proceedings before the Grand Chamber constituted to examine requests accepted by the panel.

Rule 30 – Common interest

1. If two or more applicant or respondent Contracting Parties have a common interest, the President of the Chamber may invite them to agree to appoint a single judge elected in respect of one of the Contracting Parties concerned as common-interest judge who will be called upon to sit ex officio. If the Parties are unable to agree, the President shall choose the common-interest judge by lot from the judges proposed by the Parties.

2. The President of the Chamber may decide not to invite the Contracting Parties concerned to make an appointment under paragraph 1 of this Rule until notice of the application has been given under Rule 54 § 2.

3. In the event of a dispute as to the existence of a common interest or as to any related matter, the Chamber shall decide, if necessary after obtaining written submissions from the Contracting Parties concerned.

TITLE II – PROCEDURE

Chapter I: General Rules

Rule 31 – Possibility of particular derogations

The provisions of this Title shall not prevent the Court from derogating from them for the consideration of a particular case after having consulted the parties where appropriate.

Rule 32 – Practice directions

The President of the Court may issue practice directions, notably in relation to such matters as appearance at hearings and the filing of pleadings and other documents.

Rule 33 – Public character of documents

1. All documents deposited with the Registry by the parties or by any third party in connection with an application, except those deposited within the framework of friendly-settlement negotiations as provided for in Rule 62, shall be accessible to the public in accordance with arrangements determined by the Registrar, unless the President of the Chamber, for the reasons set out in paragraph 2 of this Rule, decides otherwise, either of his or her own motion or at the request of a party or any other person concerned.

2. Public access to a document or to any part of it may be restricted in the interests of morals, public order or national security in a democratic society, where the interests of juveniles or the protection of the private life of the parties or of any person concerned so require, or to the extent strictly necessary in the opinion of the President of the Chamber in special circumstances where publicity would prejudice the interests of justice.

3. Any request for confidentiality made under paragraph 1 of this Rule must include reasons and specify whether it is requested that all or part of the documents be inaccessible to the public.

Rule 34 – Use of languages

1. The official languages of the Court shall be English and French.

2. In connection with applications lodged under Article 34 of the Convention, and for as long as no Contracting Party has been given notice of such an application in accordance with these Rules, all communications with and oral and written submissions by applicants or their representatives, if not in one of the Court's official languages, shall be in one of

the official languages of the Contracting Parties. If a Contracting Party is informed or given notice of an application in accordance with these Rules, the application and any accompanying documents shall be communicated to that State in the language in which they were lodged with the Registry by the applicant.

3. (a) All communications with and oral and written submissions by applicants or their representatives in respect of a hearing, or after notice of an application has been given to a Contracting Party, shall be in one of the Court's official languages, unless the President of the Chamber grants leave for the continued use of the official language of a Contracting Party.

(b) If such leave is granted, the Registrar shall make the necessary arrangements for the interpretation and translation into English or French of the applicant's oral and written submissions respectively, in full or in part, where the President of the Chamber considers it to be in the interests of the proper conduct of the proceedings.

(c) Exceptionally the President of the Chamber may make the grant of leave subject to the condition that the applicant bear all or part of the costs of making such arrangements.

(d) Unless the President of the Chamber decides otherwise, any decision made under the foregoing provisions of this paragraph shall remain valid in all subsequent proceedings in the case, including those in respect of requests for referral of the case to the Grand Chamber and requests for interpretation or revision of a judgment under Rules 73, 79 and 80 respectively.

4. (a) All communications with and oral and written submissions by a Contracting Party which is a party to the case shall be in one of the Court's official languages. The President of the Chamber may grant the Contracting Party concerned leave to use one of its official languages for its oral and written submissions.

(b) If such leave is granted, it shall be the responsibility of the requesting Party

(i) to file a translation of its written submissions into one of the official languages of the Court within a time-limit to be fixed by the President of the Chamber. Should that Party not file the translation within that time-limit, the Registrar may make the necessary arrangements for such translation, the expenses to be charged to the requesting Party;

(ii) to bear the expenses of interpreting its oral submissions into English or French. The Registrar shall be responsible for making the necessary arrangements for such interpretation.

(c) The President of the Chamber may direct that a Contracting Party which is a party to the case shall, within a specified time, provide a translation into, or a summary in, English or French of all or certain annexes to its written submissions or of any other relevant document, or of extracts therefrom.

(d) The preceding sub-paragraphs of this paragraph shall also apply, mutatis mutandis, to third- party intervention under Rule 44 and to the use of a non-official language by a third party.

5. The President of the Chamber may invite the respondent Contracting Party to provide a translation of its written submissions in the or an official language of that Party in order to facilitate the applicant's understanding of those submissions.

6. Any witness, expert or other person appearing before the Court may use his or her own language if he or she does not have sufficient knowledge of either of the two

official languages. In that event the Registrar shall make the necessary arrangements for interpreting or translation.

7. In respect of a request for an advisory opinion under Article 1 of Protocol No. 16 to the Convention, the requesting court or tribunal may submit the request as referred to in Rule 92 to the Court in the national official language used in the domestic proceedings. Where the language is not an official language of the Court, an English or French translation of the request shall be filed within a time-limit to be fixed by the President of the Court.

Rule 35 – Representation of Contracting Parties

The Contracting Parties shall be represented by Agents, who may have the assistance of advocates or advisers.

Rule 36 – Representation of applicants

1. Persons, non-governmental organisations or groups of individuals may initially present applications under Article 34 of the Convention themselves or through a representative.

2. Following notification of the application to the respondent Contracting Party under Rule 54 § 2 (b), the applicant should be represented in accordance with paragraph 4 of this Rule, unless the President of the Chamber decides otherwise.

3. The applicant must be so represented at any hearing decided on by the Chamber, unless the President of the Chamber exceptionally grants leave to the applicant to present his or her own case, subject, if necessary, to being assisted by an advocate or other approved representative.

4. (a) The representative acting on behalf of the applicant pursuant to paragraphs 2 and 3 of this Rule shall be an advocate authorised to practise in any of the Contracting Parties and resident in the territory of one of them, or any other person approved by the President of the Chamber.

(b) In exceptional circumstances and at any stage of the procedure, the President of the Chamber may, where he or she considers that the circumstances or the conduct of the advocate or other person appointed under the preceding sub-paragraph so warrant, direct that the latter may no longer represent or assist the applicant and that the applicant should seek alternative representation.

5. (a) The advocate or other approved representative, or the applicant in person who seeks leave to present his or her own case, must even if leave is granted under the following sub-paragraph have an adequate understanding of one of the Court's official languages.

(b) If he or she does not have sufficient proficiency to express himself or herself in one of the Court's official languages, leave to use one of the official languages of the Contracting Parties may be given by the President of the Chamber under Rule 34 § 3.

Rule 37 – Communications, notifications and summonses

1. Communications or notifications addressed to the Agents or advocates of the parties shall be deemed to have been addressed to the parties.

2. If, for any communication, notification or summons addressed to persons other than the Agents or advocates of the parties, the Court considers it necessary to have the assistance of the Government of the State on whose territory such communication, notification or summons is to have effect, the President of the Court shall apply directly to that Government in order to obtain the necessary facilities.

Rule 38 – Written pleadings

1. No written observations or other documents may be filed after the time-limit set by the President of the Chamber or the Judge Rapporteur, as the case may be, in accordance with these Rules. No written observations or other documents filed outside that time-limit or contrary to any practice direction issued under Rule 32 shall be included in the case file unless the President of the Chamber decides otherwise.

2. For the purposes of observing the time-limit referred to in paragraph 1 of this Rule, the material date is the certified date of dispatch of the document or, if there is none, the actual date of receipt at the Registry.

Rule 38A – Examination of matters of procedure

Questions of procedure requiring a decision by the Chamber shall be considered simultaneously with the examination of the case, unless the President of the Chamber decides otherwise.

Rule 39 – Interim measures

1. The Chamber or, where appropriate, the President of the Section or a duty judge appointed pursuant to paragraph 4 of this Rule may, at the request of a party or of any other person concerned, or of their own motion, indicate to the parties any interim measure which they consider should be adopted in the interests of the parties or of the proper conduct of the proceedings.

2. Where it is considered appropriate, immediate notice of the measure adopted in a particular case may be given to the Committee of Ministers.

3. The Chamber or, where appropriate, the President of the Section or a duty judge appointed pursuant to paragraph 4 of this Rule may request information from the parties on any matter connected with the implementation of any interim measure indicated.

4. The President of the Court may appoint Vice-Presidents of Sections as duty judges to decide on requests for interim measures.

Rule 40 – Urgent notification of an application

In any case of urgency the Registrar, with the authorisation of the President of the Chamber, may, without prejudice to the taking of any other procedural steps and by any available means, inform a Contracting Party concerned in an application of the introduction of the application and of a summary of its objects.

Rule 41 – Order of dealing with cases

In determining the order in which cases are to be dealt with, the Court shall have regard to the importance and urgency of the issues raised on the basis of criteria fixed by it. The Chamber, or its President, may, however, derogate from these criteria so as to give priority to a particular application.

Rule 42 – Joinder and simultaneous examination of applications (former Rule 43)

1. The Chamber may, either at the request of the parties or of its own motion, order the joinder of two or more applications.

2. The President of the Chamber may, after consulting the parties, order that the proceedings in applications assigned to the same Chamber be conducted simultaneously, without prejudice to the decision of the Chamber on the joinder of the applications.

Rule 43 – Striking out and restoration to the list (former Rule 44)

1. The Court may at any stage of the proceedings decide to strike an application out of its list of cases in accordance with Article 37 of the Convention.

2. When an applicant Contracting Party notifies the Registrar of its intention not to proceed with the case, the Chamber may strike the application out of the Court's list under Article 37 of the Convention if the other Contracting Party or Parties concerned in the case agree to such discontinuance.

3. If a friendly settlement is effected in accordance with Article 39 of the Convention, the application shall be struck out of the Court's list of cases by means of a decision. In accordance with Article 39 § 4 of the Convention, this decision shall be transmitted to the Committee of Ministers, which shall supervise the execution of the terms of the friendly settlement as set out in the decision. In other cases provided for in Article 37 of the Convention, the application shall be struck out by means of a judgment if it has been declared admissible or, if not declared admissible, by means of a decision. Where the application has been struck out by means of a judgment, the President of the Chamber shall forward that judgment, once it has become final, to the Committee of Ministers in order to allow the latter to supervise, in accordance with Article 46 § 2 of the Convention, the execution of any undertakings which may have been attached to the discontinuance or solution of the matter.

4. When an application has been struck out in accordance with Article 37 of the Convention, the costs shall be at the discretion of the Court. If an award of costs is made in a decision striking out an application which has not been declared admissible, the President of the Chamber shall forward the decision to the Committee of Ministers.

5. Where an application has been struck out in accordance with Article 37 of the Convention, the Court may restore it to its list if it considers that exceptional circumstances so justify.

Rule 44 – Third-party intervention

1. (a) When notice of an application lodged under Article 33 or 34 of the Convention is given to the respondent Contracting Party under Rules 51 § 1 or 54 § 2 (b), a copy of the application shall at the same time be transmitted by the Registrar to any other Contracting Party one of whose nationals is an applicant in the case. The Registrar shall similarly notify any such Contracting Party of a decision to hold an oral hearing in the case.

(b) If a Contracting Party wishes to exercise its right under Article 36 § 1 of the Convention to submit written comments or to take part in a hearing, it shall so advise the Registrar in writing not later than twelve weeks after the transmission or notification referred to in the preceding sub-paragraph. Another time-limit may be fixed by the President of the Chamber for exceptional reasons.

2. If the Council of Europe Commissioner for Human Rights wishes to exercise the right under Article 36 § 3 of the Convention to submit written observations or take part in a hearing, he or she shall so advise the Registrar in writing not later than twelve weeks after transmission of the application to the respondent Contracting Party or notification to it of the decision to hold an oral hearing. Another time-limit may be fixed by the President of the Chamber for exceptional reasons.

Should the Commissioner for Human Rights be unable to take part in the proceedings before the Court himself, he or she shall indicate the name of the person or persons from his or her Office whom he or she has appointed to represent him. He or she may be assisted by an advocate.

3. (a) Once notice of an application has been given to the respondent Contracting Party under Rules 51 § 1 or 54 § 2 (b), the President of the Chamber may, in the interests of the proper administration of justice, as provided in Article 36 § 2 of the Convention, invite, or grant leave to, any Contracting Party which is not a party to the proceedings, or any person concerned who is not the applicant, to submit written comments or, in exceptional cases, to take part in a hearing.

(b) Requests for leave for this purpose must be duly reasoned and submitted in writing in one of the official languages as provided in Rule 34 § 4 not later than twelve weeks after notice of the application has been given to the respondent Contracting Party. Another time-limit may be fixed by the President of the Chamber for exceptional reasons.

4. (a) In cases to be considered by the Grand Chamber, the periods of time prescribed in the preceding paragraphs shall run from the notification to the parties of the decision of the Chamber under Rule 72 § 1 to relinquish jurisdiction in favour of the Grand Chamber or of the decision of the panel of the Grand Chamber under Rule 73 § 2 to accept a request by a party for referral of the case to the Grand Chamber.

(b) The time-limits laid down in this Rule may exceptionally be extended by the President of the Chamber if sufficient cause is shown.

5. Any invitation or grant of leave referred to in paragraph 3 (a) of this Rule shall be subject to any conditions, including time-limits, set by the President of the Chamber. Where such conditions are not complied with, the President may decide not to include the comments in the case file or to limit participation in the hearing to the extent that he or she considers appropriate.

6. Written comments submitted under this Rule shall be drafted in one of the official languages as provided in Rule 34 § 4. They shall be forwarded by the Registrar to the parties to the case, who shall be entitled, subject to any conditions, including time-limits, set by the President of the Chamber, to file written observations in reply or, where appropriate, to reply at the hearing.

7. The provisions of this Rule shall apply mutatis mutandis to proceedings before the Grand Chamber constituted to deliver advisory opinions under Article 2 of Protocol No. 16 to the Convention. The President of the Court shall determine the time-limits which apply to third-party interveners.

Rule 44A – Duty to cooperate with the Court

The parties have a duty to cooperate fully in the conduct of the proceedings and, in particular, to take such action within their power as the Court considers necessary for the proper administration of justice. This duty shall also apply to a Contracting Party not party to the proceedings where such cooperation is necessary.

Rule 44B – Failure to comply with an order of the Court

Where a party fails to comply with an order of the Court concerning the conduct of the proceedings, the President of the Chamber may take any steps which he or she considers appropriate.

Rule 44C – Failure to participate effectively

1. Where a party fails to adduce evidence or provide information requested by the Court or to divulge relevant information of its own motion or otherwise fails to participate effectively in the proceedings, the Court may draw such inferences as it deems appropriate.

2. Failure or refusal by a respondent Contracting Party to participate effectively in the proceedings shall not, in itself, be a reason for the Chamber to discontinue the examination of the application.

Rule 44D – Inappropriate submissions by a party

If the representative of a party makes abusive, frivolous, vexatious, misleading or prolix submissions, the President of the Chamber may exclude that representative from the proceedings, refuse to accept all or part of the submissions or make any other order which he or she considers it appropriate to make, without prejudice to Article 35 § 3 of the Convention.

Rule 44E – Failure to pursue an application

In accordance with Article 37 § 1 (a) of the Convention, if an applicant Contracting Party or an individual applicant fails to pursue the application, the Chamber may strike the application out of the Court's list under Rule 43.

Chapter II: Institution of Proceedings

Rule 45 – Signatures

1. Any application made under Articles 33 or 34 of the Convention shall be submitted in writing and shall be signed by the applicant or by the applicant's representative.

2. Where an application is made by a non-governmental organisation or by a group of individuals, it shall be signed by those persons competent to represent that organisation or group. The Chamber or Committee concerned shall determine any question as to whether the persons who have signed an application are competent to do so.

3. Where applicants are represented in accordance with Rule 36, a power of attorney or written authority to act shall be supplied by their representative or representatives.

Rule 46 – Contents of an inter-State application

Any Contracting Party or Parties intending to bring a case before the Court under Article 33 of the Convention shall file with the Registry an application setting out

(a) the name of the Contracting Party against which the application is made;
(b) a statement of the facts;
(c) a statement of the alleged violation(s) of the Convention and the relevant arguments;
(d) a statement on compliance with the admissibility criteria (exhaustion of domestic remedies and the six-month rule) laid down in Article 35 § 1 of the Convention;
(e) the object of the application and a general indication of any claims for just satisfaction made under Article 41 of the Convention on behalf of the alleged injured party or parties; and
(f) the name and address of the person or persons appointed as Agent; and accompanied by
(g) copies of any relevant documents and in particular the decisions, whether judicial or not, relating to the object of the application.

Rule 47 – Contents of an individual application

1. An application under Article 34 of the Convention shall be made on the application form provided by the Registry, unless the Court decides otherwise. It shall contain all of the information requested in the relevant parts of the application form and set out

(a) the name, date of birth, nationality and address of the applicant and, where the applicant is a legal person, the full name, date of incorporation or registration, the official registration number (if any) and the official address;

(b) the name, address, telephone and fax numbers and e-mail address of the representative, if any;

(c) where the applicant is represented, the dated and original signature of the applicant on the authority section of the application form; the original signature of the representative showing that he or she has agreed to act for the applicant must also be on the authority section of the application form;

(d) the name of the Contracting Party or Parties against which the application is made; (e) a concise and legible statement of the facts;

(f) a concise and legible statement of the alleged violation(s) of the Convention and the relevant arguments; and

(g) a concise and legible statement confirming the applicant's compliance with the admissibility criteria laid down in Article 35 § 1 of the Convention.

2. (a) All of the information referred to in paragraph 1 (e) to (g) above that is set out in the relevant part of the application form should be sufficient to enable the Court to determine the nature and scope of the application without recourse to any other document.

(b) The applicant may however supplement the information by appending to the application form further details on the facts, alleged violations of the Convention and the relevant arguments. Such information shall not exceed 20 pages.

3.1. The application form shall be signed by the applicant or the applicant's representative and shall be accompanied by

(a) copies of documents relating to the decisions or measures complained of, judicial or otherwise;

(b) copies of documents and decisions showing that the applicant has complied with the exhaustion of domestic remedies requirement and the time-limit contained in Article 35 § 1 of the Convention;

(c) where appropriate, copies of documents relating to any other procedure of international investigation or settlement;

(d) where the applicant is a legal person as referred to in Rule 47 § 1 (a), a document or documents showing that the individual who lodged the application has the standing or authority to represent the applicant.

3.2. Documents submitted in support of the application shall be listed in order by date, numbered consecutively and be identified clearly.

4. Applicants who do not wish their identity to be disclosed to the public shall so indicate and shall submit a statement of the reasons justifying such a departure from the normal rule of public access to information in proceedings before the Court. The Court may authorise anonymity or grant it of its own motion.

5.1. Failure to comply with the requirements set out in paragraphs 1 to 3 of this Rule will result in the application not being examined by the Court, unless

(a) the applicant has provided an adequate explanation for the failure to comply;

(b) the application concerns a request for an interim measure;
(c) the Court otherwise directs of its own motion or at the request of an applicant.

5.2. The Court may in any case request an applicant to provide information or documents in any form or manner which may be appropriate within a fixed time-limit.

6. (a) The date of introduction of the application for the purposes of Article 35 § 1 of the Convention shall be the date on which an application form satisfying the requirements of this Rule is sent to the Court. The date of dispatch shall be the date of the postmark.
(b) Where it finds it justified, the Court may nevertheless decide that a different date shall be considered to be the date of introduction.

7. Applicants shall keep the Court informed of any change of address and of all circumstances relevant to the application.

Chapter III: Judge Rapporteurs

Rule 48 – Inter-State applications

1. Where an application is made under Article 33 of the Convention, the Chamber constituted to consider the case shall designate one or more of its judges as Judge Rapporteur(s), who shall submit a report on admissibility when the written observations of the Contracting Parties concerned have been received.

2. The Judge Rapporteur(s) shall submit such reports, drafts and other documents as may assist the Chamber and its President in carrying out their functions.

Rule 49 – Individual applications

1. Where the material submitted by the applicant is on its own sufficient to disclose that the application is inadmissible or should be struck out of the list, the application shall be considered by a single-judge formation unless there is some special reason to the contrary.

2. Where an application is made under Article 34 of the Convention and its examination by a Chamber or a Committee exercising the functions attributed to it under Rule 53 § 2 seems justified, the President of the Section to which the case has been assigned shall designate a judge as Judge Rapporteur, who shall examine the application.

3. In their examination of applications, Judge Rapporteurs
(a) may request the parties to submit, within a specified time, any factual information, documents or other material which they consider to be relevant;
(b) shall, subject to the President of the Section directing that the case be considered by a Chamber or a Committee, decide whether the application is to be considered by a single-judge formation, by a Committee or by a Chamber;
(c) shall submit such reports, drafts and other documents as may assist the Chamber or the Committee or the respective President in carrying out their functions.

Rule 50 – Grand Chamber proceedings

Where a case has been submitted to the Grand Chamber either under Article 30 or under Article 43 of the Convention, the President of the Grand Chamber shall designate as Judge Rapporteur(s) one or, in the case of an inter-State application, one or more of its members.

Chapter IV: Proceedings on Admissibility
Inter-State applications

Rule 51 – Assignment of applications and subsequent procedure

1. When an application is made under Article 33 of the Convention, the President of the Court shall immediately give notice of the application to the respondent Contracting Party and shall assign the application to one of the Sections.

2. In accordance with Rule 26 § 1 (a), the judges elected in respect of the applicant and respondent Contracting Parties shall sit as ex officio members of the Chamber constituted to consider the case. Rule 30 shall apply if the application has been brought by several Contracting Parties or if applications with the same object brought by several Contracting Parties are being examined jointly under Rule 42.

3. On assignment of the case to a Section, the President of the Section shall constitute the Chamber in accordance with Rule 26 § 1 and shall invite the respondent Contracting Party to submit its observations in writing on the admissibility of the application. The observations so obtained shall be communicated by the Registrar to the applicant Contracting Party, which may submit written observations in reply.

4. Before the ruling on the admissibility of the application is given, the Chamber or its President may decide to invite the Parties to submit further observations in writing.

5. A hearing on the admissibility shall be held if one or more of the Contracting Parties concerned so requests or if the Chamber so decides of its own motion.

6. Before fixing the written and, where appropriate, oral procedure, the President of the Chamber shall consult the Parties.

Individual applications

Rule 52 – Assignment of applications to the Sections

1. Any application made under Article 34 of the Convention shall be assigned to a Section by the President of the Court, who in so doing shall endeavour to ensure a fair distribution of cases between the Sections.

2. The Chamber of seven judges provided for in Article 26 § 1 of the Convention shall be constituted by the President of the Section concerned in accordance with Rule 26 § 1.

3. Pending the constitution of a Chamber in accordance with paragraph 2 of this Rule, the President of the Section shall exercise any powers conferred on the President of the Chamber by these Rules.

Rule 52A – Procedure before a single judge

1. In accordance with Article 27 of the Convention, a single judge may declare inadmissible or strike out of the Court's list of cases an application submitted under Article 34, where such a decision can be taken without further examination. The decision shall be final. It shall contain a summary reasoning. It shall be communicated to the applicant.

2. If the single judge does not take a decision of the kind provided for in the first paragraph of the present Rule, that judge shall forward the application to a Committee or to a Chamber for further examination.

Rule 53 – Procedure before a Committee

1. In accordance with Article 28 § 1 (a) of the Convention, the Committee may, by a unanimous vote and at any stage of the proceedings, declare an application inadmissible or strike it out of the Court's list of cases where such a decision can be taken without further examination.

2. If the Committee is satisfied, in the light of the parties' observations received pursuant to Rule 54 § 2 (b), that the case falls to be examined in accordance with the procedure under Article 28 § 1 (b) of the Convention, it shall, by a unanimous vote, adopt a judgment including its decision on admissibility and, as appropriate, on just satisfaction.

3. If the judge elected in respect of the Contracting Party concerned is not a member of the Committee, the Committee may at any stage of the proceedings before it, by a unanimous vote, invite that judge to take the place of one of its members, having regard to all relevant factors, including whether that Party has contested the application of the procedure under Article 28 § 1 (b) of the Convention.

4. Decisions and judgments under Article 28 § 1 of the Convention shall be final. They shall be reasoned. Decisions may contain a summary reasoning when they have been adopted following referral by a single judge pursuant to Rule 52A § 2.

5. The decision of the Committee shall be communicated by the Registrar to the applicant as well as to the Contracting Party or Parties concerned where these have previously been involved in the application in accordance with the present Rules.

6. If no decision or judgment is adopted by the Committee, the application shall be forwarded to the Chamber constituted under Rule 52 § 2 to examine the case.

7. The provisions of Rule 42 § 1 and Rules 79 to 81 shall apply, mutatis mutandis, to proceedings before a Committee.

Rule 54 – Procedure before a Chamber

1. The Chamber may at once declare the application inadmissible or strike it out of the Court's list of cases. The decision of the Chamber may relate to all or part of the application.

2. Alternatively, the Chamber or the President of the Section may decide to

(a) request the parties to submit any factual information, documents or other material considered by the Chamber or its President to be relevant;

(b) give notice of the application or part of the application to the respondent Contracting Party and invite that Party to submit written observations thereon and, upon receipt thereof, invite the applicant to submit observations in reply;

(c) invite the parties to submit further observations in writing.

3. In the exercise of the competences under paragraph 2 (b) of this Rule, the President of the Section, acting as a single judge, may at once declare part of the application inadmissible or strike part of the application out of the Court's list of cases. The decision shall be final. It shall be summarily reasoned. It shall be communicated to the applicant as well as to the Contracting Party or Parties concerned by a letter containing that reasoning.

4. Paragraph 2 of this Rule shall also apply to Vice-Presidents of Sections appointed as duty judges in accordance with Rule 39 § 4 to decide on requests for interim measures. Any decision to declare inadmissible the application shall be summarily reasoned. It shall be communicated to the applicant by a letter containing that reasoning.

5. Before taking a decision on admissibility, the Chamber may decide, either at the request of a party or of its own motion, to hold a hearing if it considers that the discharge

of its functions under the Convention so requires. In that event, unless the Chamber shall exceptionally decide otherwise, the parties shall also be invited to address the issues arising in relation to the merits of the application.

Rule 54A – Joint examination of admissibility and merits

1. When giving notice of the application to the respondent Contracting Party pursuant to Rule 54 § 2 (b), the Chamber may also decide to examine the admissibility and merits at the same time in accordance with Article 29 § 1 of the Convention. The parties shall be invited to include in their observations any submissions concerning just satisfaction and any proposals for a friendly settlement. The conditions laid down in Rules 60 and 62 shall apply, mutatis mutandis. The Court may, however, decide at any stage, if necessary, to take a separate decision on admissibility.

2. If no friendly settlement or other solution is reached and the Chamber is satisfied, in the light of the parties' arguments, that the case is admissible and ready for a determination on the merits, it shall immediately adopt a judgment including the Chamber's decision on admissibility, save in cases where it decides to take such a decision separately.

Inter-State and individual applications

Rule 55 – Pleas of inadmissibility

Any plea of inadmissibility must, in so far as its character and the circumstances permit, be raised by the respondent Contracting Party in its written or oral observations on the admissibility of the application submitted as provided in Rule 51 or 54, as the case may be.

Rule 56 – Decision of a Chamber

1. The decision of the Chamber shall state whether it was taken unanimously or by a majority and shall be reasoned.

2. The decision of the Chamber shall be communicated by the Registrar to the applicant. It shall also be communicated to the Contracting Party or Parties concerned and to any third party, including the Council of Europe Commissioner for Human Rights, where these have previously been informed of the application in accordance with the present Rules. If a friendly settlement is effected, the decision to strike an application out of the list of cases shall be forwarded to the Committee of Ministers in accordance with Rule 43 § 3.

Rule 57 – Language of the decision

Unless the Court decides that a decision shall be given in both official languages, all decisions shall be given either in English or in French. Decisions of the Grand Chamber shall, however, be given in both official languages, and both language versions shall be equally authentic.

Chapter V: Proceedings after the Admission of an Application

Rule 58 – Inter-State applications

1. Once the Chamber has decided to admit an application made under Article 33 of the Convention, the President of the Chamber shall, after consulting the Contracting Parties concerned, lay down the time-limits for the filing of written observations on the merits and

for the production of any further evidence. The President may however, with the agreement of the Contracting Parties concerned, direct that a written procedure is to be dispensed with.

2. A hearing on the merits shall be held if one or more of the Contracting Parties concerned so requests or if the Chamber so decides of its own motion. The President of the Chamber shall fix the oral procedure.

Rule 59 – Individual applications

1. Once an application made under Article 34 of the Convention has been declared admissible, the Chamber or its President may invite the parties to submit further evidence and written observations.

2. Unless decided otherwise, the parties shall be allowed the same time for submission of their observations.

3. The Chamber may decide, either at the request of a party or of its own motion, to hold a hearing on the merits if it considers that the discharge of its functions under the Convention so requires.

4. The President of the Chamber shall, where appropriate, fix the written and oral procedure.

Rule 60 – Claims for just satisfaction

1. An applicant who wishes to obtain an award of just satisfaction under Article 41 of the Convention in the event of the Court finding a violation of his or her Convention rights must make a specific claim to that effect.

2. The applicant must submit itemised particulars of all claims, together with any relevant supporting documents, within the time-limit fixed for the submission of the applicant's observations on the merits unless the President of the Chamber directs otherwise.

3. If the applicant fails to comply with the requirements set out in the preceding paragraphs the Chamber may reject the claims in whole or in part.

4. The applicant's claims shall be transmitted to the respondent Contracting Party for comment.

Rule 61 – Pilot-judgment procedure

1. The Court may initiate a pilot-judgment procedure and adopt a pilot judgment where the facts of an application reveal in the Contracting Party concerned the existence of a structural or systemic problem or other similar dysfunction which has given rise or may give rise to similar applications.

2. (a) Before initiating a pilot-judgment procedure, the Court shall first seek the views of the parties on whether the application under examination results from the existence of such a problem or dysfunction in the Contracting Party concerned and on the suitability of processing the application in accordance with that procedure.

(b) A pilot-judgment procedure may be initiated by the Court of its own motion or at the request of one or both parties.

(c) Any application selected for pilot-judgment treatment shall be processed as a matter of priority in accordance with Rule 41 of the Rules of Court.

3. The Court shall in its pilot judgment identify both the nature of the structural or systemic problem or other dysfunction as established as well as the type of remedial measures which the Contracting Party concerned is required to take at the domestic level by virtue of the operative provisions of the judgment.

4. The Court may direct in the operative provisions of the pilot judgment that the remedial measures referred to in paragraph 3 above be adopted within a specified time, bearing in mind the nature of the measures required and the speed with which the problem which it has identified can be remedied at the domestic level.

5. When adopting a pilot judgment, the Court may reserve the question of just satisfaction either in whole or in part pending the adoption by the respondent Contracting Party of the individual and general measures specified in the pilot judgment.

6. (a) As appropriate, the Court may adjourn the examination of all similar applications pending the adoption of the remedial measures required by virtue of the operative provisions of the pilot judgment.

(b) The applicants concerned shall be informed in a suitable manner of the decision to adjourn. They shall be notified as appropriate of all relevant developments affecting their cases.

(c) The Court may at any time examine an adjourned application where the interests of the proper administration of justice so require.

7. Where the parties to the pilot case reach a friendly-settlement agreement, such agreement shall comprise a declaration by the respondent Contracting Party on the implementation of the general measures identified in the pilot judgment as well as the redress to be afforded to other actual or potential applicants.

8. Subject to any decision to the contrary, in the event of the failure of the Contracting Party concerned to comply with the operative provisions of a pilot judgment, the Court shall resume its examination of the applications which have been adjourned in accordance with paragraph 6 above.

9. The Committee of Ministers, the Parliamentary Assembly of the Council of Europe, the Secretary General of the Council of Europe, and the Council of Europe Commissioner for Human Rights shall be informed of the adoption of a pilot judgment as well as of any other judgment in which the Court draws attention to the existence of a structural or systemic problem in a Contracting Party.

10. Information about the initiation of pilot-judgment procedures, the adoption of pilot judgments and their execution as well as the closure of such procedures shall be published on the Court's website.

Rule 62 – Friendly settlement

1. Once an application has been declared admissible, the Registrar, acting on the instructions of the Chamber or its President, shall enter into contact with the parties with a view to securing a friendly settlement of the matter in accordance with Article 39 § 1 of the Convention. The Chamber shall take any steps that appear appropriate to facilitate such a settlement.

2. In accordance with Article 39 § 2 of the Convention, the friendly-settlement negotiations shall be confidential and without prejudice to the parties' arguments in the contentious proceedings. No written or oral communication and no offer or concession made in the framework of the attempt to secure a friendly settlement may be referred to or relied on in the contentious proceedings.

3. If the Chamber is informed by the Registrar that the parties have agreed to a friendly settlement, it shall, after verifying that the settlement has been reached on the basis of respect for human rights as defined in the Convention and the Protocols thereto, strike the case out of the Court's list in accordance with Rule 43 § 3.

4. Paragraphs 2 and 3 apply, *mutatis mutandis*, to the procedure under Rule 54A.

Rule 62A – Unilateral declaration

1. (a) Where an applicant has refused the terms of a friendly-settlement proposal made pursuant to Rule 62, the Contracting Party concerned may file with the Court a request to strike the application out of the list in accordance with Article 37 § 1 of the Convention.

(b) Such request shall be accompanied by a declaration clearly acknowledging that there has been a violation of the Convention in the applicant's case together with an undertaking to provide adequate redress and, as appropriate, to take necessary remedial measures.

(c) The filing of a declaration under paragraph 1 (b) of this Rule must be made in public and adversarial proceedings conducted separately from and with due respect for the confidentiality of any friendly-settlement proceedings referred to in Article 39 § 2 of the Convention and Rule 62 § 2.

2. Where exceptional circumstances so justify, a request and accompanying declaration may be filed with the Court even in the absence of a prior attempt to reach a friendly settlement.

3. If it is satisfied that the declaration offers a sufficient basis for finding that respect for human rights as defined in the Convention and the Protocols thereto does not require it to continue its examination of the application, the Court may strike it out of the list, either in whole or in part, even if the applicant wishes the examination of the application to be continued.

4. This Rule applies, *mutatis mutandis*, to the procedure under Rule 54A.

Chapter VI: Hearings

Rule 63 – Public character of hearings

1. Hearings shall be public unless, in accordance with paragraph 2 of this Rule, the Chamber in exceptional circumstances decides otherwise, either of its own motion or at the request of a party or any other person concerned.

2. The press and the public may be excluded from all or part of a hearing in the interests of morals, public order or national security in a democratic society, where the interests of juveniles or the protection of the private life of the parties so require, or to the extent strictly necessary in the opinion of the Chamber in special circumstances where publicity would prejudice the interests of justice.

3. Any request for a hearing to be held in camera made under paragraph 1 of this Rule must include reasons and specify whether it concerns all or only part of the hearing.

Rule 64 – Conduct of hearings

1. The President of the Chamber shall organise and direct hearings and shall prescribe the order in which those appearing before the Chamber shall be called upon to speak.

2. Any judge may put questions to any person appearing before the Chamber.

Rule 65 – Failure to appear

Where a party or any other person due to appear fails or declines to do so, the Chamber may, provided that it is satisfied that such a course is consistent with the proper administration of justice, nonetheless proceed with the hearing.

Rules 66 to 69 deleted

Rule 70 – Verbatim record of a hearing

1. If the President of the Chamber so directs, the Registrar shall be responsible for the making of a verbatim record of the hearing. Any such record shall include:

(a) the composition of the Chamber;
(b) a list of those appearing before the Chamber;
(c) the text of the submissions made, questions put and replies given;
(d) the text of any ruling delivered during the hearing.

2. If all or part of the verbatim record is in a non-official language, the Registrar shall arrange for its translation into one of the official languages.

3. The representatives of the parties shall receive a copy of the verbatim record in order that they may, subject to the control of the Registrar or the President of the Chamber, make corrections, but in no case may such corrections affect the sense and bearing of what was said. The Registrar shall lay down, in accordance with the instructions of the President of the Chamber, the time-limits granted for this purpose.

4. The verbatim record, once so corrected, shall be signed by the President of the Chamber and the Registrar and shall then constitute certified matters of record.

Chapter VII: Proceedings before the Grand Chamber

Rule 71 (Applicability of procedural provisions)

1. Any provisions governing proceedings before the Chambers shall apply, *mutatis mutandis*, to proceedings before the Grand Chamber.

2. The powers conferred on a Chamber by Rules 54 § 5 and 59 § 3 in relation to the holding of a hearing may, in proceedings before the Grand Chamber, also be exercised by the President of the Grand Chamber.

Rule 72 – Relinquishment of jurisdiction in favour of the Grand Chamber

1. Where a case pending before a Chamber raises a serious question affecting the interpretation of the Convention or the Protocols thereto, the Chamber may relinquish jurisdiction in favour of the Grand Chamber, unless one of the parties to the case has objected in accordance with paragraph 4 of this Rule.

2. Where the resolution of a question raised in a case before the Chamber might have a result inconsistent with the Court's case-law, the Chamber shall relinquish jurisdiction in favour of the Grand Chamber, unless one of the parties to the case has objected in accordance with paragraph 4 of this Rule.

3. Reasons need not be given for the decision to relinquish.

4. The Registrar shall notify the parties of the Chamber's intention to relinquish jurisdiction. The parties shall have one month from the date of that notification within which to file at the Registry a duly reasoned objection. An objection which does not fulfil these conditions shall be considered invalid by the Chamber.

Rule 73 – Request by a party for referral of a case to the Grand Chamber

1. In accordance with Article 43 of the Convention, any party to a case may exceptionally, within a period of three months from the date of delivery of the judgment of a Chamber, file in writing at the Registry a request that the case be referred to the Grand Chamber. The party

shall specify in its request the serious question affecting the interpretation or application of the Convention or the Protocols thereto, or the serious issue of general importance, which in its view warrants consideration by the Grand Chamber.

2. A panel of five judges of the Grand Chamber constituted in accordance with Rule 24 § 5 shall examine the request solely on the basis of the existing case file. It shall accept the request only if it considers that the case does raise such a question or issue. Reasons need not be given for a refusal of the request.

3. If the panel accepts the request, the Grand Chamber shall decide the case by means of a judgment.

Chapter VIII: Judgments

Rule 74 – Contents of the judgment

1. A judgment as referred to in Articles 28, 42 and 44 of the Convention shall contain

(a) the names of the President and the other judges constituting the Chamber or the Committee concerned, and the name of the Registrar or the Deputy Registrar;
(b) the dates on which it was adopted and delivered;
(c) a description of the parties;
(d) the names of the Agents, advocates or advisers of the parties; (e) an account of the procedure followed;
(f) the facts of the case;
(g) a summary of the submissions of the parties;
(h) the reasons in point of law;
(i) the operative provisions;
(j) the decision, if any, in respect of costs;
(k) the number of judges constituting the majority;
(l) where appropriate, a statement as to which text is authentic.

2. Any judge who has taken part in the consideration of the case by a Chamber or by the Grand Chamber shall be entitled to annex to the judgment either a separate opinion, concurring with or dissenting from that judgment, or a bare statement of dissent.

Rule 75 – Ruling on just satisfaction

1. Where the Chamber or the Committee finds that there has been a violation of the Convention or the Protocols thereto, it shall give in the same judgment a ruling on the application of Article 41 of the Convention if a specific claim has been submitted in accordance with Rule 60 and the question is ready for decision; if the question is not ready for decision, the Chamber or the Committee shall reserve it in whole or in part and shall fix the further procedure.

2. For the purposes of ruling on the application of Article 41 of the Convention, the Chamber or the Committee shall, as far as possible, be composed of those judges who sat to consider the merits of the case. Where it is not possible to constitute the original Chamber or Committee, the President of the Section shall complete or compose the Chamber or Committee by drawing lots.

3. The Chamber or the Committee may, when affording just satisfaction under Article 41 of the Convention, direct that if settlement is not made within a specified time, interest is to be payable on any sums awarded.

4. If the Court is informed that an agreement has been reached between the injured party and the Contracting Party liable, it shall verify the equitable nature of the agreement and, where it finds the agreement to be equitable, strike the case out of the list in accordance with Rule 43 § 3.

Rule 76 – Language of the judgment

Unless the Court decides that a judgment shall be given in both official languages, all judgments shall be given either in English or in French. Judgments of the Grand Chamber shall, however, be given in both official languages, and both language versions shall be equally authentic.

Rule 77 – Signature, delivery and notification of the judgment

1. Judgments shall be signed by the President of the Chamber or the Committee and the Registrar.

2. The judgment adopted by a Chamber may be read out at a public hearing by the President of the Chamber or by another judge delegated by him or her. The Agents and representatives of the parties shall be informed in due time of the date of the hearing. Otherwise, and in respect of judgments adopted by Committees, the notification provided for in paragraph 3 of this Rule shall constitute delivery of the judgment.

3. The judgment shall be transmitted to the Committee of Ministers. The Registrar shall send copies to the parties, to the Secretary General of the Council of Europe, to any third party, including the Council of Europe Commissioner for Human Rights, and to any other person directly concerned. The original copy, duly signed, shall be placed in the archives of the Court.

Rule 78 deleted

Rule 79 – Request for interpretation of a judgment

1. A party may request the interpretation of a judgment within a period of one year following the delivery of that judgment.

2. The request shall be filed with the Registry. It shall state precisely the point or points in the operative provisions of the judgment on which interpretation is required.

3. The original Chamber may decide of its own motion to refuse the request on the ground that there is no reason to warrant considering it. Where it is not possible to constitute the original Chamber, the President of the Court shall complete or compose the Chamber by drawing lots.

4. If the Chamber does not refuse the request, the Registrar shall communicate it to the other party or parties and shall invite them to submit any written comments within a time-limit laid down by the President of the Chamber. The President of the Chamber shall also fix the date of the hearing should the Chamber decide to hold one. The Chamber shall decide by means of a judgment.

Rule 80 – Request for revision of a judgment

1. A party may, in the event of the discovery of a fact which might by its nature have a decisive influence and which, when a judgment was delivered, was unknown to the Court and could not reasonably have been known to that party, request the Court, within a period of six months after that party acquired knowledge of the fact, to revise that judgment.

2. The request shall mention the judgment of which revision is requested and shall contain the information necessary to show that the conditions laid down in paragraph 1 of this Rule have been complied with. It shall be accompanied by a copy of all supporting documents. The request and supporting documents shall be filed with the Registry.

3. The original Chamber may decide of its own motion to refuse the request on the ground that there is no reason to warrant considering it. Where it is not possible to constitute the original Chamber, the President of the Court shall complete or compose the Chamber by drawing lots.

4. If the Chamber does not refuse the request, the Registrar shall communicate it to the other party or parties and shall invite them to submit any written comments within a time-limit laid down by the President of the Chamber. The President of the Chamber shall also fix the date of the hearing should the Chamber decide to hold one. The Chamber shall decide by means of a judgment.

Rule 81 – Rectification of errors in decisions and judgments

Without prejudice to the provisions on revision of judgments and on restoration to the list of applications, the Court may, of its own motion or at the request of a party made within one month of the delivery of a decision or a judgment, rectify clerical errors, errors in calculation or obvious mistakes.

Chapter IX: Advisory Opinions under Articles 47, 48 and 49 of the Convention

Rule 82

In proceedings relating to advisory opinions requested by the Committee of Ministers the Court shall apply, in addition to the provisions of Articles 47, 48 and 49 of the Convention, the provisions which follow. It shall also apply the other provisions of these Rules to the extent to which it considers this to be appropriate.

Rule 83

The request for an advisory opinion shall be filed with the Registrar. It shall state fully and precisely the question on which the opinion of the Court is sought, and also

(a) the date on which the Committee of Ministers adopted the decision referred to in Article 47 § 3 of the Convention;

(b) the name and address of the person or persons appointed by the Committee of Ministers to give the Court any explanations which it may require.

The request shall be accompanied by all documents likely to elucidate the question.

Rule 84

1. On receipt of a request, the Registrar shall transmit a copy of it and of the accompanying documents to all members of the Court.

2. The Registrar shall inform the Contracting Parties that they may submit written comments on the request.

Rule 85

1. The President of the Court shall lay down the time-limits for filing written comments or other documents.

2. Written comments or other documents shall be filed with the Registrar. The Registrar shall transmit copies of them to all the members of the Court, to the Committee of Ministers and to each of the Contracting Parties.

Rule 86

After the close of the written procedure, the President of the Court shall decide whether the Contracting Parties which have submitted written comments are to be given an opportunity to develop them at an oral hearing held for the purpose.

Rule 87

1. A Grand Chamber shall be constituted to consider the request for an advisory opinion.

2. If the Grand Chamber considers that the request is not within its competence as defined in Article 47 of the Convention, it shall so declare in a reasoned decision.

Rule 88

1. Reasoned decisions and advisory opinions shall be given by a majority vote of the Grand Chamber. They shall mention the number of judges constituting the majority.

1B. Reasoned decisions and advisory opinions shall be given in both official languages of the Court, and both language versions shall be equally authentic.

2. Any judge may, if he or she so desires, attach to the reasoned decision or advisory opinion of the Court either a separate opinion, concurring with or dissenting from the reasoned decision or advisory opinion, or a bare statement of dissent.

Rule 89

The reasoned decision or advisory opinion may be read out in one of the two official languages by the President of the Grand Chamber, or by another judge delegated by the President, at a public hearing, prior notice having been given to the Committee of Ministers and to each of the Contracting Parties. Otherwise the notification provided for in Rule 90 shall constitute delivery of the opinion or reasoned decision.

Rule 90

The advisory opinion or reasoned decision shall be signed by the President of the Grand Chamber and by the Registrar. The original copy, duly signed, shall be placed in the archives of the Court. The Registrar shall send certified copies to the Committee of Ministers, to the Contracting Parties and to the Secretary General of the Council of Europe.

Chapter X: Advisory Opinions under Protocol No. 16 to the Convention

Rule 91 – General

In proceedings relating to advisory opinions requested by courts or tribunals designated by Contracting Parties pursuant to Article 10 of Protocol No. 16 to the Convention, the Court shall apply, in addition to the provisions of that Protocol, the provisions which follow. It shall also apply the other provisions of these Rules to the extent to which it considers this to be appropriate.

Rule 92 – The introduction of a request for an advisory opinion

1. In accordance with Article 1 of Protocol No. 16 to the Convention, a court or tribunal of a Contracting Party to that Protocol may request the Court to give an advisory opinion on questions of principle relating to the interpretation or application of the rights and freedoms defined in the Convention and the Protocols thereto. Any such request shall be filed with the Registrar of the Court.

2.1 The request shall be reasoned and shall set out

(a) the subject matter of the domestic case and its relevant legal and factual background;
(b) the relevant domestic legal provisions;
(c) the relevant Convention issues, in particular the rights or freedoms at stake;
(d) if relevant, a summary of the arguments of the parties to the domestic proceedings on the question; and
(e) if possible and appropriate, a statement of the requesting court's or tribunal's own views on the question, including any analysis it may itself have made of the question.

2.2. The requesting court or tribunal shall submit any further documents of relevance to the legal and factual background of the pending case.

2.3. The requesting court or tribunal shall notify the Registrar in the event of the withdrawal of its request. On receipt of such a notification the Court shall discontinue the proceedings.

Rule 93 – Examination of a request by the panel

1.1 The request for an advisory opinion shall be examined by a panel of five judges of the Grand Chamber. The panel shall be composed of

(a) the President of the Court. If the President of the Court is prevented from sitting, he or she shall be replaced by the Vice-President of the Court taking precedence;
(b) two Presidents of Sections designated by rotation. If the Presidents of the Sections so designated are prevented from sitting, they shall be replaced by the Vice-Presidents of their Sections;
(c) a judge designated by rotation from among the judges elected by the remaining Sections to serve on the panel for a period of six months;
(d) the judge elected in respect of the Contracting Party to which the requesting court or tribunal pertains or, where appropriate, a judge appointed pursuant to Rule 29; and
(e) at least two substitute judges designated in rotation from among the judges elected by the Sections to serve on the panel for a period of six months.

1.2. Judges serving on the panel shall continue to serve where they have participated in the examination of a request for an advisory opinion and no final decision has been taken on it at the date of expiry of their period of appointment to the panel.

2. Requests for advisory opinions shall be processed as a matter of priority in accordance with Rule 41.

3. The panel of the Grand Chamber shall accept the request if it considers that it fulfils the requirements of Article 1 of Protocol No. 16 to the Convention.

4. The panel shall give reasons for a refusal of a request.

5. The requesting court or tribunal and the Contracting Party to which it pertains shall be notified of the panel's decision to accept or refuse a request.

Rule 94 – Proceedings following the panel's acceptance of a request

1. Where the panel accepts a request for an advisory opinion in accordance with Rule 93, a Grand Chamber shall be constituted pursuant to Rule 24 § 2 (h) to consider the request and to deliver an advisory opinion.

2. The President of the Grand Chamber may invite the requesting court or tribunal to submit any further information which is considered necessary for clarifying the scope of the request or its own views on the question raised by the request.

3. The President of the Grand Chamber may invite the parties to the domestic proceedings to submit written observations and, if appropriate, to take part in an oral hearing.

4. Written comments or other documents shall be filed with the Registrar in accordance with the time-limits laid down by the President of the Grand Chamber.

5. Copies of any submissions filed in accordance with the provisions of Rule 44 shall be transmitted to the requesting court or tribunal, which shall have the opportunity to comment on those submissions.

6. After the close of the written procedure, the President of the Grand Chamber shall decide whether an oral hearing should be held.

7. Advisory opinions shall be given by a majority vote of the Grand Chamber. They shall mention the number of judges constituting the majority.

7B. Advisory opinions shall be given in both official languages of the Court, and both language versions shall be equally authentic.

8. Any judge may, if he or she so desires, attach to the advisory opinion of the Court either a separate opinion, concurring with or dissenting from the advisory opinion, or a bare statement of dissent.

9. The advisory opinion shall be signed by the President of the Grand Chamber and by the Registrar. The original copy, duly signed, shall be placed in the archives of the Court. The Registrar shall send certified copies to the requesting court or tribunal and to the Contracting Party to which that court or tribunal pertains.

10. Any third party who has intervened in the proceedings in accordance with Article 3 of Protocol No. 16 to the Convention and Rule 44 of the Rules of Court shall also receive a copy of the advisory opinion.

Rule 95 – Costs of the advisory-opinion proceedings and legal aid

1. Where the President of the Grand Chamber has invited a party to the domestic proceedings to intervene in the advisory opinion proceedings pursuant to Rule 44 § 7 and Rule 94 § 3, the reimbursement of that party's costs and expenses shall not be decided by the Court but shall be determined in accordance with the law and practice of the Contracting Party to which the requesting court or tribunal pertains.

2. The provisions of Chapter XII shall apply mutatis mutandis where the President of the Grand Chamber has invited pursuant to Rules 44 § 7 and 94 § 3 a party to the domestic proceedings to intervene in the advisory opinion proceedings and that party lacks sufficient means to meet all or part of the costs entailed.

Chapter XI: Proceedings under Article 46 §§ 3, 4 and 5 of the Convention

Proceedings under Article 46 § 3 of the Convention

Rule 96 (former Rule 91)

Any request for interpretation under Article 46 § 3 of the Convention shall be filed with the Registrar. The request shall state fully and precisely the nature and source of the question of interpretation that has hindered execution of the judgment mentioned in the request and shall be accompanied by

(a) information about the execution proceedings, if any, before the Committee of Ministers in respect of the judgment;
(b) a copy of the decision referred to in Article 46 § 3 of the Convention;
(c) the name and address of the person or persons appointed by the Committee of Ministers to give the Court any explanations which it may require.

Rule 97 (former Rule 92)

1. The request shall be examined by the Grand Chamber, Chamber or Committee which rendered the judgment in question.

2. Where it is not possible to constitute the original Grand Chamber, Chamber or Committee, the President of the Court shall complete or compose it by drawing lots.

Rule 98 (former Rule 93)

The decision of the Court on the question of interpretation referred to it by the Committee of Ministers is final. No separate opinion of the judges may be delivered thereto. Copies of the ruling shall be transmitted to the Committee of Ministers and to the parties concerned as well as to any third party, including the Council of Europe Commissioner for Human Rights.

Proceedings under Article 46 §§ 4 and 5 of the Convention

Rule 99 (former Rule 94)

In proceedings relating to a referral to the Court of a question whether a Contracting Party has failed to fulfil its obligation under Article 46 § 1 of the Convention the Court shall apply, in addition to the provisions of Article 31 (b) and Article 46 §§ 4 and 5 of the Convention, the provisions which follow.

It shall also apply the other provisions of these Rules to the extent to which it considers this to be appropriate.

Rule 100 (former Rule 95)

Any request made pursuant to Article 46 § 4 of the Convention shall be reasoned and shall be filed with the Registrar. It shall be accompanied by

(a) the judgment concerned;
(b) information about the execution proceedings before the Committee of Ministers in respect of the judgment concerned, including, if any, the views expressed in writing by the parties concerned and communications submitted in those proceedings;
(c) copies of the formal notice served on the respondent Contracting Party or Parties and the decision referred to in Article 46 § 4 of the Convention;
(d) the name and address of the person or persons appointed by the Committee of Ministers to give the Court any explanations which it may require;
(e) copies of all other documents likely to elucidate the question.

Rule 101 (former Rule 96)

A Grand Chamber shall be constituted, in accordance with Rule 24 § 2 (g), to consider the question referred to the Court.

Rule 102 (former Rule 97)

The President of the Grand Chamber shall inform the Committee of Ministers and the parties concerned that they may submit written comments on the question referred.

Rule 103 (former Rule 98)

1. The President of the Grand Chamber shall lay down the time-limits for filing written comments or other documents.

2. The Grand Chamber may decide to hold a hearing.

Rule 104 (former Rule 99)

The Grand Chamber shall decide by means of a judgment. Copies of the judgment shall be transmitted to the Committee of Ministers and to the parties concerned as well as to any third party, including the Council of Europe Commissioner for Human Rights.

Chapter XIA: Publication of judgments, decisions and advisory opinions

Rule 104A – Publication on the Court's case-law database

All judgments, all decisions and all advisory opinions shall be published, under the responsibility of the Registrar, on the Court's case-law database, HUDOC. However, this rule shall not apply to single judge decisions as provided by Rule 52A § 1, to decisions taken by a Section President or a Section Vice-President acting as a single judge, as provided by Rule 54 §§ 3 and 4, and to committee decisions summarily reasoned, pursuant to Rule 52A § 2; the Court shall periodically make accessible to the public general information about these decisions.

Rule 104B – Key cases

In addition, attention shall be drawn by the Registrar, in an appropriate way, to those judgments, decisions and advisory opinions that have been selected by the Bureau as key cases.

Chapter XII: Legal Aid

Rule 105 (former Rule 100)

1. The President of the Chamber may, either at the request of an applicant having lodged an application under Article 34 of the Convention or of his or her own motion, grant free legal aid to the applicant in connection with the presentation of the case from the moment when observations in writing on the admissibility of that application are received from the respondent Contracting Party in accordance with Rule 54 § 2 b, or where the time-limit for their submission has expired.

2. Subject to Rule 110, where the applicant has been granted legal aid in connection with the presentation of his or her case before the Chamber, that grant shall continue in force for the purposes of his or her representation before the Grand Chamber.

Rule 106 (former Rule 101)

Legal aid shall be granted only where the President of the Chamber is satisfied

(a) that it is necessary for the proper conduct of the case before the Chamber;

(b) that the applicant has insufficient means to meet all or part of the costs entailed.

Rule 107 (former Rule102)

1. In order to determine whether or not applicants have sufficient means to meet all or part of the costs entailed, they shall be required to complete a form of declaration stating their income, capital assets and any financial commitments in respect of dependants, or any other financial obligations. The declaration shall be certified by the appropriate domestic authority or authorities.

2. The President of the Chamber may invite the Contracting Party concerned to submit its comments in writing.

3. After receiving the information mentioned in paragraph 1 of this Rule, the President of the Chamber shall decide whether or not to grant legal aid. The Registrar shall inform the parties accordingly.

Rule 108 (former Rule 103)

1. Fees shall be payable to the advocates or other persons appointed in accordance with Rule 36 § 4. Fees may, where appropriate, be paid to more than one such representative.

2. Legal aid may be granted to cover not only representatives' fees but also travelling and subsistence expenses and other necessary expenses incurred by the applicant or appointed representative.

Rule 109 (former Rule 104)

On a decision to grant legal aid, the Registrar shall fix

(a) the rate of fees to be paid in accordance with the legal-aid scales in force;

(b) the level of expenses to be paid.

Rule 110 (former Rule 105)

The President of the Chamber may, if satisfied that the conditions stated in Rule 106 are no longer fulfilled, revoke or vary a grant of legal aid at any time.

TITLE III TRANSITIONAL RULES

Rule 111 – Relations between the Court and the Commission (former Rule 106)

1. In cases brought before the Court under Article 5 §§ 4 and 5 of Protocol No. 11 to the Convention, the Court may invite the Commission to delegate one or more of its members to take part in the consideration of the case before the Court.

2. In cases referred to in paragraph 1 of this Rule, the Court shall take into consideration the report of the Commission adopted pursuant to former Article 31 of the Convention.

3. Unless the President of the Chamber decides otherwise, the said report shall be made available to the public through the Registrar as soon as possible after the case has been brought before the Court.

4. The remainder of the case file of the Commission, including all pleadings, in cases brought before the Court under Article 5 §§ 2 to 5 of Protocol No. 11 shall remain confidential unless the President of the Chamber decides otherwise.

5. In cases where the Commission has taken evidence but has been unable to adopt a report in accordance with former Article 31 of the Convention, the Court shall take into consideration the verbatim records, documentation and opinion of the Commission's delegations arising from such investigations.

Rule 112 – Chamber and Grand Chamber proceedings (former Rule 107)

1. In cases referred to the Court under Article 5 § 4 of Protocol No. 11 to the Convention, a panel of the Grand Chamber constituted in accordance with Rule 24 § 5 shall determine, solely on the basis of the existing case file, whether a Chamber or the Grand Chamber is to decide the case.

2. If the case is decided by a Chamber, the judgment of the Chamber shall, in accordance with Article 5 § 4 of Protocol No. 11, be final and Rule 73 shall be inapplicable.

3. Cases transmitted to the Court under Article 5 § 5 of Protocol No. 11 shall be forwarded by the President of the Court to the Grand Chamber.

4. For each case transmitted to the Grand Chamber under Article 5 § 5 of Protocol No. 11, the Grand Chamber shall be completed by judges designated by rotation within one of the groups mentioned in Rule 24 § 31, the cases being allocated to the groups on an alternate basis.

Rule 113 – Grant of legal aid (former Rule 108)

Subject to Rule 101, in cases brought before the Court under Article 5 §§ 2 to 5 of Protocol No. 11 to the Convention, a grant of legal aid made to an applicant in the proceedings before the Commission or the former Court shall continue in force for the purposes of his or her representation before the Court.

Rule 114 – Request for revision of a judgment (former Rule 109)

1. Where a party requests revision of a judgment delivered by the former Court, the President of the Court shall assign the request to one of the Sections in accordance with the conditions laid down in Rule 51 or 52, as the case may be.

2. The President of the relevant Section shall, notwithstanding Rule 80 § 3, constitute a new Chamber to consider the request.

3. The Chamber to be constituted shall include as ex officio members

(a) the President of the Section;

and, whether or not they are members of the relevant Section,

(b) the judge elected in respect of any Contracting Party concerned or, if he or she is unable to sit, any judge appointed under Rule 29;

(c) any judge of the Court who was a member of the original Chamber that delivered the judgment in the former Court.

4. (a) The other members of the Chamber shall be designated by the President of the Section by means of a drawing of lots from among the members of the relevant Section.

(b) The members of the Section who are not so designated shall sit in the case as substitute judges.

TITLE IV FINAL CLAUSES

Rule 115 – Suspension of a Rule (former Rule 110)

A Rule relating to the internal working of the Court may be suspended upon a motion made without notice, provided that this decision is taken unanimously by the Chamber concerned. The suspension of a Rule shall in this case be limited in its operation to the particular purpose for which it was sought.

Rule 116 – Amendment of a Rule (former Rule 111)

1. Any Rule may be amended upon a motion made after notice where such a motion is carried at the next session of the plenary Court by a majority of all the members of the Court. Notice of such a motion shall be delivered in writing to the Registrar at least one month before the session at which it is to be discussed. On receipt of such a notice of motion, the Registrar shall inform all members of the Court at the earliest possible moment.

2. The Registrar shall inform the Contracting Parties of any proposals by the Court to amend the Rules which directly concern the conduct of proceedings before it and invite them to submit written comments on such proposals. The Registrar shall also invite written comments from organisations with experience in representing applicants before the Court as well as from relevant Bar associations.

Rule 117 – Entry into force of the Rules (former Rule 1121)

The present Rules shall enter into force on 1 November 1998.

ANNEX TO THE RULES (concerning investigations)

Rule A1 (Investigative measures)

1. The Chamber may, at the request of a party or of its own motion, adopt any investigative measure which it considers capable of clarifying the facts of the case. The Chamber may, inter alia, invite the parties to produce documentary evidence and decide to hear as a witness or expert or in any other capacity any person whose evidence or statements seem likely to assist it in carrying out its tasks.

2. The Chamber may also ask any person or institution of its choice to express an opinion or make a written report on any matter considered by it to be relevant to the case.

3. After a case has been declared admissible or, exceptionally, before the decision on admissibility, the Chamber may appoint one or more of its members or of the other judges of the Court, as its delegate or delegates, to conduct an inquiry, carry out an on-site investigation or take evidence in some other manner. The Chamber may also appoint any person or institution of its choice to assist the delegation in such manner as it sees fit.

4. The provisions of this Chapter concerning investigative measures by a delegation shall apply, mutatis mutandis, to any such proceedings conducted by the Chamber itself.

5. Proceedings forming part of any investigation by a Chamber or its delegation shall be held in camera, save in so far as the President of the Chamber or the head of the delegation decides otherwise.

6. The President of the Chamber may, as he or she considers appropriate, invite, or grant leave to, any third party to participate in an investigative measure. The President shall lay down the conditions of any such participation and may limit that participation if those conditions are not complied with.

Rule A2 (Obligations of the parties as regards investigative measures)

1. The applicant and any Contracting Party concerned shall assist the Court as necessary in implementing any investigative measures.

2. The Contracting Party on whose territory on-site proceedings before a delegation take place shall extend to the delegation the facilities and cooperation necessary for the proper conduct of the proceedings. These shall include, to the full extent necessary, freedom of movement within the territory and all adequate security arrangements for the delegation, for

the applicant and for all witnesses, experts and others who may be heard by the delegation. It shall be the responsibility of the Contracting Party concerned to take steps to ensure that no adverse consequences are suffered by any person or organisation on account of any evidence given, or of any assistance provided, to the delegation.

Rule A3 (Failure to appear before a delegation)

Where a party or any other person due to appear fails or declines to do so, the delegation may, provided that it is satisfied that such a course is consistent with the proper administration of justice, nonetheless continue with the proceedings.

Rule A4 (Conduct of proceedings before a delegation)

1. The delegates shall exercise any relevant power conferred on the Chamber by the Convention or these Rules and shall have control of the proceedings before them.

2. The head of the delegation may decide to hold a preparatory meeting with the parties or their representatives prior to any proceedings taking place before the delegation.

Rule A5 (Convocation of witnesses, experts and of other persons to proceedings before a delegation)

1. Witnesses, experts and other persons to be heard by the delegation shall be summoned by the Registrar.

2. The summons shall indicate

(a) the case in connection with which it has been issued;

(b) the object of the inquiry, expert opinion or other investigative measure ordered by the Chamber or the President of the Chamber;

(c) any provisions for the payment of sums due to the person summoned.

3. The parties shall provide, in so far as possible, sufficient information to establish the identity and addresses of witnesses, experts or other persons to be summoned.

4. In accordance with Rule 37 § 2, the Contracting Party in whose territory the witness resides shall be responsible for servicing any summons sent to it by the Chamber for service. In the event of such service not being possible, the Contracting Party shall give reasons in writing. The Contracting Party shall further take all reasonable steps to ensure the attendance of persons summoned who are under its authority or control.

5. The head of the delegation may request the attendance of witnesses, experts and other persons during on-site proceedings before a delegation. The Contracting Party on whose territory such proceedings are held shall, if so requested, take all reasonable steps to facilitate that attendance.

6. Where a witness, expert or other person is summoned at the request or on behalf of a Contracting Party, the costs of their appearance shall be borne by that Party unless the Chamber decides otherwise. The costs of the appearance of any such person who is in detention in the Contracting Party on whose territory on-site proceedings before a delegation take place shall be borne by that Party unless the Chamber decides otherwise. In all other cases, the Chamber shall decide whether such costs are to be borne by the Council of Europe or awarded against the applicant or third party at whose request or on whose behalf the person appears. In all cases, such costs shall be taxed by the President of the Chamber.

Rule A6 (Oath or solemn declaration by witnesses and experts heard by a delegation)

1. After the establishment of the identity of a witness and before testifying, each witness shall take the oath or make the following solemn declaration:

> "I swear" – or "I solemnly declare upon my honour and conscience" – "that I shall speak the truth, the whole truth and nothing but the truth."

This act shall be recorded in minutes.

2. After the establishment of the identity of the expert and before carrying out his or her task for the delegation, every expert shall take the oath or make the following solemn declaration:

> "I swear" – or "I solemnly declare" – "that I will discharge my duty as an expert honourably and conscientiously."

This act shall be recorded in minutes.

Rule A7 (Hearing of witnesses, experts and other persons by a delegation)

1. Any delegate may put questions to the Agents, advocates or advisers of the parties, to the applicant, witnesses and experts, and to any other persons appearing before the delegation.

2. Witnesses, experts and other persons appearing before the delegation may, subject to the control of the head of the delegation, be examined by the Agents and advocates or advisers of the parties. In the event of an objection to a question put, the head of the delegation shall decide.

3. Save in exceptional circumstances and with the consent of the head of the delegation, witnesses, experts and other persons to be heard by a delegation will not be admitted to the hearing room before they give evidence.

4. The head of the delegation may make special arrangements for witnesses, experts or other persons to be heard in the absence of the parties where that is required for the proper administration of justice.

5. The head of the delegation shall decide in the event of any dispute arising from an objection to a witness or expert. The delegation may hear for information purposes a person who is not qualified to be heard as a witness or expert.

Rule A8 (Verbatim record of proceedings before a delegation)

1. A verbatim record shall be prepared by the Registrar of any proceedings concerning an investigative measure by a delegation. The verbatim record shall include:

(a) the composition of the delegation;
(b) a list of those appearing before the delegation, that is to say Agents, advocates and advisers of the parties taking part;
(c) the surname, forenames, description and address of each witness, expert or other person heard;
(d) the text of statements made, questions put and replies given;
(e) the text of any ruling delivered during the proceedings before the delegation or by the head of the delegation.

2. If all or part of the verbatim record is in a non-official language, the Registrar shall arrange for its translation into one of the official languages.

3. The representatives of the parties shall receive a copy of the verbatim record in order that they may, subject to the control of the Registrar or the head of the delegation, make corrections, but in no case may such corrections affect the sense and bearing of what was said.

The Registrar shall lay down, in accordance with the instructions of the head of the delegation, the time-limits granted for this purpose.

4. The verbatim record, once so corrected, shall be signed by the head of the delegation and the Registrar and shall then constitute certified matters of record.

32.d Practice Directions*

Date: 1 April 2011
Source: https://www.echr.coe.int/documents/rules_court_eng.pdf

REQUESTS FOR INTERIM MEASURES
(Rule 39 of the Rules of Court)

By virtue of Rule 39 of the Rules of Court, the Court may issue interim measures which are binding on the State concerned. Interim measures are only applied in exceptional cases. The Court will only issue an interim measure against a Member State where, having reviewed all the relevant information, it considers that the applicant faces a real risk of serious, irreversible harm if the measure is not applied.

Applicants or their legal representatives who make a request for an interim measure pursuant to Rule 39 of the Rules of Court should comply with the requirements set out below.

I. Accompanying information

Any request lodged with the Court must state reasons. The applicant must in particular specify in detail the grounds on which his or her particular fears are based, the nature of the alleged risks and the Convention provisions alleged to have been violated.

A mere reference to submissions in other documents or domestic proceedings is not sufficient. It is essential that requests be accompanied by all necessary supporting documents, in particular relevant domestic court, tribunal or other decisions, together with any other material which is considered to substantiate the applicant's allegations.

The Court will not necessarily contact applicants whose request for interim measures is incomplete, and requests which do not include the information necessary to make a decision will not normally be submitted for a decision.

Where the case is already pending before the Court, reference should be made to the application number allocated to it.

In cases concerning extradition or deportation, details should be provided of the expected date and time of the removal, the applicant's address or place of detention and his or her official case-reference number. The Court must be notified of any change to those details (date and time of removal, address etc.) as soon as possible.

The Court may decide to take a decision on the admissibility of the case at the same time as considering the request for interim measures.

* N.B.: Footnotes and emphasis have been omitted.

II. Requests to be made by facsimile or letter

Requests for interim measures under Rule 39 should be sent by facsimile or by post. The Court will not deal with requests sent by e-mail. The request should, where possible, be in one of the official languages of the Contracting Parties. All requests should be marked as follows in bold on the face of the request:

"Rule 39 – Urgent
Person to contact (name and contact details): …
[In deportation or extradition cases]
Date and time of removal and destination: …"

III. Making requests in good time

Requests for interim measures should normally be received as soon as possible after the final domestic decision has been taken, in order to enable the Court and its Registry to have sufficient time to examine the matter. The Court may not be able to deal with requests in removal cases received less than a working day before the planned time of removal.

Where the final domestic decision is imminent and there is a risk of immediate enforcement, especially in extradition or deportation cases, applicants and their representatives should submit the request for interim measures without waiting for that decision, indicating clearly the date on which it will be taken and that the request is subject to the final domestic decision being negative.

IV. Domestic measures with suspensive effect

The Court is not an appeal tribunal from domestic tribunals, and applicants in extradition and expulsion cases should pursue domestic avenues which are capable of suspending removal before applying to the Court for interim measures. Where it remains open to an applicant to pursue domestic remedies which have suspensive effect, the Court will not apply Rule 39 to prevent removal.

V. Follow-up

Applicants who apply for an interim measure under Rule 39 should ensure that they reply to correspondence from the Court's Registry. In particular, where a measure has been refused, they should inform the Court whether they wish to pursue the application. Where a measure has been applied, they must keep the Court regularly and promptly informed about the state of any continuing domestic proceedings. Failure to do so may lead to the case being struck out of the Court's list of cases.

INSTITUTION OF PROCEEDINGS
(Individual applications under Article 34 of the Convention)

I. General

1. An application under Article 34 of the Convention must be submitted in writing. No application may be made by telephone. Except as provided otherwise by Rule 47 of the Rules of Court, only a completed application form will interrupt the running of the six-month time-limit set out in Article 35 § 1 of the Convention. An application form is available online from the Court's website. Applicants are strongly encouraged to download and print the application form instead of contacting the Court for a paper copy to be sent by post. By doing this, applicants will save time and will be in a better position to ensure that

their completed application form is submitted within the six-month time-limit. Help with the completion of the various fields is available online.

2. An application must be sent to the following address:

The Registrar
European Court of Human Rights
Council of Europe
67075 Strasbourg Cedex
FRANCE

3. Applications sent by fax will not interrupt the running of the six-month time-limit set out in Article 35 § 1 of the Convention. Applicants must also dispatch the signed original by post within the same six-month time-limit.

4. An applicant should be diligent in corresponding with the Court's Registry. A delay in replying or failure to reply may be regarded as a sign that the applicant is no longer interested in pursuing his or her application.

II. Form and contents

5. The submissions in the application form concerning the facts, complaints and compliance with the requirements of exhaustion of domestic remedies and the time-limit set out in Article 35 § 1 of the Convention must respect the conditions set out in Rule 47 of the Rules of Court. Any additional submissions, presented as a separate document, must not exceed 20 pages (see Rule 47 § 2 (b)) and should:

a) be in an A4 page format with a margin of not less than 3.5 cm wide;
b) be wholly legible and, if typed, the text should be at least 12 pt in the body of the document and 10 pt in the footnotes, with one and a half line spacing;
c) have all numbers expressed as figures;
d) have pages numbered consecutively;
e) be divided into numbered paragraphs;
f) be divided into headings corresponding to "Facts", "Complaints or statements of violations" and "Information about the exhaustion of domestic remedies and compliance with the time-limit set out in Article 35 § 1".

6. All applicable fields in the application form must be filled in by use of words. Avoid using symbols, signs or abbreviations. Explain in words, even if the answer is negative or the question does not appear relevant.

7. The applicant must set out the facts of the case, his or her complaints and the explanations as to compliance with the admissibility criteria in the space provided in the application form. The information should be enough to enable the Court to determine the nature and scope of the application and, as such, the completed application form alone should suffice. It is not acceptable merely to annex a statement of facts, complaints and compliance to the application form, with or without the mention "see attached". Filling in this information on the application form is to assist the Court in speedily assessing and allocating incoming cases. Additional explanations may be appended, if necessary, in a separate document up to a maximum of 20 pages: these only develop and cannot replace the statement of facts, complaints and compliance with the admissibility criteria that must be on the application form itself. An application form will not be regarded as compliant with Rule 47 if this information is not found on the form itself.

8. A legal person (which includes a company, non-governmental organisation or association) that applies to the Court must do so through a representative of that legal

person who is identified in the relevant section of the application form and who provides contact details and explains his or her capacity or relationship with the legal person. Proof must be supplied with the application form that the representative has authority to act on behalf of the legal person, for example an extract from the Chamber of Commerce register or minutes of the governing body. The representative of the legal person is distinct from the lawyer authorised to act before the Court as legal representative. It may be that a legal person's representative is also a lawyer or legal officer and has the capacity to act additionally as legal representative. Both parts of the application form concerning representation must still be filled in, and requisite documentary proof provided of authority to represent the legal person must be attached.

9. An applicant does not have to have legal representation at the introductory stage of proceedings. If he or she does instruct a lawyer, the authority section on the application form must be filled in. Both the applicant and the representative must sign the authority section. A separate power of attorney is not acceptable at this stage as the Court requires all essential information to be contained in its application form. If it is claimed that it is not possible to obtain the applicant's signature on the authority section in the application form due to insurmountable practical difficulties, this should be explained to the Court with any substantiating elements. The requirement of completing the application form speedily within the six-month time-limit will not be accepted as an adequate explanation.

10. An application form must be accompanied by the relevant documents

(a) relating to the decisions or measures complained of;

(b) showing that the applicant has complied with the exhaustion of available domestic remedies and the time-limit contained in Article 35 § 1 of the Convention;

(c) showing, where applicable, information regarding other international proceedings.

If the applicant is unable to provide a copy of any of these documents, he or she must provide an adequate explanation: merely stating that he or she encountered difficulties (in obtaining the documents) will not suffice if it can be reasonably expected for the explanation to be supported by documentary evidence, such as proof of indigence, a refusal of an authority to furnish a decision or otherwise demonstrating the applicant's inability to access the document. If the explanation is not forthcoming or adequate, the application will not be allocated to a judicial formation.

Where documents are provided by electronic means, they must be in the format required by this practice direction; they must also be arranged and numbered in accordance with the list of documents on the application form.

11. An applicant who has already had a previous application or applications decided by the Court or who has an application or applications pending before the Court must inform the Registry accordingly, stating the application number or numbers.

12. (a) Where an applicant does not wish to have his or her identity disclosed, he or she should state the reasons for his or her request in writing, pursuant to Rule 47 § 4.

(b) The applicant should also state whether, in the event of anonymity being authorised by the President of the Chamber, he or she wishes to be designated by his or her initials or by a single letter (e.g. "X", "Y" or "Z").

13. The applicant or the designated representative must sign the application form. If represented, both the applicant and the representative must sign the authority section of the application form. Neither the application form nor the authority section can be signed per procurationem (p.p.).

III. Grouped applications and multiple applicants

14. Where an applicant or representative lodges complaints on behalf of two or more applicants whose applications are based on different facts, a separate application form should be filled in for each individual giving all the information required. The documents relevant to each applicant should also be annexed to that individual's application form.

15. Where there are more than ten applicants, the representative should provide – in addition to the application forms and documents – a table setting out for each applicant the required personal information; this table may be downloaded from the Court's website. Where the representative is a lawyer, the table should also be provided in electronic form.

16. In cases of large groups of applicants or applications, applicants or their representatives may be directed by the Court to provide the text of their submissions or documents by electronic or other means. Other directions may be given by the Court as to steps required to facilitate the effective and speedy processing of applications.

IV. Failure to comply with requests for information or directions

17. Failure, within the specified time-limit, to provide further information or documents at the Court's request or to comply with the Court's directions as to the form or manner of the lodging of an application – including grouped applications or applications by multiple applicants – may result, depending on the stage reached in the proceedings, in the complaint(s) not being examined by the Court or the application(s) being declared inadmissible or struck out of the Court's list of cases.

WRITTEN PLEADINGS

I. Filing of pleadings

General

1. A pleading must be filed with the Registry within the time-limit fixed in accordance with Rule 38 of the Rules of Court and in the manner described in paragraph 2 of that Rule.

2. The date on which a pleading or other document is received at the Court's Registry will be recorded on that document by a receipt stamp.

3. With the exception of pleadings and documents for which a system of electronic filing has been set up (see the relevant practice directions), all other pleadings, as well as all documents annexed thereto, should be submitted to the Court's Registry in three copies sent by post or in one copy by fax, followed by three copies sent by post.

4. Pleadings or other documents submitted by electronic mail shall not be accepted. 5. Secret documents should be filed by registered post.

6. Unsolicited pleadings shall not be admitted to the case file unless the President of the Chamber decides otherwise (see Rule 38 § 1).

Filing by fax

7. A party may file pleadings or other documents with the Court by sending them by fax.

8. The name of the person signing a pleading must also be printed on it so that he or she can be identified.

Electronic filing

9. The Court may authorise the Government of a Contracting Party or, after the communication of an application, an applicant to file pleadings and other documents electronically.

In such cases, the practice direction on written pleadings shall apply in conjunction with the practice directions on electronic filing.

II. Form and contents

Form

10. A pleading should include:
   (a) the application number and the name of the case;
   (b) a title indicating the nature of the content (e.g., observations on admissibility [and the merits]; reply to the Government's/the applicant's observations on admissibility [and the merits]; observations on the merits; additional observations on admissibility [and the merits]; memorial etc.).

11. In addition, a pleading should normally:
   (a) be in an A4 page format having a margin of not less than 3.5 cm wide;
   (b) be typed and wholly legible, the text appearing in at least 12 pt in the body and 10 pt in the footnotes, with one-and-a-half line spacing;
   (c) have all numbers expressed as figures; (d) have pages numbered consecutively; (e) be divided into numbered paragraphs;
   (f) be divided into chapters and/or headings corresponding to the form and style of the Court's decisions and judgments ("Facts"/"Domestic law [and practice]"/"Complaints"/"Law"; the latter chapter should be followed by headings entitled "Preliminary objection on …", "Alleged violation of Article …", as the case may be);
   (g) place any answer to a question by the Court or to the other party's arguments under a separate heading;
   (h) give a reference to every document or piece of evidence mentioned in the pleading and annexed thereto;
   (i) if sent by post, have its text printed on one side of the page only and pages and attachments placed together in such a way as to enable them to be easily separated (they must not be glued or stapled).

12. If a pleading exceptionally exceeds thirty pages, a short summary should also be filed with it.

13. Where a party produces documents and/or other exhibits together with a pleading, every piece of evidence should be listed in a separate annex.

Contents

14. The parties' pleadings following communication of the application should include:
   (a) any comments they wish to make on the facts of the case; however,
      (i) if a party does not contest the facts as set out in the statement of facts prepared by the Registry, it should limit its observations to a brief statement to that effect;
      (ii) if a party contests only part of the facts as set out by the Registry, or wishes to supplement them, it should limit its observations to those specific points;
      (iii) if a party objects to the facts or part of the facts as presented by the other party, it should state clearly which facts are uncontested and limit its observations to the points in dispute;

(b) legal arguments relating firstly to admissibility and, secondly, to the merits of the case; however,
  (i) if specific questions on a factual or legal point were put to a party, it should, without prejudice to Rule 55, limit its arguments to such questions;
  (ii) if a pleading replies to arguments of the other party, submissions should refer to the specific arguments in the order prescribed above.

15. (a) The parties' pleadings following the admission of the application should include:
  (i) a short statement confirming a party's position on the facts of the case as established in the decision on admissibility;
  (ii) legal arguments relating to the merits of the case;
  (iii) a reply to any specific questions on a factual or legal point put by the Court.

(b) An applicant party submitting claims for just satisfaction at the same time should do so in the manner described in the practice direction on filing just satisfaction claims.

16. In view of the confidentiality of friendly-settlement proceedings (see Article 39 § 2 of the Convention and Rule 62 § 2), all submissions and documents filed as part of the attempt to secure a friendly settlement should be submitted separately from the written pleadings.

17. No reference to offers, concessions or other statements submitted in connection with the friendly settlement may be made in the pleadings filed in the contentious proceedings.

III. Time-limits General

18. It is the responsibility of each party to ensure that pleadings and any accompanying documents or evidence are delivered to the Court's Registry in time.

Extension of time-limits

19. A time-limit set under Rule 38 may be extended on request from a party.

20. A party seeking an extension of the time allowed for submission of a pleading must make a request as soon as it has become aware of the circumstances justifying such an extension and, in any event, before the expiry of the time-limit. It should state the reason for the delay.

21. If an extension is granted, it shall apply to all parties for which the relevant time-limit is running, including those which have not asked for it.

IV. Failure to comply with requirements for pleadings

22. Where a pleading has not been filed in accordance with the requirements set out in paragraphs 8 to 15 of this practice direction, the President of the Chamber may request the party concerned to resubmit the pleading in compliance with those requirements.

23. A failure to satisfy the conditions listed above may result in the pleading being considered not to have been properly lodged (see Rule 38 § 1).

JUST SATISFACTION CLAIMS

I. Introduction

1. The award of just satisfaction is not an automatic consequence of a finding by the European Court of Human Rights that there has been a violation of a right guaranteed by

the European Convention on Human Rights or its Protocols. The wording of Article 41, which provides that the Court shall award just satisfaction only if domestic law does not allow complete reparation to be made, and even then only "if necessary" (s'il y a lieu in the French text), makes this clear.

2. Furthermore, the Court will only award such satisfaction as is considered to be "just" (équitable in the French text) in the circumstances. Consequently, regard will be had to the particular features of each case. The Court may decide that for some heads of alleged prejudice the finding of violation constitutes in itself sufficient just satisfaction, without there being any call to afford financial compensation. It may also find reasons of equity to award less than the value of the actual damage sustained or the costs and expenses actually incurred, or even not to make any award at all. This may be the case, for example, if the situation complained of, the amount of damage or the level of the costs is due to the applicant's own fault. In setting the amount of an award, the Court may also consider the respective positions of the applicant as the party injured by a violation and the Contracting Party as responsible for the public interest. Finally, the Court will normally take into account the local economic circumstances.

3. When it makes an award under Article 41, the Court may decide to take guidance from domestic standards. It is, however, never bound by them.

4. Claimants are warned that compliance with the formal and substantive requirements deriving from the Convention and the Rules of Court is a condition for the award of just satisfaction.

II. Submitting claims for just satisfaction: formal requirements

5. Time-limits and other formal requirements for submitting claims for just satisfaction are laid down in Rule 60 of the Rules of Court, the relevant part of which provides as follows:

> 1. An applicant who wishes to obtain an award of just satisfaction under Article 41 of the Convention in the event of the Court finding a violation of his or her Convention rights must make a specific claim to that effect.
> 2. The applicant must submit itemised particulars of all claims, together with any relevant supporting documents, within the time-limit fixed for the submission of the applicant's observations on the merits unless the President of the Chamber directs otherwise.
> 3. If the applicant fails to comply with the requirements set out in the preceding paragraphs, the Chamber may reject the claims in whole or in part.

...

Thus, the Court requires specific claims supported by appropriate documentary evidence, failing which it may make no award. The Court will also reject claims set out on the application form but not resubmitted at the appropriate stage of the proceedings and claims lodged out of time.

III. Submitting claims for just satisfaction: substantive requirements

6. Just satisfaction may be afforded under Article 41 of the Convention in respect of:

(a) pecuniary damage;
(b) non-pecuniary damage; and
(c) costs and expenses.

1. Damage in general

7. A clear causal link must be established between the damage claimed and the violation alleged. The Court will not be satisfied by a merely tenuous connection between the alleged violation and the damage, nor by mere speculation as to what might have been.

8. Compensation for damage can be awarded in so far as the damage is the result of a violation found. No award can be made for damage caused by events or situations that have not been found to constitute a violation of the Convention, or for damage related to complaints declared inadmissible at an earlier stage of the proceedings.

9. The purpose of the Court's award in respect of damage is to compensate the applicant for the actual harmful consequences of a violation. It is not intended to punish the Contracting Party responsible. The Court has therefore, until now, considered it inappropriate to accept claims for damages with labels such as "punitive", "aggravated" or "exemplary".

2. Pecuniary damage

10. The principle with regard to pecuniary damage is that the applicant should be placed, as far as possible, in the position in which he or she would have been had the violation found not taken place, in other words, restitutio in integrum. This can involve compensation for both loss actually suffered (damnum emergens) and loss, or diminished gain, to be expected in the future (lucrum cessans).

11. It is for the applicant to show that pecuniary damage has resulted from the violation or violations alleged. The applicant should submit relevant documents to prove, as far as possible, not only the existence but also the amount or value of the damage.

12. Normally, the Court's award will reflect the full calculated amount of the damage. However, if the actual damage cannot be precisely calculated, the Court will make an estimate based on the facts at its disposal. As pointed out in paragraph 2 above, it is also possible that the Court may find reasons in equity to award less than the full amount of the loss.

3. Non-pecuniary damage

13. The Court's award in respect of non-pecuniary damage is intended to provide financial compensation for non-material harm, for example mental or physical suffering.

14. It is in the nature of non-pecuniary damage that it does not lend itself to precise calculation. If the existence of such damage is established, and if the Court considers that a monetary award is necessary, it will make an assessment on an equitable basis, having regard to the standards which emerge from its case-law.

15. Applicants who wish to be compensated for non-pecuniary damage are invited to specify a sum which in their view would be equitable. Applicants who consider themselves victims of more than one violation may claim either a single lump sum covering all alleged violations or a separate sum in respect of each alleged violation.

4. Costs and expenses

16. The Court can order the reimbursement to the applicant of costs and expenses which he or she has incurred – first at the domestic level, and subsequently in the proceedings before the Court itself – in trying to prevent the violation from occurring, or in trying to obtain redress therefor. Such costs and expenses will typically include the cost of legal assistance, court registration fees and suchlike. They may also include travel and subsistence expenses, in particular if these have been incurred by attendance at a hearing of the Court.

17. The Court will uphold claims for costs and expenses only in so far as they are referable to the violations it has found. It will reject them in so far as they relate to complaints that have not led to the finding of a violation, or to complaints declared inadmissible. This being so, applicants may wish to link separate claim items to particular complaints.

18. Costs and expenses must have been actually incurred. That is, the applicant must have paid them, or be bound to pay them, pursuant to a legal or contractual obligation. Any sums paid or payable by domestic authorities or by the Council of Europe by way of legal aid will be deducted.

19. Costs and expenses must have been necessarily incurred. That is, they must have become unavoidable in order to prevent the violation or obtain redress therefor.

20. They must be reasonable as to quantum. If the Court finds them to be excessive, it will award a sum which, on its own estimate, is reasonable.

21. The Court requires evidence, such as itemised bills and invoices. These must be sufficiently detailed to enable the Court to determine to what extent the above requirements have been met.

5. Payment information

22. Applicants are invited to identify a bank account into which they wish any sums awarded to be paid. If they wish particular amounts, for example the sums awarded in respect of costs and expenses, to be paid separately, for example directly into the bank account of their representative, they should so specify.

IV. The form of the Court's awards

23. The Court's awards, if any, will normally be in the form of a sum of money to be paid by the respondent Government to the victim or victims of the violations found. Only in extremely rare cases can the Court consider a consequential order aimed at putting an end or remedying the violation in question. The Court may, however, decide at its discretion to offer guidance for the execution of its judgment (Article 46 of the Convention).

24. Any monetary award under Article 41 will normally be in euros (EUR, €) irrespective of the currency in which the applicant expresses his or her claims. If the applicant is to receive payment in a currency other than the euro, the Court will order the sums awarded to be converted into that other currency at the exchange rate applicable on the date of payment. When formulating their claims applicants should, where appropriate, consider the implications of this policy in the light of the effects of converting sums expressed in a different currency into euros or contrariwise.

25. The Court will of its own motion set a time-limit for any payments that may need to be made, which will normally be three months from the date on which its judgment becomes final and binding. The Court will also order default interest to be paid in the event that that time-limit is exceeded, normally at a simple rate equal to the marginal lending rate of the European Central Bank during the default period plus three percentage points.

SECURED ELECTRONIC FILING BY GOVERNMENTS

I. Scope of application

1. The Governments of the Contracting Parties that have opted for the Court's system of secured electronic filing shall send all their written communications with the Court by uploading them on the secured website set up for that purpose and shall accept written

communications sent to them by the Registry of the Court by downloading them from that site, with the following exceptions:

(a) in the event of a dysfunction on the secure site, it is mandatory that the documents concerning a request for the indication of an interim measure under Rule 39 of the Rules of Court be sent by fax or email; in such cases the document must be clearly headed "Rule 39. Urgent";

(b) attachments, such as plans, manuals, etc. that may not be comprehensively viewed in an electronic format may be filed by post;

(c) the Court's Registry may request that a paper document or attachment be submitted by post.

2. If the Government have filed a document by post or fax, they shall, as soon as possible, file electronically a notice of filing by post or fax, describing the document sent, stating the date of dispatch and setting forth the reasons why electronic filing was not possible.

II. Technical requirements

3. The Government shall possess the necessary technical equipment and follow the user manual sent to them by the Court's Registry.

III. Format and naming convention

4. A document filed electronically shall be in PDF format, preferably in searchable PDF.

5. Unsigned letters and written pleadings shall not be accepted. Signed documents to be filed electronically shall be generated by scanning the original paper copy. The Government shall keep the original paper copy in their files.

6. The name of a document filed electronically shall be prefixed by the application number, followed by the name of the applicant as spelled in Latin script by the Registry of the Court, and contain an indication of the contents of the document2.

IV. Relevant date with regard to time-limits

7. The date on which the Government have successfully uploaded a document on the secured website shall be considered as the date of dispatch within the meaning of Rule 38 § 2 or the date of filing for the purposes of Rule 73 § 1.

8. To facilitate keeping track of the correspondence exchanged, every day shortly before midnight the secured server generates automatically an electronic mail message listing the documents that have been filed electronically within the past twenty-four hours.

V. Different versions of one and the same document

9. The secured website shall not permit the modification, replacement or deletion of an uploaded document. If the need arises for the Government to modify a document they have uploaded, they shall create a new document named differently (for example, by adding the word "modified" in the document name). This opportunity should only be used where genuinely necessary and should not be used to correct minor errors.

10. Where the Government have filed more than one version of the same document, only the document filed in time shall be taken into consideration. Where more than one version has been filed in time, the latest version shall be taken into consideration, unless the President of the Chamber decides otherwise.

REQUESTS FOR ANONYMITY
(Rule 33 and 47 of the Rules of Court)

General principles

The parties are reminded that, unless a derogation has been obtained pursuant to Rules 33 or 47 of the Rules of Court, documents in proceedings before the Court are public. Thus, all information that is submitted in connection with an application in both written and oral proceedings, including information about the applicant or third parties, will be accessible to the public.

The parties should also be aware that the statement of facts, decisions and judgments of the Court are usually published in HUDOC on the Court's website (Rule 78).

Requests in pending cases

Any request for anonymity should be made when completing the application form or as soon as possible thereafter. In both cases the applicant should provide reasons for the request and specify the impact that publication may have for him or her.

Retroactive requests

If an applicant wishes to request anonymity in respect of a case or cases published on HUDOC before 1 January 2010, he or she should send a letter to the Registry setting out the reasons for the request and specifying the impact that this publication has had or may have for him or her. The applicant should also provide an explanation as to why anonymity was not requested while the case was pending before the Court.

In deciding on the request the President shall take into account the explanations provided by the applicant, the level of publicity that the decision or judgment has already received and whether or not it is appropriate or practical to grant the request.

When the President grants the request, he or she shall also decide on the most appropriate steps to be taken to protect the applicant from being identified. For example, the decision or judgment could, inter alia, be removed from the Court's website or the personal data deleted from the published document.

Other measures

The President may also take any other measure he or she considers necessary or desirable in respect of any material published by the Court in order to ensure respect for private life.

ELECTRONIC FILING BY APPLICANTS

I. Scope of application

1. After the communication of a case, applicants who have opted to file pleadings electronically shall send all written communications with the Court by using the Court's Electronic Communications Service (eComms) and shall accept written communications sent to them by the Registry of the Court by means of eComms, with the following exceptions:

(a) all written communications in relation to a request for interim measures under Rule 39 of the Rules of Court shall be sent only by fax or post;

(b) attachments, such as plans, manuals, etc., that may not be comprehensively viewed in an electronic format may be filed by post;

(c) the Court's Registry may request that a paper document or attachment be submitted by post.

2. If an applicant has filed a document by post or fax, he or she shall, as soon as possible, file electronically a notice of filing by post or fax, describing the document sent, stating the date of dispatch and setting forth the reasons why electronic filing was not possible.

II. Technical requirements

3. Applicants shall possess the necessary technical equipment and follow the user manual available on the eComms site.

III. Format and naming convention

4. A document filed electronically shall be in PDF format. The PDF documents must be of the type 'text searchable PDF' rather than 'image-based' PDF.

5. Unsigned letters and written pleadings shall not be accepted. Signed documents to be filed electronically shall be generated by scanning the original paper copy. Applicants shall keep the original paper copy in their files.

6. The name of a document filed electronically shall be prefixed by the application number, followed by the name of the applicant as spelled in Latin script by the Registry of the Court, and contain an indication of the contents of the document2.

IV. Relevant date with regard to time limits

7. The date on which an applicant has successfully filed the document electronically with the Court shall be considered as the date, based on Strasbourg time, of dispatch within the meaning of Rule 38 § 2 or the date of filing for the purposes of Rule 73 § 1.

8. To facilitate keeping track of the correspondence exchanged and to ensure compliance with the time limits set by the Court, the applicant should regularly check his or her email account and eComms account.

V. Different versions of one and the same document

9. eComms shall not permit the modification, replacement or deletion of a filed document. If the need arises for the applicant to modify a document he or she has filed, they shall create a new document named differently (for example, by adding the word "modified" in the document name). This opportunity should only be used where genuinely necessary and should not be used to correct minor errors.

10. Where an applicant has filed more than one version of the same document, only the document filed in time shall be taken into consideration. Where more than one version has been filed in time, the latest version shall be taken into consideration, unless the President of the Chamber decides otherwise.

The African Regional Framework for Human Rights Protection

33.a African Charter on Human and Peoples' Rights (Banjul Charter)*

Date: 27 June 1981
Source: OAU Doc CAB/LEG/67/3 rev. 5; (1982) 21 ILM 58
https://www.achpr.org/legalinstruments/detail?id=49

...

PART II – MEASURES OF SAFEGUARD

CHAPTER I: ESTABLISHMENT AND ORGANISATION OF THE AFRICAN COMMISSION ON HUMAN AND PEOPLES' RIGHTS

ARTICLE 30

An African Commission on Human and Peoples' Rights, hereinafter called "the Commission", shall be established within the Organisation of African Unity to promote human and peoples' rights and ensure their protection in Africa.

ARTICLE 31

1. The Commission shall consist of eleven members chosen from amongst African personalities of the highest reputation, known for their high morality, integrity, impartiality and competence in matters of human and peoples' rights; particular consideration being given to persons having legal experience.
2. The members of the Commission shall serve in their personal capacity.

ARTICLE 32

The Commission shall not include more than one national of the same State.

ARTICLE 33

The members of the Commission shall be elected by secret ballot by the Assembly of Heads of State and Government, from a list of persons nominated by the State Parties to the present Charter.

ARTICLE 34

Each State Party to the present Charter may not nominate more than two candidates. The candidates must have the nationality of one of the State Parties to the present Charter. When two candidates are nominated by a State, one of them may not be a national of that State.

* N.B.: References to the Organization of African Unity (OAU) should be understood as references to the African Union in accordance with Article 33(1) of the Constitutive Act of the African Union (Document No. 46.a).

ARTICLE 35

1. The Secretary General of the Organisation of African Unity shall invite State Parties to the present Charter at least four months before the elections to nominate candidates;

2. The Secretary General of the Organisation of African Unity shall make an alphabetical list of the persons thus nominated and communicate it to the Heads of State and Government at least one month before the elections;

ARTICLE 36

The members of the Commission shall be elected for a six year period and shall be eligible for re-election. However, the term of office of four of the members elected at the first election shall terminate after two years and the term of office of three others, at the end of four years.

ARTICLE 37

Immediately after the first election, the Chairman of the Assembly of Heads of State and Government of the Organisation of African Unity shall draw lots to decide the names of those members referred to in Article 36.

ARTICLE 38

After their election, the members of the Commission shall make a solemn declaration to discharge their duties impartially and faithfully.

ARTICLE 39

1. In case of death or resignation of a member of the Commission, the Chairman of the Commission shall immediately inform the Secretary General of the Organisation of African Unity, who shall declare the seat vacant from the date of death or from the date on which the resignation takes effect.

2. If, in the unanimous opinion of other members of the Commission, a member has stopped discharging his duties for any reason other than a temporary absence, the Chairman of the Commission shall inform the Secretary General of the Organisation of African Unity, who shall then declare the seat vacant.

3. In each of the cases anticipated above, the Assembly of Heads of State and Government shall replace the member whose seat became vacant for the remaining period of his term, unless the period is less than six months.

ARTICLE 40

Every member of the Commission shall be in office until the date his successor assumes office.

ARTICLE 41

The Secretary General of the Organisation of African Unity shall appoint the Secretary of the Commission. He shall provide the staff and services necessary for the effective discharge of the duties of the Commission. The Organisation of African Unity shall bear cost of the staff and services.

ARTICLE 42

1. The Commission shall elect its Chairman and Vice Chairman for a two-year period. They shall be eligible for re-election.

2. The Commission shall lay down its rules of procedure.
3. Seven members shall form the quorum.
4. In case of an equality of votes, the Chairman shall have a casting vote.
5. The Secretary General may attend the meetings of the Commission. He shall neither participate in deliberations nor shall he be entitled to vote. The Chairman of the Commission may, however, invite him to speak.

ARTICLE 43

In discharging their duties, members of the Commission shall enjoy diplomatic privileges and immunities provided for in the General Convention on the Privileges and Immunities of the Organisation of African Unity.

ARTICLE 44

Provision shall be made for the emoluments and allowances of the members of the Commission in the Regular Budget of the Organisation of African Unity.

CHAPTER II: MANDATE OF THE COMMISSION

ARTICLE 45

The functions of the Commission shall be:

1. To promote human and peoples' rights and in particular:
   a) to collect documents, undertake studies and researches on African problems in the field of human and peoples' rights, organise seminars, symposia and conferences, disseminate information, encourage national and local institutions concerned with human and peoples' rights and, should the case arise, give its views or make recommendations to Governments.
   b) to formulae and lay down, principles and rules aimed at solving legal problems relating to human and peoples' rights and fundamental freedoms upon which African Governments may base their legislation.
   c) cooperate with other African and international institutions concerned with the promotion and protection of human and peoples' rights.
2. Ensure the protection of human and peoples' rights under conditions laid down by the present Charter.
3. Interpret all the provisions of the present Charter at the request of a State Party, an institution of the OAU or an African Organisation recognised by the OAU.
4. Perform any other tasks which may be entrusted to it by the Assembly of Heads of State and Government.

CHAPTER III: PROCEDURE OF THE COMMISSION

ARTICLE 46

The Commission may resort to any appropriate method of investigation; it may hear from the Secretary General of the Organisation of African Unity or any other person capable of enlightening it.

COMMUNICATION FROM STATES

ARTICLE 47

If a State Party to the present Charter has good reasons to believe that another State Party to this Charter has violated the provisions of the Charter, it may draw, by written communication, the attention of that State to the matter. This Communication shall also be addressed to the Secretary General of the OAU and to the Chairman of the Commission. Within three months of the receipt of the Communication, the State to which the Communication is addressed shall give the enquiring State, written explanation or statement elucidating the matter. This should include as much as possible, relevant information relating to the laws and rules of procedure applied and applicable and the redress already given or course of action available.

ARTICLE 48

If within three months from the date on which the original communication is received by the State to which it is addressed, the issue is not settled to the satisfaction of the two States involved through bilateral negotiation or by any other peaceful procedure, either State shall have the right to submit the matter to the Commission through the Chairman and shall notify the other States involved.

ARTICLE 49

Notwithstanding the provisions of Article 47, if a State Party to the present Charter considers that another State Party has violated the provisions of the Charter, it may refer the matter directly to the Commission by addressing a communication to the Chairman, to the Secretary General of the Organisation of African unity and the State concerned.

ARTICLE 50

The Commission can only deal with a matter submitted to it after making sure that all local remedies, if they exist, have been exhausted, unless it is obvious to the Commission that the procedure of achieving these remedies would be unduly prolonged.

ARTICLE 51

1. The Commission may ask the State concerned to provide it with all relevant information.
2. When the Commission is considering the matter, States concerned may be represented before it and submit written or oral representation.

ARTICLE 52

After having obtained from the States concerned and from other sources all the information it deems necessary and after having tried all appropriate means to reach an amicable solution based on the respect of human and peoples' rights, the Commission shall prepare, within a reasonable period of time from the notification referred to in Article 48, a report to the States concerned and communicated to the Assembly of Heads of State and Government.

ARTICLE 53

While transmitting its report, the Commission may make to the Assembly of Heads of State and Government such recommendations as it deems useful.

ARTICLE 54

The Commission shall submit to each Ordinary Session of the Assembly of Heads of State and Government a report on its activities.

ARTICLE 55

1. Before each Session, the Secretary of the Commission shall make a list of the Communications other than those of State Parties to the present Charter and transmit them to Members of the Commission, who shall indicate which Communications should be considered by the Commission.

2. A Communication shall be considered by the Commission if a simple majority of its members so decide.

ARTICLE 56

Communications relating to Human and Peoples' rights referred to in Article 55 received by the Commission, shall be considered if they:

1. Indicate their authors even if the latter requests anonymity,

2. Are compatible with the Charter of the Organisation of African Unity or with the present Charter,

3. Are not written in disparaging or insulting language directed against the State concerned and its institutions or to the Organisation of African Unity,

4. Are not based exclusively on news disseminated through the mass media,

5. Are sent after exhausting local remedies, if any, unless it is obvious that this procedure is unduly prolonged,

6. Are submitted within a reasonable period from the time local remedies are exhausted or from the date the Commission is seized with the matter, and

7. Do not deal with cases which have been settled by those States involved in accordance with the principles of the Charter of the United Nations, or the Charter of the Organisation of African Unity or the provisions of the present Charter.

ARTICLE 57

Prior to any substantive consideration, all communications shall be brought to the knowledge of the State concerned by the Chairman of the Commission.

ARTICLE 58

1. When it appears after deliberations of the Commission that one or more Communications apparently relate to special cases which reveal the existence of a series of serious or massive violations of human and peoples' rights, the Commission shall draw the attention of the Assembly of Heads of State and Government to these special cases.

2. The Assembly of Heads of State and Government may then request the Commission to undertake an in-depth study of these cases and make a factual report, accompanied by its finding and recommendations.

3. A case of emergency duly noticed by the Commission shall be submitted by the latter to the Chairman of the Assembly of Heads of State and Government who may request an in-depth study.

ARTICLE 59

1. All measures taken within the provisions of the present Chapter shall remain confidential until the Assembly of Heads of State and Government shall otherwise decide.

2. However the report shall be published by the Chairman of the Commission upon the decision of the Assembly of Heads of State and Government.

3. The report on the activities of the Commission shall be published by its Chairman after it has been considered by the Assembly of Heads of State and Government.

CHAPTER IV: APPLICABLE PRINCIPLES

ARTICLE 60

The Commission shall draw inspiration from international law on human and peoples' rights, particularly from the provisions of various African instruments on Human and Peoples' Rights, the Charter of the United Nations, the Charter of the Organisation of African Unity, the Universal Declaration of Human Rights, other instruments adopted by the United Nations and by African countries in the field of Human and Peoples' Rights, as well as from the provisions of various instruments adopted within the Specialised Agencies of the United Nations of which the Parties to the present Charter are members.

ARTICLE 61

The Commission shall also take into consideration, as subsidiary measures to determine the principles of law, other general or special international conventions, laying down rules expressly recognised by Member States of the Organisation of African Unity, African practices consistent with international norms on Human and Peoples' Rights, customs generally accepted as law, general principles of law recognised by African States as well as legal precedents and doctrine.

ARTICLE 62

Each State Party shall undertake to submit every two years, from the date the present Charter comes into force, a report on the legislative or other measures taken, with a view to giving effect to the rights and freedoms recognised and guaranteed by the present Charter.

ARTICLE 63

1. The present Charter shall be open to signature, ratification or adherence of the Member States of the Organisation of African Unity.

2. The instruments of ratification or adherence to the present Charter shall be deposited with the Secretary General of the Organisation of African Unity.

3. The present Charter shall come into force three months after the reception by the Secretary General of the instruments of ratification or adherence of a simple majority of the Member States of the Organisation of African Unity.

PART III – GENERAL PROVISIONS

ARTICLE 64

1. After the coming into force of the present Charter, members of the Commission shall be elected in accordance with the relevant Articles of the present Charter.

2. The Secretary General of the Organisation of African Unity shall convene the first meeting of the Commission at the Headquarters of the Organisation within three months of the constitution of the Commission. Thereafter, the Commission shall be convened by its Chairman whenever necessary but at least once a year.

...

33.b Protocol to the African Charter on Human and Peoples' Rights on the Establishment of an African Court on Human and Peoples' Rights*

Date: 9 June 1998
Source: OAU Doc CAB/LEG/665
https://www.achpr.org/legalinstruments/detail?id=45

The Member States of the Organization of African Unity hereinafter referred to as the OAU, States Parties to the African Charter on Human and Peoples' Rights.

Considering that the Charter of the Organization of African Unity recognizes that freedom, equality, justice, peace and dignity are essential objectives for the achievement of the legitimate aspirations of the African Peoples;

Noting that the African Charter on Human and Peoples` Rights reaffirms adherence to the principles of Human and Peoples' Rights, freedoms and duties contained in the declarations, conventions and other instruments adopted by the Organization of African Unity, and other international organizations;

Recognizing that the twofold objective of the African Commission on Human and Peoples' Rights is to ensure on the one hand promotion and on the other protection of Human and Peoples' Rights, freedom and duties;

Recognizing further, the efforts of the African Charter on Human and Peoples' Rights in the promotion and protection of Human and Peoples' Rights since its inception in 1987;

Recalling resolution AHGéRes.230 (XXX) adopted by the Assembly of Heads of State and Government in June 1994 in Tunis, Tunisia, requesting the Secretary-General to convene a Government experts` meeting to ponder, in conjunction with the African Commission, over the means to enhance the efficiency of the African commission and to consider in particular the establishment of an African Court on Human and Peoples' Rights;

Noting the first and second Government legal experts' meeting held respectively in Cape Town, South Africa (September, 1995) and Nouakchott, Mauritania (April 1997), and the third Government Legal Experts meeting held in Addis Ababa, Ethiopia (December, 1997), which was enlarged to include Diplomats;

Firmly convinced that the attainment of the objectives of the African Charter on Human and Peoples' Rights requires the establishment of an African Court on Human and Peoples' Rights to complement and reinforce the functions of the African Commission on Human and Peoples' Rights.

HAVE AGREED AS FOLLOWS:

* N.B.: In 2008, Member States of the African Union adopted the 'Merger Protocol' creating the African Court of Justice and Human Rights. This will incorporate the African Court on Human and Peoples' Rights and the Court of Justice of the African Union (Document No. 46.b). Further changes will be brought about by the 2014 'Malabo Protocol', which provides for the inclusion of criminal jurisdiction within the remit of the proposed African Court of Justice and Human Rights.

As at the time of editing, neither the Merger Protocol nor the Malabo Protocol have entered into force, the constituent documents of the two African Courts are reproduced here.

Article 1 ESTABLISHMENT OF THE COURT

There shall be established within the Organization of African Unity an African Court on Human and Peoples' Rights hereinafter referred to as "the Court", the organization, jurisdiction and functioning of which shall be governed by the present Protocol.

Article 2 RELATIONSHIP BETWEEN THE COURT AND THE COMMISSION

The Court shall, bearing in mind the provisions of this Protocol, complement the protective mandate of the African Commission on Human and Peoples' Rights hereinafter referred to as "the Commission", conferred upon it by the African Charter on Human and Peoples' Rights, hereinafter referred to as "the Charter".

Article 3 JURISDICTION

1. The jurisdiction of the Court shall extend to all cases and disputes submitted to it concerning the interpretation and application of the Charter, this Protocol and any other relevant Human Rights instrument ratified by the States concerned.

2. In the event of a dispute as to whether the Court has jurisdiction, the Court shall decide.

Article 4 ADVISORY OPINIONS

1. At the request of a Member State of the OAU, the OAU, any of its organs, or any African organization recognized by the OAU, the Court may provide an opinion on any legal matter relating to the Charter or any other relevant human rights instruments, provided that the subject matter of the opinion is not related to a matter being examined by the Commission.

2. The Court shall give reasons for its advisory opinions provided that every judge shall be entitled to deliver a separate of dissenting decision.

Article 5 ACCESS TO THE COURT

1. The following are entitled to submit cases to the Court:

a) The Commission
b) The State Party which had lodged a complaint to the Commission
c) The State Party against which the complaint has been lodged at the Commission
d) The State Party whose citizen is a victim of human rights violation
e) African Intergovernmental Organizations

2. When a State Party has an interest in a case, it may submit a request to the Court to be permitted to join.

3. The Court may entitle relevant Non Governmental organizations (NGOs) with observer status before the Commission, and individuals to institute cases directly before it, in accordance with article 34 (6) of this Protocol.

Article 6 ADMISSIBILITY OF CASES

1. The Court, when deciding on the admissibility of a case instituted under article 5 (3) of this Protocol, may request the opinion of the Commission which shall give it as soon as possible.

2. The Court shall rule on the admissibility of cases taking into account the provisions of article 56 of the Charter.

3. The Court may consider cases or transfer them to the Commission.

Article 7 SOURCES OF LAW

The Court shall apply the provision of the Charter and any other relevant human rights instruments ratified by the States concerned.

Article 8 CONSIDERATION OF CASES

The Rules of Procedure of the Court shall lay down the detailed conditions under which the Court shall consider cases brought before it, bearing in mind the complementarity between the Commission and the Court.

Article 9 AMICABLE SETTLEMENT

The Court may try to reach an amicable settlement in a case pending before it in accordance with the provisions of the Charter.

Article 10 HEARINGS AND REPRESENTATION

1. The Court shall conduct its proceedings in public. The Court may, however, conduct proceedings in camera as may be provided for in the Rules of Procedure.
2. Any party to a case shall be entitled to be represented by a legal representative of the party's choice. Free legal representation may be provided where the interests of justice so require.
3. Any person, witness or representative of the parties, who appears before the Court, shall enjoy protection and all facilities, in accordance with international law, necessary for the discharging of their functions, tasks and duties in relation to the Court.

Article 11 COMPOSITION

1. The Court shall consist of eleven judges, nationals of Member States of the OAU, elected in an individual capacity from among jurists of high moral character and of recognized practical, judicial or academic competence and experience in the field of human and peoples' rights.
2. No two judges shall be nationals of the same State.

Article 12 NOMINATIONS

1. States Parties to the Protocol may each propose up to three candidates, at least two of whom shall be nationals of that State.
2. Due consideration shall be given to adequate gender representation in nomination process.

Article 13 LIST OF CANDIDATES

1. Upon entry into force of this Protocol, the Secretary-general of the OAU shall request each State Party to the Protocol to present, within ninety (90) days of such a request, its nominees for the office of judge of the Court.
2. The Secretary-General of the OAU shall prepare a list in alphabetical order of the candidates nominated and transmit it to the Member States of the OAU at least thirty days prior to the next session of the Assembly of Heads of State and Government of the OAU hereinafter referred to as "the Assembly".

Article 14 ELECTIONS

1. The judges of the Court shall be elected by secret ballot by the Assembly from the list referred to in Article 13 (2) of the present Protocol.

2. The Assembly shall ensure that in the Court as a whole there is representation of the main regions of Africa and of their principal legal traditions.

3. In the election of the judges, the Assembly shall ensure that there is adequate gender representation.

Article 15 TERM OF OFFICE

1. The judges of the Court shall be elected for a period of six years and may be re-elected only once. The terms of four judges elected at the first election shall expire at the end of two years, and the terms of four more judges shall expire at the end of four years.

2. The judges whose terms are to expire at the end of the initial periods of two and four years shall be chosen by lot to be drawn by the Secretary-General of the OAU immediately after the first election has been completed.

3. A judge elected to replace a judge whose term of office has not expired shall hold office for the remainder of the predecessor's term.

4. All judges except the President shall perform their functions on a part-time basis. However, the Assembly may change this arrangement as it deems appropriate.

Article 16 OATH OF OFFICE

After their election, the judges of the Court shall make a solemn declaration to discharge their duties impartially and faithfully.

Article 17 INDEPENDENCE

1. The independence of the judges shall be fully ensured in accordance with international law.

2. No judge may hear any case in which the same judge has previously taken part as agent, counsel or advocate for one of the parties or as a member of a national or international court or a commission of enquiry or in any other capacity. Any doubt on this point shall be settled by decision of the Court.

3. The judges of the Court shall enjoy, from the moment of their election and throughout their term of office, the immunities extended to diplomatic agents in accordance with international law.

4. At no time shall the judges of the Court be held liable for any decision or opinion issued in the exercise of their functions.

Article 18 INCOMPATIBILITY

The position of judge of the court is incompatible with any activity that might interfere with the independence or impartiality of such a judge or the demands of the office as determined in the Rules of Procedure of the Court.

Article 19 CESSATION OF OFFICE

1. A judge shall not be suspended or removed from office unless, by the unanimous decision of the other judges of the Court, the judge concerned has been found to be no longer fulfilling the required conditions to be a judge of the Court.

2. Such a decision of the Court shall become final unless it is set aside by the Assembly at its next session.

Article 20 VACANCIES

1. In case of death or resignation of a judge of the Court, the President of the Court shall immediately inform the Secretary General of the Organization of African Unity, who shall declare the seat vacant from the date of death or from the date on which the resignation takes effect.

2. The Assembly shall replace the judge whose office became vacant unless the remaining period of the term is less than one hundred and eighty (180) days.

3. The same procedure and considerations as set out in Articles 12, 13 and 14 shall be followed for the filling of vacancies.

Article 21 PRESIDENCY OF THE COURT

1. The Court shall elect its President and one Vice-President for a period of two years. They may be re-elected only once.

2. The President shall perform judicial functions on a full-time basis and shall reside at the seat of the Court.

3. The functions of the President and the Vice-President shall be set out in the Rules of Procedure of the Court.

Article 22 EXCLUSION

If the judge is a national of any State which is a party to a case submitted to the Court, that judge shall not hear the case.

Article 23 QUORUM

The Court shall examine cases brought before it, if it has a quorum of at least seven judges.

Article 24 REGISTRY OF THE COURT

1. The Court shall appoint its own Registrar and other staff of the registry from among nationals of Member States of the OAU according to the Rules of Procedure.

2. The office and residence of the Registrar shall be at the place where the Court has its seat.

Article 25 SEAT OF THE COURT

1. The Court shall have its seat at the place determined by the Assembly from among States parties to this Protocol. However, it may convene in the territory of any Member State of the OAU when the majority of the Court considers it desirable, and with the prior consent of the State concerned.

2. The seat of the Court may be changed by the Assembly after due consultation with the Court.

Article 26 EVIDENCE

1. The Court shall hear submissions by all parties and if deemed necessary, hold an enquiry. The States concerned shall assist by providing relevant facilities for the efficient handling of the case.

2. The Court may receive written and oral evidence including expert testimony and shall make its decision on the basis of such evidence.

Article 27 FINDINGS

1. If the Court finds that there has been violation of a human or peoples' rights, it shall make appropriate orders to remedy the violation, including the payment of fair compensation or reparation.

2. In cases of extreme gravity and urgency, and when necessary to avoid irreparable harm to persons, the Court shall adopt such provisional measures as it deems necessary.

Article 28 JUDGMENT

1. The Court shall render its judgment within ninety (90) days of having completed its deliberations.

2. The judgment of the Court decided by majority shall be final and not subject to appeal.

3. Without prejudice to sub-article 2 above, the Court may review its decision in the light of new evidence under conditions to be set out in the Rules of Procedure.

4. The Court may interpret its own decision.

5. The judgment of the Court shall be read in open court, due notice having been given to the parties.

6. Reasons shall be given for the judgment of the Court.

7. If the judgment of the court does not represent, in whole or in part, the unanimous decision of the judges, any judge shall be entitled to deliver a separate or dissenting opinion.

Article 29 NOTIFICATION OF JUDGMENT

1. The parties to the case shall be notified of the judgment of the Court and it shall be transmitted to the Member States of the OAU and the Commission.

2. The Council of Ministers shall also be notified of the judgment and shall monitor its execution on behalf of the Assembly.

Article 30 EXECUTION OF JUDGMENT

The States Parties to the present Protocol undertake to comply with the judgment in any case to which they are parties within the time stipulated by the Court and to guarantee its execution.

Article 31 REPORT

The Court shall submit to each regular session of the Assembly, a report on its work during the previous year. The report shall specify, in particular, the cases in which a State has not complied with the Court's judgment.

Article 32 BUDGET

Expenses of the Court, emoluments and allowances for judges and the budget of its registry, shall be determined and borne by the OAU, in accordance with criteria laid down by the OAU in consultation with the Court.

Article 33 RULES OF PROCEDURE

The Court shall draw up its Rules and determine its own procedures. The Court shall consult the Commission as appropriate.

Article 34 RATIFICATION

1. This Protocol shall be open for signature and ratification or accession by any State Party to the Charter.

2. The instrument of ratification or accession to the present Protocol shall be deposited with the Secretary-General of the OAU.

3. The Protocol shall come into force thirty days after fifteen instruments of ratification or accession have been deposited.

4. For any State Party ratifying or acceding subsequently, the present Protocol shall come into force in respect of that State on the date of the deposit of its instrument of ratification or accession.

5. The Secretary-General of the OAU shall inform all Member States of the entry into force of the present Protocol.

6. At the time of the ratification of this Protocol or any time thereafter, the State shall make a declaration accepting the competence of the Court to receive cases under article 5 (3) of this Protocol. The Court shall not receive any petition under article 5 (3) involving a State Party which has not made such a declaration.

7. Declarations made under sub-article (6) above shall be deposited with the Secretary-General, who shall transmit copies thereof to the State parties.

Article 35 AMENDMENTS

1. The present Protocol may be amended if a State Party to the Protocol makes a written request to that effect to the Secretary-General of the OAU. The Assembly may adopt, by simple majority, the draft amendment after all the State Parties to the present Protocol have been duly informed of it and the Court has given its opinion on the amendment.

2. The Court shall also be entitled to propose such amendments to the present Protocol as it may deem necessary, through the Secretary-General of the OAU.

3. The amendment shall come into force for each State Party which has accepted it thirty days after the Secretary-General of the OAU has received notice of the acceptance.

The Inter-American Regional Framework for Human Rights Protection

34.a American Convention on Human Rights (Pact of San José)

Date: 22 November 1969
Source: 1144 UNTS 123
http://www.oas.org/juridico/english/treaties/b-32.html

…

PART II – MEANS OF PROTECTION

CHAPTER VI – COMPETENT ORGANS

Article 33

The following organs shall have competence with respect to matters relating to the fulfillment of the commitments made by the States Parties to this Convention:

a. the Inter-American Commission on Human Rights, referred to as "The Commission;" and
b. the Inter-American Court of Human Rights, referred to as "The Court."

CHAPTER VII – INTER-AMERICAN COMMISSION ON HUMAN RIGHTS

Section 1. Organization

Article 34

The Inter-American Commission on Human Rights shall be composed of seven members, who shall be persons of high moral character and recognized competence in the field of human rights.

Article 35

The Commission shall represent all the member countries of the Organization of American States.

Article 36

1. The members of the Commission shall be elected in a personal capacity by the General Assembly of the Organization from a list of candidates proposed by the governments of the member states.

2. Each of those governments may propose up to three candidates, who may be nationals of the states proposing them or of any other member state of the Organization of American States. When a slate of three is proposed, at least one of the candidates shall be a national of a state other than the one proposing the slate.

Article 37

1. The members of the Commission shall be elected for a term of four years and may be reelected only once, but the terms of three of the members chosen in the first election shall expire at the end of two years. Immediately following that election the General Assembly shall determine the names of those three members by lot.

2. No two nationals of the same state may be members of the Commission.

Article 38

Vacancies that may occur on the Commission for reasons other than the normal expiration of a term shall be filled by the Permanent Council of the Organization in accordance with the provisions of the Statute of the Commission.

Article 39

The Commission shall prepare its Statute, which it shall submit to the General Assembly for approval. It shall establish its own Regulations.

Article 40

Secretariat services for the Commission shall be furnished by the appropriate specialized unit of the General Secretariat of the Organization. This unit shall be provided with the resources required to accomplish the tasks assigned to it by the Commission.

Section 2. Functions

Article 41

The main function of the Commission shall be to promote respect for and defense of human rights. In the exercise of its mandate, it shall have the following functions and powers:

a. to develop an awareness of human rights among the peoples of America;
b. to make recommendations to the governments of the member states, when it considers such action advisable, for the adoption of progressive measures in favor of human rights within the framework of their domestic law and constitutional provisions as well as appropriate measures to further the observance of those rights;
c. to prepare such studies or reports as it considers advisable in the performance of its duties;
d. to request the governments of the member states to supply it with information on the measures adopted by them in matters of human rights;
e. to respond, through the General Secretariat of the Organization of American States, to inquiries made by the member states on matters related to human rights and, within the limits of its possibilities, to provide those states with the advisory services they request;
f. to take action on petitions and other communications pursuant to its authority under the provisions of Articles 44 through 51 of this Convention; and
g. to submit an annual report to the General Assembly of the Organization of American States.

Article 42

The States Parties shall transmit to the Commission a copy of each of the reports and studies that they submit annually to the Executive Committees of the Inter-American Economic and Social Council and the Inter-American Council for Education, Science, and Culture, in their respective fields, so that the Commission may watch over the promotion of the rights implicit in the economic, social, educational, scientific, and cultural standards set forth in the Charter of the Organization of American States as amended by the Protocol of Buenos Aires.

Article 43

The States Parties undertake to provide the Commission with such information as it may request of them as to the manner in which their domestic law ensures the effective application of any provisions of this Convention.

Section 3. Competence

Article 44

Any person or group of persons, or any nongovernmental entity legally recognized in one or more member states of the Organization, may lodge petitions with the Commission containing denunciations or complaints of violation of this Convention by a State Party.

Article 45

1. Any State Party may, when it deposits its instrument of ratification of or adherence to this Convention, or at any later time, declare that it recognizes the competence of the Commission to receive and examine communications in which a State Party alleges that another State Party has committed a violation of a human right set forth in this Convention.

2. Communications presented by virtue of this article may be admitted and examined only if they are presented by a State Party that has made a declaration recognizing the aforementioned competence of the Commission. The Commission shall not admit any communication against a State Party that has not made such a declaration.

3. A declaration concerning recognition of competence may be made to be valid for an indefinite time, for a specified period, or for a specific case.

4. Declarations shall be deposited with the General Secretariat of the Organization of American States, which shall transmit copies thereof to the member states of that Organization.

Article 46

1. Admission by the Commission of a petition or communication lodged in accordance with Articles 44 or 45 shall be subject to the following requirements:

a. that the remedies under domestic law have been pursued and exhausted in accordance with generally recognized principles of international law;

b. that the petition or communication is lodged within a period of six months from the date on which the party alleging violation of his rights was notified of the final judgment;

c. that the subject of the petition or communication is not pending in another international proceeding for settlement; and

d. that, in the case of Article 44, the petition contains the name, nationality, profession, domicile, and signature of the person or persons or of the legal representative of the entity lodging the petition.

2. The provisions of paragraphs 1.a and 1.b of this article shall not be applicable when:

a. the domestic legislation of the state concerned does not afford due process of law for the protection of the right or rights that have allegedly been violated;

b. the party alleging violation of his rights has been denied access to the remedies under domestic law or has been prevented from exhausting them; or

c. there has been unwarranted delay in rendering a final judgment under the aforementioned remedies.

Article 47

The Commission shall consider inadmissible any petition or communication submitted under Articles 44 or 45 if:

a. any of the requirements indicated in Article 46 has not been met;

b. the petition or communication does not state facts that tend to establish a violation of the rights guaranteed by this Convention;

c. the statements of the petitioner or of the state indicate that the petition or communication is manifestly groundless or obviously out of order; or

d. the petition or communication is substantially the same as one previously studied by the Commission or by another international organization.

Section 4. Procedure

Article 48

1. When the Commission receives a petition or communication alleging violation of any of the rights protected by this Convention, it shall proceed as follows:

a. If it considers the petition or communication admissible, it shall request information from the government of the state indicated as being responsible for the alleged violations and shall furnish that government a transcript of the pertinent portions of the petition or communication. This information shall be submitted within a reasonable period to be determined by the Commission in accordance with the circumstances of each case.

b. After the information has been received, or after the period established has elapsed and the information has not been received, the Commission shall ascertain whether the grounds for the petition or communication still exist. If they do not, the Commission shall order the record to be closed.

c. The Commission may also declare the petition or communication inadmissible or out of order on the basis of information or evidence subsequently received.

d. If the record has not been closed, the Commission shall, with the knowledge of the parties, examine the matter set forth in the petition or communication in order to verify the facts. If necessary and advisable, the Commission shall carry out an investigation, for the effective conduct of which it shall request, and the states concerned shall furnish to it, all necessary facilities.

e. The Commission may request the states concerned to furnish any pertinent information and, if so requested, shall hear oral statements or receive written statements from the parties concerned.

f. The Commission shall place itself at the disposal of the parties concerned with a view to reaching a friendly settlement of the matter on the basis of respect for the human rights recognized in this Convention.

2. However, in serious and urgent cases, only the presentation of a petition or communication that fulfills all the formal requirements of admissibility shall be necessary in order for the Commission to conduct an investigation with the prior consent of the state in whose territory a violation has allegedly been committed.

Article 49

If a friendly settlement has been reached in accordance with paragraph 1.f of Article 48, the Commission shall draw up a report, which shall be transmitted to the petitioner and to the States Parties to this Convention, and shall then be communicated to the Secretary General of the Organization of American States for publication. This report shall contain a brief statement of the facts and of the solution reached. If any party in the case so requests, the fullest possible information shall be provided to it.

Article 50

1. If a settlement is not reached, the Commission shall, within the timelimit established by its Statute, draw up a report setting forth the facts and stating its conclusions. If the report, in whole or in part, does not represent the unanimous agreement of the members of the Commission, any member may attach to it a separate opinion. The written and oral

statements made by the parties in accordance with paragraph 1.e of Article 48 shall also be attached to the report.

2. The report shall be transmitted to the states concerned, which shall not be at liberty to publish it.

3. In transmitting the report, the Commission may make such proposals and recommendations as it sees fit.

Article 51

1. If, within a period of three months from the date of the transmittal of the report of the Commission to the states concerned, the matter has not either been settled or submitted by the Commission or by the state concerned to the Court and its jurisdiction accepted, the Commission may, by the vote of an absolute majority of its members, set forth its opinion and conclusions concerning the question submitted for its consideration.

2. Where appropriate, the Commission shall make pertinent recommendations and shall prescribe a period within which the state is to take the measures that are incumbent upon it to remedy the situation examined.

3. When the prescribed period has expired, the Commission shall decide by the vote of an absolute majority of its members whether the state has taken adequate measures and whether to publish its report.

CHAPTER VIII – INTER-AMERICAN COURT OF HUMAN RIGHTS

Section 1. Organization

Article 52

1. The Court shall consist of seven judges, nationals of the member states of the Organization, elected in an individual capacity from among jurists of the highest moral authority and of recognized competence in the field of human rights, who possess the qualifications required for the exercise of the highest judicial functions in conformity with the law of the state of which they are nationals or of the state that proposes them as candidates.

2. No two judges may be nationals of the same state.

Article 53

1. The judges of the Court shall be elected by secret ballot by an absolute majority vote of the States Parties to the Convention, in the General Assembly of the Organization, from a panel of candidates proposed by those states.

2. Each of the States Parties may propose up to three candidates, nationals of the state that proposes them or of any other member state of the Organization of American States. When a slate of three is proposed, at least one of the candidates shall be a national of a state other than the one proposing the slate.

Article 54

1. The judges of the Court shall be elected for a term of six years and may be reelected only once. The term of three of the judges chosen in the first election shall expire at the end of three years. Immediately after the election, the names of the three judges shall be determined by lot in the General Assembly.

2. A judge elected to replace a judge whose term has not expired shall complete the term of the latter.

3. The judges shall continue in office until the expiration of their term. However, they shall continue to serve with regard to cases that they have begun to hear and that are still pending, for which purposes they shall not be replaced by the newly elected judges.

Article 55

1. If a judge is a national of any of the States Parties to a case submitted to the Court, he shall retain his right to hear that case.

2. If one of the judges called upon to hear a case should be a national of one of the States Parties to the case, any other State Party in the case may appoint a person of its choice to serve on the Court as an ad hoc judge.

3. If among the judges called upon to hear a case none is a national of any of the States Parties to the case, each of the latter may appoint an ad hoc judge.

4. An ad hoc judge shall possess the qualifications indicated in Article 52.

5. If several States Parties to the Convention should have the same interest in a case, they shall be considered as a single party for purposes of the above provisions. In case of doubt, the Court shall decide.

Article 56

Five judges shall constitute a quorum for the transaction of business by the Court.

Article 57

The Commission shall appear in all cases before the Court.

Article 58

1. The Court shall have its seat at the place determined by the States Parties to the Convention in the General Assembly of the Organization; however, it may convene in the territory of any member state of the Organization of American States when a majority of the Court considers it desirable, and with the prior consent of the state concerned. The seat of the Court may be changed by the States Parties to the Convention in the General Assembly by a two-thirds vote.

2. The Court shall appoint its own Secretary.

3. The Secretary shall have his office at the place where the Court has its seat and shall attend the meetings that the Court may hold away from its seat.

Article 59

The Court shall establish its Secretariat, which shall function under the direction of the Secretary of the Court, in accordance with the administrative standards of the General Secretariat of the Organization in all respects not incompatible with the independence of the Court. The staff of the Court's Secretariat shall be appointed by the Secretary General of the Organization, in consultation with the Secretary of the Court.

Article 60

The Court shall draw up its Statute which it shall submit to the General Assembly for approval. It shall adopt its own Rules of Procedure.

Section 2. Jurisdiction and Functions

Article 61

1. Only the States Parties and the Commission shall have the right to submit a case to the Court.

2. In order for the Court to hear a case, it is necessary that the procedures set forth in Articles 48 and 50 shall have been completed.

Article 62

1. A State Party may, upon depositing its instrument of ratification or adherence to this Convention, or at any subsequent time, declare that it recognizes as binding, ipso facto, and not requiring special agreement, the jurisdiction of the Court on all matters relating to the interpretation or application of this Convention.

2. Such declaration may be made unconditionally, on the condition of reciprocity, for a specified period, or for specific cases. It shall be presented to the Secretary General of the Organization, who shall transmit copies thereof to the other member states of the Organization and to the Secretary of the Court.

3. The jurisdiction of the Court shall comprise all cases concerning the interpretation and application of the provisions of this Convention that are submitted to it, provided that the States Parties to the case recognize or have recognized such jurisdiction, whether by special declaration pursuant to the preceding paragraphs, or by a special agreement.

Article 63

1. If the Court finds that there has been a violation of a right or freedom protected by this Convention, the Court shall rule that the injured party be ensured the enjoyment of his right or freedom that was violated. It shall also rule, if appropriate, that the consequences of the measure or situation that constituted the breach of such right or freedom be remedied and that fair compensation be paid to the injured party.

2. In cases of extreme gravity and urgency, and when necessary to avoid irreparable damage to persons, the Court shall adopt such provisional measures as it deems pertinent in matters it has under consideration. With respect to a case not yet submitted to the Court, it may act at the request of the Commission.

Article 64

1. The member states of the Organization may consult the Court regarding the interpretation of this Convention or of other treaties concerning the protection of human rights in the American states. Within their spheres of competence, the organs listed in Chapter X of the Charter of the Organization of American States, as amended by the Protocol of Buenos Aires, may in like manner consult the Court.

2. The Court, at the request of a member state of the Organization, may provide that state with opinions regarding the compatibility of any of its domestic laws with the aforesaid international instruments.

Article 65

To each regular session of the General Assembly of the Organization of American States the Court shall submit, for the Assembly's consideration, a report on its work during the previous year. It shall specify, in particular, the cases in which a state has not complied with its judgments, making any pertinent recommendations.

Section 3. Procedure

Article 66

1. Reasons shall be given for the judgment of the Court.

2. If the judgment does not represent in whole or in part the unanimous opinion of the judges, any judge shall be entitled to have his dissenting or separate opinion attached to the judgment.

Article 67

The judgment of the Court shall be final and not subject to appeal. In case of disagreement as to the meaning or scope of the judgment, the Court shall interpret it at the request of any of the parties, provided the request is made within ninety days from the date of notification of the judgment.

Article 68

1. The States Parties to the Convention undertake to comply with the judgment of the Court in any case to which they are parties.

2. That part of a judgment that stipulates compensatory damages may be executed in the country concerned in accordance with domestic procedure governing the execution of judgments against the state.

Article 69

The parties to the case shall be notified of the judgment of the Court and it shall be transmitted to the States Parties to the Convention.

CHAPTER IX – COMMON PROVISIONS

Article 70

1. The judges of the Court and the members of the Commission shall enjoy, from the moment of their election and throughout their term of office, the immunities extended to diplomatic agents in accordance with international law. During the exercise of their official function they shall, in addition, enjoy the diplomatic privileges necessary for the performance of their duties.

2. At no time shall the judges of the Court or the members of the Commission be held liable for any decisions or opinions issued in the exercise of their functions.

Article 71

The position of judge of the Court or member of the Commission is incompatible with any other activity that might affect the independence or impartiality of such judge or member, as determined in the respective statutes.

Article 72

The judges of the Court and the members of the Commission shall receive emoluments and travel allowances in the form and under the conditions set forth in their statutes, with due regard for the importance and independence of their office. Such emoluments and travel allowances shall be determined in the budget of the Organization of American States, which shall also include the expenses of the Court and its Secretariat. To this end, the Court shall draw up its own budget and submit it for approval to the General Assembly through the General Secretariat. The latter may not introduce any changes in it.

Article 73

The General Assembly may, only at the request of the Commission or the Court, as the case may be, determine sanctions to be applied against members of the Commission or judges of the Court when there are justifiable grounds for such action as set forth in the respective statutes. A vote of a two-thirds majority of the member states of the Organization shall be required for a decision in the case of members of the Commission and, in the case of judges of the Court, a two-thirds majority vote of the States Parties to the Convention shall also be required.

...

CHAPTER XI – TRANSITORY PROVISIONS

Section 1. Inter-American Commission on Human Rights

Article 79

Upon the entry into force of this Convention, the Secretary General shall, in writing, request each member state of the Organization to present, within ninety days, its candidates for membership on the Inter-American Commission on Human Rights. The Secretary General shall prepare a list in alphabetical order of the candidates presented, and transmit it to the member states of the Organization at least thirty days prior to the next session of the General Assembly.

Article 80

The members of the Commission shall be elected by secret ballot of the General Assembly from the list of candidates referred to in Article 79. The candidates who obtain the largest number of votes and an absolute majority of the votes of the representatives of the member states shall be declared elected. Should it become necessary to have several ballots in order to elect all the members of the Commission, the candidates who receive the smallest number of votes shall be eliminated successively, in the manner determined by the General Assembly.

Section 2. Inter-American Court of Human Rights

Article 81

Upon the entry into force of this Convention, the Secretary General shall, in writing, request each State Party to present, within ninety days, its candidates for membership on the Inter-American Court of Human Rights. The Secretary General shall prepare a list in alphabetical order of the candidates presented and transmit it to the States Parties at least thirty days prior to the next session of the General Assembly.

Article 82

The judges of the Court shall be elected from the list of candidates referred to in Article 81, by secret ballot of the States Parties to the Convention in the General Assembly.

The candidates who obtain the largest number of votes and an absolute majority of the votes of the representatives of the States Parties shall be declared elected. Should it become necessary to have several ballots in order to elect all the judges of the Court, the candidates who receive the smallest number of votes shall be eliminated successively, in the manner determined by the States Parties.

34.b Rules of Procedure of the Inter-American Court of Human Rights*

Date: 24 November 2009
Source: https://www.corteidh.or.cr/reglamento.cfm?lang=en

PRELIMINARY PROVISIONS

Article 1. Purpose

1. These Rules regulate the organization and procedure of the Inter-American Court of Human Rights.

2. The Court may adopt other Rules as may be necessary to carry out its functions.

3. In the absence of a provision in these Rules or in case of doubt as to their interpretation, the Court shall decide.

Article 2. Definitions

For the purposes of these Rules:

1. the term “Agent” refers to the person designated by a State to represent it before the Inter-American Court of Human Rights;

2. the expression “Deputy Agent” refers to the person designated by a State to assist the Agent in the discharge of his or her functions and to replace him or her during temporary absences;

3. the expression “amicus curiae” refers to the person or institution who is unrelated to the case and to the proceeding and submits to the Court reasoned arguments on the facts contained in the presentation of the case or legal considerations on the subject-matter of the proceeding by means of a document or an argument presented at a hearing;

4. the expression “General Assembly” refers to the General Assembly of the Organization of American States;

5. the term “Commission” refers to the Inter-American Commission on Human Rights;

6. the expression “Permanent Commission” refers to the Permanent Commission of the Inter-American Court of Human Rights;

7. the expression “Permanent Council” refers to the Permanent Council of the Organization of American States;

* N.B.: Footnotes omitted.

8. the term "Convention" refers to the American Convention on Human Rights (Pact of San José, Costa Rica);

9. the term "Court" refers to the Inter-American Court of Human Rights;

10. the term "declarants" refers to the alleged victims, witnesses, and expert witnesses that make declarations in a proceeding before the Court;

11. the expression "Inter-American Defender" refers to the person whom the Court designates to undertake the legal representation of an alleged victim that has not designated an advocate on his or her own accord;

12. the term "Delegates" refers to the persons designated by the Commission to represent it before the Court;

13. the term "day" shall be understood to be a natural day;

14. the expression "States Parties" refers to the States that have ratified or have adhered to the Convention;

15. the expression "Member States" refers to the States that are members of the Organization of American States;

16. the term "Statute" refers to the Statute of the Court adopted by the General Assembly of the Organization of American States on 31 October 1979 (AG/RES. 448 [IX-0/79]), as amended;

17. the term "Judge" refers to the Judges who compose the Court in each case;

18. the expression "Titular Judge" refers to any Judge selected pursuant to Articles 53 and 54 of the Convention;

19. the expression "Interim Judge" refers to any Judge appointed pursuant to Articles 6(3) and 19(4) of the Statute;

20. the expression "Judge ad hoc" refers to any Judge appointed pursuant to Article 55 of the Convention;

21. the term "month" shall be understood to be a calendar month;

22. the acronym "OAS" refers to the Organization of American States;

23. the term "expert witness" refers to the person whom, possessing particular scientific, artistic, technical, or practical knowledge or experience, informs the Court about issues in contention inasmuch as they relate to his or her special area of knowledge or experience;

24. the term "Presidency" refers to the President of the Court;

25. the expression "alleged victim" refers to the person whose rights under the Convention or another treaty of the Inter-American System have allegedly been violated;

26. the term "representatives" refers to the duly accredited legal representative or representatives of the alleged victim or victims;

27. the term "Secretariat" refers to the Secretariat of the Court;

28. the term "Secretary" refers to the Secretary of the Court;

29. the expression "Deputy Secretary" refers to the Deputy Secretary of the Court;

30. the expression "Secretary General" refers to the Secretary General of the OAS;

31. the term "Tribunal" refers to the Inter-American Court of Human Rights;

32. the term "Vice-Presidency" refers to the Vice-President of the Court;

33. the term "victim" refers to a person whose rights have been violated, according to a judgment emitted by the Court.

TITLE I
ORGANIZATION AND FUNCTIONING OF THE COURT

Chapter I
THE PRESIDENCY AND VICE-PRESIDENCY

Article 3. Election of the Presidency and the Vice-Presidency

1. The Presidency and the Vice-Presidency shall be elected by the Court for a period of two years and may be reelected. Their term shall begin on the first day of the year in question. The election shall take place during the last regular period of sessions held by the Court during the preceding year.

2. The elections referred to in this Article shall be carried out through a secret vote of the Titular Judges present, and the Judges who win four or more votes shall be elected. If no candidate receives the required number of votes, a new election shall take place between the two Judges who have received the most votes. In the event of a tie, the Judge having precedence in accordance with Article 13 of the Statute shall be deemed elected.

Article 4. Functions of the Presidency

1. The functions of the Presidency are to:
   a. represent the Court;
   b. preside over the sessions of the Court and submit the topics appearing on the agenda to its consideration;
   c. direct and promote the work of the Court;
   d. rule on the points of order that arise during the sessions of the Court. If any Judge so requests, a point of order shall be decided by a majority vote;
   e. present a biannual report to the Court on the activities he or she has carried out as President during that period;
   f. exercise such other functions as are conferred upon him or her by the Statute or these Rules, or entrusted to him or her by the Court.

2. In specific cases, the Presidency may delegate the representation referred to in paragraph 1(a) of this Article to the Vice-Presidency, to any of the Judges, or, if necessary, to the Secretary or Deputy Secretary.

Article 5. Functions of the Vice-Presidency

1. The Vice-Presidency shall replace the Presidency in the latter's temporary absence, and shall assume the Presidency when the absence is permanent. In the latter case, the Court shall elect a Vice-Presidency to serve out the rest of the term. The same procedure shall be followed if the absence of the Vice-Presidency is permanent.

2. In the absence of the Presidency and the Vice-Presidency, their functions shall be assumed by the other Judges in the order of precedence established in Article 13 of the Statute.

Article 6. Commissions

1. The Permanent Commission shall be composed of the Presidency, the VicePresidency, and any other Judges that the Presidency deems appropriate to appoint, according to the

needs of the Court. The Permanent Commission shall assist the Presidency in the exercise of his or her functions.

2. The Court may appoint other Commissions for specific matters. In urgent cases, these Commissions may be appointed by the Presidency if the Court is not in session.

3. The Commissions shall be governed by the provisions of these Rules, as applicable.

Chapter II
THE SECRETARIAT

Article 7. Election of the Secretary

1. The Court shall elect its Secretary, who must possess the legal knowledge required for the position, a command of the working languages of the Court, and the experience necessary for discharging his or her functions.

2. The Secretary shall be elected for a term of five years and may be reelected. He or she may be removed at any time if the Court so decides. A majority of no fewer than four Judges, voting by secret ballot in the presence of a quorum, is required for the appointment or removal of the Secretary.

Article 8. Deputy Secretary

1. The Deputy Secretary shall be proposed by the Secretary and appointed in the manner prescribed in the Statute. He or she shall assist the Secretary in the exercise of his or her functions and replace him or her during temporary absences.

2. If the Secretary and the Deputy Secretary are both unable to perform their functions, the Presidency may appoint an Interim Secretary.

3. If the Secretary and the Deputy Secretary are both temporarily away from the seat of the Court, the Secretary may appoint one of the Secretariat's attorneys to take charge of the Secretariat in their absence.

Article 9. Oath

1. The Secretary and the Deputy Secretary shall take an oath or make a solemn declaration before the Presidency, undertaking to discharge their duties faithfully and to respect the confidential nature of the facts that come to their attention while exercising their functions.

2. The staff of the Secretariat, including any persons called upon to perform interim or temporary duties, shall, upon assuming their functions, take an oath or make a solemn declaration before the Presidency, undertaking to discharge their duties faithfully and to respect the confidential nature of the facts that come to their attention while exercising their functions. If the Presidency is not present at the seat of the Court, the Secretary or Deputy Secretary shall administer the oath.

3. All oaths shall be recorded in a document to be signed by the person being sworn in and by the person administering the oath.

Article 10. Functions of the Secretary

The functions of the Secretary shall be to:

a. serve notice of the judgments, advisory opinions, orders, and other rulings of the Court;
b. keep the minutes of the sessions of the Court;
c. attend the meetings of the Court held at its seat or elsewhere;

d. process the correspondence of the Court;
e. certify the authenticity of documents;
f. direct the administration of the Court, pursuant to the instructions of the Presidency;
g. prepare drafts of the work schedules, rules and regulations, and budgets of the Court;
h. plan, direct, and coordinate the work of the staff of the Court;
i. carry out the tasks assigned to him or her by the Court or the Presidency;
j. perform any other duties provided for in the Statute or in these Rules.

Chapter III
FUNCTIONING OF THE COURT

Article 11. Regular Sessions

The Court shall hold the regular periods of sessions necessary for the exercise of its functions on the dates decided by the Court during the previous regular session. In exceptional circumstances, the Presidency may, in consultation with the other Judges, change the dates of the sessions.

Article 12. Extraordinary Sessions

Extraordinary sessions may be convened by the Presidency on his or her own initiative or at the request of a majority of the Judges.

Article 13. Sessions held away from the seat of the Court

The Court may convene in any Member State when a majority of the Court considers it desirable, with the prior consent of the State concerned.

Article 14. Quorum

The quorum for the deliberations of the Court shall consist of five Judges.

Article 15. Hearings, deliberations, and decisions

1. The Court shall hold hearings when it deems it appropriate to do so. Hearings shall be public, unless the Tribunal deems it appropriate that they be private.

2. The Court shall deliberate in private, and its deliberations shall remain secret. Only the Judges shall take part in the deliberations; however, the Secretary and Deputy Secretary or their substitutes, as well as the necessary staff of Secretariat, may attend. No other persons may be admitted, except by special decision of the Court and after taking an oath or making a solemn declaration.

3. Any question that calls for a vote shall be formulated in precise terms in one of the working languages. At the request of any of the Judges, the Secretariat shall translate the text thereof into the other working languages and distribute it prior to the vote.

4. The hearings and deliberations of the Court shall be kept on audio-recordings.

Article 16. Decisions and voting

1. The Presidency shall present, point by point, the matters to be voted upon. Each Judge shall vote either in the affirmative or the negative; there shall be no abstentions.

2. The votes shall be cast in reverse order of precedence as established in Article 13 of the Statute.

3. The decisions of the Court shall be adopted by a majority of the Judges present at the time of the voting.

4. In the event of a tie, the Presidency shall have a casting vote.

Article 17. Continuation in Office of the Judges

1. Judges whose terms have expired shall continue to exercise their functions in cases that they have begun to hear and that are still pending. However, in the event of death, resignation, impediment, recusal, or disqualification, the Judge in question shall be replaced by the Judge who was elected to take his or her place, if applicable, or by the Judge who has precedence among the new Judges elected upon the expiration of the term of the Judge to be replaced.

2. All matters relating to reparations and costs, as well as to the monitoring of compliance with the judgments of the Court, shall be heard by the Judges comprising the Court at that stage of the proceedings, unless a public hearing has already been held. In the latter case, those matters shall be heard by the Judges who attended the hearing.

3. All matters relating to provisional measures shall be heard by the Court composed of Titular Judges.

Article 18. Interim Judges

Interim Judges shall have the same rights and functions as Titular Judges.

Article 19. National Judges

1. In the cases referred to in Article 44 of the Convention, a Judge who is a national of the respondent State shall not be able to participate in the hearing and deliberation of the case.

2. In the cases referred to in Article 45 of the Convention, national Judges will be able to participate in the hearing and deliberation of the case. If the President is a national of one of the parties to the case, he or she will cede the exercise of his or her functions.

Article 20. Judges Ad Hoc in Interstate Cases

1. In a case arising under Article 45 of the Convention, the Presidency, acting through the Secretariat, shall inform the States referred to in that Article of their right to appoint a Judge ad hoc within 30 days following the notification of the application.

2. When it appears that two or more States have a common interest, the Presidency shall inform them that they may jointly appoint one Judge ad hoc, pursuant to Article 10 of the Statute. If those States do not communicate their agreement to the Court within 30 days of the last notification of the application, each State may propose its candidate within the following 15 days. Subsequently, if more than one candidate has been nominated, the Presidency shall choose a common Judge ad hoc by lot, and shall communicate the result to the interested parties.

3. Should the interested States fail to exercise their right within the time limits established in the preceding paragraphs, they shall be deemed to have waived that right.

4. The Secretary shall communicate the appointment of Judges ad hoc to the Inter-American Commission, the representatives of the alleged victim, and the petitioning State or respondent State, as applicable.

5. The Judge ad hoc shall take an oath at the first session devoted to the consideration of the case for which he or she has been appointed.

6. Judges ad hoc shall receive honoraria on the same terms as Titular Judges.

Article 21. Impediments, recusals, and disqualification

1. Impediments, recusals, and the disqualification of Judges shall be governed by the provisions of Article 19 of the Statute and Article 19 of these Rules of Procedure.

2. Motions for recusal or allegations of impediment must be filed prior to the first hearing of the case. However, if the grounds therefor occur or become known after that hearing, such motions may be submitted to the Court at the first possible opportunity so that it can rule on the matter immediately.

3. When, for any reason, a Judge is not present at one of the hearings or at other stages of the proceedings, the Court may decide to disqualify him from continuing to hear the case, taking into account all the circumstances it deems relevant.

TITLE II
PROCEDURE

Chapter I
GENERAL RULES

Article 22. Official Languages

1. The official languages of the Court shall be those of the OAS, to wit, Spanish, English, Portuguese, and French.

2. The working languages shall be those agreed upon by the Court each year. However, in a specific case, the language of the respondent State or, if applicable, the petitioning State may be adopted as the working language, provided it is one of the official languages.

3. The working languages for each case shall be determined at the beginning of the proceedings.

4. The Court may authorize any person appearing before it to use his or her own language if he or she does not have sufficient knowledge of the working languages. In those circumstances, the Court shall make the arrangements necessary to ensure that an interpreter is present to translate that statement into the working languages. The interpreter must take an oath or make a solemn declaration, undertaking to discharge his or her duties faithfully and to respect the confidential nature of the facts that come to his or her attention in the exercise of his or her functions.

5. When deemed necessary, the Court shall determine which text of an order is authentic.

Article 23. Representation of the States

1. States that are parties to a case shall be represented by Agents, who may be assisted by any persons of their choice.

2. Deputy Agents may be designated to assist Agents in the exercise of their functions and replace them during temporary absences.

3. If a State replaces its Agent or Agents, it shall so notify the Court; replacements shall take effect only upon said notification.

Article 24. Representation of the Commission

The Commission shall be represented by the Delegates it has designated for that purpose. Delegates may be assisted by any persons of their choice.

Article 25. Participation of the Alleged Victims or their Representatives

1. Once notice of the brief submitting a case before the Court has been served, in accordance with Article 39 of the Rules of Procedure, the alleged victims or their representatives may submit their brief containing pleadings, motions, and evidence autonomously and shall continue to act autonomously throughout the proceedings.

2. When there are several alleged victims or representatives, these shall designate a common intervener, who shall be the only person authorized to present pleadings, motions, and evidence during the proceedings, including the public hearings. Should there be no agreement as to the appointment of a common intervener in a case, the Court or its Presidency may, if appropriate, establish a deadline for the appointment of up to three representatives to act as common interveners. In the latter case, the Presidency shall establish the deadline for the submission of the respondent State's answer and the time allotted to the respondent State, the alleged victims or their representatives, and, if applicable, the petitioning State for their participation in the public hearings.

3. In case that there is disagreement among the alleged victims as to that indicated in the preceding paragraph, the Court shall make the appropriate ruling.

Article 26. Cooperation of the States

1. States that are parties to a case have the obligation to cooperate so as to ensure that all notices, communications, or summonses addressed to persons subject to their jurisdiction are duly executed. They must also facilitate compliance with summonses by persons who reside or are present in their territory.

2. The same rule shall apply to any proceeding that the Court decides to conduct or order in the territory of a State that is a party to a case.

3. When performance of any of the measures referred to in the preceding paragraphs requires the cooperation of any other State, the Presidency shall request that State to provide the assistance necessary.

Article 27. Provisional Measures

1. At any stage of proceedings involving cases of extreme gravity and urgency, and when necessary to avoid irreparable damage to persons, the Court may, on its own motion, order such provisional measures as it deems appropriate, pursuant to Article 63(2) of the Convention.

2. With respect to matters not yet submitted to it, the Court may act at the request of the Commission.

3. In contentious cases before the Court, victims or alleged victims, or their representatives, may submit to it a request for provisional measures, which must be related to the subject matter of the case.

4. The request may be submitted to the Presidency, to any Judge of the Court, or to the Secretariat, by any means of communication. In every case, the recipient of the request shall immediately bring it to the attention of the Presidency.

5. The Court, or if the Court is not sitting, the Presidency, upon considering that it is possible and necessary, may require the State, the Commission, or the representatives of the beneficiaries to provide information on a request for provisional measures before deciding on the measure requested.

6. If the Court is not sitting, the Presidency, in consultation with the Permanent Commission and, if possible, with the other Judges, shall call upon the State concerned

to adopt such urgent measures as may be necessary to ensure the effectiveness of any provisional measures that may be ordered by the Court during its next period of sessions.

7. The monitoring of urgent or provisional measures ordered shall be carried out through the submission of reports by the State and the filing of observations to those reports by the beneficiaries of the measures or their representatives. The Commission shall submit observations to the State's reports and to the observations of the beneficiaries of the measures or their representatives.

8. When the Court considers it appropriate, it may require from other sources of information any relevant data on the matter that would permit it to assess the gravity and urgency of the situation and the effectiveness of the measures. To that end, it may also require expert opinions and any other report that it considers appropriate.

9. The Court, or its Presidency if the Court is not sitting, may convene the Commission, the beneficiaries of the measures or their representatives, and the State to a public or private hearing on provisional measures.

10. In its Annual Report to the General Assembly, the Court shall include a statement concerning the provisional measures ordered during the period covered by the report. If those measures have not been duly implemented, the Court shall make such recommendations as it deems appropriate.

Article 28. Filing of Briefs

1. All briefs addressed to the Court may be presented in person or by courier, facsimile, post, or electronic mail, and must be signed in order to ensure their authenticity. If a brief is transmitted to the Court by electronic means and has not been subscribed, or in the case that a brief is not accompanied by its annexes, the original documents or missing annexes must be received by the Tribunal within a non-renewable term of 21 days from the expiration of the deadline established for the submission of that brief.

2. All briefs and annexes submitted to the Court through non-electronic means shall be accompanied by two identical copies, either on paper or in digital format, and received by the Tribunal within the term of 21 days described in the previous paragraph.

3. Annexes and copies thereof must be duly individualized and identified.

4. The Presidency may, in consultation with the Permanent Commission, reject any communication that he or she considers patently inadmissible, and shall order that it be returned to the relevant party without further action.

Article 29. Default Procedure

1. When the Commission; the victims, alleged victims, or their representatives; the respondent State; or, if applicable, the petitioning State fail to appear in or pursue a matter, the Court shall, on its own motion, take the measures necessary to conduct the proceedings to their completion.

2. When victims, alleged victims, or their representatives; the respondent State; or, if applicable, the petitioning State enter a case at a later stage in the proceedings, they shall participate in the proceedings at that stage.

Article 30. Joinder of Cases and Proceedings

1. The Court may, at any stage of the proceedings, order the joinder of related cases when there is commonality of parties, subject-matter, and applicable law.

2. The Court may also order that the written or oral proceedings of several cases, including the introduction of declarants, proceed jointly.

3. After consulting the Agents, Delegates, and alleged victims or their representatives, the Presidency may order that the proceedings of two or more cases be joined.

4. The Court may, when it deems it appropriate, order that provisional measures applications be joined when the subject-matter or the parties are identical. If such is the case, the other provisions of this Article shall be applicable.

5. The Court may join proceedings for the monitoring of compliance of two or more judgments issued with respect to a single State if it considers that the decisions set out in each judgment are closely related. In those circumstances, the victims in those cases or their representatives shall designate a common intervener in accordance with Article 25 of these Rules of Procedure.

Article 31. Decisions

1. Judgments and orders completing proceedings shall be rendered exclusively by the Court.

2. All other orders shall be rendered by the Court if it is sitting and by the Presidency if it is not, unless otherwise provided. Decisions of the Presidency that are not merely procedural may be appealed from to the Court.

3. Judgments and orders of the Court may not be contested in any way.

Article 32. Publication of Judgments and Other Decisions

1. The Court shall make public:

a. its judgments, orders, opinions, and other decisions, including separate opinions, dissenting or concurring, whenever they fulfill the requirements set forth in Article 65(2) of these Rules;

b. documents from the case file, except those considered unsuitable for publication;

c. the conduct of the hearings, except private hearings, through the appropriate means;

d. any other document that the Court considers suitable for publication.

2. Judgments shall be published in the working languages used in each case. All other documents shall be published in their original language.

3. Documents submitted to the Secretariat of the Court that relate to cases already adjudicated shall be made accessible to the public, unless the Court decides otherwise.

Article 33. Transmission of Briefs

The Court may transmit briefs, annexes, orders, judgments, advisory opinions, and other communications submitted to it by electronic means with adequate guarantees of security.

Chapter II
WRITTEN PROCEEDINGS

Article 34. Initiation of Proceedings

For a case to be referred to the Court under Article 61(1) of the Convention, a brief must be filed with the Secretariat in any of the working languages of the Tribunal. The submission of the case in only one working language shall not suspend the proceeding;

however, a translation into the language of the respondent State must be submitted within the following 21 days, as long as that language is one of the working languages of the Court.

Article 35. Filing of the case by the Commission

1. The case shall be presented to the Court through the submission of the report to which article 50 of the Convention refers, which must establish all the facts that allegedly give rise to a violation and identify the alleged victims. In order for the case to be examined, the Court shall receive the following information:

a. the names of the Delegates;

b. the names, address, telephone number, electronic address, and facsimile number of the representatives of the alleged victims, if applicable;

c. the reasons leading the Commission to submit the case before the Court and its observations on the answer of the respondent State to the recommendations of the report to which Article 50 of the Convention refers;

d. a copy of the entire case file before the Commission, including all communications following the issue of the report to which Article 50 of the Convention refers;

e. the evidence received, including the audio and the transcription, with an indication of the alleged facts and arguments on which they bear. The Commission shall indicate whether the evidence was rendered in an adversarial proceeding;

f. when the Inter-American public order of human rights is affected in a significant manner, the possible appointment of expert witnesses, the object of their statements, and their curricula vitae;

g. the claims, including those relating to reparations.

2. When it has not been possible to identify one or more of the alleged victims who figure in the facts of the case because it concerns massive or collective violations, the Tribunal shall decide whether to consider those individuals as victims.

3. The Commission shall indicate which facts contained in the report to which Article 50 of the Convention refers it is submitting to the consideration of the Court.

Article 36. Filing of the case by a State

1. A State Party may submit a case to the Court, in accordance with Article 61 of the Convention, through a reasoned brief containing the following information:

a. the names of the Agents and Alternate Agents, and the address where all relevant communications shall be deemed to have been officially received;

b. the names, address, telephone number, electronic address, and facsimile number of the duly accredited representatives of the alleged victims, if applicable;

c. the reasons leading the State to submit the case before the Court;

d. a copy of the entire case file before the Commission, including the report to which Article 50 of the Convention refers and all communications following the issue of that report;

e. the evidence offered, with an indication of the alleged facts and arguments on which they bear;

f. the identity of declarants and the object of their statements. Expert witnesses must also submit their curricula vitae and contact information.

2. Paragraphs 2 and 3 of the preceding Article are applicable in cases submitted by States before the Court.

Article 37. Inter-American Defender

In cases where alleged victims are acting without duly accredited legal representation, the Tribunal may, on its own motion, appoint an Inter-American defender to represent them during the processing of the case.

Article 38. Preliminary Review of the Presentation of the Case

When, during a preliminary review of the presentation of the case, the Presidency finds that the basic requirements have not been met, he or she shall request that its deficiencies be met within 20 days.

Article 39. Notification of the Case

1. The Secretary of the Court shall serve notice of the presentation of the case on:
   a. the Presidency and the Judges;
   b. the respondent State;
   c. the Commission, when it has not presented the case;
   d. the alleged victim, his or her representatives, or the Inter-American defender, if applicable.
2. The Secretary shall inform the other States Parties, the Permanent Council through its Presidency, and the Secretary General of the presentation of the case.
3. When giving notice, the Secretary shall request the respondent State to designate its Agent or Agents within 30 days. When appointing its Agents, the State in question shall indicate the address at which all relevant communications shall be deemed officially received.
4. Until Delegates are appointed, the Commission shall be deemed properly represented by its Presidency for all purposes of the case.
5. When giving notice, the Secretary shall request the representatives of the alleged victims to confirm, within 30 days, the address at which all relevant communications shall be deemed officially received.

Article 40. Brief containing Pleadings, Motions, and Evidence

1. Upon notice of the presentation of the case to the alleged victim or his or her representatives, these shall have a non-renewable term of two months as of receipt of that brief and its annexes to autonomously submit to the Court the brief containing pleadings, motions, and evidence.
2. The brief containing pleadings, motions, and evidence shall contain:
   a. a description of the facts within the factual framework established in the presentation of the case by the Commission;
   b. the evidence offered, properly organized, with an indication of the alleged facts and arguments that it relates to;
   c. the identities of declarants and the object of their statements. Expert witnesses must also submit their curricula vitae and contact information;
   d. all claims, including those relating to reparations and costs.

Article 41. The State's Answer

1. The respondent shall, in writing, state its position regarding the presentation of the case and, if applicable, answer the brief containing pleadings, motions, and evidence within a non-renewable term of two months from the receipt of the latter brief and its annexes, without prejudice to the term that the Presidency may establish in the circumstances

mentioned in Article 24(2) of these Rules of Procedure. In its answer, the State shall indicate:

a. whether it accepts the facts and claims or whether it contradicts them;

b. the evidence tendered, properly organized, with an indication of the facts and arguments that it relates to;

c. the identity of the declarants offered and the object of their statements. Expert witnesses must also submit their curricula vitae and contact information;

d. its legal arguments, observations on the reparations and reimbursement of costs requested, and conclusions.

2. The answer shall be communicated by the Secretary to those persons mentioned in Article 39(1)(a), 39(1)(c), and 39(1)(d) of these Rules of Procedure and to the petitioning State in the cases to which Article 45 of the Convention refers.

3. The Court may consider those facts that have not been expressly denied and those claims that have not been expressly controverted as accepted.

Article 42. Preliminary Objections

1. Preliminary objections may only be filed in the brief indicated in the preceding Article.

2. The document setting out preliminary objections shall contain the facts on which the objections are based, legal arguments and conclusions, and supporting documents, as well as any evidence to be offered.

3. The presentation of preliminary objections shall not suspend the proceedings on the merits, nor their respective deadlines.

4. The Commission, alleged victims or their representatives, and, if applicable, the petitioning State may present their observations to the preliminary objections within 30 days as of their receipt.

5. When the Court considers it necessary, it may convene a special hearing on the preliminary objections presented, after which it shall rule thereon.

6. The Court may decide upon the preliminary objections, the merits, and the reparations and costs of the case in a single judgment.

Article 43. Other Steps in the Written Proceedings

After receipt of the brief presenting the case, the brief containing pleadings, motions, and evidence, and the brief containing the answer, and before the initiation of oral proceedings, the Commission, the alleged victims or their representatives, the respondent State, and, if applicable, the petitioning State may seek the permission of the Presidency to enter additional written pleadings. In such a case, if deemed appropriate, the Presidency shall establish time limits for the presentation of the relevant documents.

Article 44. Arguments of Amicus Curiae

1. Any person or institution seeking to act as amicus curiae may submit a brief to the Tribunal, together with its annexes, by any of the means established in Article 28(1) of these Rules of Procedure, in the working language of the case and bearing the names and signatures of its authors.

2. If the amicus curiae brief is submitted by electronic means and is not signed, or if the brief is submitted without its annexes, the original and supporting documentation must be received by the Tribunal within 7 days of its transmission. If the brief is submitted out of time or is submitted without the required documentation, it shall be archived without further processing.

3. Amicus curiae briefs may be submitted at any time during contentious proceedings for up to 15 days following the public hearing. If the Court does not hold a public hearing, amicus briefs must be submitted within 15 days following the Order setting deadlines for the submission of final arguments. Following consultation with the President, the amicus curiae brief and its annexes shall be immediately transmitted to the parties, for their information.

4. Amicus curiae briefs may be submitted during proceedings for monitoring compliance of judgments and those regarding provisional measures.

Chapter III
ORAL PROCEEDINGS

Article 45. Opening

The Presidency shall announce the date on which oral proceedings will open and shall fix the necessary hearings.

Article 46. Definitive List of Declarants

1. The Court will request the Commission, the alleged victims or their representatives, the respondent State, and, if applicable, the petitioning State to submit definitive lists of declarants, in which they shall confirm or retract offers of evidence submitted within time in accordance with Articles 35(1)(f), 36(1)(f), 40(2)(c), and 41(1)(c) of these Rules of Procedure, in the form of statements of alleged victims, witnesses, or expert witnesses. Additionally, they must indicate to the Court their position as to which of the declarants offered should be summoned to the hearing, where applicable, and which declarants can render their statements through affidavits.

2. The Tribunal shall transmit the definitive list of declarants to the opposing party and shall establish a time limit in which to present, if necessary, observations, objections, or challenges.

Article 47. Objections to Witnesses

1. Any party may object to a witness within ten days of receiving the definitive list of declarants offered to the Court.

2. The Court or the Presidency, as applicable in each case, shall assess the value of statements rendered and objections thereto.

Article 48. Objections to Expert Witnesses

1. An expert witness may be disqualified based on the following grounds:

a. he or she is a relative by blood, affinity, or adoption, up to the fourth degree, of one of the alleged victims;
b. he or she is or has been a representative of one of the alleged victims in proceedings regarding the facts of the case before the Court, either at the domestic level or before the Inter-American System for the promotion and protection of human rights;
c. he or she currently has, or has had, close ties with the proposing party, or is, or has been, a subordinate of the proposing party, and the Court considers that his or her impartiality may be affected;
d. he or she is, or has been, an officer of the Inter-American Commission on Human Rights with knowledge of the contentious case in which his or her expert opinion is required;

e. he or she is or has been an Agent of the respondent State in the contentious case in which his or her expert opinion is required;

f. he or she has previously intervened, in any capacity and before any organ, whether national or international, in relation to the same case.

2. Objections shall be presented within 10 days of receipt of the definitive list of expert witnesses offered to the Court.

3. The Presidency shall communicate to the expert witness in question objections made against him or her and shall establish a time limit for the expert witness to present observations thereto. All of this shall be transmitted to those who form part of the proceedings. The Court or presiding judge shall subsequently decide on the matter.

Article 49. Substitution of Declarants Offered

Exceptionally, upon receiving a well-founded request from a party and after hearing the opinion of the opposing party, the Court may accept the replacement of a declarant, as long as his or her replacement is identified, and always respecting the object of the statement, testimony, or expert opinion originally offered.

Article 50. Offering, Convocation, and Appearance of Declarants

1. The Court or its Presidency shall issue an order deciding on the observations, objections, and challenges presented, as applicable; defining the object of the statement of each one of the declarants; requiring the submission of the affidavits deemed appropriate; and summoning all those the Court deems appropriate to a hearing, if necessary.

2. The party who has proposed a statement shall notify the declarant of the order mentioned in the preceding paragraph.

3. Statements shall be limited to the object defined by the Court in the order referred to in paragraph 1 of this Article. Exceptionally, upon receiving a wellfounded request and after hearing the opinion of the opposing party, the Court may modify the object of the statement or admit a statement that has exceeded the object established.

4. The party who offers a declarant shall be responsible for his or her appearance before the Tribunal or the submission of his or her affidavit, as applicable.

5. The alleged victims or their representatives, the respondent State, and, if applicable, the petitioning State may formulate questions in writing for the declarants offered by the opposing party and, if applicable, by the Commission who have been convened by the Court to render their statements through affidavits. The Presidency can determine the pertinence of the questions formulated and can excuse the person being questioned from responding, unless the Court determines otherwise. Leading questions and questions that do not refer to the timely established object of the statement shall not be admitted.

6. Once an affidavit is received, it shall be transmitted to the opposing party and, if applicable, to the Commission so that observations thereto may be submitted within the time limit established by the Court or its Presidency.

Article 51. Hearing

1. First, the Commission will state the grounds of the report to which Article 50 of the Convention refers and of the presentation of the case before the Court, and set out any other matter that it considers relevant for its resolution.

2. Once the Commission has concluded the statement indicated in the preceding paragraph, the Presidency shall call those declarants who have been summoned in

accordance with Article 50(1) of these Rules of Procedure so that they may be interrogated in conformity with the Article that follows. The interrogation of the declarant shall be initiated by the party that has proposed said declarant.

3. After his or her identity has been established, and before testifying, the witness shall take an oath or make a solemn declaration stating that he or she will speak the truth, the whole truth, and nothing but the truth.

4. After his or her identity has been established by the Court, and before performing his or her task, the expert witness shall take an oath or make a solemn declaration stating that he or she will discharge his or her duties honorably and conscientiously.

5. The identities of alleged victims shall be established; however, alleged victims shall not take an oath.

6. Those alleged victims and witnesses who have not rendered their statements before the Court may not be present while the statement of another alleged victim, witness, or expert witness is being delivered at the hearing.

7. Once the Court has heard the declarants summoned and the Judges have questioned them, the Presidency shall allow the victims or their representatives and the respondent State to present their oral arguments to the Tribunal. Subsequently, the Presidency shall allow the victims or their representatives and the State to present a rebuttal and surrebuttal, respectively.

8. Once the oral arguments have concluded, the Commission shall present its final observations.

9. Finally, the President shall call upon the Judges of the Tribunal, in reverse order according to the system of precedence established in Article 13 of the Statute, so that they may ask questions to the Commission, the victims or their representatives, and the State, if they so desire.

10. In cases that are not submitted to this Tribunal by the Commission, the Presidency shall conduct hearings, determine the order in which those who will intervene in the proceedings shall submit their statements to the Court, and determine the measures appropriate so that hearings are carried out in the best possible manner.

11. The Court may receive the statements of witnesses, expert witnesses, or alleged victims through the use of electronic audio-visual means.

Article 52. Questions during the debates

1. The Judges may formulate the questions they deem appropriate to all those who appear before the Court.

2. Alleged victims, witnesses, expert witnesses, and all other persons that the Court decides to hear may be interrogated by the alleged victims or their representatives, the respondent State, and, if applicable, the petitioning State. Interrogations shall be moderated by the Presidency.

3. The Commission may interrogate the expert witnesses that it has proposed in accordance with Article 35(1)(f) of these Rules of Procedure. It may also interrogate expert witnesses proposed by the alleged victims, the respondent State and, if applicable, the petitioning State, if authorized by the Court upon receiving a wellgrounded request therefor, when the Inter-American public order of human rights is affected in a significant manner and the statement in question regards a topic included in the statement of an expert witness offered by the Commission.

4. The Presidency shall have the faculty of deciding the pertinence of questions posed and of excusing the party being questioned from answering, unless the Court deems otherwise. Leading questions shall not be admitted.

Article 53. Protection of Alleged Victims, Witnesses, Expert Witnesses, Representatives, and Legal Advisers

States may not institute proceedings against witnesses, expert witnesses, or alleged victims, or their representatives or legal advisers, nor exert pressure on them or on their families on account of statements, opinions, or legal defenses presented to the Court.

Article 54. Failure to Appear or False Testimony

When a person summoned to appear or declare before the Court fails to appear or refuses to render a statement without legitimate cause, or when, in the opinion of the Court, he or she has violated his or her oath or solemn declaration, the Court shall inform the State with jurisdiction over that witness so that appropriate action may be taken under the relevant domestic legislation.

Article 55. Minutes of the Hearings

1. At each hearing, the Secretariat will keep a record of:
   a. the names of the Judges present;
   b. the names of those intervening at the hearing;
   c. the names and personal information of the declarants who have rendered statements.

2. The Secretariat shall record the hearings and annex a copy of the recording to the case file.

3. The Agents, Delegates, and victims or alleged victims, or their representatives, shall receive a copy of the recording of the public hearing as soon as possible.

Chapter IV
FINAL WRITTEN PROCEEDINGS

Article 56. Final Written Arguments

1. The alleged victims or their representatives, the respondent State, and, if applicable, the petitioning State shall have the opportunity to present final written arguments within the term established by the Presidency.

2. The Commission may submit final written observations within the term established in the previous section.

Chapter V
EVIDENCE

Article 57. Admission

1. Items of evidence tendered before the Commission will be incorporated into the case file as long as they have been received in adversarial proceedings, unless the Court considers it indispensable to duplicate them.

2. Exceptionally, and having heard the opinion of all those participating in the proceedings, the Court may admit evidence if the party that has offered it adequately explains that

the evidence was not presented or offered at the procedural moments established in Articles 35(1), 36(1), 40(2), and 41(1) of these Rules of Procedure due to force majeure or serious impediment. Additionally, the Court may admit evidence that refers to an event which occurred after the procedural moments indicated.

Article 58. Procedure for Taking Evidence

The Court may, at any stage of the proceedings:

a. Obtain, on its own motion, any evidence it considers helpful and necessary. In particular, it may hear, as an alleged victim, witness, expert witness, or in any other capacity, any person whose statement, testimony, or opinion it deems to be relevant.
b. Request the Commission; the victims or alleged victims, or their representatives; the respondent State; and, if applicable, the petitioning State to submit any evidence that they may be able to provide or any explanation or statement that, in the Court's opinion, may be useful.
c. Request any entity, office, organ, or authority of its choice to obtain information, express an opinion, or deliver a report or pronouncement on any given point. Such documents may not be published without the authorization of the Court.
d. Commission one or more of its members to take steps in the advancement of the proceedings, including hearings at the seat of the Court or at a different location.
e. If it is impossible to proceed according to the terms established in the previous paragraph, the Judges may commission the Secretariat to take necessary steps in the advancement of the proceedings.

Article 59. Incomplete or Illegible evidence

Any item of evidence submitted to the Court must be complete and intelligible. Otherwise, the Court shall grant the party that has offered the item of evidence a deadline within which to correct its defects or to submit relevant clarifications. Failure to submit the requested clarifications or corrections will result in the Court considering the evidence as not tendered.

Article 60. Cost of Evidence

Whoever offers an item of evidence shall cover the costs generated by its production.

Chapter VI
DISCONTINUANCE, ACQUIESCENCE, AND FRIENDLY SETTLEMENT

Article 61. Discontinuance of a Case

When the entity that has presented the case notifies the Court of its intention not to proceed with it, the Court shall, after hearing the opinions of all those participating in the proceedings, decide on the matter and determine the juridical effects of that decision.

Article 62. Acquiescence

If the respondent informs the Court of its acceptance of the facts or its total or partial acquiescence to the claims stated in the presentation of the case or the brief submitted by the alleged victims or their representatives, the Court shall decide, having heard the opinions of all those participating in the proceedings and at the appropriate procedural moment, whether to accept that acquiescence, and shall rule upon its juridical effects.

Article 63. Friendly Settlement

When the Commission; the victims or alleged victims, or their representatives; the respondent State; or, if applicable, the petitioning State in a case before the Court inform it of the existence of a friendly settlement, compromise, or any other occurrence likely to lead to a settlement of the dispute, the Court shall rule upon its admissibility and juridical effects at the appropriate procedural time.

Article 64. Continuation of a Case

Bearing in mind its responsibility to protect human rights, the Court may decide to continue the consideration of a case notwithstanding the existence of the conditions indicated in the preceding Articles.

Chapter VII
JUDGMENTS

Article 65. Contents of the Judgment

1. The judgment shall contain:
   a. the names of the person who presides in the Court, the Judges who rendered the decision, the Secretary, and the Deputy Secretary;
   b. the identity of those who participate in the proceedings and their representatives;
   c. a description of the proceedings;
   d. the facts of the case;
   e. the submissions of the Commission, the victims or their representatives, the respondent State, and, if applicable, the petitioning State;
   f. the legal arguments;
   g. the ruling on the case;
   h. the decision on reparations and costs, if applicable;
   i. the result of the voting;
   j. a statement indicating which text of the judgment is authentic
2. Any Judge who has taken part in the consideration of a case is entitled to append a separate reasoned opinion to the judgment, concurring or dissenting. These opinions shall be submitted within a time limit to be fixed by the Presidency so that the other Judges may take cognizance thereof before notice of the judgment is served. Said opinions shall only refer to the issues covered in the judgment.

Article 66. Judgment on reparations and costs

1. When no specific ruling on reparations and costs has been made in the judgment on the merits, the Court shall set the date and determine the procedure for the deferred decision thereon.

2. If the Court is informed that the victims or their representatives, the respondent State, and, if applicable, the petitioning State have reached an agreement with respect to the execution of the judgment on the merits, it shall verify that the agreement accords with the Convention and rule accordingly.

Article 67. Delivery and Communication of the Judgment

1. When a case is ready for judgment, the Court shall deliberate in private and approve the judgment, which shall be notified by the Secretariat to the Commission; the victims

or alleged victims, or their representatives; the respondent State; and, if applicable, the petitioning State.

2. Until notice of the judgment has been served, its text, legal arguments, and votes shall remain secret.

3. Judgments shall be signed by all of the Judges who participated in the voting and by the Secretary. However, a judgment signed by the majority of the Judges and the Secretary shall also be valid.

4. Separate opinions, concurring or dissenting, shall be signed by the Judges submitting them and by the Secretary.

5. The judgments shall conclude with an order, signed by the Presidency and the Secretary and sealed by the latter, providing for the communication and execution of the judgment.

6. The originals of the judgments shall be deposited in the archives of the Court. The Secretary shall dispatch certified copies to the States Parties; the Commission; the victims or alleged victims, or their representatives; the respondent State; the petitioning State, if applicable; the Permanent Council through its Presidency; the Secretary General of the OAS; and any other interested person who requests them.

Article 68. Request for Interpretation

1. The request for interpretation referred to in Article 67 of the Convention may be made in connection with judgments on preliminary objections, on the merits, or on reparations and costs, and shall be filed with the Secretariat. It shall state with precision questions relating to the meaning or scope of the judgment of which interpretation is requested.

2. The Secretary shall transmit the request for interpretation to all those participating in the case and shall invite them to submit any written comments they deem relevant within the time limit established by the Presidency.

3. When considering a request for interpretation, the Court shall be composed, whenever possible, of the same Judges who delivered the judgment whose interpretation is being sought. However, in the event of death, resignation, impediment, recusal, or disqualification, the judge in question shall be replaced pursuant to Article 17 of these Rules.

4. A request for interpretation shall not suspend the effect of the judgment.

5. The Court shall determine the procedure to be followed and shall render its decision in the form of a judgment.

Article 69. Procedure for Monitoring Compliance with Judgments and Other Decisions of the Court

1. The procedure for monitoring compliance with the judgments and other decisions of the Court shall be carried out through the submission of reports by the State and observations to those reports by the victims or their legal representatives. The Commission shall present observations to the State's reports and to the observations of the victims or their representatives.

2. The Court may require from other sources of information relevant data regarding the case in order to evaluate compliance therewith. To that end, the Tribunal may also request the expert opinions or reports that it considers appropriate.

3. When it deems it appropriate, the Tribunal may convene the State and the victims' representatives to a hearing in order to monitor compliance with its decisions; the Court shall hear the opinion of the Commission at that hearing.

4. Once the Tribunal has obtained all relevant information, it shall determine the state of compliance with its decisions and issue the relevant orders.

5. These rules also apply to cases that have not been submitted by the Commission.

TITLE III
ADVISORY OPINIONS

Article 70. Interpretation of the Convention

1. Requests for an advisory opinion under Article 64(1) of the Convention shall state with precision the specific questions on which the opinion of the Court is being sought.

2. Requests for an advisory opinion submitted by a Member State or by the Commission shall, in addition, identify the provisions to be interpreted, the considerations giving rise to the request, and the names and addresses of the Agent or the Delegates.

3. If the advisory opinion is sought by an OAS organ other than the Commission, the request shall also specify how it relates to the sphere of competence of the organ in question, in addition to the information listed in the preceding paragraph.

Article 71. Interpretation of Other Treaties

1. If, as provided for in Article 64(1) of the Convention, the interpretation requested refers to other treaties concerning the protection of human rights in the American States, the request shall indicate the name of the treaty and parties thereto, the specific questions on which the opinion of the Court is being sought, and the considerations giving rise to the request.

2. If the request is submitted by an OAS organ, it shall indicate how the subject of the request falls within its sphere of competence.

Article 72. Interpretation of Domestic Laws

1. A request for an advisory opinion presented pursuant to Article 64(2) of the Convention shall indicate the following:

a. the provisions of domestic law and of the Convention or of other treaties concerning the protection of human rights to which the request relates;
b. the specific questions on which the opinion of the Court is being sought;
c. the name and address of the requesting party's Agent.

2. Copies of the domestic laws referred to in the request shall accompany the application.

Article 73. Procedure

1. Upon receipt of a request for an advisory opinion, the Secretary shall transmit copies thereof to all of the Member States, the Commission, the Permanent Council through its Presidency, the Secretary General, and, if applicable, to the OAS organs whose sphere of competence is referred to in the request.

2. The Presidency shall establish a time limit for the filing of written comments by the interested parties.

3. The Presidency may invite or authorize any interested party to submit a written opinion on the issues covered by the request. If the request is governed by Article 64(2) of the Convention, the Presidency may do so after prior consultation with the Agent.

4. At the conclusion of the written proceedings, the Court shall decide whether oral proceedings should take place and shall establish the date for a hearing, unless it delegates the latter task to the Presidency. Prior consultation with the Agent is required in cases governed by Article 64(2) of the Convention.

Article 74. Application by Analogy

The Court shall apply the provisions of Title II of these Rules to advisory proceedings to the extent that it deems them to be compatible.

Article 75. Delivery and Content of Advisory Opinions

1. The delivery of advisory opinions shall be governed by Article 67 of these Rules.
2. Advisory opinions shall contain:
    a. the names of the person who presides in the Court, the Judges who rendered the opinion, the Secretary, and the Deputy Secretary;
    b. the issues presented to the Court;
    c. a description of the proceedings;
    d. the legal arguments;
    e. the opinion of the Court;
    f. a statement indicating which text of the opinion is authentic.
3. Any judge who has taken part in the delivery of an advisory opinion is entitled to append a separate reasoned opinion, concurring or dissenting, to that of the Court. These opinions shall be submitted within a time limit to be fixed by the Presidency, so that the other Judges can take cognizance thereof before the advisory opinion is served. Advisory opinions shall be published in accordance with Article 32(1)(a) of these Rules.
4. Advisory opinions may be delivered in public.

TITLE IV
RECTIFICATION OF ERRORS

Article 76. Rectification of errors in judgments and other decisions

The Court may, on its own motion or at the request of any of the parties to the case, within one month of the notice of the judgment or order, rectify obvious mistakes, clerical errors, or errors in calculation. The Commission, the victims or their representatives, the respondent State, and, if applicable, the petitioning State shall be notified if an error is rectified.

TITLE V
FINAL AND TEMPORARY PROVISIONS

Article 77. Amendments to the Rules of Procedure

These Rules of Procedure may be amended by the decision of an absolute majority of the Titular Judges of the Court. Upon their entry into force, earlier versions of the Rules of Procedure are repealed.

Article 78. Entering into force

These Rules of Procedure will enter into force on January 1, 2010.

Article 79. Application

1. Contentious cases which have been submitted for the consideration of the Court before January 1, 2010, will continue to be processed, until the issuance of a judgment, in accordance to the previous Rules of Procedure.

2. In cases in which the Commission has adopted a report under article 50 of the Convention before the these Rules of Procedure have come into force, the presentation of the case before the Court will be governed by Articles 33 and 34 of the Rules of Procedure previously in force. Statements shall be received with the aid of the Victim's Legal Assistance Fund, and the dispositions of these Rules of Procedure shall apply.

34.c Rules for the Operation of the Victims' Legal Assistance Fund of the Inter-American Court of Human Rights

Date: 4 February 2010
Source: https://corteidh.or.cr/docs/regla_victimas/victimas_eng.pdf

Considering that:

1) The General Assembly of the Organization of American States (OAS), by way of Resolution AG/RES. 2426 of June 3, 2008, provided for the "Establishment of the Legal Assistance Fund of the Inter-American Human Rights System"; and
2) Resolution CP/RES. 963 of November 11, 2009, of the Permanent Council of the OAS, approved the "Rules of Procedure for the Operation of the Legal Assistance Fund of the Inter-American Human Rights System."

RESOLVES to adopt the following Rules:

Article 1. Purpose

These Rules regulate the operation of, and access to, the Victims' Legal Assistance Fund of the Inter-American Court of Human Rights for the litigation of cases before it.

Article 2. Requests for Access to the Victims' Legal Assistance Fund

Alleged victims who wish to access the Victims' Legal Assistance Fund shall so inform the Court in the brief containing pleadings, motions, and evidence. These alleged victims must indicate, by means of a sworn affidavit and other probative evidence that will satisfy the Tribunal, that they lack the economic resources necessary to cover the cost of litigation before the Inter-American Court, and state precisely the aspects of their participation in proceedings that require use of the resources of the Victims' Legal Assistance Fund.

Article 3. Determination of the Merits of the Request

The Secretariat of the Court shall conduct a preliminary review of the request for assistance and shall require the requesting party to present the background information necessary so that the request may be submitted to the consideration of the Presidency.

The Presidency of the Court shall evaluate each request submitted, determine whether it shall be granted, and indicate the aspects of the litigation that may be funded through the Victims' Legal Assistance Fund. The Presidency's decision shall be made within three months as of the date that the background information required is received.

The Secretariat of the Court shall serve notice of the Presidency's decision on the alleged victim or his or her representative, the respondent State, and the Inter-American Commission on Human Rights.

Article 4. Administration and Assignment of Resources

The Secretariat of the Court shall administer the Victims' Legal Assistance Fund.

Once the Presidency has determined the merits of the request and that decision has been served, the Secretariat of the Court shall open a file on the costs of that particular case, which shall contain records of all expenditures made in accordance with the parameters authorized by the Presidency.

Article 5. Reimbursement of Costs to the Victims' Legal Assistance Fund

The Secretariat of the Court shall inform the respondent State of the expenditures made from the Victims' Legal Assistance Fund so that the State may submit observations thereto by the established deadline.

The Tribunal shall evaluate in its judgment whether to order the respondent State to reimburse expenditures made from the Inter-American Court of Human Rights's Legal Assistance Fund.

Article 6. Interpretation

The Court shall decide matters not governed by these Rules and questions regarding their interpretation.

Article 7. Amendments to the Rules

These Rules may be amended by decision of an absolute majority of the judges of the Court.

Article 8. Entering into Force

These Rules shall enter into force on June 1, 2010.

(c) UN Charter-based Mechanisms for Human Rights Protection

The Human Rights Council Framework

35.a GA Res 60/251 (Establishment of Human Rights Council)*

Date: 3 April 2006
Source: UN Doc A/RES/60/251
http://www2.ohchr.org/english/bodies/hrcouncil/docs/A.RES.60.251_En.pdf

The General Assembly,

Reaffirming the purposes and principles contained in the Charter of the United Nations, including developing friendly relations among nations based on respect for the principle of equal rights and self-determination of peoples, and achieving international cooperation in

* N.B.: Footnotes omitted.

solving international problems of an economic, social, cultural or humanitarian character and in promoting and encouraging respect for human rights and fundamental freedoms for all,

Reaffirming also the Universal Declaration of Human Rights and the Vienna Declaration and Programme of Action, and recalling the International Covenant on Civil and Political Rights, the International Covenant on Economic, Social and Cultural Rights and other human rights instruments,

Reaffirming further that all human rights are universal, indivisible, interrelated, interdependent and mutually reinforcing, and that all human rights must be treated in a fair and equal manner, on the same footing and with the same emphasis,

Reaffirming that, while the significance of national and regional particularities and various historical, cultural and religious backgrounds must be borne in mind, all States, regardless of their political, economic and cultural systems, have the duty to promote and protect all human rights and fundamental freedoms,

Emphasizing the responsibilities of all States, in conformity with the Charter, to respect human rights and fundamental freedoms for all, without distinction of any kind as to race, colour, sex, language or religion, political or other opinion, national or social origin, property, birth or other status,

Acknowledging that peace and security, development and human rights are the pillars of the United Nations system and the foundations for collective security and well-being, and recognizing that development, peace and security and human rights are interlinked and mutually reinforcing,

Affirming the need for all States to continue international efforts to enhance dialogue and broaden understanding among civilizations, cultures and religions, and emphasizing that States, regional organizations, non-governmental organizations, religious bodies and the media have an important role to play in promoting tolerance, respect for and freedom of religion and belief,

Recognizing the work undertaken by the Commission on Human Rights and the need to preserve and build on its achievements and to redress its shortcomings,

Recognizing also the importance of ensuring universality, objectivity and non-selectivity in the consideration of human rights issues, and the elimination of double standards and politicization,

Recognizing further that the promotion and protection of human rights should be based on the principles of cooperation and genuine dialogue and aimed at strengthening the capacity of Member States to comply with their human rights obligations for the benefit of all human beings,

Acknowledging that non-governmental organizations play an important role at the national, regional and international levels, in the promotion and protection of human rights,

Reaffirming the commitment to strengthen the United Nations human rights machinery, with the aim of ensuring effective enjoyment by all of all human rights, civil, political, economic, social and cultural rights, including the right to development, and to that end, the resolve to create a Human Rights Council,

1. *Decides* to establish the Human Rights Council, based in Geneva, in replacement of the Commission on Human Rights, as a subsidiary organ of the General Assembly; the Assembly shall review the status of the Council within five years;

2. *Decides* that the Council shall be responsible for promoting universal respect for the protection of all human rights and fundamental freedoms for all, without distinction of any kind and in a fair and equal manner;

3. *Decides also* that the Council should address situations of violations of human rights, including gross and systematic violations, and make recommendations thereon. It should also promote the effective coordination and the mainstreaming of human rights within the United Nations system;

4. *Decides further* that the work of the Council shall be guided by the principles of universality, impartiality, objectivity and non-selectivity, constructive international dialogue and cooperation, with a view to enhancing the promotion and protection of all human rights, civil, political, economic, social and cultural rights, including the right to development;

5. *Decides* that the Council shall, inter alia:

(*a*) Promote human rights education and learning as well as advisory services, technical assistance and capacity-building, to be provided in consultation with and with the consent of Member States concerned;

(*b*) Serve as a forum for dialogue on thematic issues on all human rights;

(*c*) Make recommendations to the General Assembly for the further development of international law in the field of human rights;

(*d*) Promote the full implementation of human rights obligations undertaken by States and follow-up to the goals and commitments related to the promotion and protection of human rights emanating from United Nations conferences and summits;

(*e*) Undertake a universal periodic review, based on objective and reliable information, of the fulfilment by each State of its human rights obligations and commitments in a manner which ensures universality of coverage and equal treatment with respect to all States; the review shall be a cooperative mechanism, based on an interactive dialogue, with the full involvement of the country concerned and with consideration given to its capacity-building needs; such a mechanism shall complement and not duplicate the work of treaty bodies; the Council shall develop the modalities and necessary time allocation for the universal periodic review mechanism within one year after the holding of its first session;

(*f*) Contribute, through dialogue and cooperation, towards the prevention of human rights violations and respond promptly to human rights emergencies;

(*g*) Assume the role and responsibilities of the Commission on Human Rights relating to the work of the Office of the United Nations High Commissioner for Human Rights, as decided by the General Assembly in its resolution 48/141 of 20 December 1993;

(*h*) Work in close cooperation in the field of human rights with Governments, regional organizations, national human rights institutions and civil society;

(*i*) Make recommendations with regard to the promotion and protection of human rights;

(*j*) Submit an annual report to the General Assembly;

6. *Decides also* that the Council shall assume, review and, where necessary, improve and rationalize all mandates, mechanisms, functions and responsibilities of the Commission on Human Rights in order to maintain a system of special procedures, expert advice and a complaint procedure; the Council shall complete this review within one year after the holding of its first session;

7. *Decides further* that the Council shall consist of forty-seven Member States, which shall be elected directly and individually by secret ballot by the majority of the members of the General Assembly; the membership shall be based on equitable geographical distribution, and seats shall be distributed as follows among regional groups: Group of African States, thirteen; Group of Asian States, thirteen; Group of Eastern European States, six; Group of Latin American and Caribbean States, eight; and Group of Western European and other States, seven; the members of the Council shall serve for a period of three years and shall not be eligible for immediate re-election after two consecutive terms;

8. *Decides* that the membership in the Council shall be open to all States Members of the United Nations; when electing members of the Council, Member States shall take into account the contribution of candidates to the promotion and protection of human rights and their voluntary pledges and commitments made thereto; the General Assembly, by a two-thirds majority of the members present and voting, may suspend the rights of membership in the Council of a member of the Council that commits gross and systematic violations of human rights;

9. *Decides also* that members elected to the Council shall uphold the highest standards in the promotion and protection of human rights, shall fully cooperate with the Council and be reviewed under the universal periodic review mechanism during their term of membership;

10. *Decides further* that the Council shall meet regularly throughout the year and schedule no fewer than three sessions per year, including a main session, for a total duration of no less than ten weeks, and shall be able to hold special sessions, when needed, at the request of a member of the Council with the support of one third of the membership of the Council;

11. *Decides* that the Council shall apply the rules of procedure established for committees of the General Assembly, as applicable, unless subsequently otherwise decided by the Assembly or the Council, and also decides that the participation of and consultation with observers, including States that are not members of the Council, the specialized agencies, other intergovernmental organizations and national human rights institutions, as well as non-governmental organizations, shall be based on arrangements, including Economic and Social Council resolution 1996/31 of 25 July 1996 and practices observed by the Commission on Human Rights, while ensuring the most effective contribution of these entities;

12. *Decides also* that the methods of work of the Council shall be transparent, fair and impartial and shall enable genuine dialogue, be results-oriented, allow for subsequent follow-up discussions to recommendations and their implementation and also allow for substantive interaction with special procedures and mechanisms;

13. *Recommends* that the Economic and Social Council request the Commission on Human Rights to conclude its work at its sixty-second session, and that it abolish the Commission on 16 June 2006;

14. *Decides* to elect the new members of the Council; the terms of membership shall be staggered, and such decision shall be taken for the first election by the drawing of lots, taking into consideration equitable geographical distribution;

15. *Decides also* that elections of the first members of the Council shall take place on 9 May 2006, and that the first meeting of the Council shall be convened on 19 June 2006;

16. *Decides further* that the Council shall review its work and functioning five years after its establishment and report to the General Assembly.

35.b HRC Res 5/1 (Institution-Building Package, including Rules of Procedure)

Date: 18 June 2007
Source: UN Doc A/HRC/RES/5/1 (Annex)
http://ap.ohchr.org/documents/E/HRC/resolutions/A_HRC_RES_5_1.doc

ANNEX
UNITED NATIONS HUMAN RIGHTS COUNCIL: INSTITUTION-BUILDING

I. UNIVERSAL PERIODIC REVIEW MECHANISM

A. Basis of the review

1. The basis of the review is:

(a) The Charter of the United Nations;
(b) The Universal Declaration of Human Rights;
(c) Human rights instruments to which a State is party;
(d) Voluntary pledges and commitments made by States, including those undertaken when presenting their candidatures for election to the Human Rights Council (hereinafter "the Council").

2. In addition to the above and given the complementary and mutually interrelated nature of international human rights law and international humanitarian law, the review shall take into account applicable international humanitarian law.

B. Principles and objectives

1. Principles

3. The universal periodic review should:

(*a*) Promote the universality, interdependence, indivisibility and interrelatedness of all human rights;
(*b*) Be a cooperative mechanism based on objective and reliable information and on interactive dialogue;
(*c*) Ensure universal coverage and equal treatment of all States;
(*d*) Be an intergovernmental process, United Nations Member-driven and action-oriented;
(*e*) Fully involve the country under review;
(*f*) Complement and not duplicate other human rights mechanisms, thus representing an added value;
(*g*) Be conducted in an objective, transparent, non-selective, constructive, nonconfrontational and nonpoliticized manner;
(*h*) Not be overly burdensome to the concerned State or to the agenda of the Council;
(*i*) Not be overly long; it should be realistic and not absorb a disproportionate amount of time, human and financial resources;
(*j*) Not diminish the Council's capacity to respond to urgent human rights situations;
(*k*) Fully integrate a gender perspective;
(*l*) Without prejudice to the obligations contained in the elements provided for in the basis of review, take into account the level of development and specificities of countries;

(*m*) Ensure the participation of all relevant stakeholders, including non-governmental organizations and national human rights institutions, in accordance with General Assembly resolution 60/251 of 15 March 2006 and Economic and Social Council resolution 1996/31 of 25 July 1996, as well as any decisions that the Council may take in this regard.

2. Objectives

4. The objectives of the review are:

(*a*) The improvement of the human rights situation on the ground;

(*b*) The fulfilment of the State's human rights obligations and commitments and assessment of positive developments and challenges faced by the State;

(*c*) The enhancement of the State's capacity and of technical assistance, in consultation with, and with the consent of, the State concerned;

(*d*) The sharing of best practice among States and other stakeholders;

(*e*) Support for cooperation in the promotion and protection of human rights;

(*f*) The encouragement of full cooperation and engagement with the Council, other human rights bodies and the Office of the United Nations High Commissioner for Human Rights.

C. Periodicity and order of the review

5. The review begins after the adoption of the universal periodic review mechanism by the Council.

6. The order of review should reflect the principles of universality and equal treatment.

7. The order of the review should be established as soon as possible in order to allow States to prepare adequately.

8. All member States of the Council shall be reviewed during their term of membership.

9. The initial members of the Council, especially those elected for one or two-year terms, should be reviewed first.

10. A mix of member and observer States of the Council should be reviewed.

11. Equitable geographic distribution should be respected in the selection of countries for review.

12. The first member and observer States to be reviewed will be chosen by the drawing of lots from each Regional Group in such a way as to ensure full respect for equitable geographic distribution. Alphabetical order will then be applied beginning with those countries thus selected, unless other countries volunteer to be reviewed.

13. The period between review cycles should be reasonable so as to take into account the capacity of States to prepare for, and the capacity of other stakeholders to respond to, the requests arising from the review.

14. The periodicity of the review for the first cycle will be of four years. This will imply the consideration of 48 States per year during three sessions of the working group of two weeks each.[1]

[1] The universal periodic review is an evolving process; the Council, after the conclusion of the first review cycle, may review the modalities and the periodicity of this mechanism, based on best practices and lessons learned.

D. Process and modalities of the review

1. Documentation

15. The documents on which the review would be based are:

(*a*) Information prepared by the State concerned, which can take the form of a national report, on the basis of general guidelines to be adopted by the Council at its sixth session (first session of the second cycle), and any other information considered relevant by the State concerned, which could be presented either orally or in writing, provided that the written presentation summarizing the information will not exceed 20 pages, to guarantee equal treatment to all States and not to overburden the mechanism. States are encouraged to prepare the information through a broad consultation process at the national level with all relevant stakeholders;

(*b*) Additionally a compilation prepared by the Office of the High Commissioner for Human Rights of the information contained in the reports of treaty bodies, special procedures, including observations and comments by the State concerned, and other relevant official United Nations documents, which shall not exceed 10 pages;

(*c*) Additional, credible and reliable information provided by other relevant stakehold- ers to the universal periodic review which should also be taken into consideration by the Council in the review. The Office of the High Commissioner for Human Rights will prepare a summary of such information which shall not exceed 10 pages.

16. The documents prepared by the Office of the High Commissioner for Human Rights should be elaborated following the structure of the general guidelines adopted by the Council regarding the information prepared by the State concerned.

17. Both the State's written presentation and the summaries prepared by the Office of the High Commissioner for Human Rights shall be ready six weeks prior to the review by the working group to ensure the distribution of documents simultaneously in the six official languages of the United Nations, in accordance with General Assembly resolution 53/208 of 14 January 1999.

2. Modalities

18. The modalities of the review shall be as follows:

(*a*) The review will be conducted in one working group, chaired by the President of the Council and composed of the 47 member States of the Council. Each member State will decide on the composition of its delegation;[2]

(*b*) Observer States may participate in the review, including in the interactive dialogue;

(*c*) Other relevant stakeholders may attend the review in the Working Group;

(*d*) A group of three rapporteurs, selected by the drawing of lots among the members of the Council and from different Regional Groups (*troika*) will be formed to facilitate each review, including the preparation of the report of the working group. The Office of the High Commissioner for Human Rights will provide the necessary assistance and expertise to the rapporteurs.

[2] A Universal Periodic Review Voluntary Trust Fund should be established to facilitate the participation of developing countries, particularly the Least Developed Countries, in the universal periodic review mechanism.

19. The country concerned may request that one of the rapporteurs be from its own Regional Group and may also request the substitution of a rapporteur on only one occasion.

20. A rapporteur may request to be excused from participation in a specific review process.

21. Interactive dialogue between the country under review and the Council will take place in the working group. The rapporteurs may collate issues or questions to be transmitted to the State under review to facilitate its preparation and focus the interactive dialogue, while guaranteeing fairness and transparency.

22. The duration of the review will be three hours for each country in the working group. Additional time of up to one hour will be allocated for the consideration of the outcome by the plenary of the Council.

23. Half an hour will be allocated for the adoption of the report of each country under review in the working group.

24. A reasonable time frame should be allocated between the review and the adoption of the report of each State in the working group.

25. The final outcome will be adopted by the plenary of the Council.

E. Outcome of the review

1. Format of the outcome

26. The format of the outcome of the review will be a report consisting of a summary of the proceedings of the review process; conclusions and/or recommendations, and the voluntary commitments of the State concerned.

2. Content of the outcome

27. The universal periodic review is a cooperative mechanism. Its outcome may include, inter alia:

(*a*) An assessment undertaken in an objective and transparent manner of the human rights situation in the country under review, including positive developments and the challenges faced by the country;

(*b*) Sharing of best practices;

(*c*) An emphasis on enhancing cooperation for the promotion and protection of human rights;

(*d*) The provision of technical assistance and capacity-building in consultation with, and with the consent of, the country concerned;[3]

(*e*) Voluntary commitments and pledges made by the country under review.

3. Adoption of the outcome

28. The country under review should be fully involved in the outcome.

29. Before the adoption of the outcome by the plenary of the Council, the State concerned should be offered the opportunity to present replies to questions or issues that were not sufficiently addressed during the interactive dialogue.

30. The State concerned and the member States of the Council, as well as observer States, will be given the opportunity to express their views on the outcome of the review before the plenary takes action on it.

31. Other relevant stakeholders will have the opportunity to make general comments before the adoption of the outcome by the plenary.

[3] A decision should be taken by the Council on whether to resort to existing financing mechanisms or to create a new mechanism.

32. Recommendations that enjoy the support of the State concerned will be identified as such. Other recommendations, together with the comments of the State concerned thereon, will be noted. Both will be included in the outcome report to be adopted by the Council.

F. Follow-up to the review

33. The outcome of the universal periodic review, as a cooperative mechanism, should be implemented primarily by the State concerned and, as appropriate, by other relevant stakeholders.

34. The subsequent review should focus, inter alia, on the implementation of the preceding outcome.

35. The Council should have a standing item on its agenda devoted to the universal periodic review.

36. The international community will assist in implementing the recommendations and conclusions regarding capacity-building and technical assistance, in consultation with, and with the consent of, the country concerned.

37. In considering the outcome of the universal periodic review, the Council will decide if and when any specific follow up is necessary.

38. After exhausting all efforts to encourage a State to cooperate with the universal periodic review mechanism, the Council will address, as appropriate, cases of persistent non-cooperation with the mechanism.

II. SPECIAL PROCEDURES

A. Selection and appointment of mandate-holders

39. The following general criteria will be of paramount importance while nominating, selecting and appointing mandate-holders: (a) expertise; (b) experience in the field of the mandate; (c) independence; (d) impartiality; (e) personal integrity; and (f) objectivity.

40. Due consideration should be given to gender balance and equitable geographic representation, as well as to an appropriate representation of different legal systems.

41. Technical and objective requirements for eligible candidates for mandate-holders will be approved by the Council at its sixth session (first session of the second cycle), in order to ensure that eligible candidates are highly qualified individuals who possess established competence, relevant expertise and extensive professional experience in the field of human rights.

42. The following entities may nominate candidates as special procedures mandate-holders: (a) Governments; (b) Regional Groups operating within the United Nations human rights system; (c) international organizations or their offices (e.g. the Office of the High Commissioner for Human Rights); (d) non-governmental organizations; (e) other human rights bodies; (f) individual nominations.

43. The Office of the High Commissioner for Human Rights shall immediately prepare, maintain and periodically update a public list of eligible candidates in a standardized format, which shall include personal data, areas of expertise and professional experience. Upcoming vacancies of mandates shall be publicized.

44. The principle of non-accumulation of human rights functions at a time shall be respected.

45. A mandate-holder's tenure in a given function, whether a thematic or country mandate, will be no longer than six years (two terms of three years for thematic mandate- holders).

46. Individuals holding decision-making positions in Government or in any other organization or entity which may give rise to a conflict of interest with the responsibilities inherent to the mandate shall be excluded. Mandate-holders will act in their personal capacity.

47. A consultative group would be established to propose to the President, at least one month before the beginning of the session in which the Council would consider the selection of mandate-holders, a list of candidates who possess the highest qualifications for the mandates in question and meet the general criteria and particular requirements.

48. The consultative group shall also give due consideration to the exclusion of nominated candidates from the public list of eligible candidates brought to its attention.

49. At the beginning of the annual cycle of the Council, Regional Groups would be invited to appoint a member of the consultative group, who would serve in his/her personal capacity. The Group will be assisted by the Office of the High Commissioner for Human Rights.

50. The consultative group will consider candidates included in the public list; however, under exceptional circumstances and if a particular post justifies it, the Group may consider additional nominations with equal or more suitable qualifications for the post. Recommendations to the President shall be public and substantiated.

51. The consultative group should take into account, as appropriate, the views of stakeholders, including the current or outgoing mandate-holders, in determining the necessary expertise, experience, skills, and other relevant requirements for each mandate.

52. On the basis of the recommendations of the consultative group and following broad consultations, in particular through the regional coordinators, the President of the Council will identify an appropriate candidate for each vacancy. The President will present to member States and observers a list of candidates to be proposed at least two weeks prior to the beginning of the session in which the Council will consider the appointments.

53. If necessary, the President will conduct further consultations to ensure the endorsement of the proposed candidates. The appointment of the special procedures mandate-holders will be completed upon the subsequent approval of the Council. Mandate-holders shall be appointed before the end of the session.

B. Review, rationalization and improvement of mandates

54. The review, rationalization and improvement of mandates, as well as the creation of new ones, must be guided by the principles of universality, impartiality, objectivity and non-selectivity, constructive international dialogue and cooperation, with a view to enhancing the promotion and protection of all human rights, civil, political, economic, social and cultural rights, including the right to development.

55. The review, rationalization and improvement of each mandate would take place in the context of the negotiations of the relevant resolutions. An assessment of the mandate may take place in a separate segment of the interactive dialogue between the Council and special procedures mandate-holders.

56. The review, rationalization and improvement of mandates would focus on the relevance, scope and contents of the mandates, having as a framework the internationally recognized human rights standards, the system of special procedures and General Assembly resolution 60/251.

57. Any decision to streamline, merge or possibly discontinue mandates should always be guided by the need for improvement of the enjoyment and protection of human rights.

58. The Council should always strive for improvements:
   (*a*) Mandates should always offer a clear prospect of an increased level of human rights protection and promotion as well as being coherent within the system of human rights;
   (*b*) Equal attention should be paid to all human rights. The balance of thematic mandates should broadly reflect the accepted equal importance of civil, political, economic, social and cultural rights, including the right to development;
   (*c*) Every effort should be made to avoid unnecessary duplication;
   (*d*) Areas which constitute thematic gaps will be identified and addressed, including by means other than the creation of special procedures mandates, such as by expanding an existing mandate, bringing a cross-cutting issue to the attention of mandate-holders or by requesting a joint action to the relevant mandate-holders;
   (*e*) Any consideration of merging mandates should have regard to the content and predominant functions of each mandate, as well as to the workload of individual mandate-holders;
   (*f*) In creating or reviewing mandates, efforts should be made to identify whether the structure of the mechanism (expert, rapporteur or working group) is the most effective in terms of increasing human rights protection;
   (*g*) New mandates should be as clear and specific as possible, so as to avoid ambiguity.

59. It should be considered desirable to have a uniform nomenclature of mandate-holders, titles of mandates as well as a selection and appointment process, to make the whole system more understandable.

60. Thematic mandate periods will be of three years. Country mandate periods will be of one year.

61. Mandates included in Appendix I, where applicable, will be renewed until the date on which they are considered by the Council according to the programme of work.[4]

62. Current mandate-holders may continue serving, provided they have not exceeded the sixyear term limit (Appendix II). On an exceptional basis, the term of those mandate-holders who have served more than six years may be extended until the relevant mandate is considered by the Council and the selection and appointment process has concluded.

63. Decisions to create, review or discontinue country mandates should also take into account the principles of cooperation and genuine dialogue aimed at strengthening the capacity of Member States to comply with their human rights obligations.

64. In case of situations of violations of human rights or a lack of cooperation that require the Council's attention, the principles of objectivity, non-selectivity, and the elimination of double standards and politicization should apply.

III. HUMAN RIGHTS COUNCIL ADVISORY COMMITTEE

65. The Human Rights Council Advisory Committee (hereinafter "the Advisory Committee"), composed of 18 experts serving in their personal capacity, will function as a think-tank for the Council and work at its direction. The establishment of this subsidiary body and its functioning will be executed according to the guidelines stipulated below.

[4] Country mandates meet the following criteria:
- There is a pending mandate of the Council to be accomplished; or
- There is a pending mandate of the General Assembly to be accomplished; or
- The nature of the mandate is for advisory services and technical assistance.

A. Nomination

66. All Member States of the United Nations may propose or endorse candidates from their own region. When selecting their candidates, States should consult their national human rights institutions and civil society organizations and, in this regard, include the names of those supporting their candidates.

67. The aim is to ensure that the best possible expertise is made available to the Council. For this purpose, technical and objective requirements for the submission of candidatures will be established and approved by the Council at its sixth session (first session of the second cycle). These should include:

(*a*) Recognized competence and experience in the field of human rights;

(*b*) High moral standing;

(*c*) Independence and impartiality.

68. Individuals holding decision-making positions in Government or in any other organization or entity which might give rise to a conflict of interest with the responsibilities inherent in the mandate shall be excluded. Elected members of the Committee will act in their personal capacity.

69. The principle of non-accumulation of human rights functions at the same time shall be respected.

B. Election

70. The Council shall elect the members of the Advisory Committee, in secret ballot, from the list of candidates whose names have been presented in accordance with the agreed requirements.

71. The list of candidates shall be closed two months prior to the election date. The Secretariat will make available the list of candidates and relevant information to member States and to the public at least one month prior to their election.

72. Due consideration should be given to gender balance and appropriate representation of different civilizations and legal systems.

73. The geographic distribution will be as follows: African States: 5

Asian States: 5

Eastern European States: 2

Latin American and Caribbean States: 3 Western European and other States: 3

74. The members of the Advisory Committee shall serve for a period of three years. They shall be eligible for reelection once. In the first term, one third of the experts will serve for one year and another third for two years. The staggering of terms of membership will be defined by the drawing of lots.

C. Functions

75. The function of the Advisory Committee is to provide expertise to the Council in the manner and form requested by the Council, focusing mainly on studies and research-based advice. Further, such expertise shall be rendered only upon the latter's request, in compliance with its resolutions and under its guidance.

76. The Advisory Committee should be implementation-oriented and the scope of its advice should be limited to thematic issues pertaining to the mandate of the Council; namely promotion and protection of all human rights.

77. The Advisory Committee shall not adopt resolutions or decisions. The Advisory Committee may propose within the scope of the work set out by the Council, for the latter's

consideration and approval, suggestions for further enhancing its procedural efficiency, as well as further research proposals within the scope of the work set out by the Council.

78. The Council shall issue specific guidelines for the Advisory Committee when it requests a substantive contribution from the latter and shall review all or any portion of those guidelines if it deems necessary in the future.

D. Methods of work

79. The Advisory Committee shall convene up to two sessions for a maximum of 10 working days per year. Additional sessions may be scheduled on an ad hoc basis with prior approval of the Council.

80. The Council may request the Advisory Committee to undertake certain tasks that could be performed collectively, through a smaller team or individually. The Advisory Committee will report on such efforts to the Council.

81. Members of the Advisory Committee are encouraged to communicate between sessions, individually or in teams. However, the Advisory Committee shall not establish subsidiary bodies unless the Council authorizes it to do so.

82. In the performance of its mandate, the Advisory Committee is urged to establish interaction with States, national human rights institutions, non-governmental organizations and other civil society entities in accordance with the modalities of the Council.

83. Member States and observers, including States that are not members of the Council, the specialized agencies, other intergovernmental organizations and national human rights institutions, as well as non-governmental organizations shall be entitled to participate in the work of the Advisory Committee based on arrangements, including Economic and Social Council resolution 1996/31 and practices observed by the Commission on Human Rights and the Council, while ensuring the most effective contribution of these entities.

84. The Council will decide at its sixth session (first session of its second cycle) on the most appropriate mechanisms to continue the work of the Working Groups on Indigenous Populations; Contemporary Forms of Slavery; Minorities; and the Social Forum.

IV. COMPLAINT PROCEDURE

A. Objective and scope

85. A complaint procedure is being established to address consistent patterns of gross and reliably attested violations of all human rights and all fundamental freedoms occurring in any part of the world and under any circumstances.

86. Economic and Social Council resolution 1503 (XLVIII) of 27 May 1970 as revised by resolution 2000/3 of 19 June 2000 served as a working basis and was improved where necessary, so as to ensure that the complaint procedure is impartial, objective, efficient, victims-oriented and conducted in a timely manner. The procedure will retain its confidential nature, with a view to enhancing cooperation with the State concerned.

B. Admissibility criteria for communications

87. A communication related to a violation of human rights and fundamental freedoms, for the purpose of this procedure, shall be admissible, provided that:

(*a*) It is not manifestly politically motivated and its object is consistent with the Charter of the United Nations, the Universal Declaration of Human Rights and other applicable instruments in the field of human rights law;

(*b*) It gives a factual description of the alleged violations, including the rights which are alleged to be violated;
(*c*) Its language is not abusive. However, such a communication may be considered if it meets the other criteria for admissibility after deletion of the abusive language;
(*d*) It is submitted by a person or a group of persons claiming to be the victims of violations of human rights and fundamental freedoms, or by any person or group of persons, including nongovernmental organizations, acting in good faith in accordance with the principles of human rights, not resorting to politically motivated stands contrary to the provisions of the Charter of the United Nations and claiming to have direct and reliable knowledge of the violations concerned. Nonetheless, reliably attested communications shall not be inadmissible solely because the knowledge of the individual authors is second-hand, provided that they are accompanied by clear evidence;
(*e*) It is not exclusively based on reports disseminated by mass media;
(*f*) It does not refer to a case that appears to reveal a consistent pattern of gross and reliably attested violations of human rights already being dealt with by a special procedure, a treaty body or other United Nations or similar regional complaints procedure in the field of human rights;
(*g*) Domestic remedies have been exhausted, unless it appears that such remedies would be ineffective or unreasonably prolonged.

88. National human rights institutions, established and operating under the Principles Relating to the Status of National Institutions (the Paris Principles), in particular in regard to quasi-judicial competence, may serve as effective means of addressing individual human rights violations.

C. Working groups

89. Two distinct working groups shall be established with the mandate to examine the communications and to bring to the attention of the Council consistent patterns of gross and reliably attested violations of human rights and fundamental freedoms.

90. Both working groups shall, to the greatest possible extent, work on the basis of consensus. In the absence of consensus, decisions shall be taken by simple majority of the votes. They may establish their own rules of procedure.

1. Working Group on Communications: composition, mandate and powers

91. The Human Rights Council Advisory Committee shall appoint five of its members, one from each Regional Group, with due consideration to gender balance, to constitute the Working Group on Communications.

92. In case of a vacancy, the Advisory Committee shall appoint an independent and highly qualified expert of the same Regional Group from the Advisory Committee.

93. Since there is a need for independent expertise and continuity with regard to the examination and assessment of communications received, the independent and highly qualified experts of the Working Group on Communications shall be appointed for three years. Their mandate is renewable only once.

94. The Chairperson of the Working Group on Communications is requested, together with the secretariat, to undertake an initial screening of communications received, based on the admissibility criteria, before transmitting them to the States concerned. Manifestly ill-founded or anonymous communications shall be screened out by the Chairperson and

shall therefore not be transmitted to the State concerned. In a perspective of accountability and transparency, the Chairperson of the Working Group on Communications shall provide all its members with a list of all communications rejected after initial screening. This list should indicate the grounds of all decisions resulting in the rejection of a communication. All other communications, which have not been screened out, shall be transmitted to the State concerned, so as to obtain the views of the latter on the allegations of violations.

95. The members of the Working Group on Communications shall decide on the admissibility of a communication and assess the merits of the allegations of violations, including whether the communication alone or in combination with other communications appear to reveal a consistent pattern of gross and reliably attested violations of human rights and fundamental freedoms. The Working Group on Communications shall provide the Working Group on Situations with a file containing all admissible communications as well as recommendations thereon. When the Working Group on Communications requires further consideration or additional information, it may keep a case under review until its next session and request such information from the State concerned. The Working Group on Communications may decide to dismiss a case. All decisions of the Working Group on Communications shall be based on a rigorous application of the admissibility criteria and duly justified.

2. Working Group on Situations: composition, mandate and powers

96. Each Regional Group shall appoint a representative of a member State of the Council, with due consideration to gender balance, to serve on the Working Group on Situations. Members shall be appointed for one year. Their mandate may be renewed once, if the State concerned is a member of the Council.

97. Members of the Working Group on Situations shall serve in their personal capacity. In order to fill a vacancy, the respective Regional Group to which the vacancy belongs, shall appoint a representative from member States of the same Regional Group.

98. The Working Group on Situations is requested, on the basis of the information and recommendations provided by the Working Group on Communications, to present the Council with a report on consistent patterns of gross and reliably attested violations of human rights and fundamental freedoms and to make recommendations to the Council on the course of action to take, normally in the form of a draft resolution or decision with respect to the situations referred to it. When the Working Group on Situations requires further consideration or additional information, its members may keep a case under review until its next session. The Working Group on Situations may also decide to dismiss a case.

99. All decisions of the Working Group on Situations shall be duly justified and indicate why the consideration of a situation has been discontinued or action recommended thereon. Decisions to discontinue should be taken by consensus; if that is not possible, by simple majority of the votes.

D. Working modalities and confidentiality

100. Since the complaint procedure is to be, inter alia, victims-oriented and conducted in a confidential and timely manner, both Working Groups shall meet at least twice a year for five working days each session, in order to promptly examine the communications received, including replies of States thereon, and the situations of which the Council is already seized under the complaint procedure.

101. The State concerned shall cooperate with the complaint procedure and make every effort to provide substantive replies in one of the United Nations official languages to any

of the requests of the Working Groups or the Council. The State concerned shall also make every effort to provide a reply not later than three months after the request has been made. If necessary, this deadline may however be extended at the request of the State concerned.

102. The Secretariat is requested to make the confidential files available to all members of the Council, at least two weeks in advance, so as to allow sufficient time for the consideration of the files.

103. The Council shall consider consistent patterns of gross and reliably attested violations of human rights and fundamental freedoms brought to its attention by the Working Group on Situations as frequently as needed, but at least once a year.

104. The reports of the Working Group on Situations referred to the Council shall be examined in a confidential manner, unless the Council decides otherwise. When the Working Group on Situations recommends to the Council that it consider a situation in a public meeting, in particular in the case of manifest and unequivocal lack of cooperation, the Council shall consider such recommendation on a priority basis at its next session.

105. So as to ensure that the complaint procedure is victims-oriented, efficient and conducted in a timely manner, the period of time between the transmission of the complaint to the State concerned and consideration by the Council shall not, in principle, exceed 24 months.

E. Involvement of the complainant and of the State concerned

106. The complaint procedure shall ensure that both the author of a communication and the State concerned are informed of the proceedings at the following key stages:

(*a*) When a communication is deemed inadmissible by the Working Group on Communications or when it is taken up for consideration by the Working Group on Situations; or when a communication is kept pending by one of the Working Groups or by the Council;

(*b*) At the final outcome.

107. In addition, the complainant shall be informed when his/her communication is registered by the complaint procedure.

108. Should the complainant request that his/her identity be kept confidential, it will not be transmitted to the State concerned.

F. Measures

109. In accordance with established practice the action taken in respect of a particular situation should be one of the following options:

(*a*) To discontinue considering the situation when further consideration or action is not warranted;

(*b*) To keep the situation under review and request the State concerned to provide further information within a reasonable period of time;

(*c*) To keep the situation under review and appoint an independent and highly qualified expert to monitor the situation and report back to the Council;

(*d*) To discontinue reviewing the matter under the confidential complaint procedure in order to take up public consideration of the same;

(*e*) To recommend to OHCHR to provide technical cooperation, capacity-building assistance or advisory services to the State concerned.

…

VI. METHODS OF WORK

110. The methods of work, pursuant to General Assembly resolution 60/251 should be transparent, impartial, equitable, fair, pragmatic; lead to clarity, predictability, and inclusiveness. They may also be updated and adjusted over time.

A. Institutional arrangements

1. Briefings on prospective resolutions or decisions

111. The briefings on prospective resolutions or decisions would be informative only, whereby delegations would be apprised of resolutions and/or decisions tabled or intended to be tabled. These briefings will be organized by interested delegations.

2. President's open-ended information meetings on resolutions, decisions and other related business

112. The President's open-ended information meetings on resolutions, decisions and other related business shall provide information on the status of negotiations on draft resolutions and/or decisions so that delegations may gain a bird's eye view of the status of such drafts. The consultations shall have a purely informational function, combined with information on the extranet, and be held in a transparent and inclusive manner. They shall not serve as a negotiating forum.

3. Informal consultations on proposals convened by main sponsors

113. Informal consultations shall be the primary means for the negotiation of draft resolutions and/or decisions, and their convening shall be the responsibility of the sponsor(s). At least one informal open-ended consultation should be held on each draft resolution and/or decision before it is considered for action by the Council. Consultations should, as much as possible, be scheduled in a timely, transparent and inclusive manner that takes into account the constraints faced by delegations, particularly smaller ones.

4. Role of the Bureau

114. The Bureau shall deal with procedural and organizational matters. The Bureau shall regularly communicate the contents of its meetings through a timely summary report.

5. Other work formats may include panel debates, seminars and round tables

115. Utilization of these other work formats, including topics and modalities, would be decided by the Council on a case-by-case basis. They may serve as tools of the Council for enhancing dialogue and mutual understanding on certain issues. They should be utilized in the context of the Council's agenda and annual programme of work, and reinforce and/or complement its intergovernmental nature. They shall not be used to substitute or replace existing human rights mechanisms and established methods of work.

6. High-Level Segment

116. The High-Level Segment shall be held once a year during the main session of the Council. It shall be followed by a general segment wherein delegations that did not participate in the High-Level Segment may deliver general statements.

B. Working culture

117. There is a need for:

(*a*) Early notification of proposals;

(*b*) Early submission of draft resolutions and decisions, preferably by the end of the penultimate week of a session;

(*c*) Early distribution of all reports, particularly those of special procedures, to be transmitted to delegations in a timely fashion, at least 15 days in advance of their consideration by the Council, and in all official United Nations languages;

(*d*) Proposers of a country resolution to have the responsibility to secure the broadest possible support for their initiatives (preferably 15 members), before action is taken;

(*e*) Restraint in resorting to resolutions, in order to avoid proliferation of resolutions without prejudice to the right of States to decide on the periodicity of presenting their draft proposals by:

(i) Minimizing unnecessary duplication of initiatives with the General Assembly/Third Committee;

(ii) Clustering of agenda items;

(iii) Staggering the tabling of decisions and/or resolutions and consideration of action on agenda items/issues.

C. Outcomes other than resolutions and decisions

118. These may include recommendations, conclusions, summaries of discussions and President's Statement. As such outcomes would have different legal implications, they should supplement and not replace resolutions and decisions.

D. Special sessions of the Council

119. The following provisions shall complement the general framework provided by General Assembly resolution 60/251 and the rules of procedure of the Human Rights Council.

120. The rules of procedure of special sessions shall be in accordance with the rules of procedure applicable for regular sessions of the Council.

121. The request for the holding of a special session, in accordance with the requirement established in paragraph 10 of General Assembly resolution 60/251, shall be submitted to the President and to the secretariat of the Council. The request shall specify the item proposed for consideration and include any other relevant information the sponsors may wish to provide.

122. The special session shall be convened as soon as possible after the formal request is communicated, but, in principle, not earlier than two working days, and not later than five working days after the formal receipt of the request. The duration of the special session shall not exceed three days (six working sessions), unless the Council decides otherwise.

123. The secretariat of the Council shall immediately communicate the request for the holding of a special session and any additional information provided by the sponsors in the request, as well as the date for the convening of the special session, to all United Nations Member States and make the information available to the specialized agencies, other intergovernmental organizations and national human rights institutions, as well as to non-governmental organizations in consultative status by the most expedient and expeditious means of communication. Special session documentation, in particular draft resolutions and decisions, should be made available in all official United Nations languages to all States in an equitable, timely and transparent manner.

124. The President of the Council should hold open-ended informative consultations before the special session on its conduct and organization. In this regard, the secretariat may also be requested to provide additional information, including, on the methods of work of previous special sessions.

125. Members of the Council, concerned States, observer States, specialized agencies, other intergovernmental organizations and national human rights institutions, as well as nongovernmental organizations in consultative status may contribute to the special session in accordance with the rules of procedure of the Council.

126. If the requesting or other States intend to present draft resolutions or decisions at the special session, texts should be made available in accordance with the Council's relevant rules of procedure. Nevertheless, sponsors are urged to present such texts as early as possible.

127. The sponsors of a draft resolution or decision should hold open-ended consultations on the text of their draft resolution(s) or decision(s) with a view to achieving the widest participation in their consideration and, if possible, achieving consensus on them.

128. A special session should allow participatory debate, be results-oriented and geared to achieving practical outcomes, the implementation of which can be monitored and reported on at the following regular session of the Council for possible follow-up decision.

VII. RULES OF PROCEDURE[5]

SESSIONS

Rules of procedure
Rule 1

The Human Rights Council shall apply the rules of procedure established for the Main Committees of the General Assembly, as applicable, unless subsequently otherwise decided by the Assembly or the Council.

REGULAR SESSIONS

Number of sessions
Rule 2

The Human Rights Council shall meet regularly throughout the year and schedule no fewer than three sessions per Council year, including a main session, for a total duration of no less than 10 weeks.

Assumption of membership
Rule 3

Newly-elected member States of the Human Rights Council shall assume their membership on the first day of the Council year, replacing member States that have concluded their respective membership terms.

Place of meeting
Rule 4

The Human Rights Council shall be based in Geneva.

[5] Figures indicated in square brackets refer to identical or corresponding rules of the General Assembly or its Main Committees (A/520/Rev.16).

SPECIAL SESSIONS

Convening of special sessions
Rule 5

The rules of procedure of special sessions of the Human Rights Council will be the same as the rules of procedure applicable for regular sessions of the Human Rights Council.

Rule 6

The Human Rights Council shall hold special sessions, when needed, at the request of a member of the Council with the support of one third of the membership of the Council.

PARTICIPATION OF AND CONSULTATION WITH OBSERVERS OF THE COUNCIL

Rule 7

(a) The Council shall apply the rules of procedure established for committees of the General Assembly, as applicable, unless subsequently otherwise decided by the Assembly or the Council, and the participation of and consultation with observers, including States that are not members of the Council, the specialized agencies, other intergovernmental organizations and national human rights institutions, as well as non-governmental organizations, shall be based on arrangements, including Economic and Social Council resolution 1996/31 of 25 July 1996, and practices observed by the Commission on Human Rights, while ensuring the most effective contribution of these entities.

(b) Participation of national human rights institutions shall be based on arrangements and practices agreed upon by the Commission on Human Rights, including resolution 2005/74 of 20 April 2005, while ensuring the most effective contribution of these entities.

ORGANIZATION OF WORK AND AGENDA FOR REGULAR SESSIONS

Organizational meetings
Rule 8

(a) At the beginning of each Council year, the Council shall hold an organizational meeting to elect its Bureau and to consider and adopt the agenda, programme of work, and calendar of regular sessions for the Council year indicating, if possible, a target date for the conclusion of its work, the approximate dates of consideration of items and the number of meetings to be allocated to each item.

(b) The President of the Council shall also convene organizational meetings two weeks before the beginning of each session and, if necessary, during the Council sessions to discuss organizational and procedural issues pertinent to that session.

PRESIDENT AND VICE-PRESIDENTS

Elections
Rule 9

(a) At the beginning of each Council year, at its organizational meeting, the Council shall elect, from among the representatives of its members, a President and four Vice-Presidents. The President and the VicePresidents shall constitute the Bureau. One of the Vice-Presidents shall serve as Rapporteur.

(b) In the election of the President of the Council, regard shall be had for the equitable geographical rotation of this office among the following Regional Groups: African States, Asian States, Eastern European States, Latin American and Caribbean States, and Western European and other States. The four Vice-Presidents of the Council shall be elected on the basis of equitable geographical distribution from the Regional Groups other than the one to which the President belongs. The selection of the Rapporteur shall be based on geographic rotation.

Bureau
Rule 10

The Bureau shall deal with procedural and organizational matters.

Term of office
Rule 11

The President and the Vice-Presidents shall, subject to rule 13, hold office for a period of one year. They shall not be eligible for immediate re-election to the same post.

Absence of officers
Rule 12 [105]

If the President finds it necessary to be absent during a meeting or any part thereof, he/she shall designate one of the Vice-Presidents to take his/her place. A Vice-President acting as President shall have the same powers and duties as the President. If the President ceases to hold office pursuant to rule 13, the remaining members of the Bureau shall designate one of the VicePresidents to take his/her place until the election of a new President.

Replacement of the President or a Vice-President
Rule 13

If the President or any Vice-President ceases to be able to carry out his/her functions or ceases to be a representative of a member of the Council, or if the Member of the United Nations of which he/she is a representative ceases to be a member of the Council, he/she shall cease to hold such office and a new President or Vice-President shall be elected for the unexpired term.

SECRETARIAT

Duties of the secretariat
Rule 14 [47]

The Office of the United Nations High Commissioner for Human Rights shall act as secretariat for the Council. In this regard, it shall receive, translate, print and circulate in all official United Nations languages, documents, reports and resolutions of the Council, its committees and its organs; interpret speeches made at the meetings; prepare, print and circulate the records of the session; have the custody and proper preservation of the documents in the archives of the Council; distribute all documents of the Council to the members of the Council and observers and, generally, perform all other support functions which the Council may require.

RECORDS AND REPORT

Report to the General Assembly
Rule 15

The Council shall submit an annual report to the General Assembly.

PUBLIC AND PRIVATE MEETINGS OF THE HUMAN RIGHTS COUNCIL

General principles
Rule 16 [60]

The meetings of the Council shall be held in public unless the Council decides that exceptional circumstances require the meeting be held in private.

Private meetings
Rule 17 [61]

All decisions of the Council taken at a private meeting shall be announced at an early public meeting of the Council.

CONDUCT OF BUSINESS

Working groups and other arrangements
Rule 18

The Council may set up working groups and other arrangements. Participation in these bodies shall be decided upon by the members, based on rule 7. The rules of procedure of these bodies shall follow those of the Council, as applicable, unless decided otherwise by the Council.

Quorum
Rule 19 [67]

The President may declare a meeting open and permit the debate to proceed when at least one third of the members of the Council are present. The presence of a majority of the members shall be required for any decision to be taken.

Majority required
Rule 20 [125]

Decisions of the Council shall be made by a simple majority of the members present and voting, subject to rule 19.

6 Law of the World Trade Organization

The World Trade Organization Framework

36.a Agreement Establishing the World Trade Organization

Date: 15 April 1994
Source: (1994) 33 ILM 1125
https://www.wto.org/english/docs_e/legal_e/04-wto_e.htm

The *Parties* to this Agreement,

Recognizing that their relations in the field of trade and economic endeavour should be conducted with a view to raising standards of living, ensuring full employment and a large and steadily growing volume of real income and effective demand, and expanding the production of and trade in goods and services, while allowing for the optimal use of the world's resources in accordance with the objective of sustainable development, seeking both to protect and preserve the environment and to enhance the means for doing so in a manner consistent with their respective needs and concerns at different levels of economic development,

Recognizing further that there is need for positive efforts designed to ensure that developing countries, and especially the least developed among them, secure a share in the growth in international trade commensurate with the needs of their economic development,

Being desirous of contributing to these objectives by entering into reciprocal and mutually advantageous arrangements directed to the substantial reduction of tariffs and other barriers to trade and to the elimination of discriminatory treatment in international trade relations,

Resolved, therefore, to develop an integrated, more viable and durable multilateral trading system encompassing the General Agreement on Tariffs and Trade, the results of past trade liberalization efforts, and all of the results of the Uruguay Round of Multilateral Trade Negotiations,

Determined to preserve the basic principles and to further the objectives underlying this multilateral trading system,

Agree as follows:

Article I: Establishment of the Organization

The World Trade Organization (hereinafter referred to as "the WTO") is hereby established.

Article II: Scope of the WTO

1. The WTO shall provide the common institutional framework for the conduct of trade relations among its Members in matters related to the agreements and associated legal instruments included in the Annexes to this Agreement.

2. The agreements and associated legal instruments included in Annexes 1, 2 and 3 (hereinafter referred to as "Multilateral Trade Agreements") are integral parts of this Agreement, binding on all Members.

3. The agreements and associated legal instruments included in Annex 4 (hereinafter referred to as "Plurilateral Trade Agreements") are also part of this Agreement for those Members that have accepted them, and are binding on those Members. The Plurilateral Trade Agreements do not create either obligations or rights for Members that have not accepted them.

4. The General Agreement on Tariffs and Trade 1994 as specified in Annex 1A (hereinafter referred to as "GATT 1994") is legally distinct from the General Agreement on Tariffs and Trade, dated 30 October 1947, annexed to the Final Act Adopted at the Conclusion of the Second Session of the Preparatory Committee of the United Nations Conference on Trade and Employment, as subsequently rectified, amended or modified (hereinafter referred to as "GATT 1947").

Article III: Functions of the WTO

1. The WTO shall facilitate the implementation, administration and operation, and further the objectives, of this Agreement and of the Multilateral Trade Agreements, and shall also provide the framework for the implementation, administration and operation of the Plurilateral Trade Agreements.

2. The WTO shall provide the forum for negotiations among its Members concerning their multilateral trade relations in matters dealt with under the agreements in the Annexes to this Agreement. The WTO may also provide a forum for further negotiations among its Members concerning their multilateral trade relations, and a framework for the implementation of the results of such negotiations, as may be decided by the Ministerial Conference.

3. The WTO shall administer the Understanding on Rules and Procedures Governing the Settlement of Disputes (hereinafter referred to as the "Dispute Settlement Understanding" or "DSU") in Annex 2 to this Agreement.

4. The WTO shall administer the Trade Policy Review Mechanism (hereinafter referred to as the "TPRM") provided for in Annex 3 to this Agreement.

5. With a view to achieving greater coherence in global economic policy-making, the WTO shall cooperate, as appropriate, with the International Monetary Fund and with the International Bank for Reconstruction and Development and its affiliated agencies.

Article IV: Structure of the WTO

1. There shall be a Ministerial Conference composed of representatives of all the Members, which shall meet at least once every two years. The Ministerial Conference shall carry out the functions of the WTO and take actions necessary to this effect. The Ministerial Conference shall have the authority to take decisions on all matters under any of the Multilateral Trade Agreements, if so requested by a Member, in accordance with the specific requirements for decision-making in this Agreement and in the relevant Multilateral Trade Agreement.

2. There shall be a General Council composed of representatives of all the Members, which shall meet as appropriate. In the intervals between meetings of the Ministerial Conference, its functions shall be conducted by the General Council. The General Council shall also carry out the functions assigned to it by this Agreement. The General Council shall establish its rules of procedure and approve the rules of procedure for the Committees provided for in paragraph 7.

3. The General Council shall convene as appropriate to discharge the responsibilities of the Dispute Settlement Body provided for in the Dispute Settlement Understanding. The Dispute Settlement Body may have its own chairman and shall establish such rules of procedure as it deems necessary for the fulfilment of those responsibilities.

4. The General Council shall convene as appropriate to discharge the responsibilities of the Trade Policy Review Body provided for in the TPRM. The Trade Policy Review Body may have its own chairman and shall establish such rules of procedure as it deems necessary for the fulfilment of those responsibilities.

5. There shall be a Council for Trade in Goods, a Council for Trade in Services and a Council for Trade-Related Aspects of Intellectual Property Rights (hereinafter referred to as the "Council for TRIPS"), which shall operate under the general guidance of the General Council. The Council for Trade in Goods shall oversee the functioning of the Multilateral Trade Agreements in Annex 1A. The Council for Trade in Services shall oversee the functioning of the General Agreement on Trade in Services (hereinafter referred to as "GATS"). The Council for TRIPS shall oversee the functioning of the Agreement on Trade-Related Aspects of Intellectual Property Rights (hereinafter referred to as the "Agreement on TRIPS"). These Councils shall carry out the functions assigned to them by their respective agreements and by the General Council. They shall establish their respective rules of procedure subject to the approval of the General Council. Membership in these Councils shall be open to representatives of all Members. These Councils shall meet as necessary to carry out their functions.

6. The Council for Trade in Goods, the Council for Trade in Services and the Council for TRIPS shall establish subsidiary bodies as required. These subsidiary bodies shall establish their respective rules of procedure subject to the approval of their respective Councils.

7. The Ministerial Conference shall establish a Committee on Trade and Development, a Committee on Balance-of-Payments Restrictions and a Committee on Budget, Finance and Administration, which shall carry out the functions assigned to them by this Agreement and by the Multilateral Trade Agreements, and any additional functions assigned to them by the General Council, and may establish such additional Committees with such functions as it may deem appropriate. As part of its functions, the Committee on Trade and Development shall periodically review the special provisions in the Multilateral Trade Agreements in favour of the least-developed country Members and report to the General Council for appropriate action. Membership in these Committees shall be open to representatives of all Members.

8. The bodies provided for under the Plurilateral Trade Agreements shall carry out the functions assigned to them under those Agreements and shall operate within the institutional framework of the WTO. These bodies shall keep the General Council informed of their activities on a regular basis.

Article V: Relations with Other Organizations

1. The General Council shall make appropriate arrangements for effective cooperation with other intergovernmental organizations that have responsibilities related to those of the WTO.

2. The General Council may make appropriate arrangements for consultation and cooperation with non-governmental organizations concerned with matters related to those of the WTO.

Article VI: The Secretariat

1. There shall be a Secretariat of the WTO (hereinafter referred to as "the Secretariat") headed by a Director-General.

2. The Ministerial Conference shall appoint the Director-General and adopt regulations setting out the powers, duties, conditions of service and term of office of the Director-General.

3. The Director-General shall appoint the members of the staff of the Secretariat and determine their duties and conditions of service in accordance with regulations adopted by the Ministerial Conference.

4. The responsibilities of the Director-General and of the staff of the Secretariat shall be exclusively international in character. In the discharge of their duties, the Director-General and the staff of the Secretariat shall not seek or accept instructions from any government or any other authority external to the WTO. They shall refrain from any action which might adversely reflect on their position as international officials. The Members of the WTO shall respect the international character of the responsibilities of the Director-General and of the staff of the Secretariat and shall not seek to influence them in the discharge of their duties.

Article VII: Budget and Contributions

1. The Director-General shall present to the Committee on Budget, Finance and Administration the annual budget estimate and financial statement of the WTO. The Committee on Budget, Finance and Administration shall review the annual budget estimate and the financial statement presented by the Director-General and make recommendations thereon to the General Council. The annual budget estimate shall be subject to approval by the General Council.

2. The Committee on Budget, Finance and Administration shall propose to the General Council financial regulations which shall include provisions setting out:

(a) the scale of contributions apportioning the expenses of the WTO among its Members; and

(b) the measures to be taken in respect of Members in arrears.

The financial regulations shall be based, as far as practicable, on the regulations and practices of GATT 1947.

3. The General Council shall adopt the financial regulations and the annual budget estimate by a two-thirds majority comprising more than half of the Members of the WTO.

4. Each Member shall promptly contribute to the WTO its share in the expenses of the WTO in accordance with the financial regulations adopted by the General Council.

Article VIII: Status of the WTO

1. The WTO shall have legal personality, and shall be accorded by each of its Members such legal capacity as may be necessary for the exercise of its functions.

2. The WTO shall be accorded by each of its Members such privileges and immunities as are necessary for the exercise of its functions.

3. The officials of the WTO and the representatives of the Members shall similarly be accorded by each of its Members such privileges and immunities as are necessary for the independent exercise of their functions in connection with the WTO.

4. The privileges and immunities to be accorded by a Member to the WTO, its officials, and the representatives of its Members shall be similar to the privileges and immunities stipulated in the Convention on the Privileges and Immunities of the Specialized Agencies, approved by the General Assembly of the United Nations on 21 November 1947.

5. The WTO may conclude a headquarters agreement.

Article IX: Decision-Making

1. The WTO shall continue the practice of decision-making by consensus followed under GATT 1947.[1] Except as otherwise provided, where a decision cannot be arrived at by consensus, the matter at issue shall be decided by voting. At meetings of the Ministerial Conference and the General Council, each Member of the WTO shall have one vote. Where the European Communities exercise their right to vote, they shall have a number of votes equal to the number of their member States[2] which are Members of the WTO. Decisions of the Ministerial Conference and the General Council shall be taken by a majority of the votes cast, unless otherwise provided in this Agreement or in the relevant Multilateral Trade Agreement.[3]

2. The Ministerial Conference and the General Council shall have the exclusive authority to adopt interpretations of this Agreement and of the Multilateral Trade Agreements. In the case of an interpretation of a Multilateral Trade Agreement in Annex 1, they shall exercise their authority on the basis of a recommendation by the Council overseeing the functioning of that Agreement. The decision to adopt an interpretation shall be taken by a three-fourths majority of the Members. This paragraph shall not be used in a manner that would undermine the amendment provisions in Article X.

3. In exceptional circumstances, the Ministerial Conference may decide to waive an obligation imposed on a Member by this Agreement or any of the Multilateral Trade Agreements, provided that any such decision shall be taken by three fourths[4] of the Members unless otherwise provided for in this paragraph.

(a) A request for a waiver concerning this Agreement shall be submitted to the Ministerial Conference for consideration pursuant to the practice of decision-making by consensus. The Ministerial Conference shall establish a time-period, which shall not exceed 90 days, to consider the request. If consensus is not reached during the time-period, any decision to grant a waiver shall be taken by three fourths[4] of the Members.

(b) A request for a waiver concerning the Multilateral Trade Agreements in Annexes 1A or 1B or 1C and their annexes shall be submitted initially to the Council for Trade in Goods, the Council for Trade in Services or the Council for TRIPS, respectively, for consideration during a time-period which shall not exceed 90 days. At the end of the time-period, the relevant Council shall submit a report to the Ministerial Conference.

4. A decision by the Ministerial Conference granting a waiver shall state the exceptional circumstances justifying the decision, the terms and conditions governing the application of the waiver, and the date on which the waiver shall terminate. Any waiver granted for a period of more than one year shall be reviewed by the Ministerial Conference not later than one year after it is granted, and thereafter annually until the waiver terminates. In each review, the Ministerial Conference shall examine whether the exceptional circumstances justifying the waiver still exist and whether the terms and conditions attached to the waiver

[1] The body concerned shall be deemed to have decided by consensus on a matter submitted for its consideration, if no Member, present at the meeting when the decision is taken, formally objects to the proposed decision.

[2] The number of votes of the European Communities and their member States shall in no case exceed the number of the member States of the European Communities.

[3] Decisions by the General Council when convened as the Dispute Settlement Body shall be taken only in accordance with the provisions of paragraph 4 of Article 2 of the Dispute Settlement Understanding. (N.B.: See Document No. 35.b.).

[4] A decision to grant a waiver in respect of any obligation subject to a transition period or a period for staged implementation that the requesting Member has not performed by the end of the relevant period shall be taken only by consensus.

have been met. The Ministerial Conference, on the basis of the annual review, may extend, modify or terminate the waiver.

5. Decisions under a Plurilateral Trade Agreement, including any decisions on interpretations and waivers, shall be governed by the provisions of that Agreement.

Article X: Amendments

1. Any Member of the WTO may initiate a proposal to amend the provisions of this Agreement or the Multilateral Trade Agreements in Annex 1 by submitting such proposal to the Ministerial Conference. The Councils listed in paragraph 5 of Article IV may also submit to the Ministerial Conference proposals to amend the provisions of the corresponding Multilateral Trade Agreements in Annex 1 the functioning of which they oversee. Unless the Ministerial Conference decides on a longer period, for a period of 90 days after the proposal has been tabled formally at the Ministerial Conference any decision by the Ministerial Conference to submit the proposed amendment to the Members for acceptance shall be taken by consensus. Unless the provisions of paragraphs 2, 5 or 6 apply, that decision shall specify whether the provisions of paragraphs 3 or 4 shall apply. If consensus is reached, the Ministerial Conference shall forthwith submit the proposed amendment to the Members for acceptance. If consensus is not reached at a meeting of the Ministerial Conference within the established period, the Ministerial Conference shall decide by a two-thirds majority of the Members whether to submit the proposed amendment to the Members for acceptance. Except as provided in paragraphs 2, 5 and 6, the provisions of paragraph 3 shall apply to the proposed amendment, unless the Ministerial Conference decides by a three-fourths majority of the Members that the provisions of paragraph 4 shall apply.

2. Amendments to the provisions of this Article and to the provisions of the following Articles shall take effect only upon acceptance by all Members:

Article IX of this Agreement;
Articles I and II of GATT 1994;
Article II:1 of GATS;
Article 4 of the Agreement on TRIPS.

3. Amendments to provisions of this Agreement, or of the Multilateral Trade Agreements in Annexes 1A and 1C, other than those listed in paragraphs 2 and 6, of a nature that would alter the rights and obligations of the Members, shall take effect for the Members that have accepted them upon acceptance by two thirds of the Members and thereafter for each other Member upon acceptance by it. The Ministerial Conference may decide by a three-fourths majority of the Members that any amendment made effective under this paragraph is of such a nature that any Member which has not accepted it within a period specified by the Ministerial Conference in each case shall be free to withdraw from the WTO or to remain a Member with the consent of the Ministerial Conference.

4. Amendments to provisions of this Agreement or of the Multilateral Trade Agreements in Annexes 1A and 1C, other than those listed in paragraphs 2 and 6, of a nature that would not alter the rights and obligations of the Members, shall take effect for all Members upon acceptance by two thirds of the Members.

5. Except as provided in paragraph 2 above, amendments to Parts I, II and III of GATS and the respective annexes shall take effect for the Members that have accepted them upon acceptance by two thirds of the Members and thereafter for each Member upon acceptance by it. The Ministerial Conference may decide by a three-fourths majority of the Members that any amendment made effective under the preceding provision is of such a nature

that any Member which has not accepted it within a period specified by the Ministerial Conference in each case shall be free to withdraw from the WTO or to remain a Member with the consent of the Ministerial Conference. Amendments to Parts IV, V and VI of GATS and the respective annexes shall take effect for all Members upon acceptance by two thirds of the Members.

6. Notwithstanding the other provisions of this Article, amendments to the Agreement on TRIPS meeting the requirements of paragraph 2 of Article 71 thereof may be adopted by the Ministerial Conference without further formal acceptance process.

7. Any Member accepting an amendment to this Agreement or to a Multilateral Trade Agreement in Annex 1 shall deposit an instrument of acceptance with the Director-General of the WTO within the period of acceptance specified by the Ministerial Conference.

8. Any Member of the WTO may initiate a proposal to amend the provisions of the Multilateral Trade Agreements in Annexes 2 and 3 by submitting such proposal to the Ministerial Conference. The decision to approve amendments to the Multilateral Trade Agreement in Annex 2 shall be made by consensus and these amendments shall take effect for all Members upon approval by the Ministerial Conference. Decisions to approve amendments to the Multilateral Trade Agreement in Annex 3 shall take effect for all Members upon approval by the Ministerial Conference.

9. The Ministerial Conference, upon the request of the Members parties to a trade agreement, may decide exclusively by consensus to add that agreement to Annex 4. The Ministerial Conference, upon the request of the Members parties to a Plurilateral Trade Agreement, may decide to delete that Agreement from Annex 4.

10. Amendments to a Plurilateral Trade Agreement shall be governed by the provisions of that Agreement.

Article XI: Original Membership

1. The contracting parties to GATT 1947 as of the date of entry into force of this Agreement, and the European Communities, which accept this Agreement and the Multilateral Trade Agreements and for which Schedules of Concessions and Commitments are annexed to GATT 1994 and for which Schedules of Specific Commitments are annexed to GATS shall become original Members of the WTO.

2. The least-developed countries recognized as such by the United Nations will only be required to undertake commitments and concessions to the extent consistent with their individual development, financial and trade needs or their administrative and institutional capabilities.

Article XII: Accession

1. Any State or separate customs territory possessing full autonomy in the conduct of its external commercial relations and of the other matters provided for in this Agreement and the Multilateral Trade Agreements may accede to this Agreement, on terms to be agreed between it and the WTO. Such accession shall apply to this Agreement and the Multilateral Trade Agreements annexed thereto.

2. Decisions on accession shall be taken by the Ministerial Conference. The Ministerial Conference shall approve the agreement on the terms of accession by a two-thirds majority of the Members of the WTO.

3. Accession to a Plurilateral Trade Agreement shall be governed by the provisions of that Agreement.

Article XIII: Non-Application of Multilateral Trade Agreements between Particular Members

1. This Agreement and the Multilateral Trade Agreements in Annexes 1 and 2 shall not apply as between any Member and any other Member if either of the Members, at the time either becomes a Member, does not consent to such application.

2. Paragraph 1 may be invoked between original Members of the WTO which were contracting parties to GATT 1947 only where Article XXXV of that Agreement had been invoked earlier and was effective as between those contracting parties at the time of entry into force for them of this Agreement.

3. Paragraph 1 shall apply between a Member and another Member which has acceded under Article XII only if the Member not consenting to the application has so notified the Ministerial Conference before the approval of the agreement on the terms of accession by the Ministerial Conference.

4. The Ministerial Conference may review the operation of this Article in particular cases at the request of any Member and make appropriate recommendations.

5. Non-application of a Plurilateral Trade Agreement between parties to that Agreement shall be governed by the provisions of that Agreement.

Article XIV: Acceptance, Entry into Force and Deposit

1. This Agreement shall be open for acceptance, by signature or otherwise, by contracting parties to GATT 1947, and the European Communities, which are eligible to become original Members of the WTO in accordance with Article XI of this Agreement. Such acceptance shall apply to this Agreement and the Multilateral Trade Agreements annexed hereto. This Agreement and the Multilateral Trade Agreements annexed hereto shall enter into force on the date determined by Ministers in accordance with paragraph 3 of the Final Act Embodying the Results of the Uruguay Round of Multilateral Trade Negotiations and shall remain open for acceptance for a period of two years following that date unless the Ministers decide otherwise. An acceptance following the entry into force of this Agreement shall enter into force on the 30th day following the date of such acceptance.

2. A Member which accepts this Agreement after its entry into force shall implement those concessions and obligations in the Multilateral Trade Agreements that are to be implemented over a period of time starting with the entry into force of this Agreement as if it had accepted this Agreement on the date of its entry into force.

3. Until the entry into force of this Agreement, the text of this Agreement and the Multilateral Trade Agreements shall be deposited with the Director-General to the CONTRACTING PARTIES to GATT 1947. The Director-General shall promptly furnish a certified true copy of this Agreement and the Multilateral Trade Agreements, and a notification of each acceptance thereof, to each government and the European Communities having accepted this Agreement. This Agreement and the Multilateral Trade Agreements, and any amendments thereto, shall, upon the entry into force of this Agreement, be deposited with the Director-General of the WTO.

4. The acceptance and entry into force of a Plurilateral Trade Agreement shall be governed by the provisions of that Agreement. Such Agreements shall be deposited with the Director-General to the CONTRACTING PARTIES to GATT 1947. Upon the entry into force of this Agreement, such Agreements shall be deposited with the Director-General of the WTO.

Article XV: Withdrawal

1. Any Member may withdraw from this Agreement. Such withdrawal shall apply both to this Agreement and the Multilateral Trade Agreements and shall take effect upon the expiration of six months from the date on which written notice of withdrawal is received by the Director-General of the WTO.

2. Withdrawal from a Plurilateral Trade Agreement shall be governed by the provisions of that Agreement.

Article XVI: Miscellaneous Provisions

1. Except as otherwise provided under this Agreement or the Multilateral Trade Agreements, the WTO shall be guided by the decisions, procedures and customary practices followed by the CONTRACTING PARTIES to GATT 1947 and the bodies established in the framework of GATT 1947.

2. To the extent practicable, the Secretariat of GATT 1947 shall become the Secretariat of the WTO, and the Director-General to the CONTRACTING PARTIES to GATT 1947, until such time as the Ministerial Conference has appointed a Director-General in accordance with paragraph 2 of Article VI of this Agreement, shall serve as Director-General of the WTO.

3. In the event of a conflict between a provision of this Agreement and a provision of any of the Multilateral Trade Agreements, the provision of this Agreement shall prevail to the extent of the conflict.

4. Each Member shall ensure the conformity of its laws, regulations and administrative procedures with its obligations as provided in the annexed Agreements.

5. No reservations may be made in respect of any provision of this Agreement. Reservations in respect of any of the provisions of the Multilateral Trade Agreements may only be made to the extent provided for in those Agreements. Reservations in respect of a provision of a Plurilateral Trade Agreement shall be governed by the provisions of that Agreement.

6. This Agreement shall be registered in accordance with the provisions of Article 102 of the Charter of the United Nations.

DONE at Marrakesh this fifteenth day of April one thousand nine hundred and ninety-four, in a single copy, in the English, French and Spanish languages, each text being authentic.

Explanatory Notes:

The terms "country" or "countries" as used in this Agreement and the Multilateral Trade Agreements are to be understood to include any separate customs territory Member of the WTO.

In the case of a separate customs territory Member of the WTO, where an expression in this Agreement and the Multilateral Trade Agreements is qualified by the term "national", such expression shall be read as pertaining to that customs territory, unless otherwise specified.

LIST OF ANNEXES

ANNEX 1
ANNEX 1A: Multilateral Agreements on Trade in Goods General Agreement on Tariffs and Trade 1994
Agreement on Agriculture
Agreement on the Application of Sanitary and Phytosanitary Measures
Agreement on Textiles and Clothing
Agreement on Technical Barriers to Trade
Agreement on Trade-Related Investment Measures
Agreement on Implementation of Article VI of the General
Agreement on Tariffs and Trade 1994
Agreement on Implementation of Article VII of the General
Agreement on Tariffs and Trade 1994
Agreement on Preshipment Inspection Agreement on Rules of Origin
Agreement on Import Licensing Procedures
Agreement on Subsidies and Countervailing Measures Agreement on Safeguards
ANNEX 1B: General Agreement on Trade in Services and Annexes
ANNEX 1C: Agreement on Trade-Related Aspects of Intellectual Property Rights

ANNEX 2: Understanding on Rules and Procedures Governing the Settlement of Disputes

ANNEX 3: Trade Policy Review Mechanism

ANNEX 4: Plurilateral Trade Agreements
Agreement on Trade in Civil Aircraft
Agreement on Government Procurement International Dairy
Agreement International Bovine Meat Agreement

36.b Understanding on Rules and Procedures Governing the Settlement of Disputes

Date: 15 April 1994
Source: (1994) 33 ILM 1125 (Annex 2)
http://www.wto.org/english/docs_e/legal_e/28-dsu_e.htm

Members hereby *agree* as follows:

Article 1 Coverage and Application

1. The rules and procedures of this Understanding shall apply to disputes brought pursuant to the consultation and dispute settlement provisions of the agreements listed in Appendix 1 to this Understanding (referred to in this Understanding as the "covered agreements").

The rules and procedures of this Understanding shall also apply to consultations and the settlement of disputes between Members concerning their rights and obligations under the provisions of the Agreement Establishing the World Trade Organization (referred to in this Understanding as the "WTO Agreement") and of this Understanding taken in isolation or in combination with any other covered agreement.

2. The rules and procedures of this Understanding shall apply subject to such special or additional rules and procedures on dispute settlement contained in the covered agreements as are identified in Appendix 2 to this Understanding. To the extent that there is a difference between the rules and procedures of this Understanding and the special or additional rules and procedures set forth in Appendix 2, the special or additional rules and procedures in Appendix 2 shall prevail. In disputes involving rules and procedures under more than one covered agreement, if there is a conflict between special or additional rules and procedures of such agreements under review, and where the parties to the dispute cannot agree on rules and procedures within 20 days of the establishment of the panel, the Chairman of the Dispute Settlement Body provided for in paragraph 1 of Article 2 (referred to in this Understanding as the "DSB"), in consultation with the parties to the dispute, shall determine the rules and procedures to be followed within 10 days after a request by either Member. The Chairman shall be guided by the principle that special or additional rules and procedures should be used where possible, and the rules and procedures set out in this Understanding should be used to the extent necessary to avoid conflict.

Article 2: Administration

1. The Dispute Settlement Body is hereby established to administer these rules and procedures and, except as otherwise provided in a covered agreement, the consultation and dispute settlement provisions of the covered agreements. Accordingly, the DSB shall have the authority to establish panels, adopt panel and Appellate Body reports, maintain surveillance of implementation of rulings and recommendations, and authorize suspension of concessions and other obligations under the covered agreements. With respect to disputes arising under a covered agreement which is a Plurilateral Trade Agreement, the term "Member" as used herein shall refer only to those Members that are parties to the relevant Plurilateral Trade Agreement. Where the DSB administers the dispute settlement provisions of a Plurilateral Trade Agreement, only those Members that are parties to that Agreement may participate in decisions or actions taken by the DSB with respect to that dispute.

2. The DSB shall inform the relevant WTO Councils and Committees of any developments in disputes related to provisions of the respective covered agreements.

3. The DSB shall meet as often as necessary to carry out its functions within the time-frames provided in this Understanding.

4. Where the rules and procedures of this Understanding provide for the DSB to take a decision, it shall do so by consensus.[1]

Article 3: General Provisions

1. Members affirm their adherence to the principles for the management of disputes heretofore applied under Articles XXII and XXIII of GATT 1947, and the rules and procedures as further elaborated and modified herein.

[1] The DSB shall be deemed to have decided by consensus on a matter submitted for its consideration, if no Member, present at the meeting of the DSB when the decision is taken, formally objects to the proposed decision.

2. The dispute settlement system of the WTO is a central element in providing security and predictability to the multilateral trading system. The Members recognize that it serves to preserve the rights and obligations of Members under the covered agreements, and to clarify the existing provisions of those agreements in accordance with customary rules of interpretation of public international law. Recommendations and rulings of the DSB cannot add to or diminish the rights and obligations provided in the covered agreements.

3. The prompt settlement of situations in which a Member considers that any benefits accruing to it directly or indirectly under the covered agreements are being impaired by measures taken by another Member is essential to the effective functioning of the WTO and the maintenance of a proper balance between the rights and obligations of Members.

4. Recommendations or rulings made by the DSB shall be aimed at achieving a satisfactory settlement of the matter in accordance with the rights and obligations under this Understanding and under the covered agreements.

5. All solutions to matters formally raised under the consultation and dispute settlement provisions of the covered agreements, including arbitration awards, shall be consistent with those agreements and shall not nullify or impair benefits accruing to any Member under those agreements, nor impede the attainment of any objective of those agreements.

6. Mutually agreed solutions to matters formally raised under the consultation and dispute settlement provisions of the covered agreements shall be notified to the DSB and the relevant Councils and Committees, where any Member may raise any point relating thereto.

7. Before bringing a case, a Member shall exercise its judgement as to whether action under these procedures would be fruitful. The aim of the dispute settlement mechanism is to secure a positive solution to a dispute. A solution mutually acceptable to the parties to a dispute and consistent with the covered agreements is clearly to be preferred. In the absence of a mutually agreed solution, the first objective of the dispute settlement mechanism is usually to secure the withdrawal of the measures concerned if these are found to be inconsistent with the provisions of any of the covered agreements. The provision of compensation should be resorted to only if the immediate withdrawal of the measure is impracticable and as a temporary measure pending the withdrawal of the measure which is inconsistent with a covered agreement. The last resort which this Understanding provides to the Member invoking the dispute settlement procedures is the possibility of suspending the application of concessions or other obligations under the covered agreements on a discriminatory basis vis-à-vis the other Member, subject to authorization by the DSB of such measures.

8. In cases where there is an infringement of the obligations assumed under a covered agreement, the action is considered *prima facie* to constitute a case of nullification or impairment. This means that there is normally a presumption that a breach of the rules has an adverse impact on other Members parties to that covered agreement, and in such cases, it shall be up to the Member against whom the complaint has been brought to rebut the charge.

9. The provisions of this Understanding are without prejudice to the rights of Members to seek authoritative interpretation of provisions of a covered agreement through decision-making under the WTO Agreement or a covered agreement which is a Plurilateral Trade Agreement.

10. It is understood that requests for conciliation and the use of the dispute settlement procedures should not be intended or considered as contentious acts and that, if a dispute arises, all Members will engage in these procedures in good faith in an effort to resolve the dispute. It is also understood that complaints and counter-complaints in regard to distinct matters should not be linked.

11. This Understanding shall be applied only with respect to new requests for consultations under the consultation provisions of the covered agreements made on or after the date of entry into force of the WTO Agreement. With respect to disputes for which the request for consultations was made under GATT 1947 or under any other predecessor agreement to the covered agreements before the date of entry into force of the WTO Agreement, the relevant dispute settlement rules and procedures in effect immediately prior to the date of entry into force of the WTO Agreement shall continue to apply.[2]

12. Notwithstanding paragraph 11, if a complaint based on any of the covered agreements is brought by a developing country Member against a developed country Member, the complaining party shall have the right to invoke, as an alternative to the provisions contained in Articles 4, 5, 6 and 12 of this Understanding, the corresponding provisions of the Decision of 5 April 1966 (BISD 14S/18), except that where the Panel considers that the time-frame provided for in paragraph 7 of that Decision is insufficient to provide its report and with the agreement of the complaining party, that time-frame may be extended. To the extent that there is a difference between the rules and procedures of Articles 4, 5, 6 and 12 and the corresponding rules and procedures of the Decision, the latter shall prevail.

Article 4: Consultations

1. Members affirm their resolve to strengthen and improve the effectiveness of the consultation procedures employed by Members.

2. Each Member undertakes to accord sympathetic consideration to and afford adequate opportunity for consultation regarding any representations made by another Member concerning measures affecting the operation of any covered agreement taken within the territory of the former.[3]

3. If a request for consultations is made pursuant to a covered agreement, the Member to which the request is made shall, unless otherwise mutually agreed, reply to the request within 10 days after the date of its receipt and shall enter into consultations in good faith within a period of no more than 30 days after the date of receipt of the request, with a view to reaching a mutually satisfactory solution. If the Member does not respond within 10 days after the date of receipt of the request, or does not enter into consultations within a period of no more than 30 days, or a period otherwise mutually agreed, after the date of receipt of the request, then the Member that requested the holding of consultations may proceed directly to request the establishment of a panel.

4. All such requests for consultations shall be notified to the DSB and the relevant Councils and Committees by the Member which requests consultations. Any request for consultations shall be submitted in writing and shall give the reasons for the request, including identification of the measures at issue and an indication of the legal basis for the complaint.

5. In the course of consultations in accordance with the provisions of a covered agreement, before resorting to further action under this Understanding, Members should attempt to obtain satisfactory adjustment of the matter.

[2] This paragraph shall also be applied to disputes on which panel reports have not been adopted or fully implemented.

[3] Where the provisions of any other covered agreement concerning measures taken by regional or local governments or authorities within the territory of a Member contain provisions different from the provisions of this paragraph, the provisions of such other covered agreement shall prevail.

6. Consultations shall be confidential, and without prejudice to the rights of any Member in any further proceedings.

7. If the consultations fail to settle a dispute within 60 days after the date of receipt of the request for consultations, the complaining party may request the establishment of a panel. The complaining party may request a panel during the 60-day period if the consulting parties jointly consider that consultations have failed to settle the dispute.

8. In cases of urgency, including those which concern perishable goods, Members shall enter into consultations within a period of no more than 10 days after the date of receipt of the request. If the consultations have failed to settle the dispute within a period of 20 days after the date of receipt of the request, the complaining party may request the establishment of a panel.

9. In cases of urgency, including those which concern perishable goods, the parties to the dispute, panels and the Appellate Body shall make every effort to accelerate the proceedings to the greatest extent possible.

10. During consultations Members should give special attention to the particular problems and interests of developing country Members.

11. Whenever a Member other than the consulting Members considers that it has a substantial trade interest in consultations being held pursuant to paragraph 1 of Article XXII of GATT 1994, paragraph 1 of Article XXII of GATS, or the corresponding provisions in other covered agreements,[4] such Member may notify the consulting Members and the DSB, within 10 days after the date of the circulation of the request for consultations under said Article, of its desire to be joined in the consultations. Such Member shall be joined in the consultations, provided that the Member to which the request for consultations was addressed agrees that the claim of substantial interest is well-founded. In that event they shall so inform the DSB. If the request to be joined in the consultations is not accepted, the applicant Member shall be free to request consultations under paragraph 1 of Article XXII or paragraph 1 of Article XXIII of GATT 1994, paragraph 1 of Article XXII or paragraph 1 of Article XXIII of GATS, or the corresponding provisions in other covered agreements.

Article 5: Good Offices, Conciliation and Mediation

1. Good offices, conciliation and mediation are procedures that are undertaken voluntarily if the parties to the dispute so agree.

2. Proceedings involving good offices, conciliation and mediation, and in particular positions taken by the parties to the dispute during these proceedings, shall be confidential, and without prejudice to the rights of either party in any further proceedings under these procedures.

3. Good offices, conciliation or mediation may be requested at any time by any party to a dispute. They may begin at any time and be terminated at any time. Once procedures for good offices, conciliation or mediation are terminated, a complaining party may then proceed with a request for the establishment of a panel.

[4] The corresponding consultation provisions in the covered agreements are listed hereunder: Agreement on Agriculture, Article 19; Agreement on the Application of Sanitary and Phytosanitary Measures, paragraph 1 of Article 11; Agreement on Textiles and Clothing, paragraph 4 of Article 8; Agreement on Technical Barriers to Trade, paragraph 1 of Article 14; Agreement on Trade-Related Investment Measures, Article 8; Agreement on Implementation of Article VI of GATT 1994, paragraph 2 of Article 17; Agreement on Implementation of Article VII of GATT 1994, paragraph 2 of Article 19; Agreement on Preshipment Inspection, Article 7; Agreement on Rules of Origin, Article 7; Agreement on Import Licensing Procedures, Article 6; Agreement on Subsidies and Countervailing Measures, Article 30; Agreement on Safeguards, Article 14; Agreement on Trade-Related Aspects of Intellectual Property Rights, Article 64.1; and any corresponding consultation provisions in Plurilateral Trade Agreements as determined by the competent bodies of each Agreement and as notified to the DSB.

4. When good offices, conciliation or mediation are entered into within 60 days after the date of receipt of a request for consultations, the complaining party must allow a period of 60 days after the date of receipt of the request for consultations before requesting the establishment of a panel. The complaining party may request the establishment of a panel during the 60-day period if the parties to the dispute jointly consider that the good offices, conciliation or mediation process has failed to settle the dispute.

5. If the parties to a dispute agree, procedures for good offices, conciliation or mediation may continue while the panel process proceeds.

6. The Director-General may, acting in an *ex officio* capacity, offer good offices, conciliation or mediation with the view to assisting Members to settle a dispute.

Article 6: Establishment of Panels

1. If the complaining party so requests, a panel shall be established at the latest at the DSB meeting following that at which the request first appears as an item on the DSB's agenda, unless at that meeting the DSB decides by consensus not to establish a panel.[5]

2. The request for the establishment of a panel shall be made in writing. It shall indicate whether consultations were held, identify the specific measures at issue and provide a brief summary of the legal basis of the complaint sufficient to present the problem clearly. In case the applicant requests the establishment of a panel with other than standard terms of reference, the written request shall include the proposed text of special terms of reference.

Article 7: Terms of Reference of Panels

1. Panels shall have the following terms of reference unless the parties to the dispute agree otherwise within 20 days from the establishment of the panel:

> "To examine, in the light of the relevant provisions in (name of the covered agreement(s) cited by the parties to the dispute), the matter referred to the DSB by (name of party) in document ... and to make such findings as will assist the DSB in making the recommendations or in giving the rulings provided for in that/those agreement(s)."

2. Panels shall address the relevant provisions in any covered agreement or agreements cited by the parties to the dispute.

3. In establishing a panel, the DSB may authorize its Chairman to draw up the terms of reference of the panel in consultation with the parties to the dispute, subject to the provisions of paragraph 1. The terms of reference thus drawn up shall be circulated to all Members. If other than standard terms of reference are agreed upon, any Member may raise any point relating thereto in the DSB.

Article 8: Composition of Panels

1. Panels shall be composed of well-qualified governmental and/or non-governmental individuals, including persons who have served on or presented a case to a panel, served as a representative of a Member or of a contracting party to GATT 1947 or as a representative to the Council or Committee of any covered agreement or its predecessor agreement, or in the Secretariat, taught or published on international trade law or policy, or served as a senior trade policy official of a Member.

2. Panel members should be selected with a view to ensuring the independence of the members, a sufficiently diverse background and a wide spectrum of experience.

[5] If the complaining party so requests, a meeting of the DSB shall be convened for this purpose within 15 days of the request, provided that at least 10 days' advance notice of the meeting is given.

3. Citizens of Members whose governments[6] are parties to the dispute or third parties as defined in paragraph 2 of Article 10 shall not serve on a panel concerned with that dispute, unless the parties to the dispute agree otherwise.

4. To assist in the selection of panelists, the Secretariat shall maintain an indicative list of governmental and non-governmental individuals possessing the qualifications outlined in paragraph 1, from which panelists may be drawn as appropriate. That list shall include the roster of non-governmental panelists established on 30 November 1984 (BISD 31S/9), and other rosters and indicative lists established under any of the covered agreements, and shall retain the names of persons on those rosters and indicative lists at the time of entry into force of the WTO Agreement. Members may periodically suggest names of governmental and non-governmental individuals for inclusion on the indicative list, providing relevant information on their knowledge of international trade and of the sectors or subject matter of the covered agreements, and those names shall be added to the list upon approval by the DSB. For each of the individuals on the list, the list shall indicate specific areas of experience or expertise of the individuals in the sectors or subject matter of the covered agreements.

5. Panels shall be composed of three panelists unless the parties to the dispute agree, within 10 days from the establishment of the panel, to a panel composed of five panelists. Members shall be informed promptly of the composition of the panel.

6. The Secretariat shall propose nominations for the panel to the parties to the dispute. The parties to the dispute shall not oppose nominations except for compelling reasons.

7. If there is no agreement on the panelists within 20 days after the date of the establishment of a panel, at the request of either party, the Director-General, in consultation with the Chairman of the DSB and the Chairman of the relevant Council or Committee, shall determine the composition of the panel by appointing the panelists whom the Director-General considers most appropriate in accordance with any relevant special or additional rules or procedures of the covered agreement or covered agreements which are at issue in the dispute, after consulting with the parties to the dispute. The Chairman of the DSB shall inform the Members of the composition of the panel thus formed no later than 10 days after the date the Chairman receives such a request.

8. Members shall undertake, as a general rule, to permit their officials to serve as panelists.

9. Panelists shall serve in their individual capacities and not as government representatives, nor as representatives of any organization. Members shall therefore not give them instructions nor seek to influence them as individuals with regard to matters before a panel.

10. When a dispute is between a developing country Member and a developed country Member the panel shall, if the developing country Member so requests, include at least one panelist from a developing country Member.

11. Panelists' expenses, including travel and subsistence allowance, shall be met from the WTO budget in accordance with criteria to be adopted by the General Council, based on recommendations of the Committee on Budget, Finance and Administration.

Article 9: Procedures for Multiple Complainants

1. Where more than one Member requests the establishment of a panel related to the same matter, a single panel may be established to examine these complaints taking into account the rights of all Members concerned. A single panel should be established to examine such complaints whenever feasible.

[6] In the case where customs unions or common markets are parties to a dispute, this provision applies to citizens of all member countries of the customs unions or common markets.

2. The single panel shall organize its examination and present its findings to the DSB in such a manner that the rights which the parties to the dispute would have enjoyed had separate panels examined the complaints are in no way impaired. If one of the parties to the dispute so requests, the panel shall submit separate reports on the dispute concerned. The written submissions by each of the complainants shall be made available to the other complainants, and each complainant shall have the right to be present when any one of the other complainants presents its views to the panel.

3. If more than one panel is established to examine the complaints related to the same matter, to the greatest extent possible the same persons shall serve as panelists on each of the separate panels and the timetable for the panel process in such disputes shall be harmonized.

Article 10: Third Parties

1. The interests of the parties to a dispute and those of other Members under a covered agreement at issue in the dispute shall be fully taken into account during the panel process.

2. Any Member having a substantial interest in a matter before a panel and having notified its interest to the DSB (referred to in this Understanding as a "third party") shall have an opportunity to be heard by the panel and to make written submissions to the panel. These submissions shall also be given to the parties to the dispute and shall be reflected in the panel report.

3. Third parties shall receive the submissions of the parties to the dispute to the first meeting of the panel.

4. If a third party considers that a measure already the subject of a panel proceeding nullifies or impairs benefits accruing to it under any covered agreement, that Member may have recourse to normal dispute settlement procedures under this Understanding. Such a dispute shall be referred to the original panel wherever possible.

Article 11: Function of Panels

The function of panels is to assist the DSB in discharging its responsibilities under this Understanding and the covered agreements. Accordingly, a panel should make an objective assessment of the matter before it, including an objective assessment of the facts of the case and the applicability of and conformity with the relevant covered agreements, and make such other findings as will assist the DSB in making the recommendations or in giving the rulings provided for in the covered agreements. Panels should consult regularly with the parties to the dispute and give them adequate opportunity to develop a mutually satisfactory solution.

Article 12: Panel Procedures

1. Panels shall follow the Working Procedures in Appendix 3 unless the panel decides otherwise after consulting the parties to the dispute.

2. Panel procedures should provide sufficient flexibility so as to ensure high-quality panel reports, while not unduly delaying the panel process.

3. After consulting the parties to the dispute, the panelists shall, as soon as practicable and whenever possible within one week after the composition and terms of reference of the panel have been agreed upon, fix the timetable for the panel process, taking into account the provisions of paragraph 9 of Article 4, if relevant.

4. In determining the timetable for the panel process, the panel shall provide sufficient time for the parties to the dispute to prepare their submissions.

5. Panels should set precise deadlines for written submissions by the parties and the parties should respect those deadlines.

6. Each party to the dispute shall deposit its written submissions with the Secretariat for immediate transmission to the panel and to the other party or parties to the dispute. The complaining party shall submit its first submission in advance of the responding party's first submission unless the panel decides, in fixing the timetable referred to in paragraph 3 and after consultations with the parties to the dispute, that the parties should submit their first submissions simultaneously. When there are sequential arrangements for the deposit of first submissions, the panel shall establish a firm time-period for receipt of the responding party's submission. Any subsequent written submissions shall be submitted simultaneously.

7. Where the parties to the dispute have failed to develop a mutually satisfactory solution, the panel shall submit its findings in the form of a written report to the DSB. In such cases, the report of a panel shall set out the findings of fact, the applicability of relevant provisions and the basic rationale behind any findings and recommendations that it makes. Where a settlement of the matter among the parties to the dispute has been found, the report of the panel shall be confined to a brief description of the case and to reporting that a solution has been reached.

8. In order to make the procedures more efficient, the period in which the panel shall conduct its examination, from the date that the composition and terms of reference of the panel have been agreed upon until the date the final report is issued to the parties to the dispute, shall, as a general rule, not exceed six months. In cases of urgency, including those relating to perishable goods, the panel shall aim to issue its report to the parties to the dispute within three months.

9. When the panel considers that it cannot issue its report within six months, or within three months in cases of urgency, it shall inform the DSB in writing of the reasons for the delay together with an estimate of the period within which it will issue its report. In no case should the period from the establishment of the panel to the circulation of the report to the Members exceed nine months.

10. In the context of consultations involving a measure taken by a developing country Member, the parties may agree to extend the periods established in paragraphs 7 and 8 of Article 4. If, after the relevant period has elapsed, the consulting parties cannot agree that the consultations have concluded, the Chairman of the DSB shall decide, after consultation with the parties, whether to extend the relevant period and, if so, for how long. In addition, in examining a complaint against a developing country Member, the panel shall accord sufficient time for the developing country Member to prepare and present its argumentation. The provisions of paragraph 1 of Article 20 and paragraph 4 of Article 21 are not affected by any action pursuant to this paragraph.

11. Where one or more of the parties is a developing country Member, the panel's report shall explicitly indicate the form in which account has been taken of relevant provisions on differential and more-favourable treatment for developing country Members that form part of the covered agreements which have been raised by the developing country Member in the course of the dispute settlement procedures.

12. The panel may suspend its work at any time at the request of the complaining party for a period not to exceed 12 months. In the event of such a suspension, the time-frames set out in paragraphs 8 and 9 of this Article, paragraph 1 of Article 20, and paragraph 4

of Article 21 shall be extended by the amount of time that the work was suspended. If the work of the panel has been suspended for more than 12 months, the authority for establishment of the panel shall lapse.

Article 13: Right to Seek Information

1. Each panel shall have the right to seek information and technical advice from any individual or body which it deems appropriate. However, before a panel seeks such information or advice from any individual or body within the jurisdiction of a Member it shall inform the authorities of that Member. A Member should respond promptly and fully to any request by a panel for such information as the panel considers necessary and appropriate. Confidential information which is provided shall not be revealed without formal authorization from the individual, body, or authorities of the Member providing the information.

2. Panels may seek information from any relevant source and may consult experts to obtain their opinion on certain aspects of the matter. With respect to a factual issue concerning a scientific or other technical matter raised by a party to a dispute, a panel may request an advisory report in writing from an expert review group. Rules for the establishment of such a group and its procedures are set forth in Appendix 4.

Article 14: Confidentiality

1. Panel deliberations shall be confidential.

2. The reports of panels shall be drafted without the presence of the parties to the dispute in the light of the information provided and the statements made.

3. Opinions expressed in the panel report by individual panelists shall be anonymous.

Article 15: Interim Review Stage

1. Following the consideration of rebuttal submissions and oral arguments, the panel shall issue the descriptive (factual and argument) sections of its draft report to the parties to the dispute. Within a period of time set by the panel, the parties shall submit their comments in writing.

2. Following the expiration of the set period of time for receipt of comments from the parties to the dispute, the panel shall issue an interim report to the parties, including both the descriptive sections and the panel's findings and conclusions. Within a period of time set by the panel, a party may submit a written request for the panel to review precise aspects of the interim report prior to circulation of the final report to the Members. At the request of a party, the panel shall hold a further meeting with the parties on the issues identified in the written comments. If no comments are received from any party within the comment period, the interim report shall be considered the final panel report and circulated promptly to the Members.

3. The findings of the final panel report shall include a discussion of the arguments made at the interim review stage. The interim review stage shall be conducted within the time-period set out in paragraph 8 of Article 12.

Article 16: Adoption of Panel Reports

1. In order to provide sufficient time for the Members to consider panel reports, the reports shall not be considered for adoption by the DSB until 20 days after the date they have been circulated to the Members.

2. Members having objections to a panel report shall give written reasons to explain their objections for circulation at least 10 days prior to the DSB meeting at which the panel report will be considered.

3. The parties to a dispute shall have the right to participate fully in the consideration of the panel report by the DSB, and their views shall be fully recorded.

4. Within 60 days after the date of circulation of a panel report to the Members, the report shall be adopted at a DSB meeting[7] unless a party to the dispute formally notifies the DSB of its decision to appeal or the DSB decides by consensus not to adopt the report. If a party has notified its decision to appeal, the report by the panel shall not be considered for adoption by the DSB until after completion of the appeal. This adoption procedure is without prejudice to the right of Members to express their views on a panel report.

Article 17: Appellate Review

Standing Appellate Body

1. A standing Appellate Body shall be established by the DSB. The Appellate Body shall hear appeals from panel cases. It shall be composed of seven persons, three of whom shall serve on any one case. Persons serving on the Appellate Body shall serve in rotation. Such rotation shall be determined in the working procedures of the Appellate Body.

2. The DSB shall appoint persons to serve on the Appellate Body for a four-year term, and each person may be reappointed once. However, the terms of three of the seven persons appointed immediately after the entry into force of the WTO Agreement shall expire at the end of two years, to be determined by lot. Vacancies shall be filled as they arise. A person appointed to replace a person whose term of office has not expired shall hold office for the remainder of the predecessor's term.

3. The Appellate Body shall comprise persons of recognized authority, with demonstrated expertise in law, international trade and the subject matter of the covered agreements generally. They shall be unaffiliated with any government. The Appellate Body membership shall be broadly representative of membership in the WTO. All persons serving on the Appellate Body shall be available at all times and on short notice, and shall stay abreast of dispute settlement activities and other relevant activities of the WTO. They shall not participate in the consideration of any disputes that would create a direct or indirect conflict of interest.

4. Only parties to the dispute, not third parties, may appeal a panel report. Third parties which have notified the DSB of a substantial interest in the matter pursuant to paragraph 2 of Article 10 may make written submissions to, and be given an opportunity to be heard by, the Appellate Body.

5. As a general rule, the proceedings shall not exceed 60 days from the date a party to the dispute formally notifies its decision to appeal to the date the Appellate Body circulates its report. In fixing its timetable the Appellate Body shall take into account the provisions of paragraph 9 of Article 4, if relevant. When the Appellate Body considers that it cannot provide its report within 60 days, it shall inform the DSB in writing of the reasons for the delay together with an estimate of the period within which it will submit its report. In no case shall the proceedings exceed 90 days.

6. An appeal shall be limited to issues of law covered in the panel report and legal interpretations developed by the panel.

7. The Appellate Body shall be provided with appropriate administrative and legal support as it requires.

[7] If a meeting of the DSB is not scheduled within this period at a time that enables the requirements of paragraphs 1 and 4 of Article 16 to be met, a meeting of the DSB shall be held for this purpose.

8. The expenses of persons serving on the Appellate Body, including travel and subsistence allowance, shall be met from the WTO budget in accordance with criteria to be adopted by the General Council, based on recommendations of the Committee on Budget, Finance and Administration.

Procedures for Appellate Review

9. Working procedures shall be drawn up by the Appellate Body in consultation with the Chairman of the DSB and the Director-General, and communicated to the Members for their information.

10. The proceedings of the Appellate Body shall be confidential. The reports of the Appellate Body shall be drafted without the presence of the parties to the dispute and in the light of the information provided and the statements made.

11. Opinions expressed in the Appellate Body report by individuals serving on the Appellate Body shall be anonymous.

12. The Appellate Body shall address each of the issues raised in accordance with paragraph 6 during the appellate proceeding.

13. The Appellate Body may uphold, modify or reverse the legal findings and conclusions of the panel.

Adoption of Appellate Body Reports

14. An Appellate Body report shall be adopted by the DSB and unconditionally accepted by the parties to the dispute unless the DSB decides by consensus not to adopt the Appellate Body report within 30 days following its circulation to the Members.[8] This adoption procedure is without prejudice to the right of Members to express their views on an Appellate Body report.

Article 18: Communications with the Panel or Appellate Body

1. There shall be no *ex parte* communications with the panel or Appellate Body concerning matters under consideration by the panel or Appellate Body.

2. Written submissions to the panel or the Appellate Body shall be treated as confidential, but shall be made available to the parties to the dispute. Nothing in this Understanding shall preclude a party to a dispute from disclosing statements of its own positions to the public. Members shall treat as confidential information submitted by another Member to the panel or the Appellate Body which that Member has designated as confidential. A party to a dispute shall also, upon request of a Member, provide a non-confidential summary of the information contained in its written submissions that could be disclosed to the public.

Article 19: Panel and Appellate Body Recommendations

1. Where a panel or the Appellate Body concludes that a measure is inconsistent with a covered agreement, it shall recommend that the Member concerned[9] bring the measure into conformity with that agreement.[10] In addition to its recommendations, the panel or

[8] If a meeting of the DSB is not scheduled during this period, such a meeting of the DSB shall be held for this purpose.

[9] The "Member concerned" is the party to the dispute to which the panel or Appellate Body recommendations are directed.

[10] With respect to recommendations in cases not involving a violation of GATT 1994 or any other covered agreement, see Article 26.

Appellate Body may suggest ways in which the Member concerned could implement the recommendations.

2. In accordance with paragraph 2 of Article 3, in their findings and recommendations, the panel and Appellate Body cannot add to or diminish the rights and obligations provided in the covered agreements.

Article 20: Time-frame for DSB Decisions

Unless otherwise agreed to by the parties to the dispute, the period from the date of establishment of the panel by the DSB until the date the DSB considers the panel or appellate report for adoption shall as a general rule not exceed nine months where the panel report is not appealed or 12 months where the report is appealed. Where either the panel or the Appellate Body has acted, pursuant to paragraph 9 of Article 12 or paragraph 5 of Article 17, to extend the time for providing its report, the additional time taken shall be added to the above periods.

Article 21: Surveillance of Implementation of Recommendations and Rulings

1. Prompt compliance with recommendations or rulings of the DSB is essential in order to ensure effective resolution of disputes to the benefit of all Members.

2. Particular attention should be paid to matters affecting the interests of developing country Members with respect to measures which have been subject to dispute settlement.

3. At a DSB meeting held within 30 days[11] after the date of adoption of the panel or Appellate Body report, the Member concerned shall inform the DSB of its intentions in respect of implementation of the recommendations and rulings of the DSB. If it is impracticable to comply immediately with the recommendations and rulings, the Member concerned shall have a reasonable period of time in which to do so. The reasonable period of time shall be:

(a) the period of time proposed by the Member concerned, provided that such period is approved by the DSB; or, in the absence of such approval,

(b) a period of time mutually agreed by the parties to the dispute within 45 days after the date of adoption of the recommendations and rulings; or, in the absence of such agreement,

(c) a period of time determined through binding arbitration within 90 days after the date of adoption of the recommendations and rulings.[12] In such arbitration, a guideline for the arbitrator[13] should be that the reasonable period of time to implement panel or Appellate Body recommendations should not exceed 15 months from the date of adoption of a panel or Appellate Body report. However, that time may be shorter or longer, depending upon the particular circumstances.

4. Except where the panel or the Appellate Body has extended, pursuant to paragraph 9 of Article 12 or paragraph 5 of Article 17, the time of providing its report, the period from the date of establishment of the panel by the DSB until the date of determination of the reasonable period of time shall not exceed 15 months unless the parties to the dispute agree otherwise. Where either the panel or the Appellate Body has acted to extend the time

[11] If a meeting of the DSB is not scheduled during this period, such a meeting of the DSB shall be held for this purpose.

[12] If the parties cannot agree on an arbitrator within ten days after referring the matter to arbitration, the arbitrator shall be appointed by the Director-General within ten days, after consulting the parties.

[13] The expression "arbitrator" shall be interpreted as referring either to an individual or a group.

of providing its report, the additional time taken shall be added to the 15-month period; provided that unless the parties to the dispute agree that there are exceptional circumstances, the total time shall not exceed 18 months.

5. Where there is disagreement as to the existence or consistency with a covered agreement of measures taken to comply with the recommendations and rulings such dispute shall be decided through recourse to these dispute settlement procedures, including wherever possible resort to the original panel. The panel shall circulate its report within 90 days after the date of referral of the matter to it. When the panel considers that it cannot provide its report within this time frame, it shall inform the DSB in writing of the reasons for the delay together with an estimate of the period within which it will submit its report.

6. The DSB shall keep under surveillance the implementation of adopted recommendations or rulings. The issue of implementation of the recommendations or rulings may be raised at the DSB by any Member at any time following their adoption. Unless the DSB decides otherwise, the issue of implementation of the recommendations or rulings shall be placed on the agenda of the DSB meeting after six months following the date of establishment of the reasonable period of time pursuant to paragraph 3 and shall remain on the DSB's agenda until the issue is resolved. At least 10 days prior to each such DSB meeting, the Member concerned shall provide the DSB with a status report in writing of its progress in the implementation of the recommendations or rulings.

7. If the matter is one which has been raised by a developing country Member, the DSB shall consider what further action it might take which would be appropriate to the circumstances.

8. If the case is one brought by a developing country Member, in considering what appropriate action might be taken, the DSB shall take into account not only the trade coverage of measures complained of, but also their impact on the economy of developing country Members concerned.

Article 22: Compensation and the Suspension of Concessions

1. Compensation and the suspension of concessions or other obligations are temporary measures available in the event that the recommendations and rulings are not implemented within a reasonable period of time. However, neither compensation nor the suspension of concessions or other obligations is preferred to full implementation of a recommendation to bring a measure into conformity with the covered agreements. Compensation is voluntary and, if granted, shall be consistent with the covered agreements.

2. If the Member concerned fails to bring the measure found to be inconsistent with a covered agreement into compliance therewith or otherwise comply with the recommendations and rulings within the reasonable period of time determined pursuant to paragraph 3 of Article 21, such Member shall, if so requested, and no later than the expiry of the reasonable period of time, enter into negotiations with any party having invoked the dispute settlement procedures, with a view to developing mutually acceptable compensation. If no satisfactory compensation has been agreed within 20 days after the date of expiry of the reasonable period of time, any party having invoked the dispute settlement procedures may request authorization from the DSB to suspend the application to the Member concerned of concessions or other obligations under the covered agreements.

3. In considering what concessions or other obligations to suspend, the complaining party shall apply the following principles and procedures:

(a) the general principle is that the complaining party should first seek to suspend concessions or other obligations with respect to the same sector(s) as that in which the panel or Appellate Body has found a violation or other nullification or impairment;
(b) if that party considers that it is not practicable or effective to suspend concessions or other obligations with respect to the same sector(s), it may seek to suspend concessions or other obligations in other sectors under the same agreement;
(c) if that party considers that it is not practicable or effective to suspend concessions or other obligations with respect to other sectors under the same agreement, and that the circumstances are serious enough, it may seek to suspend concessions or other obligations under another covered agreement;
(d) in applying the above principles, that party shall take into account:
    (i) the trade in the sector or under the agreement under which the panel or Appellate Body has found a violation or other nullification or impairment, and the importance of such trade to that party;
    (ii) the broader economic elements related to the nullification or impairment and the broader economic consequences of the suspension of concessions or other obligations;
(e) if that party decides to request authorization to suspend concessions or other obligations pursuant to subparagraphs (b) or (c), it shall state the reasons therefor in its request. At the same time as the request is forwarded to the DSB, it also shall be forwarded to the relevant Councils and also, in the case of a request pursuant to subparagraph (b), the relevant sectoral bodies;
(f) for purposes of this paragraph, "sector" means:
    (i) with respect to goods, all goods;
    (ii) with respect to services, a principal sector as identified in the current "Services Sectoral Classification List" which identifies such sectors;[14]
    (iii) with respect to trade-related intellectual property rights, each of the categories of intellectual property rights covered in Section 1, or Section 2, or Section 3, or Section 4, or Section 5, or Section 6, or Section 7 of Part II, or the obligations under Part III, or Part IV of the Agreement on TRIPS;
(g) for purposes of this paragraph, "agreement" means:
    (i) with respect to goods, the agreements listed in Annex 1A of the WTO Agreement, taken as a whole as well as the Plurilateral Trade Agreements in so far as the relevant parties to the dispute are parties to these agreements;
    (ii) with respect to services, the GATS;
    (iii) with respect to intellectual property rights, the Agreement on TRIPS.

4. The level of the suspension of concessions or other obligations authorized by the DSB shall be equivalent to the level of the nullification or impairment.

5. The DSB shall not authorize suspension of concessions or other obligations if a covered agreement prohibits such suspension.

6. When the situation described in paragraph 2 occurs, the DSB, upon request, shall grant authorization to suspend concessions or other obligations within 30 days of the expiry of the reasonable period of time unless the DSB decides by consensus to reject the request. However, if the Member concerned objects to the level of suspension proposed, or claims that the principles and procedures set forth in paragraph 3 have not been followed

[14] The list in document MTN.GNS/W/120 identifies eleven sectors.

where a complaining party has requested authorization to suspend concessions or other obligations pursuant to paragraph 3(b) or (c), the matter shall be referred to arbitration. Such arbitration shall be carried out by the original panel, if members are available, or by an arbitrator[15] appointed by the Director-General and shall be completed within 60 days after the date of expiry of the reasonable period of time. Concessions or other obligations shall not be suspended during the course of the arbitration.

7. The arbitrator[16] acting pursuant to paragraph 6 shall not examine the nature of the concessions or other obligations to be suspended but shall determine whether the level of such suspension is equivalent to the level of nullification or impairment. The arbitrator may also determine if the proposed suspension of concessions or other obligations is allowed under the covered agreement. However, if the matter referred to arbitration includes a claim that the principles and procedures set forth in paragraph 3 have not been followed, the arbitrator shall examine that claim. In the event the arbitrator determines that those principles and procedures have not been followed, the complaining party shall apply them consistent with paragraph 3. The parties shall accept the arbitrator's decision as final and the parties concerned shall not seek a second arbitration. The DSB shall be informed promptly of the decision of the arbitrator and shall upon request, grant authorization to suspend concessions or other obligations where the request is consistent with the decision of the arbitrator, unless the DSB decides by consensus to reject the request.

8. The suspension of concessions or other obligations shall be temporary and shall only be applied until such time as the measure found to be inconsistent with a covered agreement has been removed, or the Member that must implement recommendations or rulings provides a solution to the nullification or impairment of benefits, or a mutually satisfactory solution is reached. In accordance with paragraph 6 of Article 21, the DSB shall continue to keep under surveillance the implementation of adopted recommendations or rulings, including those cases where compensation has been provided or concessions or other obligations have been suspended but the recommendations to bring a measure into conformity with the covered agreements have not been implemented.

9. The dispute settlement provisions of the covered agreements may be invoked in respect of measures affecting their observance taken by regional or local governments or authorities within the territory of a Member. When the DSB has ruled that a provision of a covered agreement has not been observed, the responsible Member shall take such reasonable measures as may be available to it to ensure its observance. The provisions of the covered agreements and this Understanding relating to compensation and suspension of concessions or other obligations apply in cases where it has not been possible to secure such observance.[17]

Article 23: Strengthening of the Multilateral System

1. When Members seek the redress of a violation of obligations or other nullification or impairment of benefits under the covered agreements or an impediment to the attainment of any objective of the covered agreements, they shall have recourse to, and abide by, the rules and procedures of this Understanding.

[15] The expression "arbitrator" shall be interpreted as referring either to an individual or a group.

[16] The expression "arbitrator" shall be interpreted as referring either to an individual or a group or to the members of the original panel when serving in the capacity of arbitrator.

[17] Where the provisions of any covered agreement concerning measures taken by regional or local governments or authorities within the territory of a Member contain provisions different from the provisions of this paragraph, the provisions of such covered agreement shall prevail.

2. In such cases, Members shall:

(a) not make a determination to the effect that a violation has occurred, that benefits have been nullified or impaired or that the attainment of any objective of the covered agreements has been impeded, except through recourse to dispute settlement in accordance with the rules and procedures of this Understanding, and shall make any such determination consistent with the findings contained in the panel or Appellate Body report adopted by the DSB or an arbitration award rendered under this Understanding;

(b) follow the procedures set forth in Article 21 to determine the reasonable period of time for the Member concerned to implement the recommendations and rulings; and

(c) follow the procedures set forth in Article 22 to determine the level of suspension of concessions or other obligations and obtain DSB authorization in accordance with those procedures before suspending concessions or other obligations under the covered agreements in response to the failure of the Member concerned to implement the recommendations and rulings within that reasonable period of time.

Article 24: Special Procedures Involving Least-Developed Country Members

1. At all stages of the determination of the causes of a dispute and of dispute settlement procedures involving a least-developed country Member, particular consideration shall be given to the special situation of least-developed country Members. In this regard, Members shall exercise due restraint in raising matters under these procedures involving a least-developed country Member. If nullification or impairment is found to result from a measure taken by a least-developed country Member, complaining parties shall exercise due restraint in asking for compensation or seeking authorization to suspend the application of concessions or other obligations pursuant to these procedures.

2. In dispute settlement cases involving a least-developed country Member, where a satisfactory solution has not been found in the course of consultations the Director-General or the Chairman of the DSB shall, upon request by a least-developed country Member offer their good offices, conciliation and mediation with a view to assisting the parties to settle the dispute, before a request for a panel is made. The Director-General or the Chairman of the DSB, in providing the above assistance, may consult any source which either deems appropriate.

Article 25: Arbitration

1. Expeditious arbitration within the WTO as an alternative means of dispute settlement can facilitate the solution of certain disputes that concern issues that are clearly defined by both parties.

2. Except as otherwise provided in this Understanding, resort to arbitration shall be subject to mutual agreement of the parties which shall agree on the procedures to be followed. Agreements to resort to arbitration shall be notified to all Members sufficiently in advance of the actual commencement of the arbitration process.

3. Other Members may become party to an arbitration proceeding only upon the agreement of the parties which have agreed to have recourse to arbitration. The parties to the proceeding shall agree to abide by the arbitration award. Arbitration awards shall be notified to the DSB and the Council or Committee of any relevant agreement where any Member may raise any point relating thereto.

4. Articles 21 and 22 of this Understanding shall apply *mutatis mutandis* to arbitration awards.

Article 26

1. Non-Violation Complaints of the Type Described in Paragraph 1(b) of Article XXIII of GATT 1994

Where the provisions of paragraph 1(b) of Article XXIII of GATT 1994 are applicable to a covered agreement, a panel or the Appellate Body may only make rulings and recommendations where a party to the dispute considers that any benefit accruing to it directly or indirectly under the relevant covered agreement is being nullified or impaired or the attainment of any objective of that Agreement is being impeded as a result of the application by a Member of any measure, whether or not it conflicts with the provisions of that Agreement. Where and to the extent that such party considers and a panel or the Appellate Body determines that a case concerns a measure that does not conflict with the provisions of a covered agreement to which the provisions of paragraph 1(b) of Article XXIII of GATT 1994 are applicable, the procedures in this Understanding shall apply, subject to the following:

(a) the complaining party shall present a detailed justification in support of any complaint relating to a measure which does not conflict with the relevant covered agreement;

(b) where a measure has been found to nullify or impair benefits under, or impede the attainment of objectives, of the relevant covered agreement without violation thereof, there is no obligation to withdraw the measure. However, in such cases, the panel or the Appellate Body shall recommend that the Member concerned make a mutually satisfactory adjustment;

(c) notwithstanding the provisions of Article 21, the arbitration provided for in paragraph 3 of Article 21, upon request of either party, may include a determination of the level of benefits which have been nullified or impaired, and may also suggest ways and means of reaching a mutually satisfactory adjustment; such suggestions shall not be binding upon the parties to the dispute;

(d) notwithstanding the provisions of paragraph 1 of Article 22, compensation may be part of a mutually satisfactory adjustment as final settlement of the dispute.

2. Complaints of the Type Described in Paragraph 1(c) of Article XXIII of GATT 1994

Where the provisions of paragraph 1(c) of Article XXIII of GATT 1994 are applicable to a covered agreement, a panel may only make rulings and recommendations where a party considers that any benefit accruing to it directly or indirectly under the relevant covered agreement is being nullified or impaired or the attainment of any objective of that Agreement is being impeded as a result of the existence of any situation other than those to which the provisions of paragraphs 1(a) and 1(b) of Article XXIII of GATT 1994 are applicable. Where and to the extent that such party considers and a panel determines that the matter is covered by this paragraph, the procedures of this Understanding shall apply only up to and including the point in the proceedings where the panel report has been circulated to the Members. The dispute settlement rules and procedures contained in the Decision of 12 April 1989 (BISD 36S/61-67) shall apply to consideration for adoption, and surveillance and implementation of recommendations and rulings. The following shall also apply:

(a) the complaining party shall present a detailed justification in support of any argument made with respect to issues covered under this paragraph;
(b) in cases involving matters covered by this paragraph, if a panel finds that cases also involve dispute settlement matters other than those covered by this paragraph, the panel shall circulate a report to the DSB addressing any such matters and a separate report on matters falling under this paragraph.

Article 27: Responsibilities of the Secretariat

1. The Secretariat shall have the responsibility of assisting panels, especially on the legal, historical and procedural aspects of the matters dealt with, and of providing secretarial and technical support.

2. While the Secretariat assists Members in respect of dispute settlement at their request, there may also be a need to provide additional legal advice and assistance in respect of dispute settlement to developing country Members. To this end, the Secretariat shall make available a qualified legal expert from the WTO technical cooperation services to any developing country Member which so requests. This expert shall assist the developing country Member in a manner ensuring the continued impartiality of the Secretariat.

3. The Secretariat shall conduct special training courses for interested Members concerning these dispute settlement procedures and practices so as to enable Members' experts to be better informed in this regard.

APPENDIX 1: AGREEMENTS COVERED BY THE UNDERSTANDING

(A) Agreement Establishing the World Trade Organization
(B) Multilateral Trade Agreements
Annex 1A: Multilateral Agreements on Trade in Goods
Annex 1B: General Agreement on Trade in Services
Annex 1C: Agreement on Trade-Related Aspects of Intellectual Property Rights
Annex 2: Understanding on Rules and Procedures Governing the Settlement of Disputes
(C) Plurilateral Trade Agreements
Annex 4: Agreement on Trade in Civil Aircraft
Agreement on Government Procurement
International Dairy Agreement
International Bovine Meat Agreement

The applicability of this Understanding to the Plurilateral Trade Agreements shall be subject to the adoption of a decision by the parties to each agreement setting out the terms for the application of the Understanding to the individual agreement, including any special or additional rules or procedures for inclusion in Appendix 2, as notified to the DSB.

APPENDIX 2: SPECIAL OR ADDITIONAL RULES AND PROCEDURES CONTAINED IN THE COVERED AGREEMENTS

[not included]

APPENDIX 3: WORKING PROCEDURES

1. In its proceedings the panel shall follow the relevant provisions of this Understanding. In addition, the following working procedures shall apply.

2. The panel shall meet in closed session. The parties to the dispute, and interested parties, shall be present at the meetings only when invited by the panel to appear before it.

3. The deliberations of the panel and the documents submitted to it shall be kept confidential. Nothing in this Understanding shall preclude a party to a dispute from disclosing statements of its own positions to the public. Members shall treat as confidential information submitted by another Member to the panel which that Member has designated as confidential. Where a party to a dispute submits a confidential version of its written submissions to the panel, it shall also, upon request of a Member, provide a non-confidential summary of the information contained in its submissions that could be disclosed to the public.

4. Before the first substantive meeting of the panel with the parties, the parties to the dispute shall transmit to the panel written submissions in which they present the facts of the case and their arguments.

5. At its first substantive meeting with the parties, the panel shall ask the party which has brought the complaint to present its case. Subsequently, and still at the same meeting, the party against which the complaint has been brought shall be asked to present its point of view.

6. All third parties which have notified their interest in the dispute to the DSB shall be invited in writing to present their views during a session of the first substantive meeting of the panel set aside for that purpose. All such third parties may be present during the entirety of this session.

7. Formal rebuttals shall be made at a second substantive meeting of the panel. The party complained against shall have the right to take the floor first to be followed by the complaining party. The parties shall submit, prior to that meeting, written rebuttals to the panel.

8. The panel may at any time put questions to the parties and ask them for explanations either in the course of a meeting with the parties or in writing.

9. The parties to the dispute and any third party invited to present its views in accordance with Article 10 shall make available to the panel a written version of their oral statements.

10. In the interest of full transparency, the presentations, rebuttals and statements referred to in paragraphs 5 to 9 shall be made in the presence of the parties. Moreover, each party's written submissions, including any comments on the descriptive part of the report and responses to questions put by the panel, shall be made available to the other party or parties.

11. Any additional procedures specific to the panel.

12. Proposed timetable for panel work:

(a)	Receipt of first written submissions of the parties:		
	(1) complaining Party:	_____	3-6 weeks
	(2) Party complained against:	_____	2-3 weeks
(b)	Date, time and place of first substantive meeting with the parties; third party session:	_____	1-2 weeks
(c)	Receipt of written rebuttals of the parties:	_____	2-3 weeks
(d)	Date, time and place of second substantive meeting with the parties:	_____	1-2 weeks
(e)	Issuance of descriptive part of the report to the parties:	_____	2-4 weeks
(f)	Receipt of comments by the parties on the descriptive part of the report:	_____	2 weeks
(g)	Issuance of the interim report, including the		

	findings and conclusions, to the parties:	_____	2-4 weeks
(h)	Deadline for party to request review of part(s) of report:	_____	1 week
(i)	Period of review by panel, including possible additional meeting with parties:	_____	2 weeks
(j)	Issuance of final report to parties to dispute:	_____	2 weeks
(k)	Circulation of the final report to the Members:	_____	3 weeks

The above calendar may be changed in the light of unforeseen developments. Additional meetings with the parties shall be scheduled if required.

APPENDIX 4: EXPERT REVIEW GROUPS
[not included]

36.c Working Procedures for Appellate Review

Date: 16 August 2010
Source: Doc WT/AB/WP/6
http://www.wto.org/english/tratop_e/dispu_e/ab_e.htm

Definitions

1. In these *Working Procedures for Appellate Review*,

"appellant" means any party to the dispute that has filed a Notice of Appeal pursuant to Rule 20;

"appellate report" means an Appellate Body report as described in Article 17 of the DSU;

"appellee" means any party to the dispute that has filed a submission pursuant to Rule 22 or paragraph 4 of Rule 23;

"consensus" a decision is deemed to be made by consensus if no Member formally objects to it;

"covered agreements" has the same meaning as "covered agreements" in paragraph 1 of Article 1 of the DSU;

"division" means the three Members who are selected to serve on any one appeal in accordance with paragraph 1 of Article 17 of the DSU and paragraph 2 of Rule 6;

"documents" means the Notice of Appeal, any Notice of Other Appeal and the submissions and other written statements presented by the participants or third participants;

"DSB" means the Dispute Settlement Body established under Article 2 of the DSU;

"DSU" means the *Understanding on Rules and Procedures Governing the Settlement of Disputes* which is Annex 2 to the *WTO Agreement*;

"Member" means a Member of the Appellate Body who has been appointed by the DSB in accordance with Article 17 of the DSU;

"other appellant" means any party to the dispute that has filed a Notice of Other Appeal pursuant to paragraph 1 of Rule 23;

"participant" means any party to the dispute that has filed a Notice of Appeal pursuant to Rule 20, a Notice of Other Appeal pursuant to Rule 23 or a submission pursuant to Rule 22 or paragraph 4 of Rule 23;

"party to the dispute" means any WTO Member who was a complaining or defending party in the panel dispute, but does not include a third party;

"proof of service" means a letter or other written acknowledgement that a document has been delivered, as required, to the parties to the dispute, participants, third parties or third participants, as the case may be;

"Rules" means these *Working Procedures for Appellate Review;*

"*Rules of Conduct*" means the *Rules of Conduct for the Understanding on Rules and Procedures Governing the Settlement of Disputes* as attached in Annex II to these Rules;

"*SCM Agreement*" means the *Agreement on Subsidies and Countervailing Measures* which is in Annex 1A to the *WTO Agreement;*

"Secretariat" means the Appellate Body Secretariat;

"service address" means the address of the party to the dispute, participant, third party or third participant as generally used in WTO dispute settlement proceedings, unless the party to the dispute, participant, third party or third participant has clearly indicated another address;

"third participant" means any third party that has filed a written submission pursuant to Rule 24(1); or any third party that appears at the oral hearing, whether or not it makes an oral statement at that hearing;

"third party" means any WTO Member who has notified the DSB of its substantial interest in the matter before the panel pursuant to paragraph 2 of Article 10 of the DSU;

"WTO" means the World Trade Organization;

"*WTO Agreement*" means the *Marrakesh Agreement Establishing the World Trade Organization*, done at Marrakesh, Morocco on 15 April 1994;

"WTO Member" means any State or separate customs territory possessing full autonomy in the conduct of its external commercial relations that has accepted or acceded to the WTO in accordance with Articles XI, XII or XIV of the *WTO Agreement;* and

"WTO Secretariat" means the Secretariat of the World Trade Organization.

PART I – MEMBERS

Duties and Responsibilities

2. (1) A Member shall abide by the terms and conditions of the DSU, these Rules and any decisions of the DSB affecting the Appellate Body.

(2) During his/her term, a Member shall not accept any employment nor pursue any professional activity that is inconsistent with his/her duties and responsibilities.

(3) A Member shall exercise his/her office without accepting or seeking instructions from any international, governmental, or non-governmental organization or any private source.

(4) A Member shall be available at all times and on short notice and, to this end, shall keep the Secretariat informed of his/her whereabouts at all times.

Decision-Making

3. (1) In accordance with paragraph 1 of Article 17 of the DSU, decisions relating to an appeal shall be taken solely by the division assigned to that appeal. Other decisions shall be taken by the Appellate Body as a whole.

(2) The Appellate Body and its divisions shall make every effort to take their decisions by consensus. Where, nevertheless, a decision cannot be arrived at by consensus, the matter at issue shall be decided by a majority vote.

Collegiality

4. (1) To ensure consistency and coherence in decision-making, and to draw on the individual and collective expertise of the Members, the Members shall convene on a regular basis to discuss matters of policy, practice and procedure.

(2) The Members shall stay abreast of dispute settlement activities and other relevant activities of the WTO and, in particular, each Member shall receive all documents filed in an appeal.

(3) In accordance with the objectives set out in paragraph 1, the division responsible for deciding each appeal shall exchange views with the other Members before the division finalizes the appellate report for circulation to the WTO Members. This paragraph is subject to paragraphs 2 and 3 of Rule 11.

(4) Nothing in these Rules shall be interpreted as interfering with a division's full authority and freedom to hear and decide an appeal assigned to it in accordance with paragraph 1 of Article 17 of the DSU.

Chairman

5. (1) There shall be a Chairman of the Appellate Body who shall be elected by the Members.

(2) The term of office of the Chairman of the Appellate Body shall be one year. The Appellate Body Members may decide to extend the term of office for an additional period of up to one year. However, in order to ensure rotation of the Chairmanship, no Member shall serve as Chairman for more than two consecutive terms.

(3) The Chairman shall be responsible for the overall direction of the Appellate Body business, and in particular, his/her responsibilities shall include:

(a) the supervision of the internal functioning of the Appellate Body; and

(b) any such other duties as the Members may agree to entrust to him/her.

(4) Where the office of the Chairman becomes vacant due to permanent incapacity as a result of illness or death or by resignation or expiration of his/her term, the Members shall elect a new Chairman who shall serve a full term in accordance with paragraph 2.

(5) In the event of a temporary absence or incapacity of the Chairman, the Appellate Body shall authorize another Member to act as Chairman *ad interim*, and the Member so authorized shall temporarily exercise all the powers, duties and functions of the Chairman until the Chairman is capable of resuming his/her functions.

Divisions

6. (1) In accordance with paragraph 1 of Article 17 of the DSU, a division consisting of three Members shall be established to hear and decide an appeal.

(2) The Members constituting a division shall be selected on the basis of rotation, while taking into account the principles of random selection, unpredictability and opportunity for all Members to serve regardless of their national origin.

(3) A Member selected pursuant to paragraph 2 to serve on a division shall serve on that division, unless:

(a) he/she is excused from that division pursuant to Rule 9 or 10;

(b) he/she has notified the Chairman and the Presiding Member that he/she is prevented from serving on the division because of illness or other serious reasons pursuant to Rule 12; or

(c) he/she has notified his/her intentions to resign pursuant to Rule 14.

Presiding Member of the Division

7. (1) Each division shall have a Presiding Member, who shall be elected by the Members of that division.

(2) The responsibilities of the Presiding Member shall include:

(a) coordinating the overall conduct of the appeal proceeding;

(b) chairing all oral hearings and meetings related to that appeal; and

(c) coordinating the drafting of the appellate report.

(3) In the event that a Presiding Member becomes incapable of performing his/her duties, the other Members serving on that division and the Member selected as a replacement pursuant to Rule 13 shall elect one of their number to act as the Presiding Member.

Rules of Conduct

8. (1) On a provisional basis, the Appellate Body adopts those provisions of the *Rules of Conduct for the Understanding on Rules and Procedures Governing the Settlement of Disputes*, attached in Annex II to these Rules, which are applicable to it, until *Rules of Conduct* are approved by the DSB.

(2) Upon approval of *Rules of Conduct* by the DSB, such *Rules of Conduct* shall be directly incorporated and become part of these Rules and shall supersede Annex II.

9. (1) Upon the filing of a Notice of Appeal, each Member shall take the steps set out in Article VI:4(b)(i) of Annex II, and a Member may consult with the other Members prior to completing the disclosure form.

(2) Upon the filing of a Notice of Appeal, the professional staff of the Secretariat assigned to that appeal shall take the steps set out in Article VI:4(b)(ii) of Annex II.

(3) Where information has been submitted pursuant to Article VI:4(b)(i) or (ii) of Annex II, the Appellate Body shall consider whether further action is necessary.

(4) As a result of the Appellate Body's consideration of the matter pursuant to paragraph 3, the Member or the professional staff member concerned may continue to be assigned to the division or may be excused from the division.

10. (1) Where evidence of a material violation is filed by a participant pursuant to Article VIII of Annex II, such evidence shall be confidential and shall be supported by affidavits made by persons having actual knowledge or a reasonable belief as to the truth of the facts stated.

(2) Any evidence filed pursuant to Article VIII:1 of Annex II shall be filed at the earliest practicable time: that is, forthwith after the participant submitting it knew or reasonably could have known of the facts supporting it. In no case shall such evidence be filed after the appellate report is circulated to the WTO Members.

(3) Where a participant fails to submit such evidence at the earliest practicable time, it shall file an explanation in writing of the reasons why it did not do so earlier, and the Appellate Body may decide to consider or not to consider such evidence, as appropriate.

(4) While taking fully into account paragraph 5 of Article 17 of the DSU, where evidence has been filed pursuant to Article VIII of Annex II, an appeal shall be suspended for fifteen days or until the procedure referred to in Article VIII:14-16 of Annex II is completed, whichever is earlier.

(5) As a result of the procedure referred to in Article VIII:14-16 of Annex II, the Appellate Body may decide to dismiss the allegation, to excuse the Member or professional staff member concerned from being assigned to the division or make such other order as it deems necessary in accordance with Article VIII of Annex II.

11. (1) A Member who has submitted a disclosure form with information attached pursuant to Article VI:4(b)(i) or is the subject of evidence of a material violation pursuant to Article VIII:1 of Annex II, shall not participate in any decision taken pursuant to paragraph 4 of Rule 9 or paragraph 5 of Rule 10.

(2) A Member who is excused from a division pursuant to paragraph 4 of Rule 9 or paragraph 5 of Rule 10 shall not take part in the exchange of views conducted in that appeal pursuant to paragraph 3 of Rule 4.

(3) A Member who, had he/she been a Member of a division, would have been excused from that division pursuant to paragraph 4 of Rule 9, shall not take part in the exchange of views conducted in that appeal pursuant to paragraph 3 of Rule 4.

Incapacity

12. (1) A Member who is prevented from serving on a division by illness or for other serious reasons shall give notice and duly explain such reasons to the Chairman and to the Presiding Member.

(2) Upon receiving such notice, the Chairman and the Presiding Member shall forthwith inform the Appellate Body.

Replacement

13. Where a Member is unable to serve on a division for a reason set out in paragraph 3 of Rule 6, another Member shall be selected forthwith pursuant to paragraph 2 of Rule 6 to replace the Member originally selected for that division.

Resignation

14. (1) A Member who intends to resign from his/her office shall notify his/her intentions in writing to the Chairman of the Appellate Body who shall immediately inform the Chairman of the DSB, the Director-General and the other Members of the Appellate Body.

(2) The resignation shall take effect 90 days after the notification has been made pursuant to paragraph 1, unless the DSB, in consultation with the Appellate Body, decides otherwise.

Transition

15. A person who ceases to be a Member of the Appellate Body may, with the authorization of the Appellate Body and upon notification to the DSB, complete the disposition of any appeal to which that person was assigned while a Member, and that person shall, for that purpose only, be deemed to continue to be a Member of the Appellate Body.

PART II – PROCESS

General Provisions

16. (1) In the interests of fairness and orderly procedure in the conduct of an appeal, where a procedural question arises that is not covered by these Rules, a division may adopt an appropriate procedure for the purposes of that appeal only, provided that it is not inconsistent with the DSU, the other covered agreements and these Rules. Where such a procedure is adopted, the division shall immediately notify the parties to the dispute, participants, third parties and third participants as well as the other Members of the Appellate Body.

(2) In exceptional circumstances, where strict adherence to a time-period set out in these Rules would result in a manifest unfairness, a party to the dispute, a participant, a third

party or a third participant may request that a division modify a time-period set out in these Rules for the filing of documents or the date set out in the working schedule for the oral hearing. Where such a request is granted by a division, any modification of time shall be notified to the parties to the dispute, participants, third parties and third participants in a revised working schedule.

17. (1) Unless the DSB decides otherwise, in computing any time-period stipulated in the DSU or in the special or additional provisions of the covered agreements, or in these Rules, within which a communication must be made or an action taken by a WTO Member to exercise or preserve its rights, the day from which the time-period begins to run shall be excluded and, subject to paragraph 2, the last day of the time-period shall be included.

(2) The DSB Decision on "Expiration of Time-Periods in the DSU", WT/DSB/M/7, shall apply to appeals heard by divisions of the Appellate Body.

Documents

18. (1) No document is considered filed with the Appellate Body unless the document is received by the Secretariat within the time-period set out for filing in accordance with these Rules.

Official versions of documents shall be submitted in paper form to the Appellate Body Secretariat by 17:00 Geneva time on the day that the document is due. Participants, parties, third participants and third parties shall, by the same deadline, also provide to the Appellate Body Secretariat an electronic copy of each document. Such electronic copy may be sent via electronic mail to the Appellate Body Secretariat's electronic mail address, or brought to the Appellate Body Secretariat on a data storage device such as a CD-ROM or USB flash drive.

(2) Except as otherwise provided in these Rules, every document filed by a party to the dispute, a participant, a third party or a third participant shall on the same day be served on each of the other parties to the dispute, participants, third parties and third participants in the appeal, in accordance with paragraph 4.

(3) A proof of service on the other parties to the dispute, participants, third parties and third participants shall appear on, or be affixed to, each document filed with the Secretariat under paragraph 1 above.

(4) A document shall be served by the most expeditious means of delivery or communication available, including by:

(a) delivering a copy of the document to the service address of the party to the dispute, participant, third party or third participant; or

(b) sending a copy of the document to the service address of the party to the dispute, participant, third party or third participant by facsimile transmission, expedited delivery courier or expedited mail service.

Electronic copies of documents served shall also be provided on the same day, either by electronic mail, or through physical delivery of a data storage device containing an electronic copy of the document.

(5) Upon authorization by the division, a participant or a third participant may correct clerical errors in any of its documents (including typographical mistakes, errors of grammar, or words or numbers placed in the wrong order). The request to correct clerical errors shall identify the specific errors to be corrected and shall be filed with the Secretariat no later than 30 days after the date of the filing of the Notice of Appeal. A copy of the request shall be served upon the other parties to the dispute, participants, third parties and

third participants, each of whom shall be given an opportunity to comment in writing on the request. The division shall notify the parties to the dispute, participants, third parties and third participants of its decision.

Ex Parte Communications

19. (1) Neither a division nor any of its Members shall meet with or contact one party to the dispute, participant, third party or third participant in the absence of the other parties to the dispute, participants, third parties and third participants.

(2) No Member of the division may discuss any aspect of the subject matter of an appeal with any party to the dispute, participant, third party or third participant in the absence of the other Members of the division.

(3) A Member who is not assigned to the division hearing the appeal shall not discuss any aspect of the subject matter of the appeal with any party to the dispute, participant, third party or third participant.

Commencement of Appeal

20. (1) An appeal shall be commenced by notification in writing to the DSB in accordance with paragraph 4 of Article 16 of the DSU and simultaneous filing of a Notice of Appeal with the Secretariat.

(2) A Notice of Appeal shall include the following information:

- (a) the title of the panel report under appeal;
- (b) the name of the party to the dispute filing the Notice of Appeal;
- (c) the service address, telephone and facsimile numbers of the party to the dispute; and
- (d) a brief statement of the nature of the appeal, including:
  - (i) identification of the alleged errors in the issues of law covered in the panel report and legal interpretations developed by the panel;
  - (ii) a list of the legal provision(s) of the covered agreements that the panel is alleged to have erred in interpreting or applying; and
  - (iii) without prejudice to the ability of the appellant to refer to other paragraphs of the panel report in the context of its appeal, an indicative list of the paragraphs of the panel report containing the alleged errors.

Appellant's Submission

21. (1) The appellant shall, on the same day as the date of the filing of the Notice of Appeal, file with the Secretariat a written submission prepared in accordance with paragraph 2 and serve a copy of the submission on the other parties to the dispute and third parties.

(2) A written submission referred to in paragraph 1 shall:

- (a) be dated and signed by the appellant; and
- (b) set out:
  - (i) a precise statement of the grounds for the appeal, including the specific allegations of errors in the issues of law covered in the panel report and legal interpretations developed by the panel, and the legal arguments in support thereof;
  - (ii) a precise statement of the provisions of the covered agreements and other legal sources relied on; and
  - (iii) the nature of the decision or ruling sought.

Appellee's Submission

22. (1) Any party to the dispute that wishes to respond to allegations raised in an appellant's submission filed pursuant to Rule 21 may, within 18 days after the date of the filing of the Notice of Appeal, file with the Secretariat a written submission prepared in accordance with paragraph 2 and serve a copy of the submission on the appellant, other parties to the dispute and third parties.

(2) A written submission referred to in paragraph 1 shall:

(a) be dated and signed by the appellee; and

(b) set out:

(i) a precise statement of the grounds for opposing the specific allegations of errors in the issues of law covered in the panel report and legal interpretations developed by the panel raised in the appellant's submission, and the legal arguments in support thereof;

(ii) an acceptance of, or opposition to, each ground set out in the appellant's submission;

(iii) a precise statement of the provisions of the covered agreements and other legal sources relied on; and

(iv) the nature of the decision or ruling sought.

Multiple Appeals

23. (1) Within 5 days after the date of the filing of the Notice of Appeal, a party to the dispute other than the original appellant may join in that appeal or appeal on the basis of other alleged errors in the issues of law covered in the panel report and legal interpretations developed by the panel. That party shall notify the DSB in writing of its appeal and shall simultaneously file a Notice of Other Appeal with the Secretariat.

(2) A Notice of Other Appeal shall include the following information:

(a) the title of the panel report under appeal;

(b) the name of the party to the dispute filing the Notice of Other Appeal;

(c) the service address, telephone and facsimile numbers of the party to the dispute; and either

(i) a statement of the issues raised on appeal by another participant with which the party joins; or

(ii) a brief statement of the nature of the other appeal, including:

(A) identification of the alleged errors in the issues of law covered in the panel report and legal interpretations developed by the panel;

(B) a list of the legal provision(s) of the covered agreements that the panel is alleged to have erred in interpreting or applying; and

(C) without prejudice to the ability of the other appellant to refer to other paragraphs of the panel report in the context of its appeal, an indicative list of the paragraphs of the panel report containing the alleged errors.

(3) The other appellant shall, within 5 days after the date of the filing of the Notice of Appeal, file with the Secretariat a written submission prepared in accordance with paragraph 2 of Rule 21 and serve a copy of the submission on the other parties to the dispute and third parties.

(4) The appellant, any appellee and any other party to the dispute that wishes to respond to a submission filed pursuant to paragraph 3 may file a written submission within 18 days

after the date of the filing of the Notice of Appeal, and any such submission shall be in the format required by paragraph 2 of Rule 22.

(5) This Rule does not preclude a party to the dispute which has not filed a submission under Rule 21 or a Notice of Other Appeal under paragraph 1 of this Rule from exercising its right of appeal pursuant to paragraph 4 of Article 16 of the DSU.

(6) Where a party to the dispute which has not filed a submission under Rule 21 or a Notice of Other Appeal under paragraph 1 of this Rule exercises its right to appeal as set out in paragraph 5, a single division shall examine the appeals.

Amending Notices of Appeal

23*bis*. (1) The division may authorize an original appellant to amend a Notice of Appeal or an other appellant to amend a Notice of Other Appeal.

(2) A request to amend a Notice of Appeal or a Notice of Other Appeal shall be made as soon as possible in writing and shall state the reason(s) for the request and identify precisely the specific amendments that the appellant or other appellant wishes to make to the Notice. A copy of the request shall be served on the other parties to the dispute, participants, third participants and third parties, each of whom shall be given an opportunity to comment in writing on the request.

(3) In deciding whether to authorize, in full or in part, a request to amend a Notice of Appeal or Notice of Other Appeal, the division shall take into account:

(a) the requirement to circulate the appellate report within the time-period set out in Article 17.5 of the DSU or, as appropriate, Article 4.9 of the *SCM Agreement*; and,

(b) the interests of fairness and orderly procedure, including the nature and extent of the proposed amendment, the timing of the request to amend a Notice of Appeal or Notice of Other Appeal, any reasons why the proposed amended Notice of Appeal or Notice of Other Appeal was not or could not have been filed on its original date, and any other considerations that may be appropriate.

(4) The division shall notify the parties to the dispute, participants, third participants, and third parties of its decision. In the event that the division authorizes an amendment to a Notice of Appeal or a Notice of Other Appeal, it shall provide an amended copy of the Notice to the DSB.

Third Participants

24. (1) Any third party may file a written submission containing the grounds and legal arguments in support of its position. Such submission shall be filed within 21 days after the date of the filing of the Notice of Appeal.

(2) A third party not filing a written submission shall, within the same period of 21 days, notify the Secretariat in writing if it intends to appear at the oral hearing, and, if so, whether it intends to make an oral statement.

(3) Third participants are encouraged to file written submissions to facilitate their positions being taken fully into account by the division hearing the appeal and in order that participants and other third participants will have notice of positions to be taken at the oral hearing.

(4) Any third party that has neither filed a written submission pursuant to paragraph 1, nor notified the Secretariat pursuant to paragraph 2, may notify the Secretariat that it intends to appear at the oral hearing, and may request to make an oral statement at the

hearing. Such notifications and requests should be notified to the Secretariat in writing at the earliest opportunity.

Transmittal of Record

25. (1) Upon the filing of a Notice of Appeal, the Director-General of the WTO shall transmit forthwith to the Appellate Body the complete record of the panel proceeding.

(2) The complete record of the panel proceeding includes, but is not limited to:

(a) written submissions, rebuttal submissions, and supporting evidence attached thereto by the parties to the dispute and the third parties;

(b) written arguments submitted at the panel meetings with the parties to the dispute and the third parties, the recordings of such panel meetings, and any written answers to questions posed at such panel meetings;

(c) the correspondence relating to the panel dispute between the panel or the WTO Secretariat and the parties to the dispute or the third parties; and

(d) any other documentation submitted to the panel.

Working Schedule

26. (1) Forthwith after the commencement of an appeal, the division shall draw up an appropriate working schedule for that appeal in accordance with the time-periods stipulated in these Rules.

(2) The working schedule shall set forth precise dates for the filing of documents and a timetable for the division's work, including where possible, the date for the oral hearing.

(3) In accordance with paragraph 9 of Article 4 of the DSU, in appeals of urgency, including those which concern perishable goods, the Appellate Body shall make every effort to accelerate the appellate proceedings to the greatest extent possible. A division shall take this into account in drawing up its working schedule for that appeal.

(4) The Secretariat shall serve forthwith a copy of the working schedule on the appellant, the parties to the dispute and any third parties.

Oral Hearing

27. (1) A division shall hold an oral hearing, which shall be held, as a general rule, between 30 and 45 days after the date of the filing of a Notice of Appeal.

(2) Where possible in the working schedule or otherwise at the earliest possible date, the Secretariat shall notify all parties to the dispute, participants, third parties and third participants of the date for the oral hearing.

(3) (a) Any third party that has filed a submission pursuant to Rule 24(1), or has notified the Secretariat pursuant to Rule 24(2) that it intends to appear at the oral hearing, may appear at the oral hearing, make an oral statement at the hearing, and respond to questions posed by the division.

(b) Any third party that has notified the Secretariat pursuant to Rule 24(4) that it intends to appear at the oral hearing may appear at the oral hearing.

(c) Any third party that has made a request pursuant to Rule 24(4) may, at the discretion of the division hearing the appeal, taking into account the requirements of due process, make an oral statement at the hearing, and respond to questions posed by the division.

(4) The Presiding Member may set time-limits for oral arguments.

Written Responses

28. (1) At any time during the appellate proceeding, including, in particular, during the oral hearing, the division may address questions orally or in writing to, or request additional memoranda from, any participant or third participant, and specify the time-periods by which written responses or memoranda shall be received.

(2) Any such questions, responses or memoranda shall be made available to the other participants and third participants in the appeal, who shall be given an opportunity to respond.

(3) When the questions or requests for memoranda are made prior to the oral hearing, then the questions or requests, as well as the responses or memoranda, shall also be made available to the third parties, who shall also be given an opportunity to respond.

Failure to Appear

29. Where a participant fails to file a submission within the required time-periods or fails to appear at the oral hearing, the division shall, after hearing the views of the participants, issue such order, including dismissal of the appeal, as it deems appropriate.

Withdrawal of Appeal

30. (1) At any time during an appeal, the appellant may withdraw its appeal by notifying the Appellate Body, which shall forthwith notify the DSB.

(2) Where a mutually agreed solution to a dispute which is the subject of an appeal has been notified to the DSB pursuant to paragraph 6 of Article 3 of the DSU, it shall be notified to the Appellate Body.

Prohibited Subsidies

31. (1) Subject to Article 4 of the *SCM Agreement*, the general provisions of these Rules shall apply to appeals relating to panel reports concerning prohibited subsidies under Part II of that *Agreement*.

(2) The working schedule for an appeal involving prohibited subsidies under Part II of the *SCM Agreement* shall be as set out in Annex I to these Rules.

Entry into Force and Amendment

32. (1) These Rules entered into force on 15 February 1996, and have subsequently been amended as indicated in Annex III.

(2) The Appellate Body may amend these Rules in compliance with the procedures set forth in paragraph 9 of Article 17 of the DSU. The Appellate Body will announce the date on which such amendments come into force. The document number for each revised version of these Rules, and the date upon which each version entered into force and succeeded the previous version, are indicated in Annex III.

(3) Whenever there is an amendment to the DSU or to the special or additional rules and procedures of the covered agreements, the Appellate Body shall examine whether amendments to these Rules are necessary.

Annexes

[not included]

36.d General Agreement on Tariffs and Trade

Date: 30 October 1947
Source: 55 UNTS 194
http://www.wto.org/english/docs_e/legal_e/legal_e.htm#gatt47

...

Article XXII Consultation

1. Each contracting party shall accord sympathetic consideration to, and shall afford adequate opportunity for consultation regarding, such representations as may be made by another contracting party with respect to any matter affecting the operation of this Agreement.

2. The CONTRACTING PARTIES may, at the request of a contracting party, consult with any contracting party or parties in respect of any matter for which it has not been possible to find a satisfactory solution through consultation under paragraph 1.

Article XXIII Nullification or Impairment

1. If any contracting party should consider that any benefit accruing to it directly or indirectly under this Agreement is being nullified or impaired or that the attainment of any objective of the Agreement is being impeded as the result of

(*a*) the failure of another contracting party to carry out its obligations under this Agreement, or

(*b*) the application by another contracting party of any measure, whether or not it conflicts with the provisions of this Agreement, or

(*c*) the existence of any other situation,

the contracting party may, with a view to the satisfactory adjustment of the matter, make written representations or proposals to the other contracting party or parties which it considers to be concerned. Any contracting party thus approached shall give sympathetic consideration to the representations or proposals made to it.

2. If no satisfactory adjustment is effected between the contracting parties concerned within a reasonable time, or if the difficulty is of the type described in paragraph 1 (*c*) of this Article, the matter may be referred to the CONTRACTING PARTIES. The CONTRACTING PARTIES shall promptly investigate any matter so referred to them and shall make appropriate recommendations to the contracting parties which they consider to be concerned, or give a ruling on the matter, as appropriate. The CONTRACTING PARTIES may consult with contracting parties, with the Economic and Social Council of the United Nations and with any appropriate inter-governmental organization in cases where they consider such consultation necessary. If the CONTRACTING PARTIES consider that the circumstances are serious enough to justify such action, they may authorize a contracting party or parties to suspend the application to any other contracting party or parties of such concessions or other obligations under this Agreement as they determine to be appropriate in the circumstances. If the application to any contracting party of any concession or other obligation is in fact suspended, that contracting party shall then be free, not later than sixty days after such action is taken, to give written notice to the Executive Secretary[1] to the Contracting Parties of its intention to withdraw from this Agreement and such withdrawal shall take effect upon the sixtieth day following the day on which such notice is received by him.

[1] By the Decision of 23 March 1965, the CONTRACTING PARTIES changed the title of the head of the GATT secretariat from "Executive Secretary" to "Director-General".

36.e Multi-Party Interim Appeal Arbitration Arrangement Pursuant to Article 25 of the DSU

Date: 27 March 2020
Source: https://trade.ec.europa.eu/doclib/docs/2020/march/tradoc_158685.pdf

[NB: this communication will be notified to the DSB pursuant to the "Statement on a mechanism for developing, documenting and sharing practices and procedures in the conduct of WTO disputes" (JOB/DSB/1) and circulated as document JOB/DSB/1/Add.12]

[Members endorsing this communication] (hereafter the "participating Members")

Re-affirming their commitment to a multilateral rules-based trading system,

Acknowledging that a functioning dispute settlement system of the WTO is of the utmost importance for a rules-based trading system, and that an independent and impartial appeal stage must continue to be one of its essential features,

Determined to work with the whole WTO Membership to find a lasting improvement to the situation relating to the Appellate Body as a matter of priority, and to launch the selection processes as soon as possible, so that it can resume its functions as envisaged by the DSU,

Resolved, in the interim, to put in place contingency measures based on Article 25 of the DSU in order to preserve the essential principles and features of the WTO dispute settlement system which include its binding character and two levels of adjudication through an independent and impartial appellate review of panel reports, and thereby to preserve their rights and obligations under the WTO Agreement,

Desiring to also preserve the possibility of a binding resolution of disputes at panel stage, if no party chooses to appeal under this arrangement, through the adoption of panel reports by the DSB by negative consensus,

Re-affirming that consistency and predictability in the interpretation of rights and obligations under the covered agreements is of significant value to Members and that arbitration awards cannot add to or diminish the rights and obligations provided in the covered agreements,

Underlining the interim nature of this arrangement,

In view of these extraordinary circumstances, envisage resorting to the following multi-party interim appeal arbitration arrangement (hereafter the "MPIA"):

1. The participating Members indicate their intention to resort to arbitration under Article 25 of the DSU as an interim appeal arbitration procedure (hereafter the "appeal arbitration procedure"), as long as the Appellate Body is not able to hear appeals of panel reports in disputes among them due to an insufficient number of Appellate Body members.

2. In such circumstances, the participating Members will not pursue appeals under Articles 16.4 and 17 of the DSU.

3. The appeal arbitration procedure will be based on the substantive and procedural aspects of Appellate Review pursuant to Article 17 of the DSU, in order to keep its core features, including independence and impartiality, while enhancing the procedural efficiency of appeal proceedings. The appeal arbitration procedure is set out in Annex 1.

4. In particular, the participating Members envisage that, under the appeal arbitration procedure, appeals will be heard by three appeal arbitrators selected from the pool of 10 standing appeal arbitrators composed by the participating Members in accordance with

Annex 2 (hereafter the "pool of arbitrators").[1] The pool of arbitrators will comprise persons of recognized authority, with demonstrated expertise in law, international trade and the subject matter of the covered agreements generally. They will be unaffiliated with any government. They will not participate in the consideration of any disputes that would create a direct or indirect conflict of interest. The composition of the pool of arbitrators will ensure an appropriate overall balance.

5. Members of the pool of arbitrators will stay abreast of WTO dispute settlement activities and will receive all documents relating to appeal arbitration proceedings under the MPIA. In order to promote consistency and coherence in decision-making, the members of the pool of arbitrators will discuss amongst themselves matters of interpretation, practice and procedure, to the extent practicable.

6. The selection from the pool of arbitrators for a specific dispute will be done on the basis of the same principles and methods that apply to form a division of the Appellate Body under Article 17.1 of the DSU and Rule 6(2) of the Working Procedures for Appellate Review, including the principle of rotation.[2] The WTO Director General will notify the parties and third parties of the results of the selection.

7. The participating Members envisage that appeal arbitrators will be provided with appropriate administrative and legal support, which will offer the necessary guarantees of quality and independence, given the nature of the responsibilities involved. The participating Members envisage that the support structure will be entirely separate from the WTO Secretariat staff and its divisions supporting the panels and be answerable, regarding the substance of their work, only to appeal arbitrators. The participating Members request the WTO Director General to ensure the availability of a support structure meeting these criteria.

8. The participating Members also envisage limited adjustments to panel procedures in disputes covered by the MPIA, to the extent it is necessary to facilitate the proper administration of the appeal arbitration procedure, should a party decide to appeal under this procedure. If no party appeals the panel report under the appeal arbitration procedure, the participating Members envisage that the panel report will be formally circulated for adoption by the DSB by negative consensus.

9. The MPIA applies to any future dispute between any two or more participating Members, including the compliance stage of such disputes, as well as to any such dispute pending on the date of this communication, except if the interim panel report, in the relevant stage of that dispute, has already been issued on that date.[3]

10. In order to render the appeal arbitration procedure operational in particular disputes, the participating Members indicate their intention to enter into the arbitration agreement (the "appeal arbitration agreement") contained in Annex 1 to this communication and to notify that agreement pursuant to Article 25.2 of the DSU within 60 days after the

[1] Should a need arise to select arbitrators to serve on a specific dispute while the pool of arbitrators has not yet been composed, the parties to that dispute will agree on the selection procedures applicable to that dispute. This footnote will cease to apply six months after the date of the multi-party communication, unless all the participating Members agree to extend it.

[2] However, at the request of a party to a dispute, any member of the pool of arbitrators who is not a national of a participating Member will be excluded from the selection process. Two nationals of the same Member may not serve on the same case.

[3] This is without prejudice to the right of the parties to decide to apply appeal arbitration procedures, such as those contained in Annex 1, to more advanced disputes on an *ad hoc* basis.

date of the establishment of the panel. For pending disputes where, on the date of this communication, the panel has already been established but an interim report has not yet been issued, the participating Members will enter into the appeal arbitration agreement and notify that agreement pursuant to Article 25.2 of the DSU within 30 days after the date of this communication.

11. With respect to a specific dispute, parties to that dispute may, without prejudice to the principles set forth in this communication, mutually agree to depart from the procedures set out in the appeal arbitration agreement.

12. Any WTO Member is welcome to join the MPIA at any time, by notification to the DSB that it endorses this communication. In relation to disputes to which such WTO Member is a party, the date of that Member's notification to the DSB will be deemed to be the date of this communication for the purposes of paragraphs 9 and 10.

13. The participating Members will review the MPIA one year after the date of this communication. The review may concern any feature of the MPIA.

14. A participating Member may decide to cease its participation in the MPIA, by notifying to the DSB the withdrawal of its endorsement of this communication. However, subject to paragraph 9, the participating Members intend for the MPIA to continue to apply to disputes pending on the date of such withdrawal. Furthermore, any appeal arbitration agreement entered into under paragraph 10 will remain in effect.

15. The participating Members remain committed to resolving the impasse of the Appellate Body appointments as a matter of priority and envisage that the MPIA will remain in effect only until the Appellate Body is again fully functional. However, any appeal arbitration agreement entered into under paragraph 10 will remain in effect, unless the parties agree otherwise.

ANNEX 1

AGREED PROCEDURES FOR ARBITRATION UNDER ARTICLE 25 of the DSU in dispute DS X

1. In order to give effect to communication JOB/DSB/1/Add.12 in this dispute [the parties to the dispute] (hereafter the "parties") mutually agree pursuant to Article 25.2 of the Understanding on Rules and Procedures Governing the Settlement of Disputes (DSU) to enter into arbitration under Article 25 of the DSU to decide any appeal from any final panel report[4] as issued to the parties in dispute DS X. Any party to the dispute may initiate arbitration in accordance with these agreed procedures.

2. The arbitration may only be initiated if the Appellate Body is not able to hear an appeal in this dispute under Article 16.4 and 17 of the DSU. For the purposes of these agreed procedures, such situation is deemed to arise where, on the date of issuance of the final panel report to the parties, there are fewer than three Appellate Body members.

For greater certainty, if the Appellate Body is able to hear appeals at the date on which the final panel report is issued to the parties, a party may not initiate an arbitration, and the parties shall be free to consider an appeal under Articles 16.4 and 17 of the DSU.

3. In order to facilitate the proper administration of arbitration under these agreed procedures, the parties hereby jointly request the panel to notify the parties of the anticipated date of circulation of the final panel report within the meaning of Article 16 of the DSU, no later than 45 days in advance of that date.

4. Following the issuance of the final panel report to the parties, but no later than 10 days prior to the anticipated date of circulation of the final panel report to the rest of the Membership, any party may request that the panel suspend the panel proceedings with a view to initiating the arbitration under these agreed procedures. Such request by any party is deemed to constitute a joint request by the parties for suspension of the panel proceedings for 12 months pursuant to Article 12.12 of the DSU.

The parties hereby jointly request the panel to provide for the following, before the suspension takes effect:

i. the lifting of confidentiality with respect of the final panel report under the Working Procedures of the panel;
ii. the transmission of the panel record to the arbitrators upon the filing of the Notice of Appeal: Rule 25 of the Working Procedures for Appellate Review shall apply *mutatis mutandis*;
iii. the transmission of the final panel report in the working languages of the WTO to the parties and to the third parties.[5]

Except as provided in paragraphs 6 and 18, the parties shall not request the panel to resume the panel proceedings.

5. The arbitration shall be initiated by filing of a Notice of Appeal with the WTO Secretariat no later than 20 days after the suspension of the panel proceedings referred to in paragraph 4 has taken effect. The Notice of Appeal shall include the final panel report in the working languages of the WTO. The Notice of Appeal shall be simultaneously notified to the other party or parties and to the third parties in the panel proceedings. Rules 20-23 of the Working Procedures for Appellate Review shall apply *mutatis mutandis*.

6. Subject to paragraph 2, where the arbitration has not been initiated under these agreed procedures, the parties shall be deemed to have agreed not to appeal the panel report pursuant to Articles 16.4 and 17 of the DSU, with a view to its adoption by the DSB. If the panel proceedings have been suspended in accordance with paragraph 4, but no Notice of Appeal has been filed in accordance with paragraph 5, the parties hereby jointly request the panel to resume the panel proceedings.

7. The arbitrators shall be three persons selected from the pool of 10 standing appeal arbitrators composed in accordance with paragraph 4 of communication JOB/DSB/1/Add.12 (hereafter the "pool of arbitrators").[6] The selection from the pool of arbitrators will be done on the basis of the same principles and methods that apply to form a division of the Appellate Body under Article 17.1 of the DSU and Rule 6(2) of the Working Procedures for Appellate Review, including the principle of rotation.[7] The WTO Director General will notify the parties and third parties of the results of the selection. The arbitrators shall elect a Chairperson. Rule 3(2) of the Working Procedure for Appellate Review shall apply, *mutatis mutandis*, to the decision-making by the arbitrators.

[4] For greater certainty, this includes any final panel report issued in compliance proceedings pursuant to Article 21.5 of the DSU.

[5] The parties confirm that it is not their intention that the panel report be circulated within the meaning of Article 16 of the DSU.

[6] If the pool of arbitrators has not been composed, footnote 1 to paragraph 4 of communication JOB/DSB/1/Add.12 shall apply.

[7] However, at the request of a party to a dispute, any member of the pool of arbitrators who is not a national of a participating Member shall be excluded from the selection process. Two nationals of the same Member shall not serve on the same case.

8. In order to give effect to paragraph 5 of communication JOB/DSB/1/Add.12 in this dispute, the arbitrators may discuss their decisions relating to the appeal with all of the other members of the pool of arbitrators, without prejudice to the exclusive responsibility and freedom of the arbitrators with respect to such decisions and their quality. All members of the pool of arbitrators shall receive any document relating to the appeal.

9. An appeal shall be limited to issues of law covered by the panel report and legal interpretations developed by the panel. The arbitrators may uphold, modify or reverse the legal findings and conclusions of the panel. Where applicable, the arbitration award shall include recommendations, as envisaged in Article 19 of the DSU. The findings of the panel which have not been appealed shall be deemed to form an integral part of the arbitration award together with the arbitrators' own findings.

10. The arbitrators shall only address those issues that are necessary for the resolution of the dispute. They shall address only those issues that have been raised by the parties, without prejudice to their obligation to rule on jurisdictional issues.

11. Unless otherwise provided for in these agreed procedures, the arbitration shall be governed, *mutatis mutandis*, by the provisions of the DSU and other rules and procedures applicable to Appellate Review. This includes in particular the Working Procedures for Appellate Review and the timetable for appeals provided for therein as well as the Rules of Conduct.[8] The arbitrators may adapt the Working Procedures for Appellate Review and the timetable for appeals provided for therein, where justified under Rule 16 of the Working Procedures for Appellate Review, after consulting the parties.

12. The parties request the arbitrators to issue the award within 90 days following the filing of the Notice of Appeal. To that end, the arbitrators may take appropriate organizational measures to streamline the proceedings, without prejudice to the procedural rights and obligations of the parties and due process. Such measures may include decisions on page limits, time limits and deadlines as well as on the length and number of hearings required.

13. If necessary in order to issue the award within the 90 day time-period, the arbitrators may also propose substantive measures to the parties, such as an exclusion of claims based on the alleged lack of an objective assessment of the facts pursuant to Article 11 of the DSU.[9]

14. On a proposal from the arbitrators, the parties may agree to extend the 90 day time-period for the issuance of the award.

15. The parties agree to abide by the arbitration award, which shall be final. Pursuant to Article 25.3 of the DSU, the award shall be notified to, but not adopted by, the DSB and to the Council or Committee of any relevant agreement.

16. Only parties to the dispute, not third parties, may initiate the arbitration. Third parties which have notified the DSB of a substantial interest in the matter before the panel pursuant to Article 10.2 of the DSU may make written submissions to, and shall be given an opportunity to be heard by, the arbitrators. Rule 24 of the Working Procedures for Appellate Review shall apply *mutatis mutandis*.

17. Pursuant to Article 25.4 of the DSU, Articles 21 and 22 of the DSU shall apply *mutatis mutandis* to the arbitration award issued in this dispute.

[8] For greater certainty, paragraphs 14–17 of the Rules of Conduct shall apply to arbitrators.

[9] For greater certainty, the proposal of the arbitrators is not legally binding and it will be up to the party concerned to agree with the proposed substantive measures. The fact that the party concerned does not agree with the proposed substantive measures shall not prejudice the consideration of the case or the rights of the parties.

18. At any time during the arbitration, the appellant, or other appellant, may withdraw its appeal, or other appeal, by notifying the arbitrators. This notification shall also be notified to the panel and third parties, at the same time as the notification to the arbitrators. If no other appeal or appeal remains, the notification shall be deemed to constitute a joint request by the parties to resume panel proceedings under Article 12.12 of the DSU.[10] If an other appeal or appeal remains at the time an appeal or other appeal is withdrawn, the arbitration shall continue.

19. The parties shall jointly notify these agreed procedures to the panel in DS X and ask the panel to grant, where applicable, the joint requests formulated in paragraphs 3, 4, 6, and 18.[11]

ANNEX 2

COMPOSITION OF THE POOL OF ARBITRATORS PURSUANT TO PARAGRAPH 4 OF COMMUNICATION JOB/DSB/1/ADD.12

After the notification of the present communication to the DSB, the participating Members will promptly commence the composition process. The following will apply:

1. Each participating Member may nominate one candidate, by notifying the other participating Members.[12]

2. The deadline for nominations will expire 30 days after the date of this communication.

3. The candidates will undergo a pre-selection process in order to ensure that the pool of arbitrators comprises only persons of recognised authority, with demonstrated expertise in law, international trade and the subject matter of the covered agreements generally.

The participating Members envisage that this pre-selection process will be carried out by a pre- selection committee composed of the WTO Director General, and the Chairperson of the DSB, the Chairpersons of the Goods, Services, TRIPS and General Councils. The pre-selection committee will, after appropriate consultations, recommend to the participating Members the candidates who meet the above criteria.

The participating Members envisage the completion of this pre-selection process within one month following the expiry of the deadline to nominate candidates.

4. The participating Members will compose the pool of arbitrators by consensus. The participating Members will endeavour to compose the pool of arbitrators within three months following the date of this communication. They will notify the pool of arbitrators to the DSB, as addendum to this communication. The composition of the pool of arbitrators will ensure an appropriate overall balance.

5. The composition of the pool of arbitrators may be modified by agreement of all participating Members at any time. The participating Members underscore the interim nature of this arrangement. Should the conditions laid down in paragraph 15 of the communication

[10] If the authority of the panel has lapsed pursuant to Article 12.12 of the DSU, the arbitrators shall issue an award that incorporates the findings and conclusions of the panel in their entirety.

[11] For greater certainty, should any of these requests not be granted by the panel, the parties will agree on alternative procedural modalities to preserve the effects of the relevant provisions of these agreed procedures.

[12] For greater certainty, current or former Appellate Body members may be nominated as candidates. If nominated as candidates, they will not undergo the pre-selection process set out in paragraph 3 of this Annex.

remain for a longer period of time, the participating Members will, periodically, partially re-compose the pool of arbitrators, starting two years after composition, in line with the procedures established in this Annex.

6. Should a need arise to complete the pool of arbitrators, for instance following the resignation of a member of the pool, the procedure set out above will apply.

7 Investment

The International Centre for Settlement of Investment Disputes

37.a Convention on the Settlement of Investment Disputes between States and Nationals of Other States

(ICSID Convention; Washington Convention)

Date: 18 March 1965
Source: 575 UNTS 159
https://icsid.worldbank.org/sites/default/files/ICSID%20Convention%20English.pdf

PREAMBLE

The Contracting States

Considering the need for international cooperation for economic development, and the role of private international investment therein;

Bearing in mind the possibility that from time to time disputes may arise in connection with such investment between Contracting States and nationals of other Contracting States;

Recognizing that while such disputes would usually be subject to national legal processes, international methods of settlement may be appropriate in certain cases;

Attaching particular importance to the availability of facilities for international conciliation or arbitration to which Contracting States and nationals of other Contracting States may submit such disputes if they so desire;

Desiring to establish such facilities under the auspices of the International Bank for Reconstruction and Development;

Recognizing that mutual consent by the parties to submit such disputes to conciliation or to arbitration through such facilities constitutes a binding agreement which requires in particular that due consideration be given to any recommendation of conciliators, and that any arbitral award be complied with; and

Declaring that no Contracting State shall by the mere fact of its ratification, acceptance or approval of this Convention and without its consent be deemed to be under any obligation to submit any particular dispute to conciliation or arbitration,

Have agreed as follows:

CHAPTER I International Centre for Settlement of Investment Disputes

Section 1 Establishment and Organization

Article 1

(1) There is hereby established the International Centre for Settlement of Investment Disputes (hereinafter called the Centre).

(2) The purpose of the Centre shall be to provide facilities for conciliation and arbitration of investment disputes between Contracting States and nationals of other Contracting States in accordance with the provisions of this Convention.

Article 2

The seat of the Centre shall be at the principal office of the International Bank for Reconstruction and Development (hereinafter called the Bank). The seat may be moved to another place by decision of the Administrative Council adopted by a majority of two-thirds of its members.

Article 3

The Centre shall have an Administrative Council and a Secretariat and shall maintain a Panel of Conciliators and a Panel of Arbitrators.

Section 2 The Administrative Council

Article 4

(1) The Administrative Council shall be composed of one representative of each Contracting State. An alternate may act as representative in case of his principal's absence from a meeting or inability to act.

(2) In the absence of a contrary designation, each governor and alternate governor of the Bank appointed by a Contracting State shall be *ex officio* its representative and its alternate respectively.

Article 5

The President of the Bank shall be *ex officio* Chairman of the Administrative Council (hereinafter called the Chairman) but shall have no vote. During his absence or inability to act and during any vacancy in the office of President of the Bank, the person for the time being acting as President shall act as Chairman of the Administrative Council.

Article 6

(1) Without prejudice to the powers and functions vested in it by other provisions of this Convention, the Administrative Council shall:

(a) adopt the administrative and financial regulations of the Centre;

(b) adopt the rules of procedure for the institution of conciliation and arbitration proceedings;

(c) adopt the rules of procedure for conciliation and arbitration proceedings (hereinafter called the Conciliation Rules and the Arbitration Rules);

(d) approve arrangements with the Bank for the use of the Bank's administrative facilities and services;

(e) determine the conditions of service of the Secretary-General and of any Deputy Secretary-General;

(f) adopt the annual budget of revenues and expenditures of the Centre;

(g) approve the annual report on the operation of the Centre.

The decisions referred to in sub-paragraphs (a), (b), (c) and (f) above shall be adopted by a majority of two-thirds of the members of the Administrative Council.

(2) The Administrative Council may appoint such committees as it considers necessary.

(3) The Administrative Council shall also exercise such other powers and perform such other functions as it shall determine to be necessary for the implementation of the provisions of this Convention.

Article 7

(1) The Administrative Council shall hold an annual meeting and such other meetings as may be determined by the Council, or convened by the Chairman, or convened by the Secretary-General at the request of not less than five members of the Council.

(2) Each member of the Administrative Council shall have one vote and, except as otherwise herein provided, all matters before the Council shall be decided by a majority of the votes cast.

(3) A quorum for any meeting of the Administrative Council shall be a majority of its members.

(4) The Administrative Council may establish, by a majority of two-thirds of its members, a procedure whereby the Chairman may seek a vote of the Council without convening a meeting of the Council. The vote shall be considered valid only if the majority of the members of the Council cast their votes within the time limit fixed by the said procedure.

Article 8

Members of the Administrative Council and the Chairman shall serve without remuneration from the Centre.

Section 3 The Secretariat

Article 9

The Secretariat shall consist of a Secretary-General, one or more Deputy Secretaries-General and staff.

Article 10

(1) The Secretary-General and any Deputy Secretary-General shall be elected by the Administrative Council by a majority of two-thirds of its members upon the nomination of the Chairman for a term of service not exceeding six years and shall be eligible for re-election. After consulting the members of the Administrative Council, the Chairman shall propose one or more candidates for each such office.

(2) The offices of Secretary-General and Deputy Secretary-General shall be incompatible with the exercise of any political function. Neither the Secretary-General nor any Deputy Secretary-General may hold any other employment or engage in any other occupation except with the approval of the Administrative Council.

(3) During the Secretary-General's absence or inability to act, and during any vacancy of the office of Secretary-General, the Deputy Secretary-General shall act as Secretary-General. If there shall be more than one Deputy Secretary-General, the Administrative Council shall determine in advance the order in which they shall act as Secretary-General.

Article 11

The Secretary-General shall be the legal representative and the principal officer of the Centre and shall be responsible for its administration, including the appointment of staff, in accordance with the provisions of this Convention and the rules adopted by the Administrative Council. He shall perform the function of registrar and shall have the power to authenticate arbitral awards rendered pursuant to this Convention, and to certify copies thereof.

Section 4 The Panels

Article 12

The Panel of Conciliators and the Panel of Arbitrators shall each consist of qualified persons, designated as hereinafter provided, who are willing to serve thereon.

Article 13

(1) Each Contracting State may designate to each Panel four persons who may but need not be its nationals.

(2) The Chairman may designate ten persons to each Panel. The persons so designated to a Panel shall each have a different nationality.

Article 14

(1) Persons designated to serve on the Panels shall be persons of high moral character and recognized competence in the fields of law, commerce, industry or finance, who may be relied upon to exercise independent judgment. Competence in the field of law shall be of particular importance in the case of persons on the Panel of Arbitrators.

(2) The Chairman, in designating persons to serve on the Panels, shall in addition pay due regard to the importance of assuring representation on the Panels of the principal legal systems of the world and of the main forms of economic activity.

Article 15

(1) Panel members shall serve for renewable periods of six years.

(2) In case of death or resignation of a member of a Panel, the authority which designated the member shall have the right to designate another person to serve for the remainder of that member's term.

(3) Panel members shall continue in office until their successors have been designated.

Article 16

(1) A person may serve on both Panels.

(2) If a person shall have been designated to serve on the same Panel by more than one Contracting State, or by one or more Contracting States and the Chairman, he shall be deemed to have been designated by the authority which first designated him or, if one such authority is the State of which he is a national, by that State.

(3) All designations shall be notified to the Secretary-General and shall take effect from the date on which the notification is received.

Section 5 Financing the Centre

Article 17

If the expenditure of the Centre cannot be met out of charges for the use of its facilities, or out of other receipts, the excess shall be borne by Contracting States which are members of the Bank in proportion to their respective subscriptions to the capital stock of the Bank, and by Contracting States which are not members of the Bank in accordance with rules adopted by the Administrative Council.

Section 6 Status, Immunities and Privileges

Article 18

The Centre shall have full international legal personality. The legal capacity of the Centre shall include the capacity:

(a) to contract;
(b) to acquire and dispose of movable and immovable property;
(c) to institute legal proceedings.

Article 19

To enable the Centre to fulfil its functions, it shall enjoy in the territories of each Contracting State the immunities and privileges set forth in this Section.

Article 20

The Centre, its property and assets shall enjoy immunity from all legal process, except when the Centre waives this immunity.

Article 21

The Chairman, the members of the Administrative Council, persons acting as conciliators or arbitrators or members of a Committee appointed pursuant to paragraph (3) of Article 52, and the officers and employees of the Secretariat:

(a) shall enjoy immunity from legal process with respect to acts performed by them in the exercise of their functions, except when the Centre waives this immunity;
(b) not being local nationals, shall enjoy the same immunities from immigration restrictions, alien registration requirements and national service obligations, the same facilities as regards exchange restrictions and the same treatment in respect of travelling facilities as are accorded by Contracting States to the representatives, officials and employees of comparable rank of other Contracting States.

Article 22

The provisions of Article 21 shall apply to persons appearing in proceedings under this Convention as parties, agents, counsel, advocates, witnesses or experts; provided, however, that sub-paragraph (b) thereof shall apply only in connection with their travel to and from, and their stay at, the place where the proceedings are held.

Article 23

(1) The archives of the Centre shall be inviolable, wherever they may be.

(2) With regard to its official communications, the Centre shall be accorded by each Contracting State treatment not less favourable than that accorded to other international organizations.

Article 24

(1) The Centre, its assets, property and income, and its operations and transactions authorized by this Convention shall be exempt from all taxation and customs duties. The Centre shall also be exempt from liability for the collection or payment of any taxes or customs duties.

(2) Except in the case of local nationals, no tax shall be levied on or in respect of expense allowances paid by the Centre to the Chairman or members of the Administrative Council,

or on or in respect of salaries, expense allowances or other emoluments paid by the Centre to officials or employees of the Secretariat.

(3) No tax shall be levied on or in respect of fees or expense allowances received by persons acting as conciliators, or arbitrators, or members of a Committee appointed pursuant to paragraph (3) of Article 52, in proceedings under this Convention, if the sole jurisdictional basis for such tax is the location of the Centre or the place where such proceedings are conducted or the place where such fees or allowances are paid.

CHAPTER II Jurisdiction of the Centre

Article 25

(1) The jurisdiction of the Centre shall extend to any legal dispute arising directly out of an investment, between a Contracting State (or any constituent subdivision or agency of a Contracting State designated to the Centre by that State) and a national of another Contracting State, which the parties to the dispute consent in writing to submit to the Centre. When the parties have given their consent, no party may withdraw its consent unilaterally.

(2) "National of another Contracting State" means:

(a) any natural person who had the nationality of a Contracting State other than the State party to the dispute on the date on which the parties consented to submit such dispute to conciliation or arbitration as well as on the date on which the request was registered pursuant to paragraph (3) of Article 28 or paragraph (3) of Article 36, but does not include any person who on either date also had the nationality of the Contracting State party to the dispute; and

(b) any juridical person which had the nationality of a Contracting State other than the State party to the dispute on the date on which the parties consented to submit such dispute to conciliation or arbitration and any juridical person which had the nationality of the Contracting State party to the dispute on that date and which, because of foreign control, the parties have agreed should be treated as a national of another Contracting State for the purposes of this Convention.

(3) Consent by a constituent subdivision or agency of a Contracting State shall require the approval of that State unless that State notifies the Centre that no such approval is required.

(4) Any Contracting State may, at the time of ratification, acceptance or approval of this Convention or at any time thereafter, notify the Centre of the class or classes of disputes which it would or would not consider submitting to the jurisdiction of the Centre. The Secretary-General shall forthwith transmit such notification to all Contracting States. Such notification shall not constitute the consent required by paragraph (1).

Article 26

Consent of the parties to arbitration under this Convention shall, unless otherwise stated, be deemed consent to such arbitration to the exclusion of any other remedy. A Contracting State may require the exhaustion of local administrative or judicial remedies as a condition of its consent to arbitration under this Convention.

Article 27

(1) No Contracting State shall give diplomatic protection, or bring an international claim, in respect of a dispute which one of its nationals and another Contracting State shall have consented to submit or shall have submitted to arbitration under this Convention,

unless such other Contracting State shall have failed to abide by and comply with the award rendered in such dispute.

(2) Diplomatic protection, for the purposes of paragraph (1), shall not include informal diplomatic exchanges for the sole purpose of facilitating a settlement of the dispute.

CHAPTER III Conciliation

Section 1 Request for Conciliation

Article 28

(1) Any Contracting State or any national of a Contracting State wishing to institute conciliation proceedings shall address a request to that effect in writing to the Secretary-General who shall send a copy of the request to the other party.

(2) The request shall contain information concerning the issues in dispute, the identity of the parties and their consent to conciliation in accordance with the rules of procedure for the institution of conciliation and arbitration proceedings.

(3) The Secretary-General shall register the request unless he finds, on the basis of the information contained in the request, that the dispute is manifestly outside the jurisdiction of the Centre. He shall forthwith notify the parties of registration or refusal to register.

Section 2 Constitution of the Conciliation Commission

Article 29

(1) The Conciliation Commission (hereinafter called the Commission) shall be constituted as soon as possible after registration of a request pursuant to Article 28.

(2) (a) The Commission shall consist of a sole conciliator or any uneven number of conciliators appointed as the parties shall agree.

(b) Where the parties do not agree upon the number of conciliators and the method of their appointment, the Commission shall consist of three conciliators, one conciliator appointed by each party and the third, who shall be the president of the Commission, appointed by agreement of the parties.

Article 30

If the Commission shall not have been constituted within 90 days after notice of registration of the request has been dispatched by the Secretary-General in accordance with paragraph (3) of Article 28, or such other period as the parties may agree, the Chairman shall, at the request of either party and after consulting both parties as far as possible, appoint the conciliator or conciliators not yet appointed.

Article 31

(1) Conciliators may be appointed from outside the Panel of Conciliators, except in the case of appointments by the Chairman pursuant to Article 30.

(2) Conciliators appointed from outside the Panel of Conciliators shall possess the qualities stated in paragraph (1) of Article 14.

Section 3 Conciliation Proceedings

Article 32

(1) The Commission shall be the judge of its own competence.

(2) Any objection by a party to the dispute that that dispute is not within the jurisdiction of the Centre, or for other reasons is not within the competence of the Commission, shall be considered by the Commission which shall determine whether to deal with it as a preliminary question or to join it to the merits of the dispute.

Article 33

Any conciliation proceeding shall be conducted in accordance with the provisions of this Section and, except as the parties otherwise agree, in accordance with the Conciliation Rules in effect on the date on which the parties consented to conciliation. If any question of procedure arises which is not covered by this Section or the Conciliation Rules or any rules agreed by the parties, the Commission shall decide the question.

Article 34

(1) It shall be the duty of the Commission to clarify the issues in dispute between the parties and to endeavour to bring about agreement between them upon mutually acceptable terms. To that end, the Commission may at any stage of the proceedings and from time to time recommend terms of settlement to the parties. The parties shall cooperate in good faith with the Commission in order to enable the Commission to carry out its functions, and shall give their most serious consideration to its recommendations.

(2) If the parties reach agreement, the Commission shall draw up a report noting the issues in dispute and recording that the parties have reached agreement. If, at any stage of the proceedings, it appears to the Commission that there is no likelihood of agreement between the parties, it shall close the proceedings and shall draw up a report noting the submission of the dispute and recording the failure of the parties to reach agreement. If one party fails to appear or participate in the proceedings, the Commission shall close the proceedings and shall draw up a report noting that party's failure to appear or participate.

Article 35

Except as the parties to the dispute shall otherwise agree, neither party to a conciliation proceeding shall be entitled in any other proceeding, whether before arbitrators or in a court of law or otherwise, to invoke or rely on any views expressed or statements or admissions or offers of settlement made by the other party in the conciliation proceedings, or the report or any recommendations made by the Commission.

CHAPTER IV Arbitration

Section I Request for Arbitration

Article 36

(1) Any Contracting State or any national of a Contracting State wishing to institute arbitration proceedings shall address a request to that effect in writing to the Secretary-General who shall send a copy of the request to the other party.

(2) The request shall contain information concerning the issues in dispute, the identity of the parties and their consent to arbitration in accordance with the rules of procedure for the institution of conciliation and arbitration proceedings.

(3) The Secretary-General shall register the request unless he finds, on the basis of the information contained in the request, that the dispute is manifestly outside the jurisdiction of the Centre. He shall forthwith notify the parties of registration or refusal to register.

Section 2 Constitution of the Tribunal

Article 37

(1) The Arbitral Tribunal (hereinafter called the Tribunal) shall be constituted as soon as possible after registration of a request pursuant to Article 36.

(2) (a) The Tribunal shall consist of a sole arbitrator or any uneven number of arbitrators appointed as the parties shall agree.

(b) Where the parties do not agree upon the number of arbitrators and the method of their appointment, the Tribunal shall consist of three arbitrators, one arbitrator appointed by each party and the third, who shall be the president of the Tribunal, appointed by agreement of the parties.

Article 38

If the Tribunal shall not have been constituted within 90 days after notice of registration of the request has been dispatched by the Secretary-General in accordance with paragraph (3) of Article 36, or such other period as the parties may agree, the Chairman shall, at the request of either party and after consulting both parties as far as possible, appoint the arbitrator or arbitrators not yet appointed. Arbitrators appointed by the Chairman pursuant to this Article shall not be nationals of the Contracting State party to the dispute or of the Contracting State whose national is a party to the dispute.

Article 39

The majority of the arbitrators shall be nationals of States other than the Contracting State party to the dispute and the Contracting State whose national is a party to the dispute; provided, however, that the foregoing provisions of this Article shall not apply if the sole arbitrator or each individual member of the Tribunal has been appointed by agreement of the parties.

Article 40

(1) Arbitrators may be appointed from outside the Panel of Arbitrators, except in the case of appointments by the Chairman pursuant to Article 38.

(2) Arbitrators appointed from outside the Panel of Arbitrators shall possess the qualities stated in paragraph (1) of Article 14.

Section 3 Powers and Functions of the Tribunal

Article 41

(1) The Tribunal shall be the judge of its own competence.

(2) Any objection by a party to the dispute that that dispute is not within the jurisdiction of the Centre, or for other reasons is not within the competence of the Tribunal, shall be considered by the Tribunal which shall determine whether to deal with it as a preliminary question or to join it to the merits of the dispute.

Article 42

(1) The Tribunal shall decide a dispute in accordance with such rules of law as may be agreed by the parties. In the absence of such agreement, the Tribunal shall apply the law of the Contracting State party to the dispute (including its rules on the conflict of laws) and such rules of international law as may be applicable.

(2) The Tribunal may not bring in a finding of *non liquet* on the ground of silence or obscurity of the law.

(3) The provisions of paragraphs (1) and (2) shall not prejudice the power of the Tribunal to decide a dispute *ex aequo et bono* if the parties so agree.

Article 43

Except as the parties otherwise agree, the Tribunal may, if it deems it necessary at any stage of the proceedings,

(a) call upon the parties to produce documents or other evidence, and
(b) visit the scene connected with the dispute, and conduct such inquiries there as it may deem appropriate.

Article 44

Any arbitration proceeding shall be conducted in accordance with the provisions of this Section and, except as the parties otherwise agree, in accordance with the Arbitration Rules in effect on the date on which the parties consented to arbitration. If any question of procedure arises which is not covered by this Section or the Arbitration Rules or any rules agreed by the parties, the Tribunal shall decide the question.

Article 45

(1) Failure of a party to appear or to present his case shall not be deemed an admission of the other party's assertions.

(2) If a party fails to appear or to present his case at any stage of the proceedings the other party may request the Tribunal to deal with the questions submitted to it and to render an award. Before rendering an award, the Tribunal shall notify, and grant a period of grace to, the party failing to appear or to present its case, unless it is satisfied that that party does not intend to do so.

Article 46

Except as the parties otherwise agree, the Tribunal shall, if requested by a party, determine any incidental or additional claims or counterclaims arising directly out of the subject-matter of the dispute provided that they are within the scope of the consent of the parties and are otherwise within the jurisdiction of the Centre.

Article 47

Except as the parties otherwise agree, the Tribunal may, if it considers that the circumstances so require, recommend any provisional measures which should be taken to preserve the respective rights of either party.

Section 4 The Award

Article 48

(1) The Tribunal shall decide questions by a majority of the votes of all its members.

(2) The award of the Tribunal shall be in writing and shall be signed by the members of the Tribunal who voted for it.

(3) The award shall deal with every question submitted to the Tribunal, and shall state the reasons upon which it is based.

(4) Any member of the Tribunal may attach his individual opinion to the award, whether he dissents from the majority or not, or a statement of his dissent.

(5) The Centre shall not publish the award without the consent of the parties.

Article 49

(1) The Secretary-General shall promptly dispatch certified copies of the award to the parties. The award shall be deemed to have been rendered on the date on which the certified copies were dispatched.

(2) The Tribunal upon the request of a party made within 45 days after the date on which the award was rendered may after notice to the other party decide any question which it had omitted to decide in the award, and shall rectify any clerical, arithmetical or similar error in the award. Its decision shall become part of the award and shall be notified to the parties in the same manner as the award. The periods of time provided for under paragraph (2) of Article 51 and paragraph (2) of Article 52 shall run from the date on which the decision was rendered.

Section 5 Interpretation, Revision and Annulment of the Award

Article 50

(1) If any dispute shall arise between the parties as to the meaning or scope of an award, either party may request interpretation of the award by an application in writing addressed to the Secretary-General.

(2) The request shall, if possible, be submitted to the Tribunal which rendered the award. If this shall not be possible, a new Tribunal shall be constituted in accordance with Section 2 of this Chapter. The Tribunal may, if it considers that the circumstances so require, stay enforcement of the award pending its decision.

Article 51

(1) Either party may request revision of the award by an application in writing addressed to the Secretary-General on the ground of discovery of some fact of such a nature as decisively to affect the award, provided that when the award was rendered that fact was unknown to the Tribunal and to the applicant and that the applicant's ignorance of that fact was not due to negligence.

(2) The application shall be made within 90 days after the discovery of such fact and in any event within three years after the date on which the award was rendered.

(3) The request shall, if possible, be submitted to the Tribunal which rendered the award. If this shall not be possible, a new Tribunal shall be constituted in accordance with Section 2 of this Chapter.

(4) The Tribunal may, if it considers that the circumstances so require, stay enforcement of the award pending its decision. If the applicant requests a stay of enforcement of the award in his application, enforcement shall be stayed provisionally until the Tribunal rules on such request.

Article 52

(1) Either party may request annulment of the award by an application in writing addressed to the Secretary-General on one or more of the following grounds:

(a) that the Tribunal was not properly constituted;
(b) that the Tribunal has manifestly exceeded its powers;
(c) that there was corruption on the part of a member of the Tribunal;
(d) that there has been a serious departure from a fundamental rule of procedure; or
(e) that the award has failed to state the reasons on which it is based.

(2) The application shall be made within 120 days after the date on which the award was rendered except that when annulment is requested on the ground of corruption such application shall be made within 120 days after discovery of the corruption and in any event within three years after the date on which the award was rendered.

(3) On receipt of the request the Chairman shall forthwith appoint from the Panel of Arbitrators an *ad hoc* Committee of three persons. None of the members of the Committee shall have been a member of the Tribunal which rendered the award, shall be of the same nationality as any such member, shall be a national of the State party to the dispute or of the State whose national is a party to the dispute, shall have been designated to the Panel of Arbitrators by either of those States, or shall have acted as a conciliator in the same dispute. The Committee shall have the authority to annul the award or any part thereof on any of the grounds set forth in paragraph (1).

(4) The provisions of Articles 41-45, 48, 49, 53 and 54, and of Chapters VI and VII shall apply *mutatis mutandis* to proceedings before the Committee.

(5) The Committee may, if it considers that the circumstances so require, stay enforcement of the award pending its decision. If the applicant requests a stay of enforcement of the award in his application, enforcement shall be stayed provisionally until the Committee rules on such request.

(6) If the award is annulled the dispute shall, at the request of either party, be submitted to a new Tribunal constituted in accordance with Section 2 of this Chapter.

Section 6 Recognition and Enforcement of the Award

Article 53

(1) The award shall be binding on the parties and shall not be subject to any appeal or to any other remedy except those provided for in this Convention. Each party shall abide by and comply with the terms of the award except to the extent that enforcement shall have been stayed pursuant to the relevant provisions of this Convention.

(2) For the purposes of this Section, "award" shall include any decision interpreting, revising or annulling such award pursuant to Articles 50, 51 or 52.

Article 54

(1) Each Contracting State shall recognize an award rendered pursuant to this Convention as binding and enforce the pecuniary obligations imposed by that award within its territories as if it were a final judgment of a court in that State. A Contracting State with a federal constitution may enforce such an award in or through its federal courts and may provide that such courts shall treat the award as if it were a final judgment of the courts of a constituent state.

(2) A party seeking recognition or enforcement in the territories of a Contracting State shall furnish to a competent court or other authority which such State shall have designated

for this purpose a copy of the award certified by the Secretary-General. Each Contracting State shall notify the Secretary-General of the designation of the competent court or other authority for this purpose and of any subsequent change in such designation.

(3) Execution of the award shall be governed by the laws concerning the execution of judgments in force in the State in whose territories such execution is sought.

Article 55

Nothing in Article 54 shall be construed as derogating from the law in force in any Contracting State relating to immunity of that State or of any foreign State from execution.

CHAPTER V Replacement and Disqualification of Conciliators and Arbitrators

Article 56

(1) After a Commission or a Tribunal has been constituted and proceedings have begun, its composition shall remain unchanged; provided, however, that if a conciliator or an arbitrator should die, become incapacitated, or resign, the resulting vacancy shall be filled in accordance with the provisions of Section 2 of Chapter III or Section 2 of Chapter IV.

(2) A member of a Commission or Tribunal shall continue to serve in that capacity notwithstanding that he shall have ceased to be a member of the Panel.

(3) If a conciliator or arbitrator appointed by a party shall have resigned without the consent of the Commission or Tribunal of which he was a member, the Chairman shall appoint a person from the appropriate Panel to fill the resulting vacancy.

Article 57

A party may propose to a Commission or Tribunal the disqualification of any of its members on account of any fact indicating a manifest lack of the qualities required by paragraph (1) of Article 14. A party to arbitration proceedings may, in addition, propose the disqualification of an arbitrator on the ground that he was ineligible for appointment to the Tribunal under Section 2 of Chapter IV.

Article 58

The decision on any proposal to disqualify a conciliator or arbitrator shall be taken by the other members of the Commission or Tribunal as the case may be, provided that where those members are equally divided, or in the case of a proposal to disqualify a sole conciliator or arbitrator, or a majority of the conciliators or arbitrators, the Chairman shall take that decision. If it is decided that the proposal is well-founded the conciliator or arbitrator to whom the decision relates shall be replaced in accordance with the provisions of Section 2 of Chapter III or Section 2 of Chapter IV.

CHAPTER VI Cost of Proceedings

Article 59

The charges payable by the parties for the use of the facilities of the Centre shall be determined by the Secretary-General in accordance with the regulations adopted by the Administrative Council.

Article 60

(1) Each Commission and each Tribunal shall determine the fees and expenses of its members within limits established from time to time by the Administrative Council and after consultation with the Secretary-General.

(2) Nothing in paragraph (1) of this Article shall preclude the parties from agreeing in advance with the Commission or Tribunal concerned upon the fees and expenses of its members.

Article 61

(1) In the case of conciliation proceedings the fees and expenses of members of the Commission as well as the charges for the use of the facilities of the Centre, shall be borne equally by the parties. Each party shall bear any other expenses it incurs in connection with the proceedings.

(2) In the case of arbitration proceedings the Tribunal shall, except as the parties otherwise agree, assess the expenses incurred by the parties in connection with the proceedings, and shall decide how and by whom those expenses, the fees and expenses of the members of the Tribunal and the charges for the use of the facilities of the Centre shall be paid. Such decision shall form part of the award.

CHAPTER VII Place of Proceedings

Article 62

Conciliation and arbitration proceedings shall be held at the seat of the Centre except as hereinafter provided.

Article 63

Conciliation and arbitration proceedings may be held, if the parties so agree,

(a) at the seat of the Permanent Court of Arbitration or of any other appropriate institution, whether private or public, with which the Centre may make arrangements for that purpose; or

(b) at any other place approved by the Commission or Tribunal after consultation with the Secretary-General.

CHAPTER VIII Disputes Between Contracting States

Article 64

Any dispute arising between Contracting States concerning the interpretation or application of this Convention which is not settled by negotiation shall be referred to the International Court of Justice by the application of any party to such dispute, unless the States concerned agree to another method of settlement.

CHAPTER IX Amendment

Article 65

Any Contracting State may propose amendment of this Convention. The text of a proposed amendment shall be communicated to the Secretary-General not less than 90 days prior to the meeting of the Administrative Council at which such amendment is to be considered and shall forthwith be transmitted by him to all the members of the Administrative Council.

Article 66

(1) If the Administrative Council shall so decide by a majority of two-thirds of its members, the proposed amendment shall be circulated to all Contracting States for ratification, acceptance or approval. Each amendment shall enter into force 30 days after dispatch by the depositary of this Convention of a notification to Contracting States that all Contracting States have ratified, accepted or approved the amendment.

(2) No amendment shall affect the rights and obligations under this Convention of any Contracting State or of any of its constituent subdivisions or agencies, or of any national of such State arising out of consent to the jurisdiction of the Centre given before the date of entry into force of the amendment.

CHAPTER X Final Provisions

Article 67

This Convention shall be open for signature on behalf of States members of the Bank. It shall also be open for signature on behalf of any other State which is a party to the Statute of the International Court of Justice and which the Administrative Council, by a vote of two-thirds of its members, shall have invited to sign the Convention.

Article 68

(1) This Convention shall be subject to ratification, acceptance or approval by the signatory States in accordance with their respective constitutional procedures.

(2) This Convention shall enter into force 30 days after the date of deposit of the twentieth instrument of ratification, acceptance or approval. It shall enter into force for each State which subsequently deposits its instrument of ratification, acceptance or approval 30 days after the date of such deposit.

Article 69

Each Contracting State shall take such legislative or other measures as may be necessary for making the provisions of this Convention effective in its territories.

Article 70

This Convention shall apply to all territories for whose international relations a Contracting State is responsible, except those which are excluded by such State by written notice to the depositary of this Convention either at the time of ratification, acceptance or approval or subsequently.

Article 71

Any Contracting State may denounce this Convention by written notice to the depositary of this Convention. The denunciation shall take effect six months after receipt of such notice.

Article 72

Notice by a Contracting State pursuant to Articles 70 or 71 shall not affect the rights or obligations under this Convention of that State or of any of its constituent subdivisions or agencies or of any national of that State arising out of consent to the jurisdiction of the Centre given by one of them before such notice was received by the depositary.

Article 73

Instruments of ratification, acceptance or approval of this Convention and of amendments thereto shall be deposited with the Bank which shall act as the depositary of this Convention. The depositary shall transmit certified copies of this Convention to States members of the Bank and to any other State invited to sign the Convention.

Article 74

The depositary shall register this Convention with the Secretariat of the United Nations in accordance with Article 102 of the Charter of the United Nations and the Regulations thereunder adopted by the General Assembly.

Article 75

The depositary shall notify all signatory States of the following:

(a) signatures in accordance with Article 67;
(b) deposits of instruments of ratification, acceptance and approval in accordance with Article 73;
(c) the date on which this Convention enters into force in accordance with Article 68;
(d) exclusions from territorial application pursuant to Article 70;
(e) the date on which any amendment of this Convention enters into force in accordance with Article 66; and
(f) denunciations in accordance with Article 71.

DONE at Washington, in the English, French and Spanish languages, all three texts being equally authentic, in a single copy which shall remain deposited in the archives of the International Bank for Reconstruction and Development, which has indicated by its signature below its agreement to fulfil the functions with which it is charged under this Convention.

37.b Rules of Procedure for the Institution of Conciliation and Arbitration Proceedings (Institution Rules)

Date: 10 April 2006
Source: International Centre for Settlement of Investment Disputes (ed), *ICSID Convention, Regulations and Rules* (Doc ICSID/15, April 2006)
https://icsid.worldbank.org/sites/default/files/ICSID%20Convention%20English.pdf

Rule 1 The Request

(1) Any Contracting State or any national of a Contracting State wishing to institute conciliation or arbitration proceedings under the Convention shall address a request to that effect in writing to the Secretary-General at the seat of the Centre. The request shall indicate whether it relates to a conciliation or an arbitration proceeding. It shall be drawn up in an official language of the Centre, shall be dated, and shall be signed by the requesting party or its duly authorized representative.

(2) The request may be made jointly by the parties to the dispute.

Rule 2 Contents of the Request

(1) The request shall:

(a) designate precisely each party to the dispute and state the address of each;

(b) state, if one of the parties is a constituent subdivision or agency of a Contracting State, that it has been designated to the Centre by that State pursuant to Article 25(1) of the Convention;

(c) indicate the date of consent and the instruments in which it is recorded, including, if one party is a constituent subdivision or agency of a Contracting State, similar data on the approval of such consent by that State unless it had notified the Centre that no such approval is required;

(d) indicate with respect to the party that is a national of a Contracting State:

(i) its nationality on the date of consent; and

(ii) if the party is a natural person:

(A) his nationality on the date of the request; and

(B) that he did not have the nationality of the Contracting State party to the dispute either on the date of consent or on the date of the request; or

(iii) if the party is a juridical person which on the date of consent had the nationality of the Contracting State party to the dispute, the agreement of the parties that it should be treated as a national of another Contracting State for the purposes of the Convention;

(e) contain information concerning the issues in dispute indicating that there is, between the parties, a legal dispute arising directly out of an investment; and

(f) state, if the requesting party is a juridical person, that it has taken all necessary internal actions to authorize the request.

(2) The information required by subparagraphs (1)(c), (1)(d)(iii) and (1)(f) shall be supported by documentation.

(3) "Date of consent" means the date on which the parties to the dispute consented in writing to submit it to the Centre; if both parties did not act on the same day, it means the date on which the second party acted.

Rule 3 Optional Information in the Request

The request may in addition set forth any provisions agreed by the parties regarding the number of conciliators or arbitrators and the method of their appointment, as well as any other provisions agreed concerning the settlement of the dispute.

Rule 4 Copies of the Request

(1) The request shall be accompanied by five additional signed copies. The Secretary-General may require such further copies as he may deem necessary.

(2) Any documentation submitted with the request shall conform to the requirements of Administrative and Financial Regulation 30.

Rule 5 Acknowledgement of the Request

(1) On receiving a request the Secretary-General shall:

(a) send an acknowledgement to the requesting party;

(b) take no other action with respect to the request until he has received payment of the prescribed fee.

(2) As soon as he has received the fee for lodging the request, the Secretary-General shall transmit a copy of the request and of the accompanying documentation to the other party.

Rule 6 Registration of the Request

(1) The Secretary-General shall, subject to Rule 5(1)(b), as soon as possible, either:

(a) register the request in the Conciliation or the Arbitration Register and on the same day notify the parties of the registration; or

(b) if he finds, on the basis of the information contained in the request, that the dispute is manifestly outside the jurisdiction of the Centre, notify the parties of his refusal to register the request and of the reasons therefor.

(2) A proceeding under the Convention shall be deemed to have been instituted on the date of the registration of the request.

Rule 7 Notice of Registration

The notice of registration of a request shall:

(a) record that the request is registered and indicate the date of the registration and of the dispatch of that notice;

(b) notify each party that all communications and notices in connection with the proceeding will be sent to the address stated in the request, unless another address is indicated to the Centre;

(c) unless such information has already been provided, invite the parties to communicate to the Secretary-General any provisions agreed by them regarding the number and the method of appointment of the conciliators or arbitrators;

(d) invite the parties to proceed, as soon as possible, to constitute a Conciliation Commission in accordance with Articles 29 to 31 of the Convention, or an Arbitral Tribunal in accordance with Articles 37 to 40;

(e) remind the parties that the registration of the request is without prejudice to the powers and functions of the Conciliation Commission or Arbitral Tribunal in regard to jurisdiction, competence and the merits; and

(f) be accompanied by a list of the members of the Panel of Conciliators or of Arbitrators of the Centre.

Rule 8 Withdrawal of the Request

The requesting party may, by written notice to the Secretary-General, withdraw the request before it has been registered. The Secretary-General shall promptly notify the other party, unless, pursuant to Rule 5(1)(b), the request had not been transmitted to it.

Rule 9 Final Provisions

(1) The texts of these Rules in each official language of the Centre shall be equally authentic.

(2) These Rules may be cited as the "Institution Rules" of the Centre.

37.c Rules of Procedure for Arbitration Proceedings (Arbitration Rules)

Date: 10 April 2006
Source: International Centre for Settlement of Investment Disputes (ed), *ICSID Convention, Regulations and Rules* (Doc ICSID/15, April 2006)
https://icsid.worldbank.org/sites/default/files/ICSID%20Convention%20English.pdf

Chapter I Establishment of the Tribunal

Rule 1 General Obligations

(1) Upon notification of the registration of the request for arbitration, the parties shall, with all possible dispatch, proceed to constitute a Tribunal, with due regard to Section 2 of Chapter IV of the Convention.

(2) Unless such information is provided in the request, the parties shall communicate to the Secretary-General as soon as possible any provisions agreed by them regarding the number of arbitrators and the method of their appointment.

(3) The majority of the arbitrators shall be nationals of States other than the State party to the dispute and of the State whose national is a party to the dispute, unless the sole arbitrator or each individual member of the Tribunal is appointed by agreement of the parties. Where the Tribunal is to consist of three members, a national of either of these States may not be appointed as an arbitrator by a party without the agreement of the other party to the dispute. Where the Tribunal is to consist of five or more members, nationals of either of these States may not be appointed as arbitrators by a party if appointment by the other party of the same number of arbitrators of either of these nationalities would result in a majority of arbitrators of these nationalities.

(4) No person who had previously acted as a conciliator or arbitrator in any proceeding for the settlement of the dispute may be appointed as a member of the Tribunal.

Rule 2 Method of Constituting the Tribunal in the Absence of Previous Agreement

(1) If the parties, at the time of the registration of the request for arbitration, have not agreed upon the number of arbitrators and the method of their appointment, they shall, unless they agree otherwise, follow the following procedure:

- (a) the requesting party shall, within 10 days after the registration of the request, propose to the other party the appointment of a sole arbitrator or of a specified uneven number of arbitrators and specify the method proposed for their appointment;
- (b) within 20 days after receipt of the proposals made by the requesting party, the other party shall:
  - (i) accept such proposals; or
  - (ii) make other proposals regarding the number of arbitrators and the method of their appointment;
- (c) within 20 days after receipt of the reply containing any such other proposals, the requesting party shall notify the other party whether it accepts or rejects such proposals.

(2) The communications provided for in paragraph (1) shall be made or promptly confirmed in writing and shall either be transmitted through the Secretary-General or

directly between the parties with a copy to the Secretary-General. The parties shall promptly notify the Secretary-General of the contents of any agreement reached.

(3) At any time 60 days after the registration of the request, if no agreement on another procedure is reached, either party may inform the Secretary-General that it chooses the formula provided for in Article 37(2)(b) of the Convention. The Secretary-General shall thereupon promptly inform the other party that the Tribunal is to be constituted in accordance with that Article.

Rule 3 Appointment of Arbitrators to a Tribunal Constituted in Accordance with Convention Article 37(2)(b)

(1) If the Tribunal is to be constituted in accordance with Article 37(2)(b) of the Convention:

- (a) either party shall in a communication to the other party:
  - (i) name two persons, identifying one of them, who shall not have the same nationality as nor be a national of either party, as the arbitrator appointed by it, and the other as the arbitrator proposed to be the President of the Tribunal; and
  - (ii) invite the other party to concur in the appointment of the arbitrator proposed to be the President of the Tribunal and to appoint another arbitrator;
- (b) promptly upon receipt of this communication the other party shall, in its reply:
  - (i) name a person as the arbitrator appointed by it, who shall not have the same nationality as nor be a national of either party; and
  - (ii) concur in the appointment of the arbitrator proposed to be the President of the Tribunal or name another person as the arbitrator proposed to be President;
- (c) promptly upon receipt of the reply containing such a proposal, the initiating party shall notify the other party whether it concurs in the appointment of the arbitrator proposed by that party to be the President of the Tribunal.

(2) The communications provided for in this Rule shall be made or promptly confirmed in writing and shall either be transmitted through the Secretary-General or directly between the parties with a copy to the Secretary-General.

Rule 4 Appointment of Arbitrators by the Chairman of the Administrative Council

(1) If the Tribunal is not constituted within 90 days after the dispatch by the Secretary-General of the notice of registration, or such other period as the parties may agree, either party may, through the Secretary-General, address to the Chairman of the Administrative Council a request in writing to appoint the arbitrator or arbitrators not yet appointed and to designate an arbitrator to be the President of the Tribunal.

(2) The provision of paragraph (1) shall apply *mutatis mutandis* in the event that the parties have agreed that the arbitrators shall elect the President of the Tribunal and they fail to do so.

(3) The Secretary-General shall forthwith send a copy of the request to the other party.

(4) The Chairman shall use his best efforts to comply with that request within 30 days after its receipt. Before he proceeds to make an appointment or designation, with due regard to Articles 38 and 40(1) of the Convention, he shall consult both parties as far as possible.

(5) The Secretary-General shall promptly notify the parties of any appointment or designation made by the Chairman.

Rule 5 Acceptance of Appointments

(1) The party or parties concerned shall notify the Secretary-General of the appointment of each arbitrator and indicate the method of his appointment.

(2) As soon as the Secretary-General has been informed by a party or the Chairman of the Administrative Council of the appointment of an arbitrator, he shall seek an acceptance from the appointee.

(3) If an arbitrator fails to accept his appointment within 15 days, the Secretary-General shall promptly notify the parties, and if appropriate the Chairman, and invite them to proceed to the appointment of another arbitrator in accordance with the method followed for the previous appointment.

Rule 6 Constitution of the Tribunal

(1) The Tribunal shall be deemed to be constituted and the proceeding to have begun on the date the Secretary-General notifies the parties that all the arbitrators have accepted their appointment.

(2) Before or at the first session of the Tribunal, each arbitrator shall sign a declaration in the following form:

"To the best of my knowledge there is no reason why I should not serve on the Arbitral Tribunal constituted by the International Centre for Settlement of Investment Disputes with respect to a dispute between ________________ and ________________.

"I shall keep confidential all information coming to my knowledge as a result of my participation in this proceeding, as well as the contents of any award made by the Tribunal.

"I shall judge fairly as between the parties, according to the applicable law, and shall not accept any instruction or compensation with regard to the proceeding from any source except as provided in the Convention on the Settlement of Investment Disputes between States and Nationals of Other States and in the Regulations and Rules made pursuant thereto.

"Attached is a statement of (a) my past and present professional, business and other relationships (if any) with the parties and (b) any other circumstance that might cause my reliability for independent judgment to be questioned by a party. I acknowledge that by signing this declaration, I assume a continuing obligation promptly to notify the Secretary-General of the Centre of any such relationship or circumstance that subsequently arises during this proceeding."

Any arbitrator failing to sign a declaration by the end of the first session of the Tribunal shall be deemed to have resigned.

Rule 7 Replacement of Arbitrators

At any time before the Tribunal is constituted, each party may replace any arbitrator appointed by it and the parties may by common consent agree to replace any arbitrator. The procedure of such replacement shall be in accordance with Rules 1, 5 and 6.

Rule 8 Incapacity or Resignation of Arbitrators

(1) If an arbitrator becomes incapacitated or unable to perform the duties of his office, the procedure in respect of the disqualification of arbitrators set forth in Rule 9 shall apply.

(2) An arbitrator may resign by submitting his resignation to the other members of the Tribunal and the Secretary-General. If the arbitrator was appointed by one of the parties,

the Tribunal shall promptly consider the reasons for his resignation and decide whether it consents thereto. The Tribunal shall promptly notify the Secretary-General of its decision.

Rule 9 Disqualification of Arbitrators

(1) A party proposing the disqualification of an arbitrator pursuant to Article 57 of the Convention shall promptly, and in any event before the proceeding is declared closed, file its proposal with the Secretary-General, stating its reasons therefor.

(2) The Secretary-General shall forthwith:

(a) transmit the proposal to the members of the Tribunal and, if it relates to a sole arbitrator or to a majority of the members of the Tribunal, to the Chairman of the Administrative Council; and

(b) notify the other party of the proposal.

(3) The arbitrator to whom the proposal relates may, without delay, furnish explanations to the Tribunal or the Chairman, as the case may be.

(4) Unless the proposal relates to a majority of the members of the Tribunal, the other members shall promptly consider and vote on the proposal in the absence of the arbitrator concerned. If those members are equally divided, they shall, through the Secretary-General, promptly notify the Chairman of the proposal, of any explanation furnished by the arbitrator concerned and of their failure to reach a decision.

(5) Whenever the Chairman has to decide on a proposal to disqualify an arbitrator, he shall use his best efforts to take that decision within 30 days after he has received the proposal.

(6) The proceeding shall be suspended until a decision has been taken on the proposal.

Rule 10 Procedure during a Vacancy on the Tribunal

(1) The Secretary-General shall forthwith notify the parties and, if necessary, the Chairman of the Administrative Council of the disqualification, death, incapacity or resignation of an arbitrator and of the consent, if any, of the Tribunal to a resignation.

(2) Upon the notification by the Secretary-General of a vacancy on the Tribunal, the proceeding shall be or remain suspended until the vacancy has been filled.

Rule 11 Filling Vacancies on the Tribunal

(1) Except as provided in paragraph (2), a vacancy resulting from the disqualification, death, incapacity or resignation of an arbitrator shall be promptly filled by the same method by which his appointment had been made.

(2) In addition to filling vacancies relating to arbitrators appointed by him, the Chairman of the Administrative Council shall appoint a person from the Panel of Arbitrators:

(a) to fill a vacancy caused by the resignation, without the consent of the Tribunal, of an arbitrator appointed by a party; or

(b) at the request of either party, to fill any other vacancy, if no new appointment is made and accepted within 45 days of the notification of the vacancy by the Secretary-General.

(3) The procedure for filling a vacancy shall be in accordance with Rules 1, 4(4), 4(5), 5 and, *mutatis mutandis*, 6(2).

Rule 12 Resumption of Proceeding after Filling a Vacancy

As soon as a vacancy on the Tribunal has been filled, the proceeding shall continue from the point it had reached at the time the vacancy occurred. The newly appointed arbitrator may, however, require that the oral procedure be recommenced, if this had already been started.

Chapter II Working of the Tribunal

Rule 13 Sessions of the Tribunal

(1) The Tribunal shall hold its first session within 60 days after its constitution or such other period as the parties may agree. The dates of that session shall be fixed by the President of the Tribunal after consultation with its members and the Secretary-General. If upon its constitution the Tribunal has no President because the parties have agreed that the President shall be elected by its members, the Secretary-General shall fix the dates of that session. In both cases, the parties shall be consulted as far as possible.

(2) The dates of subsequent sessions shall be determined by the Tribunal, after consultation with the Secretary-General and with the parties as far as possible.

(3) The Tribunal shall meet at the seat of the Centre or at such other place as may have been agreed by the parties in accordance with Article 63 of the Convention. If the parties agree that the proceeding shall be held at a place other than the Centre or an institution with which the Centre has made the necessary arrangements, they shall consult with the Secretary-General and request the approval of the Tribunal. Failing such approval, the Tribunal shall meet at the seat of the Centre.

(4) The Secretary-General shall notify the members of the Tribunal and the parties of the dates and place of the sessions of the Tribunal in good time.

Rule 14 Sittings of the Tribunal

(1) The President of the Tribunal shall conduct its hearings and preside at its deliberations.

(2) Except as the parties otherwise agree, the presence of a majority of the members of the Tribunal shall be required at its sittings.

(3) The President of the Tribunal shall fix the date and hour of its sittings.

Rule 15 Deliberations of the Tribunal

(1) The deliberations of the Tribunal shall take place in private and remain secret.

(2) Only members of the Tribunal shall take part in its deliberations. No other person shall be admitted unless the Tribunal decides otherwise.

Rule 16 Decisions of the Tribunal

(1) Decisions of the Tribunal shall be taken by a majority of the votes of all its members. Abstention shall count as a negative vote.

(2) Except as otherwise provided by these Rules or decided by the Tribunal, it may take any decision by correspondence among its members, provided that all of them are consulted. Decisions so taken shall be certified by the President of the Tribunal.

Rule 17 Incapacity of the President

If at any time the President of the Tribunal should be unable to act, his functions shall be performed by one of the other members of the Tribunal, acting in the order in which the Secretary-General had received the notice of their acceptance of their appointment to the Tribunal.

Rule 18 Representation of the Parties

(1) Each party may be represented or assisted by agents, counsel or advocates whose names and authority shall be notified by that party to the Secretary-General, who shall promptly inform the Tribunal and the other party.

(2) For the purposes of these Rules, the expression "party" includes, where the context so admits, an agent, counsel or advocate authorized to represent that party.

Chapter III General Procedural Provisions

Rule 19 Procedural Orders

The Tribunal shall make the orders required for the conduct of the proceeding.

Rule 20 Preliminary Procedural Consultation

(1) As early as possible after the constitution of a Tribunal, its President shall endeavor to ascertain the views of the parties regarding questions of procedure. For this purpose he may request the parties to meet him. He shall, in particular, seek their views on the following matters:

(a) the number of members of the Tribunal required to constitute a quorum at its sittings;
(b) the language or languages to be used in the proceeding;
(c) the number and sequence of the pleadings and the time limits within which they are to be filed;
(d) the number of copies desired by each party of instruments filed by the other;
(e) dispensing with the written or the oral procedure;
(f) the manner in which the cost of the proceeding is to be apportioned; and
(g) the manner in which the record of the hearings shall be kept.

(2) In the conduct of the proceeding the Tribunal shall apply any agreement between the parties on procedural matters, except as otherwise provided in the Convention or the Administrative and Financial Regulations.

Rule 21 Pre-Hearing Conference

(1) At the request of the Secretary-General or at the discretion of the President of the Tribunal, a pre-hearing conference between the Tribunal and the parties may be held to arrange for an exchange of information and the stipulation of uncontested facts in order to expedite the proceeding.

(2) At the request of the parties, a pre-hearing conference between the Tribunal and the parties, duly represented by their authorized representatives, may be held to consider the issues in dispute with a view to reaching an amicable settlement.

Rule 22 Procedural Languages

(1) The parties may agree on the use of one or two languages to be used in the proceeding, provided, that, if they agree on any language that is not an official language of the Centre, the Tribunal, after consultation with the Secretary-General, gives its approval. If the parties do not agree on any such procedural language, each of them may select one of the official languages (i.e., English, French and Spanish) for this purpose.

(2) If two procedural languages are selected by the parties, any instrument may be filed in either language. Either language may be used at the hearings, subject, if the Tribunal so

requires, to translation and interpretation. The orders and the award of the Tribunal shall be rendered and the record kept in both procedural languages, both versions being equally authentic.

Rule 23 Copies of Instruments

Except as otherwise provided by the Tribunal after consultation with the parties and the Secretary-General, every request, pleading, application, written observation, supporting documentation, if any, or other instrument shall be filed in the form of a signed original accompanied by the following number of additional copies:

(a) before the number of members of the Tribunal has been determined: five;

(b) after the number of members of the Tribunal has been determined: two more than the number of its members.

Rule 24 Supporting Documentation

Supporting documentation shall ordinarily be filed together with the instrument to which it relates, and in any case within the time limit fixed for the filing of such instrument.

Rule 25 Correction of Errors

An accidental error in any instrument or supporting document may, with the consent of the other party or by leave of the Tribunal, be corrected at any time before the award is rendered.

Rule 26 Time Limits

(1) Where required, time limits shall be fixed by the Tribunal by assigning dates for the completion of the various steps in the proceeding. The Tribunal may delegate this power to its President.

(2) The Tribunal may extend any time limit that it has fixed. If the Tribunal is not in session, this power shall be exercised by its President.

(3) Any step taken after expiration of the applicable time limit shall be disregarded unless the Tribunal, in special circumstances and after giving the other party an opportunity of stating its views, decides otherwise.

Rule 27 Waiver

A party which knows or should have known that a provision of the Administrative and Financial Regulations, of these Rules, of any other rules or agreement applicable to the proceeding, or of an order of the Tribunal has not been complied with and which fails to state promptly its objections thereto, shall be deemed – subject to Article 45 of the Convention – to have waived its right to object.

Rule 28 Cost of Proceeding

(1) Without prejudice to the final decision on the payment of the cost of the proceeding, the Tribunal may, unless otherwise agreed by the parties, decide:

(a) at any stage of the proceeding, the portion which each party shall pay, pursuant to Administrative and Financial Regulation 14, of the fees and expenses of the Tribunal and the charges for the use of the facilities of the Centre;

(b) with respect to any part of the proceeding, that the related costs (as determined by the Secretary-General) shall be borne entirely or in a particular share by one of the parties.

(2) Promptly after the closure of the proceeding, each party shall submit to the Tribunal a statement of costs reasonably incurred or borne by it in the proceeding and the Secretary-General shall submit to the Tribunal an account of all amounts paid by each party to the Centre and of all costs incurred by the Centre for the proceeding. The Tribunal may, before the award has been rendered, request the parties and the Secretary-General to provide additional information concerning the cost of the proceeding.

Chapter IV Written and Oral Procedures

Rule 29 Normal Procedures

Except if the parties otherwise agree, the proceeding shall comprise two distinct phases: a written procedure followed by an oral one.

Rule 30 Transmission of the Request

As soon as the Tribunal is constituted, the Secretary-General shall transmit to each member a copy of the request by which the proceeding was initiated, of the supporting documentation, of the notice of registration and of any communication received from either party in response thereto.

Rule 31 The Written Procedure

(1) In addition to the request for arbitration, the written procedure shall consist of the following pleadings, filed within time limits set by the Tribunal:

(a) a memorial by the requesting party;
(b) a counter-memorial by the other party;
and, if the parties so agree or the Tribunal deems it necessary:
(c) a reply by the requesting party; and
(d) a rejoinder by the other party.

(2) If the request was made jointly, each party shall, within the same time limit determined by the Tribunal, file its memorial and, if the parties so agree or the Tribunal deems it necessary, its reply; however, the parties may instead agree that one of them shall, for the purposes of paragraph (1), be considered as the requesting party.

(3) A memorial shall contain: a statement of the relevant facts; a statement of law; and the submissions. A counter-memorial, reply or rejoinder shall contain an admission or denial of the facts stated in the last previous pleading; any additional facts, if necessary; observations concerning the statement of law in the last previous pleading; a statement of law in answer thereto; and the submissions.

Rule 32 The Oral Procedure

(1) The oral procedure shall consist of the hearing by the Tribunal of the parties, their agents, counsel and advocates, and of witnesses and experts.

(2) Unless either party objects, the Tribunal, after consultation with the Secretary-General, may allow other persons, besides the parties, their agents, counsel and advocates, witnesses and experts during their testimony, and officers of the Tribunal, to attend or observe all or part of the hearings, subject to appropriate logistical arrangements. The Tribunal shall for such cases establish procedures for the protection of proprietary or privileged information.

(3) The members of the Tribunal may, during the hearings, put questions to the parties, their agents, counsel and advocates, and ask them for explanations.

Rule 33 Marshalling of Evidence

Without prejudice to the rules concerning the production of documents, each party shall, within time limits fixed by the Tribunal, communicate to the Secretary-General, for transmission to the Tribunal and the other party, precise information regarding the evidence which it intends to produce and that which it intends to request the Tribunal to call for, together with an indication of the points to which such evidence will be directed.

Rule 34 Evidence: General Principles

(1) The Tribunal shall be the judge of the admissibility of any evidence adduced and of its probative value.

(2) The Tribunal may, if it deems it necessary at any stage of the proceeding:

(a) call upon the parties to produce documents, witnesses and experts; and

(b) visit any place connected with the dispute or conduct inquiries there.

(3) The parties shall cooperate with the Tribunal in the production of the evidence and in the other measures provided for in paragraph (2). The Tribunal shall take formal note of the failure of a party to comply with its obligations under this paragraph and of any reasons given for such failure.

(4) Expenses incurred in producing evidence and in taking other measures in accordance with paragraph (2) shall be deemed to constitute part of the expenses incurred by the parties within the meaning of Article 61(2) of the Convention.

Rule 35 Examination of Witnesses and Experts

(1) Witnesses and experts shall be examined before the Tribunal by the parties under the control of its President. Questions may also be put to them by any member of the Tribunal.

(2) Each witness shall make the following declaration before giving his evidence: "I solemnly declare upon my honour and conscience that I shall speak the truth, the whole truth and nothing but the truth."

(3) Each expert shall make the following declaration before making his statement: "I solemnly declare upon my honour and conscience that my statement will be in accordance with my sincere belief."

Rule 36 Witnesses and Experts: Special Rules

Notwithstanding Rule 35 the Tribunal may:

(a) admit evidence given by a witness or expert in a written deposition; and

(b) with the consent of both parties, arrange for the examination of a witness or expert otherwise than before the Tribunal itself. The Tribunal shall define the subject of the examination, the time limit, the procedure to be followed and other particulars. The parties may participate in the examination.

Rule 37 Visits and Inquiries; Submissions of Non-disputing Parties

(1) If the Tribunal considers it necessary to visit any place connected with the dispute or to conduct an inquiry there, it shall make an order to this effect. The order shall define the scope of the visit or the subject of the inquiry, the time limit, the procedure to be followed and other particulars. The parties may participate in any visit or inquiry.

(2) After consulting both parties, the Tribunal may allow a person or entity that is not a party to the dispute (in this Rule called the "non-disputing party") to file a written submission with the Tribunal regarding a matter within the scope of the dispute. In

determining whether to allow such a filing, the Tribunal shall consider, among other things, the extent to which:

(a) the non-disputing party submission would assist the Tribunal in the determination of a factual or legal issue related to the proceeding by bringing a perspective, particular knowledge or insight that is different from that of the disputing parties;
(b) the non-disputing party submission would address a matter within the scope of the dispute;
(c) the non-disputing party has a significant interest in the proceeding.

The Tribunal shall ensure that the non-disputing party submission does not disrupt the proceeding or unduly burden or unfairly prejudice either party, and that both parties are given an opportunity to present their observations on the non-disputing party submission.

Rule 38 Closure of the Proceeding

(1) When the presentation of the case by the parties is completed, the proceeding shall be declared closed.

(2) Exceptionally, the Tribunal may, before the award has been rendered, reopen the proceeding on the ground that new evidence is forthcoming of such a nature as to constitute a decisive factor, or that there is a vital need for clarification on certain specific points.

Chapter V Particular Procedures

Rule 39 Provisional Measures

(1) At any time after the institution of the proceeding, a party may request that provisional measures for the preservation of its rights be recommended by the Tribunal. The request shall specify the rights to be preserved, the measures the recommendation of which is requested, and the circumstances that require such measures.

(2) The Tribunal shall give priority to the consideration of a request made pursuant to paragraph (1).

(3) The Tribunal may also recommend provisional measures on its own initiative or recommend measures other than those specified in a request. It may at any time modify or revoke its recommendations.

(4) The Tribunal shall only recommend provisional measures, or modify or revoke its recommendations, after giving each party an opportunity of presenting its observations.

(5) If a party makes a request pursuant to paragraph (1) before the constitution of the Tribunal, the Secretary-General shall, on the application of either party, fix time limits for the parties to present observations on the request, so that the request and observations may be considered by the Tribunal promptly upon its constitution.

(6) Nothing in this Rule shall prevent the parties, provided that they have so stipulated in the agreement recording their consent, from requesting any judicial or other authority to order provisional measures, prior to or after the institution of the proceeding, for the preservation of their respective rights and interests.

Rule 40 Ancillary Claims

(1) Except as the parties otherwise agree, a party may present an incidental or additional claim or counter-claim arising directly out of the subject-matter of the dispute, provided that such ancillary claim is within the scope of the consent of the parties and is otherwise within the jurisdiction of the Centre.

(2) An incidental or additional claim shall be presented not later than in the reply and a counter-claim no later than in the counter-memorial, unless the Tribunal, upon justification by the party presenting the ancillary claim and upon considering any objection of the other party, authorizes the presentation of the claim at a later stage in the proceeding.

(3) The Tribunal shall fix a time limit within which the party against which an ancillary claim is presented may file its observations thereon.

Rule 41 Preliminary Objections

(1) Any objection that the dispute or any ancillary claim is not within the jurisdiction of the Centre or, for other reasons, is not within the competence of the Tribunal shall be made as early as possible. A party shall file the objection with the Secretary-General no later than the expiration of the time limit fixed for the filing of the counter-memorial, or, if the objection relates to an ancillary claim, for the filing of the rejoinder – unless the facts on which the objection is based are unknown to the party at that time.

(2) The Tribunal may on its own initiative consider, at any stage of the proceeding, whether the dispute or any ancillary claim before it is within the jurisdiction of the Centre and within its own competence.

(3) Upon the formal raising of an objection relating to the dispute, the Tribunal may decide to suspend the proceeding on the merits. The President of the Tribunal, after consultation with its other members, shall fix a time limit within which the parties may file observations on the objection.

(4) The Tribunal shall decide whether or not the further procedures relating to the objection made pursuant to paragraph (1) shall be oral. It may deal with the objection as a preliminary question or join it to the merits of the dispute. If the Tribunal overrules the objection or joins it to the merits, it shall once more fix time limits for the further procedures.

(5) Unless the parties have agreed to another expedited procedure for making preliminary objections, a party may, no later than 30 days after the constitution of the Tribunal, and in any event before the first session of the Tribunal, file an objection that a claim is manifestly without legal merit. The party shall specify as precisely as possible the basis for the objection. The Tribunal, after giving the parties the opportunity to present their observations on the objection, shall, at its first session or promptly thereafter, notify the parties of its decision on the objection. The decision of the Tribunal shall be without prejudice to the right of a party to file an objection pursuant to paragraph (1) or to object, in the course of the proceeding, that a claim lacks legal merit.

(6) If the Tribunal decides that the dispute is not within the jurisdiction of the Centre or not within its own competence, or that all claims are manifestly without legal merit, it shall render an award to that effect.

Rule 42 Default

(1) If a party (in this Rule called the "defaulting party") fails to appear or to present its case at any stage of the proceeding, the other party may, at any time prior to the discontinuance of the proceeding, request the Tribunal to deal with the questions submitted to it and to render an award.

(2) The Tribunal shall promptly notify the defaulting party of such a request. Unless it is satisfied that that party does not intend to appear or to present its case in the proceeding, it shall, at the same time, grant a period of grace and to this end:

(a) if that party had failed to file a pleading or any other instrument within the time limit fixed therefor, fix a new time limit for its filing; or
(b) if that party had failed to appear or present its case at a hearing, fix a new date for the hearing.

The period of grace shall not, without the consent of the other party, exceed 60 days.

(3) After the expiration of the period of grace or when, in accordance with paragraph (2) no such period is granted, the Tribunal shall resume the consideration of the dispute. Failure of the defaulting party to appear or to present its case shall not be deemed an admission of the assertions made by the other party.

(4) The Tribunal shall examine the jurisdiction of the Centre and its own competence in the dispute and, if it is satisfied, decide whether the submissions made are well-founded in fact and in law. To this end, it may, at any stage of the proceeding, call on the party appearing to file observations, produce evidence or submit oral explanations.

Rule 43 Settlement and Discontinuance

(1) If, before the award is rendered, the parties agree on a settlement of the dispute or otherwise to discontinue the proceeding, the Tribunal, or the Secretary-General if the Tribunal has not yet been constituted, shall, at their written request, in an order take note of the discontinuance of the proceeding.

(2) If the parties file with the Secretary-General the full and signed text of their settlement and in writing request the Tribunal to embody such settlement in an award, the Tribunal may record the settlement in the form of its award.

Rule 44 Discontinuance at Request of a Party

If a party requests the discontinuance of the proceeding, the Tribunal, or the Secretary-General if the Tribunal has not yet been constituted, shall in an order fix a time limit within which the other party may state whether it opposes the discontinuance. If no objection is made in writing within the time limit, the other party shall be deemed to have acquiesced in the discontinuance and the Tribunal, or if appropriate the Secretary-General, shall in an order take note of the discontinuance of the proceeding. If objection is made, the proceeding shall continue.

Rule 45 Discontinuance for Failure of Parties to Act

If the parties fail to take any steps in the proceeding during six consecutive months or such period as they may agree with the approval of the Tribunal, or of the Secretary-General if the Tribunal has not yet been constituted, they shall be deemed to have discontinued the proceeding and the Tribunal, or if appropriate the Secretary-General, shall, after notice to the parties, in an order take note of the discontinuance.

Chapter VI The Award

Rule 46 Preparation of the Award

The award (including any individual or dissenting opinion) shall be drawn up and signed within 120 days after closure of the proceeding. The Tribunal may, however, extend this period by a further 60 days if it would otherwise be unable to draw up the award.

Rule 47 The Award

(1) The award shall be in writing and shall contain:

(a) a precise designation of each party;

(b) a statement that the Tribunal was established under the Convention, and a description of the method of its constitution;

(c) the name of each member of the Tribunal, and an identification of the appointing authority of each;

(d) the names of the agents, counsel and advocates of the parties;

(e) the dates and place of the sittings of the Tribunal;

(f) a summary of the proceeding;

(g) a statement of the facts as found by the Tribunal;

(h) the submissions of the parties;

(i) the decision of the Tribunal on every question submitted to it, together with the reasons upon which the decision is based; and

(j) any decision of the Tribunal regarding the cost of the proceeding.

(2) The award shall be signed by the members of the Tribunal who voted for it; the date of each signature shall be indicated.

(3) Any member of the Tribunal may attach his individual opinion to the award, whether he dissents from the majority or not, or a statement of his dissent.

Rule 48 Rendering of the Award

(1) Upon signature by the last arbitrator to sign, the Secretary-General shall promptly:

(a) authenticate the original text of the award and deposit it in the archives of the Centre, together with any individual opinions and statements of dissent; and

(b) dispatch a certified copy of the award (including individual opinions and statements of dissent) to each party, indicating the date of dispatch on the original text and on all copies.

(2) The award shall be deemed to have been rendered on the date on which the certified copies were dispatched.

(3) The Secretary-General shall, upon request, make available to a party additional certified copies of the award.

(4) The Centre shall not publish the award without the consent of the parties. The Centre shall, however, promptly include in its publications excerpts of the legal reasoning of the Tribunal.

Rule 49 Supplementary Decisions and Rectification

(1) Within 45 days after the date on which the award was rendered, either party may request, pursuant to Article 49(2) of the Convention, a supplementary decision on, or the rectification of, the award. Such a request shall be addressed in writing to the Secretary-General. The request shall:

(a) identify the award to which it relates;

(b) indicate the date of the request;

(c) state in detail:

  (i) any question which, in the opinion of the requesting party, the Tribunal omitted to decide in the award; and

  (ii) any error in the award which the requesting party seeks to have rectified; and

(d) be accompanied by a fee for lodging the request.

(2) Upon receipt of the request and of the lodging fee, the Secretary-General shall forthwith:

(a) register the request;
(b) notify the parties of the registration;
(c) transmit to the other party a copy of the request and of any accompanying documentation; and
(d) transmit to each member of the Tribunal a copy of the notice of registration, together with a copy of the request and of any accompanying documentation.

(3) The President of the Tribunal shall consult the members on whether it is necessary for the Tribunal to meet in order to consider the request. The Tribunal shall fix a time limit for the parties to file their observations on the request and shall determine the procedure for its consideration.

(4) Rules 46-48 shall apply, *mutatis mutandis*, to any decision of the Tribunal pursuant to this Rule.

(5) If a request is received by the Secretary-General more than 45 days after the award was rendered, he shall refuse to register the request and so inform forthwith the requesting party.

Chapter VII Interpretation, Revision and Annulment of the Award

Rule 50 The Application

(1) An application for the interpretation, revision or annulment of an award shall be addressed in writing to the Secretary-General and shall:

(a) identify the award to which it relates;
(b) indicate the date of the application;
(c) state in detail:
  (i) in an application for interpretation, the precise points in dispute;
  (ii) in an application for revision, pursuant to Article 51(1) of the Convention, the change sought in the award, the discovery of some fact of such a nature as decisively to affect the award, and evidence that when the award was rendered that fact was unknown to the Tribunal and to the applicant, and that the applicant's ignorance of that fact was not due to negligence;
  (iii) in an application for annulment, pursuant to Article 52(1) of the Convention, the grounds on which it is based. These grounds are limited to the following:
    – that the Tribunal was not properly constituted;
    – that the Tribunal has manifestly exceeded its powers;
    – that there was corruption on the part of a member of the Tribunal;
    – that there has been a serious departure from a fundamental rule of procedure;
    – that the award has failed to state the reasons on which it is based;
(d) be accompanied by the payment of a fee for lodging the application.

(2) Without prejudice to the provisions of paragraph (3), upon receiving an application and the lodging fee, the Secretary-General shall forthwith:

(a) register the application;
(b) notify the parties of the registration; and
(c) transmit to the other party a copy of the application and of any accompanying documentation.

(3) The Secretary-General shall refuse to register an application for:

(a) revision, if, in accordance with Article 51(2) of the Convention, it is not made within 90 days after the discovery of the new fact and in any event within three years after the date on which the award was rendered (or any subsequent decision or correction);

(b) annulment, if, in accordance with Article 52(2) of the Convention, it is not made:

(i) within 120 days after the date on which the award was rendered (or any subsequent decision or correction) if the application is based on any of the following grounds:

– the Tribunal was not properly constituted;
– the Tribunal has manifestly exceeded its powers;
– there has been a serious departure from a fundamental rule of procedure;
– the award has failed to state the reasons on which it is based;

(ii) in the case of corruption on the part of a member of the Tribunal, within 120 days after discovery thereof, and in any event within three years after the date on which the award was rendered (or any subsequent decision or correction).

(4) If the Secretary-General refuses to register an application for revision, or annulment, he shall forthwith notify the requesting party of his refusal.

Rule 51 Interpretation or Revision: Further Procedures

(1) Upon registration of an application for the interpretation or revision of an award, the Secretary-General shall forthwith:

(a) transmit to each member of the original Tribunal a copy of the notice of registration, together with a copy of the application and of any accompanying documentation; and

(b) request each member of the Tribunal to inform him within a specified time limit whether that member is willing to take part in the consideration of the application.

(2) If all members of the Tribunal express their willingness to take part in the consideration of the application, the Secretary-General shall so notify the members of the Tribunal and the parties. Upon dispatch of these notices the Tribunal shall be deemed to be reconstituted.

(3) If the Tribunal cannot be reconstituted in accordance with paragraph (2), the Secretary-General shall so notify the parties and invite them to proceed, as soon as possible, to constitute a new Tribunal, including the same number of arbitrators, and appointed by the same method, as the original one.

Rule 52 Annulment: Further Procedures

(1) Upon registration of an application for the annulment of an award, the Secretary-General shall forthwith request the Chairman of the Administrative Council to appoint an *ad hoc* Committee in accordance with Article 52(3) of the Convention.

(2) The Committee shall be deemed to be constituted on the date the Secretary-General notifies the parties that all members have accepted their appointment. Before or at the first session of the Committee, each member shall sign a declaration conforming to that set forth in Rule 6(2).

Rule 53 Rules of Procedure

The provisions of these Rules shall apply *mutatis mutandis* to any procedure relating to the interpretation, revision or annulment of an award and to the decision of the Tribunal or Committee.

Rule 54 Stay of Enforcement of the Award

(1) The party applying for the interpretation, revision or annulment of an award may in its application, and either party may at any time before the final disposition of the application, request a stay in the enforcement of part or all of the award to which the application relates. The Tribunal or Committee shall give priority to the consideration of such a request.

(2) If an application for the revision or annulment of an award contains a request for a stay of its enforcement, the Secretary-General shall, together with the notice of registration, inform both parties of the provisional stay of the award. As soon as the Tribunal or Committee is constituted it shall, if either party requests, rule within 30 days on whether such stay should be continued; unless it decides to continue the stay, it shall automatically be terminated.

(3) If a stay of enforcement has been granted pursuant to paragraph (1) or continued pursuant to paragraph (2), the Tribunal or Committee may at any time modify or terminate the stay at the request of either party. All stays shall automatically terminate on the date on which a final decision is rendered on the application, except that a Committee granting the partial annulment of an award may order the temporary stay of enforcement of the unannulled portion in order to give either party an opportunity to request any new Tribunal constituted pursuant to Article 52(6) of the Convention to grant a stay pursuant to Rule 55(3).

(4) A request pursuant to paragraph (1), (2) (second sentence) or (3) shall specify the circumstances that require the stay or its modification or termination. A request shall only be granted after the Tribunal or Committee has given each party an opportunity of presenting its observations.

(5) The Secretary-General shall promptly notify both parties of the stay of enforcement of any award and of the modification or termination of such a stay, which shall become effective on the date on which he dispatches such notification.

Rule 55 Resubmission of Dispute after an Annulment

(1) If a Committee annuls part or all of an award, either party may request the resubmission of the dispute to a new Tribunal. Such a request shall be addressed in writing to the Secretary-General and shall:

- (a) identify the award to which it relates;
- (b) indicate the date of the request;
- (c) explain in detail what aspect of the dispute is to be submitted to the Tribunal; and
- (d) be accompanied by a fee for lodging the request.

(2) Upon receipt of the request and of the lodging fee, the Secretary-General shall forthwith:

- (a) register it in the Arbitration Register;
- (b) notify both parties of the registration;
- (c) transmit to the other party a copy of the request and of any accompanying documentation; and
- (d) invite the parties to proceed, as soon as possible, to constitute a new Tribunal, including the same number of arbitrators, and appointed by the same method, as the original one.

(3) If the original award had only been annulled in part, the new Tribunal shall not reconsider any portion of the award not so annulled. It may, however, in accordance with the procedures set forth in Rule 54, stay or continue to stay the enforcement of the unannulled portion of the award until the date its own award is rendered.

(4) Except as otherwise provided in paragraphs (1)–(3), these Rules shall apply to a proceeding on a resubmitted dispute in the same manner as if such dispute had been submitted pursuant to the Institution Rules.

Chapter VIII General Provisions

Rule 56 Final Provisions

(1) The texts of these Rules in each official language of the Centre shall be equally authentic.

(2) These Rules may be cited as the "Arbitration Rules" of the Centre.

37.d Rules Governing the Additional Facility for the Administration of Proceedings by the Secretariat of the International Centre for Settlement of Investment Disputes (Additional Facility Rules)

Date: 10 April 2006
Source: International Centre for Settlement of Investment Disputes (ed), *ICSID Additional Facility Rules* (Doc ICSID/11, April 2006)
https://icsid.worldbank.org/sites/default/files/AFR_2006%20English-final.pdf

Article 1 Definitions

(1) "Convention" means the Convention on the Settlement of Investment Disputes between States and Nationals of Other States, submitted to Governments by the Executive Directors of the International Bank for Reconstruction and Development on March 18, 1965, which entered into force on October 14, 1966.

(2) "Centre" means the International Centre for Settlement of Investment Disputes established pursuant to Article 1 of the Convention.

(3) "Secretariat" means the Secretariat of the Centre.

(4) "Contracting State" means a State for which the Convention has entered into force.

(5) "Secretary-General" means the Secretary-General of the Centre or his deputy.

(6) "National of another State" means a person who is not, or whom the parties to the proceeding in question have agreed not to treat as, a national of the State party to that proceeding.

Article 2 Additional Facility

The Secretariat of the Centre is hereby authorized to administer, subject to and in accordance with these Rules, proceedings between a State (or a constituent subdivision or agency of a State) and a national of another State, falling within the following categories:

(a) conciliation and arbitration proceedings for the settlement of legal disputes arising directly out of an investment which are not within the jurisdiction of the Centre because either the State party to the dispute or the State whose national is a party to the dispute is not a Contracting State;

(b) conciliation and arbitration proceedings for the settlement of legal disputes which are not within the jurisdiction of the Centre because they do not arise directly out of an investment, provided that either the State party to the dispute or the State whose national is a party to the dispute is a Contracting State; and

(c) fact-finding proceedings.

The administration of proceedings authorized by these Rules is hereinafter referred to as the Additional Facility.

Article 3 Convention Not Applicable

Since the proceedings envisaged by Article 2 are outside the jurisdiction of the Centre, none of the provisions of the Convention shall be applicable to them or to recommendations, awards, or reports which may be rendered therein.

Article 4 Access to the Additional Facility in Respect of Conciliation and Arbitration Proceedings Subject to Secretary-General's Approval

(1) Any agreement providing for conciliation or arbitration proceedings under the Additional Facility in respect of existing or future disputes requires the approval of the Secretary-General. The parties may apply for such approval at any time prior to the institution of proceedings by submitting to the Secretariat a copy of the agreement concluded or proposed to be concluded between them together with other relevant documentation and such additional information as the Secretariat may reasonably request.

(2) In the case of an application based on Article 2(a), the Secretary-General shall give his approval only if (a) he is satisfied that the requirements of that provision are fulfilled at the time, and (b) both parties give their consent to the jurisdiction of the Centre under Article 25 of the Convention (in lieu of the Additional Facility) in the event that the jurisdictional requirements *ratione personae* of that Article shall have been met at the time when proceedings are instituted.

(3) In the case of an application based on Article 2(b), the Secretary-General shall give his approval only if he is satisfied (a) that the requirements of that provision are fulfilled, and (b) that the underlying transaction has features which distinguish it from an ordinary commercial transaction.

(4) If in the case of an application based on Article 2(b) the jurisdictional requirements *ratione personae* of Article 25 of the Convention shall have been met and the Secretary-General is of the opinion that it is likely that a Conciliation Commission or Arbitral Tribunal, as the case may be, will hold that the dispute arises directly out of an investment, he may make his approval of the application conditional upon consent by both parties to submit any dispute in the first instance to the jurisdiction of the Centre.

(5) The Secretary-General shall as soon as possible notify the parties whether he approves or disapproves the agreement of the parties. He may hold discussions with the parties or invite the parties to a meeting with the officials of the Secretariat either at the parties' request or at his own initiative. The Secretary-General shall, upon the request of the parties or any of them, keep confidential any or all information furnished to him by such parties or party in connection with the provisions of this Article.

(6) The Secretary-General shall record his approval of an agreement pursuant to this Article together with the names and addresses of the parties in a register to be maintained at the Secretariat for that purpose.

Article 5 Administrative and Financial Provisions

The responsibilities of the Secretariat in operating the Additional Facility and the financial provisions regarding its operation shall be as those established by the Administrative and Financial Regulations of the Centre for conciliation and arbitration proceedings under the Convention. Accordingly, Regulations 14 through 16, 22 through 30 and 34(1) of the Administrative and Financial Regulations of the Centre shall apply, *mutatis mutandis*, in respect of fact-finding, conciliation and arbitration proceedings under the Additional Facility.

Article 6 Schedules

Fact-finding, conciliation and arbitration proceedings under the Additional Facility shall be conducted in accordance with the respective Fact-finding (Additional Facility), Conciliation (Additional Facility) and Arbitration (Additional Facility) Rules set forth in Schedules A, B and C.

37.e Additional Facility Arbitration Rules*

Date: 10 April 2006

Source: International Centre for Settlement of Investment Disputes (ed), *ICSID Additional Facility Rules* (Doc ICSID/11, April 2006) (Schedule C) https://icsid.worldbank.org/sites/default/files/AFR_2006%20English-final.pdf

Chapter I Introduction

Article 1 Scope of Application

Where the parties to a dispute have agreed that it shall be referred to arbitration under the Arbitration (Additional Facility) Rules, the dispute shall be settled in accordance with these Rules, save that if any of these Rules is in conflict with a provision of the law applicable to the arbitration from which the parties cannot derogate, that provision shall prevail.

Chapter II Institution of Proceedings

Article 2 The Request

(1) Any State or any national of a State wishing to institute arbitration proceedings shall send a request to that effect in writing to the Secretariat at the seat of the Centre. It shall be drawn up in an official language of the Centre, shall be dated and shall be signed by the requesting party or its duly authorized representative.

(2) The request may be made jointly by the parties to the dispute.

Article 3 Contents of the Request

(1) The request shall:

(a) designate precisely each party to the dispute and state the address of each;

(b) set forth the relevant provisions embodying the agreement of the parties to refer the dispute to arbitration;

(c) indicate the date of approval by the Secretary-General pursuant to Article 4 of the Additional Facility Rules of the agreement of the parties providing for access to the Additional Facility;

* N.B.: Annex C to Document No. 36.d.

(d) contain information concerning the issues in dispute and an indication of the amount involved, if any; and

(e) state, if the requesting party is a juridical person, that it has taken all necessary internal actions to authorize the request.

(2) The request may in addition set forth any provisions agreed by the parties regarding the number of arbitrators and the method of their appointment, as well as any other provisions agreed concerning the settlement of the dispute.

(3) The request shall be accompanied by five additional signed copies and by the fee prescribed pursuant to Regulation 16 of the Administrative and Financial Regulation of the Centre.

Article 4 Registration of the Request

As soon as the Secretary-General shall have satisfied himself that the request conforms in form and substance to the provisions of Article 3 of these Rules, he shall register the request in the Arbitration (Additional Facility) Register and on the same day dispatch to the parties a notice of registration. He shall also transmit a copy of the request and of the accompanying documentation (if any) to the other party to the dispute.

Article 5 Notice of Registration

The notice of registration of a request shall:

(a) record that the request is registered and indicate the date of the registration and of the dispatch of the notice;

(b) notify each party that all communications in connection with the proceeding will be sent to the address stated in the request, unless another address is indicated to the Secretariat;

(c) unless such information has already been provided, invite the parties to communicate to the Secretary-General any provisions agreed by them regarding the number and the method of appointment of the arbitrators;

(d) remind the parties that the registration of the request is without prejudice to the powers and functions of the Arbitral Tribunal in regard to competence and the merits; and

(e) invite the parties to proceed, as soon as possible, to constitute an Arbitral Tribunal in accordance with Chapter III of these Rules.

Chapter III The Tribunal

Article 6 General Provisions

(1) In the absence of agreement between the parties regarding the number of arbitrators and the method of their appointment, the Tribunal shall consist of three arbitrators, one arbitrator appointed by each party and the third, who shall be the President of the Tribunal, appointed by agreement of the parties, all in accordance with Article 9 of these Rules.

(2) Upon the dispatch of the notice of registration of the request for arbitration, the parties shall promptly proceed to constitute a Tribunal.

(3) The Tribunal shall consist of a sole arbitrator or any uneven number of arbitrators appointed as the parties shall agree.

(4) If the Tribunal shall not have been constituted within 90 days after the notice of registration of the request for arbitration has been dispatched by the Secretary-General,

or such other period as the parties may agree, the Chairman of the Administrative Council (hereinafter called the "Chairman") shall, at the request in writing of either party transmitted through the Secretary-General, appoint the arbitrator or arbitrators not yet appointed and, unless the President shall already have been designated or is to be designated later, designate an arbitrator to be President of the Tribunal.

(5) Except as the parties shall otherwise agree, no person who had previously acted as a conciliator or arbitrator in any proceeding for the settlement of the dispute or as a member of any fact-finding committee relating thereto may be appointed as a member of the Tribunal.

Article 7 Nationality of Arbitrators

(1) The majority of the arbitrators shall be nationals of States other than the State party to the dispute and of the State whose national is a party to the dispute, unless the sole arbitrator or each individual member of the Tribunal is appointed by agreement of the parties. Where the Tribunal is to consist of three members, a national of either of these States may not be appointed as an arbitrator by a party without the agreement of the other party to the dispute. Where the Tribunal is to consist of five or more members, nationals of either of these States may not be appointed as arbitrators by a party if appointment by the other party of the same number of arbitrators of either of these nationalities would result in a majority of arbitrators of these nationalities.

(2) Arbitrators appointed by the Chairman shall not be nationals of the State party to the dispute or of the State whose national is a party to the dispute.

Article 8 Qualifications of Arbitrators

Arbitrators shall be persons of high moral character and recognized competence in the fields of law, commerce, industry or finance, who may be relied upon to exercise independent judgment.

Article 9 Method of Constituting the Tribunal in the Absence of Agreement Between the Parties

(1) If the parties have not agreed upon the number of arbitrators and the method of their appointment within 60 days after the registration of the request, the Secretary-General shall, upon the request of either party promptly inform the parties that the Tribunal is to be constituted in accordance with the following procedure:

- (a) either party shall, in a communication to the other party:
  - (i) name two persons, identifying one of them, who shall not have the same nationality as nor be a national of either party, as the arbitrator appointed by it, and the other as the arbitrator proposed to be the President of the Tribunal; and
  - (ii) invite the other party to concur in the appointment of the arbitrator proposed to be the President of the Tribunal and to appoint another arbitrator;
- (b) promptly upon receipt of this communication the other party shall, in its reply:
  - (i) name a person as the arbitrator appointed by it, who shall not have the same nationality as nor be a national of either party; and
  - (ii) concur in the appointment of the arbitrator proposed to be the President of the Tribunal or name another person as the arbitrator proposed to be President; and
- (c) promptly upon receipt of the reply containing such a proposal, the initiating party shall notify the other party whether it concurs in the appointment of the arbitrator proposed by that party to be the President of the Tribunal.

(2) The communications provided for in paragraph (1) of this Article shall be made or promptly confirmed in writing and shall either be transmitted through the Secretary-General or directly between the parties with a copy to the Secretary-General.

Article 10 Appointment of Arbitrators and Designation of President of Tribunal by the Chairman of the Administrative Council

(1) Promptly upon receipt of a request by a party to the Chairman to make an appointment or designation pursuant to Article 6(4) of these Rules, the Secretary-General shall send a copy thereof to the other party.

(2) The Chairman shall use his best efforts to comply with that request within 30 days after its receipt. Before he proceeds to make appointments or a designation, he shall consult both parties as far as possible.

(3) The Secretary-General shall promptly notify the parties of any appointment or designation made by the Chairman.

Article 11 Acceptance of Appointments

(1) The party or parties concerned shall notify the Secretary-General of the appointment of each arbitrator and indicate the method of his appointment.

(2) As soon as the Secretary-General has been informed by a party or the Chairman of the appointment of an arbitrator, he shall seek an acceptance from the appointee.

(3) If an arbitrator fails to accept his appointment within 15 days, the Secretary-General shall promptly notify the parties, and if appropriate the Chairman, and invite them to proceed to the appointment of another arbitrator in accordance with the method followed for the previous appointment.

Article 12 Replacement of Arbitrators prior to Constitution of the Tribunal

At any time before the Tribunal is constituted, each party may replace any arbitrator appointed by it and the parties may by common consent agree to replace any arbitrator.

Article 13 Constitution of the Tribunal

(1) The Tribunal shall be deemed to be constituted and the proceeding to have begun on the date the Secretary-General notifies the parties that all the arbitrators have accepted their appointment.

(2) Before or at the first session of the Tribunal, each arbitrator shall sign a declaration in the following form:

> "To the best of my knowledge there is no reason why I should not serve on the Arbitral Tribunal constituted with respect to a dispute between ____________________ and ____________________.
>
> "I shall keep confidential all information coming to my knowledge as a result of my participation in this proceeding, as well as the contents of any award made by the Tribunal.
>
> "I shall judge fairly as between the parties and shall not accept any instruction or compensation with regard to the proceeding from any source except as provided in the Administrative and Financial Regulations of the Centre.
>
> "Attached is a statement of (a) my past and present professional, business and other relationships (if any) with the parties and (b) any other circumstance that might cause my reliability for independent judgment to be questioned by a party. I acknowledge that by signing this declaration, I assume a continuing obligation promptly to notify

the Secretary-General of the Centre of any such relationship or circumstance that subsequently arises during this proceeding."

Any arbitrator failing to sign such a declaration by the end of the first session of the Tribunal shall be deemed to have resigned.

Article 14 Replacement of Arbitrators after Constitution of the Tribunal

(1) After a Tribunal has been constituted and proceedings have begun, its composition shall remain unchanged; provided, however, that if an arbitrator should die, become incapacitated, resign or be disqualified, the resulting vacancy shall be filled as provided in this Article and Article 17 of these Rules.

(2) If an arbitrator becomes incapacitated or unable to perform the duties of his office, the procedure in respect of the disqualification of arbitrators set forth in Article 15 shall apply.

(3) An arbitrator may resign by submitting his resignation to the other members of the Tribunal and the Secretary-General. If the arbitrator was appointed by one of the parties, the Tribunal shall promptly consider the reasons for his resignation and decide whether it consents thereto. The Tribunal shall promptly notify the Secretary General of its decision.

Article 15 Disqualification of Arbitrators

(1) A party may propose to a Tribunal the disqualification of any of its members on account of any fact indicating a manifest lack of the qualities required by Article 8 of these Rules, or on the ground that he was ineligible for appointment to the Tribunal under Article 7 of these Rules.

(2) A party proposing the disqualification of an arbitrator shall promptly, and in any event before the proceeding is declared closed, file its proposal with the Secretary-General, stating its reasons therefor.

(3) The Secretary-General shall forthwith:

(a) transmit the proposal to the members of the Tribunal and, if it relates to a sole arbitrator or to a majority of the members of the Tribunal, to the Chairman; and

(b) notify the other party of the proposal.

(4) The arbitrator to whom the proposal relates may, without delay, furnish explanations to the Tribunal or the Chairman, as the case may be.

(5) The decision on any proposal to disqualify an arbitrator shall be taken by the other members of the Tribunal except that where those members are equally divided, or in the case of a proposal to disqualify a sole arbitrator, or a majority of the arbitrators, the Chairman shall take that decision.

(6) Whenever the Chairman has to decide on a proposal to disqualify an arbitrator, he shall use his best efforts to take that decision within 30 days after he has received the proposal.

(7) The proceeding shall be suspended until a decision has been taken on the proposal.

Article 16 Procedure during a Vacancy on the Tribunal

(1) The Secretary-General shall forthwith notify the parties and, if necessary, the Chairman of the disqualification, death, incapacity or resignation of an arbitrator and of the consent, if any, of the Tribunal to a resignation.

(2) Upon the notification by the Secretary-General of a vacancy on the Tribunal, the proceeding shall be or remain suspended until the vacancy has been filled.

Article 17 Filling Vacancies on the Tribunal

(1) Except as provided in paragraph (2) of this Article, a vacancy resulting from the disqualification, death, incapacity or resignation of an arbitrator shall be promptly filled by the same method by which his appointment had been made.

(2) In addition to filling vacancies relating to arbitrators appointed by him, the Chairman shall:

(a) fill a vacancy caused by the resignation, without the consent of the Tribunal, of an arbitrator appointed by a party; or

(b) at the request of either party, fill any other vacancy, if no new appointment is made and accepted within 45 days of the notification of the vacancy by the Secretary-General.

(3) In filling a vacancy the party or the Chairman, as the case may be, shall observe the provisions of these Rules with respect to the appointment of arbitrators. Article 13(2) of these Rules shall apply mutatis mutandis to the newly appointed arbitrator.

Article 18 Resumption of Proceeding after Filling a Vacancy

As soon as a vacancy on the Tribunal has been filled, the proceeding shall continue from the point it had reached at the time the vacancy occurred. The newly appointed arbitrator may, however, require that the oral procedure be recommenced, if this had already been started.

Chapter IV Place of Arbitration

Article 19 Limitation on Choice of Forum

Arbitration proceedings shall be held only in States that are parties to the 1958 UN Convention on the Recognition and Enforcement of Foreign Arbitral Awards.

Article 20 Determination of Place of Arbitration

(1) Subject to Article 19 of these Rules the place of arbitration shall be determined by the Arbitral Tribunal after consultation with the parties and the Secretariat.

(2) The Arbitral Tribunal may meet at any place it deems appropriate for the inspection of goods, other property or documents. It may also visit any place connected with the dispute or conduct inquiries there. The parties shall be given sufficient notice to enable them to be present at such inspection or visit.

(3) The award shall be made at the place of arbitration.

Chapter V Working of the Tribunal

Article 21 Sessions of the Tribunal

(1) The Tribunal shall meet for its first session within 60 days after its constitution or such other period as the parties may agree. The dates of that session shall be fixed by the President of the Tribunal after consultation with its members and the Secretariat, and with the parties as far as possible. If, upon its constitution, the Tribunal has no President, such dates shall be fixed by the Secretary-General after consultation with the members of the Tribunal, and with the parties as far as possible.

(2) Subsequent sessions shall be convened by the President within time limits determined by the Tribunal. The dates of such sessions shall be fixed by the President of the Tribunal after consultation with its members and the Secretariat, and with the parties as far as possible.

(3) The Secretary-General shall notify the members of the Tribunal and the parties of the dates and place of the sessions of the Tribunal in good time.

Article 22 Sittings of the Tribunal

(1) The President of the Tribunal shall conduct its hearings and preside at its deliberations.

(2) Except as the parties otherwise agree, the presence of a majority of the members of the Tribunal shall be required at its sittings.

(3) The President of the Tribunal shall fix the date and hour of its sittings.

Article 23 Deliberations of the Tribunal

(1) The deliberations of the Tribunal shall take place in private and remain secret.

(2) Only members of the Tribunal shall take part in its deliberations. No other person shall be admitted unless the Tribunal decides otherwise.

Article 24 Decisions of the Tribunal

(1) Any award or other decision of the Tribunal shall be made by a majority of the votes of all its members. Abstention by any member of the Tribunal shall count as a negative vote.

(2) Except as otherwise provided by these Rules or decided by the Tribunal, it may take any decisions by correspondence among its members, provided that all of them are consulted. Decisions so taken shall be certified by the President of the Tribunal.

Article 25 Incapacity of the President

If at any time the President of the Tribunal should be unable to act, his functions shall be performed by one of the other members of the Tribunal, acting in the order in which the Secretariat had received the notice of their acceptance of their appointment to the Tribunal.

Article 26 Representation of the Parties

(1) Each party may be represented or assisted by agents, counsel or advocates whose names and authority shall be notified by that party to the Secretariat, which shall promptly inform the Tribunal and the other party.

(2) For the purposes of these Rules, the expression "party" includes, where the context so admits, an agent, counsel or advocate authorized to represent that party.

Chapter VI General Procedural Provisions

Article 27 Procedural Orders

The Tribunal shall make the orders required for the conduct of the proceeding.

Article 28 Preliminary Procedural Consultation

(1) As early as possible after the constitution of a Tribunal, its President shall endeavor to ascertain the views of the parties regarding questions of procedure. For this purpose he may request the parties to meet him. He shall, in particular, seek their views on the following matters:

- (a) the number of members of the Tribunal required to constitute a quorum at its sittings;
- (b) the language or languages to be used in the proceeding;
- (c) the number and sequence of the pleadings and the time limits within which they are to be filed;

(d) the number of copies desired by each party of instruments filed by the other;
(e) dispensing with the written or oral procedure;
(f) the manner in which the cost of the proceeding is to be apportioned; and
(g) the manner in which the record of the hearings shall be kept.

(2) In the conduct of the proceeding the Tribunal shall apply any agreement between the parties on procedural matters, which is not inconsistent with any provisions of the Additional Facility Rules and the Administrative and Financial Regulations of the Centre.

Article 29 Pre-Hearing Conference

(1) At the request of the Secretary-General or at the discretion of the President of the Tribunal, a pre-hearing conference between the Tribunal and the parties may be held to arrange for an exchange of information and the stipulation of uncontested facts in order to expedite the proceeding.

(2) At the request of the parties, a pre-hearing conference between the Tribunal and the parties, duly represented by their authorized representatives, may be held to consider the issues in dispute with a view to reaching an amicable settlement.

Article 30 Procedural Languages

(1) The parties may agree on the use of one or two languages to be used in the proceeding, provided that if they agree on any language that is not an official language of the Centre, the Tribunal, after consultation with the Secretary-General, gives its approval. If the parties do not agree on any such procedural language, each of them may select one of the official languages (i.e., English, French and Spanish) for this purpose. Notwithstanding the foregoing, one of the official languages of the Centre shall be used for all communications to and from the Secretariat.

(2) If two procedural languages are selected by the parties, any instrument may be filed in either language. Either language may be used at the hearing subject, if the Tribunal so requires, to translation and interpretation. The orders and the award of the Tribunal shall be rendered and the record kept in both procedural languages, both versions being equally authentic.

Article 31 Copies of Instruments

Except as otherwise provided by the Tribunal after consultation with the parties and the Secretariat, every request, pleading, application, written observation or other instrument shall be filed in the form of a signed original accompanied by the following number of additional copies:

(a) before the number of members of the Tribunal has been determined: five; and
(b) after the number of members of the Tribunal has been determined: two more than the number of its members.

Article 32 Supporting Documentation

Supporting documentation shall ordinarily be filed together with the instrument to which it relates, and in any case within the time limit fixed for the filing of such instrument.

Article 33 Time Limits

(1) Where required, time limits shall be fixed by the Tribunal by assigning dates for the completion of the various steps in the proceeding. The Tribunal may delegate this power to its President.

(2) The Tribunal may extend any time limit that it has fixed. If the Tribunal is not in session, this power shall be exercised by its President.

(3) Any step taken after expiration of the applicable time limit shall be disregarded unless the Tribunal, in special circumstances and after giving the other party an opportunity of stating its views, decides otherwise.

Article 34 Waiver

A party which knows or ought to have known that a provision of these Rules, of any other rules or agreement applicable to the proceeding, or of an order of the Tribunal has not been complied with and which fails to state promptly its objections thereto, shall be deemed to have waived the right to object.

Article 35 Filling of Gaps

If any question of procedure arises which is not covered by these Rules or any rules agreed by the parties, the Tribunal shall decide the question.

Chapter VII Written and Oral Procedures

Article 36 Normal Procedures

Except if the parties otherwise agree, the proceeding shall comprise two distinct phases: a written procedure followed by an oral one.

Article 37 Transmission of the Request

As soon as the Tribunal is constituted, the Secretary-General shall transmit to each member of the Tribunal a copy of the request by which the proceeding was commenced, of the supporting documentation, of the notice of registration of the request and of any communication received from either party in response thereto.

Article 38 The Written Procedure

(1) In addition to the request for arbitration, the written procedure shall consist of the following pleadings, filed within time limits set by the Tribunal:

(a) a memorial by the requesting party;

(b) a counter-memorial by the other party;

and, if the parties so agree or the Tribunal deems it necessary:

(c) a reply by the requesting party; and

(d) a rejoinder by the other party.

(2) If the request was made jointly, each party shall, within the same time limit determined by the Tribunal, file its memorial. However, the parties may instead agree that one of them shall, for the purposes of paragraph (1) of this Article, be considered as the requesting party.

(3) A memorial shall contain: a statement of the relevant facts; a statement of law; and the submissions. A counter-memorial, reply or rejoinder shall contain an admission or denial of the facts stated in the last previous pleading; any additional facts, if necessary; observations concerning the statement of law in the last previous pleading; a statement of law in answer thereto; and the submissions.

Article 39 The Oral Procedure

(1) The oral procedure shall consist of the hearing by the Tribunal of the parties, their agents, counsel and advocates, and of witnesses and experts.

(2) Unless either party objects, the Tribunal, after consultation with the Secretary-General, may allow other persons, besides the parties, their agents, counsel and advocates, witnesses and experts during their testimony, and officers of the Tribunal, to attend or observe all or part of the hearings, subject to appropriate logistical arrangements. The Tribunal shall for such cases establish procedures for the protection of proprietary or privileged information.

(3) The members of the Tribunal may, during the hearings, put questions to the parties, their agents, counsel and advocates, and ask them for explanations.

Article 40 Marshalling of Evidence

Without prejudice to the rules concerning the production of documents, each party shall, within time limits fixed by the Tribunal, communicate to the Secretary-General, for transmission to the Tribunal and the other party, precise information regarding the evidence which it intends to produce and that which it intends to request the Tribunal to call for, together with an indication of the points to which such evidence will be directed.

Article 41 Evidence: General Principles

(1) The Tribunal shall be the judge of the admissibility of any evidence adduced and of its probative value.

(2) The Tribunal may, if it deems it necessary at any stage of the proceeding, call upon the parties to produce documents, witnesses and experts.

(3) After consulting both parties, the Tribunal may allow a person or entity that is not a party to the dispute (in this Article called the "non-disputing party") to file a written submission with the Tribunal regarding a matter within the scope of the dispute. In determining whether to allow such a filing, the Tribunal shall consider, among other things, the extent to which:

(a) the non-disputing party submission would assist the Tribunal in the determination of a factual or legal issue related to the proceeding by bringing a perspective, particular knowledge or insight that is different from that of the disputing parties;
(b) the non-disputing party submission would address a matter within the scope of the dispute;
(c) the non-disputing party has a significant interest in the proceeding.

The Tribunal shall ensure that the non-disputing party submission does not disrupt the proceeding or unduly burden or unfairly prejudice either party, and that both parties are given an opportunity to present their observations on the non-disputing party submission.

Article 42 Examination of Witnesses and Experts

Witnesses and experts shall be examined before the Tribunal by the parties under the control of its President. Questions may also be put to them by any member of the Tribunal.

Article 43 Witnesses and Experts: Special Rules

The Tribunal may:

(a) admit evidence given by a witness or expert in a written deposition;
(b) with the consent of both parties, arrange for the examination of a witness or expert otherwise than before the Tribunal itself. The Tribunal shall define the procedure to be followed. The parties may participate in the examination; and
(c) appoint one or more experts, define their terms of reference, examine their reports and hear from them in person.

Article 44 Closure of the Proceeding

(1) When the presentation of the case by the parties is completed, the proceeding shall be declared closed.

(2) Exceptionally, the Tribunal may, before the award has been rendered, reopen the proceeding on the ground that new evidence is forthcoming of such a nature as to constitute a decisive factor, or that there is a vital need for clarification on certain specific points.

Chapter VIII Particular Procedures

Article 45 Preliminary Objections

(1) The Tribunal shall have the power to rule on its competence. For the purposes of this Article, an agreement providing for arbitration under the Additional Facility shall be separable from the other terms of the contract in which it may have been included.

(2) Any objection that the dispute is not within the competence of the Tribunal shall be filed with the Secretary-General as soon as possible after the constitution of the Tribunal and in any event no later than the expiration of the time limit fixed for the filing of the countermemorial or, if the objection relates to an ancillary claim, for the filing of the rejoinder – unless the facts on which the objection is based are unknown to the party at that time.

(3) The Tribunal may on its own initiative consider, at any stage of the proceeding, whether the dispute before it is within its competence.

(4) Upon the formal raising of an objection relating to the dispute, the Tribunal may decide to suspend the proceeding on the merits. The President of the Tribunal, after consultation with its other members, shall fix a time limit within which the parties may file observations on the objection.

(5) The Tribunal shall decide whether or not the further procedures relating to the objection made pursuant to paragraph (2) shall be oral. It may deal with the objection as a preliminary question or join it to the merits of the dispute. If the Tribunal overrules the objection or joins it to the merits, it shall once more fix time limits for the further procedures.

(6) Unless the parties have agreed to another expedited procedure for making preliminary objections, a party may, no later than 30 days after the constitution of the Tribunal, and in any event before the first session of the Tribunal, file an objection that a claim is manifestly without legal merit. The party shall specify as precisely as possible the basis for the objection. The Tribunal, after giving the parties the opportunity to present their observations on the objection, shall, at its first session or promptly thereafter, notify the parties of its decision on the objection. The decision of the Tribunal shall be without prejudice to the right of a party to file an objection pursuant to paragraph (2) or to object, in the course of the proceeding, that a claim lacks legal merit.

(7) If the Tribunal decides that the dispute is not within its competence or that all claims are manifestly without legal merit, it shall issue an award to that effect.

Article 46 Provisional Measures of Protection

(1) Unless the arbitration agreement otherwise provides, either party may at any time during the proceeding request that provisional measures for the preservation of its rights be ordered by the Tribunal. The Tribunal shall give priority to the consideration of such a request.

(2) The Tribunal may also recommend provisional measures on its own initiative or recommend measures other than those specified in a request. It may at any time modify or revoke its recommendations.

(3) The Tribunal shall order or recommend provisional measures, or any modification or revocation thereof, only after giving each party an opportunity of presenting its observations.

(4) The parties may apply to any competent judicial authority for interim or conservatory measures. By doing so they shall not be held to infringe the agreement to arbitrate or to affect the powers of the Tribunal.

Article 47 Ancillary Claims

(1) Except as the parties otherwise agree, a party may present an incidental or additional claim or counter-claim, provided that such ancillary claim is within the scope of the arbitration agreement of the parties.

(2) An incidental or additional claim shall be presented not later than in the reply and a counter-claim no later than in the countermemorial, unless the Tribunal, upon justification by the party presenting the ancillary claim and upon considering any objection of the other party, authorizes the presentation of the claim at a later stage in the proceeding.

Article 48 Default

(1) If a party fails to appear or to present its case at any stage of the proceeding, the other party may request the Tribunal to deal with the questions submitted to it and to render an award.

(2) Whenever such a request is made by a party the Tribunal shall promptly notify the defaulting party thereof. Unless the Tribunal is satisfied that that party does not intend to appear or to present its case in the proceeding, it shall, at the same time, grant a period of grace and to this end:

(a) if that party had failed to file a pleading or any other instrument within the time limit fixed therefor, fix a new time limit for its filing; or

(b) if that party had failed to appear or present its case at a hearing, fix a new date for the hearing. The period of grace shall not, without the consent of the other party, exceed 60 days.

(3) After the expiration of the period of grace or when, in accordance with paragraph (2) of this Article, no such period is granted, the Tribunal shall examine whether the dispute is within its jurisdiction and, if it is satisfied as to its jurisdiction, decide whether the submissions made are well-founded in fact and in law. To this end, it may, at any stage of the proceeding, call on the party appearing to file observations, produce evidence or submit oral explanations.

Article 49 Settlement and Discontinuance

(1) If, before the award is rendered, the parties agree on a settlement of the dispute or otherwise to discontinue the proceeding, the Tribunal, or the Secretary-General if the Tribunal has not yet been constituted, or has not yet met, shall, at their written request, in an order take note of the discontinuance of the proceeding.

(2) If requested by both parties and accepted by the Tribunal, the Tribunal shall record the settlement in the form of an award. The Tribunal shall not be obliged to give reasons for such an award. The parties will accompany their request with the full and signed text of their settlement.

Article 50 Discontinuance at Request of a Party

If a party requests the discontinuance of the proceeding, the Tribunal, or the Secretary-General if the Tribunal has not yet been constituted, shall in an order fix a time limit with-in which the other party may state whether it opposes the discontinuance. If no objection is made in writing within the time limit, the Tribunal, or if appropriate the Secretary- General, shall in an order take note of the discontinuance of the proceeding. If objection is made, the proceeding shall continue.

Article 51 Discontinuance for Failure of Parties to Act

If the parties fail to take any steps in the proceeding during six consecutive months or such period as they may agree with the approval of the Tribunal, or of the Secretary-General if the Tribunal has not yet been constituted, they shall be deemed to have discontinued the proceeding and the Tribunal, or if appropriate the Secretary-General, shall, after notice to the parties, in an order take note of the discontinuance.

Chapter IX The Award

Article 52 The Award

(1) The award shall be made in writing and shall contain:

(a) a precise designation of each party;

(b) a statement that the Tribunal was established under these Rules, and a description of the method of its constitution;

(c) the name of each member of the Tribunal, and an identification of the appointing authority of each;

(d) the names of the agents, counsel and advocates of the parties;

(e) the dates and place of the sittings of the Tribunal;

(f) a summary of the proceeding;

(g) a statement of the facts as found by the Tribunal;

(h) the submissions of the parties;

(i) the decision of the Tribunal on every question submitted to it, together with the reasons upon which the decision is based; and

(j) any decision of the Tribunal regarding the cost of the proceeding.

(2) The award shall be signed by the members of the Tribunal who voted for it; the date of each signature shall be indicated. Any member of the Tribunal may attach his individual opinion to the award, whether he dissents from the majority or not, or a statement of his dissent.

(3) If the arbitration law of the country where the award is made requires that it be filed or registered by the Tribunal, the Tribunal shall comply with this requirement within the period of time required by law.

(4) The award shall be final and binding on the parties. The parties waive any time limits for the rendering of the award which may be provided for by the law of the country where the award is made.

Article 53 Authentication of the Award; Certified Copies; Date

(1) Upon signature by the last arbitrator to sign, the Secretary General shall promptly:

(a) authenticate the original text of the award and deposit it in the archives of the Secretariat, together with any individual opinions and statements of dissent; and

(b) dispatch a certified copy of the award (including individual opinions and statements of dissent) to each party, indicating the date of dispatch on the original text and on all copies; provided, however, that if the original text of the award must be filed or registered as contemplated by Article 52(3) of these Rules the SecretaryGeneral shall do so on behalf of the Tribunal or return the award to the Tribunal for this purpose.

(2) The award shall be deemed to have been rendered on the date on which the certified copies were dispatched.

(3) Except to the extent required for any registration or filing of the award by the Secretary-General under paragraph (1) of this Article, the Secretariat shall not publish the award without the consent of the parties. The Secretariat shall, however, promptly include in the publications of the Centre excerpts of the legal reasoning of the Tribunal.

Article 54 Applicable Law

(1) The Tribunal shall apply the rules of law designated by the parties as applicable to the substance of the dispute. Failing such designation by the parties, the Tribunal shall apply

(a) the law determined by the conflict of laws rules which it considers applicable and (b) such rules of international law as the Tribunal considers applicable.

(2) The Tribunal may decide ex aequo et bono if the parties have expressly authorized it to do so and if the law applicable to the arbitration so permits.

Article 55 Interpretation of the Award

(1) Within 45 days after the date of the award either party, with notice to the other party, may request that the Secretary-General obtain from the Tribunal an interpretation of the award.

(2) The Tribunal shall determine the procedure to be followed.

(3) The interpretation shall form part of the award, and the provisions of Articles 52 and 53 of these Rules shall apply.

Article 56 Correction of the Award

(1) Within 45 days after the date of the award either party, with notice to the other party, may request the Secretary-General to obtain from the Tribunal a correction in the award of any clerical, arithmetical or similar errors. The Tribunal may within the same period make such corrections on its own initiative.

(2) The provisions of Articles 52 and 53 of these Rules shall apply to such corrections.

Article 57 Supplementary Decisions

(1) Within 45 days after the date of the award either party, with notice to the other party may request the Tribunal, through the Secretary-General, to decide any question which it had omitted to decide in the award.

(2) The Tribunal shall determine the procedure to be followed.

(3) The decision of the Tribunal shall become part of the award and the provisions of Articles 52 and 53 of these Rules shall apply thereto.

Chapter X Costs

Article 58 Cost of Proceeding

(1) Unless the parties otherwise agree, the Tribunal shall decide how and by whom the fees and expenses of the members of the Tribunal, the expenses and charges of the Secretariat and the

expenses incurred by the parties in connection with the proceeding shall be borne. The Tribunal may, to that end, call on the Secretariat and the parties to provide it with the information it needs in order to formulate the division of the cost of the proceeding between the parties.

(2) The decision of the Tribunal pursuant to paragraph (1) of this Article shall form part of the award.

Chapter XI General Provisions

Article 59 Final Provision

The text of these Rules in each official language of the Centre shall be equally authentic.

The UNCITRAL Framework

38.a UNCITRAL Arbitration Rules

Date: 6 December 2010
Source: UN Doc A/65/17 (Annex I)
https://uncitral.un.org/sites/uncitral.un.org/files/media-documents/uncitral/en/uncitral-arbitration-rules-2013-e.pdf

Section I. Introductory rules

Scope of application[1]
Article 1

1. Where parties have agreed that disputes between them in respect of a defined legal relationship, whether contractual or not, shall be referred to arbitration under the UNCITRAL Arbitration Rules, then such disputes shall be settled in accordance with these Rules subject to such modification as the parties may agree.

2. The parties to an arbitration agreement concluded after 15 August 2010 shall be presumed to have referred to the Rules in effect on the date of commencement of the arbitration, unless the parties have agreed to apply a particular version of the Rules. That presumption does not apply where the arbitration agreement has been concluded by accepting after 15 August 2010 an offer made before that date.

3. These Rules shall govern the arbitration except that where any of these Rules is in conflict with a provision of the law applicable to the arbitration from which the parties cannot derogate, that provision shall prevail.

4. For investor-State arbitration initiated pursuant to a treaty providing for the protection of investments or investors, these Rules include the UNCITRAL Rules on Transparency in Treaty- based Investor-State Arbitration ("Rules on Transparency"), subject to article 1 of the Rules on Transparency.

Notice and calculation of periods of time
Article 2

1. A notice, including a notification, communication or proposal, may be transmitted by any means of communication that provides or allows for a record of its transmission.

[1] A model arbitration clause for contracts can be found in the annex to the Rules.

2. If an address has been designated by a party specifically for this purpose or authorized by the arbitral tribunal, any notice shall be delivered to that party at that address, and if so delivered shall be deemed to have been received. Delivery by electronic means such as facsimile or e-mail may only be made to an address so designated or authorized.

3. In the absence of such designation or authorization, a notice is:

(a) Received if it is physically delivered to the addressee; or

(b) Deemed to have been received if it is delivered at the place of business, habitual residence or mailing address of the addressee.

4. If, after reasonable efforts, delivery cannot be effected in accordance with paragraphs 2 or 3, a notice is deemed to have been received if it is sent to the addressee's last-known place of business, habitual residence or mailing address by registered letter or any other means that provides a record of delivery or of attempted delivery.

5. A notice shall be deemed to have been received on the day it is delivered in accordance with paragraphs 2, 3 or 4, or attempted to be delivered in accordance with paragraph 4. A notice transmitted by electronic means is deemed to have been received on the day it is sent, except that a notice of arbitration so transmitted is only deemed to have been received on the day when it reaches the addressee's electronic address.

6. For the purpose of calculating a period of time under these Rules, such period shall begin to run on the day following the day when a notice is received. If the last day of such period is an official holiday or a non-business day at the residence or place of business of the addressee, the period is extended until the first business day which follows. Official holidays or non-business days occurring during the running of the period of time are included in calculating the period.

Notice of arbitration
Article 3

1. The party or parties initiating recourse to arbitration (hereinafter called the "claimant") shall communicate to the other party or parties (hereinafter called the "respondent") a notice of arbitration.

2. Arbitral proceedings shall be deemed to commence on the date on which the notice of arbitration is received by the respondent.

3. The notice of arbitration shall include the following:

(a) A demand that the dispute be referred to arbitration;

(b) The names and contact details of the parties;

(c) Identification of the arbitration agreement that is invoked;

(d) Identification of any contract or other legal instrument out of or in relation to which the dispute arises or, in the absence of such contract or instrument, a brief description of the relevant relationship;

(e) A brief description of the claim and an indication of the amount involved, if any;

(f) The relief or remedy sought;

(g) A proposal as to the number of arbitrators, language and place of arbitration, if the parties have not previously agreed thereon.

4. The notice of arbitration may also include:

(a) A proposal for the designation of an appointing authority referred to in article 6, paragraph 1;

(b) A proposal for the appointment of a sole arbitrator referred to in article 8, paragraph 1;

(c) Notification of the appointment of an arbitrator referred to in article 9 or 10.

5. The constitution of the arbitral tribunal shall not be hindered by any controversy with respect to the sufficiency of the notice of arbitration, which shall be finally resolved by the arbitral tribunal.

Response to the notice of arbitration
Article 4

1. Within 30 days of the receipt of the notice of arbitration, the respondent shall communicate to the claimant a response to the notice of arbitration, which shall include:
   (a) The name and contact details of each respondent;
   (b) A response to the information set forth in the notice of arbitration, pursuant to article 3, paragraphs 3 (c) to (g).
2. The response to the notice of arbitration may also include:
   (a) Any plea that an arbitral tribunal to be constituted under these Rules lacks jurisdiction;
   (b) A proposal for the designation of an appointing authority referred to in article 6, paragraph 1;
   (c) A proposal for the appointment of a sole arbitrator referred to in article 8, paragraph 1;
   (d) Notification of the appointment of an arbitrator referred to in article 9 or 10;
   (e) A brief description of counterclaims or claims for the purpose of a set-off, if any, including where relevant, an indication of the amounts involved, and the relief or remedy sought;
   (f) A notice of arbitration in accordance with article 3 in case the respondent formulates a claim against a party to the arbitration agreement other than the claimant.
3. The constitution of the arbitral tribunal shall not be hindered by any controversy with respect to the respondent's failure to communicate a response to the notice of arbitration, or an incomplete or late response to the notice of arbitration, which shall be finally resolved by the arbitral tribunal.

Representation and assistance
Article 5

Each party may be represented or assisted by persons chosen by it. The names and addresses of such persons must be communicated to all parties and to the arbitral tribunal. Such communication must specify whether the appointment is being made for purposes of representation or assistance. Where a person is to act as a representative of a party, the arbitral tribunal, on its own initiative or at the request of any party, may at any time require proof of authority granted to the representative in such a form as the arbitral tribunal may determine.

Designating and appointing authorities
Article 6

1. Unless the parties have already agreed on the choice of an appointing authority, a party may at any time propose the name or names of one or more institutions or persons, including the Secretary-General of the Permanent Court of Arbitration at The Hague (hereinafter called the "PCA"), one of whom would serve as appointing authority.
2. If all parties have not agreed on the choice of an appointing authority within 30 days after a proposal made in accordance with paragraph 1 has been received by all other parties,

any party may request the Secretary-General of the PCA to designate the appointing authority.

3. Where these Rules provide for a period of time within which a party must refer a matter to an appointing authority and no appointing authority has been agreed on or designated, the period is suspended from the date on which a party initiates the procedure for agreeing on or designating an appointing authority until the date of such agreement or designation.

4. Except as referred to in article 41, paragraph 4, if the appointing authority refuses to act, or if it fails to appoint an arbitrator within 30 days after it receives a party's request to do so, fails to act within any other period provided by these Rules, or fails to decide on a challenge to an arbitrator within a reasonable time after receiving a party's request to do so, any party may request the Secretary-General of the PCA to designate a substitute appointing authority.

5. In exercising their functions under these Rules, the appointing authority and the Secretary-General of the PCA may require from any party and the arbitrators the information they deem necessary and they shall give the parties and, where appropriate, the arbitrators, an opportunity to present their views in any manner they consider appropriate. All such communications to and from the appointing authority and the Secretary-General of the PCA shall also be provided by the sender to all other parties.

6. When the appointing authority is requested to appoint an arbitrator pursuant to articles 8, 9, 10 or 14, the party making the request shall send to the appointing authority copies of the notice of arbitration and, if it exists, any response to the notice of arbitration.

7. The appointing authority shall have regard to such considerations as are likely to secure the appointment of an independent and impartial arbitrator and shall take into account the advisability of appointing an arbitrator of a nationality other than the nationalities of the parties.

Section II. Composition of the arbitral tribunal Number of arbitrators

Article 7

1. If the parties have not previously agreed on the number of arbitrators, and if within 30 days after the receipt by the respondent of the notice of arbitration the parties have not agreed that there shall be only one arbitrator, three arbitrators shall be appointed.

2. Notwithstanding paragraph 1, if no other parties have responded to a party's proposal to appoint a sole arbitrator within the time limit provided for in paragraph 1 and the party or parties concerned have failed to appoint a second arbitrator in accordance with article 9 or 10, the appointing authority may, at the request of a party, appoint a sole arbitrator pursuant to the procedure provided for in article 8, paragraph 2, if it determines that, in view of the circumstances of the case, this is more appropriate.

Appointment of arbitrators (articles 8 to 10)

Article 8

1. If the parties have agreed that a sole arbitrator is to be appointed and if within 30 days after receipt by all other parties of a proposal for the appointment of a sole arbitrator the parties have not reached agreement thereon, a sole arbitrator shall, at the request of a party, be appointed by the appointing authority.

2. The appointing authority shall appoint the sole arbitrator as promptly as possible. In making the appointment, the appointing authority shall use the following list-procedure,

unless the parties agree that the list-procedure should not be used or unless the appointing authority determines in its discretion that the use of the list-procedure is not appropriate for the case:

(a) The appointing authority shall communicate to each of the parties an identical list containing at least three names;

(b) Within 15 days after the receipt of this list, each party may return the list to the appointing authority after having deleted the name or names to which it objects and numbered the remaining names on the list in the order of its preference;

(c) After the expiration of the above period of time the appointing authority shall appoint the sole arbitrator from among the names approved on the lists returned to it and in accordance with the order of preference indicated by the parties;

(d) If for any reason the appointment cannot be made according to this procedure, the appointing authority may exercise its discretion in appointing the sole arbitrator.

Article 9

1. If three arbitrators are to be appointed, each party shall appoint one arbitrator. The two arbitrators thus appointed shall choose the third arbitrator who will act as the presiding arbitrator of the arbitral tribunal.

2. If within 30 days after the receipt of a party's notification of the appointment of an arbitrator the other party has not notified the first party of the arbitrator it has appointed, the first party may request the appointing authority to appoint the second arbitrator.

3. If within 30 days after the appointment of the second arbitrator the two arbitrators have not agreed on the choice of the presiding arbitrator, the presiding arbitrator shall be appointed by the appointing authority in the same way as a sole arbitrator would be appointed under article 8.

Article 10

1. For the purposes of article 9, paragraph 1, where three arbitrators are to be appointed and there are multiple parties as claimant or as respondent, unless the parties have agreed to another method of appointment of arbitrators, the multiple parties jointly, whether as claimant or as respondent, shall appoint an arbitrator.

2. If the parties have agreed that the arbitral tribunal is to be composed of a number of arbitrators other than one or three, the arbitrators shall be appointed according to the method agreed upon by the parties.

3. In the event of any failure to constitute the arbitral tribunal under these Rules, the appointing authority shall, at the request of any party, constitute the arbitral tribunal and, in doing so, may revoke any appointment already made and appoint or reappoint each of the arbitrators and designate one of them as the presiding arbitrator.

Disclosures by and challenge of arbitrators[2] (articles 11 to 13)

Article 11

When a person is approached in connection with his or her possible appointment as an arbitrator, he or she shall disclose any circumstances likely to give rise to justifiable doubts as to his or her impartiality or independence. An arbitrator, from the time of his or her appointment and throughout the arbitral proceedings, shall without delay disclose any

[2] Model statements of independence pursuant to article 11 can be found in the annex to the Rules.

such circumstances to the parties and the other arbitrators unless they have already been informed by him or her of these circumstances.

Article 12

1. Any arbitrator may be challenged if circumstances exist that give rise to justifiable doubts as to the arbitrator's impartiality or independence.

2. A party may challenge the arbitrator appointed by it only for reasons of which it becomes aware after the appointment has been made.

3. In the event that an arbitrator fails to act or in the event of the de jure or de facto impossibility of his or her performing his or her functions, the procedure in respect of the challenge of an arbitrator as provided in article 13 shall apply.

Article 13

1. A party that intends to challenge an arbitrator shall send notice of its challenge within 15 days after it has been notified of the appointment of the challenged arbitrator, or within 15 days after the circumstances mentioned in articles 11 and 12 became known to that party.

2. The notice of challenge shall be communicated to all other parties, to the arbitrator who is challenged and to the other arbitrators. The notice of challenge shall state the reasons for the challenge.

3. When an arbitrator has been challenged by a party, all parties may agree to the challenge. The arbitrator may also, after the challenge, withdraw from his or her office. In neither case does this imply acceptance of the validity of the grounds for the challenge.

4. If, within 15 days from the date of the notice of challenge, all parties do not agree to the challenge or the challenged arbitrator does not withdraw, the party making the challenge may elect to pursue it. In that case, within 30 days from the date of the notice of challenge, it shall seek a decision on the challenge by the appointing authority.

Replacement of an arbitrator
Article 14

1. Subject to paragraph 2, in any event where an arbitrator has to be replaced during the course of the arbitral proceedings, a substitute arbitrator shall be appointed or chosen pursuant to the procedure provided for in articles 8 to 11 that was applicable to the appointment or choice of the arbitrator being replaced. This procedure shall apply even if during the process of appointing the arbitrator to be replaced, a party had failed to exercise its right to appoint or to participate in the appointment.

2. If, at the request of a party, the appointing authority determines that, in view of the exceptional circumstances of the case, it would be justified for a party to be deprived of its right to appoint a substitute arbitrator, the appointing authority may, after giving an opportunity to the parties and the remaining arbitrators to express their views: (a) appoint the substitute arbitrator; or (b) after the closure of the hearings, authorize the other arbitrators to proceed with the arbitration and make any decision or award.

Repetition of hearings in the event of the replacement of an arbitrator
Article 15

If an arbitrator is replaced, the proceedings shall resume at the stage where the arbitrator who was replaced ceased to perform his or her functions, unless the arbitral tribunal decides otherwise.

Exclusion of liability
Article 16

Save for intentional wrongdoing, the parties waive, to the fullest extent permitted under the applicable law, any claim against the arbitrators, the appointing authority and any person appointed by the arbitral tribunal based on any act or omission in connection with the arbitration.

Section III. Arbitral proceedings

General provisions
Article 17

1. Subject to these Rules, the arbitral tribunal may conduct the arbitration in such manner as it considers appropriate, provided that the parties are treated with equality and that at an appropriate stage of the proceedings each party is given a reasonable opportunity of presenting its case. The arbitral tribunal, in exercising its discretion, shall conduct the proceedings so as to avoid unnecessary delay and expense and to provide a fair and efficient process for resolving the parties' dispute.
2. As soon as practicable after its constitution and after inviting the parties to express their views, the arbitral tribunal shall establish the provisional timetable of the arbitration. The arbitral tribunal may, at any time, after inviting the parties to express their views, extend or abridge any period of time prescribed under these Rules or agreed by the parties.
3. If at an appropriate stage of the proceedings any party so requests, the arbitral tribunal shall hold hearings for the presentation of evidence by witnesses, including expert witnesses, or for oral argument. In the absence of such a request, the arbitral tribunal shall decide whether to hold such hearings or whether the proceedings shall be conducted on the basis of documents and other materials.
4. All communications to the arbitral tribunal by one party shall be communicated by that party to all other parties. Such communications shall be made at the same time, except as otherwise permitted by the arbitral tribunal if it may do so under applicable law.
5. The arbitral tribunal may, at the request of any party, allow one or more third persons to be joined in the arbitration as a party provided such person is a party to the arbitration agreement, unless the arbitral tribunal finds, after giving all parties, including the person or persons to be joined, the opportunity to be heard, that joinder should not be permitted because of prejudice to any of those parties. The arbitral tribunal may make a single award or several awards in respect of all parties so involved in the arbitration.

Place of arbitration
Article 18

1. If the parties have not previously agreed on the place of arbitration, the place of arbitration shall be determined by the arbitral tribunal having regard to the circumstances of the case. The award shall be deemed to have been made at the place of arbitration.
2. The arbitral tribunal may meet at any location it considers appropriate for deliberations. Unless otherwise agreed by the parties, the arbitral tribunal may also meet at any location it considers appropriate for any other purpose, including hearings.

Language
Article 19

1. Subject to an agreement by the parties, the arbitral tribunal shall, promptly after its appointment, determine the language or languages to be used in the proceedings. This determination shall apply to the statement of claim, the statement of defence, and any further written statements and, if oral hearings take place, to the language or languages to be used in such hearings.

2. The arbitral tribunal may order that any documents annexed to the statement of claim or statement of defence, and any supplementary documents or exhibits submitted in the course of the proceedings, delivered in their original language, shall be accompanied by a translation into the language or languages agreed upon by the parties or determined by the arbitral tribunal.

Statement of claim
Article 20

1. The claimant shall communicate its statement of claim in writing to the respondent and to each of the arbitrators within a period of time to be determined by the arbitral tribunal. The claimant may elect to treat its notice of arbitration referred to in article 3 as a statement of claim, provided that the notice of arbitration also complies with the requirements of paragraphs 2 to 4 of this article.

2. The statement of claim shall include the following particulars:

(a) The names and contact details of the parties;
(b) A statement of the facts supporting the claim;
(c) The points at issue;
(d) The relief or remedy sought;
(e) The legal grounds or arguments supporting the claim.

3. A copy of any contract or other legal instrument out of or in relation to which the dispute arises and of the arbitration agreement shall be annexed to the statement of claim.

4. The statement of claim should, as far as possible, be accompanied by all documents and other evidence relied upon by the claimant, or contain references to them.

Statement of defence
Article 21

1. The respondent shall communicate its statement of defence in writing to the claimant and to each of the arbitrators within a period of time to be determined by the arbitral tribunal. The respondent may elect to treat its response to the notice of arbitration referred to in article 4 as a statement of defence, provided that the response to the notice of arbitration also complies with the requirements of paragraph 2 of this article.

2. The statement of defence shall reply to the particulars (b) to (e) of the statement of claim (art. 20, para. 2). The statement of defence should, as far as possible, be accompanied by all documents and other evidence relied upon by the respondent, or contain references to them.

3. In its statement of defence, or at a later stage in the arbitral proceedings if the arbitral tribunal decides that the delay was justified under the circumstances, the respondent may make a counterclaim or rely on a claim for the purpose of a set-off provided that the arbitral tribunal has jurisdiction over it.

4. The provisions of article 20, paragraphs 2 to 4, shall apply to a counterclaim, a claim under article 4, paragraph 2 (f), and a claim relied on for the purpose of a set-off.

Amendments to the claim or defence
Article 22

During the course of the arbitral proceedings, a party may amend or supplement its claim or defence, including a counterclaim or a claim for the purpose of a set-off, unless the arbitral tribunal considers it inappropriate to allow such amendment or supplement having regard to the delay in making it or prejudice to other parties or any other circumstances. However, a claim or defence, including a counterclaim or a claim for the purpose of a set-off, may not be amended or supplemented in such a manner that the amended or supplemented claim or defence falls outside the jurisdiction of the arbitral tribunal.

Pleas as to the jurisdiction of the arbitral tribunal
Article 23

1. The arbitral tribunal shall have the power to rule on its own jurisdiction, including any objections with respect to the existence or validity of the arbitration agreement. For that purpose, an arbitration clause that forms part of a contract shall be treated as an agreement independent of the other terms of the contract. A decision by the arbitral tribunal that the contract is null shall not entail automatically the invalidity of the arbitration clause.

2. A plea that the arbitral tribunal does not have jurisdiction shall be raised no later than in the statement of defence or, with respect to a counterclaim or a claim for the purpose of a set-off, in the reply to the counterclaim or to the claim for the purpose of a set-off. A party is not precluded from raising such a plea by the fact that it has appointed, or participated in the appointment of, an arbitrator. A plea that the arbitral tribunal is exceeding the scope of its authority shall be raised as soon as the matter alleged to be beyond the scope of its authority is raised during the arbitral proceedings. The arbitral tribunal may, in either case, admit a later plea if it considers the delay justified.

3. The arbitral tribunal may rule on a plea referred to in paragraph 2 either as a preliminary question or in an award on the merits. The arbitral tribunal may continue the arbitral proceedings and make an award, notwithstanding any pending challenge to its jurisdiction before a court.

Further written statements
Article 24

The arbitral tribunal shall decide which further written statements, in addition to the statement of claim and the statement of defence, shall be required from the parties or may be presented by them and shall fix the periods of time for communicating such statements.

Periods of time
Article 25

The periods of time fixed by the arbitral tribunal for the communication of written statements (including the statement of claim and statement of defence) should not exceed 45 days. However, the arbitral tribunal may extend the time limits if it concludes that an extension is justified.

Interim measures
Article 26

1. The arbitral tribunal may, at the request of a party, grant interim measures.

2. An interim measure is any temporary measure by which, at any time prior to the issuance of the award by which the dispute is finally decided, the arbitral tribunal orders a party, for example and without limitation, to:

(a) Maintain or restore the status quo pending determination of the dispute;

(b) Take action that would prevent, or refrain from taking action that is likely to cause, (i) current or imminent harm or (ii) prejudice to the arbitral process itself;

(c) Provide a means of preserving assets out of which a subsequent award may be satisfied; or

(d) Preserve evidence that may be relevant and material to the resolution of the dispute.

3. The party requesting an interim measure under paragraphs 2 (a) to (c) shall satisfy the arbitral tribunal that:

(a) Harm not adequately reparable by an award of damages is likely to result if the measure is not ordered, and such harm substantially outweighs the harm that is likely to result to the party against whom the measure is directed if the measure is granted; and

(b) There is a reasonable possibility that the requesting party will succeed on the merits of the claim. The determination on this possibility shall not affect the discretion of the arbitral tribunal in making any subsequent determination.

4. With regard to a request for an interim measure under paragraph 2 (d), the requirements in paragraphs 3 (a) and (b) shall apply only to the extent the arbitral tribunal considers appropriate.

5. The arbitral tribunal may modify, suspend or terminate an interim measure it has granted, upon application of any party or, in exceptional circumstances and upon prior notice to the parties, on the arbitral tribunal's own initiative.

6. The arbitral tribunal may require the party requesting an interim measure to provide appropriate security in connection with the measure.

7. The arbitral tribunal may require any party promptly to disclose any material change in the circumstances on the basis of which the interim measure was requested or granted.

8. The party requesting an interim measure may be liable for any costs and damages caused by the measure to any party if the arbitral tribunal later determines that, in the circumstances then prevailing, the measure should not have been granted. The arbitral tribunal may award such costs and damages at any point during the proceedings.

9. A request for interim measures addressed by any party to a judicial authority shall not be deemed incompatible with the agreement to arbitrate, or as a waiver of that agreement.

Evidence
Article 27

1. Each party shall have the burden of proving the facts relied on to support its claim or defence.

2. Witnesses, including expert witnesses, who are presented by the parties to testify to the arbitral tribunal on any issue of fact or expertise may be any individual, notwithstanding that the individual is a party to the arbitration or in any way related to a party. Unless otherwise directed by the arbitral tribunal, statements by witnesses, including expert witnesses, may be presented in writing and signed by them.

3. At any time during the arbitral proceedings the arbitral tribunal may require the parties to produce documents, exhibits or other evidence within such a period of time as the arbitral tribunal shall determine.

4. The arbitral tribunal shall determine the admissibility, relevance, materiality and weight of the evidence offered.

Hearings
Article 28

1. In the event of an oral hearing, the arbitral tribunal shall give the parties adequate advance notice of the date, time and place thereof.

2. Witnesses, including expert witnesses, may be heard under the conditions and examined in the manner set by the arbitral tribunal.

3. Hearings shall be held in camera unless the parties agree otherwise. The arbitral tribunal may require the retirement of any witness or witnesses, including expert witnesses, during the testimony of such other witnesses, except that a witness, including an expert witness, who is a party to the arbitration shall not, in principle, be asked to retire.

4. The arbitral tribunal may direct that witnesses, including expert witnesses, be examined through means of telecommunication that do not require their physical presence at the hearing (such as videoconference).

Experts appointed by the arbitral tribunal
Article 29

1. After consultation with the parties, the arbitral tribunal may appoint one or more independent experts to report to it, in writing, on specific issues to be determined by the arbitral tribunal. A copy of the expert's terms of reference, established by the arbitral tribunal, shall be communicated to the parties.

2. The expert shall, in principle before accepting appointment, submit to the arbitral tribunal and to the parties a description of his or her qualifications and a statement of his or her impartiality and independence. Within the time ordered by the arbitral tribunal, the parties shall inform the arbitral tribunal whether they have any objections as to the expert's qualifications, impartiality or independence. The arbitral tribunal shall decide promptly whether to accept any such objections. After an expert's appointment, a party may object to the expert's qualifications, impartiality or independence only if the objection is for reasons of which the party becomes aware after the appointment has been made. The arbitral tribunal shall decide promptly what, if any, action to take.

3. The parties shall give the expert any relevant information or produce for his or her inspection any relevant documents or goods that he or she may require of them. Any dispute between a party and such expert as to the relevance of the required information or production shall be referred to the arbitral tribunal for decision.

4. Upon receipt of the expert's report, the arbitral tribunal shall communicate a copy of the report to the parties, which shall be given the opportunity to express, in writing, their opinion on the report. A party shall be entitled to examine any document on which the expert has relied in his or her report.

5. At the request of any party, the expert, after delivery of the report, may be heard at a hearing where the parties shall have the opportunity to be present and to interrogate the expert. At this hearing, any party may present expert witnesses in order to testify on the points at issue. The provisions of article 28 shall be applicable to such proceedings.

Default
Article 30

1. If, within the period of time fixed by these Rules or the arbitral tribunal, without showing sufficient cause:

(a) The claimant has failed to communicate its statement of claim, the arbitral tribunal shall issue an order for the termination of the arbitral proceedings, unless there are remaining matters that may need to be decided and the arbitral tribunal considers it appropriate to do so;

(b) The respondent has failed to communicate its response to the notice of arbitration or its statement of defence, the arbitral tribunal shall order that the proceedings continue, without treating such failure in itself as an admission of the claimant's allegations; the provisions of this subparagraph also apply to a claimant's failure to submit a defence to a counterclaim or to a claim for the purpose of a set-off.

2. If a party, duly notified under these Rules, fails to appear at a hearing, without showing sufficient cause for such failure, the arbitral tribunal may proceed with the arbitration.

3. If a party, duly invited by the arbitral tribunal to produce documents, exhibits or other evidence, fails to do so within the established period of time, without showing sufficient cause for such failure, the arbitral tribunal may make the award on the evidence before it.

Closure of hearings
Article 31

1. The arbitral tribunal may inquire of the parties if they have any further proof to offer or witnesses to be heard or submissions to make and, if there are none, it may declare the hearings closed.

2. The arbitral tribunal may, if it considers it necessary owing to exceptional circumstances, decide, on its own initiative or upon application of a party, to reopen the hearings at any time before the award is made.

Waiver of right to object
Article 32

A failure by any party to object promptly to any non-compliance with these Rules or with any requirement of the arbitration agreement shall be deemed to be a waiver of the right of such party to make such an objection, unless such party can show that, under the circumstances, its failure to object was justified.

Section IV. The award

Decisions
Article 33

1. When there is more than one arbitrator, any award or other decision of the arbitral tribunal shall be made by a majority of the arbitrators.

2. In the case of questions of procedure, when there is no majority or when the arbitral tribunal so authorizes, the presiding arbitrator may decide alone, subject to revision, if any, by the arbitral tribunal.

Form and effect of the award
Article 34

1. The arbitral tribunal may make separate awards on different issues at different times.

2. All awards shall be made in writing and shall be final and binding on the parties. The parties shall carry out all awards without delay.

3. The arbitral tribunal shall state the reasons upon which the award is based, unless the parties have agreed that no reasons are to be given.

4. An award shall be signed by the arbitrators and it shall contain the date on which the award was made and indicate the place of arbitration. Where there is more than one arbitrator and any of them fails to sign, the award shall state the reason for the absence of the signature.

5. An award may be made public with the consent of all parties or where and to the extent disclosure is required of a party by legal duty, to protect or pursue a legal right or in relation to legal proceedings before a court or other competent authority.

6. Copies of the award signed by the arbitrators shall be communicated to the parties by the arbitral tribunal.

Applicable law, amiable compositeur
Article 35

1. The arbitral tribunal shall apply the rules of law designated by the parties as applicable to the substance of the dispute. Failing such designation by the parties, the arbitral tribunal shall apply the law which it determines to be appropriate.

2. The arbitral tribunal shall decide as amiable compositeur or ex aequo et bono only if the parties have expressly authorized the arbitral tribunal to do so.

3. In all cases, the arbitral tribunal shall decide in accordance with the terms of the contract, if any, and shall take into account any usage of trade applicable to the transaction.

Settlement or other grounds for termination
Article 36

1. If, before the award is made, the parties agree on a settlement of the dispute, the arbitral tribunal shall either issue an order for the termination of the arbitral proceedings or, if requested by the parties and accepted by the arbitral tribunal, record the settlement in the form of an arbitral award on agreed terms. The arbitral tribunal is not obliged to give reasons for such an award.

2. If, before the award is made, the continuation of the arbitral proceedings becomes unnecessary or impossible for any reason not mentioned in paragraph 1, the arbitral tribunal shall inform the parties of its intention to issue an order for the termination of the proceedings. The arbitral tribunal shall have the power to issue such an order unless there are remaining matters that may need to be decided and the arbitral tribunal considers it appropriate to do so.

3. Copies of the order for termination of the arbitral proceedings or of the arbitral award on agreed terms, signed by the arbitrators, shall be communicated by the arbitral tribunal to the parties.

Where an arbitral award on agreed terms is made, the provisions of article 34, paragraphs 2, 4 and 5, shall apply.

Interpretation of the award
Article 37

1. Within 30 days after the receipt of the award, a party, with notice to the other parties, may request that the arbitral tribunal give an interpretation of the award.

2. The interpretation shall be given in writing within 45 days after the receipt of the request. The interpretation shall form part of the award and the provisions of article 34, paragraphs 2 to 6, shall apply.

Correction of the award
Article 38

1. Within 30 days after the receipt of the award, a party, with notice to the other parties, may request the arbitral tribunal to correct in the award any error in computation, any clerical or typographical error, or any error or omission of a similar nature. If the arbitral tribunal considers that the request is justified, it shall make the correction within 45 days of receipt of the request.

2. The arbitral tribunal may within 30days after the communication of the award make such corrections on its own initiative.

3. Such corrections shall be in writing and shall form part of the award. The provisions of article 34, paragraphs 2 to 6, shall apply.

Additional award
Article 39

1. Within 30 days after the receipt of the termination order or the award, a party, with notice to the other parties, may request the arbitral tribunal to make an award or an additional award as to claims presented in the arbitral proceedings but not decided by the arbitral tribunal.

2. If the arbitral tribunal considers the request for an award or additional award to be justified, it shall render or complete its award within 60 days after the receipt of the request. The arbitral tribunal may extend, if necessary, the period of time within which it shall make the award.

3. When such an award or additional award is made, the provisions of article 34, paragraphs 2 to 6, shall apply.

Definition of costs
Article 40

1. The arbitral tribunal shall fix the costs of arbitration in the final award and, if it deems appropriate, in another decision.

2. The term "costs" includes only:

(a) The fees of the arbitral tribunal to be stated separately as to each arbitrator and to be fixed by the tribunal itself in accordance with article 41;
(b) The reasonable travel and other expenses incurred by the arbitrators;
(c) The reasonable costs of expert advice and of other assistance required by the arbitral tribunal;
(d) The reasonable travel and other expenses of witnesses to the extent such expenses are approved by the arbitral tribunal;
(e) The legal and other costs incurred by the parties in relation to the arbitration to the extent that the arbitral tribunal determines that the amount of such costs is reasonable;
(f) Any fees and expenses of the appointing authority as well as the fees and expenses of the Secretary-General of the PCA.

3. In relation to interpretation, correction or completion of any award under articles 37 to 39, the arbitral tribunal may charge the costs referred to in paragraphs 2 (b) to (f), but no additional fees.

Fees and expenses of arbitrators
Article 41

1. The fees and expenses of the arbitrators shall be reasonable in amount, taking into account the amount in dispute, the complexity of the subject matter, the time spent by the arbitrators and any other relevant circumstances of the case.

2. If there is an appointing authority and it applies or has stated that it will apply a schedule or particular method for determining the fees for arbitrators in international cases, the arbitral tribunal in fixing its fees shall take that schedule or method into account to the extent that it considers appropriate in the circumstances of the case.

3. Promptly after its constitution, the arbitral tribunal shall inform the parties as to how it proposes to determine its fees and expenses, including any rates it intends to apply. Within 15 days of receiving that proposal, any party may refer the proposal to the appointing authority for review. If, within 45 days of receipt of such a referral, the appointing authority finds that the proposal of the arbitral tribunal is inconsistent with paragraph 1, it shall make any necessary adjustments thereto, which shall be binding upon the arbitral tribunal.

4. (a) When informing the parties of the arbitrators' fees and expenses that have been fixed pursuant to article 40, paragraphs 2 (a) and (b), the arbitral tribunal shall also explain the manner in which the corresponding amounts have been calculated;
   (b) Within 15 days of receiving the arbitral tribunal's determination of fees and expenses, any party may refer for review such determination to the appointing authority. If no appointing authority has been agreed upon or designated, or if the appointing authority fails to act within the time specified in these Rules, then the review shall be made by the Secretary-General of the PCA;
   (c) If the appointing authority or the Secretary-General of the PCA finds that the arbitral tribunal's determination is inconsistent with the arbitral tribunal's proposal (and any adjustment thereto) under paragraph 3 or is otherwise manifestly excessive, it shall, within 45 days of receiving such a referral, make any adjustments to the arbitral tribunal's determination that are necessary to satisfy the criteria in paragraph 1. Any such adjustments shall be binding upon the arbitral tribunal;
   (d) Any such adjustments shall either be included by the arbitral tribunal in its award or, if the award has already been issued, be implemented in a correction to the award, to which the procedure of article 38, paragraph 3, shall apply.

5. Throughout the procedure under paragraphs 3 and 4, the arbitral tribunal shall proceed with the arbitration, in accordance with article 17, paragraph 1.

6. A referral under paragraph 4 shall not affect any determination in the award other than the arbitral tribunal's fees and expenses; nor shall it delay the recognition and enforcement of all parts of the award other than those relating to the determination of the arbitral tribunal's fees and expenses.

Allocation of costs
Article 42

1. The costs of the arbitration shall in principle be borne by the unsuccessful party or parties. However, the arbitral tribunal may apportion each of such costs between the parties if it determines that apportionment is reasonable, taking into account the circumstances of the case.

2. The arbitral tribunal shall in the final award or, if it deems appropriate, in any other award, determine any amount that a party may have to pay to another party as a result of the decision on allocation of costs.

Deposit of costs
Article 43

1. The arbitral tribunal, on its establishment, may request the parties to deposit an equal amount as an advance for the costs referred to in article 40, paragraphs 2 (a) to (c).

2. During the course of the arbitral proceedings the arbitral tribunal may request supplementary deposits from the parties.

3. If an appointing authority has been agreed upon or designated, and when a party so requests and the appointing authority consents to perform the function, the arbitral tribunal shall fix the amounts of any deposits or supplementary deposits only after consultation with the appointing authority, which may make any comments to the arbitral tribunal that it deems appropriate concerning the amount of such deposits and supplementary deposits.

4. If the required deposits are not paid in full within 30 days after the receipt of the request, the arbitral tribunal shall so inform the parties in order that one or more of them may make the required payment. If such payment is not made, the arbitral tribunal may order the suspension or termination of the arbitral proceedings.

5. After a termination order or final award has been made, the arbitral tribunal shall render an accounting to the parties of the deposits received and return any unexpended balance to the parties.

ANNEX
Model arbitration clause for contracts

Any dispute, controversy or claim arising out of or relating to this contract, or the breach, termination or invalidity thereof, shall be settled by arbitration in accordance with the UNCITRAL Arbitration Rules.

Note. Parties should consider adding:

(a) The appointing authority shall be … [name of institution or person];
(b) The number of arbitrators shall be … [one or three];
(c) The place of arbitration shall be … [town and country];
(d) The language to be used in the arbitral proceedings shall be ….

Possible waiver statement

Note. If the parties wish to exclude recourse against the arbitral award that may be available under the applicable law, they may consider adding a provision to that effect as suggested below, considering, however, that the effectiveness and conditions of such an exclusion depend on the applicable law.

Waiver

The parties hereby waive their right to any form of recourse against an award to any court or other competent authority, insofar as such waiver can validly be made under the applicable law.

Model statements of independence pursuant to article 11 of the Rules

No circumstances to disclose

I am impartial and independent of each of the parties and intend to remain so. To the best of my knowledge, there are no circumstances, past or present, likely to give rise to justifiable doubts as to my impartiality or independence. I shall promptly notify the parties and the other arbitrators of any such circumstances that may subsequently come to my attention during this arbitration.

Circumstances to disclose

I am impartial and independent of each of the parties and intend to remain so. Attached is a statement made pursuant to article 11 of the UNCITRAL Arbitration Rules of (a) my past and present professional, business and other relationships with the parties and (b) any other relevant circumstances.

[Include statement.] I confirm that those circumstances do not affect my independence and impartiality. I shall promptly notify the parties and the other arbitrators of any such further relationships or circumstances that may subsequently come to my attention during this arbitration.

Note. Any party may consider requesting from the arbitrator the following addition to the statement of independence:

I confirm, on the basis of the information presently available to me, that I can devote the time necessary to conduct this arbitration diligently, efficiently and in accordance with the time limits in the Rules.

38.b UNCITRAL Rules on Transparency in Treaty-based Investor-State Arbitration

Date: effective 1 April 2014
Source: https://uncitral.un.org/sites/uncitral.un.org/files/media-documents/uncitral/en/uncitral-arbitration-rules-2013-e.pdf

Article 1. Scope of application

Applicability of the Rules

1. The UNCITRAL Rules on Transparency in Treaty-based Investor-State Arbitration ("Rules on Transparency") shall apply to investor-State arbitration initiated under the UNCITRAL Arbitration Rules pursuant to a treaty providing for the protection of investments or investors ("treaty")* concluded on or after 1 April 2014 unless the Parties to the treaty** have agreed otherwise.

2. In investor-State arbitrations initiated under the UNCITRAL Arbitration Rules pursuant to a treaty concluded before 1 April 2014, these Rules shall apply only when:

(a) The parties to an arbitration (the "disputing parties") agree to their application in respect of that arbitration; or

(b) The Parties to the treaty or, in the case of a multilateral treaty, the State of the claimant and the respondent State, have agreed after 1 April 2014 to their application.

* For the purposes of the Rules on Transparency, a "treaty" shall be understood broadly as encompassing any bilateral or multilateral treaty that contains provisions on the protection of investments or investors and a right for investors to resort to arbitration against Parties to the treaty, including any treaty commonly referred to as a free trade agreement, economic integration agreement, trade and investment framework or cooperation agreement, or bilateral investment treaty.

** For the purposes of the Rules on Transparency, any reference to a "Party to the treaty" or a "State" includes, for example, a regional economic integration organization where it is a Party to the treaty.

Application of the Rules

3. In any arbitration in which the Rules on Transparency apply pursuant to a treaty or to an agreement by the Parties to that treaty:

(a) The disputing parties may not derogate from these Rules, by agreement or otherwise, unless permitted to do so by the treaty;

(b) The arbitral tribunal shall have the power, besides its discretionary authority under certain provisions of these Rules, to adapt the requirements of any specific provision of these Rules to the particular circumstances of the case, after consultation with the disputing parties, if such adaptation is necessary to conduct the arbitration in a practical manner and is consistent with the transparency objective of these Rules.

Discretion and authority of the arbitral tribunal

4. Where the Rules on Transparency provide for the arbitral tribunal to exercise discretion, the arbitral tribunal in exercising such discretion shall take into account:

(a) The public interest in transparency in treaty-based investor-State arbitration and in the particular arbitral proceedings; and

(b) The disputing parties' interest in a fair and efficient resolution of their dispute.

5. These Rules shall not affect any authority that the arbitral tribunal may otherwise have under the UNCITRAL Arbitration Rules to conduct the arbitration in such a manner as to promote transparency, for example by accepting submissions from third persons.

6. In the presence of any conduct, measure or other action having the effect of wholly undermining the transparency objectives of these Rules, the arbitral tribunal shall ensure that those objectives prevail.

Applicable instrument in case of conflict

7. Where the Rules on Transparency apply, they shall supplement any applicable arbitration rules. Where there is a conflict between the Rules on Transparency and the applicable arbitration rules, the Rules on Transparency shall prevail. Notwithstanding any provision in these Rules, where there is a conflict between the Rules on Transparency and the treaty, the provisions of the treaty shall prevail.

8. Where any of these Rules is in conflict with a provision of the law applicable to the arbitration from which the disputing parties cannot derogate, that provision shall prevail.

Application in non-UNCITRAL arbitrations

9. These Rules are available for use in investor-State arbitrations initiated under rules other than the UNCITRAL Arbitration Rules or in ad hoc proceedings.

Article 2. Publication of information at the commencement of arbitral proceedings

Once the notice of arbitration has been received by the respondent, each of the disputing parties shall promptly communicate a copy of the notice of arbitration to the repository referred to under article 8. Upon receipt of the notice of arbitration from the respondent, or upon receipt of the notice of arbitration and a record of its transmission to the respondent, the repository shall promptly make available to the public information regarding the name of the disputing parties, the economic sector involved and the treaty under which the claim is being made.

Article 3. Publication of documents

1. Subject to article 7, the following documents shall be made available to the public: the notice of arbitration, the response to the notice of arbitration, the statement of claim, the statement of defence and any further written statements or written submissions by any disputing party; a table listing all exhibits to the aforesaid documents and to expert reports and witness statements, if such table has been prepared for the proceedings, but not the exhibits themselves; any written submissions by the non-disputing Party (or Parties) to the treaty and by third persons, transcripts of hearings, where available; and orders, decisions and awards of the arbitral tribunal.

2. Subject to article 7, expert reports and witness statements, exclusive of the exhibits thereto, shall be made available to the public, upon request by any person to the arbitral tribunal.

3. Subject to article 7, the arbitral tribunal may decide, on its own initiative or upon request from any person, and after consultation with the disputing parties, whether and how to make available exhibits and any other documents provided to, or issued by, the arbitral tribunal not falling within paragraphs 1 or 2 above. This may include, for example, making such documents available at a specified site.

4. The documents to be made available to the public pursuant to paragraphs 1 and 2 shall be communicated by the arbitral tribunal to the repository referred to under article 8 as soon as possible, subject to any relevant arrangements or time limits for the protection of confidential or protected information prescribed under article 7. The documents to be made available pursuant to paragraph 3 may be communicated by the arbitral tribunal to the repository referred to under article 8 as they become available and, if applicable, in a redacted form in accordance with article 7. The repository shall make all documents available in a timely manner, in the form and in the language in which it receives them.

5. A person granted access to documents under paragraph 3 shall bear any administrative costs of making those documents available to that person, such as the costs of photocopying or shipping documents to that person, but not the costs of making those documents available to the public through the repository.

Article 4. Submission by a third person

1. After consultation with the disputing parties, the arbitral tribunal may allow a person that is not a disputing party, and not a non-disputing Party to the treaty ("third person(s)"), to file a written submission with the arbitral tribunal regarding a matter within the scope of the dispute.

2. A third person wishing to make a submission shall apply to the arbitral tribunal, and shall, in a concise written statement, which is in a language of the arbitration and complies with any page limits set by the arbitral tribunal:

(a) Describe the third person, including, where relevant, its membership and legal status (e.g., trade association or other non-governmental organization), its general objectives, the nature of its activities and any parent organization (including any organization that directly or indirectly controls the third person);

(b) Disclose any connection, direct or indirect, which the third person has with any disputing party;

(c) Provide information on any government, person or organization that has provided to the third person (i) any financial or other assistance in preparing the submission; or (ii) substantial assistance in either of the two years preceding the application by the third person under this article (e.g. funding around 20 per cent of its overall operations annually);

(*d*) Describe the nature of the interest that the third person has in the arbitration; and
(*e*) Identify the specific issues of fact or law in the arbitration that the third person wishes to address in its written submission.

3. In determining whether to allow such a submission, the arbitral tribunal shall take into consideration, among other factors it determines to be relevant:

(*a*) Whether the third person has a significant interest in the arbitral proceedings; and
(*b*) The extent to which the submission would assist the arbitral tribunal in the determination of a factual or legal issue related to the arbitral proceedings by bringing a perspective, particular knowledge or insight that is different from that of the disputing parties.

4. The submission filed by the third person shall:

(*a*) Be dated and signed by the person filing the submission on behalf of the third person;
(*b*) Be concise, and in no case longer than as authorized by the arbitral tribunal;
(*c*) Set out a precise statement of the third person's position on issues; and
(*d*) Address only matters within the scope of the dispute.

5. The arbitral tribunal shall ensure that any submission does not disrupt or unduly burden the arbitral proceedings, or unfairly prejudice any disputing party.

6. The arbitral tribunal shall ensure that the disputing parties are given a reasonable opportunity to present their observations on any submission by the third person.

Article 5. Submission by a non-disputing Party to the treaty

1. The arbitral tribunal shall, subject to paragraph 4, allow, or, after consultation with the disputing parties, may invite, submissions on issues of treaty interpretation from a non-disputing Party to the treaty.

2. The arbitral tribunal, after consultation with the disputing parties, may allow submissions on further matters within the scope of the dispute from a non-disputing Party to the treaty. In determining whether to allow such submissions, the arbitral tribunal shall take into consideration, among other factors it determines to be relevant, the factors referred to in article 4, paragraph 3, and, for greater certainty, the need to avoid submissions which would support the claim of the investor in a manner tantamount to diplomatic protection.

3. The arbitral tribunal shall not draw any inference from the absence of any submission or response to any invitation pursuant to paragraphs 1 or 2.

4. The arbitral tribunal shall ensure that any submission does not disrupt or unduly burden the arbitral proceedings, or unfairly prejudice any disputing party.

5. The arbitral tribunal shall ensure that the disputing parties are given a reasonable opportunity to present their observations on any submission by a non-disputing Party to the treaty.

Article 6. Hearings

1. Subject to article 6, paragraphs 2 and 3, hearings for the presentation of evidence or for oral argument ("hearings") shall be public.

2. Where there is a need to protect confidential information or the integrity of the arbitral process pursuant to article 7, the arbitral tribunal shall make arrangements to hold in private that part of the hearing requiring such protection.

3. The arbitral tribunal shall make logistical arrangements to facilitate the public access to hearings (including where appropriate by organizing attendance through video links or such other means as it deems appropriate). However, the arbitral tribunal may, after consultation with the disputing parties, decide to hold all or part of the hearings in private where this becomes necessary for logistical reasons, such as when the circumstances render any original arrangement for public access to a hearing infeasible.

Article 7. Exceptions to transparency
Confidential or protected information

1. Confidential or protected information, as defined in paragraph 2 and as identified pursuant to the arrangements referred to in paragraphs 3 and 4, shall not be made available to the public pursuant to articles 2 to 6.

2. Confidential or protected information consists of:
   (a) Confidential business information;
   (b) Information that is protected against being made available to the public under the treaty;
   (c) Information that is protected against being made available to the public, in the case of the information of the respondent State, under the law of the respondent State, and in the case of other information, under any law or rules determined by the arbitral tribunal to be applicable to the disclosure of such information; or
   (d) Information the disclosure of which would impede law enforcement.

3. The arbitral tribunal, after consultation with the disputing parties, shall make arrangements to prevent any confidential or protected information from being made available to the public, including by putting in place, as appropriate:
   (a) Time limits in which a disputing party, non-disputing Party to the treaty or third person shall give notice that it seeks protection for such information in documents;
   (b) Procedures for the prompt designation and redaction of the particular confidential or protected information in such documents; and
   (c) Procedures for holding hearings in private to the extent required by article 6, paragraph 2.

   Any determination as to whether information is confidential or protected shall be made by the arbitral tribunal after consultation with the disputing parties.

4. Where the arbitral tribunal determines that information should not be redacted from a document, or that a document should not be prevented from being made available to the public, any disputing party, non-disputing Party to the treaty or third person that voluntarily introduced the document into the record shall be permitted to withdraw all or part of the document from the record of the arbitral proceedings.

5. Nothing in these Rules requires a respondent State to make available to the public information the disclosure of which it considers to be contrary to its essential security interests.

Integrity of the arbitral process

6. Information shall not be made available to the public pursuant to articles 2 to 6 where the information, if made available to the public, would jeopardize the integrity of the arbitral process as determined pursuant to paragraph 7.

7. The arbitral tribunal may, on its own initiative or upon the application of a disputing party, after consultation with the disputing parties where practicable, take appropriate measures to restrain or delay the publication of information where such publication would jeopardize the integrity of the arbitral process because it could hamper the collection or production of evidence, lead to the intimidation of witnesses, lawyers acting for disputing parties or members of the arbitral tribunal, or in comparably exceptional circumstances.

Article 8. Repository of published information

The repository of published information under the Rules on Transparency shall be the Secretary-General of the United Nations or an institution named by UNCITRAL.

38.c United Nations Convention on Transparency in Treaty-based Investor-State Arbitration

Date: 10 December 2014
Source: https://www.uncitral.org/pdf/english/texts/arbitration/transparency-convention/Transparency-Convention-e.pdf

Preamble

The Parties to this Convention,

Recognizing the value of arbitration as a method of settling disputes that may arise in the context of international relations, and the extensive and wide-ranging use of arbitration for the settlement of investor-State disputes,

Also recognizing the need for provisions on transparency in the settlement of treaty-based investor-State disputes to take account of the public interest involved in such arbitrations,

Believing that the Rules on Transparency in Treaty-based Investor-State Arbitration adopted by the United Nations Commission on International Trade Law on 11 July 2013 ("UNCITRAL Rules on Transparency"), effective as of 1 April 2014, would contribute significantly to the establishment of a harmonized legal framework for a fair and efficient settlement of international investment disputes,

Noting the great number of treaties providing for the protection of investments or investors already in force, and the practical importance of promoting the application of the UNCITRAL Rules on Transparency to arbitration under those already concluded investment treaties,

Noting also article 1(2) and (9) of the UNCITRAL Rules on Transparency,

Have agreed as follows:

Article 1. Scope of application

1. This Convention applies to arbitration between an investor and a State or a regional economic integration organization conducted on the basis of an investment treaty concluded before 1 April 2014 ("investor-State arbitration").

2. The term "investment treaty" means any bilateral or multilateral treaty, including any treaty commonly referred to as a free trade agreement, economic integration agreement, trade and investment framework or cooperation agreement, or bilateral investment treaty, which contains provisions on the protection of investments or investors and a right for investors to resort to arbitration against contracting parties to that investment treaty.

Article 2. Application of the UNCITRAL Rules on Transparency
Bilateral or multilateral application

1. The UNCITRAL Rules on Transparency shall apply to any investor-State arbitration, whether or not initiated under the UNCITRAL Arbitration Rules, in which the respondent is a Party that has not made a relevant reservation under article 3(1)*(a)* or *(b)*, and the claimant is of a State that is a Party that has not made a relevant reservation under article 3(1)*(a)*.

Unilateral offer of application

2. Where the UNCITRAL Rules on Transparency do not apply pursuant to paragraph 1, the UNCITRAL Rules on Transparency shall apply to an investor-State arbitration, whether or not initiated under the UNCITRAL Arbitration Rules, in which the respondent is a Party that has not made a reservation relevant to that investor-State arbitration under article 3(1), and the claimant agrees to the application of the UNCITRAL Rules on Transparency.

Applicable version of the UNCITRAL Rules on Transparency

3. Where the UNCITRAL Rules on Transparency apply pursuant to paragraph 1 or 2, the most recent version of those Rules as to which the respondent has not made a reservation pursuant to article 3(2) shall apply.

Article 1(7) of the UNCITRAL Rules on Transparency

4. The final sentence of article 1(7) of the UNCITRAL Rules on Transparency shall not apply to investor-State arbitrations under paragraph 1.

Most favoured nation provision in an investment treaty

5. The Parties to this Convention agree that a claimant may not invoke a most favoured nation provision to seek to apply, or avoid the application of, the UNCITRAL Rules on Transparency under this Convention.

Article 3. Reservations

1. A Party may declare that:
   (a) It shall not apply this Convention to investor-State arbitration under a specific investment treaty, identified by title and name of the contracting parties to that investment treaty;
   (b) Article 2(1) and (2) shall not apply to investor-State arbitration conducted using a specific set of arbitration rules or procedures other than the UNCITRAL Arbitration Rules, and in which it is a respondent;
   (c) Article 2(2) shall not apply in investor-State arbitration in which it is a respondent.

2. In the event of a revision of the UNCITRAL Rules on Transparency, a Party may, within six months of the adoption of such revision, declare that it shall not apply that revised version of the Rules.

3. Parties may make multiple reservations in a single instrument. In such an instrument, each declaration made:
   (a) In respect of a specific investment treaty under paragraph (1)*(a)*;
   (b) In respect of a specific set of arbitration rules or procedures under paragraph (1)*(b)*;

(c) Under paragraph (1)*(c)*; or

(d) Under paragraph (2); shall constitute a separate reservation capable of separate withdrawal under article 4(6).

4. No reservations are permitted except those expressly authorized in this article.

Article 4. Formulation of reservations

1. Reservations may be made by a Party at any time, save for a reservation under article 3(2).

2. Reservations made at the time of signature shall be subject to confirmation upon ratification, acceptance or approval. Such reservations shall take effect simultaneously with the entry into force of this Convention in respect of the Party concerned.

3. Reservations made at the time of ratification, acceptance or approval of this Convention or accession thereto shall take effect simultaneously with the entry into force of this Convention in respect of the Party concerned.

4. Except for a reservation made by a Party under article 3(2), which shall take effect immediately upon deposit, a reservation deposited after the entry into force of the Convention for that Party shall take effect twelve months after the date of its deposit.

5. Reservations and their confirmations shall be deposited with the depositary.

6. Any Party that makes a reservation under this Convention may withdraw it at any time. Such withdrawals are to be deposited with the depositary, and shall take effect upon deposit.

Article 5. Application to investor-State arbitrations

This Convention and any reservation, or withdrawal of a reservation, shall apply only to investor-State arbitrations that are commenced after the date when the Convention, reservation, or withdrawal of a reservation, enters into force or takes effect in respect of each Party concerned.

Article 6. Depositary

The Secretary-General of the United Nations is hereby designated as the depositary of this Convention.

Article 7. Signature, ratification, acceptance, approval, accession

1. This Convention is open for signature in Port Louis, Mauritius, on 17 March 2015, and thereafter at United Nations Headquarters in New York by any *(a)* State; or *(b)* regional economic integration organization that is constituted by States and is a contracting party to an investment treaty.

2. This Convention is subject to ratification, acceptance or approval by the signatories to this Convention.

3. This Convention is open for accession by all States or regional economic integration organizations referred to in paragraph 1 which are not signatories as from the date it is open for signature.

4. Instruments of ratification, acceptance, approval or accession are to be deposited with the depositary.

Article 8. Participation by regional economic integration organizations

1. When depositing an instrument of ratification, acceptance, approval or accession, a regional economic integration organization shall inform the depositary of a specific

investment treaty to which it is a contracting party, identified by title and name of the contracting parties to that investment treaty.

2. When the number of Parties is relevant in this Convention, a regional economic integration organization does not count as a Party in addition to its member States which are Parties.

Article 9. Entry into force

1. This Convention shall enter into force six months after the date of deposit of the third instrument of ratification, acceptance, approval or accession.

2. When a State or a regional economic integration organization ratifies, accepts, approves or accedes to this Convention after the deposit of the third instrument of ratification, acceptance, approval or accession, this Convention enters into force in respect of that State or regional economic integration organization six months after the date of the deposit of its instrument of ratification, acceptance, approval or accession.

Article 10. Amendment

1. Any Party may propose an amendment to the present Convention by submitting it to the Secretary-General of the United Nations. The Secretary-General shall thereupon communicate the proposed amendment to the Parties to this Convention with a request that they indicate whether they favour a conference of Parties for the purpose of considering and voting upon the proposal. In the event that within four months from the date of such communication at least one third of the Parties favour such a conference, the Secretary-General shall convene the conference under the auspices of the United Nations.

2. The conference of Parties shall make every effort to achieve consensus on each amendment. If all efforts at consensus are exhausted and no consensus is reached, the amendment shall, as a last resort, require for its adoption a two-thirds majority vote of the Parties present and voting at the conference.

3. An adopted amendment shall be submitted by the Secretary-General of the United Nations to all the Parties for ratification, acceptance or approval.

4. An adopted amendment enters into force six months after the date of deposit of the third instrument of ratification, acceptance or approval. When an amendment enters into force, it shall be binding on those Parties which have expressed consent to be bound by it.

5. When a State or a regional economic integration organization ratifies, accepts or approves an amendment that has already entered into force, the amendment enters into force in respect of that State or that regional economic integration organization six months after the date of the deposit of its instrument of ratification, acceptance or approval.

6. Any State or regional economic integration organization which becomes a Party to the Convention after the entry into force of the amendment shall be considered as a Party to the Convention as amended.

Article 11. Denunciation of this Convention

1. A Party may denounce this Convention at any time by means of a formal notification addressed to the depositary. The denunciation shall take effect twelve months after the notification is received by the depositary.

2. This Convention shall continue to apply to investor-State arbitrations commenced before the denunciation takes effect.

DONE in a single original, of which the Arabic, Chinese, English, French, Russian and Spanish texts are equally authentic.

Dispute Settlement Provisions in Regional Frameworks: Examples

39.a North American Free Trade Agreement (NAFTA)*

Date: 17 December 1992
Source: (1993) 32 ILM 296
http://www.nafta-sec-alena.org/en/view.aspx?x=343

…

Part Five – Investment, Services and Related Matters

Chapter Eleven: Investment

Section A – Investment

Article 1101: Scope and Coverage

1. This Chapter applies to measures adopted or maintained by a Party relating to:
   (a) investors of another Party;
   (b) investments of investors of another Party in the territory of the Party; and
   (c) with respect to Articles 1106 and 1114, all investments in the territory of the Party.

2. A Party has the right to perform exclusively the economic activities set out in Annex III and to refuse to permit the establishment of investment in such activities.

3. This Chapter does not apply to measures adopted or maintained by a Party to the extent that they are covered by Chapter Fourteen (Financial Services).

4. Nothing in this Chapter shall be construed to prevent a Party from providing a service or performing a function such as law enforcement, correctional services, income security or insurance, social security or insurance, social welfare, public education, public training, health, and child care, in a manner that is not inconsistent with this Chapter.

…

Section B – Settlement of Disputes between a Party and an Investor of Another Party

Article 1115: Purpose

Without prejudice to the rights and obligations of the Parties under Chapter Twenty (Institutional Arrangements and Dispute Settlement Procedures), this Section establishes a mechanism for the settlement of investment disputes that assures both equal treatment among investors of the Parties in accordance with the principle of international reciprocity and due process before an impartial tribunal.

* NAFTA entered into force on 1 December 1994. On 30 November 2018, its three member States – the United States, Canada and Mexico – signed a Protocol of Amendment (later revised on 10 December 2019), which replaces NAFTA with a new United States-Mexico-Canada-Agreement (USMCA), which modifies the process for settling investment claims. In force from 1 July 2020, USMCA envisages investor-State proceedings under the conditions set out in Annex 14-D and 14-E. Annex 14-C of the USMCA preserves the possibility of certain 'legacy claims'. Given the parallel application, for the time being, of both treaties, the subsequent documents set out the old NAFTA regime (Document No. 39.a) alongside pertinent provisions of the new USMCA regime (Document No. 39.b).

Article 1116: Claim by an Investor of a Party on Its Own Behalf

1. An investor of a Party may submit to arbitration under this Section a claim that another Party has breached an obligation under:

(a) Section A or Article 1503(2) (State Enterprises), or

(b) Article 1502(3)(a) (Monopolies and State Enterprises) where the monopoly has acted in a manner inconsistent with the Party's obligations under Section A, and that the investor has incurred loss or damage by reason of, or arising out of, that breach.

2. An investor may not make a claim if more than three years have elapsed from the date on which the investor first acquired, or should have first acquired, knowledge of the alleged breach and knowledge that the investor has incurred loss or damage.

Article 1117: Claim by an Investor of a Party on Behalf of an Enterprise

1. An investor of a Party, on behalf of an enterprise of another Party that is a juridical person that the investor owns or controls directly or indirectly, may submit to arbitration under this Section a claim that the other Party has breached an obligation under:

(a) Section A or Article 1503(2) (State Enterprises), or

(b) Article 1502(3)(a) (Monopolies and State Enterprises) where the monopoly has acted in a manner inconsistent with the Party's obligations under Section A, and that the enterprise has incurred loss or damage by reason of, or arising out of, that breach.

2. An investor may not make a claim on behalf of an enterprise described in paragraph 1 if more than three years have elapsed from the date on which the enterprise first acquired, or should have first acquired, knowledge of the alleged breach and knowledge that the enterprise has incurred loss or damage.

3. Where an investor makes a claim under this Article and the investor or a non-controlling investor in the enterprise makes a claim under Article 1116 arising out of the same events that gave rise to the claim under this Article, and two or more of the claims are submitted to arbitration under Article 1120, the claims should be heard together by a Tribunal established under Article 1126, unless the Tribunal finds that the interests of a disputing party would be prejudiced thereby.

4. An investment may not make a claim under this Section.

Article 1118: Settlement of a Claim through Consultation and Negotiation

The disputing parties should first attempt to settle a claim through consultation or negotiation.

Article 1119: Notice of Intent to Submit a Claim to Arbitration

The disputing investor shall deliver to the disputing Party written notice of its intention to submit a claim to arbitration at least 90 days before the claim is submitted, which notice shall specify:

(a) the name and address of the disputing investor and, where a claim is made under Article 1117, the name and address of the enterprise;

(b) the provisions of this Agreement alleged to have been breached and any other relevant provisions;

(c) the issues and the factual basis for the claim; and

(d) the relief sought and the approximate amount of damages claimed.

Article 1120: Submission of a Claim to Arbitration

1. Except as provided in Annex 1120.1, and provided that six months have elapsed since the events giving rise to a claim, a disputing investor may submit the claim to arbitration under:

(a) the ICSID Convention, provided that both the disputing Party and the Party of the investor are parties to the Convention;

(b) the Additional Facility Rules of ICSID, provided that either the disputing Party or the Party of the investor, but not both, is a party to the ICSID Convention; or

(c) the UNCITRAL Arbitration Rules.

2. The applicable arbitration rules shall govern the arbitration except to the extent modified by this Section.

Article 1121: Conditions Precedent to Submission of a Claim to Arbitration

1. A disputing investor may submit a claim under Article 1116 to arbitration only if:

(a) the investor consents to arbitration in accordance with the procedures set out in this Agreement; and

(b) the investor and, where the claim is for loss or damage to an interest in an enterprise of another Party that is a juridical person that the investor owns or controls directly or indirectly, the enterprise, waive their right to initiate or continue before any administrative tribunal or court under the law of any Party, or other dispute settlement procedures, any proceedings with respect to the measure of the disputing Party that is alleged to be a breach referred to in Article 1116, except for proceedings for injunctive, declaratory or other extraordinary relief, not involving the payment of damages, before an administrative tribunal or court under the law of the disputing Party.

2. A disputing investor may submit a claim under Article 1117 to arbitration only if both the investor and the enterprise:

(a) consent to arbitration in accordance with the procedures set out in this Agreement; and

(b) waive their right to initiate or continue before any administrative tribunal or court under the law of any Party, or other dispute settlement procedures, any proceedings with respect to the measure of the disputing Party that is alleged to be a breach referred to in Article 1117, except for proceedings for injunctive, declaratory or other extraordinary relief, not involving the payment of damages, before an administrative tribunal or court under the law of the disputing Party.

3. A consent and waiver required by this Article shall be in writing, shall be delivered to the disputing Party and shall be included in the submission of a claim to arbitration.

4. Only where a disputing Party has deprived a disputing investor of control of an enterprise:

(a) a waiver from the enterprise under paragraph 1(b) or 2(b) shall not be required; and

(b) Annex 1120.1(b) shall not apply.

Article 1122: Consent to Arbitration

1. Each Party consents to the submission of a claim to arbitration in accordance with the procedures set out in this Agreement.

2. The consent given by paragraph 1 and the submission by a disputing investor of a claim to arbitration shall satisfy the requirement of:

(a) Chapter II of the ICSID Convention (Jurisdiction of the Centre) and the Additional Facility Rules for written consent of the parties;

(b) Article II of the New York Convention for an agreement in writing; and

(c) Article I of the InterAmerican Convention for an agreement.

Article 1123: Number of Arbitrators and Method of Appointment

Except in respect of a Tribunal established under Article 1126, and unless the disputing parties otherwise agree, the Tribunal shall comprise three arbitrators, one arbitrator appointed by each of the disputing parties and the third, who shall be the presiding arbitrator, appointed by agreement of the disputing parties.

Article 1124: Constitution of a Tribunal When a Party Fails to Appoint an Arbitrator or the Disputing Parties Are Unable to Agree on a Presiding Arbitrator

1. The Secretary-General shall serve as appointing authority for an arbitration under this Section.

2. If a Tribunal, other than a Tribunal established under Article 1126, has not been constituted within 90 days from the date that a claim is submitted to arbitration, the Secretary-General, on the request of either disputing party, shall appoint, in his discretion, the arbitrator or arbitrators not yet appointed, except that the presiding arbitrator shall be appointed in accordance with paragraph 3.

3. The Secretary-General shall appoint the presiding arbitrator from the roster of presiding arbitrators referred to in paragraph 4, provided that the presiding arbitrator shall not be a national of the disputing Party or a national of the Party of the disputing investor. In the event that no such presiding arbitrator is available to serve, the Secretary-General shall appoint, from the ICSID Panel of Arbitrators, a presiding arbitrator who is not a national of any of the Parties.

4. On the date of entry into force of this Agreement, the Parties shall establish, and thereafter maintain, a roster of 45 presiding arbitrators meeting the qualifications of the Convention and rules referred to in Article 1120 and experienced in international law and investment matters. The roster members shall be appointed by consensus and without regard to nationality.

Article 1125: Agreement to Appointment of Arbitrators

For purposes of Article 39 of the ICSID Convention and Article 7 of Schedule C to the ICSID Additional Facility Rules, and without prejudice to an objection to an arbitrator based on Article 1124(3) or on a ground other than nationality:

(a) the disputing Party agrees to the appointment of each individual member of a Tribunal established under the ICSID Convention or the ICSID Additional Facility Rules;

(b) a disputing investor referred to in Article 1116 may submit a claim to arbitration, or continue a claim, under the ICSID Convention or the ICSID Additional Facility Rules, only on condition that the disputing investor agrees in writing to the appointment of each individual member of the Tribunal; and

(c) a disputing investor referred to in Article 1117(1) may submit a claim to arbitration, or continue a claim, under the ICSID Convention or the ICSID Additional Facility Rules, only on condition that the disputing investor and the enterprise agree in writing to the appointment of each individual member of the Tribunal.

Article 1126: Consolidation

1. A Tribunal established under this Article shall be established under the UNCITRAL Arbitration Rules and shall conduct its proceedings in accordance with those Rules, except as modified by this Section.

2. Where a Tribunal established under this Article is satisfied that claims have been submitted to arbitration under Article 1120 that have a question of law or fact in common, the Tribunal may, in the interests of fair and efficient resolution of the claims, and after hearing the disputing parties, by order:

(a) assume jurisdiction over, and hear and determine together, all or part of the claims; or

(b) assume jurisdiction over, and hear and determine one or more of the claims, the determination of which it believes would assist in the resolution of the others.

3. A disputing party that seeks an order under paragraph 2 shall request the Secretary-General to establish a Tribunal and shall specify in the request:

(a) the name of the disputing Party or disputing investors against which the order is sought;

(b) the nature of the order sought; and

(c) the grounds on which the order is sought.

4. The disputing party shall deliver to the disputing Party or disputing investors against which the order is sought a copy of the request.

5. Within 60 days of receipt of the request, the Secretary-General shall establish a Tribunal comprising three arbitrators. The Secretary-General shall appoint the presiding arbitrator from the roster referred to in Article 1124(4). In the event that no such presiding arbitrator is available to serve, the Secretary-General shall appoint, from the ICSID Panel of Arbitrators, a presiding arbitrator who is not a national of any of the Parties. The Secretary-General shall appoint the two other members from the roster referred to in Article 1124(4), and to the extent not available from that roster, from the ICSID Panel of Arbitrators, and to the extent not available from that Panel, in the discretion of the Secretary-General. One member shall be a national of the disputing Party and one member shall be a national of a Party of the disputing investors.

6. Where a Tribunal has been established under this Article, a disputing investor that has submitted a claim to arbitration under Article 1116 or 1117 and that has not been named in a request made under paragraph 3 may make a written request to the Tribunal that it be included in an order made under paragraph 2, and shall specify in the request:

(a) the name and address of the disputing investor;

(b) the nature of the order sought; and

(c) the grounds on which the order is sought.

7. A disputing investor referred to in paragraph 6 shall deliver a copy of its request to the disputing parties named in a request made under paragraph 3.

8. A Tribunal established under Article 1120 shall not have jurisdiction to decide a claim, or a part of a claim, over which a Tribunal established under this Article has assumed jurisdiction.

9. On application of a disputing party, a Tribunal established under this Article, pending its decision under paragraph 2, may order that the proceedings of a Tribunal established under Article 1120 be stayed, unless the latter Tribunal has already adjourned its proceedings.

10. A disputing Party shall deliver to the Secretariat, within 15 days of receipt by the disputing Party, a copy of:

(a) a request for arbitration made under paragraph (1) of Article 36 of the ICSID Convention;

(b) a notice of arbitration made under Article 2 of Schedule C of the ICSID Additional Facility Rules; or

(c) a notice of arbitration given under the UNCITRAL Arbitration Rules.

11. A disputing Party shall deliver to the Secretariat a copy of a request made under paragraph 3:

(a) within 15 days of receipt of the request, in the case of a request made by a disputing investor;

(b) within 15 days of making the request, in the case of a request made by the disputing Party.

12. A disputing Party shall deliver to the Secretariat a copy of a request made under paragraph 6 within 15 days of receipt of the request.

13. The Secretariat shall maintain a public register of the documents referred to in paragraphs 10, 11 and 12.

Article 1127: Notice

A disputing Party shall deliver to the other Parties:

(a) written notice of a claim that has been submitted to arbitration no later than 30 days after the date that the claim is submitted; and

(b) copies of all pleadings filed in the arbitration.

Article 1128: Participation by a Party

On written notice to the disputing parties, a Party may make submissions to a Tribunal on a question of interpretation of this Agreement.

Article 1129: Documents

1. A Party shall be entitled to receive from the disputing Party, at the cost of the requesting Party a copy of:

(a) the evidence that has been tendered to the Tribunal; and

(b) the written argument of the disputing parties.

2. A Party receiving information pursuant to paragraph 1 shall treat the information as if it were a disputing Party.

Article 1130: Place of Arbitration

Unless the disputing parties agree otherwise, a Tribunal shall hold an arbitration in the territory of a Party that is a party to the New York Convention, selected in accordance with:

(a) the ICSID Additional Facility Rules if the arbitration is under those Rules or the ICSID Convention; or

(b) the UNCITRAL Arbitration Rules if the arbitration is under those Rules.

Article 1131: Governing Law

1. A Tribunal established under this Section shall decide the issues in dispute in accordance with this Agreement and applicable rules of international law.

2. An interpretation by the Commission of a provision of this Agreement shall be binding on a Tribunal established under this Section.

Article 1132: Interpretation of Annexes

1. Where a disputing Party asserts as a defense that the measure alleged to be a breach is within the scope of a reservation or exception set out in Annex I, Annex II, Annex III or Annex IV, on request of the disputing Party, the Tribunal shall request the interpretation of the Commission on the issue. The Commission, within 60 days of delivery of the request, shall submit in writing its interpretation to the Tribunal.

2. Further to Article 1131(2), a Commission interpretation submitted under paragraph 1 shall be binding on the Tribunal. If the Commission fails to submit an interpretation within 60 days, the Tribunal shall decide the issue.

Article 1133: Expert Reports

Without prejudice to the appointment of other kinds of experts where authorized by the applicable arbitration rules, a Tribunal, at the request of a disputing party or, unless the disputing parties disapprove, on its own initiative, may appoint one or more experts to report to it in writing on any factual issue concerning environmental, health, safety or other scientific matters raised by a disputing party in a proceeding, subject to such terms and conditions as the disputing parties may agree.

Article 1134: Interim Measures of Protection

A Tribunal may order an interim measure of protection to preserve the rights of a disputing party, or to ensure that the Tribunal's jurisdiction is made fully effective, including an order to preserve evidence in the possession or control of a disputing party or to protect the Tribunal's jurisdiction. A Tribunal may not order attachment or enjoin the application of the measure alleged to constitute a breach referred to in Article 1116 or 1117. For purposes of this paragraph, an order includes a recommendation.

Article 1135: Final Award

1. Where a Tribunal makes a final award against a Party, the Tribunal may award, separately or in combination, only:

   (a) monetary damages and any applicable interest;

   (b) restitution of property, in which case the award shall provide that the disputing Party may pay monetary damages and any applicable interest in lieu of restitution.

A tribunal may also award costs in accordance with the applicable arbitration rules.

2. Subject to paragraph 1, where a claim is made under Article 1117(1):

   (a) an award of restitution of property shall provide that restitution be made to the enterprise;

   (b) an award of monetary damages and any applicable interest shall provide that the sum be paid to the enterprise; and

(c) the award shall provide that it is made without prejudice to any right that any person may have in the relief under applicable domestic law.

3. A Tribunal may not order a Party to pay punitive damages.

Article 1136: Finality and Enforcement of an Award

1. An award made by a Tribunal shall have no binding force except between the disputing parties and in respect of the particular case.

2. Subject to paragraph 3 and the applicable review procedure for an interim award, a disputing party shall abide by and comply with an award without delay.

3. A disputing party may not seek enforcement of a final award until:

(a) in the case of a final award made under the ICSID Convention

(i) 120 days have elapsed from the date the award was rendered and no disputing party has requested revision or annulment of the award, or

(ii) revision or annulment proceedings have been completed; and

(b) in the case of a final award under the ICSID Additional Facility Rules or the UNCITRAL Arbitration Rules

(i) three months have elapsed from the date the award was rendered and no disputing party has commenced a proceeding to revise, set aside or annul the award, or

(ii) a court has dismissed or allowed an application to revise, set aside or annul the award and there is no further appeal.

4. Each Party shall provide for the enforcement of an award in its territory.

5. If a disputing Party fails to abide by or comply with a final award, the Commission, on delivery of a request by a Party whose investor was a party to the arbitration, shall establish a panel under Article 2008 (Request for an Arbitral Panel). The requesting Party may seek in such proceedings:

(a) a determination that the failure to abide by or comply with the final award is inconsistent with the obligations of this Agreement; and

(b) a recommendation that the Party abide by or comply with the final award.

6. A disputing investor may seek enforcement of an arbitration award under the ICSID Convention, the New York Convention or the InterAmerican Convention regardless of whether proceedings have been taken under paragraph 5.

7. A claim that is submitted to arbitration under this Section shall be considered to arise out of a commercial relationship or transaction for purposes of Article I of the New York Convention and Article I of the InterAmerican Convention.

Article 1137: General

Time when a Claim is Submitted to Arbitration

1. A claim is submitted to arbitration under this Section when:

(a) the request for arbitration under paragraph (1) of Article 36 of the ICSID Convention has been received by the Secretary-General;

(b) the notice of arbitration under Article 2 of Schedule C of the ICSID Additional Facility Rules has been received by the Secretary-General; or

(c) the notice of arbitration given under the UNCITRAL Arbitration Rules is received by the disputing Party.

Service of Documents

2. Delivery of notice and other documents on a Party shall be made to the place named for that Party in Annex 1137.2.

Receipts under Insurance or Guarantee Contracts

3. In an arbitration under this Section, a Party shall not assert, as a defense, counterclaim, right of setoff or otherwise, that the disputing investor has received or will receive, pursuant to an insurance or guarantee contract, indemnification or other compensation for all or part of its alleged damages.

Publication of an Award

4. Annex 1137.4 applies to the Parties specified in that Annex with respect to publication of an award.

Article 1138: Exclusions

1. Without prejudice to the applicability or non-applicability of the dispute settlement provisions of this Section or of Chapter Twenty (Institutional Arrangements and Dispute Settlement Procedures) to other actions taken by a Party pursuant to Article 2102 (National Security), a decision by a Party to prohibit or restrict the acquisition of an investment in its territory by an investor of another Party, or its investment, pursuant to that Article shall not be subject to such provisions.

2. The dispute settlement provisions of this Section and of Chapter Twenty shall not apply to the matters referred to in Annex 1138.2.

Section C – Definitions

Article 1139: Definitions

For purposes of this Chapter:

disputing investor means an investor that makes a claim under Section B;

disputing parties means the disputing investor and the disputing Party;

disputing party means the disputing investor or the disputing Party;

disputing Party means a Party against which a claim is made under Section B;

enterprise means an "enterprise" as defined in Article 201 (Definitions of General Application), and a branch of an enterprise;

enterprise of a Party means an enterprise constituted or organized under the law of a Party, and a branch located in the territory of a Party and carrying out business activities there.

equity or debt securities includes voting and non-voting shares, bonds, convertible debentures, stock options and warrants;

G7 Currency means the currency of Canada, France, Germany, Italy, Japan, the United Kingdom of Great Britain and Northern Ireland or the United States;

ICSID means the International Centre for Settlement of Investment Disputes;

ICSID Convention means the *Convention on the Settlement of Investment Disputes between States and Nationals of other States*, done at Washington, March 18, 1965;

Inter-American Convention means the *Inter-American Convention on International Commercial Arbitration*, done at Panama, January 30, 1975;

investment means:

(a) an enterprise;

(b) an equity security of an enterprise;

(c) a debt security of an enterprise
  (i) where the enterprise is an affiliate of the investor, or
  (ii) where the original maturity of the debt security is at least three years,

but does not include a debt security, regardless of original maturity, of a state enterprise;

(d) a loan to an enterprise
  (i) where the enterprise is an affiliate of the investor, or
  (ii) where the original maturity of the loan is at least three years,

but does not include a loan, regardless of original maturity, to a state enterprise;

(e) an interest in an enterprise that entitles the owner to share in income or profits of the enterprise;

(f) an interest in an enterprise that entitles the owner to share in the assets of that enterprise on dissolution, other than a debt security or a loan excluded from subparagraph (c) or (d);

(g) real estate or other property, tangible or intangible, acquired in the expectation or used for the purpose of economic benefit or other business purposes; and

(h) interests arising from the commitment of capital or other resources in the territory of a Party to economic activity in such territory, such as under
  (i) contracts involving the presence of an investor›s property in the territory of the Party, including turnkey or construction contracts, or concessions, or
  (ii) contracts where remuneration depends substantially on the production, revenues or profits of an enterprise;

but investment does not mean,

(i) claims to money that arise solely from
  (i) commercial contracts for the sale of goods or services by a national or enterprise in the territory of a Party to an enterprise in the territory of another Party, or
  (ii) the extension of credit in connection with a commercial transaction, such as trade financing, other than a loan covered by subparagraph (d); or

(j) any other claims to money,

that do not involve the kinds of interests set out in subparagraphs (a) through (h);

investment of an investor of a Party means an investment owned or controlled directly or indirectly by an investor of such Party;

investor of a Party means a Party or state enterprise thereof, or a national or an enterprise of such Party, that seeks to make, is making or has made an investment;

investor of a non-Party means an investor other than an investor of a Party, that seeks to make, is making or has made an investment;

New York Convention means the *United Nations Convention on the Recognition and Enforcement of Foreign Arbitral Awards*, done at New York, June 10, 1958;

Secretary-General means the Secretary-General of ICSID;

transfers means transfers and international payments;

Tribunal means an arbitration tribunal established under Article 1120 or 1126; and

UNCITRAL Arbitration Rules means the arbitration rules of the United Nations Commission on International Trade Law, approved by the United Nations General Assembly on December 15, 1976.

Annex 1120.1
Submission of a Claim to Arbitration
Mexico

With respect to the submission of a claim to arbitration:

(a) an investor of another Party may not allege that Mexico has breached an obligation under:
   (i) Section A or Article 1503(2) (State Enterprises), or
   (ii) Article 1502(3)(a) (Monopolies and State Enterprises) where the monopoly has acted in a manner inconsistent with the Party's obligations under Section A,

   both in an arbitration under this Section and in proceedings before a Mexican court or administrative tribunal; and

(b) where an enterprise of Mexico that is a juridical person that an investor of another Party owns or controls directly or indirectly alleges in proceedings before a Mexican court or administrative tribunal that Mexico has breached an obligation under:
   (i) Section A or Article 1503(2) (State Enterprises), or
   (ii) Article 1502(3)(a) (Monopolies and State Enterprises) where the monopoly has acted in a manner inconsistent with the Party's obligations under Section A,

   the investor may not allege the breach in an arbitration under this Section.

Annex 1137.2
Service of Documents on a Party Under Section B

Each Party shall set out in this Annex and publish in its official journal by January 1, 1994, the place for delivery of notice and other documents under this Section.

Annex 1137.4
Publication of an Award
Canada

Where Canada is the disputing Party, either Canada or a disputing investor that is a party to the arbitration may make an award public.

Mexico

Where Mexico is the disputing Party, the applicable arbitration rules apply to the publication of an award.

United States

Where the United States is the disputing Party, either the United States or a disputing investor that is a party to the arbitration may make an award public.

Annex 1138.2
Exclusions from Dispute Settlement
Canada

A decision by Canada following a review under the *Investment Canada Act*, with respect to whether or not to permit an acquisition that is subject to review, shall not be subject to the dispute settlement provisions of Section B or of Chapter Twenty (Institutional Arrangements and Dispute Settlement Procedures).

Mexico

A decision by the National Commission on Foreign Investment ("Comisión Nacional de Inversiones Extranjeras") following a review pursuant to Annex I, page I-M-4, with respect to whether or not to permit an acquisition that is subject to review, shall not be subject to the dispute settlement provisions of Section B or of Chapter Twenty.

39.b United States-Mexico-Canada Agreement (USMCA)*

Date: 30 November 2018
Source: https://ustr.gov/trade-agreements/free-trade-agreements/united-states-mexico-canada-agreement/agreement-between

ANNEX 14-C LEGACY INVESTMENT CLAIMS AND PENDING CLAIMS**

1. Each Party consents, with respect to a legacy investment, to the submission of a claim to arbitration in accordance with Section B of Chapter 11 (Investment) of NAFTA 1994 and this Annex alleging breach of an obligation under: (a) Section A of Chapter 11 (Investment) of NAFTA 1994; (b) Article 1503(2) (State Enterprises) of NAFTA 1994; and (c) Article 1502(3)(a) (Monopolies and State Enterprises) of NAFTA 1994 where the monopoly has acted in a manner inconsistent with the Party's obligations under Section A of Chapter 11 (Investment) of NAFTA 1994. 20, 21

2. The consent under paragraph 1 and the submission of a claim to arbitration in accordance with Section B of Chapter 11 (Investment) of NAFTA 1994 and this Annex shall satisfy the requirements of: (a) Chapter II of the ICSID Convention (Jurisdiction of the Centre) and the ICSID Additional Facility Rules for written consent of the parties to the dispute; (b) Article II of the New York Convention for an "agreement in writing"; and (c) Article I of the Inter-American Convention for an "agreement".

3. A Party's consent under paragraph 1 shall expire three years after the termination of NAFTA 1994.

4. For greater certainty, an arbitration initiated pursuant to the submission of a claim under paragraph 1 may proceed to its conclusion in accordance with Section B of Chapter 11 (Investment) of NAFTA 1994, the Tribunal's jurisdiction with respect to such a claim is not affected by the expiration of consent referenced in paragraph 3, and Article 1136 (Finality and Enforcement of an Award) of NAFTA 1994 (excluding paragraph 5) applies with respect to any award made by the Tribunal.

5. For greater certainty, an arbitration initiated pursuant to the submission of a claim under Section B of Chapter 11 (Investment) of NAFTA 1994 while NAFTA 1994 is in force may proceed to its conclusion in accordance with Section B of Chapter 11 (Investment) of NAFTA 1994, the Tribunal's jurisdiction with respect to such a claim is not affected by the termination of NAFTA 1994, and Article 1136 of NAFTA 1994 (excluding paragraph 5) applies with respect to any award made by the Tribunal.

* The subsequent sections set out the text of Annex 14-C, 14-D and 14-E of the USMCA. As of 1 July 2020, the USMCA replaces NAFTA in relations between the three member States. As regards the process of settling investment disputes, Chapter 14C preserves the possibility of certain 'legacy claims'. Other investor-State proceedings can be brought under the conditions set out in Annex 14-D and 14-E. For the prior NAFTA regime of investor-State dispute settlement see Document No. 39.a.

** N.B.: Footnotes have been omitted.

6. For the purposes of this Annex:
   (a) "legacy investment" means an investment of an investor of another Party in the territory of the Party established or acquired between January 1, 1994, and the date of termination of NAFTA 1994, and in existence on the date of entry into force of this Agreement;
   (b) "investment", "investor", and "Tribunal" have the meanings accorded in Chapter 11 (Investment) of NAFTA 1994; and
   (c) "ICSID Convention", "ICSID Additional Facility Rules", "New York Convention", and "Inter-American Convention" have the meanings accorded in Article 14.D.1 (Definitions).

ANNEX 14-D MEXICO-UNITED STATES INVESTMENT DISPUTES

Article 14.D.1: Definitions

For the purposes of this Annex:

Annex Party means Mexico or the United States;

Centre means the International Centre for Settlement of Investment Disputes (ICSID) established by the ICSID Convention;

claimant means an investor of an Annex Party that is a party to a qualifying investment dispute, excluding an investor that is owned or controlled by a person of a non-Annex Party that, on the date of signature of this Agreement, the other Annex Party has determined to be a non-market economy for purposes of its trade remedy laws and with which no Party has a free trade agreement;

disputing parties means the claimant and the respondent;

disputing party means either the claimant or the respondent;

ICSID Additional Facility Rules means the *Rules Governing the Additional Facility for the Administration of Proceedings by the Secretariat of the International Centre for Settlement of Investment Disputes*;

ICSID Convention means the *Convention on the Settlement of Investment Disputes between States and Nationals of other States*, done at Washington, March 18, 1965;

Inter-American Convention means the *Inter-American Convention on International Commercial Arbitration*, done at Panama, January 30, 1975;

New York Convention means the *Convention on the Recognition and Enforcement of Foreign Arbitral Awards*, done at New York, June 10, 1958;

non-disputing Annex Party means the Annex Party that is not a party to a qualifying investment dispute;

protected information means confidential business information or information that is privileged or otherwise protected from disclosure under a Party's law, including classified government information;

qualifying investment dispute means an investment dispute between an investor of an Annex Party and the other Annex Party;

respondent means the Annex Party that is a party to a qualifying investment dispute;

Secretary-General means the Secretary-General of ICSID; and

UNCITRAL Arbitration Rules means the arbitration rules of the United Nations Commission on International Trade Law.

Article 14.D.2: Consultation and Negotiation

1. In the event of a qualifying investment dispute, the claimant and the respondent should initially seek to resolve the dispute through consultation and negotiation, which may include the use of non-binding, third party procedures, such as good offices, conciliation, or mediation.

2. For greater certainty, the initiation of consultations and negotiations shall not be construed as recognition of the jurisdiction of the tribunal.

Article 14.D.3: Submission of a Claim to Arbitration

1. In the event that a disputing party considers that a qualifying investment dispute cannot be settled by consultation and negotiation:

(a) the claimant, on its own behalf, may submit to arbitration under this Annex a claim:

(i) that the respondent has breached:

(A) Article 14.4 (National Treatment) or Article 14.5 (Most-FavoredNation Treatment),[1] except with respect to the establishment or acquisition of an investment, or

(B) Article 14.8 (Expropriation and Compensation), except with respect to indirect expropriation, and

(ii) that the claimant has incurred loss or damage by reason of, or arising out of, that breach; and

(b) the claimant, on behalf of an enterprise of the respondent that is a juridical person that the claimant owns or controls directly or indirectly, may submit to arbitration under this Annex a claim:

(i) that the respondent has breached:

(A) Article 14.4 (National Treatment) or Article 14.5 (Most-FavoredNation Treatment), except with respect to the establishment or acquisition of an investment, or

(B) Article 14.8 (Expropriation and Compensation), except with respect to indirect expropriation, and

[1] For the purposes of this paragraph: (i) the "treatment" referred to in Article 14.5 (Most-Favored-Nation Treatment) excludes provisions in other international trade or investment agreements that establish international dispute resolution procedures or impose substantive obligations; and (ii) the "treatment" referred to in Article 14.5 only encompasses measures adopted or maintained by the other Annex Party, which for greater clarity may include measures adopted in connection with the implementation of substantive obligations in other international trade or investment agreements.

(ii) that the enterprise has incurred loss or damage by reason of, or arising out of, that breach.[2]

2. At least 90 days before submitting any claim to arbitration under this Annex, the claimant shall deliver to the respondent a written notice of its intention to submit a claim to arbitration (notice of intent). The notice shall specify:

(a) the name and address of the claimant and, if a claim is submitted on behalf of an enterprise, the name, address, and place of incorporation of the enterprise;

(b) for each claim, the provision of this Agreement alleged to have been breached and any other relevant provisions;

(c) the legal and factual basis for each claim; and

(d) the relief sought and the approximate amount of damages claimed.

3. The claimant may submit a claim referred to in paragraph 1 under one of the following alternatives:

(a) the ICSID Convention and the ICSID *Rules of Procedure for Arbitration Proceedings*, provided that both the respondent and the Party of the claimant are parties to the ICSID Convention;[3]

(b) the ICSID Additional Facility Rules, provided that either the respondent or the Party of the claimant is a party to the ICSID Convention;

(c) the UNCITRAL Arbitration Rules; or

(d) if the claimant and respondent agree, any other arbitral institution or any other arbitration rules.

4. A claim shall be deemed submitted to arbitration under this Annex when the claimant's notice of or request for arbitration (notice of arbitration):

(a) referred to in the ICSID Convention is received by the Secretary-General;

(b) referred to in the ICSID Additional Facility Rules is received by the SecretaryGeneral;

(c) referred to in the UNCITRAL Arbitration Rules, together with the statement of claim referred to therein, are received by the respondent; or

(d) referred to under any arbitral institution or arbitration rules selected under paragraph 3(d) is received by the respondent.

A claim asserted by the claimant for the first time after such notice of arbitration is submitted shall be deemed submitted to arbitration under this Annex on the date of its receipt under the applicable arbitration rules.

5. The arbitration rules applicable under paragraph 3 that are in effect on the date the claim or claims were submitted to arbitration under this Annex shall govern the arbitration except to the extent modified by this Agreement.

6. The claimant shall provide with the notice of arbitration:

(a) the name of the arbitrator that the claimant appoints; or

(b) the claimant's written consent for the Secretary-General to appoint that arbitrator.

[2] For greater certainty, in order for a claim to be submitted to arbitration under subparagraph (b), an investor of the Party of the claimant must own or control the enterprise on the date of the alleged breach and the date on which the claim is submitted to arbitration.

[3] For greater certainty, if a claimant submits a claim under this subparagraph, any award made by the tribunal under Article 14.D.13 (Awards) constitutes an award under Chapter IV of the ICSID Convention (Arbitration).

Article 14.D.4: Consent to Arbitration

1. Each Annex Party consents to the submission of a claim to arbitration under this Annex in accordance with this Agreement.

2. The consent under paragraph 1 and the submission of a claim to arbitration under this Annex shall be deemed to satisfy the requirements of:

(a) Chapter II of the ICSID Convention (Jurisdiction of the Centre) and the ICSID Additional Facility Rules for written consent of the parties to the dispute;

(b) Article II of the New York Convention for an "agreement in writing"; and

(c) Article I of the Inter-American Convention for an "agreement".

Article 14.D.5: Conditions and Limitations on Consent

1. No claim shall be submitted to arbitration under this Annex unless:

(a) the claimant (for claims brought under Article 14.D.3.1(a) (Submission of a Claim to Arbitration)) and the claimant or the enterprise (for claims brought under Article 14.D.3.1(b)) first initiated a proceeding before a competent court or administrative tribunal of the respondent with respect to the measures alleged to constitute a breach referred to in Article 14.D.3;

(b) the claimant or the enterprise obtained a final decision from a court of last resort of the respondent or 30 months have elapsed from the date the proceeding in subparagraph (a) was initiated;[4]

(c) no more than four years have elapsed from the date on which the claimant first acquired, or should have first acquired, knowledge of the breach alleged under Article 14.D.3.1 (Submission of a Claim to Arbitration) and knowledge that the claimant (for claims brought under Article 14.D.3.1(a)) or the enterprise (for claims brought under Article 14.D.3.1(b)) has incurred loss or damage;

(d) the claimant consents in writing to arbitration in accordance with the procedures set out in this Agreement; and

(e) the notice of arbitration is accompanied:

(i) for claims submitted to arbitration under Article 14.D.3.1(a) (Submission of a Claim to Arbitration), by the claimant's written waiver, and

(ii) for claims submitted to arbitration under Article 14.D.3.1(b) (Submission of a Claim to Arbitration), by the claimant's and the enterprise's written waivers,

of any right to initiate or continue before any court or administrative tribunal under the law of an Annex Party, or any other dispute settlement procedures, any proceeding with respect to any measure alleged to constitute a breach referred to in Article 14.D.3 (Submission of a Claim to Arbitration).

2. Notwithstanding paragraph 1(e), the claimant (for claims brought under Article 14.D.3.1(a) (Submission of a Claim to Arbitration)) and the claimant or the enterprise (for claims brought under Article 14.D.3.1(b)) may initiate or continue an action that seeks interim injunctive relief and does not involve the payment of monetary damages before a judicial or administrative tribunal of the respondent, provided that the action is brought for the sole purpose of preserving the claimant's or the enterprise's rights and interests during the pendency of the arbitration.

[4] The provisions in subparagraphs (a) and (b) do not apply to the extent recourse to domestic remedies was obviously futile.

Article 14.D.6: Selection of Arbitrators

1. Unless the disputing parties agree otherwise, the tribunal shall comprise three arbitrators, one arbitrator appointed by each of the disputing parties and the third, who shall be the presiding arbitrator, appointed by agreement of the disputing parties.

2. The Secretary-General shall serve as appointing authority for an arbitration under this Annex.

3. If a tribunal has not been constituted within a period of 75 days after the date that a claim is submitted to arbitration under this Annex, the Secretary-General, on the request of a disputing party, shall appoint, in his or her discretion, the arbitrator or arbitrators not yet appointed. The Secretary-General shall not appoint a national of either the respondent or the Party of the claimant as the presiding arbitrator unless the disputing parties agree otherwise.

4. For the purposes of Article 39 of the ICSID Convention and Article 7 of Schedule C to the ICSID Additional Facility Rules, and without prejudice to an objection to an arbitrator on a ground other than nationality:

(a) the respondent agrees to the appointment of each individual member of a tribunal established under the ICSID Convention or the ICSID Additional Facility Rules;

(b) a claimant referred to in Article 14.D.3.1(a) (Submission of a Claim to Arbitration) may submit a claim to arbitration under this Annex, or continue a claim, under the ICSID Convention or the ICSID Additional Facility Rules, only on condition that the claimant agrees in writing to the appointment of each individual member of the tribunal; and

(c) a claimant referred to in Article 14.D.3.1(b) (Submission of a Claim to Arbitration) may submit a claim to arbitration under this Annex, or continue a claim, under the ICSID Convention or the ICSID Additional Facility Rules, only on condition that the claimant and the enterprise agree in writing to the appointment of each individual member of the tribunal.

5. Arbitrators appointed to a tribunal for claims submitted under Article 14.D.3.1 shall:

(a) comply with the International Bar Association Guidelines on Conflicts of Interest in International Arbitration, including guidelines regarding direct or indirect conflicts of interest, or any supplemental guidelines or rules adopted by the Annex Parties;

(b) not take instructions from any organization or government regarding the dispute; and

(c) not, for the duration of the proceedings, act as counsel or as party-appointed expert or witness in any pending arbitration under the annexes to this Chapter.

6. Challenges to arbitrators shall be governed by the procedures in the UNCITRAL Arbitration Rules.

Article 14.D.7: Conduct of the Arbitration

1. The disputing parties may agree on the legal place of any arbitration under the arbitration rules applicable under Article 14.D.3.3 (Submission of a Claim to Arbitration). If the disputing parties fail to reach agreement, the tribunal shall determine the place in accordance with the applicable arbitration rules, provided that the place shall be in the territory of a State that is a party to the New York Convention.

2. The non-disputing Annex Party may make oral and written submissions to the tribunal regarding the interpretation of this Agreement.

3. After consultation with the disputing parties, the tribunal may accept and consider written *amicus curiae* submissions regarding a matter of fact or law within the scope of the dispute that may assist the tribunal in evaluating the submissions and arguments of the disputing parties from a person or entity that is not a disputing party but has a significant interest in the arbitral proceedings. Each submission shall identify the author; disclose any affiliation, direct or indirect, with any disputing party; and identify any person, government, or other entity that has provided, or will provide, any financial or other assistance in preparing the submission. Each submission shall be in a language of the arbitration and comply with any page limits and deadlines set by the tribunal. The tribunal shall provide the disputing parties with an opportunity to respond to such submissions. The tribunal shall ensure that the submissions do not disrupt or unduly burden the arbitral proceedings, or unfairly prejudice any disputing party.

4. Without prejudice to a tribunal's authority to address other objections as a preliminary question, such as an objection that a dispute is not within the competence of the tribunal, including an objection to the tribunal's jurisdiction, a tribunal shall address and decide as a preliminary question any objection by the respondent that, as a matter of law, a claim submitted is not a claim for which an award in favor of the claimant may be made under Article 14.D.13 (Awards) or that a claim is manifestly without legal merit.

(a) An objection under this paragraph shall be submitted to the tribunal as soon as possible after the tribunal is constituted, and in no event later than the date the tribunal fixes for the respondent to submit its counter-memorial or, in the case of an amendment to the notice of arbitration, the date the tribunal fixes for the respondent to submit its response to the amendment.

(b) On receipt of an objection under this paragraph, the tribunal shall suspend any proceedings on the merits, establish a schedule for considering the objection consistent with any schedule it has established for considering any other preliminary question, and issue a decision or award on the objection, stating the grounds therefor.

(c) In deciding an objection under this paragraph that a claim submitted is not a claim for which an award in favor of the claimant may be made under Article 14.D.13 (Awards), the tribunal shall assume to be true the claimant's factual allegations in support of any claim in the notice of arbitration (or any amendment thereof) and, in disputes brought under the UNCITRAL Arbitration Rules, the statement of claim referred to in the relevant article of the UNCITRAL Arbitration Rules. The tribunal may also consider any relevant facts not in dispute.

(d) The respondent does not waive any objection as to competence, including an objection to jurisdiction, or any argument on the merits merely because the respondent did or did not raise an objection under this paragraph or make use of the expedited procedure set out in paragraph 5.

5. In the event that the respondent so requests within 45 days after the tribunal is constituted, the tribunal shall decide on an expedited basis an objection under paragraph 4 or any objection that the dispute is not within the tribunal's competence, including an objection that the dispute is not within the tribunal's jurisdiction. The tribunal shall suspend any proceedings on the merits and issue a decision or award on the objection, stating the grounds therefor, no later than 150 days after the date of the request. However, if a disputing

party requests a hearing, the tribunal may take an additional 30 days to issue the decision or award. Regardless of whether a hearing is requested, a tribunal may, on a showing of extraordinary cause, delay issuing its decision or award by an additional brief period, which may not exceed 30 days.

6. When the tribunal decides a respondent's objection under paragraph 4 or 5, it may, if warranted, award to the prevailing disputing party reasonable costs and attorney's fees incurred in submitting or opposing the objection. In determining whether such an award is warranted, the tribunal shall consider whether either the claimant's claim or the respondent's objection was frivolous, and shall provide the disputing parties a reasonable opportunity to comment.

7. For greater certainty, if an investor of an Annex Party submits a claim under this Annex, the investor has the burden of proving all elements of its claims, consistent with general principles of international law applicable to international arbitration.

8. A respondent may not assert as a defense, counterclaim, right of set-off, or for any other reason, that the claimant has received or will receive indemnification or other compensation for all or part of the alleged damages pursuant to an insurance or guarantee contract.

9. A tribunal may order an interim measure of protection to preserve the rights of a disputing party, or to ensure that the tribunal's jurisdiction is made fully effective, including an order to preserve evidence in the possession or control of a disputing party or to protect the tribunal's jurisdiction. A tribunal may not order attachment or enjoin the application of a measure alleged to constitute a breach referred to in Article 14.D.3 (Submission of a Claim to Arbitration). For the purposes of this paragraph, an order includes a recommendation.

10. The tribunal and the disputing parties shall endeavor to conduct the arbitration in an expeditious and cost-effective manner.

11. Following the submission of a claim to arbitration under this Annex, if the disputing parties fail to take any steps in the proceedings for more than 150 days, or such period as they may agree with the approval of the tribunal, the tribunal shall notify the disputing parties that they shall be deemed to have discontinued the proceedings if the parties fail to take any steps within 30 days after the notice is received. If the parties fail to take any steps within that time period, the tribunal shall take note of the discontinuance in an order. If a tribunal has not yet been constituted, the Secretary-General shall assume these responsibilities.

12. In any arbitration conducted under this Annex, at the request of a disputing party, a tribunal shall, before issuing a decision or award on liability, transmit its proposed decision or award to the disputing parties. Within 60 days after the tribunal transmits its proposed decision or award, the disputing parties may submit written comments to the tribunal concerning any aspect of its proposed decision or award. The tribunal shall consider any comments and issue its decision or award no later than 45 days after the expiration of the 60 day comment period.

Article 14.D.8: Transparency of Arbitral Proceedings

1. Subject to paragraphs 2 and 4, the respondent shall, after receiving the following documents, promptly transmit them to the non-disputing Annex Party and make them available to the public:

(a) the notice of intent;

(b) the notice of arbitration;
(c) pleadings, memorials, and briefs submitted to the tribunal by a disputing party and any written submissions submitted pursuant to Article 14.D.7.2 and 14.D.7.3 (Conduct of the Arbitration), and Article 14.D.12 (Consolidation);
(d) minutes or transcripts of hearings of the tribunal, if available; and
(e) orders, awards, and decisions of the tribunal.

2. The tribunal shall conduct hearings open to the public and shall determine, in consultation with the disputing parties, the appropriate logistical arrangements. If a disputing party intends to use information in a hearing that is designated as protected information or otherwise subject to paragraph 3 it shall so advise the tribunal. The tribunal shall make appropriate arrangements to protect such information from disclosure which may include closing the hearing for the duration of the discussion of that information.

3. Nothing in this Annex, including paragraph 4(d), requires a respondent to make available to the public or otherwise disclose during or after the arbitral proceedings, including the hearing, protected information, or to furnish or allow access to information that it may withhold in accordance with Article 32.2 (Essential Security) or Article 32.7 (Disclosure of Information).[5]

4. Any protected information that is submitted to the tribunal shall be protected from disclosure in accordance with the following procedures:

(a) subject to subparagraph (d), neither the disputing parties nor the tribunal shall disclose to the non-disputing Annex Party or to the public any protected information if the disputing party that provided the information clearly designates it in accordance with subparagraph (b);
(b) any disputing party claiming that certain information constitutes protected information shall clearly designate the information according to any schedule set by the tribunal;
(c) a disputing party shall, according to any schedule set by the tribunal, submit a redacted version of the document that does not contain the protected information. Only the redacted version shall be disclosed in accordance with paragraph 1; and
(d) the tribunal, subject to paragraph 3, shall decide any objection regarding the designation of information claimed to be protected information. If the tribunal determines that the information was not properly designated, the disputing party that submitted the information may:
    (i) withdraw all or part of its submission containing that information, or
    (ii) agree to resubmit complete and redacted documents with corrected designations in accordance with the tribunal's determination and subparagraph (c).

    In either case, the other disputing party shall, whenever necessary, resubmit complete and redacted documents which either remove the information withdrawn under subparagraph (d)(i) by the disputing party that first submitted the information or redesignate the information consistent with the designation under subparagraph (d)(ii) of the disputing party that first submitted the information.

[5] For greater certainty, when a respondent chooses to disclose to the tribunal information that may be withheld in accordance with Article 32.2 (Essential Security) or Article 32.7 (Disclosure of Information), the respondent may still withhold that information from disclosure to the public.

5. Nothing in this Annex requires a respondent to withhold from the public information required to be disclosed by its laws. The respondent should endeavor to apply those laws in a manner sensitive to protecting from disclosure information that has been designated as protected information.

Article 14.D.9: Governing Law

1. Subject to paragraph 2, when a claim is submitted under Article 14.D.3.1 (Submission of a Claim to Arbitration), the tribunal shall decide the issues in dispute in accordance with this Agreement and applicable rules of international law.

2. A decision of the Commission on the interpretation of a provision of this Agreement under Article 30.2 (Functions of the Commission) shall be binding on a tribunal, and any decision or award issued by a tribunal must be consistent with that decision.

Article 14.D.10: Interpretation of Annexes

1. If a respondent asserts as a defense that the measure alleged to be a breach is within the scope of a non-conforming measure set out in Annex I or Annex II, the tribunal shall, on request of the respondent, request the interpretation of the Commission on the issue. The Commission shall submit in writing any decision on its interpretation under Article 30.2 (Functions of the Commission) to the tribunal within 90 days of delivery of the request.

2. A decision issued by the Commission under paragraph 1 shall be binding on the tribunal, and any decision or award issued by the tribunal must be consistent with that decision. If the Commission fails to issue such a decision within 90 days, the tribunal shall decide the issue.

Article 14.D.11: Expert Reports

Without prejudice to the appointment of other kinds of experts when authorized by the applicable arbitration rules, a tribunal, on request of a disputing party or, unless the disputing parties disapprove, on its own initiative, may appoint one or more experts to report to it in writing on any factual issue concerning scientific matters raised by a disputing party in a proceeding, subject to any terms and conditions that the disputing parties may agree.

Article 14.D.12: Consolidation

1. If two or more claims have been submitted separately to arbitration under Article 14.D.3.1 (Submission of a Claim to Arbitration) and the claims have a question of law or fact in common and arise out of the same events or circumstances, any disputing party may seek a consolidation order in accordance with the agreement of all the disputing parties sought to be covered by the order or the terms of paragraphs 2 through 10.

2. A disputing party that seeks a consolidation order under this Article shall deliver, in writing, a request to the Secretary-General and to all the disputing parties sought to be covered by the order and shall specify in the request:

(a) the names and addresses of all the disputing parties sought to be covered by the order;
(b) the nature of the order sought; and
(c) the grounds on which the order is sought.

3. Unless the Secretary-General finds within a period of 30 days after the date of receiving a request under paragraph 2 that the request is manifestly unfounded, a tribunal shall be established under this Article.

4. Unless all the disputing parties sought to be covered by the order agree otherwise, a tribunal established under this Article shall comprise three arbitrators:

(a) one arbitrator appointed by agreement of the claimants;
(b) one arbitrator appointed by the respondent; and
(c) the presiding arbitrator appointed by the Secretary-General, provided that the presiding arbitrator is not a national of the respondent or of the Party of the claimants.

5. If, within a period of 60 days after the date when the Secretary-General receives a request made under paragraph 2, the respondent fails or the claimants fail to appoint an arbitrator in accordance with paragraph 4, the Secretary-General, on request of any disputing party sought to be covered by the order, shall appoint, in his or her discretion, the arbitrator or arbitrators not yet appointed.

6. If a tribunal established under this Article is satisfied that two or more claims that have been submitted to arbitration under Article 14.D.3.1 (Submission of a Claim to Arbitration) have a question of law or fact in common, and arise out of the same events or circumstances, the tribunal may, in the interest of fair and efficient resolution of the claims, and after hearing the disputing parties, by order:

(a) assume jurisdiction over, and hear and determine together, all or part of the claims;
(b) assume jurisdiction over, and hear and determine one or more of the claims, the determination of which it believes would assist in the resolution of the others; or
(c) instruct a tribunal previously established under Article 14.D.6 (Selection of Arbitrators) to assume jurisdiction over, and hear and determine together, all or part of the claims, provided that:
    (i) that tribunal, on request of a claimant that was not previously a disputing party before that tribunal, shall be reconstituted with its original members, except that the arbitrator for the claimants shall be appointed pursuant to paragraphs 4(a) and 5, and
    (ii) that tribunal shall decide whether a prior hearing shall be repeated.

7. If a tribunal has been established under this Article, a claimant that has submitted a claim to arbitration under Article 14.D.3.1 (Submission of a Claim to Arbitration) and that has not been named in a request made under paragraph 2 may make a written request to the tribunal that it be included in any order made under paragraph 6. The request shall specify:

(a) the name and address of the claimant;
(b) the nature of the order sought; and
(c) the grounds on which the order is sought.

The claimant shall deliver a copy of its request to the Secretary-General.

8. A tribunal established under this Article shall conduct its proceedings in accordance with the UNCITRAL Arbitration Rules, except as modified by this Annex.

9. A tribunal established under Article 14.D.6 (Selection of Arbitrators) shall not have jurisdiction to decide a claim, or a part of a claim, over which a tribunal established or instructed under this Article has assumed jurisdiction.

10. On the application of a disputing party, a tribunal established under this Article, pending its decision under paragraph 6, may order that the proceedings of a tribunal established under Article 14.D.6 (Selection of Arbitrators) be stayed, unless the latter tribunal has already adjourned its proceedings.

Article 14.D.13: Awards

1. When a tribunal makes a final award, the tribunal may award, separately or in combination, only:
   (a) monetary damages and any applicable interest; and
   (b) restitution of property, in which case the award shall provide that the respondent may pay monetary damages and any applicable interest in lieu of restitution.[6]

2. For greater certainty, if an investor of an Annex Party submits a claim to arbitration under Article 14.D.3.1 (Submission of a Claim to Arbitration), it may recover only for loss or damage that is established on the basis of satisfactory evidence and that is not inherently speculative.

3. For greater certainty, if an investor of an Annex Party submits a claim to arbitration under Article 14.D.3.1(a) (Submission of a Claim to Arbitration), it may recover only for loss or damage incurred in its capacity as an investor of an Annex Party.

4. A tribunal may also award costs and attorney's fees incurred by the disputing parties in connection with the arbitral proceedings, and shall determine how and by whom those costs and attorney's fees shall be paid, in accordance with this Annex and the applicable arbitration rules.

5. Subject to paragraph 1, if a claim is submitted to arbitration under Article 14.D.3.1(b) (Submission of a Claim to Arbitration) and an award is made in favor of the enterprise:
   (a) an award of restitution of property shall provide that restitution be made to the enterprise;
   (b) an award of monetary damages and any applicable interest shall provide that the sum be paid to the enterprise; and
   (c) the award shall provide that it is made without prejudice to any right that any person may have under applicable domestic law with respect to the relief provided in the award.

6. A tribunal shall not award punitive damages.

7. An award made by a tribunal has no binding force except between the disputing parties and in respect of the particular case.

8. Subject to paragraph 9 and the applicable review procedure for an interim award, a disputing party shall abide by and comply with an award without delay.

9. A disputing party shall not seek enforcement of a final award until:
   (a) in the case of a final award made under the ICSID Convention:
      (i) 120 days have elapsed from the date the award was rendered and no disputing party has requested revision or annulment of the award, or
      (ii) revision or annulment proceedings have been completed; and

[6] For greater certainty, in the final award the tribunal may not order the respondent to take or not to take other actions, including the amendment, repeal, adoption, or implementation of a law or regulation.

(b) in the case of a final award under the ICSID Additional Facility Rules, the UNCITRAL Arbitration Rules, or the rules selected pursuant to Article 14.D.3.3(d) (Submission of a Claim to Arbitration):
   (i) 90 days have elapsed from the date the award was rendered and no disputing party has commenced a proceeding to revise, set aside or annul the award, or
   (ii) a court has dismissed or allowed an application to revise, set aside or annul the award and there is no further appeal.

10. Each Annex Party shall provide for the enforcement of an award in its territory.

11. If the respondent fails to abide by or comply with a final award, on delivery of a request by the Party of the claimant, a panel shall be established under Article 31.6 (Establishment of a Panel). The requesting Party may seek in those proceedings:

(a) a determination that the failure to abide by or comply with the final award is inconsistent with the obligations of this Agreement; and
(b) in accordance with Article 31.17 (Panel Report), a recommendation that the respondent abide by or comply with the final award.

12. A disputing party may seek enforcement of an arbitration award under the ICSID Convention, the New York Convention, or the Inter-American Convention regardless of whether proceedings have been taken under paragraph 11.

13. A claim that is submitted to arbitration under this Annex shall be considered to arise out of a commercial relationship or transaction for the purposes of Article I of the New York Convention and Article I of the Inter-American Convention.

Article 14.D.14: Service of Documents

Delivery of notice and other documents to an Annex Party shall be made to the place named for that Annex Party in Appendix 1 (Service of Documents on an Annex Party). An Annex Party shall promptly make publicly available and notify the other Annex Party of any change to the place referred to in that Appendix.

Appendices to Annex 14-D*

Appendix 2: PUBLIC DEBT

1. For greater certainty, no award shall be made in favor of a claimant for a claim under Article 14.D.3.1 (Submission of a Claim to Arbitration) with respect to default or non-payment of debt issued by a Party[7] unless the claimant meets its burden of proving that such default or nonpayment constitutes a breach of a relevant obligation in the Chapter.

2. No claim that a restructuring of debt issued by a Party, standing alone, breaches an obligation in this Chapter shall be submitted to arbitration under Article 14.D.3.1 (Submission of a Claim to Arbitration), provided that the restructuring is effected as provided for under the debt instrument's terms, including the debt instrument's governing law.

* N.B.: Appendix 1, detailing the proper recipient for the service of document, has been omitted.

[7] For purposes of this Annex, "debt issued by a Party" includes, in the case of Mexico, "public debt" of Mexico as defined in Article 1 of the Federal Law on Public Debt (*Ley Federal de Deuda Pública*).

Appendix 3: SUBMISSION OF A CLAIM TO ARBITRATION

An investor of the United States may not submit to arbitration a claim that Mexico has breached an obligation under this Chapter either:

(a) on its own behalf under Article 14.D.3.1(a) (Submission of a Claim to Arbitration); or

(b) on behalf of an enterprise of Mexico that is a juridical person that the investor owns or controls directly or indirectly under Article 14.D.3.1(b) (Submission of a Claim to Arbitration),

if the investor or the enterprise, respectively, has alleged that breach of an obligation under this Chapter, as distinguished from breach of other obligations under Mexican law, in proceedings before a court or administrative tribunal of Mexico.

ANNEX 14-E MEXICO-UNITED STATES INVESTMENT DISPUTES RELATED TO COVERED GOVERNMENT CONTRACTS

1. Annex 14-D (Mexico-United States Investment Disputes) applies as modified by this Annex to the settlement of a qualifying investment dispute under this Chapter in the circumstances set out in paragraph 2.[8]

2. In the event that a disputing party considers that a qualifying investment dispute cannot be settled by consultation and negotiation:

(a) the claimant, on its own behalf, may submit to arbitration under Annex 14-D (Mexico-United States Investment Disputes) a claim:

(i) that the respondent has breached any obligation under this Chapter,[9] provided that:

(A) the claimant is:

(1) a party to a covered government contract, or

(2) engaged in activities in the same covered sector in the territory of the respondent as an enterprise of the respondent that the claimant owns or controls directly or indirectly and that is a party to a covered government contract, and

(B) the respondent is a party to another international trade or investment agreement that permits investors to initiate dispute settlement procedures to resolve an investment dispute with a government, and

(ii) that the claimant has incurred loss or damage by reason of, or arising out of, that breach;

(b) the claimant, on behalf of an enterprise of the respondent that is a juridical person that the claimant owns or controls directly or indirectly, may submit to arbitration under Annex 14-D (Mexico-United States Investment Disputes) a claim:

[8] For greater certainty, Annex 14-D (Mexico-United States Investment Disputes) includes its appendices.

[9] For the purposes of this paragraph: (i) the "treatment" referred to in Article 14.5 (Most-Favored-Nation Treatment) excludes provisions in other international trade or investment agreements that establish international dispute resolution procedures or impose substantive obligations; (ii) the "treatment" referred to in Article 14.5 only encompasses measures adopted or maintained by the other Annex Party, which for greater clarity may include measures adopted in connection with the implementation of substantive obligations in other international trade or investment agreements.

(i) that the respondent has breached any obligation under this Chapter, provided that:

(A) the enterprise is:

(1) a party to a covered government contract,

(2) engaged in activities in the same covered sector in the territory of the respondent as the claimant and the claimant is a party to a covered government contract, or

(3) engaged in activities in the same covered sector in the territory of the respondent as another enterprise of the respondent that the claimant owns or controls directly or indirectly and that is a party to a covered government contract, and

(B) the respondent is a party to another international trade or investment agreement that permits investors to initiate dispute settlement procedures to resolve an investment dispute with a government, and

(ii) that the enterprise has incurred loss or damage by reason of, or arising out of, that breach.[10]

3. For the purposes of paragraph 2, if a covered government contract is terminated in a manner inconsistent with an obligation under this Chapter, the claimant or enterprise that was previously a party to the contract shall be deemed to remain a party for the duration of the contract, as if it had not been terminated.

4. No claim shall be submitted to arbitration under paragraph 2 if:

(a) less than six months have elapsed from the events giving rise to the claim; and

(b) more than three years have elapsed from the date on which the claimant first acquired, or should have first acquired, knowledge of the breach alleged under paragraph 2 and knowledge that the claimant (for claims brought under paragraph 2(a)) or the enterprise (for claims brought under paragraph 2(b)) has incurred loss or damage.[11]

5. For greater certainty, the Annex Parties may agree to modify or eliminate this Annex.

6. For the purposes of this Annex:

(a) "covered government contract" means a written agreement between a national authority of an Annex Party and a covered investment or investor of the other Annex Party, on which the covered investment or investor relies in establishing or acquiring a covered investment other than the written agreement itself, that grants rights to the covered investment or investor in a covered sector;

(b) "covered sector" means:

(i) activities with respect to oil and natural gas that a national authority of an Annex Party controls, such as exploration, extraction, refining, transportation, distribution, or sale,

(ii) the supply of power generation services to the public on behalf of an Annex Party,

(iii) the supply of telecommunications services to the public on behalf of an Annex Party,

(iv) the supply of transportation services to the public on behalf of an Annex Party, or

[10] For greater certainty, in order for a claim to be submitted to arbitration under subparagraph (b), an investor of the Party of the claimant must own or control the enterprise on the date of the alleged breach and the date on which the claim is submitted to arbitration.

[11] For greater certainty, Article 14.D.5.1(a)-(c) does not apply to claims under paragraph 2.

(v) the ownership or management of roads, railways, bridges, or canals that are not for the exclusive or predominant use and benefit of the government of an Annex Party;

(c) "national authority" means an authority at the central level of government;[12] and

(d) "written agreement" means an agreement in writing, negotiated, and executed by two or more parties, whether in a single instrument or in multiple instruments.[13]

40 Comprehensive Economic and Trade Agreement (CETA) between Canada, of the one part, and the European Union and its Member States, of the other part

Date: 30 October 2016

Source: https://trade.ec.europa.eu/doclib/docs/2014/september/tradoc_152806.pdf

...

Article 13.20 Dispute settlement

1. Chapter Twenty-Nine (Dispute Settlement) applies as modified by this Article to the settlement of disputes arising under this Chapter.

2. If the Parties are unable to agree on the composition of the arbitration panel established for the purposes of a dispute arising under this Chapter, Article 29.7 (Composition of the arbitration panel) applies. However, all references to the list of arbitrators established under Article 29.8 (List of arbitrators) shall be understood to refer to the list of arbitrators established under this Article.

3. The CETA Joint Committee may establish a list of at least 15 individuals, chosen on the basis of objectivity, reliability, and sound judgement, who are willing and able to serve as arbitrators. The list shall be composed of three sub-lists: one sub-list for each Party and one sub-list of individuals, who are not nationals of either Party, to act as chairpersons. Each sub-list shall include at least five individuals. The CETA Joint Committee may review the list at any time and shall ensure that the list conforms with this Article.

4. The arbitrators included on the list must have expertise or experience in financial services law or regulation or in the practice thereof, which may include the regulation of financial service suppliers. The arbitrators acting as chairpersons must also have experience as counsel, panellist, or arbitrator in dispute settlement proceedings. Arbitrators shall be independent, serve in their individual capacity, and shall not take instructions from any organisation or government. They shall comply with the Code of Conduct in Annex 29-B (Code of conduct).

[12] For greater certainty, an authority at the central level of government includes any person, including a state enterprise or another body, when it exercises governmental authority delegated to it by an authority at the central level of government.

[13] For greater certainty, (a) a unilateral act of an administrative or judicial authority, such as a permit, license, certificate, approval, or similar instrument issued by an Annex Party in its regulatory capacity, or a subsidy or grant, or a decree, order or judgment, standing alone; and (b) an administrative or judicial consent decree or order, shall not be considered a written agreement.

5. If an arbitration panel finds that a measure is inconsistent with this Agreement and the measure affects:

(a) the financial services sector and any other sector, the complaining Party may suspend benefits in the financial services sector that have an effect equivalent to the effect of the measure in the Party's financial services sector; or

(b) only a sector other than the financial services sector, the complaining Party shall not suspend benefits in the financial services sector.

CHAPTER TWENTY-NINE. Dispute settlement

Section A
Initial provisions

Article 29.1 Cooperation

The Parties shall, at all times, endeavour to agree on the interpretation and application of this Agreement, and shall make every attempt through cooperation and consultations to arrive at a mutually satisfactory resolution of any matter that might affect its operation.

Article 29.2 Scope

Except as otherwise provided in this Agreement, this Chapter applies to any dispute concerning the interpretation or application of the provisions of this Agreement.

Article 29.3 Choice of forum

1. Recourse to the dispute settlement provisions of this Chapter is without prejudice to recourse to dispute settlement under the WTO Agreement or under any other agreement to which the Parties are party.

2. Notwithstanding paragraph 1, if an obligation is equivalent in substance under this Agreement and under the WTO Agreement, or under any other agreement to which the Parties are party, a Party may not seek redress for the breach of such an obligation in the two fora. In such case, once a dispute settlement proceeding has been initiated under one agreement, the Party shall not bring a claim seeking redress for the breach of the substantially equivalent obligation under the other agreement, unless the forum selected fails, for procedural or jurisdictional reasons, other than termination under paragraph 20 of Annex 29-A, to make findings on that claim.

3. For the purposes of paragraph 2:

(a) dispute settlement proceedings under the WTO Agreement are deemed to be initiated by a Party's request for the establishment of a panel under Article 6 of the DSU;

(b) dispute settlement proceedings under this Charter are deemed to be initiated by a Party's request for the establishment of an arbitration panel under Article 29.6; and

(c) dispute settlement proceedings under any other agreement are deemed to be initiated by a Party's request for the establishment of a dispute settlement panel or tribunal in accordance with the provisions of that agreement.

4. Nothing in this Agreement shall preclude a Party from implementing the suspension of obligations authorised by the WTO Dispute Settlement Body. A Party may not invoke the WTO Agreement to preclude the other Party from suspending obligations pursuant to this Chapter.

Section B
Consultations and mediation

Article 29.4 Consultations

1. A Party may request in writing consultations with the other Party regarding any matter referred to in Article 29.2.

2. The requesting Party shall transmit the request to the responding Party, and shall set out the reasons for the request, including the identification of the specific measure at issue and the legal basis for the complaint.

3. Subject to paragraph 4, the Parties shall enter into consultations within 30 days of the date of receipt of the request by the responding Party.

4. In cases of urgency, including those involving perishable or seasonal goods, or services that rapidly lose their trade value, consultations shall commence within 15 days of the date of receipt of the request by the responding Party.

5. The Parties shall make every attempt to arrive at a mutually satisfactory resolution of the matter through consultations. To this end, each Party shall:

(a) provide sufficient information to enable a full examination of the matter at issue;

(b) protect any confidential or proprietary information exchanged in the course of consultations as requested by the Party providing the information; and

(c) make available the personnel of its government agencies or other regulatory bodies who have expertise in the matter that is the subject of the consultations.

6. Consultations are confidential and without prejudice to the rights of the Parties in proceedings under this Chapter.

7. Consultations shall take place in the territory of the responding Party unless the Parties agree otherwise. Consultations may be held in person or by any other means agreed to by the Parties.

8. A Party's proposed measure may be the subject of consultations under this Article but may not be the subject of mediation under Article 29.5 or the dispute settlement procedures under Section C.

Article 29.5 Mediation

The Parties may have recourse to mediation with regard to a measure if the measure adversely affects trade and investment between the Parties. Mediation procedures are set out in Annex 29-C.

Section C
Dispute settlement procedures and compliance

Sub-section A
Dispute settlement procedures

Article 29.6 Request for the establishment of an arbitration panel

1. Unless the Parties agree otherwise, if a matter referred to in Article 29.4 has not been resolved within:

(a) 45 days of the date of receipt of the request for consultations; or

(b) 25 days of the date of receipt of the request for consultations for matters referred to in Article 29.4.4, the requesting Party may refer the matter to an arbitration panel by providing its written request for the establishment of an arbitration panel to the responding Party.

2. The requesting Party shall identify in its written request the specific measure at issue and the legal basis for the complaint, including an explanation of how such measure constitutes a breach of the provisions referred to in Article 29.2.

Article 29.7 Composition of the arbitration panel

1. The arbitration panel shall be composed of three arbitrators.

2. The Parties shall consult with a view to reaching an agreement on the composition of the arbitration panel within 10 working days of the date of receipt by the responding Party of the request for the establishment of an arbitration panel.

3. In the event that the Parties are unable to agree on the composition of the arbitration panel within the time frame set out in paragraph 2, either Party may request the Chair of the CETA Joint Committee, or the Chair's delegate, to draw by lot the arbitrators from the list established under Article 29.8. One arbitrator shall be drawn from the sub-list of the requesting Party, one from the sub-list of the responding Party and one from the sub-list of chairpersons. If the Parties have agreed on one or more of the arbitrators, any remaining arbitrator shall be selected by the same procedure in the applicable sub-list of arbitrators. If the Parties have agreed on an arbitrator, other than the chairperson, who is not a national of either Party, the chairperson and other arbitrator shall be selected from the sub-list of chairpersons.

4. The Chair of the CETA Joint Committee, or the Chair's delegate, shall select the arbitrators as soon as possible and normally within five working days of the request referred to in paragraph 3 by either Party. The Chair, or the Chair's delegate, shall give a reasonable opportunity to representatives of each Party to be present when lots are drawn. One of the Chairpersons can perform the selection by lot alone if the other Chairperson was informed about the date, time and place of the selection by lot and did not accept to participate within five working days of the request referred to in paragraph 3.

5. The date of establishment of the arbitration panel shall be the date on which the last of the three arbitrators is selected.

6. If the list provided for in Article 29.8 is not established or if it does not contain sufficient names at the time a request is made pursuant to paragraph 3, the three arbitrators shall be drawn by lot from the arbitrators who have been proposed by one or both of the Parties in accordance with Article 29.8.1.

7. Replacement of arbitrators shall take place only for the reasons and according to the procedure set out in paragraphs 21 through 25 of Annex 29-A.

Article 29.8 List of arbitrators

1. The CETA Joint Committee shall, at its first meeting after the entry into force of this Agreement, establish a list of at least 15 individuals, chosen on the basis of objectivity, reliability and sound judgment, who are willing and able to serve as arbitrators. The list shall be composed of three sub-lists: one sub-list for each Party and one sub-list of individuals who are not nationals of either Party to act as chairpersons. Each sub-list shall include at least five individuals. The CETA Joint Committee may review the list at any time and shall ensure that the list conforms with this Article.

2. The arbitrators must have specialised knowledge of international trade law. The arbitrators acting as chairpersons must also have experience as counsel or panellist in dispute settlement proceedings on subject matters within the scope of this Agreement. The

arbitrators shall be independent, serve in their individual capacities and not take instructions from any organisation or government, or be affiliated with the government of any of the Parties, and shall comply with the Code of Conduct in Annex 29-B.

Article 29.9 Interim panel report

1. The arbitration panel shall present to the Parties an interim report within 150 days of the establishment of the arbitration panel. The report shall contain:

(a) findings of fact; and

(b) determination as to whether the responding Party has conformed with its obligations under this Agreement.

2. Each Party may submit written comments to the arbitration panel on the interim report, subject to any time limits set by the arbitration panel. After considering any such comments, the arbitration panel may:

(a) reconsider its report; or

(b) make any further examination that it considers appropriate.

3. The interim report of the arbitration panel shall be confidential.

Article 29.10 Final panel report

1. Unless the Parties agree otherwise, the arbitration panel shall issue a report in accordance with this Chapter. The final panel report shall set out the findings of fact, the applicability of the relevant provisions of this Agreement and the basic rationale behind any findings and conclusions that it makes. The ruling of the arbitration panel in the final panel report shall be binding on the Parties.

2. The arbitration panel shall issue to the Parties and to the CETA Joint Committee a final report within 30 days of the interim report.

3. Each Party shall make publicly available the final panel report, subject to paragraph 39 of Annex 29-A.

Article 29.11 Urgent proceedings

In cases of urgency, including those involving perishable or seasonal goods, or services that rapidly lose their trade value, the arbitration panel and the Parties shall make every effort to accelerate the proceedings to the greatest extent possible. The arbitration panel shall aim at issuing an interim report to the Parties within 75 days of the establishment of the arbitration panel, and a final report within 15 days of the interim report. Upon request of a Party, the arbitration panel shall make a preliminary ruling within 10 days of the request on whether it deems the case to be urgent.

41 Agreement on Promotion, Protection and Guarantee of Investments amongst the Member States of the Organization of the Islamic Conference

Date: 5 June 1981

Source: https://investmentpolicy.unctad.org/international-investment-agreements/treaties/otheriia/3092/oic-investment-agreement-1981-

Article 16

The host state undertakes to allow the investor the right to resort to its national judicial system to complain against a measure adopted by its authorities against him, or to contest the extent of its conformity with the provisions of the regulations and laws in force in its territory, or to complain against the non-adoption by the host state of a certain measure which is in the interest of the investor, and which the state should have adopted, irrespective of whether the complaint is related, or otherwise, to the implementation of the provisions of the Agreement to the relationship between the investor and the host state.

Provided that if the investor chooses to raise the complaint before the national courts or before an arbitral tribunal then having done so before one of the two quarters he loses the right of recourse to the other.

Article 17

1. Until an Organ for the settlement of disputes arising under the Agreement is established, disputes that may arise shall be entitled through conciliation or arbitration in accordance with the following rules and procedures:

1. Conciliation

a) In case the parties to the dispute agree on conciliation, the agreement shall include a description of the dispute, the claims of the parties to the dispute and the name of the conciliator whom they have chosen. The parties concerned may request the Secretary General to choose the conciliator. The General Secretariat shall forward to the conciliator a copy of the conciliation agreement so that he may assume his duties.

b) The task of the conciliator shall be confined to bringing the different view points closer and making proposals which may lead to a solution that may be acceptable to the parties concerned. The conciliator shall, within the period assigned for the completion of his task, submit a report thereon to be communicated to the parties concerned. This report shall have no legal authority before a court should the dispute be referred to it.

2. Arbitration

a) If the two parties to the dispute do not reach an agreement as a result of their resort to conciliation, or if the conciliator is unable to issue his report within the prescribed period, or if the two parties do not accept the solutions proposed therein, then each party has the right to resort to the Arbitration Tribunal for a final decision on the dispute.

b) The arbitration procedure begins with a notification by the party requesting the arbitration to the other party to the dispute, clearly explaining the nature of the dispute and the name of the arbitrator he has appointed. The other party must, within sixty days from the date on which such notification was given, inform the party requesting arbitration of the name of the arbitrator appointed by him. The two arbitrators are to choose, within sixty days from the date on which the last of them was appointed arbitrator, an umpire who shall have a casting vote in case of equality of votes. If the second party does not appoint an arbitrator, or if the two arbitrators do not agree on the appointment of an Umpire within the prescribed time, either party may request the Secretary General to complete the composition of the Arbitration Tribunal.

c) The Arbitration Tribunal shall hold its first meeting at the time and place specified by the Umpire. Thereafter the Tribunal will decide on the venue and time of its meetings as well as other matters pertaining to its functions.

d) The decisions of the Arbitration Tribunal shall be final and cannot be contested. They are binding on both parties who must respect and implement them.

They shall have the force of judicial decisions. The contracting parties are under an obligation to implement them in their territory, no matter whether it be a party to the dispute or not and irrespective of whether the investor against whom the decision was passed is one of its nationals or residents or not, as if it were a final and enforceable decision of its national courts.

42 The Energy Charter Treaty

Date: 17 December 1994
Source: 2080 UNTS 100
https://www.energychartertreaty.org/treaty/energy-charter-treaty/

PART I – DEFINITIONS AND PURPOSE

Article 1 Definitions

As used in this Treaty:

. . .

6. 'Investment' means every kind of asset, owned or controlled directly or indirectly by an investor and includes:

(a) tangible and intangible, and moveable and immovable, property, and any property rights such as leases, mortgages, liens, and pledges;
(b) a company or business enterprise, or shares, stock, or other forms of equity participation in a company or business enterprise, and bonds and other debt of a company or business enterprise;
(c) claims to money and claims to performance pursuant to contract having an economic value and associated with investment;
(d) intellectual property;
(e) returns;
(f) any right conferred by law or contract or by virtue of any licences and permits granted pursuant to law to undertake any economic activity in the energy sector;

A change in the form in which assets are invested does not affect their character as investments and the term 'investment' includes all investments whether existing at or made after the later of date of entry into force of this Treaty for the Contracting Party of the investor making the investment and that for the Contracting Party in the area of which the investment is made hereinafter referred to as the 'effective date') provided that the Treaty shall only apply to matters affecting such investments after the effective date.

'Investment' refers to any investment associated with an economic activity in the energy sector and to investments or classes of investments designated by a Contracting Party in its area as 'Charter Efficiency projects' and so notified to the Secretariat.

7. 'Investor' means:

(a) with respect to a Contracting Party:
 (i) a natural person having the citizenship or nationality of or who is permanently residing in that Contracting Party in accordance with its applicable law;
 (ii) a company or other organisation organized in accordance with the law applicable in that Contracting Party;

(b) with respect to a 'third State', a natural person, company or other mutatis mutandis, the conditions specified in subparagraph (a) for the Contracting Party.

…

PART II – COMMERCE

…

Article 7 Transit

…

6. A Contracting Party through whose Area Energy Materials and Products transit shall not, in the event of a dispute over any matter arising from that Transit, interrupt or reduce, permit any entity subject to its control to interrupt or reduce, or require any entity subject to its jurisdiction to interrupt or reduce the existing flow of Energy Materials and Products prior to the conclusion of the dispute resolution procedures set out in paragraph (7), except where this is specifically provided for in a contract or other agreement governing such Transit or permitted in accordance with the conciliator's decision.

7. The following provisions shall apply to a dispute described in paragraph (6), but only following the exhaustion of all relevant contractual or other dispute resolution remedies previously agreed between the Contracting Parties party to the dispute or between any entity referred to in paragraph (6) and an entity of another Contracting Party party to the dispute:

(a) A Contracting Party party to the dispute may refer it to the Secretary-General by a notification summarizing the matters in dispute. The Secretary-General shall notify all Contracting Parties of any such referral.

(b) Within 30 days of receipt of such a notification, the Secretary-General, in consultation with the parties to the dispute and the other Contracting Parties concerned, shall appoint a conciliator. Such a conciliator shall have experience in the matters subject to dispute and shall not be a national or citizen of or permanently resident in a party to the dispute or one of the other Contracting Parties concerned.

(c) The conciliator shall seek the agreement of the parties to the dispute to a resolution thereof or upon a procedure to achieve such resolution. If within 90 days of his appointment he has failed to secure such agreement, he shall recommend a resolution to the dispute or a procedure to achieve such resolution and shall decide the interim tariffs and other terms and conditions to be observed for Transit from a date which he shall specify until the dispute is resolved.

(d) The Contracting Parties undertake to observe and ensure that the entities under their control or jurisdiction observe any interim decision under subparagraph (c) on tariffs, terms and conditions for 12 months following the conciliator's decision or until resolution of the dispute, whichever is earlier.

(e) Notwithstanding subparagraph (b) the Secretary-General may elect not to appoint a conciliator if in his judgement the dispute concerns Transit that is or has been the subject of the dispute resolution procedures set out in subparagraphs (a) to (d) and those proceedings have not resulted in a resolution of the dispute.

(f) The Charter Conference shall adopt standard provisions concerning the conduct of conciliation and the compensation of conciliators.

… ###

PART V – DISPUTE SETTLEMENT

Article 26 Settlement of disputes between an investor and a Contracting Party

1. Disputes between a Contracting Party and an investor of another Contracting Party relating to an investment of the latter in the area of the former, which concerned an alleged breach of an obligation under the former under Part III shall, if possible, be settled amicably.

2. If such disputes cannot be settled according to the provision of paragraph 1 within a period of three months from the date on which either party to the dispute requested amicable settlement, the investor party to the dispute may choose to settle submit it for resolution:

(a) to the courts or administrative tribunals of the Contracting Party to the dispute;

(b) in accordance with any applicable, previously agreed dispute settlement procedure; or

(c) in accordance with the following paragraphs of this Article.

3. (a) Subject only to paragraphs (b) and (c), each Contracting Party hereby gives its unconditional consent to the submission of a dispute to arbitration or conciliation in accordance with the provisions of this Article.

(b) (i) The Contracting Parties listed in Annex ID does not give unconditional consent where the investor has previously submitted the disputes under subparagraph 2(a) or (b).

(ii) For the sake of transparency, each Contracting Party that is listed in Annex ID shall provide a written statement of its policies, practices and conditions in this regard to the Secretariat no later than the date of the deposit of its instrument of ratification, acceptance or approval in accordance with Article 39 or the deposit of its instrument of accession in accordance with Article 41.

(c) A Contracting Party listed in Annex IA does not give such unconditional consent with respect to a dispute arising under the last sentence of Article 10 (1).

4. In the event that the investor chooses to submit the dispute for resolution under subparagraph 2(c), the investor shall further provide its consent in writing for the dispute to be submitted to:

(a) (i) the International Centre for the Settlement of Investment Disputes, established pursuant to the Convention on the Settlement of Investment Disputes between States and Nationals of other States opened for signature at Washington, 18 March 1965 (hereinafter referred to as the 'Icsid Convention') if the Contracting Party of the Investor and the Contracting Party party to the dispute are both Parties to the Icsid Convention, or

(ii) The International Centre for the Settlement of Investment Disputes, established pursuant to the Convention referred to in subparagraph (a)(i), under the rules governing the Additional Facility for the Administration of Proceedings by the Secretariat of the Centre (hereinafter referred to as the 'Additional Facility Rules') if the Contracting Party of the Investor or the Contracting Party party to the dispute, but not both, is a party to the Icsid Convention;

(b) A sole arbitrator or ad hoc arbitration tribunal established under the Arbitration Rules of the United Nations Commission on International Trade Law (hereinafter referred to as 'UNCITRAL'); or

(c) An arbitral proceeding under the Arbitration Institute of the Stockholm Chamber of Commerce.

5. (a) The consent given in paragraph 3 together with the written consent of the investor given pursuant to paragraph 4 shall be considered to satisfy the requirement for:
(i) Written consent of the partied to a dispute for the purposes of Chapter II of the ICSID Convention and for purposes of the Additional Facility Rules;
(ii) An 'agreement in writing' for the purposes of Article II of the United Nations Convention on the Recognition and Enforcement of Foreign Arbitral Awards, done at New York, 10 June 1958 (hereinafter referred to at the 'New York Convention'); and
(iii) 'the parties to a contract (to) have agreed in writing' for the purposes of Article 1 of the UNCITRAL Arbitration Rules.
(b) Any arbitration request pursuant to this Article shall at the request of any party to the dispute be held in a State that is a party to the New York Convention. Claims submitted to arbitration hereunder shall be considered to arise out of a commercial relationship or transaction for the purposes of Article I of that Convention.

6. A tribunal established pursuant to paragraph 4 shall decide the issues in dispute in accordance with this Treaty and applicable rules and principles of international law.

7. An investor other than a natural person which has the nationality of a Contracting Party party to the dispute on the date of consent in writing referred to in paragraph 4 and which, before a dispute between it and that Contracting Party arises, is controlled by investors of another Contracting Party, shall for the purpose of Article 25 (2) (b) of the ICSID Convention be treated as a 'national of another Contracting State' and shall for the purpose of Article 1 (6) of the Additional Facility Rules be treated as a 'national of another State.'

8. The awards of arbitration, which may include an award of interest, shall be final and binding upon the parties to the dispute. An award of arbitration concerning a measure of a sub-national government or authority of the disputing Contracting Party shall provide that the Contracting Party may pay monetary damages in lieu of any other remedy granted. Each Contracting Party shall carry out without any delay such award and shall make provision for the effective enforcement in its area of such awards.

Article 27 Settlement of disputes between Contracting Parties

1. Contracting Parties shall endeavour to settle disputes concerning the application or interpretation of this Treaty through diplomatic channels.

2. If a dispute has not been settled in accordance with paragraph 1 within a reasonable period of time, either party thereto may, except as otherwise provided in this Treaty or agreed in writing by the Contracting Parties, and except as concerns the application or interpretation of Article 6 or Article 19 or, for Contracting Partied listed in Annex IA, the last sentence of Article 10(1), upon written notice to the other party to the dispute submit the matter to and *ad hoc* tribunal pursuant to this Article.

3. Such an *ad hoc* tribunal shall be constituted as follows:
(a) The Contracting Party instituting the proceedings shall appoint one member of the tribunal and inform the other Contracting Party to the dispute of its appointment within 30 days of receipt of the notice referred to in paragraph 2 by the other Contracting Party.
(b) Within 60 days of the receipt of the written notice referred to in paragraph 2, the other Contracting Party party to the dispute shall appoint one member. If the appointment is not made within the time limit prescribed, the Contracting Party having instituted the proceedings may, within 90 days of the receipt of the

written notice referred to in paragraph 2, request that the appointment be made in accordance with subparagraph (d).

(c) A third member, who may not be a national or citizen of a Contracting Party party to the dispute, shall be appointed by the Contracting Party parties to the dispute. That member shall be the President of the Tribunal. If, within 150 days of the receipt of the notice referred to in paragraph 2, the Contracting Parties are unable to agree on the appointment of a third member, that appointment shall be made, in accordance with subparagraph (d), at the request of either Contracting Party submitted within 180 days of the receipt of that notice.

(d) Appointments requested to be made in accordance with this paragraph shall be made by the Secretary-General of the Permanent Court of International Arbitration within 30 days of the receipt of a request to do so. If the Secretary-General is prevented from discharging this task, the appointments shall be made by the First Secretary of the Bureau. If the latter, in turn, is prevented from discharging this task, the appointments shall be made by the most senior deputy.

(e) Appointments made in accordance with subparagraphs (a) to (d) shall be made with regard to the qualifications and experience, particularly in matters covered by this Treaty, of the members to be appointed.

(f) In the absence of agreement to the contrary between the Contracting Parties, the Arbitration Rules of UNCITRAL shall govern, except to the extent modified by the Contracting Parties parties to the dispute or by the arbitrators. The tribunal shall take its decisions by a majority vote of its members.

(g) The tribunal shall deicide the dispute in accordance with this Treaty and applicable rules and principles of international law.

(h) The arbitral award shall be final and binding upon the Contracting Parties parties to the dispute.

(i) Where, in making an award, a tribunal finds that a measure of a regional or local government or authority within the area of a Contracting Party listed in Part I of Annex P is not in conformity with this Treaty, either party to the dispute may invoke the provisions of Part II of Annex P.

(j) The expenses of the tribunal, including the remuneration of its members, shall be borne in equal shares by the Contracting Parties parties to the dispute. The tribunal may, however, at its discretion direct that a higher proportion of the costs be paid by one of the Contracting Partied parties to the dispute.

(k) Unless the Contracting Parties parties to the dispute agree otherwise, the tribunal shall sit in The Hague, and use the premises and facilities of the Permanent Court of Arbitration.

(l) A copy of the award shall be deposited with the Secretariat which will make it generally available.

Article 28 Non-application of Article 27 to certain disputes

A dispute between Contracting Parties with respect to the application or interpretation of Article 5 or 29 shall not be settled pursuant to Article 27 unless the Contracting Parties parties to the dispute so agree.

…

UNDERSTANDINGS

…

3. With respect to Article 1(6)

For greater clarity as to whether an Investment made in the Area of one Contracting Party is controlled, directly or indirectly, by an Investor of any other Contracting Party, control of an Investment means control in fact, determined after an examination of the actual circumstances in each situation. In any such examination, all relevant factors should be considered, including the Investor's

(a) financial interest, including equity interest, in the Investment;
(b) ability to exercise substantial influence over the management and operation of the Investment; and
(c) ability to exercise substantial influence over the selection of members of the board of directors or any other managing body.

Where there is doubt as to whether an Investor controls, directly or indirectly, an Investment, an Investor claiming such control has the burden of proof that such control exists.

…

16. With respect to Article 26(2)(a)

Article 26(2)(a) should not be interpreted to require a Contracting Party to enact Part III of the Treaty into its domestic law.

17. With respect to Articles 26 and 27

The reference to treaty obligations in the penultimate sentence of Article 10(1) does not include decisions taken by international organizations, even if they are legally binding, or treaties which entered into force before 1 January 1970.

…

ANNEX P: SPECIAL SUB-NATIONAL DISPUTE PROCEDURE (IN ACCORDANCE WITH ARTICLE 27(3)(I))

…

PART II

(1) Where, in making an award, the tribunal finds that a measure of a regional or local government or authority of a Contracting Party (hereinafter referred to as the "Responsible Party") is not in conformity with a provision of this Treaty, the Responsible Party shall take such reasonable measures as may be available to it to ensure observance of the Treaty in respect of the measure.

(2) The Responsible Party shall, within 30 days from the date the award is made, provide to the Secretariat written notice of its intentions as to ensuring observance of the Treaty in respect of the measure. The Secretariat shall present the notification to the Charter Conference at the earliest practicable opportunity, and no later than the meeting of the Charter Conference following receipt of the notice. If it is impracticable to ensure observance immediately, the Responsible Party shall have a reasonable period of time in which to do so. The reasonable period of time shall be agreed by both parties to the dispute. In the event that such agreement is not reached, the Responsible Party shall propose a reasonable period for approval by the Charter Conference.

(3) Where the Responsible Party fails, within the reasonable period of time, to ensure observance in respect of the measure, it shall at the request of the other Contracting Party

party to the dispute (hereinafter referred to as the "Injured Party") endeavour to agree with the Injured Party on appropriate compensation as a mutually satisfactory resolution of the dispute.

(4) If no satisfactory compensation has been agreed within 20 days of the request of the Injured Party, the Injured Party may with the authorization of the Charter Conference suspend such of its obligations to the Responsible Party under the Treaty as it considers equivalent to those denied by the measure in question, until such time as the Contracting Parties have reached agreement on a resolution of their dispute or the non-conforming measure has been brought into conformity with the Treaty.

(5) In considering what obligations to suspend, the Injured Party shall apply the following principles and procedures:

(a) The Injured Party should first seek to suspend obligations with respect to the same Part of the Treaty as that in which the tribunal has found a violation.

(b) If the Injured Party considers that it is not practicable or effective to suspend obligations with respect to the same Part of the Treaty, it may seek to suspend obligations in other Parts of the Treaty. If the Injured Party decides to request authorization to suspend obligations under this subparagraph, it shall state the reasons therefor in its request to the Charter Conference for authorization.

(6) On written request of the Responsible Party, delivered to the Injured Party and to the President of the tribunal that rendered the award, the tribunal shall determine whether the level of obligations suspended by the Injured Party is excessive, and if so, to what extent. If the tribunal cannot be reconstituted, such determination shall be made by one or more arbitrators appointed by the Secretary-General. Determinations pursuant to this paragraph shall be completed within 60 days of the request to the tribunal or the appointment by the Secretary-General. Obligations shall not be suspended pending the determination, which shall be final and binding.

(7) In suspending any obligations to a Responsible Party, an Injured Party shall make every effort not to affect adversely the rights under the Treaty of any other Contracting Party.

ANNEX D: INTERIM PROVISIONS FOR TRADE DISPUTE SETTLEMENT (IN ACCORDANCE WITH ARTICLE 29(7))

(1) (a) In their relations with one another, Contracting Parties shall make every effort through co-operation and consultations to arrive at a mutually satisfactory resolution of any dispute about existing measures that might materially affect compliance with the provisions applicable to trade under Article 5 or 29.

(b) A Contracting Party may make a written request to any other Contracting Party for consultations regarding any existing measure of the other Contracting Party that it considers might affect materially compliance with provisions applicable to trade under Article 5 or 29. A Contracting Party which requests consultations shall to the fullest extent possible indicate the measure complained of and specify the provisions of Article 5 or 29 and of the GATT and Related Instruments that it considers relevant. Requests to consult pursuant to this paragraph shall be notified to the Secretariat, which shall periodically inform the Contracting Parties of pending consultations that have been notified.

(c) A Contracting Party shall treat any confidential or proprietary information identified as such and contained in or received in response to a written request, or received in the course of consultations, in the same manner in which it is treated by the Contracting Party providing the information.

(d) In seeking to resolve matters considered by a Contracting Party to affect compliance with provisions applicable to trade under Article 5 or 29 as between itself and another Contracting Party, the Contracting Parties participating in consultations or other dispute settlement shall make every effort to avoid a resolution that adversely affects the trade of any other Contracting Party.

(2) (a) If, within 60 days from the receipt of the request for consultation referred to in subparagraph (1)(b), the Contracting Parties have not resolved their dispute or agreed to resolve it by conciliation, mediation, arbitration or other method, either Contracting Party may deliver to the Secretariat a written request for the establishment of a panel in accordance with subparagraphs (b) to (f). In its request the requesting Contracting Party shall state the substance of the dispute and indicate which provisions of Article 5 or 29 and of the GATT and Related Instruments are considered relevant. The Secretariat shall promptly deliver copies of the request to all Contracting Parties.

(b) The interests of other Contracting Parties shall be taken into account during the resolution of a dispute. Any other Contracting Party having a substantial interest in a matter shall have the right to be heard by the panel and to make written submissions to it, provided that both the disputing Contracting Parties and the Secretariat have received written notice of its interest no later than the date of establishment of the panel, as determined in accordance with subparagraph (c).

(c) A panel shall be deemed to be established 45 days after the receipt of the written request of a Contracting Party by the Secretariat pursuant to subparagraph (a).

(d) A panel shall be composed of three members who shall be chosen by the Secretary-General from the roster described in paragraph (7). Except where the disputing Contracting Parties agree otherwise, the members of a panel shall not be citizens of Contracting Parties which either are party to the dispute or have notified their interest in accordance with subparagraph (b), or citizens of states members of a Regional Economic Integration Organization which either is party to the dispute or has notified its interest in accordance with subparagraph (b).

(e) The disputing Contracting Parties shall respond within ten working days to the nominations of panel members and shall not oppose nominations except for compelling reasons.

(f) Panel members shall serve in their individual capacities and shall neither seek nor take instruction from any government or other body. Each Contracting Party undertakes to respect these principles and not to seek to influence panel members in the performance of their tasks. Panel members shall be selected with a view to ensuring their independence, and that a sufficient diversity of backgrounds and breadth of experience are reflected in a panel.

(g) The Secretariat shall promptly notify all Contracting Parties that a panel has been constituted.

(3) (a) The Charter Conference shall adopt rules of procedure for panel proceedings consistent with this Annex. Rules of procedure shall be as close as possible to those of the GATT and Related Instruments. A panel shall also have the right to adopt additional rules of procedure not inconsistent with the rules of procedure adopted by the Charter Conference or with this Annex. In a proceeding before a panel each disputing Contracting Party and any other Contracting Party which has notified its interest in accordance with subparagraph (2)(b), shall have the right to at least one hearing before the panel and to provide a written submission. Disputing

Contracting Parties shall also have the right to provide a written rebuttal. A panel may grant a request by any other Contracting Party which has notified its interest in accordance with subparagraph (2)(b) for access to any written submission made to the panel, with the consent of the Contracting Party which has made it.

The proceedings of a panel shall be confidential. A panel shall make an objective assessment of the matters before it, including the facts of the dispute and the compliance of measures with the provisions applicable to trade under Article 5 or 29. In exercising its functions, a panel shall consult with the disputing Contracting Parties and give them adequate opportunity to arrive at a mutually satisfactory solution. Unless otherwise agreed by the disputing Contracting Parties, a panel shall base its decision on the arguments and submissions of the disputing Contracting Parties. Panels shall be guided by the interpretations given to the GATT and Related Instruments within the framework of the GATT, and shall not question the compatibility with Article 5 or 29 of practices applied by any Contracting Party which is a party to the GATT to other parties to the GATT to which it applies the GATT and which have not been taken by those other parties to dispute resolution under the GATT. Unless otherwise agreed by the disputing Contracting Parties, all procedures involving a panel, including the issuance of its final report, should be completed within 180 days of the date of establishment of the panel; however, a failure to complete all procedures within this period shall not affect the validity of a final report.

(b) A panel shall determine its jurisdiction; such determination shall be final and binding. Any objection by a disputing Contracting Party that a dispute is not within the jurisdiction of the panel shall be considered by the panel, which shall decide whether to deal with the objection as a preliminary question or to join it to the merits of the dispute.

(c) In the event of two or more requests for establishment of a panel in relation to disputes that are substantively similar, the Secretary-General may with the consent of all the disputing Contracting Parties appoint a single panel.

(4) (a) After having considered rebuttal arguments, a panel shall submit to the disputing Contracting Parties the descriptive sections of its draft written report, including a statement of the facts and a summary of the arguments made by the disputing Contracting Parties. The disputing Contracting Parties shall be afforded an opportunity to submit written comments on the descriptive sections within a period set by the panel.

Following the date set for receipt of comments from the Contracting Parties, the panel shall issue to the disputing Contracting Parties an interim written report, including both the descriptive sections and the panel's proposed findings and conclusions. Within a period set by the panel a disputing Contracting Party may submit to the panel a written request that the panel review specific aspects of the interim report before issuing a final report. Before issuing a final report the panel may, in its discretion, meet with the disputing Contracting Parties to consider the issues raised in such a request.

The final report shall include descriptive sections (including a statement of the facts and a summary of the arguments made by the disputing Contracting Parties), the panel's findings and conclusions, and a discussion of arguments made on specific aspects of the interim report at the stage of its review. The final report shall deal with every substantial issue raised before the panel and necessary to the resolution of the dispute and shall state the reasons for the panel's conclusions. A panel shall issue its final report by providing it promptly to the Secretariat and to the disputing Contracting Parties. The Secretariat shall at the earliest practicable opportunity distribute the final report, together with any written views that a disputing Contracting Party desires to have appended, to all Contracting Parties.

(b) Where a panel concludes that a measure introduced or maintained by a Contracting Party does not comply with a provision of Article 5 or 29 or with a provision of the GATT or a Related Instrument that applies under Article 29, the panel may recommend in its final report that the Contracting Party alter or abandon the measure or conduct so as to be in compliance with that provision.

(c) Panel reports shall be adopted by the Charter Conference. In order to provide sufficient time for the Charter Conference to consider panel reports, a report shall not be adopted by the Charter Conference until at least 30 days after it has been provided to all Contracting Parties by the Secretariat. Contracting Parties having objections to a panel report shall give written reasons for their objections to the Secretariat at least 10 days prior to the date on which the report is to be considered for adoption by the Charter Conference, and the Secretariat shall promptly provide them to all Contracting Parties. The disputing Contracting Parties and Contracting Parties which notified their interest in accordance with subparagraph (2)(b) shall have the right to participate fully in the consideration of the panel report on that dispute by the Charter Conference, and their views shall be fully recorded.

(d) In order to ensure effective resolution of disputes to the benefit of all Contracting Parties, prompt compliance with rulings and recommendations of a final panel report that has been adopted by the Charter Conference is essential. A Contracting Party which is subject to a ruling or recommendation of a final panel report that has been adopted by the Charter Conference shall inform the Charter Conference of its intentions regarding compliance with such ruling or recommendation. In the event that immediate compliance is impracticable, the Contracting Party concerned shall explain its reasons for non-compliance to the Charter Conference and, in light of this explanation, shall have a reasonable period of time to effect compliance. The aim of dispute resolution is the modification or removal of inconsistent measures.

(5) (a) Where a Contracting Party has failed within a reasonable period of time to comply with a ruling or recommendation of a final panel report that has been adopted by the Charter Conference, a Contracting Party to the dispute injured by such non-compliance may deliver to the non-complying Contracting Party a written request that the non-complying Contracting Party enter into negotiations with a view to agreeing upon mutually acceptable compensation. If so requested the non-complying Contracting Party shall promptly enter into such negotiations.

(b) If the non-complying Contracting Party refuses to negotiate, or if the Contracting Parties have not reached agreement within 30 days after delivery of the request for negotiations, the injured Contracting Party may make a written request for authorization of the Charter Conference to suspend obligations owed by it to the non-complying Contracting Party under Article 5 or 29.

(c) The Charter Conference may authorize the injured Contracting Party to suspend such of its obligations to the non-complying Contracting Party, under provisions of Article 5 or 29 or under provisions of the GATT or Related Instruments that apply under Article 29, as the injured Contracting Party considers equivalent in the circumstances.

(d) The suspension of obligations shall be temporary and shall be applied only until such time as the measure found to be inconsistent with Article 5 or 29 has been removed, or until a mutually satisfactory solution is reached.

(6) (a) Before suspending such obligations the injured Contracting Party shall inform the non-complying Contracting Party of the nature and level of its proposed suspension. If the non-complying Contracting Party delivers to the Secretary-General a written objection to the level of suspension of obligations proposed by the injured Contracting Party, the objection shall be referred to arbitration as provided below. The proposed suspension of obligations shall be stayed until the arbitration has been completed and the determination of the arbitral panel has become final and binding in accordance with subparagraph (e).

(b) The Secretary-General shall establish an arbitral panel in accordance with subparagraphs (2)(d) to (f), which if practicable shall be the same panel which made the ruling or recommendation referred to in subparagraph (4)(d), to examine the level of obligations that the injured Contracting Party proposes to suspend. Unless the Charter Conference decides otherwise the rules of procedure for panel proceedings shall be adopted in accordance with subparagraph (3)(a).

(c) The arbitral panel shall determine whether the level of obligations proposed to be suspended by the injured Contracting Party is excessive in relation to the injury it experienced, and if so, to what extent. It shall not review the nature of the obligations suspended, except insofar as this is inseparable from the determination of the level of suspended obligations.

(d) The arbitral panel shall deliver its written determination to the injured and the non-complying Contracting Parties and to the Secretariat within 60 days of the establishment of the panel or within such other period as may be agreed by the injured and the non-complying Contracting Parties. The Secretariat shall present the determination to the Charter Conference at the earliest practicable opportunity, and no later than the meeting of the Charter Conference following receipt of the determination.

(e) The determination of the arbitral panel shall become final and binding 30 days after the date of its presentation to the Charter Conference, and any level of suspension of benefits allowed thereby may thereupon be put into effect by the injured Contracting Party in such manner as that Contracting Party considers equivalent in the circumstances, unless prior to the expiration of the 30 days period the Charter Conference decides otherwise.

(f) In suspending any obligations to a non-complying Contracting Party, an injured Contracting Party shall make every effort not to affect adversely the trade of any other Contracting Party.

(7) Each Contracting Party may designate two individuals who shall, in the case of Contracting Parties which are also party to the GATT, if they are willing and able to serve as panellists under this Annex, be panellists currently nominated for the purpose of GATT dispute panels. The Secretary-General may also designate, with the approval of the Charter Conference, not more than ten individuals, who are willing and able to serve as panellists for purposes of dispute resolution in accordance with paragraphs (2) to (4). The Charter Conference may in addition decide to designate for the same purposes up to 20 individuals,

who serve on dispute settlement rosters of other international bodies, who are willing and able to serve as panellists. The names of all of the individuals so designated shall constitute the dispute settlement roster. Individuals shall be designated strictly on the basis of objectivity, reliability and sound judgement and, to the greatest extent possible, shall have expertise in international trade and energy matters, in particular as relates to provisions applicable under Article 29. In fulfilling any function under this Annex, designees shall not be affliated with or take instructions from any Contracting Party. Designees shall serve for renewable terms of five years and until their successors have been designated. A designee whose term expires shall continue to fulfil any function for which that individual has been chosen under this Annex. In the case of death, resignation or incapacity of a designee, the Contracting Party or the Secretary-General, whichever designated said designee, shall have the right to designate another individual to serve for the remainder of that designee's term, the designation by the Secretary-General being subject to approval of the Charter Conference.

(8) Notwithstanding the provisions contained in this Annex, Contracting Parties are encouraged to consult throughout the dispute resolution proceeding with a view to settling their dispute.

(9) The Charter Conference may appoint or designate other bodies or fora to perform any of the functions delegated in this Annex to the Secretariat and the Secretary-General.

Dispute Settlement Provisions in BITs and FTAs: Examples

43.a Treaty between the Federal Republic of Germany and Pakistan for the Promotion and Protection of Investments

Date: 25 November 1959
Source: 457 UNTS 23
http://treaties.un.org/doc/Publication/UNTS/Volume%20457/v457.pdf

The Federal Republic of Germany and Pakistan,

Desiring to intensify economic co-operation between the two States,

Intending to create favourable conditions for investments by nationals and companies of either State in the territory of the other State, and

Recognizing that an understanding reached between the two States likely to promote investment, encourage private industrial and financial enterprise and to create increase the prosperity of both of the States, have agreed as follows:

…

Article 8

(1) (a) The term "investment" shall compromise capital brought into the territory of the other party for investment in various forms in the shape of assets such as foreign exchange, goods, property rights, patents, and technical knowledge. The term "investment" shall also include returns derived from and ploughed back into such "investment".

(b) Any partnerships, companies or assets of similar kind, created by the utilisation of the above mentioned assets shall be regarded as "investment".

(2) The term "return" shall mean the amounts derived from investments as profits or interest in a specified period.

(3) The term "nationals" shall mean

(a) in respect of the Federal Republic of Germany, within the meaning of the Basic Law for the Federal Republic of Germany;

(b) in respect of Pakistan, a person who is a citizen of Pakistan according to its laws.

(4) The term "companies" shall comprise

(a) in respect of the Federal Republic of Germany, any juridical person, any commercial company or any other company or association, with or without legal personality, having seat in the territory of the Federal Republic of Germany and lawfully existing in accordance with its legislation, irrespective of whether the liability of its partners, associates or members is limited or unlimited and whether or not its activities are directed to pecuniary gain;

(b) in respect to Pakistan, any juridical person or company or association, incorporated in the territory of Pakistan and lawfully existing in accordance with its legislation.

…

Article 11

1. In the event of disputes as to the interpretation or application of the present treaty, the Parties shall enter into consultation for the purpose of finding a solution in the spirit of friendship.

2. If no such solution is forthcoming, the dispute shall be submitted

(a) To the International Court of Justice if both Parties so agree or

(b) If they do not so agree to an arbitration tribunal upon the request of either Party

3. (a) The Tribunal referred to in paragraph 2(b) above shall be formed in respect of each specific case and it shall consist of three arbitrators. Each Party shall appoint on arbitrator and the two members so appointed shall appoint a chairman who shall be a national of a third country.

(b) Each party shall appoint its arbitrator within two months after a request to this effect has been made by either Party. If either Party fails to comply with this obligation the arbitrator shall be appointed upon the request of the other Party by the President of the International Court of Justice.

(c) If within one month of the date of their appointment the arbitrators are unable to agree on the chairman of the arbitration tribunal such chairman shall be appointed upon the request of either Party by the President of the International Court of Justice.

(d) If the President of the International Court of Justice is prevented from acting upon a request under sub-paragraph (b) or (c) of the present paragraph or if the President is a national of either Party the Vice-President shall make the appointment. If the Vice-President is prevented or if he is a national of either Party the appointment shall be made by the seniormost member of the International Court of Justice who is not a national of either Party.

(e) Unless the Parties otherwise decide, the arbitration tribunal shall determine its own rules of procedure.

(f) The arbitration tribunal shall take its decision by a majority of votes. Such decision shall be binding upon the Parties and shall be carried out by them.

…

43.b Agreement between the Federal Republic of Germany and the Islamic Republic of Pakistan on the Encouragement and Reciprocal Protection of Investments

Date: 1 December 2009
Source: https://oxia.ouplaw.com/view/10.1093/law:iic/bt1582.regGroup.1/law-iic-bt1582?prd=IC

The Federal Republic of Germany
and
The Islamic Republic of Pakistan
Hereinafter referred to individually as "Contracting State" and collectively as "Contracting States",
Desiring to intensify economic co-operation between both States,
Intending to create favourable conditions for investments by investors of either State in the territory of the other State,
Recognizing that the encouragement and protection of such investments can stimulate private business initiative and increase the prosperity of both Contracting States,
Have agreed as follows:

Article 1 Definitions

For the purposes of this Agreement

(1) the term "investments" comprises every kind of asset, established or acquired by an investor of one Contracting State in the territory of the other Contracting State in accordance with the laws and regulations of the latter Contracting State, in particular:

(a) movable and immovable property, as well as other rights in rem, such as mortgages, liens and pledges;
(b) shares of companies and other kinds of interest in companies;
(c) claims to money or to any other performance having an economic value associated with an investment;
(d) intellectual property rights, in particular copyrights, patents, utility model patents, industrial designs, trade marks, trade names, trade and business secrets, technical processes, know how, and good will;
(e) business concessions under public law, including concessions to search for, extract and exploit natural resources;

any alteration of the form in which assets are invested shall not affect their classification as investment;

mere construction and service contracts that do not include an investment component do not fall under the definition of investment under this Agreement;

(2) the term "investor" means

(a) in respect of the Federal Republic of Germany:
- Germans within the meaning of the Basic Law of the Federal Republic of Germany,
- any juridical person as well as any commercial or other company or association With or without legal personality having its seat in the territory of the Federal Republic of Germany, irrespective of whether or not its activities are directed at profit,

(b) in respect of the Islamic Republic of Pakistan:
- Pakistanis within the meaning of the laws of the Islamic Republic of Pakistan,
- any juridical person or any company or association, incorporated in the territory of the Islamic Republic of Pakistan and lawfully existing in accordance with its legislation;

(3) The term "company" or "companies" of a Contracting State means corporations, firms and associations incorporated or constituted or established under the law in force in the territory of a Contracting State whether privately or state owned;

without prejudice to any other method of determining nationality, in particular any person in possession of a national passport issued by the competent authorities of the Contracting State concerned shall be deemed to be a national of that Contracting State;

(4) the term "returns" means the amount yielded by an investment for a definite period, such as profit, dividends, interest, royalties or fees;

(5) the term "territory" means the land and territorial sea as well as the exclusive economic zone and the continental shelf where a Contracting State exercises sovereign rights or jurisdiction in accordance with the provisions of international law and its domestic law.

...

Article 9 Settlement of Disputes between the Contracting States

(1) Any dispute between the Contracting States concerning the interpretation or application of this Agreement should as far as possible be settled by the governments of the two Contracting States.

(2) If the dispute cannot thus be settled, it shall upon the request of either Contracting State be submitted to an arbitration tribunal.

(3) Such arbitration tribunal shall be constituted ad hoc as follows: each Contracting State shall appoint one member, and these two members shall agree upon a national of a third State as their chairman to be appointed by the governments of the two Contracting States. Such members shall be appointed within two months, and such chairman within three months from the date on which either Contracting State has informed the other Contracting State that it intends to submit the dispute to an arbitration tribunal.

(4) If the periods specified in paragraph 3 above have not been observed, either Contracting State may, in the absence of any other arrangement, invite the President of the International Court of Justice to make the necessary appointments. If the President is a national of either Contracting State or if he is otherwise prevented from discharging the said function, the Vice-President should make the necessary appointments. If the Vice-President is a national of either Contracting State or if he, too, is prevented from discharging the said function, the member of the Court next in seniority who is not a national of either Contracting State should make the necessary appointments.

(5) The arbitration tribunal shall reach its decisions by a majority of votes. Such decisions shall be binding. Each Contracting State shall bear the cost of its own member and of its representatives in the arbitration proceedings. The cost of the chairman and the remaining costs shall be borne in equal parts by the Contracting States. The arbitration tribunal may make a different regulation concerning costs. In all other respects, the arbitration tribunal shall determine its own procedure.

Article 10 Settlement of Disputes between a Contracting State and an Investor of the other Contracting State

(1) Disputes arising from an investment between a Contracting State and an investor of the other Contracting State which concern an alleged breach of an obligation of a Contracting State under this Agreement should as far as possible be settled amicably between the parties in dispute.

(2) If the dispute cannot be settled within six months of the date when it has been raised in writing by one of the parties in dispute, it shall, at the request of the investor be submitted to:

(a) the competent court in the Contracting State in whose territory the investment has been made; or

(b) international arbitration under either:

- the Convention of 18 March 1965 on the Settlement of Investment Disputes between States and Nationals of Other States (ICSID), or
- the rules of arbitration of the United Nations Commission on International Trade Law (UNCITRAL), or
- the rules of arbitration of the International Chamber of Commerce (ICC), or
- any other form of dispute settlement agreed upon by the parties to the dispute.
- Each Contracting State herewith declares its acceptance of such international arbitral procedures.

(3) The award shall be binding and shall not be subject to any appeal or remedy other than those provided for in the said Convention. The award shall be enforced in accordance with domestic law.

(4) During arbitration proceedings or the enforcement of an award, the Contracting State involved in the dispute shall not raise the objection that the investor of the other Contracting State has received compensation under an insurance contract in respect of all or part of the damage.

(5) If a contract between an investor and a Contracting State provides a dispute resolution mechanism, the investor can invoke only that dispute resolution mechanism concerning the issues arising under that contract. However, in case of issues arising under this Agreement including Article 7 (2), he is entitled to utilize the dispute settlement procedures provided under this Article.

…

43.c Treaty between United States of America and the Argentine Republic Concerning the Reciprocal Encouragement and Protection of Investment

Date: 14 November 1991
Source: (1992) 31 ILM 124
https://docs.pca-cpa.org/2016/01/Treaty-Concerning-the-Reciprocal-Encouragement-and-Protection-of-Investment-Argentina-United-States-of-America.pdf

The United States of America and the Argentine Republic, hereinafter referred to as the Parties;

Desiring to promote greater economic cooperation between them, with respect to investment by nationals and companies of one Party in the territory of the other Party;

Recognizing that agreement upon the treatment to be accorded such investment will stimulate the flow of private capital and the economic development of the Parties;

Agreeing that fair and equitable treatment of investment is desirable in order to maintain a stable framework for investment and maximum effective use of economic resources;

Recognizing that the development of economic and business ties can contribute to the well-being of workers in both Parties and promote respect for internationally recognized worker rights; and having resolved to conclude a Treaty concerning the encouragement and reciprocal protection of investment;

Have agreed as follows:

ARTICLE I

1. For the purposes of this Treaty,

a) "investment" means every kind of investment in the territory of one Party owned or controlled directly or indirectly by nationals or companies of the other Party, such as equity, debt, and service and investment contracts; and includes without limitation:
   (i) tangible and intangible property, including rights, such as mortgages, liens and pledges;
   (ii) a company or shares of stock or other interests in a company or interests in the assets thereof;
   (iii) a claim to money or a claim to performance having economic value and directly related to an investment;
   (iv) intellectual property which includes, inter alia, rights relating to: literary and artistic works, including sound recordings, inventions in all fields of human endeavor, industrial designs, semiconductor mask works, trade secrets, know-how, and confidential business information, and trademarks, service marks, and trade names; and
   (v) any right conferred by law or contract, and any licenses and permits pursuant to law;

b) "company" of a Party means any kind of corporation, company, association, state enterprise, or other organization, legally constituted under the laws and regulations of a Party or a political subdivision thereof whether or not organized for pecuniary gain, and whether privately or governmentally owned;

c) "national" of a Party means a natural person who is a national of a Party under its applicable law;

...

ARTICLE VI

The Parties agree to consult promptly, on the request of either, to resolve any disputes in connection with the Treaty, or to discuss any matter relating to the interpretation or application of the Treaty.

ARTICLE VII

1. For purposes of this Article, an investment dispute is a dispute between a Party and a national or company of the other Party arising out of or relating to (a) an investment agreement between that Party and such national or company; (b) an investment authorization granted by that Party's foreign investment authority (if any such authorization exists) to such national or company; or (c) an alleged breach of any right conferred or created by this Treaty with respect to an investment.

2. In the event of an investment dispute, the parties to the dispute should initially seek a resolution through consultation and negotiation. If the dispute cannot be settled

amicably, the national or company concerned may choose to submit the dispute for resolution:

(a) to the courts or administrative tribunals of the Party that is a party to the dispute; or

(b) in accordance with any applicable, previously agreed dispute-settlement procedures; or

(c) in accordance with the terms of paragraph 3.

3. (a) Provided that the national or company concerned has not submitted the dispute for resolution under paragraph 2 (a) or (b) and that six months have elapsed from the date on which the dispute arose, the national or company concerned may choose to consent in writing to the submission of the dispute for settlement by binding arbitration:

(i) to the International Centre for the Settlement of Investment Disputes ("Centre") established by the Convention on the Settlement of Investment Disputes between States and Nationals of other States, done at Washington, March 18, 1965 ("ICSID Convention"), provided that the Party is a party to such convention: or

(ii) to the Additional Facility of the Centre, if the Centre is not available; or

(iii) in accordance with the Arbitration Rules of the United Nations Commission on International Trade Law (UNICTRAL): or

(iv) to any other arbitration institution, or in accordance with any other arbitration rules, as may be mutually agreed between the parties to the dispute.

(b) Once the national or company concerned has so consented, either party to the dispute may initiate arbitration in accordance with the choice so specified in the consent.

4. Each Party hereby consents to the submission of any investment dispute for settlement by binding arbitration in accordance with the choice specified in the written consent of the national or company under paragraph 3. Such consent, together with the written consent of the national or company when given under paragraph 3 shall satisfy the requirement for:

(a) written consent of the parties to the dispute for purposes of Chapter II of the ICSID Convention (Jurisdiction of the Centre) and for purposes of the Additional Facility Rules; and

(b) an "agreement in writing" for purposes of Article II of the United Nations Convention on the Recognition and Enforcement of Foreign Arbitral Awards, done at New York, June 10, 1958 ("New York Convention").

5. Any arbitration under paragraph 3(a)(ii), (iii) or (iv) of this Article shall be held in a state that is a party to the New York Convention.

6. Any arbitral award rendered pursuant to this Article shall be final and binding on the parties to the dispute. Each Party undertakes to carry out without delay the provisions of any such award and to provide in its territory for its enforcement.

7. In any proceeding involving an investment dispute, a Party shall not assert, as a defense, counterclaim, right of set-off or otherwise, that the national or company concerned has received or will receive, pursuant to an insurance or guarantee contract, indemnification or other compensation for all or part of its alleged damages.

8. For purposes of an arbitration held under paragraph 3 of this Article, any company legally constituted under the applicable laws and regulations of a Party or a political subdivision thereof but that, immediately before the occurrence of the event or events giving rise to the dispute, was an investment of nationals or companies of the other Party, shall be treated as a national or company of such other Party in accordance with Article 25(2)(b) of the ICSID Convention.

ARTICLE VIII

1. Any dispute between the Parties concerning the interpretation or application of the Treaty which is not resolved through consultations or other diplomatic channels, shall be submitted, upon the request of either Party, to an arbitral tribunal for binding decision in accordance with the applicable rules of international law. In the absence of an agreement by the Parties to the contrary, the arbitration rules of the United Nations Commission on International Trade Law (UNCITRAL), except to the extent modified by the Parties or by the arbitrators, shall govern.

2. Within two months of receipt of a request, each Party shall appoint an arbitrator. The two arbitrators shall select a third arbitrator as Chairman, who is a national of a third State. The UNCITRAL Rules for appointing members of three member panels shall apply mutatis mutandis to the appointment of the arbitral panel except that the appointing authority referenced in those rules shall be the Secretary General of the Permanent Court of Arbitration.

3. Unless otherwise agreed, all submissions shall be made and all hearings shall be completed within six months of the date of selection of the third arbitrator, and the Tribunal shall render its decisions within two months of the date of the final submissions or the date of the closing of the hearings, whichever is later.

4. Expenses incurred by the Chairman, the other arbitrators, and other costs of the proceedings shall be paid for equally by the Parties.

ARTICLE IX

The provisions of Article VII and VIII shall not apply to a dispute arising (a) under the export credit, guarantee or insurance programs of the Export-Import Bank of the United States or (b) under other official credit, guarantee or insurance arrangements pursuant to which the Parties have agreed to other means of settling disputes.

...

43.d United States Model Bilateral Investment Treaty

Date: 2012

Source: https://ustr.gov/sites/default/files/BIT%20text%20for%20ACIEP%20Meeting.pdf

TREATY BETWEEN THE GOVERNMENT OF THE UNITED STATES OF AMERICA AND THE GOVERNMENT OF [Country] CONCERNING THE ENCOURAGEMENT AND RECIPROCAL PROTECTION OF INVESTMENT

SECTION A

Article 1: Definitions

For purposes of this Treaty:

...

"investment" means every asset that an investor owns or controls, directly or indirectly, that has the characteristics of an investment, including such characteristics as the commitment of capital or other resources, the expectation of gain or profit, or the assumption of risk. Forms that an investment may take include:

(a) an enterprise;
(b) shares, stock, and other forms of equity participation in an enterprise;
(c) bonds, debentures, other debt instruments, and loans;[1]
(d) futures, options, and other derivatives;
(e) turnkey, construction, management, production, concession, revenue-sharing, and other similar contracts;
(f) intellectual property rights;
(g) licenses, authorizations, permits, and similar rights conferred pursuant to domestic law;[2] 2,[3] and
(h) other tangible or intangible, movable or immovable property, and related property rights, such as leases, mortgages, liens, and pledges.

"investment agreement" means a written agreement[4] between a national authority[5] of a Party and a covered investment or an investor of the other Party, on which the covered investment or the investor relies in establishing or acquiring a covered investment other than the written agreement itself, that grants rights to the covered investment or investor:

(a) with respect to natural resources that a national authority controls, such as for their exploration, extraction, refining, transportation, distribution, or sale;
(b) to supply services to the public on behalf of the Party, such as power generation or distribution, water treatment or distribution, or telecommunications; or
(c) to undertake infrastructure projects, such as the construction of roads, bridges, canals, dams, or pipelines, that are not for the exclusive or predominant use and benefit of the government.

...

SECTION B

Article 23: Consultation and Negotiation

In the event of an investment dispute, the claimant and the respondent should initially seek to resolve the dispute through consultation and negotiation, which may include the use of non-binding, third-party procedures.

[1] Some forms of debt, such as bonds, debentures, and long-term notes, are more likely to have the characteristics of an investment, while other forms of debt, such as claims to payment that are immediately due and result from the sale of goods or services, are less likely to have such characteristics.

[2] Whether a particular type of license, authorization, permit, or similar instrument (including a concession, to the extent that it has the nature of such an instrument) has the characteristics of an investment depends on such factors as the nature and extent of the rights that the holder has under the law of the Party. Among the licenses, authorizations, permits, and similar instruments that do not have the characteristics of an investment are those that do not create any rights protected under domestic law. For greater certainty, the foregoing is without prejudice to whether any asset associated with the license, authorization, permit, or similar instrument has the characteristics of an investment.

[3] The term "investment" does not include an order or judgment entered in a judicial or administrative action.

[4] "Written agreement" refers to an agreement in writing, executed by both parties, whether in a single instrument or in multiple instruments, that creates an exchange of rights and obligations, binding on both parties under the law applicable under Article 30[Governing Law](2). For greater certainty, (a) a unilateral act of an administrative or judicial authority, such as a permit, license, or authorization issued by a Party solely in its regulatory capacity, or a decree, order, or judgment, standing alone; and (b) an administrative or judicial consent decree or order, shall not be considered a written agreement.

[5] For purposes of this definition, "national authority" means (a) for the United States, an authority at the central level of government; and (b) for [Country], [].

Article 24: Submission of a Claim to Arbitration

1. In the event that a disputing party considers that an investment dispute cannot be settled by consultation and negotiation:

(a) the claimant, on its own behalf, may submit to arbitration under this Section a claim
 (i) that the respondent has breached
  (A) an obligation under Articles 3 through 10,
  (B) an investment authorization, or
  (C) an investment agreement;
 and
 (ii) that the claimant has incurred loss or damage by reason of, or arising out of, that breach; and

(b) the claimant, on behalf of an enterprise of the respondent that is a juridical person that the claimant owns or controls directly or indirectly, may submit to arbitration under this Section a claim
 (i) that the respondent has breached
  (A) an obligation under Articles 3 through 10,*
  (B) an investment authorization, or
  (C) an investment agreement;
 and
 (ii) that the enterprise has incurred loss or damage by reason of, or arising out of, that breach,

provided that a claimant may submit pursuant to subparagraph (a)(i)(C) or (b)(i)(C) a claim for breach of an investment agreement only if the subject matter of the claim and the claimed damages directly relate to the covered investment that was established or acquired, or sought to be established or acquired, in reliance on the relevant investment agreement.

2. At least 90 days before submitting any claim to arbitration under this Section, a claimant shall deliver to the respondent a written notice of its intention to submit the claim to arbitration ("notice of intent"). The notice shall specify:

(a) the name and address of the claimant and, where a claim is submitted on behalf of an enterprise, the name, address, and place of incorporation of the enterprise;
(b) for each claim, the provision of this Treaty, investment authorization, or investment agreement alleged to have been breached and any other relevant provisions;
(c) the legal and factual basis for each claim; and
(d) the relief sought and the approximate amount of damages claimed.

3. Provided that six months have elapsed since the events giving rise to the claim, a claimant may submit a claim referred to in paragraph 1:

(a) under the ICSID Convention and the ICSID Rules of Procedure for Arbitration Proceedings, provided that both the respondent and the non-disputing Party are parties to the ICSID Convention;
(b) under the ICSID Additional Facility Rules, provided that either the respondent or the non-disputing Party is a party to the ICSID Convention;

* N.B.: Articles 3-10 refer to substantive protections of investments under the Model BIT, namely national treatment, most favoured nation treatment, minimum standard of treatment, protection from expropriation, transfers, performance requirements, senior management and board of directors protection, and publication of laws and decisions respecting investment.

(c) under the UNCITRAL Arbitration Rules; or
(d) if the claimant and respondent agree, to any other arbitration institution or under any other arbitration rules.

4. A claim shall be deemed submitted to arbitration under this Section when the claimant's notice of or request for arbitration ("notice of arbitration"):

(a) referred to in paragraph 1 of Article 36 of the ICSID Convention is received by the Secretary-General;
(b) referred to in Article 2 of Schedule C of the ICSID Additional Facility Rules is received by the Secretary-General;
(c) referred to in Article 3 of the UNCITRAL Arbitration Rules, together with the statement of claim referred to in Article 18 of the UNCITRAL Arbitration Rules, are received by the respondent; or
(d) referred to under any arbitral institution or arbitral rules selected under paragraph 3(d) is received by the respondent.

A claim asserted by the claimant for the first time after such notice of arbitration is submitted shall be deemed submitted to arbitration under this Section on the date of its receipt under the applicable arbitral rules.

5. The arbitration rules applicable under paragraph 3, and in effect on the date the claim or claims were submitted to arbitration under this Section, shall govern the arbitration except to the extent modified by this Treaty.

6. The claimant shall provide with the notice of arbitration:

(a) the name of the arbitrator that the claimant appoints; or
(b) the claimant's written consent for the Secretary-General to appoint that arbitrator.

Article 25: Consent of Each Party to Arbitration

1. Each Party consents to the submission of a claim to arbitration under this Section in accordance with this Treaty.

2. The consent under paragraph 1 and the submission of a claim to arbitration under this Section shall satisfy the requirements of:

(a) Chapter II of the ICSID Convention (Jurisdiction of the Centre) and the ICSID Additional Facility Rules for written consent of the parties to the dispute; [and]
(b) Article II of the New York Convention for an "agreement in writing[."] [;" and
(c) Article I of the Inter-American Convention for an "agreement."]

Article 26: Conditions and Limitations on Consent of Each Party

1. No claim may be submitted to arbitration under this Section if more than three years have elapsed from the date on which the claimant first acquired, or should have first acquired, knowledge of the breach alleged under Article 24(1) and knowledge that the claimant (for claims brought under Article 24(1)(a)) or the enterprise (for claims brought under Article 24(1)(b)) has incurred loss or damage.

2. No claim may be submitted to arbitration under this Section unless:

(a) the claimant consents in writing to arbitration in accordance with the procedures set out in this Treaty; and
(b) the notice of arbitration is accompanied,
    (i) for claims submitted to arbitration under Article 24(1)(a), by the claimant's written waiver, and

(ii) for claims submitted to arbitration under Article 24(1)(b), by the claimant's and the enterprise's written waivers of any right to initiate or continue before any administrative tribunal or court under the law of either Party, or other dispute settlement procedures, any proceeding with respect to any measure alleged to constitute a breach referred to in Article 24.

3. Notwithstanding paragraph 2(b), the claimant (for claims brought under Article 24(1)(a)) and the claimant or the enterprise (for claims brought under Article 24(1)(b)) may initiate or continue an action that seeks interim injunctive relief and does not involve the payment of monetary damages before a judicial or administrative tribunal of the respondent, provided that the action is brought for the sole purpose of preserving the claimant's or the enterprise's rights and interests during the pendency of the arbitration.

Article 27: Selection of Arbitrators

1. Unless the disputing parties otherwise agree, the tribunal shall comprise three arbitrators, one arbitrator appointed by each of the disputing parties and the third, who shall be the presiding arbitrator, appointed by agreement of the disputing parties.

2. The Secretary-General shall serve as appointing authority for an arbitration under this Section.

3. Subject to Article 20(3), if a tribunal has not been constituted within 75 days from the date that a claim is submitted to arbitration under this Section, the Secretary-General, on the request of a disputing party, shall appoint, in his or her discretion, the arbitrator or arbitrators not yet appointed.

4. For purposes of Article 39 of the ICSID Convention and Article 7 of Schedule C to the ICSID Additional Facility Rules, and without prejudice to an objection to an arbitrator on a ground other than nationality:

(a) the respondent agrees to the appointment of each individual member of a tribunal established under the ICSID Convention or the ICSID Additional Facility Rules;

(b) a claimant referred to in Article 24(1)(a) may submit a claim to arbitration under this Section, or continue a claim, under the ICSID Convention or the ICSID Additional Facility Rules, only on condition that the claimant agrees in writing to the appointment of each individual member of the tribunal; and

(c) a claimant referred to in Article 24(1)(b) may submit a claim to arbitration under this Section, or continue a claim, under the ICSID Convention or the ICSID Additional Facility Rules, only on condition that the claimant and the enterprise agree in writing to the appointment of each individual member of the tribunal.

Article 28: Conduct of the Arbitration

1. The disputing parties may agree on the legal place of any arbitration under the arbitral rules applicable under Article 24(3). If the disputing parties fail to reach agreement, the tribunal shall determine the place in accordance with the applicable arbitral rules, provided that the place shall be in the territory of a State that is a party to the New York Convention.

2. The non-disputing Party may make oral and written submissions to the tribunal regarding the interpretation of this Treaty.

3. The tribunal shall have the authority to accept and consider *amicus curiae* submissions from a person or entity that is not a disputing party.

4. Without prejudice to a tribunal's authority to address other objections as a preliminary question, a tribunal shall address and decide as a preliminary question any objection by the

respondent that, as a matter of law, a claim submitted is not a claim for which an award in favor of the claimant may be made under Article 34.

(a) Such objection shall be submitted to the tribunal as soon as possible after the tribunal is constituted, and in no event later than the date the tribunal fixes for the respondent to submit its counter-memorial (or, in the case of an amendment to the notice of arbitration, the date the tribunal fixes for the respondent to submit its response to the amendment).

(b) On receipt of an objection under this paragraph, the tribunal shall suspend any proceedings on the merits, establish a schedule for considering the objection consistent with any schedule it has established for considering any other preliminary question, and issue a decision or award on the objection, stating the grounds therefor.

(c) In deciding an objection under this paragraph, the tribunal shall assume to be true claimant's factual allegations in support of any claim in the notice of arbitration (or any amendment thereof) and, in disputes brought under the UNCITRAL Arbitration Rules, the statement of claim referred to in Article 18 of the UNCITRAL Arbitration Rules. The tribunal may also consider any relevant facts not in dispute.

(d) The respondent does not waive any objection as to competence or any argument on the merits merely because the respondent did or did not raise an objection under this paragraph or make use of the expedited procedure set out in paragraph 5.

5. In the event that the respondent so requests within 45 days after the tribunal is constituted, the tribunal shall decide on an expedited basis an objection under paragraph 4 and any objection that the dispute is not within the tribunal's competence. The tribunal shall suspend any proceedings on the merits and issue a decision or award on the objection(s), stating the grounds therefor, no later than 150 days after the date of the request. However, if a disputing party requests a hearing, the tribunal may take an additional 30 days to issue the decision or award. Regardless of whether a hearing is requested, a tribunal may, on a showing of extraordinary cause, delay issuing its decision or award by an additional brief period, which may not exceed 30 days.

6. When it decides a respondent's objection under paragraph 4 or 5, the tribunal may, if warranted, award to the prevailing disputing party reasonable costs and attorney's fees incurred in submitting or opposing the objection. In determining whether such an award is warranted, the tribunal shall consider whether either the claimant's claim or the respondent's objection was frivolous, and shall provide the disputing parties a reasonable opportunity to comment.

7. A respondent may not assert as a defense, counterclaim, right of set-off, or for any other reason that the claimant has received or will receive indemnification or other compensation for all or part of the alleged damages pursuant to an insurance or guarantee contract.

8. A tribunal may order an interim measure of protection to preserve the rights of a disputing party, or to ensure that the tribunal's jurisdiction is made fully effective, including an order to preserve evidence in the possession or control of a disputing party or to protect the tribunal's jurisdiction. A tribunal may not order attachment or enjoin the application of a measure alleged to constitute a breach referred to in Article 24. For purposes of this paragraph, an order includes a recommendation.

9. (a) In any arbitration conducted under this Section, at the request of a disputing party, a tribunal shall, before issuing a decision or award on liability, transmit its proposed decision or award to the disputing parties and to the non-disputing Party. Within 60 days after the tribunal transmits its proposed decision or award,

the disputing parties may submit written comments to the tribunal concerning any aspect of its proposed decision or award. The tribunal shall consider any such comments and issue its decision or award not later than 45 days after the expiration of the 60-day comment period.

(b) Subparagraph (a) shall not apply in any arbitration conducted pursuant to this Section for which an appeal has been made available pursuant to paragraph 10 or Annex D.

10. If a separate, multilateral agreement enters into force between the Parties that establishes an appellate body for purposes of reviewing awards rendered by tribunals constituted pursuant to international trade or investment arrangements to hear investment disputes, the Parties shall strive to reach an agreement that would have such appellate body review awards rendered under Article 34 in arbitrations commenced after the multilateral agreement enters into force between the Parties.

Article 29: Transparency of Arbitral Proceedings

1. Subject to paragraphs 2 and 4, the respondent shall, after receiving the following documents, promptly transmit them to the non-disputing Party and make them available to the public:

(a) the notice of intent;

(b) the notice of arbitration;

(c) pleadings, memorials, and briefs submitted to the tribunal by a disputing party and any written submissions submitted pursuant to Article 28(2) [Non-Disputing Party submissions] and (3) [*Amicus* Submissions] and Article 33 [Consolidation];

(d) minutes or transcripts of hearings of the tribunal, where available; and

(e) orders, awards, and decisions of the tribunal.

2. The tribunal shall conduct hearings open to the public and shall determine, in consultation with the disputing parties, the appropriate logistical arrangements. However, any disputing party that intends to use information designated as protected information in a hearing shall so advise the tribunal. The tribunal shall make appropriate arrangements to protect the information from disclosure.

3. Nothing in this Section requires a respondent to disclose protected information or to furnish or allow access to information that it may withhold in accordance with Article 18 [Essential Security Article] or Article 19 [Disclosure of Information Article].

4. Any protected information that is submitted to the tribunal shall be protected from disclosure in accordance with the following procedures:

(a) Subject to subparagraph (d), neither the disputing parties nor the tribunal shall disclose to the non-disputing Party or to the public any protected information where the disputing party that provided the information clearly designates it in accordance with subparagraph (b);

(b) Any disputing party claiming that certain information constitutes protected information shall clearly designate the information at the time it is submitted to the tribunal;

(c) A disputing party shall, at the time it submits a document containing information claimed to be protected information, submit a redacted version of the document that does not contain the information. Only the redacted version shall be provided to the non-disputing Party and made public in accordance with paragraph 1; and

(d) The tribunal shall decide any objection regarding the designation of information claimed to be protected information. If the tribunal determines that such information was not properly designated, the disputing party that submitted the information may
  (i) withdraw all or part of its submission containing such information, or
  (ii) agree to resubmit complete and redacted documents with corrected designations in accordance with the tribunal's determination and subparagraph (c). In either case, the other disputing party shall, whenever necessary, resubmit complete and redacted documents which either remove the information withdrawn under (i) by the disputing party that first submitted the information or redesignate the information consistent with the designation under (ii) of the disputing party that first submitted the information.

5. Nothing in this Section requires a respondent to withhold from the public information required to be disclosed by its laws.

Article 30: Governing Law

1. Subject to paragraph 3, when a claim is submitted under Article 24(1)(a)(i)(A) or Article 24(1)(b)(i)(A), the tribunal shall decide the issues in dispute in accordance with this Treaty and applicable rules of international law.

2. Subject to paragraph 3 and the other terms of this Section, when a claim is submitted under Article 24(1)(a)(i)(B) or (C), or Article 24(1)(b)(i)(B) or (C), the tribunal shall apply:
(a) the rules of law specified in the pertinent investment authorization or investment agreement, or as the disputing parties may otherwise agree; or
(b) if the rules of law have not been specified or otherwise agreed:
  (i) the law of the respondent, including its rules on the conflict of laws;[6] and
  (ii) such rules of international law as may be applicable.

3. A joint decision of the Parties, each acting through its representative designated for purposes of this Article, declaring their interpretation of a provision of this Treaty shall be binding on a tribunal, and any decision or award issued by a tribunal must be consistent with that joint decision.

Article 31: Interpretation of Annexes

1. Where a respondent asserts as a defense that the measure alleged to be a breach is within the scope of an entry set out in Annex I, II, or III, the tribunal shall, on request of the respondent, request the interpretation of the Parties on the issue. The Parties shall submit in writing any joint decision declaring their interpretation to the tribunal within 60 days of delivery of the request.

2. A joint decision issued under paragraph 1 by the Parties, each acting through its representative designated for purposes of this Article, shall be binding on the tribunal, and any decision or award issued by the tribunal must be consistent with that joint decision. If the Parties fail to issue such a decision within 60 days, the tribunal shall decide the issue.

Article 32: Expert Reports

Without prejudice to the appointment of other kinds of experts where authorized by the applicable arbitration rules, a tribunal, at the request of a disputing party or, unless

[6] The "law of the respondent" means the law that a domestic court or tribunal of proper jurisdiction would apply in the same case.

the disputing parties disapprove, on its own initiative, may appoint one or more experts to report to it in writing on any factual issue concerning environmental, health, safety, or other scientific matters raised by a disputing party in a proceeding, subject to such terms and conditions as the disputing parties may agree.

Article 33: Consolidation

1. Where two or more claims have been submitted separately to arbitration under Article 24(1) and the claims have a question of law or fact in common and arise out of the same events or circumstances, any disputing party may seek a consolidation order in accordance with the agreement of all the disputing parties sought to be covered by the order or the terms of paragraphs 2 through 10.

2. A disputing party that seeks a consolidation order under this Article shall deliver, in writing, a request to the Secretary-General and to all the disputing parties sought to be covered by the order and shall specify in the request:

(a) the names and addresses of all the disputing parties sought to be covered by the order;

(b) the nature of the order sought; and

(c) the grounds on which the order is sought.

3. Unless the Secretary-General finds within 30 days after receiving a request under paragraph 2 that the request is manifestly unfounded, a tribunal shall be established under this Article.

4. Unless all the disputing parties sought to be covered by the order otherwise agree, a tribunal established under this Article shall comprise three arbitrators:

(a) one arbitrator appointed by agreement of the claimants;

(b) one arbitrator appointed by the respondent; and

(c) the presiding arbitrator appointed by the Secretary-General, provided, however, that the presiding arbitrator shall not be a national of either Party.

5. If, within 60 days after the Secretary-General receives a request made under paragraph 2, the respondent fails or the claimants fail to appoint an arbitrator in accordance with paragraph 4, the Secretary-General, on the request of any disputing party sought to be covered by the order, shall appoint the arbitrator or arbitrators not yet appointed. If the respondent fails to appoint an arbitrator, the Secretary-General shall appoint a national of the disputing Party, and if the claimants fail to appoint an arbitrator, the Secretary-General shall appoint a national of the non-disputing Party.

6. Where a tribunal established under this Article is satisfied that two or more claims that have been submitted to arbitration under Article 24(1) have a question of law or fact in common, and arise out of the same events or circumstances, the tribunal may, in the interest of fair and efficient resolution of the claims, and after hearing the disputing parties, by order:

(a) assume jurisdiction over, and hear and determine together, all or part of the claims;

(b) assume jurisdiction over, and hear and determine one or more of the claims, the determination of which it believes would assist in the resolution of the others; or

(c) instruct a tribunal previously established under Article 27 [Selection of Arbitrators] to assume jurisdiction over, and hear and determine together, all or part of the claims, provided that

(i) that tribunal, at the request of any claimant not previously a disputing party before that tribunal, shall be reconstituted with its original members, except that the arbitrator for the claimants shall be appointed pursuant to paragraphs 4(a) and 5; and
(ii) that tribunal shall decide whether any prior hearing shall be repeated.

7. Where a tribunal has been established under this Article, a claimant that has submitted a claim to arbitration under Article 24(1) and that has not been named in a request made under paragraph 2 may make a written request to the tribunal that it be included in any order made under paragraph 6, and shall specify in the request:

(a) the name and address of the claimant;
(b) the nature of the order sought; and
(c) the grounds on which the order is sought.

The claimant shall deliver a copy of its request to the Secretary-General.

8. A tribunal established under this Article shall conduct its proceedings in accordance with the UNCITRAL Arbitration Rules, except as modified by this Section.

9. A tribunal established under Article 27 [Selection of Arbitrators] shall not have jurisdiction to decide a claim, or a part of a claim, over which a tribunal established or instructed under this Article has assumed jurisdiction.

10. On application of a disputing party, a tribunal established under this Article, pending its decision under paragraph 6, may order that the proceedings of a tribunal established under Article 27 [Selection of Arbitrators] be stayed, unless the latter tribunal has already adjourned its proceedings.

Article 34: Awards

1. Where a tribunal makes a final award against a respondent, the tribunal may award, separately or in combination, only:

(a) monetary damages and any applicable interest; and
(b) restitution of property, in which case the award shall provide that the respondent may pay monetary damages and any applicable interest in lieu of restitution.

A tribunal may also award costs and attorney's fees in accordance with this Treaty and the applicable arbitration rules.

2. Subject to paragraph 1, where a claim is submitted to arbitration under Article 24(1)(b):

(a) an award of restitution of property shall provide that restitution be made to the enterprise;
(b) an award of monetary damages and any applicable interest shall provide that the sum be paid to the enterprise; and
(c) the award shall provide that it is made without prejudice to any right that any person may have in the relief under applicable domestic law.

3. A tribunal may not award punitive damages.

4. An award made by a tribunal shall have no binding force except between the disputing parties and in respect of the particular case.

5. Subject to paragraph 6 and the applicable review procedure for an interim award, a disputing party shall abide by and comply with an award without delay.

6. A disputing party may not seek enforcement of a final award until:

(a) in the case of a final award made under the ICSID Convention,
(i) 120 days have elapsed from the date the award was rendered and no disputing party has requested revision or annulment of the award; or

(ii) revision or annulment proceedings have been completed; and

(b) in the case of a final award under the ICSID Additional Facility Rules, the UNCITRAL Arbitration Rules, or the rules selected pursuant to Article 24(3)(d),

(i) 90 days have elapsed from the date the award was rendered and no disputing party has commenced a proceeding to revise, set aside, or annul the award; or

(ii) a court has dismissed or allowed an application to revise, set aside, or annul the award and there is no further appeal.

7. Each Party shall provide for the enforcement of an award in its territory.

8. If the respondent fails to abide by or comply with a final award, on delivery of a request by the non-disputing Party, a tribunal shall be established under Article 37 [State-State Dispute Settlement]. Without prejudice to other remedies available under applicable rules of international law, the requesting Party may seek in such proceedings:

(a) a determination that the failure to abide by or comply with the final award is inconsistent with the obligations of this Treaty; and

(b) a recommendation that the respondent abide by or comply with the final award.

9. A disputing party may seek enforcement of an arbitration award under the ICSID Convention or the New York Convention [or the Inter-American Convention] regardless of whether proceedings have been taken under paragraph 8.

10. A claim that is submitted to arbitration under this Section shall be considered to arise out of a commercial relationship or transaction for purposes of Article I of the New York Convention [and Article I of the Inter-American Convention].

44 Free Trade Agreement between the Government of New Zealand and the Government of the People's Republic of China

Date: 7 April 2008

Source: https://www.wipo.int/edocs/lexdocs/treaties/en/cn-nz/trt_cn_nz.pdf

Chapter 11 – Investment Section 1: Investment

Article 135 Definitions

For the purposes of this Chapter:

...

investment means every kind of asset invested, directly or indirectly, by the investors of a Party in the territory of the other Party including, but not limited to, the following:

a. movable and immovable property and other property rights such as mortgages and pledges;

b. shares, debentures, stock and any other kind of participation in companies;

c. claims to money or to any other contractual performance having an economic value associated with an investment;

d. intellectual property rights, in particular, copyrights, patents and industrial designs, trade-marks, trade-names, technical processes, trade and business secrets, know-how and good-will;

e. concessions conferred by law or under contract permitted by law, including concessions to search for, cultivate, extract or exploit natural resources;

f. bonds, including government issued bonds, debentures, loans other forms of debt,[1] and rights derived therefrom;

g. any right conferred by law or under contract and any licences and permits pursuant to law;

Any change in the form in which assets are invested does not affect their character as investments;

investments includes investments of legal persons of a third country which are owned or controlled by investors of one Party and which have been made in the territory of the other Party. The relevant provisions of this Agreement shall apply to such investments only when such third country has no right or abandons the right to claim compensation after the investments have been expropriated by the other Party;

investor of a Party means a natural person or enterprise of a Party who seeks to make, is making, or has made an investment in the territory of another Party[2]

...

Section 2: Investor – State Dispute Settlement

Article 152 Consultation and Negotiation

Any legal dispute arising under this Chapter between an investor of one Party and the other Party, directly concerning an investment by that investor in the territory of that other Party, shall, as far as possible, be settled amicably through consultations and negotiations between the investor and that other Party, which may include the use of non-binding third-party procedures, where this is acceptable to both parties to the dispute. A request for consultations and negotiations shall be made in writing and shall state the nature of the dispute.

Article 153 Consent to Submission of a Claim

1. If the dispute cannot be settled as provided for in Article 152 within 6 months from the date of request for consultations and negotiations then, unless the parties to the dispute agree otherwise, it shall, by the choice of the investor, be submitted to:

a. conciliation or arbitration by the International Centre for the Settlement of Investment Disputes ("ICSID") under the Convention on the Settlement of Disputes between States and Nationals of Other States, done at Washington on March 18, 1965; or

b. arbitration under the rules of the United Nations Commission on International Trade Law ("UNCITRAL");

provided that the investor shall give the state party 3 months' notice prior to submitting the claim to arbitration under paragraph 1(a) or 1(b).

2. Upon the receipt of a notice referred to in paragraph 1, the state party may require the investor concerned to go through any applicable domestic administrative review procedures specified by the laws and regulations of the state party, which may not exceed 3 months, before the submission of the claim to arbitration under paragraph 1(a) or 1(b).

[1] Loans and other forms of debt, which have been registered to the competent authority of a Party, do not mean trade debts where the debts would be non-interest earning if paid on time without penalty.

[2] For greater certainty, the elements of the definition of investor of a Party that relate to the establishment of investment are only applicable to Article 139 and Article 142. [N.B.: Articles 139-142 lay down rules on most-favoured nations treatment, performance requirements, non-conforming measures and transfers.]

3. In case a dispute has been submitted to a competent domestic court, it may be submitted to international dispute settlement, on the condition that the investor concerned has withdrawn its case from the domestic courts before a final judgment has been reached in the case.

4. The arbitration rules applicable under paragraph 1, and in effect on the date the claim or claims were submitted to arbitration under this Section, shall govern the arbitration except to the extent modified by this Section.

5. The arbitration award shall be final and binding upon both parties to the dispute. Each party shall commit itself to the enforcement of the award.

Article 154 Admissibility of Claims and Preliminary Objections

1. No claim may be submitted to arbitration under this Chapter if more than 3 years have elapsed between the time at which the disputing investor became aware, or should reasonably have become aware, of a breach of obligation under this Chapter causing loss or damage to the investor or its investments and the date of submission of the request for consultations and negotiations referred to in Article 152.

2. A state party may, no later than 30 days after the constitution of the tribunal, file an objection that a claim is manifestly without merit or is otherwise outside the jurisdiction or competence of the tribunal. The state party shall specify as precisely as possible the basis for the objection.

3. The tribunal shall address any such objection as a preliminary question apart from the merits of the claim. The parties shall be given a reasonable opportunity to present their views and observations to the tribunal. If the tribunal decides that the claim is manifestly without merit, or is otherwise not within the jurisdiction or competence of the tribunal, it shall render a decision to that effect.

4. The tribunal may, if warranted, award the prevailing party reasonable costs and fees incurred in submitting or opposing the objection. In determining whether such an award is warranted, the tribunal shall consider whether either the claim or the objection was frivolous or manifestly without merit, and shall provide the parties a reasonable opportunity to comment.

Article 155 Interpretation of Agreement

1. The tribunal shall, on request of the state party, request a joint interpretation of the Parties of any provision of this Agreement that is in issue in a dispute. The Parties shall submit in writing any joint decision declaring their interpretation to the tribunal within 60 days of delivery of the request.

2. A joint decision issued under paragraph 1 by the Parties shall be binding on the tribunal, and any award must be consistent with that joint decision. If the Parties fail to issue such a decision within 60 days, the tribunal shall decide the issue on its own account.

Article 156 Consolidation of Claims

Where two or more investors notify an intention to submit claims to arbitration which have a question of law or fact in common and arise out of the same events or circumstances, the disputing parties shall consult with a view to harmonising the procedures to apply, where all disputing parties agree to the consolidation of the claims, including with respect to the forum chosen to hear the dispute.

Article 157 Publication of Information and Documents Relating to Arbitral Proceedings

1. Subject to paragraph 2, the state party may, as it considers appropriate, ensure public availability of all tribunal documents.

2. Any information that is submitted to the tribunal and that is specifically designated as confidential information shall be protected from disclosure.

Article 158 Awards

1. Where a tribunal makes a final award against a state party, the tribunal may award, separately or in combination, only:

   a. monetary damages and any applicable interest;
   b. restitution of property, in which case the award shall provide that the state party may pay monetary damages and any applicable interest in lieu of restitution.

2. A tribunal may also award costs and fees in accordance with this Chapter and the applicable arbitration rules.

3. A tribunal may not award punitive damages.

4. An award made by a tribunal shall have no binding force except between the disputing parties and in respect of the particular case.

5. A disputing party may not seek enforcement of a final award until all applicable review procedures have been completed.

6. Subject to paragraph 5, a disputing party shall abide by and comply with an award without delay.

8 Regional (and Sub-Regional) Integration

The European Union Framework

45.a Treaty on European Union

Date: 13 December 2007
Source: Official Journal of the European Union 2008/C 115/01
https://eur-lex.europa.eu/legal-content/EN/TXT/?uri=celex%3A12012M%2FTXT

...

Article 19

1. The Court of Justice of the European Union shall include the Court of Justice, the General Court and specialised courts. It shall ensure that in the interpretation and application of the Treaties the law is observed.

Member States shall provide remedies sufficient to ensure effective legal protection in the fields covered by Union law.

2. The Court of Justice shall consist of one judge from each Member State. It shall be assisted by Advocates-General.

The General Court shall include at least one judge per Member State.

The Judges and Advocates-General of the Court of Justice and the Judges of the General Court shall be chosen from persons whose independence is beyond doubt and who satisfy the conditions set out in Articles 253 and 254 of the Treaty on the Functioning of the European Union. They shall be appointed by common accord of the governments of the Member States for six years. Retiring Judges and Advocates-General may be re-appointed.

3. The Court of Justice in the European Union shall, in accordance with the Treaties:

(a) rule on actions brought by a Member State, an institution or natural or legal person;

(b) give preliminary rulings, at the request of courts or tribunals of the Member States, on the interpretation of Union Law or the validity of acts adopted by the institutions;

(c) rule in other cases provided for in the Treaties.

Article 24 (ex Article 11 TEU)

1. The Union's competence in matters of common foreign and security policy shall cover all areas of foreign policy and all questions relating to the Union's security including the progressive framing of a common defence policy that might lead to a common defence.

The common foreign and security policy is subject to specific rules and procedures. It shall be defined and implemented by the European Council and the Council acting unanimously, except where the treaties provide otherwise. The adoption of legislative acts shall be excluded. The common foreign and security policy shall be put into effect by the High Representative of the Union for Foreign Affairs and Security Policy and by Member States, in accordance with Treaties. The Court of Justice of the European Union shall not have jurisdiction with respect to these provisions, with the exception of its jurisdiction to monitor compliance with Article 40 of this Treaty and to review the legality of certain decisions as provided for by the second paragraph of Article 275 of the Treaty on the Functioning of the European Union.

...

45.b Treaty on the Functioning of the European Union

Date: 13 December 2007
Source: Official Journal of the European Union 2008/C 115/47
https://eur-lex.europa.eu/legal-content/EN/TXT/HTML/?uri=CELEX:12012E/TXT&from=EN

...

Article 218

1. Without prejudice to the specific provisions laid down in Article 207 [dealing with the common commercial policy], agreements between the Union and third countries or international organisations shall be negotiated and concluded in accordance with the following procedure.

...

11. A Member State, the European Parliament, the Council or the Commission may obtain the opinion of the Court of Justice as to whether an agreement envisaged is compatible with the Treaties. Where the opinion of the court is so adverse, the agreement envisaged may not enter into force unless it is amended or the treaties are revised.

...

SECTION 5 – THE COURT OF JUSTICE OF THE EUROPEAN UNION

Article 251

The Court of Justice shall sit in chambers or in a Grand Chamber, in accordance with the rules laid down for that purpose in the Statute of the Court of Justice of the European Union.

When provided for in the Statute, the Court of Justice may also sit as a full Court.

Article 252

The Court of Justice shall be assisted by eight Advocates-General. Should the Court of Justice so request, the Council, acting unanimously, may increase the number of Advocates-General.

It shall be the duty of the Advocate-General, acting with complete impartiality and independence, to make, in open court, reasoned submissions on cases which, in accordance with the Statute of the Court of Justice of the European Union, require his involvement.

Article 253

The Judges and Advocates-General of the Court of Justice shall be chosen from persons whose independence is beyond doubt and who possess the qualifications required for appointment to the highest judicial offices in their respective countries or who are jurisconsults of recognised competence; they shall be appointed by common accord of the governments of the Member States for a term of six years, after consultation of the panel provided for in Article 255.

Every three years there shall be a partial replacement of the Judges and Advocates-General, in accordance with the conditions laid down in the Statute of the Court of Justice of the European Union.

The Judges shall elect the President of the Court of Justice from among their number for a term of three years. He may be re-elected.

Retiring Judges and Advocates-General may be reappointed.

The Court of Justice shall appoint its Registrar and lay down the rules governing his service.

The Court of Justice shall establish its Rules of Procedure. Those Rules shall require the approval of the Council.

Article 254

The number of Judges of the General Court shall be determined by the Statute of the Court of Justice of the European Union. The Statute may provide for the General Court to be assisted by Advocates-General.

The members of the General Court shall be chosen from persons whose independence is beyond doubt and who possess the ability required for appointment to high judicial office. They shall be appointed by common accord of the governments of the Member States for a term of six years, after consultation of the panel provided for in Article 255. The membership shall be partially renewed every three years. Retiring members shall be eligible for reappointment.

The Judges shall elect the President of the General Court from among their number for a term of three years. He may be re-elected.

The General Court shall appoint its Registrar and lay down the rules governing his service.

The General Court shall establish its Rules of Procedure in agreement with the Court of Justice. Those Rules shall require the approval of the Council.

Unless the Statute of the Court of Justice of the European Union provides otherwise, the provisions of the Treaties relating to the Court of Justice shall apply to the General Court.

Article 255

A panel shall be set up in order to give an opinion on candidates' suitability to perform the duties of Judge and Advocate-General of the Court of Justice and the General Court before the governments of the Member States make the appointments referred to in Articles 253 and 254.

The panel shall comprise seven persons chosen from among former members of the Court of Justice and the General Court, members of national supreme courts and lawyers of recognised competence, one of whom shall be proposed by the European Parliament. The Council shall adopt a decision establishing the panel's operating rules and a decision appointing its members. It shall act on the initiative of the President of the Court of Justice.

Article 256

1. The General Court shall have jurisdiction to hear and determine at first instance actions or proceedings referred to in Articles 263, 265, 268, 270 and 272, with the exception of those assigned to a specialised court set up under Article 257 and those reserved in the

Statute for the Court of Justice. The Statute may provide for the General Court to have jurisdiction for other classes of action or proceeding.

Decisions given by the General Court under this paragraph may be subject to a right of appeal to the Court of Justice on points of law only, under the conditions and within the limits laid down by the Statute.

2. The General Court shall have jurisdiction to hear and determine actions or proceedings brought against decisions of the specialised courts.

Decisions given by the General Court under this paragraph may exceptionally be subject to review by the Court of Justice, under the conditions and within the limits laid down by the Statute, where there is a serious risk of the unity or consistency of Union law being affected.

3. The General Court shall have jurisdiction to hear and determine questions referred for a preliminary ruling under Article 267, in specific areas laid down by the Statute.

Where the General Court considers that the case requires a decision of principle likely to affect the unity or consistency of Union law, it may refer the case to the Court of Justice for a ruling.

Decisions given by the General Court on questions referred for a preliminary ruling may exceptionally be subject to review by the Court of Justice, under the conditions and within the limits laid down by the Statute, where there is a serious risk of the unity or consistency of Union law being affected.

Article 257

The European Parliament and the Council, acting in accordance with the ordinary legislative procedure, may establish specialised courts attached to the General Court to hear and determine at first instance certain classes of action or proceeding brought in specific areas. The European Parliament and the Council shall act by means of regulations either on a proposal from the Commission after consultation of the Court of Justice or at the request of the Court of Justice after consultation of the Commission.

The regulation establishing a specialised court shall lay down the rules on the organisation of the court and the extent of the jurisdiction conferred upon it.

Decisions given by specialised courts may be subject to a right of appeal on points of law only or, when provided for in the regulation establishing the specialised court, a right of appeal also on matters of fact, before the General Court.

The members of the specialised courts shall be chosen from persons whose independence is beyond doubt and who possess the ability required for appointment to judicial office. They shall be appointed by the Council, acting unanimously.

The specialised courts shall establish their Rules of Procedure in agreement with the Court of Justice. Those Rules shall require the approval of the Council.

Unless the regulation establishing the specialised court provides otherwise, the provisions of the Treaties relating to the Court of Justice of the European Union and the provisions of the Statute of the Court of Justice of the European Union shall apply to the specialised courts. Title I of the Statute and Article 64 thereof shall in any case apply to the specialised courts.

Article 258

If the Commission considers that a Member State has failed to fulfil an obligation under the Treaties, it shall deliver a reasoned opinion on the matter after giving the State concerned the opportunity to submit its observations.

If the State concerned does not comply with the opinion within the period laid down by the Commission, the latter may bring the matter before the Court of Justice of the European Union.

Article 259

A Member State which considers that another Member State has failed to fulfil an obligation under the Treaties may bring the matter before the Court of Justice of the European Union.

Before a Member State brings an action against another Member State for an alleged infringement of an obligation under the Treaties, it shall bring the matter before the Commission.

The Commission shall deliver a reasoned opinion after each of the States concerned has been given the opportunity to submit its own case and its observations on the other party's case both orally and in writing.

If the Commission has not delivered an opinion within three months of the date on which the matter was brought before it, the absence of such opinion shall not prevent the matter from being brought before the Court.

Article 260

1. If the Court of Justice of the European Union finds that a Member State has failed to fulfil an obligation under the Treaties, the State shall be required to take the necessary measures to comply with the judgment of the Court.

2. If the Commission considers that the Member State concerned has not taken the necessary measures to comply with the judgment of the Court, it may bring the case before the Court after giving that State the opportunity to submit its observations. It shall specify the amount of the lump sum or penalty payment to be paid by the Member State concerned which it considers appropriate in the circumstances.

If the Court finds that the Member State concerned has not complied with its judgment it may impose a lump sum or penalty payment on it.

This procedure shall be without prejudice to Article 259.

3. When the Commission brings a case before the Court pursuant to Article 258 on the grounds that the Member State concerned has failed to fulfil its obligation to notify measures transposing a directive adopted under a legislative procedure, it may, when it deems appropriate, specify the amount of the lump sum or penalty payment to be paid by the Member State concerned which it considers appropriate in the circumstances.

If the Court finds that there is an infringement it may impose a lump sum or penalty payment on the Member State concerned not exceeding the amount specified by the Commission. The payment obligation shall take effect on the date set by the Court in its judgment.

Article 261

Regulations adopted jointly by the European Parliament and the Council, and by the Council, pursuant to the provisions of the Treaties, may give the Court of Justice of the European Union unlimited jurisdiction with regard to the penalties provided for in such regulations.

Article 262

Without prejudice to the other provisions of the Treaties, the Council, acting unanimously in accordance with a special legislative procedure and after consulting the European

Parliament, may adopt provisions to confer jurisdiction, to the extent that it shall determine, on the Court of Justice of the European Union in disputes relating to the application of acts adopted on the basis of the Treaties which create European intellectual property rights. These provisions shall enter into force after their approval by the Member States in accordance with their respective constitutional requirements.

Article 263

The Court of Justice of the European Union shall review the legality of legislative acts, of acts of the Council, of the Commission and of the European Central Bank, other than recommendations and opinions, and of acts of the European Parliament and of the European Council intended to produce legal effects *vis-à-vis* third parties. It shall also review the legality of acts of bodies, offices or agencies of the Union intended to produce legal effects *vis-à-vis* third parties.

It shall for this purpose have jurisdiction in actions brought by a Member State, the European Parliament, the Council or the Commission on grounds of lack of competence, infringement of an essential procedural requirement, infringement of the Treaties or of any rule of law relating to their application, or misuse of powers.

The Court shall have jurisdiction under the same conditions in actions brought by the Court of Auditors, by the European Central Bank and by the Committee of the Regions for the purpose of protecting their prerogatives.

Any natural or legal person may, under the conditions laid down in the first and second paragraphs, institute proceedings against an act addressed to that person or which is of direct and individual concern to them, and against a regulatory act which is of direct concern to them and does not entail implementing measures.

Acts setting up bodies, offices and agencies of the Union may lay down specific conditions and arrangements concerning actions brought by natural or legal persons against acts of these bodies, offices or agencies intended to produce legal effects in relation to them.

The proceedings provided for in this Article shall be instituted within two months of the publication of the measure, or of its notification to the plaintiff, or, in the absence thereof, of the day on which it came to the knowledge of the latter, as the case may be.

Article 264

If the action is well founded, the Court of Justice of the European Union shall declare the act concerned to be void.

However, the Court shall, if it considers this necessary, state which of the effects of the act which it has declared void shall be considered as definitive.

Article 265

Should the European Parliament, the European Council, the Council, the Commission or the European Central Bank, in infringement of the Treaties, fail to act, the Member States and the other institutions of the Union may bring an action before the Court of Justice of the European Union to have the infringement established. This Article shall apply, under the same conditions, to bodies, offices and agencies of the Union which fail to act.

The action shall be admissible only if the institution, body, office or agency concerned has first been called upon to act. If, within two months of being so called upon, the institution, body, office or agency concerned has not defined its position, the action may be brought within a further period of two months.

Any natural or legal person may, under the conditions laid down in the preceding paragraphs, complain to the Court that an institution, body, office or agency of the Union has failed to address to that person any act other than a recommendation or an opinion.

Article 266

The institution whose act has been declared void or whose failure to act has been declared contrary to the Treaties shall be required to take the necessary measures to comply with the judgment of the Court of Justice of the European Union.

This obligation shall not affect any obligation which may result from the application of the second paragraph of Article 340.*

Article 267

The Court of Justice of the European Union shall have jurisdiction to give preliminary rulings concerning:

(a) the interpretation of the Treaties;

(b) the validity and interpretation of acts of the institutions, bodies, offices or agencies of the Union;

Where such a question is raised before any court or tribunal of a Member State, that court or tribunal may, if it considers that a decision on the question is necessary to enable it to give judgment, request the Court to give a ruling thereon.

Where any such question is raised in a case pending before a court or tribunal of a Member State against whose decisions there is no judicial remedy under national law, that court or tribunal shall bring the matter before the Court.

If such a question is raised in a case pending before a court or tribunal of a Member State with regard to a person in custody, the Court of Justice of the European Union shall act with the minimum of delay.

Article 268

The Court of Justice of the European Union shall have jurisdiction in disputes relating to compensation for damage provided for in the second and third paragraphs of Article 340.**

Article 269

The Court of Justice shall have jurisdiction to decide on the legality of an act adopted by the European Council or by the Council pursuant to Article 7 of the Treaty on European Union*** solely at the request of the Member State concerned by a determination of the

* N.B.: Art 340, para. 2 provides: 'In the case of non-contractual liability, the Union shall, in accordance with the general principles common to the laws of the Member States, make good any damage caused by its institutions or by its servants in the performance of their duties.'

** N.B.: For Article 340, para. 2 see the last footnote. Article 340, para. 3: 'the European Central Bank shall, in accordance with the general principles common to the laws of the Member States, make good any damage caused by it or by its servants in the performance of their duties.'

*** N.B.: Article 7 TEU provides in its relevant parts: '1. On a reasoned proposal by one third of the Member States, by the European Parliament or by the European Commission, the Council, acting by a majority of four fifths of its members after obtaining the consent of the European Parliament, may determine that there is a clear risk of a serious breach by a Member State of the values referred to in Article 2. Before making such a determination, the Council shall hear the Member State in question and may address recommendations to it, acting in accordance

European Council or of the Council and in respect solely of the procedural stipulations contained in that Article.

Such a request must be made within one month from the date of such determination. The Court shall rule within one month from the date of the request.

Article 270

The Court of Justice of the European Union shall have jurisdiction in any dispute between the Union and its servants within the limits and under the conditions laid down in the Staff Regulations of Officials and the Conditions of Employment of other servants of the Union.

Article 271

The Court of Justice of the European Union shall, within the limits hereinafter laid down, have jurisdiction in disputes concerning:

(a) the fulfilment by Member States of obligations under the Statute of the European Investment Bank. In this connection, the Board of Directors of the Bank shall enjoy the powers conferred upon the Commission by Article 258;

(b) measures adopted by the Board of Governors of the European Investment Bank. In this connection, any Member State, the Commission or the Board of Directors of the Bank may institute proceedings under the conditions laid down in Article 263;

(c) measures adopted by the Board of Directors of the European Investment Bank. Proceedings against such measures may be instituted only by Member States or by the Commission, under the conditions laid down in Article 263, and solely on the grounds of non-compliance with the procedure provided for in Article 19(2), (5), (6) and (7) of the Statute of the Bank;

(d) the fulfilment by national central banks of obligations under the Treaties and the Statute of the ESCB and of the ECB. In this connection the powers of the Governing Council of the European Central Bank in respect of national central banks shall be the same as those conferred upon the Commission in respect of Member States by Article 258. If the Court finds that a national central bank has failed to fulfil an obligation under the Treaties, that bank shall be required to take the necessary measures to comply with the judgment of the Court.

Article 272

The Court of Justice of the European Union shall have jurisdiction to give judgment pursuant to any arbitration clause contained in a contract concluded by or on behalf of the Union, whether that contract be governed by public or private law.

with the same procedure. The Council shall regularly verify that the grounds on which such a determination was made continue to apply.

2. The European Council, acting by unanimity on a proposal by one third of the Member States or by the Commission and after obtaining the consent of the European Parliament, may determine the existence of a serious and persistent breach by a Member State of the values referred to in Article 2 [i.e. human dignity, freedom, democracy, equality, the rule of law and respect for human rights, including the rights of persons belonging to minorities], after inviting the Member State in question to submit its observations.

3. Where a determination under paragraph 2 has been made, the Council, acting by a qualified majority, may decide to suspend certain of the rights deriving from the application of the Treaties to the Member State in question, including the voting rights of the representative of the government of that Member State in the Council. In doing so, the Council shall take into account the possible consequences of such a suspension on the rights and obligations of natural and legal persons.'

Article 273

The Court of Justice shall have jurisdiction in any dispute between Member States which relates to the subject matter of the Treaties if the dispute is submitted to it under a special agreement between the parties.

Article 274

Save where jurisdiction is conferred on the Court of Justice of the European Union by the Treaties, disputes to which the Union is a party shall not on that ground be excluded from the jurisdiction of the courts or tribunals of the Member States.

Article 275

The Court of Justice of the European Union shall not have jurisdiction with respect to the provisions relating to the common foreign and security policy nor with respect to acts adopted on the basis of those provisions.

However, the Court shall have jurisdiction to monitor compliance with Article 40 of the Treaty on European Union and to rule on proceedings, brought in accordance with the conditions laid down in the fourth paragraph of Article 263 of this Treaty, reviewing the legality of decisions providing for restrictive measures against natural or legal persons adopted by the Council on the basis of Chapter 2 of Title V of the Treaty on European Union.

Article 276

In exercising its powers regarding the provisions of Chapters 4 and 5 of Title V of Part Three relating to the area of freedom, security and justice, the Court of Justice of the European Union shall have no jurisdiction to review the validity or proportionality of operations carried out by the police or other law-enforcement services of a Member State or the exercise of the responsibilities incumbent upon Member States with regard to the maintenance of law and order and the safeguarding of internal security.

Article 277

Notwithstanding the expiry of the period laid down in Article 263, sixth paragraph, any party may, in proceedings in which an act of general application adopted by an institution, body, office or agency of the Union is at issue, plead the grounds specified in Article 263, second paragraph, in order to invoke before the Court of Justice of the European Union the inapplicability of that act.

Article 278

Actions brought before the Court of Justice of the European Union shall not have suspensory effect. The Court may, however, if it considers that circumstances so require, order that application of the contested act be suspended.

Article 279

The Court of Justice of the European Union may in any cases before it prescribe any necessary interim measures.

Article 280

The judgments of the Court of Justice of the European Union shall be enforceable under the conditions laid down in Article 299.*

Article 281

The Statute of the Court of Justice of the European Union shall be laid down in a separate Protocol.

The European Parliament and the Council, acting in accordance with the ordinary legislative procedure, may amend the provisions of the Statute, with the exception of Title I and Article 64. The European Parliament and the Council shall act either at the request of the Court of Justice and after consultation of the Commission, or on a proposal from the Commission and after consultation of the Court of Justice.

...

Article 344

Member States undertake not to submit a dispute concerning the interpretation or application of Treaties to any method of settlement other than those provided for therein.

45.c Protocol (No 3) on the Statute of the Court of Justice of the European Union

Date: 13 December 2007
Source: Official Journal of the European Union 2008/C 115/210
https://curia.europa.eu/jcms/upload/docs/application/pdf/2016-08/tra-doc-en-div-c-0000-2016-201606984-05_00.pdf

THE HIGH CONTRACTING PARTIES,

DESIRING to lay down the Statute of the Court of Justice of the European Union provided for in Article 281 of the Treaty on the Functioning of the European Union,

HAVE AGREED UPON the following provisions, which shall be annexed to the Treaty on European Union, the Treaty on the Functioning of the European Union and the Treaty establishing the European Atomic Energy Community:

Article 1

The Court of Justice of the European Union shall be constituted and shall function in accordance with the provisions of the Treaties, of the Treaty establishing the European Atomic Energy Community (EAEC Treaty) and of this Statute.

* N.B.: Article 299 provides: 'Acts of the Council, the Commission or the European Central Bank which impose a pecuniary obligation on persons other than States, shall be enforceable. Enforcement shall be governed by the rules of civil procedure in force in the State in the territory of which it is carried out. The order for its enforcement shall be appended to the decision, without other formality than verification of the authenticity of the decision, by the national authority which the government of each Member State shall designate for this purpose and shall make known to the Commission and to the Court of Justice of the European Union.'

TITLE I – JUDGES AND ADVOCATES-GENERAL

Article 2

Before taking up his duties each Judge shall, before the Court of Justice sitting in open court, take an oath to perform his duties impartially and conscientiously and to preserve the secrecy of the deliberations of the Court.

Article 3

The Judges shall be immune from legal proceedings. After they have ceased to hold office, they shall continue to enjoy immunity in respect of acts performed by them in their official capacity, including words spoken or written.

The Court of Justice, sitting as a full Court, may waive the immunity. If the decision concerns a member of the General Court or of a specialised court, the Court shall decide after consulting the court concerned.

Where immunity has been waived and criminal proceedings are instituted against a Judge, he shall be tried, in any of the Member States, only by the court competent to judge the members of the highest national judiciary.

Articles 11 to 14 and Article 17 of the Protocol on the privileges and immunities of the European Union* shall apply to the Judges, Advocates-General, Registrar and Assistant Rapporteurs of the Court of Justice of the European Union, without prejudice to the provisions relating to immunity from legal proceedings of Judges which are set out in the preceding paragraphs.

Article 4

The Judges may not hold any political or administrative office.

They may not engage in any occupation, whether gainful or not, unless exemption is exceptionally granted by the Council, acting by a simple majority.

When taking up their duties, they shall give a solemn undertaking that, both during and after their term of office, they will respect the obligations arising therefrom, in particular the duty to behave with integrity and discretion as regards the acceptance, after they have ceased to hold office, of certain appointments or benefits.

Any doubt on this point shall be settled by decision of the Court of Justice. If the decision concerns a member of the General Court or of a specialised court, the Court shall decide after consulting the court concerned.

Article 5

Apart from normal replacement, or death, the duties of a Judge shall end when he resigns. Where a Judge resigns, his letter of resignation shall be addressed to the President of the Court of Justice for transmission to the President of the Council. Upon this notification a vacancy shall arise on the bench.

Save where Article 6 applies, a Judge shall continue to hold office until his successor takes up his duties.

Article 6

A Judge may be deprived of his office or of his right to a pension or other benefits in its stead only if, in the unanimous opinion of the Judges and Advocates-General of the Court

* N.B.: Protocol No 7 to the Treaties of the European Union (Official Journal of the European Union 2008/C 115/266).

of Justice, he no longer fulfils the requisite conditions or meets the obligations arising from his office. The Judge concerned shall not take part in any such deliberations. If the person concerned is a member of the General Court or of a specialised court, the Court shall decide after consulting the court concerned.

The Registrar of the Court shall communicate the decision of the Court to the President of the European Parliament and to the President of the Commission and shall notify it to the President of the Council.

In the case of a decision depriving a Judge of his office, a vacancy shall arise on the bench upon this latter notification.

Article 7

A Judge who is to replace a member of the Court whose term of office has not expired shall be appointed for the remainder of his predecessor's term.

Article 8

The provisions of Articles 2 to 7 shall apply to the Advocates-General.

TITLE II – ORGANISATION OF THE COURT OF JUSTICE

Article 9*

When, every three years, the Judges are partially replaced, one half of the number of Judges shall be replaced. If the number of Judges is an uneven number, the number of Judges who shall be replaced shall alternately be the number which is the next above one half of the number of Judges and the number which is next below one half.

The first paragraph shall also apply when the Advocates-General are partially replaced, every three years.

Article 10

The Registrar shall take an oath before the Court of Justice to perform his duties impartially and conscientiously and to preserve the secrecy of the deliberations of the Court of Justice.

Article 11

The Court of Justice shall arrange for replacement of the Registrar on occasions when he is prevented from attending the Court of Justice.

Article 12

Officials and other servants shall be attached to the Court of Justice to enable it to function. They shall be responsible to the Registrar under the authority of the President.

Article 13

At the request of the Court of Justice, the European Parliament and the Council may, acting in accordance with the ordinary legislative procedure, provide for the appointment

* N.B.: Article 9 was amended on 16 December 2015 by Regulation (EU, Euratom) 2015/2422 of the European Parliament and of the Council amending Protocol No 3 on the Statute of the Court of Justice of the European Union. Previous text:

When, every three years, the Judges are partially replaced, 14 and 13 Judges shall be replaced alternately.

When, every three years, the Advocates-General are partially replaced, four Advocates-General shall be replaced on each occasion.

of Assistant Rapporteurs and lay down the rules governing their service. The Assistant Rapporteurs may be required, under conditions laid down in the Rules of Procedure, to participate in preparatory inquiries in cases pending before the Court and to cooperate with the Judge who acts as Rapporteur.

The Assistant Rapporteurs shall be chosen from persons whose independence is beyond doubt and who possess the necessary legal qualifications; they shall be appointed by the Council, acting by a simple majority. They shall take an oath before the Court to perform their duties impartially and conscientiously and to preserve the secrecy of the deliberations of the Court.

Article 14

The Judges, the Advocates-General and the Registrar shall be required to reside at the place where the Court of Justice has its seat.

Article 15

The Court of Justice shall remain permanently in session. The duration of the judicial vacations shall be determined by the Court with due regard to the needs of its business.

Article 16

The Court of Justice shall form chambers consisting of three and five Judges. The Judges shall elect the Presidents of the chambers from among their number. The Presidents of the chambers of five Judges shall be elected for three years. They may be re-elected once.

The Grand Chamber shall consist of 13 Judges. It shall be presided over by the President of the Court. The Presidents of the chambers of five Judges and other Judges appointed in accordance with the conditions laid down in the Rules of Procedure shall also form part of the Grand Chamber.

The Court shall sit in a Grand Chamber when a Member State or an institution of the Union that is party to the proceedings so requests.

The Court shall sit as a full Court where cases are brought before it pursuant to Article 228(2), Article 245(2), Article 247 or Article 286(6) of the Treaty on the Functioning of the European Union.*

Moreover, where it considers that a case before it is of exceptional importance, the Court may decide, after hearing the Advocate-General, to refer the case to the full Court.

Article 17

Decisions of the Court of Justice shall be valid only when an uneven number of its members is sitting in the deliberations.

Decisions of the chambers consisting of either three or five Judges shall be valid only if they are taken by three Judges.

Decisions of the Grand Chamber shall be valid only if nine Judges are sitting. Decisions of the full Court shall be valid only if 15 Judges are sitting.

In the event of one of the Judges of a chamber being prevented from attending, a Judge of another chamber may be called upon to sit in accordance with conditions laid down in the Rules of Procedure.

* N.B.: These envisage sanctions applied against the European Ombudsman, members of the Commission, and members of the Court of Auditors, respectively.

Article 18

No Judge or Advocate-General may take part in the disposal of any case in which he has previously taken part as agent or adviser or has acted for one of the parties, or in which he has been called upon to pronounce as a member of a court or tribunal, of a commission of inquiry or in any other capacity.

If, for some special reason, any Judge or Advocate-General considers that he should not take part in the judgment or examination of a particular case, he shall so inform the President. If, for some special reason, the President considers that any Judge or Advocate-General should not sit or make submissions in a particular case, he shall notify him accordingly.

Any difficulty arising as to the application of this Article shall be settled by decision of the Court of Justice.

A party may not apply for a change in the composition of the Court or of one of its chambers on the grounds of either the nationality of a Judge or the absence from the Court or from the chamber of a Judge of the nationality of that party.

TITLE III – PROCEDURE BEFORE THE COURT OF JUSTICE

Article 19

The Member States and the institutions of the Union shall be represented before the Court of Justice by an agent appointed for each case; the agent may be assisted by an adviser or by a lawyer.

The States, other than the Member States, which are parties to the Agreement on the European Economic Area and also the EFTA Surveillance Authority referred to in that Agreement shall be represented in same manner.

Other parties must be represented by a lawyer.

Only a lawyer authorised to practise before a court of a Member State or of another State which is a party to the Agreement on the European Economic Area may represent or assist a party before the Court.

Such agents, advisers and lawyers shall, when they appear before the Court, enjoy the rights and immunities necessary to the independent exercise of their duties, under conditions laid down in the Rules of Procedure.

As regards such advisers and lawyers who appear before it, the Court shall have the powers normally accorded to courts of law, under conditions laid down in the Rules of Procedure.

University teachers being nationals of a Member State whose law accords them a right of audience shall have the same rights before the Court as are accorded by this Article to lawyers.

Article 20

The procedure before the Court of Justice shall consist of two parts: written and oral.

The written procedure shall consist of the communication to the parties and to the institutions of the Union whose decisions are in dispute, of applications, statements of case, defences and observations, and of replies, if any, as well as of all papers and documents in support or of certified copies of them.

Communications shall be made by the Registrar in the order and within the time laid down in the Rules of Procedure.

The oral procedure shall consist of the reading of the report presented by a Judge acting as Rapporteur, the hearing by the Court of agents, advisers and lawyers and of the submissions of the Advocate-General, as well as the hearing, if any, of witnesses and experts.

Where it considers that the case raises no new point of law, the Court may decide, after hearing the Advocate-General, that the case shall be determined without a submission from the Advocate-General.

Article 21

A case shall be brought before the Court of Justice by a written application addressed to the Registrar. The application shall contain the applicant's name and permanent address and the description of the signatory, the name of the party or names of the parties against whom the application is made, the subject-matter of the dispute, the form of order sought and a brief statement of the pleas in law on which the application is based.

The application shall be accompanied, where appropriate, by the measure the annulment of which is sought or, in the circumstances referred to in Article 265 of the Treaty on the Functioning of the European Union, by documentary evidence of the date on which an institution was, in accordance with those Articles, requested to act. If the documents are not submitted with the application, the Registrar shall ask the party concerned to produce them within a reasonable period, but in that event the rights of the party shall not lapse even if such documents are produced after the time limit for bringing proceedings.

Article 22

A case governed by Article 18 of the EAEC Treaty* shall be brought before the Court of Justice by an appeal addressed to the Registrar. The appeal shall contain the name and permanent address of the applicant and the description of the signatory, a reference to the decision against which the appeal is brought, the names of the respondents, the subject-matter of the dispute, the submissions and a brief statement of the grounds on which the appeal is based.

The appeal shall be accompanied by a certified copy of the decision of the Arbitration Committee which is contested.

If the Court rejects the appeal, the decision of the Arbitration Committee shall become final.

If the Court annuls the decision of the Arbitration Committee, the matter may be re-opened, where appropriate, on the initiative of one of the parties in the case, before the Arbitration Committee. The latter shall conform to any decisions on points of law given by the Court.

Article 23

In the cases governed by Article 267 of the Treaty on the Functioning of the European Union, the decision of the court or tribunal of a Member State which suspends its proceedings and refers a case to the Court of Justice shall be notified to the Court by the court or tribunal concerned. The decision shall then be notified by the Registrar of the Court to the parties, to the Member States and to the Commission, and to the institution, body, office or agency of the Union which adopted the act the validity or interpretation of which is in dispute.

Within two months of this notification, the parties, the Member States, the Commission and, where appropriate, the institution, body, office or agency which adopted the act the validity or interpretation of which is in dispute, shall be entitled to submit statements of case or written observations to the Court.

In the cases governed by Article 267 of the Treaty on the Functioning of the European Union, the decision of the national court or tribunal shall, moreover, be notified by the

* N.B.: Article 18 envisages appeals to the Court against decisions of the Arbitration Committee established by the EAEC Treaty.

Registrar of the Court to the States, other than the Member States, which are parties to the Agreement on the European Economic Area and also to the EFTA Surveillance Authority referred to in that Agreement which may, within two months of notification, where one of the fields of application of that Agreement is concerned, submit statements of case or written observations to the Court.

Where an agreement relating to a specific subject matter, concluded by the Council and one or more non-member States, provides that those States are to be entitled to submit statements of case or written observations where a court or tribunal of a Member State refers to the Court of Justice for a preliminary ruling a question falling within the scope of the agreement, the decision of the national court or tribunal containing that question shall also be notified to the non-member States concerned. Within two months from such notification, those States may lodge at the Court statements of case or written observations.

Article 23a

The Rules of Procedure may provide for an expedited or accelerated procedure and, for references for a preliminary ruling relating to the area of freedom, security and justice, an urgent procedure.

Those procedures may provide, in respect of the submission of statements of case or written observations, for a shorter period than that provided for by Article 23, and, in derogation from the fourth paragraph of Article 20, for the case to be determined without a submission from the Advocate General.

In addition, the urgent procedure may provide for restriction of the parties and other interested persons mentioned in Article 23, authorised to submit statements of case or written observations and, in cases of extreme urgency, for the written stage of the procedure to be omitted.

Article 24

The Court of Justice may require the parties to produce all documents and to supply all information which the Court considers desirable. Formal note shall be taken of any refusal. The Court may also require the Member States and institutions, bodies, offices and agencies not being parties to the case to supply all information which the Court considers necessary for the proceedings.

Article 25

The Court of Justice may at any time entrust any individual, body, authority, committee or other organisation it chooses with the task of giving an expert opinion.

Article 26

Witnesses may be heard under conditions laid down in the Rules of Procedure.

Article 27

With respect to defaulting witnesses the Court of Justice shall have the powers generally granted to courts and tribunals and may impose pecuniary penalties under conditions laid down in the Rules of Procedure.

Article 28

Witnesses and experts may be heard on oath taken in the form laid down in the Rules of Procedure or in the manner laid down by the law of the country of the witness or expert.

Article 29

The Court of Justice may order that a witness or expert be heard by the judicial authority of his place of permanent residence.

The order shall be sent for implementation to the competent judicial authority under conditions laid down in the Rules of Procedure. The documents drawn up in compliance with the letters rogatory shall be returned to the Court under the same conditions.

The Court shall defray the expenses, without prejudice to the right to charge them, where appropriate, to the parties.

Article 30

A Member State shall treat any violation of an oath by a witness or expert in the same manner as if the offence had been committed before one of its courts with jurisdiction in civil proceedings. At the instance of the Court of Justice, the Member State concerned shall prosecute the offender before its competent court.

Article 31

The hearing in court shall be public, unless the Court of Justice, of its own motion or on application by the parties, decides otherwise for serious reasons.

Article 32

During the hearings the Court of Justice may examine the experts, the witnesses and the parties themselves. The latter, however, may address the Court of Justice only through their representatives.

Article 33

Minutes shall be made of each hearing and signed by the President and the Registrar.

Article 34

The case list shall be established by the President.

Article 35

The deliberations of the Court of Justice shall be and shall remain secret.

Article 36

Judgments shall state the reasons on which they are based. They shall contain the names of the Judges who took part in the deliberations.

Article 37

Judgments shall be signed by the President and the Registrar. They shall be read in open court.

Article 38

The Court of Justice shall adjudicate upon costs.

Article 39

The President of the Court of Justice may, by way of summary procedure, which may, in so far as necessary, differ from some of the rules contained in this Statute and which shall be laid down in the Rules of Procedure, adjudicate upon applications to suspend execution, as provided for in Article 278 of the Treaty on the Functioning of the European Union and Article 157 of the EAEC Treaty, or to prescribe interim measures pursuant to Article 279 of the Treaty on the Functioning of the European Union, or to suspend enforcement in accordance with the fourth paragraph of Article 299 of the Treaty on the Functioning of the European Union or the third paragraph of Article 164 of the EAEC Treaty.

Should the President be prevented from attending, his place shall be taken by another Judge under conditions laid down in the Rules of Procedure.

The ruling of the President or of the Judge replacing him shall be provisional and shall in no way prejudice the decision of the Court on the substance of the case.

Article 40

Member States and institutions of the Union may intervene in cases before the Court of Justice.

The same right shall be open to the bodies, offices and agencies of the Union and to any other person which can establish an interest in the result of a case submitted to the Court. Natural or legal persons shall not intervene in cases between Member States, between institutions of the Union or between Member States and institutions of the Union.

Without prejudice to the second paragraph, the States, other than the Member States, which are parties to the Agreement on the European Economic Area, and also the EFTA Surveillance Authority referred to in that Agreement, may intervene in cases before the Court where one of the fields of application of that Agreement is concerned.

An application to intervene shall be limited to supporting the form of order sought by one of the parties.

Article 41

Where the defending party, after having been duly summoned, fails to file written submissions in defence, judgment shall be given against that party by default. An objection may be lodged against the judgment within one month of it being notified. The objection shall not have the effect of staying enforcement of the judgment by default unless the Court of Justice decides otherwise.

Article 42

Member States, institutions, bodies, offices and agencies of the Union and any other natural or legal persons may, in cases and under conditions to be determined by the Rules of Procedure, institute third-party proceedings to contest a judgment rendered without their being heard, where the judgment is prejudicial to their rights.

Article 43

If the meaning or scope of a judgment is in doubt, the Court of Justice shall construe it on application by any party or any institution of the Union establishing an interest therein.

Article 44

An application for revision of a judgment may be made to the Court of Justice only on discovery of a fact which is of such a nature as to be a decisive factor, and which, when the judgment was given, was unknown to the Court and to the party claiming the revision. The revision shall be opened by a judgment of the Court expressly recording the existence of a new fact, recognising that it is of such a character as to lay the case open to revision and declaring the application admissible on this ground.

No application for revision may be made after the lapse of 10 years from the date of the judgment.

Article 45

Periods of grace based on considerations of distance shall be determined by the Rules of Procedure.

No right shall be prejudiced in consequence of the expiry of a time limit if the party concerned proves the existence of unforeseeable circumstances or of *force majeure*.

Article 46

Proceedings against the Union in matters arising from non-contractual liability shall be barred after a period of five years from the occurrence of the event giving rise thereto. The period of limitation shall be interrupted if proceedings are instituted before the Court of Justice or if prior to such proceedings an application is made by the aggrieved party to the relevant institution of the Union. In the latter event the proceedings must be instituted within the period of two months provided for in Article 263 of the Treaty on the Functioning of the European Union; the provisions of the second paragraph of Article 265 of the Treaty on the Functioning of the European Union shall apply where appropriate.

This Article shall also apply to proceedings against the European Central Bank regarding non- contractual liability.

TITLE IV – GENERAL COURT

Article 47

The first paragraph of Article 9, Articles 14 and 15, the first, second, fourth and fifth paragraphs of Article 17 and Article 18 shall apply to the General Court and its members.

The fourth paragraph of Article 3 and Articles 10, 11 and 14 shall apply to the Registrar of the General Court *mutatis mutandis*.

Article 48*

The General Court shall consist of:

(a) 40 Judges as from 25 December 2015;

(b) 47 Judges as from 1 September 2016;

(c) two Judges per Member State as from 1 September 2019.

Article 49

The Members of the General Court may be called upon to perform the task of an Advocate-General.

It shall be the duty of the Advocate-General, acting with complete impartiality and independence, to make, in open court, reasoned submissions on certain cases brought before the General Court in order to assist the General Court in the performance of its task. The criteria for selecting such cases, as well as the procedures for designating the Advocates-General, shall be laid down in the Rules of Procedure of the General Court.

A Member called upon to perform the task of Advocate-General in a case may not take part in the judgment of the case.

* Article 48 was amended on 16 December 2015 by Regulation (EU, Euratom) 2015/2422 of the European Parliament and of the Council amending Protocol No 3 on the Statute of the Court of Justice of the European Union. Previous text:

The General Court shall consist of 27 Judges.

Article 50

The General Court shall sit in chambers of three or five Judges. The Judges shall elect the Presidents of the chambers from among their number. The Presidents of the chambers of five Judges shall be elected for three years. They may be re-elected once.

The composition of the chambers and the assignment of cases to them shall be governed by the Rules of Procedure. In certain cases governed by the Rules of Procedure, the General Court may sit as a full court or be constituted by a single Judge.

The Rules of Procedure may also provide that the General Court may sit in a Grand Chamber in cases and under the conditions specified therein.

Article 51

By way of derogation from the rule laid down in Article 256(1) of the Treaty on the Functioning of the European Union, jurisdiction shall be reserved to the Court of Justice in the actions referred to in Articles 263 and 265 of the Treaty on the Functioning of the European Union when they are brought by a Member State against:

(a) an act of or failure to act by the European Parliament or the Council, or by those institutions acting jointly, except for:
- — decisions taken by the Council under the third subparagraph of Article 108(2) of the Treaty on the Functioning of the European Union [declaring aid to be compatible with the internal market];
- — acts of the Council adopted pursuant to a Council regulation concerning measures to protect trade within the meaning of Article 207 of the Treaty on the Functioning of the European Union [common commercial policy];
- — acts of the Council by which the Council exercises implementing powers in accordance with the second paragraph of Article 291 of the Treaty on the Functioning of the European Union [where uniform conditions for implementing legally binding Union acts are needed];

(b) against an act of or failure to act by the Commission under the first paragraph of Article 331 of the Treaty on the Functioning of the European Union [confirmation of a Member State's participation in enhanced cooperation].

Jurisdiction shall also be reserved to the Court of Justice in the actions referred to in the same Articles when they are brought by an institution of the Union against an act of or failure to act by the European Parliament, the Council, both those institutions acting jointly, or the Commission, or brought by an institution of the Union against an act of or failure to act by the European Central Bank.

Article 52

The President of the Court of Justice and the President of the General Court shall determine, by common accord, the conditions under which officials and other servants attached to the Court of Justice shall render their services to the General Court to enable it to function. Certain officials or other servants shall be responsible to the Registrar of the General Court under the authority of the President of the General Court.

Article 53

The procedure before the General Court shall be governed by Title III.

Such further and more detailed provisions as may be necessary shall be laid down in its Rules of Procedure. The Rules of Procedure may derogate from the fourth paragraph of

Article 40 and from Article 41 in order to take account of the specific features of litigation in the field of intellectual property.

Notwithstanding the fourth paragraph of Article 20, the Advocate-General may make his reasoned submissions in writing.

Article 54

Where an application or other procedural document addressed to the General Court is lodged by mistake with the Registrar of the Court of Justice, it shall be transmitted immediately by that Registrar to the Registrar of the General Court; likewise, where an application or other procedural document addressed to the Court of Justice is lodged by mistake with the Registrar of the General Court, it shall be transmitted immediately by that Registrar to the Registrar of the Court of Justice.

Where the General Court finds that it does not have jurisdiction to hear and determine an action in respect of which the Court of Justice has jurisdiction, it shall refer that action to the Court of Justice; likewise, where the Court of Justice finds that an action falls within the jurisdiction of the General Court, it shall refer that action to the General Court, whereupon that Court may not decline jurisdiction.

Where the Court of Justice and the General Court are seised of cases in which the same relief is sought, the same issue of interpretation is raised or the validity of the same act is called in question, the General Court may, after hearing the parties, stay the proceedings before it until such time as the Court of Justice has delivered judgment or, where the action is one brought pursuant to Article 263 of the Treaty on the Functioning of the European Union, may decline jurisdiction so as to allow the Court of Justice to rule on such actions. In the same circumstances, the Court of Justice may also decide to stay the proceedings before it; in that event, the proceedings before the General Court shall continue.

Where a Member State and an institution of the Union are challenging the same act, the General Court shall decline jurisdiction so that the Court of Justice may rule on those applications.

Article 55

Final decisions of the General Court, decisions disposing of the substantive issues in part only or disposing of a procedural issue concerning a plea of lack of competence or inadmissibility, shall be notified by the Registrar of the General Court to all parties as well as all Member States and the institutions of the Union even if they did not intervene in the case before the General Court.

Article 56

An appeal may be brought before the Court of Justice, within two months of the notification of the decision appealed against, against final decisions of the General Court and decisions of that Court disposing of the substantive issues in part only or disposing of a procedural issue concerning a plea of lack of competence or inadmissibility.

Such an appeal may be brought by any party which has been unsuccessful, in whole or in part, in its submissions. However, interveners other than the Member States and the institutions of the Union may bring such an appeal only where the decision of the General Court directly affects them.

With the exception of cases relating to disputes between the Union and its servants, an appeal may also be brought by Member States and institutions of the Union which did not intervene in the proceedings before the General Court. Such Member States and institutions shall be in the same position as Member States or institutions which intervened at first instance.

Article 57

Any person whose application to intervene has been dismissed by the General Court may appeal to the Court of Justice within two weeks from the notification of the decision dismissing the application.

The parties to the proceedings may appeal to the Court of Justice against any decision of the General Court made pursuant to Article 278 or Article 279 or the fourth paragraph of Article 299 of the Treaty on the Functioning of the European Union or Article 157 or the third paragraph of Article 164 of the EAEC Treaty within two months from their notification.

The appeal referred to in the first two paragraphs of this Article shall be heard and determined under the procedure referred to in Article 39.

Article 58

An appeal to the Court of Justice shall be limited to points of law. It shall lie on the grounds of lack of competence of the General Court, a breach of procedure before it which adversely affects the interests of the appellant as well as the infringement of Union law by the General Court.

No appeal shall lie regarding only the amount of the costs or the party ordered to pay them.

Article 59

Where an appeal is brought against a decision of the General Court, the procedure before the Court of Justice shall consist of a written part and an oral part. In accordance with conditions laid down in the Rules of Procedure, the Court of Justice, having heard the Advocate-General and the parties, may dispense with the oral procedure.

Article 60

Without prejudice to Articles 278 and 279 of the Treaty on the Functioning of the European Union or Article 157 of the EAEC Treaty, an appeal shall not have suspensory effect.

By way of derogation from Article 280 of the Treaty on the Functioning of the European Union, decisions of the General Court declaring a regulation to be void shall take effect only as from the date of expiry of the period referred to in the first paragraph of Article 56 of this Statute or, if an appeal shall have been brought within that period, as from the date of dismissal of the appeal, without prejudice, however, to the right of a party to apply to the Court of Justice, pursuant to Articles 278 and 279 of the Treaty on the Functioning of the European Union or Article 157 of the EAEC Treaty, for the suspension of the effects of the regulation which has been declared void or for the prescription of any other interim measure.

Article 61

If the appeal is well founded, the Court of Justice shall quash the decision of the General Court. It may itself give final judgment in the matter, where the state of the proceedings so permits, or refer the case back to the General Court for judgment.

Where a case is referred back to the General Court, that Court shall be bound by the decision of the Court of Justice on points of law.

When an appeal brought by a Member State or an institution of the Union, which did not intervene in the proceedings before the General Court, is well founded, the Court of Justice may, if it considers this necessary, state which of the effects of the decision of the General Court which has been quashed shall be considered as definitive in respect of the parties to the litigation.

Article 62

In the cases provided for in Article 256(2) and (3) of the Treaty on the Functioning of the European Union, where the First Advocate-General considers that there is a serious risk of the unity or consistency of Union law being affected, he may propose that the Court of Justice review the decision of the General Court.

The proposal must be made within one month of delivery of the decision by the General Court. Within one month of receiving the proposal made by the First Advocate-General, the Court of Justice shall decide whether or not the decision should be reviewed.

Article 62a

The Court of Justice shall give a ruling on the questions which are subject to review by means of an urgent procedure on the basis of the file forwarded to it by the General Court.

Those referred to in Article 23 of this Statute and, in the cases provided for in Article 256(2) of the EC Treaty, the parties to the proceedings before the General Court shall be entitled to lodge statements or written observations with the Court of Justice relating to questions which are subject to review within a period prescribed for that purpose. The Court of Justice may decide to open the oral procedure before giving a ruling.

Article 62b

In the cases provided for in Article 256(2) of the Treaty on the Functioning of the European Union, without prejudice to Articles 278 and 279 of the Treaty on the Functioning of the European Union, proposals for review and decisions to open the review procedure shall not have suspensory effect. If the Court of Justice finds that the decision of the General Court affects the unity or consistency of Union law, it shall refer the case back to the General Court which shall be bound by the points of law decided by the Court of Justice; the Court of Justice may state which of the effects of the decision of the General Court are to be considered as definitive in respect of the parties to the litigation. If, however, having regard to the result of the review, the outcome of the proceedings flows from the findings of fact on which the decision of the General Court was based, the Court of Justice shall give final judgment.

In the cases provided for in Article 256(3) of the Treaty on the Functioning of the European Union, in the absence of proposals for review or decisions to open the review procedure, the answer(s) given by the General Court to the questions submitted to it shall take effect upon expiry of the periods prescribed for that purpose in the second paragraph of Article 62. Should a review procedure be opened, the answer(s) subject to review shall take effect following that procedure, unless the Court of Justice decides otherwise. If the Court of Justice finds that the decision of the General Court affects the unity or consistency of Union law, the answer given by the Court of Justice to the questions subject to review shall be substituted for that given by the General Court.

TITLE IVa – SPECIALISED COURTS

Article 62c

The provisions relating to the jurisdiction, composition, organisation and procedure of the specialised courts established under Article 257 of the Treaty on the Functioning of the European Union are set out in an Annex to this Statute.

TITLE V – FINAL PROVISIONS

Article 63

The Rules of Procedure of the Court of Justice and of the General Court shall contain any provisions necessary for applying and, where required, supplementing this Statute.

Article 64

The rules governing the language arrangements applicable at the Court of Justice of the European Union shall be laid down by a regulation of the Council acting unanimously. This regulation shall be adopted either at the request of the Court of Justice and after consultation of the Commission and the European Parliament, or on a proposal from the Commission and after consultation of the Court of Justice and of the European Parliament. Until those rules have been adopted, the provisions of the Rules of Procedure of the Court of Justice and of the Rules of Procedure of the General Court governing language arrangements shall continue to apply. By way of derogation from Articles 253 and 254 of the Treaty on the Functioning of the European Union, those provisions may only be amended or repealed with the unanimous consent of the Council.

Annex I – THE EUROPEAN UNION CIVIL SERVICE TRIBUNAL

[not included]

45.d Agreement on the withdrawal of the United Kingdom of Great Britain and Northern Ireland from the European Union and the European Atomic Energy Community

Date: 12 November 2019
Source: Official Journal of the European Union
https://eur-lex.europa.eu/legal-content/EN/TXT/HTML/?uri=CELEX:12019W/TXT(02)&from=EN#d1e8217-1-1

PART SIX
INSTITUTIONAL AND FINAL PROVISIONS
TITLE III
DISPUTE SETTLEMENT

Article 167 Cooperation

The Union and the United Kingdom shall at all times endeavour to agree on the interpretation and application of this Agreement, and shall make every attempt, through cooperation and consultations, to arrive at a mutually satisfactory resolution of any matter that might affect its operation.

Article 168 Exclusivity

For any dispute between the Union and the United Kingdom arising under this Agreement, the Union and the United Kingdom shall only have recourse to the procedures provided for in this Agreement.

Article 169 Consultations and communications within the Joint Committee

1. The Union and the United Kingdom shall endeavour to resolve any dispute regarding the interpretation and application of the provisions of this Agreement by entering into consultations in the Joint Committee in good faith, with the aim of reaching a mutually agreed solution. A party wishing to commence consultations shall provide written notice to the Joint Committee.

2. Any communication or notification between the Union and the United Kingdom provided for in this Title shall be made within the Joint Committee.

Article 170 Initiation of the arbitration procedure

1. Without prejudice to Article 160, if no mutually agreed solution has been reached within 3 months after a written notice has been provided to the Joint Committee in accordance with Article 169(1), the Union or the United Kingdom may request the establishment of an arbitration panel. Such request shall be made in writing to the other party and to the International Bureau of the Permanent Court of Arbitration. The request shall identify the subject matter of the dispute to be brought before the arbitration panel and a summary of the legal arguments in support of the request.

2. The Union and the United Kingdom may agree that the establishment of an arbitration panel may be requested before the expiry of the time limit laid down in paragraph 1.

Article 171 Establishment of the arbitration panel

1. The Joint Committee shall, no later than by the end of the transition period, establish a list of 25 persons who are willing and able to serve as members of an arbitration panel. To that end, the Union and the United Kingdom shall each propose ten persons. The Union and the United Kingdom shall also jointly propose five persons to act as chairperson of the arbitration panel. The Joint Committee shall ensure that the list complies with these requirements at any moment in time.

2. The list established pursuant to paragraph 1 shall only comprise persons whose independence is beyond doubt, who possess the qualifications required for appointment to the highest judicial office in their respective countries or who are jurisconsults of recognised competence, and who possess specialised knowledge or experience of Union law and public international law. That list shall not comprise persons who are members, officials or other servants of the Union institutions, of the government of a Member State, or of the government of the United Kingdom.

3. An arbitration panel shall be composed of five members.

4. Within 15 days of the date of a request in accordance with Article 170, the panel shall be established in accordance with paragraphs 5 and 6.

5. The Union and the United Kingdom shall each nominate two members from among the persons on the list established under paragraph 1. The chairperson shall be selected by consensus by the members of the panel from the persons jointly nominated by the Union and the United Kingdom to serve as a chairperson.

In the event that the members of the panel are unable to agree on the selection of the chairperson within the time limit laid down in paragraph 4, the Union or the United Kingdom may request the Secretary-General of the Permanent Court of Arbitration to select the chairperson by lot from among the persons jointly proposed by the Union and the United Kingdom to act as chairperson.

6. The Secretary-General of the Permanent Court of Arbitration shall make the selection referred to in second subparagraph of paragraph 5 within 5 days of the request referred to in paragraph 5. Representatives of the Union and of the United Kingdom shall be entitled to be present at the selection.

7. The date of establishment of the arbitration panel shall be the date on which the selection procedure is completed.

8. In the event that the list referred to in paragraph 1 has not been established by expiry of the time limit laid down in paragraph 4, the Union and the United Kingdom shall within 5 days each nominate two persons to serve as members of the panel. If persons have been proposed under paragraph 1, the nominations shall be made from among those persons. The chairperson shall then be appointed in accordance with the procedure set out in paragraph 5. In the event that the Union and the United Kingdom have not, within a further 5 days, jointly proposed at least one person to serve as chairperson, the Secretary-General of the Permanent Court of Arbitration shall within five days, after consultation with the Union and the United Kingdom, propose a chairperson who fulfils the requirements of paragraph 2. Unless either the Union or the United Kingdom objects to that proposal within 5 days, the person proposed by the Secretary-General of the Permanent Court of Arbitration shall be appointed.

9. In the event of failure to establish an arbitration panel within 3 months from the date of the request made pursuant to Article 170, the Secretary-General of the Permanent Court of Arbitration shall, upon request by either the Union or the United Kingdom, within 15 days of such request, after consultation with the Union and the United Kingdom, appoint persons who fulfil the requirements of paragraph 2 of this Article to constitute the arbitration panel.

Article 172 Rules of procedure

Dispute settlement procedures set out in this Title shall be governed by the rules of procedure set out in Part A of Annex IX ("Rules of Procedure"), the Joint Committee shall keep the functioning of those dispute settlement procedures under constant review and may amend the Rules of Procedure.

Article 173 Time-frame of the procedure before the arbitration panel

1. The arbitration panel shall notify its ruling to the Union, the United Kingdom and the Joint Committee within 12 months from the date of establishment of the arbitration panel. Where the arbitration panel considers that it cannot comply with this time limit, its chairperson shall notify the Union and the United Kingdom in writing, stating the reasons for the delay and the date on which the panel intends to conclude its work.

2. Within 10 days of the establishment of the arbitration panel the Union or the United Kingdom may submit a reasoned request to the effect that the case is urgent. In that case, the arbitration panel shall give a ruling on the urgency within 15 days from the receipt of such request. If it has determined the urgency of the case, the arbitration panel shall make every effort to notify its ruling to the Union and the United Kingdom within 6 months from the date of its establishment.

Article 174 Disputes raising questions of Union law

1. Where a dispute submitted to arbitration in accordance with this Title raises a question of interpretation of a concept of Union law, a question of interpretation of a provision of Union law referred to in this Agreement or a question of whether the United Kingdom has complied with its obligations under Article 89(2), the arbitration panel shall not decide on any such question. In such case, it shall request the Court of Justice of the European Union to give a ruling on the question. The Court of Justice of the European Union shall have jurisdiction to give such a ruling which shall be binding on the arbitration panel.

The arbitration panel shall make the request referred to in the first subparagraph after having heard the parties.

2. Without prejudice to the first sentence of the first subparagraph of paragraph 1, if the Union or the United Kingdom considers that a request in accordance with paragraph 1 is to be made, it may make submissions to the arbitration panel to that effect. In such case, the arbitration panel shall submit the request in accordance with paragraph 1 unless the question raised does not concern the interpretation of a concept of Union law, interpretation of a provision of Union law referred to in this Agreement, or does not concern whether the United Kingdom has complied with its obligations under Article 89(2). The arbitration panel shall provide reasons for its assessment. Within 10 days following the assessment, either party may request the arbitration panel to review its assessment, and a hearing shall be organised within 15 days of the request for the parties to be heard on the matter. The arbitration panel shall provide reasons for its assessment.

3. In the cases referred to in paragraphs 1 and 2, the time limits laid down in Article 173 shall be suspended until the Court of Justice of the European Union has given its ruling. The arbitration panel shall not be required to give its ruling less than 60 days from the date on which the Court of Justice of the European Union has given its ruling.

4. The first subparagraph of Article 161(2) and Article 161(3) shall apply mutatis mutandis to the procedures brought before the Court of Justice of the European Union in accordance with this Article.

Article 175 Compliance with the arbitration panel ruling

The arbitration panel ruling shall be binding on the Union and the United Kingdom. The Union and the United Kingdom shall take any measures necessary to comply in good faith with the arbitration panel ruling and shall endeavour to agree on the period of time to comply with the ruling in accordance with the procedure in Article 176.

Article 176 Reasonable period of time for compliance

1. No later than 30 days after the notification of the arbitration panel ruling to the Union and the United Kingdom, the respondent shall, if the panel has ruled in favour of the complainant, notify the complainant of the time it considers it will require for compliance (the "reasonable period of time").

2. If there is disagreement between the Union and the United Kingdom on the reasonable period of time to comply with the arbitration panel ruling, the complainant shall, within 40 days of the notification by the respondent under paragraph 1, request the original arbitration panel in writing to determine the length of the reasonable period of time. Such request shall be notified simultaneously to the respondent. The arbitration panel shall notify its decision on the period for compliance to the Union and the United Kingdom within 40 days of the date of submission of the request.

3. In the event of the original arbitration panel, or some of its members, being unable to reconvene to consider a request under paragraph 2, a new arbitration panel shall be established as set out in Article 171. The time limit for notifying the decision shall be 60 days from the date of establishment of the new arbitration panel.

4. The respondent shall inform the complainant in writing of its progress in complying with the arbitration panel ruling referred to in Article 173 at least 1 month before the expiry of the reasonable period of time.

5. The reasonable period of time may be extended by mutual agreement of the Union and the United Kingdom.

Article 177 Review of any measure taken to comply with the arbitration panel ruling

1. The respondent shall notify the complainant before the end of the reasonable period of time of any measure that it has taken to comply with the arbitration panel ruling.

2. If, at the end of the reasonable period, the complainant considers that the respondent has failed to comply with the arbitration panel ruling referred to in Article 173, the complainant may request the original arbitration panel in writing to rule on the matter. The arbitration panel shall notify its ruling to the Union and the United Kingdom within 90 days of the date of submission of the request.

3. In the event of the original arbitration panel, or some of its members, being unable to reconvene to consider a request under paragraph 2, a new arbitration panel shall be established as set out in Article 171. The time limit for notifying the ruling shall be 60 days from the date of establishment of the new arbitration panel.

4. Where a case referred to the arbitration panel pursuant to paragraph 2 raises a question of interpretation of a concept of Union law or a question of interpretation of a provision of Union law referred to in this Agreement, Article 174 shall apply mutatis mutandis.

Article 178 Temporary remedies in case of non-compliance

1. If the arbitration panel rules in accordance with Article 177(2) that the respondent has failed to comply with the arbitration panel ruling referred to in Article 173, at the request of the complainant it may impose a lump sum or penalty payment to be paid to the complainant. In determining the lump sum or penalty payment, the arbitration panel shall take into account the seriousness of the non-compliance and underlying breach of obligation, the duration of the non-compliance and underlying breach of obligation.

2. If, 1 month after the arbitration panel ruling referred to in paragraph 1, the respondent has failed to pay any lump sum or penalty payment imposed on it, or if, 6 months after the arbitration panel ruling referred to in Article 177(2), the respondent persists in not complying with the arbitration panel ruling referred to in Article 173, the complainant shall be entitled, upon notification to the respondent, to suspend obligations arising from:

(a) any provision of this Agreement other than those contained in Part Two; or

(b) parts of any other agreement between the Union and the United Kingdom under the conditions set out in that agreement.

The notification shall specify the provisions which the complainant intends to suspend. Before deciding to suspend parts of an agreement referred to in point (b) the complainant shall first consider whether the suspension of the provision of this Agreement in accordance with point (a) would be an appropriate response to the breach. Any suspension shall be proportionate to the breach of obligation concerned, taking into account the gravity of the breach and the rights in question and, where the suspension is based on the fact that the respondent persists in not complying with the arbitration panel ruling referred to in Article 173, whether a penalty payment has been imposed on the respondent and has been paid or is still being paid by the latter.

The complainant may implement the suspension at any moment but not earlier than 10 days after the date of the notification, unless the respondent has requested arbitration under paragraph 3.

3. If the respondent considers that the extent of the suspension set out in the notification referred to in paragraph 2 is not proportionate, it may request the original arbitration panel in writing to rule on the matter. Such request shall be notified to the complainant before the expiry of the 10-day period referred to in paragraph 2. The arbitration panel shall notify its ruling to the Union and the United Kingdom within 60 days of the date of submission of the request. Obligations shall not be suspended until the arbitration panel has notified its ruling, and any suspension shall be consistent with the arbitration panel ruling.

4. In the event of the original arbitration panel, or some of its members, being unable to reconvene to consider a request under paragraph 2, a new arbitration panel shall be established as set out in Article 171. In such cases, the period for notifying the ruling shall be 90 days from the date of establishment of the new arbitration panel.

5. The suspension of obligations shall be temporary and shall be applied only until any measure found to be inconsistent with the provisions of this Agreement has been withdrawn or amended, so as to achieve conformity with the provisions of this Agreement, or until the Union and the United Kingdom have agreed to otherwise settle the dispute.

Article 179 Review of any measure taken after temporary remedies

1. Where the complainant has suspended obligations in accordance with Article 178 or where the arbitration panel has imposed a penalty payment on the respondent in accordance with Article 178(1), the respondent shall notify the complainant of any measure it has taken to comply with the ruling of the arbitration panel and of its request for an end to the suspension of obligations applied by the complainant or to the penalty payment.

2. If the Union and the United Kingdom do not reach an agreement on whether the notified measure brings the respondent into conformity with the provisions of this Agreement within 45 days of the date of submission of the notification, either party may request the original arbitration panel in writing to rule on the matter. Such request shall be notified simultaneously to the other party. The arbitration panel ruling shall be notified to the Union and the United Kingdom and to the Joint Committee within 75 days of the date of submission of the request.

If the arbitration panel rules that the respondent has brought itself into conformity with this Agreement, or if the complainant does not, within 45 days of the submission of the notification referred to in paragraph 1, request that the original arbitration panel rule on the matter:

(a) the suspension of obligations shall be terminated within 15 days of either the ruling of the arbitration panel or the end of the 45-day period;

(b) the penalty payment shall be terminated on the day after either the ruling of the arbitration panel or the end of the 45-day period.

3. In the event of the original arbitration panel, or some of its members, being unable to reconvene to consider a request under paragraph 2, a new arbitration panel shall be established as set out in Article 171. The period for notifying the ruling shall in that case be 90 days from the date of establishment of the new arbitration panel.

4. Where a case referred to the arbitration panel pursuant to paragraph 2 raises a question of interpretation of a concept of Union law or a question of interpretation of a provision of Union law referred to in this Agreement, Article 174 shall apply mutatis mutandis.

Article 180 Arbitration panel decisions and rulings

1. The arbitration panel shall make every effort to take decisions by consensus. Where, nevertheless, a decision cannot be arrived at by consensus, the matter at issue shall be decided by majority vote. However, in no case dissenting opinions of members of an arbitration panel shall be published.

2. Any ruling of the arbitration panel shall be binding on the Union and the United Kingdom. The ruling shall set out the findings of fact, the applicability of the relevant provisions of this Agreement, and the reasoning behind any findings and conclusions. The Union and the United Kingdom shall make the arbitration panel rulings and decisions publicly available in their entirety, subject to the protection of confidential information.

Article 181 Members of an arbitration panel

1. The members of an arbitration panel shall be independent, shall serve in their individual capacity and shall not take instructions from any organisation or government, and shall comply with the Code of Conduct set out in Part B of Annex IX. The Joint Committee may amend that Code of Conduct.

2. The members of an arbitration panel shall, as from the establishment thereof, enjoy immunity from legal proceedings in the Union and the United Kingdom with respect to acts performed by them in the exercise of their functions on that arbitration panel.

45.e Trade and Cooperation – Agreement between the European Union and the European Atomic Energy Community, of the one part, and the United Kingdom of Great Britain and Northern Ireland, of the other part

Date: 30 April 2021
Source: Official Journal of the European Union
https://eur-lex.europa.eu/legal-content/EN/TXT/HTML/?uri=CELEX:22021A0430(01)&from=EN

PART SIX
DISPUTE SETTLEMENT AND HORIZONTAL PROVISIONS
TITLE I
DISPUTE SETTLEMENT
CHAPTER 1 GENERAL PROVISIONS

Article 734 Objective

The objective of this Title is to establish an effective and efficient mechanism for avoiding and settling disputes between the Parties concerning the interpretation and application of this Agreement and supplementing agreements with a view to reaching, where possible, a mutually agreed solution.

Article 735 Scope

1. This Title applies, subject to paragraphs 2, 3, 4 and 5, to disputes between the Parties concerning the interpretation and application of the provisions of this Agreement or of any supplementing agreement ("covered provisions").

2. The covered provisions shall include all provisions of this Agreement and of any supplementing agreement with the exception of:

(a) Article 32(1) to (6) and Article 36;
(b) Annex 12;
(c) Title VII of Heading one of Part Two;
(d) Title X of Heading One of Part Two;
(e) Article 355(1), (2) and (4), Article 356(1) and (3), Chapter 2 of Title XI of Heading One of Part Two, Articles 371 and 372, Chapter 5 of Title XI of Heading One of Part Two, and Article 411(4) to (9);
(f) Part Three, including when applying in relation to situations governed by other provisions of this Agreement;
(g) Part Four;
(h) Title II of Part Six;
(i) Article 782; and
(j) the Agreement on security procedures for exchanging and protecting classified information.

3. The Partnership Council may be seized by a Party with a view to resolving a dispute with respect to obligations arising from the provisions referred to in paragraph 2.

4. Article 736 applies to the provisions referred to in paragraph 2 of this Article.

5. Notwithstanding paragraphs 1 and 2, this Title shall not apply with respect to disputes concerning the interpretation and application of the provisions of the Protocol on Social Security Coordination or its annexes in individual cases.

Article 736 Exclusivity

The Parties undertake not to submit a dispute between them regarding the interpretation or application of provisions of this Agreement or of any supplementing agreement to a mechanism of settlement other than those provided for in this Agreement.

Article 737 Choice of forum in case of a substantially equivalent obligation under another international agreement

1. If a dispute arises regarding a measure allegedly in breach of an obligation under this Agreement or any supplementing agreement and of a substantially equivalent obligation under another international agreement to which both Parties are party, including the WTO Agreement, the Party seeking redress shall select the forum in which to settle the dispute.

2. Once a Party has selected the forum and initiated dispute settlement procedures either under this Title or under another international agreement, that Party shall not initiate such procedures under the other international agreement with respect to the particular measure referred to in paragraph 1, unless the forum selected first fails to make findings for procedural or jurisdictional reasons.

3. For the purposes of this Article:

(a) dispute settlement procedures under this Title are deemed to be initiated by a Party's request for the establishment of an arbitration tribunal under Article 739;

(b) dispute settlement procedures under the WTO Agreement are deemed to be initiated by a Party's request for the establishment of a panel under Article 6 of the Understanding on Rules and Procedure Governing the Settlement of Disputes of the WTO; and

(c) dispute settlement procedures under any other agreement are deemed to be initiated if they are initiated in accordance with the relevant provisions of that agreement.

4. Without prejudice to paragraph 2, nothing in this Agreement or any supplementing agreement shall preclude a Party from suspending obligations authorised by the Dispute Settlement Body of the WTO or authorised under the dispute settlement procedures of another international agreement to which the Parties are party. The WTO Agreement or any other international agreement between the Parties shall not be invoked to preclude a Party from suspending obligations under this Title.

CHAPTER 2
PROCEDURE

Article 738 Consultations

1. If a Party (the "complaining Party") considers that the other Party (the "respondent Party") has breached an obligation under this Agreement or under any supplementing agreement, the Parties shall endeavour to resolve the matter by entering into consultations in good faith, with the aim of reaching a mutually agreed solution.

2. The complaining Party may seek consultations by means of a written request delivered to the respondent Party. The complaining Party shall specify in its written request the reasons for the request, including the identification of the measures at issue and the legal basis for the request, and the covered provisions it considers applicable.

3. The respondent Party shall reply to the request promptly, and in any case no later than 10 days after the date of its delivery. Consultations shall be held within 30 days of the date of delivery of the request in person or by any other means of communication agreed by the Parties. If held in person, consultations shall take place in the territory of the respondent Party, unless the Parties agree otherwise.

4. The consultations shall be deemed concluded within 30 days of the date of delivery of the request, unless the Parties agree to continue consultations.

5. Consultations on matters of urgency, including those regarding perishable goods or seasonal goods or services, shall be held within 20 days of the date of delivery of the request. The consultations shall be deemed concluded within those 20 days unless the Parties agree to continue consultations.

6. Each Party shall provide sufficient factual information to allow a complete examination of the measure at issue, including an examination of how that measure could affect the application of this Agreement or any supplementing agreement. Each Party shall endeavour to ensure the participation of personnel of their competent authorities who have expertise in the matter subject to the consultations.

7. For any dispute concerning an area other than Titles I to VII, Chapter 4 of Title VIII, Titles IX to XII of Heading One or Heading Six of Part Two, at the request of the complaining Party, the consultations referred to in paragraph 3 of this Article shall be held in the framework of a Specialised Committee or of the Partnership Council. The Specialised Committee may at any time decide to refer the matter to the Partnership Council. The Partnership Council may also seize itself of the matter. The Specialised Committee, or, as

the case may be, the Partnership Council, may resolve the dispute by a decision. The time periods referred to in paragraph 3 of this Article shall apply. The venue of meetings shall be governed by the rules of procedure of the Specialised Committee or, as the case may be, the Partnership Council.

8. Consultations, and in particular all information designated as confidential and positions taken by the Parties during consultations, shall be confidential, and shall be without prejudice to the rights of either Party in any further proceedings.

Article 739 Arbitration procedure

1. The complaining Party may request the establishment of an arbitration tribunal if:
   (a) the respondent Party does not respond to the request for consultations within 10 days of the date of its delivery;
   (b) consultations are not held within the time periods referred to in Article 738(3), (4) or (5);
   (c) the Parties agree not to have consultations; or
   (d) consultations have been concluded without a mutually agreed solution having been reached.

2. The request for the establishment of the arbitration tribunal shall be made by means of a written request delivered to the respondent Party. In its request, the complaining Party shall explicitly identify the measure at issue and explain how that measure constitutes a breach of the covered provisions in a manner sufficient to present the legal basis for the complaint clearly.

Article 740 Establishment of an arbitration tribunal

1. An arbitration tribunal shall be composed of three arbitrators.

2. No later than 10 days after the date of delivery of the request for the establishment of an arbitration tribunal, the Parties shall consult with a view to agreeing on the composition of the arbitration tribunal.

3. If the Parties do not agree on the composition of the arbitration tribunal within the time period provided for in paragraph 2 of this Article, each Party shall appoint an arbitrator from the sub-list for that Party established pursuant to Article 752 no later than five days after the expiry of the time period provided for in paragraph 2 of this Article. If a Party fails to appoint an arbitrator from its sub-list within that time period, the co-chair of the Partnership Council from the complaining Party shall select, no later than five days after the expiry of that time period, an arbitrator by lot from the sub-list of the Party that has failed to appoint an arbitrator. The co-chair of the Partnership Council from the complaining Party may delegate such selection by lot of the arbitrator.

4. If the Parties do not agree on the chairperson of the arbitration tribunal within the time period provided for in paragraph 2 of this Article, the co-chair of the Partnership Council from the complaining Party shall select, no later than five days after the expiry of that time period, the chairperson of the arbitration tribunal by lot from the sub-list of chairpersons established pursuant to Article 752. The co-chair of the Partnership Council from the complaining Party may delegate such selection by lot of the chairperson of the arbitration tribunal.

5. Should any of the lists provided for in Article 752 not be established or not contain sufficient names at the time a selection is made pursuant to paragraph 3 or 4 of this Article, the arbitrators shall be selected by lot from the individuals who have been formally proposed by one Party or both Parties in accordance with Annex 48.

6. The date of establishment of the arbitration tribunal shall be the date on which the last of the three arbitrators has notified to the Parties the acceptance of his or her appointment in accordance with Annex 48.

Article 741 Requirements for arbitrators

1. All arbitrators shall:

(a) have demonstrated expertise in law and international trade, including on specific matters covered by Titles I to VII, Chapter 4 of Title VIII, Titles IX to XII of Heading One of Part Two or Heading Six of Part Two, or in law and any other matter covered by this Agreement or by any supplementing agreement and, in the case of a chairperson, also have experience in dispute settlement procedures;

(b) not be affiliated with or take instructions from either Party;

(c) serve in their individual capacities and not take instructions from any organisation or government with regard to matters related to the dispute; and

(d) comply with Annex 49.

2. All arbitrators shall be persons whose independence is beyond doubt, who possess the qualifications required for appointment to high judicial office in their respective countries or who are jurisconsults of recognised competence.

3. In view of the subject-matter of a particular dispute, the Parties may agree to derogate from the requirements listed in point (a) of paragraph 1.

Article 742 Functions of the arbitration tribunal

The arbitration tribunal:

(a) shall make an objective assessment of the matter before it, including an objective assessment of the facts of the case and the applicability of, and conformity of the measures at issue with, the covered provisions;

(b) shall set out, in its decisions and rulings, the findings of facts and law and the rationale behind any findings that it makes; and

(c) should consult regularly with the Parties and provide adequate opportunities for the development of a mutually agreed solution.

Article 743 Terms of reference

1. Unless the Parties agree otherwise no later than five days after the date of the establishment of the arbitration tribunal, the terms of reference of the arbitration tribunal shall be:

"to examine, in the light of the relevant covered provisions of this Agreement or of a supplementing agreement, the matter referred to in the request for the establishment of the arbitration tribunal, to decide on the conformity of the measure at issue with the provisions referred to in Article 735 and to issue a ruling in accordance with Article 745".

2. If the Parties agree on terms of reference other than those referred to in paragraph 1, they shall notify the agreed terms of reference to the arbitration tribunal within the time period referred to in paragraph 1.

Article 744 Urgent proceedings

1. If a Party so requests, the arbitration tribunal shall decide, no later than 10 days after the date of its establishment, whether the case concerns matters of urgency.

2. In cases of urgency, the applicable time periods set out in Article 745 shall be half the time prescribed therein.

Article 745 Ruling of the arbitration tribunal

1. The arbitration tribunal shall deliver an interim report to the Parties within 100 days after the date of establishment of the arbitration tribunal. If the arbitration tribunal considers that this deadline cannot be met, the chairperson of the arbitration tribunal shall notify the Parties in writing, stating the reasons for the delay and the date on which the arbitration tribunal plans to deliver its interim report. The arbitration tribunal shall not deliver its interim report later than 130 days after the date of establishment of the arbitration tribunal under any circumstances.

2. Each Party may deliver to the arbitration tribunal a written request to review precise aspects of the interim report within 14 days of its delivery. A Party may comment on the other Party's request within six days of the delivery of the request.

3. If no written request to review precise aspects of the interim report is delivered within the time period referred to in paragraph 2, the interim report shall become the ruling of the arbitration tribunal.

4. The arbitration tribunal shall deliver its ruling to the Parties within 130 days of the date of establishment of the arbitration tribunal. When the arbitration tribunal considers that that deadline cannot be met, its chairperson shall notify the Parties in writing, stating the reasons for the delay and the date on which the arbitration tribunal plans to deliver its ruling. The arbitration tribunal shall not deliver its ruling later than 160 days after the date of establishment of the arbitration tribunal under any circumstances.

5. The ruling shall include a discussion of any written request by the Parties on the interim report and clearly address the comments of the Parties.

6. For greater certainty, a "ruling" or "rulings" as referred to in Articles 742, 743 and 753 and Article 754(1), (3), (4) and (6) shall be understood to refer also to the interim report of the arbitration tribunal.

CHAPTER 3
COMPLIANCE

Article 746 Compliance measures

1. If, in its ruling referred to in Article 745(4), the arbitration tribunal finds that the respondent Party has breached an obligation under this Agreement or under any supplementing agreement, that Party shall take the necessary measures to comply immediately with the ruling of the arbitration tribunal in order to bring itself in compliance with the covered provisions.

2. The respondent Party, no later than 30 days after delivery of the ruling, shall deliver a notification to the complaining Party of the measures which it has taken or which it envisages to take in order to comply.

Article 747 Reasonable period of time

1. If immediate compliance is not possible, the respondent Party, no later than 30 days after delivery of the ruling referred to in Article 745(4), shall deliver a notification to the complaining Party of the length of the reasonable period of time it will require for compliance with the ruling referred to in Article 745(4). The Parties shall endeavour to agree on the length of the reasonable period of time to comply.

2. If the Parties have not agreed on the length of the reasonable period of time, the complaining Party may, at the earliest 20 days after the delivery of the notification referred to in paragraph 1, request in writing that the original arbitration tribunal determines the length of the reasonable period of time. The arbitration tribunal shall deliver its decision to the Parties within 20 days of the date of delivery of the request.

3. The respondent Party shall deliver a written notification of its progress in complying with the ruling referred to in Article 745(4) to the complaining Party at least one month before the expiry of the reasonable period of time.

4. The Parties may agree to extend the reasonable period of time.

Article 748 Compliance review

1. The respondent Party shall, no later than the date of expiry of the reasonable period of time, deliver a notification to the complaining Party of any measure that it has taken to comply with the ruling referred to in Article 745(4).

2. When the Parties disagree on the existence of, or the consistency with the covered provisions of, any measure taken to comply, the complaining Party may deliver a request, which shall be in writing, to the original arbitration tribunal to decide on the matter. The request shall identify any measure at issue and explain how that measure constitutes a breach of the covered provisions in a manner sufficient to present the legal basis for the complaint clearly. The arbitration tribunal shall deliver its decision to the Parties within 45 days of the date of delivery of the request.

Article 749 Temporary remedies

1. The respondent Party shall, at the request of and after consultations with the complaining Party, present an offer for temporary compensation if:

(a) the respondent Party delivers a notification to the complaining Party that it is not possible to comply with the ruling referred to in Article 745(4); or

(b) the respondent Party fails to deliver a notification of any measure taken to comply within the deadline referred to in Article 746 or before the date of expiry of the reasonable period of time; or

(c) the arbitration tribunal finds that no measure taken to comply exists or that the measure taken to comply is inconsistent with the covered provisions.

2. In any of the conditions referred to in points (a), (b) and (c) of paragraph 1, the complaining Party may deliver a written notification to the respondent Party that it intends to suspend the application of obligations under the covered provisions if:

(a) the complaining Party decides not to make a request under paragraph 1; or

(b) the Parties do not agree on the temporary compensation within 20 days after the expiry of the reasonable period of time or the delivery of the arbitration tribunal decision under Article 748 if a request under paragraph 1 of this Article is made.

The notification shall specify the level of intended suspension of obligations.

3. Suspension of obligations shall be subject to the following conditions:

(a) obligations under Heading Four of Part Two, the Protocol on Social Security Coordination or its annexes or Part Five may not be suspended under this Article;

(b) by way of derogation from point (a), obligations under Part Five may be suspended only where the ruling referred to in Article 745(4) concerns the interpretation and implementation of Part Five;

(c) obligations outside Part Five may not be suspended where the ruling referred to in Article 745(4) concerns the interpretation and implementation of Part Five; and
(d) obligations under Title II of Heading One of Part Two in respect of financial services may not be suspended under this Article, unless the ruling referred to in Article 745(4) concerns the interpretation and application of obligations under Title II of Heading One of Part two in respect of financial services.

4. Where a Party persists in not complying with a ruling of an arbitration panel established under an earlier agreement concluded between the Parties, the other Party may suspend obligations under the covered provisions referred to in Article 735. With the exception of the rule in point (a) of paragraph 3 of this Article, all rules relating to temporary remedies in case of non-compliance and to review of any such measures shall be governed by the earlier agreement.

5. The suspension of obligations shall not exceed the level equivalent to the nullification or impairment caused by the violation.

6. If the arbitration tribunal has found the violation in Heading One or Heading Three of Part Two, the suspension may be applied in another Title of the same Heading as that in which the tribunal has found the violation, in particular if the complaining party is of the view that such suspension is effective in inducing compliance.

7. If the arbitration tribunal has found the violation in Heading Two of Part Two:
(a) the complaining party should first seek to suspend obligations in the same Title as that in which the arbitration tribunal has found the violation;
(b) if the complaining party considers that it is not practicable or effective to suspend obligations with respect to the same Title as that in which the tribunal has found the violation, it may seek to suspend obligations in the other Title under the same Heading.

8. If the arbitration tribunal has found the violation in Heading One, Heading Two, Heading Three or Heading Five of Part Two, and if the complaining party considers that it is not practicable or effective to suspend obligations within the same Heading as that in which the arbitration tribunal has found the violation, and that the circumstances are serious enough, it may seek to suspend obligations under other covered provisions.

9. In the case of point (b) of paragraph 7 and paragraph 8, the complaining Party shall state the reasons for its decision.

10. The complaining Party may suspend the obligations 10 days after the date of delivery of the notification referred to in paragraph 2 unless the respondent Party made a request under paragraph 11.

11. If the respondent Party considers that the notified level of suspension of obligations exceeds the level equivalent to the nullification or impairment caused by the violation or that the principles and procedures set forth in point (b) of paragraph 7, paragraph 8 or paragraph 9 have not been followed, it may deliver a written request to the original arbitration tribunal before the expiry of the 10 day period set out in paragraph 10 to decide on the matter. The arbitration tribunal shall deliver its decision on the level of the suspension of obligations to the Parties within 30 days of the date of the request. Obligations shall not be suspended until the arbitration tribunal has delivered its decision. The suspension of obligations shall be consistent with that decision.

12. The arbitration tribunal acting pursuant to paragraph 11 shall not examine the nature of the obligations to be suspended but shall determine whether the level of such

suspension exceeds the level equivalent to the nullification or impairment caused by the violation. However, if the matter referred to arbitration includes a claim that the principles and procedures set forth in point (b) of paragraph 7, paragraph 8 or paragraph 9 have not been followed, the arbitration tribunal shall examine that claim. In the event the arbitration tribunal determines that those principles and procedures have not been followed, the complaining party shall apply them consistently with point (b) of paragraph 7, paragraph 8 and paragraph 9. The parties shall accept the arbitration tribunal's decision as final and shall not seek a second arbitration procedure. This paragraph shall under no circumstances delay the date as of which the complaining Party is entitled to suspend obligations under this Article.

13. The suspension of obligations or the compensation referred to in this Article shall be temporary and shall not be applied after:

(a) the Parties have reached a mutually agreed solution pursuant to Article 756;

(b) the Parties have agreed that the measure taken to comply brings the respondent Party into compliance with the covered provisions; or

(c) any measure taken to comply which the arbitration tribunal has found to be inconsistent with the covered provisions has been withdrawn or amended so as to bring the respondent Party into compliance with those covered provisions.

Article 750 Review of any measure taken to comply after the adoption of temporary remedies

1. The respondent Party shall deliver a notification to the complaining Party of any measure it has taken to comply following the suspension of obligations or following the application of temporary compensation, as the case may be. With the exception of cases under paragraph 2, the complaining Party shall terminate the suspension of obligations within 30 days from the delivery of the notification. In cases where compensation has been applied, with the exception of cases under paragraph 2, the respondent Party may terminate the application of such compensation within 30 days from the delivery of its notification that it has complied.

2. If the Parties do not reach an agreement on whether the notified measure brings the respondent Party into compliance with the covered provisions within 30 days of the date of delivery of the notification, the complaining Party shall deliver a written request to the original arbitration tribunal to decide on the matter. The arbitration tribunal shall deliver its decision to the Parties within 46 days of the date of the delivery of the request. If the arbitration tribunal finds that the measure taken to comply is in conformity with the covered provisions, the suspension of obligations or compensation, as the case may be, shall be terminated. When relevant, the level of suspension of obligations or of compensation shall be adjusted in light of the arbitration tribunal decision.

CHAPTER 4
COMMON PROCEDURAL PROVISIONS

Article 751 Receipt of information

1. On request of a Party, or on its own initiative, the arbitration tribunal may seek from the Parties relevant information it considers necessary and appropriate. The Parties shall respond promptly and fully to any request by the arbitration tribunal for such information.

2. On request of a Party, or on its own initiative, the arbitration tribunal may seek from any source any information it considers appropriate. The arbitration tribunal may also seek the opinion of experts as it considers appropriate and subject to any terms and conditions agreed by the Parties, where applicable.

3. The arbitration tribunal shall consider amicus curiae submissions from natural persons of a Party or legal persons established in a Party in accordance with Annex 48.

4. Any information obtained by the arbitration tribunal under this Article shall be made available to the Parties and the Parties may submit comments on that information to the arbitration tribunal.

Article 752 Lists of arbitrators

1. The Partnership Council shall, no later than 180 days after the date of entry into force of this Agreement, establish a list of individuals with expertise in specific sectors covered by this Agreement or its supplementing agreements who are willing and able to serve as members of an arbitration tribunal. The list shall comprise at least 15 persons and shall be composed of three sub-lists:

(a) one sub-list of individuals established on the basis of proposals by the Union;

(b) one sub-list of individuals established on the basis of proposals by the United Kingdom; and

(c) one sub-list of individuals who are not nationals of either Party who shall serve as chairperson to the arbitration tribunal.

Each sub-list shall include at least five individuals. The Partnership Council shall ensure that the list is always maintained at this minimum number of individuals.

2. The Partnership Council may establish additional lists of individuals with expertise in specific sectors covered by this Agreement or by any supplementing agreement. Subject to the agreement of the Parties, such additional lists may be used to compose the arbitration tribunal in accordance with the procedure set out in Article 740(3) and (5). Additional lists shall be composed of two sub-lists:

(a) one sub-list of individuals established on the basis of proposals by the Union; and

(b) one sub-list of individuals established on the basis of proposals by the United Kingdom.

3. The lists referred to in paragraphs 1 and 2 shall not comprise persons who are members, officials or other servants of the Union institutions, of the Government of a Member State, or of the Government of the United Kingdom.

Article 753 Replacement of arbitrators

If during dispute settlement procedures under this Title, an arbitrator is unable to participate, withdraws, or needs to be replaced because that arbitrator does not comply with the requirements of the Code of Conduct, the procedure set out in Article 740 shall apply. The time period for the delivery of the ruling or decision shall be extended for the time necessary for the appointment of the new arbitrator.

Article 754 Arbitration tribunal decisions and ruling

1. The deliberations of the arbitration tribunal shall be kept confidential. The arbitration tribunal shall make every effort to draft rulings and take decisions by consensus. If this is not possible, the arbitration tribunal shall decide the matter by majority vote. In no case shall separate opinions of arbitrators be disclosed.

2. The decisions and rulings of the arbitration tribunal shall be binding on the Union and on the United Kingdom. They shall not create any rights or obligations with respect to natural or legal persons.

3. Decisions and rulings of the arbitration tribunal cannot add to or diminish the rights and obligations of the Parties under this Agreement or under any supplementing agreement.

4. For greater certainty, the arbitration tribunal shall have no jurisdiction to determine the legality of a measure alleged to constitute a breach of this Agreement or of any supplementing agreement, under the domestic law of a Party. No finding made by the arbitration tribunal when ruling on a dispute between the Parties shall bind the domestic courts or tribunals of either Party as to the meaning to be given to the domestic law of that Party.

5. For greater certainty, the courts of each Party shall have no jurisdiction in the resolution of disputes between the Parties under this Agreement.

6. Each Party shall make the rulings and decisions of the arbitration tribunal publicly available, subject to the protection of confidential information.

7. The information submitted by the Parties to the arbitration tribunal shall be treated in accordance with the confidentiality rules laid down in Annex 48.

Article 755 Suspension and termination of the arbitration proceedings

At the request of both Parties, the arbitration tribunal shall suspend its work at any time for a period agreed by the Parties and not exceeding 12 consecutive months. The arbitration tribunal shall resume its work before the end of the suspension period at the written request of both Parties, or at the end of the suspension period at the written request of either Party. The requesting Party shall deliver a notification to the other Party accordingly. If a Party does not request the resumption of the arbitration tribunal's work at the expiry of the suspension period, the authority of the arbitration tribunal shall lapse and the dispute settlement procedure shall be terminated. In the event of a suspension of the work of the arbitration tribunal, the relevant time periods shall be extended by the same time period for which the work of the arbitration tribunal was suspended.

Article 756 Mutually agreed solution

1. The Parties may at any time reach a mutually agreed solution with respect to any dispute referred to in Article 735.

2. If a mutually agreed solution is reached during panel proceedings, the Parties shall jointly notify the agreed solution to the chairperson of the arbitration tribunal. Upon such notification, the arbitration proceedings shall be terminated.

3. The solution may be adopted by means of a decision of the Partnership Council. Mutually agreed solutions shall be made publicly available. The version disclosed to the public shall not contain any information either Party has designated as confidential.

4. Each Party shall take the measures necessary to implement the mutually agreed solution within the agreed time period.

5. No later than the date of expiry of the agreed time period, the implementing Party shall inform the other Party in writing of any measures thus taken to implement the mutually agreed solution.

Article 757 Time periods

1. All time periods laid down in this Title shall be counted in days from the day following the act to which they refer.

2. Any time period referred to in this Title may be modified by mutual agreement of the Parties.

3. The arbitration tribunal may at any time propose to the Parties to modify any time period referred to in this Title, stating the reasons for the proposal.

Article 758 Costs

1. Each Party shall bear its own expenses derived from the participation in the arbitration tribunal procedure.

2. The Parties shall share jointly and equally the expenses derived from organisational matters, including the remuneration and expenses of the members of the arbitration tribunal. The remuneration of the arbitrators shall be in accordance with Annex 48.

Article 759 Annexes

1. Dispute settlement procedures set out in this Title shall be governed by the rules of procedure set out in Annex 48 and conducted in accordance with Annex 49.

2. The Partnership Council may amend Annexes 48 and 49.

The African Union Framework

46.a Constitutive Act of the African Union

Date: 11 July 2000
Source: 2158 UNTS 3
https://au.int/sites/default/files/pages/34873-file-constitutiveact_en.pdf

...

Article 5 Organs of the Union

1. The organs of the Union shall be:

(a) *The Assembly of the Union;*
(b) *The Executive Council;*
(c) *The Pan-African Parliament;*
(d) *The Court of Justice;*
(e) *The Commission;*
(f) *The Permanent Representatives Committee;*
(g) *The Specialized Technical Committees;*
(h) *The Economic, Social and Cultural Council;*
(i) *The Financial Institutions;*

...

Article 18 The Court of Justice

1. A Court of Justice of the Union shall be established;

2. The statute, composition and functions of the Court of Justice shall be defined in a protocol relating thereto.

...

Article 26 Interpretation

The Court shall be seized with matters of interpretation arising from the application or implementation of this Act. Pending its establishment, such matters shall be submitted to the Assembly of the Union, which shall decide by a two-thirds majority.

...

46.b Protocol of the Court of Justice of the African Union*

Date: 11 July 2003

Source: https://au.int/sites/default/files/treaties/36395-treaty-0026_-_protocol_of_the_court_of_justice_of_the_african_union_e.pdf

The Member States of the African Union:

Considering that the Constitutive Act established the Court of Justice of the African Union;

Firmly convinced that the attainment of the objectives of the African Union requires the establishment of the Court of Justice of the African Union;

HAVE AGREED AS FOLLOWS:

CHAPTER I

Article 1 DEFINITIONS

In this Protocol unless otherwise specifically stated:

"**Act**" means the Constitutive Act of the Union;

"**Assembly**" means the Assembly of Heads of State and Government of the Union;

"**Commission**" means the Commission of the Union;

"**Court**" means the Court of Justice of the Union;

"**ECOSOCC**" means the Economic, Social and Cultural Council of the Union;

"**Executive Council**" means the Executive Council of Ministers of the Union;

"**Financial Institutions**" means the Financial Institutions established by the Constitutive Act;

"Judge" means a judge of the Court;

"**Member State**" means a Member State of the Union;

* N.B.: In 2008, Member States of the African Union adopted the 'Merger Protocol' creating the African Court of Justice and Human Rights. This will incorporate the African Court on Human and Peoples' Rights and the Court of Justice of the African Union (Document No. 33.b). Further changes will be brought about with the entry into force of the 2014 'Malabo Protocol', which provides for the inclusion of criminal jurisdiction within the remit of the proposed African Court of Justice and Human Rights.

As at the time of editing neither the Merger Protocol nor the Malabo Protocol have entered into force, the constituent documents of the two African Courts are reproduced in this volume separately.

"**Parliament**" means the Pan-African Parliament of the Union;
"**Peace and Security Council**" means the Peace and Security Council of the Union;
"**President**" means the President of the Court;
"**Protocol**" means this Protocol defining the composition, powers and functions of the Court;
"**Regions**" means the geographical regions into which the continent of Africa, at any time, is divided pursuant to a decision of the Assembly;
"**Rules of Court**" means the Rules of Court under Article 58;
"**Registrar**" means the Registrar of the Court;
"**States Parties**" means the Member States that have ratified or acceded to this Protocol;
"**Union**" means the African Union established by the Act;
"**Vice President**" means the Vice President of the Court;

Article 2 ESTABLISHMENT OF THE COURT

1. The Court established by the Act shall function in accordance with the provisions of the Act and this Protocol.
2. The Court shall be the principal judicial organ of the Union.

Article 3 COMPOSITION

1. The Court shall consist of eleven (11) Judges who are nationals of States Parties.
2. The Assembly may, when it deems it necessary, review the number of Judges.
3. The Judges shall be assisted by the necessary staff for the smooth functioning of the Court.
4. No two (2) Judges shall be nationals of the same State Party.
5. In the Court as a whole, the representation of the principal legal traditions of Africa shall be assured.
6. Each region shall be represented by no less than two (2) Judges.

CHAPTER II

Article 4 QUALIFICATIONS

The Court shall be composed of impartial and independent Judges elected from among persons of high moral character, who possess the necessary qualifications required in their respective countries for appointment to the highest judicial offices, or are jurists of recognized competence in international law.

Article 5 SUBMISSION OF CANDIDATES

1. Upon entry into force of this Protocol, the Chairperson of the Commission shall request each State Party to submit in writing within ninety (90) days of such a request, its nomination for the office of a Judge of the Court.
2. Each State Party may nominate only one (1) candidate having the qualifications prescribed in Article 4 of this Protocol.
3. Due consideration shall be given to adequate gender representation in the nomination process.

Article 6 LIST OF CANDIDATES

The Chairperson of the Commission shall prepare a list of the candidates nominated, in alphabetical order and transmit it to the Member States at least thirty (30) days prior to the ordinary session of 4 Member States at least thirty (30) days prior to the ordinary session of the Assembly at which the Judges are to be elected.

Article 7 ELECTION OF JUDGES OF THE COURT

1. The Assembly shall elect the Judges by secret ballot and by two-thirds majority of the Member States eligible to vote.

2. Where one or more candidates fail to obtain the two-thirds majority required for an election, the balloting shall continue until the required number of Judges has been elected. However, the next ballots shall be restricted to the candidates who obtain the greatest number of votes.

3. In the election of the Judges, the Assembly shall ensure that there is equal gender representation.

Article 8 TENURE OF OFFICE

1. The Judges shall be elected for a period of six (6) years and may be re-elected only once. The term of five (5) Judges elected at the first election shall expire at the end of four (4) years and the other Judges shall serve the full term.

2. The Judges whose terms are to expire at the end of the initial period of four (4) years shall be chosen by lot to be drawn by the Chairperson of the Assembly immediately after the first election has been completed.

3. A Judge elected to replace another Judge whose term of office has not expired shall be from the same region and shall hold office for the remainder of the predecessor's term.

Article 9 OATH OF OFFICE

1. Before taking up his or her duties each Judge shall in open court take the following oath: "I .... do solemnly swear (or affirm or declare) that I shall faithfully exercise the duties of my office as Judge of the Court of Justice of the African Union impartially and conscientiously, without fear or favour, affection or ill-will and that I will preserve the secrecy of the deliberations of the Court."

2. The oath of office shall be administered by the Chairperson of the Assembly or his or her duly authorized representative.

Article 10 PRESIDENCY OF THE COURT

1. The Court shall elect its President and Vice-President for a period of three (3) years. The President and Vice-President may be re–elected once.

2. The President shall reside at the seat of the Court.

3. The modalities for elections of the President and the Vice-President and their functions shall be set out in the Rules of Court.

Article 11 RESIGNATION, SUSPENSION AND REMOVAL FROM OFFICE

1. A Judge may resign his or her position in writing addressed to the President for transmission to the Chairperson of the Assembly.

2. A Judge shall not be suspended or removed from office save where, on the unanimous recommendation of the other Judges, he or she no longer fulfils the requisite conditions to be a Judge.

3. The President shall communicate the recommendation for the suspension or removal of a judge to the Chairperson of the Assembly and the Chairperson of the Commission.

4. Such a recommendation of the Court shall become final upon its adoption by the Assembly.

Article 12 VACANCIES

1. A vacancy shall arise in the Court under the following circumstances:
   (a) death;
   (b) resignation;
   (c) removal from office.
2. In the case of death or resignation of a Judge, the President shall immediately inform the Chairperson of the Assembly in writing, who shall declare the seat vacant.
3. The same procedure and consideration for the election of a Judge shall also be followed in filling vacancies.

Article 13 INDEPENDENCE

1. The independence of the Judges shall be fully ensured in accordance with international law.
2. No Judge may participate in the decision of any case in which he or she has previously taken part as agent, counsel or advocate for one of the parties, or as a member of a national or international court, or commission of inquiry, or in any other capacity.
3. Any doubt on this point shall be settled by decision of the Court.

Article 14 PRIVILEGES AND IMMUNITIES

1. The Judges shall enjoy, from the time of their election and throughout their term of office, the full privileges and immunities extended to diplomatic agents in accordance with international law.
2. The Judges shall be immune from legal proceedings for any act or omission committed in the discharge of their judicial functions.
3. The Judges shall continue, after they have ceased to hold office, to enjoy immunity in respect of acts performed by them when engaged in their official capacity.

Article 15 INCOMPATIBILITY

1. The position of a Judge shall be incompatible with any activity that might interfere with the independence or impartiality of such a judge or the demands of the office, as determined in the Rules of Court.
2. Any doubt on this point shall be settled by the Court.

Article 16 QUORUM

1. The full Court shall sit except where it is expressly provided otherwise in this Protocol;
2. Except when sitting in Chamber, the Court shall only examine cases brought before it, if it has a quorum of at least seven (7) Judges;
3. The quorum for a Special Chamber shall be set out in the Rule s of Court.

Article 17 REMUNERATION OF JUDGES

1. A Judge shall receive an annual allowance and, for each day on which he or she exercises his or her functions, a special allowance, provided that in any year the total sum payable to any Judge as special allowance shall not exceed the amount of the annual allowance.

2. The President shall receive an additional special annual allowance.

3. The Vice-President shall receive an additional special allowance for each day on which he or she acts as President.

4. The allowances shall be determined from time to time by the Assembly upon the recommendation of the Executive Council, taking into account the workload of the Court. They may not be decreased during the term of office.

5. Regulations adopted by the Assembly upon the recommendation of the Executive Council shall determine the conditions under which retirement pensions shall be given to the Judges and the terms and conditions under which their travel expenses shall be paid or refunded.

6. The allowances shall be free of all taxation.

Article 18 ELIGIBILITY TO SUBMIT CASES

1. The following are entitled to submit cases to the Court:

(a) States Parties to this Protocol;

(b) The Assembly, the Parliament and other organs of the Union authorised by the Assembly;

(c) The Commission or a member of staff of the Commission in a dispute between them within the limits and under the conditions laid down in the Staff Rules and Regulations of the Union;

(d) Third Parties under conditions to be determined by the Assembly and with the consent of the State Party concerned.

2. The conditions under which the Court shall be open to third parties shall, subject to the special provisions contained in treaties in force, be laid down by the Assembly, but in no case shall such conditions place the parties in a position of inequality before the Court.

3. The States which are not members of the Union shall not be allowed to submit cases to the Court. The Court shall have no jurisdiction to deal with a dispute involving a Member State that has not ratified this Protocol.

Article 19 COMPETENCE/JURISDICTION

1. The Court shall have jurisdiction over all disputes and applications referred to it in accordance with the Act and this Protocol which relate to:

(a) the interpretation and application of the Act;

(b) the interpretation, application or validity of Union treaties and all subsidiary legal instruments adopted within the framework of the Union;

(c) any question of international law;

(d) all acts, decisions, regulations and directives of the organs of the Union;

(e) all matters specifically provided for in any other agreements that States Parties may conclude among themselves or with the Union and which confer jurisdiction on the Court;

(f) the existence of any fact which, if established, would constitute a breach of an obligation owed to a State Party or to the Union;

(g) the nature or extent of the reparation to be made for the breach of an obligation.

2. The Assembly may confer on the Court power to assume jurisdiction over any dispute other than those referred to in this Article.

CHAPTER III

Article 20 SOURCES OF LAW

1. The Court, whose function is to decide in accordance with international law such disputes, as are submitted to it, shall have regard to:

(a) The Act

(b) International treaties whether general or particular, establishing rules expressly recognized by the contesting states;

(c) International custom, as evidence of a general practice accepted as law;

(d) The general principles of law recognized universally or by African States;

(e) Subject to Article 37 of this Protocol, judicial decisions and the writings of the most highly qualified publicists of various nations as well as the regulations, directives and decisions of the Union as subsidiary means for the determination of the rules of law.

2. This provision shall not prejudice the power of the Court to decide a case *ex aequo et bono*, if the parties, agree thereto.

CHAPTER IV

Article 21 SUBMISSION OF A DISPUTE

1. Disputes shall be submitted to the Court by a written application to the Registrar. The subject of the dispute, the applicable law and basis of the jurisdiction shall be indicated.

2. The Registrar shall forthwith give notice of the application to all concerned parties.

3. The Registrar shall also notify all Member States, the Chairperson of the Commission and any third parties entitled to appear before the Court.

Article 22 PROVISIONAL MEASURES

1. The Court shall have the power, on its own motion or on application by the parties, to indicate, if it considers that circumstances so require any provisional measures which ought to be taken to preserve the respective rights of the parties.

2. Pending the final decision, notice of the provisional measures shall forthwith be given to the parties and to the Chairperson of the Commission.

Article 23 REPRESENTATION OF PARTIES

1. The parties may be represented before the Court by agents.

2. An agent or party may have the assistance of counsel or advocate before the Court.

3. The organs of the Union, where relevant, shall be represented by the Chairperson of the Commission or his or her representative.

4. The agents, counsel and advocates of the parties before the Court shall enjoy the privileges and immunities necessary to the independent exercise of their duties.

Article 24 PROCEDURE BEFORE THE COURT

1. The procedure before the Court shall consist of two parts: written and oral.

2. The written procedure shall consist of the communications to the Court, the parties and the institutions of the Union whose decisions are in dispute, of applications, statements of the case, defences and observations and of replies if any, as well as all papers and documents in support, or of certified copies thereof.

3. The communications shall be made through the Registrar, in the order and time fixed by the Court either in the Rules or the case.

4. A certified copy of every document produced by one party shall be communicated to the other party.

5. The oral proceedings shall, if necessary, consist of hearing by the Court of witnesses, experts, agents, counsels and advocates.

Article 25 SERVICE OF NOTICE

1. For the service of all notices upon persons other than parties, agents, counsel and advocates, the Court shall apply direct to the government of the State upon whose territory the notice has to be served.

2. The same provision shall apply whenever steps are to be taken to procure evidence locally in the territory of the State concerned.

Article 26 PUBLIC HEARING

The hearing in Court shall be public, unless the Court, on its own motion or upon application by the parties, decides that the public not be admitted.

Article 27 RECORD OF PROCEEDINGS

1. A record of proceedings shall be made at each hearing and shall be signed by the presiding Judge and the Registrar of the session.

2. Such a record shall be kept by the Registrar and shall be the authentic record of the case.

Article 28 REGULATION OF PROCEEDINGS

1. The Court shall have the power to regulate its own proceedings. It shall have the power to make orders for the conduct of the case before it.

2. It shall decide the form and time in which each party must conclude its arguments, and make all arrangements connected with the taking of evidence.

Article 29 PRODUCTION OF DOCUMENTS

The Court may, before the hearing begins, call upon the agents to produce any relevant document or to supply any relevant explanation. Formal note shall be taken of any refusal to produce documents or supply an explanation requested by it.

Article 30 ENQUIRIES

The Court may, at any time, entrust any individual, body, bureau, commission, or other organisation that it may select, and accepted by the parties to the dispute, with the task of carrying out an enquiry or giving an expert opinion.

Article 31 REFUSAL OF EVIDENCE

After the Court has received the proofs and evidence within the time specified for the purpose, it may, unless it decides that the interests of justice so require, refuse to accept any further oral or written evidence that any party may desire to present.

Article 32 DEFAULT JUDGMENTS

1. Whenever one of the parties does not appear before the Court, or fails to defend the case against it, the other party may call upon the Court to give its judgment.

2. The Court must before doing so, satisfy itself, not only that it has jurisdiction in accordance with Article 19, but also that the claim is well founded in fact and in law and that the other party had due notice.

3. An objection by the party concerned may be lodged against the judgment within ninety (90) days of it being notified of the default judgment. The objection shall not have the effect of staying the enforcement of the judgment by default

Article 33 CONSIDERATION OF THE JUDGMENT

1. When, subject to the control of the Court, the agent, counsel and advocates have completed their submissions of the case, the President shall declare the hearing closed.

2. The Court shall adjourn to consider its judgment.

3. The deliberations of the Court shall take place in private and shall remain secret at all times.

Article 34 MAJORITY NECESSARY FOR DECISION

1. All questions shall be decided by a majority of the Judges present.

2. In the event of equality of votes, the presiding Judge shall have a casting vote.

Article 35 JUDGMENT

1. The judgment shall state the reasons on which it is based.

2. The judgment shall state the names of Judges who have taken part in the decision.

3. The judgment shall be signed by all the Judges and certified by the President and the Registrar. It shall be read in open session, due notice having been given to the agents.

4. Subject to Article 32 and 41 of this Protocol, the judgment shall be final.

Article 36 SEPARATE OR DISSENTING OPINION

If the judgment does not represent in whole or in part the unanimous opinion of the Judges, any Judge shall be entitled to deliver a separate or dissenting opinion.

Article 37 BINDING FORCE OF JUDGMENTS

The judgments of the Court shall be binding on the parties and in respect of that particular case.

Article 38 DECISIONS ON INTERPRETATION AND APPLICATION OF THE ACT

1. Decisions of the Court on the interpretation and application of the Act shall be binding on Member States and organs of the Union notwithstanding the provisions of Article 37 of this Protocol.

2. Whenever questions of interpretation of the Act arise in a case in which States other than those concerned have expressed an interest, the Registrar shall notify all such States and organs of the Union forthwith.

3. Every Member State and organ of the Union so notified has the right to intervene in the proceedings.

4. Any decision taken in application of Articles 38 and 39 of this Protocol shall be by a qualified majority of at least two (2) votes and in the presence of at least nine (9) Judges.

Article 39 INTERPRETATION OF OTHER TREATIES

1. Whenever the question of interpretation of a treaty arises in a case in which States other than those concerned have expressed an interest, the Registrar shall notify all such States and organs of the Union forthwith.

2. Every State Party and organ of the Union so notified has the right to intervene in the proceedings and the interpretation given by the judgment will be equally binding upon it.

Article 40 INTERPRETATION OF A JUDGEMENT

In the event of any dispute as to the meaning or scope of the judgment, the Court shall construe it upon the request of any of the parties.

Article 41 REVISION

1. An application for revision of a judgment may be made only when it is based upon discovery of a new fact of such nature as to be a decisive factor, which fact was, when the judgment was given, unknown to the Court and also to the party claiming revision, provided that such ignorance was not due to negligence.

2. The proceedings for revision shall be opened by a ruling of the Court expressly recording the existence of the new fact, recognizing that it has such a character as to lay the case open to revision, and declaring the revision admissible on this ground.

3. The Court may require prior compliance with the terms of the judgment before it admits proceedings in revision.

4. The application for revision shall be made within six (6) months of the discovery of the new fact.

5. No application may be made after the lapse of ten (10) years from the date of the judgment.

Article 42 INTERVENTION

1. Any Member State that has an interest of a legal nature, which may be affected by the decision in the case, may submit a request to the Court to be permitted to intervene.

2. The Court shall decide upon the request.

Article 43 COSTS

Unless otherwise decided by the Court, each party shall bear its own costs.

Article 44 ADVISORY OPINION

1. The Court may give an advisory opinion on any legal question at the request of the Assembly, the Parliament, the Executive Council, the Peace and Security Council, the ECOSOCC, any of the Financial Institutions, a Regional Economic Community or such other organs of the Union as may be authorized by the Assembly.

2. A request for an advisory opinion under paragraph 1 of this Article shall be in writing and shall contain an exact statement of the question upon which the opinion is required and shall be accompanied by all relevant documents.

CHAPTER V

Article 45 PROCEDURE FOR AMENDMENTS

1. This Protocol may be amended if a State Party makes a written request to that effect to the Chairperson of the Assembly.

2. Proposals for amendment shall be submitted to the Chairperson of the Commission who shall transmit same to Member States within thirty (30) days of receipt thereof.

3. The Assembly may adopt by a simple majority, the draft amendment after the Court has given its opinion on the amendment.

Article 46 POWER OF THE COURT TO PROPOSE AMENDMENTS

The Court shall have the power to propose such amendments to this Protocol as it may deem necessary to the Assembly through written communication to the Chairperson of the Commission for consideration in conformity with Article 45 of this Protocol.

CHAPTER VI

Article 47 SEAT AND SEAL OF THE COURT

1. The seat of the Court shall be determined by the Assembly from among States Parties. However, the Court may sit in any other Member State if circumstances warrant and with the consent of the Member State concerned. The seat of the Court may be changed by the Assembly after due consultations with the Court.

2. The Court shall have a seal bearing the inscription "The Court of Justice of the African Union".

CHAPTER VII

Article 48 APPOINTMENT OF REGISTRAR

1. The Court shall appoint the Registrar and Deputy Registrar(s) from amongst candidates proposed by the Judges of the Court, as it considers necessary, in accordance with the Rules of Court.

2. The Registrar and Deputy Registrar(s) shall be elected for a term of four (4) years. They may be re-appointed once. They shall reside at the seat of the Court.

3. The salary and conditions of service of the Registrar and Deputy Registrar(s) shall be determined by the Assembly upon recommendation of the Court through the Executive Council.

Article 49 APPOINTMENT AND TERMS OF SERVICE OF OTHER STAFF

1. The Court shall employ such staff as may be required to enable the Court to perform its functions and who shall hold office in the service of the Court.

2. The salary and other allowances of the other staff of the Court shall be determined by the Assembly upon the recommendation of the Court through the Executive Council.

Article 50 OFFICIAL LANGUAGES OF THE COURT

The official and working languages of the Court shall be those of the Union.

CHAPTER VIII

Article 51 EXECUTION OF JUDGMENT

The State Parties shall comply with the judgment in any dispute to which they are parties within the time stipulated by the Court and shall guarantee its execution.

Article 52 NON-COMPLIANCE WITH JUDGMENT

1. Where a party has failed to comply with a judgment, the Court may, upon application by either party, refer the matter to the Assembly, which may decide upon measures to be taken to give effect to the judgment.

2. The Assembly may impose sanctions under paragraph 2 of Article 23 of the Act.

Article 53 REPORT TO THE ASSEMBLY

The Court shall submit to each ordinary session of the Assembly, a report on its work during the previous year. The report shall specify, in particular, the cases in which a State has not complied with the Court's judgment.

CHAPTER IX

Article 54 BUDGET

1. The Court shall elaborate its draft annual budget and shall submit it to the Assembly through the Executive Council.

2. The budget of the Court shall be borne by the Member States. Article 55

SUMMARY PROCEDURE

With a view to the speedy dispatch of business, the Court shall form annually a chamber composed of five (5) Judges, which, at the request of the parties, may hear and determine cases by summary procedure in accordance with the Rules of Court. In addition, two (2) Judges shall be selected from among themselves for the purpose of replacing Judges who find it impossible to sit.

Article 56 SPECIAL CHAMBERS

The Court may from time to time form one or more chambers, composed of three (3) or more Judges as the Court may determine, for dealing with particular categories of cases.

Article 57 JUDGMENT GIVEN BY A CHAMBER

A judgment given by any of the chambers provided for in Articles 55 and 56 of this Protocol shall be considered as rendered by the Court.

CHAPTER X

Article 58 RULES OF COURT

The Court shall frame rules for carrying out its functions and generally for giving effect to this Protocol. In particular, it shall lay down rules of procedure in conformity with this Protocol.

Article 59 SIGNATURE, RATIFICATION AND ACCESSION

1. This Protocol shall be open to signature, ratification and accession by Member States in accordance with their respective constitutional procedures.

2. The instruments of ratification shall be deposited with the Chairperson of the Commission.

3. Any Member State acceding to this Protocol after its entry into force shall deposit the instrument of accession with the Chairperson of the Commission.

Article 60 ENTRY INTO FORCE

This Protocol shall enter into force thirty (30) days after the deposit of the instruments of ratification by fifteen (15) Member States.

Adopted by the 2nd Ordinary Session of the Assembly of the Union Maputo, 11 July 2003

The ECOWAS Framework

47.a Revised Treaty of the Economic Community of West African States

Date: 24 July 1993
Source: (1996) 35 ILM 660
https://www.ecowas.int/wp-content/uploads/2015/01/Revised-treaty.pdf

…

ARTICLE 6 INSTITUTIONS

1. The Institutions of the Community shall be:
   a) the Authority of Heads of State and Government;
   b) the Council of Ministers;
   c) the Community Parliament;
   d) the Economic and Social Council;
   e) the Community Court of Justice;
   f) the Executive Secretariat;
   g) the Fund for Co-operation, Compensation and Development;
   h) Specialised Technical Commissions; and
   i) Any other institutions that may be established by the Authority.

…

ARTICLE 15 THE COURT OF JUSTICE: ESTABLISHMENT AND FUNCTIONS

1. There is hereby established a Court of Justice of the Community.

2. The status, composition, powers, procedure and other issues concerning the Court of Justice shall be as set out in a Protocol relating thereto.

3. The Court of Justice shall carry out the functions assigned to it independently of the Member States and the institutions of the Community.

4. Judgements of the, Court of Justice shall be binding on the Member States, the Institutions of the Community and on individuals and corporate bodies.

ARTICLE 16 ARBITRATION TRIBUNAL ESTABLISHMENT AND FUNCTIONS

1. There is hereby established an Arbitration Tribunal of the Community.

2. The status, composition, powers, procedure and other issues concerning the Arbitration Tribunal shall be as set out in a Protocol relating thereto.*

…

* N.B.: The Protocol relating to the Arbitration Tribunal has not yet been adopted.

ARTICLE 76 SETTLEMENT OF DISPUTES

1. Any dispute regarding the interpretation or the application of the provisions of this Treaty shall he amicably settled through direct agreement without prejudice to the provisions of this Treaty and relevant Protocols.

2. Failing this, either party or any other Member States or the Authority may refer the matter to the Court of the Community whose decision shall be final and shall not be subject to appeal.

…

47.b Protocol on the Community Court of Justice (ECOWAS)*

Date: 6 July 1991 / 19 January 2005
Source: Protocol A/P.1/7/91 as amended by Protocol A/SP.1/01/05
http://www.courtecowas.org/wp-content/uploads/2018/11/Protocol_AP1791_ENG.pdf

…

Article 2: Establishment of the Court

1. The Community Court of Justice established under Article [15] of the Treaty as the principal legal organ of the Community shall be constituted and execute its functions in accordance with the provisions of this protocol.

Article 3: Composition

1. The Court shall be composed of independent judges selected and appointed from nationals of the Member States who are persons of high moral character, and possess the qualification required in their respective countries for appointment to the highest judicial officers, or are jurisconsults of recognized competence in international law.

2. The Court shall consist of seven (7) members, no two of whom may be nationals of the same state. The members of the Court shall elect a President and Vice President from among their number who shall serve in that capacity for a term of three (3) years.

3. A person who for the purpose of membership of the Court could be regarded as a national of more than one Member State shall be a national of the one in which he originally exercises civil and political rights.

4. The members of the Court shall be appointed by the Authority and selected from a list of persons nominated by Member States. No Member State shall appoint more than two persons.

5. The Executive Secretary shall prepare a list in alphabetical order of all the persons thus nominated which he shall forward to the Council.

6. The Authority shall appoint the member of the Court from a shortlist of fourteen persons proposed by the Council.

7. No person below the age of 40 years and above the age of 60 years shall be eligible for appointment as a member of the Court. A member of the Court shall not be eligible for reappointment after the age of 65 years.

* N.B.: This is a consolidated version of the 1991 Protocol as amended by the 2005 Protocol, which is provisionally applied from the date of its adoption, in accordance with its Art 11(1). Amended sections are indicated in square brackets.

Article 4: Terms of Office of Members of the Court

1. [Members of the Court shall be appointed for a period of five (5) years. Their term of office may be renewed for another term of five (5) years only, except that for members of the Court appointed for the first time, the terms of office of the three (3) members shall expire at the end of three (3) years and the term of the other four (4) members shall expire at the end of five (5) years.]

2. The members of the Court whose terms are to expire at the end of the above-mentioned initial periods of three and five years shall be chosen by lot to be drawn by the Chairman of the Authority immediately after the first appointments have been made.

3. At the expiration of the term of a member of the Court, the said member shall remain in office until the appointment and assumption of office of his successor. Though replaced, he shall finish any cases which he may have begun.

4. In the absence of the President, or where it becomes impossible for the President to continue to carry out his duties and functions, the Vice President shall assume these assignments of the President.

5. In the temporary absence of a member of the Court, another member shall be nominated to replace him in accordance with the provisions of the Rules of Procedure.

6. Where a member of the court can no longer perform his duties, the Executive Secretary shall inform Council thereof, Council shall then propose to the Authority that a new member be appointed to replace him.

7. In the event of gross misconduct, inability to exercise his functions or physical or mental disability on the part of one of its members, the Court shall meet in plenary session to take cognizance of the fact. The Court shall then draw up a report which will be promptly transmitted to the Authority which may decide to relieve the member in question of his post.

8. Where the President of the Court cannot participate in the proceedings of a given case, he shall be replaced by the Vice President or where the latter is absent be replaced by another member of the Court appointed in accordance with the Rules of Procedure of the Court.

9. Where a member of the Court cannot participate in the proceedings of a given case, he shall inform the President of the Court who shall replace him with another member of the Court for the purpose of that case.

10. Whenever the Vice President or any member of the Court replaces the President in accordance with the provisions of paragraph 8 of this Article, he shall exercise all the authority and powers vested in the office of the President of the Court.

11. No member of the Court may exercise any political or administrative function or engage in any other occupation of a professional nature.

…

Article 9: [Jurisdiction of the Court]

[1. The Court has competence to adjudicate on any dispute relating to the following:

(a) The interpretation and application of the Treaty, Conventions and Protocols of the Community;

(b) The interpretation and application of the regulations, directives, decisions and other subsidiary legal instruments adopted by ECOWAS;

(c) The legality of regulations, directives, decisions and other legal instruments adopted by ECOWAS;

(d) The failure by Member States to honor their obligations under the Treaty, Conventions and Protocols, regulations, directives, or decisions of ECOWAS;

(e) The provisions of the Treaty, Conventions and Protocols, regulations, directives or decisions of ECOWAS Member States;
(f) The Community and its officials; and
(g) The action for damages against a Community institution or an official of the Community for any action or omission in the exercise of official functions.

2. The Court shall have the power to determine any non-contractual liability of the Community and may order the Community to pay damages or make reparation for official acts or omissions of any Community institution or Community officials in the performance of official duties or functions.

3. Any action by or against a Community Institution or any Member of the Community shall be statute barred after three (3) years from the date when the right of action arose.

4. The Court has jurisdiction to determine case of violation of human rights that occur in any Member State.

5. Pending the establishment of the Arbitration Tribunal provided for under Article 16 of the Treaty, the Court shall have the power to act as arbitrator for the purpose of Article 16 of the Treaty.

6. The Court shall have jurisdiction over any matter provided for in an agreement where the parties provide that the Court shall settle disputes arising from the agreement.

7. The Court shall have the powers conferred upon it by the provisions of this Protocol as well as any other powers that may be conferred by subsequent Protocols and Decisions of the Community.

8. The Authority of Heads of State and Government shall have the power to grant the Court the power to adjudicate on any specific dispute that it may refer to the Court other than those specified in this Article.]

[Article 10: Access to the Court]

[Access to the Court is open to the following:

(a) Member States, and unless otherwise provided in a Protocol, the Executive Secretary, where action is brought for failure by a Member state to fulfill an obligation;
(b) Member States, the Council of Ministers and the Executive Secretary in proceeding for the determination of the legality of an action in relation to any community text;
(c) Individuals and corporate bodies in proceedings for the determination of an act or inaction of a Community official which violates the rights of the individuals or corporate bodies;
(d) Individuals on application for relief for violation of their human rights; the submission of application for which shall:
    (i) Not be anonymous; nor
    (ii) Be made whilst the same matter has been instituted before another International Court for adjudication;
(e) Staff of any Community institution, after the Staff Member has exhausted all appeal processes available to the officer under the ECOWAS Staff Rules and Regulations;
(f) Where in any action before a court of a Member State, an issue arises as to the interpretation of a provision of the Treaty, or the other Protocols or Regulations, the national court may on its own or at the request of any of the parties to the action refer the issue to the Court for interpretation.]

Article [11]: Advisory Opinion

1. The Court may, at the request of the Authority, Council one or more Member States, or the Executive Secretary and any other institution of the Community, express in an advisory, a legal opinion on requests of the Treaty.

2. Requests for advisory opinion as contained in paragraph 1 of this Article shall be made in writing and shall contain a statement of the questions upon which advisory opinion is required. They must be accompanied by all relevant documents likely to throw light upon the question.

3. Upon receipt of the request referred to in paragraph 2 of this Article the Chief Registrar shall immediately inform Member States, notify them of the time limit fixed by the President for the receipt of their written observations or for hearing their oral declarations.

4. The Court shall give the advisory opinion in public.

5. In the exercise of its advisory functions, the Court shall be governed by the provisions of this Protocol which apply in contentions cases, where the Court recognizes them to be applicable.

Article [12]: Application to the Tribunal

1. Cases may be brought before the Court by an application addressed to the Court Registry. This application shall set out the subject matter of the dispute and the parties involved and shall contain a summary of the argument put forward as well as the plea of the plaintiff.

2. The Chief Registrar of the Court shall immediately serve notice of the application and of all documents relating to the subject matter of the dispute to the other party, who shall make known his grounds for defense, within the time limit stipulated by the rules of procedure of the Court.

Article [13]: Representation before the Court

Each party to a dispute shall be represented before the Court by one or more agents nominated by the party concerned for this purpose. The agents may, where necessary, request the assistance of one or more Advocates or Counsels who are recognized by the laws and regulations of the Member States as being empowered to appear in Court in their area of jurisdiction.

Article [14]: Proceedings before the Court

1. Proceedings before the Court shall consist of two parts: written and oral.

2. Written proceedings shall consist of the application entered in the Court, notification of the application, the defense, the reply or counter statement, the rejoinder and any other briefs or documents in support.

3. Documents comprising the written proceedings shall be addressed to the Chief Registrar of the Court in the order and within the limit fixed by the Rules of Procedure of the Court. A copy of each document produced by one party shall be communicated to the other party.

4. The oral proceedings shall consist of the hearing of parties, agent's witnesses, advocates or counsels.

Article [15]: Sittings of the Court

1. The President shall issue summons to the parties to appear before the Court. He shall determine the roll at the Court and preside over its sittings.

2. Sittings and deliberations of the Court shall be valid when the President and at least two judges are present, but such that any sitting of the Court shall compromise of an uneven number of its members.

3. Sittings of the Court shall be public. The Court may however sit in camera at the request of one of the parties or for reasons which only the Court may determine.

Article [16]: Production of Documents

1. At any time, the Court may request the parties to produce any documents and provide any information or explanation which it may deem useful. Formal note shall be taken of any refusal.

2. The Court may, in any circumstance, and, in accordance with its Rules and Procedure, order any manner of judicial enquiry summon any person, organization or institution to carry out any enquiry or give an expert opinion.

...

Article [18]: Examination and Expert Opinion

1. Witnesses upon whom a summon has been served must appear before the Court. They shall be heard under conditions specified in the Rules of Procedure of the Court.

2. Experts may testify as witnesses under oath, in accordance with the provisions of the Rules of Procedure of the Court.

3. All hearings shall be recorded and signed by the President and the Chief Registrar of the Court.

Article [19]: Deposition upon Request

1. The Court may request the judicial authority of his place of residence to hear the evidence of a witness or an expert.

2. Such a request shall be made to the judicial authority in accordance with the conditions stipulated in the Rules of Procedure of the Court. Documents emanating from such hearing shall be transmitted to the Court under the same conditions.

3. Expenses incurred by this procedure shall be borne by the parties.

4. The oral proceedings shall consist of the hearing of parties, agent's witnesses, advocates or counsels.

...

[Article 24: Method of implementation of Judgments of the Court]

[1. Judgments of the Court that have financial implications for nationals of Member States or Member States are binding.

2. Execution of any decision of the Court shall be in form of a writ of execution, which shall be submitted by the Registrar of the Court to the relevant Member State for execution according to the rules of civil procedure of that Member State.

3. Upon the verification by the appointed authority of the recipient Member State that the writ is from the Court, the writ shall be enforced.

4. All Member States shall determine the competent national authority for the purpose of recipient and processing of execution and notify the Court accordingly.

5. The writ of execution issued by the Community Court may be suspended only by a decision of the Community Court of Justice.]

...

Article [30]: [Budget of the Court]

[The budget of the Community Court of Justice shall be dealt with in accordance with the relevant provisions of the Revised Treaty.]

Article [31]: [Official languages]

[The Official languages of the Court shall be English, French, and Portuguese.]

The Gulf Cooperation Council Framework

48.a Charter of the Cooperation Council for the Arab States of the Gulf

Date: 25 May 1981
Source: 1288 UNTS 3
https://www.gcc-sg.org/en-us/AboutGCC/Pages/Primarylaw.aspx

…

ARTICLE SIX Organization of the Cooperation Council

The Cooperation Council shall have the following main organizations:

1. The Supreme Council to which shall be attached the Commission for Settlement of Disputes.
2. The Ministerial Council.
3. The Secretariat General.

Each of these organizations may establish sub-agencies as may be necessary.

ARTICLE EIGHT The Functions of the Supreme Council

The Supreme Council shall endeavour to realize the objectives of the Cooperation Council, particularly as concerns the following:

…

Approve the rules of procedure of the Commission for the Settlement of Disputes and nominate its members.

…

ARTICLE TEN Commission for the Settlement of Disputes

The Cooperation Council shall have a commission called "The Commission for the Settlement of Disputes" which shall be attached to the Supreme Council. The Supreme Council shall establish the composition of the Commission for every case on an "ad hoc" basis in accordance with the nature of the dispute. If a dispute arises over interpretation or implementation of the Charter and such dispute is not resolved within the Ministerial Council or the Supreme Council, the Supreme Council may refer such dispute to the Commission for the Settlement of Disputes. The Commission shall submit its recommendations or opinion, as applicable, to the Supreme Council for such action as the Supreme Council deems appropriate.

…

48.b Rules of Procedure of the Commission for the Settlement of Disputes

Date: 25 May 1981
Source: 1288 UNTS 3

Preamble

In accordance with the provisions of Article Six of the Charter of the Gulf Arab States Cooperation Council; and in implementation of the Provisions of Article Ten of the Cooperation Council Charter,

A Commission for Settlement of Disputes, hereinafter referred to as Commission, shall be set up and its jurisdiction and rules for its proceedings shall be as follows:

ARTICLE ONE Terminology

Terms used in these Rules of Procedure shall have the same meanings as those established in the Charter of the Gulf Arab States Cooperation Council.

ARTICLE TWO Location and Session of the Commission

The Commission shall have its headquarters at Riyadh, Saudi Arabia, and shall hold its meetings on the territory of the state where its headquarters is located, but may hold its meetings elsewhere, when necessary.

ARTICLE THREE Jurisdiction

The Commission shall, once installed, have jurisdiction to consider the following matters referred to it by the Supreme Council:

a. disputes between member states.

b. Differences of opinion as to the interpretation or implementation of the Cooperation Council Charter.

ARTICLE FOUR Membership of the Commission

a. The Commission shall be formed of an appropriate number of citizens of member states not involved in the dispute. The Council shall select members of the Commission in every case separately depending on the nature of the dispute, provided that the number shall be no less than three.

b. The Commission may seek the advice of such experts and consultants as it may deem necessary.

c. Unless the Supreme Council resolves otherwise, the Commission's task shall end with the submission of its recommendations or opinion to the Supreme Council which, after the conclusion of the Commission's task, may summon it at any time to explain or elaborate on its recommendations or opinions.

ARTICLE FIVE Meetings and Internal Procedures

a. A meeting of the Commission shall be valid if attended by all members.

b. The Secretariat-General of the Cooperation Council shall prepare procedures required to conduct the Commission's affairs, and such procedures shall go in to effect as of the date of approval by the Ministerial Council.

c. Each party to the dispute shall send representatives to the Commission who shall be entitled to follow proceedings and present their defence.

ARTICLE SIX Chairmanship

The Commission shall select a chairman from among its members.

ARTICLE SEVEN Voting

Every member of the Commission shall have one vote, and shall issue its recommendations or opinions on matters referred to it by a majority of the members. In the event of an indecisive vote the party with whom the chairman has voted shall prevail.

ARTICLE EIGHT The Secretariat of the Commission

a. The Secretary-General shall appoint a Secretary for the Commission, and a sufficient number of officials to carry out the work of the Commission's Secretariat.

b. The Supreme Council may if necessary create an independent organization to carry out the work of the Secretariat of the Commission.

ARTICLE NINE Recommendations & Opinions

a. The Commission shall issue its recommendations or opinions in accordance with the Cooperation Council's Charter, with international laws and practices, and the principles of Islamic Shari'ah. The Commission shall submit its findings on the case in hand to the Supreme Council for appropriate action.

b. The Commission may, while considering any dispute referred to it and pending the issue of its final recommendations thereon, ask the Supreme Council to take interim action called for by necessity or circumstances.

c. The Commission's recommendations or opinions shall specify the reasons on which they were based and shall be signed by the Chairman and the Secretary.

d. If an opinion is not passed wholly or partially by unanimous vote of the members, the dissenting members shall be entitled to record their dissenting opinion.

ARTICLE TEN Immunities and Privileges

The Commission and its members shall enjoy such immunities and privileges in the territories of the member states as are required to realize its objectives in accordance with Article Seventeen of the Cooperation Council Charter.

ARTICLE ELEVEN The Budget of the Commission

The Commission's budget shall be considered part of the Secretariat-General's budget. Remunerations of the Commission's members shall be established by the Supreme Council.

ARTICLE TWELVE Amendments

a. Any member state may request for amendments to these Rules of Procedure.

b. Requests for amendments shall be submitted to the Secretary-General who shall relay them to the member states at least four months before submission to the Ministerial Council.

c. An amendment shall be effective if approved unanimously by the Supreme Council.

ARTICLE THIRTEEN Effective Date

These Rules of Procedure shall go into effect as of the date of approval by the Supreme Council. These Rules of Procedure were signed at Abu Dhabi City, United Arab Emirates on 21 Rajab 1401 AH corresponding to 25 May 1981 AD.

9 Law of the Sea*

49 Optional Protocol of Signature concerning the Compulsory Settlement of Disputes (The 1958 Geneva Conventions Optional Protocol)

Date: 29 April 1958
Source: 450 UNTS 169
https://legal.un.org/ilc/texts/instruments/english/conventions/8_1_1958_optional_protocol.pdf

The States Parties to this Protocol and to any one or more of the Conventions on the Law of the Sea adopted by the United Nations Conference on the Law of the Sea held at Geneva from 24 February to 27 April 1958**,

EXPRESSING their wish to resort, in all matters concerning them in respect of any dispute arising out of the interpretation or application of any article of any Convention on the Law of the Sea of 29 April 1958, to the compulsory jurisdiction of the International Court of Justice, unless some other form of settlement is provided in the Convention or has been agreed upon by the Parties within a reasonable period,

Have agreed as follows:

Article I

Disputes arising out of the interpretation or application of any Convention on the Law of the Sea shall lie within the compulsory jurisdiction of the International Court of Justice, and may accordingly be brought before the Court by an application made by any party to the dispute being a Party to this Protocol.

Article II

This undertaking relates to all the provisions of any Convention on the Law of the Sea except, in the Convention on Fishing and Conservation of the Living Resources of the High Seas, articles 4, 5, 6, 7 and 8, to which articles 9, 10, 11 and 12 of that Convention remain applicable.

Article III

The Parties may agree, within a period of two months after one party has notified its opinion to the other that a dispute exists, to resort not to the International Court of Justice but to an arbitral tribunal. After the expiry of the said period, either Party to this Protocol may bring the dispute before the Court by an application.

* N.B.: See further Document Nos. 56.a and 56.b on protection of the marine environment.

** N.B.: This refers to the following four Conventions adopted during the United Nations Conference on the Law of the Sea of 1958: (i) Convention on the Territorial Sea and the Contiguous Zone (516 UNTS 205); (ii) Convention on the High Seas (450 UNTS 11); (iii) Convention on Fishing and Conservation of the Living Resources of the High Seas (559 UNTS 285); (iv) Convention on the Continental Shelf (499 UNTS 311).

Article IV

1. Within the same period of two months, the Parties to this Protocol may agree to adopt a conciliation procedure before resorting to the International Court of Justice.

2. The conciliation commission shall make its recommendations within five months after its appointment. If its recommendations are not accepted by the parties to the dispute within two months after they have been delivered, either party may bring the dispute before the Court by an application.

Article V

This Protocol shall remain open for signature by all States who become Parties to any Convention on the Law of the Sea adopted by the United Nations Conference on the Law of the Sea and is subject to ratification, where necessary, according to the constitutional requirements of the signatory States.

...

Dispute Settlement under the 1982 UN Convention on the Law of the Sea

50.a United Nations Convention on the Law of the Sea

Date: 10 December 1982
Source: 1833 UNTS 397
https://www.un.org/Depts/los/convention_agreements/texts/unclos/unclos_e.pdf

...

PART XI: THE AREA

...

SECTION 5. SETTLEMENT OF DISPUTES AND ADVISORY OPINIONS

Article 186 Seabed Disputes Chamber of the International Tribunal for the Law of the Sea

The establishment of the Seabed Disputes Chamber and the manner in which it shall exercise its jurisdiction shall be governed by the provisions of this section, of Part XV and of Annex VI.

Article 187 Jurisdiction of the Seabed Disputes Chamber

The Seabed Disputes Chamber shall have jurisdiction under this Part and the Annexes relating thereto in disputes with respect to activities in the Area falling within the following categories:

(a) disputes between States Parties concerning the interpretation or application of this Part and the Annexes relating thereto;

(b) disputes between a State Party and the Authority concerning:

   (i) acts or omissions of the Authority or of a State Party alleged to be in violation of this Part or the Annexes relating thereto or of rules, regulations and procedures of the Authority adopted in accordance therewith; or

(ii) acts of the Authority alleged to be in excess of jurisdiction or a misuse of power;

(c) disputes between parties to a contract, being States Parties, the Authority or the Enterprise, state enterprises and natural or juridical persons referred to in article 153, paragraph 2(b), concerning:

(i) the interpretation or application of a relevant contract or a plan of work; or

(ii) acts or omissions of a party to the contract relating to activities in the Area and directed to the other party or directly affecting its legitimate interests;

(d) disputes between the Authority and a prospective contractor who has been sponsored by a State as provided in article 153, paragraph 2(b), and has duly fulfilled the conditions referred to in Annex III, article 4, paragraph 6, and article 13, paragraph 2, concerning the refusal of a contract or a legal issue arising in the negotiation of the contract;

(e) disputes between the Authority and a State Party, a state enterprise or a natural or juridical person sponsored by a State Party as provided for in article 153, paragraph 2(b), where it is alleged that the Authority has incurred liability as provided in Annex III, article 22;

(f) any other disputes for which the jurisdiction of the Chamber is specifically provided in this Convention.

Article 188 Submission of disputes to a special chamber of the International Tribunal for the Law of the Sea or an ad hoc chamber of the Seabed Disputes Chamber or to binding commercial arbitration

1. Disputes between States Parties referred to in article 187, subparagraph (a), may be submitted:

(a) at the request of the parties to the dispute, to a special chamber of the International Tribunal for the Law of the Sea to be formed in accordance with Annex VI, articles 15 and 17; or

(b) at the request of any party to the dispute, to an ad hoc chamber of the Seabed Disputes Chamber to be formed in accordance with Annex VI, article 36.

2. (a) Disputes concerning the interpretation or application of a contract referred to in article 187, subparagraph (c)(i), shall be submitted, at the request of any party to the dispute, to binding commercial arbitration, unless the parties otherwise agree. A commercial arbitral tribunal to which the dispute is submitted shall have no jurisdiction to decide any question of interpretation of this Convention. When the dispute also involves a question of the interpretation of Part XI and the Annexes relating thereto, with respect to activities in the Area, that question shall be referred to the Seabed Disputes Chamber for a ruling.

(b) If, at the commencement of or in the course of such arbitration, the arbitral tribunal determines, either at the request of any party to the dispute or *proprio motu*, that its decision depends upon a ruling of the Seabed Disputes Chamber, the arbitral tribunal shall refer such question to the Seabed Disputes Chamber for such ruling. The arbitral tribunal shall then proceed to render its award in conformity with the ruling of the Seabed Disputes Chamber.

(c) In the absence of a provision in the contract on the arbitration procedure to be applied in the dispute, the arbitration shall be conducted in accordance with the UNCITRAL Arbitration Rules or such other arbitration rules as may be prescribed in the rules, regulations and procedures of the Authority, unless the parties to the dispute otherwise agree.

Article189 Limitation on jurisdiction with regard to decisions of the Authority

The Seabed Disputes Chamber shall have no jurisdiction with regard to the exercise by the Authority of its discretionary powers in accordance with this Part; in no case shall it substitute its discretion for that of the Authority. Without prejudice to article 191, in exercising its jurisdiction pursuant to article 187, the Seabed Disputes Chamber shall not pronounce itself on the question of whether any rules, regulations and procedures of the Authority are in conformity with this Convention, nor declare invalid any such rules, regulations and procedures. Its jurisdiction in this regard shall be confined to deciding claims that the application of any rules, regulations and procedures of the Authority in individual cases would be in conflict with the contractual obligations of the parties to the dispute or their obligations under this Convention, claims concerning excess of jurisdiction or misuse of power, and to claims for damages to be paid or other remedy to be given to the party concerned for the failure of the other party to comply with its contractual obligations or its obligations under this Convention.

Article190 Participation and appearance of sponsoring States Parties in proceedings

1. If a natural or juridical person is a party to a dispute referred to in article 187, the sponsoring State shall be given notice thereof and shall have the right to participate in the proceedings by submitting written or oral statements.
2. If an action is brought against a State Party by a natural or juridical person sponsored by another State Party in a dispute referred to in article 187, subparagraph (c), the respondent State may request the State sponsoring that person to appear in the proceedings on behalf of that person. Failing such appearance, the respondent State may arrange to be represented by a juridical person of its nationality.

Article191 Advisory opinions

The Seabed Disputes Chamber shall give advisory opinions at the request of the Assembly or the Council on legal questions arising within the scope of their activities. Such opinions shall be given as a matter of urgency.

...

PART XV: SETTLEMENT OF DISPUTES

SECTION 1. GENERAL PROVISIONS

Article 279 Obligation to settle disputes by peaceful means

States Parties shall settle any dispute between them concerning the interpretation or application of this Convention by peaceful means in accordance with Article 2, paragraph 3, of the Charter of the United Nations and, to this end, shall seek a solution by the means indicated in Article 33, paragraph 1, of the Charter.

Article 280 Settlement of disputes by any peaceful means chosen by the parties

Nothing in this Part impairs the right of any States Parties to agree at any time to settle a dispute between them concerning the interpretation or application of this Convention by any peaceful means of their own choice.

Article 281 Procedure where no settlement has been reached by the parties

1. If the States Parties which are parties to a dispute concerning the interpretation or application of this Convention have agreed to seek settlement of the dispute by a peaceful means of their own choice, the procedures provided for in this Part apply only where no settlement has been reached by recourse to such means and the agreement between the parties does not exclude any further procedure.

2. If the parties have also agreed on a time-limit, paragraph 1 applies only upon the expiration of that time-limit.

Article 282 Obligations under general, regional or bilateral agreements

If the States Parties which are parties to a dispute concerning the interpretation or application of this Convention have agreed, through a general, regional or bilateral agreement or otherwise, that such dispute shall, at the request of any party to the dispute, be submitted to a procedure that entails a binding decision, that procedure shall apply in lieu of the procedures provided for in this Part, unless the parties to the dispute otherwise agree.

Article 283 Obligation to exchange views

1. When a dispute arises between States Parties concerning the interpretation or application of this Convention, the parties to the dispute shall proceed expeditiously to an exchange of views regarding its settlement by negotiation or other peaceful means.

2. The parties shall also proceed expeditiously to an exchange of views where a procedure for the settlement of such a dispute has been terminated without a settlement or where a settlement has been reached and the circumstances require consultation regarding the manner of implementing the settlement.

Article 284 Conciliation

1. A State Party which is a party to a dispute concerning the interpretation or application of this Convention may invite the other party or parties to submit the dispute to conciliation in accordance with the procedure under Annex V, section 1, or another conciliation procedure.

2. If the invitation is accepted and if the parties agree upon the conciliation procedure to be applied, any party may submit the dispute to that procedure.

3. If the invitation is not accepted or the parties do not agree upon the procedure, the conciliation proceedings shall be deemed to be terminated.

4. Unless the parties otherwise agree, when a dispute has been submitted to conciliation, the proceedings may be terminated only in accordance with the agreed conciliation procedure.

Article 285 Application of this section to disputes submitted pursuant to Part XI

This section applies to any dispute which pursuant to Part XI, section 5, is to be settled in accordance with procedures provided for in this Part. If an entity other than a State Party is a party to such a dispute, this section applies *mutatis mutandis.*

SECTION 2. COMPULSORY PROCEDURES ENTAILING BINDING DECISIONS

Article 286 Application of procedures under this section

Subject to section 3, any dispute concerning the interpretation or application of this Convention shall, where no settlement has been reached by recourse to section 1, be submitted at the request of any party to the dispute to the court or tribunal having jurisdiction under this section.

Article 287 Choice of procedure

1. When signing, ratifying or acceding to this Convention or at any time thereafter, a State shall be free to choose, by means of a written declaration, one or more of the following means for the settlement of disputes concerning the interpretation or application of this Convention:

(a) the International Tribunal for the Law of the Sea established in accordance with Annex VI;

(b) the International Court of Justice;

(c) an arbitral tribunal constituted in accordance with Annex VII;

(d) a special arbitral tribunal constituted in accordance with Annex VIII for one or more of the categories of disputes specified therein.

2. A declaration made under paragraph 1 shall not affect or be affected by the obligation of a State Party to accept the jurisdiction of the Seabed Disputes Chamber of the International Tribunal for the Law of the Sea to the extent and in the manner provided for in Part XI, section 5.

3. A State Party, which is a party to a dispute not covered by a declaration in force, shall be deemed to have accepted arbitration in accordance with Annex VII.

4. If the parties to a dispute have accepted the same procedure for the settlement of the dispute, it may be submitted only to that procedure, unless the parties otherwise agree.

5. If the parties to a dispute have not accepted the same procedure for the settlement of the dispute, it may be submitted only to arbitration in accordance with Annex VII, unless the parties otherwise agree.

6. A declaration made under paragraph 1 shall remain in force until three months after notice of revocation has been deposited with the Secretary-General of the United Nations.

7. A new declaration, a notice of revocation or the expiry of a declaration does not in any way affect proceedings pending before a court or tribunal having jurisdiction under this article, unless the parties otherwise agree.

8. Declarations and notices referred to in this article shall be deposited with the Secretary-General of the United Nations, who shall transmit copies thereof to the States Parties.

Article 288 Jurisdiction

1. A court or tribunal referred to in article 287 shall have jurisdiction over any dispute concerning the interpretation or application of this Convention which is submitted to it in accordance with this Part.

2. A court or tribunal referred to in article 287 shall also have jurisdiction over any dispute concerning the interpretation or application of an international agreement related to the purposes of this Convention, which is submitted to it in accordance with the agreement.

3. The Seabed Disputes Chamber of the International Tribunal for the Law of the Sea established in accordance with Annex VI, and any other chamber or arbitral tribunal

referred to in Part XI, section 5, shall have jurisdiction in any matter which is submitted to it in accordance therewith.

4. In the event of a dispute as to whether a court or tribunal has jurisdiction, the matter shall be settled by decision of that court or tribunal.

Article 289 Experts

In any dispute involving scientific or technical matters, a court or tribunal exercising jurisdiction under this section may, at the request of a party or *proprio motu*, select in consultation with the parties no fewer than two scientific or technical experts chosen preferably from the relevant list prepared in accordance with Annex VIII, article 2, to sit with the court or tribunal but without the right to vote.

Article 290 Provisional measures

1. If a dispute has been duly submitted to a court or tribunal which considers that *prima facie* it has jurisdiction under this Part or Part XI, section 5, the court or tribunal may prescribe any provisional measures which it considers appropriate under the circumstances to preserve the respective rights of the parties to the dispute or to prevent serious harm to the marine environment, pending the final decision.

2. Provisional measures may be modified or revoked as soon as the circumstances justifying them have changed or ceased to exist.

3. Provisional measures may be prescribed, modified or revoked under this article only at the request of a party to the dispute and after the parties have been given an opportunity to be heard.

4. The court or tribunal shall forthwith give notice to the parties to the dispute, and to such other States Parties as it considers appropriate, of the prescription, modification or revocation of provisional measures.

5. Pending the constitution of an arbitral tribunal to which a dispute is being submitted under this section, any court or tribunal agreed upon by the parties or, failing such agreement within two weeks from the date of the request for provisional measures, the International Tribunal for the Law of the Sea or, with respect to activities in the Area, the Seabed Disputes Chamber, may prescribe, modify or revoke provisional measures in accordance with this article if it considers that *prima facie* the tribunal which is to be constituted would have jurisdiction and that the urgency of the situation so requires. Once constituted, the tribunal to which the dispute has been submitted may modify, revoke or affirm those provisional measures, acting in conformity with paragraphs 1 to 4.

6. The parties to the dispute shall comply promptly with any provisional measures prescribed under this article.

Article 291 Access

1. All the dispute settlement procedures specified in this Part shall be open to States Parties.

2. The dispute settlement procedures specified in this Part shall be open to entities other than States Parties only as specifically provided for in this Convention.

Article 292 Prompt release of vessels and crews

1. Where the authorities of a State Party have detained a vessel flying the flag of another State Party and it is alleged that the detaining State has not complied with the provisions

of this Convention for the prompt release of the vessel or its crew upon the posting of a reasonable bond or other financial security, the question of release from detention may be submitted to any court or tribunal agreed upon by the parties or, failing such agreement within 10 days from the time of detention, to a court or tribunal accepted by the detaining State under article 287 or to the International Tribunal for the Law of the Sea, unless the parties otherwise agree.

2. The application for release may be made only by or on behalf of the flag State of the vessel.

3. The court or tribunal shall deal without delay with the application for release and shall deal only with the question of release, without prejudice to the merits of any case before the appropriate domestic forum against the vessel, its owner or its crew. The authorities of the detaining State remain competent to release the vessel or its crew at any time.

4. Upon the posting of the bond or other financial security determined by the court or tribunal, the authorities of the detaining State shall comply promptly with the decision of the court or tribunal concerning the release of the vessel or its crew.

Article 293 Applicable law

1. A court or tribunal having jurisdiction under this section shall apply this Convention and other rules of international law not incompatible with this Convention.

2. Paragraph 1 does not prejudice the power of the court or tribunal having jurisdiction under this section to decide a case *ex aequo et bono*, if the parties so agree.

Article 294 Preliminary proceedings

1. A court or tribunal provided for in article 287 to which an application is made in respect of a dispute referred to in article 297 shall determine at the request of a party, or may determine *proprio motu*, whether the claim constitutes an abuse of legal process or whether *prima facie* it is well founded. If the court or tribunal determines that the claim constitutes an abuse of legal process or is *prima facie* unfounded, it shall take no further action in the case.

2. Upon receipt of the application, the court or tribunal shall immediately notify the other party or parties of the application, and shall fix a reasonable time-limit within which they may request it to make a determination in accordance with paragraph 1.

3. Nothing in this article affects the right of any party to a dispute to make preliminary objections in accordance with the applicable rules of procedure.

Article 295 Exhaustion of local remedies

Any dispute between States Parties concerning the interpretation or application of this Convention may be submitted to the procedures provided for in this section only after local remedies have been exhausted where this is required by international law.

Article 296 Finality and binding force of decisions

1. Any decision rendered by a court or tribunal having jurisdiction under this section shall be final and shall be complied with by all the parties to the dispute.

2. Any such decision shall have no binding force except between the parties and in respect of that particular dispute.

SECTION 3. LIMITATIONS AND EXCEPTIONS TO APPLICABILITY OF SECTION 2

Article 297 Limitations on applicability of section 2

1. Disputes concerning the interpretation or application of this Convention with regard to the exercise by a coastal State of its sovereign rights or jurisdiction provided for in this Convention shall be subject to the procedures provided for in section 2 in the following cases:
   (a) when it is alleged that a coastal State has acted in contravention of the provisions of this Convention in regard to the freedoms and rights of navigation, overflight or the laying of submarine cables and pipelines, or in regard to other internationally lawful uses of the sea specified in article 58;
   (b) when it is alleged that a State in exercising the aforementioned freedoms, rights or uses has acted in contravention of this Convention or of laws or regulations adopted by the coastal State in conformity with this Convention and other rules of international law not incompatible with this Convention; or
   (c) when it is alleged that a coastal State has acted in contravention of specified international rules and standards for the protection and preservation of the marine environment which are applicable to the coastal State and which have been established by this Convention or through a competent international organization or diplomatic conference in accordance with this Convention.
2. (a) Disputes concerning the interpretation or application of the provisions of this Convention with regard to marine scientific research shall be settled in accordance with section 2, except that the coastal State shall not be obliged to accept the submission to such settlement of any dispute arising out of:
      (i) the exercise by the coastal State of a right or discretion in accordance with article 246; or
      (ii) a decision by the coastal State to order suspension or cessation of a research project in accordance with article 253.
   (b) A dispute arising from an allegation by the researching State that with respect to a specific project the coastal State is not exercising its rights under articles 246 and 253 in a manner compatible with this Convention shall be submitted, at the request of either party, to conciliation under Annex V, section 2, provided that the conciliation commission shall not call in question the exercise by the coastal State of its discretion to designate specific areas as referred to in article 246, paragraph 6, or of its discretion to withhold consent in accordance with article 246, paragraph 5.
3. (a) Disputes concerning the interpretation or application of the provisions of this Convention with regard to fisheries shall be settled in accordance with section 2, except that the coastal State shall not be obliged to accept the submission to such settlement of any dispute relating to its sovereign rights with respect to the living resources in the exclusive economic zone or their exercise, including its discretionary powers for determining the allowable catch, its harvesting capacity, the allocation of surpluses to other States and the terms and conditions established in its conservation and management laws and regulations.
   (b) Where no settlement has been reached by recourse to section 1 of this Part, a dispute shall be submitted to conciliation under Annex V, section 2, at the request of any party to the dispute, when it is alleged that:

(i) a coastal State has manifestly failed to comply with its obligations to ensure through proper conservation and management measures that the maintenance of the living resources in the exclusive economic zone is not seriously endangered;

(ii) a coastal State has arbitrarily refused to determine, at the request of another State, the allowable catch and its capacity to harvest living resources with respect to stocks which that other State is interested in fishing; or

(iii) a coastal State has arbitrarily refused to allocate to any State, under articles 62, 69 and 70 and under the terms and conditions established by the coastal State consistent with this Convention, the whole or part of the surplus it has declared to exist.

(c) In no case shall the conciliation commission substitute its discretion for that of the coastal State.

(d) The report of the conciliation commission shall be communicated to the appropriate international organizations.

(e) In negotiating agreements pursuant to articles 69 and 70, States Parties, unless they otherwise agree, shall include a clause on measures which they shall take in order to minimize the possibility of a disagreement concerning the interpretation or application of the agreement, and on how they should proceed if a disagreement nevertheless arises.

Article 298 Optional exceptions to applicability of section 2

1. When signing, ratifying or acceding to this Convention or at any time thereafter, a State may, without prejudice to the obligations arising under section 1, declare in writing that it does not accept any one or more of the procedures provided for in section 2 with respect to one or more of the following categories of disputes:

(a) (i) disputes concerning the interpretation or application of articles 15, 74 and 83 relating to sea boundary delimitations, or those involving historic bays or titles, provided that a State having made such a declaration shall, when such a dispute arises subsequent to the entry into force of this Convention and where no agreement within a reasonable period of time is reached in negotiations between the parties, at the request of any party to the dispute, accept submission of the matter to conciliation under Annex V, section 2; and provided further that any dispute that necessarily involves the concurrent consideration of any unsettled dispute concerning sovereignty or other rights over continental or insular land territory shall be excluded from such submission;

(ii) after the conciliation commission has presented its report, which shall state the reasons on which it is based, the parties shall negotiate an agreement on the basis of that report; if these negotiations do not result in an agreement, the parties shall, by mutual consent, submit the question to one of the procedures provided for in section 2, unless the parties otherwise agree;

(iii) this subparagraph does not apply to any sea boundary dispute finally settled by an arrangement between the parties, or to any such dispute which is to be settled in accordance with a bilateral or multilateral agreement binding upon those parties;

(b) disputes concerning military activities, including military activities by government vessels and aircraft engaged in non-commercial service, and disputes concerning law enforcement activities in regard to the exercise of sovereign rights or jurisdiction excluded from the jurisdiction of a court or tribunal under article 297, paragraph 2 or 3;

(c) disputes in respect of which the Security Council of the United Nations is exercising the functions assigned to it by the Charter of the United Nations, unless the Security Council decides to remove the matter from its agenda or calls upon the parties to settle it by the means provided for in this Convention.

2. A State Party which has made a declaration under paragraph 1 may at any time withdraw it, or agree to submit a dispute excluded by such declaration to any procedure specified in this Convention.

3. A State Party which has made a declaration under paragraph 1 shall not be entitled to submit any dispute falling within the excepted category of disputes to any procedure in this Convention as against another State Party, without the consent of that party.

4. If one of the States Parties has made a declaration under paragraph 1(a), any other State Party may submit any dispute falling within an excepted category against the declarant party to the procedure specified in such declaration.

5. A new declaration, or the withdrawal of a declaration, does not in any way affect proceedings pending before a court or tribunal in accordance with this article, unless the parties otherwise agree.

6. Declarations and notices of withdrawal of declarations under this article shall be deposited with the Secretary-General of the United Nations, who shall transmit copies thereof to the States Parties.

Article 299 Right of the parties to agree upon a procedure

1. A dispute excluded under article 297 or excepted by a declaration made under article 298 from the dispute settlement procedures provided for in section 2 may be submitted to such procedures only by agreement of the parties to the dispute.

2. Nothing in this section impairs the right of the parties to the dispute to agree to some other procedure for the settlement of such dispute or to reach an amicable settlement.

…

50.b Statute of the International Tribunal for the Law of the Sea (United Nations Convention on the Law of the Sea Annex VI)

Date: 10 December 1982
Source: 1833 UNTS 397
https://www.itlos.org/fileadmin/itlos/documents/basic_texts/statute_en.pdf

Article 1 General provisions

1. The International Tribunal for the Law of the Sea is constituted and shall function in accordance with the provisions of this Convention and this Statute.

2. The seat of the Tribunal shall be in the Free and Hanseatic City of Hamburg in the Federal Republic of Germany.

3. The Tribunal may sit and exercise its functions elsewhere whenever it considers this desirable.

4. A reference of a dispute to the Tribunal shall be governed by the provisions of Parts XI and XV.

SECTION 1. ORGANIZATION OF THE TRIBUNAL

Article 2 Composition

1. The Tribunal shall be composed of a body of 21 independent members, elected from among persons enjoying the highest reputation for fairness and integrity and of recognized competence in the field of the law of the sea.

2. In the Tribunal as a whole the representation of the principal legal systems of the world and equitable geographical distribution shall be assured.

Article 3 Membership

1. No two members of the Tribunal may be nationals of the same State. A person who for the purposes of membership in the Tribunal could be regarded as a national of more than one State shall be deemed to be a national of the one in which he ordinarily exercises civil and political rights.

2. There shall be no fewer than three members from each geographical group as established by the General Assembly of the United Nations.

Article 4 Nominations and elections

1. Each State Party may nominate not more than two persons having the qualifications prescribed in article 2 of this Annex. The members of the Tribunal shall be elected from the list of persons thus nominated.

2. At least three months before the date of the election, the Secretary-General of the United Nations in the case of the first election and the Registrar of the Tribunal in the case of subsequent elections shall address a written invitation to the States Parties to submit their nominations for members of the Tribunal within two months. He shall prepare a list in alphabetical order of all the persons thus nominated, with an indication of the States Parties which have nominated them, and shall submit it to the States Parties before the seventh day of the last month before the date of each election.

3. The first election shall be held within six months of the date of entry into force of this Convention.

4. The members of the Tribunal shall be elected by secret ballot. Elections shall be held at a meeting of the States Parties convened by the Secretary-General of the United Nations in the case of the first election and by a procedure agreed to by the States Parties in the case of subsequent elections. Two thirds of the States Parties shall constitute a quorum at that meeting. The persons elected to the Tribunal shall be those nominees who obtain the largest number of votes and a two-thirds majority of the States Parties present and voting, provided that such majority includes a majority of the States Parties.

Article 5 Term of office

1. The members of the Tribunal shall be elected for nine years and may be re-elected; provided, however, that of the members elected at the first election, the terms of seven members shall expire at the end of three years and the terms of seven more members shall expire at the end of six years.

2. The members of the Tribunal whose terms are to expire at the end of the above-mentioned initial periods of three and six years shall be chosen by lot to be drawn by the Secretary-General of the United Nations immediately after the first election.

3. The members of the Tribunal shall continue to discharge their duties until their places have been filled. Though replaced, they shall finish any proceedings which they may have begun before the date of their replacement.

4. In the case of the resignation of a member of the Tribunal, the letter of resignation shall be addressed to the President of the Tribunal. The place becomes vacant on the receipt of that letter.

Article 6 Vacancies

1. Vacancies shall be filled by the same method as that laid down for the first election, subject to the following provision: the Registrar shall, within one month of the occurrence of the vacancy, proceed to issue the invitations provided for in article 4 of this Annex, and the date of the election shall be fixed by the President of the Tribunal after consultation with the States Parties.

2. A member of the Tribunal elected to replace a member whose term of office has not expired shall hold office for the remainder of his predecessor's term.

Article 7 Incompatible activities

1. No member of the Tribunal may exercise any political or administrative function, or associate actively with or be financially interested in any of the operations of any enterprise concerned with the exploration for or exploitation of the resources of the sea or the seabed or other commercial use of the sea or the seabed.

2. No member of the Tribunal may act as agent, counsel or advocate in any case.

3. Any doubt on these points shall be resolved by decision of the majority of the other members of the Tribunal present.

Article 8 Conditions relating to participation of members in a particular case

1. No member of the Tribunal may participate in the decision of any case in which he has previously taken part as agent, counsel or advocate for one of the parties, or as a member of a national or international court or tribunal, or in any other capacity.

2. If, for some special reason, a member of the Tribunal considers that he should not take part in the decision of a particular case, he shall so inform the President of the Tribunal.

3. If the President considers that for some special reason one of the members of the Tribunal should not sit in a particular case, he shall give him notice accordingly.

4. Any doubt on these points shall be resolved by decision of the majority of the other members of the Tribunal present.

Article 9 Consequence of ceasing to fulfil required conditions

If, in the unanimous opinion of the other members of the Tribunal, a member has ceased to fulfil the required conditions, the President of the Tribunal shall declare the seat vacant.

Article 10 Privileges and immunities

The members of the Tribunal, when engaged on the business of the Tribunal, shall enjoy diplomatic privileges and immunities.

Article 11 Solemn declaration by members

Every member of the Tribunal shall, before taking up his duties, make a solemn declaration in open session that he will exercise his powers impartially and conscientiously.

Article 12 President, Vice-President and Registrar

1. The Tribunal shall elect its President and Vice-President for three years; they may be re-elected.

2. The Tribunal shall appoint its Registrar and may provide for the appointment of such other officers as may be necessary.

3. The President and the Registrar shall reside at the seat of the Tribunal.

Article 13 Quorum

1. All available members of the Tribunal shall sit; a quorum of 11 elected members shall be required to constitute the Tribunal.

2. Subject to article 17 of this Annex, the Tribunal shall determine which members are available to constitute the Tribunal for the consideration of a particular dispute, having regard to the effective functioning of the chambers as provided for in articles 14 and 15 of this Annex.

3. All disputes and applications submitted to the Tribunal shall be heard and determined by the Tribunal, unless article 14 of this Annex applies, or the parties request that it shall be dealt with in accordance with article 15 of this Annex.

Article 14 Seabed Disputes Chamber

A Seabed Disputes Chamber shall be established in accordance with the provisions of section 4 of this Annex. Its jurisdiction, powers and functions shall be as provided for in Part XI, section 5.

Article 15 Special chambers

1. The Tribunal may form such chambers, composed of three or more of its elected members, as it considers necessary for dealing with particular categories of disputes.

2. The Tribunal shall form a chamber for dealing with a particular dispute submitted to it if the parties so request. The composition of such a chamber shall be determined by the Tribunal with the approval of the parties.

3. With a view to the speedy dispatch of business, the Tribunal shall form annually a chamber composed of five of its elected members which may hear and determine disputes by summary procedure. Two alternative members shall be selected for the purpose of replacing members who are unable to participate in a particular proceeding.

4. Disputes shall be heard and determined by the chambers provided for in this article if the parties so request.

5. A judgment given by any of the chambers provided for in this article and in article 14 of this Annex shall be considered as rendered by the Tribunal.

Article 16 Rules of the Tribunal

The Tribunal shall frame rules for carrying out its functions. In particular it shall lay down rules of procedure.

Article 17 Nationality of members

1. Members of the Tribunal of the nationality of any of the parties to a dispute shall retain their right to participate as members of the Tribunal.

2. If the Tribunal, when hearing a dispute, includes upon the bench a member of the nationality of one of the parties, any other party may choose a person to participate as a member of the Tribunal.

3. If the Tribunal, when hearing a dispute, does not include upon the bench a member of the nationality of the parties, each of those parties may choose a person to participate as a member of the Tribunal.

4. This article applies to the chambers referred to in articles 14 and 15 of this Annex. In such cases, the President, in consultation with the parties, shall request specified members of the Tribunal forming the chamber, as many as necessary, to give place to the members of the Tribunal of the nationality of the parties concerned, and, failing such, or if they are unable to be present, to the members specially chosen by the parties.

5. Should there be several parties in the same interest, they shall, for the purpose of the preceding provisions, be considered as one party only. Any doubt on this point shall be settled by the decision of the Tribunal.

6. Members chosen in accordance with paragraphs 2, 3 and 4 shall fulfil the conditions required by articles 2, 8 and 11 of this Annex. They shall participate in the decision on terms of complete equality with their colleagues.

Article 18 Remuneration of members

1. Each elected member of the Tribunal shall receive an annual allowance and, for each day on which he exercises his functions, a special allowance, provided that in any year the total sum payable to any member as special allowance shall not exceed the amount of the annual allowance.

2. The President shall receive a special annual allowance.

3. The Vice-President shall receive a special allowance for each day on which he acts as President.

4. The members chosen under article 17 of this Annex, other than elected members of the Tribunal, shall receive compensation for each day on which they exercise their functions.

5. The salaries, allowances and compensation shall be determined from time to time at meetings of the States Parties, taking into account the workload of the Tribunal. They may not be decreased during the term of office.

6. The salary of the Registrar shall be determined at meetings of the States Parties, on the proposal of the Tribunal.

7. Regulations adopted at meetings of the States Parties shall determine the conditions under which retirement pensions may be given to members of the Tribunal and to the Registrar, and the conditions under which members of the Tribunal and Registrar shall have their travelling expenses refunded.

8. The salaries, allowances, and compensation shall be free of all taxation.

Article 19 Expenses of the Tribunal

1. The expenses of the Tribunal shall be borne by the States Parties and by the Authority on such terms and in such a manner as shall be decided at meetings of the States Parties.

2. When an entity other than a State Party or the Authority is a party to a case submitted to it, the Tribunal shall fix the amount which that party is to contribute towards the expenses of the Tribunal.

SECTION 2. COMPETENCE

Article 20 Access to the Tribunal

1. The Tribunal shall be open to States Parties.

2. The Tribunal shall be open to entities other than States Parties in any case expressly provided for in Part XI or in any case submitted pursuant to any other agreement conferring jurisdiction on the Tribunal which is accepted by all the parties to that case.

Article 21 Jurisdiction

The jurisdiction of the Tribunal comprises all disputes and all applications submitted to it in accordance with this Convention and all matters specifically provided for in any other agreement which confers jurisdiction on the Tribunal.

Article 22 Reference of disputes subject to other agreements

If all the parties to a treaty or convention already in force and concerning the subject-matter covered by this Convention so agree, any disputes concerning the interpretation or application of such treaty or convention may, in accordance with such agreement, be submitted to the Tribunal.

Article 23 Applicable law

The Tribunal shall decide all disputes and applications in accordance with article 293.

SECTION 3. PROCEDURE

Article 24 Institution of proceedings

1. Disputes are submitted to the Tribunal, as the case may be, either by notification of a special agreement or by written application, addressed to the Registrar. In either case, the subject of the dispute and the parties shall be indicated.

2. The Registrar shall forthwith notify the special agreement or the application to all concerned.

3. The Registrar shall also notify all States Parties.

Article 25 Provisional measures

1. In accordance with article 290, the Tribunal and its Seabed Disputes Chamber shall have the power to prescribe provisional measures.

2. If the Tribunal is not in session or a sufficient number of members is not available to constitute a quorum, the provisional measures shall be prescribed by the chamber of summary procedure formed under article 15, paragraph 3, of this Annex. Notwithstanding article 15, paragraph 4, of this Annex, such provisional measures may be adopted at the request of any party to the dispute. They shall be subject to review and revision by the Tribunal.

Article 26 Hearing

1. The hearing shall be under the control of the President or, if he is unable to preside, of the Vice-President. If neither is able to preside, the senior judge present of the Tribunal shall preside.

2. The hearing shall be public, unless the Tribunal decides otherwise or unless the parties demand that the public be not admitted.

Article 27 Conduct of case

The Tribunal shall make orders for the conduct of the case, decide the form and time in which each party must conclude its arguments, and make all arrangements connected with the taking of evidence.

Article 28 Default

When one of the parties does not appear before the Tribunal or fails to defend its case, the other party may request the Tribunal to continue the proceedings and make its decision. Absence of a party or failure of a party to defend its case shall not constitute a bar to the proceedings. Before making its decision, the Tribunal must satisfy itself not only that it has jurisdiction over the dispute, but also that the claim is well founded in fact and law.

Article 29 Majority for decision

1. All questions shall be decided by a majority of the members of the Tribunal who are present.
2. In the event of an equality of votes, the President or the member of the Tribunal who acts in his place shall have a casting vote.

Article 30 Judgment

1. The judgment shall state the reasons on which it is based.
2. It shall contain the names of the members of the Tribunal who have taken part in the decision.
3. If the judgment does not represent in whole or in part the unanimous opinion of the members of the Tribunal, any member shall be entitled to deliver a separate opinion.
4. The judgment shall be signed by the President and by the Registrar. It shall be read in open court, due notice having been given to the parties to the dispute.

Article 31 Request to intervene

1. Should a State Party consider that it has an interest of a legal nature which may be affected by the decision in any dispute, it may submit a request to the Tribunal to be permitted to intervene.
2. It shall be for the Tribunal to decide upon this request.
3. If a request to intervene is granted, the decision of the Tribunal in respect of the dispute shall be binding upon the intervening State Party in so far as it relates to matters in respect of which that State Party intervened.

Article 32 Right to intervene in cases of interpretation or application

1. Whenever the interpretation or application of this Convention is in question, the Registrar shall notify all States Parties forthwith.
2. Whenever pursuant to article 21 or 22 of this Annex the interpretation or application of an international agreement is in question, the Registrar shall notify all the parties to the agreement.
3. Every party referred to in paragraphs 1 and 2 has the right to intervene in the proceedings; if it uses this right, the interpretation given by the judgment will be equally binding upon it.

Article 33 Finality and binding force of decisions

1. The decision of the Tribunal is final and shall be complied with by all the parties to the dispute.

2. The decision shall have no binding force except between the parties in respect of that particular dispute.

3. In the event of dispute as to the meaning or scope of the decision, the Tribunal shall construe it upon the request of any party.

Article 34 Costs

Unless otherwise decided by the Tribunal, each party shall bear its own costs.

SECTION 4. SEABED DISPUTES CHAMBER

Article 35 Composition

1. The Seabed Disputes Chamber referred to in article 14 of this Annex shall be composed of 11 members, selected by a majority of the elected members of the Tribunal from among them.

2. In the selection of the members of the Chamber, the representation of the principal legal systems of the world and equitable geographical distribution shall be assured. The Assembly of the Authority may adopt recommendations of a general nature relating to such representation and distribution.

3. The members of the Chamber shall be selected every three years and may be selected for a second term.

4. The Chamber shall elect its President from among its members, who shall serve for the term for which the Chamber has been selected.

5. If any proceedings are still pending at the end of any three-year period for which the Chamber has been selected, the Chamber shall complete the proceedings in its original composition.

6. If a vacancy occurs in the Chamber, the Tribunal shall select a successor from among its elected members, who shall hold office for the remainder of his predecessor's term.

7. A quorum of seven of the members selected by the Tribunal shall be required to constitute the Chamber.

Article 36 Ad hoc chambers

1. The Seabed Disputes Chamber shall form an ad hoc chamber, composed of three of its members, for dealing with a particular dispute submitted to it in accordance with article 188, paragraph 1(b). The composition of such a chamber shall be determined by the Seabed Disputes Chamber with the approval of the parties.

2. If the parties do not agree on the composition of an ad hoc chamber, each party to the dispute shall appoint one member, and the third member shall be appointed by them in agreement. If they disagree, or if any party fails to make an appointment, the President of the Seabed Disputes Chamber shall promptly make the appointment or appointments from among its members, after consultation with the parties.

3. Members of the ad hoc chamber must not be in the service of, or nationals of, any of the parties to the dispute.

Article 37 Access

The Chamber shall be open to the States Parties, the Authority and the other entities referred to in Part XI, section 5.

Article 38 Applicable law

In addition to the provisions of article 293, the Chamber shall apply:

(a) the rules, regulations and procedures of the Authority adopted in accordance with this Convention; and

(b) the terms of contracts concerning activities in the Area in matters relating to those contracts.

Article 39 Enforcement of decisions of the Chamber

The decisions of the Chamber shall be enforceable in the territories of the States Parties in the same manner as judgments or orders of the highest court of the State Party in whose territory the enforcement is sought.

Article 40 Applicability of other sections of this Annex

1. The other sections of this Annex which are not incompatible with this section apply to the Chamber.

2. In the exercise of its functions relating to advisory opinions, the Chamber shall be guided by the provisions of this Annex relating to procedure before the Tribunal to the extent to which it recognizes them to be applicable.

SECTION 5. AMENDMENTS

Article 41 Amendments

1. Amendments to this Annex, other than amendments to section 4, may be adopted only in accordance with article 313 or by consensus at a conference convened in accordance with this Convention.

2. Amendments to section 4 may be adopted only in accordance with article 314.

3. The Tribunal may propose such amendments to this Statute as it may consider necessary, by written communications to the States Parties for their consideration in conformity with paragraphs 1 and 2.

50.c Rules of the Tribunal

Date: 28 October 1997 (last amended 25 March 2021)
Source: Doc ITLOS/8
https://www.itlos.org/fileadmin/itlos/documents/basic_texts/ITLOS_8_25.03.21.pdf

Preamble

The Tribunal,

Acting pursuant to article 16 of the Statute of the International Tribunal for the Law of the Sea, Annex VI to the United Nations Convention on the Law of the Sea,

Adopts the following Rules of the Tribunal.

PART I USE OF TERMS

Article 1

For the purposes of these Rules:

(a) "Convention" means the United Nations Convention on the Law of the Sea of 10 December 1982, together with the Agreement of 28 July 1994 relating to the implementation of Part XI of the Convention;

(b) "Statute" means the Statute of the International Tribunal for the Law of the Sea, Annex VI to the Convention;

(c) "States Parties" has the meaning set out in article 1, paragraph 2, of the Convention and includes, for the purposes of Part XI of the Convention, States and entities which are members of the Authority on a provisional basis in accordance with section 1, paragraph 12, of the Annex to the Agreement relating to the implementation of Part XI;

(d) "international organization" has the meaning set out in Annex IX, article 1, to the Convention, unless otherwise specified;

(e) "Member" means an elected judge;

(f) "judge" means a Member as well as a judge *ad hoc;*

(g) "judge *ad hoc*" means a person chosen under article 17 of the Statute for the purposes of a particular case;

(h) "Authority" means the International Seabed Authority;

(i) "certified copy" means a copy of a document bearing an attestation by or on behalf of the custodian of the original or the party submitting it that it is a true and accurate copy thereof.

PART II ORGANIZATION

Section A. The Tribunal

Subsection 1. The Members

Article 2

1. The term of office of Members elected at a triennial election shall begin to run from 1 October following the date of the election.

2. The term of office of a Member elected to replace a Member whose term of office has not expired shall run from the date of the election for the remainder of that term.

Article 3

The Members, in the exercise of their functions, are of equal status, irrespective of age, priority of election or length of service.

Article 4

1. The Members shall, except as provided in paragraphs 3 and 4, take precedence according to the date on which their respective terms of office began.

2. Members whose terms of office began on the same date shall take precedence in relation to one another according to seniority of age.

3. A Member who is re-elected to a new term of office which is continuous with her or his previous term shall retain her or his precedence.

4. The President and the Vice-President of the Tribunal, while holding these offices, shall take precedence over the other Members.

5. The Member who, in accordance with the foregoing paragraphs, takes precedence next after the President and the Vice-President of the Tribunal is in these Rules designated the "Senior Member". If that Member is unable to act, the Member who is next after her or him in precedence and able to act is considered as Senior Member.

Article 5

1. The solemn declaration to be made by every Member in accordance with article 11 of the Statute shall be as follows: "I solemnly declare that I will perform my duties and exercise my powers as judge honourably, faithfully, impartially and conscientiously".

2. This declaration shall be made at the first public sitting at which the Member is present. Such sitting shall be held as soon as practicable after her or his term of office begins and, if necessary, a special sitting shall be held for the purpose.

3. A Member who is re-elected shall make a new declaration only if her or his new term is not continuous with her or his previous one.

Article 6

1. In the case of the resignation of a Member, the letter of resignation shall be addressed to the President of the Tribunal. The place becomes vacant on the receipt of the letter.

2. In the case of the resignation of the President of the Tribunal, the letter of resignation shall be addressed to the Vice-President of the Tribunal or, failing her or him, the Senior Member. The place becomes vacant on the receipt of the letter.

Article 7

In any case in which the application of article 9 of the Statute is under consideration, the Member concerned shall be so informed by the President of the Tribunal or, if the circumstances so require, by the Vice-President of the Tribunal, in a written statement which shall include the grounds therefor and any relevant evidence. The Member concerned shall subsequently, at a private meeting of the Tribunal specially convened for the purpose, be afforded an opportunity of making a statement, of furnishing any information or explanations she or he wishes to give and of supplying answers, orally or in writing, to any questions put to her or him. The Member concerned may be assisted or represented by counsel or any other person of her or his choice. At a further private meeting, at which the Member concerned shall not be present, the matter shall be discussed; each Member shall state her or his opinion, and if requested a vote shall be taken.

Subsection 2. Judges *ad hoc*

Article 8

1. Judges *ad hoc* shall participate in the case in which they sit on terms of complete equality with the other judges.

2. Judges *ad hoc* shall take precedence after the Members and in order of seniority of age.

3. In the case of the resignation of a judge *ad hoc*, the letter of resignation shall be addressed to the President of the Tribunal. The place becomes vacant on the receipt of the letter.

Article 9

1. The solemn declaration to be made by every judge *ad hoc* in accordance with articles 11 and 17, paragraph 6, of the Statute shall be as set out in article 5, paragraph 1, of these Rules.

2. This declaration shall be made at a public sitting in the case in which the judge *ad hoc* is participating.

3. Judges *ad hoc* shall make the declaration in relation to each case in which they are participating.

Subsection 3. President and Vice-President

Article 10

1. The term of office of the President and that of the Vice-President of the Tribunal shall begin to run from the date on which the term of office of the Members elected at a triennial election begins.

2. The elections of the President and the Vice-President of the Tribunal shall be held on that date or shortly thereafter. The former President, if still a Member, shall continue to exercise the functions of President of the Tribunal until the election to this position has taken place.

Article 11

1. If, on the date of the election to the presidency, the former President of the Tribunal is still a Member, she or he shall conduct the election. If she or he has ceased to be a Member, 6 or is unable to act, the election shall be conducted by the Member exercising the functions of the presidency.

2. The election shall take place by secret ballot, after the presiding Member has declared the number of affirmative votes necessary for election; there shall be no nominations. The Member obtaining the votes of the majority of the Members composing the Tribunal at the time of the election shall be declared elected and shall enter forthwith upon her or his functions.

3. The new President of the Tribunal shall conduct the election of the Vice-President of the Tribunal either at the same or at the following meeting. Paragraph 2 applies to this election.

Article 12

1. The President of the Tribunal shall preside at all meetings of the Tribunal. She or he shall direct the work and supervise the administration of the Tribunal.

2. The President shall represent the Tribunal in its relations with States and other entities.

Article 13

1. In the event of a vacancy in the presidency or of the inability of the President of the Tribunal to exercise the functions of the presidency, these shall be exercised by the VicePresident of the Tribunal or, failing her or him, by the Senior Member.

2. When the President of the Tribunal is precluded by a provision of the Statute or of these Rules either from sitting or from presiding in a particular case, she or he shall continue to exercise the functions of the presidency for all purposes save in respect of that case.

3. The President of the Tribunal shall take the measures necessary in order to ensure the continuous exercise of the functions of the presidency at the seat of the Tribunal. In the

event of her or his absence, she or he may, so far as is compatible with the Statute and these Rules, arrange for these functions to be exercised by the Vice-President of the Tribunal or, failing her or him, by the Senior Member.

4. If the President of the Tribunal decides to resign the presidency, she or he shall communicate her or his decision in writing to the Tribunal through the Vice-President of the Tribunal or, failing her or him, the Senior Member. If the Vice-President of the Tribunal decides to resign the vice-presidency, she or he shall communicate her or his decision in writing to the President of the Tribunal.

Article 14

If a vacancy in the presidency or the vice-presidency occurs before the date when the current term is due to expire, the Tribunal shall decide whether or not the vacancy shall be filled during the remainder of the term.

Subsection 4. Experts appointed under article 289 of the Convention

Article 15

1. A request by a party for the selection by the Tribunal of scientific or technical experts under article 289 of the Convention shall, as a general rule, be made not later than the closure of the written proceedings. The Tribunal may consider a later request made prior to the closure of the oral proceedings, if appropriate in the circumstances of the case.

2. When the Tribunal decides to select experts, at the request of a party or *proprio motu*, it shall select such experts upon the proposal of the President of the Tribunal, who shall consult the parties before making such a proposal.

3. Experts shall be independent and enjoy the highest reputation for fairness, competence and integrity. An expert in a field mentioned in Annex VIII, article 2, to the Convention shall be chosen preferably from the relevant list prepared in accordance with that annex.

4. This article applies *mutatis mutandis* to any chamber and its President.

5. Before entering upon their duties, such experts shall make the following solemn declaration at a public sitting:

> "I solemnly declare that I will perform my duties as an expert honourably, impartially and conscientiously and that I will faithfully observe all the provisions of the Statute and of the Rules of the Tribunal".

Subsection 5. The composition of the Tribunal for particular cases

Article 16

1. No Member who is a national of a party in a case, a national of a State member of an international organization which is a party in a case or a national of a sponsoring State of an entity other than a State which is a party in a case, shall exercise the functions of the presidency in respect of the case.

2. The Member who is presiding in a case on the date on which the Tribunal meets in accordance with article 68 shall continue to preside in that case until completion of the current phase of the case, notwithstanding the election in the meantime of a new President or Vice-President of the Tribunal. If she or he should become unable to act, the presidency for the case shall be determined in accordance with article 13 and on the basis of the composition of the Tribunal on the date on which it met in accordance with article 68.

Article 17

Members who have been replaced following the expiration of their terms of office shall continue to sit in a case until the completion of any phase in respect of which the Tribunal has met in accordance with article 68.

Article 18

1. Whenever doubt arises on any point in article 8 of the Statute, the President of the Tribunal shall inform the other Members. The Member concerned shall be afforded an opportunity of furnishing any information or explanations.

2. If a party desires to bring to the attention of the Tribunal facts which it considers to be of possible relevance to the application of article 8 of the Statute, but which it believes may not be known to the Tribunal, that party shall communicate confidentially such facts to the President of the Tribunal in writing.

Article 19

1. If a party intends to choose a judge ad hoc in a case, it shall notify the Tribunal of its intention as soon as possible. It shall inform the Tribunal of the name, nationality and brief biographical details of the person chosen, preferably at the same time but in any event not later than two months before the time-limit fixed for the filing of the counter-memorial. The judge ad hoc may be of a nationality other than that of the party which chooses her or him.

2. If a party proposes to abstain from choosing a judge ad hoc, on condition of a like abstention by the other party, it shall so notify the Tribunal, which shall inform the other party. If the other party thereafter gives notice of its intention to choose, or chooses, a judge ad hoc, the time-limit for the party which had previously abstained from choosing a judge may be extended up to 30 days by the President of the Tribunal.

3. A copy of any notification relating to the choice of a judge ad hoc shall be communicated by the Registrar to the other party, which shall be requested to furnish, within a time-limit not exceeding 30 days to be fixed by the President of the Tribunal, such observations as it may wish to make. If within the said time-limit no objection is raised by the other party, and if none appears to the Tribunal itself, the parties shall be so informed. In the event of any objection or doubt, the matter shall be decided by the Tribunal, if necessary after hearing the parties.

4. A judge ad hoc who becomes unable to sit may be replaced.

5. If the Tribunal finds that the reasons for the participation of a judge ad hoc no longer exist, that judge shall cease to sit on the bench.

Article 20

1. If the Tribunal finds that two or more parties are in the same interest and are therefore to be considered as one party only, and that there is no Member of the nationality of any one of these parties upon the bench, the Tribunal shall fix a time-limit within which they may jointly choose a judge *ad hoc*.

2. Should any party among those found by the Tribunal to be in the same interest allege the existence of a separate interest of its own or put forward any other objection, the matter shall be decided by the Tribunal, if necessary after hearing the parties.

Article 21

1. If a Member having the nationality of one of the parties is or becomes unable to sit in any phase of a case, that party is entitled to choose a judge *ad hoc* within a time-limit to be fixed by the Tribunal, or by the President of the Tribunal if the Tribunal is not sitting.

2. Parties in the same interest shall be deemed not to have a Member of one of their nationalities upon the bench if every Member having one of their nationalities is or becomes unable to sit in any phase of the case.

3. If a Member having the nationality of one of the parties becomes able to sit not later than the closure of the written proceedings in that phase of the case, that Member shall resume the seat on the bench in the case.

Article 22

1. An entity other than a State may choose a judge *ad hoc* only if:

(a) one of the other parties is a State Party and there is upon the bench a judge of its nationality or, where such party is an international organization, there is upon the bench a judge of the nationality of one of its member States or the State Party has itself chosen a judge *ad hoc*; or

(b) there is upon the bench a judge of the nationality of the sponsoring State of one of the other parties.

2. However, an international organization or a natural or juridical person or state enterprise is not entitled to choose a judge *ad hoc* if there is upon the bench a judge of the nationality of one of the member States of the international organization or a judge of the nationality of the sponsoring State of such natural or juridical person or state enterprise.

3. Where an international organization is a party to a case and there is upon the bench a judge of the nationality of a member State of the organization, the other party may choose a judge *ad hoc*.

4. Where two or more judges on the bench are nationals of member States of the international organization concerned or of the sponsoring States of a party, the President may, after consulting the parties, request one or more of such judges to withdraw from the bench.

Section B. The Seabed Disputes Chamber

Subsection 1. The members and judges *ad hoc*

Article 23

The members of the Seabed Disputes Chamber shall be selected following each triennial election to the Tribunal as soon as possible after the term of office of Members elected at such election begins. The term of office of members of the Chamber shall begin to run from the date of their selection. The term of office of members selected at the first selection shall expire on 30 September 1999; the terms of office of members selected at subsequent triennial selections shall expire on 30 September every three years thereafter. Members of the Chamber who remain on the Tribunal after the expiry of their term of office shall continue to serve on the Chamber until the next selection.

Article 24

The President of the Chamber, while holding that office, takes precedence over the other members of the Chamber. The other members take precedence according to their precedence in the Tribunal in the case where the President and Vice-President of the Tribunal are not exercising the functions of those offices.

Article 25

Articles 8 and 9 apply *mutatis mutandis* to the judges *ad hoc* of the Chamber.

Subsection 2. The presidency

Article 26

1. The Chamber shall elect its President by secret ballot and by a majority vote of its members.

2. The President shall preside at all meetings of the Chamber.

3. In the event of a vacancy in the presidency or of the inability of the President of the Chamber to exercise the functions of the presidency, these shall be exercised by the member of the Chamber who is senior in precedence and able to act.

4. In other respects, articles 10 to 14 apply *mutatis mutandis*.

Subsection 3. *Ad hoc* chambers of the Seabed Disputes Chamber

Article 27

1. Any request for the formation of an *ad hoc* chamber of the Seabed Disputes Chamber in accordance with article 188, paragraph 1 (b), of the Convention shall be made within three months from the date of the institution of proceedings.

2. If, within a time-limit fixed by the President of the Seabed Disputes Chamber, the parties do not agree on the composition of the chamber, the President shall establish time-limits for the parties to make the necessary appointments.

Section C. Special chambers

Article 28

1. The Chamber of Summary Procedure shall be composed of the President and Vice-President of the Tribunal, acting ex officio, and three other Members. In addition, two Members shall be selected to act as alternates.

2. The members and alternates of the Chamber shall be selected by the Tribunal upon the proposal of the President of the Tribunal.

3. The selection of members and alternates of the Chamber shall be made as soon as possible after 1 October in each year. The members of the Chamber and the alternates shall enter upon their functions on their selection and serve until 30 September of the following year. Members of the Chamber and alternates who remain on the Tribunal after that date shall continue to serve on the Chamber until the next selection.

4. If a member of the Chamber is unable, for whatever reason, to sit in a given case, that member shall be replaced for the purposes of that case by the senior in precedence of the two alternates.

5. If a member of the Chamber resigns or otherwise ceases to be a member, the place of that member shall be taken by the senior in precedence of the two alternates, who shall thereupon become a full member of the Chamber and be replaced by the selection of another alternate.

6. The quorum for meetings of the Chamber is three members.

Article 29

1. Whenever the Tribunal decides to form a standing special chamber provided for in article 15, paragraph 1, of the Statute, it shall determine the particular category of disputes for which it is formed, the number of its members, the period for which they will serve, the date when they will enter upon their duties and the quorum for meetings.

2. The members of such chamber shall be selected by the Tribunal upon the proposal of the President of the Tribunal from among the Members, having regard to any special knowledge, expertise or previous experience which any of the Members may have in relation to the category of disputes the chamber deals with.

3. The Tribunal may decide to dissolve a standing special chamber. The chamber shall finish any cases pending before it.

Article 30

1. A request for the formation of a special chamber to deal with a particular dispute, as provided for in article 15, paragraph 2, of the Statute, shall be made within two months from the date of the institution of proceedings. Upon receipt of a request made by one party, the President of the Tribunal shall ascertain whether the other party assents.

2. When the parties have agreed, the President of the Tribunal shall ascertain their views regarding the composition of the chamber and shall report to the Tribunal accordingly.

3. The Tribunal shall determine, with the approval of the parties, the Members who are to constitute the chamber. The same procedure shall be followed in filling any vacancy. The Tribunal shall also determine the quorum for meetings of the chamber.

4. Members of a chamber formed under this article who have been replaced, in accordance with article 5 of the Statute, following the expiration of their terms of office, shall continue to sit in all phases of the case, whatever the stage it has then reached.

Article 31

1. If a chamber when formed includes the President of the Tribunal, the President shall preside over the chamber. If it does not include the President but includes the Vice-President, the Vice-President shall preside. In any other event, the chamber shall elect its own President by secret ballot and by a majority of votes of its members. The member who, under this paragraph, presides over the chamber at the time of its formation shall continue to preside so long as she or he remains a member of that chamber.

2. Subject to paragraph 3, the President of a chamber shall exercise, in relation to cases being dealt with by that chamber and from the time it begins dealing with the case, the functions of the President of the Tribunal in relation to cases before the Tribunal.

3. The President of the Tribunal shall take such steps as may be necessary to give effect to article 17, paragraph 4, of the Statute.

4. If the President of a chamber is prevented from sitting or acting as President of the chamber, the functions of the presidency of the chamber shall be assumed by the member of the chamber who is the senior in precedence and able to act.

Section D. The Registry

Article 32

1. The Tribunal shall elect its Registrar by secret ballot from among candidates nominated by Members. The Registrar shall be elected for a term of five years and may be re-elected.

2. The President of the Tribunal shall give notice of a vacancy or impending vacancy to Members, either forthwith upon the vacancy arising or, where the vacancy will arise on the expiration of the term of office of the Registrar, not less than three months prior thereto. The President of the Tribunal shall fix a date for the closure of the list of candidates so as to enable nominations and information concerning the candidates to be received in sufficient time.

3. Nominations shall be accompanied by the relevant information concerning the candidates, in particular information as to age, nationality, present occupation, academic and other qualifications, knowledge of languages and any previous experience in law, especially the law of the sea, diplomacy or the work of international organizations.

4. The candidate obtaining the votes of the majority of the Members composing the Tribunal at the time of the election shall be declared elected.

Article 33

The Tribunal shall elect a Deputy Registrar; it may also elect an Assistant Registrar. Article 32 applies to their election and terms of office.

Article 34

Before taking up their duties, the Registrar, the Deputy Registrar and the Assistant Registrar shall make the following solemn declaration at a meeting of the Tribunal:

> "I solemnly declare that I will perform my duties as Registrar (Deputy Registrar or Assistant Registrar as the case may be) of the International Tribunal for the Law of the Sea in all loyalty, discretion and good conscience and that I will faithfully observe all the provisions of the Statute and of the Rules of the Tribunal".

Article 35

1. The staff of the Registry, other than the Registrar, the Deputy Registrar and the Assistant Registrar, shall be appointed by the Tribunal on proposals submitted by the Registrar. Appointments to such posts as the Tribunal shall determine may, however, be made by the Registrar with the approval of the President of the Tribunal.

2. The paramount consideration in the recruitment and employment of the staff and in the determination of the conditions of service shall be the necessity of securing the highest standards of efficiency, competence and integrity. Due regard shall be paid to the importance of recruiting the staff on as wide a geographical basis as possible.

3. Before taking up their duties, the staff shall make the following solemn declaration before the President of the Tribunal, the Registrar being present:

> "I solemnly declare that I will perform my duties as an official of the International Tribunal for the Law of the Sea in all loyalty, discretion and good conscience and that I will faithfully observe all the provisions of the Statute and of the Rules of the Tribunal".

Article 36

1. The Registrar, in the discharge of her or his functions, shall:

(a) be the regular channel of communications to and from the Tribunal and in particular shall effect all communications, notifications and transmission of documents required by the Convention, the Statute, these Rules or any other relevant international agreement and ensure that the date of dispatch and receipt thereof may be readily verified;

(b) keep, under the supervision of the President of the Tribunal, and in such form as may be laid down by the Tribunal, a List of cases, entered and numbered in the order in which the documents instituting proceedings or requesting an advisory opinion are received in the Registry;

(c) keep copies of declarations and notices of revocation or withdrawal thereof deposited with the Secretary-General of the United Nations under articles 287 and 298 of the Convention or Annex IX, article 7, to the Convention;

(d) keep copies of agreements conferring jurisdiction on the Tribunal;

(e) keep notifications received under article 110, paragraph 2;

(f) transmit to the parties certified copies of pleadings and annexes upon receipt thereof in the Registry;

(g) communicate to the Government of the State in which the Tribunal or a chamber is sitting, or is to sit, and any other Governments which may be concerned, the necessary information as to the persons from time to time entitled, under the Statute and the relevant agreements, to privileges, immunities or facilities;

(h) be present in person or represented by the Deputy Registrar, the Assistant Registrar or in their absence by a senior official of the Registry designated by her or him, at meetings of the Tribunal, and of the chambers, and be responsible for preparing records of such meetings;

(i) make arrangements for such provision or verification of translations and interpretations into the Tribunal's official languages as the Tribunal may require;

(j) sign all judgments, advisory opinions and orders of the Tribunal and the records referred to in subparagraph (h);

(k) be responsible for the reproduction, printing and publication of the Tribunal's judgments, advisory opinions and orders, the pleadings and statements and the minutes of public sittings in cases and of such other documents as the Tribunal may direct to be published;

(l) be responsible for all administrative work and in particular for the accounts and financial administration in accordance with the financial procedures of the Tribunal;

(m) deal with inquiries concerning the Tribunal and its work;

(n) assist in maintaining relations between the Tribunal and the Authority, the International Court of Justice and the other organs of the United Nations, its related agencies, the arbitral and special arbitral tribunals referred to in article 287 of the Convention and international bodies and conferences concerned with the codification and progressive development of international law, in particular the law of the sea;

(o) ensure that information concerning the Tribunal and its activities is accessible to Governments, the highest national courts of justice, professional and learned societies, legal faculties and schools of law and public information media;

(p) have custody of the seals and stamps of the Tribunal, of the archives of the Tribunal and of such other archives as may be entrusted to the Tribunal.

2. The Tribunal may at any time entrust additional functions to the Registrar.

3. In the discharge of her or his functions the Registrar shall be responsible to the Tribunal.

Article 37

1. The Deputy Registrar shall assist the Registrar, act as Registrar in the latter's absence and, in the event of the office becoming vacant, exercise the functions of Registrar until the office has been filled.

2. If the Registrar, the Deputy Registrar and the Assistant Registrar are unable to carry out the duties of Registrar, the President of the Tribunal shall appoint an official of the Registry to discharge those duties for such time as may be necessary. If the three offices are vacant at the same time, the President, after consulting the Members, shall appoint an official of the Registry to discharge the duties of Registrar pending an election to that office.

Article 38

1. The Registry consists of the Registrar, the Deputy Registrar, the Assistant Registrar and such other staff as required for the efficient discharge of its functions.

2. The Tribunal shall determine the organization of the Registry and shall for this purpose request the Registrar to make proposals.

3. Instructions for the Registry shall be drawn up by the Registrar and approved by the Tribunal.

4. The staff of the Registry shall be subject to Staff Regulations drawn up by the Registrar and approved by the Tribunal.

Article 39

1. The Registrar may resign from office with two months' notice tendered in writing to the President of the Tribunal. The Deputy Registrar and the Assistant Registrar may resign from office with one month's notice tendered in writing to the President of the Tribunal through the Registrar.

2. The Registrar may be removed from office only if, in the opinion of two thirds of the Members, she or he has either committed a serious breach of her or his duties or become permanently incapacitated from exercising her or his functions. Before a decision to remove the Registrar is taken under this paragraph, she or he shall be informed by the President of the Tribunal of the action contemplated, in a written statement which shall include the grounds therefor and any relevant evidence. When the action contemplated concerns permanent incapacity, relevant medical information shall be included. The Registrar shall subsequently, at a private meeting of the Tribunal, be afforded an opportunity of making a statement, of furnishing any information or explanations she or he wishes to give and of supplying answers, orally or in writing, to any questions put to her or him. The Registrar may be assisted or represented at such meeting by counsel or any other person of her or his choice.

3. The Deputy Registrar and the Assistant Registrar may be removed from office only on the same grounds and by the same procedure as specified in paragraph 2.

Section E. Internal functioning of the Tribunal

Article 40

The internal judicial practice of the Tribunal shall, subject to the Convention, the Statute and these Rules, be governed by any resolutions on the subject adopted by the Tribunal.

Article 41

1. The quorum specified by article 13, paragraph 1, of the Statute applies to all meetings of the Tribunal. The quorum specified in article 35, paragraph 7, of the Statute applies to all meetings of the Seabed Disputes Chamber. The quorum specified for a special chamber applies to all meetings of that chamber.

2. Members shall hold themselves permanently available to exercise their functions and shall attend all such meetings, unless they are absent on leave as provided for in paragraph 4

or prevented from attending by illness or for other serious reasons duly explained to the President of the Tribunal, who shall inform the Tribunal.

3. Judges *ad hoc* are likewise bound to hold themselves at the disposal of the Tribunal and to attend all meetings held in the case in which they are participating unless they are prevented from attending by illness or for other serious reasons duly explained to the President of the Tribunal, who shall inform the Tribunal. They shall not be taken into account for the calculation of the quorum.

4. The Tribunal shall fix the dates and duration of the judicial vacations and the periods and conditions of leave to be accorded to individual Members, having regard in both cases to the state of the List of cases and to the requirements of its current work.

5. Subject to the same considerations, the Tribunal shall observe the public holidays customary at the place where the Tribunal is sitting.

6. In case of urgency the President of the Tribunal may convene the Tribunal at any time.

7. Upon consultations with the Members of the Tribunal, the President may decide, as an exceptional measure, for public health, security or other compelling reasons, to hold meetings entirely or in part by video link.

Article 42

1. The deliberations of the Tribunal shall take place in private and remain secret. The Tribunal may, however, at any time decide in respect of its deliberations on other than judicial matters to publish or allow publication of any part of them.

2. Only judges and any experts appointed in accordance with article 289 of the Convention take part in the Tribunal's judicial deliberations. The Registrar, or the Deputy Registrar, and other members of the staff of the Registry as may be required shall be present. No other person shall be present except by permission of the Tribunal.

3. The records of the Tribunal's judicial deliberations shall contain only the title or nature of the subjects or matters discussed and the results of any vote taken. They shall not contain any details of the discussions nor the views expressed, provided however that any judge is entitled to require that a statement made by her or him be inserted in the records.

Section F. Official languages

Article 43

The official languages of the Tribunal are English and French.

PART III PROCEDURE

Section A. General provisions

Article 44

1. The proceedings consist of two parts: written and oral.

2. The written proceedings shall consist of the communication to the Tribunal and to the parties of memorials, counter-memorials and, if the Tribunal so authorizes, replies and rejoinders, as well as all documents in support.

3. The oral proceedings shall consist of the hearing by the Tribunal of agents, counsel, advocates, witnesses and experts.

Article 45

In every case submitted to the Tribunal, the President shall ascertain the views of the parties with regard to questions of procedure. For this purpose, the President may summon the agents of the parties to meet her or him as soon as possible after their appointment and whenever necessary thereafter, or use other appropriate means of communication.

Article 46

Time-limits for the completion of steps in the proceedings may be fixed by assigning a specified period but shall always indicate definite dates. Such time-limits shall be as short as the character of the case permits.

Article 47

The Tribunal may at any time direct that the proceedings in two or more cases be joined. It may also direct that the written or oral proceedings, including the calling of witnesses, be in common; or the Tribunal may, without effecting any formal joinder, direct common action in any of these respects.

Article 48

The parties may jointly propose particular modifications or additions to the Rules contained in this Part, which may be applied by the Tribunal or by a chamber if the Tribunal or the chamber considers them appropriate in the circumstances of the case.

Article 49

The proceedings before the Tribunal shall be conducted without unnecessary delay or expense.

Article 50

The Tribunal may issue guidelines consistent with these Rules concerning any aspect of its proceedings, including the length, format and presentation of written and oral pleadings and the use of electronic means of communication.

Article 51

All communications to the Tribunal under these Rules shall be addressed to the Registrar unless otherwise stated. Any request made by a party shall likewise be addressed to the Registrar unless made in open court in the course of the oral proceedings.

Article 52

1. All communications to the parties shall be sent to their agents.

2. The communications to a party before it has appointed an agent and to an entity other than a party shall be sent as follows:

(a) in the case of a State, the Tribunal shall direct all communications to its Government;

(b) in the case of the International Seabed Authority or the Enterprise, any international organization and any other intergovernmental organization, the Tribunal shall direct all communications to the competent body or executive head of such organization at its headquarters location;

(c) in the case of state enterprises or natural or juridical persons referred to in article 153, paragraph 2 (b), of the Convention, the Tribunal shall direct all communications through the Government of the sponsoring or certifying State, as the case may be;

(d) in the case of a group of States, state enterprises or natural or juridical persons referred to in article 153, paragraph 2 (b), of the Convention, the Tribunal shall direct all communications to each member of the group according to subparagraphs (a) and (c) above;

(e) in the case of other natural or juridical persons, the Tribunal shall direct all communications through the Government of the State in whose territory the communication has to be received.

3. The same provisions apply whenever steps are to be taken to procure evidence on the spot.

Article 53

1. The parties shall be represented by agents.
2. The parties may have the assistance of counsel or advocates before the Tribunal.

Section B. Proceedings before the Tribunal

Subsection 1. Institution of proceedings

Article 54

1. When proceedings before the Tribunal are instituted by means of an application, the application shall indicate the party making it, the party against which the claim is brought and the subject of the dispute.

2. The application shall specify as far as possible the legal grounds upon which the jurisdiction of the Tribunal is said to be based; it shall also specify the precise nature of the claim, together with a succinct statement of the facts and grounds on which the claim is based.

3. The original of the application shall be signed by the agent of the party submitting it or by the diplomatic representative of that party in the country in which the Tribunal has its seat or by some other duly authorized person. If the application bears the signature of someone other than such diplomatic representative, the signature must be authenticated by the latter or by the competent governmental authority.

4. The Registrar shall forthwith transmit to the respondent a certified copy of the application.

5. When the applicant proposes to found the jurisdiction of the Tribunal upon a consent thereto yet to be given or manifested by the party against which the application is made, the application shall be transmitted to that party. It shall not however be entered in the List of cases, nor any action be taken in the proceedings, unless and until the party against which such application is made consents to the jurisdiction of the Tribunal for the purposes of the case.

Article 55

1. When proceedings are brought before the Tribunal by the notification of a special agreement, the notification may be effected by the parties jointly or by any one or more of them. If the notification is not a joint one, a certified copy of it shall forthwith be communicated by the Registrar to any other party.

2. In each case the notification shall be accompanied by an original or certified copy of the special agreement. The notification shall also, insofar as this is not already apparent from the agreement, indicate the precise subject of the dispute and identify the parties to it.

Article 56

1. Except in the circumstances contemplated by article 54, paragraph 5, all steps on behalf of the parties after proceedings have been instituted shall be taken by agents. Agents shall have an address for service at the seat of the Tribunal or in the capital of the country where the seat is located, to which all communications concerning the case are to be sent.

2. When proceedings are instituted by means of an application, the name of the agent for the applicant shall be stated. The respondent, upon receipt of the certified copy of the application, or as soon as possible thereafter, shall inform the Tribunal of the name of its agent.

3. When proceedings are brought by notification of a special agreement, the party or parties making the notification shall state the name of its agent or the names of their agents, as the case may be. Any other party to the special agreement, upon receiving from the Registrar a certified copy of such notification, or as soon as possible thereafter, shall inform the Tribunal of the name of its agent if it has not already done so.

Article 57

1. Whenever proceedings are instituted on the basis of an agreement other than the Convention, the application or the notification shall be accompanied by a certified copy of the agreement in question.

2. In a dispute to which an international organization is a party, the Tribunal may, at the request of any other party or *proprio motu*, request the international organization to provide, within a reasonable time, information as to which, as between the organization and its member States, has competence in respect of any specific question which has arisen. If the Tribunal considers it necessary, it may suspend the proceedings until it receives such information.

Article 58

In the event of a dispute as to whether the Tribunal has jurisdiction, the matter shall be decided by the Tribunal.

Subsection 2. The written proceedings

Article 59

1. In the light of the views of the parties ascertained by the President of the Tribunal, the Tribunal shall make the necessary orders to determine, *inter alia*, the number and the order of filing of the pleadings and the time-limits within which they must be filed. The time-limits for each pleading shall not exceed six months.

2. The Tribunal may at the request of a party extend any time-limit or decide that any step taken after the expiration of the time-limit fixed therefor shall be considered as valid. It may not do so, however, unless it is satisfied that there is adequate justification for the request. In either case the other party shall be given an opportunity to state its views within a time-limit to be fixed by the Tribunal.

3. If the Tribunal is not sitting, its powers under this article may be exercised by the President of the Tribunal, but without prejudice to any subsequent decision of the Tribunal.

Article 60

1. The pleadings in a case begun by means of an application shall consist, in the following order, of: a memorial by the applicant and a counter-memorial by the respondent.

2. The Tribunal may authorize or direct that there shall be a reply by the applicant and a rejoinder by the respondent if the parties are so agreed or if the Tribunal decides, at the

request of a party or *proprio motu*, that these pleadings are necessary. If the Tribunal is not sitting, its powers under this article may be exercised by the President of the Tribunal, but without prejudice to any subsequent decision of the Tribunal.

Article 61

1. In a case begun by the notification of a special agreement, the number and order of the pleadings shall be governed by the provisions of the agreement, unless the Tribunal, after ascertaining the views of the parties, decides otherwise.

2. If the special agreement contains no such provision, and if the parties have not subsequently agreed on the number and order of pleadings, they shall each file a memorial and counter-memorial, within the same time-limits.

3. The Tribunal shall not authorize the presentation of replies and rejoinders unless it finds them to be necessary. If the Tribunal is not sitting, its powers under this article may be exercised by the President of the Tribunal, but without prejudice to any subsequent decision of the Tribunal.

Article 62

1. A memorial shall contain: a statement of the relevant facts, a statement of law and the submissions.

2. A counter-memorial shall contain: an admission or denial of the facts stated in the memorial; any additional facts, if necessary; observations concerning the statement of law in the memorial; a statement of law in answer thereto; and the submissions.

3. A reply and rejoinder shall not merely repeat the parties' contentions, but shall be directed to bringing out the issues that still divide them.

4. Every pleading shall set out the party's submissions at the relevant stage of the case, distinctly from the arguments presented, or shall confirm the submissions previously made.

Article 63

1. There shall be annexed to the original of every pleading certified copies of any relevant documents adduced in support of the contentions contained in the pleading. Parties need not annex or certify copies of documents which have been published and are readily available to the Tribunal and the other party.

2. If only parts of a document are relevant, only such extracts as are necessary for the purpose of the pleading in question or for identifying the document need be annexed. A copy of the whole document shall be filed in the Registry, unless it has been published and is readily available to the Tribunal and the other party.

3. A list of all documents annexed to a pleading shall be furnished at the time the pleading is filed.

Article 64

1. The parties shall submit any pleading or any part of a pleading in one or both of the official languages.

2. A party may use a language other than one of the official languages for its pleadings. A translation into one of the official languages, certified as accurate by the party submitting it, shall be submitted together with the original of each pleading.

3. When a document annexed to a pleading is not in one of the official languages, it shall be accompanied by a translation into one of these languages certified as accurate by the party submitting it. The translation may be confined to part of an annex, or to extracts therefrom, but in this case it must be accompanied by an explanatory note indicating what

passages are translated. The Tribunal may, however, require a more extensive or a complete translation to be furnished.

4. When a language other than one of the official languages is chosen by the parties and that language is an official language of the United Nations, the decision of the Tribunal shall, at the request of any party, be translated into that official language of the United Nations at no cost for the parties.

Article 65

1. The original of every pleading shall be signed by the agent and filed in the Registry. It shall be accompanied by a certified copy of the pleading, any document annexed thereto and any translations, for communication to the other party. It shall also be accompanied by the number of additional copies required by the Registry; further copies may be required should the need arise later.

2. All pleadings shall be dated. When a pleading has to be filed by a certain date, it is the date of receipt of the pleading in the Registry which will be regarded by the Tribunal as the material date.

3. If the Registrar arranges for the reproduction of a pleading at the request of a party, the text must be supplied in sufficient time to enable the pleading to be filed in the Registry before expiration of any time-limit which may apply to it. The reproduction is done under the responsibility of the party in question.

4. The correction of a slip or error in any document which has been filed may be made at any time with the consent of the other party or by leave of the President of the Tribunal. Any correction so effected shall be notified to the other party in the same manner as the pleading to which it relates.

Article 66

A certified copy of every pleading and any document annexed thereto produced by one party shall be communicated by the Registrar to the other party upon receipt.

Article 67

1. Copies of the pleadings and documents annexed thereto shall, as soon as possible after their filing, be made available by the Tribunal to a State or other entity entitled to appear before the Tribunal and which has asked to be furnished with such copies. However, if the party submitting the memorial so requests, the Tribunal shall make the memorial available at the same time as the counter-memorial.

2. Copies of the pleadings and documents annexed thereto shall be made accessible to the public on the opening of the oral proceedings, or earlier if the Tribunal or the President if the Tribunal is not sitting so decides after ascertaining the views of the parties.

3. However, the Tribunal, or the President if the Tribunal is not sitting, may, at the request of a party, and after ascertaining the views of the other party, decide otherwise than as set out in this article.

Subsection 3. Initial deliberations

Article 68

After the closure of the written proceedings and prior to the opening of the oral proceedings, the Tribunal shall meet in private to enable judges to exchange views concerning the written pleadings and the conduct of the case.

Subsection 4. Oral proceedings

Article 69

1. Upon the closure of the written proceedings, the date for the opening of the oral proceedings shall be fixed by the Tribunal. Such date shall fall within a period of six months from the closure of the written proceedings unless the Tribunal is satisfied that there is adequate justification for deciding otherwise. The Tribunal may also decide, when necessary, that the opening or the continuance of the oral proceedings be postponed.

2. When fixing the date for the opening of the oral proceedings or postponing the opening or continuance of such proceedings, the Tribunal shall have regard to:
   (a) the need to hold the hearing without unnecessary delay;
   (b) the priority required by articles 90 and 112;
   (c) any special circumstances, including the urgency of the case or other cases on the List of cases; and
   (d) the views expressed by the parties.

3. When the Tribunal is not sitting, its powers under this article shall be exercised by the President.

Article 70

The Tribunal may, if it considers it desirable, decide pursuant to article 1, paragraph 3, of the Statute that all or part of the further proceedings in a case shall be held at a place other than the seat of the Tribunal. Before so deciding, it shall ascertain the views of the parties.

Article 71

1. After the closure of the written proceedings, no further documents may be submitted to the Tribunal by either party except with the consent of the other party or as provided in paragraph 2. The other party shall be held to have given its consent if it does not lodge an objection to the production of the document within 15 days of receiving it.

2. In the event of objection, the Tribunal, after hearing the parties, may authorize production of the document if it considers production necessary.

3. The party desiring to produce a new document shall file the original or a certified copy thereof, together with the number of copies required by the Registry, which shall be responsible for communicating it to the other party and shall inform the Tribunal.

4. If a new document is produced under paragraph 1 or 2, the other party shall have an opportunity of commenting upon it and of submitting documents in support of its comments.

5. No reference may be made during the oral proceedings to the contents of any document which has not been produced as part of the written proceedings or in accordance with this article, unless the document is part of a publication readily available to the Tribunal and the other party.

6. The application of this article shall not in itself constitute a ground for delaying the opening or the course of the oral proceedings.

Article 72

Without prejudice to the provisions of these Rules concerning the production of documents, each party shall communicate to the Registrar, in sufficient time before the opening of the oral proceedings, information regarding any evidence which it intends to produce or which it intends to request the Tribunal to obtain. This communication shall contain a list of the surnames, first names, nationalities, descriptions and places of residence of the witnesses and experts whom the party intends to call, with indications of the point or points to which their evidence will be directed. A certified copy of the communication shall also be furnished for transmission to the other party.

Article 73

1. The Tribunal shall determine whether the parties should present their arguments before or after the production of the evidence; the parties shall, however, retain the right to comment on the evidence given.

2. The Tribunal, after ascertaining the views of the parties, shall determine the order in which the parties will be heard, the method of handling the evidence and examining any witnesses and experts and the number of counsel and advocates to be heard on behalf of each party.

Article 74

1. The hearing shall, in accordance with article 26, paragraph 2, of the Statute, be public, unless the Tribunal decides otherwise or unless the parties request that the public be not admitted. Such a decision or request may concern either the whole or part of the hearing, and may be made at any time.

2. The Tribunal may decide, as an exceptional measure, for public health, security or other compelling reasons, to hold a hearing entirely or in part by video link.

Article 75

1. The oral statements made on behalf of each party shall be as succinct as possible within the limits of what is requisite for the adequate presentation of that party's contentions at the hearing. Accordingly, they shall be directed to the issues that still divide the parties, and shall not go over the whole ground covered by the pleadings or merely repeat the facts and arguments these contain.

2. At the conclusion of the last statement made by a party at the hearing, its agent, without recapitulation of the arguments, shall read that party's final submissions. A copy of the written text of these, signed by the agent, shall be communicated to the Tribunal and transmitted to the other party.

Article 76

1. The Tribunal may at any time prior to or during the hearing indicate any points or issues which it would like the parties specially to address, or on which it considers that there has been sufficient argument.

2. The Tribunal may, during the hearing, put questions to the agents, counsel and advocates, and may ask them for explanations.

3. Each judge has a similar right to put questions, but before exercising it the judge should make her or his intention known to the President of the Tribunal.

4. The agents, counsel and advocates may answer either immediately or within a timelimit fixed by the President of the Tribunal.

Article 77

1. The Tribunal may at any time call upon the parties to produce such evidence or to give such explanations as the Tribunal may consider to be necessary for the elucidation of any aspect of the matters in issue, or may itself seek other information for this purpose.

2. The Tribunal may, if necessary, arrange for the attendance of a witness or expert to give evidence in the proceedings.

Article 78

1. The parties may call any witnesses or experts appearing on the list communicated to the Tribunal pursuant to article 72. If at any time during the hearing a party wishes to call a witness or expert whose name was not included in that list, it shall make a request therefor to the Tribunal and inform the other party, and shall supply the information required by article 72. The witness or expert may be called either if the other party raises no objection or, in the event of objection, if the Tribunal so authorizes after hearing the other party.

2. The Tribunal may, at the request of a party or *proprio motu*, decide that a witness or expert be examined otherwise than before the Tribunal itself. The President of the Tribunal shall take the necessary steps to implement such a decision.

Article 79

Unless on account of special circumstances the Tribunal decides on a different form of words,

(a) every witness shall make the following solemn declaration before giving any evidence:
"I solemnly declare upon my honour and conscience that I will speak the truth, the whole truth and nothing but the truth";

(b) every expert shall make the following solemn declaration before making any statement:
"I solemnly declare upon my honour and conscience that I will speak the truth, the whole truth and nothing but the truth, and that my statement will be in accordance with my sincere belief".

Article 80

Witnesses and experts shall, under the control of the President of the Tribunal, be examined by the agents, counsel or advocates of the parties starting with the party calling the witness or expert. Questions may be put to them by the President of the Tribunal and by the judges. Before testifying, witnesses and experts other than those appointed under article 289 of the Convention shall remain out of court.

Article 81

The Tribunal may at any time decide, at the request of a party or *proprio motu*, to exercise its functions with regard to the obtaining of evidence at a place or locality to which the case relates, subject to such conditions as the Tribunal may decide upon after ascertaining the views of the parties. The necessary arrangements shall be made in accordance with article 52.

Article 82

1. If the Tribunal considers it necessary to arrange for an inquiry or an expert opinion, it shall, after hearing the parties, issue an order to this effect, defining the subject of the inquiry or expert opinion, stating the number and mode of appointment of the persons to hold the inquiry or of the experts and laying down the procedure to be followed. Where appropriate, the Tribunal shall require persons appointed to carry out an inquiry, or to give an expert opinion, to make a solemn declaration.

2. Every report or record of an inquiry and every expert opinion shall be communicated to the parties, which shall be given the opportunity of commenting upon it.

Article 83

Witnesses and experts who appear at the instance of the Tribunal under article 77, paragraph 2, and persons appointed by the Tribunal under article 82, paragraph 1, to carry out an inquiry or to give an expert opinion, shall, where appropriate, be paid out of the funds of the Tribunal.

Article 84

1. The Tribunal may, at any time prior to the closure of the oral proceedings, at the request of a party or *proprio motu*, request an appropriate intergovernmental organization to furnish information relevant to a case before it. The Tribunal, after consulting the chief administrative officer of the organization concerned, shall decide whether such information shall be presented to it orally or in writing and fix the time-limits for its presentation.

2. When such an intergovernmental organization sees fit to furnish, on its own initiative, information relevant to a case before the Tribunal, it shall do so in the form of a memorial to be filed in the Registry before the closure of the written proceedings. The Tribunal may require such information to be supplemented, either orally or in writing, in the form of answers to any questions which it may see fit to formulate, and also authorize the parties to comment, either orally or in writing, on the information thus furnished.

3. Whenever the construction of the constituent instrument of such an intergovernmental organization or of an international convention adopted thereunder is in question in a case before the Tribunal, the Registrar shall, on the instructions of the Tribunal, or of the President if the Tribunal is not sitting, so notify the intergovernmental organization concerned and shall communicate to it copies of all the written proceedings. The Tribunal, or the President if the Tribunal is not sitting, may, as from the date on which the Registrar has communicated copies of the written proceedings and after consulting the chief administrative officer of the intergovernmental organization concerned, fix a time-limit within which the organization may submit to the Tribunal its observations in writing. These observations shall be communicated to the parties and may be discussed by them and by the representative of the said organization during the oral proceedings.

4. In the foregoing paragraphs, "intergovernmental organization" means an intergovernmental organization other than any organization which is a party or intervenes in the case concerned.

Article 85

1. Unless the Tribunal decides otherwise, all speeches and statements made and evidence given at the hearing in one of the official languages of the Tribunal shall be interpreted into the other official language. If they are made or given in any other language, they shall be interpreted into the two official languages of the Tribunal.

2. Whenever a language other than an official language is used, the necessary arrangements for interpretation into one of the official languages shall be made by the party concerned. The Registrar shall make arrangements for the verification of the interpretation provided by a party at the expense of that party. In the case of witnesses or experts who appear at the instance of the Tribunal, arrangements for interpretation shall be made by the Registrar.

3. A party on behalf of which speeches or statements are to be made, or evidence is to be given, in a language which is not one of the official languages of the Tribunal shall so notify the Registrar in sufficient time for the necessary arrangements to be made, including verification.

4. Before entering upon their duties in the case, interpreters provided by a party shall make the following solemn declaration:

> "I solemnly declare upon my honour and conscience that my interpretation will be faithful and complete".

Article 86

1. Minutes shall be made of each hearing. For this purpose, a verbatim record shall be made by the Registrar of every hearing, in the official language or languages of the Tribunal used during the hearing. When another language is used, the verbatim record shall be prepared in one of the official languages of the Tribunal.

2. In order to prepare such a verbatim record, the party on behalf of which speeches or statements are made in a language which is not one of the official languages shall supply to the Registry in advance a text thereof in one of the official languages.

3. The transcript of the verbatim record shall be preceded by the names of the judges present, and those of the agents, counsel and advocates of the parties.

4. Copies of the transcript shall be circulated to the judges sitting in the case and to the parties. The latter may, under the supervision of the Tribunal, correct the transcripts of speeches and statements made on their behalf, but in no case may such corrections affect the meaning and scope thereof. The judges may likewise make corrections in the transcript of anything they have said.

5. Witnesses and experts shall be shown that part of the transcript which relates to the evidence given or the statements made by them, and may correct it in like manner as the parties.

6. One certified copy of the corrected transcript, signed by the President of the Tribunal and the Registrar, shall constitute the authentic minutes of the hearing. The minutes of public hearings shall be printed and published by the Tribunal.

Article 87

Any written reply by a party to a question put under article 76 or any evidence or explanation supplied by a party under article 77 received by the Tribunal after the closure of the oral proceedings shall be communicated to the other party, which shall be given the opportunity of commenting upon it. The oral proceedings may be reopened for that purpose, if necessary.

Article 88

1. When, subject to the control of the Tribunal, the agents, counsel and advocates have completed their presentation of the case, the President of the Tribunal shall declare the oral proceedings closed. The agents shall remain at the disposal of the Tribunal.

2. The Tribunal shall withdraw to consider the judgment.

Section C. Incidental proceedings

Subsection 1. Provisional measures

Article 89

1. A party may submit a request for the prescription of provisional measures under article 290, paragraph 1, of the Convention at any time during the course of the proceedings in a dispute submitted to the Tribunal.

2. Pending the constitution of an arbitral tribunal to which a dispute is being submitted, a party may submit a request for the prescription of provisional measures under article 290, paragraph 5, of the Convention:

(a) at any time if the parties have so agreed;

(b) at any time after two weeks from the notification to the other party of a request for provisional measures if the parties have not agreed that such measures may be prescribed by another court or tribunal.

3. The request shall be in writing and specify the measures requested, the reasons therefor and the possible consequences, if it is not granted, for the preservation of the respective rights of the parties or for the prevention of serious harm to the marine environment.

4. A request for the prescription of provisional measures under article 290, paragraph 5, of the Convention shall also indicate the legal grounds upon which the arbitral tribunal which is to be constituted would have jurisdiction and the urgency of the situation. A certified copy of the notification or of any other document instituting the proceedings before the arbitral tribunal shall be annexed to the request.

5. When a request for provisional measures has been made, the Tribunal may prescribe measures different in whole or in part from those requested and indicate the parties which are to take or to comply with each measure.

Article 90

1. Subject to article 112, paragraph 1, a request for the prescription of provisional measures has priority over all other proceedings before the Tribunal.

2. The Tribunal, or the President if the Tribunal is not sitting, shall fix the earliest possible date for a hearing.

3. The Tribunal shall take into account any observations that may be presented to it by a party before the closure of the hearing.

4. Pending the meeting of the Tribunal, the President of the Tribunal may call upon the parties to act in such a way as will enable any order the Tribunal may make on the request for provisional measures to have its appropriate effects.

Article 91

1. If the President of the Tribunal ascertains that at the date fixed for the hearing referred to in article 90, paragraph 2, a sufficient number of Members will not be available to constitute a quorum, the Chamber of Summary Procedure shall be convened to carry out the functions of the Tribunal with respect to the prescription of provisional measures.

2. The Tribunal shall review or revise provisional measures prescribed by the Chamber of Summary Procedure at the written request of a party within 15 days of the prescription of the measures. The Tribunal may also at any time decide *proprio motu* to review or revise the measures.

Article 92

The rejection of a request for the prescription of provisional measures shall not prevent the party which made it from making a fresh request in the same case based on new facts.

Article 93

A party may request the modification or revocation of provisional measures. The request shall be submitted in writing and shall specify the change in, or disappearance of, the circumstances considered to be relevant. Before taking any decision on the request, the Tribunal shall afford the parties an opportunity of presenting their observations on the subject.

Article 94

Any provisional measures prescribed by the Tribunal or any modification or revocation thereof shall forthwith be notified to the parties and to such other States Parties as the Tribunal considers appropriate in each case.

Article 95

1. Each party shall inform the Tribunal as soon as possible as to its compliance with any provisional measures the Tribunal has prescribed. In particular, each party shall submit an initial report upon the steps it has taken or proposes to take in order to ensure prompt compliance with the measures prescribed.

2. The Tribunal may request further information from the parties on any matter connected with the implementation of any provisional measures it has prescribed.

Subsection 2. Preliminary proceedings

Article 96

1. When an application is made in respect of a dispute referred to in article 297 of the Convention, the Tribunal shall determine at the request of the respondent or may determine *proprio motu*, in accordance with article 294 of the Convention, whether the claim constitutes an abuse of legal process or whether *prima facie* it is well founded.

2. The Registrar, when transmitting an application to the respondent under article 54, paragraph 4, shall notify the respondent of the time-limit fixed by the President of the Tribunal for requesting a determination under article 294 of the Convention.

3. The Tribunal may also decide, within two months from the date of an application, to exercise *proprio motu* its power under article 294, paragraph 1, of the Convention.

4. The request by the respondent for a determination under article 294 of the Convention shall be in writing and shall indicate the grounds for a determination by the Tribunal that:

(a) the application is made in respect of a dispute referred to in article 297 of the Convention; and

(b) the claim constitutes an abuse of legal process or is *prima facie* unfounded.

5. Upon receipt of such a request or *proprio motu*, the Tribunal, or the President if the Tribunal is not sitting, shall fix a time-limit not exceeding 60 days within which the parties may present their written observations and submissions. The proceedings on the merits shall be suspended.

6. Unless the Tribunal decides otherwise, the further proceedings shall be oral.

7. The written observations and submissions referred to in paragraph 5, and the statements and evidence presented at the hearings contemplated by paragraph 6, shall be confined to

those matters which are relevant to the determination of whether the claim constitutes an abuse of legal process or is *prima facie* unfounded, and of whether the application is made in respect of a dispute referred to in article 297 of the Convention. The Tribunal may, however, request the parties to argue all questions of law and fact, and to adduce all evidence, bearing on the issue.

8. The Tribunal shall make its determination in the form of a judgment.

Subsection 3. Preliminary objections

Article 97

1. Any objection to the jurisdiction of the Tribunal or to the admissibility of the application, or other objection the decision upon which is requested before any further proceedings on the merits, shall be made in writing within 90 days from the institution of proceedings.

2. The preliminary objection shall set out the facts and the law on which the objection is based, as well as the submissions.

3. Upon receipt by the Registry of a preliminary objection, the proceedings on the merits shall be suspended and the Tribunal, or the President if the Tribunal is not sitting, shall fix a time-limit not exceeding 60 days within which the other party may present its written observations and submissions. It shall fix a further time-limit not exceeding 60 days from the receipt of such observations and submissions within which the objecting party may present its written observations and submissions in reply. Copies of documents in support shall be annexed to such statements and evidence which it is proposed to produce shall be mentioned.

4. Unless the Tribunal decides otherwise, the further proceedings shall be oral.

5. The written observations and submissions referred to in paragraph 3, and the statements and evidence presented at the hearings contemplated by paragraph 4, shall be confined to those matters which are relevant to the objection. Whenever necessary, however, the Tribunal may request the parties to argue all questions of law and fact and to adduce all evidence bearing on the issue.

6. The Tribunal shall give its decision in the form of a judgment, by which it shall uphold the objection or reject it or declare that the objection does not possess, in the circumstances of the case, an exclusively preliminary character. If the Tribunal rejects the objection or declares that it does not possess an exclusively preliminary character, it shall fix time-limits for the further proceedings.

7. The Tribunal shall give effect to any agreement between the parties that an objection submitted under paragraph 1 be heard and determined within the framework of the merits.

Subsection 4. Counter-claims

Article 98

1. A party may present a counter-claim provided that it is directly connected with the subject-matter of the claim of the other party and that it comes within the jurisdiction of the Tribunal.

2. A counter-claim shall be made in the counter-memorial of the party presenting it and shall appear as part of the submissions of that party.

3. In the event of doubt as to the connection between the question presented by way of counter-claim and the subject-matter of the claim of the other party the Tribunal shall, after

hearing the parties, decide whether or not the question thus presented shall be joined to the original proceedings.

Subsection 5. Intervention

Article 99

1. An application for permission to intervene under the terms of article 31 of the Statute shall be filed not later than 30 days after the counter-memorial becomes available under article 67, paragraph 1, of these Rules. In exceptional circumstances, an application submitted at a later stage may however be admitted.

2. The application shall be signed in the manner provided for in article 54, paragraph 3, and state the name and address of an agent. It shall specify the case to which it relates and shall set out:

(a) the interest of a legal nature which the State Party applying to intervene considers may be affected by the decision in that case;

(b) the precise object of the intervention.

3. Permission to intervene under the terms of article 31 of the Statute may be granted irrespective of the choice made by the applicant under article 287 of the Convention.

4. The application shall contain a list of the documents in support, copies of which documents shall be annexed.

Article 100

1. A State Party or an entity other than a State Party referred to in article 32, paragraphs 1 and 2, of the Statute which desires to avail itself of the right of intervention conferred upon it by article 32, paragraph 3, of the Statute shall file a declaration to that effect. The declaration shall be filed not later than 30 days after the counter-memorial becomes available under article 67, paragraph 1, of these Rules. In exceptional circumstances, a declaration submitted at a later stage may, however, be admitted.

2. The declaration shall be signed in the manner provided for in article 54, paragraph 3, and state the name and address of an agent. It shall specify the case to which it relates and shall:

(a) identify the particular provisions of the Convention or of the international agreement the interpretation or application of which the declaring party considers to be in question;

(b) set out the interpretation or application of those provisions for which it contends;

(c) list the documents in support, copies of which documents shall be annexed.

Article 101

1. Certified copies of the application for permission to intervene under article 31 of the Statute, or of the declaration of intervention under article 32 of the Statute, shall be communicated forthwith to the parties to the case, which shall be invited to furnish their written observations within a time-limit to be fixed by the Tribunal or by the President if the Tribunal is not sitting.

2. The Registrar shall also transmit copies to: (a) States Parties; (b) any other parties which have to be notified under article 32, paragraph 2, of the Statute; (c) the Secretary-General of the United Nations; (d) the Secretary-General of the Authority when the proceedings are before the Seabed Disputes Chamber.

Article 102

1. The Tribunal shall decide whether an application for permission to intervene under article 31 of the Statute should be granted or whether an intervention under article 32 of the Statute is admissible as a matter of priority unless in view of the circumstances of the case the Tribunal determines otherwise.

2. If, within the time-limit fixed under article 101, an objection is filed to an application for permission to intervene, or to the admissibility of a declaration of intervention, the Tribunal shall hear the State Party or entity other than a State Party seeking to intervene and the parties before deciding.

Article 103

1. If an application for permission to intervene under article 31 of the Statute is granted, the intervening State Party shall be supplied with copies of the pleadings and documents annexed and shall be entitled to submit a written statement within a time-limit to be fixed by the Tribunal. A further time-limit shall be fixed within which the parties may, if they so desire, furnish their written observations on that statement prior to the oral proceedings. If the Tribunal is not sitting, these time-limits shall be fixed by the President.

2. The time-limits fixed according to paragraph 1 shall, so far as possible, coincide with those already fixed for the pleadings in the case.

3. The intervening State Party shall be entitled, in the course of the oral proceedings, to submit its observations with respect to the subject-matter of the intervention.

4. The intervening State Party shall not be entitled to choose a judge *ad hoc* or to object to an agreement to discontinue the proceedings under article 105, paragraph 1.

Article 104

1. If an intervention under article 32 of the Statute is admitted, the intervenor shall be supplied with copies of the pleadings and documents annexed and shall be entitled, within a time-limit to be fixed by the Tribunal, or the President if the Tribunal is not sitting, to submit its written observations on the subject-matter of the intervention.

2. These observations shall be communicated to the parties and to any other State Party or entity other than a State Party admitted to intervene. The intervenor shall be entitled, in the course of the oral proceedings, to submit its observations with respect to the subject-matter of the intervention.

3. The intervenor shall not be entitled to choose a judge *ad hoc* or to object to an agreement to discontinue the proceedings under article 105, paragraph 1.

Subsection 6. Discontinuance

Article 105

1. If at any time before the final judgment on the merits has been delivered the parties, either jointly or separately, notify the Tribunal in writing that they have agreed to discontinue the proceedings, the Tribunal shall make an order recording the discontinuance and directing the Registrar to remove the case from the List of cases.

2. If the parties have agreed to discontinue the proceedings in consequence of having reached a settlement of the dispute and if they so desire, the Tribunal shall record this fact in the order for the removal of the case from the List, or indicate in, or annex to, the order the terms of the settlement.

3. If the Tribunal is not sitting, any order under this article may be made by the President.

Article 106

1. If, in the course of proceedings instituted by means of an application, the applicant informs the Tribunal in writing that it is not going on with the proceedings, and if, at the date on which this communication is received by the Registry, the respondent has not yet taken any step in the proceedings, the Tribunal shall make an order officially recording the discontinuance of the proceedings and directing the removal of the case from the List of cases. A copy of this order shall be sent by the Registrar to the respondent.

2. If, at the time when the notice of discontinuance is received, the respondent has already taken some step in the proceedings, the Tribunal shall fix a time-limit within which the respondent may state whether it opposes the discontinuance of the proceedings. If no objection is made to the discontinuance before the expiration of the time-limit, acquiescence will be presumed and the Tribunal shall make an order recording the discontinuance of the proceedings and directing the Registrar to remove the case from the List of cases. If objection is made, the proceedings shall continue.

3. If the Tribunal is not sitting, its powers under this article may be exercised by the President.

Section D. Proceedings before special chambers

Article 107

Proceedings before the special chambers mentioned in article 15 of the Statute shall, subject to the provisions of the Convention, the Statute and these Rules relating specifically to the special chambers, be governed by the Rules applicable in contentious cases before the Tribunal.

Article 108

1. When it is desired that a case should be dealt with by one of the chambers which has been formed in accordance with article 15, paragraph 1 or 3, of the Statute, a request to this effect shall either be made in the document instituting the proceedings or accompany it. Effect shall be given to the request if the parties are in agreement.

2. Upon receipt by the Registry of this request, the President of the Tribunal shall communicate it to the members of the chamber concerned.

3. Effect shall be given to a request that a case be brought before a chamber to be formed in accordance with article 15, paragraph 2, of the Statute as soon as the chamber has been formed in accordance with article 30 of these Rules.

4. The President of the Tribunal shall convene the chamber at the earliest date compatible with the requirements of the procedure.

Article 109

1. Written proceedings in a case before a chamber shall consist of a single pleading by each party. The time-limits concerning the filing of written pleadings shall be fixed by the chamber, or its President if the chamber is not sitting.

2. The chamber may authorize or direct the filing of further pleadings if the parties are so agreed, or if the chamber decides, *proprio motu* or at the request of one of the parties, that such pleadings are necessary.

3. Oral proceedings shall take place unless the parties agree to dispense with them and the chamber consents. Even when no oral proceedings take place, the chamber may call upon the parties to supply information or furnish explanations orally.

Section E. Prompt release of vessels and crews

Article 110

1. An application for the release of a vessel or its crew from detention may be made in accordance with article 292 of the Convention by or on behalf of the flag State of the vessel.

2. A State Party may at any time notify the Tribunal of:
   (a) the State authorities competent to authorize persons to make applications on its behalf under article 292 of the Convention;
   (b) the name and address of any person who is authorized to make an application on its behalf;
   (c) the office designated to receive notice of an application for the release of a vessel or its crew and the most expeditious means for delivery of documents to that office;
   (d) any clarification, modification or withdrawal of such notification.

3. An application on behalf of a flag State shall be accompanied by an authorization under paragraph 2, if such authorization has not been previously submitted to the Tribunal, as well as by documents stating that the person submitting the application is the person named in the authorization. It shall also contain a certification that a copy of the application and all supporting documentation has been delivered to the flag State.

Article 111

1. The application shall contain a succinct statement of the facts and legal grounds upon which the application is based.

2. The statement of facts shall:
   (a) specify the time and place of detention of the vessel and the present location of the vessel and crew, if known;
   (b) contain relevant information concerning the vessel and crew including, where appropriate, the name, flag and the port or place of registration of the vessel and its tonnage, cargo capacity and data relevant to the determination of its value, the name and address of the vessel owner and operator and particulars regarding its crew;
   (c) specify the amount, nature and terms of the bond or other financial security that may have been imposed by the detaining State and the extent to which such requirements have been complied with;
   (d) contain any further information the applicant considers relevant to the determination of the amount of a reasonable bond or other financial security and to any other issue in the proceedings.

3. Supporting documents shall be annexed to the application.

4. A certified copy of the application shall forthwith be transmitted by the Registrar to the detaining State, which may submit a statement in response with supporting documents annexed, to be filed as soon as possible but not later than 96 hours before the hearing referred to in article 112, paragraph 3.

5. The Tribunal may, at any time, require further information to be provided in a supplementary statement.

6. The further proceedings relating to the application shall be oral.

Article 112

1. The Tribunal shall give priority to applications for release of vessels or crews over all other proceedings before the Tribunal. However, if the Tribunal is seized of an application for release of a vessel or its crew and of a request for the prescription of provisional measures, it shall take the necessary measures to ensure that both the application and the request are dealt with without delay.

2. If the applicant has so requested in the application, the application shall be dealt with by the Chamber of Summary Procedure, provided that, within five days of the receipt of notice of the application, the detaining State notifies the Tribunal that it concurs with the request.

3. The Tribunal, or the President if the Tribunal is not sitting, shall fix the earliest possible date, within a period of 15 days commencing with the first working day following the date on which the application is received, for a hearing at which each of the parties shall be accorded, unless otherwise decided, one day to present its evidence and arguments.

4. The decision of the Tribunal shall be in the form of a judgment. The judgment shall be adopted as soon as possible and shall be read at a public sitting of the Tribunal to be held not later than 14 days after the closure of the hearing. The parties shall be notified of the date of the sitting.

5. The Tribunal may decide, as an exceptional measure, for public health, security or other compelling reasons, that the judgment shall be read at a sitting of the Tribunal accessible to the parties and the public by video link.

Article 113

1. The Tribunal shall in its judgment determine in each case in accordance with article 292 of the Convention whether or not the allegation made by the applicant that the detaining State has not complied with a provision of the Convention for the prompt release of the vessel or the crew upon the posting of a reasonable bond or other financial security is well-founded.

2. If the Tribunal decides that the allegation is well-founded, it shall determine the amount, nature and form of the bond or financial security to be posted for the release of the vessel or the crew.

3. Unless the parties agree otherwise, the Tribunal shall determine whether the bond or other financial security shall be posted with the Registrar or with the detaining State.

Article 114

1. If the bond or other financial security has been posted with the Registrar, the detaining State shall be promptly notified thereof.

2. The Registrar shall endorse or transmit the bond or other financial security to the detaining State to the extent that it is required to satisfy the final judgment, award or decision of the competent authority of the detaining State.

3. The bond or other financial security shall be endorsed or transmitted, to the extent that it is not required to satisfy the final judgment, award or decision, to the party at whose request the bond or other financial security is issued.

Section F. Proceedings in contentious cases before the Seabed Disputes Chamber

Article 115

Proceedings in contentious cases before the Seabed Disputes Chamber and its *ad hoc* chambers shall, subject to the provisions of the Convention, the Statute and these Rules relating specifically to the Seabed Disputes Chamber and its *ad hoc* chambers, be governed by the Rules applicable in contentious cases before the Tribunal.

Article 116

Articles 117 to 121 apply to proceedings in all disputes before the Chamber with the exception of disputes exclusively between States Parties and between States Parties and the Authority.

Article 117

When proceedings before the Chamber are instituted by means of an application, the application shall indicate:

(a) the name of the applicant and, where the applicant is a natural or juridical person, the permanent residence or address or registered office address thereof;
(b) the name of the respondent and, where the respondent is a natural or juridical person, the permanent residence or address or registered office address thereof;
(c) the sponsoring State, in any case where the applicant is a natural or juridical person or a state enterprise;
(d) the sponsoring State of the respondent, in any case where the party against which the claim is brought is a natural or juridical person or state enterprise;
(e) an address for service at the seat of the Tribunal;
(f) the subject of the dispute and the legal grounds on which jurisdiction is said to be based; the precise nature of the claim, together with a statement of the facts and legal grounds on which the claim is based;
(g) the decision or measure sought by the applicant;
(h) the evidence on which the application is founded.

Article 118

1. The application shall be served on the respondent. The application shall also be served on the sponsoring State in any case where the applicant or respondent is a natural or juridical person or a state enterprise.

2. Within two months after service of the application, the respondent shall lodge a defence, stating:

(a) the name of the respondent and, where the respondent is a natural or juridical person, the permanent residence or address or registered office address thereof;
(b) an address for service at the seat of the Tribunal;
(c) the matters in issue between the parties and the facts and legal grounds on which the defence is based;
(d) the decision or measure sought by the respondent;
(e) the evidence on which the defence is founded.

3. At the request of the respondent, the President of the Chamber may extend the time-limit referred to in paragraph 2, if satisfied that there is adequate justification for the request.

Article 119

1. Within two months after service of the application in accordance with article 118, paragraph 1, where the respondent is a State Party in a case brought by a natural or juridical person sponsored by another State Party in a dispute referred to in article 187, subparagraph (c), of the Convention, the respondent State may make an application in

accordance with article 190, paragraph 2, of the Convention for the sponsoring State of the applicant to appear in the proceedings on behalf of the applicant.

2. Notice of an application under paragraph 1 shall be communicated to the applicant and its sponsoring State. If, within a time-limit fixed by the President of the Chamber, the sponsoring State does not indicate it will appear in the proceedings on behalf of the applicant, the respondent State may designate a juridical person of its nationality to represent it.

3. Within two months after service of the application in accordance with article 118, paragraph 1, on the sponsoring State of a party, such State may give written notice of its intention to submit written or oral statements in accordance with article 190, paragraph 1, of the Convention.

4. Upon receipt of such a notice, the President of the Chamber shall fix the time-limit within which the sponsoring State may submit its written statements. The sponsoring State shall be notified of such time-limit. It shall also be notified of the date of the hearing. The written statements shall be communicated to the parties and to any other sponsoring State of a party.

5. At the request of the respondent or a sponsoring State, the President of the Chamber may extend a time-limit referred to in this article, if satisfied that there is adequate justification for the request.

Article 120

1. When proceedings are brought before the Chamber by the notification of a special agreement, the notification shall indicate:

(a) the parties to the case and any sponsoring States of the parties;

(b) the subject of the dispute and the precise nature of the claims of the parties, together with a statement of the facts and legal grounds on which the claims are based;

(c) the decisions or measures sought by the parties;

(d) the evidence on which the claims are founded.

2. The notification shall also provide information regarding participation and appearance in the proceedings by sponsoring States Parties in accordance with article 190 of the Convention.

Article 121

1. The Chamber may authorize or direct the filing of further pleadings if the parties are so agreed or the Chamber decides, *proprio motu* or at the request of a party, that these pleadings are necessary.

2. The President of the Chamber shall fix the time-limits within which these pleadings are to be filed.

Article 122

Proceedings by the Council on behalf of the Authority under article 185, paragraph 2, of the Convention shall be instituted by means of an application in accordance with article 162, paragraph 2 (u), of the Convention. The application shall be accompanied by a certified copy of the decision or resolution of the Council upon which it is based and the full records of all discussions within the Authority on the matter.

Article 123

1. When a commercial arbitral tribunal, pursuant to article 188, paragraph 2, of the Convention, refers to the Chamber a question of interpretation of Part XI of the Convention and the annexes relating thereto upon which its decision depends, the document submitting

the question to the Chamber shall contain a precise statement of the question and be accompanied by all relevant information and documents.

2. Upon receipt of the document, the President of the Chamber shall fix a time-limit not exceeding three months within which the parties to the proceedings before the arbitral tribunal and the States Parties may submit their written observations on the question. The parties to the proceedings and the States Parties shall be notified of the time-limit. The States Parties shall be informed of the contents of the submission.

3. The President of the Chamber shall fix a date for a hearing if, within one month from the expiration of the time-limit for submitting written observations, a party to the proceedings before the arbitral tribunal or a State Party gives written notice of its intention to submit oral observations.

4. The Chamber shall give its ruling in the form of a judgment.

Section G. Judgments, interpretation and revision

Subsection 1. Judgments

Article 124

1. When the Tribunal has completed its deliberations and adopted its judgment, the parties shall be notified of the date on which it will be read.

2. The judgment shall be read at a public sitting of the Tribunal and shall become binding on the parties on the day of the reading.

3. The Tribunal may decide, as an exceptional measure, for public health, security or other compelling reasons, that the judgment shall be read at a sitting of the Tribunal accessible to the parties and the public by video link.

Article 125

1. The judgment, which shall state whether it is given by the Tribunal or by a chamber, shall contain:

(a) the date on which it is read;
(b) the names of the judges participating in it;
(c) the names of the parties;
(d) the names of the agents, counsel and advocates of the parties;
(e) the names of the experts, if any, appointed under article 289 of the Convention;
(f) a summary of the proceedings;
(g) the submissions of the parties;
(h) a statement of the facts;
(i) the reasons of law on which it is based;
(j) the operative provisions of the judgment;
(k) the decision, if any, in regard to costs;
(l) the number and names of the judges constituting the majority and those constituting the minority, on each operative provision;
(m) a statement as to the text of the judgment which is authoritative.

2. Any judge may attach a separate or dissenting opinion to the judgment; a judge may record concurrence or dissent without stating reasons in the form of a declaration. The same applies to orders.

3. One copy of the judgment, signed by the President and by the Registrar and sealed, shall be placed in the archives of the Tribunal and other copies shall be transmitted to each party. Copies shall be sent to: (a) States Parties; (b) the Secretary-General of the United Nations; (c) the Secretary-General of the Authority; (d) in a case submitted under an agreement other than the Convention, the parties to such agreement.

Subsection 2. Requests for the interpretation or revision of a judgment

Article 126

1. In the event of dispute as to the meaning or scope of a judgment, any party may make a request for its interpretation.

2. A request for the interpretation of a judgment may be made either by an application or by the notification of a special agreement to that effect between the parties; the precise point or points in dispute as to the meaning or scope of the judgment shall be indicated.

3. If the request for interpretation is made by an application, the requesting party's contentions shall be set out therein, and the other party shall be entitled to file written observations thereon within a time-limit fixed by the Tribunal or by the President if the Tribunal is not sitting.

4. Whether the request is made by an application or by notification of a special agreement, the Tribunal may, if necessary, afford the parties the opportunity of furnishing further written or oral explanations.

Article 127

1. A request for revision of a judgment may be made only when it is based upon the discovery of some fact of such a nature as to be a decisive factor, which fact was, when the judgment was given, unknown to the Tribunal and also to the party requesting revision, always provided that such ignorance was not due to negligence. Such request must be made at the latest within six months of the discovery of the new fact and before the lapse of ten years from the date of the judgment.

2. The proceedings for revision shall be opened by a decision of the Tribunal in the form of a judgment expressly recording the existence of the new fact, recognizing that it has such a character as to lay the case open to revision, and declaring the application admissible on this ground.

Article 128

1. A request for the revision of a judgment shall be made by an application containing the particulars necessary to show that the conditions specified in article 127, paragraph 1, are fulfilled. Any document in support of the application shall be annexed to it.

2. The other party shall be entitled to file written observations on the admissibility of the application within a time-limit fixed by the Tribunal or by the President if the Tribunal is not sitting. These observations shall be communicated to the party making the application.

3. The Tribunal, before giving its judgment on the admissibility of the application, may afford the parties a further opportunity of presenting their views thereon.

4. If the Tribunal decides to make the admission of the proceedings in revision conditional on previous compliance with the judgment, it shall make an order accordingly.

5. If the Tribunal finds that the application is admissible it shall fix time-limits for such further proceedings on the merits of the application as, after ascertaining the views of the parties, it considers necessary.

Article 129

1. If the judgment to be revised or to be interpreted was given by the Tribunal, the request for its revision or interpretation shall be dealt with by the Tribunal.

2. If the judgment was given by a chamber, the request for its revision or interpretation shall, if possible, be dealt with by that chamber. If that is not possible, the request shall be dealt with by a chamber composed in conformity with the relevant provisions of the Statute and these Rules. If, according to the Statute and these Rules, the composition of the chamber requires the approval of the parties which cannot be obtained within time-limits fixed by the Tribunal, the request shall be dealt with by the Tribunal.

3. The decision on a request for interpretation or revision of a judgment shall be given in the form of a judgment.

Section H. Advisory proceedings

Article 130

1. In the exercise of its functions relating to advisory opinions, the Seabed Disputes Chamber shall apply this section and be guided, to the extent to which it recognizes them to be applicable, by the provisions of the Statute and of these Rules applicable in contentious cases.

2. The Chamber shall consider whether the request for an advisory opinion relates to a legal question pending between two or more parties. When the Chamber so determines, article 17 of the Statute applies, as well as the provisions of these Rules concerning the application of that article.

Article 131

1. A request for an advisory opinion on a legal question arising within the scope of the activities of the Assembly or the Council of the Authority shall contain a precise statement of the question. It shall be accompanied by all documents likely to throw light upon the question.

2. The documents shall be transmitted to the Chamber at the same time as the request or as soon as possible thereafter in the number of copies required by the Registry.

Article 132

If the request for an advisory opinion states that the question necessitates an urgent answer the Chamber shall take all appropriate steps to accelerate the procedure.

Article 133

1. The Registrar shall forthwith give notice of the request for an advisory opinion to all States Parties.

2. The Chamber, or its President if the Chamber is not sitting, shall identify the intergovernmental organizations which are likely to be able to furnish information on the question. The Registrar shall give notice of the request to such organizations.

3. States Parties and the organizations referred to in paragraph 2 shall be invited to present written statements on the question within a time-limit fixed by the Chamber or its President if the Chamber is not sitting. Such statements shall be communicated to States Parties and organizations which have made written statements. The Chamber, or its President if the Chamber is not sitting, may fix a further time-limit within which such States Parties and organizations may present written statements on the statements made.

4. The Chamber, or its President if the Chamber is not sitting, shall decide whether oral proceedings shall be held and, if so, fix the date for the opening of such proceedings.

States Parties and the organizations referred to in paragraph 2 shall be invited to make oral statements at the proceedings.

Article 134

The written statements and documents annexed shall be made accessible to the public as soon as possible after they have been presented to the Chamber.

Article 135

1. When the Chamber has completed its deliberations and adopted its advisory opinion, the opinion shall be read at a public sitting of the Chamber.

1*bis*. The Chamber may decide, as an exceptional measure, for public health, security or other compelling reasons, that the advisory opinion shall be read at a sitting of the Chamber accessible to the parties and the public by video link.

2. The advisory opinion shall contain:

(a) the date on which it is delivered;
(b) the names of the judges participating in it;
(c) the question or questions on which the advisory opinion of the Chamber is requested;
(d) a summary of the proceedings;
(e) a statement of the facts;
(f) the reasons of law on which it is based;
(g) the reply to the question or questions put to the Chamber;
(h) the number and names of the judges constituting the majority and those constituting the minority, on each question put to the Chamber;
(i) a statement as to the text of the opinion which is authoritative.

3. Any judge may attach a separate or dissenting opinion to the advisory opinion of the Chamber; a judge may record concurrence or dissent without stating reasons in the form of a declaration.

Article 136

The Registrar shall inform the Secretary-General of the Authority as to the date and the time fixed for the public sitting to be held for the reading of the opinion. The Registrar shall also inform the States Parties and the intergovernmental organizations immediately concerned.

Article 137

One copy of the advisory opinion, signed by the President and by the Registrar and sealed, shall be placed in the archives of the Tribunal, others shall be sent to the Secretary- General of the Authority and to the Secretary-General of the United Nations. Copies shall be sent to the States Parties and the intergovernmental organizations immediately concerned.

Article 138

1. The Tribunal may give an advisory opinion on a legal question if an international agreement related to the purposes of the Convention specifically provides for the submission to the Tribunal of a request for such an opinion.

2. A request for an advisory opinion shall be transmitted to the Tribunal by whatever body is authorized by or in accordance with the agreement to make the request to the Tribunal.

3. The Tribunal shall apply *mutatis mutandis* articles 130 to 137.

50.d Resolution on the Internal Judicial Practice of the Tribunal

Date: 31 October 1997
Source: Doc ITLOS/10
https://www.itlos.org/fileadmin/itlos/documents/basic_texts/Itlos.10.E.27.04.05.pdf

The Tribunal,
Acting in accordance with article 40 of the Rules,
Adopts this Resolution.

Article 1 Use of terms

In this Resolution:
(a) "President" means the person presiding over the Tribunal in a particular case;
(b) "Rules" means the Rules of the Tribunal;
(c) references to the "Tribunal" include any chamber of the Tribunal.

Article 2 Preparatory documentation

1. After the closure of the written proceedings, each judge may within five weeks prepare a brief written note identifying without further elaboration:
   (a) the principal issues for decision as they emerge from the written pleadings; and
   (b) points, if any, which should be clarified during the oral proceedings.
2. Notes received by the Registry are circulated to the other judges.
3. On the basis of the written pleadings and the judges' notes, the President draws up a working paper containing:
   (a) a summary of the facts and the principal contentions of the parties advanced in their written pleadings; and
   (b) proposals concerning:
      (i) indications to be given, or questions to be put, to the parties in accordance with article 76 of the Rules;
      (ii) evidence or explanations to be requested from the parties in accordance with article 77 of the Rules; and
      (iii) issues which, in the opinion of the President, should be discussed and decided by the Tribunal.
4. The Registrar shall send the working paper to the judges as soon as possible and normally within eight weeks after the closure of the written proceedings.

Article 3 Deliberations before the oral proceedings

After the circulation of the working paper and before the date fixed for the opening of the oral proceedings, the Tribunal deliberates in private, as provided for in article 68 of the Rules, in order to allow the judges an opportunity to:
(a) exchange views concerning the written pleadings and the conduct of the case;
(b) consider whether to give any indications, or put any questions, to the parties in accordance with article 76 of the Rules;
(c) consider whether to call upon the parties to produce any evidence or to give any explanations in accordance with article 77 of the Rules; and
(d) consider the nature, scope and terms of the questions and issues which will have to be decided by the Tribunal.

Article 4 Deliberations during oral proceedings

During the course of the oral proceedings, the President may convene brief meetings in order to permit the judges to exchange views concerning the case and to inform each other of possible questions which judges may wish to put to the parties in accordance with article 76 of the Rules.

Article 5 Initial deliberations after oral proceedings

1. Unless the Tribunal decides otherwise, the judges have four working days after the closure of the oral proceedings in order to study the arguments presented to the Tribunal in the case. During this time, judges may also summarize their tentative opinions in writing in the form of speaking notes.

2. If the President considers it appropriate in the light of the oral proceedings, a revised list of issues for examination is circulated.

3. During its initial deliberations after the closure of the oral proceedings, the Tribunal reaches conclusions on what are the issues which need to be decided and then hears the tentative opinions of the judges on those issues, as well as on the correct disposal of the case.

4. The Tribunal next deliberates on each issue in turn, addressing also the question of the disposal of the case and the main reasons for the decision to be given.

5. During these deliberations, judges will be called upon by the President in the order in which they signify their wish to speak.

6. The President may seek to establish a majority opinion as it appears then to exist on each issue and on the reasons to be given.

7. Instead of establishing majority opinions at that stage, the Tribunal may decide that every judge should prepare a brief written note, expressing the judge's tentative opinion on the issues and the correct disposal of the case, for circulation to the other judges before a specified date. The Tribunal resumes its deliberations as soon as possible on the basis of the written notes.

Article 6 Establishment of a Drafting Committee

1. As soon as possible during the deliberations, the Tribunal sets up a Drafting Committee for the case, composed of five judges belonging to the majority as it appears then to exist. Subject to paragraph 2, the members of the Committee are selected on the proposal of the President by an absolute majority of the judges present, taking into account the need to select judges who, from their statements, clearly support the opinion of the majority as it appears then to exist.

2. The President is a member ex officio of the Committee unless the President does not share the opinion of the majority as it appears then to exist, in which case the Vice-President acts instead. If the Vice-President is ineligible for the same reason, all the members of the Committee are selected by the Tribunal.

3. Unless the Tribunal or the members of the Committee decide otherwise, the judge who is senior in precedence among the members of the Committee acts as its chairman.

Article 7 Work of the Drafting Committee

1. The Drafting Committee meets immediately after its establishment in order to prepare a first draft of the judgment, for completion normally within three weeks. To this end, any

member of the Committee may send written proposals for its consideration and inclusion in the draft.

2. The Drafting Committee should prepare a draft judgment which not only states the opinion of the majority as it appears then to exist but which may also attract wider support within the Tribunal.

3. The first draft of the judgment shall be distributed to all the judges in the case. Any judge who wishes to offer amendments or comments submits them in writing to the Committee within three weeks from the date of circulation.

4. After the members of the Committee have received the comments, they will normally meet in order to revise the draft, unless they decide a meeting is not required.

5. When the members of the Committee have completed the second draft of the judgment, the Registrar shall circulate copies to all judges.

6. If the President is not a member of the Committee, its chairman keeps the President informed of work on the draft judgment, as well as its terms.

Article 8 Deliberations on the draft judgment

1. Deliberations on the draft judgment are held as soon as possible after its circulation and in principle not later than three months after the closure of the oral proceedings.

2. The chairman of the Drafting Committee introduces the draft.

3. The draft is examined by the Tribunal in first reading. A judge wishing to modify the draft proposes amendments in writing.

4. At this stage, a judge who, after taking cognizance of the draft judgment, wishes to deliver a separate or dissenting opinion so informs the other judges and puts forward at least an outline of the opinion, making the text available within a time-limit fixed by the Tribunal before the second reading. Such a judge continues to participate in the examination of the draft judgment and cognizance is taken by the Tribunal of such opinions.

5. The Drafting Committee circulates a revised draft judgment for consideration at a second reading, during the course of which the President asks if the judges wish to propose new amendments.

6. Separate or dissenting opinions, which may be individual or collective, should be submitted within a time-limit fixed by the Tribunal. They should take account of any changes made to the draft judgment pursuant to paragraphs 4 and 5 and should concentrate on the remaining points of difference with the judgment.

Article 9 Voting

1. After the Tribunal has completed its second reading of the draft judgment, the President takes the vote in accordance with article 29 of the Statute in order to adopt the judgment. A separate vote is normally taken on each operative provision in the judgment. Any judge may request a separate vote on issues which are separable. Each judge votes by means solely of an affirmative or a negative vote, cast in person and in inverse order of seniority, provided that in exceptional circumstances accepted by the Tribunal an absent judge may vote by appropriate means of communications.

2. A judge who has been absent, because of illness or other reason duly explained to the President, from any part of the hearing or the deliberations may vote provided the Tribunal accepts that the judge has taken a sufficient part in the hearing and the deliberations to be able to reach a judicial determination of all issues of fact and law material to the decision to be given in the case.

Article 10 Experts appointed under article 289 of the Convention

Experts appointed under article 289 of the Convention for a particular case before the Tribunal shall be sent copies of the written pleadings and other documents in the case in good time before the beginning of the deliberations. They sit with the judges during the oral proceedings and take part in the deliberations in accordance with article 42 of the Rules. They receive the written notes and other documents. They may be consulted by the Drafting Committee, as appropriate.

Article 11 Procedures in particular instances

1. The Tribunal may decide to vary the procedures and arrangements set out above in a particular case for reasons of urgency or if circumstances so justify.
2. Deliberations concerning applications for provisional measures and applications for the prompt release of a vessel or crew are conducted in accordance with the principles and procedures set out in this Resolution, taking account of the nature and urgency of the case.
3. The Chamber for Summary Procedure deliberates in accordance with the principles and procedures set out in this Resolution, taking account of the summary nature of the proceedings and the urgency of the case.

Article 12 Application

The foregoing provisions apply whether the proceedings before the Tribunal are contentious or advisory.

Article 13 Review

This Resolution may be reviewed in the light of experience and revised whenever considered appropriate.

50.e Arbitration under UNCLOS Annex VII

Date: 10 December 1982
Source: 1833 UNTS 397
https://www.un.org/Depts/los/convention_agreements/texts/unclos/annex7.htm

Article 1 Institution of proceedings

Subject to the provisions of Part XV, any party to a dispute may submit the dispute to the arbitral procedure provided for in this Annex by written notification addressed to the other party or parties to the dispute. The notification shall be accompanied by a statement of the claim and the grounds on which it is based.

Article 2 List of arbitrators

1. A list of arbitrators shall be drawn up and maintained by the Secretary-General of the United Nations. Every State Party shall be entitled to nominate four arbitrators, each of whom shall be a person experienced in maritime affairs and enjoying the highest reputation for fairness, competence and integrity. The names of the persons so nominated shall constitute the list.

2. If at any time the arbitrators nominated by a State Party in the list so constituted shall be fewer than four, that State Party shall be entitled to make further nominations as necessary.

3. The name of an arbitrator shall remain on the list until withdrawn by the State Party which made the nomination, provided that such arbitrator shall continue to serve on any arbitral tribunal to which that arbitrator has been appointed until the completion of the proceedings before that arbitral tribunal.

Article 3 Constitution of arbitral tribunal

For the purpose of proceedings under this Annex, the arbitral tribunal shall, unless the parties otherwise agree, be constituted as follows:

(a) Subject to subparagraph (g), the arbitral tribunal shall consist of five members.

(b) The party instituting the proceedings shall appoint one member to be chosen preferably from the list referred to in article 2 of this Annex, who may be its national. The appointment shall be included in the notification referred to in article 1 of this Annex.

(c) The other party to the dispute shall, within 30 days of receipt of the notification referred to in article 1 of this Annex, appoint one member to be chosen preferably from the list, who may be its national. If the appointment is not made within that period, the party instituting the proceedings may, within two weeks of the expiration of that period, request that the appointment be made in accordance with subparagraph (e).

(d) The other three members shall be appointed by agreement between the parties. They shall be chosen preferably from the list and shall be nationals of third States unless the parties otherwise agree. The parties to the dispute shall appoint the President of the arbitral tribunal from among those three members. If, within 60 days of receipt of the notification referred to in article 1 of this Annex, the parties are unable to reach agreement on the appointment of one or more of the members of the tribunal to be appointed by agreement, or on the appointment of the President, the remaining appointment or appointments shall be made in accordance with subparagraph (e), at the request of a party to the dispute. Such request shall be made within two weeks of the expiration of the aforementioned 60-day period.

(e) Unless the parties agree that any appointment under subparagraphs (c) and (d) be made by a person or a third State chosen by the parties, the President of the International Tribunal for the Law of the Sea shall make the necessary appointments. If the President is unable to act under this subparagraph or is a national of one of the parties to the dispute, the appointment shall be made by the next senior member of the International Tribunal for the Law of the Sea who is available and is not a national of one of the parties. The appointments referred to in this subparagraph shall be made from the list referred to in article 2 of this Annex within a period of 30 days of the receipt of the request and in consultation with the parties. The members so appointed shall be of different nationalities and may not be in the service of, ordinarily resident in the territory of, or nationals of, any of the parties to the dispute.

(f) Any vacancy shall be filled in the manner prescribed for the initial appointment.

(g) Parties in the same interest shall appoint one member of the tribunal jointly by agreement. Where there are several parties having separate interests or where there is disagreement as to whether they are of the same interest, each of them shall appoint one member of the tribunal. The number of members of the tribunal appointed separately by the parties shall always be smaller by one than the number of members of the tribunal to be appointed jointly by the parties.

(h) In disputes involving more than two parties, the provisions of subparagraphs (a) to (f) shall apply to the maximum extent possible.

Article 4 Functions of arbitral tribunal

An arbitral tribunal constituted under article 3 of this Annex shall function in accordance with this Annex and the other provisions of this Convention.

Article 5 Procedure

Unless the parties to the dispute otherwise agree, the arbitral tribunal shall determine its own procedure, assuring to each party a full opportunity to be heard and to present its case.

Article 6 Duties of parties to a dispute

The parties to the dispute shall facilitate the work of the arbitral tribunal and, in particular, in accordance with their law and using all means at their disposal, shall:

(a) provide it with all relevant documents, facilities and information; and

(b) enable it when necessary to call witnesses or experts and receive their evidence and to visit the localities to which the case relates.

Article 7 Expenses

Unless the arbitral tribunal decides otherwise because of the particular circumstances of the case, the expenses of the tribunal, including the remuneration of its members, shall be borne by the parties to the dispute in equal shares.

Article 8 Required majority for decisions

Decisions of the arbitral tribunal shall be taken by a majority vote of its members. The absence or abstention of less than half of the members shall not constitute a bar to the tribunal reaching a decision. In the event of an equality of votes, the President shall have a casting vote.

Article 9 Default of appearance

If one of the parties to the dispute does not appear before the arbitral tribunal or fails to defend its case, the other party may request the tribunal to continue the proceedings and to make its award. Absence of a party or failure of a party to defend its case shall not constitute a bar to the proceedings. Before making its award, the arbitral tribunal must satisfy itself not only that it has jurisdiction over the dispute but also that the claim is well founded in fact and law.

Article 10 Award

The award of the arbitral tribunal shall be confined to the subject-matter of the dispute and state the reasons on which it is based. It shall contain the names of the members who have participated and the date of the award. Any member of the tribunal may attach a separate or dissenting opinion to the award.

Article 11 Finality of award

The award shall be final and without appeal, unless the parties to the dispute have agreed in advance to an appellate procedure. It shall be complied with by the parties to the dispute.

Article 12 Interpretation or implementation of award

1. Any controversy which may arise between the parties to the dispute as regards the interpretation or manner of implementation of the award may be submitted by either party for decision to the arbitral tribunal which made the award. For this purpose, any vacancy in the tribunal shall be filled in the manner provided for in the original appointments of the members of the tribunal.

2. Any such controversy may be submitted to another court or tribunal under article 287 by agreement of all the parties to the dispute.

Article 13 Application to entities other than States Parties

The provisions of this Annex shall apply *mutatis mutandis* to any dispute involving entities other than States Parties.

50.f Special Arbitration under UNCLOS Annex VIII

Date: 10 December 1982
Source: 1833 UNTS 397
https://www.un.org/depts/los/convention_agreements/texts/unclos/closindx.htm

Article 1 Institution of proceedings

Subject to Part XV, any party to a dispute concerning the interpretation or application of the articles of this Convention relating to (1) fisheries, (2) protection and preservation of the marine environment, (3) marine scientific research, or (4) navigation, including pollution from vessels and by dumping, may submit the dispute to the special arbitral procedure provided for in this Annex by written notification addressed to the other party or parties to the dispute. The notification shall be accompanied by a statement of the claim and the grounds on which it is based.

Article 2 Lists of experts

1. A list of experts shall be established and maintained in respect of each of the fields of (1) fisheries, (2) protection and preservation of the marine environment, (3) marine scientific research, and (4) navigation, including pollution from vessels and by dumping.

2. The lists of experts shall be drawn up and maintained, in the field of fisheries by the Food and Agriculture Organization of the United Nations, in the field of protection and preservation of the marine environment by the United Nations Environment Programme, in the field of marine scientific research by the Intergovernmental Oceanographic Commission, in the field of navigation, including pollution from vessels and by dumping, by the International Maritime Organization, or in each case by the appropriate subsidiary body concerned to which such organization, programme or commission has delegated this function.

3. Every State Party shall be entitled to nominate two experts in each field whose competence in the legal, scientific or technical aspects of such field is established and generally recognized and who enjoy the highest reputation for fairness and integrity. The names of the persons so nominated in each field shall constitute the appropriate list.

4. If at any time the experts nominated by a State Party in the list so constituted shall be fewer than two, that State Party shall be entitled to make further nominations as necessary.

5. The name of an expert shall remain on the list until withdrawn by the State Party which made the nomination, provided that such expert shall continue to serve on any special arbitral tribunal to which that expert has been appointed until the completion of the proceedings before that special arbitral tribunal.

Article 3 Constitution of special arbitral tribunal

For the purpose of proceedings under this Annex, the special arbitral tribunal shall, unless the parties otherwise agree, be constituted as follows:

(a) Subject to subparagraph (g), the special arbitral tribunal shall consist of five members.

(b) The party instituting the proceedings shall appoint two members to be chosen preferably from the appropriate list or lists referred to in article 2 of this Annex relating to the matters in dispute, one of whom may be its national. The appointments shall be included in the notification referred to in article 1 of this Annex.

(c) The other party to the dispute shall, within 30 days of receipt of the notification referred to in article 1 of this Annex, appoint two members to be chosen preferably from the appropriate list or lists relating to the matters in dispute, one of whom may be its national. If the appointments are not made within that period, the party instituting the proceedings may, within two weeks of the expiration of that period, request that the appointments be made in accordance with subparagraph (e).

(d) The parties to the dispute shall by agreement appoint the President of the special arbitral tribunal, chosen preferably from the appropriate list, who shall be a national of a third State, unless the parties otherwise agree. If, within 30 days of receipt of the notification referred to in article l of this Annex, the parties are unable to reach agreement on the appointment of the President, the appointment shall be made in accordance with subparagraph (e), at the request of a party to the dispute. Such request shall be made within two weeks of the expiration of the aforementioned 30-day period.

(e) Unless the parties agree that the appointment be made by a person or a third State chosen by the parties, the Secretary-General of the United Nations shall make the necessary appointments within 30 days of receipt of a request under subparagraphs (c) and (d). The appointments referred to in this subparagraph shall be made from the appropriate list or lists of experts referred to in article 2 of this Annex and in consultation with the parties to the dispute and the appropriate international organization. The members so appointed shall be of different nationalities and may not be in the service of, ordinarily resident in the territory of, or nationals of, any of the parties to the dispute.
(f) Any vacancy shall be filled in the manner prescribed for the initial appointment.
(g) Parties in the same interest shall appoint two members of the tribunal jointly by agreement. Where there are several parties having separate interests or where there is disagreement as to whether they are of the same interest, each of them shall appoint one member of the tribunal.
(h) In disputes involving more than two parties, the provisions of subparagraphs (a) to (f) shall apply to the maximum extent possible.

Article 4 General provisions

Annex VII, articles 4 to 13, apply *mutatis mutandis* to the special arbitration proceedings in accordance with this Annex.

Article 5 Fact finding

1. The parties to a dispute concerning the interpretation or application of the provisions of this Convention relating to (1) fisheries, (2) protection and preservation of the marine environment, (3) marine scientific research, or (4) navigation, including pollution from vessels and by dumping, may at any time agree to request a special arbitral tribunal constituted in accordance with article 3 of this Annex to carry out an inquiry and establish the facts giving rise to the dispute.

2. Unless the parties otherwise agree, the findings of fact of the special arbitral tribunal acting in accordance with paragraph 1, shall be considered as conclusive as between the parties.

3. If all the parties to the dispute so request, the special arbitral tribunal may formulate recommendations which, without having the force of a decision, shall only constitute the basis for a review by the parties of the questions giving rise to the dispute.

4. Subject to paragraph 2, the special arbitral tribunal shall act in accordance with the provisions of this Annex, unless the parties otherwise agree.

50.g Participation by International Organisations (UNCLOS Annex IX)

Source: 1833 UNTS 397
https://www.un.org/depts/los/convention_agreements/texts/unclos/unclos_e.pdf

...

Article 5 Declarations, notifications and communications

1. The instrument of formal confirmation or of accession of an international organization shall contain a declaration specifying the matters governed by this Convention in respect

of which competence has been transferred to the organization by its member States which are Parties to this Convention.

2. A member State of an international organization shall, at the time it ratifies or accedes to this Convention or at the time when the organization deposits its instrument of formal confirmation or of accession, whichever is later, make a declaration specifying the matters governed by this Convention in respect of which it has transferred competence to the organization.

3. States Parties which are member States of an international organization which is a Party to this Convention shall be presumed to have competence over all matters governed by this Convention in respect of which transfers of competence to the organization have not been specifically declared, notified or communicated by those States under this article.

4. The international organization and its member States which are States Parties shall promptly notify the depositary of this Convention of any changes to the distribution of competence, including new transfers of competence, specified in the declarations under paragraphs 1 and 2.

5. Any State Party may request an international organization and its member States which are States Parties to provide information as to which, as between the organization and its member States, has competence in respect of any specific question which has arisen. The organization and the member States concerned shall provide this information within a reasonable time. The international organization and the member States may also, on their own initiative, provide this information.

6. Declarations, notifications and communications of information under this article shall specify the nature and extent of the competence transferred.

Article 6 Responsibility and liability

1. Parties which have competence under article 5 of this Annex shall have responsibility for failure to comply with obligations or for any other violation of this Convention.

2. Any State Party may request an international organization or its member States which are States Parties for information as to who has responsibility in respect of any specific matter. The organization and the member States concerned shall provide this information. Failure to provide this information within a reasonable time or the provision of contradictory information shall result in joint and several liability.

Article 7 Settlement of disputes

1. At the time of deposit of its instrument of formal confirmation or of accession, or at any time thereafter, an international organization shall be free to choose, by means of a written declaration, one or more of the means for the settlement of disputes concerning the interpretation or application of this Convention, referred to in article 287, paragraph 1(a), (c) or (d).

2. Part XV applies mutatis mutandis to any dispute between Parties to this Convention, one or more of which are international organizations.

3. When an international organization and one or more of its member States are joint parties to a dispute, or parties in the same interest, the organization shall be deemed to have accepted the same procedures for the settlement of disputes as the member States; when, however, a member State has chosen only the International Court of Justice under article 287, the organization and the member State concerned shall be deemed to have accepted arbitration in accordance with Annex VII, unless the parties to the dispute otherwise agree.

…

51 Agreement for the Implementation of the United Nations Convention on the Law of the Sea of 10 December 1982 relating to the Conservation and Management of Straddling Fish Stocks and Highly Migratory Fish Stocks (Fish Stocks Agreement)

Date: 4 December 1995
Source: 2167 UNTS 3
https://treaties.un.org/doc/Treaties/1995/08/19950804%2008-25%20AM/Ch_XXI_07p.pdf

...

PART VIII: PEACEFUL SETTLEMENT OF DISPUTES

Article 27 Obligation to settle disputes by peaceful means

States have the obligation to settle their disputes by negotiation, inquiry, mediation, conciliation, arbitration, judicial settlement, resort to regional agencies or arrangements, or other peaceful means of their own choice.

Article 28 Prevention of disputes

States shall cooperate in order to prevent disputes. To this end, States shall agree on efficient and expeditious decision-making procedures within subregional and regional fisheries management organizations and arrangements and shall strengthen existing decision-making procedures as necessary.

Article 29 Disputes of a technical nature

Where a dispute concerns a matter of a technical nature, the States concerned may refer the dispute to an ad hoc expert panel established by them. The panel shall confer with the States concerned and shall endeavour to resolve the dispute expeditiously without recourse to binding procedures for the settlement of disputes.

Article 30 Procedures for the settlement of disputes

1. The provisions relating to the settlement of disputes set out in Part XV of the Convention apply *mutatis mutandis* to any dispute between States Parties to this Agreement concerning the interpretation or application of this Agreement, whether or not they are also Parties to the Convention.

2. The provisions relating to the settlement of disputes set out in Part XV of the Convention apply *mutatis mutandis* to any dispute between States Parties to this Agreement concerning the interpretation or application of a subregional, regional or global fisheries agreement relating to straddling fish stocks or highly migratory fish stocks to which they are parties, including any dispute concerning the conservation and management of such stocks, whether or not they are also Parties to the Convention.

3. Any procedure accepted by a State Party to this Agreement and the Convention pursuant to article 287 of the Convention shall apply to the settlement of disputes under this Part, unless that State Party, when signing, ratifying or acceding to this Agreement, or at any time thereafter, has accepted another procedure pursuant to article 287 for the settlement of disputes under this Part.

4. A State Party to this Agreement which is not a Party to the Convention, when signing, ratifying or acceding to this Agreement, or at any time thereafter, shall be free to choose, by means of a written declaration, one or more of the means set out in article 287, paragraph 1, of the Convention for the settlement of disputes under this Part. Article 287 shall apply to such a declaration, as well as to any dispute to which such State is a party which is not covered by a declaration in force. For the purposes of conciliation and arbitration in accordance with Annexes V, VII and VIII to the Convention, such State shall be entitled to nominate conciliators, arbitrators and experts to be included in the lists referred to in Annex V, article 2, Annex VII, article 2, and Annex VIII, article 2, for the settlement of disputes under this Part.

5. Any court or tribunal to which a dispute has been submitted under this Part shall apply the relevant provisions of the Convention, of this Agreement and of any relevant subregional, regional or global fisheries agreement, as well as generally accepted standards for the conservation and management of living marine resources and other rules of international law not incompatible with the Convention, with a view to ensuring the conservation of the straddling fish stocks and highly migratory fish stocks concerned.

Article 31 Provisional measures

1. Pending the settlement of a dispute in accordance with this Part, the parties to the dispute shall make every effort to enter into provisional arrangements of a practical nature.

2. Without prejudice to article 290 of the Convention, the court or tribunal to which the dispute has been submitted under this Part may prescribe any provisional measures which it considers appropriate under the circumstances to preserve the respective rights of the parties to the dispute or to prevent damage to the stocks in question, as well as in the circumstances referred to in article 7, paragraph 5, and article 16, paragraph 2.

3. A State Party to this Agreement which is not a Party to the Convention may declare that, notwithstanding article 290, paragraph 5, of the Convention, the International Tribunal for the Law of the Sea shall not be entitled to prescribe, modify or revoke provisional measures without the agreement of such State.

Article 32 Limitations on applicability of procedures for the settlement of disputes

Article 297, paragraph 3, of the Convention applies also to this Agreement.

…

52 Convention for the Conservation of Southern Bluefin Tuna

Date: 10 May 1993
Source: 1819 UNTS 360
https://treaties.un.org/doc/Publication/UNTS/Volume%201819/volume-1819-I-31155-English.pdf

…

Article 6

1. The Parties hereby establish and agree to maintain the Commission for the Conservation of Southern Bluefin Tuna (hereinafter referred to as "the Commission").

2. Each Party shall be represented on the Commission by not more than three delegates who may be accompanied by experts and advisers.

3. The Commission shall hold an annual meeting before 1 August each year or at such other time as it may determine.

4. At each annual meeting the Commission shall elect from among the delegates a Chair and a Vice-Chair. The Chair and the Vice-Chair shall be elected from different Parties and shall remain in office until the election of their successors at the next annual meeting. A delegate, when acting as Chair, shall not vote.

5. Special meetings of the Commission shall be convened by the Chair at the request of a Party supported by at least two other Parties.

6. A special meeting may consider any matter of relevance to this Convention.

7. Two-thirds of the Parties shall constitute a quorum.

8. The rules of procedure of the Commission and other internal administrative regulations as may be necessary to carry out its functions shall be decided upon at the first meeting of the Commission and may be amended by the Commission as occasion may require.

9. The Commission shall have legal personality and shall enjoy in its relations with other international organisations and in the territories of the Parties such legal capacity as may be necessary to perform its functions and achieve its ends. The immunities and privileges which the Commission and its officers shall enjoy in the territory of a Party shall be subject to agreement between the Commission and the Party concerned.

10. The Commission shall determine the location of its headquarters at such time as a Secretariat is established pursuant to paragraph 1 of Article 10.

11. The official languages of the Commission shall be Japanese and English. Proposals and data may be submitted to the Commission in either language.

Article 7

Each Party shall have one vote in the Commission. Decisions of the Commission shall be taken by a unanimous vote of the Parties present at the Commission meeting.

Article 8

1. The Commission shall collect and accumulate information described below:
   (a) scientific information, statistical data and other information relating to southern bluefin tuna and ecologically related species;
   (b) information relating to laws, regulations and administrative measures on southern bluefin tuna fisheries;
   (c) any other information relating to southern bluefin tuna.
2. The Commission shall consider matters described below:
   (a) interpretation or implementation of this Convention and measures adopted pursuant to it;
   (b) regulatory measures for conservation, management and optimum utilisation of southern bluefin tuna;
   (c) matters which shall be reported by the Scientific Committee prescribed in Article 9;
   (d) matters which may be entrusted to the Scientific Committee prescribed in Article 9;
   (e) matters which may be entrusted to the Secretariat prescribed in Article 10;
   (f) other activities necessary to carry out the provisions of this Convention.

3. For the conservation, management and optimum utilisation of southern bluefin tuna:
   (a) the Commission shall decide upon a total allowable catch and its allocation among the Parties unless the Commission decides upon other appropriate measures on the basis of the report and recommendations of the Scientific Committee referred to in paragraph 2(c) and (d) of Article 9; and
   (b) the Commission may, if necessary, decide upon other additional measures.

4. In deciding upon allocations among the Parties under paragraph 3 above the Commission shall consider:
   (a) relevant scientific evidence;
   (b) the need for orderly and sustainable development of southern bluefin tuna fisheries;
   (c) the interests of Parties through whose exclusive economic or fishery zones southern bluefin tuna migrates;
   (d) the interests of Parties whose vessels engage in fishing for southern bluefin tuna including those which have historically engaged in such fishing and those which have southern bluefin tuna fisheries under development;
   (e) the contribution of each Party to conservation and enhancement of, and scientific research on, southern bluefin tuna;
   (f) any other factors which the Commission deems appropriate.

5. The Commission may decide upon recommendations to the Parties in order to further the attainment of the objective of this Convention.

6. In deciding upon measures under paragraph 3 above and recommendations under paragraph 5 above, the Commission shall take full account of the report and recommendations of the Scientific Committee under paragraph 2(c) and (d) of Article 9.

7. All measures decided upon under paragraph 3 above shall be binding on the Parties.

8. The Commission shall notify all Parties promptly of measures and recommendations decided upon by the Commission.

9. The Commission shall develop, at the earliest possible time and consistent with international law, systems to monitor all fishing activities related to southern bluefin tuna in order to enhance scientific knowledge necessary for conservation and management of southern bluefin tuna and in order to achieve effective implementation of this Convention and measures adopted pursuant to it.

10. The Commission may establish such subsidiary bodies as it considers desirable for the exercise of its duties and functions.

…

Article 16

1. If any dispute arises between two or more of the Parties concerning the interpretation or implementation of this Convention, those Parties shall consult among themselves with a view to having the dispute resolved by negotiation, inquiry, mediation, conciliation, arbitration, judicial settlement or other peaceful means of their own choice.

2. Any dispute of this character not so resolved shall, with the consent in each case of all parties to the dispute, be referred for settlement to the International Court of Justice or to arbitration; but failure to reach agreement on reference to the International Court of Justice or to arbitration shall not absolve parties to the dispute from the responsibility of continuing to seek to resolve it by any of the various peaceful means referred to in paragraph 1 above.

3. In cases where the dispute is referred to arbitration, the arbitral tribunal shall be constituted as provided in the Annex to this Convention. The Annex forms an integral part of this Convention.

...

ANNEX FOR AN ARBITRAL TRIBUNAL

1. The arbitral tribunal referred to in paragraph 3 of Article 16 shall be composed of three arbitrators who shall be appointed as follows:

(a) The party commencing proceedings shall communicate the name of an arbitrator to the other party which, in turn, within a period of forty days following such notification, shall communicate the name of the second arbitrator. The parties shall, within a period of sixty days following the appointment of the second arbitrator, appoint the third arbitrator, who shall not be a national of either party and shall not be of the same nationality as either of the first two arbitrators. The third arbitrator shall preside over the tribunal.

(b) If the second arbitrator has not been appointed within the prescribed period, or if the parties have not reached agreement within the prescribed period on the appointment of the third arbitrator, that arbitrator shall be appointed, at the request of either party, by the Secretary-General of the Permanent Court of Arbitration, from among persons of international standing not having the nationality of a State which is a Party to this Convention.

2. The arbitral tribunal shall decide where its headquarters will be located and shall adopt its own rules of procedure.

3. The award of the arbitral tribunal shall be made by a majority of its members, who may not abstain from voting.

4. Any Party which is not a party to the dispute may intervene in the proceedings with the consent of the arbitral tribunal.

5. The award of the arbitral tribunal shall be final and binding on all parties to the dispute and on any party which intervenes in the proceedings and shall be complied with without delay. The arbitral tribunal shall interpret the award at the request of one of the parties to the dispute or of any intervening party.

6. Unless the arbitral tribunal determines otherwise because of the particular circumstances of the case, the expenses of the tribunal, including the remuneration of its members, shall be borne by the parties to the dispute in equal shares.

10 Environment

Climate Change

53.a United Nations Framework Convention on Climate Change

Date: 9 May 1992
Source: 1771 UNTS 107
http://unfccc.int/resource/docs/convkp/conveng.pdf

...

ARTICLE 13 RESOLUTION OF QUESTIONS REGARDING IMPLEMENTATION

The Conference of the Parties shall, at its first session, consider the establishment of a multilateral consultative process, available to Parties on their request, for the resolution of questions regarding the implementation of the Convention.

ARTICLE 14 SETTLEMENT OF DISPUTES

1. In the event of a dispute between any two or more Parties concerning the interpretation or application of the Convention, the Parties concerned shall seek a settlement of the dispute through negotiation or any other peaceful means of their own choice.

2. When ratifying, accepting, approving or acceding to the Convention, or at any time thereafter, a Party which is not a regional economic integration organization may declare in a written instrument submitted to the Depositary that, in respect of any dispute concerning the interpretation or application of the Convention, it recognizes as compulsory ipso facto and without special agreement, in relation to any Party accepting the same obligation:

(a) Submission of the dispute to the International Court of Justice; and/or

(b) Arbitration in accordance with procedures to be adopted by the Conference of the Parties as soon as practicable, in an annex on arbitration.

A Party which is a regional economic integration organization may make a declaration with like effect in relation to arbitration in accordance with the procedures referred to in subparagraph (b) above.

3. A declaration made under paragraph 2 above shall remain in force until it expires in accordance with its terms or until three months after written notice of its revocation has been deposited with the Depositary.

4. A new declaration, a notice of revocation or the expiry of a declaration shall not in any way affect proceedings pending before the International Court of Justice or the arbitral tribunal, unless the parties to the dispute otherwise agree.

5. Subject to the operation of paragraph 2 above, if after twelve months following notification by one Party to another that a dispute exists between them, the Parties concerned have not been able to settle their dispute through the means mentioned in paragraph 1 above, the dispute shall be submitted, at the request of any of the parties to the dispute, to conciliation.

6. A conciliation commission shall be created upon the request of one of the parties to the dispute. The commission shall be composed of an equal number of members appointed by each party concerned and a chairman chosen jointly by the members appointed by each party. The commission shall render a recommendatory award, which the parties shall consider in good faith.

7. Additional procedures relating to conciliation shall be adopted by the Conference of the Parties, as soon as practicable, in an annex on conciliation.

8. The provisions of this Article shall apply to any related legal instrument which the Conference of the Parties may adopt, unless the instrument provides otherwise.

…

53.b Kyoto Protocol to the United Nations Framework Convention on Climate Change

Date: 11 December 1997
Source: (1998) 37 ILM 22
http://unfccc.int/resource/docs/convkp/kpeng.pdf

…

Article 16

The Conference of the Parties serving as the meeting of the Parties to this Protocol shall, as soon as practicable, consider the application to this Protocol of, and modify as appropriate, the multilateral consultative process referred to in Article 13 of the Convention, in the light of any relevant decisions that may be taken by the Conference of the Parties. Any multilateral consultative process that may be applied to this Protocol shall operate without prejudice to the procedures and mechanisms established in accordance with Article 18.

…

Article 18

The Conference of the Parties serving as the meeting of the Parties to this Protocol shall, at its first session, approve appropriate and effective procedures and mechanisms to determine and to address cases of non-compliance with the provisions of this Protocol, including through the development of an indicative list of consequences, taking into account the cause, type, degree and frequency of non-compliance. Any procedures and mechanisms under this Article entailing binding consequences shall be adopted by means of an amendment to this Protocol.

Article 19

The provisions of Article 14 of the Convention on settlement of disputes shall apply *mutatis mutandis* to this Protocol.

…

53.c Procedures and Mechanisms Relating to Compliance under the Kyoto Protocol

Date: 9–10 December 2005
Source: Decision 27/CMP.1 (Annex) in Doc FCCC/KP/CMP/2005/8/Add.3
http://unfccc.int/resource/docs/2005/cmp1/eng/08a03.pdf#page=92

In pursuit of the ultimate objective of the United Nations Framework Convention on Climate Change, hereinafter referred to as "the Convention", as stated in its Article 2,

Recalling the provisions of the United Nations Framework Convention on Climate Change, and the Kyoto Protocol to the Convention, herein after referred to as "the Protocol",

Being guided by Article 3 of the Convention,

Pursuant to the mandate adopted in decision 8/CP.4 by the Conference of the Parties at its fourth session,

The following procedures and mechanisms have been adopted:

I. Objective

The objective of these procedures and mechanisms is to facilitate, promote and enforce compliance with the commitments under the Protocol.

II. Compliance Committee

1. A compliance committee, hereinafter referred to as "the Committee", is hereby established.

2. The Committee shall function through a plenary, a bureau and two branches, namely, the facilitative branch and the enforcement branch.

3. The Committee shall consist of twenty members elected by the Conference of the Parties serving as the meeting of the Parties to the Protocol, ten of whom are to be elected to serve in the facilitative branch and ten to be elected to serve in the enforcement branch.

4. Each branch shall elect, from among its members and for a term of two years, a chairperson and a vice-chairperson, one of whom shall be from a Party included in Annex I and one from a Party not included in Annex I. These persons shall constitute the bureau of the Committee. The chairing of each branch shall rotate between Parties included in Annex I and Parties not included in Annex I in such a manner that at any time one chairperson shall be from among the Parties included in Annex I and the other chairperson shall be from among the Parties not included in Annex I.

5. For each member of the Committee, the Conference of the Parties serving as the meeting of the Parties to the Protocol shall elect an alternate member.

6. Members of the Committee and their alternates shall serve in their individual capacities. They shall have recognized competence relating to climate change and in relevant fields such as the scientific, technical, socio-economic or legal fields.

7. The facilitative branch and the enforcement branch shall interact and cooperate in their functioning and, as necessary, on a case-by-case basis, the bureau of the Committee may designate one or more members of one branch to contribute to the work of the other branch on a non-voting basis.

8. The adoption of decisions by the Committee shall require a quorum of at least three fourths of the members to be present.

9. The Committee shall make every effort to reach agreement on any decisions by consensus. If all efforts at reaching consensus have been exhausted, the decisions shall as a last resort be adopted by a majority of at least three fourths of the members present and voting. In addition, the adoption of decisions by the enforcement branch shall require a majority of members from Parties included in Annex I present and voting, as well as a majority of members from Parties not included in Annex I present and voting. "Members present and voting" means members present and casting an affirmative or a negative vote.

10. The Committee shall, unless it decides otherwise, meet at least twice each year, taking into account the desirability of holding such meetings in conjunction with the meetings of the subsidiary bodies under the Convention.

11. The Committee shall take into account any degree of flexibility allowed by the Conference of the Parties serving as the meeting of the Parties to the Protocol, pursuant to Article 3, paragraph 6, of the Protocol and taking into account Article 4, paragraph 6, of the Convention, to the Parties included in Annex I undergoing the process of transition to a market economy.

III. Plenary of the Committee

1. The plenary shall consist of the members of the facilitative branch and the enforcement branch. The chairpersons of the two branches shall be the co-chairpersons of the plenary.

2. The functions of the plenary shall be:

(a) To report on the activities of the Committee, including a list of decisions taken by the branches, to each ordinary session of the Conference of the Parties serving as the meeting of the Parties to the Protocol;

(b) To apply the general policy guidance referred to in section XII (c) below, received from the Conference of the Parties serving as the meeting of the Parties to the Protocol;

(c) To submit proposals on administrative and budgetary matters to the Conference of the Parties serving as the meeting of the Parties to the Protocol for the effective functioning of the Committee;

(d) To develop any further rules of procedure that may be needed, including rules on confidentiality, conflict of interest, submission of information by intergovernmental and non-governmental organizations, and translation, for adoption by the Conference of the Parties serving as the meeting of the Parties to the Protocol by consensus; and

(e) To perform such other functions as may be requested by the Conference of the Parties serving as the meeting of the Parties to the Protocol for the effective functioning of the Committee.

IV. Facilitative Branch

1. The facilitative branch shall be composed of:

(a) One member from each of the five regional groups of the United Nations and one member from the small island developing States, taking into account the interest groups as reflected by the current practice in the Bureau of the Conference of the Parties;

(b) Two members from Parties included in Annex I; and

(c) Two members from Parties not included in Annex I.

2. The Conference of the Parties serving as the meeting of the Parties to the Protocol shall elect five members for a term of two years and five members for a term of four years. Each time thereafter, the Conference of the Parties serving as the meeting of the Parties to the Protocol shall elect five new members for a term of four years. Members shall not serve for more than two consecutive terms.

3. In electing the members of the facilitative branch, the Conference of the Parties serving as the meeting of the Parties to the Protocol shall seek to reflect competences in a balanced manner in the fields referred to in section II, paragraph 6, above.

4. The facilitative branch shall be responsible for providing advice and facilitation to Parties in implementing the Protocol, and for promoting compliance by Parties with their commitments under the Protocol, taking into account the principle of common

but differentiated responsibilities and respective capabilities as contained in Article 3, paragraph 1, of the Convention. It shall also take into account the circumstances pertaining to the questions before it.

5. Within its overall mandate, as specified in paragraph 4 above, and falling outside the mandate of the enforcement branch, as specified in section V, paragraph 4, below, the facilitative branch shall be responsible for addressing questions of implementation:

(a) Relating to Article 3, paragraph 14, of the Protocol, including questions of implementation arising from the consideration of information on how a Party included in Annex I is striving to implement Article 3, paragraph 14, of the Protocol; and

(b) With respect to the provision of information on the use by a Party included in Annex I of Articles 6, 12 and 17 of the Protocol as supplemental to its domestic action, taking into account any reporting under Article 3, paragraph 2, of the Protocol.

6. With the aim of promoting compliance and providing for early warning of potential non-compliance, the facilitative branch shall be further responsible for providing advice and facilitation for compliance with:

(a) Commitments under Article 3, paragraph 1, of the Protocol, prior to the beginning of the relevant commitment period and during that commitment period;

(b) Commitments under Article 5, paragraphs 1 and 2, of the Protocol, prior to the beginning of the first commitment period; and

(c) Commitments under Article 7, paragraphs 1 and 4, of the Protocol prior to the beginning of the first commitment period.

7. The facilitative branch shall be responsible for applying the consequences set out in section XIV below.

V. Enforcement Branch

1. The enforcement branch shall be composed of:

(a) One member from each of the five regional groups of the United Nations and one member from the small island developing States, taking into account the interest groups as reflected by the current practice in the Bureau of the Conference of the Parties;

(b) Two members from Parties included in Annex I; and

(c) Two members from Parties not included in Annex I.

2. The Conference of the Parties serving as the meeting of the Parties to the Protocol shall elect five members for a term of two years and five members for a term of four years. Each time thereafter, the Conference of the Parties serving as the meeting of the Parties to the Protocol shall elect five new members for a term of four years. Members shall not serve for more than two consecutive terms.

3. In electing the members of the enforcement branch, the Conference of the Parties serving as the meeting of the Parties to the Protocol shall be satisfied that the members have legal experience.

4. The enforcement branch shall be responsible for determining whether a Party included in Annex I is not in compliance with:

(a) Its quantified emission limitation or reduction commitment under Article 3, paragraph 1, of the Protocol;

(b) The methodological and reporting requirements under Article 5, paragraphs 1 and 2, and Article 7, paragraphs 1 and 4, of the Protocol; and

(c) The eligibility requirements under Articles 6, 12 and 17 of the Protocol.

5. The enforcement branch shall also determine whether to apply:

(a) Adjustments to inventories under Article 5, paragraph 2, of the Protocol, in the event of a disagreement between an expert review team under Article 8 of the Protocol and the Party involved; and

(b) A correction to the compilation and accounting database for the accounting of assigned amounts under Article 7, paragraph 4, of the Protocol, in the event of a disagreement between an expert review team under Article 8 of the Protocol and the Party involved concerning the validity of a transaction or such Party's failure to take corrective action.

6. The enforcement branch shall be responsible for applying the consequences set out in section XV below for the cases of non-compliance mentioned in paragraph 4 above. The consequences of non-compliance with Article 3, paragraph 1, of the Protocol to be applied by the enforcement branch shall be aimed at the restoration of compliance to ensure environmental integrity, and shall provide for an incentive to comply.

VI. Submissions

1. The Committee shall receive, through the secretariat, questions of implementation indicated in reports of expert review teams under Article 8 of the Protocol, together with any written comments by the Party which is subject to the report, or questions of implementation submitted by:

(a) Any Party with respect to itself; or

(b) Any Party with respect to another Party, supported by corroborating information.

2. The secretariat shall forthwith make available to the Party in respect of which the question of implementation is raised, hereinafter referred to as "the Party concerned", any question of implementation submitted under paragraph 1 above.

3. In addition to the reports referred to in paragraph 1 above, the Committee shall also receive, through the secretariat, other final reports of expert review teams.

VII. Allocation and preliminary examination

1. The bureau of the Committee shall allocate questions of implementation to the appropriate branch in accordance with the mandates of each branch set out in section IV, paragraphs 4–7, and Section V, paragraphs 4–6.

2. The relevant branch shall undertake a preliminary examination of questions of implementation to ensure that, except in the case of a question raised by a Party with respect to itself, the question before it:

(a) Is supported by sufficient information;

(b) Is not *de minimis* or ill-founded; and

(c) Is based on the requirements of the Protocol.

3. The preliminary examination of questions of implementation shall be completed within three weeks from the date of receipt of these questions by the relevant branch.

4. After the preliminary examination of questions of implementation, the Party concerned shall, through the secretariat, be notified in writing of the decision and, in the event of a decision to proceed, be provided with a statement identifying the question of implementation, the information on which the question is based and the branch that will consider the question.

5. In the event of the review of eligibility requirements for a Party included in Annex I under Articles 6, 12 and 17 of the Protocol, the enforcement branch shall also, through the secretariat, notify forthwith the Party concerned, in writing, of the decision not to proceed with questions of implementation relating to eligibility requirements under those articles.

6. Any decision not to proceed shall be made available by the secretariat to other Parties and to the public.

7. The Party concerned shall be given an opportunity to comment in writing on all information relevant to the question of implementation and the decision to proceed.

VIII. General procedures

1. Following the preliminary examination of questions of implementation, the procedures set out in this section shall apply to the Committee, except where otherwise provided in these procedures and mechanisms.

2. The Party concerned shall be entitled to designate one or more persons to represent it during the consideration of the question of implementation by the relevant branch. This Party shall not be present during the elaboration and adoption of a decision of the branch.

3. Each branch shall base its deliberations on any relevant information provided by:

(a) Reports of the expert review teams under Article 8 of the Protocol;

(b) The Party concerned;

(c) The Party that has submitted a question of implementation with respect to another Party;

(d) Reports of the Conference of the Parties, the Conference of the Parties serving as the meeting of the Parties to the Protocol, and the subsidiary bodies under the Convention and the Protocol; and

(e) The other branch.

4. Competent intergovernmental and non-governmental organizations may submit relevant factual and technical information to the relevant branch.

5. Each branch may seek expert advice.

6. Any information considered by the relevant branch shall be made available to the Party concerned. The branch shall indicate to the Party concerned which parts of this information it has considered. The Party concerned shall be given an opportunity to comment in writing on such information. Subject to any rules relating to confidentiality, the information considered by the branch shall also be made available to the public, unless the branch decides, of its own accord or at the request of the Party concerned, that information provided by the Party concerned shall not be made available to the public until its decision has become final.

7. Decisions shall include conclusions and reasons. The relevant branch shall forthwith, through the secretariat, notify the Party concerned in writing of its decision, including conclusions and reasons therefor. The secretariat shall make final decisions available to other Parties and to the public.

8. The Party concerned shall be given an opportunity to comment in writing on any decision of the relevant branch.

9. If the Party concerned so requests, any question of implementation submitted under section VI, paragraph 1; any notification under section VII, paragraph 4; any information under paragraph 3 above; and any decision of the relevant branch, including conclusions and reasons therefor, shall be translated into one of the six official languages of the United Nations.

IX. Procedures for the Enforcement Branch

1. Within ten weeks from the date of receipt of the notification under section VII, paragraph 4, the Party concerned may make a written submission to the enforcement branch, including rebuttal of information submitted to the branch.

2. If so requested in writing by the Party concerned within ten weeks from the date of receipt of the notification under section VII, paragraph 4, the enforcement branch shall hold a hearing at which the Party concerned shall have the opportunity to present its views. The hearing shall take place within four weeks from the date of receipt of the request or of the written submission under paragraph 1 above, whichever is the later. The Party concerned may present expert testimony or opinion at the hearing. Such a hearing shall be held in public, unless the enforcement branch decides, of its own accord or at the request of the Party concerned, that part or all of the hearing shall take place in private.

3. The enforcement branch may put questions to and seek clarification from the Party concerned, either in the course of such a hearing or at any time in writing, and the Party concerned shall provide a response within six weeks thereafter.

4. Within four weeks from the date of receipt of the written submission of the Party concerned under paragraph 1 above, or within four weeks from the date of any hearing pursuant to paragraph 2 above, or within fourteen weeks from the notification under section VII, paragraph 4, if the Party has not provided a written submission, whichever is the latest, the enforcement branch shall:

(a) Adopt a preliminary finding that the Party concerned is not in compliance with commitments under one or more of the articles of the Protocol referred to in section V, paragraph 4; or

(b) Otherwise determine not to proceed further with the question.

5. The preliminary finding, or the decision not to proceed, shall include conclusions and reasons therefor.

6. The enforcement branch shall forthwith, through the secretariat, notify the Party concerned in writing of its preliminary finding or decision not to proceed. The secretariat shall make the decision not to proceed available to the other Parties and to the public.

7. Within ten weeks from the date of receipt of the notification of the preliminary finding, the Party concerned may provide a further written submission to the enforcement branch. If the Party concerned does not do so within that period of time, the enforcement branch shall forthwith adopt a final decision confirming its preliminary finding.

8. If the Party concerned provides a further written submission, the enforcement branch shall, within four weeks from the date it received the further submission, consider it and adopt a final decision, indicating whether the preliminary finding, as a whole or any part of it to be specified, is confirmed.

9. The final decision shall include conclusions and reasons therefor.

10. The enforcement branch shall forthwith, through the secretariat, notify the Party concerned in writing of its final decision. The secretariat shall make the final decision available to the other Parties and to the public.

11. The enforcement branch, when the circumstances of an individual case so warrant, may extend any time frames provided for in this section.

12. Where appropriate, the enforcement branch may, at any time, refer a question of implementation to the facilitative branch for consideration.

X. Expedited procedures for the Enforcement Branch

1. Where a question of implementation relates to eligibility requirements under Articles 6, 12 and 17 of the Protocol, sections VII to IX shall apply, except that:

(a) The preliminary examination referred to in section VII, paragraph 2, shall be completed within two weeks from the date of receipt of the question of implementation by the enforcement branch;

(b) The Party concerned may make a written submission within four weeks from the date of receipt of the notification under section VII, paragraph 4;

(c) If so requested in writing by the Party concerned within two weeks from the date of receipt of the notification under section VII, paragraph 4, the enforcement branch shall hold a hearing as referred to in section IX, paragraph 2, that shall take place within two weeks from the date of receipt of the request or of the written submission under subparagraph (b) above, whichever is the later;

(d) The enforcement branch shall adopt its preliminary finding or a decision not to proceed within six weeks of the notification under section VII, paragraph 4, or within two weeks of a hearing under section IX, paragraph 2, whichever is the shorter;

(e) The Party concerned may make a further written submission within four weeks from the date of receipt of the notification referred to in section IX, paragraph 6;

(f) The enforcement branch shall adopt its final decision within two weeks from the date of receipt of any further written submission referred to in section IX, paragraph 7; and

(g) The periods of time stipulated in section IX shall apply only if, in the opinion of the enforcement branch, they do not interfere with the adoption of decisions in accordance with subparagraphs (d) and (f) above.

2. Where the eligibility of a Party included in Annex I under Articles 6, 12 and 17 of the Protocol has been suspended under section XV, paragraph 4, the Party concerned may submit a request to reinstate its eligibility, either through an expert review team or directly to the enforcement branch. If the enforcement branch receives a report from the expert review team indicating that there is no longer a question of implementation with respect to the eligibility of the Party concerned, it shall reinstate that Party's eligibility, unless the enforcement branch considers that there continues to be such a question of implementation, in which case the procedure referred to in paragraph 1 above shall apply. In response to a request submitted to it directly by the Party concerned, the enforcement branch shall decide as soon as possible, either that there no longer continues to be a question of implementation with respect to that Party's eligibility in which case it shall reinstate that Party's eligibility, or that the procedure referred to in paragraph 1 above shall apply.

3. Where the eligibility of a Party to make transfers under Article 17 of the Protocol has been suspended under section XV, paragraph 5 (c), the Party may request the enforcement branch to reinstate that eligibility. On the basis of the compliance action plan submitted by the Party in accordance with section XV, paragraph 6, and any progress reports submitted by the Party including information on its emissions trends, the enforcement branch shall reinstate that eligibility, unless it determines that the Party has not demonstrated that it will meet its quantified emission limitation or reduction commitment in the commitment period subsequent to the one for which the Party was determined to be in non-compliance, hereinafter referred to as "the subsequent commitment period". The enforcement branch shall apply the procedure referred to in paragraph 1 above, adapted insofar as necessary for the purposes of the procedure in the present paragraph.

4. Where the eligibility of a Party to make transfers under Article 17 of the Protocol has been suspended under section XV, paragraph 5 (c), the enforcement branch shall reinstate that eligibility forthwith if the Party demonstrates that it has met its quantified emission limitation or reduction commitment in the subsequent commitment period, either through the report of the expert review team under Article 8 of the Protocol for the final year of the subsequent commitment period or through a decision of the enforcement branch.

5. In the event of a disagreement whether to apply adjustments to inventories under Article 5, paragraph 2, of the Protocol, or whether to apply a correction to the compilation and accounting database for the accounting of assigned amounts under Article 7, paragraph 4, of the Protocol, the enforcement branch shall decide on the matter within twelve weeks of being informed in writing of such disagreement. In doing so, the enforcement branch may seek expert advice.

XI. Appeals

1. The Party in respect of which a final decision has been taken may appeal to the Conference of the Parties serving as the meeting of the Parties to the Protocol against a decision of the enforcement branch relating to Article 3, paragraph 1, of the Protocol if that Party believes it has been denied due process.

2. The appeal shall be lodged with the secretariat within 45 days after the Party has been informed of the decision of the enforcement branch. The Conference of the Parties serving as the meeting of the Parties to the Protocol shall consider the appeal at its first session after the lodging of the appeal.

3. The Conference of the Parties serving as the meeting of the Parties to the Protocol may agree by a three-fourths majority vote of the Parties present and voting at the meeting to override the decision of the enforcement branch, in which event the Conference of the Parties serving as the meeting of the Parties to the Protocol shall refer the matter of the appeal back to the enforcement branch.

4. The decision of the enforcement branch shall stand pending the decision on appeal. It shall become definitive if, after 45 days, no appeal has been made against it.

XII. Relationship with the Conference of the Parties serving as the meeting of the Parties to the Protocol

The Conference of the Parties serving as the meeting of the Parties to the Protocol shall:

(a) In considering the reports of the expert review teams in accordance with Article 8, paragraphs 5 and 6 of the Protocol, identify any general problems that should be addressed in the general policy guidance referred to in subparagraph (c) below;

(b) Consider the reports of the plenary on the progress of its work;

(c) Provide general policy guidance, including on any issues regarding implementation that may have implications for the work of the subsidiary bodies under the Protocol;

(d) Adopt decisions on proposals on administrative and budgetary matters; and

(e) Consider and decide appeals in accordance with section XI.

XIII. Additional period for fulfilling commitments

For the purpose of fulfilling commitments under Article 3, paragraph 1, of the Protocol, a Party may, until the hundredth day after the date set by the Conference of the Parties serving as the meeting of the Parties to the Protocol for the completion of the expert review process under Article 8 of the Protocol for the last year of the commitment period, continue to acquire, and other Parties may transfer to such Party, emission reduction units, certified emission reductions, assigned amount units and removal units under Articles 6, 12 and 17 of the Protocol, from the preceding commitment period, provided the eligibility of any such Party has not been suspended in accordance with section XV, paragraph 4.

XIV. Consequences applied by the Facilitative Branch

The facilitative branch, taking into account the principle of common but differentiated responsibilities and respective capabilities, shall decide on the application of one or more of the following consequences:

(a) Provision of advice and facilitation of assistance to individual Parties regarding the implementation of the Protocol;

(b) Facilitation of financial and technical assistance to any Party concerned, including technology transfer and capacity building from sources other than those established under the Convention and the Protocol for the developing countries;

(c) Facilitation of financial and technical assistance, including technology transfer and capacity building, taking into account Article 4, paragraphs 3, 4 and 5, of the Convention; and

(d) Formulation of recommendations to the Party concerned, taking into account Article 4, paragraph 7, of the Convention.

XV. Consequences applied by the Enforcement Branch

1. Where the enforcement branch has determined that a Party is not in compliance with Article 5, paragraph 1 or paragraph 2, or Article 7, paragraph 1 or paragraph 4, of the Protocol, it shall apply the following consequences, taking into account the cause, type, degree and frequency of the non-compliance of that Party:

(a) Declaration of non-compliance; and

(b) Development of a plan in accordance with paragraphs 2 and 3 below.

2. The Party not in compliance under paragraph 1 above, shall, within three months after the determination of non-compliance, or such longer period that the enforcement branch considers appropriate, submit to the enforcement branch for review and assessment a plan that includes:

(a) An analysis of the causes of non-compliance of the Party;

(b) Measures that the Party intends to implement in order to remedy the non-compliance; and

(c) A timetable for implementing such measures within a time frame not exceeding twelve months which enables the assessment of progress in the implementation.

3. The Party not in compliance under paragraph 1 above shall submit to the enforcement branch progress reports on the implementation of the plan on a regular basis.

4. Where the enforcement branch has determined that a Party included in Annex I does not meet one or more of the eligibility requirements under Articles 6, 12 and 17 of the Protocol, it shall suspend the eligibility of that Party in accordance with relevant provisions under those articles. At the request of the Party concerned, eligibility may be reinstated in accordance with the procedure in section X, paragraph 2.

5. Where the enforcement branch has determined that the emissions of a Party have exceeded its assigned amount, calculated pursuant to its quantified emission limitation

or reduction commitment inscribed in Annex B to the Protocol and in accordance with the provisions of Article 3 of the Protocol as well as the modalities for the accounting of assigned amounts under Article 7, paragraph 4, of the Protocol, taking into account emission reduction units, certified emission reductions, assigned amount units and removal units the Party has acquired in accordance with section XIII, it shall declare that that Party is not in compliance with its commitments under Article 3, paragraph 1, of the Protocol, and shall apply the following consequences:

(a) Deduction from the Party's assigned amount for the second commitment period of a number of tonnes equal to 1.3 times the amount in tonnes of excess emissions;

(b) Development of a compliance action plan in accordance with paragraphs 6 and 7 below; and

(c) Suspension of the eligibility to make transfers under Article 17 of the Protocol until the Party is reinstated in accordance with section X, paragraph 3 or paragraph 4.

6. The Party not in compliance under paragraph 5 above shall, within three months after the determination of non-compliance or, where the circumstances of an individual case so warrant, such longer period that the enforcement branch considers appropriate, submit to the enforcement branch for review and assessment a compliance action plan that includes:

(a) An analysis of the causes of the non-compliance of the Party;

(b) Action that the Party intends to implement in order to meet its quantified emission limitation or reduction commitment in the subsequent commitment period, giving priority to domestic policies and measures; and

(c) A timetable for implementing such action, which enables the assessment of annual progress in the implementation, within a time frame that does not exceed three years or up to the end of the subsequent commitment period, whichever occurs sooner. At the request of the Party, the enforcement branch may, where the circumstances of an individual case so warrant, extend the time for implementing such action for a period which shall not exceed the maximum period of three years mentioned above.

7. The Party not in compliance under paragraph 5 above shall submit to the enforcement branch a progress report on the implementation of the compliance action plan on an annual basis.

8. For subsequent commitment periods, the rate referred to in paragraph 5 (a) above shall be determined by an amendment.

XVI. Relationship with Articles 16 and 19 of the Protocol

The procedures and mechanisms relating to compliance shall operate without prejudice to Articles 16 and 19 of the Protocol.

XVII. Secretariat

The secretariat referred to in Article 14 of the Protocol shall serve as the secretariat of the Committee.

53.d Rules of Procedure of the Compliance Committee of the Kyoto Protocol

Date: 3 February 2014
Source: Informal Consolidated Text Combining the Committee's Rules of Procedure, as contained in the Annex to Decision 4/CMP.2 and the Amendments, as contained in the Annexes to Decisions 4/CMP.4 and 8/CMP.9
https://unfccc.int/files/kyoto_protocol/compliance/application/pdf/consolidated_rop_with_cmp_4&cmp9_amend_2014feb03.pdf

Part 1: Conduct of Business

1. SCOPE

Rule 1

These rules of procedure shall apply to the Compliance Committee, including its enforcement branch and facilitative branch, as defined in the "Procedures and mechanisms relating to compliance under the Kyoto Protocol", contained in the annex to decision 27/CMP.1. They shall be read together with and in furtherance of these procedures and mechanisms.

2. DEFINITIONS

Rule 2

For the purposes of these rules section numbers refer to the section so numbered in the annex to decision 27/CMP.1, unless otherwise noted, and:

(a) "Committee" means the Compliance Committee established by section II, paragraph 1;
(b) "Plenary" means the plenary of the Committee as set out in section III;
(c) "Branch" means the facilitative branch or the enforcement branch as set out in sections IV and V;
(d) "Bureau" means the bureau of the Committee constituted in accordance with section II, paragraph 4;
(e) "Co-chairpersons" means the chairperson of the enforcement branch and the chairperson of the facilitative branch acting together in the plenary of the Committee in accordance with section III, paragraph 1;
(f) "Member" means a member of the Committee elected under section II, paragraph 3;
(g) "Alternate member" means an alternate member elected under section II, paragraph 5;
(h) "Party" means a Party to the Kyoto Protocol to the United Nations Framework Convention on Climate Change;
(i) "Party concerned" means a Party in respect of which a question of implementation is raised, as set out in section VI, paragraph 2;
(i bis) "Party involved" means a Party that disagrees with adjustments to its inventory under Article 5, paragraph 2, of the Kyoto Protocol, as calculated and

recommended by an expert review team in accordance with the procedures set out in paragraphs 79 and 80 of the "Guidelines for review under Article 8 of the Kyoto Protocol" contained in the annex to decision 22/CMP.1;

(j) "Diplomatic agent" means the head of the mission or a designated member of the diplomatic staff of the mission of a Party who is accredited to the host country of the secretariat;

(k) "Agent" means the Head of State or Government, the Minister of Foreign Affairs, the diplomatic agent or another person duly authorized by the Head of State or Government or by the Minister of Foreign Affairs or, in the case of a regional economic integration organization, by the competent authority of that organization;

(l) "Representative" means a person designated by the Party concerned to represent it during the consideration of a question of implementation, in accordance with section VIII, paragraph 2;

(m) "Secretariat" means the secretariat referred to in section XVII.

3. MEMBERS

Rule 3

1. The term of service of each member and alternate member shall start on 1 January of the calendar year immediately following his or her election and shall end on 31 December, two or four years thereafter, as applicable.

2. Subject to these rules, alternate members are entitled to participate in the proceedings of the plenary or the respective branch to which they belong, without the right to vote. An alternate member may cast a vote only if serving as the member.

3. During the absence of a member from all or part of a meeting of the plenary or of the branch to which he or she has been elected, his or her alternate shall serve as the member.

4. When a member resigns or is otherwise unable to complete the assigned term or the functions of a member, his or her alternate shall serve as a member for the same branch, ad interim.

5. When a member or alternate member resigns or is otherwise unable to complete the assigned term or the functions of a member or alternate member, the Committee shall request the Conference of the Parties serving as the meeting of the Parties to the Kyoto Protocol to elect a new member or alternate member for the remainder of the term at its next session.

Rule 4

1. Each member and alternate member shall serve in his or her individual capacity and, with respect to any matter that is under consideration by the Committee, act in an independent and impartial manner and avoid real or apparent conflicts of interest.

2. Each member and alternate member shall take and agree to respect a written oath of service before assuming his or her service. The oath of service shall read as follows:

> "I solemnly declare that I will perform my duties and exercise my authority as member/alternate member of the Compliance Committee of the Kyoto Protocol established in decision 27/CMP.1 honourably, faithfully, impartially and conscientiously.
>
> "I further solemnly declare that, subject to my responsibilities within the Compliance Committee, I shall not disclose, even after the termination of my functions, any confidential information coming to my knowledge by reason of my duties in the Compliance Committee.

"I shall disclose immediately to the Executive Secretary of the United Nations Framework Convention on Climate Change any interest in any matter under discussion before the Compliance Committee which may constitute a conflict of interest or which might be incompatible with the requirements of independence and impartiality expected of a member or alternate member of the Compliance Committee and I shall refrain from participating in the work of the Compliance Committee in relation to such matter."

3. Where the Executive Secretary of the United Nations Framework Convention on Climate Change receives any disclosure made in accordance with paragraph 2, he or she shall forthwith notify the bureau. The bureau shall inform the plenary that the member or alternate member will refrain from participating in the work of the Committee in relation to the matter that is the subject of the disclosure.

4. Where the Executive Secretary of the United Nations Framework Convention on Climate Change receives evidence from a Party on circumstances which may indicate a conflict of interest or which might be incompatible with the requirements of independence and impartiality expected of a member or alternate member of the Committee, he or she shall forthwith notify the bureau as well as the member or alternate member concerned. The evidence shall be submitted to the plenary for its consideration, unless the member or alternate member informs the bureau that he or she will refrain from participating in the work of the Committee in relation to the matter to which the evidence relates. The bureau shall inform the plenary that the member or alternate member will refrain from participating in the work of the Committee in relation to the matter that is the subject of the disclosure. Otherwise, the plenary may decide to excuse the member or alternate member from consideration of one or more questions of implementation and the elaboration and adoption of a decision of a branch, after having provided a reasonable opportunity for the member or alternate member to be heard.

5. If the plenary considers that a material violation of the requirements of independence and impartiality expected of a member or alternate member of the Committee has occurred, it may decide to suspend, or recommend to the Conference of the Parties serving as the meeting of the Parties to the Kyoto Protocol to revoke, the membership of any member or alternate member concerned, after having provided a reasonable opportunity for the member or alternate member to be heard.

6. All decisions of the Committee taken under this rule shall be noted in the annual report of the Committee to the Conference of the Parties serving as the meeting of the Parties to the Kyoto Protocol.

4. OFFICERS

Rule 5

1. In addition to exercising the powers conferred upon him or her elsewhere in these rules, an officer chairing a meeting shall:

(a) Declare the opening and closure of the meeting;
(b) Preside over the meeting;
(c) Ensure the observance of these rules;
(d) Accord the right to speak;
(e) Put questions to the vote and announce decisions;
(f) Rule on any points of order;
(g) Subject to these rules, have complete control over the proceedings and maintain order.

2. An officer chairing a meeting may also propose:

(a) The closure of the list of speakers;

(b) A limitation on the time to be allowed to speakers and on the number of times they may speak on an issue;

(c) The adjournment or closure of debate on an issue;

(d) The suspension or adjournment of the meeting.

3. Any officer chairing a meeting, in the exercise of his or her functions, remains under the authority of the plenary or, as the case may be, of the enforcement branch or facilitative branch.

Rule 6

1. If a chairperson is temporarily unable to fulfil the functions of his or her office, the vice-chairperson of the relevant branch shall act as chairperson of that branch and co-chairperson of the plenary ad interim.

2. If the chairperson and the vice-chairperson of the same branch are temporarily unable to fulfil the functions of their offices at the same time, the branch shall elect a chairperson for that branch ad interim having regard to section II, paragraph 4.

3. If a chairperson or vice-chairperson of a branch resigns or is otherwise unable to complete the assigned term or the functions of his or her office, the branch shall elect, in accordance with section II, paragraph 4, a replacement from among its members for the remainder of the term of that officer.

5. AGENDA

Rule 7

1. In agreement with the bureau, the secretariat shall draft the provisional agenda for each meeting of the plenary.

2. In agreement with the chairperson and vice-chairperson of the relevant branch, the secretariat shall draft the provisional agenda of each meeting of that branch.

3. The provisional agenda and draft schedule for each meeting as well as the draft report on the previous meeting shall be circulated to members and alternate members at least four weeks before the opening of the meeting, to the extent possible under the applicable time frames.

4. The proposed agenda of each meeting of the plenary and each meeting of a branch shall include any item proposed by a member.

5. The plenary or a branch, when adopting its agenda, may decide to add urgent and important items and to delete, defer or amend items.

6. MEETINGS AND DELIBERATIONS

Rule 8

Notice of meetings shall be sent to the members and alternate members, as well as any representative, as the case may be, at least four weeks before the opening of the meeting, to the extent possible under the applicable time frames.

Rule 9

1. Subject to paragraph 2, meetings of the plenary and the branches shall be held in public, unless the plenary or branch of its own accord or at the request of the Party concerned decides, for overriding reasons, that part or all of the meeting shall be held in private.

2. Only members and alternate members of the Committee and secretariat officials may be present during the elaboration and adoption of a decision of a branch.

Rule 10

1. With respect to a notification or document sent by the secretariat to a Party, the date of receipt shall be deemed to be the date indicated in a written confirmation from the Party or the date indicated in a written confirmation of receipt by the expedited delivery courier, whichever comes first.

2. With respect to a submission, request, or other document intended for the Committee, the date of receipt by the Committee shall be deemed to be the first business day after receipt by the secretariat.

7. USE OF ELECTRONIC MEANS

Rule 11

1. The Committee may use electronic means for transmission, distribution and storage of documentation, without prejudice to normal means of circulation of the documentation, as the case may be.

2. The Committee may elaborate and take decisions in a written procedure using electronic means, where possible.

3. Any decision in accordance with paragraph 2 of this rule shall be deemed to be taken at the headquarters of the secretariat.

8. SECRETARIAT

Rule 12

1. The secretariat shall make arrangements for meetings of the Committee and provide it with services as required.

2 The secretariat shall make all documents of the plenary and the branches available to the public, subject to section VIII, paragraph 6, as well as any guidance provided by the Committee.

3. In addition, the secretariat shall perform any other functions assigned that the Committee may require or that the Conference of the Parties serving as the meeting of the Parties to the Kyoto Protocol may direct with respect to the work of the Committee.

9. LANGUAGES

Rule 13

1. Without prejudice to section VIII, paragraph 9, the working language of the Committee shall be English.

2. A representative taking part in the proceedings of a branch may speak in a language other than the working language of the Committee if the Party provides for interpretation.

3. Decisions of the branches that are final shall be made available in all official languages of the United Nations, taking into account the provisions of rule 22, paragraph 1.

9 bis. CALCULATION OF TIME PERIODS

Rule 13 bis

For the purposes of calculating time periods:

(a) The day of the act or event from which the period of time begins to run shall not be included. The last day of the period so calculated shall be included, unless it is a Saturday, Sunday or official UNFCCC holiday, or official national holiday in the case of a time limit applicable to a Party concerned, in which case the period shall be deemed to run until the end of the next working day;

(b) Subject to subparagraph (a) above, where a period of time is expressed in weeks, months or years, the day on which the period of time expires shall be the same day of the week, month or year as the day from which the period of time begins to run, or if the month does not have such a date, the last day of that month.

Part 2: Procedures for the Branches

10. GENERAL PROCEDURES FOR THE BRANCHES

Rule 14

1. A submission by any Party raising a question of implementation with respect to itself shall set out:

   (a) The name of the Party making the submission;
   (b) A statement identifying the question of implementation;
   (c) A reference to the provisions of the Kyoto Protocol and decision 27/CMP.1 that form the basis for raising the question of implementation.

2. The submission should also set out:

   (a) Any provisions of the decisions of the Conference of the Parties serving as the meeting of the Parties to the Kyoto Protocol and the reports of the subsidiary bodies that are applicable to the question of implementation;
   (b) The information that is material to the question of implementation;
   (c) The branch from which action is sought;
   (d) The action requested from the branch;
   (e) A list of all documents annexed to the submission.

Rule 15

1. A submission by any Party raising a question of implementation with respect to another Party shall set out:

   (a) The name of the Party making the submission;
   (b) A statement identifying the question of implementation;
   (c) The name of the Party concerned;
   (d) A reference to the provisions of the Kyoto Protocol and decision 27/CMP.1 that form the basis for raising the question of implementation;
   (e) Corroborating information supporting the question of implementation.

2. The submission should also set out:

   (a) Any provisions of the decisions of the Conference of the Parties serving as the meeting of the Parties to the Kyoto Protocol and the reports of the subsidiary bodies that are applicable to the question of implementation;
   (b) The branch from which action is sought;
   (c) A list of all documents annexed to the submission.

Rule 16

The secretariat shall make the submission and any supporting information submitted under rule 15 available to the agent of that Party.

Rule 17

Comments and written submissions by the Party concerned in accordance with the provisions of sections VII to X should include:

(a) A statement of the position of the Party concerned on the information, decision or question of implementation under consideration, including the grounds therefor;

(b) An identification of any information provided by the Party that it requests not to be made available to the public in accordance with section VIII, paragraph 6;

(c) A list of all documents annexed to the submission or comment.

Rule 18

1. Any submission or comment under rules 14, 15, 17 and 25 bis shall be signed by the agent of the Party and be delivered to the secretariat in hard copy and by electronic means.

2. Any relevant documents in support of the submission or comment shall be annexed to it.

Rule 19

1. The bureau shall, within seven days from receipt of a question of implementation, decide on its allocation to the appropriate branch. The bureau may allocate questions of implementation by employing electronic means in accordance with rule 11.

2. The secretariat shall forthwith notify members and alternate members of the branch of the question of implementation and send them all available materials.

3. The secretariat shall also notify members and alternate members of the other branch of the question of implementation.

Rule 20

1. Following the preliminary examination, subject to section VIII, paragraph 4, competent intergovernmental organizations and nongovernmental organizations that wish to submit relevant factual and technical information to the relevant branch shall do so in writing.

2. The secretariat shall forthwith notify members and alternate members of the branch of the submission of such information and send it to them.

3. The secretariat shall also notify members and alternate members of the other branch of the submission of such information.

Rule 21

If a branch decides to seek expert advice, it shall:

(a) Define the question on which expert opinion is sought;

(b) Identify the experts to be consulted;

(c) Lay down the procedures to be followed.

Rule 22

1. A preliminary finding or a final decision shall contain, mutatis mutandis:

(a) The name of the Party concerned;

(b) A statement identifying the question of implementation addressed;

(c) The provisions of the Kyoto Protocol and decision 27/CMP.1 and other relevant decisions of the Conference of the Parties serving as the meeting of the Parties to the Kyoto Protocol that form the basis of the preliminary finding or final decision;
(d) A description of the information considered in the deliberations, including in the case of a final decision, a confirmation that the Party concerned was given an opportunity to comment in writing on all information considered;
(e) A summary of the proceedings, including an indication, in the case of a final decision of the enforcement branch, of whether its preliminary finding or any part of it as specified is confirmed;
(f) The substantive decision of the question of implementation, including the consequences applied, if any;
(g) Conclusions and reasons for the decision;
(h) The place and date of the decision;
(i) The names of the members who participated in the consideration of the question of implementation, as well as the elaboration and adoption of the decision.

2. Comments in writing on a final decision submitted within 45 days from the receipt of that decision by the Party concerned shall be circulated by the secretariat to the members and alternate members of the relevant branch and shall be included in the Committee's annual report to the Conference of the Parties serving as the meeting of the Parties to the Kyoto Protocol.

Rule 23

1. Any referral of a question of implementation to the facilitative branch in accordance with section IX, paragraph 12, shall be made through a decision by the enforcement branch with a statement identifying the question of implementation and the information on which the question is based.

2. The secretariat shall forthwith notify the Party concerned of the decision.

3. A question of implementation referred by the enforcement branch to the facilitative branch shall not require a preliminary examination.

11. PROCEDURES FOR THE FACILITATIVE BRANCH

Rule 24

1. Subject to section VI and without prejudice to section XVI, the facilitative branch may have a dialogue with the representative of the Party concerned.

2. Subject to sections VI and VII, the representative of the Party concerned may enter into a dialogue with the facilitative branch in order to seek advice and facilitation.

3. The facilitative branch shall receive, through the secretariat, information as required under relevant decisions of the Conference of the Parties serving as the meeting of the Parties to the Kyoto Protocol.

12. PROCEDURES FOR THE ENFORCEMENT BRANCH

Rule 25

1. In its request for a hearing, the Party concerned may identify:
(a) The issues that the Party proposes to raise and any documents that it intends to discuss during the hearing;

(b) Any individuals whose expert testimony or opinion it will present at the hearing.

2. The Party concerned, when choosing individuals to represent it during the hearing, should refrain from nominating individuals who were members or alternate members of the Committee in the two years preceding the date of the submission.

3. The entitlement of the Party concerned to designate one or more persons to represent it during the consideration of a question of implementation pursuant to paragraph 2 of section VIII extends to any meeting convened:

(a) To consider reinstatement of eligibility under paragraphs 2, 3 and 4 of section X;
(b) To consider adjustments and corrections under paragraph 5 of section X;
(c) To review and assess any plan submitted to the enforcement branch under paragraph 2 or paragraph 6 of section XV;
(d) To consider any progress report on the implementation of this plan submitted to the enforcement branch under paragraph 3 or paragraph 7 of section XV.

Rule 25 bis

1. A plan to be submitted by the Party concerned to the enforcement branch under paragraph 2 or paragraph 6 of section XV shall explicitly:

(a) Address, in separate sections, each of the elements specified in paragraph 2 or paragraph 6 of section XV;
(b) Respond to any specific issues raised in the part of the final decision of the enforcement branch applying the consequences.

2. The enforcement branch shall endeavour to conduct the review and assessment of the plan under paragraph 2 or paragraph 6 of section XV within four weeks from the date of receipt of the plan.

3. In its review and assessment, the enforcement branch shall assess whether the plan submitted:

(a) Sets out and adequately addresses the elements and issues referred to in paragraph 1 above;
(b) If implemented, is expected to remedy the non-compliance or to meet the quantified emission limitation or reduction commitment of the Party concerned in the subsequent commitment period, as envisaged in paragraph 2 and paragraph 6 of section XV, respectively.

Rule 25 ter

1. Where there is a disagreement on whether to apply adjustments to inventories under Article 5, paragraph 2, of the Kyoto Protocol under section X, paragraph 5, this rule shall apply. In addition, the other relevant rules and other relevant provisions contained in the annex to decision 27/CMP.1 shall be applied mutatis mutandis, as appropriate.

2. Within seven days of having received, through the secretariat, a report of an expert review team under Article 8 of the Kyoto Protocol in accordance with section VI, paragraph 1 or 3, that includes a disagreement on whether to apply adjustments to an inventory under Article 5, paragraph 2, of the Kyoto Protocol, the bureau shall request the secretariat to notify forthwith:

(a) Members and alternate members of the enforcement branch of the disagreement and send them all available materials;
(b) Members and alternate members of the facilitative branch of the disagreement;

(c) The Party involved that the disagreement will be considered by the enforcement branch.

3. The Party involved may make a written submission within four weeks from the date of receipt of the notification referred to in paragraph 2 (c) above, including rebuttal of information submitted to the enforcement branch.

4. If so requested in writing by the Party involved within four weeks from the date of receipt of the notification referred to in paragraph 2 (c) above, the enforcement branch shall hold a hearing, which shall take place within four weeks from the date of receipt of the request or the written submission referred to in paragraph 3 above, whichever is the later. The Party involved may present expert testimony or opinion at the hearing. Such a hearing shall be held in public, unless the enforcement branch decides, of its own accord or at the request of the Party involved, that part or all of the hearing shall take place in private.

5. The enforcement branch shall adopt its decision on the disagreement referred to in paragraph 2 above within 11 weeks of the notification referred to in paragraph 2 (c) above or within three weeks of the hearing as referred to in paragraph 4 above, whichever is the shorter.

6. The Party involved may, at any time before the adoption of the decision referred to in paragraph 5 above, accept, at the hearing referred to in paragraph 4 above or in writing, the adjustments as calculated and recommended by the expert review team referred to in paragraph 2 above. Such acceptance shall result in the resolution of the disagreement referred to in paragraph 2 above and shall be noted by the enforcement branch in its decision on the matter.

7. If the report referred to in paragraph 2 above also indicates a question of implementation that is allocated to the enforcement branch and to which the expedited procedure set out in section X, paragraph 1, applies, the enforcement branch may extend any time frames provided for in this rule to align both procedures. The enforcement branch shall make every effort to minimize any resulting delay and, in any event, shall decide on the disagreement referred to in paragraph 2 above no later than at the time of the adoption of the final decision on the question of implementation in accordance with section X, paragraph 1 (f).

8. The period of time stipulated in section IX, paragraph 3, shall apply only if, in the opinion of the enforcement branch, it does not interfere with the adoption of the decision in accordance with paragraph 5 above.

Part 3: General Provisions

13. AMENDMENTS

Rule 26

1. These rules of procedure may be amended by a decision of the Conference of the Parties serving as the meeting of the Parties to the Kyoto Protocol in terms of section III, paragraph 2 (d) after the plenary has approved the proposed amendment and reported on the matter to the Conference of the Parties serving as the meeting of the Parties to the Kyoto Protocol.

2. Any amendment of these rules approved by the plenary shall be provisionally applied pending their adoption by the Conference of the Parties serving as the meeting of the Parties to the Kyoto Protocol.

14. OVERRIDING AUTHORITY

Rule 27

In the event of a conflict between any provision in these rules and any provision in the Kyoto Protocol or decision 27/CMP.1, the provision of the Protocol or the decision, as the case may be, shall prevail.

53.e Paris Agreement

Date: 4 November 2016 (entry into force)
Source: UN Doc FCCC/CP/2015/L.9/Rev/1
https://unfccc.int/sites/default/files/english_paris_agreement.pdf

...

Article 13

1. In order to build mutual trust and confidence and to promote effective implementation, an enhanced transparency framework for action and support, with built-in flexibility which takes into account Parties' different capacities and builds upon collective experience is hereby established.

2. The transparency framework shall provide flexibility in the implementation of the provisions of this Article to those developing country Parties that need it in the light of their capacities. The modalities, procedures and guidelines referred to in paragraph 13 of this Article shall reflect such flexibility.

3. The transparency framework shall build on and enhance the transparency arrangements under the Convention, recognizing the special circumstances of the least developed countries and small island developing States, and be implemented in a facilitative, non-intrusive, non-punitive manner, respectful of national sovereignty, and avoid placing undue burden on Parties.

4. The transparency arrangements under the Convention, including national communications, biennial reports and biennial update reports, international assessment and review and international consultation and analysis, shall form part of the experience drawn upon for the development of the modalities, procedures and guidelines under paragraph 13 of this Article.

5. The purpose of the framework for transparency of action is to provide a clear understanding of climate change action in the light of the objective of the Convention as set out in its Article 2, including clarity and tracking of progress towards achieving Parties' individual nationally determined contributions under Article 4, and Parties' adaptation actions under Article 7, including good practices, priorities, needs and gaps, to inform the global stocktake under Article 14.

6. The purpose of the framework for transparency of support is to provide clarity on support provided and received by relevant individual Parties in the context of climate change actions under Articles 4, 7, 9, 10 and 11, and, to the extent possible, to provide a full overview of aggregate financial support provided, to inform the global stocktake under Article 14.

7. Each Party shall regularly provide the following information:
   (a) A national inventory report of anthropogenic emissions by sources and removals by sinks of greenhouse gases, prepared using good practice methodologies accepted by the Intergovernmental Panel on Climate Change and agreed upon by the Conference of the Parties serving as the meeting of the Parties to this Agreement; and
   (b) Information necessary to track progress made in implementing and achieving its nationally determined contribution under Article 4.

8. Each Party should also provide information related to climate change impacts and adaptation under Article 7, as appropriate.

9. Developed country Parties shall, and other Parties that provide support should, provide information on financial, technology transfer and capacity-building support provided to developing country Parties under Articles 9, 10 and 11.

10. Developing country Parties should provide information on financial, technology transfer and capacity-building support needed and received under Articles 9, 10 and 11.

11. Information submitted by each Party under paragraphs 7 and 9 of this Article shall undergo a technical expert review, in accordance with decision 1/CP.21. For those developing country Parties that need it in the light of their capacities, the review process shall include assistance in identifying capacity-building needs. In addition, each Party shall participate in a facilitative, multilateral consideration of progress with respect to efforts under Article 9, and its respective implementation and achievement of its nationally determined contribution.

12. The technical expert review under this paragraph shall consist of a consideration of the Party's support provided, as relevant, and its implementation and achievement of its nationally determined contribution. The review shall also identify areas of improvement for the Party, and include a review of the consistency of the information with the modalities, procedures and guidelines referred to in paragraph 13 of this Article, taking into account the flexibility accorded to the Party under paragraph 2 of this Article. The review shall pay particular attention to the respective national capabilities and circumstances of developing country Parties.

13. The Conference of the Parties serving as the meeting of the Parties to this Agreement shall, at its first session, building on experience from the arrangements related to transparency under the Convention, and elaborating on the provisions in this Article, adopt common modalities, procedures and guidelines, as appropriate, for the transparency of action and support.

14. Support shall be provided to developing countries for the implementation of this Article.

15. Support shall also be provided for the building of transparency-related capacity of developing country Parties on a continuous basis.

Article 14

1. The Conference of the Parties serving as the meeting of the Parties to this Agreement shall periodically take stock of the implementation of this Agreement to assess the collective progress towards achieving the purpose of this Agreement and its long-term goals (referred to as the "global stocktake"). It shall do so in a comprehensive and facilitative manner, considering mitigation, adaptation and the means of implementation and support, and in the light of equity and the best available science.

2. The Conference of the Parties serving as the meeting of the Parties to this Agreement shall undertake its first global stocktake in 2023 and every five years thereafter unless otherwise decided by the Conference of the Parties serving as the meeting of the Parties to this Agreement.

3. The outcome of the global stocktake shall inform Parties in updating and enhancing, in a nationally determined manner, their actions and support in accordance with the relevant provisions of this Agreement, as well as in enhancing international cooperation for climate action.

Article 15

1. A mechanism to facilitate implementation of and promote compliance with the provisions of this Agreement is hereby established.

2. The mechanism referred to in paragraph 1 of this Article shall consist of a committee that shall be expert-based and facilitative in nature and function in a manner that is transparent, non-adversarial and non-punitive. The committee shall pay particular attention to the respective national capabilities and circumstances of Parties.

3. The committee shall operate under the modalities and procedures adopted by the Conference of the Parties serving as the meeting of the Parties to this Agreement at its first session and report annually to the Conference of the Parties serving as the meeting of the Parties to this Agreement.

Article 16

1. The Conference of the Parties, the supreme body of the Convention, shall serve as the meeting of the Parties to this Agreement.

2. Parties to the Convention that are not Parties to this Agreement may participate as observers in the proceedings of any session of the Conference of the Parties serving as the meeting of the Parties to this Agreement. When the Conference of the Parties serves as the meeting of the Parties to this Agreement, decisions under this Agreement shall be taken only by those that are Parties to this Agreement.

3. When the Conference of the Parties serves as the meeting of the Parties to this Agreement, any member of the Bureau of the Conference of the Parties representing a Party to the Convention but, at that time, not a Party to this Agreement, shall be replaced by an additional member to be elected by and from amongst the Parties to this Agreement.

4. The Conference of the Parties serving as the meeting of the Parties to this Agreement shall keep under regular review the implementation of this Agreement and shall make, within its mandate, the decisions necessary to promote its effective implementation. It shall perform the functions assigned to it by this Agreement and shall:

(a) Establish such subsidiary bodies as deemed necessary for the implementation of this Agreement; and

(b) Exercise such other functions as may be required for the implementation of this Agreement.

5. The rules of procedure of the Conference of the Parties and the financial procedures applied under the Convention shall be applied *mutatis mutandis* under this Agreement, except as may be otherwise decided by consensus by the Conference of the Parties serving as the meeting of the Parties to this Agreement.

6. The first session of the Conference of the Parties serving as the meeting of the Parties to this Agreement shall be convened by the secretariat in conjunction with the first session

of the Conference of the Parties that is scheduled after the date of entry into force of this Agreement. Subsequent ordinary sessions of the Conference of the Parties serving as the meeting of the Parties to this Agreement shall be held in conjunction with ordinary sessions of the Conference of the Parties, unless otherwise decided by the Conference of the Parties serving as the meeting of the Parties to this Agreement.

7. Extraordinary sessions of the Conference of the Parties serving as the meeting of the Parties to this Agreement shall be held at such other times as may be deemed necessary by the Conference of the Parties serving as the meeting of the Parties to this Agreement or at the written request of any Party, provided that, within six months of the request being communicated to the Parties by the secretariat, it is supported by at least one third of the Parties.

8. The United Nations and its specialized agencies and the International Atomic Energy Agency, as well as any State member thereof or observers thereto not party to the Convention, may be represented at sessions of the Conference of the Parties serving as the meeting of the Parties to this Agreement as observers. Any body or agency, whether national or international, governmental or non-governmental, which is qualified in matters covered by this Agreement and which has informed the secretariat of its wish to be represented at a session of the Conference of the Parties serving as the meeting of the Parties to this Agreement as an observer, may be so admitted unless at least one third of the Parties present object. The admission and participation of observers shall be subject to the rules of procedure referred to in paragraph 5 of this Article.

Article 17

1. The secretariat established by Article 8 of the Convention shall serve as the secretariat of this Agreement.

2. Article 8, paragraph 2, of the Convention on the functions of the secretariat, and Article 8, paragraph 3, of the Convention, on the arrangements made for the functioning of the secretariat, shall apply *mutatis mutandis* to this Agreement. The secretariat shall, in addition, exercise the functions assigned to it under this Agreement and by the Conference of the Parties serving as the meeting of the Parties to this Agreement.

Article 18

1. The Subsidiary Body for Scientific and Technological Advice and the Subsidiary Body for Implementation established by Articles 9 and 10 of the Convention shall serve, respectively, as the Subsidiary Body for Scientific and Technological Advice and the Subsidiary Body for Implementation of this Agreement. The provisions of the Convention relating to the functioning of these two bodies shall apply *mutatis mutandis* to this Agreement. Sessions of the meetings of the Subsidiary Body for Scientific and Technological Advice and the Subsidiary Body for Implementation of this Agreement shall be held in conjunction with the meetings of, respectively, the Subsidiary Body for Scientific and Technological Advice and the Subsidiary Body for Implementation of the Convention.

2. Parties to the Convention that are not Parties to this Agreement may participate as observers in the proceedings of any session of the subsidiary bodies. When the subsidiary bodies serve as the subsidiary bodies of this Agreement, decisions under this Agreement shall be taken only by those that are Parties to this Agreement.

3. When the subsidiary bodies established by Articles 9 and 10 of the Convention exercise their functions with regard to matters concerning this Agreement, any member of the bureaux of those subsidiary bodies representing a Party to the Convention but, at that time, not a Party to this Agreement, shall be replaced by an additional member to be elected by and from amongst the Parties to this Agreement.

Article 19

1. Subsidiary bodies or other institutional arrangements established by or under the Convention, other than those referred to in this Agreement, shall serve this Agreement upon a decision of the Conference of the Parties serving as the meeting of the Parties to this Agreement. The Conference of the Parties serving as the meeting of the Parties to this Agreement shall specify the functions to be exercised by such subsidiary bodies or arrangements.

2. The Conference of the Parties serving as the meeting of the Parties to this Agreement may provide further guidance to such subsidiary bodies and institutional arrangements.

…

Article 24

The provisions of Article 14 of the Convention[1] on settlement of disputes shall apply *mutatis mutandis* to this Agreement.

Article 25

1. Each Party shall have one vote, except as provided for in paragraph 2 of this Article.

2. Regional economic integration organizations, in matters within their competence, shall exercise their right to vote with a number of votes equal to the number of their member States that are Parties to this Agreement. Such an organization shall not exercise its right to vote if any of its member States exercises its right, and vice versa.

…

The Ozone Layer

54.a Vienna Convention for the Protection of the Ozone Layer

Date: 22 March 1985
Source: 1513 UNTS 293
https://ozone.unep.org/sites/default/files/2019-12/The%20Ozone%20Treaties%20EN%20-%20WEB_final.pdf

…

Article 6: Conference of the Parties

1. A Conference of the Parties is hereby established. The first meeting of the Conference of the Parties shall be convened by the secretariat designated on an interim basis under

[1] [N.B.: This footnote merely reproduces Article 14 of the UNFCCC, which is reproduced in this volume as Document No. 53.a].

article 7 not later than one year after entry into force of this Convention. Thereafter, ordinary meetings of the Conference of the Parties shall be held at regular intervals to be determined by the Conference at its first meeting.

2. Extraordinary meetings of the Conference of the Parties shall be held at such other times as may be deemed necessary by the Conference, or at the written request of any Party, provided that, within six months of the request being communicated to them by the secretariat, it is supported by at least one third of the Parties.

3. The Conference of the Parties shall by consensus agree upon and adopt rules of procedure and financial rules for itself and for any subsidiary bodies it may establish, as well as financial provisions governing the functioning of the secretariat.

4. The Conference of the Parties shall keep under continuous review the implementation of this Convention, and, in addition, shall:

a. Establish the form and the intervals for transmitting the information to be submitted in accordance with article 5 and consider such information as well as reports submitted by any subsidiary body;
b. Review the scientific information on the ozone layer, on its possible modification and on possible effects of any such modification;
c. Promote, in accordance with article 2, the harmonization of appropriate policies, strategies and measures for minimizing the release of substances causing or likely to cause modification of the ozone layer, and make recommendations on any other measures relating to this Convention;
d. Adopt, in accordance with articles 3 and 4, programmes for research, systematic observations, scientific and technological co-operation, the exchange of information and the transfer of technology and knowledge;
e. Consider and adopt, as required, in accordance with articles 9 and 10, amendments to this Convention and its annexes;
f. Consider amendments to any protocol, as well as to any annexes thereto, and, if so decided, recommend their adoption to the parties to the protocol concerned;
g. Consider and adopt, as required, in accordance with article 10, additional annexes to this Convention;
h. Consider and adopt, as required, protocols in accordance with article 8;
i. Establish such subsidiary bodies as are deemed necessary for the implementation of this Convention;
j. Seek, where appropriate, the services of competent international bodies and scientific committees, in particular the World Meteorological Organization and the World Health Organization as well as the Co-ordinating Committee on the Ozone Layer, in scientific research, systematic observations and other activities pertinent to the objectives of this Convention, and make use as appropriate of information from these bodies and committees;
k. Consider and undertake any additional action that may be required for the achievement of the purposes of this Convention.

5. The United Nations, its specialized agencies and the International Atomic Energy Agency, as well as any State not party to this Convention, may be represented at meetings of the Conference of the Parties by observers. Any body or agency, whether national or international, governmental or non-governmental, qualified in fields relating to the protection of the ozone layer which has informed the secretariat of its wish to be represented

at a meeting of the Conference of the Parties as an observer may be admitted unless at least one-third of the Parties present object. The admission and participation of observers shall be subject to the rules of procedure adopted by the Conference of the Parties.

...

Article 11: Settlement of disputes

1. In the event of a dispute between Parties concerning the interpretation or application of this Convention, the parties concerned shall seek solution by negotiation.

2. If the parties concerned cannot reach agreement by negotiation, they may jointly seek the good offices of, or request mediation by, a third party.

3. When ratifying, accepting, approving or acceding to this Convention, or at any time thereafter, a State or regional economic integration organization may declare in writing to the Depositary that for a dispute not resolved in accordance with paragraph 1 or paragraph 2 above, it accepts one or both of the following means of dispute settlement as compulsory:

a. Arbitration in accordance with procedures to be adopted by the Conference of the Parties at its first ordinary meeting;

b. Submission of the dispute to the International Court of Justice.

4. If the parties have not, in accordance with paragraph 3 above, accepted the same or any procedure, the dispute shall be submitted to conciliation in accordance with paragraph 5 below unless the parties otherwise agree.

5. A conciliation commission shall be created upon the request of one of the parties to the dispute. The commission shall be composed of an equal number of members appointed by each party concerned and a chairman chosen jointly by the members appointed by each party. The commission shall render a final and recommendatory award, which the parties shall consider in good faith.

6. The provisions of this Article shall apply with respect to any protocol except as provided in the protocol concerned.

...

54.b Decision VCI/7 on Arbitration Procedure under the Vienna Convention on the Protection of the Ozone Layer

Date: 28 April 1989
Source: Doc UNEP/OzL.Conv.1/5 (Annex II)
https://ozone.unep.org/meetings/first-conference-parties-vienna-convention/decisions/annex-ii-arbitration-procedure-under

Article 1

This procedure is adopted as required by Article 11, paragraph 3 (a), of the Vienna Convention for the Protection of the Ozone Layer. Unless the Parties to a dispute otherwise agree the arbitration procedure shall be conducted in accordance with articles 2 to 16 below.

Article 2

The claimant Party shall notify the Secretariat that the Parties are referring a dispute to arbitration pursuant to Article 11, paragraph 3, of the Convention. The notification shall state the subject-matter of arbitration and include in particular the articles of the Convention or the Protocol, the interpretation or application of which are at issue. The Secretariat shall forward the information thus received to all Contracting Parties to the Convention or to the Protocol concerned.

Article 3

1. In disputes between two Parties, the arbitral tribunal shall consist of three members. Each of the Parties to the dispute shall appoint an arbitrator and the two arbitrators so appointed shall designate by common agreement the third arbitrator who shall be the chairman of the tribunal. The latter shall not be a national of one of the Parties to the dispute, nor have his usual place of residence in the territory of one of these Parties, nor be employed by any of them, nor have dealt with the case in any other capacity.
2. In disputes between more than two Parties, Parties in the same interest shall appoint one member of the tribunal jointly by agreement.
3. Any vacancy shall be filled in the manner prescribed for the initial appointment.

Article 4

1. If the chairman of the arbitral tribunal has not been designated within two months of the appointment of the second arbitrator, the Secretary General of the United Nations shall, at the request of a Party, designate him within a further two month's period.
2. If one of the Parties to the dispute does not appoint an arbitrator within two months of receipt of the request, the other Party may inform the Secretary-General of the United Nations who shall designate the other arbitrator within a further two months' period.

Article 5

The arbitral tribunal shall render its decisions in accordance with international law, as well as the provisions of this Convention and any protocols concerned.

Article 6

Unless the Parties to the dispute otherwise agree, the arbitral tribunal shall determine its own procedure, assuring that each Party has a full opportunity to be heard and to present its case.

Article 7

The Parties to the dispute shall facilitate the work of the arbitral tribunal and, in particular, using all means at their disposal, shall:

a. Provide it with all relevant documents, facilities and information; and
b. Enable it when necessary to call witnesses or experts and receive their evidence.

Article 7 bis

The Parties and the arbitrators are under an obligation to protect the confidentiality of any information they receive in confidence during the proceedings of the arbitral tribunal.

Article 8

Unless the arbitral tribunal determines otherwise because of the particular circumstances of the case, the costs of the tribunal shall be borne by the Parties to the dispute in equal shares. The tribunal shall keep a record of all its costs, and shall furnish a final statement thereof to the Parties.

Article 9

Any Contracting Party that has an interest of a legal nature in the subject-matter of the dispute which may be affected by the decision in the case, may intervene in the proceedings with the consent of the tribunal.

Article 10

The tribunal may hear and determine counterclaims arising directly out of the subject-matter of the dispute.

Article 11

Decisions both on procedure and substance of the arbitral tribunal shall be taken by a majority vote of its members.

Article 12

If one of the Parties to the dispute does not appear before the arbitral tribunal or fails to defend its case, the other Party may request the tribunal to continue the proceedings and to make its award. Absence of a Party or failure of a Party to defend its case shall not constitute a bar to the proceedings. Before rendering its final decision, the arbitral tribunal must satisfy itself that the claim is well founded in fact and law.

Article 13

The tribunal shall render its final decision within five months of the date on which it is fully constituted unless it finds it necessary to extend the time-limit for a period which should not exceed five months.

Article 14

The final decision of the arbitral tribunal shall be confined to the subject-matter of the dispute and shall state the reasons on which it is based. It shall contain the names of the members who have participated and the date of the final decision. Any member of the tribunal may attach a separate or dissenting opinion to the final decision.

Article 15

The final decision shall be without appeal unless the Parties to the dispute have agreed in advance to an appellate procedure. It shall be complied with by the Parties to the dispute.

Article 16

Any controversy which may arise between the Parties to the dispute as regards the interpretation or manner of implementation of the final decision may be submitted by either Party for decision to the arbitral tribunal which rendered it.

54.c Montreal Protocol on Substances that Deplete the Ozone Layer

Date: 16 September 1987
Source: 1522 UNTS 28
https://ozone.unep.org/sites/default/files/2019-12/The%20Ozone%20Treaties%20EN%20-%20WEB_final.pdf

...

Article 8: Non-compliance

The Parties, at their first meeting, shall consider and approve procedures and institutional mechanisms for determining non-compliance with the provisions of this Protocol and for treatment of Parties found to be in non-compliance.

...

54.d Non-Compliance Procedure under the Montreal Protocol*

Date: 3 December 1998
Source: Doc UNEP/OzL.Pro.10/9 (Annex II)
https://ozone.unep.org/node/2078

The following procedure has been formulated pursuant to Article 8 of the Montreal Protocol. It shall apply without prejudice to the operation of the settlement of disputes procedure laid down in Article 11 of the Vienna Convention.

1. If one or more Parties have reservations regarding another Party's implementation of its obligations under the Protocol, those concerns may be addressed in writing to the Secretariat. Such a submission shall be supported by corroborating information.

2. The Secretariat shall, within two weeks of its receiving a submission, send a copy of that submission to the Party whose implementation of a particular provision of the Protocol is at issue. Any reply and information in support thereof are to be submitted to the Secretariat and to the Parties involved within three months of the date of the despatch or such longer period as the circumstances of any particular case may require. **If the Secretariat has not received a reply from the Party three months after sending it the original submission, the Secretariat shall send a reminder to the Party that it has yet to provide its reply. The Secretariat shall, as soon as the reply and information from the Party are available, but not later than six months after receiving the submission, transmit the submission, the reply and the information, if any, provided by the Parties to the Implementation Committee referred to in paragraph 5, which shall consider the matter as soon as practicable.**

3. Where the Secretariat, during the course of preparing its report, becomes aware of possible non-compliance by any Party with its obligations under the Protocol, it may request the Party concerned to furnish necessary information about the matter. If there is no response from the Party concerned within three months of such longer period as the

* N.B.: As amended after review. Amendments indicated in bold.

circumstances of the matter may require of the matter is not resolved through administrative action or through diplomatic contacts, the Secretariat shall include the matter in its report to the Meeting of the Parties pursuant to Article 12 (c) of the Protocol and inform the Implementation Committee**, which shall consider the matter as soon as practicable.**

4. Where a Party concludes that, despite having made its best, bona fide efforts, it is unable to comply fully with its obligations under the Protocol, it may address to the Secretariat a submission in writing, explaining, in particular, the specific circumstances that it considers to be the cause of its non-compliance. The Secretariat shall transmit such submission to the Implementation Committee which shall consider it as soon as practicable.

5. An Implementation Committee is hereby established. It shall consist of 10 Parties elected by the Meeting of the Parties for two years, based on equitable geographical distribution. **Each Party so elected to the Committee shall be requested to notify the Secretariat, within two months of its election, of the name of the individual who is to represent it and shall endeavour to ensure that the same individual remains its representative throughout the entire term of office.** Outgoing Parties may be re-elected for one immediate consecutive term. **A Party that has completed a second consecutive two-year term as a Committee member shall be eligible for election again only after an absence of one year from the Committee.** The Committee shall elect its own President and Vice-President. Each shall serve for one year at a time. The Vice-President shall, in addition, serve as the rapporteur of the Committee.

6. The Implementation Committee shall, unless it decides otherwise, meet twice a year. The Secretariat shall arrange for and service its meetings.

7. The functions of the Implementation Committee shall be:

(a) To receive, consider and report on any submission in accordance with paragraphs 1, 2 and 4;

(b) To receive, consider and report on any information or observations forwarded by the Secretariat in connection with the preparation of the reports referred to in Article 12 (c) of the Protocol and on any other information received and forwarded by the Secretariat concerning compliance with the provisions of the Protocol;

(c) To request, where it considers necessary, through the Secretariat, further information on matters under its consideration;

(d) To identify the facts and possible causes relating to individual cases of non-compliance referred to the Committee and make appropriate recommendations to the Meeting of the Parties;

(e) To undertake, upon the invitation of the Party concerned, information-gathering in the territory of that Party for fulfilling the functions of the Committee;

(f) To maintain, in particular for the purposes of drawing up its recommendations, an exchange of information with the Executive Committee of the Multilateral Fund related to the provision of financial and technical cooperation, including the transfer of technologies to Parties operating under Article 5, paragraph 1, of the Protocol.

8. The Implementation Committee shall consider the submissions, information and observations referred to in paragraph 7 with a view to securing an amicable solution of the matter on the basis of respect for the provisions of the Protocol.

9. The Implementation Committee shall report to the Meeting of the Parties, including any recommendations it considers appropriate. The report shall be made available to the Parties

not later than six weeks before their meeting. After receiving a report by the Committee the Parties may, taking into consideration the circumstances of the matter, decide upon and call for steps to bring about full compliance with the Protocol, including measures to assist the Parties' compliance with the Protocol, and to further the Protocol's objectives.

10. Where a Party that is not a member of the Implementation Committee is identified in a submission under paragraph 1, or itself makes such a submission, it shall be entitled to participate in the consideration by the Committee of that submission.

11. No Party, whether or not a member of the Implementation Committee, involved in a matter under consideration by the Implementation Committee, shall take part in the elaboration and adoption of recommendations on that matter to be included in the report of the Committee.

12. The Parties involved in a matter referred to in paragraphs 1, 3 or 4 shall inform, through the Secretariat, the Meeting of the Parties of the results of proceedings taken under Article 11 of the Convention regarding possible non-compliance, about implementation of those results and about implementation of any decision of the Parties pursuant to paragraph 9.

13. The Meeting of the Parties may, pending completion of proceedings initiated under Article 11 of the Convention, issue an interim call and/or recommendations.

14. The Meeting of the Parties may request the Implementation Committee to make recommendations to assist the Meeting's consideration of matters of possible non-compliance.

15. The members of the Implementation Committee and any Party involved in its deliberations shall protect the confidentiality of information they receive in confidence.

16. The report, which shall not contain any information received in confidence, shall be made available to any person upon request. All information exchanged by or with the Committee that is related to any recommendation by the Committee to the Meeting of the Parties shall be made available by the Secretariat to any Party upon its request; that party shall ensure the confidentiality of the information it has received in confidence.

Trade in Endangered Species

55.a Convention on International Trade in Endangered Species of Wild Fauna and Flora (CITES)

Date: 3 March 1973
Source: 993 UNTS 243
http://www.cites.org/eng/disc/text.php#texttop

...

Article VIII Measures to Be Taken by the Parties

1. The Parties shall take appropriate measures to enforce the provisions of the present Convention and to prohibit trade in specimens in violation thereof. These shall include measures:

(a) to penalize trade in, or possession of, such specimens, or both; and
(b) to provide for the confiscation or return to the State of export of such specimens.

2. In addition to the measures taken under paragraph 1 of this Article, a Party may, when it deems it necessary, provide for any method of internal reimbursement for expenses incurred as a result of the confiscation of a specimen traded in violation of the measures taken in the application of the provisions of the present Convention.

3. As far as possible, the Parties shall ensure that specimens shall pass through any formalities required for trade with a minimum of delay. To facilitate such passage, a Party may designate ports of exit and ports of entry at which specimens must be presented for clearance. The Parties shall ensure further that all living specimens, during any period of transit, holding or shipment, are properly cared for so as to minimize the risk of injury, damage to health or cruel treatment.

4. Where a living specimen is confiscated as a result of measures referred to in paragraph 1 of this Article:

(a) the specimen shall be entrusted to a Management Authority of the State of confiscation;

(b) the Management Authority shall, after consultation with the State of export, return the specimen to that State at the expense of that State, or to a rescue centre or such other place as the Management Authority deems appropriate and consistent with the purposes of the present Convention; and

(c) the Management Authority may obtain the advice of a Scientific Authority, or may, whenever it considers it desirable, consult the Secretariat in order to facilitate the decision under sub-paragraph (b) of this paragraph, including the choice of a rescue centre or other place.

5. A rescue centre as referred to in paragraph 4 of this Article means an institution designated by a Management Authority to look after the welfare of living specimens, particularly those that have been confiscated.

6. Each Party shall maintain records of trade in specimens of species included in Appendices I, II and III which shall cover:

(a) the names and addresses of exporters and importers; and

(b) the number and type of permits and certificates granted; the States with which such trade occurred; the numbers or quantities and types of specimens, names of species as included in Appendices I, II and III and, where applicable, the size and sex of the specimens in question.

7. Each Party shall prepare periodic reports on its implementation of the present Convention and shall transmit to the Secretariat:

(a) an annual report containing a summary of the information specified in sub-paragraph (b) of paragraph 6 of this Article; and

(b) a biennial report on legislative, regulatory and administrative measures taken to enforce the provisions of the present Convention.

8. The information referred to in paragraph 7 of this Article shall be available to the public where this is not inconsistent with the law of the Party concerned.

Article IX Management and Scientific Authorities

1. Each Party shall designate for the purposes of the present Convention:

(a) one or more Management Authorities competent to grant permits or certificates on behalf of that Party; and

(b) one or more Scientific Authorities.

2. A State depositing an instrument of ratification, acceptance, approval or accession shall at that time inform the Depositary Government of the name and address of the Management Authority authorized to communicate with other Parties and with the Secretariat.

3. Any changes in the designations or authorizations under the provisions of this Article shall be communicated by the Party concerned to the Secretariat for transmission to all other Parties.

4. Any Management Authority referred to in paragraph 2 of this Article shall, if so requested by the Secretariat or the Management Authority of another Party, communicate to it impression of stamps, seals or other devices used to authenticate permits or certificates.

...

Article XI Conference of the Parties

1. The Secretariat shall call a meeting of the Conference of the Parties not later than two years after the entry into force of the present Convention.

2. Thereafter the Secretariat shall convene regular meetings at least once every two years, unless the Conference decides otherwise, and extraordinary meetings at any time on the written request of at least one-third of the Parties.

3. At meetings, whether regular or extraordinary, the Parties shall review the implementation of the present Convention and may:

(a) make such provision as may be necessary to enable the Secretariat to carry out its duties, and adopt financial provisions;

(b) consider and adopt amendments to Appendices I and II in accordance with Article XV;

(c) review the progress made towards the restoration and conservation of the species included in Appendices I, II and III;

(d) receive and consider any reports presented by the Secretariat or by any Party; and

(e) where appropriate, make recommendations for improving the effectiveness of the present Convention.

4. At each regular meeting, the Parties may determine the time and venue of the next regular meeting to be held in accordance with the provisions of paragraph 2 of this Article.

5. At any meeting, the Parties may determine and adopt rules of procedure for the meeting.

6. The United Nations, its Specialized Agencies and the International Atomic Energy Agency, as well as any State not a Party to the present Convention, may be represented at meetings of the Conference by observers, who shall have the right to participate but not to vote.

7. Any body or agency technically qualified in protection, conservation or management of wild fauna and flora, in the following categories, which has informed the Secretariat of its desire to be represented at meetings of the Conference by observers, shall be admitted unless at least one-third of the Parties present object:

(a) international agencies or bodies, either governmental or non-governmental, and national governmental agencies and bodies; and

(b) national non-governmental agencies or bodies which have been approved for this purpose by the State in which they are located. Once admitted, these observers shall have the right to participate but not to vote.

Article XII The Secretariat

1. Upon entry into force of the present Convention, a Secretariat shall be provided by the Executive Director of the United Nations Environment Programme. To the extent and

in the manner he considers appropriate, he may be assisted by suitable inter-governmental or non-governmental international or national agencies and bodies technically qualified in protection, conservation and management of wild fauna and flora.

2. The functions of the Secretariat shall be:
   (a) to arrange for and service meetings of the Parties;
   (b) to perform the functions entrusted to it under the provisions of Articles XV and XVI of the present Convention;
   (c) to undertake scientific and technical studies in accordance with programmes authorized by the Conference of the Parties as will contribute to the implementation of the present Convention, including studies concerning standards for appropriate preparation and shipment of living specimens and the means of identifying specimens;
   (d) to study the reports of Parties and to request from Parties such further information with respect thereto as it deems necessary to ensure implementation of the present Convention;
   (e) to invite the attention of the Parties to any matter pertaining to the aims of the present Convention;
   (f) to publish periodically and distribute to the Parties current editions of Appendices I, II and III together with any information which will facilitate identification of specimens of species included in those Appendices;
   (g) to prepare annual reports to the Parties on its work and on the implementation of the present Convention and such other reports as meetings of the Parties may request;
   (h) to make recommendations for the implementation of the aims and provisions of the present Convention, including the exchange of information of a scientific or technical nature;
   (i) to perform any other function as may be entrusted to it by the Parties.

Article XIII International Measures

1. When the Secretariat in the light of information received is satisfied that any species included in Appendix I or II is being affected adversely by trade in specimens of that species or that the provisions of the present Convention are not being effectively implemented, it shall communicate such information to the authorized Management Authority of the Party or Parties concerned.

2. When any Party receives a communication as indicated in paragraph 1 of this Article, it shall, as soon as possible, inform the Secretariat of any relevant facts insofar as its laws permit and, where appropriate, propose remedial action. Where the Party considers that an inquiry is desirable, such inquiry may be carried out by one or more persons expressly authorized by the Party.

3. The information provided by the Party or resulting from any inquiry as specified in paragraph 2 of this Article shall be reviewed by the next Conference of the Parties which may make whatever recommendations it deems appropriate.

…

Article XVIII Resolution of Disputes

1. Any dispute which may arise between two or more Parties with respect to the interpretation or application of the provisions of the present Convention shall be subject to negotiation between the Parties involved in the dispute.

2. If the dispute can not be resolved in accordance with paragraph 1 of this Article, the Parties may, by mutual consent, submit the dispute to arbitration, in particular that of the Permanent Court of Arbitration at The Hague, and the Parties submitting the dispute shall be bound by the arbitral decision.

...

55.b Guide to CITES Compliance Procedures

Date: March 2004
Source: CITES Resolution Conf. 14.3 (Annex)
http://www.cites.org/eng/res/14/14-03C15.php

Objective and scope

1. The objective of this Guide is to inform Parties and others of CITES procedures concerning promoting, facilitating and achieving compliance with obligations under the Convention and, in particular, assisting Parties in meeting their obligations regarding such compliance.

Specifically, the Guide describes existing procedures in order to facilitate consistent and effective handling of compliance matters relating to obligations under the Convention, taking into account relevant Resolutions and Decisions, in both specific and general compliance matters.

This Guide is non-legally binding.

2. This Guide addresses compliance matters relating to the obligations under the Convention, taking into account relevant Resolutions and Decisions. Particular attention should be paid to the following:

a) designating Management Authority(ies) and Scientific Authority(ies) (Article IX);
b) permitting trade in CITES-listed specimens only to the extent consistent with the procedures laid down in the Convention (Articles III, IV, V, VI, VII and XV);
c) taking appropriate domestic measures to enforce the provisions of the Convention and prohibit trade in violation thereof (Article VIII, paragraph 1);
d) maintaining records of trade and submitting periodic reports (Article VIII, paragraphs 7 and 8); and
e) responding as soon as possible to communications of the Secretariat related to information that a species included in Appendix I or II is being adversely affected by trade in specimens of that species or that the provisions of the Convention are not being effectively implemented (Article XIII).

3. The procedures described in this Guide are without prejudice to any rights and obligations and to any dispute settlement procedure under the Convention.

General principles

4. A supportive and non-adversarial approach is taken towards compliance matters, with the aim of ensuring long-term compliance.

5. Compliance matters are handled as quickly as possible. Such matters are considered and ensuing compliance measures are applied in a fair, consistent and transparent manner.

6. Generally, findings, reports and communications in compliance matters are not treated confidentially.

However, communications between the Secretariat and individual Parties on specific compliance matters are generally confidential.

7. Decisions on whether to close or keep open debates in compliance matters are taken according to the Rules of Procedure of the body considering the matter and generally reasons are given.

8. The Secretariat communicates compliance-related decisions to the relevant authorities.

The various bodies and their compliance-related tasks

9. Compliance matters are handled by the following CITES bodies. Their main compliance-related tasks are listed below.

10. The Conference of the Parties:

a) provides general policy guidance on compliance issues;

b) directs and oversees the handling of compliance matters particularly through the identification of key obligations and procedures;

c) reviews as needed decisions of the Standing Committee related to specific compliance matters; and

d) may delegate certain authority to the Standing Committee or other CITES bodies in accordance with the Convention.

11. When the Conference of the Parties decides to carry out itself the tasks delegated to the Standing Committee, it follows the same procedures as those described below for the Standing Committee.

12. The Standing Committee[*], acting in accordance with instructions from and authority delegated by the Conference of the Parties, handles general and specific compliance matters, including:

a) monitoring and assessing overall compliance with obligations under the Convention;

b) advising and assisting Parties in complying with obligations under the Convention;

c) verifying information; and

d) taking compliance measures as described below.

13. The Animals and Plants Committees, acting in accordance with instructions from and authority delegated by the Conference of the Parties, advise and assist the Standing Committee and the Conference of the Parties with regard to compliance matters, *inter alia*, by undertaking necessary reviews, consultations, assessments and reporting. These Committees are entrusted with specific tasks in the handling of matters related to the Review of Significant Trade.

14. The Secretariat:

a) assists and supports the Animals and Plants Committees, the Standing Committee and the Conference of the Parties in carrying out their functions concerning compliance matters as described in this Guide and, where applicable, according to the procedures set out in relevant Resolutions and Decisions;

b) receives, assesses and communicates to the Parties information on compliance matters;

c) advises and assists Parties in complying with obligations under the Convention;

d) makes recommendations for achieving compliance; and

e) monitors the implementation of compliance-related decisions.

* N.B.: The Standing Committee (which is not mentioned in the Convention itself) was established by CITES Resolution Conf. 2.2, 'Establishment of the Standing Committee of the Conference of the Parties' (1979).

Handling of specific compliance matters

A. Identification of potential compliance matters

15. Annual and biennial reports, legislative texts as well as other special reports and responses to information requests, for example within the Review of Significant Trade or the National Legislation Project, provide the primary, but not exclusive, means of monitoring compliance with obligations under the Convention.

16. The Secretariat provides a Party concerned with information it receives about that Party's compliance, and communicates with the Party regarding this matter.

17. In response, the Party informs the Secretariat as soon as possible of any relevant facts in so far as its laws permit and, where appropriate, proposes remedial action. Where the Party considers that an inquiry is desirable, such inquiry may be carried out by one or more persons expressly authorized by the Party.

18. Any Party concerned over matters related to trade in specimens of CITES-listed species by another Party may bring the matter up directly with that Party and/or call upon the Secretariat for assistance.

19. Parties themselves are encouraged to give the Secretariat early warning of any compliance matter, including the inability to provide information by a certain deadline, and indicate the reasons and any need for assistance.

20. Where compliance matters are identified, the Parties concerned are given every opportunity to correct them within reasonable time limits, if necessary with the assistance of the Secretariat.

B. Consideration of compliance matters

21. If the Party fails to take sufficient remedial action within a reasonable time limit, the compliance matter is brought to the attention of the Standing Committee by the Secretariat, in direct contact with the Party concerned.

22. If a compliance matter is otherwise brought to the attention of the Standing Committee in accordance with the Rules of Procedure, the Standing Committee:

a) refers the matter to the Secretariat for action according to the procedure in paragraphs 16–20 above; or
b) rejects it as trivial or ill-founded; or
c) in exceptional circumstances, after consultation with the Party concerned, follows the procedures as described below.

23. When compliance matters are brought to the attention of the Standing Committee, it is generally done in writing and includes details as to which specific obligations are concerned and an assessment of the reasons why the Party concerned may be unable to meet those obligations.

24. When a compliance matter is brought to the attention of the Standing Committee, the Secretariat immediately informs the Party or Parties concerned.

25. The Standing Committee rejects compliance matters which it considers are trivial or ill-founded.

Where the Standing Committee has decided that the submission is not trivial or ill-founded, the Party concerned is given the opportunity to provide comments within a reasonable time limit.

26. The Standing Committee decides whether to gather or request further information on a compliance matter whenever such information may be found and whether to seek

an invitation from the Party concerned to undertake the gathering and verification of information in the territory of that Party or wherever such information may be found.

27. The Party concerned has the right to participate in discussions with respect to its own compliance, in accordance with the Rules of Procedure of the relevant body.

28. If a Party cannot access the financial resources needed to participate in CITES meetings where its own compliance is being considered, it is able to request assistance from the Secretariat or the Standing Committee in identifying such resources.

C. Measures to achieve compliance

29. If a compliance matter has not been resolved, the Standing Committee decides to take one or more of the following measures:

a) provide advice, information and appropriate facilitation of assistance and other capacity-building support to the Party concerned;
b) request special reporting from the Party concerned;
c) issue a written caution, requesting a response and offering assistance;
d) recommend specific capacity-building actions to be undertaken by the Party concerned;
e) provide in-country assistance, technical assessment and a verification mission, upon the invitation of the Party concerned;
f) send a public notification of a compliance matter through the Secretariat to all Parties advising that compliance matters have been brought to the attention of a Party and that, up to that time, there has been no satisfactory response or action;
g) issue a warning to the Party concerned that it is in non-compliance, e.g. in relation to national reporting and/or the National Legislation Project; and
h) request a compliance action plan to be submitted to the Standing Committee by the Party concerned identifying appropriate steps, a timetable for when those steps should be completed and means to assess satisfactory completion.

30. In certain cases, the Standing Committee decides to recommend the suspension of commercial or all trade in specimens of one or more CITES-listed species, consistent with the Convention. Such a recommendation may be made in cases where a Party's compliance matter is unresolved and persistent and the Party is showing no intention to achieve compliance or a State not a Party is not issuing the documentation referred to in Article X of the Convention. Such a recommendation is always specifically and explicitly based on the Convention and on any applicable Resolutions and Decisions of the Conference of the Parties[1].

31. The list of measures above is not necessarily an exhaustive list of measures applied to date.

32. When the Standing Committee decides upon one or more of the measures mentioned above, it takes into account:

a) the capacity of the Party concerned, especially developing countries, and in particular the least developed and small island developing States and Parties with economies in transition;

[1] These currently include: Resolution Conf. 11.17 (Rev. CoP14) (National reports); Resolution Conf. 8.4 (Rev. CoP15) (National laws for implementation of the Convention); Decision 14.29 (National laws for implementation of the Convention); Resolution Conf. 12.8 (Rev. CoP13) (Review of Significant trade in specimens of Appendix-II species); Convention Article XIII and Resolution Conf. 11.3 (Rev. CoP15) (Compliance and enforcement); and Resolution Conf 11.1 (Rev. CoP15) (Establishment of committees).

[N.B.: Excerpts of Resolution Conf. 11.3 (Rev. CoP15) (Compliance and enforcement) are included as Document No 55.d below. All resolutions are available at http://www.cites.org/.]

b) such factors as the cause, type, degree and frequency of the compliance matters;
c) the appropriateness of the measures so that they are commensurate with the gravity of the compliance matter; and
d) the possible impact on conservation and sustainable use with a view to avoiding negative results.

These considerations are clearly set out in the Standing Committee's recommendations.

D. Monitoring and implementation of measures to achieve compliance

33. The Standing Committee, with the assistance of the Secretariat, monitors the actions taken by the Party concerned to implement measures taken. In this regard, the Standing Committee may, *inter alia*:

a) request the Party concerned to submit progress reports in accordance with a schedule; and
b) arrange, upon the invitation of the Party concerned, for an in-country technical assessment and for a verification mission.

In the light of progress, the Standing Committee decides whether to adjust the measures it has taken, or to take other measures.

34. Existing recommendations to suspend trade are generally reviewed at each Standing Committee meeting. They are also monitored intersessionally by the Secretariat. A recommendation to suspend trade is withdrawn as soon as the compliance matter has been resolved or sufficient progress has been made. The Secretariat notifies Parties of any such withdrawal as soon as possible.

35. The general guidelines in paragraphs 33 and 34 above are in some cases supplemented by more precise provisions regarding specific categories of compliance matters, e.g. in the case of significant trade in specimens of Appendix-II species, as laid out in the Resolutions and Decisions related thereto.

Reporting and reviews

36. The Standing Committee reports to the Conference of the Parties on compliance matters. The Secretariat reports to the Standing Committee and the Conference of the Parties on compliance matters.

37. The Conference of the Parties may review this document periodically and revise it where appropriate.

55.c Resolution on Annual Reports

Date: (as amended) August 2019
Source: Resolutions Conf. 11.17 (Rev. CoP18)[2]
https://cites.org/sites/default/files/document/E-Res-11-17-R18.pdf

...

CONSIDERING the obligation of Parties to submit periodic reports on their implementation of the Convention under the provisions of Article VIII, paragraph 7, of the Convention;

[2] Amended at the 12th, 13th and 14th meetings of the Conference of the Parties; and corrected by the Secretariat following the 15th meeting; subsequently amended at the 16th, 17th and 18th meetings of the Conference of the Parties.

RECOGNIZING the importance of the national reports as a tool for monitoring the implementation of the Convention and the level of legal and illegal international trade in specimens of species included in the Appendices;

ACKNOWLEDGING the necessity for the national reports of the Parties to be as complete as possible and to be comparable;

CONSIDERING that the provisions of Article XII, paragraph 2 (d), of the Convention require the Secretariat to study the periodic reports of Parties;

APPRECIATING the valuable assistance in meeting this responsibility provided by the UNEP World Conservation Monitoring Centre under contract to the Secretariat;

NOTING that the use of computers can help to ensure that trade statistics and information on Convention implementation are dealt with more effectively;

THE CONFERENCE OF THE PARTIES TO THE CONVENTION

1. URGES all Parties to submit their annual reports required under the provisions of Article VIII, paragraph 7 (a), by 31 October following the year for which they are due and in accordance with the most recent version of the *Guidelines for the preparation and submission of CITES annual reports* distributed by the Secretariat, as may be amended with the concurrence of the Standing Committee;

2. URGES all Parties to submit their reports required under the provisions of Article VIII, paragraph 7 (b), one year before each meeting of the Conference of the Parties, beginning with the 17th meeting of the Conference of the Parties and in accordance with the *report format* distributed by the Secretariat, as may be amended by the Secretariat from time to time with the concurrence of the Standing Committee;

3. URGES all Parties to submit an annual illegal trade report by 31 October each year covering actions in the preceding year and in accordance with the report format distributed by the Secretariat, as may be amended by the Secretariat from time to time with the concurrence of the Standing Committee;

4. AGREES that, unless otherwise specified by the reporting Party, data collected in the annual illegal trade report and included in the database should be made available to Parties for research and analysis of wildlife and forest crime as it affects them, and to the members of the International Consortium on Combating Wildlife Crime (ICCWC) for ICCWC global research and analysis studies on wildlife and forest crime;

5. ALSO URGES Parties with multiple Management Authorities to submit coordinated national reports to the extent possible;

6. ACKNOWLEDGES that the Conference of the Parties may request that Parties provide special reports not required by the Convention, if additional information is needed that cannot be sought via the national reports required under Article VIII, paragraph 7, of the Convention;

7. RECOGNIZES that the Conference of the Parties, when requesting special reports, should give consideration to making those special reports time-limited, where this is appropriate, to avoid the potential for unnecessarily increasing reporting burdens;

8. RECOMMENDS that each Party to the Convention, if a member of a regional trade agreement within the meaning of Article XIV, paragraph 3, of the Convention, include in its annual reports information on trade in specimens of species included in Appendices I, II and III with other member States of that regional trade agreement, unless the record-keeping and reporting duties of Article VIII are in direct and irreconcilable conflict with the provisions of the regional trade agreement;

9. RECOMMENDS that, when compiling their annual reports in accordance with Article VIII, paragraph 7, of the Convention and this Resolution, Parties pay particular attention to the reporting of trade in specimens of species subject to annual export quotas. For these species, the report should indicate the level of the quota and the amount actually exported. In cases where trade is authorized in the reporting year in specimens obtained under a quota for the previous year, this should be reflected in the annual report;

10. URGES every Party to consider whether the preparation of its national reports could be computerized and the submission of such reports made in electronic format;

11. FURTHER URGES Parties experiencing problems with the regular preparation and submission of national reports to seek assistance from the Secretariat to produce those reports;

12. RECOMMENDS that Parties studying or developing computer programmes for licensing and reporting trade as well as managing other information under the Convention consult with each other, and with the Secretariat, in order to ensure optimal harmonization and compatibility of systems;

13. DECIDES that:

a) failure to submit an annual report by 31 October of the year following the year for which the report was due constitutes a major problem with the implementation of the Convention, which the Secretariat shall refer to the Standing Committee for a solution in accordance with Resolution Conf. 11.3 (Rev. CoP18)[1] on *Compliance and enforcement*; and

b) the Secretariat may approve a valid request from a Party for a reasonable extension of time to the 31 October deadline for the submission of national reports provided the Party submits to the Secretariat a written request, containing adequate justification, before that deadline;

14. INSTRUCTS the Standing Committee to determine, on the basis of reports presented by the Secretariat, which Parties have failed, for three consecutive years and without having provided adequate justification, to provide the annual reports required under Article VIII, paragraph 7 (a), of the Convention within the deadline (or any extended deadline) provided in the present Resolution;

15. RECOMMENDS that Parties not authorize trade in specimens of CITES-listed species with any Party that the Standing Committee has determined has failed, for three consecutive years and without having provided adequate justification, to provide the annual reports required under Article VIII, paragraph 7 (a), of the Convention within the deadline (or any extended deadline) provided in the present Resolution;

16. APPEALS to all Parties, and to intergovernmental organizations and non-governmental organizations interested in furthering the objectives of the Convention, to make financial contributions to the Secretariat to support the trade and other monitoring work of the Secretariat and that of the UNEP World Conservation Monitoring Centre undertaken under contract to the Secretariat; and

17. REPEALS Resolution Conf. 9.4 (Rev.) (Fort Lauderdale, 1994, as amended at Harare, 1997) – *Annual reports and monitoring of trade.*

...

[1] Corrected by the Secretariat following the 18th meeting of the Conference of the Parties.

55.d Resolution on Compliance and Enforcement

Date: (as amended) August 2019
Source: Resolution Conf. 11.3 (Rev. CoP18)
https://cites.org/sites/default/files/document/E-Res-11-03-R18.pdf

... THE CONFERENCE OF THE PARTIES TO THE CONVENTION

...

Exercising due diligence

...

3. URGES all Parties to strengthen, as soon as possible, the controls on trade in wildlife in the territories under their jurisdiction, and in particular controls on shipments from source countries, including neighbouring countries, and to verify the validity of documents originating from such countries with the respective Management Authorities;

...

Regarding application of Article XIII

5. RECOMMENDS that:

a) when, in application of Article XIII of the Convention and Resolution Conf. 14.3 (Rev. CoP18), the Secretariat requests information on a potential compliance matter, Parties reply within one month or, if this is impossible, provide within the month an approximate date by which they consider it will be possible to provide the information requested;
b) when, within six months, the information requested has not been provided, Parties provide the Secretariat with justification of the reasons for which they have not been able to respond;
c) if major compliance matters concerning particular Parties are brought to the attention of the Secretariat, the Secretariat, in consultation with the Chair of the Standing Committee and as expeditiously as possible, work with the Parties concerned to try to solve the matter and offer advice or technical assistance as required;
d) if it does not appear a solution can be readily achieved, the Secretariat bring the matter to the attention of the Standing Committee, which may pursue the matter in direct contact with the Party concerned with a view to helping to find a solution; and
e) the Secretariat keep the Parties informed as fully as possible, through Notifications to the Parties, of such compliance matters and of actions taken to solve them, and include such matters in its reports for meetings of the Standing Committee and the Conference of the Parties;

Regarding enforcement activities of the Secretariat

6. URGES the Parties, intergovernmental and non-governmental organizations to provide additional financial support for the enforcement of the Convention, by providing funds for the enforcement assistance work of the Secretariat;

7. DIRECTS the Secretariat to utilize such funds towards the following priorities:

a) the appointment of additional officers to the Secretariat to work on enforcement-related matters;

b) assistance in the development and implementation of regional and subregional law-enforcement agreements; and

c) training and technical assistance to the Parties;

8. URGES the Parties to offer secondment of enforcement officers to assist the Secretariat in addressing law-enforcement issues; and

9. DIRECTS the Secretariat to:

a) pursue closer international liaison between the Convention's institutions, regional and subregional wildlife enforcement networks and national enforcement agencies, and to work in close cooperation with ICPO-INTERPOL, the United Nations Office on Drugs and Crime, the World Bank and the World Customs Organization as ICCWC partner organizations;

b) submit a report on activities that have been conducted under the auspices of ICCWC at each Standing Committee meeting and each regular meeting of the Conference of the Parties and consult with the Standing Committee on the development of the ICCWC Programme of Work to ensure CITES Parties' needs are adequately addressed; and

c) maintain the dedicated portal on ICCWC, in the official languages of the Convention, on the CITES website to enable Parties to identify the opportunities and support available through ICCWC;

d) in close collaboration with forensic experts from relevant ICCWC partner agencies and the Society for Wildlife Forensics Science as the professional body engaged by ICCWC to advise the Consortium on wildlife forensic science matters, consider annually any new applications from laboratories for inclusion in the electronic directory of laboratories that conduct wildlife forensic testing and, further, to review existing listings every two years;

...

The Marine Environment*

56.a Convention for the Protection of the Marine Environment of the North-East Atlantic** (OSPAR Convention)

Date: 22 September 1992
Source: (1993) 32 ILM 1069
https://www.ospar.org/site/assets/files/1290/ospar_convention-1.pdf

...

ARTICLE 10 COMMISSION

1. A Commission, made up of representatives of each of the Contracting Parties, is hereby established. The Commission shall meet at regular intervals and at any time when, due to special circumstances, it is so decided in accordance with the Rules of Procedure.

* See also Documents No. 49-51 on dispute settlement in the law of the sea.
** N.B.: as amended.

2. It shall be the duty of the Commission:
   (a) to supervise the implementation of the Convention;
   (b) generally to review the condition of the maritime area, the effectiveness of the measures being adopted, the priorities and the need for any additional or different measures;
   (c) to draw up, in accordance with the General Obligations of the Convention, programmes and measures for the prevention and elimination of pollution and for the control of activities which may, directly or indirectly, adversely affect the maritime area; such programmes and measure may, when appropriate, include economic instruments;
   (d) to establish at regular intervals its programme of work;
   (e) to set up such subsidiary bodies as it considers necessary and to define their terms of reference;
   (f) to consider and, where appropriate, adopt proposals for the amendment of the Convention in accordance with Articles 15, 16, 17, 18, 19 and 27;
   (g) to discharge the functions conferred by Articles 21 and 23 and such other functions as may be appropriate under the terms of the Convention;

3. To these ends the Commission may, *inter alia*, adopt decisions and recommendations in accordance with Article 13.

4. The Commission shall draw up its Rules of Procedure which shall be adopted by unanimous vote of the Contracting Parties.

5. The Commission shall draw up its Financial Regulations which shall be adopted by unanimous vote of the Contracting Parties.

…

ARTICLE 22 REPORTING TO THE COMMISSION

The Contracting Parties shall report to the Commission at regular intervals on:
   (a) the legal, regulatory, or other measures taken by them for the implementation of the provisions of the Convention and of decisions and recommendations adopted thereunder, including in particular measures taken to prevent and punish conduct in contravention of those provisions;
   (b) the effectiveness of the measures referred to in subparagraph (a) of this Article;
   (c) problems encountered in the implementation of the provisions referred to in subparagraph (a) of this Article.

ARTICLE 23 COMPLIANCE

The Commission shall:
   (a) on the basis of the periodical reports referred to in Article 22 and any other report submitted by the Contracting Parties, assess their compliance with the Convention and the decisions and recommendations adopted thereunder;
   (b) when appropriate, decide upon and call for steps to bring about full compliance with the Convention, and decisions adopted thereunder, and promote the implementation of recommendations, including measures to assist a Contracting Party to carry out its obligations.

…

ARTICLE 32 SETTLEMENT OF DISPUTES

1. Any disputes between Contracting Parties relating to the interpretation or application of the Convention, which cannot be settled otherwise by the Contracting Parties concerned, for instance by means of inquiry or conciliation within the Commission, shall at the request of any of those Contracting Parties, be submitted to arbitration under the conditions laid down in this Article.

2. Unless the parties to the dispute decide otherwise, the procedure of the arbitration referred to in paragraph 1 of this Article shall be in accordance with paragraphs 3 to 10 of this Article.

3. (a) At the request addressed by one Contracting Party to another Contracting Party in accordance with paragraph 1 of this Article, an arbitral tribunal shall be constituted. The request for arbitration shall state the subject matter of the application including in particular the Articles of the Convention, the interpretation or application of which is in dispute.

(b) The applicant party shall inform the Commission that it has requested the setting up of an arbitral tribunal, stating the name of the other party to the dispute and the Articles of the Convention the interpretation or application of which, in its opinion, is in dispute. The Commission shall forward the information thus received to all Contracting Parties to the Convention.

4. The arbitral tribunal shall consist of three members: each of the parties to the dispute shall appoint an arbitrator; the two arbitrators so appointed shall designate by common agreement the third arbitrator who shall be the chairman of the tribunal. The latter shall not be a national of one of the parties to the dispute, nor have his usual place of residence in the territory of one of these parties, nor be employed by any of them, nor have dealt with the case in any other capacity.

5. (a) If the chairman of the arbitral tribunal has not been designated within two months of the appointment of the second arbitrator, the President of the International Court of Justice shall, at the request of either party, designate him within a further two months' period.

(b) If one of the parties to the dispute does not appoint an arbitrator within two months of receipt of the request, the other party may inform the President of the International Court of Justice who shall designate the chairman of the arbitral tribunal within a further two months' period. Upon designation, the chairman of the arbitral tribunal shall request the party which has not appointed an arbitrator to do so within two months. After such period, he shall inform the President of the International Court of Justice who shall make this appointment within a further two months' period.

6. (a) The arbitral tribunal shall decide according to the rules of international law and, in particular, those of the Convention.

(b) Any arbitral tribunal constituted under the provisions of this Article shall draw up its own rules of procedure.

(c) In the event of a dispute as to whether the arbitral tribunal has jurisdiction, the matter shall be decided by the decision of the arbitral tribunal.

7. (a) The decisions of the arbitral tribunal, both on procedure and on substance, shall be taken by majority voting of its members.

(b) The arbitral tribunal may take all appropriate measures in order to establish the facts. It may, at the request of one of the parties, recommend essential interim measures of protection.

(c) If two or more arbitral tribunals constituted under the provisions of this Article are seized of requests with identical or similar subjects, they may inform themselves of the procedures for establishing the facts and take them into account as far as possible.

(d) The parties to the dispute shall provide all facilities necessary for the effective conduct of the proceedings.

(e) The absence or default of a party to the dispute shall not constitute an impediment to the proceedings.

8. Unless the arbitral tribunal determines otherwise because of the particular circumstances of the case, the expenses of the tribunal, including the remuneration of its members, shall be borne by the parties to the dispute in equal shares. The tribunal shall keep a record of all its expenses, and shall furnish a final statement thereof to the parties.

9. Any Contracting Party that has an interest of a legal nature in the subject matter of the dispute which may be affected by the decision in the case, may intervene in the proceedings with the consent of the tribunal.

10.(a) The award of the arbitral tribunal shall be accompanied by a statement of reasons. It shall be final and binding upon the parties to the dispute.

(b) Any dispute which may arise between the parties concerning the interpretation or execution of the award may be submitted by either party to the arbitral tribunal which made the award or, if the latter cannot be seized thereof, to another arbitral tribunal constituted for this purpose in the same manner as the first.

...

56.b Rules of Procedure of the OSPAR Commission

Date: 2005

Source: https://www.ospar.org/site/assets/files/1202/rules_of_procedure.pdf

A. Definitions

Rule 1

1. For the purposes of these Rules of Procedure:

(a) **"the Convention"** means the Convention for the Protection of the Marine Environment of the North-East Atlantic, Paris, 22 September 1992 (OSPAR Convention);

(b) **"the Commission"** means the Commission established by Article 10.1 of the Convention;

(c) **"Decision"** means a Decision as described in Article 13 of the Convention;

(d) **"document"** means any information, whether recorded in writing or in a form for reproduction by aural, electronic, or visual means, to which Article 9 of the Convention applies;

(e) "**main committee"** means the Biodiversity Committee, the Environmental Monitoring and Assessment Committee, the Eutrophication Committee, the Hazardous Substances Committee, the Offshore Industry Committee or the Radioactive Substances Committee;

(f) **"Recommendation"** means a Recommendation as described in Article 13 of the Convention;

(g) **"delegations present and voting at the meeting"** means delegations present at the meeting casting an affirmative or negative vote; delegations abstaining from voting shall be considered as not voting;

(h) in computing any period of time which is less than a year, no account shall be taken of the period between 25 December and 1 January, inclusive.

B. Composition of the Commission

Rules 2–3

2. The Commission shall consist of representatives of each of the Contracting Parties.

3. Each Contracting Party shall designate a Head of Delegation to the Commission and as many other delegates to each meeting as it considers appropriate.

C. Meetings of the Commission

Rules 4–9

4. Ordinary meetings of the Commission shall take place at least once a year. The time and place of such meetings shall be decided either by the Commission at the preceding meeting or by correspondence between the Executive Secretary and the Contracting Parties.

5. On the request of at least three Contracting Parties, the Chairman of the Commission shall convene an extraordinary meeting in accordance with Article 10(1) of the Convention as soon as practicable after the request. An extraordinary meeting shall only take place if the Contracting Parties requesting it provide the necessary facilities, unless the Commission has made other provision for it.

6. Each Contracting Party should give the Secretariat the number and names of its delegates, if possible two weeks before the opening of an ordinary meeting.

7. The presence of delegations representing at least three-quarters of the Contracting Parties shall constitute a quorum for ordinary and extraordinary meetings. In the absence of a quorum, the meeting may not take a valid decision, except to fix a date for the next meeting.

8. The meetings of the Commission and its subsidiary bodies shall be held in private unless the Commission unanimously decides otherwise.

9. In accordance with Article 11 of the Convention, the Commission may unanimously decide to admit

(a) any state which is not a Contracting Party to the Convention;

(b) any international Governmental organisation; and

(c) any international non-Governmental organisation (NGO);

to be represented by observers at its meetings. If need be, the Commission may restrict the participation in a specified meeting of observers in any category. The participation of NGO observers in the work of the Commission shall be governed by the Criteria and Procedures set out in Annex 2.

D. Chairman and Vice-Chairmen of the Commission

Rules 10–14

10. The Commission shall elect a Chairman and two Vice-Chairmen by the unanimous vote of the Contracting Parties present and voting at the meeting.

11. The Chairman and Vice-Chairmen shall serve for a period of two years. In exceptional cases their term of office may be extended, in the case of any of them, for a further period of two years.

12. In electing the Chairman and Vice-Chairmen the Commission will seek to ensure rotation amongst the Contracting Parties and an equitable geographical representation of the Contracting Parties.

13. Should the Chairmanship fall vacant, or should the Chairman be temporarily unable to perform his/her functions, the two Vice-Chairmen shall agree which shall act as Chairman until a successor is elected. Failing such agreement, the elder shall act as Chairman. A Chairman or a Vice-Chairman who is a delegate shall not act as a delegate as long as he/she is sitting as Chairman.

14. The duties of the Chairman shall be to preside over the meetings of the Commission, to take initiatives and put forward proposals to the Commission which could promote the efficient operation of the Commission, and to perform any other tasks that may be entrusted to him/her by the Commission.

E. Secretariat

Rules 15–18

15. The Commission shall appoint its Executive Secretary by consensus.

16. The Commission shall decide on the location of the Secretariat.

17. The Executive Secretary shall be the Commission's executive official and shall be responsible to the Commission for the administration of the Secretariat, for drawing up budgets and calculating contributions and for the income and expenditure of the Commission. He/she shall perform any other tasks that may be entrusted to him/her by the Commission or by the Chairman.

18. All communications addressed to or emanating from the Commission shall be sent to or despatched by the Secretariat. The Secretariat shall be charged with receiving, translating and distributing to participants all the reports, resolutions, proposals for decisions and recommendations, summary records and other documents of the meetings of the Commission and its subsidiary bodies.

F. Subsidiary Bodies

Rules 19–42

19. The Commission may by the unanimous vote of delegations present and voting at a meeting set up, for such period as it thinks fit, such subsidiary bodies as it considers necessary and determine their terms of reference.

20. Unless the Commission makes special provision to meet a particular need, the subsidiary bodies shall be:

- (i) the main committees;
- (ii) the Coordination Group
- (iii) working groups;
- (iv) the Meeting of Heads of Delegation to the Commission and the Committee of Chairmen and Vice-Chairmen;
- (v) the Group of Jurists and Linguists;
- (vi) intersessional correspondence groups;
- (vii) *ad hoc* meetings included in the schedule of meetings.

21. At each annual meeting, and in the light of proposals from the main committees, the Commission shall establish a schedule of meetings of subsidiary bodies for the ensuing year. The precise date and location of each meeting shall be fixed by the Secretariat, in agreement with any Contracting Party that has agreed to host the meeting.

22. Unless otherwise specified, each Contracting Party may send to any meeting of a subsidiary body a delegation consisting of as many delegates as it considers appropriate.

23. States and intergovernmental organisations which have been admitted as observers may be represented at meetings of the main committees and working groups, and may participate in intersessional correspondence groups, on the same basis as for meetings of the Commission. By special invitation of the Chairman, they may also participate in meetings of Heads of Delegation and meetings of the Committee of Chairmen and Vice-Chairmen and the Group of Jurists and Linguists.

24. Representatives of non-governmental organisations admitted as observers may participate in the work of subsidiary bodies in accordance with the criteria and procedures set out in Annex 2.

25. Each subsidiary body shall decide on its own working procedures to carry out tasks, including, *inter alia*, the establishment of parallel working groups during a meeting. Any conclusions from a parallel working group shall be considered by the plenary session of the subsidiary body and an opportunity given for discussion.

26. All proposals by subsidiary bodies with financial implications for the Commission shall be subject to approval by the Commission.

(i) Main committees

27. The terms of reference of the main committees shall be adopted by the Commission.

28. Each main committee shall elect its chairman by the unanimous vote of the delegations present and voting at the meeting at which the election is made. In making an election, the subsidiary body should bear in mind, *inter alia*, the need to ensure rotation amongst the Contracting Parties and an equitable geographical representation of Contracting Parties.

29. Chairmen shall hold office for two years, unless the main committee decides otherwise when making an election. One of the chairman's tasks shall be the reporting as specified in that main committee's terms of reference. If a chairman ceases to hold office before his or her successor has been elected, the Secretariat shall nevertheless consult him or her on the agenda and arrangements for the next-following meeting of the subsidiary body, unless the Commission has nominated a successor, in which case that person shall be consulted.

30. Each main committee may also elect one or two vice-chairmen by the unanimous vote of delegations present and voting at the meeting. A vice-chairman shall hold office for two years, unless the main committee decides otherwise when making an election. A vice-chairman shall assist the chairman and shall replace him/her if he/she is not available. If there are two vice-chairmen and if the chairmanship falls vacant, or if the chairman is temporarily unable to perform his/her functions, rule 13 shall apply as it applies to Vice-Chairmen of the Commission.

31. The heads of the delegations of Contracting Parties to main committees shall hold a preliminary meeting, under the chairmanship of the chairman of the committee, before the start of the committee meeting, to agree the working arrangements for the ensuing meeting. This preliminary meeting shall also agree under rule 50 which documents proposed to be circulated at the committee meeting shall be discussed.

32. Where appropriate, each main committee shall consider each year what changes in the work programme should be proposed for the approval of the Commission.

(ii) Working Groups

33. On the proposal of the main committee responsible for an activity, the Commission may establish a working group to carry out specific parts of that activity. In addition, a main committee may, as an exception, decide on the establishment of *ad hoc* working groups if this is necessary to fulfil its work programme in due time, and if the working group needs to meet for this purpose before the next Commission meeting. In such cases, the chairman of the relevant main committee shall make a written proposal to the Heads of Delegation to the Commission. If no Contracting Party objects to the proposal within two weeks after the date on which the proposal was sent, the proposal shall be regarded as accepted. The relevant main committee shall review the output of all working groups in its field of activity.

34. Rules 28 and 29 shall apply in respect of the chairmen of working groups as they apply in respect of chairmen of main committees, except that the relevant main committee may provide for its chairman or one of its vice-chairmen to be the chairman of a working group which it has recommended the Commission to establish. The relevant main committee may nominate a chairman for a working group where the chairman has ceased to hold that office before his/her successor has been elected. In that case, the nominee shall be consulted in place of the former chairman.

35. Rule 31 (heads of delegation to agree working arrangements and what late documents are to be discussed) shall apply to working groups as it applies to main committees.

(iii) Meetings of Heads of Delegation to the Commission and the Committee of Chairmen and Vice-Chairmen

36. The meeting of Heads of Delegation to the Commission shall:

(a) ensure that the material to be presented to meetings of the Commission is properly prepared;

(b) advise on the management of the administrative, budgetary, contractual and personnel issues of the Commission and the Secretariat;

(c) oversee the development and implementation of the decisions, recommendations and other agreements (including the strategies and work programmes) adopted by the Commission.

It shall have no powers of decision on behalf of the Commission.

37. The Committee of Chairmen and Vice-Chairmen shall consist of the Chairman and Vice-Chairmen of the Commission and the Chairmen of two main committees designated by the Commission. It shall advise the Chairman of the Commission and the Executive Secretary on the discharge of their functions.

38. The Chairman of the Commission shall be the chairman both of the Meetings of the Heads of Delegation to the Commission and of the Committee of Chairmen and Vice-Chairmen. These bodies may establish their own procedures. Subject to other express provision elsewhere in these Rules, and to any decisions by these bodies to the contrary, these Rules shall apply to meetings of these bodies as they apply to meetings of a main committee.

(iv) Group of Jurists and Linguists

39. In relation to the formulation of advice on draft OSPAR Decisions and Recommendations, the procedure of the Group of Jurists and Linguists shall be that:

(a) in a preliminary written procedure a copy of every draft Decision and Recommendation shall be sent by the Secretariat to the Group as soon as a working group or main committee has agreed that a proposal for such a measure shall be put to the relevant main committee or to the Commission, as the case may be, with an invitation to comment on the formulation; the Secretariat may add any suggestions that it wishes to make to the Group;

(b) in the case of a draft to be submitted to a main committee, the Secretariat shall submit the comments made by the Group to the next meeting of the relevant main committee;

(c) in the case of a draft to be submitted to the Commission, the Secretariat shall submit to the annual meeting of the Group of Jurists and Linguists the comments received, together with any further suggestions that it may wish to add; the advice of the Group shall be submitted to the Meeting of Heads of Delegation to the Commission and to the heads of the delegations to the relevant main committee;

(d) as far as possible, arrangements should be made for a representative of the lead Contracting Party, or for the chairman or a vice-chairman of the relevant main committee, to attend the annual meeting of the Group of Jurists and Linguists to advise on the technical content of the drafts;

(e) as far as possible, the annual meeting of the Group of Jurists and Linguists shall be held between the last meeting of a main committee in each cycle of meetings and the Meeting of the Heads of Delegation to the Commission which will review the material to be submitted to the next meeting of the Commission;

39(bis). In relation to the formulation of legal advice on the interpretation and application of the Convention, the procedure shall be that:

(a) a request for the formulation of legal advice by the Group of Jurists and Linguists on the interpretation and application of the Convention shall be addressed to the Commission through a main committee;

(b) the relevant main committee shall:

(i) prepare a clear outline of the issue under consideration;

(ii) prepare draft Terms of Reference on the issue under consideration for the Group of Jurists and Linguists to be submitted to the Commission;

(iii) submit the documentation specified in subparagraphs (i) and (ii) in accordance with Rule 46.

39(ter). Notwithstanding Rule 39(bis), no legal advice on the interpretation and application of the Convention provided collectively by the Group of Jurists and Linguists is to be taken as definitive or as binding Contracting Parties as a matter of international law.

39(quarter). If the amount of business does not justify it, the Chairman of the Commission may decide that the annual meeting of the Group of Jurists and Linguists shall not be held, and that any business shall instead be dealt with by a written procedure.

40. The Chairman of the Commission, or a person appointed by him/her, shall be the chairman of the Group of Jurists and Linguists. Subject to other express provision elsewhere in these Rules, these Rules shall apply to the meetings of the Group as they apply to meetings of a main committee.

(v) Intersessional correspondence groups

41. Any subsidiary body, other than an intersessional correspondence group, may establish an intersessional correspondence group to take forward an issue on which work

has not been completed at the meeting which decides to set up that group. The meeting establishing the group shall appoint a convenor of the group, who shall be responsible for

(a) ensuring that all documents for the group are circulated to all members of the group;

(b) arranging any informal meetings which the members of the group agree by consensus to hold;

(c) reporting the outcome of the work of the group to the next meeting of the subsidiary body that established the group or to another meeting identified in the decision to set up the group.

42. Subject to any decision to the contrary by the subsidiary body establishing the intersessional correspondence group, any Contracting Party and any observer shall be entitled to nominate a person to receive the documents of the group and to circulate documents as part of the group's work. The Secretariat shall assist the convenor of an intersessional correspondence group as far as resources allow.

G. Documents

Rules 43–62

Meeting agendas

43. For ordinary meetings of the Commission, the Executive Secretary shall, in agreement with the Chairman, circulate a proposed draft agenda at least two months before the opening of meeting. Each delegation shall be entitled, up to five weeks before the opening of the meeting, to ask for subjects to be placed on the draft agenda; delegations requesting such additions should submit an explanatory memorandum in support of their request. The draft agenda shall be sent to all Contracting Parties at least one month before the opening of the meeting. The agenda shall be adopted at the beginning of the meeting, and at that stage items may only be added with the unanimous approval of all delegations present.

44. For extraordinary meetings of the Commission (see rule 5 above), the agenda shall be limited to the matters specified in the request from the Contracting Parties for the calling of the meeting and such other matters as the Contracting Parties agree unanimously to add to the agenda. The Secretariat shall distribute without delay all papers which it receives relating to the matters specified in that request and other matters which a Contracting Party intends to propose to be added to the agenda.

45. For meetings of subsidiary bodies, the Secretariat shall, in agreement with the Chairman of the body, prepare a draft agenda reflecting the work programme approved by the Commission. The draft agenda shall be sent to all Contracting Parties at least six weeks before the commencement of the meeting. The agenda shall be adopted at the beginning of the meeting, and at that stage items may only be added with the unanimous approval of all delegations present.

Proposals for Decisions and Recommendations

46. For meetings of the Commission, proposals for Decisions or Recommendations to be adopted by the Commission shall be received by the Secretariat in at least one of the official languages at least five weeks before the opening of an ordinary meeting of the Commission and shall be distributed by the Secretariat without delay. The translated version of the proposal into the other official language shall be distributed by the Secretariat as soon

as practicable. If the five-week deadline is not met, the proposal will only be discussed if the Commission unanimously so decides. Contracting Parties which wish to have written comments on such proposals circulated to other Contracting Parties before the opening of the ordinary meeting should ensure that they are received by the Secretariat at least two weeks before the opening of that meeting.

47. For meetings of a subsidiary body, proposals for Decisions and Recommendations shall be received by the Secretariat in at least one of the official languages at least twelve weeks before the opening of a meeting of that subsidiary body and shall be distributed by the Secretariat without delay. The version of the proposal translated into the other official language shall be distributed by the Secretariat as soon as practicable. If the twelve-week deadline is not met, the proposal will only be discussed if the subsidiary body unanimously so decides. Contracting Parties which wish to have written comments on such proposals circulated to the other Contracting Parties before the meeting should ensure that they are received by the Secretariat at least two weeks before opening of the meeting.

Other meeting documents

48. All other documents submitted for discussion or information at a meeting shall be received by the Secretariat at least three weeks before the opening of a meeting of the Commission or of a subsidiary body and, subject to the next rule, shall be circulated by the Secretariat as soon as possible.

49. No documents shall be circulated by the Secretariat two weeks before a meeting, except where:

(a) the chairman of the meeting, or, where there is no chairman, the person to be consulted on the agenda or, if he/she cannot act, the Executive Secretary, considers that the document is essential for the meeting to deliver its intended results;

(b) the document comments on a document already circulated.

50. Documents circulated at a meeting shall only be discussed if agreed under Rule 31.

Reports of meetings

51. Reports of the meetings of the Commission, of the main committees and, subject to rule 52, of working groups shall be prepared by the Secretariat and shall be amended and adopted in a plenary session before the close of the meeting. Such reports, including, as appropriate, any Decisions and Recommendations adopted by the Commission or proposed for adoption by a subsidiary body, shall be distributed by the Secretariat without delay.

52. The reports of Meetings of Heads of Delegation to the Commission, the Committee of Chairmen and Vice-Chairmen and the Group of Jurists and Linguists shall be adopted under a written procedure after the close of the meeting. The Commission, or the main committee establishing an *ad hoc* working group, may decide that the report of a working group shall be adopted in a written procedure after the close of the meeting.

53. Where there is a written procedure under Rule 52, the meeting shall agree the procedure to be adopted, including the deadlines for comments, taking into account any general advice from the Commission. Unless some other period is agreed, one week shall be the period allowed under the written procedure for comment on drafts. All comments shall be sent by e-mail or fax. The Secretariat shall acknowledge the receipt of all comments. When the chairman of the meeting is satisfied that a report has been agreed, the Secretariat shall distribute it without delay.

54. Contracting Parties shall ensure that they have arrangements to make any necessary comments on draft reports to be adopted under a written procedure by the agreed deadlines, even if their head of delegation is absent following a meeting where the report is to be adopted in that way.

Annual Reports

55. The Executive Secretary shall prepare and circulate not later than six weeks after the first ordinary meeting of each calendar year a draft report giving an account of the activities in the intersessional period and at that meeting. Contracting Parties shall be allowed at least six weeks to comment on that draft report, following which the report shall be made available to the public. If any comments received conflict, they shall be resolved by the Executive Secretary in consultation with the Contracting Parties concerned.

Availability of Documents

56. Subject to Rule 57, all documents which represent the considered views of the Commission, a main committee or a working group (including summary records of meetings) shall be made available by the Secretariat to any person on request (with a payment towards the costs of making them available, when appropriate).

57. Rule 56 shall not apply to:

(a) proposals and drafts submitted to the Commission, a main committee or working group, unless the originator agrees that they should be made publicly available;

(b) documents of a management nature (such as those dealing with budgetary, contractual or personnel issues);

(c) documents formally restricted by the originator (such as those containing commercially confidential information);

(d) documents of the Meeting of Heads of Delegation to the Commission and the Committee of Chairmen and Vice-Chairmen.

58. Documents formally restricted by the originator shall:

(a) be made available only to Contracting Parties, observer states and, to the extent that they are involved, intergovernmental observers.

(b) be clearly marked as "RESTRICTED*" and shall carry a footnote "*The Commission has decided that documents marked as "RESTRICTED" shall only be made available to Contracting Parties, observer states and, to the extent that they are involved, intergovernmental observers".

Documents of a management nature and documents of the Meeting of Heads of Delegation to the Commission and the Committee of Chairmen and Vice-Chairmen shall be made available to Contracting Parties, and to observers of States or intergovernmental organisations. In addition, documents of the Meeting of Heads of Delegation to the Commission shall be made available to observers of non-Governmental organisations, except where they are of a management nature or are formally restricted by the originator.

59. In the case of documents prepared by the Secretariat, the Executive Secretary shall exercise the discretion given to the originator until the document is submitted to the Commission or the subsidiary body for which it was prepared. If the Executive Secretary decides that it is not appropriate to make such a document available, the body to which it was submitted, or the Commission, may alter that decision after it has been submitted.

60. The circulation of documents shall be by means of:
   a. placing the documents on the OSPAR website; the Secretariat shall ensure that documents which are not to be made available to the general public, or which are only to be made available to Contracting Parties, observer states and intergovernmental observers are protected by appropriate measures;
   b. sending one paper copy to the official contact point for each Contracting Party which states in writing to the Secretariat that it wishes to receive such copies.

Where it is not practicable to circulate a document by electronic means, the Secretariat shall send a paper copy to each Contracting Party, and to each observer that requests it, and up to three additional paper copies to those Contracting Parties that so request.

Format of documents

61. Any document submitted to the Commission or a subsidiary body shall, as far as possible, start with a short summary of its contents, and conclude with a clear statement of the action requested to be taken by the body to which it is submitted.

62. Any proposal for a Decision or Recommendation shall, as far as possible, follow the Guidelines on the Preparation of Draft Measures, as from time to time adopted by the Commission.

H. Voting Procedures

Rules 63–70

63. Subject to the provisions of Article 20 of the Convention, each Contracting Party shall have one vote at the Commission.

64. Decisions and Recommendations shall be adopted in accordance with the procedure specified in Article 13 of the Convention (that is unanimity or three-quarters majority of the Contracting Parties).

65. Substantive issues, other than issues for which the Convention or these Rules prescribe some other procedures, shall be determined by a three-quarters majority of the votes of the Contracting Parties present and voting at the meeting. Procedural questions, other than questions for which the Convention or these Rules prescribe some other procedures, shall be decided by a simple majority of the votes of the Contracting Parties present and voting at the meeting.

66. Disputes as to whether a specific question is procedural or substantive shall be decided by the Chairman. Such a ruling may be challenged by a Contracting Party and over-ruled by a simple majority of the votes of the Contracting Parties present and voting at the meeting. If such a vote is requested, it shall be taken before the vote on the question itself.

67. Decisions under Regulations 2.1(c) and 2.1(e) of the Financial Regulations at Annex 1 shall be taken by unanimous vote of the Contracting Parties present and voting at the meeting.

68. If there is an equal vote on a subject for which a simple majority is required, the Chairman shall have a casting vote.

69. Amendments to a proposal shall be voted upon before the proposal itself.

70. Unless other Rules/Regulations apply, in exceptional cases, on a proposal by the Chairman, a written vote may be held between meetings. The rules applicable to a vote

at a meeting of the Commission shall apply to such a written vote, with the following modifications:

a. references to Contracting Parties present and voting at the meeting shall be understood as references to all Contracting Parties;

b. a letter shall be sent to the head of the delegation of each Contracting Party to the Convention, by e-mail and by post, setting out the proposal on which the Contracting Parties are asked to vote. Except where the Contracting Party has notified the Secretariat that a new head of delegation has been appointed, the head of delegation of a Contracting Party shall be taken to be the person or persons who attended the last meeting of the Commission or the Meeting of Heads of Delegation (whichever is more recent) as head(s) of the delegation from that Contracting Party;

c. the letter setting out the proposal shall indicate the date and time by which a vote must be received by the Secretariat. This date and time shall be at least three weeks after the end of business at the Secretariat on the day that the letter is sent by e-mail;

d. if the Chairman agrees, the letter setting out the proposal may indicate that, if no contrary view has been received by the Secretariat from the Contracting Party by the date and time by which a vote must be received, that Contracting Party will be taken to have accepted the proposal, except in the case of written votes on proposals for Decisions or Recommendations where the provisions of Article 13 of the Convention apply;

e. any proposal by a Contracting Party to amend the proposal contained in the letter shall be taken to be a vote against the proposal. Nevertheless, an amended proposal may subsequently be made by a further written procedure in accordance with this rule;

f. copies of the letter setting out the proposal shall be sent at the same time to all observers who have relevant specialised technical, scientific or other expertise relating to the proposals, with an invitation to make any comments on the proposal to the heads of delegation;

g. the Secretariat shall write to each head of delegation setting out the result of the vote. A copy of this letter shall be sent to the observers to which a copy of the letter setting out the proposal was sent.

I. Press Notices

Rule 71

71. A press notice about the results of meetings of the Commission may be prepared by the Chairman of the Commission and the Executive Secretary at the end of the Commission's meetings. Press statements may also be issued at other times on the responsibility of the Executive Secretary.

J. Languages

Rules 72–73

72. The official languages of the Commission are English and French. A Contracting Party desiring to use any other language shall be entitled to do so if, at its own expense, it provides for translation or interpretation into at least one of the official languages.

73. The host country shall be responsible for ensuring adequate interpretation into both official languages at the plenary sessions of meetings of:
- the Commission;
- the main committees, and
- as far as possible, any working group.

Nevertheless, where the Secretariat:

(a) at a date six weeks before the commencement of a meeting of a main committee or a working group, has received no notification from any Contracting Party that its delegation would wish to use interpretation facilities; and

(b) considers that the meeting of the main committee can effectively be conducted in a single specified language,

there shall be no requirement to provide interpretation at that meeting of that committee or working group.

K. Other

Rules 74–82

74. The Commission may nominate members of the Secretariat or delegates of Contracting Parties as representatives to meetings organised by other international organisations. Between meetings of the Commission, the Chairman of the Commission may make such nominations after consulting the Heads of Delegation to the Commission. Where such a representative may have to express views on behalf of the Commission, the Secretariat shall ensure that agreed guidance is provided to him/her. The representative shall follow such guidance.

75. The Commission may, where it so decides, seek expert advice from competent scientific authorities or international organisations.

76. Where more than three Contracting Parties agree to share the lead on any issue, their cooperation shall be organised in the form of an intersessional correspondence group limited to those Contracting Parties.

77. The Commission may agree that a workshop to be organised by a Contracting Party may be described as an OSPAR workshop. When this is done, the Contracting Party organising the workshop should ensure that:

(a) all Contracting Parties are invited to send participants to the workshop;

(b) States, intergovernmental organisations and international non-governmental organisations which have been admitted as observers and which have expressed an interest in the workshop are invited to participate; the number of places allocated to such observers should be at least one-eighth of the places available for Contracting Parties;

(c) the Secretariat is invited to participate;

(d) a report on the outcome of the workshop is submitted to the appropriate main committee or working group.

78. If a Contracting Party is more than 12 months in arrears with its contribution to the budget:

(a) this shall be mentioned in the annual report;

(b) its delegates shall not be eligible to be Chairman or Vice-Chairman of the Commission or any subsidiary body.

79. The Commission shall decide what other action shall be taken in respect of a Contracting Party more than 12 months in arrears with its contribution.

80. The Financial Regulations of the Commission are set out in Annex 1.

81. The principles and arrangements set out in Annex 3 shall be applied to all decisions on the release of monitoring data held by, or on behalf of, OSPAR.

82. These Rules including their annexes may be amended at any meeting of the Commission by a unanimous vote of the Contracting Parties present and voting at the meeting. Proposals for amendment of these Rules shall be circulated to Contracting Parties at least five weeks before a meeting of the Commission.

11 Disarmament, Arms Control, Non-Proliferation

57 Convention on the Prohibition of the Development, Production and Stockpiling of Bacteriological (Biological) and Toxin Weapons and on Their Destruction

Date: 10 April 1972
Source: 1015 UNTS 163
https://front.un-arm.org/wp-content/uploads/2020/12/BWC-text-English-1.pdf

…

ARTICLE V

The States Parties to this Convention undertake to consult one another and to cooperate in solving any problems which may arise in relation to the objective of, or in the application of the provisions of, the Convention. Consultation and cooperation pursuant to this Article may also be undertaken through appropriate international procedures within the framework of the United Nations and in accordance with its Charter.

ARTICLE VI

1. Any State Party to this Convention which finds that any other State Party is acting in breach of obligations deriving from the provisions of the Convention may lodge a complaint with the Security Council of the United Nations. Such a complaint should include all possible evidence confirming its validity, as well as a request for its consideration by the Security Council.

2. Each State Party to this Convention undertakes to cooperate in carrying out any investigation which the Security Council may initiate, in accordance with the provisions of the Charter of the United Nations, on the basis of the complaint received by the Council. The Security Council shall inform the States Parties to the Convention of the results of the investigation.

ARTICLE VII

Each State Party to this Convention undertakes to provide or support assistance, in accordance with the United Nations Charter, to any Party to the Convention which so requests, if the Security Council decides that such Party has been exposed to danger a result of violation of the Convention.

…

The Chemical Weapons Convention Framework

58.a Convention on the Prohibition of the Development, Production, Stockpiling and Use of Chemical Weapons and on Their Destruction

Date: 13 January 1993
Source: 1974 UNTS 317
http://www.opcw.org/chemical-weapons-convention/download-the-cwc/

...

ARTICLE IX CONSULTATIONS, COOPERATION AND FACT-FINDING

1. States Parties shall consult and cooperate, directly among themselves, or through the Organization or other appropriate international procedures, including procedures within the framework of the United Nations and in accordance with its Charter, on any matter which may be raised relating to the object and purpose, or the implementation of the provisions, of this Convention.

2. Without prejudice to the right of any State Party to request a challenge inspection, States Parties should, whenever possible, first make every effort to clarify and resolve, through exchange of information and consultations among themselves, any matter which may cause doubt about compliance with this Convention, or which gives rise to concerns about a related matter which may be considered ambiguous. A State Party which receives a request from another State Party for clarification of any matter which the requesting State Party believes causes such a doubt or concern shall provide the requesting State Party as soon as possible, but in any case not later than 10 days after the request, with information sufficient to answer the doubt or concern raised along with an explanation of how the information provided resolves the matter. Nothing in this Convention shall affect the right of any two or more States Parties to arrange by mutual consent for inspections or any other procedures among themselves to clarify and resolve any matter which may cause doubt about compliance or gives rise to a concern about a related matter which may be considered ambiguous. Such arrangements shall not affect the rights and obligations of any State Party under other provisions of this Convention.

Procedure for requesting clarification

3. A State Party shall have the right to request the Executive Council to assist in clarifying any situation which may be considered ambiguous or which gives rise to a concern about the possible noncompliance of another State Party with this Convention. The Executive Council shall provide appropriate information in its possession relevant to such a concern.

4. A State Party shall have the right to request the Executive Council to obtain clarification from another State Party on any situation which may be considered ambiguous or which gives rise to a concern about its possible noncompliance with this Convention. In such a case, the following shall apply:

(a) The Executive Council shall forward the request for clarification to the State Party concerned through the Director General not later than 24 hours after its receipt;

(b) The requested State Party shall provide the clarification to the Executive Council as soon as possible, but in any case not later than 10 days after the receipt of the request;

(c) The Executive Council shall take note of the clarification and forward it to the requesting State Party not later than 24 hours after its receipt;
(d) If the requesting State Party deems the clarification to be inadequate, it shall have the right to request the Executive Council to obtain from the requested State Party further clarification;
(e) For the purpose of obtaining further clarification requested under subparagraph (d), the Executive Council may call on the Director General to establish a group of experts from the Technical Secretariat, or if appropriate staff are not available in the Technical Secretariat, from elsewhere, to examine all available information and data relevant to the situation causing the concern. The group of experts shall submit a factual report to the Executive Council on its findings;
(f) If the requesting State Party considers the clarification obtained under subparagraphs (d) and (e) to be unsatisfactory, it shall have the right to request a special session of the Executive Council in which States Parties involved that are not members of the Executive Council shall be entitled to take part. In such a special session, the Executive Council shall consider the matter and may recommend any measure it deems appropriate to resolve the situation.

5. A State Party shall also have the right to request the Executive Council to clarify any situation which has been considered ambiguous or has given rise to a concern about its possible noncompliance with this Convention. The Executive Council shall respond by providing such assistance as appropriate.

6. The Executive Council shall inform the States Parties about any request for clarification provided in this Article.

7. If the doubt or concern of a State Party about a possible noncompliance has not been resolved within 60 days after the submission of the request for clarification to the Executive Council, or it believes its doubts warrant urgent consideration, notwithstanding its right to request a challenge inspection, it may request a special session of the Conference in accordance with Article VIII, paragraph 12 (c). At such a special session, the Conference shall consider the matter and may recommend any measure it deems appropriate to resolve the situation.

Procedures for challenge inspections

8. Each State Party has the right to request an onsite challenge inspection of any facility or location in the territory or in any other place under the jurisdiction or control of any other State Party for the sole purpose of clarifying and resolving any questions concerning possible noncompliance with the provisions of this Convention, and to have this inspection conducted anywhere without delay by an inspection team designated by the Director General and in accordance with the Verification Annex.

9. Each State Party is under the obligation to keep the inspection request within the scope of this Convention and to provide in the inspection request all appropriate information on the basis of which a concern has arisen regarding possible noncompliance with this Convention as specified in the Verification Annex. Each State Party shall refrain from unfounded inspection requests, care being taken to avoid abuse. The challenge inspection shall be carried out for the sole purpose of determining facts relating to the possible noncompliance.

10. For the purpose of verifying compliance with the provisions of this Convention, each State Party shall permit the Technical Secretariat to conduct the onsite challenge inspection pursuant to paragraph 8.

11. Pursuant to a request for a challenge inspection of a facility or location, and in accordance with the procedures provided for in the Verification Annex, the inspected State Party shall have:

(a) The right and the obligation to make every reasonable effort to demonstrate its compliance with this Convention and, to this end, to enable the inspection team to fulfil its mandate;
(b) The obligation to provide access within the requested site for the sole purpose of establishing facts relevant to the concern regarding possible noncompliance; and
(c) The right to take measures to protect sensitive installations, and to prevent disclosure of confidential information and data, not related to this Convention.

12. With regard to an observer, the following shall apply:

(a) The requesting State Party may, subject to the agreement of the inspected State Party, send a representative who may be a national either of the requesting State Party or of a third State Party, to observe the conduct of the challenge inspection.
(b) The inspected State Party shall then grant access to the observer in accordance with the Verification Annex.
(c) The inspected State Party shall, as a rule, accept the proposed observer, but if the inspected State Party exercises a refusal, that fact shall be recorded in the final report.

13. The requesting State Party shall present an inspection request for an onsite challenge inspection to the Executive Council and at the same time to the Director General for immediate processing.

14. The Director-General shall immediately ascertain that the inspection request meets the requirements specified in Part X, paragraph 4, of the Verification Annex, and, if necessary, assist the requesting State Party in filing the inspection request accordingly. When the inspection request fulfils the requirements, preparations for the challenge inspection shall begin.

15. The Director-General shall transmit the inspection request to the inspected State Party not less than 12 hours before the planned arrival of the inspection team at the point of entry.

16. After having received the inspection request, the Executive Council shall take cognizance of the Director-General's actions on the request and shall keep the case under its consideration throughout the inspection procedure. However, its deliberations shall not delay the inspection process.

17. The Executive Council may, not later than 12 hours after having received the inspection request, decide by a three-quarter majority of all its members against carrying out the challenge inspection, if it considers the inspection request to be frivolous, abusive or clearly beyond the scope of this Convention as described in paragraph 8. Neither the requesting nor the inspected State Party shall participate in such a decision. If the Executive Council decides against the challenge inspection, preparations shall be stopped, no further action on the inspection request shall be taken, and the States Parties concerned shall be informed accordingly.

18. The Director-General shall issue an inspection mandate for the conduct of the challenge inspection. The inspection mandate shall be the inspection request referred to in paragraphs 8 and 9 put into operational terms, and shall conform with the inspection request.

19. The challenge inspection shall be conducted in accordance with Part X or, in the case of alleged use, in accordance with Part XI of the Verification Annex. The inspection team

shall be guided by the principle of conducting the challenge inspection in the least intrusive manner possible, consistent with the effective and timely accomplishment of its mission.

20. The inspected State Party shall assist the inspection team throughout the challenge inspection and facilitate its task. If the inspected State Party proposes, pursuant to Part X, Section C, of the Verification Annex, arrangements to demonstrate compliance with this Convention, alternative to full and comprehensive access, it shall make every reasonable effort, through consultations with the inspection team, to reach agreement on the modalities for establishing the facts with the aim of demonstrating its compliance.

21. The final report shall contain the factual findings as well as an assessment by the inspection team of the degree and nature of access and cooperation granted for the satisfactory implementation of the challenge inspection. The Director-General shall promptly transmit the final report of the inspection team to the requesting State Party, to the inspected State Party, to the Executive Council and to all other States Parties. The Director General shall further transmit promptly to the Executive Council the assessments of the requesting and of the inspected States Parties, as well as the views of other States Parties which may be conveyed to the Director General for that purpose, and then provide them to all States Parties.

22. The Executive Council shall, in accordance with its powers and functions, review the final report of the inspection team as soon as it is presented, and address any concerns as to:

(a) Whether any noncompliance has occurred;

(b) Whether the request had been within the scope of this Convention; and

(c) Whether the right to request a challenge inspection had been abused.

23. If the Executive Council reaches the conclusion, in keeping with its powers and functions, that further action may be necessary with regard to paragraph 22, it shall take the appropriate measures to redress the situation and to ensure compliance with this Convention, including specific recommendations to the Conference. In the case of abuse, the Executive Council shall examine whether the requesting State Party should bear any of the financial implications of the challenge inspection.

24. The requesting State Party and the inspected State Party shall have the right to participate in the review process. The Executive Council shall inform the States Parties and the next session of the Conference of the outcome of the process.

25. If the Executive Council has made specific recommendations to the Conference, the Conference shall consider action in accordance with Article XII.

...

ARTICLE XII MEASURES TO REDRESS A SITUATION AND TO ENSURE COMPLIANCE, INCLUDING SANCTIONS

1. The Conference shall take the necessary measures, as set forth in paragraphs 2, 3 and 4, to ensure compliance with this Convention and to redress and remedy any situation which contravenes the provisions of this Convention. In considering action pursuant to this paragraph, the Conference shall take into account all information and recommendations on the issues submitted by the Executive Council.

2. In cases where a State Party has been requested by the Executive Council to take measures to redress a situation raising problems with regard to its compliance, and where the State Party fails to fulfil the request within the specified time, the Conference may, *inter alia*, upon the recommendation of the Executive Council, restrict or suspend the State Party's rights and privileges under this Convention until it undertakes the necessary action to conform with its obligations under this Convention.

3. In cases where serious damage to the object and purpose of this Convention may result from activities prohibited under this Convention, in particular by Article I, the Conference may recommend collective measures to States Parties in conformity with international law.

4. The Conference shall, in cases of particular gravity, bring the issue, including relevant information and conclusions, to the attention of the United Nations General Assembly and the United Nations Security Council.

ARTICLE XIV SETTLEMENT OF DISPUTES

1. Disputes that may arise concerning the application or the interpretation of this Convention shall be settled in accordance with the relevant provisions of this Convention and in conformity with the provisions of the Charter of the United Nations.

2. When a dispute arises between two or more States Parties, or between one or more States Parties and the Organization, relating to the interpretation or application of this Convention, the parties concerned shall consult together with a view to the expeditious settlement of the dispute by negotiation or by other peaceful means of the parties' choice, including recourse to appropriate organs of this Convention and, by mutual consent, referral to the International Court of Justice in conformity with the Statute of the Court. The States Parties involved shall keep the Executive Council informed of actions being taken.

3. The Executive Council may contribute to the settlement of a dispute by whatever means it deems appropriate, including offering its good offices, calling upon the States Parties to a dispute to start the settlement process of their choice and recommending a timelimit for any agreed procedure.

4. The Conference shall consider questions related to disputes raised by States Parties or brought to its attention by the Executive Council. The Conference shall, as it finds necessary, establish or entrust organs with tasks related to the settlement of these disputes in conformity with Article VIII, paragraph 21 (f).

5. The Conference and the Executive Council are separately empowered, subject to authorization from the General Assembly of the United Nations, to request the International Court of Justice to give an advisory opinion on any legal question arising within the scope of the activities of the Organization. An agreement between the Organization and the United Nations shall be concluded for this purpose in accordance with Article VIII, paragraph 34 (a).

6. This Article is without prejudice to Article IX or to the provisions on measures to redress a situation and to ensure compliance, including sanctions.

...

58.b Annex on Implementation and Verification

Date: 13 January 1993
Source: http://www.opcw.org/chemical-weapons-convention/verification-annex/

...

Part X. Challenge Inspections Pursuant to Article IX
A. Designation and Selection of Inspectors and Inspection

1. Challenge inspections pursuant to Article IX shall only be performed by inspectors and inspection assistants especially designated for this function. In order to designate

inspectors and inspection assistants for challenge inspections pursuant to Article IX, the Director General shall, by selecting inspectors and inspection assistants from among the inspectors and inspection assistants for routine inspection activities, establish a list of proposed inspectors and inspection assistants. It shall comprise a sufficiently large number of inspectors and inspection assistants having the necessary qualification, experience, skill and training, to allow for flexibility in the selection of the inspectors, taking into account their availability, and the need for rotation. Due regard shall be paid also to the importance of selecting inspectors and inspection assistants on as wide a geographical basis as possible. The designation of inspectors and inspection assistants shall follow the procedures provided for under Part II, Section A, of this Annex.

2. The Director-General shall determine the size of the inspection team and select its members taking into account the circumstances of a particular request. The size of the inspection team shall be kept to a minimum necessary for the proper fulfilment of the inspection mandate. No national of the requesting State Party or the inspected State Party shall be a member of the inspection team.

B. Pre-Inspection Activities

3. Before submitting the inspection request for a challenge inspection, the State Party may seek confirmation from the Director-General that the Technical Secretariat is in a position to take immediate action on the request. If the Director-General cannot provide such confirmation immediately, he shall do so at the earliest opportunity, in keeping with the order of requests for confirmation. He shall also keep the State Party informed of when it is likely that immediate action can be taken. Should the Director-General reach the conclusion that timely action on requests can no longer be taken, he may ask the Executive Council to take appropriate action to improve the situation in the future.

Notification

4. The inspection request for a challenge inspection to be submitted to the Executive Council and the Director-General shall contain at least the following information:

(a) The State Party to be inspected and, if applicable, the Host State;
(b) The point of entry to be used;
(c) The size and type of the inspection site;
(d) The concern regarding possible non compliance with this Convention including a specification of the relevant provisions of this Convention about which the concern has arisen, and of the nature and circumstances of the possible non compliance as well as all appropriate information on the basis of which the concern has arisen; and
(e) The name of the observer of the requesting State Party.

The requesting State Party may submit any additional information it deems necessary.

5. The Director-General shall within one hour acknowledge to the requesting State Party receipt of its request.

6. The requesting State Party shall notify the Director-General of the location of the inspection site in due time for the Director-General to be able to provide this information to the inspected State Party not less than 12 hours before the planned arrival of the inspection team at the point of entry.

7. The inspection site shall be designated by the requesting State Party as specifically as possible by providing a site diagram related to a reference point with geographic coordinates, specified to the nearest second if possible. If possible, the requesting State

Party shall also provide a map with a general indication of the inspection site and a diagram specifying as precisely as possible the requested perimeter of the site to be inspected.

8. The requested perimeter shall:

(a) Run at least a 10 metre distance outside any buildings or other structures;

(b) Not cut through existing security enclosures; and

(c) Run at least a 10 metre distance outside any existing security enclosures that the requesting State Party intends to include within the requested perimeter.

9. If the requested perimeter does not conform with the specifications of paragraph 8, it shall be redrawn by the inspection team so as to conform with that provision.

10. The Director-General shall, not less than 12 hours before the planned arrival of the inspection team at the point of entry, inform the Executive Council about the location of the inspection site as specified in paragraph 7.

11. Contemporaneously with informing the Executive Council according to paragraph 10, the Director-General shall transmit the inspection request to the inspected State Party including the location of the inspection site as specified in paragraph 7. This notification shall also include the information specified in Part II, paragraph 32, of this Annex.

12. Upon arrival of the inspection team at the point of entry, the inspected State Party shall be informed by the inspection team of the inspection mandate.

Entry into the territory of the inspected State Party or the Host State

13. The Director-General shall, in accordance with Article IX, paragraphs 13 to 18, dispatch an inspection team as soon as possible after an inspection request has been received. The inspection team shall arrive at the point of entry specified in the request in the minimum time possible, consistent with the provisions of paragraphs 10 and 11.

14. If the requested perimeter is acceptable to the inspected State Party, it shall be designated as the final perimeter as early as possible, but in no case later than 24 hours after the arrival of the inspection team at the point of entry. The inspected State Party shall transport the inspection team to the final perimeter of the inspection site. If the inspected State Party deems it necessary, such transportation may begin up to 12 hours before the expiry of the time period specified in this paragraph for the designation of the final perimeter. Transportation shall, in any case, be completed not later than 36 hours after the arrival of the inspection team at the point of entry.

15. For all declared facilities, the procedures in subparagraphs (a) and (b) shall apply. (For the purposes of this Part, "declared facility" means all facilities declared pursuant to Articles III, IV, and V. With regard to Article VI, "declared facility" means only facilities declared pursuant to Part VI of this Annex, as well as declared plants specified by declarations pursuant to Part VII, paragraphs 7 and 10 (c), and Part VIII, paragraphs 7 and 10 (c), of this Annex.)

(a) If the requested perimeter is contained within or conforms with the declared perimeter, the declared perimeter shall be considered the final perimeter. The final perimeter may, however, if agreed by the inspected State Party, be made smaller in order to conform with the perimeter requested by the requesting State Party.

(b) The inspected State Party shall transport the inspection team to the final perimeter as soon as practicable, but in any case shall ensure their arrival at the perimeter not later than 24 hours after the arrival of the inspection team at the point of entry.

Alternative determination of final perimeter

16. At the point of entry, if the inspected State Party cannot accept the requested perimeter, it shall propose an alternative perimeter as soon as possible, but in any case not

later than 24 hours after the arrival of the inspection team at the point of entry. In case of differences of opinion, the inspected State Party and the inspection team shall engage in negotiations with the aim of reaching agreement on a final perimeter.

17. The alternative perimeter should be designated as specifically as possible in accordance with paragraph 8. It shall include the whole of the requested perimeter and should, as a rule, bear a close relationship to the latter, taking into account natural terrain features and man made boundaries. It should normally run close to the surrounding security barrier if such a barrier exists. The inspected State Party should seek to establish such a relationship between the perimeters by a combination of at least two of the following means:

(a) An alternative perimeter that does not extend to an area significantly greater than that of the requested perimeter;

(b) An alternative perimeter that is a short, uniform distance from the requested perimeter;

(c) At least part of the requested perimeter is visible from the alternative perimeter.

18. If the alternative perimeter is acceptable to the inspection team, it shall become the final perimeter and the inspection team shall be transported from the point of entry to that perimeter. If the inspected State Party deems it necessary, such transportation may begin up to 12 hours before the expiry of the time period specified in paragraph 16 for proposing an alternative perimeter. Transportation shall, in any case, be completed not later than 36 hours after the arrival of the inspection team at the point of entry.

19. If a final perimeter is not agreed, the perimeter negotiations shall be concluded as early as possible, but in no case shall they continue more than 24 hours after the arrival of the inspection team at the point of entry. If no agreement is reached, the inspected State Party shall transport the inspection team to a location at the alternative perimeter. If the inspected State Party deems it necessary, such transportation may begin up to 12 hours before the expiry of the time period specified in paragraph 16 for proposing an alternative perimeter. Transportation shall, in any case, be completed not later than 36 hours after the arrival of the inspection team at the point of entry.

20. Once at the location, the inspected State Party shall provide the inspection team with prompt access to the alternative perimeter to facilitate negotiations and agreement on the final perimeter and access within the final perimeter.

21. If no agreement is reached within 72 hours after the arrival of the inspection team at the location, the alternative perimeter shall be designated the final perimeter.

Verification of location

22. To help establish that the inspection site to which the inspection team has been transported corresponds to the inspection site specified by the requesting State Party, the inspection team shall have the right to use approved location finding equipment and have such equipment installed according to its directions. The inspection team may verify its location by reference to local landmarks identified from maps. The inspected State Party shall assist the inspection team in this task.

Securing the site, exit monitoring

23. Not later than 12 hours after the arrival of the inspection team at the point of entry, the inspected State Party shall begin collecting factual information of all vehicular exit activity from all exit points for all land, air, and water vehicles of the requested perimeter. It shall provide this information to the inspection team upon its arrival at the alternative or final perimeter, whichever occurs first.

24. This obligation may be met by collecting factual information in the form of traffic logs, photographs, video recordings, or data from chemical evidence equipment provided by the inspection team to monitor such exit activity. Alternatively, the inspected State Party may also meet this obligation by allowing one or more members of the inspection team independently to maintain traffic logs, take photographs, make video recordings of exit traffic, or use chemical evidence equipment, and conduct other activities as may be agreed between the inspected State Party and the inspection team.

25. Upon the inspection team's arrival at the alternative perimeter or final perimeter, whichever occurs first, securing the site, which means exit monitoring procedures by the inspection team, shall begin.

26. Such procedures shall include: the identification of vehicular exits, the making of traffic logs, the taking of photographs, and the making of video recordings by the inspection team of exits and exit traffic. The inspection team has the right to go, under escort, to any other part of the perimeter to check that there is no other exit activity.

27. Additional procedures for exit monitoring activities as agreed upon by the inspection team and the inspected State Party may include, inter alia:

(a) Use of sensors;
(b) Random selective access;
(c) Sample analysis.

28. All activities for securing the site and exit monitoring shall take place within a band around the outside of the perimeter, not exceeding 50 metres in width, measured outward.

29. The inspection team has the right to inspect on a managed access basis vehicular traffic exiting the site. The inspected State Party shall make every reasonable effort to demonstrate to the inspection team that any vehicle, subject to inspection, to which the inspection team is not granted full access, is not being used for purposes related to the possible non compliance concerns raised in the inspection request.

30. Personnel and vehicles entering and personnel and personal passenger vehicles exiting the site are not subject to inspection.

31. The application of the above procedures may continue for the duration of the inspection, but may not unreasonably hamper or delay the normal operation of the facility.

Pre-inspection briefing and inspection plan

32. To facilitate development of an inspection plan, the inspected State Party shall provide a safety and logistical briefing to the inspection team prior to access.

33. The pre-inspection briefing shall be held in accordance with Part II, paragraph 37, of this Annex. In the course of the pre-inspection briefing, the inspected State Party may indicate to the inspection team the equipment, documentation, or areas it considers sensitive and not related to the purpose of the challenge inspection. In addition, personnel responsible for the site shall brief the inspection team on the physical layout and other relevant characteristics of the site. The inspection team shall be provided with a map or sketch drawn to scale showing all structures and significant geographic features at the site. The inspection team shall also be briefed on the availability of facility personnel and records.

34. After the pre-inspection briefing, the inspection team shall prepare, on the basis of the information available and appropriate to it, an initial inspection plan which specifies the activities to be carried out by the inspection team, including the specific areas of the site to which access is desired. The inspection plan shall also specify whether the inspection team will be divided into subgroups. The inspection plan shall be made available to the

representatives of the inspected State Party and the inspection site. Its implementation shall be consistent with the provisions of Section C, including those related to access and activities.

Perimeter activities

35. Upon the inspection team's arrival at the final or alternative perimeter, whichever occurs first, the team shall have the right to commence immediately perimeter activities in accordance with the procedures set forth under this Section, and to continue these activities until the completion of the challenge inspection.

36. In conducting the perimeter activities, the inspection team shall have the right to:

(a) Use monitoring instruments in accordance with Part II, paragraphs 27 to 30, of this Annex;

(b) Take wipes, air, soil or effluent samples; and

(c) Conduct any additional activities which may be agreed between the inspection team and the inspected State Party.

37. The perimeter activities of the inspection team may be conducted within a band around the outside of the perimeter up to 50 metres in width measured outward from the perimeter. If the inspected State Party agrees, the inspection team may also have access to any building or structure within the perimeter band. All directional monitoring shall be oriented inward. For declared facilities, at the discretion of the inspected State Party, the band could run inside, outside, or on both sides of the declared perimeter.

C. Conduct of Inspections

General rules

38. The inspected State Party shall provide access within the requested perimeter as well as, if different, the final perimeter. The extent and nature of access to a particular place or places within these perimeters shall be negotiated between the inspection team and the inspected State Party on a managed access basis.

39. The inspected State Party shall provide access within the requested perimeter as soon as possible, but in any case not later than 108 hours after the arrival of the inspection team at the point of entry in order to clarify the concern regarding possible non compliance with this Convention raised in the inspection request.

40. Upon the request of the inspection team, the inspected State Party may provide aerial access to the inspection site.

41. In meeting the requirement to provide access as specified in paragraph 38, the inspected State Party shall be under the obligation to allow the greatest degree of access taking into account any constitutional obligations it may have with regard to proprietary rights or searches and seizures. The inspected State Party has the right under managed access to take such measures as are necessary to protect national security. The provisions in this paragraph may not be invoked by the inspected State Party to conceal evasion of its obligations not to engage in activities prohibited under this Convention.

42. If the inspected State Party provides less than full access to places, activities, or information, it shall be under the obligation to make every reasonable effort to provide alternative means to clarify the possible non compliance concern that generated the challenge inspection.

43. Upon arrival at the final perimeter of facilities declared pursuant to Articles IV, V and VI, access shall be granted following the pre inspection briefing and discussion of the inspection plan which shall be limited to the minimum necessary and in any event shall

not exceed three hours. For facilities declared pursuant to Article III, paragraph 1 (d), negotiations shall be conducted and managed access commenced not later than 12 hours after arrival at the final perimeter.

44. In carrying out the challenge inspection in accordance with the inspection request, the inspection team shall use only those methods necessary to provide sufficient relevant facts to clarify the concern about possible non compliance with the provisions of this Convention, and shall refrain from activities not relevant thereto. It shall collect and document such facts as are related to the possible non compliance with this Convention by the inspected State Party, but shall neither seek nor document information which is clearly not related thereto, unless the inspected State Party expressly requests it to do so. Any material collected and subsequently found not to be relevant shall not be retained.

45. The inspection team shall be guided by the principle of conducting the challenge inspection in the least intrusive manner possible, consistent with the effective and timely accomplishment of its mission. Wherever possible, it shall begin with the least intrusive procedures it deems acceptable and proceed to more intrusive procedures only as it deems necessary.

Managed access

46. The inspection team shall take into consideration suggested modifications of the inspection plan and proposals which may be made by the inspected State Party, at whatever stage of the inspection including the pre inspection briefing, to ensure that sensitive equipment, information or areas, not related to chemical weapons, are protected.

47. The inspected State Party shall designate the perimeter entry/exit points to be used for access. The inspection team and the inspected State Party shall negotiate: the extent of access to any particular place or places within the final and requested perimeters as provided in paragraph 48; the particular inspection activities, including sampling, to be conducted by the inspection team; the performance of particular activities by the inspected State Party; and the provision of particular information by the inspected State Party.

48. In conformity with the relevant provisions in the Confidentiality Annex the inspected State Party shall have the right to take measures to protect sensitive installations and prevent disclosure of confidential information and data not related to chemical weapons. Such measures may include, inter alia:

(a) Removal of sensitive papers from office spaces;
(b) Shrouding of sensitive displays, stores, and equipment;
(c) Shrouding of sensitive pieces of equipment, such as computer or electronic systems;
(d) Logging off of computer systems and turning off of data indicating devices;
(e) Restriction of sample analysis to presence or absence of chemicals listed in Schedules 1, 2 and 3 or appropriate degradation products;
(f) Using random selective access techniques whereby the inspectors are requested to select a given percentage or number of buildings of their choice to inspect; the same principle can apply to the interior and content of sensitive buildings;
(g) In exceptional cases, giving only individual inspectors access to certain parts of the inspection site.

49. The inspected State Party shall make every reasonable effort to demonstrate to the inspection team that any object, building, structure, container or vehicle to which the inspection team has not had full access, or which has been protected in accordance with paragraph 48, is not used for purposes related to the possible non compliance concerns raised in the inspection request.

50. This may be accomplished by means of, inter alia, the partial removal of a shroud or environmental protection cover, at the discretion of the inspected State Party, by means of a visual inspection of the interior of an enclosed space from its entrance, or by other methods.

51. In the case of facilities declared pursuant to Articles IV, V and VI, the following shall apply:

(a) For facilities with facility agreements, access and activities within the final perimeter shall be unimpeded within the boundaries established by the agreements;

(b) For facilities without facility agreements, negotiation of access and activities shall be governed by the applicable general inspection guidelines established under this Convention;

(c) Access beyond that granted for inspections under Articles IV, V and VI shall be managed in accordance with procedures of this section.

52. In the case of facilities declared pursuant to Article III, paragraph 1 (d), the following shall apply: if the inspected State Party, using procedures of paragraphs 47 and 48, has not granted full access to areas or structures not related to chemical weapons, it shall make every reasonable effort to demonstrate to the inspection team that such areas or structures are not used for purposes related to the possible non compliance concerns raised in the inspection request.

Observer

53. In accordance with the provisions of Article IX, paragraph 12, on the participation of an observer in the challenge inspection, the requesting State Party shall liaise with the Technical Secretariat to coordinate the arrival of the observer at the same point of entry as the inspection team within a reasonable period of the inspection team's arrival.

54. The observer shall have the right throughout the period of inspection to be in communication with the embassy of the requesting State Party located in the inspected State Party or in the Host State or, in the case of absence of an embassy, with the requesting State Party itself. The inspected State Party shall provide means of communication to the observer.

55. The observer shall have the right to arrive at the alternative or final perimeter of the inspection site, wherever the inspection team arrives first, and to have access to the inspection site as granted by the inspected State Party. The observer shall have the right to make recommendations to the inspection team, which the team shall take into account to the extent it deems appropriate. Throughout the inspection, the inspection team shall keep the observer informed about the conduct of the inspection and the findings.

56. Throughout the in country period, the inspected State Party shall provide or arrange for the amenities necessary for the observer such as communication means, interpretation services, transportation, working space, lodging, meals and medical care. All the costs in connection with the stay of the observer on the territory of the inspected State Party or the Host State shall be borne by the requesting State Party.

Duration of inspection

57. The period of inspection shall not exceed 84 hours, unless extended by agreement with the inspected State Party.

D. Post-Inspection Activities

Departure

58. Upon completion of the post-inspection procedures at the inspection site, the inspection team and the observer of the requesting State Party shall proceed promptly to a point of entry and shall then leave the territory of the inspected State Party in the minimum time possible.

Reports

59. The inspection report shall summarize in a general way the activities conducted by the inspection team and the factual findings of the inspection team, particularly with regard to the concerns regarding possible non-compliance with this Convention cited in the request for the challenge inspection, and shall be limited to information directly related to this Convention. It shall also include an assessment by the inspection team of the degree and nature of access and cooperation granted to the inspectors and the extent to which this enabled them to fulfil the inspection mandate. Detailed information relating to the concerns regarding possible non-compliance with this Convention cited in the request for the challenge inspection shall be submitted as an Appendix to the final report and be retained within the Technical Secretariat under appropriate safeguards to protect sensitive information.

60. The inspection team shall, not later than 72 hours after its return to its primary work location, submit a preliminary inspection report, having taken into account, inter alia, paragraph 17 of the Confidentiality Annex, to the Director-General. The Director-General shall promptly transmit the preliminary inspection report to the requesting State Party, the inspected State Party and to the Executive Council.

61. A draft final inspection report shall be made available to the inspected State Party not later than 20 days after the completion of the challenge inspection. The inspected State Party has the right to identify any information and data not related to chemical weapons which should, in its view, due to its confidential character, not be circulated outside the Technical Secretariat. The Technical Secretariat shall consider proposals for changes to the draft final inspection report made by the inspected State Party and, using its own discretion, wherever possible, adopt them. The final report shall then be submitted not later than 30 days after the completion of the challenge inspection to the Director-General for further distribution and consideration in accordance with Article IX, paragraphs 21 to 25.

Part XI. Investigations in Cases of Alleged Use of Chemical Weapons

A. General

1. Investigations of alleged use of chemical weapons, or of alleged use of riot control agents as a method of warfare, initiated pursuant to Articles IX or X, shall be conducted in accordance with this Annex and detailed procedures to be established by the Director-General.

2. The following additional provisions address specific procedures required in cases of alleged use of chemical weapons.

B. Pre-Inspection Activities

Request for an investigation

3. The request for an investigation of an alleged use of chemical weapons to be submitted to the Director-General, to the extent possible, should include the following information:

(a) The State Party on whose territory use of chemical weapons is alleged to have taken place;

(b) The point of entry or other suggested safe routes of access;

(c) Location and characteristics of the areas where chemical weapons are alleged to have been used;

(d) When chemical weapons are alleged to have been used;
(e) Types of chemical weapons believed to have been used;
(f) Extent of alleged use;
(g) Characteristics of the possible toxic chemicals;
(h) Effects on humans, animals and vegetation;
(i) Request for specific assistance, if applicable.

4. The State Party which has requested an investigation may submit at any time any additional information it deems necessary.

Notification

5. The Director-General shall immediately acknowledge receipt to the requesting State Party of its request and inform the Executive Council and all States Parties.

6. If applicable, the Director-General shall notify the State Party on whose territory an investigation has been requested. The Director-General shall also notify other States Parties if access to their territories might be required during the investigation.

Assignment of inspection team

7. The Director-General shall prepare a list of qualified experts whose particular field of expertise could be required in an investigation of alleged use of chemical weapons and constantly keep this list updated. This list shall be communicated, in writing, to each State Party not later than 30 days after entry into force of this Convention and after each change to the list. Any qualified expert included in this list shall be regarded as designated unless a State Party, not later than 30 days after its receipt of the list, declares its non-acceptance in writing.

8. The Director-General shall select the leader and members of an inspection team from the inspectors and inspection assistants already designated for challenge inspections taking into account the circumstances and specific nature of a particular request. In addition, members of the inspection team may be selected from the list of qualified experts when, in the view of the Director-General, expertise not available among inspectors already designated is required for the proper conduct of a particular investigation.

9. When briefing the inspection team, the Director-General shall include any additional information provided by the requesting State Party, or any other sources, to ensure that the inspection can be carried out in the most effective and expedient manner.

Dispatch of inspection team

10. Immediately upon the receipt of a request for an investigation of alleged use of chemical weapons the Director-General shall, through contacts with the relevant States Parties, request and confirm arrangements for the safe reception of the team.

11. The Director-General shall dispatch the team at the earliest opportunity, taking into account the safety of the team.

12. If the inspection team has not been dispatched within 24 hours from the receipt of the request, the Director-General shall inform the Executive Council and the States Parties concerned about the reasons for the delay.

Briefings

13. The inspection team shall have the right to be briefed by representatives of the inspected State Party upon arrival and at any time during the inspection.

14. Before the commencement of the inspection the inspection team shall prepare an inspection plan to serve, inter alia, as a basis for logistic and safety arrangements. The inspection plan shall be updated as need arises.

C. Conduct of Inspections

Access

15. The inspection team shall have the right of access to any and all areas which could be affected by the alleged use of chemical weapons. It shall also have the right of access to hospitals, refugee camps and other locations it deems relevant to the effective investigation of the alleged use of chemical weapons. For such access, the inspection team shall consult with the inspected State Party.

Sampling

16. The inspection team shall have the right to collect samples of types, and in quantities it considers necessary. If the inspection team deems it necessary, and if so requested by it, the inspected State Party shall assist in the collection of samples under the supervision of inspectors or inspection assistants. The inspected State Party shall also permit and cooperate in the collection of appropriate control samples from areas neighbouring the site of the alleged use and from other areas as requested by the inspection team.

17. Samples of importance in the investigation of alleged use include toxic chemicals, munitions and devices, remnants of munitions and devices, environmental samples (air, soil, vegetation, water, snow, etc.) and biomedical samples from human or animal sources (blood, urine, excreta, tissue etc.).

18. If duplicate samples cannot be taken and the analysis is performed at off-site laboratories, any remaining sample shall, if so requested, be returned to the inspected State Party after the completion of the analysis.

Extension of inspection site

19. If the inspection team during an inspection deems it necessary to extend the investigation into a neighbouring State Party, the Director-General shall notify that State Party about the need for access to its territory and request and confirm arrangements for the safe reception of the team.

Extension of inspection duration

20. If the inspection team deems that safe access to a specific area relevant to the investigation is not possible, the requesting State Party shall be informed immediately. If necessary, the period of inspection shall be extended until safe access can be provided and the inspection team will have concluded its mission.

Interviews

21. The inspection team shall have the right to interview and examine persons who may have been affected by the alleged use of chemical weapons. It shall also have the right to interview eyewitnesses of the alleged use of chemical weapons and medical personnel, and other persons who have treated or have come into contact with persons who may have been affected by the alleged use of chemical weapons. The inspection team shall have access to medical histories, if available, and be permitted to participate in autopsies, as appropriate, of persons who may have been affected by the alleged use of chemical weapons.

D. Reports

Procedures

22. The inspection team shall, not later than 24 hours after its arrival on the territory of the inspected State Party, send a situation report to the Director-General. It shall further throughout the investigation send progress reports as necessary.

23. The inspection team shall, not later than 72 hours after its return to its primary work location, submit a preliminary report to the Director-General. The final report shall be submitted to the Director-General not later than 30 days after its return to its primary work location. The Director-General shall promptly transmit the preliminary and final reports to the Executive Council and to all States Parties.

Contents

24. The situation report shall indicate any urgent need for assistance and any other relevant information. The progress reports shall indicate any further need for assistance that might be identified during the course of the investigation.

25. The final report shall summarize the factual findings of the inspection, particularly with regard to the alleged use cited in the request. In addition, a report of an investigation of an alleged use shall include a description of the investigation process, tracing its various stages, with special reference to:

(a) The locations and time of sampling and on-site analyses; and
(b) Supporting evidence, such as the records of interviews, the results of medical examinations and scientific analyses, and the documents examined by the inspection team.

26. If the inspection team collects through, inter alia, identification of any impurities or other substances during laboratory analysis of samples taken, any information in the course of its investigation that might serve to identify the origin of any chemical weapons used, that information shall be included in the report.

E. States Not Party to this Convention

27. In the case of alleged use of chemical weapons involving a State not Party to this Convention or in territory not controlled by a State Party, the Organization shall closely cooperate with the Secretary-General of the United Nations. If so requested, the Organization shall put its resources at the disposal of the Secretary-General of the United Nations.

58.c Summary Report of the Work of the OPCW Fact-Finding Mission in Syria Covering the Period from 3 to 31 May 2014

Date: 16 June 2014
Source: S/1191/2014
https://www.opcw.org/sites/default/files/documents/S_series/2014/en/s-1191-2014_e_.pdf

Introduction

1. With repeated allegations of the use of toxic chemicals for hostile purposes at a number of locations in the Syrian Arab Republic, on 29 April 2014 the Director-General

announced the formation of a Fact-Finding Mission (FFM), "to establish facts surrounding allegations of use of chlorine in the Syrian Arab Republic". The allegations mainly referred to the use of chlorine in a number of provinces that the Syrian Government does not consider to be under its effective control, more specifically, in Hama, Idlib, and Rif Damascus.

2. The Syrian Government, which had given its consent for the FFM, also agreed to the "terms of reference" that would govern its work. Apart from the necessary legal guarantees that would allow the FFM to execute its mandate, including security assurances for areas under governmental control, the terms of reference outlined the activities that the FFM was expected to undertake.

3. The FFM was set up with the full awareness that, being the first OPCW-led mission that would physically cross confrontational lines, it would face unprecedented security risks. The official OPCW press release regarding the FFM stated that "[t]he mission will carry out its work in the most challenging circumstances."

Basis for the FFM

4. While offering a constructive means of clarifying the aforementioned allegations, the establishment of the FFM was based on the general authority of the OPCW Director-General to seek to uphold at all times the object and purpose of the Chemical Weapons Convention; this authority is reinforced in the present instance by the relevant decisions of the OPCW Executive Council and the United Nations Security Council resolution (UNSCR) 2118 (2013); the general endorsement by the Executive Council of the FFM; and its acceptance by the State Party concerned through an exchange of letters on the subject between the Director-General and the Government of the Syrian Arab Republic, dated 1 and 10 May 2014, respectively.

Cooperation with the United Nations

5. Following consultations with the Director-General, on 26 April 2014, the United Nations Secretary-General pledged full support for the FFM by the United Nations. The modalities of this support are outlined in letters between the Director-General and the Secretary-General dated 25 April, and 2 and 5 May.

6. The support by the United Nations encompasses: the provision of safety and security support and advice to the OPCW; the provision of logistical support; and assistance with liaising and coordinating, in particular, with opposition representatives on the security, logistical, and operational aspects of the OPCW FFM, as may be required, for the safe access and movement of OPCW personnel, any accompanying United Nations personnel, and their equipment and samples within the areas to be visited in the Syrian Arab Republic, including liaising with the opposition representatives for the purposes of making available persons for interviews.

7. The FFM received the full cooperation and support of the United Nations, and the staff assigned to work with the Team displayed a high standard of professionalism and commitment.

FFM Strategic Concept of Operations

8. In order to state unambiguously the aims and objectives of the FFM and to create a framework for the FFM's operational concept, planning, and implementation, including the possibility of field visits, an internal document entitled "FFM Strategic Concept of Operations (CONOPS)" was drafted and finalised.

9. The CONOPS describes the establishment by the Director-General of the FFM as signaling "the determination of the OPCW that, despite the difficult security situation prevailing in the SAR, it will take serious notice of allegations of use of chemical weapons. By making every effort to bring to light the facts surrounding these allegations, the international community can bring to bear its influence on those who might consider such actions immune from censure".

The Non-Proliferation Treaty Framework

59.a Treaty on the Non-Proliferation of Nuclear Weapons

Date: 1 July 1968
Source: 729 UNTS 161
http://www.un.org/disarmament/WMD/Nuclear/NPTtext.shtml

...

Article III

1. Each non-nuclear-weapon State Party to the Treaty undertakes to accept safeguards, as set forth in an agreement to be negotiated and concluded with the International Atomic Energy Agency in accordance with the Statute of the International Atomic Energy Agency and the Agency's safeguards system, for the exclusive purpose of verification of the fulfilment of its obligations assumed under this Treaty with a view to preventing diversion of nuclear energy from peaceful uses to nuclear weapons or other nuclear explosive devices. Procedures for the safeguards required by this Article shall be followed with respect to source or special fissionable material whether it is being produced, processed or used in any principal nuclear facility or is outside any such facility. The safeguards required by this Article shall be applied on all source or special fissionable material in all peaceful nuclear activities within the territory of such State, under its jurisdiction, or carried out under its control anywhere.

...

3. The safeguards required by this Article shall be implemented in a manner designed to comply with Article IV of this Treaty, and to avoid hampering the economic or technological development of the Parties or international co-operation in the field of peaceful nuclear activities, including the international exchange of nuclear material and equipment for the processing, use or production of nuclear material for peaceful purposes in accordance with the provisions of this Article and the principle of safeguarding set forth in the Preamble of the Treaty.

4. Non-nuclear-weapon States Party to the Treaty shall conclude agreements with the International Atomic Energy Agency to meet the requirements of this Article either individually or together with other States in accordance with the Statute of the International Atomic Energy Agency. Negotiation of such agreements shall commence within 180 days from the original entry into force of this Treaty. For States depositing their instruments of ratification or accession after the 180-day period, negotiation of such agreements shall

commence not later than the date of such deposit. Such agreements shall enter into force not later than eighteen months after the date of initiation of negotiations.

Article IV

1. Nothing in this Treaty shall be interpreted as affecting the inalienable right of all the Parties to the Treaty to develop research, production and use of nuclear energy for peaceful purposes without discrimination and in conformity with Articles I and II of this Treaty.

2. All the Parties to the Treaty undertake to facilitate, and have the right to participate in, the fullest possible exchange of equipment, materials and scientific and technological information for the peaceful uses of nuclear energy. Parties to the Treaty in a position to do so shall also co-operate in contributing alone or together with other States or international organizations to the further development of the applications of nuclear energy for peaceful purposes, especially in the territories of non-nuclear-weapon States Party to the Treaty, with due consideration for the needs of the developing areas of the world.

Article V

Each Party to the Treaty undertakes to take appropriate measures to ensure that, in accordance with this Treaty, under appropriate international observation and through appropriate international procedures, potential benefits from any peaceful applications of nuclear explosions will be made available to non-nuclear-weapon States Party to the Treaty on a non-discriminatory basis and that the charge to such Parties for the explosive devices used will be as low as possible and exclude any charge for research and development. Non-nuclear-weapon States Party to the Treaty shall be able to obtain such benefits, pursuant to a special international agreement or agreements, through an appropriate international body with adequate representation of non-nuclear-weapon States. Negotiations on this subject shall commence as soon as possible after the Treaty enters into force. Non-nuclear-weapon States Party to the Treaty so desiring may also obtain such benefits pursuant to bilateral agreements.

Article VI

Each of the Parties to the Treaty undertakes to pursue negotiations in good faith on effective measures relating to cessation of the nuclear arms race at an early date and to nuclear disarmament, and on a treaty on general and complete disarmament under strict and effective international control.

Article VII

Nothing in this Treaty affects the right of any group of States to conclude regional treaties in order to assure the total absence of nuclear weapons in their respective territories.

...

Note:

On 11 May 1995, in accordance with article X, paragraph 2, the Review and Extension Conference of the Parties to the Treaty on the Non-Proliferation of Nuclear Weapons decided that the Treaty should continue in force indefinitely (see decision 3).

59.b The Structure and Content of Agreements between the Agency and States Required in Connection with the Treaty on the Non-Proliferation of Nuclear Weapons*

Date: June 1972
Source: IAEA INFCIRC/153 (Corr.)
http://www.iaea.org/Publications/Documents/Infcircs/Others/infcirc153.pdf

PART I

BASIC UNDERTAKING

1. The Agreement should contain, in accordance with Article III.1 of the Treaty on the Non-Proliferation of Nuclear Weapons[1], an undertaking by the State to accept safeguards, in accordance with the terms of the Agreement, on all source or special fissionable material in all peaceful nuclear activities within its territory, under its jurisdiction or carried out under its control anywhere, for the exclusive purpose of verifying that such material is not diverted to nuclear weapons or other nuclear explosive devices.

APPLICATION OF SAFEGUARDS

2. The Agreement should provide for the Agency's right and obligation to ensure that safeguards will be applied, in accordance with the terms of the Agreement, on all source or special fissionable material in all peaceful nuclear activities within the territory of the State, under its jurisdiction or carried out under its control anywhere, for the exclusive purpose of verifying that such material is not diverted to nuclear weapons or other nuclear explosive devices.

CO-OPERATION BETWEEN THE AGENCY AND THE STATE

3. The Agreement should provide that the Agency and the State shall co-operate to facilitate the implementation of the safeguards provided for therein.

IMPLEMENTATION OF SAFEGUARDS

4. The Agreement should provide that safeguards shall be implemented in a mariner designed:

(a) To avoid hampering the economic and technological development of the State or international co-operation in the field of peaceful nuclear activities, including international exchange of *nuclear material*[2];

(b) To avoid undue interference in the State's peaceful nuclear activities, and in particular in the operation of *facilities;* and

(c) To be consistent with prudent management practices required for the economic and safe conduct of nuclear activities.

* N.B.: The following document has served as the basis for comprehensive safeguards agreements concluded pursuant to Art III NPT (see Document No. 59.a). In the individual agreements, the provisions based on the 'model paragraphs' appear as articles. The text of agreements concluded on the basis of the model safeguards agreement is available at http://www.iaea.org/Publications/Documents/Infcircs/part13.shtml.

[1] Reproduced in [Document No. 59.a].

[2] Terms in italics have specialized meanings, which are defined in paragraphs 98–116 below.

5. The Agreement should provide that the Agency shall take every precaution to protect commercial and industrial secrets and other confidential information coming to its knowledge in the implementation of the Agreement.

The Agency shall not publish or communicate to any State, organization or person any information obtained by it in connection with the implementation of the Agreement, except that specific information relating to such implementation in the State may be given to the Board of Governors and to such Agency staff members as require such knowledge by reason of their official duties in connection with safeguards, but only to the extent necessary for the Agency to fulfil its responsibilities in implementing the Agreement.

Summarized information on *nuclear material* being safeguarded by the Agency under the Agreement may be published upon decision of the Board if the States directly concerned agree.

6. The Agreement should provide that in implementing safeguards pursuant thereto the Agency shall take full account of technological developments in the field of safeguards, and shall make every effort to ensure optimum cost-effectiveness and the application of the principle of safeguarding effectively the flow of *nuclear material* subject to safeguards under the Agreement by use of instruments and other techniques at certain *strategic points* to the extent that present or future technology permits. In order to ensure optimum cost-effectiveness, use should be made, for example, of such means as:

(a) Containment as a means of defining *material balance areas* for accounting purposes;
(b) Statistical techniques and random sampling in evaluating the flow of *nuclear material;* and
(c) Concentration of verification procedures on those stages in the nuclear fuel cycle involving the production, processing, use or storage of *nuclear material* from which nuclear weapons or other nuclear explosive devices could readily be made, and minimization of verification procedures in respect of other *nuclear material,* on condition that this does not hamper the Agency in applying safeguards under the Agreement.

NATIONAL SYSTEM OF ACCOUNTING FOR AND CONTROL OF NUCLEAR MATERIAL

7. The Agreement should provide that the State shall establish and maintain a system of accounting for and control of all *nuclear material* subject to safeguards under the Agreement, and that such safeguards shall be applied in such a manner as to enable the Agency to verify, in ascertaining that there has been no diversion of *nuclear material* from peaceful uses to nuclear weapons or other nuclear explosive devices, findings of the State's system. The Agency's verification shall include, inter alia, independent measurements and observations conducted by the Agency in accordance with the procedures specified in Part II below. The Agency, in its verification, shall take due account ofthe technical effectiveness of the State's system.

PROVISION OF INFORMATION TO THE AGENCY

8. The Agreement should provide that to ensure the effective implementation of safeguards thereunder the Agency shall be provided, in accordance with the provisions set out in Part II below, with information concerning *nuclear material* subject to safeguards under the Agreement and the features of *facilities* relevant to safeguarding such material. The Agency

shall require only the minimum amount of information and data consistent with carrying out its responsibilities under the Agreement. Information pertaining to *facilities* shall be the minimum necessary for safeguarding *nuclear material* subject to safeguards under the Agreement. In examining design information, the Agency shall, at the request of the State, be prepared to examine on premises of the State design information which the State regards as being of particular sensitivity.

Such information would not have to be physically transmitted to the Agency provided that it remained available for ready further examination by the Agency on premises of the State.

AGENCY INSPECTORS

9. The Agreement should provide that the State shall take the necessary steps to ensure that Agency inspectors can effectively discharge their functions under the Agreement. The Agency shall secure the consent of the State to the designation of Agency inspectors to that State. If the State, either upon proposal of a designation or at any other time after a designation has been made, objects to the designation, the Agency shall propose to the State an alternative designation or designations. The repeated refusal of a State to accept the designation of Agency inspectors which would impede the inspections conducted under the Agreement would be considered by the Board upon referral by the Director General with a view to appropriate action. The visits and activities of Agency inspectors shall be so arranged as to reduce to a minimum the possible inconvenience and disturbance to the State and to the peaceful nuclear activities inspected, as well as to ensure protection of industrial secrets or any other confidential information coming to the inspectors' knowledge.

PRIVILEGES AND IMMUNITIES

10. The Agreement should specify the privileges and immunities which shall be granted to the Agency and its staff in respect of their functions under the Agreement. In the case of a State party to the Agreement on the Privileges and Immunities of the Agency[3] the provisions thereof, as in force for such State, shall apply. In the case of other States, the privileges and immunities granted should be such as to ensure that:

(a) The Agency and its staff will be in a position to discharge their functions under the Agreement effectively; and

(b) No such State will be placed thereby in a more favourable position than States party to the Agreement on the Privileges and Immunities of the Agency.

TERMINATION OF SAFEGUARDS

Consumption or dilution of nuclear material

11. The Agreement should provide that safeguards shall terminate on *nuclear material* subject to safeguards thereunder upon determination by the Agency that it has been consumed, or has been diluted in such a way that it is no longer usable for any nuclear activity relevant from the point of view of safeguards, or has become practicably irrecoverable.

Transfer of nuclear material out of the State

12. The Agreement should provide, with respect to *nuclear material* subject to safeguards thereunder, for notification of transfers of such material out of the State, in accordance

[3] Reproduced in document INFCIRC/9/Rev. 2.

with the provisions set out in paragraphs 92–94 below. The Agency shall terminate safeguards under the Agreement on *nuclear material* when the recipient State has assumed responsibility therefor, as provided for in paragraph 91. The Agency shall maintain records indicating each transfer and, where applicable, the re-application of safeguards to the transferred *nuclear material.*

Provisions relating to nuclear material to be used in non-nuclear activities

13. The Agreement should provide that if the State wishes to use *nuclear material* subject to safeguards thereunder in non-nuclear activities, such as the production of alloys or ceramics, it shall agree with the Agency on the circumstances under which the safeguards on such *nuclear material* may be terminated.

NON-APPLICATION OF SAFEGUARDS TO NUCLEAR MATERIAL TO BE USED IN NON-PEACEFUL ACTIVITIES

14. The Agreement should provide that if the State intends to exercise its discretion to use *nuclear material* which is required to be safeguarded thereunder in a nuclear activity which does not require the application of safeguards under the Agreement, the following procedures will apply:

(a) The State shall inform the Agency of the activity, making it clear:

  (i) That the use *of* the *nuclear material m* a non-proscribed military activity will not be in conflict with an undertaking the State may have given and in respect of which Agency safeguards apply, that the *nuclear material* will be used only in a peaceful nuclear activity; and

  (ii) That during the period of non-application of safeguards the *nuclear material* will not be used for the production of nuclear weapons or other nuclear explosive devices;

(b) The Agency and the State shall make an arrangement so that, only while the *nuclear material* is in such an activity, the safeguards provided for in the Agreement will not be applied. The arrangement shall identify, to the extent possible, the period or circumstances during which safeguards will not be applied. In any event, the safeguards provided for in the Agreement shall again apply as soon as the *nuclear material* is reintroduced into a peaceful nuclear activity. The Agency shall be kept informed of the total quantity and composition of such unsafeguarded *nuclear material* in the State and of any exports of such material; and

(c) Each arrangement shall be made in agreement with the Agency. The Agency's agreement shall be given as promptly as possible; it shall only relate to die temporal and procedural provisions, reporting arrangements, etc., but shall not involve any approval or classified knowledge of the military activity or relate to the use of the *nuclear material* therein.

FINANCE

15. The Agreement should contain one of the following sets of provisions:

(a) An agreement with a Member of the Agency should provide that each party thereto shall bear the expenses it incurs in implementing its responsibilities thereunder. However, if the State or persons under its jurisdiction incur extraordinary expenses as a result of a specific request by the Agency, the

Agency shall reimburse such expenses provided that it has agreed in advance to do so. In any case the Agency shall bear the cost of any additional measuring or sampling which inspectors may request; or

(b) An agreement with a party not a Member of the Agency should in application of the provisions of Article XIV.C of the Statute, provide that the party shall reimburse fully to the Agency the safeguards expenses the Agency incurs thereunder. However, if the party or persons under its jurisdiction incur extraordinary expenses as a result of a specific request by the Agency, the Agency shall reimburse such expenses provided that it has agreed in advance to do so.

THIRD PARTY LIABILITY FOR NUCLEAR DAMAGE

16. The Agreement should provide that the State shall ensure that any protection against third party liability in respect of nuclear damage, including any insurance or other financial security, which may be available under its laws or regulations shall apply to the Agency and its officials for the purpose of the implementation of the Agreement, in the same way as that protection applies to nationals of the State.

INTERNATIONAL RESPONSIBILITY

17. The Agreement should provide that any claim by one party thereto against the other in respect of any damage, other than damage arising out of a nuclear incident, resulting from the implementation of safeguards under the Agreement, shall be settled in accordance with international law.

MEASURES IN RELATION TO VERIFICATION OF NON-DIVERSION

18. The Agreement should provide that if the Board, upon report of the Director General, decides that an action by the State is essential and urgent in order to ensure verification that *nuclear material* subject to safeguards under the Agreement is not diverted to nuclear weapons or other nuclear explosive devices the Board shall be able to call upon the State to take the required action without delay, irrespective of whether procedures for the settlement of a dispute have been invoked.

19. The Agreement should provide that if the Board upon examination of relevant information reported to it by the Director General finds that the Agency is not able to verify that there has been no diversion of *nuclear material* required to be safeguarded under the Agreement to nuclear weapons or other nuclear explosive devices, it may make the reports provided for in paragraph C of Article XII of the Statute and may also take, where applicable, the other measures provided for in that paragraph. In taking such action the Board shall take account of the degree of assurance provided by the safeguards measures that have been applied and shall afford the State every reasonable opportunity to furnish the Board with any necessary reassurance.

INTERPRETATION AND APPLICATION OF THE AGREEMENT AND SETTLEMENT OF DISPUTES

20. The Agreement should provide that the parties thereto shall, at the request of either, consult about any question arising out of the interpretation or application thereof.

21. The Agreement should provide that the State shall have the right to request that any question arising out of the interpretation or application thereof be considered by the

Board; and that the State shall be invited by the Board to participate in the discussion of any such question by the Board.

22. The Agreement should provide that any dispute arising out of the interpretation or application thereof except a dispute with regard to a finding by the Board under paragraph 19 above or an action taken by the Board pursuant to such a finding which is not settled by negotiation or another procedure agreed to by the parties should, on the request of either party, be submitted to an arbitral tribunal composed as follows: each party would designate one arbitrator, and the two arbitrators so designated would elect a third, who would be the Chairman. If, within 30 days of the request for arbitration, either party has not designated an arbitrator, either party to the dispute may request the President of the International Court of Justice to appoint an arbitrator.

The same procedure would apply if, within 30 days of the designation or appointment of the second arbitrator, the third arbitrator had not been elected. A majority of the members of the arbitral tribunal would constitute a quorum, and all decisions would require the concurrence of two arbitrators. The arbitral procedure would be fixed by the tribunal. The decisions of the tribunal would be binding on both parties.

FINAL CLAUSES

Amendment of the Agreement

23. The Agreement should provide that the parties thereto shall, at the request of either of them, consult each other on amendment of the Agreement. All amendments shall require the agreement of both parties. It might additionally be provided, if convenient to the State, that the agreement of the parties on amendments to Part II of the Agreement could be achieved by recourse to a simplified procedure. The Director General shall promptly inform all Member States of any amendment to the Agreement.

Suspension of application of Agency safeguards under other agreements

24. Where applicable and where the State desires such a provision to appear, the Agreement should provide that the application of Agency safeguards in the State under other safeguards agreements with the Agency shall be suspended while the Agreement is in force. If the State has received assistance from the Agency for a project, the State's undertaking in the Project Agreement not to use items subject thereto in such a way as to further any military purpose shall continue to apply.

Entry into force and duration

25. The Agreement should provide that it shall enter into force on the date on which the Agency receives from the State written notification that the statutory and constitutional requirements for entry into force have been met.

The Director General shall promptly inform all Member States of the entry into force.

26. The Agreement should provide for it to remain in force as long as the State is party to the Treaty on the Non-Proliferation of Nuclear Weapons).

PART II

INTRODUCTION

27. The Agreement should provide that the purpose of Part II thereof is to specify the procedures to be applied for the implementation of the safeguards provisions of Part I.

OBJECTIVE OF SAFEGUARDS

28. The Agreement should provide that the objective of safeguards is the timely detection of diversion of significant quantities of *nuclear material* from peaceful nuclear activities to the manufacture of nuclear weapons or of other nuclear explosive devices or for purposes unknown, and deterrence of such diversion by the risk of early detection.

29. To this end the Agreement should provide for the use of material accountancy as a safeguards measure of fundamental importance, with containment and surveillance as important complementary measures.

30. The Agreement should provide that the technical conclusion of the Agency's verification activities shall be a statement, in respect of each *material balance area*, of the amount of *material unaccounted for* over a specific period, giving the limits of accuracy of the amounts stated.

NATIONAL SYSTEM OF ACCOUNTING FOR AND CONTROL OF NUCLEAR MATERIAL

31. The Agreement should provide that pursuant to paragraph 7 above the Agency, in carrying out its verification activities, shall make full use of the State's system of accounting for and control of all *nuclear material* subject to safeguards under the Agreement, and shall avoid unnecessary duplication of the State's accounting and control activities.

32. The Agreement should provide that the State's system of accounting for and control of all *nuclear material* subject to safeguards under the Agreement shall be based on a structure of material balance areas, and shall make provision as appropriate and specified in the Subsidiary Arrangements for the establishment of such measures as:

(a) A measurement system for the determination of the quantities of *nuclear material* received, produced, shipped, lost or otherwise removed from inventory, and the quantities on inventory;
(b) The evaluation of precision and accuracy of measurements and the estimation of measurement uncertainty;
(c) Procedures for identifying, reviewing and evaluating differences in shipper/receiver measurements;
(d) Procedures for taking a *physical inventory;*
(e) Procedures for the evaluation of accumulations of unmeasured inventory and unmeasured losses;
(f) A system of records and reports showing, for each *material balance area*, the inventory of *nuclear material* and the changes in that inventory including receipts into and transfers out of the *material balance area;*
(g) Provisions to ensure that the accounting procedures and arrangements are being operated correctly; and
(h) Procedures for the provisions of reports to the Agency in accordance with paragraphs 59–69 below.

STARTING POINT OF SAFEGUARDS

33. The Agreement should provide that safeguards shall not apply thereunder to material in mining or ore processing activities.

34. The Agreement should provide that:

(a) When any material containing uranium or thorium which has not reached the stage of the nuclear fuel cycle described in subparagraph (c) below is directly or indirectly exported to a non-nuclear-weapon State, the State shall inform the Agency of its quantity, composition and destination, unless the material is exported for specifically non-nuclear purposes;

(b) When any material containing uranium or thorium which has not reached the stage of the nuclear fuel cycle described in sub-paragraph (c) below is imported, the State shall inform the Agency of its quantity and composition, unless the material is imported for specifically nonnuclear purposes; and

(c) When any *nuclear material* of a composition and purity suitable for fuel fabrication or for being isotopically enriched leaves the plant or the process stage in which it has been produced, or when such *nuclear material*, or any other *nuclear material* produced at a later stage in the nuclear fuel cycle, is imported into the State, the *nuclear material* shall become subject to the other safeguards procedures specified in the Agreement.

TERMINATION OF SAFEGUARDS

35. The Agreement should provide that safeguards shall terminate on *nuclear material* subject to safeguards thereunder under the conditions set forth in paragraph 11 above. Where the conditions of that paragraph are not met, but the State considers that the recovery of safeguarded *nuclear material* from residues is not for the time being practicable or desirable, the Agency and the State shall consult on the appropriate safeguards measures to be applied. It should further be provided that safeguards shall terminate on *nuclear material* subject to safeguards under the Agreement under the conditions set forth in paragraph 13 above, provided that the State and the Agency agree that such *nuclear material* is practicably irrecoverable.

EXEMPTIONS FROM SAFEGUARDS

36. The Agreement should provide that the Agency shall, at the request of the State, exempt *nuclear material* from safeguards, as follows:

(a) Special fissionable material, when it is used in gram quantities or less as a sensing component in instruments;

(b) *Nuclear material*, when it is used in non-nuclear activities in accordance with paragraph 13 above, if such *nuclear material* is recoverable; and

(c) Plutonium with an isotopic concentration of plutonium-238 exceeding 80%.

37. The Agreement should provide that *nuclear material* that would otherwise be subject to safeguards shall be exempted from safeguards at the request of the State, provided that *nuclear material* so exempted in the State may not at any time exceed:

(a) One kilogram in total of special fissionable material, which may consist of one of more of the following:

(i) Plutonium;

(ii) Uranium with an *enrichment* of 0.2 (20%) and above, taken account of by multiplying its weight by its *enrichment;* and

(iii) Uranium with an *enrichment* below 0.2 (20%) and above that of natural uranium, taken account of by multiplying its weight by five times the square of its *enrichment;*

(b) Ten metric tons in total of natural uranium and depleted uranium with an *enrichment* above 0.005 (0.5%);

(c) Twenty metric tons of depleted uranium with an *enrichment* of 0.005 (0.5%) or below; and

(d) Twenty metric tons of thorium; or such greater amounts as may be specified by the Board of Governors for uniform application.

38. The Agreement should provide that if exempted *nuclear material* is to be processed or stored together with safeguarded *nuclear material*, provision should be made for the re-application of safeguards thereto.

SUBSIDIARY ARRANGEMENTS

39. The Agreement should provide that the Agency and the State shall make Subsidiary Arrangements which shall specify in detail, to the extent necessary to permit the Agency to fulfil its responsibilities under the Agreement in an effective and efficient manner, how the procedures laid down in the Agreement are to be applied. Provision should be made for the possibility of an extension or change of the Subsidiary Arrangements by agreement between the Agency and the State without amendment of the Agreement.

40. It should be provided that the Subsidiary Arrangements shall enter into force at the same time as, or as soon as possible after, the entry into force of the Agreement. The State and the Agency shall make every effort to achieve their entry into force within 90 days of the entry into force of the Agreement, a later date being acceptable only with the agreement of both parties. The State shall provide the Agency promptly with the information required for completing the Subsidiary Arrangements. The Agreement should also provide that, upon its entry into force, the Agency shall be entitled to apply the procedures laid down therein in respect of the *nuclear material* listed in the inventory provided for in paragraph 41 below.

INVENTORY

41. The Agreement should provide that, on the basis of the initial report referred to in paragraph 62 below, the Agency shall establish a unified inventory of all *nuclear material* in the State subject to safeguards under the Agreement, irrespective of its origin, and maintain this inventory on the basis of subsequent reports and of the results of its verification activities. Copies of the inventory shall be made available to the State at agreed intervals.

DESIGN INFORMATION

General

42. Pursuant to paragraph 8 above, the Agreement should stipulate that design information in respect of existing *facilities* shall be provided to the Agency during the discussion of the Subsidiary Arrangements, and that the time limits for the provision of such information in respect of new *facilities* shall be specified in the Subsidiary Arrangements. It should further be stipulated that such information shall be provided as early as possible before *nuclear material* is introduced into a new *facility*.

43. The Agreement should specify that the design information in respect of each *facility* to be made available to the Agency shall include, when applicable:

(a) The identification of the *facility*, stating its general character, purpose, nominal capacity and geographic location, and the name and address to be used for routine business purposes;

(b) A description of the general arrangement of the *facility* with reference, to the extent feasible, to the form, location and flow of *nuclear material* and to the general layout of important items of equipment which use, produce or process *nuclear material;*

(c) A description of features of *the facility* relating to material accountancy, containment and surveillance; and

(d) A description of the existing and proposed procedures at the *facility* for *nuclear material* accountancy and control, with special reference to *material balance areas* established by the operator, measurements of flow and procedures for *physical inventory* taking.

44. The Agreement should further provide that other information relevant to the application of safeguards shall be made available to the Agency in respect of each *facility*, in particular on organizational responsibility for material accountancy and control. It should also be provided that the State shall make available to the Agency supplementary information on the health and safety procedures which the Agency shall observe and with which the inspectors shall comply at *the facility.*

45. The Agreement should stipulate that design information in respect of a modification relevant for safeguards purposes shall be provided for examination sufficiently in advance for the safeguards procedures to be adjusted when necessary.

Purposes of examination of design information

46. The Agreement should provide that the design information made available to the Agency shall be used for the following purposes:

(a) To identify the features of *facilities* and *nuclear material* relevant to the application of safeguards to *nuclear material* in sufficient detail to facilitate verification;

(b) To determine *material balance areas* to be used for Agency accounting purposes and to select those *strategic points* which are *key measurement points* and which will be used to determine the *nuclear material* flows and inventories; in determining such *material balance areas* the Agency shall, inter alia, use the following criteria:

(i) The size of the *material balance area* should be related to the accuracy with which the material balance can be established;

(ii) In determining the *material balance area* advantage should be taken of any opportunity to use containment and surveillance to help ensure the completeness of flow measurements and thereby simplify the application of safeguards and concentrate measurement efforts at *key measurement points;*

(iii) A number of *material balance areas* in use at a *facility* or at distinct sites may be combined in one *material balance area* to be used for Agency accounting purposes when the Agency determines that this is consistent with its verification requirements; and

(iv) If the State so requests, a special *material balance area* around a process step involving commercially sensitive information may be established;

(c) To establish the nominal timing and procedures for taking of *physical inventory* for Agency accounting purposes;

(d) To establish the records and reports requirements and records evaluation procedures;
(e) To establish requirements and procedures for verification of the quantity and location of *nuclear material;* and
(f) To select appropriate combinations of containment and surveillance methods and techniques and the *strategic points* at which they are to be applied.

It should further be provided that the results of the examination of the design information shall be included in the Subsidiary Arrangements.

Re-examination of design information

47. The Agreement should provide that design information shall be re-examined in the light of changes in operating conditions, of developments in safeguards technology or of experience in the application of verification procedures, with a view to modifying the action the Agency has taken pursuant to paragraph 46 above.

Verification of design information

48. The Agreement should provide that the Agency, in co-operation with the State, may send inspectors to *facilities* to verify the design information provided to the Agency pursuant to paragraphs 42–45 above for the purposes stated in paragraph 46.

INFORMATION IN RESPECT OF NUCLEAR MATERIAL OUTSIDE FACILITIES

49. The Agreement should provide that the following information concerning *nuclear material* customarily used outside *facilities* shall be provided as applicable to the Agency:

(a) A general description of the use of the *nuclear material*, its geographic location, and the user's name and address for routine business purposes; and
(b) A general description of the existing and proposed procedures for *nuclear material* accountancy and control, including organizational responsibility for material accountancy and control.

The Agreement should further provide that the Agency shall be informed on a timely basis of any change in the information provided to it under this paragraph.

50. The Agreement should provide that the information made available to the Agency in respect of *nuclear material* customarily used outside *facilities* may be used, to the extent relevant, for the purposes set out in subparagraphs 46(b)–(f) above.

RECORDS SYSTEM

General

51. The Agreement should provide that in establishing a national system of accounting for and control of *nuclear material* as referred to in paragraph 7 above, the State shall arrange that records are kept in respect of each *material balance area.* Provision should also be made that the Subsidiary Arrangements shall describe the records to be kept in respect of each *material balance area.*

52. The Agreement should provide that the State shall make arrangements to facilitate the examination of records by inspectors, particularly if the records are not kept in English, French, Russian or Spanish.

53. The Agreement should provide that the records shall be retained for at least five years.

54. The Agreement should provide that the records shall consist, as appropriate, of:
   (a) Accounting records of all *nuclear material* subject to safeguards under the Agreement; and
   (b) Operating records *lor facilities* containing such *nuclear material.*

55. The Agreement should provide that the system of measurements on which the records used for the preparation of reports are based shall either conform to the latest international standards or be equivalent in quality to such standards.

Accounting records

56. The Agreement should provide that the accounting records shall set forth the following in respect of each *material balance area:*
   (a) All *inventory changes*, so as to permit a determination of the *book inventory* at any time;
   (b) All measurement results that are used for determination of the *physical inventory;* and
   (c) All *adjustments* and *corrections* that have been made in respect of *inventory changes, book inventories* and *physical inventories.*

57. The Agreement should provide that for all *inventory changes* and *physical inventories* the records shall show, in respect of each *batch* of *nuclear material*, material identification, *batch data* and *source data.* Provision should further be included that records shall account for uranium, thorium and plutonium separately in each *batch* of *nuclear material.* Furthermore, the date of the *inventory change* and, when appropriate, the originating *material balance area* and the receiving *material balance area* or the recipient, shall be indicated for each *inventory change.*

Operating records

58. The Agreement should provide that the operating records shall set forth as appropriate in respect of each *material balance area:*
   (a) Those operating data which are used to establish changes in the quantities and composition of *nuclear material;*
   (b) The data obtained from the calibration of tanks and instruments and from sampling and analyses, the procedures to control the quality of measurements and the derived estimates of random and systematic error;
   (c) A description of the sequence of the actions taken in preparing for, and in taking, a *physical inventory*, in order to ensure that it is correct and complete; and
   (d) A description of the actions taken in order to ascertain the cause and magnitude of any accidental or unmeasured loss that might occur.

REPORTS SYSTEM

General

59. The Agreement should specify that the State shall provide the Agency with reports as detailed in paragraphs 60–69 below in respect of *nuclear material* subject to safeguards thereunder.

60. The Agreement should provide that reports shall be made in English, French, Russian or Spanish, except as otherwise specified in the Subsidiary Arrangements.

61. The Agreement should provide that reports shall be based on the records kept in accordance with paragraphs 51–58 above and shall consist, as appropriate, of accounting reports and special reports.

Accounting reports

62. The Agreement should stipulate that the Agency shall be provided with an initial report on all *nuclear material* which is to be subject to safeguards thereunder. It should also be provided that the initial report shall be dispatched by the State to the Agency within 30 days of the last day of the calendar month in which the Agreement enters into force, and shall reflect the situation as of the last day of that month.

63. The Agreement should stipulate that for each *material balance area* the State shall provide the Agency with the following accounting reports:

(a) *Inventory change* reports showing changes in the inventory of *nuclear material.* The reports shall be dispatched as soon as possible and in any event within 30 days after the end of the month in which the *inventory changes* occurred or were established; and

(b) Material balance reports showing the material balance based on a *physical inventory* of *nuclear material* actually present in the *material balance area.* The reports shall be dispatched as soon as possible and in any event within 30 days after the *physical inventory* has been taken.

The reports shall be based on data available as of the date of reporting and may be corrected at a later date as required.

64. The Agreement should provide that *inventory change* reports shall specify identification and *batch data* for each *batch* of *nuclear material*, the date of the *inventory change* and, as appropriate, the originating *material balance area* and the receiving *material balance area* or the recipient. These reports shall be accompanied by concise notes:

(a) Explaining the *inventory changes*, on the basis of the operating data contained in the operating records provided for under subparagraph 58(a) above; and

(b) Describing, as specified in the Subsidiary Arrangements, the anticipated operational programme, particularly the taking of a *physical inventory.*

65. The Agreement should provide that the State shall report each *inventory change, adjustment* and *correction* either periodically in a consolidated list or individually.

The *inventory changes* shall be reported in terms of *batches;* small amounts, such as analytical samples, as specified in the Subsidiary Arrangements, may be combined and reported as one *inventory change.*

66. The Agreement should stipulate that the Agency shall provide the State with semi-annual statements of *book inventory* of *nuclear material* subject to safeguards, for each *material balance area*, as based on the *inventory change* reports for the period covered by each such statement.

67. The Agreement should specify that the material balance reports shall include the following entries, unless otherwise agreed by the Agency and the State:

(a) Beginning *physical inventory;*
(b) *Inventory changes* (first increases, then decreases);
(c) Ending *book inventory;*
(d) *Shipper I receiver differences;*
(e) Adjusted ending *book inventory;*
(f) Ending *physical inventory;* and
(g) *Material unaccounted for.*

A statement of the *physical inventory*, listing all *batches* separately and specifying material identification and *batch data* for each *batch*, shall be attached to each material balance report.

Special reports

68. The Agreement should provide that the State shall make special reports without delay:

(a) If any unusual incident or circumstances lead the State to believe that there is or may have been loss of *nuclear material* that exceeds the limits to be specified for this purpose in the Subsidiary Arrangements; or

(b) If the containment has unexpectedly changed from that specified in the Subsidiary Arrangements to the extent that unauthorized removal of *nuclear material* has become possible.

Amplification and clarification of reports

69. The Agreement should provide that at the Agency's request the State shall supply amplifications or clarifications of any report, in so far as relevant for the purpose of safeguards.

INSPECTIONS

General

70. The Agreement should stipulate that the Agency shall have the right to make inspections as provided for in paragraphs 71–82 below.

Purposes of inspections

71. The Agreement should provide that the Agency may make ad hoc inspections in order to:

(a) Verify the information contained in the initial report on the *nuclear material* subject to safeguards under the Agreement;

(b) Identify and verify changes in the situation which have occurred since the date of the initial report; and

(c) Identify, and if possible verify the quantity and composition of, *nuclear material* in accordance with paragraphs 93 and 96 below, before its transfer out of or upon its transfer into the State.

72. The Agreement should provide that the Agency may make routine inspections in order to:

(a) Verify that reports are consistent with records;

(b) Verify the location, identity, quantity and composition of all *nuclear material* subject to safeguards under the Agreement; and

(c) Verify information on the possible causes of *material unaccounted for, shipper I receiver differences* and uncertainties in the *book inventory.*

73. The Agreement should provide that the Agency may make special inspections subject to the procedures laid down in paragraph 77 below:

(a) In order to verify the information contained in special reports; or

(b) If the Agency considers that information made available by the State, including explanations from the State and information obtained from routine inspections, is not adequate for the Agency to fulfil its responsibilities under the Agreement.

An inspection shall be deemed to be special when it is either additional to the routine inspection effort provided for in paragraphs 78–82 below, or involves access to information or locations in addition to the access specified in paragraph 76 for ad hoc and routine inspections, or both.

Scope of inspections

74. The Agreement should provide that for the purposes stated in paragraphs 71–73 above the Agency may:

(a) Examine the records kept pursuant to paragraphs 51–58;
(b) Make independent measurements of all *nuclear material* subject to safeguards under the Agreement;
(c) Verify the functioning and calibration of instruments and other measuring and control equipment;
(d) Apply and make use of surveillance and containment measures; and
(e) Use other objective methods which have been demonstrated to be technically feasible.

75. It should further be provided that within the scope of paragraph 74 above the Agency shall be enabled:

(a) To observe that samples at *key measurement points* for material balance accounting are taken in accordance with procedures which produce representative samples, to observe the treatment and analysis of the samples and to obtain duplicates of such samples;
(b) To observe that the measurements of *nuclear material* at *key measurement points* for material balance accounting are representative, and to observe the calibration of the instruments and equipment involved;
(c) To make arrangements with the State that, if necessary:
  (i) Additional measurements are made and additional samples taken for the Agency's use;
  (ii) The Agency's standard analytical samples are analysed;
  (iii) Appropriate absolute standards are used in calibrating instruments and other equipment; and
  (iv) Other calibrations are carried out;
(d) To arrange to use its own equipment for independent measurement and surveillance, and if so agreed and specified in the Subsidiary Arrangements, to arrange to install such equipment;
(e) To apply its seals and other identifying and tamper-indicating devices to containments, if so agreed and specified in the Subsidiary Arrangements; and
(f) To make arrangements with the State for the shipping of samples taken for the Agency's use.

Access for inspections

76. The Agreement should provide that:

(a) For the purposes specified in sub-paragraphs 71(a) and (b) above and until such time as the *strategic points* have been specified in the Subsidiary Arrangements, the Agency's inspectors shall have access to any location where the initial report or any inspections carried out in connection with it indicate that *nuclear material* is present;
(b) For the purposes specified in sub-paragraph 71(c) above the inspectors shall have access to any location of which the Agency has been notified in accordance with sub-paragraphs 92(c) or 95(c) below;
(c) For the purposes specified in paragraph 72 above the Agency's inspectors shall have access only to the *strategic points* specified in the Subsidiary Arrangements and to the records maintained pursuant to paragraphs 51–58; and

(d) In the event of the State concluding that any unusual circumstances require extended limitations on access by the Agency, the State and the Agency shall promptly make arrangements with a view to enabling the Agency to discharge its safeguards responsibilities in the light of these limitations. The Director General shall report each such arrangement to the Board.

77. The Agreement should provide that in circumstances which may lead to special inspections for the purposes specified in paragraph 73 above the State and the Agency shall consult forthwith. As a result of such consultations the Agency may make inspections in addition to the routine inspection effort provided for in paragraphs 78–82 below, and may obtain access in agreement with the State to information or locations in addition to the access specified in paragraph 76 above for ad hoc and routine inspections. Any disagreement concerning the need for additional access shall be resolved in accordance with paragraphs 21 and 22; in case action by the State is essential and urgent, paragraph 18 above shall apply.

Frequency and intensity of routine inspections

78. The Agreement should provide that the number, intensity, duration and timing of routine inspections shall be kept to the minimum consistent with the effective implementation of the safeguards procedures set forth therein, and that the Agency shall make the optimum and most economical use of available inspection resources.

79. The Agreement should provide that in the case of *facilities* and *material balance areas* outside *facilities* with a content or *annual throughput*, whichever is greater, of *nuclear material* not exceeding five *effective kilograms*, routine inspections shall not exceed one per year. For other *facilities* the number, intensity, duration, timing and mode of inspections shall be determined on the basis that in the maximum or limiting case the inspection regime shall be no more intensive than is necessary and sufficient to maintain continuity of knowledge of the flow and inventory of *nuclear material.*

80. The Agreement should provide that the maximum routine inspection effort in respect of *facilities* with a content or *annual throughput* of *nuclear material* exceeding five *effective kilograms* shall be determined as follows:

(a) For reactors and sealed stores, the maximum total of routine inspection per year shall be determined by allowing one sixth of a *man-year of inspection* for each such *facility* in the State;

(b) For other *facilities* involving plutonium or uranium enriched to more than 5%, the maximum total of routine inspection per year shall be determined by allowing for each such *facility* 30 X $\sqrt{E}$ man-days of inspection per year, where E is the inventory or *annual throughput* of *nuclear material*, whichever is greater, expressed in *effective kilograms.* The maximum established for any such *facility* shall not, however, be less than 1.5 *man-years of inspection;* and

(c) For all other *facilities*, the maximum total of routine inspection per year shall be determined by allowing for each such *facility* one third of a *man-year of inspection* plus 0.4 X E man-days of inspection per year, where E is the inventory or *annual throughput* of *nuclear material*, whichever is greater, expressed in *effective kilograms.*

The Agreement should further provide that the Agency and the State may agree to amend the maximum figures specified in this paragraph upon determination by the Board that such amendment is reasonable.

81. Subject to paragraphs 78–80 above the criteria to be used for determining the actual number, intensity, duration, timing and mode of routine inspections of any *facility* shall include:

(a) The form of *nuclear material*, in particular, whether the material is in bulk form or contained in a number of separate items; its chemical composition and, in the case of uranium, whether it is of low or high *enrichment;* and its accessibility;

(b) The effectiveness of the State's accounting and control system, including the extent to which the operators of *facilities* are functionally independent of the State's accounting and control system; the extent to which the measures specified in paragraph 32 above have been implemented by the State; the promptness of reports submitted to the Agency; their consistency with the Agency's independent verification; and the amount and accuracy of the *material unaccounted for*, as verified by the Agency;

(c) Characteristics of the State's nuclear fuel cycle, in particular, the number and types of *facilities* containing *nuclear material* subject to safeguards, the characteristics of such *facilities* relevant to safeguards, notably the degree of containment; the extent to which the design of such *facilities* facilitates verification of the flow and inventory of *nuclear material;* and the extent to which information from different *material balance areas* can be correlated;

(d) International interdependence, in particular, the extent to which *nuclear material* is received from or sent to other States for use or processing; any verification activity by the Agency in connection therewith; and the extent to which the State's nuclear activities are interrelated with those of other States; and

(e) Technical developments in the field of safeguards, including the use of statistical techniques and random sampling in evaluating the flow of *nuclear material.*

82. The Agreement should provide for consultation between the Agency and the State if the latter considers that the inspection effort is being deployed with undue concentration on particular *facilities.*

Notice of inspections

83. The Agreement should provide that the Agency shall give advance notice to the State before arrival of inspectors at *facilities* or *material balance areas* outside *facilities*, as follows:

(a) For ad hoc inspections pursuant to sub-paragraph 71(c) above, at least 24 hours, for those pursuant to sub-paragraphs 71(a) and (b), as well as the activities provided for in paragraph 48, at least one week;

(b) For special inspections pursuant to paragraph 73 above, as promptly as possible after the Agency and the State have consulted as provided for in paragraph 77, it being understood that notification of arrival normally will constitute part of the consultations; and

(c) For routine inspections pursuant to paragraph 72 above, at least 24 hours in respect of the *facilities* referred to in sub-paragraph 80(b) and sealed stores containing plutonium or uranium enriched to more than 596, and one week in all other cases.

Such notice of inspections shall include the names of the inspectors and shall indicate the *facilities* and the *material balance areas* outside *facilities* to be visited and the periods during which they will be visited. If the inspectors are to arrive from outside the State the Agency shall also give advance notice of the place and time of their arrival in the State.

84. However, the Agreement should also provide that, as a supplementary measure, the Agency may carry out without advance notification a portion of the routine inspections pursuant to paragraph 80 above in accordance with the principle of random sampling.

In performing any unannounced inspections, the Agency shall fully take into account any operational programme provided by the State pursuant to paragraph 64(b). Moreover, whenever practicable, and on the basis of the operational programme, it shall advise the State periodically of its general programme of announced and unannounced inspections, specifying the general periods when inspections are foreseen. In carrying out any unannounced inspections, the Agency shall make every effort to minimize any practical difficulties for *facility* operators and the State, bearing in mind the relevant provisions of paragraphs 44 above and 89 below. Similarly the State shall make every effort to facilitate the task of the inspectors.

Designation of inspectors

85. The Agreement should provide that:

(a) The Director General shall inform the State in writing of the name, qualifications, nationality, grade and such other particulars as may be relevant, of each Agency official he proposes for designation as an inspector for the State;

(b) The State shall inform the Director General within 30 days of the receipt of such a proposal whether it accepts the proposal;

(c) The Director General may designate each official who has been accepted by the State as one of the inspectors for the State, and shall inform the State of such designations; and

(d) The Director General, acting in response to a request by the State or on his own initiative, shall immediately inform the State of the withdrawal of the designation of any official as an inspector for the State.

The Agreement should also provide, however, that in respect of inspectors needed for the purposes stated in paragraph 48 above and to carry out ad hoc inspections pursuant to sub-paragraphs 71(a) and (b) the designation procedures shall be completed if possible within 30 days after the entry into force of the Agreement. If such designation appears impossible within this time limit, inspectors for such purposes shall be designated on a temporary basis.

86. The Agreement should provide that the State shall grant or renew as quickly as possible appropriate visas, where required, for each inspector designated for the State.

Conduct and visits of inspectors

87. The Agreement should provide that inspectors, in exercising their functions under paragraphs 48 and 71–75 above, shall carry out their activities in a manner designed to avoid hampering or delaying the construction, commissioning or operation of *facilities*, or affecting their safety. In particular inspectors shall not operate *any facility* themselves or direct the staff of a *facility* to carry out any operation. If inspectors consider that in pursuance of paragraphs 74 and 75, particular operations in a *facility* should be carried out by the operator, they shall make a request therefor.

88. When inspectors require services available in the State, including the use of equipment, in connection with the performance of inspections, the State shall facilitate the procurement of such services and the use of such equipment by inspectors.

89. The Agreement should provide that the State shall have the right to have inspectors accompanied during their inspections by representatives of the State, provided that inspectors shall not thereby be delayed or otherwise impeded in the exercise of their functions.

STATEMENTS ON THE AGENCY'S VERIFICATION ACTIVITIES

90. The Agreement should provide that the Agency shall inform the State of:

(a) The results of inspections, at intervals to be specified in the Subsidiary Arrangements; and

(b) The conclusions it has drawn from its verification activities in the State, in particular by means of statements in respect of each *material balance area*, which shall be made as soon as possible after a *physical inventory* has been taken and verified by the Agency and a material balance has been struck.

INTERNATIONAL TRANSFERS

General

91. The Agreement should provide that *nuclear material* subject or required to be subject to safeguards thereunder which is transferred internationally shall, for purposes of the Agreement, be regarded as being the responsibility of the State:

(a) In the case of import, from the time that such responsibility ceases to lie with the exporting State, and no later than the time at which the *nuclear material* reaches its destination; and

(b) In the case of export, up to the time at which the recipient State assumes such responsibility, and no later than the time at which the *nuclear material* reaches its destination. The Agreement should provide that the States concerned shall make suitable arrangements to determine the point at which the transfer of responsibility will take place. No State shall be deemed to have such responsibility for *nuclear material* merely by reason of the fact that the *nuclear material* is in transit on or over its territory or territorial waters, or that it is being transported under its flag or in its aircraft.

Transfers out of the State

92. The Agreement should provide that any intended transfer out of the State of safeguarded *nuclear material* in an amount exceeding one *effective kilogram*, or by successive shipments to the same State within a period of three months each of less than one *effective kilogram* but exceeding in total one *effective kilogram*, shall be notified to the Agency after the conclusion of the contractual arrangements leading to the transfer and normally at least two weeks before the *nuclear material* is to be prepared for shipping. The Agency and the State may agree on different procedures for advance notification. The notification shall specify:

(a) The identification and, if possible, the expected quantity and composition of the *nuclear material* to be transferred, and the *material balance area* from which it will come;

(b) The State for which the *nuclear material* is destined;

(c) The dates on and locations at which the *nuclear material* is to be prepared for shipping;

(d) The approximate dates of dispatch and arrival of the *nuclear material;* and

(e) At what point of the transfer the recipient State will assume responsibility for the *nuclear material*, and the probable date on which this point will be reached.

93. The Agreement should further provide that the purpose of this notification shall be to enable the Agency if necessary to identify, and if possible verify the quantity and composition of, *nuclear material* subject to safeguards under the Agreement before it is

transferred out of the State and, if the Agency so wishes or the State so requests, to affix seals to the *nuclear material* when it has been prepared for shipping. However, the transfer of the *nuclear material* shall not be delayed in any way by any action taken or contemplated by the Agency pursuant to this notification.

94. The Agreement should provide that, if the *nuclear material* will not be subject to Agency safeguards in the recipient State, the exporting State shall make arrangements for the Agency to receive, within three months of the time when the recipient State accepts responsibility for the *nuclear material* from the exporting State, confirmation by the recipient State of the transfer.

Transfers into the State

95. The Agreement should provide that the expected transfer into the State of *nuclear material* required to be subject to safeguards in an amount greater than one *effective kilogram*, or by successive shipments from the same State within a period of three months each of less than one *effective kilogram* but exceeding in total one *effective kilogram*, shall be notified to the Agency as much in advance as possible of the expected arrival of the *nuclear material*, and in any case not later than the date on which the recipient State assumes responsibility therefor. The Agency and the State may agree on different procedures for advance notification. The notification shall specify:

(a) The identification and, if possible, the expected quantity and composition of the *nuclear material;*

(b) At what point of the transfer responsibility for the *nuclear material* will be assumed by the State for the purposes of the Agreement, and the probable date on which this point will be reached; and

(c) The expected date of arrival, the location to which the *nuclear material* is to be delivered and the date on which it is intended that the *nuclear material* should be unpacked.

96. The Agreement should provide that the purpose of this notification shall be to enable the Agency if necessary to identify, and if possible verify the quantity and composition of, *nuclear material* subject to safeguards which has been transferred into the State, by means of inspection of the consignment at the time it is unpacked. However, unpacking shall not be delayed by any action taken or contemplated by the Agency pursuant to this notification.

Special reports

97. The Agreement should provide that in the case of international transfers a special report as envisaged in paragraph 68 above shall be made if any unusual incident or circumstances lead the State to believe that there is or may have been loss of *nuclear material*, including the occurrence of significant delay during the transfer.

DEFINITIONS

98. "Adjustment" means an entry into an accounting record or a report showing *2. shipper I receiver difference* or *material unaccounted for.*

99. "Annual throughput" means, for the purposes of paragraphs 79 and 80 above, the amount of *nuclear material* transferred annually out of a *facility* working at nominal capacity.

100. "Batch" means a portion of *nuclear material* handled as a unit for accounting purposes at a *key measurement point* and for which the composition and quantity are defined by a single set of specifications or measurements. The *nuclear material* may be in bulk form or contained in a number of separate items.

101. "Batch data" means the total weight of each element of *nuclear material* and, in the case of plutonium and uranium, the isotopic composition when appropriate. The units of account shall be as follows:

(a) Grams of contained plutonium;
(b) Grams of total uranium and grams of contained uranium-235 plus uranium-233 for uranium enriched in these isotopes; and
(c) Kilograms of contained thorium, natural uranium or depleted uranium.

For reporting purposes the weights of individual items in the *batch* shall be added together before rounding to the nearest unit.

102. "Book inventory" of a *material balance area* means the algebraic sum of the most recent *physical inventory* of that *material balance area* and of all *inventory changes* that have occurred since *that physical inventory was* taken.

103. "Correction" means an entry into an accounting record or a report to rectify an identified mistake or to reflect an improved measurement of a quantity previously entered into the record or report. Each correction must identify the entry to which it pertains.

104. "Effective kilogram" means a special unit used in safeguarding *nuclear material.* The quantity in "effective kilograms" is obtained by taking:

(a) For plutonium, its weight in kilograms;
(b) For uranium with an *enrichment oi 0.01 (1%)* and above, its weight in kilograms multiplied by the square of its *enrichment;*
(c) For uranium with an *enrichment* below 0.01 *(1%)* and above 0.005 (0.5 %), its weight in kilograms multiplied by 0.0001; and
(d) For depleted uranium with an *enrichment* of 0.005 (0.595) or below, and for thorium, its weight in kilograms multiplied by 0.00005.

105. "Enrichment" means the ratio of the combined weight of the isotopes uranium-233 and uranium-235 to that of the total uranium in question.

106. "Facility" means:

(a) A reactor, a critical facility, a conversion plant, a fabrication plant, a reprocessing plant, an isotope separation plant or a separate storage installation; or
(b) Any location where *nuclear material* in amounts greater than one *effective kilogram* is customarily used.

107. "Inventory change" means an increase or decrease, in terms of *batches*, of *nuclear material* in a *material balance area;* such a change shall involve one of the following:

(a) Increases:
  (i) Import;
  (ii) Domestic receipt: receipts from other *material balance areas*, receipts from a non-safeguarded (non-peaceful) activity or receipts at the starting point of safeguards;
  (iii) Nuclear production: production of special fissionable material in a reactor; and
  (iv) De-exemption: reapplication of safeguards *on nuclear material* previously exempted therefrom on account of Its use or quantity.
(b) Decreases:
  (i) Export;
  (ii) Domestic shipment: shipments to other *material balance areas* or shipments for a non-safeguarded (non-peaceful) activity;
  (iii) Nuclear loss: loss of *nuclear material due* to its transformation into other element(s) or isotope(s) as a result of nuclear reactions;

(iv) Measured discard: *nuclear material* which has been measured, or estimated on the basis of measurements, and disposed of in such a way that it is not suitable for further nuclear use;
(v) Retained waste: *nuclear material* generated from processing or from an operational accident, which is deemed to be unrecoverable for the time being but which is stored;
(vi) Exemption: exemption of *nuclear material* from safeguards on account of its use or quantity; and
(vii) Other loss: for example, accidental loss (that is, irretrievable and inadvertent loss of *nuclear material* as the result of an operational accident) or theft.

108. "Key measurement point" means a location where *nuclear material* appears in such a form that it may be measured to determine material flow or inventory. "Key measurement points" thus include, but are not limited to, the inputs and outputs (including measured discards) and storages in *material balance areas.*

109. "Man-year of inspection" means, for the purposes of paragraph 80 above, 300 man-days of inspection, a man-day being a day during which a single inspector has access to a *facility* at any time for a total of not more than eight hours.

110. "Material balance area" means an area in or outside of a *facility* such that:
(a) The quantity of *nuclear material* in each transfer into or out of each "material balance area" can be determined; and
(b) The *physical inventory* of *nuclear material* in each "material balance area" can be determined when necessary, in accordance with specified procedures, in order that the material balance for Agency safeguards purposes can be established.

111. "Material unaccounted for" means the difference between *book inventory* and *physical inventory.*

112. "Nuclear material" means any source or any special fissionable material as defined in Article XX of the Statute. The term source material shall not be interpreted as applying to ore or ore residue. Any determination by the Board under Article XX of the Statute after the entry into force of this Agreement which adds to the materials considered to be source material or special fissionable material shall have effect under this Agreement only upon acceptance by the State.

113. "Physical inventory" means the sum of all the measured or derived estimates of *batch* quantities of *nuclear material* on hand at a given time within a *material balance area,* obtained in accordance with specified procedures.

114. "Shipper/receiver difference" means the difference between the quantity of *nuclear material* in a *batch* as stated by the shipping *material balance area* and as measured at the receiving *material balance area.*

115. "Source data" means those data, recorded during measurement or calibration or used to derive empirical relationships, which identify *nuclear material* and provide *batch data.* "Source data" may include, for example, weight of compounds, conversion factors to determine weight of element, specific gravity, element concentration, isotopic ratios, relationship between volume and manometer readings and relationship between plutonium produced and power generated.

116. "Strategic point" means a location selected during examination of design information where, under normal conditions and when combined with the information from all "strategic points" taken together, the information necessary and sufficient for the implementation of safeguards measures is obtained and verified; a "strategic point" may

include any location where key measurements related to material balance accountancy are made and where containment and surveillance measures are executed.

59.c Model Protocol Additional to the Agreement(s) between State(s) and the International Atomic Energy Agency for the Application of Safeguards*

Date: June 1972
Source: IAEA INFCIRC/540 (Corr.)
http://www.iaea.org/Publications/Documents/Infcircs/1997/infcirc540c.pdf

Preamble

WHEREAS … … …. (hereinafter referred to as " … … … … ") is a party to (an) Agreement(s) between … … … … and the International Atomic Energy Agency (hereinafter referred to as the "Agency") for the application of safeguards [full title of the Agreement(s) to be inserted] (hereinafter referred to as the "Safeguards Agreement(s)"), which entered into force on … … ….;

AWARE OF the desire of the international community to further enhance nuclear non-proliferation by strengthening the effectiveness and improving the efficiency of the Agency's safeguards system;

RECALLING that the Agency must take into account in the implementation of safeguards the need to: avoid hampering the economic and technological development of … … …. or international co-operation in the field of peaceful nuclear activities; respect health, safety, physical protection and other security provisions in force and the rights of individuals; and take every precaution to protect commercial, technological and industrial secrets as well as other confidential information coming to its knowledge;

WHEREAS the frequency and intensity of activities described in this Protocol shall be kept to the minimum consistent with the objective of strengthening the effectiveness and improving the efficiency of Agency safeguards;

NOW THEREFORE .... and the Agency have agreed as follows:

RELATIONSHIP BETWEEN THE PROTOCOL AND THE SAFEGUARDS AGREEMENT

Article 1

The provisions of the Safeguards Agreement shall apply to this Protocol to the extent that they are relevant to and compatible with the provisions of this Protocol. In case of conflict between the provisions of the Safeguards Agreement and those of this Protocol, the provisions of this Protocol shall apply.

* N.B.: The following Model Additional Protocol is designed for States that already have entered into a safeguards agreement (see Document No. 59.b) pursuant to Art III of the Non-Proliferation Treaty (see Document No. 59.a). The Model Addition Protocol is designed to strengthen the effectiveness of the safeguards system. The text of Additional Protocols concluded on the basis of the Model reproduced here is available at http://www.iaea.org/Publications/Documents/Infcircs/part13.shtml.

PROVISION OF INFORMATION

Article 2

a. .... shall provide the Agency with a declaration containing:

(i) A general description of and information specifying the location of *nuclear fuel cycle-related research and development activities*[1] not involving *nuclear material* carried out anywhere that are funded, specifically authorized or controlled by, or carried out on behalf of,..........

(ii) Information identified by the Agency on the basis of expected gains in effectiveness or efficiency, and agreed to by, on operational activities of safeguards relevance at *facilities* and at *locations outside facilities* where *nuclear material* is customarily used.

(iii) A general description of each building on each *site*, including its use and, if not apparent from that description, its contents. The description shall include a map of the *site*.

(iv) A description of the scale of operations for each location engaged in the activities specified in Annex I to this Protocol.

(v) Information specifying the location, operational status and the estimated annual production capacity of uranium mines and concentration plants and thorium concentration plants, and the current annual production of such mines and concentration plants for .... as a whole. shall provide, upon request by the Agency, the current annual production of an individual mine or concentration plant. The pro-vision of this information does not require detailed *nuclear material* accountancy.

(vi) Information regarding source material which has not reached the composition and purity suitable for fuel fabrication or for being isotopically enriched, as follows:

(a) The quantities, the chemical composition, the use or intended use of such material, whether in nuclear or non-nuclear use, for each location in .... at which the material is present in quantities exceeding ten metric tons of uranium and/or twenty metric tons of thorium, and for other locations with quantities of more than one metric ton, the aggregate for .... as a whole if the aggregate exceeds ten metric tons of uranium or twenty metric tons of thorium. The provision of this information does not require detailed *nuclear material* accountancy;

(b) The quantities, the chemical composition and the destination of each export out of ...., of such material for specifically non-nuclear purposes in quantities exceeding:

(1) Ten metric tons of uranium, or for successive exports of uranium from .... to the same State, each of less than ten metric tons, but exceeding a total of ten metric tons for the year;

[1] Terms in italics have specialized meanings, which are defined in Article 18 below.

(2) Twenty metric tons of thorium, or for successive exports of thorium from .... to the same State, each of less than twenty metric tons, but exceeding a total of twenty metric tons for the year;

(c) The quantities, chemical composition, current location and use or intended use of each import into .... of such material for specifically non-nuclear purposes in quantities exceeding:

(1) Ten metric tons of uranium, or for successive imports of uranium into .... each of less than ten metric tons, but exceeding a total of ten metric tons for the year;

(2) Twenty metric tons of thorium, or for successive imports of thorium into .... each of less than twenty metric tons,

but exceeding a total of twenty metric tons for the year; it being understood that there is no requirement to provide information on such material intended for a non-nuclear use once it is in its non-nuclear end-use form.

(vii) (a) Information regarding the quantities, uses and locations of *nuclear material* exempted from safeguards pursuant to [paragraph 37 of INFCIRC/153][2];

(b) Information regarding the quantities (which may be in the form of estimates) and uses at each location, of *nuclear material* exempted from safeguards pursuant to [paragraph 36(b) of INFCIRC/153]2/ but not yet in a non-nuclear end-use form, in quantities exceeding those set out in [paragraph 37 of INFCIRC/153]2/. The provision of this information does not require detailed *nuclear material* accountancy.

(viii) Information regarding the location or further processing of intermediate or high-level waste containing plutonium, *high enriched uranium* or uranium-233 on which safeguards have been terminated pursuant to [paragraph 11 of INFCIRC/153]2/. For the purpose of this paragraph, "further processing" does not include repackaging of the waste or its further conditioning not involving the separation of elements, for storage or disposal.

(ix) The following information regarding specified equipment and non-nuclear material listed in Annex II:

(a) For each export out of .... of such equipment and material: the identity, quantity, location of intended use in the receiving State and date or, as appropriate, expected date, of export;

(b) Upon specific request by the Agency, confirmation by, as importing State, of information provided to the Agency by another State concerning the export of such equipment and material to ....".

(x) General plans for the succeeding ten-year period relevant to the development of the nuclear fuel cycle (including planned *nuclear fuel cycle-related research and development activities*) when approved by the appropriate authorities in ....

[2] The reference to the corresponding provision of the relevant Safeguards Agreement should be inserted where bracketed references to INFCIRC/153 are made.

b. .... shall make every reasonable effort to provide the Agency with the following information:
   (i) A general description of and information specifying the location of *nuclear fuel cycle-related research and development activities* not involving *nuclear material* which are specifically related to enrichment, reprocessing of nuclear fuel or the processing of intermediate or high-level waste containing plutonium, *high enriched uranium* or uranium-233 that are carried out anywhere in but which are not funded, specifically authorized or controlled by, or carried out on behalf of, ... For the purpose of this paragraph, "processing" of intermediate or high-level waste does not include repackaging of the waste or its conditioning not involving the separation of elements, for storage or disposal.
   (ii) A general description of activities and the identity of the person or entity carrying out such activities, at locations identified by the Agency outside a *site* which the Agency considers might be functionally related to the activities of that *site*. The provision of this information is subject to a specific request by the Agency. It shall be provided in consultation with the Agency and in a timely fashion.

c. Upon request by the Agency, ... shall provide amplifications or clarifications of any information it has provided under this Article, in so far as relevant for the purpose of safeguards.

Article 3

a. .... shall provide to the Agency the information identified in Article 2.a.(i), (iii), (iv), (v), (vi)(a), (vii) and (x) and Article 2.b.(i) within 180 days of the entry into force of this Protocol.

b. .... shall provide to the Agency, by 15 May of each year, updates of the information referred to in paragraph a. above for the period covering the previous calendar year. If there has been no change to the information previously provided, shall so indicate.

c. .... shall provide to the Agency, by 15 May of each year, the information identified in Article 2.a.(vi)(b) and (c) for the period covering the previous calendar year.

d. .... shall provide to the Agency on a quarterly basis the information identified in Article 2.a.(ix)(a). This information shall be provided within sixty days of the end of each quarter.

e. .... shall provide to the Agency the information identified in Article 2.a.(viii) 180 days before further processing is carried out and, by 15 May of each year, information on changes in location for the period covering the previous calendar year.

f. .... and the Agency shall agree on the timing and frequency of the provision of the information identified in Article 2.a.(ii).

g. .... shall provide to the Agency the information in Article 2.a.(ix)(b) within sixty days of the Agency's request.

COMPLEMENTARY ACCESS

Article 4

The following shall apply in connection with the implementation of complementary access under Article 5 of this Protocol:

a. The Agency shall not mechanistically or systematically seek to verify the information referred to in Article 2; however, the Agency shall have access to:
   (i) Any location referred to in Article 5.a.(i) or (ii) on a selective basis in order to assure the absence of undeclared *nuclear material* and activities;
   (ii) Any location referred to in Article 5.b. or c. to resolve a question relating to the correctness and completeness of the information provided pursuant to Article 2 or to resolve an inconsistency relating to that information;
   (iii) Any location referred to in Article 5.a.(iii) to the extent necessary for the Agency to confirm, for safeguards purposes, ...'s declaration of the decommissioned status of a *facility* or of a *location outside facilities* where *nuclear material* was customarily used.

b. (i) Except as provided in paragraph (ii) below, the Agency shall give .... advance notice of access of at least 24 hours;
   (ii) For access to any place on a *site* that is sought in conjunction with design information verification visits or ad hoc or routine inspections on that *site*, the period of advance notice shall, if the Agency so requests, be at least two hours but, in exceptional circumstances, it may be less than two hours.

c. Advance notice shall be in writing and shall specify the reasons for access and the activities to be carried out during such access.

d. In the case of a question or inconsistency, the Agency shall provide .... with an opportunity to clarify and facilitate the resolution of the question or inconsistency. Such an opportunity will be provided before a request for access, unless the Agency considers that delay in access would prejudice the purpose for which the access is sought. In any event, the Agency shall not draw any conclusions about the question or inconsistency until .... has been provided with such an opportunity.

e. Unless otherwise agreed to by ...., access shall only take place during regular working hours.

f. shall have the right to have Agency inspectors accompanied during their access by representatives of ...., provided that the inspectors shall not thereby be delayed or otherwise impeded in the exercise of their functions.

Article 5

.... shall provide the Agency with access to:

a. (i) Any place on a *site*;
   (ii) Any location identified by ....under Article 2.a.(v)–(viii);
   (iii) Any *decommissioned facility* or *decommissioned location outside facilities* where *nuclear material* was customarily used.

b. Any location identified by .... under Article 2.a.(i), Article 2.a.(iv), Article 2.a.(ix)(b) or Article 2.b, other than those referred to in paragraph a.(i) above, provided that if .... is unable to provide such access, shall make every reasonable effort to satisfy Agency requirements, without delay, through other means.

c. Any location specified by the Agency, other than locations referred to in paragraphs a. and b. above, to carry out *location-specific environmental sampling*, provided that if .... is unable to provide such access, shall make every reasonable effort to satisfy Agency requirements, without delay, at adjacent locations or through other means.

Article 6

When implementing Article 5, the Agency may carry out the following activities:

a. For access in accordance with Article 5.a.(i) or (iii): visual observation; collection of environmental samples; utilization of radiation detection and measurement devices; application of seals and other identifying and tamper indicating devices specified in Subsidiary Arrangements; and other objective measures which have been demonstrated to be technically feasible and the use of which has been agreed by the Board of Governors (hereinafter referred to as the "Board") and following consultations between the Agency and ....

b. For access in accordance with Article 5.a.(ii): visual observation; item counting of *nuclear material*; non-destructive measurements and sampling; utilization of radiation detection and measurement devices; examination of records relevant to the quantities, origin and disposition of the material; collection of environmental samples; and other objective measures which have been demonstrated to be technically feasible and the use of which has been agreed by the Board and following consultations between the Agency and ....

c. For access in accordance with Article 5.b.: visual observation; collection of environmental samples; utilization of radiation detection and measurement devices; examination of safeguards relevant production and shipping records; and other objective measures which have been demonstrated to be technically feasible and the use of which has been agreed by the Board and following consultations between the Agency and ....

d. For access in accordance with Article 5.c.: collection of environmental samples and, in the event the results do not resolve the question or inconsistency at the location specified by the Agency pursuant to Article 5.c., utilization at that location of visual observation, radiation detection and measurement devices, and, as agreed by and the Agency, other objective measures.

Article 7

a. Upon request by ...., the Agency and shall make arrangements for managed access under this Protocol in order to prevent the dissemination of proliferation sensitive information, to meet safety or physical protection requirements, or to protect proprietary or commercially sensitive information. Such arrangements shall not preclude the Agency from conducting activities necessary to provide credible assurance of the absence of undeclared *nuclear material* and activities at the location in question, including the resolution of a question relating to the correctness and completeness of the information referred to in Article 2 or of an inconsistency relating to that information.

b. .... may, when providing the information referred to in Article 2, inform the Agency of the places at a *site* or location at which managed access may be applicable.

c. Pending the entry into force of any necessary Subsidiary Arrangements, ... may have recourse to managed access consistent with the provisions of paragraph a. above.

Article 8

Nothing in this Protocol shall preclude .... from offering the Agency access to locations in addition to those referred to in Articles 5 and 9 or from requesting the Agency to conduct verification activities at a particular location. The Agency shall, without delay, make every reasonable effort to act upon such a request.

Article 9

.... shall provide the Agency with access to locations specified by the Agency to carry out *wide-area environmental sampling*, provided that if ....is unable to provide such access it shall make every reasonable effort to satisfy Agency requirements at alternative locations. The Agency shall not seek such access until the use of *wide-area environmental sampling* and the procedural arrangements therefor have been approved by the Board and following consultations between the Agency and ....

Article 10

The Agency shall inform ....of:

a. The activities carried out under this Protocol, including those in respect of any questions or inconsistencies the Agency had brought to the attention of ...., within sixty days of the activities being carried out by the Agency.

b. The results of activities in respect of any questions or inconsistencies the Agency had brought to the attention of ...., as soon as possible but in any case within thirty days of the results being established by the Agency.

c. The conclusions it has drawn from its activities under this Protocol. The conclusions shall be provided annually.

DESIGNATION OF AGENCY INSPECTORS

Article 11

a. (i) The Director General shall notify ....of the Board's approval of any Agency official as a safeguards inspector. Unless ....advises the Director General of its rejection of such an official as an inspector for ....within three months of receipt of notification of the Board's approval, the inspector so notified to ....shall be considered designated to ....;

(ii) The Director General, acting in response to a request by .... or on his own initiative, shall immediately inform of the withdrawal of the designation of any official as an inspector for ....

b. A notification referred to in paragraph a. above shall be deemed to be received by .... seven days after the date of the transmission by registered mail of the notification by the Agency to ....

VISAS

Article 12

……… shall, within one month of the receipt of a request therefor, provide the designated inspector specified in the request with appropriate multiple entry/exit and/or transit visas, where required, to enable the inspector to enter and remain on the territory of ……….for the purpose of carrying out his/her functions. Any visas required shall be valid for at least one year and shall be renewed, as required, to cover the duration of the inspector's designation to ……….

SUBSIDIARY ARRANGEMENTS

Article 13

a. Where ………. or the Agency indicates that it is necessary to specify in Subsidiary Arrangements how measures laid down in this Protocol are to be applied, ………. and the Agency shall agree on such Subsidiary Arrangements within ninety days of the entry into force of this Protocol or, where the indication of the need for such Subsidiary Arrangements is made after the entry into force of this Protocol, within ninety days of the date of such indication.
b. Pending the entry into force of any necessary Subsidiary Arrangements, the Agency shall be entitled to apply the measures laid down in this Protocol.

COMMUNICATIONS SYSTEMS

Article 14

a. ……… shall permit and protect free communications by the Agency for official purposes between Agency inspectors in ………. and Agency Headquarters and/or Regional Offices, including attended and unattended transmission of information generated by Agency containment and/or surveillance or measurement devices. The Agency shall have, in consultation with ………., the right to make use of internationally established systems of direct communications, including satellite systems and other forms of telecommunication, not in use in ………. At the request of ……….or the Agency, details of the implementation of this paragraph with respect to the attended or unattended transmission of information generated by Agency containment and/or surveillance or measurement devices shall be specified in the Subsidiary Arrangements.
b. Communication and transmission of information as provided for in paragraph a. above shall take due account of the need to protect proprietary or commercially sensitive information or design information which regards as being of particular sensitivity.

PROTECTION OF CONFIDENTIAL INFORMATION

Article 15

a. The Agency shall maintain a stringent regime to ensure effective protection against disclosure of commercial, technological and industrial secrets and other confidential information coming to its knowledge, including such information coming to the Agency's knowledge in the implementation of this Protocol.

b. The regime referred to in paragraph a. above shall include, among others, provisions relating to:
   (i) General principles and associated measures for the handling of confidential information;
   (ii) Conditions of staff employment relating to the protection of confidential information;
   (iii) Procedures in cases of breaches or alleged breaches of confidentiality.
c. The regime referred to in paragraph a. above shall be approved and periodically reviewed by the Board.

ANNEXES

Article 16

a. The Annexes to this Protocol shall be an integral part thereof. Except for the purposes of amendment of the Annexes, the term "Protocol" as used in this instrument means the Protocol and the Annexes together.
b. The list of activities specified in Annex I, and the list of equipment and material specified in Annex II, may be amended by the Board upon the advice of an open-ended working group of experts established by the Board. Any such amendment shall take effect four months after its adoption by the Board.

ENTRY INTO FORCE

Article 17

a. This Protocol shall enter into force on the date on which the Agency receives from ………. written notification that ……….'s
statutory and/or constitutional requirements for entry into force have been met.

OR[3]

upon signature by the representatives of ……….and the Agency.
b. ……….may, at any date before this Protocol enters into force, declare that it will apply this Protocol provisionally.
c. The Director General shall promptly inform all Member States of the Agency of any declaration of provisional application of, and of the entry into force of, this Protocol.

DEFINITIONS

Article 18

For the purpose of this Protocol:
a. *Nuclear fuel cycle-related research and development activities* means those activities which are specifically related to any process or system development aspect of any of the following:
   – conversion of *nuclear material*,
   – enrichment of *nuclear material*,

[3] The choice of alternative depends on the preference of the State concerned according to its internal legal requirements.

- nuclear fuel fabrication,
- reactors,
- critical facilities,
- reprocessing of nuclear fuel,
- processing (not including repackaging or conditioning not involving the separation of elements, for storage or disposal) of intermediate or high-level waste containing plutonium, *high enriched uranium* or uranium-233,

but do not include activities related to theoretical or basic scientific research or to research and development on industrial radioisotope applications, medical, hydrological and agricultural applications, health and environmental effects and improved maintenance.

b. *Site* means that area delimited by … … …. in the relevant design information for a *facility*, including a *closed-down facility*, and in the relevant information on a *location outside facilities* where *nuclear material* is customarily used, including a *closed-down location outside facilities* where *nuclear material* was customarily used (this is limited to locations with hot cells or where activities related to conversion, enrichment, fuel fabrication or reprocessing were carried out). It shall also include all installations, co-located with the *facility* or location, for the provision or use of essential services, including: hot cells for processing irradiated materials not containing *nuclear material*; installations for the treatment, storage and disposal of waste; and buildings associated with specified activities identified by under Article 2.a.(iv) above.

c. *Decommissioned facility* or *decommissioned location outside facilities* means an installation or location at which residual structures and equipment essential for its use have been removed or rendered inoperable so that it is not used to store and can no longer be used to handle, process or utilize *nuclear material.*

d. *Closed-down facility* or *closed-down location outside facilities* means an installation or location where operations have been stopped and the *nuclear material* removed but which has not been decommissioned.

e. *High enriched uranium* means uranium containing 20 percent or more of the isotope uranium-235.

f. *Location-specific environmental sampling* means the collection of environmental samples (e.g., air, water, vegetation, soil, smears) at, and in the immediate vicinity of, a location specified by the Agency for the purpose of assisting the Agency to draw conclusions about the absence of undeclared *nuclear material* or nuclear activities at the specified location.

g. *Wide-area environmental sampling* means the collection of environmental samples (e.g., air, water, vegetation, soil, smears) at a set of locations specified by the Agency for the purpose of assisting the Agency to draw conclusions about the absence of undeclared *nuclear material* or nuclear activities over a wide area.

h. *Nuclear material* means any source or any special fissionable material as defined in Article XX of the Statute. The term source material shall not be interpreted as applying to ore or ore residue. Any determination by the Board under Article XX of the Statute of the Agency after the entry into force of this Protocol which adds to the materials considered to be source material or special fissionable material shall have effect under this Protocol only upon acceptance by ……….

i. *Facility* means:
   (i) A reactor, a critical facility, a conversion plant, a fabrication plant, a reprocessing plant, an isotope separation plant or a separate storage installation; or
   (ii) Any location where *nuclear material* in amounts greater than one effective kilogram is customarily used.

j. *Location outside facilities* means any installation or location, which is not a *facility*, where *nuclear material* is customarily used in amounts of one effective kilogram or less.

ANNEX I: LIST OF ACTIVITIES REFERRED TO IN ARTICLE 2.a.(iv) OF THE PROTOCOL
ANNEX II: LIST OF SPECIFIED EQUIPMENT AND NON-NUCLEAR MATERIAL FOR THE REPORTING OF EXPORTS AND IMPORTS ACCORDING TO ARTICLE 2.a.(ix)

[not included]

60 Treaty on the Prohibition of Nuclear Weapons

Date: 7 July 2017
Source: A/CONF.229/2017/8
https://treaties.un.org/doc/Treaties/2017/07/20170707%2003-42%20PM/Ch_XXVI_9.pdf

…

Article 2 Declarations

1. Each State Party shall submit to the Secretary-General of the United Nations, not later than 30 days after this Treaty enters into force for that State Party, a declaration in which it shall:
   (a) Declare whether it owned, possessed or controlled nuclear weapons or nuclear explosive devices and eliminated its nuclear-weapon programme, including the elimination or irreversible conversion of all nuclear-weapons-related facilities, prior to the entry into force of this Treaty for that State Party;
   (b) Notwithstanding Article 1 (a), declare whether it owns, possesses or controls any nuclear weapons or other nuclear explosive devices;
   (c) Notwithstanding Article 1 (g), declare whether there are any nuclear weapons or other nuclear explosive devices in its territory or in any place under its jurisdiction or control that are owned, possessed or controlled by another State.

2. The Secretary-General of the United Nations shall transmit all such declarations received to the States Parties.

Article 3 Safeguards

1. Each State Party to which Article 4, paragraph 1 or 2, does not apply shall, at a minimum, maintain its International Atomic Energy Agency safeguards obligations in

force at the time of entry into force of this Treaty, without prejudice to any additional relevant instruments that it may adopt in the future.

2. Each State Party to which Article 4, paragraph 1 or 2, does not apply that has not yet done so shall conclude with the International Atomic Energy Agency and bring into force a comprehensive safeguards agreement (INFCIRC/153 (Corrected)). Negotiation of such agreement shall commence within 180 days from the entry into force of this Treaty for that State Party. The agreement shall enter into force no later than 18 months from the entry into force of this Treaty for that State Party. Each State Party shall thereafter maintain such obligations, without prejudice to any additional relevant instruments that it may adopt in the future.

Article 4 Towards the total elimination of nuclear weapons

1. Each State Party that after 7 July 2017 owned, possessed or controlled nuclear weapons or other nuclear explosive devices and eliminated its nuclear-weapon programme, including the elimination or irreversible conversion of all nuclear- weapons-related facilities, prior to the entry into force of this Treaty for it, shall cooperate with the competent international authority designated pursuant to paragraph 6 of this Article for the purpose of verifying the irreversible elimination of its nuclear-weapon programme. The competent international authority shall report to the States Parties. Such a State Party shall conclude a safeguards agreement with the International Atomic Energy Agency sufficient to provide credible assurance of the non-diversion of declared nuclear material from peaceful nuclear activities and of the absence of undeclared nuclear material or activities in that State Party as a whole. Negotiation of such agreement shall commence within 180 days from the entry into force of this Treaty for that State Party. The agreement shall enter into force no later than 18 months from the entry into force of this Treaty for that State Party. That State Party shall thereafter, at a minimum, maintain these safeguards obligations, without prejudice to any additional relevant instruments that it may adopt in the future.

2. Notwithstanding Article 1 (a), each State Party that owns, possesses or controls nuclear weapons or other nuclear explosive devices shall immediately remove them from operational status, and destroy them as soon as possible but not later than a deadline to be determined by the first meeting of States Parties, in accordance with a legally binding, time-bound plan for the verified and irreversible elimination of that State Party's nuclear-weapon programme, including the elimination or irreversible conversion of all nuclear-weapons-related facilities. The State Party, no later than 60 days after the entry into force of this Treaty for that State Party, shall submit this plan to the States Parties or to a competent international authority designated by the States Parties. The plan shall then be negotiated with the competent international authority, which shall submit it to the subsequent meeting of States Parties or review conference, whichever comes first, for approval in accordance with its rules of procedure.

3. A State Party to which paragraph 2 above applies shall conclude a safeguards agreement with the International Atomic Energy Agency sufficient to provide credible assurance of the non-diversion of declared nuclear material from peaceful nuclear activities and of the absence of undeclared nuclear material or activities in the State as a whole. Negotiation of such agreement shall commence no later than the date upon which implementation of the plan referred to in paragraph 2 is completed. The agreement shall enter into force no later than 18 months after the date of initiation of negotiations. That State Party shall thereafter, at a minimum, maintain these safeguards obligations, without prejudice to any additional

relevant instruments that it may adopt in the future. Following the entry into force of the agreement referred to in this paragraph, the State Party shall submit to the Secretary-General of the United Nations a final declaration that it has fulfilled its obligations under this Article.

4. Notwithstanding Article 1 (b) and (g), each State Party that has any nuclear weapons or other nuclear explosive devices in its territory or in any place under its jurisdiction or control that are owned, possessed or controlled by another State shall ensure the prompt removal of such weapons, as soon as possible but not later than a deadline to be determined by the first meeting of States Parties. Upon the removal of such weapons or other explosive devices, that State Party shall submit to the Secretary-General of the United Nations a declaration that it has fulfilled its obligations under this Article.

5. Each State Party to which this Article applies shall submit a report to each meeting of States Parties and each review conference on the progress made towards the implementation of its obligations under this Article, until such time as they are fulfilled.

6. The States Parties shall designate a competent international authority or authorities to negotiate and verify the irreversible elimination of nuclear-weapons programmes, including the elimination or irreversible conversion of all nuclear- weapons-related facilities in accordance with paragraphs 1, 2 and 3 of this Article. In the event that such a designation has not been made prior to the entry into force of this Treaty for a State Party to which paragraph 1 or 2 of this Article applies, the Secretary-General of the United Nations shall convene an extraordinary meeting of States Parties to take any decisions that may be required.

Article 5 National implementation

1. Each State Party shall adopt the necessary measures to implement its obligations under this Treaty.

2. Each State Party shall take all appropriate legal, administrative and other measures, including the imposition of penal sanctions, to prevent and suppress any activity prohibited to a State Party under this Treaty undertaken by persons or on territory under its jurisdiction or control.

Article 6 Victim assistance and environmental remediation

1. Each State Party shall, with respect to individuals under its jurisdiction who are affected by the use or testing of nuclear weapons, in accordance with applicable international humanitarian and human rights law, adequately provide age- and gender-sensitive assistance, without discrimination, including medical care, rehabilitation and psychological support, as well as provide for their social and economic inclusion.

2. Each State Party, with respect to areas under its jurisdiction or control contaminated as a result of activities related to the testing or use of nuclear weapons or other nuclear explosive devices, shall take necessary and appropriate measures towards the environmental remediation of areas so contaminated.

3. The obligations under paragraphs 1 and 2 above shall be without prejudice to the duties and obligations of any other States under international law or bilateral agreements.

Article 7 International cooperation and assistance

1. Each State Party shall cooperate with other States Parties to facilitate the implementation of this Treaty.

2. In fulfilling its obligations under this Treaty, each State Party shall have the right to seek and receive assistance, where feasible, from other States Parties.

3. Each State Party in a position to do so shall provide technical, material and financial assistance to States Parties affected by nuclear-weapons use or testing, to further the implementation of this Treaty.

4. Each State Party in a position to do so shall provide assistance for the victims of the use or testing of nuclear weapons or other nuclear explosive devices.

5. Assistance under this Article may be provided, inter alia, through the United Nations system, international, regional or national organizations or institutions, non-governmental organizations or institutions, the International Committee of the Red Cross, the International Federation of Red Cross and Red Crescent Societies, or national Red Cross and Red Crescent Societies, or on a bilateral basis.

6. Without prejudice to any other duty or obligation that it may have under international law, a State Party that has used or tested nuclear weapons or any other nuclear explosive devices shall have a responsibility to provide adequate assistance to affected States Parties, for the purpose of victim assistance and environmental remediation.

Article 8 Meeting of States Parties

1. The States Parties shall meet regularly in order to consider and, where necessary, take decisions in respect of any matter with regard to the application or implementation of this Treaty, in accordance with its relevant provisions, and on further measures for nuclear disarmament, including:

(a) The implementation and status of this Treaty;

(b) Measures for the verified, time-bound and irreversible elimination of nuclear-weapon programmes, including additional protocols to this Treaty;

(c) Any other matters pursuant to and consistent with the provisions of this Treaty.

2. The first meeting of States Parties shall be convened by the Secretary- General of the United Nations within one year of the entry into force of this Treaty. Further meetings of States Parties shall be convened by the Secretary-General of the United Nations on a biennial basis, unless otherwise agreed by the States Parties. The meeting of States Parties shall adopt its rules of procedure at its first session.

Pending their adoption, the rules of procedure of the United Nations conference to negotiate a legally binding instrument to prohibit nuclear weapons, leading towards their total elimination, shall apply.

3. Extraordinary meetings of States Parties shall be convened, as may be deemed necessary, by the Secretary-General of the United Nations, at the written request of any State Party provided that this request is supported by at least one third of the States Parties.

4. After a period of five years following the entry into force of this Treaty, the Secretary-General of the United Nations shall convene a conference to review the operation of the Treaty and the progress in achieving the purposes of the Treaty. The Secretary-General of the United Nations shall convene further review conferences at intervals of six years with the same objective, unless otherwise agreed by the States Parties.

5. States not party to this Treaty, as well as the relevant entities of the United Nations system, other relevant international organizations or institutions, regional organizations, the International Committee of the Red Cross, the International Federation of Red Cross and Red Crescent Societies and relevant non-governmental organizations, shall be invited to attend the meetings of States Parties and the review conferences as observers.

Article 9 Costs

1. The costs of the meetings of States Parties, the review conferences and the extraordinary meetings of States Parties shall be borne by the States Parties and States not party to this Treaty participating therein as observers, in accordance with the United Nations scale of assessment adjusted appropriately.

2. The costs incurred by the Secretary-General of the United Nations in the circulation of declarations under Article 2, reports under Article 4 and proposed amendments under Article 10 of this Treaty shall be borne by the States Parties in accordance with the United Nations scale of assessment adjusted appropriately.

3. The cost related to the implementation of verification measures required under Article 4 as well as the costs related to the destruction of nuclear weapons or other nuclear explosive devices, and the elimination of nuclear-weapon programmes, including the elimination or conversion of all nuclear-weapons-related facilities, should be borne by the States Parties to which they apply.

Article 10 Amendments

1. At any time after the entry into force of this Treaty, any State Party may propose amendments to the Treaty. The text of a proposed amendment shall be communicated to the Secretary-General of the United Nations, who shall circulate it to all States Parties and shall seek their views on whether to consider the proposal. If a majority of the States Parties notify the Secretary-General of the United Nations no later than 90 days after its circulation that they support further consideration of the proposal, the proposal shall be considered at the next meeting of States Parties or review conference, whichever comes first.

2. A meeting of States Parties or a review conference may agree upon amendments which shall be adopted by a positive vote of a majority of two thirds of the States Parties. The Depositary shall communicate any adopted amendment to all States Parties.

3. The amendment shall enter into force for each State Party that deposits its instrument of ratification or acceptance of the amendment 90 days following the deposit of such instruments of ratification or acceptance by a majority of the States Parties at the time of adoption. Thereafter, it shall enter into force for any other State Party 90 days following the deposit of its instrument of ratification or acceptance of the amendment.

Article 11 Settlement of disputes

1. When a dispute arises between two or more States Parties relating to the interpretation or application of this Treaty, the parties concerned shall consult together with a view to the settlement of the dispute by negotiation or by other peaceful means of the parties' choice in accordance with Article 33 of the Charter of the United Nations.

2. The meeting of States Parties may contribute to the settlement of the dispute, including by offering its good offices, calling upon the States Parties concerned to start the settlement procedure of their choice and recommending a time limit for any agreed procedure, in accordance with the relevant provisions of this Treaty and the Charter of the United Nations.

Article 12 Universality

Each State Party shall encourage States not party to this Treaty to sign, ratify, accept, approve or accede to the Treaty, with the goal of universal adherence of all States to the Treaty.

...

The Framework of the Bangkok Treaty on the Southeast Asia Nuclear Weapon-Free Zone

61.a Treaty on the Southeast Asia Nuclear Weapon-Free Zone (The Bangkok Treaty)

Date: 15 December 1995
Source: (1996) 35 ILM 635
https://asean.org/treaty-on-the-southeast-asia-nuclear-weapon-free-zone/

...

Article 5: IAEA SAFEGUARDS

Each State Party which has not done so shall conclude an agreement with the IAEA for the application of full scope safeguards to its peaceful nuclear activities not later than eighteen months after the entry into force for that State Party of this Treaty.

...

Article 8: ESTABLISHMENT OF THE COMMISSION FOR THE SOUTHEAST ASIA NUCLEAR WEAPON-FREE ZONE

1. There is hereby established a Commission for the Southeast Asia Nuclear Weapon-Free Zone, hereinafter referred to as the "Commission".

2. All States Parties are ipso facto members or the Commission. Each State Party shall be represented by its Foreign Minister or his representative accompanied by alternates and advisers.

3. The function of the Commission shall be to oversee the implementation of this Treaty and ensure compliance with its provisions.

4. The Commission shall meet as and when necessary in accordance with the provisions of this Treaty including upon the request of any State Party. As far as possible, the Commission shall meet in conjunction with the ASEAN Ministerial Meeting.

5. At the beginning of each meeting, the Commission shall elect its Chairman and such other officers as may be required. They shall hold office until a new Chairman and other officers are elected at the next meeting.

6. Unless otherwise provided for in this Treaty, two-thirds of the members of the Commission shall be present to constitute a quorum.

7. Each member of the Commission shall have one vote.

8. Except as provided for in this Treaty, decisions of the Commission shall be taken by consensus or, failing consensus, by a two-thirds majority of the members present and voting.

9. The Commission shall, by consensus, agree upon and adopt rules of procedure for itself as well as financial rules governing its funding and that of its subsidiary organs.

Article 9: THE EXECUTIVE COMMITTEE

1. There is hereby established, as a subsidiary organ of the Commission, the Executive Committee.

2. The Executive Committee shall be composed of all States Parties to this Treaty. Each State Party shall be represented by one senior official as its representative, who may be accompanied by alternates and advisers.

3. The functions of the Executive Committee shall be to:
   (a) ensure the proper operation of verification measures in accordance with the provisions on the control system as stipulated in Article 10;
   (b) consider and decide on requests for clarification and for a fact-finding mission;
   (c) set up a fact-finding mission in accordance with the Annex of this Treaty;
   (d) consider and decide on the findings of a fact-finding mission and report to the Commission;
   (e) request the Commission to convene a meeting when appropriate and necessary;
   (f) conclude such agreements with the IAEA or other international organizations as referred to in Article 18 on behalf of the Commission after being duly authorized to do so by the Commission; and
   (g) carry out such other tasks as may, from time to time, be assigned by the Commission.

4. The Executive Committee shall meet as and when necessary for the efficient exercise of its functions. As far as possible, the Executive Committee shall meet in conjunction with the ASEAN Senior Officials Meeting.

5. The Chairman of the Executive Committee shall be the representative of the Chairman of the Commission. Any submission or communication made by a State Party to the Chairman of the Executive Committee shall be disseminated to the other members of the Executive Committee.

6. Two-thirds of the members of the Executive Committee shall be present to constitute a quorum.

7. Each member of the Executive Committee shall have one vote.

8. Decisions of the Executive Committee shall be taken by consensus or, failing consensus, by a two-thirds majority of the members present and voting.

Article 10: CONTROL SYSTEM

1. There is hereby established a control system for the purpose of verifying compliance with the obligations of the States Parties under this Treaty.

2. The Control System shall comprise:
   (a) the IAEA safeguards system as provided for in Article 5;
   (b) report and exchange of information as provided for in Article 11;
   (c) request for clarification as provided for in Article 12; and
   (d) request and procedures for a fact-finding mission as provided for in Article 13.

Article 11: REPORT AND EXCHANGE OF INFORMATION

1. Each State Party shall submit reports to the Executive Committee on any significant event within its territory and areas under its jurisdiction and control affecting the implementation of this Treaty.

2. The States Parties may exchange information on matters arising under or in relation to this Treaty.

Article 12: REQUEST FOR CLARIFICATION

1. Each State Party shall have the right to request another State Party for clarification concerning any situation which may be considered ambiguous or which may give rise to doubts about the compliance of that State Party with this Treaty. It shall inform the

Executive Committee of such a request. The requested State Party shall duly respond by providing without delay the necessary information and inform the Executive Committee of its reply to the requesting State Party.

2. Each State Party shall have the right to request the Executive committee to seek clarification from another State Party concerning any situation which may be considered ambiguous or which may give rise to doubts about compliance of that State-Party with this Treaty. Upon receipt of such a request, the Executive Committee shall consult the State Party from which clarification is sought for the purpose of obtaining the clarification requested.

Article 13: REQUEST FOR A FACT-FINDING MISSION

A State Party shall have the right to request the Executive Committee to send a fact-finding mission to another State Party in order to clarify and resolve a situation which may be considered ambiguous or which may give rise to doubts about compliance with the provisions of this Treaty, in accordance with the procedure contained in the Annex to this Treaty.

Article 14: REMEDIAL MEASURES

1. In case the Executive Committee decides in accordance with the Annex that there is a breach of this Treaty by a State Party, that State Party shall, within a reasonable time, take all steps necessary to bring itself in full compliance with this Treaty and shall promptly inform the Executive Committee of the action taken or proposed to be taken by it.

2. Where a State Party fails or refuses to comply with the provisions of Paragraph 1 of this Article, the Executive Committee shall request the commission to convene a meeting in accordance with the provisions of Paragraph 3(e) of Article 9.

3. At the meeting convened pursuant to Paragraph 2 of this Article, the Commission shall consider the emergent situation and shall decide on any measure it deems appropriate to cope with the situation, including the submission of the matter to the IAEA and, where the situation might endanger international peace and security, the Security council and the General Assembly of the United Nations.

4. In the event of breach of the Protocol attached to this Treaty by a State Party to the Protocol, the Executive Committee shall convene a special meeting of the Commission to decide on appropriate measures to be taken.

...

Article 21: SETTLEMENT OF DISPUTES

Any dispute arising from the interpretation of the provisions of this Treaty shall be settled by peaceful means as may be agreed upon by the States Parties to the dispute. If within one month, the parties to the dispute are unable to achieve a peaceful settlement of the dispute by negotiation, mediation, enquiry or conciliation, any of the parties concerned shall, with the prior consent of the other parties concerned, refer the dispute to arbitration or to the International Court of Justice.

61.b Procedure for a Fact-Finding Mission (Annex to the Bangkok Treaty)

Date: 15 December 1995
Source: (1996) 35 ILM 635
http://disarmament.un.org/treaties/t/bangkok/text

1. The State Party requesting a fact-finding mission as provided in Article 13, hereinafter referred to as the "requesting State", shall submit the request to the Executive Committee specifying the following:

(*a*) the doubts or concerns and the reasons for such doubts or concerns;

(*b*) the location in which the situation which gives rise to doubts has allegedly occurred;

(*c*) the relevant provisions of this Treaty about which doubts of compliance have arisen; and

(*d*) any other relevant information.

2. Upon receipt of a request for a fact-finding mission, the Executive Committee shall:

(*a*) immediately inform the State Party to which the fact-finding mission is requested to be sent, hereinafter referred to as the "receiving State", about the receipt of the request; and

(*b*) not later than 3 weeks after receiving the request, decide if the request complies with the provisions of Paragraph l and whether or not it is frivolous, abusive or clearly beyond the scope of this Treaty. Neither the requesting nor receiving State Party shall participate in such decisions.

3. In case the Executive Committee decides that the request does not comply with the provisions of Paragraph 1, or that it is frivolous, abusive or clearly beyond the scope of this Treaty, it shall take no further action on the request and inform the requesting State and the receiving State accordingly.

4. In the event that the Executive Committee decides that the request complies with the provisions of Paragraph l, and that it is not frivolous, abusive or clearly beyond the scope of this Treaty, it shall immediately forward the request for a fact-finding mission to the receiving State, indicating, *inter alia*, the proposed date for sending the mission. The proposed date shall not be later than 3 weeks from the time the receiving State receives the request for a fact-finding mission. The Executive Committee shall also immediately set up a fact-finding mission consisting of 3 inspectors from the IAEA who are neither nationals of the requesting nor receiving State.

5. The receiving State shall comply with the request for a fact-finding mission referred to in Paragraph 4. It shall cooperate with the Executive Committee in order to facilitate the effective functioning of the fact-finding mission, *inter alia*, by promptly providing unimpeded access of the fact-finding mission to the location in question. The receiving State shall accord to the members of the fact-finding mission such privileges and immunities as are necessary for them to exercise their functions effectively, including inviolability of all papers and documents and immunity from arrest, detention and legal process for acts done and words spoken for the purpose of the mission.

6. The receiving State shall have the right to take measures to protect sensitive installations and to prevent disclosures of confidential information and data not related to this Treaty.

7. The fact-finding mission, in the discharge of its functions, shall:
   (*a*) respect the laws and regulations of the receiving State;
   (*b*) refrain from activities inconsistent with the objectives and purposes of this Treaty;
   (*c*) submit preliminary or interim reports to the Executive Committee; and
   (*d*) complete its task without undue delay and shall submit its final report to the Executive Committee within a reasonable time upon completion of its work.

8. The Executive Committee shall:
   (*a*) consider the reports submitted by the fact-finding mission and reach a decision on whether or not there is a breach of this Treaty;
   (*b*) immediately communicate its decision to the requesting State and the receiving State; and
   (*c*) present a full report on its decision to the Commission.

9. In the event that the receiving State refuses to comply with the request for a fact-finding mission in accordance with Paragraph 4, the requesting State through the Executive Committee shall have the right to request for a meeting of the Commission. The Executive Committee shall immediately request the Commission to convene a meeting in accordance with Paragraph 3(*e*) of Article 9.

62 Convention on the Prohibition of the Use, Stockpiling, Production and Transfer of Anti-Personnel Mines and on Their Destruction (The Ottawa Convention)

Date: 18 September 1997
Source: 2056 UNTS 211
https://treaties.un.org/doc/Treaties/1997/09/19970918%2007-53%20AM/Ch_XXVI_05p.pdf

…

Article 7 Transparency measures

1. Each State Party shall report to the Secretary-General of the United Nations as soon as practicable, and in any event not later than 180 days after the entry into force of this Convention for that State Party on:
   a) The national implementation measures referred to in Article 9;
   b) The total of all stockpiled anti-personnel mines owned or possessed by it, or under its jurisdiction or control, to include a breakdown of the type, quantity and, if possible, lot numbers of each type of anti-personnel mine stockpiled;
   c) To the extent possible, the location of all mined areas that contain, or are suspected to contain, anti-personnel mines under its jurisdiction or control, to include as much detail as possible regarding the type and quantity of each type of anti- personnel mine in each mined area and when they were emplaced;
   d) The types, quantities and, if possible, lot numbers of all anti-personnel mines retained or transferred for the development of and training in mine detection, mine clearance or mine destruction techniques, or transferred for the purpose of destruction, as well as the institutions authorized by a State Party to retain or transfer anti-personnel mines, in accordance with Article 3;

e) The status of programs for the conversion or de-commissioning of anti-personnel mine production facilities;

f) The status of programs for the destruction of anti-personnel mines in accordance with Articles 4 and 5, including details of the methods which will be used in destruction, the location of all destruction sites and the applicable safety and environmental standards to be observed;

g) The types and quantities of all anti-personnel mines destroyed after the entry into force of this Convention for that State Party, to include a breakdown of the quantity of each type of anti-personnel mine destroyed, in accordance with Articles 4 and 5, respectively, along with, if possible, the lot numbers of each type of anti-personnel mine in the case of destruction in accordance with Article 4;

h) The technical characteristics of each type of anti-personnel mine produced, to the extent known, and those currently owned or possessed by a State Party, giving, where reasonably possible, such categories of information as may facilitate identification and clearance of anti-personnel mines; at a minimum, this information shall include the dimensions, fusing, explosive content, metallic content, colour photographs and other information which may facilitate mine clearance; and

i) The measures taken to provide an immediate and effective warning to the population in relation to all areas identified under paragraph 2 of Article 5.

2. The information provided in accordance with this Article shall be updated by the States Parties annually, covering the last calendar year, and reported to the Secretary- General of the United Nations not later than 30 April of each year.

3. The Secretary-General of the United Nations shall transmit all such reports received to the States Parties.

Article 8 Facilitation and clarification of compliance

1. The States Parties agree to consult and cooperate with each other regarding the implementation of the provisions of this Convention, and to work together in a spirit of cooperation to facilitate compliance by States Parties with their obligations under this Convention.

2. If one or more States Parties wish to clarify and seek to resolve questions relating to compliance with the provisions of this Convention by another State Party, it may submit, through the Secretary-General of the United Nations, a Request for Clarification of that matter to that State Party. Such a request shall be accompanied by all appropriate information. Each State Party shall refrain from unfounded Requests for Clarification, care being taken to avoid abuse. A State Party that receives a Request for Clarification shall provide, through the Secretary-General of the United Nations, within 28 days to the requesting State Party all information which would assist in clarifying this matter.

3. If the requesting State Party does not receive a response through the Secretary-General of the United Nations within that time period, or deems the response to the Request for Clarification to be unsatisfactory, it may submit the matter through the Secretary-General of the United Nations to the next Meeting of the States Parties. The Secretary-General of the United Nations shall transmit the submission, accompanied by all appropriate information pertaining to the Request for Clarification, to all States Parties. All such information shall be presented to the requested State Party which shall have the right to respond.

4. Pending the convening of any meeting of the States Parties, any of the States Parties concerned may request the Secretary-General of the United Nations to exercise his or her good offices to facilitate the clarification requested.

5. The requesting State Party may propose through the Secretary-General of the United Nations the convening of a Special Meeting of the States Parties to consider the matter. The Secretary-General of the United Nations shall thereupon communicate this proposal and all information submitted by the States Parties concerned, to all States Parties with a request that they indicate whether they favour a Special Meeting of the States Parties, for the purpose of considering the matter. In the event that within 14 days from the date of such communication, at least one-third of the States Parties favours such a Special Meeting, the Secretary-General of the United Nations shall convene this Special Meeting of the States Parties within a further 14 days. A quorum for this Meeting shall consist of a majority of States Parties.

6. The Meeting of the States Parties or the Special Meeting of the States Parties, as the case may be, shall first determine whether to consider the matter further, taking into account all information submitted by the States Parties concerned. The Meeting of the States Parties or the Special Meeting of the States Parties shall make every effort to reach a decision by consensus. If despite all efforts to that end no agreement has been reached, it shall take this decision by a majority of States Parties present and voting.

7. All States Parties shall cooperate fully with the Meeting of the States Parties or the Special Meeting of the States Parties in the fulfilment of its review of the matter, including any fact-finding missions that are authorized in accordance with paragraph 8.

8. If further clarification is required, the Meeting of the States Parties or the Special Meeting of the States Parties shall authorize a fact-finding mission and decide on its mandate by a majority of States Parties present and voting. At any time the requested State Party may invite a fact-finding mission to its territory. Such a mission shall take place without a decision by a Meeting of the States Parties or a Special Meeting of the States Parties to authorize such a mission. The mission, consisting of up to 9 experts, designated and approved in accordance with paragraphs 9 and 10, may collect additional information on the spot or in other places directly related to the alleged compliance issue under the jurisdiction or control of the requested State Party.

9. The Secretary-General of the United Nations shall prepare and update a list of the names, nationalities and other relevant data of qualified experts provided by States Parties and communicate it to all States Parties. Any expert included on this list shall be regarded as designated for all fact-finding missions unless a State Party declares its non-acceptance in writing. In the event of non-acceptance, the expert shall not participate in fact-finding missions on the territory or any other place under the jurisdiction or control of the objecting State Party, if the non-acceptance was declared prior to the appointment of the expert to such missions.

10. Upon receiving a request from the Meeting of the States Parties or a Special Meeting of the States Parties, the Secretary-General of the United Nations shall, after consultations with the requested State Party, appoint the members of the mission, including its leader. Nationals of States Parties requesting the fact-finding mission or directly affected by it shall not be appointed to the mission. The members of the fact-finding mission shall enjoy privileges and immunities under Article VI of the Convention on the Privileges and Immunities of the United Nations, adopted on 13 February 1946.

11. Upon at least 72 hours notice, the members of the fact-finding mission shall arrive in the territory of the requested State Party at the earliest opportunity. The requested State Party

shall take the necessary administrative measures to receive, transport and accommodate the mission, and shall be responsible for ensuring the security of the mission to the maximum extent possible while they are on territory under its control.

12. Without prejudice to the sovereignty of the requested State Party, the fact-finding mission may bring into the territory of the requested State Party the necessary equipment which shall be used exclusively for gathering information on the alleged compliance issue. Prior to its arrival, the mission will advise the requested State Party of the equipment that it intends to utilize in the course of its fact-finding mission.

13. The requested State Party shall make all efforts to ensure that the fact-finding mission is given the opportunity to speak with all relevant persons who may be able to provide information related to the alleged compliance issue.

14. The requested State Party shall grant access for the fact-finding mission to all areas and installations under its control where facts relevant to the compliance issue could be expected to be collected. This shall be subject to any arrangements that the requested State Party considers necessary for:

a) The protection of sensitive equipment, information and areas;
b) The protection of any constitutional obligations the requested State Party may have with regard to proprietary rights, searches and seizures, or other constitutional rights; or
c) The physical protection and safety of the members of the fact-finding mission.

In the event that the requested State Party makes such arrangements, it shall make every reasonable effort to demonstrate through alternative means its compliance with this Convention.

15. The fact-finding mission may remain in the territory of the State Party concerned for no more than 14 days, and at any particular site no more than 7 days, unless otherwise agreed.

16. All information provided in confidence and not related to the subject matter of the fact-finding mission shall be treated on a confidential basis.

17. The fact-finding mission shall report, through the Secretary-General of the United Nations, to the Meeting of the States Parties or the Special Meeting of the States Parties the results of its findings.

18. The Meeting of the States Parties or the Special Meeting of the States Parties shall consider all relevant information, including the report submitted by the fact-finding mission, and may request the requested State Party to take measures to address the compliance issue within a specified period of time. The requested State Party shall report on all measures taken in response to this request.

19. The Meeting of the States Parties or the Special Meeting of the States Parties may suggest to the States Parties concerned ways and means to further clarify or resolve the matter under consideration, including the initiation of appropriate procedures in conformity with international law. In circumstances where the issue at hand is determined to be due to circumstances beyond the control of the requested State Party, the Meeting of the States Parties or the Special Meeting of the States Parties may recommend appropriate measures, including the use of cooperative measures referred to in Article 6.

20. The Meeting of the States Parties or the Special Meeting of the States Parties shall make every effort to reach its decisions referred to in paragraphs 18 and 19 by consensus, otherwise by a two-thirds majority of States Parties present and voting.

Article 9 National implementation measures

Each State Party shall take all appropriate legal, administrative and other measures, including the imposition of penal sanctions, to prevent and suppress any activity prohibited to a State Party under this Convention undertaken by persons or on territory under its jurisdiction or control.

Article 10 Settlement of disputes

1. The States Parties shall consult and cooperate with each other to settle any dispute that may arise with regard to the application or the interpretation of this Convention. Each State Party may bring any such dispute before the Meeting of the States Parties.

2. The Meeting of the States Parties may contribute to the settlement of the dispute by whatever means it deems appropriate, including offering its good offices, calling upon the States parties to a dispute to start the settlement procedure of their choice and recommending a time-limit for any agreed procedure.

3. This Article is without prejudice to the provisions of this Convention on facilitation and clarification of compliance.

Article 11 Meetings of the States Parties

1. The States Parties shall meet regularly in order to consider any matter with regard to the application or implementation of this Convention, including:

a) The operation and status of this Convention;
b) Matters arising from the reports submitted under the provisions of this Convention;
c) International cooperation and assistance in accordance with Article 6;
d) The development of technologies to clear anti-personnel mines;
e) Submissions of States Parties under Article 8; and
f) Decisions relating to submissions of States Parties as provided for in Article 5.

2. The First Meeting of the States Parties shall be convened by the Secretary-General of the United Nations within one year after the entry into force of this Convention. The subsequent meetings shall be convened by the Secretary-General of the United Nations annually until the first Review Conference.

3. Under the conditions set out in Article 8, the Secretary-General of the United Nations shall convene a Special Meeting of the States Parties.

4. States not parties to this Convention, as well as the United Nations, other relevant international organizations or institutions, regional organizations, the International Committee of the Red Cross and relevant non-governmental organizations may be invited to attend these meetings as observers in accordance with the agreed Rules of Procedure.

...

12 The Aftermath of Crises

63 The Treaty of Peace between the Allied and Associated Powers and Germany (Versailles Treaty)

Date: 28 June 1919
Source: C Parry, *Consolidated Treaty Series* (vol 225, 1969) 188

...

PART X. ECONOMIC CLAUSES

...

SECTION VI. MIXED ARBITRAL TRIBUNAL

ARTICLE 304

a. Within three months from the date of the coming into force of the present Treaty, a Mixed Arbitral Tribunal shall be established between each of the Allied and Associated Powers on the one hand and Germany on the other hand. Each such Tribunal shall consist of three members. Each of the Governments concerned shall appoint one of these members. The President shall be chosen by agreement between the two Governments concerned.

In case of failure to reach agreement, the President of the Tribunal and two other persons, either of whom may in case of need take his place, shall be chosen by the Council of the League of Nations, or, until this is set up, by M. Gustave Ador if he is willing. These persons shall be nationals of Powers that have remained neutral during the war.

If any Government does not proceed within a period of one month in case there is a vacancy to appoint a member of the Tribunal, such member shall be chosen by the other Government from the two persons mentioned above other than the President.

The decision of the majority of the members of the Tribunal shall be the decision of the Tribunal.

b. The Mixed Arbitral Tribunals established pursuant to paragraph (a), shall decide all questions within their competence under Sections III, IV, V and VII.[*]

In addition, all questions, whatsoever their nature, relating to contracts concluded before the coming into force of the present Treaty between nationals of the Allied and Associated Powers and German nationals shall be decided by the Mixed Arbitral Tribunal, always excepting questions which, under the laws of the Allied, Associated or Neutral Powers, are within the jurisdiction of the National Courts of those Powers. Such questions shall be decided by the National Courts in question, to the exclusion of the Mixed Arbitral Tribunal. The party who is a national of an Allied or Associated Power may nevertheless bring the case before the Mixed Arbitral Tribunal if this is not prohibited by the laws of his country.

c. If the number of cases justifies it, additional members shall be appointed and each Mixed Arbitral Tribunal shall sit in divisions. Each of these divisions will be constituted as above.

* N.B.: These dealt with questions relating to debts (section III), property, rights and interests (section IV), contracts, prescriptions and judgments (section V) and industrial, literary and artistic property (section VII). The jurisdiction of Mixed Arbitral Tribunals established pursuant to Article 304 was further defined in their respective constituent documents, which are reprinted in GC Gidel (ed), *Recueil des décisions des tribunaux arbitraux mixtes institués par les traités de paix* (vol 1, 1922).

d. Each Mixed Arbitral Tribunal will settle its own procedure except in so far as it is provided in the following Annex, and is empowered to award the sums to be paid by the loser in respect of the costs and expenses of the proceedings.

e. Each Government will pay the remuneration of the member of the Mixed Arbitral Tribunal appointed by it and of any agent whom it may appoint to represent it before the Tribunal. The remuneration of the President will be determined by special agreement between the Governments concerned; and this remuneration and the joint expenses of each Tribunal will be paid by the two Governments in equal moieties.

f. The High Contracting Parties agree that their courts and authorities shall render to the Mixed Arbitral Tribunals direct all the assistance in their power, particularly as regards transmitting notices and collecting evidence.

g. The High Contracting Parties agree to regard the decisions of the Mixed Arbitral Tribunal as final and conclusive, and to render them binding upon their nationals.

ARTICLE 305

Whenever a competent court has given or gives a decision in a case covered by Sections III, IV, V or VII,[*] and such decision is inconsistent with the provisions of such Sections, the party who is prejudiced by the decision shall be entitled to obtain redress which shall be fixed by the Mixed Arbitral Tribunal. At the request of the national of an Allied or Associated Power, the redress may, whenever possible, be effected by the Mixed Arbitral Tribunal directing the replacement of the parties in the position occupied by them before the judgment was given by the German court.

Annex to Article 304

1. Should one of the members of the Tribunal either die, retire, or be unable for any reason whatever to discharge his function, the same procedure will be followed for filling the vacancy as was followed for appointing him.

2. The Tribunal may adopt such rules of procedure as shall be in accordance with justice and equity and decide the order and time at which each party must conclude its arguments, and may arrange all formalities required for dealing with the evidence.

3. The agent and counsel of the parties on each side are authorised to present orally and in writing to the Tribunal arguments in Support or in defence of each case.

4. The Tribunal shall keep record of the questions and cases submitted and the proceedings thereon, with the dates of such proceedings.

5. Each of the Powers concerned may appoint a secretary. These secretaries shall act together as joint secretaries of the Tribunal and shall be subject to its direction. The Tribunal may appoint and employ any other necessary officer or officers to assist in the performance of its duties.

6. The Tribunal shall decide all questions and matters submitted upon such evidence and information as may be furnished by the parties concerned.

7. Germany agrees to give the Tribunal all facilities and information required by it for carrying out its investigations.

8. The language in which the proceedings shall be conducted shall, unless otherwise agreed, be English, French, Italian or Japanese, as may be determined by the Allied or Associated Power concerned.

9. The place and time for the meetings of each Tribunal shall be determined by the President of the Tribunal.

...

* N.B.: See the last footnote.

64 Treaty of Peace with Italy 1947

Date: 10 February 1947
Source: 49 UNTS 50

…

PART IX
SETTLEMENT OF DISPUTES

Article 83

1. Any disputes which may arise in giving effect to Articles 75 and 78 and Annexes XIV, XV, XVI and XVII, part B, of the present Treaty[*] shall be referred to a Conciliation Commission consisting of one representative of the Government of the United Nation concerned and one representative of the Government of Italy, having equal status. If within three months after the dispute has been referred to the Conciliation Commission no agreement has been reached, either Government may ask for the addition to the Commission of a third member selected by mutual agreement of the two Governments from nationals of a third country. Should the two Governments fail to agree within two months on the selection of a third member of the Commission, the Governments shall apply to the Ambassadors in Rome of the Soviet Union, of the United Kingdom, of the United States of America, and of France, who will appoint the third member of the Commission. If the Ambassadors are unable to agree within a period of one month upon the appointment of the third member, the Secretary-General of the United Nations may be requested by either party to make the appointment.

2. When any Conciliation Commission is established under paragraph 1 above, it shall have jurisdiction over all disputes which may thereafter arise between the United Nation concerned and Italy in the application or interpretation of Articles 75 and 78 and Annexes XIV, XV, XVI, and XVII, part B, of the present Treaty, and shall perform the functions attributed to it by those provisions.

3. Each Conciliation Commission shall determine its own procedure, adopting rules conforming to justice and equity.

4. Each Government shall pay the salary of the member of the Conciliation Commission whom it appoints and of any agent whom it may designate to represent it before the Commission. The salary of the third member shall be fixed by special agreement between the Governments concerned and this salary, together with the common expenses of each Commission, shall be paid in equal shares by the two Governments.

5. The parties undertake that their authorities shall furnish directly to the Conciliation Commission all assistance which may be within their power.

6. The decision of the majority of the members of the Commission shall be the decision of the Commission, and shall be accepted by the parties as definitive and binding.

* N.B.: These provisions notably required Italy to restore 'property removed from the territory of any of the United Nations' (within the meaning of the 1943 United Nations Declaration), as well as 'all legal rights and interests in Italy of the United Nations and their nationals as they existed on 10 June 1940'; and to transfer without compensation property located in the ceded territories.

The Framework Established by the 1979 Israel-Egypt Peace Treaty

65.a Peace Treaty between Israel and Egypt

Date: 26 March 1979
Source: (1979) 18 ILM 362

...

Article IV

1. In order to provide maximum security for both Parties on the basis of reciprocity, agreed security arrangements will be established including limited force zones in Egyptian and Israeli territory, and United Nations forces and observers, described in detail as to nature and timing in Annex I, and other security arrangements the Parties may agree upon.

2. The Parties agree to the stationing of United Nations personnel in areas described in Annex I. The Parties agree not to request withdrawal of the United Nations personnel and that these personnel will not be removed unless such removal is approved by the Security Council of the United Nations, with the affirmative vote of the five Permanent Members, unless the Parties otherwise agree.

3. A Joint Commission will be established to facilitate the implementation of the Treaty, as provided for in Annex I.

4. The security arrangements provided for in paragraphs 1 and 2 of this Article may at the request of either party be reviewed and amended by mutual agreement of the Parties.

...

Article VII

1. Disputes arising out of the application or interpretation of this Treaty shall be resolved by negotiations.

2. Any such disputes which cannot be settled by negotiations shall be resolved by conciliation or submitted to arbitration.

Article VIII

The Parties agree to establish a claims commission for the mutual settlement of all financial claims.

...

65.b Protocol Concerning Israeli Withdrawal and Security Agreements (Annex I and Appendix thereto)

Date: 26 March 1979
Source: (1979) 18 ILM 362

Article I: Concept of Withdrawal

1. Israel will complete withdrawal of all its armed forces and civilians from the Sinai not later than three years from the date of exchange of instruments of ratification of this Treaty.

2. To ensure the mutual security of the Parties, the implementation of phased withdrawal will be accompanied by the military measures and establishment of zones set out in this Annex and in Map 1, hereinafter referred to as "the Zones."

3. The withdrawal from the Sinai will be accomplished in two phases:

a. The interim withdrawal behind the line from east of El-Arish to Ras Mohammed as delineated on Map 2 within nine months from the date of exchange of instruments of ratification of this Treaty.

b. The final withdrawal from the Sinai behind the international boundary not later than three years from the date of exchange of instruments of ratification of this Treaty.

4. A Joint Commission will be formed immediately after the exchange of instruments of ratification of this Treaty in order to supervise and coordinate movements and schedules during the withdrawal, and to adjust plans and timetables as necessary within the limits established by paragraph 3, above. Details relating to the Joint Commission are set out in Article IV of the attached Appendix. The Joint Commission will be dissolved upon completion of final Israeli withdrawal from the Sinai.

…

Article VI: United Nations Operations

1. The Parties will request the United Nations to provide forces and observers to supervise the implementation of this Annex and employ their best efforts to prevent any violation of its terms.

2. With respect to these United Nations forces and observers, as appropriate, the Parties agree to request the following arrangements:

a. Operation of check points, reconnaissance patrols, and observation posts along the international boundary and line B, and within Zone C.

b. Periodic verification of the implementation of the provisions of this Annex will be carried out not less than twice a month unless otherwise agreed by the Parties.

c. Additional verifications within 48 hours after the receipt of a request from either Party.

d. Ensuring the freedom of navigation through the Strait of Tiran in accordance with Article V of the Treaty of Peace.

3. The arrangements described in this article for each zone will be implemented in ones A, B, and C by the United Nations Force and in Zone D by the United Nations Observers.

4. United Nations verification teams shall be accompanied by liaison officers of the respective Party.

5. The United Nations Force and observers will report their findings to both Parties.

6. The United Nations Force and Observers operating in the Zones will enjoy freedom of movement and other facilities necessary for the performance of their tasks.

7. The United Nations Force and Observers are not empowered to authorize the crossing of the international boundary.

8. The Parties shall agree on the nations from which the United Nations Force and Observers will be drawn. They will be drawn from nations other than those which are permanent members of the United Nations Security Council.

9. The Parties agree that the United Nations should make those command arrangements that will best assure the effective implementation of its responsibilities.

Article VII: Liaison System

1. Upon dissolution of the Joint Commission, a liaison system between the Parties will be established. This liaison system is intended to provide an effective method to assess progress in the implementation of obligations under the present Annex and to resolve any problem that may arise in the course of implementation, and refer other unresolved matters to the higher military authorities of the two countries respectively for consideration. It is also intended to prevent situations resulting from errors or misinterpretation on the part of either Party.

2. An Egyptian liaison office will be established in the city of El-Arish and an Israeli liaison office will be established in the city of Beer-Sheba. Each office will be headed by an officer of the respective country, and assisted by a number of officers.

3. A direct telephone link between the two offices will be set up and also direct telephone lines with the United Nations command will be maintained by both offices.

...

Appendix to Annex I: Organization of Movements in the Sinai

Article I: Principles of Withdrawal

1. The withdrawal of Israeli armed forces and civilians from the Sinai will be accomplished in two phases as described in Article I of Annex I. The description and timing of the withdrawal are included in this Appendix. The Joint Commission will develop and present to the Chief Coordinator of the United Nations forces in the Middle East the details of these phases not later than one month before the initiation of each phase of withdrawal.

2. Both parties agree on the following principles for the sequences of military movements.

...

Article III: United Nations Forces

1. The Parties shall request that United Nations forces be deployed as necessary to perform the functions described in the Appendix up to the time of completion of final Israeli withdrawal. For that purpose, the Parties agree to the redeployment of the United Nations Emergency Force.

2. United Nations forces will supervise the implementation of this Appendix and will employ their best efforts to prevent any violation of its terms.

3. When United Nations forces deploy in accordance with the provisions of Article I and II of this Appendix, they will perform the functions of verification in limited force zones in accordance with Article VI of Annex I, and will establish check points, reconnaissance patrols, and observation posts in the temporary buffer zones described in Article II above. Other functions of the United Nations forces which concern the interim buffer zone are described in Article V of this Appendix.[*]

Article IV: Joint Commission and Liaison

1. The Joint Commission referred to in Article IV of this Treaty will function from the date of exchange of instruments of ratification of this Treaty up to the date of completion of final Israeli withdrawal from the Sinai.

* N.B.: Art V of Appendix I to Annex I envisages the creation of an interim buffer zone in which the UN Forces were to operate check points, reconnaissance patrols, and observation posts.

2. The Joint Commission will be composed of representatives of each Party headed by senior officers. This Commission shall invite a representative of the United Nations when discussing subjects concerning the United Nations, or when either Party requests United Nations presence. Decisions of the Joint Commission will be reached by agreement of Egypt and Israel.

3. The Joint Commission will supervise the implementation of the arrangements described in Annex I and this Appendix. To this end, and by agreement of both Parties, it will:

a. coordinate military movements described in this Appendix and supervise their implementation;
b. address and seek to resolve any problem arising out of the implementation of Annex I and this Appendix, and discuss any violations reported by the United Nations Force and Observers and refer to the Governments of Egypt and Israel any unresolved problems;
c. assist the United Nations Force and Observers in the execution of their mandates, and deal with the timetables of the periodic verification when referred to it by the Parties as provided for in Annex I and this Appendix;
d. organize the demarcation of the international boundary and all lines and zones described in Annex I and this Appendix;
e. supervise the handing over of the main installations in the Sinai from Israel to Egypt;
f. agree on necessary arrangements for finding and returning missing bodies of Egyptian and Israeli soldiers;
g. organize the setting up and operation of entry check points along the El Arish-Ras Mohammed line in accordance with the provisions of Article 4 of Annex III;
h. conduct its operations through the use of joint liaison teams consisting of one Israeli representative and one Egyptian representative, provided from a standing Liaison Group, which will conduct activities as directed by the Joint Commission;
i. provide liaison and coordination to the United Nations command implementing provisions of the Treaty, and, through the joint liaison teams, maintain local coordination and cooperation with the United Nations Force stationed in specific areas or United Nations Observers monitoring specific areas for any assistance as needed;
j. discuss any other matters which the Parties by agreement may place before it.

4. Meetings of the Joint Commission shall be held at least once a month. In the event that either Party of the Command of the United Nations Force requests a specific meeting, it will be convened within 24 hours.

5. The Joint Committee will meet in the buffer zone until the completion of the interim withdrawal and in El Arish and Beer-Sheba alternately afterwards. The first meeting will be held not later than two weeks after the entry into force of this Treaty.

…

The Iran-US Claims Tribunal Framework*

66.a Declaration of the Government of the Democratic and Popular Republic of Algeria Concerning the Settlement of Claims by the Government of the United States of America and the Government of the Islamic Republic of Iran (The Claims Settlement Declaration)

Date: 19 January 1981
Source: (1981) 20 ILM 224
https://iusct.com/wp-content/uploads/2021/02/2-Claims-Settlement-Declaration.pdf

The Government of the Democratic and Popular Republic of Algeria, on the basis of formal notice of adherence received from the Government of the Islamic Republic of Iran and the Government of the United States of America, now declares that Iran and the United States have agreed as follows:

Article I

Iran and the United States will promote the settlement of the claims described in Article II by the parties directly concerned. Any such claims not settled within six months from the date of entry into force of this agreement shall be submitted to binding third-party arbitration in accordance with the terms of this agreement. The aforementioned six months' period may be extended once by three months at the request of either party.

Article II

1. An International Arbitral Tribunal (the Iran-United States Claims Tribunal) is hereby established for the purpose of deciding claims of nationals of the United States against Iran and claims of nationals of Iran against the United States, and any counterclaim which arises out of the same contract, transaction or occurrence that constitutes the subject matter of that national's claim, if such claims and counterclaims are outstanding on the date of this agreement, whether or not filed with any court, and arise out of debts, contracts (including transactions which are the subject of letters of credit or bank guarantees), expropriations or other measures affecting property rights, excluding claims described in Paragraph 11 of the Declaration of the Government of Algeria of January 19, 1981, and claims arising out of the actions of the United States in response to the conduct described in such paragraph, and excluding claims arising under a binding contract between the parties specifically providing that any disputes thereunder shall be within the sole jurisdiction of the competent Iranian courts in response to the Majlis position.

2. The Tribunal shall also have jurisdiction over official claims of the United States and Iran against each other arising out of contractual arrangements between them for the purchase and sale of goods and services.

3. The Tribunal shall have jurisdiction, as specified in Paragraphs 16–17 of the Declaration of the Government of Algeria of January 19, 1981, over any dispute as to the interpretation or performance of any provision of that declaration.

* N.B.: The Iran-US Claims Tribunal was established on the basis of the 'Mediated Algiers Accords' (Document No. 13), of which the Claims Settlement Declaration (Document No. 66.a) forms part.

Article III

1. The Tribunal shall consist of nine members or such larger multiple of three as Iran and the United States may agree are necessary to conduct its business expeditiously. Within ninety days after the entry into force of this agreement, each government shall appoint one-third of the members. Within thirty days after their appointment, the members so appointed shall by mutual agreement select the remaining third of the members and appoint one of the remaining third President of the Tribunal.

Claims may be decided by the full Tribunal or by a panel of three members of the Tribunal as the President shall determine. Each such panel shall be composed by the President and shall consist of one member appointed by each of the three methods set forth above.

2. Members of the Tribunal shall be appointed and the Tribunal shall conduct its business in accordance with the arbitration rules of the United Nations Commission on International Trade Law (UNCITRAL) except to the extent modified by the parties or by the Tribunal to ensure that this agreement can be carried out. The UNCITRAL rules for appointing members of three-member Tribunals shall apply mutatis mutandis to the appointment of the Tribunal.

3. Claims of nationals of the United States and Iran that are within the scope of this agreement shall be presented to the Tribunal either by claimants themselves, or, in the case of claims of less than $250,000, by the Government of such national.

4. No claim may be filed with the Tribunal more than one year after the entry into force of this agreement or six months after the date the President is appointed, whichever is later. These deadlines do not apply to the procedures contemplated by Paragraphs 16 and 17 of the Declaration of the Government of Algeria of January 19, 1981.[*]

Article IV

1. All decisions and awards of the Tribunal shall be final and binding.

2. The President of the Tribunal shall certify, as prescribed in Paragraph 7 of the Declaration of the Government of Algeria of January 19, 1981, when all arbitral awards under this agreement have been satisfied.

3. Any award which the Tribunal may render against either government shall be enforceable against such government in the courts of any nation in accordance with its laws.

Article V

The Tribunal shall decide all cases on the basis of respect for law, applying such choice of law rules and principles of commercial and international law as the Tribunal determines to be applicable, taking into account relevant usages of the trade, contract provisions and changed circumstances.

Article VI

1. The seat of the Tribunal shall be The Hague, The Netherlands, or any other place agreed by Iran and the United States.

2. Each government shall designate an agent at the seat of the Tribunal to represent it to the Tribunal and to receive notices or other communications directed to it or to its nationals, agencies, instrumentalities, or entities in connection with proceedings before the Tribunal.

3. The expenses of the Tribunal shall be borne equally by the two governments.

* N.B.: See Document No. 13.

4. Any question concerning the interpretation or application of this agreement shall be decided by the Tribunal upon the request of either Iran or the United States.

Article VII

For the purposes of this agreement:

1. A "national" of Iran or of the United States, as the case may be, means (a) a natural person who is a citizen of Iran or the United States; and (b) a corporation or other legal entity which is organized under the laws of Iran or the United States or any of its states or territories, the District of Columbia or the Commonwealth of Puerto Rico, if, collectively, natural persons who are citizens of such country hold, directly or indirectly, an interest in such corporation or entity equivalent to fifty per cent or more of its capital stock.

2. "Claims of nationals" of Iran or the United States, as the case may be, means claims owned continuously, from the date on which the claim arose to the date on which this agreement enters into force, by nationals of that state, including claims that are owned indirectly by such nationals through ownership of capital stock or other proprietary interests in juridical persons, provided that the ownership interests of such nationals, collectively, were sufficient at the time the claim arose to control the corporation or other entity, and provided, further, that the corporation or other entity is not itself entitled to bring a claim under the terms of this agreement. Claims referred to the Arbitral Tribunal shall, as of the date of filing of such claims with the Tribunal, be considered excluded from the jurisdiction of the courts of Iran, or of the United States, or of any other court.

3. "Iran" means the Government of Iran, any political subdivision of Iran, and any agency, instrumentality, or entity controlled by the Government of Iran or any political subdivision thereof.

4. The "United States" means the Government of the United States, any political subdivision of the United States, any agency, instrumentality or entity controlled by the Government of the United States or any political subdivision thereof.

Article VIII

This agreement shall enter into force when the Government of Algeria has received from both Iran and the United States a notification of adherence to the agreement.

66.b Tribunal Rules of Procedure

Date: 3 May 1983
Source: (1983-I) 2 Iran-USCTR 405
https://iusct.com/wp-content/uploads/2018/10/5-TRIBUNAL-RULES-OF-PROCEDURE.pdf

DEFINITIONS

The following definitions apply for the purpose of the Tribunal Rules:

(a) "Algiers Declarations" means the two Declarations of the Government of the Democratic and Popular Republic of Algeria, dated 19 January 1981.

(b) "Arbitral tribunal" means either the Full Tribunal or a Chamber, depending on whichever is seised of a particular case or issue.

(c) "Arbitrating party" means, in a particular case, the party or parties initiating recourse to arbitration (the claimant), or the other party or parties (the respondent). The term "arbitrating party" also means one of the two Governments when, in a particular case, it *is* a claimant or respondent, or when it refers a dispute or question to the Tribunal pursuant to the Algiers Declarations.

(d) "Chamber" means a panel of three members composed by the President of the Tribunal from among the nine members of the Full Tribunal, pursuant to his powers under Article Ill, paragraph 1 of the Claims Settlement Declaration.

(e) "Claims Settlement Declaration It means the Declaration of the Democratic and Popular Republic of Algeria concerning the Settlement of Claims by the Government of the United States and the Government of the Islamic Republic of Iran", dated 19 January 1981.

(f) "Full Tribunal" means the nine member Tribunal.

(g) "Member" as used in the Tribunal Rules shall have the same meaning as "arbitrator" where used in the UNCITRAL Rules.

(h) "National", "Iran", and the "United States" shall have the same meanings as defined in Article VII of the Claims Settlement Declaration.

(i) "President" means the President of the Tribunal.

(j) "Presiding arbitrator" or "presiding member" means the President of the Tribunal or the Chairman of a Chamber, as the case may be.

(k) "Registrar" means the Registrar of the Tribunal and includes any deputy of, or other person authorized by, the Registrar, the President, or the Full Tribunal to perform a function for which the Registrar is responsible.

(l) "Secretary-General" means the Secretary-General of the Tribunal and includes any deputy of, or other person authorized by, the Secretary-General, the President, or the Full Tribunal to perform a function for which the Secretary-General is responsible.

(m) "Tribunal" means the Iran-United States Claims Tribunal established within the framework of and pursuant to the Algiers Declarations.

(n) "Tribunal Rules" means these Rules, as they may from time to time be modified or supplemented by the Full Tribunal or the two Governments.

(o) "The two Governments" means the Government of the Islamic Republic of Iran and the Government of the United States of America.

(p) "UNCITRAL Arbitration Rules" and "UNCITRAL Rules" mean the Arbitration Rules of the United Nations Commission on International Trade Law which are the subject of Resolution 31/98 adopted by the General Assembly of the United Nations on 15 December 1976.

SECTION I: INTRODUCTORY RULES
SCOPE OF APPLICATION

Article 1

1. Within the framework of the Algiers Declarations, the initiation and conduct of proceedings before the arbitral tribunal shall be subject to the following Tribunal Rules which may be modified by the Full Tribunal or the two Governments.

2. These Rules shall govern the arbitration except that where any of these Rules is in conflict with a provision of the law applicable to the arbitration from which the parties cannot derogate, that provision shall prevail.

3. The Claims Settlement Declaration constitutes an agreement in writing by Iran and the United States, on their own behalf and on behalf of their nationals submitting to arbitration within the framework of the Algiers Declarations and in accordance with the Tribunal Rules.

NOTICE, CALCULATION OF PERIODS OF TIME

Article 2

1. All documents must be filed with the Tribunal. Filing of a document with the Tribunal shall be deemed to have been made when it is physically received by the Registrar.

2. All documents filed in a particular case shall be served upon all arbitrating parties in that case through the Agents. The Registrar shall promptly deliver copies to the offices of each of the two Agents in The Hague, except for a filing Agent. Each Agent shall be responsible for transmitting one copy to each concerned arbitrating party in his country or to the representative designated by each such arbitrating party to receive documents on its behalf.

3. The filing of documents with the Tribunal shall constitute service on all of the other arbitrating parties in the case and shall be deemed to have been received by said arbitrating parties when it is received by the Agent of their Government.

4. Notwithstanding the provisions of paragraphs 1-3 of Article 2, when the arbitral tribunal has so permitted in a particular case, service of written evidence may be effected by actual delivery to the representative of an arbitrating party during a hearing or a pre-hearing conference in that case. The Secretary-General shall make a record of such service which shall be signed by him. A copy of each document so served, together with such record of service, shall be delivered by the Secretary-general to the Registrar after the hearing or pre-hearing conference at which service was so made.

5. The Registrar may refuse to accept any document which is not received within the required time period or which does not comply with the Algiers Declarations or with the Tribunal Rules. Any such refusal by the Registrar is, upon objection by an arbitrating party concerned within thirty days of notification of refusal, subject to review by the arbitral tribunal.

Notes to Article 2

1. For the purposes of calculating a period of time under these Rules, such period shall begin to run on the day following the day when the document is received. If the last day of such a period is an official holiday or a non-business day at the seat of the arbitral tribunal, the period is extended until the first business day which follows. Official holidays and non-business days occurring during the running of the period of time are included in calculating the period. The Secretary-General will issue a list of such days.

2. Twenty copies of all documents shall be filed with the Registrar, unless a smaller number is determined by the arbitral tribunal. In the event that there are more than two arbitrating parties in a case, a sufficient number of additional copies shall be filed to permit service on all arbitrating parties in the case. Also, the arbitral tribunal, or the Registrar, may at any time require a party which files a document to submit additional copies.

3. Exhibits and written evidence, other than those annexed to the Statement of Claim or Statement of Defence, shall be submitted in such manner and number of copies as the arbitral tribunal may determine in each case based on the nature and volume of the particular exhibit or written evidence and any other relevant circumstances.

4. Upon the filing of a document, the Registrar shall note on all copies the date received. The Registrar shall issue a receipt to the arbitrating party which filed the document. In all instances in which the Registrar is required to deliver copies to the Agents, he will secure a written receipt of such delivery, which will be kept in the case file and be available for inspection or copying by any arbitrating party in that case.

5. All documents filed with the Registrar are to be submitted on paper 8 inches x 11 inches or on A-4 size paper (21 cm x 29.5 cm), or on paper no longer than A-4. If a document, exhibit or other written evidence cannot conveniently be reproduced on paper no larger than A-4, it is be folded to A-4 size, unless the Registrar permits otherwise in special circumstances.

6. Upon filing a Statement of Claim, the Registrar shall assign an identifying number to the claim, and the case shall be assigned to the Full Tribunal, or by lot to a Chamber. Thereafter, all documents filed in the case, including the award, shall have a caption stating:

(i) the names of the parties,

(ii) the case number assigned by the Registrar, and

(iii) the number of the Chamber seised of the case; otherwise the caption shall state "Full Tribunal."

7. At least two copies in English and two copies in Persian of all documents mentioned in Article 17, Note 3 and filed with the Tribunal shall be manually signed by the arbitrating party submitting them or by its representative. Exhibits and annexes to documents need not be signed. If a document is presented without such signatures, it shall be accepted for filing, but the filing party shall be notified and required promptly to submit two manually signed copies in each language.

NOTICE OF ARBITRATION

Article 3

No Notice of Arbitration pursuant to Article 3 of the UNCITRAL Rules is to be given.

REPRESENTATION AND ASSISTANCE

Article 4

The Parties may be represented or assisted by persons of their choice. The names and addresses of such persons must be communicated in writing to the other party: such communication must specify whether the appointment is being made for purposes of representation or assistance.

Notes to Article 4

1. As used in Article 4 the terms "parties" means the arbitrating parties.

2. For the purpose of a particular case, the two Governments may each appoint representatives in addition to their Agents and each of the other arbitrating parties may appoint representatives. An appointed representative shall be deemed to be authorized to act before the arbitral tribunal on behalf of the appointing party for all purposes of the case and the acts of the representative shall be binding upon the appointing party. A representative is not required to be licensed to practice law. Parties who appoint a representative shall file with the Registrar notice of appointment in such form as the Registrar may require.

3. Arbitrating parties may also be assisted in proceedings before the arbitral tribunal by one or more persons of their choice. Persons chosen to assist who are not also appointed as representatives are not deemed to be authorized to act before the arbitral tribunal on behalf of the appointing party, to bind the appointing party or to receive notices, communications or documents on behalf of the appointing party. Any such assistant is not required to be licensed to practice law.

SECTION II: COMPOSITION OF THE ARBITRAL TRIBUNAL NUMBER OF MEMBERS

Article 5

The composition of Chambers, the assignment of cases to various Chambers, the transfer of cases among Chambers and the relinquishment by Chambers of certain cases to the Full Tribunal will be provided for in orders issued by the President pursuant to his powers under Article III, paragraph 1 of the Claims Settlement Declaration.

APPOINTMENT OF MEMBERS: ARTICLES 6–8

Article 6

1. If a sole arbitrator is to be appointed, either party may propose to the other:
   (a) The names of one or more persons, one of whom would serve as the sole arbitrator; and
   (b) If no appointing authority has been agreed upon by the parties, the name or names of one or more institutions or persons, one of whom would serve as appointing authority.

2. If within thirty days after receipt by a party of a proposal made in accordance with paragraph 1 the parties have not reached agreement on the choice of a sole arbitrator, the sole arbitrator shall be appointed by the appointing authority agreed upon by the parties. If no appointing authority has been agreed upon by the parties, or if the appointing authority agreed upon refuses to act or fails to appoint the arbitrator within sixty days of the receipt of a party's request therefor, either party may request the Secretary-General of the Permanent Court of Arbitration at The Hague to designate an appointing authority.

3. The appointing authority shall, at the request of one of the parties, appoint the sole arbitrator as promptly as possible. In making the appointment the appointing authority shall use the following list-procedure, unless both parties agree that the list-procedure should not be used or unless the appointing authority determines in its discretion that the use of the list-procedure is not appropriate for the case:
   (a) At the request of one of the parties the appointing authority shall communicate to both parties an identical list containing at least three names;
   (b) Within fifteen days after the receipt of this list, each party may return the list to the appointing authority after having deleted the name or names to which he objects and numbered the remaining names on the list in the order of his preference;
   (c) After the expiration of the above period of time the appointing authority shall appoint the sole arbitrator from among the names approved on the lists returned to it and in accordance with the order of preference indicated by the parties;
   (d) If for any reason the appointment cannot be made according to this procedure, the appointing authority may exercise its discretion in appointing the sole arbitrator.

4. In making the appointment, the appointing authority shall have regard to such considerations as are likely to secure the appointment of an independent and impartial arbitrator and shall take into account as well the advisability of appointing an arbitrator of a nationality other than the nationalities of the parties.

Article 7

1. If three arbitrators are to be appointed, each party shall appoint one arbitrator. The two arbitrators thus appointed shall choose the third arbitrator who will act as the presiding arbitrator of the tribunal.

2. If within thirty days after the receipt of a party notification of the appointment of an arbitrator the other party has not notified the first party of the arbitrator he has appointed:

(a) The first party may request the appointing authority previously designated by the parties to appoint the second arbitrator; or

(b) If no such authority has been previously designated by the parties, or if the appointing authority previously designated refuses to act or fails to appoint the arbitrator within thirty days after receipt of a party's I s request therefor, the first party may request the Secretary-General of the Permanent Court of Arbitration at The Hague to designate the appointing authority. The first party may then request the appointing authority so designated to appoint the second arbitrator. In either case, the appointing authority may exercise its discretion in appointing the arbitrator.

3. If within thirty days after the appointment of the second arbitrator the two arbitrators have not agreed on the choice of the presiding arbitrator, the presiding arbitrator shall be appointed by an appointing authority in the same way as a sole arbitrator would be appointed under article 6.

Article 8

1. When an appointing authority is requested to appoint an arbitrator pursuant to article 6 or article 7, the party which makes the request shall send to the appointing authority a copy of the notice of arbitration, a copy of the contract out of or in relation to which the dispute has arisen and a copy of the arbitration agreement if it is not contained in the contract. The appointing authority may require from either party such information as it deems necessary to fulfil its function.

2. Where the names of one or more persons are proposed for appointment as arbitrators, their full names, addresses and nationalities shall be indicated, together with a description of their qualifications.

Note to Articles 6–8

As used in Articles 6, 7 and 8 of the Tribunal Rules the terms "party" and "parties" refer to the one or both of the two Governments, as the case may be.

**CHALLENGE OF MEMBERS:
ARTICLES 9–12**

Article 9

A prospective arbitrator shall disclose to those who approach him in connexion with his possible appointment any circumstances likely to give rise to justifiable doubts as to his impartiality or independence. An arbitrator, once appointed or chosen, shall disclose such circumstances to the parties unless they have already been informed by him of these circumstances.

When any member of the arbitral tribunal obtains knowledge that any particular case before the arbitral tribunal involves circumstances likely to give rise to justifiable doubts as to his impartiality or independence with respect to that case, he shall disclose such circumstances to the President and, if the President so determines, to the arbitrating parties in the case and, if appropriate, shall disqualify himself as to that case.

Article 10

1. Any arbitrator may be challenged if circumstances exist that give rise to justifiable doubts as to the arbitrator's impartiality or independence.

2. A party may challenge the arbitrator appointed by him only for reasons of which he becomes aware after the appointment has been made.

Article 11

1. A party who intends to challenge an arbitrator shall send notice of his challenge within fifteen days after the appointment of the challenged arbitrator has been notified to the challenging party or within fifteen days after the circumstances mentioned in articles 9 and 10 became known to that party.

2. The challenge shall be notified to the other party, to the arbitrator who is challenged and to the other members of the arbitral tribunal. The notification shall be in writing and shall state the reasons for the challenge.

3. When an arbitrator has been challenged by one party, the other party may agree to the challenge. The arbitrator may also, after the challenge, withdraw from his office. In neither case does this imply acceptance of the validity of the grounds for the challenge. In both cases the procedure provided in article 6 or 7 shall be used in full for the appointment of the substitute arbitrator, even if during the process of appointing the challenged arbitrator a party had failed to exercise his right to appoint or to participate in the appointment.

Article 12

1. If the other party does not agree to the challenge and the challenged arbitrator does not withdraw, the decision on the challenge will be made:

a) When the initial appointment was made by an appointing authority, by that authority;

b) When the initial appointment was not made by an appointing authority, but an appointing authority has been previously designated, by that authority;

c) In all other cases, by the appointing authority to be designated in accordance with the procedure for an appointing authority as provided for in article 6.

2. If the appointing authority sustains the challenge, a substitute arbitrator shall be appointed or chosen pursuant to the procedure applicable to the appointment or choice of an arbitrator as provided in articles 6 to 9 except that, when this procedure would call for the designation of an appointing authority, the appointment of the arbitrator shall be made by the appointing authority which decided on the challenge.

Notes to Articles 9–12

1. As used in Articles 9, 10, 11 and 12 of the Tribunal Rules, with respect to the initial appointment of a member the terms "party" and "parties" mean one or both of the two Governments, as the case may be. After the initial appointment, the terms "party" and "parties" mean the arbitrating party or parties, as the case may be. Arbitrating parties may challenge a member only on the basis of the existence of circumstances which give rise to justifiable doubts as to the member's impartiality or independence with respect to the particular case involved, and not upon any general grounds which may also relate to other cases. Challenges on such general grounds may only be made by one of the two Governments.

2. In applying paragraph 1 of Article 11 of the Tribunal Rules, the period for making a challenge to a member of a Chamber to which a case has been assigned shall be fifteen days after the challenging party is given notice of the circumstances mentioned in Articles 9 and 10 of Tribunal Rules became known to that party. In the event the case is relinquished by the Chamber to the Full Tribunal, the period for challenging a member who is not a member of the relinquishing Chamber shall be fifteen days after the challenging party *is* given notice of the relinquishment, or after the circumstances mentioned in Articles 9 and 10 of the Tribunal Rules became known to that party.

3. In the event a member withdraws with respect to a particular case or if the challenge is sustained, he shall continue to exercise his functions as a member for all other cases and purposes except in respect of that particular case.

4. In the event that a member of a Chamber is challenged with respect to a particular case and withdraws, or if the challenge is sustained, the President will order the transfer of the case to another Chamber.

5. In the event the Full Tribunal is seised of a particular case and a member is challenged with respect to that case and withdraws, or if the challenge is sustained, a substitute member shall be appointed to the Full Tribunal for the purposes of that case in accordance with the procedure set forth in Article III of the Claims Settlement Declaration as was used in appointing the member being substituted. An appointing authority, if needed, shall be designated as provided in Article 12 of the Tribunal Rules.

6. Disclosure statements filed as to each member shall be made available by the Registrar to each arbitrating party in each case.

REPLACEMENT OF A MEMBER

Article 13

1. In the event of the death or resignation of an arbitrator during the course of the arbitral proceedings, a substitute arbitrator shall be appointed or chosen pursuant to the procedure provided for in articles 6 to 9 that was applicable to the appointment or choice of the arbitrator being replaced.

2. In the event that an arbitrator fails to act or in the event of the de jure or de facto impossibility of his performing his functions, the procedure in respect of the challenge and replacement of an arbitrator as provided in the preceding articles shall apply.

In applying the provisions of this paragraph, if the President, after consultation with the other members of the Full Tribunal, determines that the failure of a member to act or his impossibility to perform his functions is due to a temporary illness or other circumstance expected to be of relatively short duration, the member shall not be replaced but a substitute member shall be appointed for the temporary period in accordance with the same procedures as are described in Note 5 to Articles 9–12.

3. In the event of the temporary absence of the President, the senior other member of the Tribunal not appointed by either of the two Governments shall act as President of the Tribunal and as Chairman at the meetings of the Full Tribunal. Seniority shall be based on the date of appointment, or for members appointed on the same date shall be based on age.

4. A substitute member appointed for a temporary period shall continue to serve with respect to any case in which he has participated in the hearing, notwithstanding the member for whom he is a substitute is again available and may work on other Tribunal cases and matters.

5. After the effective date of a member's resignation he shall continue to serve as a member of the Tribunal with respect to all cases in which he had participated in a hearing on the merits, and for that purpose shall be considered a member of the Tribunal instead of the person who replaces him.

Note to Article 13

Iran may, in advance, appoint up to three persons, to be available to act as a substitute member for a temporary period for a specified member, or members, of the Tribunal appointed by Iran and the United States may, in advance, appoint up to three persons, to be available to act as a substitute member for a temporary period for a specified member, or members of the Tribunal appointed by the United States. The members of the Tribunal appointed by Iran and the United States may select, in advance, by mutual agreement, a person to act as substitute for a temporary period for any of the remaining one third of the members of the Tribunal.

REPETITION OF HEARINGS IN THE EVENT OF REPLACEMENT OR SUBSTITUTION OF A MEMBER

Article 14

If a member of the Full Tribunal or of a Chamber is replaced or if a substitute is appointed for him, the arbitral tribunal shall determine whether all, any part or none of any previous hearings shall be repeated.

SECTION III: ARBITRAL PROCEEDINGS GENERAL PROVISIONS

Article 15

1. Subject to these Rules, the arbitral tribunal may conduct the arbitration in such manner as it considers appropriate, provided that the parties are treated with equality and that at any stage of the proceedings each party is given a full opportunity of presenting his case.

2. If either party so requests at any stage of the proceedings, the arbitral tribunal shall hold hearings for the presentation of evidence by witnesses, including expert witnesses, or for oral argument. In the absence of such a request, the arbitral tribunal shall decide whether to hold such hearings or whether the proceedings shall be conducted on the basis of documents and other materials.

3. All documents or information supplied to the arbitral tribunal by one party shall at the same time be communicated by that party to the other party.

Notes to Article 15

1. As used in Article 15, the terms "party" and "parties" If mean the arbitrating party or parties, as the case may be.

2. In applying paragraph 2 of Article 15, the arbitral tribunal shall determine without hearing any written requests or objections of the concerned arbitrating parties with respect to procedural matters unless it grants or invites oral argument in special circumstances.

3. In complying with paragraph 3 of Article 15, an arbitrating party shall follow the procedures set forth in Article 2 of the Tribunal Rules.

4. The arbitral tribunal may make an order directing the arbitrating parties to appear for a pre-hearing conference. The pre-hearing conference will normally be held only after the Statement of Defence in the case has been received. The order will state the matters to be considered at the pre-hearing conference.

5. The arbitral tribunal may, having satisfied itself that the statement of one of the two Governments – or, under special circumstances, any other person – who is not an arbitrating party in a particular case is likely to assist the tribunal in carrying out its task, permit such Government or person to assist the tribunal by presenting oral or written statements.

PLACE OF ARBITRATION

Article 16

1. Unless the parties have agreed upon the place where the arbitration is to be held, such place shall be determined by the arbitral tribunal, having regard to the circumstances of the arbitration.

2. The arbitral tribunal may determine the locale of the arbitration within the country agreed upon by the parties. It may hear witnesses and hold meetings for consultation among its members at any place it deems appropriate, having regard to the circumstances of the arbitration.

3. The arbitral tribunal may meet at any place it deems appropriate for the inspection of goods, other property or documents. The parties shall be given sufficient notice to enable them to be present at such inspection.

4. The award shall be made at the place of arbitration.

Note to Article 16

As used in Article 16, paragraphs 1 and 2 of the Tribunal Rules, the term "parties" means the two Governments. As used in Article 16, paragraph 3 of the Tribunal Rules, the term "parties" means the arbitrating parties.

LANGUAGE

Article 17

1. Subject to an agreement by the parties, the arbitral tribunal shall, promptly after its appointment, determine the language or languages to be used in the proceedings.

This determination shall apply to the statement of claim, the statement of defence, and any further written statements and, if oral hearings take place, to the language or languages to be used in such hearings.

2. The arbitral tribunal may order that any documents annexed to the statement of claim or statement of defence, and any supplementary documents or exhibits submitted in the course of the proceedings, delivered in their original language, shall be accompanied by a translation into the language or languages agreed upon by the parties or determined by the arbitral tribunal.

Notes to Article 17

1. As used in Article 17 of the Tribunal Rules, the term "parties" means the two Governments.

2. In accordance with an agreement of the Agents, English and Persian shall be the two official languages to be used in the arbitration proceedings, and these languages shall be used for all oral hearings, decisions and awards.

3. In accordance with the provisions of Article 17 of the Tribunal Rules, the following documents filed with the Tribunal shall be submitted in both English and Persian, unless otherwise agreed by the arbitrating parties:

(a) The Statement of Claim and its annexes.
(b) The Statement of Defence, and any counter-claim, including any annexes.
(c) The reply (including any annexes) to any counter-claim.
(d) Any further written statement (e.g. reply, rejoinder, brief), including any annexes, which the arbitral tribunal may require or permit an arbitrating party to be present.
(e) Any written request to the arbitral tribunal to take action or any objection thereto.
(f) Any challenge to a member.

4. The arbitral tribunal shall determine in each particular case what other documents, documentary exhibits and written evidence, or what parts thereof, shall be submitted in both English and Persian.

5. Any disputes or difficulties regarding translations shall be resolved by the arbitral tribunal.

STATEMENT OF CLAIM

Article 18

1. A party initiating recourse to arbitration before the Tribunal (the "claimant") shall do so by filing a Statement of Claim. Each Statement of Claim shall contain the following particulars:

(a) A demand that the dispute be referred to arbitration by the Tribunal;
(b) The names, nationalities and last known addresses of the parties;
(c) A reference to the debt, contract (including transactions which are the subject of letters of credit or bank guarantees), expropriations or other measures affecting property rights out of or in relation to which the dispute arises and as to which the Tribunal has jurisdiction pursuant to Article II, paragraphs 1 and 2 of the Claims Settlement Declaration;
(d) The general nature of the claim and an indication of the amount involved, if any;
(e) A statement of the facts supporting the claim;
(f) The points at issue;
(g) The relief or remedy sought;
(h) If the claimant has appointed a lawyer or other person for purposes of representation or assistance in connection with the claim, the name and address

of such person and an indication whether the appointment is for purposes of representation or assistance;

(i) The name and address of the person to whom communications should be sent on behalf of the claimant (only one such person shall be entitled to be sent communications).

2. It is advisable that claimants (i) annex to their Statements of Claim such documents as will serve to clearly establish the basis of the claim, and/or (ii) add a reference and a summary of relevant portions of such documents, and/or (iii) include in the Statement of Claim quotations of relevant portions of such documents.

3. No priority for the scheduling of hearings or the making of awards shall be based on the date of filing the Statement of Claim.

Notes to Article 18

1. No claims with respect to which the Tribunal has jurisdiction within the framework of the Algiers Declarations and pursuant to paragraphs 1 and 2 of Article II of the Claims Settlement Declaration may be filed before October 20, 1981.

2. All Statements of Claim with respect to matters as to which the Tribunal has jurisdiction pursuant to paragraphs 1 and 2 of Article II of the Claims Settlement Declaration which are filed between October 20, 1981 and November 19, 1981 will be deemed to have been filed simultaneously as of October 20, 1981. All such claims filed between November 20, 1981 and December 19, 1981 will be deemed to have been filed simultaneously as of November 20, 1981. All such claims filed between December 20, 1981 and January 19, 1982 will be deemed to have been filed simultaneously as of December 20, 1981.

STATEMENT OF DEFENCE

Article 19

1. Within a period of time to be determined by the arbitral tribunal with respect to each case, which should not exceed 135 days, the respondent shall file its Statement of Defence. However, the arbitral tribunal may extend the time-limits if it concludes that such an extension is justified.

2. The Statement of Defence shall reply to the particulars (e), (f) and (g) and include the information required in (h) and (i) of the Statement of Claim (see Article 18, paragraph 1 of the Tribunal Rules). It is advisable that Respondents (i) annex to their Statement of Defence such documents as will clearly serve to establish the basis of the defence, and/or (ii) add a reference and summary of the relevant portions of such documents, and/or (iii) include in the Statement of Defence quotations of relevant portions of such documents.

3. In the Statement of Defence, or at a later stage in the arbitral proceedings if the arbitral tribunal decides that the delay was justified under the circumstances, the respondent may make a counterclaim or rely on a claim for the purpose of a set-off, if such counter-claim or set-off is allowed under the Claims Settlement Declaration.

4. The provisions of Article 18, paragraph 1 shall apply to a counter-claim or claim relied on for purpose of a set-off.

Notes to Article 19

1. In determining and extending periods of time pursuant to this Article, the arbitral tribunal will take into account:

(i) the complexity of the case,

(ii) any special circumstances, including demonstrated hardship to a claimant or respondent, and

(iii) such other circumstances as it considers appropriate. In the event that the arbitral tribunal determines that a requirement to file a large number of Statements of Defence in any particular period would impose an unfair burden on a respondent to a claim or counter-claim, it will in some cases extend the time periods based on the above-mentioned factors or by lot.

2. In the event of a counter-claim or claim relied on for the purpose of a set-off, the claimant against whom it is made will be given the right of reply, and the provisions of paragraph 2 of Article 19 of the Tribunal Rules shall apply.

AMENDMENTS TO THE CLAIM OR DEFENCE

Article 20

During the course of the arbitral proceedings either party may amend or supplement his claim or defence unless the arbitral tribunal considers it inappropriate to allow such amendment having regard to the delay in making it or prejudice to the other party or any other circumstances.

However, a claim may not be amended in such a manner that the amended claim falls outside the jurisdiction of the arbitral tribunal.

Note to Article 20

As used in Article 20 of the Tribunal Rules, the term "party" means the arbitrating party.

PLEAS AS TO THE JURISDICTION OF THE ARBITRAL TRIBUNAL

Article 21

1. The arbitral tribunal shall have the power to rule on objections that it has no jurisdiction, including any objections with respect to the existence or validity of the arbitration clause or of the separate arbitration agreement.

2. The arbitral tribunal shall have the power to determine the existence or the validity of the contract of which an arbitration clause forms a part. For the purposes of article 21, an arbitration clause which forms part of a contract and which provides for arbitration under these Rules shall be treated as an agreement independent of the other terms of the contract. A decision by the arbitral tribunal that the contract is null and void shall not entail ipso jure the invalidity of the arbitration clause.

3. A plea that the arbitral tribunal does not have jurisdiction shall be raised not later than in the statement of defence or, with respect to a counter-claim, in the reply to the counter-claim.

4. In general, the arbitral tribunal should rule on a plea concerning its jurisdiction as a preliminary question. However, the arbitral tribunal may proceed with the arbitration and rule on such a plea in their final award.

FURTHER WRITTEN STATEMENTS

Article 22

The arbitral tribunal shall decide which further written statements, in addition to the statement of claim and the statement of defence, shall be required from the parties or may be presented by them and shall fix the periods of time for communicating such statements.

Note to Article 22

As used in Article 22 of the Tribunal Rules, the term "parties" means the arbitrating parties.

PERIODS OF TIME

Article 23

The periods of time fixed by the arbitral tribunal for the communication of written statements (excluding the Statement of Defence) should not exceed 90 days. However, the arbitral tribunal may extend the time-limits if it concludes that an extension is justified.

EVIDENCE AND HEARINGS: Articles 24–25

Article 24

1. Each party shall have the burden of proving the facts relied on to support his claim or defence.

2. The arbitral tribunal may, if it considers it appropriate, require a party to deliver to the tribunal and to the other party, within such a period of time as the arbitral tribunal shall decide, a summary of the documents and other evidence which that party intends to present in support of the facts in issue set out in his statement of claim or statement of defence.

3. At any time during the arbitral proceedings the arbitral tribunal may require the parties to produce documents, exhibits or other evidence within such a period of time as the tribunal shall determine.

Note to Article 24

As used in Article 24 of the Tribunal Rules, the terms "party" and "parties" mean the arbitrating party or parties, as the case may be.

Article 25

1. In the event of an oral hearing, the arbitral tribunal shall give the parties adequate advance notice of the date, time and place thereof.

2. If witnesses are to be heard, at least thirty days before the hearing each party shall communicate to the arbitral tribunal and to the other party the names and addresses of the witnesses he intends to present, the subject upon and the languages in which such witnesses will give their testimony.

3. The arbitral tribunal shall make arrangements for the translation of oral statements made at a hearing and for a record of the hearing if either is deemed necessary by the tribunal under the circumstances of the case, or if the parties have agreed thereto and have communicated such agreement to the tribunal at least fifteen days before the hearing.

4. Hearings shall be held in camera unless the parties agree otherwise. The arbitral tribunal may require the retirement of any witness or witnesses during the testimony of other witnesses. The arbitral tribunal is free to determine the manner in which witnesses are examined.

5. Evidence of witnesses may also be presented in the form of written statements signed by them.

6. The arbitral tribunal shall determine the admissibility, relevance, materiality and weight of the evidence offered.

Notes to Article 25

1. As used in Article 25 of the Tribunal Rules, the terms "party" and "parties" mean the arbitrating party or parties, as the case may be, except that, as used in paragraph 4 of Article 25, the term "parties" means the two Governments and the arbitrating parties.

2. The information concerning witnesses which an arbitrating party must communicate pursuant to paragraph 2 of Article 25 of the Tribunal Rules is not required with respect to any witnesses which an arbitrating party may later decide to present to rebut evidence presented by the other arbitrating party. However, such information concerning any rebuttal witness shall be communicated to the arbitral tribunal and the other arbitrating parties as far in advance of hearing the witness as is reasonably possible.

3. With respect to paragraph 3 of Article 25 of the Tribunal Rules, the Secretary-General shall make arrangements for a tape-recording or stenographic record of hearings or parts of hearings if the arbitral tribunal so determines. If the arbitral tribunal determines that a transcript shall be made of any such tape-recording or stenographic record, the arbitrating parties in that case, or their authorized representatives, shall be permitted to read the transcript.

4. Any arbitrating party in the case may make a stenographic record of the hearings, or parts of the hearings, and, in that event, shall make a transcript thereof available to the arbitral tribunal without charge. Arbitrating parties are not permitted to make tape-recordings of hearings or other proceedings.

5. Notwithstanding the provisions of paragraph 4 of Article 25, the arbitral tribunal may at its discretion permit representatives of arbitrating parties in other cases which present similar issues of fact or law to be present to observe all or part of the hearing in a particular case, subject to the prior approval of the arbitrating parties in the particular case. The Agents of the two Governments are permitted to be present at pre-hearing conferences and hearings.

6. In applying paragraph 4 of Article 25 of the Tribunal Rules, the following provisions shall determine the manner in which witnesses are examined.

(a) Before giving any evidence each witness shall make the following declaration: "I solemnly declare upon my honour and conscience that I will speak the truth, the whole truth and nothing but the truth."

(b) Witnesses may be examined by the presiding member and the other members of the arbitral tribunal. Also, when permitted by the arbitral tribunal, the representatives of the arbitrating parties in the case may ask questions, subject to the control of the presiding member.

7. The Secretary-General shall draft minutes of each hearing. After each member of the arbitral tribunal present at the hearing has been given the opportunity to comment on the draft minutes, the minutes, with any corrections approved by a majority of members who were present, shall be signed by the presiding member and the Secretary-general. The arbitrating parties in the case, or their representatives, shall be permitted to read such minutes.

INTERIM MEASURES OF PROTECTION

Article 26

1. At the request of either party, the arbitral tribunal may take any interim measures it deems necessary in respect of the subject-matter of the dispute, including measures for the conservation of the goods forming the subject-matter in dispute, such as ordering their deposit with a third person or the sale of perishable goods.

2. Such interim measures may be established in the form of an interim award. The arbitral tribunal shall be entitled to require security for the costs of such measures.

3. A request for interim measures addressed by any party to a judicial authority shall not be deemed incompatible with the agreement to arbitrate, or as a waiver of that agreement.

Note to Article 26

As used in Article 26 of the Tribunal Rules, the term "party" means the arbitrating party.

EXPERTS

Article 27

1. The arbitral tribunal may appoint one or more experts to report to it, in writing, on specific issues to be determined by the tribunal. A copy of the expert's terms of reference, established by the arbitral tribunal, shall be communicated to the parties.

2. The parties shall give the expert any relevant information or produce for his inspection any relevant documents or goods that he may require of them. Any dispute between a party and such expert as to the relevance of the required information or production shall be referred to the arbitral tribunal for decision.

The expert shall invite a representative of each arbitrating party to attend any site inspection, and, when the arbitral tribunal so determines, a representative of each arbitrating party shall be invited to attend other inspections made by the expert.

3. Upon receipt of the expert's report, the arbitral tribunal shall communicate a copy of the report to the parties who shall be given the opportunity to express, in writing, their opinion on the report. A party shall be entitled to examine any document on which the expert has relied in *his* report.

4. At the request of either party the expert, after delivery of the report, may be heard at a hearing where the parties shall have the opportunity to be present and to interrogate the expert. At this hearing either party may present expert witnesses in order to testify on the points at *issue.* The provisions of article 25 shall be applicable to such proceedings.

Notes to Article 27

1. As used in Article 27 of the Tribunal Rules, the terms "party" and "parties" mean the arbitrating party or parties, as the case may be.

2. Every expert, before beginning the performance of his duties, shall make the following declaration:

DEFAULT

"I solemnly declare upon my honour and conscience that I will perform my duties in accordance with my sincere belief and will keep confidential all matters relating to the performance of my task."

Article 28

1. If, within the period of time fixed by the arbitral tribunal, the claimant has failed to communicate his claim without showing sufficient cause for such failure, the arbitral tribunal shall issue an order for the termination of the arbitral proceedings. If, within the period of time fixed by the arbitral tribunal, the respondent has failed to communicate his statement of defence without showing sufficient cause for such failure, the arbitral tribunal shall order that the proceedings continue.

2. If one of the parties, duly notified under these Rules, fails to appear at a hearing, without showing sufficient cause for such failure, the arbitral tribunal. may proceed with the arbitration.

3. If one of the parties, duly invited to produce documentary evidence, fails to do so within the established period of time without showing sufficient cause for such failure, the arbitral tribunal may make the award on the evidence before it.

Note to Article 28

As used in Article 28 of the Tribunal Rules, the term “parties” means the arbitrating parties.

CLOSURE OF HEARINGS

Article 29

1. The arbitral tribunal may inquire of the parties if they have any further proof to offer or witnesses to be heard or submissions to make and, if there are none, it may declare the hearings closed.

2. The arbitral tribunal may, if it considers it necessary owing to exceptional circumstances, decide, on its own motion or upon application of a party, to reopen the hearings at any time before the award is made.

Note to Article 29

As used in Article 29 of the Tribunal Rules, the terms “party” and “parties” mean the arbitrating party or parties, as the case may be.

WAIVER OF RULES

Article 30

A party who knows that any provision of, or requirement under, these Rules has not been complied with and yet proceeds with the arbitration without promptly stating his objection to such non-compliance, shall be deemed to have waived his right to object.

Note to Article 30

As used in Article 30 of the Tribunal Rules, the term “party” means the arbitrating party.

DECISIONS

Article 31

1. When there are three arbitrators, any award or other decision of the arbitral tribunal shall be made by a majority of the arbitrators.

2. In the case of questions of procedure, when there is no majority or when the arbitral tribunal so authorizes, the presiding arbitrator may decide on his own, subject to revision, if any, by the arbitral tribunal.

Notes to Article 31

1. Any award or other decision of the arbitral tribunal pursuant to paragraph 1 of Article 31 shall be made by a majority of its members.

2. The arbitral tribunal shall deliberate in private. Its deliberations shall be and remain secret. Only the members of the arbitral tribunal shall take part in the deliberations. The Secretary-General may be present. No other person may be admitted except by special decision of the arbitral tribunal. Any question which is to be voted upon shall be formulated in precise terms in English and Persian and the text shall, if a member so requests, be distributed before the vote is taken. The minutes of the private sittings of the arbitral tribunal shall be secret.

FORM AND EFFECT OF AWARD

Article 32

1. In addition to making a final award, the arbitral tribunal shall be entitled to make interim, interlocutory, or partial awards.

2. The award shall be made in writing and shall be final and binding on the parties. The parties undertake to carry out the award without delay.

3. The arbitral tribunal shall state the reasons upon which the award is based, unless the parties have agreed that no reasons are to be given. Any arbitrator may request that his dissenting vote or his dissenting vote and the reasons therefor be recorded.

4. An award shall be signed by the arbitrators and it shall contain the date on which and the place where the award was made. When there are three arbitrators and one of them fails to sign, the award shall state the reason for the absence of the signature.

5. All awards and other decisions shall be made available to the public, except that upon the request of one or more arbitrating parties, the arbitral tribunal may determine that it will not make the entire award or other decision public, but will make public only portions thereof from which the identity of the parties, other identifying facts and trade or military secrets have been deleted.

6. Copies of the award signed by the arbitrators shall be communicated to the parties by the arbitral tribunal.

7. If the arbitration law of the country where the award is made requires that the award be filed or registered by the arbitral tribunal, the tribunal shall comply with this requirement within the period of time required by law.

Note to Article 32

As used in Article 32 of the Tribunal Rules, the term "parties" means the arbitrating parties.

APPLICABLE LAW

Article 33

1. The arbitral tribunal shall decide all cases on the basis of respect for law, applying such choice of law rules and principles of commercial and international law as the arbitral

tribunal determines to be applicable, taking into account relevant usages of the trade, contract provisions and changed circumstances.

2. The arbitral tribunal shall decide ex aequo et bono only if the arbitrating parties have expressly and in writing authorized it to do so.

Note to Article 33

Paragraph 1 of Article 33 corresponds to Article V of the Claims Settlement Declaration.

SETTLEMENT OR OTHER GROUNDS FOR TERMINATION

Article 34

1. If, before the award is made, the parties agree on a settlement of the dispute, the arbitral tribunal shall either issue an order for the termination of the arbitral proceedings or, if requested by both parties and accepted by the tribunal, record the settlement in the form of an arbitral award on agreed terms. The arbitral tribunal is not obliged to give reasons for such an award.

2. If, before the award is made, the continuation of the arbitral proceedings becomes unnecessary or impossible for any reason not mentioned in paragraph 1, the arbitral tribunal shall inform the parties of its intention to issue an order for the termination of the proceedings. The arbitral tribunal shall have the power to issue such an order unless a party raises justifiable grounds for objection.

3. Copies of the order for termination of the arbitral proceedings or of the arbitral award on agreed terms, signed by the arbitrators, shall be communicated by the arbitral tribunal to the parties. Where an arbitral award on agreed terms is made, the provisions of article 32, paragraphs 2 and 4 to 7, shall apply.

Note to Article 34

As used in Article 34 of the Tribunal Rules, the terms "party" and "parties" mean the arbitrating party or parties, as the case may be.

INTERPRETATION OF THE AWARD

Article 35

1. Within thirty days after the receipt of the award, either party, with notice to the other party, may request that the arbitral tribunal give an interpretation of the award.

2. The interpretation shall be given forty-five days after the receipt of interpretation shall form part of the in writing within the request. The award and the provisions of article 32, paragraphs 2 to 7, shall apply.

Note to Article 35

As used in Article 35 of the Tribunal Rules, the term "party" means the arbitrating party.

CORRECTION OF THE AWARD

Article 36

1. Within thirty days after the receipt of the award, either party, with notice to the other party, may request the arbitral tribunal to correct in the award any errors in computation,

any clerical or typographical errors, or any errors of similar nature. The arbitral tribunal may within thirty days after the communication of the award make such corrections on its own initiative.

2. Such corrections shall be in writing, and the provisions of article 32, paragraphs 2 to 7, shall apply.

Note to Article 36

As used in Article 36 of the Tribunal Rules, the term "party" means the arbitrating party.

ADDITIONAL AWARD

Article 37

1. Within thirty days after the receipt of the award, either party, with notice to the other party, may request the arbitral tribunal to make an additional award as to claims presented in the arbitral proceedings but omitted from the award.

2. If the arbitral tribunal considers the request for an additional award to be justified and considers that the omission can be rectified without any further hearings or evidence, it shall complete its award within sixty days after the receipt of the request.

3. When an additional award is made, the provisions of article 32, paragraphs 2 to 7, shall apply.

Note to Article 37

As used in Article 37 of the Tribunal Rules, the term "party" means the arbitrating party.

Articles 38–40 COSTS

Article 38

1. The arbitral tribunal shall fix the costs of arbitration in its award. The term "costs" includes only:

(a) The costs of expert advice and of other special assistance required for a particular case by the arbitral tribunal;

(b) The travel and other expenses of witnesses to the extent such expenses are approved by the arbitral tribunal;

(c) The costs for legal representation and assistance of the successful party if such costs were claimed during the arbitral proceedings, and only to the extent that the arbitral tribunal determines that the amount of such costs is reasonable.

2. The Full Tribunal shall fix the fees and expenses of the Tribunal which, in accordance with Article VI, paragraph 3 of the Claims Settlement Declaration, shall be borne equally by the two Governments.

Note to Article 38

As used in Article 38 of the Tribunal Rules, the term "party" means the arbitrating party.

Article 39

1. The fees of the arbitral tribunal shall be reasonable in amount, taking into account the amount in dispute, the complexity of the subject-matter, the time spent by the arbitrators and any other relevant circumstances of the case.

2. If an appointing authority has been agreed upon by the parties or designated by the Secretary-General of the Permanent Court of Arbitration at The Hague, and if that authority has issued a schedule of fees for arbitrators in international cases which it administers, the arbitral tribunal in fixing its fees shall take that schedule of fees into account to the extent that it considers appropriate in the circumstances of the case.

3. If such appointing authority has not issued a schedule of fees for arbitration in international cases, any party may at any time request the appointing authority to furnish a statement setting forth the basis for establishing fees which is customarily followed in international cases in which the authority appoints arbitrators. If the appointing authority consents to provide such a statement, the arbitral tribunal in fixing its fees shall take such information into account to the extent that it considers appropriate in the circumstances of that case.

4. In cases referred to in paragraphs 2 and 3, when a party so requests and the appointing authority consents to perform the function, the arbitral tribunal shall fix its fees only after consultation with the appointing authority which may make any comment it deems appropriate to the arbitral tribunal concerning the fees.

Note to Article 39

As used in Article 39 of the Tribunal Rules, the terms "party" and "parties" mean one or both of the two Governments, as the case may be.

Article 40

1. Except as provided in paragraph 2, the costs of arbitration referred to in paragraphs 1 (a) and 1. (b) of Article 38 shall in principle be borne by the unsuccessful party. However, the arbitral tribunal may apportion each of such costs between the parties if it determines that apportionment is reasonable, taking into account the circumstances of the case.

2. With respect to the costs of legal representation and assistance referred to in article 38, paragraph 1 (c), the arbitral tribunal, taking into account the circumstances of the case, shall be free to determine which party shall bear such costs or may apportion such costs between the parties if it determines that apportionment is reasonable.

3. When the arbitral tribunal issues an order for the termination of the arbitral proceedings it shall fix the costs of arbitration referred to in article 38 of the text of that order.

4. No additional fees may be charged by an arbitral tribunal for interpretation or correction or completion of its award under articles 35 to 37.

Note to Article 40

As used in Article 40 of the Tribunal Rules, the terms "party" and "parties" mean the arbitrating party or parties as the case may be.

DEPOSIT OF COSTS

Article 41

1. During the course of its proceedings the Full Tribunal may from time to time determine the costs referred to in paragraph 2 of Article 38 and may request each of the two Governments to deposit equal amounts as advances for such costs.

2. The arbitral tribunal may request each arbitrating party to deposit an amount determined by it as advances for the costs referred to in paragraph l(a) of Article 38.

3. If the required deposits are not paid in full within the time fixed by the arbitral tribunal, the arbitral tribunal shall inform the parties in order that one or another of them may make the required payment. If such payment is not made, the arbitral tribunal may order the suspension or termination of the arbitral proceedings or may take such action to permit continuation of the proceedings as is appropriate under the circumstances of the case.

4. The Secretary-General shall transmit monthly, quarterly and annual financial statements to the Full Tribunal and to the Agents. The accounts of the Tribunal shall be audited annually by an independent qualified accountant approved by the Full Tribunal. The Secretary-General shall transmit copies of the audit report to the Full Tribunal and to the Agents. At the request of either Agent, the annual audit shall be reviewed by an Audit Committee composed of three professionally qualified persons, one appointed by each Agent and one by the President. The Audit Committee shall submit its report to the Full Tribunal, to the Agents, and to the Secretary-General.

5. After the termination of the work of the Tribunal, it shall, after a final audit render an accounting to the two Governments of the deposits received and return any unexpended balance to the two Governments.

Note to Article 41

As used in paragraph 3, insofar as it refers to the deposits made pursuant to paragraph 1 of Article 41 of the Tribunal Rules, the term "parties" means the two Governments insofar as it refers to deposits made pursuant to paragraph 2 that term means the arbitrating parties.

The Settlement of Mixed Claims After the Second Gulf War

67.a SC Res 687 (1991) (Iraq-Kuwait)

Date: 3 April 1991
Source: UN Doc S/Res/687 (1991)
https://undocs.org/en/S/RES/687%20(1991)

The Security Council,

...

16. *Reaffirms* that Iraq, without prejudice to the debts and obligations of Iraq arising prior to 2 August 1990, which will be addressed through the normal mechanisms, is liable under international law for any direct loss, damage, including environmental damage and the depletion of natural resources, or injury to foreign Governments, nationals and corporations, as a result of Iraq's unlawful invasion and occupation of Kuwait;

17. *Decides* that all Iraqi statements made since 2 August 1990 repudiating its foreign debt are null and void, and demands that Iraq adhere scrupulously to all of its obligations concerning servicing and repayment of its foreign debt;

18. *Decides also* to create a fund to pay compensation for claims that fall within paragraph 16 above and to establish a Commission that will administer the fund;

19. *Directs* the Secretary-General to develop and present to the Security Council for decision, no later than thirty days following the adoption of the present resolution, recommendations for the fund to meet the requirement for the payment of claims established in accordance with paragraph 18 above and for a programme to implement the decisions in paragraphs 16, 17 and 18 above, including: administration of the fund; mechanisms for determining the appropriate level of Iraq's contribution to the fund based on a percentage of the value of the exports of petroleum and petroleum products from Iraq not to exceed a figure to be suggested to the Council by the Secretary-General, taking into account the requirements of the people of Iraq, Iraq's payment capacity as assessed in conjunction with the international financial institutions taking into consideration external debt service, and the needs of the Iraqi economy; arrangements for ensuring that payments are made to the fund; the process by which funds will be allocated and claims paid; appropriate procedures for evaluating losses, listing claims and verifying their validity and resolving disputed claims in respect of Iraq's liability as specified in paragraph 16 above; and the composition of the Commission designated above;

…

67.b Report of the Secretary-General Pursuant to Paragraph 19 of Security Council Resolution 687 (1991)

Date: 2 May 1991
Source: UN Doc S/22559
https://digitallibrary.un.org/record/114005?ln=en

…

C. Claims Procedure

20. The process by which funds will be allocated and claims paid, the appropriate procedure for evaluating losses, the listing of claims and the verification of their validity and the resolution of disputed claims as set out in paragraph 19 of resolution 687 (1991) – the claims procedure – is the central purpose and object of paragraphs 16 to 19 of resolution 687 (1991). It is in this area of the Commission's work that the distinction between policy-making and function is most important. The Commission is not a court or an arbitral tribunal before which the parties appear; it is a political organ that performs an essentially fact-finding function of examining claims, verifying their validity, evaluating losses, assessing payments and resolving disputed claims. It is only in this last respect that a quasi-judicial function may be involved. Given the nature of the Commission, it is all the more important that some element of due process be built into the procedure. It will be the function of the commissioners to provide this element. As the policy-making organ of the Commission, it will fall to the Governing Council to establish the guidelines in respect of claims that are presented and in resolving disputed claims. They will make the appropriate recommendations to the Governing Council, which will in turn make the final determination. The recommendations that follow have been divided for the sake of convenience under three main headings: the filing of claims; the processing of claims; and the payments of claims.

1. Filing of claims

21. With regard to the filing of claims, the Governing Council must first decide in what manner the claims of foreign Governments, nationals and corporations are to be filed with the Commission. It is recommended that the Commission should entertain, as a general rule, only consolidated claims filed by individual Governments on their own behalf or on behalf of their nationals and corporations. The filing of individual claims would entail tens of thousands of claims to be processed by the Commission, a task which could take a decade of more and could lead to inequalities in the filing of claims disadvantaging small claimants. It will be for each individual Government to decide on the procedures to be followed internally in respect of the consolidation of the claim having regard to its own legal system, practice and procedures. The Governing Council may, in addition, consider whether, in exceptional circumstances involving very large and complex claims, a somewhat different procedure could apply. The question might be considered whether such claims, the character of which, of course, would have to be defined by the Governing Council, could be filled individually with the Commission by Governments, nationals or corporations and whether the individual Government, national or corporation could be authorized to present those claims.

22. In this context, there is another matter that requires consideration by the Commission and regarding which the Governing Council should establish guidelines, namely the question of the exclusivity or non-exclusivity of the claims procedure foreseen in paragraph 19 of the resolution. It is clear from paragraph 16 of the resolution that the debts and obligations or Iraq arising prior to 2 August 1990 are an entirely separate issue and will be addressed "through the normal mechanisms". It is also clear from paragraph 16 that the resolution and the procedure foreseen in paragraph 19 relate to liability under international law. Resolution 687 (1991) could not, and does not, establish the Commission as an organ with exclusive competence to consider claims arising from Iraq's unlawful invasion and occupation of Kuwait. In other words, it is entirely possible, indeed probable, that individual claimants will proceed with claims against Iraq in their domestic legal systems. The likelihood of parallel actions taking place on the international level in the Commission and on the domestic level in the Commission and on the domestic level in national courts cannot be ignored. It is, therefore, recommended that the Governing Council establish guidelines regarding the non-exclusivity of claims and the appropriate mechanisms for coordination of actions at the international and domestic levels in order to ensure that the aggregate of compensation awarded by the Commission and a national court or commission does not exceed the amount of the loss. A particular problem might arise in this regard concerning default judgements obtained in national courts.

23. In addition to deciding on the consolidation of claims, the Governing Council may also wish to establish a organization of claims according to both type and size. The categorization of claims according to type might, for example, distinguish between claims for loss of life or personal injury and property damage, environmental damage or damage due to the depletion of natural resources. The categorization of claims by size might for example, differentiate between small-, medium- and large-sized claims. A further categorization might be to distinguish between losses incurred by Governments, on the one hand, and losses incurred by nationals and corporations, on the other hand.

24. Governments could be requested by the Governing Council to use these categorizations when filing their consolidated claims. The Governing Council should also establish guidelines regarding the formal requirements for the presentation of claims such

as the type of documentation to be presented in support of the claim and the time-delays for the filing of claims. The time-delays should be of sufficient length to permit Governments to establish and implement an internal procedure to establish and implement an internal procedure for the assembling and consolidation of claims. It is recommended that a fixed time period be established for the filing of all claims. A period of two years from the adoption of the filing guidelines would appear to be adequate. Alternatively, the Governing Council could set different filing periods for different types of claims in order to ensure that priority is given to certain claims, for example, loss of life of personal injury. In this respect, I am of the opinion that there would be some merit in providing for a priority consideration of small claims relating to losses by individuals so that these are disposed of before the consideration of claims relating to losses by foreign Governments and by corporations.

2. Processing of claims

25. The processing of claims will entail the verification of claims and evaluation of losses and the resolution of losses and the resolution of any disputed claims. The major part of this task is not of a judicial nature; the resolution of disputed claims would, however, be quasi-judicial. It is envisaged that the processing of claims would be carried out principally by the commissioners. Before proceeding to the verification of claims and evaluation of losses, however, a determination will have to be made as to whether the losses for which claims are presented fall within the meaning of paragraph 16 of resolution 687 (1991), that is to say, whether the loss, damage or injury is direct and as a result of Iraq's unlawful invasion and occupation of Kuwait. It is recommended that the Governing Council establish detailed guidelines regarding what constitutes such direct loss for the guidance of all claimants as well as the commissioners.

26. Claims will be addressed to the Commission. The Commission will make a preliminary assessment of the claims, which will be carried out by the Secretariat, to determine whether they meet the formal requirements established by the Governing Council. The claims would then be submitted to verification and evaluation by panels normally comprised of three commissioners for this purpose. In carrying out these tasks, it is recommended that the commissioners be given the necessary powers to request additional evidence, to hold hearings in which individual Governments, nationals and corporations can present their views and to hear expert testimony. The Governing Council might wish to address the question of possible assistance to ensure the adequacy of the representation of countries of limited financial means. Iraq will be informed of all claims and will have the right to present its comments to the commissioners within time-delays to be fixed by the Governing Council or the Panel dealing with the individual claim. Recommendations of the commissioners regarding the verification and evaluation of claims will be final and subject only to the approval of the Governing Council, which shall make the final determination. The Governing Council should have the power to return claims to the commissioners for further revision if it so decides.

27. Where a dispute arises out of the allegation made by a claimant that the Panel of Commissioners, in dealing with its claims, has made an error, whether on a point of law and procedure or on a point of fact, such disputes will be dealt with by a board of commissioners who for this purposes should be guided by such guidelines as have been established by the Governing Council and the Arbitration Rules of the United Nations Commission on International Trade Law (UNCITRAL). The UNCITRAL Arbitration Rules will be modified as necessary. The final decision will be made by the Governing Council.

3. Payment of Claims

28. It is to be anticipated that the value of claims approved by the Commission will at any given time far exceed the resources of the Fund. It will, therefore, be incumbent upon the Commission to decide on an allocation of funds and a procedure for the payment of claims. It is recommended that the Governing Council establish criteria for the allocation of funds, taking into account the size of claims, the scope of the losses sustained by the country concerned and any other relevant factors. In this connection, it might be necessary to distinguish between Kuwait, on the one hand, and other countries on the other hand. As far as the payment of claims is concerned, it follows from the consolidation of the claims and their filing by individual Governments that payments will be made exclusively to Governments. Individual Governments will be responsible for the appropriate distribution to individual claimants. The Governing Council should establish further guidelines regarding the payment of claims, for example, whether claims should be paid in full or whether percentages should be paid. In the latter case, the unsatisfied portions of the claims will remain as outstanding obligations.

D. Expenses of the Commission

29. The expenses of the Commission, including those of the Governing Council, the commissioners and the secretariat, should in principle be paid from the Fund. However, as some time will elapse before the Fund is adequately financed, consideration must be given to the financial implications of the programme outlined. It is recommended that urgent consideration be given to the means by which the initial costs of the Commission will be met.

…

67.c United Nations Compensation Commission Provisional Rules for Claims Procedures

Date: 26 June 1992

Source: (1992) 31 ILM 1053

https://uncc.ch/sites/default/files/attachments/S-AC.26-DEC%2010%20%5B1992%5D.pdf

I. GENERAL PROVISIONS

Article 1. Use of terms

The following definitions apply for the purpose of these Rules:

1. "Commission" means the United Nations Compensation Commission.

2. "Compensation Fund" or "Fund" means the United Nations Compensation Fund, created by paragraph 18 of Security Council resolution 687 (1991) and established by paragraph 3 of Security Council resolution 692 (1991) in accordance with section I of the Secretary-General's report (S/22559) dated 2 May 1991.

3. "Secretary-General" means the Secretary-General of the United Nations.

4. "Governing Council" or "Council" means the Governing Council of the Commission.

5. "Commissioners" means experts appointed by the Governing Council for the verification and evaluation of claims.

6. "Executive Secretary" means the Executive Secretary of the Commission and includes any Deputy of, or other person authorized by, the Executive Secretary.

7. "Secretariat" means the secretariat of the Commission.

8. "Standard forms" means claim forms prepared and distributed to Governments by the Executive Secretary for claims under claims criteria adopted by the Governing Council.

9. "Claim forms" means standard forms and any other form agreed between the Executive Secretary and the Government or international organization in question for filing claims.

10. "Rules" means the Commission's Provisional Rules for Claims Procedure.

11. "Criteria" means criteria for expedited processing of urgent claims (Governing Council's decision S/AC.26/1991/I dated 2 August 1991), and criteria for additional categories of claims (Governing Council's decision S/AC.26/1991/7 dated 4 December 1991) as well as any other criteria that the Governing Council may adopt.

12. "Claimant" means any individual, corporation or other private legal entity, public sector entity, Government, or international organization that files a claim with the Commission.

13. "Person or body" means an individual, corporation or other private legal entity, public sector entity, Government, or international organization.

14. "International organization" means an international organization of States.

15. "Documents" means all submissions and evidence presented by a claimant in support of a claim, in whatever form, including statements of claim in categories E and F.

16. "Database" means computerized information, pertaining to individual claimants and claims, kept by the Commission to assist in the processing of claims.

Article 2. Scope of the Rules

These Rules apply to processing of claims submitted to the Commission under the criteria adopted by the Governing Council.

Article 3. Calculation of periods of time

For the purposes of calculating a period of time under these Rules, such period shall begin to run on the day following the day when the document is received or a notification is made. If the last day of such period is an official holiday or a non-business day at the headquarters of the Commission, the period is extended until the first business day that follows. Official holidays and non-business days occurring during the running of the period of time are included in calculating the period. The Executive Secretary will issue a list of such days.

II. SUBMISSION AND FILING OF CLAIMS

Article 4. Submission of claims

1. Claim forms and documents are to be submitted to the Commission at the Secretariat's headquarters (Palais des Nations, Villa La Pelouse, Geneva, Switzerland).

2. Claim forms shall be deemed to have been submitted when they are physically delivered to and received by the Secretariat.

Article 5. Who may submit claims

1. Governments and international organizations are entitled to submit claims to the Commission.

(a) A Government may submit claims on behalf of its nationals and, at its discretion, of other persons resident in its territory. In the case of Governments existing in the territory of a former federal state, one such Government may submit claims on behalf of nationals, corporations or other entities of another such Government, if both Governments agree.

(b) A Government may submit claims on behalf of corporations or other entities that, on the date on which the claim arose, were incorporated or organized under the law of that State. If the Governments concerned agree, one Government may submit claims in respect of joint ventures on behalf of the nationals, corporations or other entities of other Governments.

(c) Claims may be submitted on behalf of an individual, corporation or other entity by only one Government.

(d) International organizations may submit claims only on their own behalf.

2. An appropriate person, authority, or body appointed by the Governing Council may submit claims on behalf of persons who are not in a position to have their claims submitted by a Government.

3. A corporation or other private legal entity is required to request the State of its corporation or organization to submit its claim to the Commission. In the case of a corporation or other private legal entity whose State of incorporation or organization fails to submit, within the time-limit established by the Governing Council, such claims falling within the applicable criteria, the corporation or other private legal entity may itself make a claim to the Commission within three months thereafter. It must provide at the same time an explanation as to why its claim is not being submitted by a Government.

Article 6. Claim forms and language

1. Except as may otherwise be agreed between the Executive Secretary and the Government or international organization in question, claims must be submitted on the standard forms prepared and distributed by the Secretariat.

2. Owing to the fact that the Commission's computerized software and database system, which is technically required for the processing of a large number of claims, has been designed in English, the working language of the claims procedure before the Commission will be English.

3. Claim forms can be submitted in any of the official languages of the United Nations. However, since English is the working language of the claims procedure and of the Commission's computerized database, in cases where claim forms are not submitted in English, an English translation of the form must be provided. The translation, as submitted, will serve as the basis for the evaluation of the claim.

4. With respect to claims in categories A, B and C, the documents supporting the claims are not required to be translated into English at the stage of the submission of the claims. The secretariat, on the basis of methods adopted for processing and evaluation of claims, will notify each Government as to the extent of the translation required and the time-limit for providing it.

5. With respect to claims in categories D, E and F, all documents supporting the claims must also be submitted in English or be accompanied by an English translation.

6. In the case of oral proceedings, the Executive Secretary shall arrange for interpretation as necessary into and from other official languages of the United Nations.

Article 7. Format of claims

1. Claim forms in category A must be submitted only in the computer format distributed by the secretariat. Governments will maintain custody of the original paper copies of form A and supporting documents and will make them available to the Commission upon request.

2. Claim forms and documents in all other categories must be submitted on paper. In addition to filing claims in these categories on paper, Governments may also submit them in a computer format.

3. All claim forms and documents filed with the Commission on paper are to be submitted on paper 8 1/2 inches x 11 inches or on A-4 size paper (21 centimetres x 29.5 centimetres) or on paper no larger than A-4. If a document cannot conveniently be reproduced on paper no larger than A-4, it is to be folded to A-4 size, unless the Executive Secretary agrees otherwise in special circumstances.

4. Claims and documents filed with the Commission in a computer format are to be submitted on MS/DOS or UNIX compatible formats, or in such other format as may be agreed to by the Executive Secretary.

Article 8. Copies

1. Except as otherwise agreed to by the Executive Secretary, claim forms and documents must be submitted with the following number of copies:

For category A: 3 copies of micro floppy disk

For categories B and C: 1 original and 2 copies

For D and other categories: 1 original and 8 copies.

2. The secretariat, or the Commissioners, may request additional copies or accept a smaller number in exceptional circumstances.

Article 9. Representatives

For the purpose of these Rules, all communications between the Commission's secretariat and a Government concerning claims shall take place through its Permanent Mission at Geneva. Further, except in cases where a specially authorized representative is designated by a Government and notified to the Executive Secretary, the head of the Permanent Mission of a Government shall be considered as its representative before the Commission. Governments that do not maintain Permanent Missions at Geneva and international organizations shall notify the name of their duly authorized representatives to the Executive Secretary.

Article 10. The Registry

A registry will be set up within the secretariat. A member of the secretariat will be designated by the Executive Secretary as Registry Officer. The Registry Officer will receive the claims and register them.

Article 11. Receipt of claims

1. Upon the submission of a claim, the Registry Officer will issue a delivery receipt identifying the parcel received and confirming the date it was received and the person who presented it.

2. The Registry Officer will in due course verify:

(a) That the claim has been submitted by a person or body who, in accordance with the decisions of the Governing Council, has a right to file claims with the Commission;

(b) That the claim has been submitted within the relevant time-limit established by the Governing Council;

(c) That, in the case of a corporation or other private legal entity making a claim directly to the Commission in accordance with article 5, paragraph 3, above:

(i) Evidence is attached indicating that a request was made by the entity concerned to the State of its incorporation or organization to submit its claim to the Commission;

(ii) Explanation is provided as to why the claim was not submitted by a Government.

Article 12. Unauthorized or late submissions

1. in the case of claims submitted by an unauthorized person or entity, including claims presented by a corporation or other private legal entity without showing that a previous request has been made to the State of its incorporation or organization, the Executive Secretary will return the documents received, and inform the person or entity concerned of the reasons why the claim cannot be registered.

2. In the case of claims submitted by an authorized person or body after the expiration of the time-limit set by the Governing Council for a given category of claims, the Executive Secretary will report to the Governing Council. The Governing Council will decide whether to accept the late-filed claims or not.

Article 13. Filing receipt

If the claim is submitted by an authorized person or body within the established time-limit, the Registry Officer will register the claim and issue a filing receipt indicating:

(a) The claim and its category;

(b) The party who presented the claim;

(c) The number of claims contained in a consolidated claim;

(d) The number assigned to the claim for identification.

Article 14. Preliminary assessment

1. The secretariat will make a preliminary assessment of the claims received in order to determine whether they meet the formal requirements established by the Governing Council. To this end the secretariat will verify:

(a) That the claims have been submitted on the appropriate claim forms with the required number of copies, and in English or with an English translation;

(b) That the claims contain the names and addresses of the claimants and, where applicable, evidence of the amount, type and causes of losses;

(c) That the affirmation by the Government has been included in respect of each consolidated claim stating that, to the best of the information available to it, the claimants are its nationals or residents, and that it has no reason to believe that the information stated in the claims is incorrect;

(d) That all required affirmations have been given by each claimant.

2. In the case of claims of corporations and other legal entities the secretariat will also verify that each separate claim contains:

(a) Documents evidencing the name, address and place of incorporation or organization of the entity;

(b) Evidence that the corporation or the legal entity was, on the date on which the claim arose, incorporated or organized under the law of the State the Government of which has submitted the claim;

(c) A general description of the legal structure of the entity;

(d) An affirmation by the authorized official for each corporation or other entity that the information contained in the claim is correct.

Article 15. Claims not meeting the formal requirements

If it is found that the claim does not meet the formal requirements established by the Governing Council, the secretariat will notify the person or body that submitted the claim about that circumstance and will give it 60 days from the date of that notification to remedy the defect. If the formal requirements are not met within this period, the claim shall not be considered as filed.

Article 16. Reports and views on claims

1. The Executive Secretary will make periodic reports to the Governing Council concerning claims received. These reports shall be made as frequently as required to inform the Council of the Commission's case load but not less than quarterly. The reports shall indicate:

(a) Governments, international organizations or other eligible parties that have submitted claims;
(b) The categories of claims submitted;
(c) The number of claimants in each consolidated claim;
(d) The total amount of compensation sought in each consolidated claim.

In addition, each report may indicate significant legal and factual issues raised by the claims, if any.

2. The Executive Secretary's report will be promptly circulated to the Government of Iraq as well as to all Governments and international organizations that have submitted claims.

3. Within 30 days in case of claims in categories A, B and C, and 90 days in case of claims in other categories, of the date of the circulation of the Executive Secretary's report, the Government of Iraq as well as Governments and international organizations that have submitted claims, may present their additional information and views concerning the report to the Executive Secretary for transmission to panels of Commissioners in accordance with article 32. There shall be no extensions of the time-limits specified in this paragraph.

4. Requirements set forth in articles 3, 4, 6 (3), 7, 8 and 11 (1) shall apply to such additional information and views.

Article 17. Categorization of claims

In order to facilitate the work of Commissioners and to ensure uniformity in the treatment of similar claims, the secretariat will proceed to categorize claims according to, inter alia, the type or size of the claims and the similarity of legal and factual issues.

III. COMMISSIONERS

Article 18. Appointment

1. Commissioners shall be appointed for specific tasks and terms by the Governing Council upon nomination by the Secretary-General on the basis of recommendations of the Executive Secretary.

2. The Secretary-General has established a Register of Experts which, as stated in his invitation of 12 June 1991 for the submission of names of experts, while not limiting his selection, might be drawn upon when Commissioners are nominated for appointment. The Executive Secretary will keep and update the Register.

Article 19. Qualifications

1. In nominating and appointing the Commissioners, due regard shall be paid to the need for geographical representation, professional qualifications, experience and integrity.

2. Commissioners will be experts in fields such as finance, law, accounting, insurance, environmental damage assessment, oil, trade and engineering.

3. Nominations and appointments of Commissioners shall be made paying due regard to the nature of the claims and categories of claims to be assigned to them.

Article 20. Procedure for appointment

1. The Executive Secretary will transmit to the Governing Council the nominations for Commissioners proposed by the Secretary-General, indicating which Commissioners are to serve on each panel and who, within each panel, will act as a Chairman.

2. The Executive Secretary will recommend to the Secretary-General for nomination as many panels of Commissioners as necessary to process claims in an expeditious manner.

3. When transmitting to the Governing Council the nominations for Commissioners, the Executive Secretary will specify the claims or categories of claims to be assigned to each panel, indicating the expertise and the number of Commissioners required.

4. If the Governing Council does not agree on the appointment of a nominee for a panel, it will request the Secretary-General, through the Executive Secretary, to submit a new nomination.

5. If, at the time the Executive Secretary transmits the new nomination the Governing Council is not in session, the new nomination will be communicated to the members of the Governing Council. The Governing Council may approve replacement Commissioners at intersessional meetings.

6. The same procedure will apply whenever a new Commissioner must be nominated.

Article 21. Requirements

1. Commissioners will act in their personal capacity. Commissioners shall not have financial interests in any of the claims submitted to them or to the panel to which they belong. They may not be associated with or have financial interests in any corporations whose claims have been submitted to them or to the panel to which they belong.

2. Commissioners shall not represent or advise any party or claimant concerning the preparation or presentation of their claims to the Commission during their service as Commissioner or for two years thereafter.

Article 22. Disclosure

1. All prospective Commissioners shall file a statement that shall disclose to the Executive Secretary any prior or actual relationship with Governments, corporations or individuals, or any other circumstances, that are likely to give rise to justifiable doubts as to his impartiality or independence with respect to his prospective tasks. This information will be provided to the Governing Council at the time the nomination of the prospective Commissioner is transmitted.

2. A Commissioner, once appointed, shall disclose to the Executive Secretary any new circumstances likely to give rise to justifiable doubts as to his impartiality or independence.

3. When any Commissioner obtains knowledge that any particular claim before his panel involves circumstances likely to give rise to justifiable doubts as to his impartiality or independence with respect to that claim or group of claims, he shall disclose such

circumstances to the Executive Secretary and, if appropriate, shall disqualify himself as to that case.

4. If any Government, international organization, individual claimant, or Commissioner becomes aware of circumstances that give rise to justifiable doubts as to a Commissioner's impartiality or independence, such circumstances must be communicated to the Executive Secretary not later than 15 days after they became known.

5. The Executive Secretary will inform the Governing Council about the circumstances brought to his attention or of which he learns that are likely to give rise to justifiable doubts as to the impartiality or independence of a Commissioner, transmitting a statement of the Commissioner concerned.

6. In any case in which such circumstances are disclosed to the Governing Council, it may determine whether the Commissioner should cease to act, either generally or with respect to a particular claim or claims. Pending such a determination by the Governing Council, the Commissioner concerned will continue to perform his tasks.

Article 23. Resignation

1. A Commissioner who intends to resign from his office shall communicate his decision, through the Executive Secretary, to the Governing Council.

2. A Commissioner who has submitted his resignation shall continue to perform his functions until such time as his resignation is accepted by the Governing Council.

Article 24. Completion of work

If a Commissioner resigns during the course of consideration of any particular claim or group of claims, the Commissioner will continue to serve for the limited purpose of completing work on that particular claim or group of claims, unless excused by the Governing Council.

Article 25. Failure to act

In the event that a Commissioner fails to act or in the event of de jure or de facto impossibility of his performing his functions, the Executive Secretary shall inform the Governing Council, which may decide to replace the Commissioner in accordance with the procedures set forth in article 20, paragraph:6.

Article 26. Privileges and immunities

Commissioners, when performing functions for the Commission, will have the status of experts on mission within the meaning of article VI of the Convention on the Privileges and Immunities of the United Nations of 13 February 1946.

Article 27. Declaration

Every Commissioner shall, before taking up his duties, make the following declaration:

"I solemnly declare that I will perform my duties and exercise my position as Commissioner honourably, faithfully, independently, impartially and conscientiously."

This declaration shall be signed and delivered to the Executive Secretary, and attached to the documents pertaining to the Commissioner's appointment.

IV. PROCEDURES GOVERNING THE WORK OF THE PANELS

Article 28. Constitution of panels

1. Unless otherwise decided by the Governing Council, Commissioners will work in panels of three members. Each of the members of a panel shall be of different nationality.

2. Priority is to be given to the establishment of panels of Commissioners to deal with claims in categories A, B and C.

Article 29. Organization of work

Chairmen of the panels will organize the work of their respective panels so as to ensure the expeditious processing of the claims and the consistent application of the relevant criteria and these Rules.

Article 30. Confidentiality

1. Unless otherwise provided in these procedures or decided by the Governing Council, all records received or developed by the Commission will be confidential, but the secretariat may provide status reports to Governments, international organizations or corporations making claims directly to the Commission in accordance with article 5, paragraph 3, regarding claims that they have submitted.

2. Panels will conduct their work in private.

3. Commissioners shall not disclose, even after the termination of their functions, any information not in the public domain that has come to their knowledge by reason of their working for the Commission.

Article 31. Applicable law

In considering the claims, Commissioners will apply Security Council resolution 687 (1991) and other relevant Security Council resolutions, the criteria established by the Governing Council for particular categories of claims, and any pertinent decisions of the Governing Council. In addition, where necessary, Commissioners shall apply other relevant rules of international law.

Article 32. Submission of claims to panels

1. Following the appointment of Commissioners by the Governing Council, the Executive Secretary will submit to panels of Commissioners the single claims or categories of claims assigned to each of them together with the related documentation, containing the results of the preliminary assessment made by the secretariat and any other information deemed to be useful for the work of the Commissioners, as well as the additional information and views submitted in accordance with article 16.

2. Any information received by the secretariat after the expiration of the time-limits as established in article 16 will be submitted when received, but the work of the panel will not be delayed pending receipt or consideration of such information.

3. The Executive Secretary may, after consulting the relevant panel chairmen, reallocate a claim or claims from one panel to another in order to ensure the efficient processing of claims.

Article 33. Work of the panels

1. After receiving claims from the Executive Secretary, Commissioners will examine them and meet to deliberate and prepare their recommendations to the Governing Council.

2. Panels of Commissioners will normally meet at the headquarters of the secretariat. Meetings will be held to the extent deemed necessary by the Chairman of each panel. Commissioners will continue their work on the claims while away from the headquarters of the secretariat, conducting the necessary communications among themselves and with the secretariat.

3. Any recommendation or other decision of the panel shall be made by a majority of the Commissioners.

Article 34. Assistance by the Executive Secretary

1. The Executive Secretary and the staff of the secretariat will provide administrative, technical and legal support to the Commissioners, including the development and maintenance of a computerized database for claims and assistance in obtaining additional information.

2. In considering the claims, the Commissioners will take into account the results of the preliminary assessment of claims made by the secretariat in accordance with article 14, as well as other information and views that the Executive Secretary may provide in accordance with article 32.

3. A member of the secretariat may attend sessions of the panel and may, if required, provide information to the Commissioners.

Article 35. Evidence

1. Each claimant is responsible for submitting documents and other evidence which demonstrate satisfactorily that a particular claim or group of claims is eligible for compensation pursuant to Security Council resolution 687 (1991). Each panel will determine the admissibility, relevance, materiality and weight of any documents and other evidence submitted.

2. With respect to claims received under the criteria for expedited processing of. urgent claims (S/AC.26/1991/l), the following guidelines will apply:

(a) For the payment of fixed amounts in the case of departures, claimants are required to provide simple documentation of the fact and date of departure from Iraq or Kuwait. Documentation of the actual amount of loss will not be required;

(b) For the payment of fixed amounts in the case of serious personal injury not resulting in death, claimants are required to provide simple documentation of the fact and date of the injury; in the case of death, claimants are required to provide simple documentation of the death and family relationship. Documentation of the actual amount of loss will not be required;

(c) For consideration of claims up to US$ 100,000 of actual losses, such claims must be documented by appropriate evidence of the circumstances and amount of claimed loss. Documents and other evidence required will be the reasonable minimum that is appropriate under the particular circumstances of the case. A lesser degree of documentary evidence ordinarily will be sufficient for smaller claims such as those below US$ 20,000.

3. With respect to claims received under the criteria for processing claims of individuals not otherwise covered, claims of corporations and other entities, and claims of governments and international organizations (S/AC.26/1991/7/Rev.I), such claims must be supported by documentary and other appropriate evidence sufficient to demonstrate the circumstances and amount of the claimed loss.

4. A panel of Commissioners may request evidence required under this Article.

Article 36. Additional information

A panel of Commissioners may:

(a) In unusually large or complex cases, request further written submissions and invite individuals, corporations or other entities, Governments or international organizations to present their views in oral proceedings;

(b) Request additional information from any other source, including expert advice, as necessary.

Article 37. Review by Commissioners of urgent claims

With respect to claims received under the criteria for expedited processing of urgent claims (S/AC.26/1991/I), the following expedited procedures may be used:

(a) The secretariat will proceed to check individual claims by matching them, in so far as possible, against the information in its computerized database. The results of the database analysis may be cross-checked by the panel;

(b) With respect to claims that cannot be completely verified through the computerized database, if the volume of claims is large, the panel may check individual claims on the basis of a sampling with further verification only as circumstances warrant;

(c) Each panel will make its recommendations on the basis of the documents submitted, taking into account the preliminary assessment conducted in accordance with article 14, any other information and views submitted in accordance with article 32 and any information submitted in accordance with article 34. Each panel will normally make its recommendations without holding an oral proceeding. The panel may determine that special circumstances warrant holding an oral proceeding concerning a particular claim or claims;

(d) Each panel will complete its review of the claims assigned to it and issue its-report as soon as possible but no later than 120 days from the date the claims in question are submitted to the panel;

(e) Each panel will report in writing through the Executive Secretary to the Governing Council on the claims received and the amount recommended to be allocated to each Government or other entity for each consolidated claim.

Each report will briefly explain the reasons for the recommendations and, to the extent practicable within the time-limit, contain a breakdown of the recommendations in respect of individual claims within each consolidated claim.

Article 38. Review by Commissioners of other claims

With respect to claims received under the criteria for processing of claims of individuals not otherwise covered, claims of corporations and other entities, and claims of Governments and international organizations (S/AC.26/1991/7/Rev.l), the following procedures will be used:

(a) In so far as possible, claims with significant common legal and factual issues will be processed together;

(b) Panels may adopt special procedures appropriate to the character, amount and subject-matter of the particular types of claims under consideration;

(c) Each panel will complete its review of any claim or group of claims and report in writing through the Executive Secretary to the Governing Council within 180 days of the date the claims in question are submitted to the panel, except for any unusually large or complex claims referred for detailed review, as described below. Each panel will make its recommendations on the basis of the documents submitted, taking into account the preliminary assessment conducted in accordance with article 14, any other information and views submitted in accordance with article 32 and any information submitted in accordance with article 34;

(d) Unusually large or complex claims may receive detailed review, as appropriate. If so, the panel considering such a claim may, in its discretion, ask for additional written submissions and hold oral proceedings. In such a case, the individual, corporation, Government, international organization or other entity making the claim may present the case directly to the panel, and may be assisted by an attorney or other representative of choice. The panel will complete its review of the case and report in writing through the Executive Secretary its recommendations to the Governing Council within 12 months of the date the claim was submitted to the panel;

(e) Each panel will report in writing through the Executive Secretary to the Governing Council on the claims received and the amount recommended to be awarded for each claimant. Each report will briefly explain the reasons for the recommendations.

Article 39. Additional time

If a panel considering a claim or group of claims cannot complete its work within the allotted time, the panel will notify the Governing Council through the Executive Secretary of the estimated additional time required. The Governing Council will decide whether the panel should continue its work on the claims or group of claims, with a time-limit to be decided by the Council, or should be discharged of the claim or group of claims, which would be given to another panel.

Article 40. Decisions

1. The amounts recommended by the panels of Commissioners will be subject to approval by the Governing Council. The Governing Council may review the amounts recommended and, where it determines circumstances require, increase or reduce them.

2. The Governing Council may, in its discretion, return a particular claim or group of claims for further review by the Commissioners.

3. The Governing Council will make its decisions on amounts to be awarded at each session with respect to claims covered in any reports of Commissioners circulated to members of the Governing Council at least 30 days in advance of the session.

4. Decisions of the Governing Council will be final and are not subject to appeal or review on procedural, substantive or other grounds.

5. Decisions of the Governing Council and, after the relevant decision is made, the associated report of the panels of Commissioners, will be made public, except the Executive Secretary will delete from the reports of panels of Commissioners the identities of individual claimants or other information determined by the panels to be confidential or privileged.

Article 41. Correction of decisions

1. Computational, clerical, typographical or other errors brought to the attention of the Executive Secretary within 60 days from the publication of the decisions and reports will be reported by the Executive Secretary to the Governing Council.

2. The Governing Council will decide whether any action is necessary. If it is determined that a correction must be made, the Governing Council will direct the Executive Secretary as to the proper method of correction.

Article 42. Withdrawal of claims

A claim pending before the Commission may be withdrawn at any time by the Government or entity that submitted the claim to the Commission. In any case where the claim has been paid, settled or otherwise resolved, it shall be withdrawn.

Article 43. Additional procedural rulings

Subject to the provisions of these procedures, Commissioners may make such additional procedural rulings as may be necessary to complete work on particular cases or categories of cases. In so doing, the Commissioners may rely on the relevant rules of the United Nations Commission on International Trade Law for guidance. Commissioners may request the Governing Council to provide further guidance with respect to these procedures at any time. The Governing Council may adopt further procedures or revise these rules when circumstances warrant.

Dispute Settlement After the Eritrean-Ethiopian War

68.a Agreement between the Government of the Federal Democratic Republic of Ethiopia and the Government of the State of Eritrea (The Algiers Agreement)

Date: 12 December 2000
Source: (2001) 40 ILM 260
https://pcacases.com/web/sendAttach/786

The Government of the State of Eritrea and the Government of the Federal Democratic Republic of Ethiopia (the "parties"),

REAFFIRMING their acceptance of the Organization of African Unity ("OAU") Framework Agreement and the Modalities for its Implementation, which have been endorsed by the 35th ordinary session of the Assembly of Heads of State and Government, held in Algiers, Algeria, from 12 to 14 July 1999,

RECOMMITTING themselves to the Agreement on Cessation of Hostilities, signed in Algiers on 18 June 2000,

WELCOMING the commitment of the OAU and the United Nations, through their endorsement of the Framework Agreement and Agreement on Cessation of Hostilities, to work closely with the international community to mobilize resources for the resettlement of displaced persons, as well as rehabilitation and peacebuilding in both countries,

Have agreed as follows:

Article 1

1. The parties shall permanently terminate hostilities between themselves. Each party shall refrain from the threat or use of force against the other.

2. The parties shall respect and fully implement the provisions of the Agreement on Cessation of Hostilities.

…

Article 3

1. In order to determine the origins of the conflict, an investigation will be carried out on the incidents of 6 May 1998 and on any other incident prior to that date which could have contributed to a misunderstanding between the parties regarding their common border, including the incidents of July and August 1997.

2. The investigation will be carried out by an independent, impartial body appointed by the Secretary General of the OAU, in consultation with the Secretary General of the United Nations and the two parties.

3. The independent body will endeavor to submit its report to the Secretary General of the OAU in a timely fashion.

4. The parties shall cooperate fully with the independent body.

5. The Secretary General of the OAU will communicate a copy of the report to each of the two parties, which shall consider it in accordance with the letter and spirit of the Framework Agreement and the Modalities.

Article 4

1. Consistent with the provisions of the Framework Agreement and the Agreement on Cessation of Hostilities, the parties reaffirm the principle of respect for the borders existing at independence as stated in resolution AHG/Res. 16(1) adopted by the OAU Summit in Cairo in 1964, and, in this regard, that they shall be determined on the basis of pertinent colonial treaties and applicable international law.

2. The parties agree that a neutral Boundary Commission composed of five members shall be established with a mandate to delimit and demarcate the colonial treaty border based on pertinent colonial treaties (1900, 1902 and 1908) and applicable international law. The Commission shall not have the power to make decisions ex aequo et bono.

3. The Commission shall be located in the Hague.

4. Each party shall, by written notice to the United Nations Secretary General, appoint two commissioners within 45 days from the effective date of this agreement, neither of whom shall be nationals or permanent residents of the party making the appointment. In the event that a party fails to name one or both of its party-appointed commissioners within the specified time, the Secretary-General of the United Nations shall make the appointment.

5. The president of the Commission shall be selected by the party-appointed commissioners or, failing their agreement within 30 days of the date of appointment of the latest party-appointed commissioner, by the Secretary-General of the United Nations after consultation with the parties. The president shall be neither a national nor permanent resident of either party.

6. In the event of the death or resignation of a commissioner in the course of the proceedings, a substitute commissioner shall be appointed or chosen pursuant to the procedure set forth in this paragraph that was applicable to the appointment or choice of the commissioner being replaced.

7. The UN Cartographer shall serve as Secretary to the Commission and undertake such tasks as assigned to him by the Commission, making use of the technical expertise of the UN Cartographic Unit. The Commission may also engage the services of additional experts as it deems necessary.

8. Within 45 days after the effective date of this Agreement, each party shall provide to the Secretary its claims and evidence relevant to the mandate of the Commission. These shall be provided to the other party by the Secretary.

9. After reviewing such evidence and within 45 days of its receipt, the Secretary shall subsequently transmit to the Commission and the parties any materials relevant to the mandate of the Commission as well as his findings identifying those portions of the border as to which there appears to be no dispute between the parties. The Secretary shall also transmit to the Commission all the evidence presented by the parties.

10. With regard to those portions of the border about which there appears to be controversy, as well as any portions of the border identified pursuant to paragraph 9 with respect to which either party believes there to be controversy, the parties shall present their written and oral submissions and any additional evidence directly to the Commission, in accordance with its procedures.

11. The Commission shall adopt its own rules of procedure based upon the 1992 Permanent Court of Arbitration Option Rules for Arbitrating Disputes Between Two States. Filing deadlines for the parties' written submissions shall be simultaneous rather than consecutive. All decisions of the Commission shall be made by a majority of the commissioners.

12. The Commission shall commence its work not more than 15 days after it is constituted and shall endeavor to make its decision concerning delimitation of the border within six months of its first meeting. The Commission shall take this objective into consideration when establishing its schedule. At its discretion, the Commission may extend this deadline.

13. Upon reaching a final decision regarding delimitation of the borders, the Commission shall transmit its decision to the parties and Secretaries General of the OAU and the United Nations for publication, and the Commission shall arrange for expeditious demarcation.

14. The parties agree to cooperate with the Commission, its experts and other staff in all respects during the process of delimitation and demarcation, including the facilitation of access to territory they control. Each party shall accord to the Commission and its employees the same privileges and immunities as are accorded to diplomatic agents under the Vienna Convention on Diplomatic Relations.

15. The parties agree that the delimitation and demarcation determinations of the Commission shall be final and binding. Each party shall respect the border so determined, as well as the territorial integrity and sovereignty of the other party.

16. Recognizing that the results of the delimitation and demarcation process are not yet known, the parties request the United Nations to facilitate resolution of problems which may arise due to the transfer of territorial control, including the consequences for individuals residing in previously disputed territory.

17. The expenses of the Commission shall be borne equally by the two parties. To defray its expenses, the Commission may accept donations from the United Nations Trust Fund established under paragraph 8 of Security Council Resolution 1177 of 26 June 1998.

Article 5

1. Consistent with the Framework Agreement, in which the parties commit themselves to addressing the negative socio-economic impact of the crisis on the civilian population, including the impact on those persons who have been deported, a neutral Claims Commission shall be established. The mandate of the Commission is to decide through binding arbitration all claims for loss, damage or injury by one Government against the other, and by nationals (including both natural and juridical persons) of one party against the Government of the other party or entities owned or controlled by the other party that are (a) related to the conflict that was the subject of the Framework Agreement, the Modalities

for its Implementation and the Cessation of Hostilities Agreement, and (b) result from violations of international humanitarian law, including the 1949 Geneva Conventions, or other violations of international law. The Commission shall not hear claims arising from the cost of military operations, preparing for military operations, or the use of force, except to the extent that such claims involve violations of international humanitarian law.

2. The Commission shall consist of five arbitrators. Each party shall, by written notice to the United Nations Secretary General, appoint two members within 45 days from the effective date of this agreement, neither of whom shall be nationals or permanent residents of the party making the appointment. In the event that a party fails to name one or both of its party-appointed arbitrators within the specified time, the Secretary-General of the United Nations shall make the appointment.

3. The president of the Commission shall be selected by the party-appointed arbitrators or, failing their agreement within 30 days of the date of appointment of the latest party-appointed arbitrator, by the Secretary-General of the United Nations after consultation with the parties. The president shall be neither a national nor permanent resident of either party.

4. In the event of the death or resignation of a member of the Commission in the course of the proceedings, a substitute member shall be appointed or chosen pursuant to the procedure set forth in this paragraph that was applicable to the appointment or choice of the arbitrator being replaced.

5. The Commission shall be located in The Hague. At its discretion it may hold hearings and conduct investigations in the territory of either party, or at such other location as it deems expedient.

6. The Commission shall be empowered to employ such professional, administrative and clerical staff as it deems necessary to accomplish its work, including establishment of a Registry. The Commission may also retain consultants and experts to facilitate the expeditious completion of its work.

7. The Commission shall adopt its own rules of procedure based upon the 1992 Permanent Court of Arbitration Option Rules for Arbitrating Disputes Between Two States. All decisions of the Commission shall be made by a majority of the commissioners.

8. Claims shall be submitted to the Commission by each of the parties on its own behalf and on behalf of its nationals, including both natural and juridical persons. All claims submitted to the Commission must be filed no later than one year from the effective date of this agreement. Except for claims submitted to another mutually agreed settlement mechanism in accordance with paragraph 17 or filed in another forum prior to the effective date of this agreement, the Commission shall be the sole forum for adjudicating claims described in paragraph 1 or filed under paragraph 9 of this Article, and any such claims which could have been and not submitted by that deadline shall be extinguished, in accordance with international law.

9. In appropriate cases, each party may file claims on behalf of persons of Eritreans or Ethiopian origin who may not be its nationals. Such claims shall be considered by the Commission on the same basis as claims submitted on behalf of that party's nationals.

10. In order to facilitate the expeditious resolution of these disputes, the Commission shall be authorized to adopt such methods of efficient case management and mass claims processing as it deems appropriate, such as expedited procedures for processing claims and checking claims on a sample basis for further verification only if circumstances warrant.

11. Upon application of either of the parties, the Commission may decide to consider specific claims, or categories of claims, on a priority basis.

12. The Commission shall commence its work not more than 15 days after it is constituted and shall endeavor to complete its work within three years of the date when the period for filing claims closes pursuant to paragraph 8.

13. In considering claims, the Commission shall apply relevant rules of international law. The Commission shall not have the power to make decisions ex aequo et bono.

14. Interest, costs and fees may be awarded.

15. The expenses of the Commission shall be borne equally by the parties. Each party shall pay any invoice from the Commission within 30 days of its receipt.

16. The parties may agree at any time to settle outstanding claims, individually or by categories, through direct negotiation or by reference to another mutually agreed settlement mechanism.

17. Decisions and awards of the Commission shall be final and binding. The parties agree to honor all decisions and to pay any monetary awards rendered against them promptly.

18. Each party shall accord to members of the Commission and its employees the privileges and immunities that are accorded to diplomatic agents under the Vienna Convention on Diplomatic Relations.

68.b Eritrea-Ethiopia Claims Commission Rules of Procedure

Date: October 2001
Source: https://pcacases.com/web/sendAttach/774

CHAPTER ONE: RULES APPLICABLE TO ALL PROCEEDINGS
SECTION I – INTRODUCTORY RULES

Scope of Application

Article 1

1. Pursuant to Article 5, paragraph 7, of the Agreement between the Government of the Federal Democratic Republic of Ethiopia and the Government of the State of Eritrea concluded in Algiers on 12 December 2000 [the "Agreement"], the conduct of proceedings before the Commission shall be subject to the following Rules, which have been based upon the Permanent Court of Arbitration Optional Rules for Arbitrating Disputes Between Two States and have been adopted by the Commission after consultation with the two parties.

2. The Commission may modify these Rules after consultation with the two parties.

3. The Agreement constitutes an agreement in writing by Ethiopia and Eritrea, on their own behalf and on behalf of their nationals, submitting to arbitration pursuant to the Agreement and these Rules.

4. These Rules contain three Chapters: Chapter One (Rules Applicable For All Proceedings), Chapter Two (Procedures For Individual Consideration Of Claims) and Chapter Three (Mass Claims Procedures).

Notice, Calculation of Periods of Time

Article 2

1. The Commission intends to utilize e-mail or fax to the greatest extent possible. Any communication to the Commission shall be deemed to have been made at the time and place it was transmitted by e-mail or fax to the Commission's Registrar. The Registrar shall promptly retransmit such communication to each arbitrator and to the contact person of the other party designated pursuant to Article 3.

2. Any communications or documents that cannot reasonably be submitted to the Commission by e-mail or fax shall be delivered to the Registrar in nine copies. Such communications or documents shall be deemed to have been made at the time they are received by the Registrar. The Registrar shall promptly send one copy of such communications or documents to each arbitrator and two copies of such communications or documents to the contact person of the other party designated pursuant to Article 3 by a rapid and reliable means.

3. Any period of time established under these Rules shall be calculated beginning on the day after a communication establishing that period is made. If the period ends on an official holiday or a non-work day in the State of the recipient, the period is extended until the next working day. Official holidays or non-work days occurring during any period of time are included in calculating the period.

Representation and Assistance

Article 3

Each party shall appoint an Agent and if so desired a Co-Agent. The parties may also be assisted by counsel or other persons of their choice. Each party must communicate in writing to the other party and to the Registrar the name, telephone number, mailing address and e-mail address of the counsel or other person to whom all communications to that party are to be sent.

SECTION II – COMPOSITION OF THE COMMISSION

Appointment of Arbitrators

Article 4

The Commission consists of five arbitrators, one of whom is its President. The President and the other arbitrators are appointed as provided in Article 5 of the Agreement.

Challenge of Arbitrators

Article 5

A prospective arbitrator shall disclose to those who approach him/her in connection with his/her possible appointment any circumstances likely to give rise to justifiable doubts as to his/her impartiality or independence. An arbitrator, once appointed or chosen, shall disclose such circumstances to the parties unless they have already been informed by him/her of these circumstances.

Article 6

1. Any arbitrator may be challenged if circumstances exist that give rise to justifiable doubts as to the arbitrator's impartiality or independence.

2. A party may challenge the arbitrator appointed by it only for reasons of which it becomes aware after the appointment has been made.

3. A party who intends to challenge an arbitrator shall send notice of its challenge within thirty days after the appointment of the challenged arbitrator or, following that appointment, within thirty days after the circumstances mentioned in Articles 5 and 6 became known to that party.

4. The challenge shall be notified to the other party, to the arbitrator who is challenged and to the other arbitrators. The notification shall be in writing and shall state the reasons for the challenge.

5. When an arbitrator has been challenged by one party, the other party may agree to the challenge. The arbitrator may also, after the challenge, withdraw from his/her office. In neither case does this imply acceptance of the validity of the grounds for the challenge. In both cases the procedure provided in Article 5 of the Agreement shall be used in full for the appointment of the substitute arbitrator, even if during the process of appointing the challenged arbitrator a party had failed to exercise its right to appoint or to participate in the appointment.

6. If the other party does not agree to the challenge and the challenged arbitrator does not withdraw, the decision on the challenge will be made by an Appointing Authority designated by the Secretary General of the United Nations. Pending the Appointing Authority's decision, the challenged arbitrator shall continue to serve as an arbitrator of the Commission, and the Commission shall continue to perform its duties under the Agreement.

7. If the Appointing Authority sustains the challenge, a substitute arbitrator shall be appointed or chosen pursuant to the procedure applicable to the appointment or choice of an arbitrator as provided in Article 5 of the Agreement.

Replacement of an Arbitrator

Article 7

1. In the event of the death or resignation of an arbitrator during the course of the work of the Commission, a substitute arbitrator shall be appointed or chosen as provided in the Agreement. Any resignation of an arbitrator shall be addressed to the Commission and shall not be effective unless the Commission determines that there are sufficient reasons to accept the resignation, and if the Commission so determines the resignation shall become effective on the date designated by the Commission.

2. In the event that an arbitrator fails to act or in the event of the *de jure* or *de facto* impossibility of his/her performing his/her functions, the procedure in respect of the challenge and replacement of an arbitrator as provided in the preceding Articles shall apply.

Repetition of Hearings in the Event of the Replacement of an Arbitrator

Article 8

If any arbitrator of the Commission is replaced, the Commission shall determine whether all, any part of or none of the previous hearings shall be repeated. All prior decisions by the Commission remain in effect.

Registrar

Article 9

The Commission shall have a Registrar. The Registrar shall maintain the archives of the Commission for further disposition as the Commission may direct, and shall act as a channel of communication between the parties and the Commission as directed by the Commission.

SECTION III – ARBITRAL PROCEEDINGS

General Provisions

Article 10

1. Subject to these Rules, the Commission may conduct the arbitration in such manner as it considers appropriate, provided that the parties are treated with equality and that each party is given a full opportunity of presenting its case in accordance with these rules.

2. The Commission shall decide whether to hold hearings for the presentation of evidence by witnesses, including expert witnesses, or for oral argument, or whether the proceedings shall be conducted on the basis of documents and other materials.

Place of Arbitration

Article 11

1. As specified in the Agreement, the Commission shall be located in The Hague. At its discretion it may hold meetings and hearings and conduct investigations in the territory of either party, or at such other location as it deems expedient. All awards shall be made at The Hague.

2. Any person or persons appointed by the Commission may enter the territory of either party for the purpose of obtaining information related to the Commission's work. The Commission shall give the parties sufficient notice to enable both to be present at such visits or inspections. Each party shall take all necessary measures to permit and facilitate such visits or inspections, including any measures required to permit the participation of appropriate representatives of the other party.

Language

Article 12

The language to be used in the proceedings of the Commission is English, and any documents in other languages should be accompanied by English translations, except as the Commission may otherwise permit.

Hearings

Article 13

1. In the event of an oral hearing, the Commission shall give the parties adequate advance notice of the date, time and place thereof.

2. If witnesses are to be heard, at least thirty days before the hearing, each party shall communicate to the Commission and to the other party the names and addresses of the witnesses it intends to present, and the subject upon and the languages in which such witnesses will testify. As necessary, the Commission shall make arrangements for translation into English of oral statements to be made at a hearing.

3. The Commission may arrange for a record of the hearing if it deems this necessary, or if the parties have agreed thereto and have so informed the Commission at least thirty days before the hearing.

4. Any documents or other written information that the Commission permits a party to introduce at a hearing shall at the same time or earlier be supplied to the other party, and a copy shall be filed with the Registrar.

5. Hearings shall be held *in camera* unless the parties agree otherwise. The Commission may require the retirement of any witness or witnesses during the testimony of other witnesses. The Commission is free to determine the manner in which witnesses are examined and shall take appropriate measures as required for the protection of the security and privacy of witnesses.

6. Evidence of witnesses may also be presented in the form of written statements signed by them.

7. The Commission may inquire of the parties if they have any further proof to offer or witnesses to be heard or submissions to make and, if there are none, it may declare the hearings closed.

8. If one of the parties, duly notified under these Rules, fails to appear at a hearing without showing sufficient cause for such failure, the Commission may proceed with the hearing and decision of the matter involved.

9. The Commission may, if it considers it necessary owing to exceptional circumstances, decide, on its own motion or upon application of a party, to reopen the hearings at any time before the award is made.

Evidence

Article 14

1. Each party shall have the burden of proving the facts it relies on to support its claim or defense.

2. The Commission shall determine the admissibility, relevance, materiality and weight of the evidence offered.

3. The Commission may require a party to deliver to the Commission and to the other party, within such time as the Commission shall decide, a summary of the documents and other evidence which that party intends to present in support of the facts in issue.

4. At any time, the Commission may request the parties to produce documents, exhibits or other evidence within a specified time. The Commission shall take note of any failure to do so, as well as any reason given for such failure. Where circumstances warrant, the Commission may draw adverse inferences from any failure by a party to produce evidence.

5. If one of the parties, duly invited to produce documentary evidence, fails to do so within the established period of time, without showing sufficient cause for such failure, the Commission may make the award on the evidence before it.

Interim Measures of Protection

Article 15

1. The Commission may, at the request of either party or on its own initiative, take any interim measures it deems necessary to preserve the respective rights of either party. Such interim measures may be established in the form of interim awards.

2. In taking such interim measures, the Commission must determine that it has *prima facie* jurisdiction, that the interim measures are necessary to avoid irreparable harm, and that they would not constitute a final decision of the issues in dispute.

Consultants and Experts

Article 16

1. The Commission may appoint one or more consultants to advise it.

2. The Commission may also appoint experts to examine and report on particular matters with the parties' assistance. The Commission shall establish an expert's terms of reference, which shall be communicated to the parties.

3. The parties shall assist the expert as requested. They shall provide any relevant information or produce for the expert, or permit the expert's inspection of, any relevant documents, data or location requested by the expert. Any disagreement between a party and the expert regarding the expert's requests for assistance may be referred to the Commission for decision.

4. The expert shall prepare a written report to the Commission. The Commission shall communicate copies of this report to the parties, who may state their views in writing on it and on the expert's conclusions and recommendations.

5. The Commission may in its sole discretion decide to hold a hearing on an expert's report so that the expert may be heard and asked questions by the Commission and the parties. At such a hearing, either party may present expert witnesses to testify on points at issue. The provisions of these Rules relating to hearings shall apply.

Waiver of Rules

Article 17

A party who knows that any provision of, or requirement under, these Rules has not been complied with and yet proceeds with the arbitration without promptly stating its objection to such non-compliance shall be deemed to have waived its right to object.

Decisions and Awards

Article 18

1. The Commission may make final awards, interlocutory awards, interim awards, partial awards and decisions. The Commission may designate as "decisions" significant actions it takes regarding jurisdiction, procedure or other matters that are not related to the legal and factual merits of particular claims.

2. The Commission shall endeavor to decide questions unanimously. When the Commission is not unanimous, it shall decide by a majority of the arbitrators.

3. In the case of questions of procedure, when there is no majority or when the Commission so authorizes, the President may decide on his/her own, subject to revision, if any, by the Commission.

4. Decisions and awards shall be made in writing. As provided in Article 5(17) of the Agreement, they shall be final and binding on the parties. The parties agree to honor all decisions and to pay any monetary awards rendered against them promptly.

5. The Commission shall state the reasons upon which awards are based, unless the parties have agreed that no reasons are to be given.

6. Awards shall be signed by each arbitrator. Each shall contain the date and the place where it was made. If any arbitrator fails to sign an award after being given opportunity to do so, the award shall state the reasons for the absence of signature.

7. All awards shall be made available to the public, including by posting on an appropriate Internet website. The Commission may, at the request of a party or on its own initiative,

determine that it will not make an entire award public, but will make public only portions from which the identity of individuals, other identifying facts or trade or military secrets have been deleted.

8. Copies of each award signed by the arbitrators shall be communicated to the parties by the Registrar.

Applicable Law

Article 19

1. As specified in the Agreement, the Commission shall apply relevant rules of international law, and the Commission shall not have the power to make decisions *ex aequo et bono*.

2. In reaching its decisions, the Commission shall look to:

a. International conventions, whether general or particular, establishing rules expressly recognized by the parties;

b. International custom, as evidence of a general practice accepted as law;

c. The general principles of law recognized by civilized nations;

d. Judicial and arbitral decisions and the teachings of the most highly qualified publicists of the various nations, as subsidiary means for the determination of rules of law.

3. The Commission may also refer to national laws in appropriate circumstances.

Settlement or Other Grounds for Termination

Article 20

1. If, before an award in a claim or group of claims is made, the parties agree on a settlement of that claim or claims, the Commission shall either issue an order terminating the relevant arbitral proceedings or, if requested by both parties and accepted by the Commission, record the settlement as an arbitral award on agreed terms. The Commission need not give reasons for such an award. The provisions of these Rules regarding the form and effect of awards shall apply.

2. If continuation of the arbitral proceedings under the Agreement, or any portion of them, becomes unnecessary or impossible for any reason, the Commission shall inform the parties of its intention to issue an order terminating such proceedings. The Commission shall issue such an order unless a party establishes justifiable grounds not to do so.

3. Copies of any award on agreed terms or order terminating arbitral proceedings shall be communicated to the parties by the Registrar.

Interpretation or Correction of the Award; Additional Award

Article 21

1. Within sixty days after receiving the award, either party, with notice to the other party, may request that the Commission:

(a) give an interpretation of the award. Any such interpretation shall be in the sole discretion of the Commission and shall be given in writing within forty-five days after receipt of the request. The interpretation shall form part of the award.

(b) correct in the award any errors in computation, any clerical or typographical errors, or any errors of similar nature. The Commission may also within thirty days after the communication of the award make such corrections on its own initiative. Corrections shall be in writing.

(c) make an additional award as to claims presented in the arbitral proceedings but omitted from the award. If the Commission considers the request for an additional award to be justified and considers that the omission can be rectified without any further hearings or evidence, it shall complete its award within sixty days after the receipt of the request.

2. The provisions of these Rules regarding the form and effect of awards shall apply to interpretations, corrections and additional awards.

Expenses of the Commission

Article 22

1. The Commission shall determine its own expenses after consultation with the parties. These expenses will include the fees of the arbitrators, the costs of the Commission staff, the costs of the facilities and equipment used by the Commission, the costs of expert advice and of any other assistance required by the Commission and any fees or expenses of the Appointing Authority, as well any related expenses of the Permanent Court of Arbitration.

2. As provided in Article 5(15) of the Agreement, the expenses of the Commission shall be borne equally by the parties. At any time, the Commission may request each party to deposit equal amounts as an advance for the Commission's costs. Each party shall pay any such request from the Commission within thirty days of its receipt.

3. All amounts deposited by the parties pursuant to this Article shall be directed to the Registrar for disbursement for the Commission's costs under direction of the President of the Commission.

4. If the requested deposits are not paid in full within sixty days after the receipt of the request, the Commission shall so inform the parties in order that one or another of them may make the required payment. If such payment is not made, the Commission may order the suspension or termination of the proceedings. If such payment is made by the party that is not in default, the Commission shall suspend proceedings related to the claims filed by the party that is in default until such time as it has made the required payments.

CHAPTER TWO: PROCEDURES FOR INDIVIDUAL CONSIDERATION OF CLAIMS

Application of this Chapter

Article 23

This Chapter applies to all claims that are to be individually arbitrated. These claims include all claims by the government of one party on its own behalf against the government of the other party, all claims for compensation in excess of US$100,000 on behalf of persons, and any other claims for which individual treatment is required by Chapter Three.

Statement of Claim

Article 24

1. Claims to be individually considered under this Chapter shall be submitted to the Commission by filing a Statement of Claim for each claim with the Registrar. As specified in the Agreement, Statements of Claim are to be filed by 12 December 2001. The claimant may annex to its Statement of Claim all documents it deems relevant or it may add a reference to documents or other evidence it may submit.

2. Statements of Claim and any annexed documents or other evidence shall be filed by delivering a signed original and nine copies to the Registrar at the premises of the

Permanent Court of Arbitration at The Hague. The text of the Statement of Claim and as much supporting documentation or evidence as is reasonably practicable shall at the same time be delivered to the Registrar on computer discs or other electronic media to be prescribed by the Commission.

3. Statements of Claim shall include a precise statement of the following particulars:
   (a) The names and addresses of the parties;
   (b) If the claimant is the government of a Party or an agency of such government, whether the claim is solely of that government or agency or whether it includes the claims of persons, and, if the latter, the identification of such persons, including their names, places of residence and nationalities;
   (c) A statement of the facts supporting the claim or claims;
   (d) The violation or violations of international law on the basis of which the claim or claims are alleged to have arisen;
   (e) Any other points at issue;
   (f) The relief or remedy sought;
   (g) The Commission's jurisdiction over the claim or claims;
   (h) Whether the claim or claims have been filed in any other forum.

Statement of Defense

Article 25

1. Within a period of time to be determined by the Commission, the respondent in each claim under this Chapter shall file its Statement of Defense. Statements of Defense shall be filed utilizing in all respects the procedure for filing Statements of Claim under the previous Article.

2. The Statement of Defense shall reply to the particulars of the Statement of Claim. The respondent may annex to its statement the documents or evidence on which it relies for its defense or may add a reference to the documents or other evidence it will submit.

3. If, within the period of time fixed by the Commission, the respondent has not filed its Statement of Defense without showing sufficient cause for such failure, the Commission shall order that the proceedings continue.

Amendments to the Claim or Defense

Article 26

Either party may amend or supplement its claim or defense unless the Commission considers it inappropriate to allow such amendment having regard to the delay in making it or prejudice to the other party or any other circumstances. However, a claim may not be amended in such a manner as to state a new claim, or so that the amended claim falls outside the jurisdiction of the Commission.

Pleas as to the Jurisdiction of the Commission

Article 27

1. The Commission shall have the power to rule on objections that it has no jurisdiction. A plea that the Commission does not have jurisdiction shall be raised not later than in the Statement of Defense.

2. The Commission should consider whether, in the interests of economy and efficiency, it should rule on a plea concerning its jurisdiction as a preliminary question. However, the Commission may proceed with the arbitration and rule on such a plea in its final award.

Further Written Statements

Article 28

The Commission shall decide which further written statements, in addition to the Statement of Claim and the Statement of Defense, shall be required from the parties or may be presented by them and shall fix the period of time for filing such statements. The Commission may seek the views of the parties in this regard.

Interest and Costs

Article 29

Interest and costs may be awarded.

CHAPTER THREE: MASS CLAIMS PROCEDURES

Filing of Claims

Article 30

1. Claims covered by this Chapter are claims for fixed amount compensation in one of the following categories:
   (a) Category 1 – Claims of natural persons for unlawful expulsion from the country of their residence;
   (b) Category 2 – Claims of natural persons for unlawful displacement from their residence;
   (c) Category 3 – Claims of prisoners of war for injuries suffered from unlawful treatment;
   (d) Category 4 – Claims of civilians for unlawful detention and for injuries suffered from unlawful treatment during detention; and
   (e) Category 5 – Claims of persons for loss, damage or injury other than those covered by the other categories.
2. Other claims in the above categories that do not seek fixed amount compensation, including claims that seek to prove actual damages, must be filed as claims for individual compensation pursuant to Chapter Two of these rules. Taking into account the number and nature of such claims filed pursuant to Chapter Two, the Commission may establish a separate process to expedite their resolution.
3. Claims to be considered under Chapter Three shall be filed with the Commission on the claims forms approved by the Commission in both electronic and paper copies. As specified in the Agreement, all claims are to be filed by 12 December 2001.

Sub-Categories of Claims

Article 31

In due course after the claims covered by this Chapter have been filed and following further instructions by the Commission, each party shall group its claims in each category in sub-categories that it selects in such a manner that each sub-category contains claims in that category alleged to arise from a particular violation of international law.

Decisions on Sub-Categories

Article 32

For each sub-category, the Commission shall make its decision as follows:

1. Following consideration of the evidence and pleadings submitted by each party, the Commission shall determine whether the acts or omissions alleged to have been in violation of international law have been proved to have occurred, to be attributable to the other party and to have constituted a violation of international law.

2. If the Commission finds that one or more of these determinations cannot be made for lack of proof, it shall issue an award dismissing all claims in that sub-category.

3. If the Commission makes all of the determinations in paragraph 1, the claims in that sub-category for each of the two levels of compensation shall be subject to random sampling of their evidence to ascertain the percentage of such claims for which the evidence is inadequate to establish the claim. The compensation for all claims in that compensation level of that sub-category is automatically reduced by that percentage, and the Commission shall issue an award of such compensation for all claims in that sub-category.

Other Claims

Article 33

Any claims filed pursuant to Chapter Three that are not subsequently included in a sub-category and are not withdrawn by the filing party shall be dismissed by the Commission.

68.c Eritrea-Ethiopia Boundary Commission Rules of Procedure

Date: 11 April 2002
Source: https://pcacases.com/web/sendAttach/787

SECTION I – INTRODUCTORY RULES

Scope of Application

Article 1

1. These Rules of Procedure are adopted pursuant to Article 4, paragraph 11 of the Agreement signed in Algiers on 12 December 2000 between the Governments of the State of Eritrea and the Federal Democratic Republic of Ethiopia (the "Agreement"). As provided therein, they are based on the 1992 Permanent Court of Arbitration Optional Rules for Arbitrating Disputes between Two States.[1]

2. These Rules are supplementary to the Agreement and must be read therewith. In the event of a conflict between the provisions of the Agreement and the provisions of these Rules, the provisions of the Agreement shall prevail. Any differences or uncertainties regarding these Rules will, upon application by the interested Party, be determined by the Commission.

Notice, Calculation of Periods of Time

Article 2

1. For the purposes of these Rules, any notice, including a notification, communication or proposal, is deemed to have been received when it has been delivered to the addressee. Notice shall be deemed to have been received on the day it is so delivered.

[1] The words "him" or "his" shall, as appropriate, also mean "her" or "hers".

2. For the purposes of calculating a period of time under these Rules, such period shall begin to run on the day following the day when a notice, notification, communication or proposal is received. If the last day of such period is an official holiday or a non-work day in the Party addressed, the period is extended until the first work day which follows. Official holidays or non-work days occurring during the running of the period of time are included in calculating the period.

Support and Assistance

Article 3

1. The Commission may engage such staff and secure such services and equipment as it deems necessary in order to perform its functions.

2. As provided in Article 4, paragraph 7 of the Agreement, the United Nations Cartographer shall serve as Secretary to the Commission. The Secretary shall perform those tasks that the Commission may assign to him, as well as those set out in paragraphs 8 and 9 of Article 4 of the Agreement. These may include the following:

a) preparation or acquisition of, or arrangements for the preparation of, such maps, aerial and satellite photographs and aerial and ground surveys as the Commission may request;

b) preparation of such reports as the Commission may request in connection with the technical aspects of the delimitation and demarcation of the border;

c) provision of assistance to the Commission, and conclusion of such arrangements as the Commission may direct, in relation to the demarcation on the ground of the border, including demining and other necessary measures related thereto.

3. The Registrar of the Commission shall be the Principal Legal Counsel of the Permanent Court of Arbitration. The Registrar shall perform such tasks as shall be assigned to him by the Commission, which may include the following:

a) acting as the sole channel for communications between the Commission and the Parties and vice versa and, to the extent that such assistance may be requested, between the Parties, and amongst the Members of the Commission;

b) assisting the Commission in making arrangements for hearings, giving such advance notice thereof to the Parties as the Commission may determine, and arranging for all hearing facilities;

c) making arrangements for stenographic transcripts and/or tape recordings of hearings, and for any necessary translations or interpretation;

d) assisting the Commission in the organisation of its deliberations and drafting activities;

e) receiving, holding and disbursing deposits from the Parties for costs of the Commission, as well as any donations from the United Nations Trust Fund established pursuant to paragraph 8 of Security Council Resolution 1177 of 26 June 1998 (the "Trust Fund"), and accounting for the same;

f) maintaining the archives of the Commission, including copies of all communications passing between the Secretary of the Commission and other persons relating to the work of the Commission.

4. The Secretary and the Registrar shall keep each other fully informed of all aspects of their work, in particular by the transmission to each other of copies of all documents and correspondence that either produces or receives.

Representation and Assistance

Article 4

Each Party shall appoint an Agent. The Parties may also be assisted by persons of their choice. The name and address of the Agent must be communicated in writing to the other Party, and to the Secretary and Registrar. The Agent, or someone duly authorised by him, shall be the sole representative of a Party for the purpose of all communication with the Commission or the other Party, save for hearings before, or meetings with, the Commission, at which the Agent may be assisted by Counsel or other representatives.

SECTION II – COMPOSITION OF THE COMMISSION

Number of Commissioners

Article 5

As provided in Article 4, paragraph 2 of the Agreement, the Commission shall be composed of five Commissioners.

Appointment of Commissioners

Article 6

1. The Commissioners shall be appointed by the Parties as provided in Article 4, paragraph 4 of the Agreement.
2. The President of the Commission shall be appointed as provided in Article 4, paragraph 5 of the Agreement.

Challenge to Commissioners

Article 7

A prospective Commissioner shall disclose to those who approach him on behalf of a Party in connection with his possible appointment any circumstances that may give rise to justifiable doubts as to his impartiality or independence. A Commissioner, once appointed or chosen, shall disclose such circumstances to the Parties unless they have already received such disclosure.

Article 8

1. Any Commissioner may be challenged if circumstances exist that give rise to justifiable doubts as to his impartiality or independence.
2. A Party may challenge a Commissioner appointed by it only for reasons of which it becomes aware after the appointment has been made.

Article 9

1. Challenge to a Commissioner shall be made by notice sent to the Registrar, who shall communicate it forthwith to the other members of the Commission, to the Commissioner who is challenged, to the Secretary and to the other Party. The notice shall be in writing and shall state the reasons for the challenge.
2. When a Commissioner has been challenged by one Party, the other Party may agree to the challenge. The Commissioner may also, after the challenge, withdraw from his office. In neither case does this imply acceptance of the validity of the grounds for the challenge. In such cases, a substitute Commissioner shall be appointed pursuant to the procedure applicable to the original appointment of the Commissioner being replaced.

3. A Commissioner who has been challenged remains a Commissioner unless and until the challenge is upheld or the Commissioner resigns.

Article 10

1. If, within thirty days of the date of the dispatch of the notice of challenge referred to in Article 9, paragraph 1, above, the other Party does not agree to the challenge and the challenged Commissioner does not withdraw, the challenge shall be decided by those Commissioners whose appointments are not challenged; provided that there are at least three of them. If there are less than three, the President shall refer the challenge to the Secretary-General of the United Nations for decision. The Commissioners shall endeavour to render such decision within thirty days following a request thereof.

2. Both Parties, as well as the challenged Commissioner, may, without delay, submit comments or furnish explanations to the remaining Commissioners who are not challenged concerning the challenge, provided that there are at least three of them.

3. If the remaining Commissioners uphold the challenge, a substitute Commissioner shall be appointed pursuant to the procedure that was applicable to the original appointment of the Commissioner being replaced.

4. If for any reason the remaining Commissioners are unable to reach a decision on the challenge within the period of thirty days mentioned in paragraph 1 of this Article, the President shall immediately refer the challenge to the Secretary-General of the United Nations with a request that he should decide thereon, if possible within thirty days, and communicate his decision to the President of the Commission (or, in the case of a challenge to the President, to the Registrar). If the Secretary-General upholds the challenge, the Commissioner shall cease to be a Commissioner from the date of the Secretary-General's decision and the procedure prescribed in paragraph 3 of this Article shall be followed and completed within thirty days.

5. The Interim Rule of Procedure adopted by the Commission on 5 April 2001 is withdrawn.

Replacement of a Commissioner

Article 11

As provided in Article 4, paragraph 6 of the Agreement, in the event of the death or resignation of a Commissioner in the course of the proceedings, a substitute Commissioner shall be appointed pursuant to the procedure that was applicable to the original appointment of the Commissioner being replaced. Any resignation by a Commissioner shall be addressed to the President of the Commission and shall not be effective unless the Commission determines that there are sufficient reasons to accept the resignation. If the Commission so determines, the resignation shall become effective on the date designated by the Commission.

Repetition of Hearings in the Event of the Replacement of a Commissioner

Article 12

1. If the President of the Commission is replaced, any hearings held previously relating to matters still unresolved shall be repeated; if any other Commissioner is replaced, such prior hearings may be repeated at the discretion of the Commission.

2. The Parties may jointly or separately take out insurance to cover the additional cost of any proceedings in respect of the possible application of the proceeding paragraph.

SECTION III – PROCEEDINGS BEFORE THE COMMISSION

General Provisions

Article 13

1. Subject to these Rules and the provisions of the Agreement, the Commission may conduct its proceedings in such manner as it considers appropriate, provided that the Parties are treated with equality and that, at every stage of the proceedings, each Party is given a full opportunity of presenting its case.

2. The proceedings shall consist of both a written and an oral phase, as further set forth below.

3. All documents or information to be sent to the Commission by a Party shall be communicated by that Party's Agent to the Commission through the Registrar who will send a copy to the other Party.

Location of Commission

Article 14

1. As provided in Article 4, paragraph 3 of the Agreement, the Commission shall be located in The Hague.

2. The Commission will meet in The Hague at the seat of the Permanent Court of Arbitration. The Commissioners may hold meetings amongst themselves at any place they deem appropriate or by telephone consultation.

3. After inviting the views of the Parties, the Commission may meet with them for any purpose at any place it deems appropriate. The Parties shall be given sufficient notice to enable them to be present at such meetings.

4. The decisions of the Commission delimiting the border and the subsequent formal promulgation of the demarcation thereof shall be made at The Hague.

Language

Article 15

1. Both the written and the oral phase of the proceedings shall be conducted in English.

2. Any documents annexed to the written pleadings, and any supplementary documents or exhibits submitted in the course of the proceedings, delivered in their original language, shall be accompanied by a translation into English.

Written phase

Article 16

1. As provided in Article 4, paragraph 11 of the Agreement, the written submissions of the Parties shall be filed simultaneously.

2. The written submissions shall consist of:

a) a Memorial to be filed by each Party by 30 June 2001;

b) a Counter-Memorial to be filed by each Party not later than 22 September 2001;

c) any other pleading that the Commission deems necessary after consulting the Parties, such pleading to be filed not later than one month after filing of the Counter-Memorials.

3. Each stage of the written submissions shall be filed with the Registrar for onward transmission, after the submissions of both Parties have been received, to the Commissioners and the other Party.

4. Upon the filing of the last of the written submissions directed by the Commission, the written phase of the proceedings will close.

5. The written submissions shall be confidential until such time as the Commission, after consultation with the Parties, may decide otherwise.

Pleas as to the Jurisdiction of the Commission

Article 17

1. The Commission shall have the power to rule on any questions relating to its own jurisdiction.

2. The Commission shall rule on a plea concerning its jurisdiction as a preliminary question unless the Commission decides to defer such ruling until its final decision.

Evidence and Hearings

Article 18

1. Each Party shall have the burden of proving the facts it relies on to support its claims.

2. The Commission shall determine the admissibility, relevance, materiality and weight of the evidence offered.

3. At any time during the proceedings, the Commission may call upon the Parties to produce documents, exhibits or other evidence within such a period of time as the Commission shall determine. The Commission shall take note of any refusal to do so as well as the reasons that must be given for such refusal.

Article 19

1. Upon the closure of the written phase of the proceedings, the Commission shall give the Parties adequate advance notice of the date, time and place of the hearings.

2. With a view to the expeditious and efficient conduct of the hearings, not less than twenty-eight days before the date set for their opening, the Commission or, if all the Commissioners cannot be present and so request, the President alone, will hold a pre-hearing consultation with the Parties at which the following matters will be considered:

a) the order of speaking and the allocation of time at the hearings;

b) the number and names of any witnesses that either Party may wish to call at the hearings and the subjects upon, and the languages in which, such witnesses will give their evidence;

c) the manner in which any such evidence would be presented at the hearings;

d) the indication by the Commission of any points or issues to which it would like the Parties, or either of them, specially to address themselves, or on which it considers that there has been sufficient argument.

3. The Registrar shall make arrangements for the translation of statements made at a hearing and for a record of the hearing if either is deemed necessary by the Commission under the circumstances of the case, or if the Parties have agreed thereto and have communicated such agreement to the Commission at least thirty days before the hearing or such longer period before the hearing as the Commission may determine.

4. Hearings shall be held *in camera* unless the Parties agree otherwise.

Interim Measures of Protection

Article 20

1. Unless the Parties otherwise agree, the Commission may, at the request of either Party, prescribe any interim measures it deems necessary to preserve the respective rights of either Party.

2. Such interim measures may be prescribed in the form of an interim decision, which shall be binding on the Parties.

Experts

Article 21

As provided in Article 4, paragraph 7 of the Agreement, the Secretary to the Commission shall make use of the technical expertise of the United Nations Cartographic Unit. The Commission may also engage the services of additional experts as it deems necessary.

Failure to Appear or to Make Submissions

Article 22

1. If a Party, duly notified under these Rules, fails to file any of its written submissions in a timely manner or to appear at a hearing, without showing sufficient cause for such failure, the Commission may continue with the proceedings.

2. If a Party, duly invited to produce documentary evidence, fails to do so within the established period of time, without showing sufficient cause for such failure, the Commission may make its decision on the evidence before it.

Closure of Hearings

Article 23

1. At the end of the hearings, the Commission will declare the hearings closed.

2. The Commission may, if it considers it necessary, decide, on its own motion or upon application of a Party, to re-open the hearings at any time before its decision is rendered.

Waiver of Rules

Article 24

A Party which knows that any provision of, or requirement under, these Rules has not been complied with and yet proceeds without promptly stating its objection to such noncompliance shall be deemed to have waived its right to object.

SECTION IV – DECISIONS OF THE COMMISSION

Applicable Law

Article 25

As provided in Article 4, paragraph 2 of the Agreement, the Commission's decision on delimitation shall be based on pertinent colonial treaties (1900, 1902 and 1908) and applicable international law. The Commission shall not have the power to make a decision *ex aequo et bono*.

Decisions

Article 26

1. As provided in Article 4, paragraph 11 of the Agreement, all decisions of the Commission shall be made by a majority of the Commissioners.

2. In the case of an even division of votes, the President shall have the casting vote.

3. In the case of questions of procedure, when there is no majority or when the Commission so authorises, the President may decide on his own, subject to revision, if any, by the Commission.

Form and effect of the Decision Delimiting the Border

Article 27

1. In addition to making a final decision regarding the delimitation of the border, the Commission shall be entitled to make any necessary interim, interlocutory, or partial decisions.

2. All decisions shall be made in writing and shall be final and binding on the Parties.

3. The Commission shall state the reasons upon which any decision is based.

4. All decisions shall be signed by the President, the Secretary and the Registrar, and shall contain the date on which, and the place where, the decision was made.

5. Any Commissioner may attach to the decision a concurring or dissenting opinion.

6. The border delimitation shall be accompanied by maps drawn to such scale as is necessary to illustrate the line described in the decision. In the central sector, this map shall be on a scale of 1:50,000; in the western and eastern sectors this map shall be on a scale no smaller than 1:1,000,000. The Commission shall state in its decision whether the line on the map is illustrative or definitive.

7. As provided in Article 4, paragraph 13 of the Agreement, the Commission shall transmit its final decision regarding delimitation of the borders to the Parties and Secretaries-General of the Organization of African Unity and the United Nations for publication.

Interpretation of the Decision

Article 28

1. Within thirty days after the receipt of the decision on delimitation or the decision promulgating the demarcation, either Party, with notice to the other Party, may request the Commission to give an interpretation of the decision.

2. The interpretation shall be given in writing within forty-five days after the receipt of the request. The interpretation shall form part of the decision and the provisions of Article 27, paragraphs 2 to 6, shall apply.

Correction of the Decision

Article 29

1. Within thirty days after the receipt of the decision, either Party, with notice to the other Party, may request the Commission to correct in the decision any errors in computation, any clerical or typographical errors, or any errors of similar nature. The Commission may within thirty days after the communication of the decision make such corrections on its own initiative.

2. Such corrections shall be in writing, and the provisions of Article 28, paragraphs 2 to 6, shall apply.

Demarcation of the Border

Article 30

1. In consultation with, and with the co-operation of, the Secretary-General of the United Nations, the Commission shall arrange for the expeditious demarcation of the border as delimited. Without prejudice to paragraph 2 hereof, the procedure relating thereto shall be adopted by the Commission at an appropriate moment after consultation with the Parties. If the circumstances so permit, the border may be demarcated in such stages as the Commission may from time to time determine.

2. The Commission may, at any time, take, or direct the taking of, such preparatory steps as it considers desirable to expedite completion of its task and the prompt demarcation of the border. If any such steps are taken or prescribed before the delimitation decision is given, they shall be strictly without prejudice to that decision and may be disregarded, overridden, or discounted in such decision. The Parties shall, to such extent as the Commission may direct, co-operate fully with the Secretary or any other personnel involved in such preparatory steps.

3. Upon the conclusion of the demarcation, the Commission will render a decision formally promulgating the boundary as demarcated. The Parties will ensure the prompt implementation of the decision and will render all assistance required by the United Nations in carrying out paragraph 16 of Article 4 of the Agreement.

Costs

Article 31

1. (a) As provided in Article 4, paragraph 17 of the Agreement, the costs of the Commission shall be borne equally by the Parties.
   (b) With a view to reducing as much as possible the costs to be borne by the Parties, the Commission shall enter into arrangements with the United Nations regarding the manner in which the Trust Fund shall be used to meet the costs of the delimitation and demarcation phases of the task of the Commission.

2. The costs of the Commission shall include the remuneration of the members of the Commission and of the Registrar, as well as their expenses and those of the Secretary, together with such expenses of demarcation as are not borne by the United Nations.

3. Each Party shall bear all the expenses incurred by it in the preparation and conduct of its case.

Deposit of Costs

Article 32

1. The Commission may request each Party to deposit an equal amount as an advance for the costs referred to in Article 32, paragraph 2. All amounts deposited by the Parties pursuant to this paragraph and paragraph 2 of this Article shall be paid to the Registrar, and shall be disbursed by him for such expenses.

2. During the course of the proceedings, the Commission may request supplementary deposits from the Parties.

3. If the requested deposits are not paid in full within sixty days after the receipt of the request, the Commission shall so inform the Parties in order that one or another of them may make the required payment. If such payment is not made, the Commission may suspend or terminate the proceedings.

4. After the demarcation has been concluded, the Registrar shall render an accounting to the Parties and to the Trust Fund of the deposits and contributions received and return any unexpended balance to the Parties and to the Trust Fund in proportion to the amounts of their respective contributions.

Fact-Finding under Additional Protocol I to the Geneva Conventions 1949

69.a Protocol Additional to the Geneva Conventions of 12 August 1949, and relating to the Protection of Victims of International Armed Conflicts (Additional Protocol I)

Date: 8 June 1977
Source: 1125 UNTS 3
http://www.icrc.org/ihl.nsf/FULL/470?OpenDocument

...

Article 90. International Fact-Finding Commission

1. (a) An International Fact-Finding Commission (hereinafter referred to as "the Commission") consisting of fifteen members of high moral standing and acknowledged impartiality shall be established.
   (b) When not less than twenty High Contracting Parties have agreed to accept the competence of the Commission pursuant to paragraph 2, the depositary shall then, and at intervals of five years thereafter, convene a meeting of representatives of those High Contracting Parties for the purpose of electing the members of the Commission. At the meeting, the representatives shall elect the members of the Commission by secret ballot from a list of persons to which each of those High Contracting Parties may nominate one person.
   (c) The members of the Commission shall serve in their personal capacity and shall hold office until the election of new members at the ensuing meeting.
   (d) At the election, the High Contracting Parties shall ensure that the persons to be elected to the Commission individually possess the qualifications required and that, in the Commission as a whole, equitable geographical representation is assured.
   (e) In the case of a casual vacancy, the Commission itself shall fill the vacancy, having due regard to the provisions of the preceding sub-paragraphs.
   (f) The depositary shall make available to the Commission the necessary administrative facilities for the performance of its functions.
2. (a) The High Contracting Parties may at the time of signing, ratifying or acceding to the Protocol, or at any other subsequent time, declare that they recognize ipso facto and without special agreement, in relation to any other High Contracting Party accepting the same obligation, the competence of the Commission to enquire into allegations by such other Party, as authorized by this Article.
   (b) The declarations referred to above shall be deposited with the depositary, which shall transmit copies thereof to the High Contracting Parties.

c) The Commission shall be competent to:
   (i) enquire into any facts alleged to be a grave breach as defined in the Conventions and this Protocol or other serious violation of the Conventions or of this Protocol;
   (ii) facilitate, through its good offices, the restoration of an attitude of respect for the Conventions and this Protocol.

(d) In other situations, the Commission shall institute an enquiry at the request of a Party to the conflict only with the consent of the other Party or Parties concerned.

(e) Subject to the foregoing provisions of this paragraph, the provisions of Article 52 of the First Convention, Article 53 of the Second Convention, Article 132 of the Third Convention and Article 149 of the Fourth Convention shall continue to apply to any alleged violation of the Conventions and shall extend to any alleged violation of this Protocol.

3. (a) Unless otherwise agreed by the Parties concerned, all enquiries shall be undertaken by a Chamber consisting of seven members appointed as follows:
   (i) five members of the Commission, not nationals of any Party to the conflict, appointed by the President of the Commission on the basis of equitable representation of the geographical areas, after consultation with the Parties to the conflict;
   (ii) two 'ad hoc' members, not nationals of any Party to the conflict, one to be appointed by each side.

(b) Upon receipt of the request for an enquiry, the President of the Commission shall specify an appropriate time limit for setting up a Chamber. If any 'ad hoc' member has not been appointed within the time limit, the President shall immediately appoint such additional member or members of the Commission as may be necessary to complete the membership of the Chamber.

4. (a) The Chamber set up under paragraph 3 to undertake an enquiry shall invite the Parties to the conflict to assist it and to present evidence. The Chamber may also seek such other evidence as it deems appropriate and may carry out an investigation of the situation 'in loco'.

(b) All evidence shall be fully disclosed to the Parties, which shall have the right to comment on it to the Commission.

(c) Each Party shall have the right to challenge such evidence.

5. (a) The Commission shall submit to the Parties a report on the findings of fact of the Chamber, with such recommendations as it may deem appropriate.

(b) If the Chamber is unable to secure sufficient evidence for factual and impartial findings, the Commission shall state the reasons for that inability.

(c) The Commission shall not report its findings publicly, unless all the Parties to the conflict have requested the Commission to do so.

6. The Commission shall establish its own rules, including rules for the presidency of the Commission and the presidency of the Chamber. Those rules shall ensure that the functions of the President of the Commission are exercised at all times and that, in the case of an enquiry, they are exercised by a person who is not a national of a Party to the conflict.

7. The administrative expenses of the Commission shall be met by contributions from the High Contracting Parties which made declarations under paragraph 2, and by voluntary contributions. The Party or Parties to the conflict requesting an enquiry shall advance the necessary funds for expenses incurred by a Chamber and shall be reimbursed by the Party

or Parties against which the allegations are made to the extent of fifty percent of the costs of the Chamber. Where there are counter-allegations before the Chamber each side shall advance fifty per cent of the necessary funds.

...

69.b Rules of the International Humanitarian Fact-Finding Commission

Date: 8 July 1992 (as amended 26 March 2014)
Source: http://www.ihffc.org/index.asp?Language=EN&page=rules_of_commission

PREAMBLE

The Commission:

Having regard to Protocol I Additional to the Geneva Conventions of 1949 for the protection of the victims of armed conflicts, hereinafter referred to as "the Protocol",

Bearing in mind its competence in respect of enquiry as well as of good offices, recognised for the purpose of obtaining the observation of the principles and rules of international law applicable in armed conflict,

Convinced of the need to take all appropriate initiatives as necessary in cooperation with other international bodies, in particular the United Nations, with the purpose of carrying out its functions in the interest of the victims of armed conflict,

Acting under article 90 of the Protocol,

Adopts the present Rules:

PART I – ORGANISATION OF THE COMMISSION

Chapter I – Members of the Commission

Rule 1 – Independence and Solemn Declaration

1. In the performance of their functions, the Members of the Commission (hereinafter referred to as the "Members") shall accept no instructions from any authority or person whatsoever and serve in their personal capacity.

2. Before taking up his duties, each Member shall make the following solemn declaration: "I will exercise my functions as a Member of this Commission impartially, conscientiously and in accordance with the provisions of the Protocol and these Rules, including those concerning secrecy".

Rule 2 – Availability

Unless prevented by serious reasons duly justified to the President, Members shall at all times be able to respond to a call by the President or, as the case may be, by the Head of a Chamber in order to ensure the accomplishment of the Commission's functions under the Protocol.

Rule 3 – Incompatibilities

During their term of office, Members shall not engage in any occupation or make any public statement that may cast a legitimate doubt on their morality and impartiality required by the Protocol. In case of doubt, the Commission shall decide on the proper measures to take.

Rule 4 – Resignation

1. The resignation of a Member shall be addressed to the President, who shall communicate it without delay to the secretariat of the Commission (hereinafter referred to as the "Secretariat"). The Secretariat shall register the resignation under Rule 37 (1).

2. The President shall address his resignation to the first Vice-President.

3. The resignation shall take effect on the day of its registration by the Secretariat who shall without delay inform the Members of the date.

Rule 5 – The filling of casual vacancies

1. The Commission shall ensure that each candidate possesses the qualifications required by article 90 of the Protocol and that, in the Commission as a whole, equitable geographical representation is maintained.

2. In the absence of a consensus among the Members, the following provisions shall apply:

a. When no candidate obtains in the first ballot the majority required, a second ballot, restricted to the two candidates who obtained the highest number of votes, shall be taken.

b. If the second ballot is inconclusive and a majority vote of Members present is required, a third ballot shall be taken in which votes may be cast for any eligible candidate. If the third ballot is inconclusive, the next ballot shall be restricted to the two candidates who obtained the highest number of votes in the third ballot and so on, with unrestricted and restricted ballots alternating, until a Member is elected.

c. The elections referred to in this Rule shall be held by secret ballot. Election shall be by a majority of the Members present.

3. A Member elected under this Rule shall serve for the remainder of the term of his predecessor.

Chapter II – Presidency and precedence

Rule 6 – Election of the President, the first Vice-President and other Vice-Presidents

1. The Commission shall elect from among its Members a President, a first Vice-President as well as three other Vice-Presidents who together shall constitute the Bureau.

2. The President, the first Vice-President and the three other Vice-Presidents shall be elected for an initial term of three years. The term starts on the first annual meeting of the Commission following the elections of the Members of the Commission by the High Contracting Parties. At the fourth annual meeting of the Commission following the elections of the Members of the Commission by the High Contracting Parties, new elections will take place for a further term of two years.

3. The President and the Vice-Presidents may be re-elected. However, the term of office of the President or of a Vice-President shall end if he ceases to be a Member.

4. If the President or a Vice-President ceases to be a Member or resigns his office of President or Vice-President before its normal expiry, the Commission may elect a successor for the remainder of the term of that office.

5. The elections referred to in this Rule shall be held by secret ballot. Election shall be by a majority of the Members.

Rule 7 – Precedence

1. The first Vice-President shall take precedence over the three other Vice-Presidents.

2. The second, third and fourth Vice-Presidents shall take precedence according to the duration of their term of office.

3. The second, third and fourth Vice-Presidents having the same length of time in office shall take precedence according to age.

4. The Members shall take precedence after the President and Vice-Presidents according to the duration of their term of office.

5. Members having the same length of time in office shall take precedence according to age.

Rule 8 – Functions of the President

1. The President shall chair the meetings of the Commission and perform all other functions conferred upon him by the Protocol, these Rules and by the Commission.

2. In exercising his functions, the President shall remain under the authority of the Commission.

3. The President may delegate some of his functions to one of the Vice-Presidents.

4. In co-operation with the Vice-Presidents and the Secretariat, the President shall take the necessary measures to ensure that the functions of the Commission can be exercised at all times and expeditiously.

Rule 9 – Temporary replacement of the President

The first Vice-President shall take the place of the President if the presidency is vacant or the President is prevented from carrying out his duties, especially if, in the case of an enquiry, he is a national of a party to the conflict. The second Vice-President shall replace the first Vice-President if the latter is prevented from carrying out his duties or if the office of first Vice-President is vacant. The third Vice-President shall replace the second Vice-President if the latter is prevented from carrying out his duties or if the office of second Vice-President is vacant.

Rule 10 – Replacement of the President and Vice-Presidents

If the President and Vice-Presidents are at the same time prevented from carrying out their duties or if their offices are vacant at the same time, the duties of President shall be carried out by another Member according to the order of precedence established by Rule 7.

PART II – WORKING OF THE COMMISSION

Chapter I – Seat of the Commission, Secretariat and languages

Rule 11 – Seat of the Commission

The seat of the Commission shall be in Berne, Switzerland.

Rule 12 – Secretariat

The functions of the Secretariat of the Commission shall be assumed by the Depositary State of the Geneva Conventions and the Protocol.

Rule 13 – Languages

The official and working languages of the Commission shall be English and French.

Chapter II – Meetings of the Commission

Rule 14 – Holding of meetings

1. The Commission shall hold such meetings as it considers necessary to perform its functions. It shall meet at least once a year. The Commission shall also meet if at least one third of the Members so request or the Bureau so decides.

2. The Commission shall hold its meetings at its seat, unless the Commission or the Bureau decides otherwise.

3. Commission meetings shall be convened at dates set by the Commission or by the Bureau.

4. The Secretariat shall notify the Members of the date, time and place of each Commission meeting. Whenever possible, such notification shall be given at least six weeks in advance.

Rule 15 – Agenda

1. Following consultation with the President, the Secretariat shall transmit a draft agenda to the Members of the Commission, whenever possible at least six weeks before a meeting.

2. The agenda shall be adopted by the Commission at the beginning of the meeting.

Rule 16 – Documentation

The Secretariat shall transmit to the Members the working documents relating to the different agenda items, whenever possible at least four weeks in advance.

Rule 17 – Quorum

Eight Members shall constitute a quorum.

Rule 18 – Privacy of meetings

1. The Commission shall meet in camera. Its deliberations shall remain confidential.

2. Apart from Members, only members of the Secretariat, interpreters and persons assisting the Commission may attend its meetings, unless the Commission determines otherwise.

Rule 19 – Hearings

The Commission may hear any person whom it considers to be in a position to assist it in the performance of its functions.

PART III – ENQUIRIES

Chapter I – Enquiry request

Rule 20 – Lodging the request

1. The request for an enquiry shall be addressed to the Secretariat.

2. It shall state the facts that, in the opinion of the requesting party, constitute a grave breach or a serious violation, as well as the date and the place of their occurrence.

3. It shall list the evidence the requesting party wishes to present in support of its allegations.

4. It shall name the authority to which all communications concerning the enquiry shall be addressed, as well as the most expedient means of contacting that authority.

5. Where applicable and to the extent possible, it shall contain, in the enclosure, the original or a certified copy of any document cited in the list of evidence.

6. If the Commission receives a request for an enquiry under article 90(2)(d), and the consent of the other party or parties concerned has not yet been indicated, the Commission shall refer the request to that party or those parties with a request that it or they indicate its or their consent.

Rule 21 – Examination of the request for an enquiry

1. On receiving a request for an enquiry, the President shall without delay advise the interested party or parties of it. He shall send them, as soon as possible, a copy of the request as well as its enclosures and, subject to Rule 20(6), advise them of their right to submit, within a fixed time period, their observations concerning the admissibility of the request. The setting of that time limit does not however prevent the Commission from opening the enquiry at once.

2. The Commission may ask the requesting party to supply additional information within a fixed time limit.

3. If the competence of the Commission is contested, the latter shall decide by means of speedy consultation.

4. The Commission shall inform the requesting party if the request does not meet the conditions described in Rule 20, or if an enquiry cannot be conducted for any other reason.

5. All parties to the conflict shall be informed of the Commission's decision to open an enquiry.

6. If, in the course of an enquiry, the requesting party communicates to the Commission the withdrawal of its request, the Chamber shall cease its enquiry only with the consent of the other parties to the conflict. The withdrawal does not affect the payment of the costs of the enquiry in accordance with article 90 (7) of the Protocol.

Rule 22 – Expenses of the enquiry

The President, in consultation with the Secretariat, shall determine the amount to be advanced by the requesting party to cover the expenses of the enquiry.

Chapter II – The Chamber

Rule 23 – Formation of the Chamber

Unless the interested parties agree otherwise, the following provisions apply:

a. The President shall appoint, after consultation with the Bureau and the parties to the conflict, and on the basis of equitable geographical representation, five Members of the Chamber, not nationals of any party to the conflict.

b. The President shall invite the parties concerned to appoint, within a fixed time period, two additional persons, not nationals of any party to the conflict, as ad hoc Members of the Chamber.

c. If one or both of the ad hoc Members have not been appointed within the time limit set under Rule 23(b), the President shall immediately make the appointments necessary to fill the seats of the Chamber.
d. The President of the Commission shall appoint the Head of the Chamber.
e. If a Member appointed as a member of a Chamber believes that there are reasons disqualifying him from participating in the enquiry, he shall immediately impart them to the President, who may appoint another member.

Rule 24 – Custody of documents

All documents relating to an enquiry shall, as soon as possible, be handed over to the Head of the Chamber who shall be responsible for their registration and custody until the conclusion of the enquiry. They shall then be put in the custody of the Secretariat.

Rule 25 – Assistants

1. The Chamber may decide that it shall be assisted by one or more experts or interpreters.

2. All persons assisting the Chamber shall act on the instructions and under the authority of the Head of the Chamber.

Chapter III – Enquiry procedure

Rule 26 – Instructions

The Commission may establish general or specific instructions or guidelines concerning the enquiry.

Rule 27 – Procedure

1. The Chamber shall invite the parties to the conflict to assist it and to present evidence within a fixed time period. It may also seek any other evidence it considers relevant and may carry out an enquiry in loco.

2. The Chamber shall determine the admissibility and the weight of the evidence presented by the parties to the conflict, and the conditions under which witnesses shall be heard.

3. The President shall remind the interested parties that, during an enquiry in loco, they must assure to the members of the Chamber and all persons accompanying them the privileges and immunities necessary for the discharge of their functions which shall not be less extensive than those accorded to the experts on mission under the 1946 Convention on Privileges and Immunities of the United Nations, as well as their adequate protection.

4. During an enquiry in loco, the members of the Chamber shall be issued a document stating their capacity, as well as a white badge displaying in clearly visible black letters the name of the Commission in the local language.

5. The members of the Chamber may separate in order to conduct simultaneous enquiries at different places. In particular, the Chamber may, at any time, detach two or more of its members for an urgent enquiry on the spot and, if necessary, to ensure the preservation of evidence.

6. The quorum of the Chamber shall be fixed by the Commission in its instructions to the Chamber.

7. The Chamber shall, as soon as possible, communicate the results of its enquiry to the Commission in accordance with the instructions given to it.

8. All the evidence shall be fully disclosed to the parties concerned who shall be informed of their right to comment on it to the Commission.

9. If necessary, the Commission may instruct the Chamber to undertake a complementary enquiry.

Chapter IV – Report and Obligation of Confidentiality

Rule 28 – Preparation of the Commission's report

1. After each enquiry the Commission shall draw up, in the light of the Chamber's findings, a report to be transmitted to the parties concerned. In particular, the Commission shall consider, as appropriate, whether it should take steps to facilitate, through its good offices, the restoration of an attitude of respect for the Geneva Conventions and the Protocol.

2. The President shall transmit the report together with any recommendations the Commission considers appropriate to the parties concerned.

3. The President shall have the date on which the Commission's report was sent to the interested parties duly registered. The Secretariat shall keep in its archives copies of the communications of the Chambers and the reports of the Commission in its custody. These records are accessible only to Members while in office.

Rule 29 – Confidentiality

1. No personal data shall be published without the express consent of the person concerned.

2. Members of the Commission, ad hoc members of the Chambers, experts and other persons assisting the Commission or a Chamber are under an obligation, during and after their terms of office, to keep secret the facts or information of which they have become aware during the discharge of their functions.

3. The experts and other persons hired to assist the Commission or a Chamber shall, as a condition of their engagement, be required to agree, as a rule in writing, to comply with paragraph 2.

PART IV – METHODS OF WORK

Chapter I – Conduct of business

Rule 30 – Powers of the President

The President shall declare the opening and closing of each meeting of the Commission, direct the discussion, ensure observance of these Rules, accord the right to speak, put questions to the vote and announce decisions. The President, subject to these Rules, shall have control over the proceedings of the Commission and over the maintenance of order at its meetings. The President may, in the course of the discussion of an item, propose to the Commission the limitation of the time to be allowed to speakers, the limitation of the number of times each speaker may speak on any question and the closure of the list of speakers. He shall rule on points of order. He shall also have the power to propose adjournment or closure of the debate or adjournment or suspension of a meeting.

Rule 31 – Proposals

A proposal must be submitted in writing, if a Member so requests.

Rule 32 – Order of voting on proposals and amendments

1. Where a number of proposals relate to the same subject, they shall be put to the vote in the order in which they were submitted. In case of doubt about priority, the President shall decide.

2. Where a proposal is the subject of an amendment, the amendment shall be put to the vote first. Where two or more amendments to the same proposal are presented, the Commission shall vote first on whichever departs furthest in substance from the original proposal, and so on until all the amendments have been put to the vote. However, where the acceptance of one amendment necessarily entails rejection of another, the latter shall not be put to the vote. The final vote shall then be taken on the proposal as amended or not amended. In case of doubt as to the order of priority, the President shall decide.

3. A motion may be withdrawn by the Member who proposed it at any time before voting on it has commenced, provided that the motion has not been amended. A motion which has thus been withdrawn may be reintroduced by any Member.

Rule 33 – Order of procedural motions

Procedural motions shall take precedence over all other proposals.

Rule 34 – Voting

As a rule, the Commission decides by consensus. In the absence of consensus, the following provisions apply:

a. Subject to the provisions of Rules 6(4), 39 and 40, the decisions of the Commission shall be taken by a majority of the Members present.

b. In matters other than elections, a proposal shall be regarded as rejected if the majority referred to under letter (a) heretofore is not obtained.

c. Subject to Rules 5 (2)(d) and 6 (4), the Commission shall vote by show of hands, unless a Member requests a roll call vote.

d. After a vote has commenced, there shall be no interruption of the voting except on a point of order by a Member in connection with the actual conduct of the voting.

Chapter II – Working modalities

Rule 35 – Reports of Meetings

1. The Secretariat shall prepare a draft report of the Commission's deliberations and decisions following each meeting. The draft report shall be circulated as soon as possible to the Members of the Commission, who will be given the opportunity to submit corrections within a prescribed time-limit.

2. If no corrections are submitted, the meeting report shall be deemed adopted. If corrections are submitted, they shall be consolidated in a single document and circulated to all Members. In this latter case, the adoption of the report of the meeting shall be taken up at the next meeting of the Commission.

Rule 36 – Working groups

The Commission may set up ad hoc working groups comprising a limited number of its Members. The terms of reference of such working groups shall be defined by the Commission.

Rule 37 – Communications

1. The Secretariat shall register and bring to the Commission's attention communications received containing information which may be of interest to the Members.
2. Such communications received by a Member shall be forwarded to the Secretariat.
3. The Secretariat shall acknowledge receipt of the communications to their authors.

Rule 38 – Report of activities

Subject to the obligation of confidentiality stated in Rule 29, the Commission shall issue, whenever it considers it useful, a general report on its activities to the governments of the High Contracting Parties to the Geneva Conventions. The Commission may also prepare such reports and make such public statements relating to its functions as it considers appropriate and in conformity with the provisions of the Protocol and these Rules concerning confidentiality.

PART V – AMENDMENTS AND SUSPENSION

Rule 39 – Amendments of the Rules

The present Rules may be amended by a decision taken by a majority of the Members, subject to the provisions of the Protocol.

Rule 40 – Suspension of a provision of the Rules

Upon the proposal of a Member, the application of a provision of these Rules may be suspended by a decision taken by a majority of the Members, subject to the provisions of the Protocol. The suspension of a provision shall be limited in its operation to the particular purpose for which such suspension has been sought.

Index